E-Health, Privacy, and Security Law

Second Edition

Publications From BNA Books on Related Topics

Managed Care Litigation

Health Care Fraud and Abuse: Practical Perspectives

Prosecuting and Defending Health Care Fraud Cases

E-Health Business & Transactional Law

Pharmaceutical Law: Regulation of Research, Development, and Marketing

Supreme Court Practice

Federal Appellate Practice

BNA's Directory of State and Federal Courts, Judges and Clerks

Medical Ethics: Analysis of the Issues Raised by the Codes, Opinions, and Statements

Medical Ethics: Codes, Opinions, and Statements

Occupational Safety and Health Law

For details on these and other related titles, please visit the BNA Books Web site at **bna.com/bnabooks** or call **1-800-960-1220** to request a catalog. All books are available on a 30-day free examination period.

E-Health, Privacy, and Security Law

Second Edition

Editor-in-Chief
W. Andrew H. Gantt III
COOLEY LLP
Washington, D.C.

The American Bar Association
Health Law Section

BNA Books, *A Division of BNA*, Arlington, VA

Copyright © 2011
The American Bar Association

All rights reserved. No copyright claimed on U.S. government materials.

Library of Congress Cataloging-in-Publication Data

E-health, privacy, and security law / editor-in-chief, W. Andrew H. Gantt III. -- 2nd ed.
   p. cm.
   Includes bibliographical references and index.
   ISBN 978-1-57018-992-0 (alk. paper)
   1. Medical informatics--Law and legislation--United States. 2. Data protection--Law and legislation--United States. 3. Medical records--Access control--United States. 4. Medical records--Law and legislation--United States. I. Gantt, W. Andrew H.

KF3827.R4E34 2011
344.7304'1--dc23

2011047481

The materials contained in this work represent the opinions of the individual authors and should not be construed to be those of either the American Bar Association (ABA) or the ABA Health Law Section, or any other person or entity. The authors expressly reserve the right to freely advocate other positions on behalf of clients. Nothing contained herein is to be considered the rendering of legal advice for specific cases, and readers are responsible for obtaining such advice from their own legal counsel. These materials are intended for educational and informational purposes only.

Published by BNA Books
1801 S. Bell Street, Arlington, VA 22202
bna.com/bnabooks

ISBN 978-1-57018-992-0
Printed in the United States of America

Contributors

W. Andrew H. Gantt III
Cooley LLP
Washington, D.C.

Adrienne Belyea
Cooley LLP
Reston, Virginia

John Healey
The Blue Cross & Blue Shield Ass'n
Chicago, Illinois

Robyn S. Shapiro
Drinker Biddle & Reath
Milwaukee, Wisconsin

Leslie M. Tector
Drinker Biddle & Reath
Milwaukee, Wisconsin

Lisa L. Dahm
South Texas College of Law
Houston, Texas

Amy Taylor
Latham & Watkins LLP
London, England

Gail Crawford
Latham & Watkins LLP
London, England

John R. Christiansen
Christiansen IT Law
Seattle, Washington

Alan S. Goldberg
Attorney & Counsellor at Law
McLean, Virginia

Adam Greene
Davis Wright Tremaine
Washington, D.C.

Daphne D. Walker
Fulbright & Jaworski
Dallas, Texas

J. Benneville Haas
Latham & Watkins LLP
Washington, D.C.

Eric C. Greig
Latham & Watkins LLP
Washington, D.C.

Mark Faccenda
Fulbright & Jaworski LLP
Washington, D.C.

L. Robert Guenthner III
SNR Denton
Chicago, Illinois

Arthur G. House
Paley Rothman Goldstein
Rosenberg Eig & Cooper
Bethesda, Maryland

Arthur E. Peabody
BlueCross BlueShield Ass'n
Washington, D.C.

Patricia M. Wagner
Epstein Becker & Green
Washington, D.C.

Paul Roberts
Foley & Lardner
Washington, D.C.

Brian R. Balow
Dickinson Wright
Troy, Michigan

Sheryl Tatar Dasco
Seyfarth Shaw LLP
Houston, Texas

Kari K. Loeser
Genentech, Inc.
San Francisco, California

Amy Jurevic Sokol
Tulsa, Oklahoma

Foreword

The American Bar Association (ABA) Health Law Section proudly presents the *Second Edition* of *E-Health, Privacy, and Security Law*—a book that has helped lawyers and their clients better understand and find solutions to the legal issues arising from the integration of the Internet and other technology into the health care delivery system. The *Second Edition* puts a new focus on patient privacy and information security issues that are undergoing massive change with new government regulations, the inclusion of social media into the health care delivery mix, and redoubled enforcement initiatives.

The new *Second Edition* continues to cover developments in business and transactional issues of e-health, but a number of new chapters have been added to increase the coverage and analysis of privacy and security law and regulation. The Health Law Section expresses its appreciation to Andrew Gantt for his role as Editor-in-Chief of the new edition and to Barbara Bennett and June Sullivan for their contributions and leadership during the formative first edition and its numerous annual supplements. Thanks also to Jim Fattibene and Elizabeth Turqman at BNA Books and, particularly, to the Section member authors for their hard work on this project and their service to the profession.

On behalf of the ABA and its Health Law Section, we are pleased to have this continuing opportunity to share our members' collective experience in the dynamic area of e-health, privacy and security law. We believe you will find this *Second Edition* to be a continuing valuable resource. We welcome your thoughts about how the Section can further use its BNA book series to address your practice needs.

DAVID H. JOHNSON
SECTION CHAIR
DAVID L. DOUGLASS
CHAIR-ELECT
MICHAEL E. CLARK
CHAIR
PUBLICATIONS COMMITTEE

HEALTH LAW SECTION
AMERICAN BAR ASSOCIATION

December 2011

Preface

The universe of e-health, including electronic health records (EHR) and other health information technology, has experienced unprecedented expansion. This expansion, spurred particularly by the federal government's incentives tied to "meaningful use" of EHR technology, has come with new regulations and legal challenges. Keeping up-to-date can be a tremendous burden for anyone working in this area. With these significant changes, and aggressive enforcement actions by the Department of Health and Human Services on the rise, health lawyers and others who work with the electronic transmission of health information need to be well-informed about the current legal climate now more than ever. For that reason, it is essential to have a reference guide to keep abreast of these changes.

In order to advise clients, those who practice in this area need to be knowledgeable and have the state-of-the-art information. The *Second Edition* of *E-Health, Privacy, and Security Law*, previously titled *E-Health Business and Transactional Law*, is an indispensable means to accomplish this goal. The *Second Edition* includes recent changes that are vital to you as well as your clients. The important updates contained in the *Second Edition* include such areas as: e-health legal and market trends including the role of social media; current U.S. and European privacy regulation and related enforcement; other government regulation highlights such as antitrust and FDA; proprietary rights in technology and information; unique liability issues in the e-health industry; contracting principles for e-health transactions; due diligence; and litigation and ethical considerations. The breadth and depth of topics makes the *Second Edition* of *E-Health, Privacy, and Security Law* a valuable reference and guide.

You may wonder what makes this book stand apart from others. It is substantially different because it is written by authors who are highly regarded and valued for their expertise in their respective areas. These authors carefully research and analyze the current law, the new laws, and the recent changes to the laws. Their exceptional skills make *E-Health, Privacy, and Security Law* distinct from all other publications. We are grateful for their contributions.

The authors made every attempt to provide the most recent updates available for this 2011 *Second Edition*. However, the reader should be aware that the nature of the e-health law lends itself to rapid transformation and change. It was not always possible to include the most recent information in this *Second Edition*. Also, the reader should be aware that this *Second Edition* is for general information purposes only, and should not be considered legal advice or opinion.

Lastly, the views expressed in this book are those of the individual authors and do not reflect the views of their firms, their clients, or other authors of this book. We wholeheartedly thank James Fattibene for his input and hard work to bring this *Second Edition* to its final print. But most importantly, we acknowledge you, the reader, for having the insight to seek the very best resource for your practice and to stay abreast of the recent changes of the laws pertaining to the e-health industry. *E-Health, Privacy, and Security Law* is an invaluable means for you to increase your knowledge base and properly advise your clients.

W. ANDREW H. GANTT III
COOLEY LLP
Editor-in-Chief

December 2011

The American Bar Association Health Law Section 2011–2012 Officers & Council

Chair
David H. Johnson
Albuquerque, NM

Secretary
Michael E. Clark
Houston, TX

Chair-Elect
David L. Douglass
Washington, D.C.

Budget Officer
Daniel A. Cody
San Francisco, CA

Financial Officer-Elect
Alexandria Hien McCombs,
Addison, TX

Vice Chair
Kathleen Scully-Hayes
Baltimore, MD

Immediate Past Chair
Linda A. Baumann
Washington, D.C.

Council Members at Large

Gregory E. Demske
Washington, D.C.

Robert W. Friz
Philadelphia, PA

C. Joyce Hall
Jackson, MS

Eugene Holmes
Washington, D.C.

William W. Horton
Birmingham, AL

Priscilla D. Keith
Indianapolis, IN

Charity Scott
Atlanta, GA

Robyn S. Shapiro
Milwaukee, WI

Hilary Young
Austin, TX

Section Delegates to the House of Delegates

J.A. (Tony) Patterson, Jr.
Kalispell, MT

Gregory L. Pemberton
Indianapolis, IN

Young Lawyers Division Liaison
Marc Meyer
Magnolia, TX

Law Student Division Liaison
Carrie Wallace
Northwood, ND

Board of Governors Liaison
R. Kinnan Golemon
Austin, TX

Publications Co-Chairs

Michael E. Clark
Houston, TX

Charles M. Key
Memphis, TN

Section Director
Wanda Workman
Chicago, IL

About the Contributors

Andrew Gantt (Editor-in-Chief; Chapter 1: The E-Health Explosion: An Overview of Legal and Market Trends)

Andrew Gantt is a partner at Cooley LLP and practices in the firm's Washington, D.C. office. He is a member of the Life Sciences Practice Group and leads Cooley's Health Care Regulatory Practice. Mr. Gantt represents a wide variety of health care providers, manufacturers, suppliers, and e-health companies in corporate and regulatory matters. In addition, Mr. Gantt advises venture capital groups, private equity funds and underwriters on health care regulatory issues in connection with health care and life sciences financings and investments. Mr. Gantt has a particular expertise in e-health, privacy, and security issues, and has advised a wide variety of e-health clients on a wide variety of business transactions and regulatory issues. Mr. Gantt serves as Chair of the ABA eHealth, Privacy & Security Law Interest Group. He was named an "Outstanding Healthcare IT Lawyer" in by Nightingale's HEALTHCARE News and has been recommended as a Health Care and Life Sciences attorney by THE LEGAL 500: UNITED STATES 2011 EDITION.

Adrienne Belyea (Chapter 1: The E-Health Explosion: An Overview of Legal and Market Trends)

Adrienne M. Belyea is an associate at Cooley LLP in its Reston, Virginia office. She is a member of the Technology Transactions group and of Cooley's Business Department. Ms. Belyea's practice focuses primarily on technology licensing involving clients ranging from emerging companies to large public companies. She counsels clients in the energy, high-tech, software, medical device, health care, and Internet industries regarding the structuring and negotiation of their technology related deals to develop, license, and commercialize their intellectual property assets. Her practice involves negotiating and drafting a range of technology agreements including software licensing agreements, consulting agreements, strategic collaboration agreements, application service provider agreements, distribution/reseller agreements, services agreements, and content licensing and hosting arrangements.

John Healey (Chapter 2: E-Health Industry Overview; Chapter 3: Health Information Technology)

John Healey serves as in-house counsel for the Blue Cross and Blue Shield Association (BCBSA) in Chicago, Illinois. Prior to joining BCBSA, he practiced in the Health Law Department of McDermott Will & Emery's Chicago office. Mr. Healey focuses his practice on information technology and health care regulatory matters. Before earning his law degree, Mr. Healey gained extensive health care and information technology experience while performing multiple roles in a start-up company and managing worldwide product line responsibilities in established companies. As a legal advisor and as a line executive, he has been responsible for negotiating contracts and licenses, resolving commercial disputes, developing regulatory compliance approaches and policies, planning security and privacy measures, and protecting intellectual property assets. Mr. Healey possesses credentials as a Certified Information Systems Security Professional (CISSP) and is admitted to practice in Illinois.

Robyn S. Shapiro (Chapter 4: Privacy, PHRs, and Social Media)

Robyn S. Shapiro is a health law partner and Regional Partner in Charge in the Milwaukee office of Drinker Biddle & Reath. She has worked extensively in health law matters involving clinical research, genetics, biotechnology, treatment decision-making, bioethics issues, medical staff matters, health information privacy issues, informed consent, regulatory and licensing matters, and employment and other business issues. Ms. Shapiro is listed in the BEST LAWYERS IN AMERICA and a number of WHO'S WHO publications, she was included in Nightingale's 2006 list of "Outstanding Hospital Lawyers" in the nation, and in 2011 she was named Milwaukee's "Health Care Lawyer of the Year" by BEST LAWYERS. Ms. Shapiro has written more than 50 articles and book chapters on health law topics that have been published in peer-reviewed journals and books, and she has lectured on a wide variety of health law and bioethics topics throughout the world. She recently completed her service as an appointed member of the U.S. Department of Health and Human Services, NIH Recombinant DNA Advisory Committee (RAC), and the RAC Clinical Trials Working Group, and she currently serves on the RAC Bio-safety Working Group. She also has served as an appointed member of the U.S. Food and Drug Administration Drug Safety and Risk Management Advisory Committee and appointed member of the U.S. Department of Health and Human Services Secretary's Advisory Committee on Xeno-transplantation. Ms. Shapiro has been named an ABA Fellow and she served as Chair of the ABA Individual Rights and Responsibilities Section, and currently she serves as Chair of the ABA Special Committee on Bioethics and the Law, Chair of the ABA Health Law Section's Health Policy Task Force, and Council Member of the ABA Health Law Section. Ms. Shapiro earned her J.D. from Harvard Law School, and her B.A., summa cum laude with Highest Distinction from the University of Michigan, where she was Phi Beta Kappa. She is admitted to the bars of the District of Columbia, the State of Wisconsin, and the U.S. Supreme Court.

Leslie M. Tector (Chapter 4: Privacy, PHRs, and Social Media)

Leslie M. Tector is counsel in Drinker Biddle & Reath's Health Law Practice Group in Milwaukee, Wisconsin. Her practice focuses on research compliance, regulatory health care and general corporate matters. Ms. Tector provides clients with guidance on research compliance, regulatory health care and general corporate matters. With a broad and diverse client base that includes health care systems, hospitals, academic medical centers, physician groups, device manufacturers, and pharmaceutical companies, she has significant experience drafting compliance policies and related documents for sponsors and research sites that relate to clinical trials, human subject protection, conflicts of interest, grant reviews and approvals, and audits. Ms. Tector has taught health law classes at Marquette University Law School and the Medical College of Wisconsin. She has lectured at conferences throughout the nation, and has published a number of articles on cutting-edge health law issues. Prior to entering law school, Ms. Tector received a B.S. in Nursing and practiced for a brief period as a registered nurse with an emphasis on cardiac intensive care. She holds a B.S.N., *cum laude*, from Georgetown University, a J.D. from Boston College Law School, and an LL.M. in Health Law *with distinction* from DePaul University College of Law.

Lisa L. Dahm (Chapter 5: Privacy Issues in U.S. Health Care)

Lisa Dahm currently practices health care law as a solo practitioner in Houston, and also serves as the Director of Continuing Legal Education and an Adjunct Professor at South Texas College of Law where she teaches the Privacy Law Seminar, Health Law, Forensic Medicine, Legal Medicine, Contract Negotiations and Drafting, and Contract Building Blocks courses. Ms. Dahm has extensive and comprehensive knowledge and understanding of health care laws and regulations with particular emphasis on privacy and confidentiality (including HIPAA and the HITECH Act), corporate compliance, fraud and abuse, physician transactions, and Stark statutes and regulations. Prior to graduation from law school, Ms. Dahm worked for health care information systems vendors, health care providers, and her own and another Big Four consulting firm. Following law school, Ms. Dahm spent three years as in-house counsel for a major integrated delivery system located in Houston, Texas, where she helped draft the System's corporate compliance program, served on the Corporate Compliance Committee, responded to requests and subpoenas for business and health information, served on the System's Institutional Review Board, and advised the System on and drafted required policies, procedures, credentialing activities, and all types of contracts. She then joined Deloitte & Touche as a Senior Manager, serving as a member of the National HIPAA Advisory Services Task Force and assisted in creating the firm's approach to providing HIPAA services to its health care clients. She conducted numerous executive briefings for Deloitte's health care clients to raise awareness of HIPAA, and managed and participated in HIPAA Privacy and other health care risk assessments. Ms. Dahm received her J.D. magna cum laude from South Texas College of Law in 1995, and was admitted to the Bar in Texas the same year. In 2005, she received her LL.M. in Health Law from the University of Houston. Ms. Dahm is the Chair of the editorial board of THE HEALTH LAWYER and a member of the ABA Health Law Section's Publications Committee. She authored a monograph on patient confidentiality laws (American Health Lawyers Ass'n June 1999) and has written numerous articles and papers on HIPAA and other legal topics. Ms. Dahm is a recognized expert on privacy and confidentiality, and a frequent speaker at health care, HIPAA, and legal regional and national conferences. Her experience in the health care industry spans more than 25 years.

Amy Taylor (Chapter 6: The European Data Privacy Regime)

Amy Taylor is an associate in the London office of Latham & Watkins, focusing primarily on data privacy and commercial law, technology transactions and intellectual property. Amy has experience in advising various global clients on complex data privacy and e-commerce issues and compliance projects, as well as advising on broader data privacy and commercial aspects of operations in the UK. She also advises clients in relation to global technology focused transactions and intellectual property matters, in both a transactional and intellectual property litigation context. Amy is also a frequent contributor to the Latham & Watkins Global Privacy & Security Compliance Law Blog (http://www.globalprivacyblog.com), writing on the latest privacy and security law developments across Europe.

Gail Crawford (Chapter 6: The European Data Privacy Regime)

Gail Crawford is a partner in the London office of Latham & Watkins. Her practice focuses primarily on technology, intellectual property and commercial and data privacy law and includes advising on data protection issues and e-commerce and communications regulation, technology licensing agreements and joint ventures and technology procurement. She also advises both customers and suppliers on multi-jurisdictional IT, business process and transformation outsourcing transactions. Gail has extensive experience advising on data protection issues including advising a global corporation with operations in over 100 countries on its compliance strategy and advising a number of US e-commerce and web 2.0 businesses as they expand into Europe and beyond. She also advises online business and providers of communications services on the impact of the UK and European restrictions on interception and disclosure of communications data. Gail is also an editor of the Latham & Watkins Global Privacy & Security Compliance Law Blog (http://www.globalprivacyblog.com) and has contributed to a number of publications and conferences in the area of data privacy and security.

John R. Christiansen (Chapter 7: Information Security and Breach Notification Under HIPAA and HITECH)

John R. Christiansen practices law at Christiansen IT Law, based in Seattle, Washington. He founded Christiansen IT Law in 2005, after 20 years in law firm practice and a stint leading HIPAA security risk assessments of Fortune 100 companies for a Big Four consulting firm. Mr. Christiansen's practice has focused on health care information technology law since the early 1990s, including privacy and security assessment, planning, policy and procedures development, and risk management; information technology and services development, acquisition, licensing and management; incident response; due diligence support in transactions involving information technologies or protected information; and expert support and expert witness services in litigation involving information technology-, privacy-, and security-related issues. Christiansen IT Law clients include health care organizations ranging from multi-state hospital systems and regional medical centers to physician practices, as well as information technology products and services vendors serving health care providers. Mr. Christiansen is a frequent national speaker and author, and wrote one of the first major monographs on HIPAA and a treatise on information security standards of care. Mr. Christiansen is a past Co-Chair of the American Bar Association's Healthcare Informatics Committee and Committee on Healthcare Privacy, Security and Information Technology, and past Chair of the Contractual and Regulatory Principle Work Group of the Generally Accepted Information Security Principles project. He is currently a member of the Technical Advisory Panel of the Health Information Security and Privacy Collaboration, a 34-state study of business practices and legal standards affecting health information sharing funded by the U.S. Department of Health and Human Services Office, the National Coordinator for Health Information Technology, and the Agency for Healthcare Research and Quality.

Alan S. Goldberg (Chapter 8: Enforcement of the Health Insurance Portability and Accountability Act of 1996; and Appendix E)

Alan S. Goldberg, Attorney & Counsellor-at-Law, McLean, Virginia, and Adjunct Professor of Health Law at George Mason University and American University, Washington College of Law, practices business law, including health care, information technology, and tax law. Mr. Goldberg joined Goulston & Storrs in Boston, Massachusetts in 1967 upon graduation from Boston College Law School, where he was a member of the BOSTON COLLEGE LAW REVIEW, and in 2002 Mr. Goldberg relocated to the District of Columbia office of the firm and disembarked in 2006 to become a solo practitioner. Mr. Goldberg received an LL.M. in Taxation from Boston University School of Law and served on the Adjunct Faculty of Boston College Law School, Suffolk Law School, and University of Maryland School of Law. He was a member of the Council of the ABA Health Law Section and is a Past President and Inaugural Fellow of the American Health Lawyers Association and he is the founding Moderator of AHLA's Health & Information Technology listserv. Mr. Goldberg co-chairs the National HIPAA Summit series of events and is Secretary/Treasurer of the Virginia Bar Association Health Law Section, and he is a Past Chair of the Board of Governors of the Health Law Section and Vice-Chair of the Special Committee of Law and Technology and a member of the Mandatory Continuing Legal Education Committee and a member of the Education of Lawyers Section of the Virginia State Bar. He served as a Member of the Rules of Professional

Conduct Review Committee and is a Past Co-Chair of the Steering Committee of the Health Law Section of the District of Columbia Bar. He maintains HEALTHLAWYERBLOG at http://healthlawyer.typepad.com/healthlawyer/ for the education of health law and other students. Mr. Goldberg served in the Judge Advocate's General Corps of the U.S. Navy. Mr. Goldberg has published extensively on a wide range of health law and other legal issues and is a frequent lecturer. Mr. Goldberg is a member of the bars of the Commonwealth of Pennsylvania, the Commonwealth of Virginia, the District of Columbia, the Commonwealth of Massachusetts, and the States of New York and Florida, and he is admitted to the U.S. Court of Appeals for Veterans Claims and he is a U.S. Department of Veterans Affairs accredited attorney

Adam Greene (Chapter 8: Enforcement of the Health Insurance Portability and Accountability Act of 1996; and Appendix E)

Adam Greene is a partner in the Washington, D.C. office of Davis Wright Tremaine, where he primarily counsels health care providers and technology companies on compliance with the HIPAA privacy, security, and breach notification rules. Previously, Adam was a regulator at the U.S. Department of Health and Human Services, where he played a fundamental role in administering and enforcing the HIPAA rules. At HHS, Adam was responsible for determining how HIPAA rules apply to new and emerging health information technologies, and he was instrumental in the development of the current HIPAA enforcement process.

Daphne D. Walker (Chapter 9: Professional Licensure and Liability Issues)

Daphne D. Walker is a Senior Counsel in the regulatory group at Tenet Healthcare Corporation in Dallas, Texas, where she advises Tenet and its subsidiaries on health care regulatory matters. Ms. Walker received her B.S.N., cum laude, from West Texas A&M University in 1997 and her J.D. from Southern Methodist University Dedman School of Law in 2006. Prior to joining Tenet, Ms. Walker practiced as a registered nurse for nine years and practiced health care law at Fulbright & Jaworski L.L.P. for five years. Ms. Walker has given several presentations on nursing peer review matters. She is a past Sarah T. Hughes Diversity Law Scholarship Fellow and currently Treasurer of the Dallas Bar Association Health Law Section.

J. Benneville Haas (Chapter10: FDA Regulation of E-Health and Technology)

J. Ben Haas practices in the Washington, D.C. office of Latham & Watkins LLP, where he is a corporate partner in the firm's Health Care and Life Sciences Practice Group. Mr. Haas focuses his practice on regulatory, transactional, and legislative matters involving the medical device, pharmaceutical, biotechnology, tobacco, food, cosmetic, and dietary supplement industries. Mr. Haas has counseled clients on a wide variety of regulatory matters involving the FDA, including, among others, pre-market product development and clinical and pre-clinical testing; FDA submissions; product promotion and labeling; compliance with good manufacturing practice requirements; agency inspections; and recalls. Mr. Haas has also counseled clients on legislative and administrative rulemaking proceedings relating to the FDA, including matters involving the implementation of the Family Smoking Prevention and Tobacco Control Act. Mr. Haas has authored and co-authored articles on FDA regulatory matters, and has been a featured speaker and lecturer on FDA regulatory and policy matters at several industry-sponsored events.

Eric C. Greig (Chapter 10: FDA Regulation of E-Health and Technology)

Eric Greig is an associate in the Washington, D.C. office of Latham & Watkins LLP. He focuses his practice on health care regulatory and transactional matters involving the medical device, pharmaceutical, tobacco, and health care provider industries. Mr. Greig has advised on a variety of issues involving the FDA and the Centers for Medicare & Medicaid Services, including clinical testing; product promotion and labeling; third-party reimbursement strategies for new and existing technologies; and Medicare and Medicaid coverage, payment, and compliance. Mr. Greig has also assisted clients on a number of privacy and security matters, such as implementing a coordinated response to a large-scale data breach and counseling a mobile medical device company as to its federal reporting and record maintenance responsibilities. Mr. Greig attended the University of Texas School of Law, graduating with high honors and Order of the Coif. He graduated cum laude with a B.S. in microbiology and philosophy from The Ohio State University, where he was a Presidential Scholar.

Mark Faccenda (Chapter 11: Obligations in Response to a Health Care Data Security Breach)

Mark Faccenda is an associate in Fulbright & Jaworski LLP's Washington, D.C. office. As part of the firm's Health Care Practice Group, Mr. Faccenda has represented health care industry clients on regulatory and transactional matters including federal health care program reimbursement, fraud and abuse, and privacy issues. He advises clients including academic medical centers, health systems, physician/hospital joint ventures, pharmaceutical manufacturers, physician groups, long term care facilities, and durable medical equipment suppliers. Mr. Faccenda received his law degree from the University of Pittsburgh School of Law. He also received his Masters in Health Administration from the University of Pittsburgh Graduate School of Public Health.

L. Robert Guenthner III (Chapter 12: Due Diligence in E-Health Transactions)

Robert Guenthner is a partner with SNR Denton in Chicago, Illinois. His practice includes the representation of diversified health systems, managed care organizations, medical equipment manufacturers, and various other health care and general corporate entities. He concentrates his practice in the areas of mergers and acquisitions, divestitures, joint ventures, corporate reorganizations, and other commercial transactions. He has substantial experience in the acquisition and divestiture of various types of regulated and non-regulated entities, both publicly traded and privately held. Mr. Guenthner received his law degree from Washington University School of Law in Saint Louis, where he was inducted into the Order of the Coif, a national honor society for law school graduates. He also received his Masters in Business Administration with a joint concentration in finance and organizational behavior from Washington University's John M. Olin School of Business, and his B.S. from the University of Dayton.

Arthur G. House (Chapter 12: Due Diligence in E-Health Transactions)

Arthur House is a principal in Paley Rothman Goldstein Rosenberg Eig & Cooper in Bethesda, Maryland. Mr. House's practice is focused on licensing and venture formation in biotech and other technology areas, including license, distribution, storage and assignment transactions, strategic alliance agreements, and litigation. He has overseen the growth and development of a number of technology and science-based clients from start-up through venture capital, merger, acquisition, and IPO stages. He received his B.A., cum laude, from Tufts University in Medford, Massachusetts, and his J.D. from the University of Virginia School of Law in Charlottesville, Virginia.

Arthur E. Peabody (Chapter 13: Contracts in the Digital Age: Adapting to Changing Times)

Arthur E. Peabody, Jr. is the Lead Medicare Counsel for the BlueCross BlueShield Association in Washington, D.C. He litigates complex, multi-million dollar Medicare reimbursement cases brought by hospitals, nursing homes, and rehabilitation facilities. He has coordinated a demonstration project to evaluate arbitration as a means to resolve disputes over Medicare coverage of home health care benefits. As an Assistant U.S. Attorney for the Eastern District of Virginia (the "rocket docket"), Mr. Peabody litigated civil cases representing federal agencies as both plaintiff and defendant, including health care fraud actions including misbilling, kickbacks, and regulatory noncompliance. He spearheaded an initiative to improve conditions in Virginia's worst nursing homes by creative use of the False Claims Act. For the past 15 years he has served a volunteer mediator for the U.S. District Court for the District of Columbia. For many years, Mr. Peabody served as Chief of the Special Litigation Section of the Civil Rights Division at the U.S. Department of Justice. He manages all aspects of the investigation and litigation of novel federal court actions brought to vindicate the constitutional and federal statutory rights of juveniles and elderly and disabled persons. Many of these cases formed the basis for statutes, regulations, and the development of Supreme Court precedents. He has appeared in 34 different federal courts across the nation. Mr. Peabody is completing his second term as an elected member of the Alexandria City School Board. He earned his J.D. degree from the Cornell Law School.

Patricia M. Wagner (Chapter 14: Evaluating Antitrust Concerns in the Electronic Marketplace)

Patricia M. Wagner is a Member of Epstein Becker Green in the Health Care and Life Sciences Practice in the firm's Washington, DC office. She has experience representing a wide range of clients in all aspects of antitrust counseling and has worked with clients to develop general strategies to achieve corporate antitrust compliance in all aspects of their business processes, including advising clients on antitrust issues that arise in contracting or other business ventures, and assisting clients in developing protocols to foster antitrust compliance. In addition, she has extensive experience representing clients in front of the Federal Trade Commission and the Department of Justice. She recently participated on a panel hosted by the FTC related to the FTC/DOJ Proposed Statement on antitrust compliance for Accountable Care Organizations participating in the Medicare Shared Savings Program.

Paul Roberts (Chapter 15: The Intersection of Health Law and Intellectual Property Law)

Paul Roberts is attorney at Foley and Lardner in Washington, DC. Trained in both bio-medical engineering and computer science at Johns Hopkins University, and a graduate of Rutgers Law School *magna cum laude*, Paul's practice focuses on intellectual property counseling, prosecution, and litigation of electronics, software, medical treatment, and health related patents. Paul is an active member of the American Bar Association (ABA) Intellectual Property Section, where he is vice-chair of the online data committee, co-chair of the non-practicing entity subcommittee for IP Litigation. He has spoken on topics such as privacy concerns in electronic media; transferability of software; and ownership and transferability of electronic information. In addition, Paul is the principle author of SECRETS FOR EFFECTIVE PATENT DRAFTING AND PROSECUTION, a book, in development and published through the ABA, that provides strategy considerations for filing and effectively prosecuting patent applications from the view of both an attorney and a patent examiner.

Brian R. Balow (Chapter 16: Allocation and Mitigation of Liability)

Brian R. Balow is a Member of Dickinson Wright in Troy, Michigan. He has served as Practice Director of Dickinson Wright's IP, Business Technology, Telecommunications, and Energy Practice, and as outside general counsel to tax-exempt nonprofit corporation delivering broad range of senior services, including nursing, assisted living, independent living, memory care, rehabilitation, home health, and wellness services. Mr. Balow represented an international magazine publisher in connection with data security breach involving customer personally identifiable information, including compliance with breach notification statutes and PCI standards, and represented a Fortune 100 company in negotiation and documentation of IT transactions (including global enterprise solution and outsourcing deals), aggregating more than one billion dollars, with vendors including IBM, Hewlett Packard, Oracle, SAP, PeopleSoft, Microsoft, and EDS. Mr. Balow holds a B.A. in Urban Planning from Western Michigan University and a J.D., cum laude, from the University of Georgia, where he was Managing Editor of the GEORGIA JOURNAL OF INTERNATIONAL AND COMPARATIVE LAW.

Sheryl Tatar Dasco (Chapter 18: Legal Ethics and E-Health)

Sheryl Tatar Dacso, J.D., Dr.P.H. is senior counsel in the Corporate & Finance Practice Group of Seyfarth Shaw LLP. Dr. Dacso has represented health care organizations, individual physicians and physician groups for over 30 years. She is Board Certified in Health Care Law by the Texas Board of Legal Specialization and certified in health care compliance by the Health Care Compliance Association. Dr. Dacso concentrates her practice on health care compliance, regulations and transactions, including physician practice mergers, acquisitions and business ventures. Dr. Dacso is an AHLA trained negotiator/mediator for resolution of health care disputes and has handled many complex transactions involving health care organizations. In November 2002, she was named by Texas Lawyer as the number one "Top Notch Lawyer" in health care law in Texas. In 2011, she was listed in TEXAS BEST LAWYERS. She has written several text books and articles on a broad range of health care topics ranging from managed care contracting to virtual practice arrangements among physician practices. Dr. Dacso holds a faculty appointment at the University of Houston where she teaches at the Law School in the Health Law Institute and in the College of Technology.

Kari K. Loeser (Chapter 18: Legal Ethics and E-Health)

Kari Karsjens Loeser is a Manager at Genentech, Inc., a member of the Roche Group, located in South San Francisco, CA. She previously worked at the United States Department of Health and Human Services, Office for Civil Rights, Region IX, in San Francisco. She has published articles and presented at conferences on various topics in health law including bioethics, health care compliance, and health policy. Mrs. Loeser received her B.A., with honors, from the University of Iowa, and her J.D. degree from DePaul University College of Law, with a specialization in health law. She is also holds a Certification in Healthcare Compliance from the Health Care Compliance Association (HCCA).

Amy Jurevic Sokol (Appendices A, B, C, and D)

Amy Jurevic Sokol has been the Vice President and General Counsel for St. John Health System in Tulsa, Oklahoma and Carondelet Health in Kansas

City, Missouri. Ms. Sokol also practiced at Shughart Thomson & Kilroy PC (now Polsinelli Shughart PC) and was an adjunct assistant professor at Rockhurst University and Kansas University. Ms. Sokol received her J.D. degree, cum laude, from St. Louis University School of Law, where she was the executive managing editor of the ST. LOUIS-WARSAW TRANSATLANTIC LAW JOURNAL. She received her Master's degree in Health Administration with Great Distinction from St. Louis University School of Public Health.

Summary Table of Contents

Foreword		vii
Preface		ix
About the Contributors		xiii
Detailed Table of Contents		xxvii
Chapter 1.	The E-Health Explosion—An Analysis of Legal and Market Trends	1
Chapter 2.	E-Health Industry Overview	19
Chapter 3.	Health Information Technology	43
Chapter 4.	Privacy, PHRs, and Social Media	63
Chapter 5.	Privacy Issues in U.S. Health Care	85
Chapter 6.	The European Data Privacy Regime	127
Chapter 7.	Information Security and Breach Notification Under HIPAA and HITECH	157
Chapter 8.	Enforcement of the Health Insurance Portability and Accountability Act of 1996	207
Chapter 9.	E-Health Liability	251
Chapter 10.	FDA Regulation of E-Health Technology and Services	287
Chapter 11.	Obligations in Response to a Health Care Data Security Breach	315
Chapter 12.	Due Diligence in E-Health Transactions	343
Chapter 13.	Contracts in the Digital Age: Adapting to Changing Times	377
Chapter 14.	Evaluating Antitrust Concerns in the Electronic Marketplace	425
Chapter 15.	The Intersection of Health Law and Intellectual Property Law	455
Chapter 16.	Allocation and Mitigation of Liability	547

Chapter 17.	Discovery and Admission of Electronic Information as Evidence...	597
Chapter 18.	Legal Ethics and E-Health	621
Appendix A:	**Internet Health Sites**	657
Appendix B:	**Government Agencies**	681
Appendix C:	**E-Health Glossary**	695
Appendix D:	**Health Insurance Portability and Accountability Act (HIPAA) Glossary**	717
Appendix E:	**Documenting the Deal [Forms]**	767
Appendix F:	**Selected HIPAA Materials**....................................	827
Table of Cases		829
Index		839

Detailed Table of Contents

Foreword vii
Preface ix
About the Contributors xiii
Summary Table of Contents xxv

Chapter 1. **The E-Health Explosion—An Analysis of Legal and Market Trends** 1

    I. Introduction 1
   II. What Is E-Health? 2
  III. Growth of the E-Health Industry 3
       A. E-Health Product Developments 4
           1. Wireless Medical Devices and Mobile Applications 4
           2. Social Media 6
           3. Cloud Computing 7
       B. Corporate Transactions 8
           1. Government and Venture Capital Investment in E-Health Innovation 8
           2. Recent E-Health Merger and Acquisition Activity 10
       C. Other Government Support 12
  IV. Privacy Concerns and Enforcement 15
   V. Conclusion 17

Chapter 2. **E-Health Industry Overview** 19

    I. Introduction to E-Health 19
   II. The E-Health Industry 21
       A. Traditional Health Care Delivery Model 21
       B. E-Health's Underlying Technology 23
       C. Participants in E-Health Industry 23
           1. Web Site Operators 23
           2. Providers 24
           3. Internet Pharmacies 25
           4. Vendors of Health Information Technology 26
       D. E-Health Business Industry Models 27
       E. State of Electronic Health Records Adoption 28

	F.	Improvement for E-Health..	29
	G.	Challenges Confronting E-Health..	30
III.	Government Role in E-Health..		30
	A.	HITECH Act and Health Care Reform...	30
	B.	EHR, E-Prescribing Incentives, and Key Regulations...................	33
	C.	Government Role as a Payor..	35
IV.	E-Health Improvement to Health Care Delivery.................................		36
V.	Conclusion		41

Chapter 3.   Health Information Technology.. 43

I.	Introduction...	43
II.	Government Health Information Technology Initiatives	44
III.	Development of Standards for Electronic Health Records	46
	A. Standards Development for Electronic Health Records	46
	B. Barriers to Adoption of Electronic Health Records.......................	50
IV.	Health Information Exchanges	51
	A. Implementation of RHIOs	52
	B. Lessons Learned From Early RHIO Efforts	53
	C. RHIO Technology Providers Are Fragmented..............................	56
V.	Accountable Care Organizations	56
VI.	Analysis of Health Care Data to Support Improvements and Comparative Effectiveness...	57
	A. Data Aggregation for Analysis..	57
	B. Issues With Aggregation	58
	C. Interoperability and the Aggregation of Data	59
	D. Risks of Electronic Health Care Data..	60
VII.	Conclusions..	61

Chapter 4.   Privacy, PHRs, and Social Media 63

I.	Introduction...	64
II.	What Is a Personal Health Record?	64
III.	Background..	65
	A. Paradigm Shift to Electronic Health Records	65
	B. Market Forces Spurring the Use of Electronic Personal Health Records	67
	C. Web 2.0—What Is Social Media?..	67
IV.	Types of PHRs	69
	A. Untethered Versus Tethered	69
	B. Attributes of PHRs...	70
	C. PHRs Distinguished From EMRs and EHRs.................................	70
V.	Unique Risks Associated With Internet-Based PHRs	72
VI.	Federal Privacy and Breach Notification Protections of PHRs............	73
	A. Privacy Statutes...	73
	1. HIPAA Entities	73
	2. Privacy Protection for Non-HIPAA Vendor Information.........	74
	B. Security/Breach Notification	76
	1. HIPAA Breach Notification Rule	76
	a. What Is a Breach?...	76
	b. Did the Breach Cause Threshold Harm?....................	77
	c. To Whom Must the Breach Be Reported, and When?......	77
	d. Enforcement	78

		2.	HITECH Health Breach Notification Rule for Non-HIPAA Vendors	78
			a. What Is a Reportable Breach?	79
			b. To Whom Must the Breach Be Reported, and When?	79
			i. Vendors	79
			ii. Individuals	79
			iii. Media Outlets	79
			iv. Federal Trade Commission	79
			v. Third-Party Service Providers	80
	C.	Content of Notice of Disclosure		80
	D.	Dual Reporting Obligations under HIPAA Breach Notification Rule and Health Breach Notification Rule		81
	E.	Enforcement		81
VII.	State Privacy Statutes			81
	A.	Confidentiality of Patient Medical Records		81
	B.	State Breach Notification Statutes		82
VIII.	Conclusion and Recommendations			82

Chapter 5. Privacy Issues in U.S. Health Care 85

I.	Introduction			86
	A.	Privacy Laws and Standards—Domestic and International		86
II.	Federal Privacy Protections			88
	A.	U.S. Constitution		89
		1. Fourteenth Amendment		89
		2. *Whalen v. Roe*		89
		3. Scope of Constitutional Protection		89
	B.	Statutes and Regulations		90
		1. Protection of Specified Health Information		90
			a. Freedom of Information Act	90
			b. Confidentiality of Records	90
			c. Medicare/Medicaid Conditions of Participation	91
		2. Protection of Specified Groups		92
			a. Children's Online Privacy Protection Act of 1998	92
			b. Human Subjects in Research	93
			c. Public Health Service Act	93
		3. Protection of Specific Segments of the Health Care Industry		94
			a. Privacy Act of 1974	94
			b. Gramm-Leach-Bliley Act	94
			c. Health Insurance Portability and Accountability Act of 1996—Privacy Regulations	95
			i. Individual Rights	97
			ii. Required and Permitted Uses and Disclosures	101
			iii. "Minimum Necessary" Standard	102
			iv. De-Identified Information and Limited Data Sets	103
			v. Business Associates and Business Associate Agreements	104
			vi. Enforcement	106
			vii. Conflicts With State Law	106
			d. Health Information Technology for Economic and Clinical Health (HITECH) Act	107
			i. Summary of Subtitles A, B, and C	107

			ii.	Subtitle D—Amendments to HIPAA's Privacy Rule	110
				(a) Definitions	110
				(b) Breach and Notification of Breach	111
				(c) Business Associates and Business Associate Agreements	113
				(d) Changes to Individual Rights Granted Under HIPAA's Privacy Rule	115
				(e) Changes to Marketing and Fundraising Provisions	116
				(f) Prohibition on the Sale or Marketing of EHRs and PHI	117
				(g) Improved Enforcement	118

III. State Privacy Protections 119
    A. Model Privacy Laws 119
        1. Health Information Privacy Model Act 120
        2. Uniform Health Care Information Act 120
    B. State Laws and Regulations 120
        1. Common Privacy Protections 121
            a. Consents and Authorizations 121
            b. Individual's Right of Access 121
            c. Individual's Cause of Action for Unauthorized Disclosures 122
        2. Common Disclosure Restrictions and Their Effects 122
            a. What Type of Entity Is Disclosing? 123
            b. What Type of Health Information Is to Be Disclosed? 123
            c. Mandatory Versus Permitted Disclosures 124

IV. Professional Organizations and Groups 125
    A. Professional Organizations 125
        1. American Medical Association 125
        2. American Hospital Association 125
        3. JCAHO/Joint Commission on Accreditation of Healthcare Organizations 126
    B. Other Privacy Protection Guidelines 126

V. Conclusion 126

Chapter 6. The European Data Privacy Regime 127

I. Introduction 128
    A. European Union Legislation 129
    B. The Importance of National Laws 130
    C. National Regulators and the Article 29 Working Party 131

II. Key Concepts 132
    A. Personal Data 132
    B. Processing 133
    C. Data Controller and Data Processors 134

III. Jurisdiction 134
    A. EEA Establishment 134
    B. Non-EEA Established Entities 135

IV. The European Data Protection Principles 136
    A. Fair and Lawful Processing 136
    B. Particular Conditions for Sensitive Personal Data 137
    C. Valid Consent and Explicit Consent 139

	D. Data Subject Rights	140
	E. Data Security	141
V.	Appointing a Data Processor	142
VI.	Export of Personal Data Outside the EEA	143
	A. Adequate Level of Protection	144
	1. European Commission Findings of Adequacy	144
	2. U.S. Safe Harbor	144
	B. Adequate Safeguards	145
	1. Model Clauses	145
	2. Binding Corporate Rules	146
	C. Exceptions to the General Prohibition	147
	D. Personal Data Export Flow Chart	149
VII.	Administrative Requirements	150
VIII.	The E-Privacy Directive	151
IX.	On the Horizon	153
X.	Consumer Laws and Other Relevant Laws	155

Chapter 7. Information Security and Breach Notification Under HIPAAA and HITECH 157

I.	Introduction	158
II.	HIPAA Security Requirements	158
	A. Information Security Program Development and Management	162
	1. Confidentiality	164
	2. Integrity and Availability	164
	3. Accountability	164
	4. Balancing the Objectives	165
	B. Implementing HIPAA Security Safeguards	167
	C. HIPAA Security Investigations	167
	D. HIPAA Security Violation Penalty Risks	170
	E. Business Associates and Business Associate Contracts Under the Security Rule	172
III.	HITECH Amendments to HIPAA: Security Implications	174
IV.	HITECH Security Breach Requirements	177
V.	State Security Breach Notification Legislation	179
	A. The Economic Logic of Information Security Breach Disclosure	180
	B. A Brief History of Information Security Breach Notification Laws	181
	C. Analysis of a Representative Information Security Breach Notification Law	183
	1. The Problem of Encryption	184
	2. The Complexities of Notification	185
	3. The Scope of Regulation	187
	D. State Security Breach Notification Laws as of August 2011	189
Appendix 7-A: Sample HITECH/HIPAA Security Gap Analysis Checklist		191

Chapter 8. Enforcement of the Health Insurance Portability and Accountability Act of 1996 207

I.	Introduction	208
II.	Key HIPAA Features	210
	A. Standards and Requirements	210

		B.	Guidance	214
		C.	Violations	214
	III.	Investigations, Breach Reports, and Audits		215
		A.	Complaint Process and Compliance Reviews	216
		B.	Breach Reports	217
		C.	HHS Audits of HIPAA Compliance	218
		D.	Voluntary Compliance and Resolution Agreements	219
	IV.	HIPAA Civil Monetary Penalties		220
		A.	In General	220
		B.	The Enforcement Rule	222
		C.	CMP Limitations and Lenience Provisions	222
		D.	What Is a "Violation"?	224
		E.	Industry-Wide HIPAA Compliance	226
		F.	Procedures for Imposition of Civil Monetary Penalties	227
		G.	Distinctive Features in the Imposition of Civil Monetary Penalties	229
			1. Imposition of Penalties	229
			2. Public Notice	230
			3. Statistical Sampling	230
			4. Liability for Violations by Agents	230
			5. Aggravating and Mitigating Factors	231
		H.	Actions by State Attorneys General	233
	V.	HIPAA Criminal Provisions		234
		A.	In General	234
		B.	Intent Standard	236
		C.	Aiding and Abetting	239
		D.	Conspiracy	239
		E.	Other Potential Theories of Indirect Criminal Liability of Business Associates	240
		F.	Statute of Limitations	240
	VI.	Enforcement Under Other Federal Statutes		241
		A.	Federal Trade Commission Act	241
		B.	False Claims and False Statements Statutes	242
		C.	Mail and Wire Fraud	243
		D.	RICO	244
		E.	HIPAA as a Standard of Care	244
	VII.	State-Law Preemption		245
	VIII.	Compliance: Establishing a Plan to Avoid Enforcement Actions		247
	IX.	Conclusion		249

Chapter 9. E-Health Liability 251

I.	Introduction		252
II.	Professional Licensure and Credentialing		254
	A.	Licensure Generally	254
	B.	Penalties for Violating Licensure Laws	257
	C.	Pharmacogenetics	259
	D.	Public Health Emergencies	260
	E.	Practice of Telemedicine Without Full Licensure	261
		1. The Consultation Exception	261
		2. Endorsement	262
		3. Reciprocity	262
		4. Special License	263

		5. Telehealth Networks	263
	F.	Credentialing	264
III.	Initiatives Regarding Regulation of Telemedicine		264
	A.	Joint Working Group on Telemedicine	265
	B.	Federation of State Medical Boards	266
	C.	Nurse Licensure Compact	267
IV.	Malpractice		268
	A.	Existence of Physician-Patient Relationship	268
	B.	What Is the Legal Duty?	271
	C.	Informed Consent and the Duty to Disclose	272
	D.	Vicarious Liability	274
	E.	Patient Abandonment	275
	F.	Availability of Insurance for Telemedicine Encounters	276
		1. Malpractice Insurance and Gaps in Coverage	276
		2. Disclaimers of Liability	277
		3. What Malpractice Does Cover	277
		a. "Specified-Risk" or "Specified-Perils" Coverage	277
		b. "All-Risk" or "Open-Perils" Coverage	277
		c. Recommendation	278
V.	International Practice of Medicine		278
	A.	Telemedicine	278
	B.	Medical Tourism	278
	C.	Medicaid and Medicare Reimbursement	279
	D.	International Legal and Licensing Issues	280
VI.	Electronic Health Information		281
	A.	Physician-Patient Relationship	282
	B.	Standard of Care	283
	C.	Certifications	283
	D.	Liability	284
VII.	Conclusion		286

Chapter 10. FDA Regulation of E-Health Technology and Services 287

I.	Introduction		288
II.	FDA Regulation of Online Activities		289
	A.	Internet Drug Sales	289
		1. FDA Enforcement Activities	290
		2. Consumer Education	290
	B.	Online Direct-to-Consumer Advertising	291
		1. Sponsored Links	291
		2. DTC Promotion of Genetic Testing Services	292
III.	FDA and Electronic Health Records		293
	A.	FDA Authority to Regulate EHR	293
	B.	ONC Regulation of EHR	294
	C.	Increased Scrutiny and Oversight of EHR Systems	294
		1. FDA Working Group	294
		2. Legislative Inquiries	295
	D.	FDA and ONC Collaboration	295
		1. HIT Policy Committee Recommendation	296
		2. Concerns	296
		3. Future Collaboration	296
IV.	FDA Regulation of Telemedicine		297
	A.	What Is Telemedicine?	297

	B.	mHealth Technologies	298
	C.	FDA Regulation of Mobile Medical Devices	299
		1. Overview	299
		2. "Intended Use" of Mobile Medical Devices	299
		a. "Accessory" and "Component" Devices	300
		b. Regulatory Class	300
	D.	Why Regulate Telemedicine?	301
		1. Safety Concerns	301
		2. Legislative Interest	301
		3. Industry Growth	302
	E.	The FDA and Telemedicine in the Early 2000s	302
		1. Early Guidance	303
		2. Further Guidance Documents	303
	F.	Recent Developments in FDA Telemedicine Regulation	304
	G.	FDA Final Rule on Medical Device Data Systems	304
		1. Exclusion of EHR	305
		2. Uncertain Applications	305
	H.	Draft Guidance: Mobile Medical Applications	306
		1. Scope	306
		2. Classification of Mobile Platforms and Applications	306
		3. Definition of Mobile Application "Manufacturer"	307
	I.	Future Direction of Telemedicine Regulation	307
	J.	Possible Collaboration with the Federal Communications Commission	309
V.	The Sentinel Initiative		309
	A.	Structure and Objective of the Initiative	310
	B.	Current Status and Future Plans	311
	C.	Privacy and Security Concerns	312

Chapter 11. Obligations in Response to a Health Care Data Security Breach 315

I.	Introduction		316
II.	Breach Defined		318
III.	Risk Assessment		320
	A.	Nature of Breach	321
	B.	Identity of Any Known Recipient	323
	C.	Mitigating Actions	323
	D.	Covered Entity Obligations When Risk of Individual Harm is Small	324
IV.	Exceptions to the Definition of Breach		325
	A.	Good-Faith Disclosures Within the Scope of Employment	325
	B.	Inadvertent Disclosures by Otherwise Authorized Individuals	326
	C.	Information Disclosed Not Reasonably Retained	328
	D.	Disclosures of the Limited Data Set Excluding Certain Identifiers	329
V.	Identity of Breaching Party		330
	A.	Obligations for Covered Entities When Multiple Entities Transfer PHI and/or Breach Security Requirements	330
	B.	Business Associate Requirements	331
VI.	Notification Requirements		335
	A.	Timing Requirements	335

		B.	Method of Providing Notice	336
		C.	Contents of Notice	338
	VII.	Potential Liabilities Created by the HITECH Act		339
		A.	Civil Penalties	340
		B.	Criminal Penalties	341
	VIII.	Conclusion		342

Chapter 12. Due Diligence in E-Health Transactions 343

	I.	Introduction		344
	II.	The Nature of Due Diligence and Its Purposes		345
	III.	Standard for Due Diligence Review		347
	IV.	Composition of the Due Diligence Team		348
	V.	Procedure for the Due Diligence Review		349
		A.	Planning	349
		B.	Confidentiality Agreements	350
		C.	Checklists	350
		D.	Location	351
		E.	Reporting the Results	352
	VI.	Contents of the Due Diligence Review		353
		A.	Disclosure Controls	354
		B.	Internal Controls	354
		C.	Audit Committee Activities	355
		D.	Code of Ethics	356
		E.	Off-Balance-Sheet Transactions	356
		F.	Implications of Sarbanes-Oxley for the Due Diligence Review	356
		G.	Certification of EHR Products	357
		H.	Data Security and Privacy	357
	VII.	Focus of the Due Diligence Review		358
		A.	Assets	359
		B.	Liability	360
		C.	Agreements	363
		D.	Capabilities and Liabilities	364
		E.	Interviews	364
	VIII.	Common Pitfalls in Due Diligence		365
	IX.	Understanding Health Care Entities and Operations		366
		A.	Tax-Exempt Status	367
		B.	Accreditation and Certification Issues	368
		C.	Protected Health Care Information	368
		D.	Health Planning Approvals	369
		E.	Conditions for Reimbursement	370
		F.	Research or Grant Considerations	370
		G.	Obligations to Provide Notice	370
	X.	Laws and Regulations Specific to the Health Care Industry		370
	XI.	Conclusion		376

Chapter 13. Contracts in the Digital Age: Adapting to Changing Times 377

	I.	Introduction	378
	II.	Jurisdiction	380
	III.	The Relevant Statutes and Principles of Contract Law	385

A.	Electronic Signatures in Global and National Commerce Act (E-SIGN)	386
B.	Uniform Electronic Transactions Act (UETA)	389
C.	Uniform Computer Information Transactions Act (UCITA)	394
IV. Litigation: Courts Coping With a New Means of Contracting		398
A.	Browse Wrap Agreements	400
B.	Click Wrap Agreements	403
C.	Shrink Wrap Agreements	405
D.	Common Principles	408
V. HIPAA/HITECH Business Associate Agreements		408
A.	Introduction	408
B.	Statutory and Regulatory Requirements	410
	1. Business Associate	410
	2. HITECH Mandated Changes to Privacy Rule	413
	a. Minimum Necessary	414
	b. Logging and Auditing	415
	c. Restricted Disclosures	415
	d. Fundraising and Marketing	416
	e. Access to Patient Record	418
	f. Role of State Law	418
	3. HITECH Mandated Changes to Security Rule	418
	a. Administrative Safeguards	419
	b. Physical Safeguards	419
	c. Technical Safeguards	419
	d. Breach Reporting Requirement	420
	e. Additional Responsibilities	423
	f. Monetary Penalties	423
VI. Conclusion		424

Chapter 14. Evaluating Antitrust Concerns in the Electronic Marketplace 425

I. Introduction		426
A.	Electronic Marketplaces	426
B.	Overview of Antitrust Law	426
C.	Antitrust Issues in the E-Commerce Setting	429
II. Collaborations With Competitors		430
A.	Guidance	430
B.	Market Definition	431
C.	Facilitating Collusion	432
	1. Inherent Risks of Sharing Information	432
	2. Controlling the Risks	433
	3. Heightened Standard for Circumstantial Evidence	436
D.	Group Boycott	436
E.	Group Purchasing and Sales	437
	1. Traditional Analysis	437
	2. New Issues Created by the Electronic Marketplace	438
III. Legal Analysis of Vertical Integration Issues		439
A.	Competitor Control of Vertically Related Entity	439
B.	Practical Limitations of the Theory	441
IV. Exclusionary Practices		443
A.	Network Effects	443
B.	Exclusive Use Requirements	444

		C. Most-Favored-Nation Requirements	445
V.	Standards and Certification..		447
	A.	Significance to Electronic Health Care...	447
	B.	Historical Analysis...	448
	C.	Health Care Experience With Private Standard-Setting	450
VI.	Conclusion		452

Chapter 15. The Intersection of Health Law and Intellectual Property Law 455

I.	Introduction...				458
II.	Federal Acts and Agencies				459
	A.	HIPAA			459
		1.	Background...		459
		2.	Privacy and Security Rules		460
		3.	Identifier Standards..		460
		4.	TCS Standards		460
		5.	Enforcement Rule		461
	B	HITECH Act			461
		1.	Background...		461
		2.	Health Information Technology Standards...................		462
		3.	Incentive Payments		462
		4.	Strengthened Privacy Rules and Breach Notification....		463
		5.	Strengthened Penalties...		463
	C.	Standards for Privacy of Individually Identifiable Health Information			464
		1.	Background...		464
		2.	What Is Protected		464
		3.	Who Is Subject to the Privacy Rule		465
		4.	Disclosures of PHI..		466
			a. Required Disclosures...		466
			b. Permissible Disclosures for Public Health, Law Enforcement, and Oversight Purposes		467
			c. Disclosures for Research Purposes...................		467
			d. Disclosures for Marketing Purposes..................		468
			e. Minimum Necessary Requirement.....................		468
		5.	Administrative Safeguards of the Privacy Rule		469
	D.	The Hatch-Waxman Act...			469
		1.	Introduction		469
		2.	Abbreviated New Drug Application		470
		3.	Generic Drugs and Patent Infringement		471
		4.	Safe Harbor..		472
		5.	Patent Term Extension and Market Exclusivity for Pioneer Drug Companies...		472
III.	Copyrights and Health Law				473
	A.	What Is a Copyright?...			473
	B.	Exclusive Rights of Copyright Ownership			474
	C.	Derivative Works and Substantial Similarity			474
	D.	Obtaining a Copyright			475
	E.	Duration of Copyrights			475
	F.	Berne Convention			476
	G.	Section 117 of the Copyright Act: Computer Programs			476

H.	Medical Materials and Copyright Law	476
	1. Protection for Medical Documents and Images	477
	2. European and U.S. Database Protection	477
I.	Proprietary Databases and Copyright	478

IV. Impact of Computer-Related Legislation on Medical Record Privacy 478
    A. Computer Privacy Acts 478
    B. Health Insurance Portability and Accountability Act 479
    C. Computer Fraud and Abuse Act 480
    D. Digital Millennium Copyright Act 482
    E. Other Relevant Computer Privacy Acts 485
        1. Electronic Communications Privacy Act 485
        2. Semiconductor Chip Protection Act 485
        3. Children's Online Privacy Protection Act 486

V. Medical Codes and How They Affect Privacy 486
    A. HCPCS/CPT 487
    B. ICD-9-CM 489
    C. DRG 490
    D. Medical Codes and the Re-identification Problem 491

VI. Trademark—Protecting Indicia of Ownership 493
    A. Trademarks in General and Identification With a Source of Goods 493
        1. What Can Be Trademarked? 494
        2. Trademark Remedies 495
        3. Trademark Laws 496
        4. Dilution 496
    B. How Are Trademarks Used? 499
        1. Purple Gloves 499
        2. How Trademarks Can Protect a Surgical Product or Medicine 500
        3. The Aspirin Story 500
    C. Domain Names 501
        1. Protect Domain Name 501
        2. Secure Domain Name 501

VII. Patents and Patent Law for the Health Attorney 502
    A. Patent Drafting, Patent Prosecution, and Patent Rights and Enforcement 503
        1. The Parts of a Patent Application 503
        2. Patent Prosecution 506
        3. Patent Rights and Enforcement 506
    B. The Patent Statutes in Detail and Some Commonly Misunderstood Concepts of Patent Law 507
        1. The Four Requirements for Obtaining a Patent: "Idea" Versus "Invention" 507
        2. Section 112, First Paragraph: Written Description and Enablement 507
        3. Section 101: Statutory Class of the Invention 508
        4. Section 102: Novelty Versus Originality 509
        5. Unobviousness and Invalidity 510
    C. Bringing a Product to Market 512
        1. Freedom to Operate 512
        2. Filing and Acquiring Patents 514

		D.	Nuances in the Medical Field	516
			1. Enablement Requirements for Claiming Multiple Configurations of Drugs and Materials	516
			2. HIPAA Regulations and Patent Claim Strategy	519
VIII.	Trade Secrets—Protecting Essential Information			521
	A.	Sources of Trade Secret Law		522
	B.	Uniform Trade Secrets Act		522
	C.	Establishing Ownership of a Trade Secret		523
		1. The Nature of the Information		523
		2. Preserving Secrecy		523
		3. Proper and Improper Means of Acquisition of a Trade Secret		524
IX.	Preliminary Transactional Agreements and Proprietary Rights			524
	A.	Modern Applications in the Health Care Industry		524
		1. Protected Health Information and Electronic Health Records		525
			a. Health Services Contracting	525
			i. Software Vendors	527
			ii. Warranties in Technology Transfers	528
			iii. Regulatory Compliance Covenants	528
			iv. Foreign Contractors	529
			b. Health Research	529
			c. Health Information Exchange and State Practices	530
			d. ACOs and Data Sharing	531
		2. Proprietary Rights in Product Development		531
			a. Collaboration Agreements	531
			b. Trade Secrets	532
	B.	Suggested Drafting Provisions for the Creation of Effective Nondisclosure Agreements		533
		1. Access to Confidential Information		533
		2. Restricted Use of Confidential Information		534
		3. Nondisclosure of Confidential Information		534
		4. Nonsolicitation of Customers and Employees		534
		5. Reservation of Proprietary Rights		534
X.	Managing Exposure to Intellectual Property Litigation			534
	A.	Due Diligence		535
		1. Identifying Potential Rights Holders		535
		2. Identifying the Scope of Existing Rights		536
		3. Determining How to Proceed: Licenses, Workarounds, and Declaratory Relief		536
	B.	Strategic Intellectual Property Acquisitions		538
		1. Strategic Intellectual Property Filings		538
		2. Cross-Licensing Agreements and Patent Pools		539
	C.	Corporate Policies and Employee Education		540
		1. Policies for Existing Employees and Independent Contractors		540
		2. Policies Addressing Concerns Relating to Nonemployees		542
		3. Ensuring Policies Are Properly Implemented		543
	D.	Minimizing Exposure to Unavoidable Intellectual Property Litigation		543
		1. Insurance		544
		2. Industry and Government Outreach		544

		3.	Alternative Dispute Resolution...	545
	E.	Conclusion		546

Chapter 16. Allocation and Mitigation of Liability.................................. 547

- I. Introduction... 548
- II. Category-Based Risks 549
  - A. E-Content Providers... 549
    - 1. Consumer-Oriented E-Content Providers........................... 549
      - a. Unauthorized Use of Copyrighted Material 550
      - b. Unauthorized Use of a Trademark or Service Mark......... 553
      - c. Liability for Erroneous Information/Defamation 557
      - d. Unlicensed/Unauthorized Practice of Medicine............... 562
    - 2. Provider-Oriented E-Content Providers 563
  - B. E-Product Providers.. 564
    - 1. Consumer-Oriented E-Product Providers............................. 564
      - a. E-Prescribing Risks 565
      - b. Privacy and Data Security Issues—Excluding HIPAA 568
        - i. State Data Breach Notification Statutes 569
        - ii. PCI Data Security Standard 569
        - iii. Federal Trade Commission Section 5 Actions 570
        - iv. The Red Flags Rule... 572
    - 2. Provider/Business-Oriented E-Product Providers 573
      - a. Employee Access to Health Insurance Accounts 573
      - b. Provider Publication Tools 574
  - C. E-Connection Providers.. 574
    - 1. Unauthorized Use of Copyrighted Material 574
    - 2. Unauthorized Use of Trademark/Service Mark...................... 575
    - 3. Infringement of Proprietary Rights in Technology.................. 575
    - 4. Privacy and Data Security... 576
    - 5. Liability for Erroneous Information/Defamation 576
  - D. E-Care Providers... 577
    - 1. Unlicensed/Unauthorized Practice of Medicine...................... 577
    - 2. Malpractice 578
    - 3. Technology Performance Issues 578
    - 4. Privacy and Data Security... 579
    - 5. FDA Regulation of Telemedicine 579
  - E. EHR System Providers 580
    - 1. Privacy and Data Security—HIPAA and HITECH 580
    - 2. Medicare and Medicaid Incentive Programs and Achievement of Meaningful Use 582
    - 3. Allocation of Rights and Obligations Among HIE Participants 583
- III. Allocation and Mitigation of Risk 585
  - A. The Risk: Unauthorized Use of Copyrighted Material.................... 585
    - 1. Before a Claim Occurs—Mitigation.. 585
    - 2. Before a Claim Occurs—Allocation 586
    - 3. When a Claim Occurs—Mitigation.. 587
  - B. The Risk: Unauthorized Use of a Trademark or Service Mark 588
    - 1. Before a Claim Occurs—Mitigation.. 588
    - 2. Before a Claim Occurs—Allocation 588
    - 3. After a Claim Occurs—Mitigation 589

C. The Risk: Publication of Erroneous or Defamatory Information 590
    1. Before a Claim Occurs—Mitigation 590
    2. Before a Claim Occurs—Allocation 590
    3. When a Claim Occurs—Mitigation 590
D. The Risk: Unlicensed or Unauthorized Practice of Medicine 591
    1. Before a Claim Occurs—Mitigation 591
    2. Before a Claim Occurs—Allocation 592
E. The Risk: E-Prescribing and Malpractice 592
    1. Before a Claim Occurs—Mitigation 592
    2. Before a Claim Occurs—Allocation 593
F. The Risk: Privacy and Data Security Compliance 593
    1. Before a Claim Occurs—Mitigation 593
    2. Before a Claim Occurs—Allocation 594
    3. When a Claim Occurs—Mitigation 595

Chapter 17. Discovery and Admission of Electronic Information as Evidence 597

I. Introduction 597
II. Background of the Development of Rules and Standards for Electronic Evidence 598
III. Technology Implications for Electronic Evidence: An Electronic Medical Record Information Ecosystem 601
IV. The 2006 Amendments to the Federal Rules of Civil Procedure 604
  A. Spoliation and the Obligation to Preserve ESI 606
  B. Production of ESI 608
  C. Inadvertent Disclosure of Privileged or Protected Health Information 610
V. Admission of ESI 611
VI. Special Problems 614
  A. Electronic Signatures and Electronic Medical Records 614
  B. Electronic Health Records and Health Information Exchange 618

Chapter 18. Legal Ethics and E-Health 621

I. Introduction 623
II. Use of Technology in the Practice of Health Law 623
  A. Attorney E-Competence in Managing Technology 623
    1. Confidentiality and Privacy of Electronic Information 624
      a. Misdirected Facsimiles or E-Mail 624
      b. Managing Compliance with HIPAA and the HITECH Act 624
    2. Security of Electronic Information 625
      a. Back Up 625
      b. Viruses 625
      c. Internet E-Mail and Encryption 625
        i. Duty of Confidentiality 626
        ii. Waiver of Attorney-Client Privilege 626
        iii. Malpractice Liability 627
        iv. HITECH Act Violations 627
      d. Hardware Risks 627
        i. Hard Drive or Remote Disk Drive Use 627

			ii. Deleting Data	628
		e.	E-Mailed Documents	628
		f.	Other Issues	628
	3.	E-Discovery		628
		a.	Scope of Discovery	629
		b.	Ethical Requirements	629
		c.	Social Media and Professional Communications	629
			i. Ethical Considerations	630
			ii. Admissibility	630
			iii. Special Issues	630
	4.	Electronic Filings		630
		a	Affecting the Practice of Law	630
		b.	Affecting Health Care Laws	630
	5.	Use of Cellular Phones, PDAs, and Other Devices		631
	6.	Cloud Computing		631
B.	Ethical Issues with Technology Use			631
	1.	Web Sites.		631
	2.	Social Media		632
		a.	Blogs	632
		b.	Wiki Pages	633
		c.	Facebook	633
		d.	Myspace and LinkedIn	634
		e.	Twitter	634
		f.	Use of Social Media by Attorneys—Use Caution	635
	3.	Corporate Family Conflict Issues		635
C.	Other Ethical Considerations			635
	1.	Solicitation of Business.		635
	2.	Researching Potential Jurors or Witnesses		636
	3.	Ex Parte Communications		637

III. Knowledge of Client Misconduct 637
   A. Attorney-Client Privilege 639
   B. Ethics Rules on Confidentiality 640

	1.	Confidentiality.		640
	2.	Assisting a Client's Crime or Fraud		640
	3.	Audits and Investigations		641
		a.	Hiring Consultants	642
		b.	Crime/Fraud Exception to the Attorney-Client Privilege	642
	4.	Representing the Organization		642
		a.	"Climbing the Corporate Ladder"	642
		b.	Preventing Misunderstandings About Who Represents Whom	643
		c.	Causing a Constituent to Be Fired	643

IV. Conflicts of Interest 643
   A. Joint Representation 644

1.	Model Rule 2.2.	644
2.	Model Rule 2.2 and the Ethics 2000 Commission	644
3.	Restatement	645
4.	Joint Confidences and the Ethics 2000 Commission	645
5.	Recommendation	645
6.	Joint Representation in Commercial Negotiations	646
7.	"Unintentional" Joint Representation	647

		8. Litigation and Joint Representation	648
	B.	Close Corporations	649
	C.	Partnerships and Limited Partnerships	651
		1. General Partnerships	651
		2. Limited Partnerships	652
	D.	Conflicts and Malpractice Liability	653

Appendices 655

Appendix A:	**Internet Health Sites**	657
Appendix B:	**Government Agencies**	681
Appendix C:	**E-Health Glossary**	695
Appendix D:	**Health Insurance Portability and Accountability Act (HIPAA) Glossary**	717
Appendix E:	**Documenting the Deal [Forms]**	767

E-1 HIPAA Business Associate Agreement Forms 769

    E-1.1 Business Associate Agreement [HIPAA Administrative Simplification Subtitle]: General Form 769

    E-1.2 Business Associate Agreement [HIPAA Administrative Simplification Subtitle]: Addendum 779

E-2 Resolution Agreement 783

    E-2.1 Example of Resolution Agreement and Corrective Action Plan (Without External Monitoring) 787

    E-2.2 Example of Resolution Agreement and Corrective Action Plan (With External Monitoring) 803

Appendix F:	**Selected HIPAA Materials**	827

F-1 HHS, Security and Electronic Signature Standards; Proposed Rule, 63 Fed. Reg. 43,242 (Aug. 12, 1998) .... (on CD only)

F-2 HHS, Office of Civil Rights, Guidance on Risk Analysis Requirements Under the HIPAA Security Rule (July 14, 2010) .... (on CD only)

F-3 HHS, Educational Materials for State Attorney General Educational Event on Enforcement of Health Privacy Laws, etc. (2011) .... (on CD only)

Table of Cases 829

Index 839

1

The E-Health Explosion—An Analysis of Legal and Market Trends*

I.	Introduction	1
II.	What Is E-Health?	2
III.	Growth of the E-Health Industry	3
	A. E-Health Product Developments	4
	1. Wireless Medical Devices and Mobile Applications	4
	2. Social Media	6
	3. Cloud Computing	7
	B. Corporate Transactions	8
	1. Government and Venture Capital Investment in E-Health Innovation	8
	2. Recent E-Health Merger and Acquisition Activity	10
	C. Other Government Support	12
IV.	Privacy Concerns and Enforcement	15
V.	Conclusion	17

I. Introduction

Spurred by both government support and private innovation, e-health is entering a new frontier. This technological evolution of health care promises efficiencies and savings that will benefit patients, doctors, and insurance companies alike. Of course, with such rapid growth into uncharted territory come ethical, legal, and financial risks, as well as particular privacy and security issues. The remaining chapters of this book highlight these risks and recommend ways to comply with applicable regulations and avoid common pitfalls in this nascent industry. This chapter provides a snapshot of the legal and market trends in the

---

*Drew Gantt, Cooley LLP, Washington, D.C., and Adrienne Belyea, Cooley LLP, Reston, Virginia.

industry, focusing on recent developments that may provide a glimpse of the direction of the industry in years to come.

II. WHAT IS E-HEALTH?

As discussed in Chapter 2, many experts in the health care industry have grappled with defining "e-health."[1] The Department of Health and Human Services (HHS) defines e-health as "the use of digital information and communication technologies to improve people's health and health care."[2] E-health generally melds health care and technology, and traditional e-health products and services include electronic health records, electronic prescribing capabilities, electronic medical devices, and telemedicine services. Newer e-health modalities include smart phones, tablet computers, other mobile media devices, and the cloud.

An electronic health record (EHR) is an electronic version of a patient's medical history that is maintained by the provider over time, and may include all of the key administrative clinical data relevant to that person's care under a particular provider, including demographics, progress notes, problems, medications, vital signs, past medical history, immunizations, laboratory data, and radiology reports.[3] The EHR automates access to information and has the potential to streamline the clinician's workflow.[4] The EHR also has the ability to support other care-related activities directly or indirectly through various interfaces, including evidence-based decision support, quality management, and outcomes reporting.[5]

Electronic prescribing, or e-prescribing, is a prescriber's ability to electronically send an accurate, error-free, and understandable prescription directly to a pharmacy from the point of care.[6] As discussed in Chapter 10,[7] electronic medical devices are products that fall within the FDA's definition of a medical device largely based on the "intended use" of the product. Electronic medical devices include home health monitoring equipment such as wireless blood pressure monitors and weight scales. These devices also play an active role in telemedicine. Telemedicine and telehealth both describe the use of medical information exchanged from one site to another via electronic communications to improve patients' health status.[8] Telemedicine sometimes is associated with

---

[1] See Chapter 2 (Healey, E-Health Industry Overview).

[2] U.S. Dep't of Health & Human Servs., Health Communication, *Health Literacy & e-health* (Oct. 6, 2011), *available at* http://www.health.gov/communication/ehealth/.

[3] U.S. Dep't of Health & Human Servs., Centers for Medicare & Medicaid Servs., Electronic Health Records: Overview (June 13, 2011), *available at* https://www.cms.gov/ehealthrecords/. See also Chapter 3 (Healey, Health Information Technology).

[4] *Electronic Health Records: Overview.*

[5] *Id.*

[6] Centers for Medicare & Medicaid Servs., E-Prescribing: Overview (June 13, 2011), *available at* https://www.cms.gov/eprescribing/.

[7] See Chapter 10 (Hass, FDA Regulation of E-Health Technology and Services).

[8] *See* American Telemedicine Ass'n, Telemedicine Technology Summit, Telemedicine/Telehealth Terminology, *available at* http://www.americantelemed.org/files/public/about telemedicine/Terminology.pdf.

direct patient clinical services, and telehealth sometimes is associated with a broader definition of remote health care and is often perceived to be more focused on other health related services.[9]

With the widespread use of smart phones and tablet computers, e-health has expanded into the world of social media and mobile applications, ranging from applications that help people with home disease monitoring of chronic diseases such as diabetes[10] to applications that keep soon-to-be parents informed about their pregnancy progress and allow sharing the experience with friends, family, and an online community of mothers.[11] The breadth of e-health products will undoubtedly continue to expand for so long as the industry enjoys the government advocacy and private funding described below.

III. Growth of the E-Health Industry

The annual health care spending of the United States reached around $2.6 trillion in 2010, and is expected to soar to $3.4 trillion by 2015.[12] The rising cost of health care is a problem that continues to affect both the public and private sectors, and e-health undoubtedly represents a part of the solution. The variety of e-health products and services can reduce the costs of health care in a number of ways. In an article published by Healthcare IT News, Jamie Thompson highlighted the five following ways e-health will reduce the cost of health care:

- *Improving standards of care.* Analyzing outcomes data collected by electronic health records can lead to identifying the best treatment methods, leading to a healthier population.
- *Increasing patient involvement and collaboration.* America's health expenditure is in a large part due to chronic health issues, many of which can be mitigated through better lifestyle choices. Health information technology (IT) can provide disease management and wellness solutions to address these issues. EHR data could also be useful in determining ways to stem costs associated with chronic illness.
- *Putting information at the forefront.* The health care industry is constantly changing, which results in an overwhelming amount of information to distill and absorb. E-health offers a way to bring critical information to the forefront.
- *Focusing on outcomes.* Electronic clinical data provides an opportunity to replace the volume-based, fee-for-service business model with one that is evidence based and focused on quality.
- *Transparency to the patient.* E-health should be used as a tool to include the patient in his or her own care. One expert states, "Our current system of financing health care leaves patients completely insulated from

---

[9] *See id.*

[10] *See, e.g.,* CareLogger, *available at* http://carelogger.com/.

[11] *See, e.g.,* Baby Bump, *available at* http://babybump.alt12.com/community/groups.

[12] Veronica Franco, *E-Health Market to Grow 13% Annually Through 2015*, Market Research.com (Sept. 6, 2011), *available at* http://www.marketwire.com/press-release/e-health-market-to-grow-13-annually-through-2015-1557266.htm.

the cost of their care. Until we find a means for patients to educate themselves and question services, quality and price, the market forces that can naturally contain rising healthcare costs will never have an opportunity to work."[13]

These benefits, among many others, have led the e-health market to evolve as one of the fastest growing U.S. industries, even in recent difficult economic times.[14] The widespread adoption of e-health products and services will open market opportunities for the health care sector, which is poised to grow at a compound annual growth rate (CAGR) of around 13 percent during the period 2010–2015.[15] The sections below briefly describe a sample of recent e-health product developments, commercial transactions illustrating the burgeoning e-health market, and the latest measures of executive and legislative support that incentivize the implementation of e-health measures.

A. E-Health Product Developments

1. *Wireless Medical Devices and Mobile Applications*

Although e-health products are still a budding industry, a new wave of such products has appeared in the market that take advantage of the popular advancements in the technology sphere, such as mobile applications, social media, and cloud computing. An estimated 40 million medical devices currently include Bluetooth, the wireless technology that allows many of our mobile devices to communicate with each other.[16] In a June 2011 press release from the Bluetooth Special Interest Group (SIG), it was announced that medical devices would be the first to use the new Bluetooth 4.0 technology, featuring lower power and higher speed transmission.[17] Specifically, the Bluetooth SIG approved a Health Thermometer Profile and a Heart Rate Profile as the first mobile health profiles built on Bluetooth 4.0.[18]

In addition to wireless medical devices, the increasing adoption of smartphones and tablet computers during the past few years has also led to growth in mobile health applications. More than 72 percent of physicians were reported to be smartphone users, and mobile health applications embedded in smartphones were a significant reason for this increased usage.[19] For example, as of October 1, 2011, the Department of Veterans Affairs (VA) allows its employees

---

[13]Jamie Thompson, *Five Ways Health IT will Reduce Cost of Care*, HEALTHCARE IT NEWS (Feb. 10, 2011), *available at* http://healthcareitnews.com/news/five-ways-health-it-will-reduce-cost-care.

[14]Franco, *E-Health Market to Grow 13% Annually Through 2015*.

[15]*Id.*

[16]Scott Jung, *Bluetooth 4.0 Adds Special Support for Medical Devices*, MEDGADGET (June 9, 2011), *available at* http://medgadget.com/2011/06/bluetooth-4-0-adds-special-support-for-medical-devices.html.

[17]Press Release, Bluetooth Special Interest Group, *Mobile Health Device Manufacturers Ramp Up New Products Using Bluetooth Technology Version 4.0* (June 7, 2011), *available at* http://www.bluetooth.com/Pages/Press-Releases-Detail.aspx?ItemID=131.

[18]*Id.*

[19]*Id.*

and clinicians in its hospitals to use their iPhones and iPads.[20] The portability, flexible computing power, and connectivity of smartphones enables less expensive designs for home health devices, and several companies are entering the market.[21]

The FDA in 2011 approved a device created by Withings (a French consumer electronics company) that is a simple cuff that plugs directly into an Apple, Inc., iPod, iPad, or iTouch device, using an application available in the app store. The free app reads the wearer's blood pressure and heart rate and then sends the data to a doctor or synchronizes directly with electronic medical record systems like Microsoft HealthVault.[22] Remote medical monitoring could save the U.S. nearly $200 billion in health costs over 25 years, according to a 2009 study.[23] That is, in part, because devices like the cuff let people relay frequent medical data to health care providers to track problems before they get serious and require more drastic interventions. However, the success of these devices depends on the patient's consistent and compliant use of the application. Surveys have shown that 74 percent of people who confirm use of mobile health apps drop out by the tenth use.[24] A startup spun out of the MIT Media Lab, Ginger.io, aimed to avoid this issue with its DailyData app, which automatically collects data from mobile phones to warn users and their physicians that they may be on the verge of a manic episode or a bout of debilitating illness.[25] Other mobile apps, designed for physicians, include the Handyscope, from FotoFinder, which turns an iPhone into a digital dermascope helping doctors diagnose skin disease, and the LifeLens, still in the prototype stage, which lets doctors diagnose malaria in the field from a blood sample. The VA and Department of Defense (DOD) jointly created a free application, PTSD Coach, which enables users to track symptoms of post traumatic stress disorder (PTSD), find local support sources, individualize strategies for managing PTSD, and get anonymous assistance.[26]

The explosion of mobile health apps caught the eye of federal regulators early in 2011, and in July 2011, the Food and Drug Administration (FDA) released its first guidelines related to mobile health applications, targeting mobile apps that are similar to medical devices.[27] Specifically, the guidelines suggested

---

[20] Mary Mosquera, *Info Security Is Critical When VA Allows iPhone, iPad*, GOVERNMENT HEALTH IT (July 28, 2011), *available at* http://www.govhealthit.com/news/info-security-critical-when-va-allows-iphone-ipad.

[21] Peter Ferenczi, *Iphone Blood Pressure Cuff Gets FDA Approval*, MOBILEDIA (June 21, 2011), *available at* http://www.mobiledia.com/news/94750.html.

[22] *Id.*; *see also* Withings.com, Blood Pressure Monitor, *available at* http://www.withings.com/en/bloodpressuremonitor.

[23] Ferenczi, *Iphone Blood Pressure Cuff Gets FDA Approval*.

[24] *Do Patients Really Use Smartphone Health Apps?*, GOVERNMENT HEALTH IT (Apr. 27, 2011), *available at* http://govhealthit.com/news/do-patients-really-use-smartphone-health-apps.

[25] Emily Singer, *An App That Looks for Signs of Sickness*, TECHNOLOGY REVIEW (June 21, 2011), *available at* http://www.technologyreview.com/biomedicine/37866/?nlid=4631.

[26] Tom Sullivan, *Smartphone PTSD App from VA, DOD "Coaches" Vets*, GOVERNMENT HEALTH IT (Apr. 20, 2011), *available at* http://www.govhealthit.com/news/smartphone-ptsd-app-va-dod-coaches-vets.

[27] Steven Overly, *FDA Moves to Regulate Mobile Health Applications*, WASHINGTON POST (July 19, 2011), *available at* http://www.washingtonpost.com/business/capitalbusiness/fda-moves-to-regulate-mobile-health-applications/2011/07/18/gIQApwLdNI_story.html.

that three types of applications require FDA approval: a mobile application that acts as an accessory to a regulated medical device, turns a mobile gadget into such a device, or makes suggestions regarding a patient's diagnosis or treatment.[28] Chapter 10 provides more information regarding the FDA's regulation of e-health products.[29]

2. Social Media

As further discussed in Chapter 4, the health care industry is continuing to utilize the benefits of social media.[30] Examples include patient community sites like patientslikeme.com® that has the following "Promise" on its Web site: "PatientsLikeMe is committed to putting patients first. We do this by providing a better, more effective way for you to share your real-world health experiences in order to help yourself, other patients like you and organizations that focus on your conditions."[31] Hospitals and academic medical centers are also diving into the social media mix with more than 300 YouTube channels and 500 Twitter accounts.[32]

The Mayo Clinic Center for Social Media, which boasts the most popular medical provider channel on YouTube and more than 175,000 "followers" on Twitter, as well as an active Facebook page with over 50,000 connections, celebrated its first anniversary in August 2011.[33] The Center's mission is to improve health globally by accelerating effective application of social media tools throughout Mayo Clinic and spurring broader and deeper engagement in social media by hospitals, medical professionals, and patients.[34] A recent study of a rare heart disease brought this mission to life. Cardiologists at the Mayo Clinic were able to track down patient participants for a study of spontaneous coronary artery dissection through WomenHeart, a patient-run social media site.[35] Dr. Sharonne Hayes stated that it was a novel way to track down patients who are notoriously hard to reach.[36]

The federal government also began encouraging its employees to take advantage of the benefits of social media. In 2011, the VA released a policy promoting the use of social media by employees "to enhance communication, stakeholder outreach collaboration, and information exchange; streamline processes;

---

[28] *Id.*

[29] See Chapter 10 (Haas & Greig, FDA Regulation of E-Health Technology and Services).

[30] See Chapter 4 (Tector & Shapiro, Privacy, PHRs, and Social Media).

[31] *See* Patients Like Me, *available at* http://www.patientslikeme.com/about.

[32] John Sharp, *Social Media in Healthcare: Barriers and Future Trends*, iHEALTH BEAT (May 6, 2010), *available at* http://www.ihealthbeat.org/perspectives/2010/social-media-in-health-care-barriers-and-future-trends.aspx#ixzz1Z5Kfa0mv.

[33] Mayo Clinic Center for Social Media, Background, *available at* http://socialmedia.mayoclinic.org/about-3/home/.

[34] Mayo Clinic Center for Social Media, About, *available at* http://socialmedia.mayoclinic.org/about-3/.

[35] Elizabeth Armstrong Moore, *How Social Media Helps Us Study Rare Diseases*, CNET NEWS (Aug. 30, 2011), *available at* http://news.cnet.com/8301-27083_3-20099540-247/how-social-media-helps-us-study-rare-diseases/.

[36] *Id.*

and foster productivity improvements."[37] In addition, HHS challenged developers to create an application that uses Facebook to better prepare individuals for disasters. The winning app of the "Lifeline Facebook App Challenge" will enable a Facebook user to invite three Facebook friends to become "lifelines," points of contact who agree to act as a source of support during disasters.[38]

Social media is here to stay in health care. Patient engagement, tactical use of social media within organizational marketing and communications efforts, and online patient communities will continue to thrive, and medical research will hopefully progress even more with increased use of social media by health care providers.[39]

3. Cloud Computing

Where is all the data that is transferred through wireless medical devices, mobile health apps, and social media stored? According to the Federal Cloud Computing Strategy released by former U.S. Chief Information Officer Vivek Kundra in February 2011, it should be in the cloud. The Strategy sets forth the "Cloud First" policy, which requires all federal agencies to evaluate cloud computing options before making any further IT investments. "Cloud computing" is a model for enabling ubiquitous, convenient, on-demand network access to a shared pool of configurable computing resources (e.g., networks, servers, storage, applications, and services) that can be rapidly provisioned and released with minimal management effort or service provider interaction.[40] The Strategy states that one quarter of federal IT spending will be dedicated to migrating to cloud computing solutions to enable the government to be more efficient, agile, and innovative.[41] The General Services Administration (GSA) has estimated that cloud computing will save the GSA alone $2 billion per year.[42]

Health care IT professionals in the commercial sector agree with Kundra: the benefits and cost savings that the cloud offers currently appear to outweigh the security and privacy risks inherent in health care data storage. Nearly one-third of health care sector decision makers said they are using cloud applications, and 73 percent said they are planning to move more applications to the

---

[37]Tom Sullivan, *VA Tells Its Own to Interact with the Public via Blogs, Facebook, Twitter*, GOVERNMENT HEALTH IT (Aug. 16, 2011), *available at* http://govhealthit.com/news/va-tells-its-own-interact-public-blogs-facebook-twitter.

[38]Mary Mosquera, *HHS Seeks Facebook App for Disaster Preparedness*, GOVERNMENT HEALTH IT (Aug. 10, 2011), *available at* http://govhealthit.com/news/hhs-wants-facebook-app-disaster-preparedness.

[39]John Sharp, *Social Media in Healthcare: Barriers and Future Trends*, iHEALTH BEAT (May 6, 2010), *available at* http://www.ihealthbeat.org/perspectives/2010/social-media-in-health-care-barriers-and-future-trends.aspx#ixzz1Z5Kfa0mv.

[40]U.S. Dep't of Commerce, National Institute of Standards and Technology, Definition of Cloud Computing, *available at* http://csrc.nist.gov/publications/drafts/800-145/Draft-SP-800-145_cloud-definition.pdf.

[41]VIVEK KUNDRA, U.S. CHIEF INFORMATION OFFICER, FEDERAL CLOUD COMPUTING STRATEGY (Feb. 8, 2011), *available at* http://www.cio.gov/documents/Federal-Cloud-Computing-Strategy.pdf.

[42]Bob Violino, *Cloud Computing Thunders into the Government*, GOVERNMENT HEALTH IT (June 2, 2011) *available at* http://govhealthit.com/news/cloud-computing-thunders-government?page=0,0.

cloud, according to a recent report by Accenture.⁴³ Many of those reasons boil down to cost advantages and flexibility that cloud computing offers health care organizations, especially as they implement plans to meet the federal government's $20 billion-plus HITECH financial incentive programs for the meaningful use of IT. Put simply, the cloud makes it much easier and less costly to store large quantities of health care data. An Accenture expert stated that cloud models—in which third parties host applications, storage, and access to computing power via the Web—provide "economies of scale," often giving 2 to 10 times the cost advantages of other computing models, which would otherwise require health care providers to host servers on site or hire in-house technical support to keep systems running.⁴⁴

B. Corporate Transactions

1. Government and Venture Capital Investment in E-Health Innovation

The current rate of innovation in e-health products and services, the increasing use of social media and cloud computing, which lower the costs of health IT, and the government incentives discussed in this section have made e-health an industry ripe with investors, even in tough economic times. The number of health care technology financing transactions doubled from 2005 to 2010.⁴⁵ A number of seed accelerator programs have emerged, such as Rock Health and Healthbox, organized by venture capital funds anxious to provide financing to the next big e-health start-up.

The federal government also has directly invested in e-health companies by issuing grants or contracts. For example, the Agency for Healthcare Research and Quality (AHRQ), a division of HHS, invested more than $300 million in contracts and grants to over 200 communities, hospitals, providers, and health care systems in 48 states to promote access to and encourage the adoption of health IT.⁴⁶ AHRQ stated that these projects constitute a real-world laboratory for examining health IT at work and aim to achieve the following: (1) help clinicians provide higher quality, safer health care; (2) put the patient at the center of health care; (3) stimulate the implementation of health IT, especially in rural and underserved areas; (4) identify the most successful approaches and barriers to health IT implementation; and (5) make the business case for health IT by evaluating costs and benefits.⁴⁷ The Health Information Exchange Challenge Grant Program, administered by the Office of the National Coordinator for Health IT (ONC), also awarded over $16 million in new grants to encourage breakthrough

---

⁴³Marianne Kolbasuk McGee, *Healthcare Taking Computing to the Cloud*, INFORMATION WEEK (June 21, 2010), *available at* http://www.informationweek.com/news/healthcare/interoperability/225700843.

⁴⁴*Id.*

⁴⁵Rock Health, Rock Report: State of Digital Health (Aug. 1, 2011), *available at* http://www.slideshare.net/RockHealth/rock-report-state-of-digital-health.

⁴⁶Agency for Healthcare Research and Quality, About, *available at* http://healthit.ahrq.gov/portal/server.pt/community/about/562.

⁴⁷*Id.*

innovations for health information exchange that can be leveraged widely to support nationwide health information exchange and interoperability.[48]

There are also various contests sponsored by both public and private organizations to stimulate further innovation. These include HHS's i2 program, conducted under the America Competes Reauthorization Act of 2010. The goal of i2 is "supporting innovations in research and encouraging health IT development through open-innovation mechanisms like prizes and challenges," the agency said in a news release.[49] HHS awarded nearly $5 million to the Capital Consulting Corp. of Rockville, Md., and to Health 2.0 LLC of San Francisco to fund application development projects supporting specific health IT goals.[50] In June 2011, U.S. Chief Technology Officer Aneesh Chopra announced StartUp Health, a strategic initiative designed to improve access to capital, education, and resources for health and wellness entrepreneurs. The goal of StartUp Health is to help entrepreneurs create, fund, and build sustainable health and wellness companies by improving access to (1) long-term support, guidance, and mentoring; (2) data, technology, tools, and other required resources; (3) sector-specific investors and stage-appropriate capital; (4) a collaborative community of like-minded people and organizations; and (5) a talent pool of people dedicated to meaningful innovation in health and wellness.[51]

At the May 2011 IBM SmartCamp in Austin, Texas, which connects start-up firms with venture capitalists and industry leaders to provide coaching and support, three of the five finalists focused on empowering patient-driven health care.[52] Also, the second annual DC to VC: HIT Startup Showcase, a nationwide contest to find the best startup ideas in health IT, was held in September 2011. The 10 winners presented their ideas to influential health IT venture capital funds and angel investors. New events, such as the National E-Health Innovation Series, which bring together e-health entrepreneurs to further accelerate our nation's progress toward efficient health care technologies are frequently being announced.[53]

---

[48] U.S. Dep't of Health & Human Servs., Office of the National Coordinator of Health IT, Health Information Exchange Challenge Grant Program, *available at* http://healthit.hhs.gov/portal/server.pt?open=512&mode=2&objID=3378.

[49] Alice Lipowicz, *HHS Kicks Off $5Million "i2" Health IP App Development Program*, WASHINGTON TECHNOLOGY (July 11, 2011), *available at* http://washingtontechnology.com/articles/2011/07/11/hhs-kicks-off-5m-i2-health-it-app-development-program.aspx.

[50] *Id.*

[51] Molly Merrill, *Startup Health Initiative Launches to Spur Innovation*, GOVERNMENT HEALTH IT (June 13, 2011), *available at* http://govhealthit.com/news/startup-health-initiative-launched-spur-innovation.

[52] Mike Miliard, *VC Opportunities for an "Explosion of Bright Young Companies,"* HEALTHCARE IT NEWS (May 18, 2011), *available at* http://www.healthcareitnews.com/news/vc-opportunities-explosion-bright-young-companies.

[53] *See* MedCity Hospitals, Health IT Innovators and Providers Collide at eHealth Summits (Sept. 8, 2011), *available at* http://www.medcitynews.com/2011/09/health-it-innovators-and-providers-collide-at-ehealth-summits/?edition=hospitals.

2. Recent E-Health Merger and Acquisition Activity

Mergers and acquisitions in the health care industry[54] surged in the second quarter of 2011, setting a pace to break all previous records in the sector as measured by dollars, according to Irving Levin Associates, Inc., based in Norwalk, Connecticut.[55] In the second quarter of 2011, a total of $73.5 billion was spent to finance 243 mergers and acquisitions (M&A) in the health care industry, up 44 percent from the $51.1 billion spent in the first quarter of 2011, and up 61 percent from the $45.7 billion spent in the second quarter of 2010.[56] E-health accounted for $639 million of the mergers and acquisitions in the second quarter.[57] However, in August 2011 alone, 11 deals worth a combined $4.0 billion were posted in the e-health market, accounting for 42 percent of the $9.5 billion spent in the entire health care M&A market to finance 67 deals.[58] The largest deal of August 2011 for both e-health and the entire health care industry was The Blackstone Group's proposed $3.0 billion leveraged buy-out of Emdeon, Inc.[59] Based in Nashville, Tennessee, Emdeon provides revenue and payment cycle management solutions that connect payors, providers, and patients. The company's software is used to manage patient lists and claims, among other functions. Another significant transaction is General Dynamics IT's acquisition of Vangent Holding, which closed September 30, 2011.[60] For the nearly $1 billion ticket, GDIT obtained Vangent, its 7,500 employees, and a line-up of products including electronic health records, data analytics, health informatics, and business process outsourcing solutions. In short, e-health is big business, and a number of big players are entering the market.[61]

In February 2010, Microsoft supplemented its Healthcare Solutions sector with the purchase of Sentillion Inc., a privately held company specializing in software for the health care industry. Microsoft's press release regarding the acquisition stated, "Microsoft will add Sentillion's technologies to its portfolio of health solutions to make it easier for doctors and nurses worldwide to deliver better patient care by streamlining access to multiple health IT applications and data."[62] In the same month, IBM expanded its health care IT offerings with the

---

[54] See generally Chapter 12 (House & Guenthner, Due Diligence in E-Health Transactions).

[55] John Commins, *Healthcare M&A Activity Hits Record Pace*, HEALTHLEADERS MEDIA (July 18, 2011), *available at* http://www.healthleadersmedia.com/content/LED-268639/Healthcare-MA-Activity-Hits-Record-Pace.html.

[56] *Id.*

[57] *Id.*

[58] Irvin Levin Associates, Inc., *e-Health Posts Strong Numbers—11 Deals Worth $4.0 Billion*, HEALTHCARE M&A MONTHLY (Sept. 2011), *available at* http://www.levinassociates.com/1109mamhead.

[59] *Id.* The Blackstone Group's designation on the New York Stock Exchange (NYSE) is "BX." The NYSE designation for Emdeon is "EM."

[60] Tom Sullivan, *General Dynamics Scoops Up Vangent With an Eye on Health IT*, GOVERNMENT HEALTH IT (Aug. 16, 2011), *available at* http://govhealthit.com/news/general-dynamics-scoops-vangent-eye-health-it. *See also* Jeff Clabaugh, *General Dynamics Completes Vangent Acquisition*, WASHINGTON BUS. J. (Sept. 30, 2011), *available at* http://www.bizjournals.com/washington/news/2011/09/30/general-dynamics-complete-vangent.html.

[61] *Id.*

[62] Press Release, *Microsoft Corp., Microsoft Completes Acquisition of Healthcare Provider Sentillion* (Feb. 2, 2010), *available at* http://www.microsoft.com/presspass/press/2010/feb10/02-02sentillionpr.mspx.

purchase of Initiate Systems, a market leader in data integrity software for information sharing among health care and government organizations.[63] Initiate's software helps health care clients work more intelligently and efficiently with timely access to patient and clinical data. It also enables governments to share information across multiple agencies to better serve citizens. IBM's slogan for its health care solutions is "Smarter Healthcare," and IBM messaging states, "To build a smarter system, healthcare solutions need to be instrumented, interconnected and intelligent." In April 2010, Oracle acquired Phase Forward, the leader in the e-clinical data management market, having as much as 70 percent market share, including as many as 15 out of 20 of the top pharma and biotech companies, for $685 million.[64]

With the flurry of acquisition activity and involvement of giant corporations in the emerging e-health industry, antitrust concerns are top of mind. Chapter 14 evaluates the particular antitrust concerns in the e-health industry, focusing on the regulatory aspects of both the e-commerce market and the health care industry.[65] However, simultaneously with the consolidation and innovation in the e-health market, some large corporations such as Thomson Reuters and Google have decided to exit the market. In June 2011, Thomson Reuters announced that it would sell its health care unit, which had $450 million in revenues in 2010.[66] Thomson's announcement surprised many in the industry, because the market is booming and some even postulated that the complexity and immaturity of the market is what led Thomson to exit,[67] but Thomson publicly stated that was opting to focus on its other sectors. Thomson released the following statement: "While a growing and profitable unit, our Healthcare business lacks the integration with and global scale of our other units, and our disciplined approach to capital allocation convinced us that the expected proceeds from a sale into a consolidating market could be better applied elsewhere in our portfolio."[68] Later in the same month, Google announced the retirement of its Google Health product, effective January 1, 2012. Google Health allowed users to, among other things, create a personal health record to organize, track, and monitor their health information. Google ended the service due to slow public adoption of the initiative, stating,

> Now, with a few years of experience, we've observed that Google Health is not having the broad impact that we hoped it would. There has been adoption among certain groups of users like tech-savvy patients and their caregivers, and more recently fitness and wellness enthusiasts. But we haven't found a way to translate

---

[63]Press Release, *IBM, IBM to Acquire Initiate Systems* (Feb. 3, 2010), *available at* http://www-03.ibm.com/press/us/en/pressrelease/29305.wss.

[64]Ahsan Awan, *Health IT M&A: Impact of Oracle Acquisition of Phase Forward*, SACRAMENTO PRESS (Apr. 19, 2010), *available at* http://www.sacramentopress.com/headline/25072/Health_IT_MA_Impact_of_Oracle_Acquisition_of_Phase_Forward.

[65]See Chapter 14 (Wagner, Evaluating Antitrust Concerns in the Electronic Marketplace).

[66]Press Release, *Thomson Reuters, Thomson Reuters to Sell Its Healthcare Business*, REUTERS (June 6, 2011), *available at* http://www.reuters.com/article/2011/06/06/idUS184504+06-Jun-2011+HUG20110606.

[67]John Moore, *Additional Thoughts on Thomson Reuters*, CHILMARK RESEARCH (June 13, 2011), *available at* http://chilmarkresearch.com/2011/06/13/additional-thoughts-on-thomson-reuters/.

[68]*Thomson Reuters to Sell Its Healthcare Business*.

that limited usage into widespread adoption in the daily health routines of millions of people.[69]

Although the market is growing at a rapid pace, uncertainty looms regarding the viability of the e-health market due to consumers' apprehension about adopting e-health products and services. As discussed above, if widely adopted by all players in the industry, the innovations developed by the private sector will fundamentally change the way health care is provided. The business world has demonstrated its interest in the market, even in these poor economic times. With that interest and with the government support described in the next section, it is to be hoped that consumers will gain confidence in e-health innovations and that uncertainty will disappear.

C. Other Government Support

In addition to the government-sponsored innovation initiatives described in the previous section, many more traditional federal government measures aim to balance the endless possibilities that e-health products and services offer regarding cost savings and improved care with the protection of patient privacy and maintenance of quality health care. This additional federal government support of the emerging e-health industry ranges from executive proclamations to legislation and even leading by example through a number of VA initiatives.

The Health Information Technology for Economic and Clinical Health Act (HITECH Act), enacted as part of the American Recovery and Reinvestment Act of 2009 (ARRA), was signed into law on February 17, 2009, to promote the adoption and meaningful use of health information technology.[70] The HITECH Act established Medicare and Medicaid EHR Incentive Programs that provide incentive payments to eligible professionals, eligible hospitals, and critical access hospitals as they adopt, implement, upgrade, or demonstrate "meaningful use" of certified EHR technology.[71] "Meaningful use" includes the use of EHR technology (1) in a meaningful manner, such as e-prescribing; (2) for electronic exchange of health information to improve quality of health care, and (3) to submit clinical quality and other measures. Simply put, "meaningful use" means providers need to show they are using certified EHR technology in ways that can be measured significantly in quality and in quantity.[72] By October 2011, the ONC had certified more than 1,100 complete EHR and EHR modules.[73]

Physicians may receive $18,000 if they qualify in 2011 or 2012 and up to a total of $44,000 through 2015 if they continue to qualify. Hospitals begin with base payments of $2 million a year through 2015 if they qualify. The HHS

---

[69]*An Update on Google Health and Google Power Meter*, GOOGLE BLOG (June 24, 2011), *available at* http://googleblog.blogspot.com/2011/06/update-on-google-health-and-google.html.

[70]HITECH, div. A, tit. XIII, and div. B, tit. IV, Pub. L. No. 111-005, 123 Stat. 115, 226–79, 467–96 (2009), §§13301 *et seq.*

[71]*Id.*

[72]Centers for Medicare & Medicaid Servs., EHR Incentive Programs, CMS EHR Meaningful Use Overview, *available at* https://www.cms.gov/EHRIncentivePrograms/30_Meaningful_Use.asp#BOOKMARK1.

[73]The Office of National Coordinator for Health IT, Certified Health IT Product List, *available at* http://onc-chpl.force.com/ehrcert/CHPLHome.

Centers for Medicare and Medicaid Services (CMS) launched the attestation process on April 18, 2011, through which eligible professionals, eligible hospitals, and critical access hospitals will have to demonstrate meaningful use through CMS' Web-based registration and attestation system and legally *attest* that they have successfully demonstrated meaningful use. As of August 31, 2011, over 90,650 physicians and hospitals have completed the CMS attestation process and over $264 million incentive payments have been distributed.[74] Therefore, it seems clear that HHS, through the ONC and CMS, is making strides towards achieving the mission of HITECH. In fact, a recent survey found that 64 percent of all physicians consider meaningful use incentives one of the strongest drivers to implement EHR.[75]

Despite the incentives of the meaningful use programs, the cost, physician practice size, and lack of technical resources still present barriers for small health care providers in adopting electronic health records.[76] In an effort to assist small health care providers with the challenges of adopting EHR, the ONC offers a number of other programs, including the extension program, that (1) provides training and support services to assist doctors and other providers in adopting EHRs, (2) offers information and guidance to help with EHR implementation, and (3) gives technical assistance as needed.[77] The ONC established over 60 regional extension centers. Also, the Beacon Community Cooperative Agreement Program provides funding to 17 selected communities throughout the United States that have already made inroads in the development of secure, private, and accurate systems of EHR adoption and health information exchange.[78] The Beacon Program will support these communities to build and strengthen their health information technology infrastructure and exchange capabilities to improve care coordination, increase the quality of care, and slow the growth of health care spending.[79] Therefore, it appears that for the momentum of EHR adoption in both large hospitals and small health care providers to progress, the federal government will need to continue to offer hands-on assistance like the extension programs and Beacon Communities in addition to financial incentives.

The government support for adoption of e-health measures and further innovation in the industry also came directly from the White House. President Obama proclaimed September 11–September 17, 2011, to be National Health

---

[74]Centers for Medicare & Medicaid Servs., EHR Incentive Programs, Spotlight and Upcoming Events, *available at* http://www.cms.gov/EHRIncentivePrograms/50_Spotlight.asp#TopOfPage.

[75]*Survey: Meaningful Use Driving Physicians to Adopt Electronic Health Records*, iHEALTH BEAT (Aug. 9, 2011), *available at* http://www.ihealthbeat.org/articles/2011/8/9/survey-meaningful-use-driving-physicians-to-adopt-ehealth-records.aspx.

[76]Mary Mosquera, *Despite Incentives, Cost is a Barrier to Small Provider EHR Use*, GOVERNMENT HEALTH IT (June 2, 2011), *available at* http://govhealthit.com/news/congressional-panel-explores-barriers-small-provider-ehr-use.

[77]U.S. Dep't of Health & Human Servs., Office of the National Coordinator of Health IT, Regional Extension Program, *available at* http://healthit.hhs.gov/portal/server.pt?open=512&objID=1495&parentname=CommunityPage&parentid=58&mode=2&in_hi_userid=11113&cached=true.

[78]*Id.*

[79]U.S. Dep't of Health & Human Servs., Office of the National Coordinator of Health IT, Beacon Program, *available at* http://healthit.hhs.gov/portal/server.pt?open=512&objID=1805&parentname=CommunityPage&parentid=2&mode=2&cached=true.

Information Technology Week.[80] The proclamation stated, "I urge all Americans to learn more about the benefits of Health IT by visiting HealthIT.gov, take action to increase adoption and meaningful use of Health IT, and utilize the information Health IT provides to improve the quality, safety, and cost effectiveness of health care in the United States."[81]

The government was doing more than just talking about e-health. Innovative e-health measures were adopted to provide health care to the members of the American armed forces and veterans. For example, the Air Force instituted a digital dental radiography system that can transmit digital x rays across 80 Air Force dental clinics treating active duty and Air Reserve and Air National Guard personnel worldwide.[82] This technology assists the military's overall need for force readiness and compliance with the DOD's 2006 standard that at least 65 percent of all service members must be orally healthy.[83] Because dental problems are one of the top causes of non-battle-related disease that troops have in the field and require significant resources to address the problem, the Army and Navy each planned to roll out similar digital dental radiography systems in the short term.[84]

In addition, the VA fervently supports telehealth measures. A group of VA researchers found that using telehealth services to monitor intensive care unit (ICU) patients could reduce mortality rates by 20 percent and decrease length of stay by nearly 1.3 days.[85] The VA budget for telehealth doubled from 2009 to 2010, and in April 2011, the VA awarded $1.38 billion in telehealth contracts to six vendors.[86] Also, similar to HHS's i2 program, described in III.B.1., above, the VA administers the VA Innovation Initiative (VAi2), which

> invites employees, private sector companies, entrepreneurs, and academic leaders to contribute their best ideas for innovations that increase Veterans' access to VA services, improve the quality of services delivered, enhance the performance of VA operations, and reduce or control the cost of delivering those services that Veterans and their families receive.[87]

---

[80] Press Release, The White House, *President Proclamation: National Health Information Technology Week* (Sept. 12, 2011), *available at* http://www.whitehouse.gov/the-press-office/2011/09/12/presidential-proclamation-national-health-information-technology-week.

[81] *Id.*

[82] Heather B. Hayes, *Military Dental Records Going Digital*, GOVERNMENT HEALTH IT (Jan. 1, 2011), *available at* http://govhealthit.com/news/military-dental-records-going-digital-0.

[83] U.S. Dep't of Defense, Memorandum—Policy on Oral Health and Readiness (Jan. 9, 2006), *available at* http://www.health.mil/libraries/HA_Policies_and_Guidelines/06-001.pdf.

[84] Hayes, *Military Dental Records Going Digital.*

[85] Sara Jackson, *Telehealth Prevents ICU Deaths, Research Shows*, FIERCE MOBILE HEALTHCARE (Apr. 5, 2011), *available at* http://www.fiercemobilehealthcare.com/story/telehealth-prevents-icu-deaths-research-shows/2011-04-05.

[86] Sara Jackson, *VA Awards $1.38 Billion in Telehealth Contracts*, FIERCE MOBILE HEALTHCARE (Apr. 14, 2011), *available at* http://www.fiercemobilehealthcare.com/story/va-awards-138-billion-telehealth-contracts-six-contractors/2011-04-14.

[87] U.S. Dep't of Veterans Affairs, vai2 Innovation Initiative, About, *available at* http://www.va.gov/vai2/About_Home.asp.

IV. PRIVACY CONCERNS AND ENFORCEMENT

Even with the exciting innovation and strong public and private sector incentives and support in the United States, the adoption of e-health measures, particularly EHR, by doctors, patients, and payors in Europe is four times higher than the adoption rate in the United States.[88] This slow adoption rate could be due to a variety of factors, which certainly include a general resistance to change (especially among less tech-savvy individuals) and privacy concerns.[89] This section highlights, and the rest of this book further analyzes, additional legal concerns applicable to the e-health industry and the ways in which the government tries to balance the potential improvement to health care efficiency and cost savings that e-health initiatives offer with patient privacy and safety.

Health care information undeniably encompasses some of the most private information about individuals, so people naturally are wary of adopting a system whereby that information is so easily transmitted. Patient trust in e-health technology is an important key that will further open the health care industry to the benefits of e-health.[90] Privacy is important to regulators as well. As discussed further in Chapters 5 and 7, the government has instituted a number of regulations to protect health-related information and to require those that collect such information to keep it secure.[91]

As discussed in III.C., above, the HITECH Act was enacted on February 17, 2009, to promote the adoption and meaningful use of e-health technology. Legislators realized that in order to promote the adoption of e-health, they must also include regulations regarding privacy and security to provide patients with adequate comfort regarding their personal information. Therefore, the HITECH Act broadened the penalties applicable to violations of the privacy and security provisions of Health Information Portability and Accountability Act (HIPAA). For example, the Act created (1) four categories of violations that reflect increasing levels of culpability, (2) four corresponding tiers of penalty amounts that significantly increase the minimum penalty amount for each violation, and (3) a maximum penalty amount of $1.5 million for all violations of an identical provision in any one year.[92] HITECH also removed the previous bar on the

---

[88] Mary Mosquera, *US, Europe will Cooperate on EHR Exchange Standards*, GOVERNMENT HEALTH IT (Dec. 21, 2010), *available at* http://govhealthit.com/news/us-europe-will-cooperate-ehr-exchange-standards.

[89] *See* John Przybys, *Internet Personal Health Record Services Slow to Catch On*, LAS VEGAS REVIEW J. (Sept. 18, 2011), *available at* http://www.lvrj.com/health/internet-personal-health-record-services-slow-to-catch-on-130098668.html?ref=668; Lucas Mearian, *Consumers Remain Wary of Personal Health Records*, COMPUTERWORLD (Apr. 21, 2011), *available at* http://www.computerworld.com/s/article/9215996/Consumers_remain_wary_of_personal_health_records?taxonomyId=17.

[90] Mary Mosquera, *Consumer Confidence about Health Data Safety is Key EHR Adoption*, GOVERNMENT HEALTH IT (June 14, 2011), *available at* http://govhealthit.com/news/consumer-confidence-about-health-data-safety-key-ehr-adoption.

[91] See Chapter 5 (Dahm, Privacy Issues in U.S. Health Care); Chapter 7 (Christiansen, Information Security and Security Breach Notification Under HIPAA and HITECH).

[92] U.S. Dep't of Health & Human Servs., Health Information Privacy, HIPAA Administrative Simplification Statute and Rules, *available at* http://www.hhs.gov/ocr/privacy/hipaa/administrative/enforcementrule/hitechenforcementifr.html.

imposition of penalties if the covered entity did not know and with the exercise of reasonable diligence would not have known of the violation.[93]

Chapter 8 delves deeply into the enforcement of HIPAA and the potential penalties.[94] Soon after the enactment of the HITECH Act, HHS's Office of Civil Rights (OCR) stepped up enforcement activity. As of June 6, 2011, HHS published reports of 281 breaches affecting 10.4 million in total.[95] HHS issued its first civil monetary penalty in February 2011 under the HIPAA Privacy Rule since that rule took effect in 2003 when it issued Cignet Health of Temple Hills, Maryland, a $4.3 million fine for denying patients access to their records and subsequently refusing to cooperate with investigations.[96] Two days later, HHS settled potential privacy violations with Massachusetts General Hospital, which agreed to pay the U.S. government $1 million and establish more stringent policies and procedures to safeguard the privacy of its patients.[97] Also, in one of the first criminal cases involving federal medical privacy laws, a researcher at UCLA Health System in Los Angeles pled guilty to four counts of viewing confidential patient medical records, including those of high-profile celebrities, in early 2010.[98]

Another significant change in the HITECH Act is that it provides state attorneys general with authority to bring civil actions for violations of HIPAA. In March 2010, HHS invited the 50 state attorneys general for in-person training on HIPAA privacy and security rules, at the agency's expense, so they would be better prepared to take on expanded enforcement roles to safeguard health information privacy.[99] In July 2010, the Connecticut Attorney General became the first state attorney general to exercise this authority by entering into a settlement agreement with Health Net, a health insurer, related to its loss of a computer disk drive that contained unencrypted protected health information such as claim forms, health plan appeals information, and other sensitive data relating to approximately 1.5 million health plan participants.[100]

HHS also reached out to the private sector for assistance with streamlining HIPAA enforcement. In July 2011, HHS awarded a $9 million contract to

---

[93] *Id.*

[94] See Chapter 8 (Goldberg & Greene, Enforcement of HIPAA).

[95] Mosquera, *Consumer Confidence about Health Data Safety is Key EHR Adoption*.

[96] Mary Mosquera, *HHS Slaps $4.3 Million on Cignet for HIPAA Privacy Violations*, GOVERNMENT HEALTH IT (Feb. 24, 2011), *available at* http://govhealthit.com/news/hhs-slaps-43m-fine-cignet-hipaa-privacy-violations.

[97] Mary Mosquera, *Mass General Pays $1 Million to Settle Potential Privacy Violations*, GOVERNMENT HEALTH IT (Feb. 25, 2011), *available at* http://govhealthit.com/news/mass-general-pays-1m-settle-potential-privacy-violations.

[98] Associated Press, *Snooping Celebrity Medical Records Cases Settled*, CBC NEWS (July 8, 2011), *available at* http://www.cbc.ca/news/arts/story/2011/07/08/medical-records-celebrities-snooping.html.

[99] Mary Mosquera, *OCR Will Train State AGs to Enforce HIPAA*, GOVERNMENT HEALTH IT (Mar. 10, 2011), *available at* http://govhealthit.com/news/ocr-will-train-state-ags-enforce-hipaa.

[100] Colin J. Zick, *Connecticut Attorney General Reaches First State HIPAA Settlement with Health Net*, SECURITY, PRIVACY & L. (July 7, 2010), *available at* http://www.securityprivacyandthelaw.com/2010/07/articles/government-enforcement/connecticut-attorney-general-reaches-first-state-hipaa-settlement-with-health-net/.

accounting firm KPMG to help HHS create an audit program to verify that covered entities adhere to HIPAA privacy and security standards.[101] KPMG also committed to visit and audit up to 150 covered organizations by the end of 2012 to make sure they have consistently put their privacy and security policies into practice.[102] Such visits will include interviews with senior officers, such as chief information officers, privacy officers, and legal counsel; examination of the organizations' physical features and operations; and observation of whether the organizations follow HIPAA requirements.[103]

Given these aggressive enforcement efforts and increased penalties, it is even more important for covered entities and their business associates to comply with HIPAA and the HITECH Act. In early 2011, the National Institute of Standards and Technology (NIST) awarded a contract to Exeter Government Services to develop an online toolkit and electronic user manual to help providers and health plans understand and comply with the requirements of the HIPAA Security Rule.[104] When complete, NIST will post the toolkit on its Web site. Private companies such as ID Experts also offer tools to help companies ensure compliance with HIPAA's privacy and security standards.[105] Chapter 11 provides further insight regarding ways e-health players should prepare for and respond to security breaches.[106]

V. Conclusion

The e-health industry, while still emerging, is growing at a rapid pace. The potential benefits that various e-health products and services offer, from convenience to cost savings to reduction in medical errors, are inspiring entrepreneurs to further innovate and maintaining the interest of investors in these tumultuous economic times. The major hurdle that these innovators face is the apprehension of patients, health care providers, and insurance companies about adoption of e-health initiatives. The federal government, mainly through the implementation of the HITECH Act, is trying to promote the advancement of health information technology while easing constituents' fears, particularly regarding privacy and safety, about this powerful movement. This effort has led the government to spend millions of dollars investing in e-health companies and supporting the adoption of e-health measures across the nation, while also aggressively enforcing the stringent privacy and security rules set forth in HIPAA against those

---

[101] Mary Mosquera, *HHS Taps KPMG to Perform HIPAA Audits*, GOVERNMENT HEALTH IT (July 6, 2011), *available at* http://govhealthit.com/news/hhs-taps-kpmg-perform-hipaa-audits.

[102] Fed Biz Opps, OCR HIPAA Audit Protocol and Program Performance (June 20, 2011), *available at* https://www.fbo.gov/index?s=opportunity&mode=form&id=9e045aa4f7e6f8499c5b6f74d5b211e9&tab=core&_cview=0%20.

[103] *Id.*

[104] Mary Mosquera, *NIST Will Offer Online Tool to Help Providers Comply with HIPAA Security*, GOVERNMENT HEALTH IT (Feb. 1, 2011), *available at* http://govhealthit.com/news/nist-will-offer-online-tool-help-providers-comply-hipaa-security.

[105] *See, e.g.*, ID Experts, OCR Survival Tool, *available at* http://www2.idexpertscorp.com/breach-tools/ocr-survival-tool/.

[106] See Chapter 11 (Faccenda, Obligations in Response to a Health Care Data Security Breach).

same companies. The budding industry, new regulations, and aggressive enforcement of privacy and security regulations create the perfect recipe for compliance issues. The following chapters highlight a number of legal issues as they particularly relate to the e-health industry and include guidance on how parties can avoid liability in this exciting and evolving market.

2

E-Health Industry Overview*

I.	Introduction to E-Health	19
II.	The E-Health Industry	21
	A. Traditional Health Care Delivery Model	21
	B. E-Health's Underlying Technology	23
	C. Participants in E-Health Industry	23
	1. Web Site Operators	23
	2. Providers	24
	3. Internet Pharmacies	25
	4. Vendors of Health Information Technology	26
	D. E-Health Business Industry Models	27
	E. State of Electronic Health Records Adoption	28
	F. Improvement for E-Health	29
	G. Challenges Confronting E-Health	30
III.	Government Role in E-Health	30
	A. HITECH Act and Health Care Reform	30
	B. EHR, E-Prescribing Incentives, and Key Regulations	33
	C. Government Role as a Payor	35
IV.	E-Health Improvement to Health Care Delivery	36
V.	Conclusion	41

I. Introduction to E-Health

"E-Health" is a relatively new term that entered industry usage in the late 1990s.[1] The prefix "e-" frequently designates activities that are performed electronically, and often over the Internet, such as "e-mail," "e-business," and "e-commerce." A systematic review of "e-health" usage in industry literature concluded that no universally agreed definition existed, but that "technology" was a component of virtually every definition and the Internet was referenced in

---

*John Healey, JD, CISSP, Blue Cross and Blue Shield Association, Chicago, Illinois.
[1] Gunther Eysenbach, *What is E-health?*, J. Med. Internet Res. 3(2):e20 (2001), *available at* http://www.jmir.org/2001/2/e20.

over half.² The Health Information and Management Systems Society (HIMSS) has proposed defining e-health as "the application of Internet and other related technologies in the health care industry to improve the access, efficiency, effectiveness, and quality of clinical and business processes utilized by health care organizations, practitioners, patients, and consumers in an effort to improve the health status of patients."³ Others have suggested viewing e-health as an umbrella term for "the combined use of electronic communication and information technology in the health sector."⁴ The term continues to evolve and means much more than simply incorporating technology into medical devices or using computerized systems to record patient data more efficiently. As the HIMSS definition suggests, e-health applies technology to health care to improve the overall health care delivery system and patient health. The definition implies that practitioners of e-health will capture information about patients and treatments, analyze the data, and take action based on the evidence.

As an umbrella term, e-health encompasses the concept of telemedicine, which had focused on the use in health care delivery of communication technologies such as cellular networks, teleconferencing between patients and health care providers, remote physiological monitoring, and e-mail. E-health also includes certain electronic medical devices that are subject to extensive regulation by the Food and Drug Administration (FDA). For regulatory purposes, the Food, Drug, and Cosmetic Act defines a medical device as:

> [A]n instrument, apparatus, implement, machine, contrivance, implant, in vitro reagent, or other similar or related article, including any component, part, or accessory, which is—
>
> (1) recognized in the official National Formulary, or the United States Pharmacopeia, or any supplement to them,
>
> (2) intended for use in the diagnosis of disease or other conditions, or in the cure, mitigation, treatment, or prevention of disease, in man or other animals, or
>
> (3) intended to affect the structure or any function of the body of man or other animals, and which does not achieve its primary intended purposes through chemical action within or on the body of man or other animals and which is not dependent upon being metabolized for the achievement of its primary intended purposes.⁵

The distinction between products used for e-health applications and medical devices depends largely upon the function being performed. Many medical devices now have communications and processing capabilities designed into them that enable them to communicate via network connections, wireless or physical Internet connections, or cellular systems and to perform analysis rather than merely collect data. An application that simply records patient data would generally not be a medical device, but if that application analyzes that same

---

²Hans Oh, et al., *What is e-Health (3): A Systematic Review of Published Definitions*, J. MED. INTERNET RES. 7(1):e1 (2005), *available at* http://www.jmir.org/2005/1/e1.

³HEALTHCARE INFORMATION AND MANAGEMENT SYSTEMS SOCIETY, HIMSS E-HEALTH SIG WHITE PAPER (2003), *available at* http://www.himss.org/content/files/ehealth_whitepaper.pdf.

⁴Vincenzo Della Mea, *What is e-Health (2): The death of telemedicine?*, J. MED. INTERNET RES. 3(2):e22 (2001), *available at* http://www.jmir.org/2001/2/e22/.

⁵Food, Drug, and Cosmetic Act §201(h) (codified at 21 U.S.C. §321(h)).

patient data and displays a possible diagnosis, it may meet Section 2 of the medical device definition above and be regulated as a medical device. Designation as a medical device can have a significant impact in terms of the applicable rules and regulations and in the cost of bringing a product to market. Among other requirements, development of a regulated medical device requires formal design and production processes, product service, complaint histories, and extensive recordkeeping in addition to making the developer subject to on-site inspection by the Food and Drug Administration.[6] Developers of e-health products and services need to ensure that they do not unintentionally meet the definition of a medical device and become subject to the extensive regulatory obligations associated with medical devices.

Within the e-health industry, electronic prescribing capabilities and electronic health records (EHR) systems are of particular interest and are receiving significant attention, both from the government and from private entities. E-prescribing capabilities are being promoted in conjunction with the Medicare Part D Prescription Drug Benefit, and for their promise of medical error reduction relative to written prescription scripts and manual checking for drug interactions. As more activities within health care are performed electronically, EHR could serve as a single repository of the various health records associated with an individual that are now maintained by individual health care providers. The EHR could serve as the central control point at which decisions to disclose such information to authorized entities within the continuum of care would be made and to aggregate such information for research and analytics purposes. The current structure of health care delivery in the U.S. inhibits the development of such a repository, but certain government and private initiatives are working to promote widespread adoption of EHR and to create an infrastructure under which information sharing could readily occur. Theoretically, the widespread utilization of EHR could be exploited to achieve medical error reduction, cost controls, quality improvements, and increased treatment effectiveness, as will be discussed later in this chapter.

II. The E-Health Industry

A. Traditional Health Care Delivery Model

A brief overview of the traditional health care delivery model is helpful in order to understand the contributions that e-health could make. The traditional health care delivery model typically consists of a primary care physician who conducts face-to-face examinations of the patient, prescribes drugs and treatment, and makes referrals to specialists and treatment facilities as required. Approximately 50 percent of health care is delivered in primary care physicians' offices. Patients typically rely on the recommendations of the primary care physician, in part because of limited access to information concerning treatment alternatives and a lack of transparency regarding price and quality of medical services. In many cases, the patient's choices of treatment are also influenced

---

[6]*See generally* 21 C.F.R. §§820 *et seq.*

by an insurance plan, sponsored either by a private employer or a government entity.

In many respects, there are two groups of consumers of medical services in the traditional health care delivery model: the patient who actually receives the services and the payor (the health plan sponsor or insurance company) that pays some or all of the health care service's cost. Generally, the patient has limited advance knowledge of the price of health care services and performs little or no comparison shopping. The payor attempts to manage health care service costs by negotiating rates in advance and creating networks of providers who have consented to policies set by the payor regarding pricing and treatment. Both patients and payors are seeking more insight into the quality and outcomes achieved by providers. Such information is available to a degree, but its creation is hampered by the difficulty of assembling reliable data in a form that permits direct comparison.

Health care services are provided by a variety of independent organizations, such as the primary care physician, a specialist to whom the patient was referred, any additional specialists such as anesthesiologists or therapists who may perform supporting services, a hospital or surgical care center at which services may be delivered, and others. Coordination among these service providers and the sharing of information among them is often performed on an ad hoc basis, with portions of the patient's records being copied, faxed, or otherwise manually communicated among providers. The decisions regarding what information to provide is often made by the referring provider, and the receiving provider may follow up with specific additional requests or may generate desired information by conducting more tests and examinations, possibly duplicating material already available at another entity providing care. Records resulting from tests and prior care may reside in the files of each provider, rather than being in the patient's possession or with the primary care physician, and are often in varying formats. The patient is often largely responsible for carrying through with the recommended course of treatment by coordinating his or her own care with each provider, with some subsequent follow-up with the primary care physician.

The fragmentation of health care delivery affects the business practices of entities within the e-health industry. For example, although there are approximately 5,815 hospitals in the United States,[7] the largest hospital chain in the United States, the Hospital Corporation of America (HCA), controls less than 3 percent of the total.[8] Adoption of standardized practices can be very slow in a highly fragmented market. Even in those cases in which a hospital belongs to a larger system, the individual member hospitals are not necessarily obligated to adopt the policies of the parent organization, and may maintain incompatible records systems even within a single health care system.

---

[7] American Hospital Association, Fast Facts on U.S. Hospitals (Nov. 11, 2009), *available at* http://www.aha.org/research/rc/stat-studies/fast-facts.shtml.

[8] HCA, About Our Company, *available at* http://hcahealthcare.com/about/.

B. E-Health's Underlying Technology

The underlying technology that supports e-health became widely available in the mid-1990s and is evolving at a rapid rate. Wireless devices have advanced in speed, capability, and reliability to the point at which sizable applications can be run on truly portable devices, such as "smart" phones and tablet computers, that are far less cumbersome and fragile than the laptop and notebook computers they are rapidly supplanting. Nearly global connectivity is available through wireless cellular networks and Internet access providers. Communication methods are converging, with voice telephone, faxes, voice mail, and e-mail communications all being delivered to the recipient in various forms and on various devices, the choice of which the sender does not control. Use of the Internet, now commonly termed "cloud computing," has transitioned from being viewed as a unique capability to being viewed as another standard communication channel managed by corporate information technology (IT) departments and fully integrated into the corporate network infrastructure. Companies have made large amounts of internal corporate systems' functionality and information available through remote access portals, increasing the productivity of their mobile work force and reducing the need to physically connect to the traditional corporate network. Developers of Web sites are making medical information easily accessible to health care providers and to consumers of health care.

As noted above, integration of medical devices with cellular and Internet communication capabilities is expanding, allowing vital signs, test results, and other information to be submitted to physicians and other health care providers, who, in some cases, can adjust medical devices remotely. Prescription changes can be sent by pharmacists electronically to automated drug dispensers located in residential care facilities, speeding execution of prescription changes and reducing waste. Electronic health records and electronic health care insurance claims have contributed to the growth of health care data warehouses containing medical information for tens of millions of people, permitting data mining and trend analysis on a huge scale and offering opportunities to compare treatments and medications for effectiveness and safety, even for rare conditions that previously had been difficult to study. The e-health industry continues to grow and mature and to become less and less distinct from the overall health information technology industry.

C. Participants in E-Health Industry

1. Web Site Operators

Web site operators in the e-health industry include a wide variety of entities, such as providers of Web sites that furnish content to consumers and health care professionals; established vendors of health care products that have enabled such products to interact electronically via the Internet with other products, patients, and health care providers; health care providers who provide Internet functionality related to their practice; insurers and other payors; and third parties that offer supporting services, such as clearinghouse functions for claims processing or analytics services. Many operators of Web sites provide content that typically includes access to information repositories and community support functions like bulletin boards and chat rooms, through which a user can discuss topics related to health care with persons of similar interests. Consumer-oriented content providers generally provide members of the public with access to health news and information. These content providers may connect users to other sites with specialized information on diseases, drugs, insurance, or other health-related topics, or they may provide information directly on a range of topics. Other content providers seek to deliver information to health care providers rather than patients. Through desktop computers or wireless, hand-held devices that receive and transmit information over the Internet, such businesses offer health care professionals access to up-to-date information on health plan formularies of requirements, drug interaction data, medical research, reference material, and other data. Directory Web sites can provide physicians and other health care providers with direct, real-time access to other health care providers, facilities, or payors. These Web sites develop networks of participating providers and may provide search capabilities that assist patients, family members, and providers to identify, select, and communicate with health care providers who provide needed services, such as nursing homes, home health services, and durable medical equipment suppliers. Many health care providers operate Web sites to provide functionality by which patients and potential patients may set up appointments, select physicians, obtain health information, and seek help with questions. These Web sites frequently perform a mix of services, providing content, providing directory services, and performing transactions for patients and providers.

2. *Providers*

With inexpensive and even free access to electronic mail accounts, many businesses and individuals now rely on e-mail as one of their methods of communication. Despite several polls indicating that patients would be more likely to choose a doctor who offered electronic communications, most physicians do not do so.[9] Physicians' widespread use of e-mail to communicate with patients would present both benefits and risks. For instance, e-mail is a self-documenting form of communication that is easily retained and incorporated into a medical record. It provides evidence of a communication and can be relied upon to document a physician's advice. In addition, e-mail is convenient and quick, making it a logical choice for overburdened physicians and their busy patients, who may have difficulty finding a mutually agreeable time to communicate via telephone.

Yet, e-mail presents its own challenges. For instance, physicians are rarely compensated for e-mail communications. In addition, it can be difficult for either party to the communication to verify the identity of the parties involved. It can also be hard for physicians to verify the information that is communicated to them. In addition, concerns regarding the security of e-mail transmissions (including the use of encryption) and technical complications such as downtime of an e-mail system remain front and center in a covered entity's risk assessment

---

[9]*Patients Seeking More Interactive Contact With Providers, but Providers Still Resistant,* HEALTH CARE STRATEGIC MGMT. (Oct. 1, 2000).

for compliance with the Health Insurance Portability and Accountability Act (HIPAA) Security Standards.[10] Moreover, there are largely unresolved questions regarding the standard of care attributed to e-mail communications.

Accordingly, the Council on Ethical and Judicial Affairs of the American Medical Association (AMA) and others have recommended that health care providers establish policies and procedures relating to the use of e-mail in communicating with patients.[11] To the extent e-mail is permitted by state laws regulating the practice of medicine, the policies should require physicians to discuss the use of e-mail with patients and inform them of the associated risks and benefits. Most authors have recommended that because of the inherent limitations of e-mail, physicians should never use e-mail to establish a patient-physician relationship. Instead, e-mail should be seen as a useful tool for supplementing personal encounters. In addition, physicians should be held to the same ethical responsibilities in their e-mails that they are during other encounters. Patients should be made aware of the inherent limitations of e-mail, including potential breaches of confidentiality and privacy, difficulties in validating the identity of the parties, the possibility that others will process messages and view the content, and potential delays in responses. Accordingly, patients should be advised never to use e-mail for urgent or emergency conditions. Moreover, patients should understand that the content of any e-mail communication will likely be incorporated into their medical records.[12]

To address some of these risks, vendors of electronic medical records and other clinical systems now offer secure patient portals through which physicians with established doctor-patient relationships may communicate with their patients. These portals provide a forum by which patients may access clinical information regarding their lab results; request prescription refills; study information forwarded by a physician regarding a particular disease, condition, or symptom; or communicate inquiries or requests, such as a request for referral. In addition, these portals are used to interface with the administrative staff to track reimbursement from third-party payors and to schedule and change office appointments. These systems have an additional benefit in that they often integrate seamlessly with patients' electronic medical records. Because these patient portals typically exist within a secure environment, they may provide a meaningful alternative to e-mail communication.

3. Internet Pharmacies

Although the use of Internet pharmacies has reached public acceptance and is often an insurance company's preferred method for covering prescription medications, some online pharmacies attempt to use the anonymity of the Internet to elude FDA jurisdiction. The Drug Enforcement Administration (DEA)

---

[10] Security Standards; Final Rule, 68 Fed. Reg. 8334, 8374–81 (Feb. 20, 2003).

[11] A.M. Bovi & Council on Ethical and Judicial Affairs, *Ethical Guidelines for Use of Electronic Mail Between Patients and Physicians,* AM. J. BIOETHICS, at W43, W47 (Summer 2003).

[12] *Id.*; Elisabeth Belmont, *Clinical Encounters in Cyberspace: Minimizing Liability Exposure for "Mouse Calls,"* MEDICAL MALPRACTICE L. & STRATEGY 1 (Sept. 2000); *Using E-Mail to Communicate With Patients Offers Both Benefits and Risks,* HEALTH CARE STRATEGIC MGMT. (June 1, 2000).

recognizes online pharmacies as a major contributing factor to the high level of prescription drug abuse occurring in the United States.[13] Through online companies engaging in unlawful practices, consumers have purchased prescription drugs without prescriptions, unapproved new drugs, and products labeled with fraudulent health claims. Although the FDA, Federal Trade Commission (FTC), and several states have conducted investigations and brought lawsuits against Web site operators engaging in these practices, such practices continue.[14] In response, the FDA has conducted a consumer education program to alert the public about potential risks. The National Association of Boards of Pharmacy (NABP) has developed the Verified Internet Pharmacy Practice Sites (VIPPS) program to certify online pharmacies that have complied with the licensing and inspection requirements of their states and the states to which they dispense pharmaceuticals. In addition, pharmacies displaying the VIPPS seal have demonstrated to NABP their compliance with VIPPS criteria, including patient rights to privacy, authentication, and security of prescription orders; adherence to a recognized quality assurance policy; and provision of meaningful consultation between patients and pharmacists. In 2009, the DEA published an interim rule effective April 13, 2009, intended to prevent the illegal dispensing of prescription substances by means of the Internet, and envisions publishing future regulations that will create a special registration for the practice of telemedicine.[15] The interim rule makes it a per se violation of the Controlled Substances Act for a practitioner to prescribe a controlled substance by means of the Internet without having conducted at least one in-person medical evaluation except in certain circumstances, and requires a modified DEA pharmacy registration that expressly permits online operations.[16]

4. Vendors of Health Information Technology

Some established vendors of health information technology products have expanded their products to incorporate a communication module or portal that permits online or wireless access. Some e-health companies have developed case management and documentation software that also integrates decision support protocols aimed at reducing medical errors. This software not only provides a means for inputting and managing patient data, it also prompts the care provider with suggestions or questions at various times during patient care based on an integrated set of medical protocols. These systems can be expensive and time-consuming to implement and require provider review and annotation. For example, documentation software may automatically collect various vital signs via interfaces with patient monitors, but the values may be inaccurate due to patient repositioning, temporary disconnection, or other reasons. The provider needs to review the recorded results for artifacts and annotate the record with manual readings or explanations before adding the information to the medical

---

[13] U.S. Dep't of Justice, Implementation of the Ryan Haight Online Pharmacy Consumer Protection Act of 2008; Final Rule, 74 Fed. Reg. 15,596, 15,597 (Apr. 6, 2009) (codified at 21 C.F.R. pts. 1300, 1301, 1304, 1306).

[14] *On-Line Pharmacies Settle FTC Charges*, MARKETLETTER (July 24, 2000).

[15] 74 Fed. Reg. at 15,596–97.

[16] *Id.* at 15,599.

record. Additionally, vendors of information technology products sometimes attempt to transition their products into the health care industry, sometimes with inadequate knowledge of the health care industry.[17]

Many health care providers themselves offer Web sites featuring information about their products and services. Another category of e-health businesses includes those that provide electronic means for health care professionals to provide care to their patients. Telemedicine, in which a physician or other health care professional uses electronic means to interact with a patient or to review data or images, allows the professional to remotely monitor a patient or make a diagnosis or treatment decision. With the expansion of communication capabilities built into medical devices, telemedicine has become a mainstream issue rather than a hypothetical exercise. However, the capability to perform such interaction is not sufficient by itself to ensure adoption. E-health businesses need to ensure that the provider can be compensated for services delivered via an e-health device. Such compensation generally requires that reimbursement codes exist and that the payor recognizes the service as a covered benefit. One successful example of telemedicine involves the ability of certain implantable pacemakers to transmit data at any time (using a portable monitor attached to a standard telephone line or with built-in cellular calling capability) through the Medtronic CareLink Network for review by physicians and nurses on a secure Web site.[18] The physician can access the diagnostic reports, containing information comparable to an office visit, via a secure Web site on a 24/7 basis and can export the data to a hospital network or EHR system.[19] The CareLink Network has operated in the U.S. since 2002, and more than 250,000 patients in 20 countries have been monitored remotely.[20] Established methods are available to obtain reimbursement for such remote monitoring, such as the AMA's CPT Code No. 93294, "Interrogation device evaluation(s), (remote) up to 90 days; single, dual, or multiple lead pacemaker system with interim physician analysis, review(s) and report(s)."[21]

D. E-Health Industry Business Models

The business models of e-health industry participants vary. Often, there is no charge to the consumer to access such information or other content rooms. In some cases, the Web site is provided as a public service, a community outreach initiative, an effort to promote policy positions, or as advertising for products and services. In other cases, the Web site generates revenue by selling advertise-

---

[17] TripleTree Research, *Don't Jump to Conclusions as Thomson Cries "Uncle" on Healthcare,* UNCOMMON CLARITY BLOG (June 8, 2011), *available at* http://blog.triple-tree.com/.

[18] Medtronic, Medtronic CareLink Network for Cardiac Patients, *available at* http://www.medtronic.com/for-healthcare-professionals/products-therapies/cardiac-rhythm/patient-management-carelink/medtronic-carelink-network-for-cardiac-device-patients/index.htm.

[19] *Id.*

[20] Press Release, MTB Europe, *Remote Monitoring of Pacemaker Patients Improves Detection of Serious Events* (May 21, 2008), *available at* http://mtbeurope.info/news/2008/ 805027.htm.

[21] Medtronic, Inc., 2010 CPT Codes for Cardiac Device Monitoring (2009), *available at* http://www.medtronic.com/wcm/groups/mdtcom_sg/@mdt/@crdm/documents/documents/2010cpt-codes.pdf.

ments that are often displayed to match the information sought by the user, or by selling detailed listings in health care provider directories that facilitate contact between site users and subscribing providers. Other content providers may be subscription services that implement access accounts for health care providers. The individual consumer must evaluate all Web site content for accuracy and reliability. Additionally, many Web sites prominently disclaim any liability for the information presented and disclaim the formation of a physician-patient relationship, instructing Web site visitors to refer their specific situation to a qualified physician.

E. State of Electronic Health Records Adoption

Electronic health records currently experience a low level of adoption within the United States, particularly when defined as electronic systems that capture more than just demographic data. As published in April 2009, on the basis of responses from approximately 3,000 acute care hospitals that belong to the American Hospital Association, a survey that assessed the availability of certain EHR functionality determined that only 1.5 percent of U.S. hospitals have a comprehensive EHR system present in all clinical units; an additional 7.6 percent have a basic system featuring physician's notes and nursing assessments in at least one clinical unit.[22] Only 17 percent of hospitals have implemented Computerized Provider-Order Entry (CPOE) for medications.[23] Forty-four percent of the hospitals reported being in the initial stages of implementation of physician's notes online, and 38 percent reported early stage activity in the implementation of CPOE in one or more units.[24] The implementation of such systems is concentrated among larger hospitals, those serving urban areas, and teaching hospitals.[25] Among hospitals without electronic health records, 74 percent cited capital purchase requirements, 44 percent cited high maintenance costs, 36 percent cited physician resistance, 32 percent cited unclear return on investment, and 30 percent cited lack of adequate IT staff as barriers to implementation.[26] Those hospitals that had implemented electronic health records were less likely to cite any of the five preceding reasons except for physician resistance as major barriers to adoption.[27] The survey also noted that certain other functionality that could help support electronic health records was present, such as electronic lab and radiologic reports, radiologic images, medication lists, and some decision-support systems.[28]

With respect to ambulatory care organizations, a national survey of 4,484 physicians in late 2007 and 2008 received approximately 2,758 responses.[29] The

---

[22] Ashish Jha, et al., *Use of Electronic Health Records in U.S. Hospitals*, 360 N. ENG. J. MED. 1628 (2009), *available at* http://www.nejm.org/doi/pdf/10.1056/NEJMsa0900592.
[23] *Id.*
[24] *Id.*
[25] *Id.*
[26] *Id.*
[27] *Id.*
[28] *Id.*
[29] Catherine DesRoches, et al., *Use of Electronic Health Records in Ambulatory Care*, 359 N. ENG. J. MED. 50 (2008), *available at* http://www.nejm.org/doi/full/10.1056/NEJMsa0802005.

survey sponsor, working with a panel of experts drawn from survey research, representatives of hospital and physician organizations, health information technology, and health care management, defined an electronic health records system using the Institutes of Medicine's framework, which defined the possible functions of such a system.[30] Only 4 percent of the physicians reported having a fully functional EHR system, defined as the ability to record patients' clinical and demographic data, to view and manage the results of laboratory tests and imaging, to manage order entry including electronic prescriptions, and to support clinical decisions, including warnings about drug interactions or contraindications.[31] Thirteen percent of the physicians reported having a basic system that lacked certain order entry capabilities and clinical decision support.[32] Of the 4 percent of physicians who had a fully functional system, 71 percent reported that their system was integrated with the electronic system at the hospital where they admitted patients, while only 56 percent of the physicians with a basic system had such integration.[33] Physicians without access to an EHR system cited capital costs (66 percent), not finding a system to meet their needs (54 percent), uncertainty about the return on investment (50 percent), and concern that a system would become obsolete (44 percent) as the most common barriers to adoption.[34]

F. Improvement for E-Health

One of the first actions of the Office of the National Coordinator for Health Information Technology (ONCHIT) was to issue a report assessing the use and promotion of health information technology. Citing studies conducted by the Institute of Medicine, ONCHIT reported that up to 98,000 Americans die each year from hospital inpatient medical errors. In addition, more than 770,000 people are injured or die annually in hospitals from adverse drug events.[35] High costs and medical errors are connected to the inadequate use and low implementation rate of appropriate e-health tools.

For instance, CPOE systems can reduce the likelihood of errors caused by illegible handwriting or the use of "dangerous" abbreviations easily mistaken for others. In addition, these systems can reduce adverse drug interactions by notifying physicians of a patient's complete pharmaceutical history. The implementation of e-health tools such as longitudinal EHR and real-time clinical support tools can eliminate duplicative and unnecessary medical care, help disseminate breakthroughs in medical knowledge, reduce the variations in quality of care by geographic location, and promote a more consumer-centric approach to health care by making information more readily available to patients on demand. In

---

[30]*Id.*
[31]*Id.*
[32]*Id.*
[33]*Id.*
[34]*Id.*
[35]Tommy G. Thompson & David J. Brailer, The Decade of Health Information Technology: Delivering Consumer-Centric and Information-Rich Health Care, Framework for Strategic Action 2 (July 21, 2004), *available at* http://www.providersedge.com/ehdocs/ehr_articles/The_Decade_of_HIT-Delivering_Customer-centric_and_Info-rich_HC.pdf.

addition, with the appropriate protections in place, an interoperable EHR could be used to identify public health trends and provide the necessary information to sound an early warning against bioterrorist threats.[36]

Despite common public misperceptions and recent high-profile security breaches, e-health tools may, in fact, increase the privacy and security of patient information.[37] For instance, most EHR systems include an audit trail function that can be used to track who has viewed records and to verify that only appropriate personnel have access to patients' medical records. The system can document the purposes for access, such as for treatment, billing, or research. In contrast, with paper-based records, particularly in smaller offices, there is no automated logging of physicians each time they access records. These e-tools not only promote the privacy and security of patient information, but they also can assist providers in complying with certain regulatory requirements, including HIPAA's privacy and security regulations. Under HIPAA, lawful and appropriate access to patient information depends on and varies according to who is accessing what information and for what purposes.

G. Challenges Confronting E-Health

As the general population ages, there will be an increased demand for health care services, a likely increase in the number of companies responding to the demand, and intense debate over how to pay the costs of such health care. E-health products are currently viewed as providing a number of advantages, both on their own and as a complement to traditional information technology infrastructure. Certain products, in particular EHR and electronic prescribing applications, are being actively subsidized by the government under aggressive implementation schedules. The e-health industry needs to prove that it can contribute to quality care and reduce costs. The experience to date with implementing standard transactions and health information exchanges has been enormously expensive, and more effort is needed to create truly interoperable systems and to establish methods for using the information once collected. The e-health industry must also address its weaknesses, such as security and authentication measures.

III. GOVERNMENT ROLE IN E-HEALTH

A. HITECH Act and Health Care Reform

The passage of the Health Information Technology for Economic and Clinical Health (HITECH) Act as Title XIII of the American Recovery and Reinvestment Act of 2009 (ARRA) will provide approximately $19 billion to support and promote the adoption of health information technology. The HITECH Act provides that incentive payments may be made commencing in 2011 for

---

[36] *Id.* at 2–5.
[37] Jennifer Lubell, *VA Theft Included Medical Data*, MODERN HEALTHCARE (May 29, 2006), at 12.

the meaningful use of EHR technology by eligible professionals and hospitals, and that reduced reimbursement payments may be made to eligible professionals and hospitals beginning in 2015,[38] but provides few specifics concerning implementation.

The Department of Health and Human Services (HHS) issued a Final Rule setting forth the Centers for Medicare and Medicaid Services (CMS) Electronic Health Record Incentive Program (EHR Incentive Program).[39] The EHR Incentive Program defines "meaningful use" for 2011 (Stage 1) as satisfying certain objectives and associated measures, which vary according to whether the recipient is an eligible professional, eligible hospital, or critical access hospital, and which generally include, among others, the recording of specified demographic and vital signs data, the use of CPOE, provision of health information and discharge instructions to patients, incorporation of lab test results, submission of electronic claims to payors, reporting of specified quality measures to CMS, and electronic prescribing.[40] CMS intends to propose criteria and measures for Stage 2 and Stage 3 that promote information exchange and improvements in quality, safety, and effectiveness, respectively.[41]

A recipient could qualify for payments for meeting Stage 1 requirements at any time during the first year through the fifth year of the EHR Incentive Program, but all recipients need to satisfy Stage 2 and then Stage 3 requirements to continue receiving payments in subsequent years.[42] The incentive payments are calculated by a formula that provides greater benefits to providers that qualify as meaningful users of EHR technology earlier in the program[43] and for certain other criteria, such as eligible professionals who deliver services in a geographic Health Professional Shortage Area (HPSA).[44] Maximum payments are specified for eligible professionals, such as $18,000 for a non-HPSA-eligible professional who first qualifies as a meaningful user in 2011 and $12,000 for the same professional who first qualifies in 2014.[45] The maximum an eligible professional could receive under the program from 2011 to 2016 is a total of $44,000; by comparison, a professional who first qualifies in 2014 could receive a maximum of $24,000.[46] The formula for hospital incentive payments relies on a variety of factors, with some estimates ranging from $8 to $14 million in total payments.[47] Public comments on the EHR Incentive Program recommended a number of changes, including expanding the providers eligible for incentive payments to represent a broader section of the health care continuum, easing the criteria for meaningful use, and clarifying that each hospital within a system

---

[38] U.S. Dep't Health & Human Servs., Medicare and Medicaid Programs; Electronic Health Record Incentive Program; Final Rule, 75 Fed. Reg. 44,314 (July 28, 2010).
[39] *Id.*
[40] *Id.* at 44,321.
[41] *Id.* at 44,321–22.
[42] *Id.*
[43] *Id.* at 44,443–44.
[44] *Id.*
[45] *Id.*
[46] *Id.*
[47] Christopher Weaver, *Figuring Out What a Hospital Can Get for Switching to Electronic Records*, KAISER HEALTH NEWS (Mar. 19, 2010), *available at* http://www.kaiserhealthnews.org/Stories/2010/March/19/hospital-electronic-records.aspx.

can individually qualify for incentive payments.[48] Investors will need to assess how a company's products could be helped or hindered by the HITECH Act and its implementation details. In addition, investors must consider how well a company's product will succeed given the many competing health care budget priorities. For example, the revised HIPAA transaction standards must be implemented by January 1, 2012, for most organizations at an estimated cost of $6 to $14 billion,[49] and the ICD-10 codes must be implemented by October 1, 2013, at an estimated cost of approximately $2 billion.[50] Both the HIPAA modifications and the ICD-10 codes will require significant enhancements to health information technology systems over the next few years, and these enhancements will compete with new e-health initiatives for budget dollars, even as the economic downturn reduces revenues.

After some initial setbacks, health care reform legislation, in the form of the Patient Protection and Affordable Care Act and the Health Care and Education Reconciliation Act of 2010 (collectively, PPACA), was passed by both houses of Congress in highly partisan votes and signed into law by President Obama on March 23, 2010.[51] To promote uniformity in the HIPAA standard transactions, PPACA provides for the enactment of "operating rules," envisioned as the necessary business rules and guidelines for electronic exchange of information that are not defined by the standards and implementation specifications.[52] Such operating rules are to be recommended by a nonprofit entity that has an administrative simplification focus, consensus-based process with multiple stakeholders, a public set of guiding principles, public review and updates of the rules, and other qualifying criteria.[53] The National Committee on Vital and Health Statistics (NCVHS) was directed to advise the Secretary of HHS on the qualifications of nonprofit entities for the role, and to review and validate such nonprofit entity's recommendations.[54] After the nonprofit entity's recommendation and NCVHS's concurrence with such recommendations, the Secretary of HHS was directed to expedite adoption of the operating rules as interim final rules followed by a 60-day public comment period.[55]

PPACA adds electronic funds transfers (EFT) to the list of HIPAA standard transactions and directs the Secretary of HHS to ensure that standards and operating rules permit determination of eligibility and financial responsibility prior to or at the point of service, provide for a timely and transparent claims and denial management process, including appeals and adjudication, describe all data

---

[48] Letter from Healthcare Information and Management Systems Society (HIMSS) (Mar. 15, 2010).

[49] U.S. Dep't of Health & Human Servs., Health Insurance Reform: Modifications to the Health Insurance Portability and Accountability Act (HIPAA); Final Rule 74 Fed. Reg. 3323 (Jan. 16, 2009).

[50] U.S. Dep't of Health & Human Servs., HIPAA Administrative Simplification: Modifications to Medical Data Code Set Standards to Adopt ICD-10-CM and ICD-10-PCS, 74 Fed. Reg. 3361 (Jan. 16, 2009).

[51] Pub. L. No. 111-148, 124 Stat. 119 (Mar. 23, 2010), as amended by Pub. L. No. 111-152, 124 Stat. 1029 (Mar. 23, 2010) [hereinafter PPACA].

[52] *Id.* at §1104, as amended by Pub. L. No. 111-152, 124 Stat. 1029 (2010).

[53] *Id.*

[54] *Id.*

[55] *Id.*

elements and codes in unambiguous terms, and prohibit additional conditions except when necessary to implement state or federal requirements or to protect against fraud and abuse.[56] Operating rules for eligibility for a health plan and for health claim status transactions shall be adopted no later than July 1, 2011, and effective no later than January 1, 2013.[57] Operating rules for EFT and health care and payments remittance advice shall allow for automated reconciliation of payment with remittance advice, shall be adopted no later than July 1, 2012, and shall be effective no later than January 1, 2014.[58] Operating rules for (1) health claims or equivalent encounter information; (2) enrollment and disenrollment in a health plan; (3) health plan premium payments; (4) health claims attachments; and (5) referral certification and authorization shall be adopted no later than July 1, 2014, and effective no later than January 1, 2016.[59] By the respective effective dates of the new or revised standards and operating rules, health plans must submit documentation to the Secretary of HHS that demonstrates full compliance with the standard transactions and completion of end-to-end testing with physicians, hospitals, and others, and must ensure that entities contracted to provide services to the health plan also provide such documentation to the Secretary of HHS.[60] Penalties of $1 per day per covered life (indexed to the annual percentage increase in national health care expenditures) may be assessed for noncompliance up to $20 per covered life annually, and these penalties may be doubled for knowingly misrepresenting compliance in the required certification or documentation up to $40 per covered life annually.[61] Investors must deal with the uncertainty represented by the comprehensive PPACA and the as-yet unwritten implementing regulations.[62] Congress will likely pass additional legislation that will shape and modify the reforms. Additionally, court challenges are underway that may eliminate some provisions or at least modify their implementation.[63] Until the uncertainty is resolved, e-health strategy decisions will need to estimate what the positive and negative potential impacts of PPACA will be.

B. EHR, E-Prescribing Incentives, and Key Regulations

Congress recognized that proliferation of electronic prescribing (e-prescribing) technology important to the Medicare Part D program could not occur without an anti-kickback safe harbor and Stark law exception for donations of such technology to prescribing practitioners and others in a position to steer Medicare Part D business to particular plans. Thus, the Medicare Prescription Drug, Improvement and Modernization Act of 2003 (MMA)[64] required the HHS

---

[56] *Id.*
[57] *Id.*
[58] *Id.*
[59] *Id.*
[60] *Id.*
[61] *Id.*
[62] *Id.*
[63] *Id.*
[64] Pub. L. No. 108-173, 117 Stat. 2066 (2003).

Secretary to adopt such a safe harbor and Stark law exception. However, Congress directed HHS to limit the exceptions to technology *necessary* to and *used solely* for e-prescribing. Under the statutory approach Congress previously adopted, a physician practice could not use such donated technology for other health information purposes, such as use with an EHR system in connection with the delivery of day-to-day patient care.

Recognizing the need for an exception to address donation of EHR technology as well as e-prescribing technology by hospitals and health plans, in August 2006, the HHS Office of Inspector General (OIG) and CMS issued final regulations to promote the adoption and implementation of EHR and e-prescribing technology.[65] The regulations, effective October 10, 2006, provide Stark exceptions and anti-kickback safe harbors that are designed to permit specified individuals or entities to donate e-prescribing and EHR items and services to referral sources. In comments released with the rules, CMS and OIG emphasized that they will work to ensure that the new donation rules do not foster illegal remuneration. Provisions have been written into the rules to prevent program or patient abuse.[66]

The 2006 Stark exceptions identify parties that can donate e-prescribing or EHR software, information technology, and training services to physicians in specified relationships with the donor. Hardware donations are allowed only for e-prescribing purposes. The final regulations for EHR arrangements permit the donation of software and information technology services that are necessary and used predominantly to create, maintain, or receive EHRs. For e-prescribing arrangements, the items and services must be used *solely* for e-prescribing purposes. In all cases, the items and services must be nonmonetary.

The EHR software must be interoperable or deemed as such by a recognized certifying body at the time the donation is made and contain electronic prescribing capability that meets Medicare Part D standards. The items and services donated may not include staffing of the recipient's office and may not be used primarily to conduct personal business or business unrelated to the recipient's clinical practice or clinical operations. The arrangement must be set forth in a written agreement that (a) specifies the items and services being provided, (b) specifies the donor's cost of those items and services, (c) specifies the amount of the recipient's contribution, and (d) covers all of the items and services to be provided by the donor. For EHR arrangements, the recipient must pay 15 percent of the donor's cost of the items and services before receiving the items and services.

For EHR arrangements, the donor may not select recipients in a manner that *directly* takes into account volume or value of referrals or other business between the parties. For e-prescribing arrangements, the donor may not select recipients in a manner that takes into account volume or value of referrals or other business between the parties at all. In addition, the recipient may not make

---

[65] Safe Harbors for Certain Electronic Prescribing and Electronic Health Records Arrangements Under the Anti-Kickback Statute; Final Rule, 71 Fed. Reg. 45,110 (Aug. 8, 2006); Exceptions for Certain Electronic Prescribing and Electronic Health Records Arrangements; Final Rule, 71 Fed. Reg. 45,140 (Aug. 8, 2006).

[66] 71 Fed. Reg. at 45,148.

receipt of the technology a condition of doing business with the donor, the donor may not limit the technology's interoperability or compatibility with other EHR or e-prescribing systems, the donor may not knowingly provide technology equivalent to that already possessed by the recipient, and the donor may not restrict the recipient's ability to use the technology for any patient without regard to payor status. Finally, the transfer of technology and all requirements for EHR arrangements must be met before December 31, 2013. The anti-kickback safe harbor is essentially identical to the Stark exception, aside from the fact that it addresses donations to other recipients in addition to physicians.

The necessity of maintaining a manual system for the prescribing of controlled substances presented a barrier to the adoption of e-prescribing systems. Approximately 11 percent of all United States prescriptions are written for controlled substances, and DEA regulatory requirements prevented the use of e-prescribing technology.[67] In 2008, the DEA issued a proposed rule that permitted using e-prescribing systems to prescribe controlled substances, provided that prescribers performed certain additional measures unique to the controlled substance prescriptions.[68] Although additional record-keeping requirements decrease the benefits and increase the cost of adopting an e-prescribing system, prescribers can at least choose to move all their prescribing activity to an e-prescribing system. An interim final rule and request for comment was published in the *Federal Register*.[69] The Interim Final Rule requires authentication and other security measures, audit trails, and functionality that archives records of controlled substances prescriptions.[70] The Interim Final Rule requests comment on "identity proofing, access control, authentication, biometric subsystems and testing of those subsystems, internal audit trails for electronic prescription applications, and third-party auditors and certification organizations."[71] The DEA will likely incorporate such comments into a Final Rule to replace the interim regulation.

C. Government Role as a Payor

The health care industry represents a substantial segment of the U.S. economy. In 2009, the United States spent approximately $2.5 trillion on health care, or approximately $8,086 per person, representing 17.6 percent of the U.S. gross domestic product (GDP).[72] Health care spending growth slowed to 4.0 percent in 2009, compared to a 4.7 percent increase in the previous year.[73] Federal, state, and local government spending is dominated by Medicare, which accounted for

---

[67] Drug Enforcement Agency, Electronic Prescriptions for Controlled Substances; Proposed Rule, 73 Fed. Reg. 36,722 (June 27, 2008).

[68] *Id.*

[69] 21 C.F.R. pts. 1300, 1304, 1306 and 1311; Electronic Prescriptions for Controlled Substances; Final Rule, 75 Fed. Reg. 16,236 (Mar. 31, 2010).

[70] *Id.* at 16,241–44.

[71] *Id.* at 16,236.

[72] *See* CENTERS FOR MEDICARE & MEDICAID SERVS., NATIONAL HEALTH EXPENDITURES 2009 HIGHLIGHTS, *available at* http://www.cms.gov/NationalHealthExpendData/downloads/highlights.pdf.

[73] *Id.*

approximately $502.3 billion in total spending. Medicare Part D spending for prescription drug benefits and administration is approximately $54.5 billion.[74] Medicaid spending grew to $373.9 billion. Government programs, including Medicare, Medicaid, and others, accounted for more than 40 percent of total U.S. health care expenditures.[75] Private insurance premiums grew 1.3 percent in 2009[76] and accounted for 32 percent of total U.S. expenditures, with the remainder coming from out-of-pocket payments (12 percent) and other private sources, including philanthropy.[77] CMS projections indicate that health care spending growth will average 5.8 percent per year and will rise to $4.6 trillion, or 19.8 percent of the GDP, by 2019.[78] Nearly 50 percent of the total expenditure will be public spending.[79]

The reasons for implementing e-health solutions are critical to the health industry as a whole: improving patient care by reducing medical errors and increasing efficiency by reducing costs in providing patient care. However, one factor in the slow adoption of e-health technology may be that the parties that bear the direct costs of implementing e-health systems are not necessarily the parties that realize the benefits of such adoption. Government subsidies, incentives, and the easing of certain regulatory constraints on technology donations attempt to address this situation.

IV. E-HEALTH IMPROVEMENT TO HEALTH CARE DELIVERY

Potentially, adoption of e-health technology could reduce errors, simplify data exchange, reduce cost, and provide transparency to consumers of health care products. Many electronic health records provide a medical record program, clinical support tools, real-time access to patient records across providers within a system, the capability for patients to interface with the physician to request services or information, and often integration with billing and administrative staff. The federal government has supported certain e-health initiatives as a way to improve the quality of health care and realize certain efficiencies in delivery. Specifically, President George W. Bush, in April 2004, set a goal that every American would have an interoperable EHR within 10 years.[80] However, the implementation of an interoperable EHR systems is proving to be very difficult.

---

[74] *Id.*

[75] *See* CENTERS FOR MEDICARE & MEDICAID SERVS., NATIONAL HEALTH EXPENDITURE DATA, HISTORICAL: NATION'S HEALTH DOLLAR, CALENDAR YEAR 2009: WHERE IT CAME FROM, WHERE IT WENT (July 2011), *available at* http://www.cms.gov/NationalHealthExpendData/downloads/PieChartSourcesExpenditures2009.pdf.

[76] *See* NATIONAL HEALTH EXPENDITURES 2009 HIGHLIGHTS.

[77] *See* NATION'S HEALTH DOLLAR, CALENDAR YEAR 2009—WHERE IT CAME FROM, WHERE IT WENT.

[78] *See* CENTERS FOR MEDICARE & MEDICAID SERVS., NATIONAL HEALTH EXPENDITURE PROJECTIONS, 2010–2020, FORECAST SUMMARY AND SELECTED TABLES, *available at* http://www.cms.gov/NationalHealthExpendData/Downloads/proj2010.pdf.

[79] *Id.*

[80] Exec. Order No. 13,335, 69 Fed. Reg. 24,059 (2004).

A key element of the HHS Framework for Strategic Action[81] is the establishment of Regional Health Information Organizations (RHIOs) throughout the country to coordinate an interoperable electronic health record system. ONCHIT believes that RHIOs are critical to health information exchange because they "reflect health care priorities of a local area as well as the legitimacy and trustworthiness of this activity to clinicians and consumers."[82] The office has provided little detail, however, about how a RHIO should be structured or how it would function. Although ONCHIT's report cited examples of existing collaboratives that coordinate the flow of data in some regions (such as the Santa Barbara County Care Data Exchange (SBCCDE) and the Share Health Information Across Regional Entities project in Massachusetts), the office did not endorse any of these organizations as models for other regions. Any model will need to establish contracts with its participants and be structured in a pro-competitive manner. It is interesting to note that after eight years of operation, the SBCCDE ceased its operations in late 2006. Phil Greene, chair of SBCCDE for most of its life, cited privacy and security concerns raised by participants, technology challenges, lack of community participation, and cynicism regarding SBCCDE's prospects for success as the major reasons for its failure.[83]

For an interoperable EHR to reach its potential, there must be common standards of what to include in the medical record and common technical standards. Therefore, while lawyers continue to struggle with the numerous complex legal issues surrounding implementation of an interoperable EHR, organizations such as the American Health Information Management Association (AHIMA) and American Medical Informatics Association (AMIA) have focused on the practical and technical issues.[84]

Implementation of these systems will require the investment of significant financial resources to license software and purchase hardware. In addition, the health care providers and possibly patients will need training in how to use the system. It is not clear who will be funding these initiatives or how much of the total expense will be borne by the government or, ultimately, the patients. To date, large-scale investment in the promotion of electronic health record systems on a regional basis has come largely from payors or major health systems rolling out EHR systems to their physicians, corporations, and government entities. For instance, Blue Cross Blue Shield of Massachusetts pledged $50 million to help fund pilot programs that will purchase and install EHR in participants' office settings and provide the systems with interoperability with other systems

---

[81] TOMMY G. THOMPSON & DAVID J. BRAILER, THE DECADE OF HEALTH INFORMATION TECHNOLOGY: DELIVERING CONSUMER-CENTRIC AND INFORMATION-RICH HEALTH CARE, FRAMEWORK FOR STRATEGIC ACTION 2 (July 21, 2004), *available at* http://www.providersedge.com/ehdocs/ehr_articles/The_Decade_of_HIT-Delivering_Customer-centric_and_Info-rich_HC.pdf.

[82] *Id.* at 17.

[83] Bruce Merlin Fried, *What Killed the Santa Barbara County Care Data Exchange,* iHEALTHBEAT (Mar. 12, 2007), *available at* http://www.ihealthbeat.org/Perspectives/2007/What-Killed-the-Santa-Barbara-County-Care-Data-Exchange.aspx.

[84] AMERICAN HEALTH INFORMATION MANAGEMENT ASSOCIATION, ET AL., THE COLLABORATIVE RESPONSE TO THE ONCHIT REQUEST FOR INFORMATION (Jan. 18, 2005), *available at* http://www.markle.org/sites/default/files/collaborative_response.pdf.

to allow data exchange.⁸⁵ Conducted by the Massachusetts e-Health Collaborative (MAeHC), these pilot programs collected valuable insight into the issues and barriers associated with developing an interoperable information exchange. The MAeHC is working to transition itself to a self-sustaining model. Large corporations, including, without limitation, AT&T, Wal-Mart, and Intel, formed a not-for-profit consortium, Dossia, to provide life-long electronic personal health records to their employees.⁸⁶ Government entities, such as the District of Columbia Department of Health, have sponsored EHR in the hopes of improving care and health among their citizens.⁸⁷ It remains to be seen whether such efforts can be integrated into a truly interoperable system in which patient information can be made available when needed and in a format compatible at the point of care where needed.

The provision of and payment for health care services require the creation and maintenance of vast amounts of information, as well as the communication of that information among many entities. Individuals' health care is paid for largely by government programs, private health plans contracting with employers or individuals, and employers or employer groups that self-insure. Unfortunately, the systems for processing health care claims can be complex and inefficient. Historically, there were few industry-wide standards, and individual providers used a range of paper and electronic systems to comply with varying and numerous information submission requirements and waded through voluminous lists (paper or electronic) to determine whether specific procedures or prescriptions would be reimbursed by the applicable payor.

However, as of October 16, 2003, another component of HIPAA⁸⁸—implemented through the transaction and code set regulations and other Medicare regulations—required that health care providers of a certain size and payors communicate most transactions electronically using common codes and standards to facilitate more efficient flow of reimbursement and related health care information. A May 2006 study found that 75 percent of all health insurance claims were submitted electronically, up from 44 percent in 2002 and 24 percent in 1995.⁸⁹ The implications of moving virtually all health care reimbursement (governmental and private) to electronic means could potentially have a dramatic impact on health care finance. This shift has also spawned significant growth in and innovation by e-commerce providers with specialties associated with every single point along the communication chain, such as biometric identification keys, secure e-mail gateways, "scrubbers" for identifiable health information, remote charge entry capture, and so on.

In 2009, revised HIPAA regulations corrected many problems and omissions in the original standard transactions.⁹⁰ These new HIPAA regulations must

---

⁸⁵Marianne Kolbasuk McGee, *Massachusetts Flips the Switch on $50 Million Health IT Test*, INFORMATIONWEEK (May 13, 2005), *available at* http://www.informationweek.com/news/163102079.

⁸⁶Dossia, Member Companies, *available at* http://www.dossia.org/about-dossia/member-companies.

⁸⁷DC RHIO, Frequently Asked Questions, *available at* http://www.dc-rhio.org/faq.

⁸⁸Standards for Electronic Transactions; Announcement of Designated Standard Maintenance Organizations; Final Rule and Notice, 65 Fed. Reg. 50,312 (Aug. 17, 2000).

⁸⁹Laura B. Benko, *E-claims Now the Norm,* MODERN HEALTHCARE, May 29, 2006, at 12.

⁹⁰45 C.F.R. §162.

be implemented by January 1, 2012. Also, one of the code sets used in the HIPAA standard transactions is being upgraded to a new version, ICD-10.[91] The adoption of ICD-10 codes will require extensive modification or replacement of existing e-health systems, as well as extensive training and policy development. The codes are a different length than the existing ICD-09 codes and are sufficiently different that implementation cannot be achieved by simply mapping ICD-09 codes to ICD-10 counterparts; in fact, there are about 68,000 ICD-10-CM codes used for documenting diagnoses versus about 14,000 ICD-9-CM codes, and about 87,000 ICD-10-PCS codes used for documenting procedures, versus about 4,000 ICD-9 codes.[92] The ICD-10 codes tend to convey greater specificity; for example, an ICD-9 code might only have identified the subject body part, whereas the related ICD-10 codes will specify the left or right body part and/or other details. Implementation of the revised HIPAA regulations and the ICD-10 codes is projected to range in total cost from $9 billion to $16 billion, with offsetting savings expected in later years.[93]

An incremental step in the implementation of the standard transactions is the replacement of payor-assigned identification numbers with a single National Provider Identifier (NPI). In reality, under various federal program rules and within the latitude granted providers under the NPI rule, each provider will likely have a number of NPIs rather than one single NPI. The NPI was scheduled to be the exclusive identifier allowed in standard transactions beginning in 2007. Implementation was delayed for one year due to industry's low level of compliance and to permit creation of a central database of NPIs. The original planned approach of having each payor compile its own list of NPIs was replaced by centralized dissemination of an NPI database by the National Plan and Provider Enumeration System. The revised due date for the exclusive use of the NPI on standard transactions was May 23, 2008. Most providers were providing both their NPI number and their legacy identification number on claims for months prior to the deadline, but few had submitted claims containing only the NPI. CMS did not postpone the May 23, 2008, deadline, and some observers anticipated a dramatic slowdown in claims payment due to difficulties and delays associated with matching (cross walking) each NPI to the appropriate legacy account number. However, the changeover to NPI-only claims did not create major disruption of claims processing.

Another incremental step in the implementation of the standard transactions will be the publication of a final regulation for claims attachments. A Notice of Proposed Rule Making was published in 2005, and comments were solicited on the proposed rule. The claims attachment final rule, when published,

---

[91]*Id.*

[92]American Medical Ass'n, ICD-10 Code Set, *available at* http://www.ama-assn.org/ama/pub/physician-resources/solutions-managing-your-practice/coding-billing-insurance/hipaa-health-insurance-portability-accountability-act/transaction-code-set-standards/icd10-code-set.page.

[93]*See* U.S. Dep't of Health & Human Servs., Health Insurance Reform: Modifications to the Health Insurance Portability and Accountability Act (HIPAA); Final Rule, 74 Fed. Reg. 3323 (Jan. 16, 2009); U.S. Dep't Health & Human Servs., HIPAA Administrative Simplification: Modifications to Medical Data Code Set Standards to Adopt ICD-10-CM and ICD-10-PCS; Final Rule, 74 Fed. Reg. 3361 (Jan. 16, 2009). Statistics are aggregated from the analysis of costs and benefits published as comments to the two Final Rules.

could result in extensive revision of the standard transactions, in part because attachments are being proposed for six areas—Ambulance Services, Emergency Department, Rehabilitation Services, Clinical Reports, Laboratory Results, and Medications—and in part because of likely pressure to incorporate any routinely attached information into a revised set of base transactions. In 2008, HHS indicated that a draft final rule was being circulated internally at HHS for approval, but the date that a final rule would be available was unknown. In the response to public comments in the January 16, 2009 *Federal Register,* HHS agreed to consider not requiring implementation of the claims attachments at the same time that the health care industry was implementing the revised HIPAA standards, but no commitment was set forth and no date for release of the claims attachment rule was provided at that time.[94] PPACA directed the Secretary of HHS to publish a final rule to establish a standard and operating rules for health claims attachments by January 1, 2014, to be effective not later than January 1, 2016.[95]

In addition, as EHR and CPOE systems are implemented and become more widely accepted, buttressed by the new federal regulations permitting donations and providing subsidies of such systems, consumers' expectations regarding both the availability of their medical records and the speed at which health care is delivered will also increase. Patients may expect same-day access to their medical records; online availability of lab results and appointment information; printable, on-demand drug interaction information; disease management services; and regular e-mail correspondence with their physicians.

It seems that the increased emphasis on health information technology means that more providers are starting to implement appropriate e-tools. For example, a June 2006 study by the Center for Studying Health System Change reported that nearly 21 percent of doctors interviewed in 2004–2005 said they had access to technology for four of five clinical tasks that have been shown to improve patient care. The tasks include obtaining information about treatment alternatives or guidelines, accessing patient information, writing prescriptions, exchanging clinical data with other physicians, and generating reminders for doctors to complete certain tasks.[96] Nevertheless, in 2004–2005, nearly 17 percent did not have access to e-tools for any of the five activities and 20 percent had access for only one activity.[97] Although health care providers have historically been slow to adopt such technologies, with federal and state attention focused on these initiatives, there is no shortage of e-health vendors offering an array of products to raise consumer expectations and prove to health care providers that technology can make the delivery of health care safer and more efficient.

---

[94] 74 Fed. Reg. 3306 (Jan. 16, 2009).

[95] PPACA §1104, Pub. L. No. 111-148, 124 Stat. 119 (Mar, 23, 2010), as amended by Pub. L. No. 111-152, 124 Stat. 1029 (Mar. 23, 2010).

[96] Marie C. Reed & Joy M. Grossman, *Growing Availability of Clinical Information Technology in Physician Practices,* DATA BULLETIN NO. 31 (Center for Studying Health System Change June 2006).

[97] *Id.*

V. Conclusion

Adoption of e-health practices presents numerous challenges, especially within the extensive regulatory framework that permeates every aspect of health care. Collecting, using, disclosing, and safeguarding health care information present challenges that greatly exceed the challenges involved in conducting most other businesses. Developing the value proposition for one's e-health product requires an understanding of reimbursement methods, practice of medicine regulations, anti-kickback prohibitions, and other rules that are not immediately obvious to the outsider. The government interest in e-health has potentially beneficial effects, such as incentives that could accelerate investment in e-health products, but also creates uncertainties, as additional legislation and regulations can instantly alter the business environment. The e-health industry needs to overcome major obstacles including security and authentication measures, standardization of data, interoperability rules and practices, and liability concerns. E-health counsel must draw upon diverse expertise to develop workable strategies for success and compliance in the health care environment, and to help make the case to investors that they can successfully invest in the evolving e-health field.

E-health companies have come to combine health care and all aspects of information technology, not just the Internet and communications capabilities. Although e-health companies continue to offer content, products, and connection services online, the offerings of e-health have vastly enlarged. Electronic prescribing has become commonplace, as is the availability of prescription information nationwide. Remote communication with medical devices and the presentation of analysis results online to physicians is growing, enabling more convenient follow-up. Remote health care services are becoming more accepted, as more products become available and reimbursement programs authorize more health care to be delivered remotely. The business of e-health is growing as the Internet's capabilities are integrated more closely with health care products and practices.

3

Health Information Technology*

I.	Introduction	43
II.	Government Health Information Technology Initiatives	44
III.	Development of Standards for Electronic Health Records	46
	A. Standards Development for Electronic Health Records	46
	B. Barriers to Adoption of Electronic Health Records	50
IV.	Health Information Exchanges	51
	A. Implementation of RHIOs	52
	B. Lessons Learned From Early RHIO Efforts	53
	C. RHIO Technology Providers Are Fragmented	56
V.	Accountable Care Organizations	56
VI.	Analysis of Health Care Data to Support Improvements and Comparative Effectiveness	57
	A. Data Aggregation for Analysis	57
	B. Issues With Aggregation	58
	C. Interoperability and the Aggregation of Data	59
	D. Risks of Electronic Health Care Data	60
VII.	Conclusions	61

I. INTRODUCTION

Health information technology (HIT) is an application of information technology capabilities and practices to health care. More than mere automation of health care administrative functions, HIT is the cornerstone of the federal government's health care improvement initiatives, which aim to improve the population's health and reduce costs by promoting broader use of electronic health records, facilitating sharing of such records among providers and patients, and employing statistical data analysis methods to assess the quality, safety, and efficiency of providers and treatment alternatives.

---

*John Healey, JD, CISSP, Blue Cross and Blue Shield Association, Chicago, Illinois.

II. Government Health Information Technology Initiatives

The federal government supports certain e-health initiatives as a way to improve the quality of health care and the health of the population. In April 2004, President George W. Bush issued an executive order that set a goal for the majority of Americans to have interoperable electronic health records (EHR) within 10 years.[1] In the same order, President Bush established the Office of the National Coordinator for Health Information Technology (ONCHIT) to develop and oversee a strategic plan for nationwide adoption of health information technology in the private and public sectors.[2] ONCHIT was tasked with delivering a report within 90 days of appointment discussing development of such a strategic plan.[3] In that initial report, ONCHIT identified four critical goals: (1) to inform clinical practice by introducing EHR directly into clinical practice; (2) to interconnect clinicians by developing an interoperable infrastructure that makes critical health care information accessible when clinical and/or treatment decisions are being made; (3) to personalize care to assist individuals to manage their health care and participate in their health care decisions; and (4) to improve population health by collecting timely, accurate, and detailed clinical information for evaluating health care delivery and to report critical findings to public health officials, researchers, and others.[4] Each of the four goals was supported by various strategies set forth in the report.

Subsequently, ONCHIT elaborated on those goals when it published and updated the Federal Health Information Technology Strategic Plan (HIT Plan).[5] The current HIT Plan (2011 through 2015) has evolved the original four goals into five new goals that reflect progress and experience gained over the past several years. The five goals are: (1) Achieve Adoption and Information Exchange through Meaningful Use of Health IT; (2) Improve Care, Improve Population Health, and Reduce Health Care Costs Through the Use of Health IT; (3) Inspire Confidence and Trust in Health IT; (4) Empower Individuals with Health IT to Improve their Health and the Health Care System; and (5) Achieve Rapid Learning and Technological Advancement.[6] ONCHIT recognizes that to obtain benefits from health IT, the first priority is to achieve nationwide adoption of EHR and widespread information exchange.[7]

---

[1] Exec. Order No. 13,335, 69 Fed. Reg. 24,059 (Apr. 30, 2004).

[2] *Id.*

[3] *Id.*

[4] Tommy Thompson and David Brailer, The Decade of Health Information Technology: Delivering Consumer-Centric and Information-rich Health Care, Framework for Strategic Action (July 21, 2004), *available at* http://healthit.hhs.gov/portal/server.pt/community/healthit_hhs_gov_home/1204.

[5] Office of the National Coordinator for Health Information Technology (ONC), Federal Health Information Technology Strategic Plan 2011–2015 (2011), *available at* http://healthit.hhs.gov/portal/server.pt/community/fed_health_it_strategic_plan/1211/home/15583.

[6] *Id.* at 4–5.

[7] *Id.* at 8.

The HIT Plan sets forth the strategies that ONCHIT plans to pursue to achieve its stated goals.[8] ONCHIT plans to rely on private markets to accomplish these objectives, although it recognizes it may need to intervene to correct what it perceives as market failures when necessary.[9] As discussed in Chapter 2,[10] EHR technology currently has a low level of adoption in the U.S. health care system. To promote introduction of EHR into clinical practice, ONCHIT's current strategy involves creating incentives to promote EHR adoption, reducing the risk of the investment in EHR technology, and promoting EHR adoption in rural and underserved areas.[11] ONCHIT and other government actors will eventually use reimbursement penalties to help promote adoption of HIT. Implementation support will be made available through Regional Extension Centers.[12] Additional HIT professionals will be trained through grants intended to support training and development of more than 50,000 new HIT professionals and meaningful-use measures for EHR will be incorporated into the U.S. medical education and certification processes.[13]

To interconnect providers and enable sharing of the EHR data, ONCHIT's strategy includes encouraging locally managed health information exchanges by incrementally including information sharing in incentive programs while also collaboratively developing national health information exchange models and eliminating regulatory barriers to implementation.[14] An additional strategy for interconnecting providers would require making federal health information systems interoperable and consistent with the Nationwide Health Information Network (NHIN), a standards-based collection of capabilities that creates an interoperable infrastructure to permit secure health information sharing among diverse networks and systems.[15] ONCHIT is also supporting the Direct Project to extend the NHIN to provide for simple, standards-based health information exchange between authorized care providers in support of meaningful use.[16] Once health information is electronically recorded and available for exchange, ONCHIT's strategy is to seek additional applications, including, among others, greater involvement by individuals in their own care. Personalizing care would require encouraging use of personal health records that contain not only an individual's health records but also customized information and guidance to help them understand their care and gain control over their health care activities. It would also involve supplying adequate information to enable consumers to select providers and institutions based on their values and information on the quality of care experienced at a given provider or institution.

---

[8] *Id.* at 10–48.

[9] *Id.* at 7.

[10] See Chapter 2 (Healey, E-Health Industry Overview).

[11] *Id.* at 8.

[12] *Id.* at 10.

[13] *Id.* at 10–11.

[14] *Id.* at 14.

[15] ONCHIT, Nationwide Health Information Network: History & Background, *available at* http://healthit.hhs.gov/portal/server.pt/community/healthit_hhs_gov__nhin_historical__background_information/1409.

[16] Dep't of Health & Human Servs., Direct Project FAQ, *available at* http://directproject.org/faq.php?key_faq.

Improving population health would require unifying public health surveillance architectures, streamlining quality and health status monitoring, and accelerating research and distribution of evidence concerning medical conditions and treatment. The federal HIT strategy envisions ensuring government and research access to aggregated EHR data and the development of sophisticated analytics programs that can be used to direct the health care delivery system.

III. Development of Standards for Electronic Health Records

A. Standards Development for Electronic Health Records

Initiatives by the federal government, including the establishment of ONCHIT within the U.S. Department of Health and Human Services (HHS) and the release of EHR and e-prescribing regulations, have focused on local efforts to promote the nationwide adoption of interoperable electronic health records for all Americans.[17] In 2005, HHS convened the American Health Information Community (AHIC), a federal advisory body, to make recommendations to HHS on how to accelerate the development and adoption of health information technology.[18] AHIC was composed of seven workgroups that addressed the following topics: (1) chronic care; (2) confidentiality, privacy, and security; (3) consumer empowerment; (4) EHR; (5) personalized health care; (6) population health (formerly biosurveillance); and (7) quality.

Each of the AHIC workgroups was tasked with providing recommendations to HHS that were designed to promote the adoption of interoperable electronic health records while protecting patient privacy and the security of the records. In particular, AHIC attempted to identify breakthrough areas that would produce tangible, specific benefits to health care consumers within two to three years.[19] The recommendations were developed into Use Cases, which described

---

[17] The mission of ONCHIT is to implement the President's vision for widespread adoption of interoperable electronic health records within 10 years. Via Executive Order No. 13,335, 69 Fed. Reg. 24,059 (Apr. 30, 2004), the national coordinator was charged with four primary responsibilities:
- to serve as the senior advisor to the Secretary of HHS and the President of the United States on all health information technology programs and initiatives;
- to develop and maintain a strategic plan to guide the nationwide implementation of interoperable electronic health records in both public and private health care sectors that will "reduce medical errors, improve quality, and produce greater value for health care expenditures";
- to coordinate health information technology programs and initiatives across the federal enterprise with a goal of avoiding duplication of efforts; and
- to coordinate all outreach activities to public and private industry.

See Office of the National Coordinator for Health Information Technology; Statement of Organization, Functions, and Delegation of Authoriy, 70 Fed. Reg. 48,718 (Aug. 19, 2005).

[18] See U.S. Dep't Health & Human Servs., Office of National Coordinator for Health Information Technology, American Health Information Community, *available at* http://www.hhs.gov/healthit/community/background.

[19] See U.S. Dep't Health & Human Servs., Office of National Coordinator for Health Information Technology, American Health Information Community: Breakthroughs, *available at* http://www.hhs.gov/healthit/community/breakthroughs.

affected stakeholders, information flow, issues, and system needs in sufficient detail and context for standards harmonization, certification considerations, architecture specifications, and detailed policy discussions. In 2007, Use Cases for Consumer Access to Clinical Information, Medication Management, and Quality were added to the initial Use Cases developed in 2006 on Biosurveillance, Electronic Health Record (Lab Results Reporting), Consumer Empowerment, and Emergency Responder Electronic Health Record. Six additional Use Cases were selected for development in 2008: Remote Monitoring, Patient-Provider Secure Messaging, Personalized Healthcare, Consultations and Transfers of Care, Public Health Case Reporting, and Immunizations & Response Management.[20] Upon approval, Use Cases served as input to the Health Information Technology Standards Panel (HITSP) for the development of Interoperability Specifications, which in turn were input for the development by the Certification Commission for Health Information Technology (CCHIT) of certification criteria and test scripts. Ultimately, the expanding number of Use Cases was expected to result in an increasingly detailed interoperability certification process. AHIC was also intended to serve as a forum for participation for key stakeholders regarding achieving interoperability of health information technology.[21] In 2008, AHIC transitioned from a federal advisory body to a successor entity, the National e-Health Collaborative (NeHC), a public-private partnership.[22] The NeHC was established by a grant from ONCHIT and serves as a forum for collaboratively setting priorities and initiatives for universal health IT adoption.[23]

The American National Standards Institute (ANSI) administered HITSP, which, under contract to ONCHIT, acted as a coordinating body to enable affected parties to identify and harmonize standards for performing health information technology tasks described in the Use Cases. HITSP defined "standards" as specifications, code sets, or other guidelines that are produced through a well-defined approach; have been agreed upon by a group of experts; have been publicly vetted; provide rules, guidelines, or characteristics; help to ensure that materials, products, processes, and services are fit for their intended purpose; are available in an accessible format; and are subject to an ongoing review and revision process.[24]

In practice, HITSP has typically selected well recognized and widely used standards, including Health Level 7 communication protocols, CPT-4, ICD-9 CM, and ICD-10 CM codes, and other standards that are already familiar in

---

[20]*See* U.S. Dep't Health & Human Servs., Office of the National Coordinator for Health Information Technology, Consultations and Transfers of Care Detailed Use Case, *available at* http://www.hhs.gov/healthit/usecases/reftx.html.

[21]*See* Office of the National Coordinator for Health Information Technology, Health IT Home, *available at* http://www.hhs.gov/healthit/documents/hitframework.pdf.

[22]*See* News Release, U.S. Dep't of Health & Human Servs., *HHS Secretary Highlights Contributions of Health IT Advisory Panel* (Nov. 12, 2008), *available at* http://www.hhs.gov/news/press/2008pres/11/20081112a.html.

[23]National e-Health Collaborative, About Us, *available at* http://www.nationalehealth.org/AboutUS.

[24]*See* Health Information Technology Standards Panel [HITSP], Interoperability Specification Overview, *available at* http://publicaa.ansi.org/sites/apdl/hitspadmin/Reference Documents/HITSP Interoperability Specification Overview.pdf.

the health care environment, thereby simplifying adoption and avoiding the overhead of rolling out new standards. Using the identified standards, HITSP created Interoperability Specifications that address the core requirements of one or more Use Cases. Due to limitations of the standards, the Interoperability Specifications may not define all the functions necessary in a real-world system. Interoperability Specifications are not intended to serve as what software practitioners would commonly refer to as "functional specifications" that describe all system functions in detail. The implementer of the system must provide the infrastructure, features, and functionality to meet legal, regulatory, best-practice, and business requirements. Interoperability Specifications are intended to be architecturally neutral and to undergo review, comment, and testing by interested parties prior to release. The Interoperability Specifications serve as input to CCHIT for development into criteria and test scripts for assessment of interoperability under the Stark physician self-referral exceptions[25] and anti-kickback safe harbors,[26] as well as the contracting preferences set forth in Executive Order 13,410.[27] HITSP's contract with HHS expired on April 30, 2010.[28]

Originally a public-private entity but now an independent nonprofit organization, CCHIT incorporates the HITSP standards as criteria for product certification on an ongoing basis to promote interoperability.[29] CCHIT offers three distinct certification programs: (1) the CCHIT Certified® program; (2) the ONC-ATCB Certification; and (3) the EHR Alternative Certification. CCHIT Certified® is a certification program that assesses EHR for integrated functionality, interoperability, and security using CCHIT's independently developed criteria.[30] Within the CCHIT Certified® program, CCHIT offers multiple tracks for obtaining certification: Ambulatory, Emergency Department, and Inpatient, plus an Enterprise certification that demonstrates interoperability within those three settings, and also offers various optional add-on certifications.[31] CCHIT schedules certification efforts for specific product types during each year and grants a three-year certification. However, for the Stark exception and safe harbors, discussed above, to apply to donations of HIT, the certification must have been performed within one year prior to the donation.

The CCHIT criteria are written to implement the Interoperability Specification but also incorporate a road map that discusses planned criteria for the following two years. CCHIT envisions updating the criteria each year to fully

---

[25] Safe Harbors for Certain Electronic Prescribing and Electronic Health Records Arrangements Under the Anti-Kickback Statute, 72 Fed. Reg. 45,110 (Aug. 8, 2006).

[26] Physicians' Referrals to Health Care Entities With Which They Have Financial Relationships; Exceptions for Certain Electronic Prescribing and Electronic Health Records Arrangements; Final Rule, 71 Fed. Reg. 45,140 (Aug. 8, 2006).

[27] News Release, Dep't of Health & Human Servs., *Executive Order Is Helping "Change the Culture" in Health Care to Achieve Better Quality, Value, and Affordability, HHS Secretary Leavitt Reports* (Aug. 23, 2007), *available at* http://www.hhs.gov/news/press/2007pres/08/20070823a.html.

[28] *See* HITSP, Welcome to www.HITSP.org, *available at* http://www.hitsp.org/default.aspx.

[29] *See* News Release, U.S. Dep't of Health & Human Servs., *American Health Information Community Approves First Set of Recommendations* (May 17, 2006), *available at* http://archive.hhs.gov/news/press/2006pres/20060517a.html.

[30] *See* Certification Commission for Health Information Technology, Get Certified, *available at* http://www.cchit.org/get_certified/cchit-certified-2011.

[31] *Id.*

implement the HITSP standards and to incorporate any newly revised HITSP standards. The evolving standards and planned yearly updates have drawn some criticism from the HIT industry, which notes, among other issues, that the one-year certification period may expire in the midst of a donating entity's program and/or force the entity to donate a variety of product versions; that planning to implement new CCHIT technical requirements each year may disrupt product development efforts that typically have longer revision cycles; and that the CCHIT certification process consumes excessive amounts of resources.[32] CCHIT's second certification program certifies that EHR are capable of meeting government-defined "meaningful use" criteria to qualify for incentive payments under the American Recovery and Reinvestment Act of 2009 (ARRA).[33] CCHIT is recognized by ONCHIT as an Authorized Testing and Certification Body (an ONC-ATCB) for performing such certifications.[34] CCHIT offers a third certification program, the EHR Alternative Certification, a simplified, low-cost certification for providers and hospitals that develop or assemble EHR technologies themselves and should enable such providers and hospitals to qualify for ARRA incentives.[35]

The Health Information Technology for Economic and Clinical Health Act (HITECH Act)[36] established a successor to the Office of the National Coordinator of Health Information Technology, an HIT Policy Committee, and an HIT Standards Committee, each similar in function to the previously existing ONCHIT, AHIC, and HITSP entities, respectively. Although there is a certification function in the HITECH Act, it does not set forth a counterpart to CCHIT. Appointments to the HIT Policy and Standards Committees included at least nine members of the NeHC Board of Directors,[37] thereby ensuring some level of continuity between the old and successor organizations.

The HIT Policy and Standards Committees are now operational and have been delivering recommendations to ONCHIT. As required by the HITECH Act, ONCHIT has issued an interim final rule and final rule establishing an initial set of standards, implementation specifications, and certification criteria for electronic health records technology, a first step towards enhancing the interoperability, functionality, utility, and security of health information technology and to support its meaningful use.[38] In part, the interim final rule was intended to support the first stage of the Medicare and Medicaid EHR Incentive Programs.[39] The Incentive Programs have three planned stages of meaningful use. Stage 1

---

[32]Letter from Electronic Health Record Vendors Association (Mar. 17, 2007).

[33]*Get Certified.*

[34]*Id.*

[35]*Id.*

[36]American Recovery and Reinvestment Act of 2009, Health Information Technology for Economic and Clinical Health Act (HITECH Act), §13001 *et seq.,* Pub. L. No. 111-05, 123 Stat. 115 (Feb. 17, 2009).

[37]Press Release, National e-Health Collaborative, *National e-Health Collaborative Regarding the Announcement of Appointments to the HHS HIT Policy and Standards Committees* (May 8, 2009), *available at* http://www.nationalehealth.org/ShowContent.aspx?id=269.

[38]Health Information Technology: Initial Set of Standards, Implementation Specifications, and Certification Criteria for Electronic Health Record Technology; Final Rule, 75 Fed. Reg. 44,590 (July 28, 2010).

[39]*Id.* at 44,591.

began in 2011 and focuses on capturing health information electronically, using such information to track key clinical conditions, communicating such information for care coordination, implementing clinical decision support tools, and reporting clinical quality measures and public health information. Stages 2 and 3 will add functionality. Stage 2 begins in 2013 and may encourage the use of health information technology for continuous quality improvement at the point of care, exchange of information in structured format (such as Computerized Provider Order Entry (CPOE)), and the electronic transmission of diagnostic test results. Stage 3 begins in 2015 and may promote quality improvements, safety, and efficiency, with an emphasis on decision support for national high priority conditions, patient access to self-management tools, access to comprehensive patient data, and improving population health.[40]

B. Barriers to Adoption of Electronic Health Records

Barriers, including financial considerations, regulatory concerns, workflow concerns, and ease-of-use issues, continue to inhibit adoption of EHR. Purchasing and implementing an EHR system can require a significant up-front expenditure, including the purchase or license cost and the fees for services to set up the product and populate it with existing patient information. While incentives may be available, they are paid over a period of time, and small health care providers may not be able to afford the up-front expenditure. Selecting a hosted application, such as an Internet-based product from an application service provider, may reduce the up-front expenditure and make the EHR system more affordable. Cost is a particular concern to the health care provider, because the benefits of an EHR system are likely to accrue not to the provider but to the consumer and to other providers and payors that use the data collected by the EHR purchaser. The provider may not want to pay for ongoing support or to hire additional technical staff to maintain the EHR.

In some cases, large providers such as hospitals may choose to donate EHR technology to providers with whom they share patients. Such a donation policy may be justified from the hospitals' perspective due to expected savings from more efficient communication of patient records during referrals from participating providers to the hospital. Current regulations prohibit health care providers from participating in certain financial dealings that might lead to inappropriate remuneration, such as the Stark law and the anti-kickback regulations, discussed in III.A., above, and the False Claims Act.[41] The Centers for Medicare and Medicaid Services (CMS) and the HHS Office of Inspector General (OIG) have issued final regulations that are intended to promote the widespread use of e-prescribing and interoperable EHR systems by permitting donation of EHR technology under certain conditions.[42] Even with the new regulations, it is a

---

[40]Health Information Technology: Initial Set of Standards Implementation Specifications, and Configuration Criteria for Electronic Health Record Technology; Interim Final Rule, 75 Fed. Reg. 2016 (Jan. 13, 2010).

[41]31 U.S.C. §3829–3733.

[42]Safe Harbors for Certain Electronic Prescribing and Electronic Health Records Arrangements Under the Anti-Kickback Statute; Final Rule, 71 Fed. Reg. 45,110 (Aug. 8, 2006); Exceptions for Certain Electronic Prescribing and Electronic Health Records Arrangements; Final Rule, 71 Fed. Reg. 45,140 (Aug. 8, 2006).

challenging task for any health system to manage an EHR donation program that remains compliant. In addition, use of an EHR system needs to be coordinated with the existing, complex federal and state legal landscape surrounding privacy and security, including the Health Information Portability and Accountability Act (HIPAA),[43] the HITECH Act, and implementing regulations. Health care providers will need to adopt and implement policies and procedures that maintain the privacy and security of patients' health information.

The use of an EHR system may require that the provider change its established work processes. Using EHR may require that certain additional steps be performed or may require additional documentation that the provider had not previously collected. In a fee-for-service environment where the provider desires to minimize unproductive uses of time, any disruption of established work processes is a barrier to adoption. Customization of the EHR workflow to suit established patterns and preimplementation training may help reduce the disruption of workflow and any attendant loss of productivity.

IV. HEALTH INFORMATION EXCHANGES

ONCHIT's objective with respect to health information exchange is to incorporate more rigorous interoperability and exchange requirements into subsequent stages of meaningful use, thus ensuring that patient information follows the patient to the point of care and informs critical health decisions.[44] A key element of the HHS Framework for Strategic Action[45] is the establishment of Regional Health Information Organizations (RHIOs) throughout the country to coordinate an interoperable electronic health record system. ONCHIT believes that RHIOs are critical to health information exchange because they "reflect health care priorities of a local area as well as the legitimacy and trustworthiness of this activity to clinicians and consumers."[46] ONCHIT has provided little detail, however, about how a RHIO should be structured or how it would function. For an interoperable EHR to reach its potential, there must be common standards of what to include in the medical record and common technical standards. Therefore, while lawyers continue to struggle with the numerous complex legal issues surrounding implementation of interoperable EHR, organizations such as the American Health Information Management Association (AHIMA) and American Medical Informatics Association (AMIA) have focused on the practical and technical issues.[47]

---

[43] Pub. L. No. 104-191, 110 Stat. 1936 (Aug. 21, 1996).

[44] OFFICE OF THE NATIONAL COORDINATOR FOR HEALTH INFORMATION TECHNOLOGY, FEDERAL HEALTH INFORMATION TECHNOLOGY STRATEGIC PLAN 2011–2015, at 13 (2011), available at http://healthit.hhs.gov/portal/server.pt/community/fed_health_it_strategic_plan/1211/home/15583.

[45] U.S. DEP'T OF HEALTH & HUMAN SERVS., THE DECADE OF HEALTH INFORMATION TECHNOLOGY: DELIVERING CONSUMER-CENTRIC AND INFORMATION-RICH HEALTH CARE: FRAMEWORK FOR STRATEGIC ACTION (July 21, 2004), available at http://www.hhs.gov/healthit/documents/hitframework.pdf.

[46] Id. at 17.

[47] AMERICAN HEALTH INFORMATION MANAGEMENT ASSOCIATION, ET AL., THE COLLABORATIVE RESPONSE TO THE ONCHIT REQUEST FOR INFORMATION (Jan. 18, 2005), available at http://www.markle.org/sites/default/files/collaborative_response.pdf.

A. Implementation of RHIOs

Implementation of RHIOs will require the investment of significant financial resources to license software and purchase hardware. In addition, the health care providers and possibly patients will need training in how to use the system. It is not clear who will be funding these initiatives and how much of the total expense will be borne by the government or, ultimately, the patients. To date, large-scale investment in the promotion of electronic health record systems on a regional basis has come largely from payors or major health systems rolling out EHR systems to their physicians, corporations, and government entities. For instance, Blue Cross Blue Shield of Massachusetts has pledged $50 million to help fund pilot programs that will purchase and install EHR systems in participants' office settings and provide the systems with interoperability with other functions to allow data exchange.[48] Conducted by the Massachusetts e-Health Collaborative (MAeHC), these pilot programs were expected to be completed in mid-2010, and the MAeHC was working to transition itself to a self-sustaining model. Large corporations, including without limitation AT&T, Wal-Mart, and Intel, formed a not-for-profit consortium, Dossia, to provide life-long electronic personal health records to their employees.[49] Government entities, such as the District of Columbia Department of Health, have sponsored EHR systems in the hopes of improving care and health among their citizens.[50] It remains to be seen whether such efforts can be integrated into a truly interoperable system in which patient information can be made available when needed and in a format compatible at the point of care where needed.

Although collaboratives exist that coordinate the flow of data in some regions (such as the Santa Barbara County Care Data Exchange (SBCCDE), discussed in IV.B., below, and the Share Health Information Across Regional Entities project in Massachusetts), ONCHIT did not endorse any of these organizations as models for other regions. Any model will need to establish contracts with its participants and be structured in a procompetitive manner. However, the experience with Health Information Exchanges (HIEs) demonstrates the difficulty of implementing and maintaining an exchange.

Exchanges can be divided into two types—a "closed" system and an "open" system.[51] An example of a closed system is the Veterans Health Administration's VISTA system, which exchanges information among VA facilities.[52] An "open" system is exemplified by the RHIOs, community-based HIE initiatives that support the exchange of health information among independent entities within a geographic region. Open systems must overcome more issues such as technological and administrative hurdles associated with integrating technology from

---

[48]Marianne Kolbasuk McGee, *Massachusetts Flips the Switch on $50 Million Health IT Test,* INFORMATIONWEEK (May 13, 2005), *available at* http://www.informationweek.com/news/163102079.

[49]Dossia, Member Companies, *available at* http://www.dossia.org/about-dossia/member-companies.

[50]*See, e.g.*, DC RHIO, Frequently Asked Questions, *available at* http://www.dc-rhio.org/faq.

[51]Fontaine, Patricia, et al., *Systematic Review of Health Information Exchange in Primary Care Practices*, 23(5) J. AMER. BD. FAM. MED. 655 (Sept.–Oct. 2010).

[52]*Id.*

different vendors, organizational concerns, and less clear incentives to share data.[53] A survey of RHIOs conducted in 2007 identified 138 organizations that promoted clinical data exchange, of which approximately one quarter were determined to be defunct.[54] Of the 83 respondents to the survey, 32 reported facilitating health information exchange among independent entities and 3 reported facilitating health information exchange among physicians and hospitals that were part of the same integrated network as of January 1, 2007. Forty-five of the RHIOs were still in the planning stages.[55] Of the RHIOs that reported successfully exchanging health information, only 15 conducted such exchange across a range of patient populations totaling more than 5,000 patients, while the others were limited to specific target populations such as Medicaid enrollees, uninsured populations, and chronically ill patients or were limited in scope to fewer than 5,000 patients.[56] Of those RHIOs that were exchanging data, 40 percent were still heavily dependent upon grants, and only 5 percent earned enough revenue to be profitable.[57]

An annual survey of RHIOs revealed that the number of health information exchanges had grown to 255 in 2011, including 46 new initiatives.[58] At least 10 initiatives had closed or consolidated since the previous year.[59] Only 24 initiatives reported that they had sustainable business models, up from 18 in 2010.[60] Key findings of the survey indicated that health information exchanges continue to experience technological problems and systems integration issues, that the exchanges are developing more complex privacy controls for patients, even in the absence of new federal requirements, and that the federal Nationwide Health Information Network's Direct Project is being incorporated into over half of the exchanges.[61] Despite the current uncertainty over the requirements of accountable care organizations (ACOs), a quarter of the exchanges indicated that they will support an ACO, and about one-third are offering services that support meaningful use requirements.[62]

B. Lessons Learned From Early RHIO Efforts

Perhaps one of the most visible examples of the difficulties confronting RHIOs was the experience of the Santa Barbara County Care Data Exchange

---

[53]*Id.*

[54]Julia Adler-Milstein, *The State of Regional Health Information Organizations: Current Activities and Financing*, 27 HEALTH AFFAIRS (2008), *available at* http://content.healthaffairs.org/content/27/1/w60.full?sid=21336488-e04f-498e-a851-8a17abd51347.

[55]*Id.*

[56]*Id.*

[57]*Id.*

[58]Press Release, eHealth Initiative, *New National Survey Shows Increased Privacy Controls, Concerns with Systems Integration and Participation in Accountable Care* (July 14, 2011), *available at* http://www.ehealthinitiative.org/about-us/press/press-releases/647-new-national-survey-shows-increased-privacy-controls-concerns-with-systems-integration-and-participation-in-accountable-care.html.

[59]*Id.*

[60]*Id.*

[61]*Id.*

[62]*Id.*

(SBCCDE). Launched in 1998, the SBCCDE sought to create an exchange that would serve the 400,000 residents of Santa Barbara County, California.[63] The initial funding of $10 million dollars was supplied by the California Health-Care Foundation (CHCF).[64] Initially, SBCCDE attempted to use off-the-shelf technology to construct the infrastructure necessary to exchange health information.[65] However, it encountered technical difficulties that impeded progress and decided to develop custom software to implement its own concepts.[66] Prototyping proceeded slowly, and integration of the software with the legacy software systems of the participants was a formidable challenge.[67] SBCCDE decided to change its solution architecture and to create a repository for each participant's data to handle retrieval and standardization of data from source systems and delivery of data to requestors.[68] Costs soared, and the software developer invested its own funds—estimated at $5 to $11 million dollars—after CHCF's $10 million dollars in grant money was exhausted.[69] Further modifications were made to the software, and by 2006, 28 project interfaces to 10 types of data in 8 participating organizations had been built and tested.[70] In concert with the software development, the participating organizations had been addressing the HIE's business issues, including what data would be exchanged or excluded from exchange, who was authorized to receive data, who would be liable for data breaches, and who would pay for the HIE once the grant funding was exhausted.[71] In 2004, the participants had formed a not-for-profit entity to oversee governance and administration of the SBCCDE.[72] This not-for-profit entity began to revise or renew the participation agreements with data submitters and recipients.[73] Liability issues emerged as a key obstacle to progress, as none of the parties wanted liability for HIE mistakes.[74] By the fall of 2006, only the vendor and four Santa Barbara organizations had signed data agreements, and only two organizations were actually supplying data for users.[75] In addition to negotiating the data agreements, the SBCCDE attempted to negotiate funding arrangements for ongoing operations and software enhancements, estimated at around $500,000 per year.[76] SBCCDE was only able to raise a portion of

---

[63] Robert H. Miller & Bradley S. Miller, *The Santa Barbara County Care Data Exchange: What Happened?*, 26 HEALTH AFFAIRS (Aug. 1, 2007), *available at* http://healthaffairs.org/content/26/5/w568.full.html.

[64] *Id.* at w570.
[65] *Id.*
[66] *Id.* at w571.
[67] *Id.*
[68] *Id.*
[69] *Id.*
[70] *Id.* at w572.
[71] *Id.*
[72] *Id.*
[73] *Id.*
[74] *Id.*
[75] *Id.*
[76] *Id.* at w573.

the money, and the SBCCDE board voted to cease operations as of December 2006.[77]

The termination of the SBCCDE illustrates a number of important considerations that RHIOs must address from their inception. SBCCDE personnel identify the following factors as having doomed the effort: (1) funding source, (2) lack of community leadership, (3) lack of momentum and credibility, (4) vendor limitations, and (5) lack of a compelling value proposition. Of the various causes, the main underlying cause was the lack of a compelling value proposition for the SBCCDE.

The availability of the $10 million in grant money from CHCF motivated participants to engage in the project when they night otherwise not have, had they been required to supply the financing, or a significant portion of the financing, from the beginning.[78] The foundation money was given in recognition that the benefits of the project might accrue to the larger community beyond the actual SBCCDE participants.[79] Organizations may have accepted greater risk in the SBCCDE's approach due to the CHCF grant, whereas they would likely have tailored the effort to deliver a greater tangible return to their operations if their own resources had been at risk.[80]

The SBCCDE also experienced a lack of community participation in the decision-making processes.[81] In part, the passive demeanor of the participating organizations was due to the fact that grant money, instead of their own resources, was at risk, and because the superior expertise of the software developer led the participating organizations not to participate actively in the development decisions.[82] For their part, the CHCF and software developer anticipated that community involvement would grow over time.[83] As a result, the HIE structures and business cases did not necessarily address the participating organizations' business needs.[84]

The lack of momentum brought about by the frequent delays and re-engineering of portions of the software dulled interest among the participating organizations. Delays created doubts about the project and diluted the vision of what would be delivered. Additionally, the delays in implementation prevented a learning and refinement process from improving the software.[85] This lack of momentum also dimmed the expectation among participants of receiving more robust and valuable services over time.[86]

The vendor encountered a number of difficulties related to the software. The initial off-the-shelf approach was abandoned, and subsequent efforts to

---

[77] Id.
[78] Id.
[79] Id.
[80] Id. at w573–w574.
[81] Id. at w574.
[82] Id.
[83] Id.
[84] Id.
[85] Id.
[86] Id.

create a custom software application required repeated rework.[87] The technical risks undertaken by the software developer were huge, and the delays and staff turnover disillusioned the participants.[88]

Lack of a compelling value proposition was the most important factor in the demise of the SBCCDE. Much of the data that would have been handled by the SBCCDE was already available through Internet portals run by the individual provider organizations[89] or through existing internal electronic systems.[90] In addition, SBCCDE had not been able, after two years of negotiations,[91] to finalize a data agreement with the dominant lab service, which would have represented a value to the other participants.[92]

C. RHIO Technology Providers Are Fragmented

The market for health information exchange technology is served by over 35 companies that provide health information technology to data-sharing initiatives.[93] In a 2011 survey, 196 of 255 health data exchanges responded, and the largest HIE vendor was Axolotl, providing products and services to 22 of the respondents.[94] Second was Medicity, serving 14 HIEs.[95] Cerner and Mirth were tied for third-largest vendor, with 9 HIEs each.[96] The survey also found that more than 12 vendors serve only 1 HIE, and that at least 8 exchanges use self-developed products.[97] Fragmentation among the vendors supplying the HIE technology may lead to difficulties developing standards and disruption among the existing HIEs if the market consolidates.

V. Accountable Care Organizations

CMS published its proposed rule regarding accountable care organizations in March 2011. ACOs are voluntary organizations in which the providers agree to share the risks of patient outcomes. ACOs are required to operate for not less than three years, must treat at least 5,000 Medicare beneficiaries, and must have a sufficient number of primary care physicians to treat the ACO beneficiary population.[98] The ACO is required to implement evidence-based medicine or clinical practice guidelines and processes in an effort to improve individual

---

[87] *Id.*
[88] *Id.*
[89] *Id.* at w575.
[90] *Id.*
[91] *Id.* at w573.
[92] *Id.* at w575.
[93] Marianne Kolbasuk McGee, *HIE Vendor Market Poised for Shakeup*, Information Week (Sept. 7, 2011), *available at* http://www.informationweek.com/news/healthcare/interoperability/231600849.
[94] *Id.*
[95] *Id.*
[96] *Id.*
[97] *Id.*
[98] Accountable Care Organizations, 42 C.F.R. §425.18 (proposed Mar. 31, 2011).

care, improve the health of the population, and lower the growth of health care expenditures.[99] ACOs are required to have an infrastructure that enables the ACO to collect and evaluate data and provide feedback to ACO participants and ACPO providers and suppliers across the entire ACO, including providing information to influence care at the point of care.[100]

The required infrastructure for an ACO may be a certified EHR system that satisfies meaningful-use requirements. Details concerning ACOs are sketchy at best, and some clarification is expected in the final rule. Already, over a dozen organizations have submitted applications to become ACOs at the start of 2012. The creation of ACOs may contribute to the advancement of EHR and health care analytics programs as a means of satisfying the requirement for an infrastructure to collect and evaluate data and to provide feedback to inform the providing of care.

VI. Analysis of Health Care Data to Support Improvements and Comparative Effectiveness

A. Data Aggregation for Analysis

Local EHR systems and HIEs offer limited analytical benefit for several reasons: they are typically limited in size as represented by the number of patients whose data is being exchanged, and the data may be present in incompatible formats. As discussed in IV.A., above, as of 2007, only 15 RHIOs were exchanging information on more than 5,000 patients. A typical primary care physician may have 1,500 patients or more in his or her practice. Deriving data points from 5,000 records is of limited use. Ideally, one would want to have a much larger population from which to draw benchmarks that account for variables among the population, and then to compare an individual provider's experience against a statistically valid benchmark that was adjusted to reflect similar populations. For example, drawing benchmarks from the Medicare data that the U.S. government is making available for analytics may be of limited use to a provider whose patient population is women of child-bearing age; the primarily elderly Medicare population does not manifest many of the same concerns associated with the younger group, including the potential for concerns about the effect of drugs and treatment regimens on reproduction.

Tracking quality metrics in health care has been a difficult endeavor. The fragmented delivery system means that it is difficult to aggregate enough records to create valid benchmarks. Even when such benchmarks can be created, some of the organizations being evaluated object on the basis that their patient population is "different" from the population underlying the benchmark. Typical objections are based on populations that are sicker than the benchmark due to lower access to preventive care; a lack of health insurance that results in delaying treatment until symptoms are severe; demographic factors such as poverty that contributes to poorer nutrition; and a higher rate of co-morbidities.

---

[99] *Id.* §425.5.
[100] *Id.* §§425.5, .11.

Ideally, to obtain the benefit of health care analytics, one would want a large sample population so that benchmarks could be adjusted to account for such differences.

Typically, when an organization aggregates data for use in analytics, it makes an up-front decision concerning what data to incorporate and sets a standard for how that data may validly be represented. As a simple example, an aggregator may determine that the data item for "patient gender" may be specified as either "M" for male or "F" for female. As the aggregator incorporates available data sets from participants, it may find that some use the full words "male" and "female" in their data. Others use codes, such as 0 for male and 1 for female. Still others may use an extended set of codes, including codes for transgender individuals. Some of the data collectors will not make patient gender a required field, so blanks or null values may be encountered. Still others may require that a value be entered for the data item but not validate its value against a list of allowed values, so random entries such as UNK, N/A, TBD, or 999 may be present. This example addresses only one data item, but the described practices are likely present in each of the data items being shared. As a result, an effort to analyze data across all these different sources must either account for the differences in the data or disregard data that does not conform, risking biasing the results.

Typically, to create a data set that is useful for analysis, an aggregator will undertake a number of data validation and cleansing steps. As in the above example, the aggregator may determine the allowed values for each data item. When adding data to the aggregated set, the aggregator may then examine each of the values to ensure it is one of the allowed choices.

B. Issues With Aggregation

The availability of an EHR for every American would give health care providers access to an unprecedented amount of information. It is unclear whether access to this information would raise the standard of care or if providers would be able to evaluate the relevant information in a reasonable time, given current reimbursement models and the possible distribution of the information among a personal health record and multiple EHR maintained by various sources. In addition, it is unclear how providers would be able to assess the reliability of the data and whether providers would be responsible if they relied on potentially inaccurate or incomplete information.

Moreover, the participants in an EHR project would need to address the competing intellectual property rights among the members. Although a provider might ultimately own the medical records and patients would have certain access rights, an interoperable system would provide opportunities to track and create valuable aggregated data. Questions regarding ownership of such data and who should have access to the medical record and for what purposes would require consideration and agreement before an interoperable EHR system could be fully implemented. The owner of the technology used to store and maintain EHR would be understandably protective of its intellectual property rights in the technology, and the use of the data contained therein would require a balancing of the intellectual property rights among the technology provider, health care providers, and patients.

Currently, HIPAA permits unlimited use of information de-identified by certain statistical methods or by removal of 18 specified data elements. The current HIPAA approach is unsatisfactory both to privacy advocates and advocates of wider use of health data. Privacy advocates challenge de-identification by removal of the 18 data elements because certain subjects could be re-identified on the basis of the remaining data. Those who want to use de-identified information more freely argue that allowing de-identification to the level of Metropolitan Statistical Area (rather than state) would permit correlation of health studies to other population demographic information. HHS conducted a workshop in March 2010 to bring together stakeholders and to begin preparing guidance on the acceptable re-identification risk for health data, currently defined as "very small" in the HIPAA Privacy Rule. Such guidance was expected to be published in 2010 but has not yet been released.

The existence of large quantities of electronic health information offers new positive capabilities but also presents risks. The U.S. Food and Drug Administration (FDA) launched the Sentinel Initiative in 2008 in response to the FDA Amendment Act (FDAAA),[101] which directed the FDA to establish an active monitoring system for monitoring drugs using electronic data.[102] The FDA envisioned monitoring all FDA-regulated products by linking multiple existing databases[103] and was surveying health care data systems to identify potential data sources.[104] The stated aim was to better track the safety and effectiveness of drugs, biologics, and medical devices, but the FDA recognized that such an effort poses governance, privacy, data standards, and public availability concerns.[105]

Finally, before a national electronic health infrastructure can be successfully implemented, Americans will have to overcome cultural barriers regarding its use. Patients are concerned about the privacy, security, and accuracy of their data. A full-fledged educational program that demonstrates to the public that electronic health records are as secure and accurate as paper records—or more so—will be a crucial first step in overcoming cultural misgivings regarding a paperless medical record. Similarly, physicians and patients alike must be convinced that the benefits of an interoperable EHR system will merit the time and money required to implement a workable system.

C. Interoperability and the Aggregation of Data

To exploit the value of interoperable systems, health care data need to be aggregated together for large-scale analysis and reporting. Currently, donation of EHR is often by individual health system, RHIOs are local, and ACOs need

---

[101] Pub. L. No. 110-85, 121 Stat. 823 (Sept. 27, 2007).

[102] FDA, FDA's Sentinel Initiative—Background, *available at* http://www.fda.gov/Safety/FDAsSentinelInitiative/ucm149340.htm.

[103] *Id.*

[104] FDA, FDA's Sentinel Initiative—Ongoing Projects, *available at* http://www.fda.gov/Safety/FDAsSentinelInitiative/ucm203500.htm.

[105] FDA, FDA's Sentinel Initiative—Background, *available at* http://www.fda.gov/Safety/FDAsSentinelInitiative/ucm149340.htm.

only be in the thousands or tens of thousands of patients (although some actual proposals are for much larger systems). The HIT Strategy envisions aggregating vast data sets for the application of analytics, which could provide the statistically valid population sizes needed for meaningful research. Previously difficult and time-consuming collection of paper records could be avoided once EHR systems and HIEs are in widespread operation, especially if they adopt the Nationwide Health Information Network standards for communicating health care information.

Common data elements and rules could permit development of huge data warehouses for research and analysis. There are existing analytics vendors that purchase and aggregate large amounts of data, and there are insurers who handle such data sets, numbering in the tens of millions of individuals. Collecting the data is not sufficient, however, as it needs to be grouped into useful episodes of care that reflect the treatment of a particular condition. As an example, when an individual breaks a hip, that person may have records distributed among many different providers, each of which has portions of the data relevant to the episode of care for the broken hip—the emergency room physician, the radiologist, the hospital, the primary care physician, the orthopedic surgeon, the anesthesiologist, and others. To understand the course of treatment for the broken hip, one needs to collect all the relevant records and identify the treatment as related to a single episode, and also look for subsequent complications such as infection or rehabilitation difficulties that can be tied back to the episode. The data elements need to be consistently defined so that analytics queries can be efficient and accurate, without having to accommodate varying data definitions used by each provider for common terms.

In Chapter 2,[106] we noted that there are multiple consumers in health care—the patient and the insurance company and/or health plan sponsor. Some insurers already perform quality reviews of their networks to examine cost and quality and to compare the effectiveness of various treatments. Sponsors of health plans often desire not only to see the statistics of their own transactions but also to understand whether their plan's performance is better or worse that the experience nationally and when compared to other enterprises with shared characteristics, such as industry or population of insured. The health care industry has been much slower than the property and casualty industry and the retail industry to adopt analytics or "business intelligence," but the proliferation of EHR systems, HIEs, and communication standards may enable the health care industry to make significant advances in the near future.

D. Risks of Electronic Health Care Data

As more health care data becomes stored electronically and shared with HIEs, the risk of abuse will also increase. It is difficult to say whether electronic records are at greater risk of breach than paper records. Electronic systems may provide for more secure communication of health care data than paper records, which are forwarded as hard copies, faxed, or e-mailed between parties. The increasing scale of electronic records, however, presents the risk that massive

---

[106] See Chapter 2 (Healey, E-Health Industry Overview).

breaches may result from unauthorized access through flaws in commercial systems, of which the data holder may have little awareness or control. The FDA reports that there have been 30,000 data breaches of health care information, most limited to far fewer than 500 records; however, a few breaches have involved tens of thousands of records.

In addition to the risk of a breach, the risk of re-identification of de-identified data exists. Debate continues over the level of protection offered by current de-identification methods. The ability to re-identify data based on comparison to other data sources continues to be a concern. The FDA has conducted a workshop to try to develop guidance concerning what constitutes a "small risk" when using statistical methods to de-identify protected health information. The concept of "small risk" has been the standard in the HIPAA Rule from the outset, but it has never been defined in greater particularity. As the use of health care data for analytics increases, the need for some level of geographic specificity below the state level, and for tying patients to demographic information for more complete analysis, could potentially provide more data with which to re-identify individuals. Such guidance was expected to be published at the end of 2010 but had not been released as of August 2011. The trade-off of privacy risk and the value of the analytics continues to provide for heated exchange and polarized views.

In some cases, the use of large data aggregations has resulted in regulatory action. The Ingenix database, used by certain insurance companies to calculate "usual, customary, and reasonable" (UCR) pricing for out-of-pocket medical service fees, was sued by the Attorney General of New York and a class of providers adversely affected by the resulting pricing. The plaintiffs alleged that the data used in the database was inaccurate and resulted in UCR fee calculations that were much lower than actual market prices. In a settlement, Ingenix agreed to discontinue use of the database and to pay $50 million to set up an independent database for the purpose of calculating UCR fees.

VII. Conclusions

The U.S. health care system has embarked on a course that could deliver enormous benefits. The growing use of electronic health records and the development of health information exchanges could make the delivery of health care much more efficient and provide better information for individuals to manage their care. It is to be hoped that greater transparency regarding treatment options and pricing will help reduce the cost of health care to a more sustainable level. With the generation of large amounts of electronic health care data, the development of large databases of health care information may enable the creation of meaningful analytics that will enable the comparison of the effectiveness of different treatment options among different populations.

Barriers to these advancements continue, however. Funding continues to be an issue, as the benefits do not necessarily accrue to the parties that must make the investment. Privacy concerns continue to be raised and are in conflict with the need for specificity in the research. Concerns over the disruption of established provider work flows have been raised, and the need for incentives and training has been recognized. Cooperation among providers in the continuum of care is needed to promote the collection of useful data, but such cooperation must accommodate legal restrictions concerning antitrust, anti-kickback, and illegal remuneration regulations. The federal government is attempting to take a collaborative approach with the health care industry and has created an advisory infrastructure rather than engaging in proscriptive rule-making. Significant results of the initiatives should be observed over the next five years, and the incentive timetables spur action.

4

Privacy, PHRs, and Social Media*

I.	Introduction	64
II.	What Is a Personal Health Record?	64
III.	Background	65
	A. Paradigm Shift to Electronic Health Records	65
	B. Market Forces Spurring the Use of Electronic Personal Health Records	67
	C. Web 2.0—What Is Social Media?	67
IV.	Types of PHRs	69
	A. Untethered Versus Tethered	69
	B. Attributes of PHRs	70
	C. PHRs Distinguished From EMRs and EHRs	70
V.	Unique Risks Associated With Internet-Based PHRs	72
VI.	Federal Privacy and Breach Notification Protections of PHRs	73
	A. Privacy Statutes	73
	1. HIPAA Entities	73
	2. Privacy Protection for Non-HIPAA Vendor Information	74
	B. Security/Breach Notification	76
	1. HIPAA Breach Notification Rule	76
	a. What Is a Breach?	76
	b. Did the Breach Cause Threshold Harm?	77
	c. To Whom Must the Breach Be Reported, and When?	77
	d. Enforcement	78
	2. HITECH Health Breach Notification Rule for Non-HIPAA Vendors	78
	a. What Is a Reportable Breach?	79
	b. To Whom Must the Breach Be Reported, and When?	79
	i. Vendors	79
	ii. Individuals	79
	iii. Media Outlets	79
	iv. Federal Trade Commission	79

---

*Leslie M. Tector and Robyn Shapiro, Drinker Biddle & Reath, LLP, Milwaukee, Wisconsin. The authors gratefully acknowledge the substantial assistance provided by their colleague Eric Berman.

		v. Third-Party Service Providers	80
	C.	Content of Notice of Disclosure	80
	D.	Dual Reporting Obligations under HIPAA Breach Notification Rule and Health Breach Notification Rule	81
	E.	Enforcement	81
VII.	State Privacy Statutes		81
	A.	Confidentiality of Patient Medical Records	81
	B.	State Breach Notification Statutes	82
VIII.	Conclusion and Recommendations		82

I. Introduction

Electronic patient health care records (PHRs), which have been in existence for at least a decade,[1] are a powerful tool with the capacity to transform and enhance the delivery of health care.[2] Some commentators have suggested that PHRs may be a consumer- and market-driven attempt to correct the health care system's fragmented and failed attempts to create effective electronic health record databases.[3] However, PHRs are not without risks to consumers, the most significant being the risk of public disclosure or access to important and sensitive health information.[4] This chapter defines PHRs, provides historical background as to the development of PHRs, describes types and features of PHRs, discusses unique privacy risks related to internet-based PHRs, provides an overview of applicable U.S. federal and state statutes related to privacy and breach notification, and discusses other relevant legal and ethical concerns.

II. What Is a Personal Health Record?

There is no single, universally recognized definition of the term "personal health record."[5] In the infancy of the development of PHRs, such records were

---

[1] AMERICAN HEALTH LAWYERS ASS'N, HEALTH INFORMATION TECHNOLOGY PRACTICE GROUP, PERSONAL HEALTH RECORDS: HISTORY, EVOLUTION AND THE IMPLICATIONS OF ARRA, MEMBERSHIP BRIEFING (2011) [hereinafter AHLA REPORT], *available at* http://www.healthlawyers.org/Members/PracticeGroups/HIT/memberbriefings/Pages/Personal_Health_Records_History_Evolution_and_the_Implications_of_ARRA.aspx.

[2] Kuang-Y. Wen et al., *Consumer Perceptions about the Use of the Internet for Personal Health and Health Information Exchange: Analysis of the 2007 Health Information Nations Survey Trends Survey*, J. MED. INTERNET. RES. (Dec. 18, 2010), *available at* http://www.ncbi.nlm.gov/pmc/articles/PMC30565301/tool=pubmed.

[3] *See* Nicolas P. Terry, *Personal Health Records: Directing More Costs and Risks to Consumers?* 1 DREXEL L. REV. 216, 220 (2009)

[4] *See* Bernard Lo & Lindsay Parham, *The Impact of Web 2.0 on the Doctor-Patient Relationship*, J.L. MED. & ETHICS 17, 21 (Spring 2010) [hereinafter Lo & Parham].

[5] *See, e.g.*, U.S. Dep't of Health and Human Servs., Office of Civil Rights, Personal Health Records and the HIPAA Privacy Rule [hereinafter PHR Privacy Rule], *available at* http://www.hhs.gov/ocr/privacy/hipaa/understanding/special/healthit/phrs.pdf ("In general, a PHR is an electronic record of an individual's health information by which the individual controls access to the information and may have the ability to manage, track, and participate in his or her own health care."); *Frequently Asked Questions about Medicare: What is a Personal Health Record*, U.S. DEP'T OF HEALTH AND HUMAN SERVS. (Feb. 23, 2010), *available at* https://questions.

designed to allow individuals to monitor their own health status and chronic conditions as well as services and tests received.[6] Advances in Web technologies have enhanced the functionality of PHRs, and consequently they have evolved into interactive databases that may improve the quality and outcome of care and enhance continuity of care.[7] The basic premise of an Internet-based PHR is an application provided by a PHR vendor to health care consumers that enables them to collect, view, manage, or share health information and conduct health-related electronic transactions.[8]

III. BACKGROUND

For the past several years, national attention and market influences have called for a reduction in health care costs through the use of electronic medical records.[9] These factors, in addition to advances in Internet technologies, have created the perfect storm from which PHRs have emerged.

A. Paradigm Shift to Electronic Health Records

In the last decade, the United States has participated in a massive transition from paper-based medical records to electronic medical records.[10] This movement has been a vision and a priority of the last two presidential administrations. In 2006, President George W. Bush committed to assuring that Americans had access to secure electronic health care records via the Internet within ten years.[11] This goal was based on the belief that electronic medical records would be easier for patients to access and share, improve the continuity of care, and reduce medical costs by providing health care professionals easier access to

---

medicare.gov/app/answers/detail/a_id/1912/related/1/session/L2F2LzEvc21kL2dveXRZWkFr ("A [PHR] is generally understood to be a collection of information about an individual's health or health care services, such as hospitalizations, doctor visits, medications (prescriptions and over-the-counter drugs), allergies and medical conditions that can be stored on an individual's behalf for as long as he or she chooses."); DEPARTMENT OF HEALTH & HUMAN SERVS., OFFICE OF THE NAT'L COORDINATOR FOR HEALTH INFORMATION TECHNOLOGY, NATIONAL ALLIANCE FOR HEALTH INFORMATION TECHNOLOGY REPORT TO THE OFFICE OF THE NATIONAL COORDINATOR FOR HEALTH INFORMATION TECHNOLOGY ON: DEFINING KEY HEALTH INFORMATION TECHNOLOGY TERMS 1, 19 (Apr. 28, 2008) [hereinafter NAHIT REPORT], *available at* http://healthit.hhs.gov/portal/server.pt/gateway/PTARGS_0_10741_848133_0_0_18/10_2_hit_terms.pdf ("An electronic record of health-related information on an individual that conforms to nationally recognized interoperability standards that can be drawn from multiple sources while being managed, shared, and controlled by the individual.").

[6] *See* AHLA REPORT at 5.

[7] *See* Lo & Parham at 20.

[8] *See* PHR Privacy Rule.

[9] As an example of national influences, see the American Recovery and Reinvestment Act of 2009 (ARRA), which provided for over $20 billion allocated for health care information technology infrastructure. *See* HIMSS, The American Recovery and Reinvestment Act of 2009 Summary of Key Health Information Technology Provisions (July 1, 2009), *available at* http://www.himss.org/content/files/HIMSS_SummaryOfARRA.pdf.

[10] *Id.*

[11] The White House, Transforming HealthCare: The President's Health Information Technology Plan, (2004), *available at* http://georgewbush-whitehouse.archives.gov/infocus/technology/economic_policy200404/chap3.html.

vital health information.[12] In 2009, President Obama also expressed his support of electronic medical records generally, to allow for easy access to patient information and to reduce costly medical errors.[13]

In response to President Bush's declaration, in 2006 the U.S. Department of Health and Human Services (HHS) National Committee on Vital and Health Statistics (NCVHS) issued a report specifically relating to various aspects of electronic patient health care records.[14] This report was based on six hearings held between 2002 and 2005 to analyze the use of PHRs and PHR systems.[15] The NCVHS issued 20 recommendations in the report to identify areas for further exploration, based upon the belief that PHRs may play a role in improving health and health care outcomes.[16] Four of the 20 recommendations were aimed at federal agencies, urging them to conduct various pilot studies related to PHR usages, metrics on patient safety, quality of care and patient outcomes, and cost effectiveness related to management of chronic diseases.[17] As a result, numerous federal initiatives creating publically sponsored PHR system pilot programs have emerged to assess the overall effectiveness of using PHRs to track health in federal health programs.[18]

One unique approach aimed at encouraging the adoption of PHRs was the Personalized Health Information Act of 2007, which was proposed but never enacted.[19] The proposed bill contemplated providing physicians with incentive payments set at three dollars per patient to enroll their qualifying patients into the PHRs that qualified under the Act.[20] Under the bill, "qualified patients" included Medicare patients, as well as those patients receiving benefits under another health sponsor participating in the fund created under the Act.[21] Although the Act died in the House of Representatives, the concept of creating incentives for health care professionals and health care consumers to adopt PHR technology is also an objective of the American Recovery and Reinvestment Act of 2009 (ARRA).[22]

---

[12]*Id.*

[13]Robert Pear, *Privacy Issue Complicates Push to Link Medical Data*, N.Y. TIMES, Jan. 18, 2009, at A16.

[14]U.S. DEP'T OF HEALTH & HUMAN SERVS., NATIONAL COMMITTEE ON VITAL HEALTH STATS., REPORT: RECOMMENDATION ON PERSONAL HEALTH RECORDS AND PERSONAL HEALTH SYSTEMS (Comm. Print, Feb. 2006), *available at* http://www.ncvhs.hhs.gov/0602nhiirpt.pdf.

[15]*See id.* at 6.

[16]*See id.* at 11.

[17]*Id.* at 30.

[18]*See, e.g.*, Dep't of Health & Human Servs., Centers for Medicare & Medicaid Servs., CMS Personal Health Record Pilots in South Carolina, Arizona and Utah (Sept. 8, 2011), *available at* https://www.cms.gov/PerHealthRecords/02_PHR_Pilots.asp.

[19]Personalized Health Information Act of 2007, H.R. 1368, 110th Cong. (2007). The Act was introduced to the House Ways and Means Committee in March 2007 but was never enacted. *See* http://www.govtrack.us/congress/bill.xpd?=hl10-1368.

[20]*Id.* at §2(b).

[21]*Id.* at §2(d), 2(f)(2)(A).

[22]HIMSS, The American Recovery and Reinvestment Act of 2009 Summary of Key Health Information Technology Provisions (July 1, 2009), *available at* http://www.himss.org/content/files/HIMSS_SummaryOfARRA.pdf.

B. Market Forces Spurring the Use of Electronic Personal Health Records

The cost of U.S. health care and increases in health care spending have fueled the desire to identify ways to reduce health care costs.[23] Fragmented health care systems and costly medical errors have been identified as significant factors that contribute to increases in health care spending.[24] One proposed solution was the use of paperless health information technology to increase efficiency by payors and reduce costly medical errors caused by health care providers who lacked access to relevant medical information at the time of treatment.[25] Also, studies have suggested that use of computers reduces errors related to illegible physician handwriting and prescription errors, which increase national health care costs.[26] The mobility of U.S. health care consumers who change or lose their jobs and thus change health plans or doctors at a high rate also underlies the need for portable health care records.[27] Further, Internet technology continued to advance in the early years of the twenty-first century, allowing patients and health care consumers to not only obtain information on the Internet (Web 1.0) but also interact with health care providers and other health-related Web sites on the Internet (Web 2.0) through the use of social media.[28]

C. Web 2.0—What Is Social Media?

"Social media" is the term applied to "a group of Internet-based applications that build upon the ideological and technical foundations of Web 2.0, and that allow the creation and exchange of User Generated Content."[29] The term "Web 2.0" "describe[s][sic] a new way in which software developers and end-users started to utilize the World Wide Web; that is, as a platform whereby content and applications are no longer created and published by individuals, but instead, modified by all users in a participatory and collaborative fashion."[30] Web 2.0 technologies are used in social networking sites such as Facebook and YouTube, which have become enormously popular.[31] Social networking in health care, through the use of social media, promotes collaboration between patients, health care providers, medical professionals, and other stakeholders

---

[23] *See* The White House, Transforming HealthCare: The President's Health Information Technology Plan (2004), *available at* http://georgewbush-whitehouse.archives.gov/infocus/technology/economic_policy200404/chap3.html.

[24] *Id.*

[25] *See generally* Patricia Sanchez Abril & Anita Cava, *Health Privacy in a Techno-Social World: A Cyber–Patient's Bill of Rights*, 6 Nw. J. Tech. & Intell. Prop. 244, 245 (2008) [hereinafter Abril & Cava].

[26] For further discussion related to the market forces that drove demand for electronic health care records, see Juliana Bell, *Privacy at Risk: Patients Use New Web Products to Store and Share Personal Health Records*, 38 U. Balt. L. Rev. 485, 497–501 (2009).

[27] *Id.* at 499.

[28] *See id.*

[29] Andreas M. Kaplan & Michael Hanenlein, *Users of the world unite! The challenges and opportunities of Social Media*, 53 Bus. Horizons 59, 61 (2010).

[30] *Id.* at 60–61.

[31] *See generally, id.* at 59.

in health.[32] Web 2.0 social networking sites also allow online communities to form around a common disease state or medical condition.[33] Through the use of online networking, patients share health information and personal experiences, obtain educational information on disease states, and gain access to others with the same conditions.[34]

Other social media technologies, including blogs, wikis, video sharing sites, pod casts, and hosted services, also connect patients with other health care consumers and allow patients to share personal experiences related to an illness or treatment.[35] Web 2.0 sites have the capacity to track the individual's characteristics, preferences, navigation patterns, and decisions.[36] "Cloud computing" is another technology that is being used more commonly with Internet-based PHRs.[37] Cloud computing provides applications via the Internet, while the business, software, and data stored on servers are in a remote location.[38]

Web 2.0-based PHRs may improve access to health care services by allowing patients to interact with physicians, receive prescriptions or have tests ordered without a visit or telephone call.[39] Hand-held mobile applications are being used on smart phones, tablet computers and personal digital assistants, which can interface with Internet-based PHRs.[40] Some of these applications are targeted at assisting consumers in their own health and wellness management.[41] Other mobile applications are targeted to health care providers as tools to improve and facilitate the delivery of patient care.[42]

Following the advent of Web 2.0 in 2007, two Internet giants, Google and Microsoft, launched Internet-based PHR systems to subscribers, and they continue to provide additional health care-related applications and social network-

---

[32] *See, generally*, Lo & Parham at 18–22.

[33] *See, e.g.*, Revolution Health, *available at* http://www.revolutionhealth.com (a Web site dedicated to wellness and health care information and products for health care consumers on a myriad of topics); Organized Wisdom, *available at* http://www.organizedwisdom.com/about_us/an/med (allowing physicians to create an online presence and build a digital office accessible to patients; patients can access health information, schedule physician appointments, and receive health alerts); PatientsLikeMe, *available at* http://www.patientslikeme.com (a health data-sharing platform for patient and families to allow interaction among patients with same or similar conditions).

[34] *See* Abril & Cava, 6 Nw. J. Tech. & Intell. Prop. at 245.

[35] *See, e.g.*, PatientsLikeMe, *available at* http://www.PatientsLikeMe.com.

[36] *See* Abril & Cava at 245.

[37] AHLA Report at 10.

[38] Health Breach Notification Rule; Final Rule, 74 Fed. Reg. 42,962, 42,970 n.85 (Aug. 25, 2009) (to be codified at 6 C.F.R. pt. 318).

[39] *See* Abril & Cava at 248.

[40] *See* Draft Guidance for Industry and Food Administration Staff-and on Mobile Medical Applications, Draft Guidance (July 21, 2011), *available at* http://www.fda.gov/NewsEvents/Newsroom/PressAnnouncements/UCM263340.htm.

[41] *See id.*

[42] *See id.*

ing capabilities.[43] Since that time, other large vendors with varying business models and motivations have also entered the market place.[44]

IV. TYPES OF PHRs

A. Untethered Versus Tethered

PHRs typically fall within one of two categories: "untethered" or "tethered."[45] PHRs are considered "untethered" (i.e., stand-alone, free-standing) databases when purchased by individuals for use on a personal computer or subscribed to via a commercially available Web-based service.[46] Untethered PHRs allow individuals to gather and input their own historical health information across their life spans and their family histories.[47] In some cases, the PHR may include variables of behavioral health information related to the individual's lifestyle choices, such as exercise, diet, and smoking.[48] In the case of a Web-based, untethered PHR, information can be accessed remotely anywhere as long as the user has Internet coverage.[49]

In contrast, a "tethered PHR" is a subset of an individual's health information compiled by a health care provider,[50] health insurer,[51] or employer that is aimed at promoting greater health preventative engagement by the individual.[52] Tethered PHRs allow individuals to access and update their PHRs with varying

---

[43] *See* AHLA REPORT. Recently, however, Google announced retirement of Google Health on January 1, 2012, based upon the failure of wide-spread adoption of PHRs by health care consumers. *An Important Update About Google Health*, GOOGLE (2011), *available at* http://www.google.com/intl/en-US/health/about/.

[44] One such company is Dossia, a large consortium of employers providing PHRs to their employees directed at wellness management and preventative health care. *See, e.g.*, Dossia, *Dossia Personal Health Platform*, (2011), *available at* http://www.dossia.org (employer-members of Dossia provide their employees with access to and control over their personal health information and empower their employees to be more discerning health care consumers).

[45] *Personal Health Records Increasingly Being Stored in Tethered or Untethered Cloud Solutions: companiesandmarkets.com,* BUSINESS WIRE, July 26, 2011, at 1 [hereinafter *Personal Health Records Increasingly Being Stored in Tethered or Untethered Cloud Solutions*], *available at* http://www.businesswire.com/news/hom/20110726006432/en/Personal-Health-Records-Increasingly-Stored-Tethered-Untethered. For an example of an Untethered PHR, go to WebMD Health Record, *available at* http://www.webmd.com/phr.

[46] *See Personal Health Records Increasingly Being Stored in Tethered or Untethered Cloud Solutions* at 1.

[47] *Id.*

[48] *See, e.g.*, WebMD, Web MD Health Manager (2011), *available at* http://www.webmd.com/phr.

[49] *See Personal Health Records Increasingly Being Stored in Tethered or Untethered Cloud Solutions* at 1.

[50] *See, e.g.*, MyChart (a PHR provided by Froedtert and The Medical College of Wisconsin & Community Memorial Hospital), *available at* http://tpcaruso.com/phrs/.

[51] *See, e.g.*, Kaiser Permanente, My Health Manager (2011), *available at* http://healthplans.kaiserpermanente.org/federalemployees/why-kp/complete-health/mhm/.

[52] *See Personal Health Records Increasingly Being Stored in Tethered or Untethered Cloud Solutions* at 1.

degrees of privacy and control.[53] Examples of such tethered PHR providers include Kaiser Permanente[54] and Dossia.[55]

B. Attributes of PHRs

The fundamental attributes of a PHR (untethered and tethered) include the following:

(1) comprised of individually identifiable health information of a person;
(2) drawn from multiple sources;
(3) managed, shared, and controlled by an individual health care consumer or his or her surrogate; and
(4) accessible by various third parties, including but not limited to health care providers, payors, and employers.

In some cases, the lines of distinction between an untethered and tethered PHR can become blurred. For example, an untethered PHR can provide PHR services to a health care provider or health plan, although it is not considered "tethered" to that entity.[56] These distinctions are helpful in understanding the PHR vendors' role in the Breach Notification Rules that are promulgated under the Health Information Technology for Economic and Clinical Health (HITECH) Act and the Federal Trade Commission's Health Breach Notification Rule, discussed further in Section VI.B., below.

C. PHRs Distinguished From EMRs and EHRs

The PHR platforms are electronic in nature, and a subset of PHR is comprised of Electronic Medical Records (EMRs) and/or Electronic Health Records (EHRs).[57] An EMR contains health-related information on an individual *patient* that can be created, gathered, managed, and consulted by authorized clinicians and staff within one health care organization.[58] An EHR differs from an EMR in that the EHR has operability:[59] the EHR can be created, managed, and consulted by authorized clinicians and staff across *more than one* health organization.[60] PHRs are different from EMRs and EHRs in four distinct respects.

First, the goal of the design of PHRs is to include all health information of an individual; the EMR or EHR is just once source of health data.[61] PHRs may

---

[53] *Id.*

[54] *See, e.g.*, Kaiser Permanente PHR (2011), *available at* https://members.kaiserpermanente.org/kpweb/about/yourhealthrecord.do?rop+HAW (an insurer-tethered PHR).

[55] *See* e.g., Dossia Health Management System, *available at* http://www.dossia.org//.

[56] For a full explanation of breach notification analysis based on the nature of a PHS vendor, see Health Breach Notification Rule; Final Rule, 74 Fed. Reg. 42,964 (Aug. 25, 2011) (to be codified at 16 C.F.R. pt. 318).

[57] *See* NAHIT REPORT at 15–16, *available at* http://healthit.hhs.gov/portal/server.pt/gateway/PTARGS_0_10741_848133_0_0_18/10_2_hit_terms.pdf.

[58] *Id.*

[59] The term "interoperable" means the ability to exchange or use information among systems. *See id.* at 12–13.

[60] AHLA REPORT.

[61] *Id.*

contain wellness or behavioral health information, prescription data, familial information, and payor information data from mobile devices used at home, and emergency contact information may also be included.[62] The sources of information in a PHR are much more expansive than for EMRs and EHRs.

Second, PHRs are created, managed, and modified by or at the direction of the individual rather than the health care provider.[63] In contrast, all entries and the content of an EMR and EHR are controlled or managed by health care providers. Under state and federal laws governing confidentiality of medical records, patients may have limited access and rights to request modifications to the content of their EMRs and EHRs.[64]

Third, EMRs and EHRs are created to memorialize the medical treatment and medical conditions of patients while they are an inpatient or outpatient in one or more health care facilities.[65] EMRs and EHRs are not designed to interface with applications contained on the Web.[66] Therefore, the functionality of EMRs and EHRs is more limited. In contrast, the Web 2.0 PHR has the capacity to:

(1) organize in one place individual health information (lab tests, diagnoses, images, hospitalizations, surgeries, vaccination/immunizations, allergies, and drug reactions) from various health care providers;
(2) provide quick access to emergency information, including contact information, medications, allergies, chronic health conditions, and related recent test values;
(3) organize health information for family members;
(4) connect with mobile devices that monitor health states such as blood pressure monitors, glucometers, and peak/flow meters;
(5) connect with online pharmacies that are members of the PHR system to import prescription histories or link with health tools to monitor drug interactions and side effects;
(6) manage chronic illnesses (e.g., diabetes) and access Internet-targeted advice on such illnesses and links to health Web sites and social networking sites; and
(7) interface with mobile applications to electronically upload behavioral health or wellness behaviors such as diet and exercise.

---

[62] *See generally* Microsoft, Microsoft HealthVault (2011), *available at* http://www.microsoft.com/en-us/healthvault/.

[63] *See* Lo & Parham, J.L. MED. & ETHICS at 24.

[64] *See* 45 C.F.R. §164.

[65] NAHIT REPORT at 15–16, *available at* http://healthit.hhs.gov/portal/server.pt/gateway/PTARGS_0_10741_848133_0_0_18/10_2_hit_terms.pdf .

[66] *But see* Lo & Parham at 18 ("Currently there are technical problems with this model of PCHRs because health records from different organizations are in incompatible formats and there are no standards for interoperability.").

V. UNIQUE RISKS ASSOCIATED WITH INTERNET-BASED PHRs

Unique risks arise with the use of Internet-based PHRs, which have the capacity to intersect with online technologies.[67] First, PHRs are controlled by the patient, thus giving the patient the ability to omit important relevant medical information vital to proper diagnoses and treatment decisions.[68] For example, alcohol abuse, mental health issues, or drug abuse may be significant information to the health care provider in providing treatment, but patients with control over content of the PHR may omit such vital information.[69] In addition, some patients might suffer psychological harm if they directly access test results revealing a serious health problem, rather than learn about the information from their physician.[70] Another concern is that patients may rely on information from other nonmedical-expert patients when dealing with complex medical information, rather than interacting with their own physicians.[71] This type of consumer influence may have the effect of degrading or undermining the physician-patient relationship.[72] The issue arises as to whether the use of Web sites, blogs, or Twitter encroaches upon state laws' prohibition against the practice of medicine by unlicensed individuals.[73]

Electronic surveillance by means of an Internet site allows tracking of the individual user's research patterns, personal preferences, and online activity.[74] Such tracked information is used by third parties to conduct "behavioral advertising" that bases advertisements on user online activity.[75] Sensitive information about the individual may be revealed through these advertisements, which has the potential to cause embarrassment, damage to reputation, and discrimination, which may impact insurability or employment.[76] In addition, individuals who use social networking sites may run the risk that they disclose information that is sensitive in nature without fully understanding the magnitude of the communication.[77] For example, family members who disclose family histories on an Internet-based PHR may inadvertently reveal personal health information about another blood relative, in the case of a genetically based disorder.[78] Another risk with an Internet-based PHR is that it may be impossible to completely erase or delete networking files that were used to connect with health-related social net-

---

[67] *See* Abril & Cava, 6 Nw. J. TECH. & INTELL. PROP. at 249–57.
[68] *See* Lo & Parham at 24.
[69] *See id.*
[70] *Id.* at 21.
[71] *Id.* at 20–21.
[72] *Id.*
[73] This question is beyond the scope of this chapter, although the authors believe this is an issue that merits further analysis.
[74] *See generally*, Abril & Cava, 6 Nw. J. TECH. & INTELL. PROP. at 249–51.
[75] *See id.*
[76] *See id.*
[77] *Id.* at 254–55.
[78] *Id* at 254.

working sites and other public fora.[79] Finally, PHR system vendors using cloud computing may reside and store data outside of the United States, where local privacy laws may not be as restrictive as those in the United States.[80]

VI. Federal Privacy and Breach Notification Protections of PHRs

Commentators have noted that the potential benefits to consumers from the creation and use of Internet-based PHR systems must be balanced against the heightened risk associated with public disclosure of health information on such systems.[81] Numerous articles have been written on the deficiencies of U.S. laws in protecting health information in PHRs in the age of social media. The following sections discuss the disjointed federal protection of PHRs related to privacy and breach notification.

A. Privacy Statutes

1. HIPAA Entities

PHRs that are provided by either a "covered entity" as defined by the Health Insurance Portability and Accountability Act (HIPAA) or a "business associate" of a covered entity are regulated under HIPAA.[82] For purposes of this analysis, to be a "covered entity's PHR system," the PHR system would have to be provided by a "health care provider"[83] or a health care provider's business associate, or under a "health plan."[84] These types of PHR systems would have to comply with the requirements imposed under HIPAA's Privacy Rule.[85]

Specifically, the HIPAA Privacy Rule applies to PHRs provided by covered entities or their business associates with respect to (1) the use and disclosure of individually identifiable health information in the PHRs; (2) the individual's right to access and modify the contents of the PHR; (3) the covered entity's obligations to provide a Notice of Privacy Practice; and (4) the covered entity's obligations to account for certain permissible disclosures of protected individual health information.[86]

---

[79] *See id.* at 253.

[80] AHLA Report at 10.

[81] *See generally* Peter S. Rank, Comment, *Co-Regulation of Online Consumer Personal Health Records: Breaking Through the Privacy Logjam to Increase the Adoption of a Long Overdue Technology*, 5 Wis. L. Rev. 1169 (2009) [hereinafter Rank].

[82] *See* Dep't of Health & Human Servs., Office for Civil Rights, Personal Health Records and the HIPAA Privacy Rule, *available at* www.hhs.gov/ocr/privacy/hipaa/understanding/special/healthit/phrs.pdf [hereinafter PHR Privacy Rule].

[83] 45 C.F.R. §160.103.

[84] *Id.*

[85] *See* PHR Privacy Rule.

[86] *Id.*

With respect to use and disclosure[87] of an individual's protected health information contained within the PHR, the covered entity may use and disclose such information as permitted[88] or required by law,[89] or in accordance with a written authorization of the subject of the PHR.[90] Regarding the individual's rights to access the PHR contents, under the Privacy Rule, individuals have the right to view and obtain a copy of portions of the designated record to the extent allowed by the covered entity. In addition, individuals have the right to have corrections and amendments made.[91] Covered entities that provide PHRs are also required to comply with HIPAA Notice of Privacy Practices requirements.[92]

The covered entity must also account for certain disclosures of the PHR for a period of six years prior to the request for accounting,[93] so that individuals are aware of how their information has been shared.[94] The Office of Civil Rights does not anticipate that the accounting provisions will be burdensome for PHR vendors, since the typical disclosures associated with a PHR are unlikely to be subject to the accounting rules.[95] Instead, typical disclosures by a covered entity will be to the individual or for limited purposes, such as administering the PHR pursuant to a HIPAA-compliant authorization, and thus not subject to the accounting rules.[96]

Any service provider for a covered entity's PHRs must also comply with the requirements for business associates under HIPAA[97] and the HITECH Act.[98]

2. Privacy Protection for Non-HIPAA Vendor Information

For PHRs that are not subject to HIPAA, the consumer is afforded much less protection and must rely on general privacy statutes related to online privacy[99] or consumer protection laws that may protect against breaches of PHR vendors' posted privacy practices.[100]

Many authors have opined on the adequacy of privacy protections afforded to health information such as PHRs stored within or transmitted by online net-

---

[87] A "disclosure" is defined as the "release, transfer, provision of access, to, or divulging in any manner of information outside the entity holding the information." 45 C.F.R. §160.103.

[88] See PHR Privacy Rule.

[89] Id.

[90] Id.

[91] Id.

[92] Id.

[93] Id.

[94] Id.

[95] Id.

[96] Id.

[97] Id.

[98] American Recovery and Reinvestment Act of 2009 (ARRA), Pub. L. No. 111-5 (Feb. 17, 2009), Title XIII of Div. A and Title IV of Div. B.

[99] See Abril & Cava, 6 Nw. J. Tech. & Intell. Prop. at 244.

[100] See Rank, 5 Wis. L. Rev. at 1181.

works.[101] One source in particular discusses the applicability of two federal privacy statutes: the Electronic Communications Privacy Act of 1986 (ECPA)[102] and the Children's Online Privacy Protection Act of 1998 (COPPA),[103] which tangentially provide limited protection to health data that are transmitted or stored on the Internet.[104] ECPA, an extension of the 1968 Wiretap Act, prohibits the interception and knowing intentional disclosure of information transmitted or stored by a "wire, radio, electromagnetic, photoelectric or photooptical system...."[105] The limited scope of the protection has been well articulated:

> The statute covers any communication by a person who exhibits a reasonable expectation that the communication is not subject to interception....
>
> [T]he ECPA seems to prohibit entities such as social networking websites from knowingly divulging the contents of any private electronic communication or posting. The exact confines of the prohibition, however, are dictated by the extent to which the user's behavior evinces a reasonable expectation of privacy. ECPA prohibitions do not apply to conduct authorized by the service provider or user. Moreover, the statute's legislative history states that "a subscriber who places a communication on a computer 'electronic bulletin board,' with a reasonable basis for knowing that such communications are freely made available to the public, should be considered to have given consent to the disclosure or use of the communication." The ECPA only bars disclosure of the content of private communications. In other words, non-content information is fair game. For example, a transcript of a cyber-patient's posting on a private online support group may be protected, but not the fact the cyber-patient participated in an HIV support group. Given the abilities discussed above to aggregate and reverse engineer identity, the ECPA provides very little solace or redress for an aggrieved cyber-patient. Whether content or non-content information is disclosed, a health networker's privacy would be similarly compromised.[106]

Similarly, the protections afforded under COPPA are minimal at best with regard to protecting privacy of PHRs. COPPA prohibits Web site operators from collecting personal health information[107] of a child, 13 years of age or younger, unless (1) the Web site operator provides notice of its privacy practices, indicating what information is collected and the disclosure practices of the Web site operator; and (2) with a few exceptions, the Web site operator has obtained parental consent for the collection, use, or disclosure of personal health information

---

[101] *Id.* at 1188–1202; *see also* Colin P. McCarthy, *Paging Dr. Google: Personal Health Records and Patient Privacy.* 51 WM. & MARY L. REV 2243, 2258–62 (2010).

[102] 18 U.S.C. §§2510–2522; *see* Abril & Cava, 6 NW. J. TECH. & INTELL. PROP. at 258.

[103] 15 U.S.C. §§6501–6506 (2000); *see* Abril & Cava at 258 (citing H.R. No. 99-647, at 66 (1986)).

[104] *See* Abril & Cava at 258.

[105] 18 U.S.C. §2510.

[106] *See* Abril & Cava at 257–58.

[107] The term "personal health information" means (1) individually identifiable information about an individual collected online, including the child's first name, home or other physical address that includes street name and city and town, an e-mail address, a telephone number, a Social Security number, and any other identifier that the Federal Trade Commission determines permits the physical or online contacting of a specific individual, or (2) information concerning the child or the parents of that child that the Web site collects online from the child and combines with an identifier described above. 15 U.S.C. §§6501(8)(2000).

about their children.[108,] The shortcomings in COPPA[109] with respect to protecting online personal health information are summarized as follows:

> While COPPA is the strongest consumer privacy law, its effectiveness in the social networking arena is limited. The statute only protects minors under thirteen, leaving the great majority of social networking teens to fend for themselves. Moreover, COPPA protects the child-user from predatory practices originating with the ISP or website operator, not from any other privacy violators.[110]

When consumers rely on consumer protection laws to address the failure of an Internet site to comply with the site's written privacy policies, they should be aware that this form of protection presumes that there is a written policy, and that the written policy adequately protects the individual's health information. For example, consumers' only protection may be inadequate privacy policies of the vendor's third-party service providers. Consumers should carefully evaluate privacy policies to determine the adequacy of those protections. To address this problem, in lieu of expanding privacy protections to non-HIPAA-covered PHRs, one proposed solution is to enact regulations setting a minimum or floor for privacy policies of PHR vendors.[111]

B. Security/Breach Notification

The following section addresses HIPAA's Breach Notification Rule, issued under the Health Information Technology for Economic and Clinical Health Act of 2010 (HITECH Act),[112] and the Health Breach Notification Rule, issued by the Federal Trade Commission under the HITECH Act, which applies to non-HIPAA-covered vendors of PHRs. Both rules implement provisions of the American Recovery and Reinvestment Act of 2009.[113] As explained more fully below, both rules have been criticized for adopting a privacy/security enforcement paradigm that is based on voluntary self-regulation by the PHR vendors.[114]

1. HIPAA Breach Notification Rule

a. What Is a Breach?

PHRs provided by a covered entity or a business associate of a covered entity are subject to HIPAA's Breach Notification Rule.[115] The HIPAA Breach

---

[108] *See* Abril & Cava, 6 Nw. J. Tech. & Intell. Prop. at 258 n.94:
No consent is required when the child's information is used to respond directly to a one-time request from the child, when the information is used to obtain parental consent and is not maintained thereafter, or the collection is necessary to protect the security or integrity of a website, to take precautions against liability, or to respond to judicial process, among other things.
[109] Children's Online Privacy Protection Act of 1998, 15 U.S.C. §§6501–6506 (2000).
[110] Abril & Cava at 258–59.
[111] *See* Rank, 5 Wis. L. Rev. at 1188.
[112] 45 C.F.R. pts. 160 and 164.
[113] Pub. L. No. 111-5, 123 Stat. 115. *See* 16 C.F.R. §318 *et seq.*
[114] *See* Rank, 5 Wis. L. Rev. at 1193–94.
[115] *See* Breach Notification for Unsecured Protected Health Information; Interim Final Rule, 74 Fed. Reg. 42,740 (Aug. 24, 2009) (codified at 45 C.F.R. pts. 160 and 164).

Notification Rule is triggered when a HIPAA-covered entity or its business associate discovers a breach of unsecured PHI.[116] "Unsecured protected health information" means protected health information that was not secured through the use of technology or methodology specified by HHS in published guidance. HHS's interim final rule specifies encryption and destruction technology as the "safe harbor" methods for securing PHI. Therefore, disclosure of PHI that is secured by encryption or destruction technology does not trigger the Breach Notification Rule.

b. Did the Breach Cause Threshold Harm?

Once the Breach Notification Rule is triggered, the covered entity must determine whether the breach meets the reporting threshold by analyzing whether the breach created a "significant risk of financial, reputational or other harm" to one or more individuals.[117] The regulations specifically exempt certain disclosures as falling outside of the reporting threshold. For example, under the Breach Notification Rule, use or disclosure of protected health information that does not include date of birth and zip code does not meet the minimum threshold and thus would not require reporting.[118]

c. To Whom Must the Breach Be Reported, and When?

If the Breach Notification Rule is triggered and the reporting threshold is met, the covered entity is required to report the breach to affected individuals within 60 calendar days of the date on which the covered entity or its business associate discovered the breach.[119] In the event the breach affects 500 or more individuals in a state or jurisdiction, the covered entity must notify an appropriate prominent media outlet within the state or jurisdiction.[120] The covered entity must also notify HHS at the same time that notices to individuals are released.[121] If the breach affects fewer than 500 individuals, then the Secretary of HHS can be notified annually of all breaches occurring in the calendar year in which the breach occurred.[122] Business associates of the HIPAA covered entity are required to provide notice to the covered entity of a reportable breach without unreasonable delay, and in no case more than 60 days after the discovery of the breach.[123]

---

[116] 45 C.F.R. §164.404(a)(1).

[117] *See* Breach Notification for Unsecured Protected Health Information; Interim Final Rule, 74 Fed. Reg. at 42,744; *see also* Memorandum from Clay Johnson III, Deputy Director for Management, Executive Office of the President, Memorandum for the Heads of Executive Departments and Agencies re Safeguarding Against and Responding to the Breach of Personally Identifiable Information (May 22, 2007), *available at* http://www.whitehouse.gov/sites/default/files/OMB/fy207/m07-16.pdf.

[118] 45 C.F.R. §164.402(2)(i)-(ii).

[119] 45 C.F.R. §164.404(a).

[120] *Id.*

[121] 45 C.F.R. §164.408(b).

[122] 45 C.F.R. §164.408(c); *see* Breach Notification for Unsecured Protected Health Information; Interim Rule, 74 Fed. Reg. 42,740, 42,753 (Aug. 24, 2009) (codified at 45 pts. 160 and 164).

[123] 45 C.F.R. §164.410(a)(1).

Notice may be delayed by enforcement officials if compliance with the Breach Notification Rule would impede a criminal investigation or proceeding.[124]

d. Enforcement

Violators of the HIPAA Breach Notification Rule are subject to the civil monetary penalties imposed under HIPAA.[125] The amount of the monetary penalties is dependent on the knowledge and willfulness of the violator.[126] A violator who does not know, and by exercising reasonable diligence would not have known, that the Rule was violated, is subject to a penalty of not less than $100 for each violation.[127] If the person knew or should have known that the Rule was violated, but there is reasonable cause for the violation and the violation is not attributable to willful neglect, the minimum penalty is $1,000 per violation.[128] In the case of willful neglect, the penalties start at $10,000 per violation if the violation is corrected within 30 days, and at $50,000 per violation otherwise, up to a maximum of $1.5 million per calendar year for all violations of the same requirement.[129]

Most PHR vendors are not subject to HIPAA or the HIPAA Breach Notification Rule because they are neither a covered entity nor a business associate of a covered entity.[130] Such PHR systems are not protected under the Privacy Rule, nor are those vendors or their subcontractors required to comply with HIPAA's Breach Notification Rule.

2. HITECH Health Breach Notification Rule for Non-HIPAA Vendors

Pursuant to the HITECH Act, as of February 22, 2010, vendors of PHRs that are not covered under HIPAA are required to comply with the Health Breach Notification Rule published by the FTC.[131] Under the Health Breach Notification Rule, PHR vendors,[132] PHR related entities,[133] and third-party service

---

[124] 45 C.F.R. §164.528(a)(2).
[125] 42 U.S.C. §1320d-5(a).
[126] *See id.*
[127] 42 U.S.C. §1320d-5(a).
[128] *See id.*
[129] *See id.*
[130] *See* Rank, 5 WIS. L. REV. at 1185.
[131] *See* Health Breach Notification Rule; Final Rule, 74 Fed. Reg. 42,962 (Aug. 25, 2009) (codified at 16 C.F.R. pt. 318).
[132] A "PHR Vendor" is "an entity other than a HIPAA-covered entity or an entity to the extent it engages in activities as a business associate of a HIPAA-covered entity, that offers or maintains a personal health record." 16 C.F.R. §318(f). It includes foreign vendors who provide PHRs to U.S. customers. *See* Health Breach Notification Rule; Final Rule, 74 Fed. Reg. at 42,965 (codified at 16 C.F.R. pt. 318).
[133] A "PHR related entity" is defined as "an entity, other than a HIPAA-covered entity or an entity to the extent that it engages in activities as a business associate of a HIPAA-covered entity, that (1) offers products or services through the Web site of a vendor of personal health records; (2) offers products or services through the Web site of HIPAA-covered entities that offer individuals personal health records; (3) accesses information in a personal heath record or sends information to a personal health record." 16 C.F.R. §318.2(f)(1)–(3).

providers[134] of PHR vendors that have access to PHRs are obligated to make breach notifications.

a. What Is a Reportable Breach?

The regulations define a "breach of security" of a PHR as an unauthorized acquisition of "unsecured PHR identifiable health information" of an individual.[135] A vendor, a PHR-related entity, or a third-party service provider can rebut a claim of breach by producing evidence showing that no unauthorized acquisition could reasonably have occurred.[136]

b. To Whom Must the Breach Be Reported, and When?

i. Vendors

The Health Breach Notification Rule requires PHR vendors to provide notification of the breach to PHR customers who are directly affected by the breach, to the FTC, and in cases discussed below, to prominent media outlets.[137]

ii. Individuals

All notices of breach of security must be sent to individuals 60 calendar days after the discovery of the breach.[138] A breach is treated as discovered on the first day on which the breach is known by the reporting entity or should reasonably have been known by the reporting entity.[139]

iii. Media Outlets

In the event of a breach affecting 500 or more residents of a state or jurisdiction, the PHR vendor must also notify "prominent media outlets" serving the state or jurisdiction.[140]

iv. Federal Trade Commission

PHR vendors as well as third parties are required to report breaches to the FTC following discovery of a breach. If the breach involves fewer than 500 individuals, the reporting may be done on an annual basis within 60 days of the end of the calendar year and may include all breaches occurring that calendar year.[141] If the breach involves 500 individuals or more, the reporting requirements must occur within 10 business days following the date of discovery.[142]

---

[134] A third-party service provider that provides services to a PHR vendor or PHR related entity in connection with offering or maintaining the PHR, and that accesses, maintains, retains, modifies, records, stores, destroys, or otherwise holds, uses or discloses PHR identifiable health information must notify the PHR vendor (or PHR-related entity) of a breach of such information.

[135] See 16 C.F.R. §318.2(a).

[136] Id.

[137] 16 C.F.R. §318.3(a).

[138] 16 C.F.R. §318.4(a).

[139] 16 C.F.R. §318.3(c).

[140] 16 C.F.R. §318.5(b).

[141] 16 C.F.R. §318.5(c).

[142] Id.

v. Third-Party Service Providers

Third-party service providers are obligated to report discovery of a breach of PHR security to the vendor's designated official in accordance with the written agreement between the PHR vendor and the service provider.[143] The notice should identify each customer who is the subject of the alleged breach.[144] PHR vendors are obligated to notify their third-party providers of their status as a vendor of PHR to ensure the third-party service provider is on notice of its obligation to comply with the Health Breach Notification Rule.[145] PHR vendors may opt to include the third-party service provider's compliance as a contractual obligation in the written contract between the parties.

C. Content of Notice of Disclosure

The notice to individuals should at a minimum contain: (1) a brief description of what happened, including the date of the breach and date of discovery of the breach; (2) a description of the types of nonsecured PHR identifiable health information that were involved in the breach (name, Social Security number, date of birth, home address, account number, or disability code); (3) steps individuals should take to protect themselves from potential harm resulting from the breach; (4) a brief description of what the entity that suffered the breach is doing to investigate the breach, mitigate harm, and protect against any further breaches; and (5) contact procedures for individuals to use to ask questions or to learn additional information, which must include a toll-free telephone number and e-mail address, Web site, or postal address.[146]

The notices provided by PHR vendors or PHR-related entities can be sent to individuals by first class mail at the individual's last known address.[147] However, if the individual has clearly opted out of notice by first class mail, then an e-mail notice may suffice.[148] In addition, if an individual receiving notice is deceased, the next of kin must be notified.[149] Finally, if, after making reasonable efforts to notify individuals, the PHR vendor finds that the contact information of ten or more individuals is incomplete, there are three alternative service methods available to provide notice: 90-day posting on the homepage of a PHR website; use of a regional newspaper or other media outlet; and in cases when contact is required immediately because of imminent use of identifiable information, the PHR vendor can contact individuals by telephone.[150]

Law enforcement officials can delay notice under this rule if such notice would impede a criminal investigation or proceeding.[151]

---

[143] 16 C.F.R. §318.3(b).
[144] *See id.*
[145] *Id.*
[146] 16 C.F.R. §318.6.
[147] 16 C.F.R. §318.5(a).
[148] 16 C.F.R. §318.5(a)(1).
[149] *Id.*
[150] *Id.*
[151] 16 C.F.R. §318.4 (c).

D. Dual Reporting Obligations Under HIPAA Breach Notification Rule and Health Breach Notification Rule

In some cases, an entity may be subject to requirements of both the HIPAA Breach Notification Rule and the Health Breach Notification Rule.[152] For example, a PHR vendor that is a business associate of a HIPAA-covered entity may have a dual reporting obligation if a breach occurs that triggers reporting under both rules.[153] In that case, the PHR vendor must provide notice to the individuals and report to the FTC under the Health Breach Notification Rule and to the covered entity under the HIPAA Breach Notification Rule.[154] The FTC recommends that the PHR vendor and the HIPAA-covered entity enter into a contractual agreement authorizing the vendor to notify individuals on the covered entity's behalf so that individuals only receive one consistent notice from both obligated parties.[155]

E. Enforcement

Violations of the Health Breach Notification Rule are treated as unfair and deceptive acts or practices under the Federal Trade Commission Act.[156]

VII. STATE PRIVACY STATUTES

The privacy protection of individually identifiable health information contained in PHRs falls under two types of state statutes: (1) those protecting confidentiality of patient health care records, and (2) other breach notification state statutes that apply to sensitive information.

A. Confidentiality of Patient Medical Records

State statutes addressing the confidentiality of patient health care records theoretically may provide some privacy protection for the individually identifiable health information contained in PHRs. However, there are limitations to the protections afforded by these statutes as applied to PHRs. First, it is not always clear whether these provisions apply to health information in an electronic format that is voluntarily stored, for example, on Internet Web-based media.[157] For example, Wisconsin's state statute governing confidentiality of health records fails to address whether the provisions apply to those records stored in an electronic media format,[158] thus leaving the matter open to interpretation by courts of

---

[152] Health Breach Notification Rule; Final Rule, 74 Fed. Reg. 42,965 (Aug. 25, 2009) (codified at 16 C.F.R. pt. 318).
[153] *Id.*
[154] *Id.*
[155] *Id.*
[156] *See* 16 C.F.R. §318.7; *see also* Federal Trade Commission Act, 15 U.S.C. §57a(a)(1)(B).
[157] *See, e.g.*, WIS. STAT. §146.81(4) (The definition does not specifically include electronic records or PHRs.).
[158] *Id.*

that state. In contrast, the California legislature has explicitly extended its state health record confidentiality protections to clinical laboratory test results that are communicated to the patient by Internet posting or other electronic means.[159] Further, the statute prohibits electronic communications between health care providers and patients of clinical test results that are related to sensitive health information, such as HIV or Hepatitis C test results, which require greater confidentiality protection under the law.[160]

Another shortcoming of state confidentiality statutes is that they protect health care records created by or under the supervision of a health care provider in the context of providing inpatient or outpatient health care services.[161] Therefore, the protections potentially apply only to portions of the PHR that meet such criteria. As noted above, PHRs are more expansive than traditional health care records and may contain information uploaded from a mobile medical device or other sensitive information that does not meet this standard.

Finally, it can be inferred that an individual patient who voluntarily posts his or her health information on a Web-based PHR system has impliedly waived some or all protections related to confidentiality of the health care records.[162]

B. State Breach Notification Statutes

At least 48 states have adopted laws aimed at providing breach notification to affected individuals for unauthorized disclosure of personal information such as names, Social Security numbers, driver's license numbers, or financial information.[163] Most such state statutes do not specifically address breach notification related to health information contained in PHRs.[164]

VIII. Conclusion and Recommendations

The interaction between PHRs and other Web 2.0 technologies is rapidly changing the role of health care providers, health care consumers, and the doctor-patient relationship. In this new Web-based world, consumers are gaining more control over their medical and health information but are potentially subjected to additional risks. Many of the changes may have a positive impact on an individual's knowledge base and access to health information. However, technology has outpaced the law's ability to provide uniform and adequate privacy protections for health information contained in Internet-based PHRs.

---

[159]CAL. HEALTH & SAFETY CODE §123148 (2002).

[160]*See id.* §123148(f)(1)–(j).

[161]*See, e.g.*, WIS. STAT. §146.81(4).

[162]Nathan Andersen, *Patient Blogs, PHI and HIPAA-Social Networking and Patient Self-Disclosures as Waiver of PHI*, HEALTH LAW PERSPECTIVES (Nov. 2008), *available at* http://www.law.uh.edu/healthlaw/perspectives/homepage.asp (exploring the theory of waiver of protections afforded under HIPAA by a patient who self-discloses individually identifiable health information on a blog).

[163]*See, e.g.*, WIS. STAT. §134.98; *see also* National Conference State Legislatures, State Breach Notification Laws (Oct. 12, 2010), *available at* http://www.ncsl.org/default.aspx?tabid=13489.

[164]*See id.*

On a federal level, PHRs provided by HIPAA-covered entities are subject to restrictions applied to all electronic medical records. There is greater protection over use *and* disclosure of such PHRs, as compared to PHRs provided by vendors that are not subject to HIPAA requirements.

With respect to PHRs that are not regulated by HIPAA, some federal and state protections are available, but they were not drafted to address privacy concerns relative to health information in PHRs, and the standards may vary from state to state. The FTC's Health Breach Notification Rule and ensuing enforcement activity may assist the legislatures in pursuing appropriate privacy legislation based on existing risks and issues that have been self-reported. In the meantime, to enhance the benefits of PHRs and minimize related privacy and other risks:

(1) Patients and physicians should make efforts to assure that the information in PHRs is accurate and sufficiently complete.
(2) Providers should develop procedures for optimizing privacy protection for communication of particularly sensitive health information.
(3) Federal legislation that comprehensively protects the privacy of personal health records regardless of the type of organization that developed or holds it should be drafted and enacted; and drafting should be informed by analysis of risks and issues identified through breach notification enforcement activities.
(4) Technology advances that improve online data protection should be pursued.

# 5

Privacy Issues in U.S. Health Care*

I.	Introduction	86
	A. Privacy Laws and Standards—Domestic and International	86
II.	Federal Privacy Protections	88
	A. U.S. Constitution	89
	1. Fourteenth Amendment	89
	2. *Whalen v. Roe*	89
	3. Scope of Constitutional Protection	89
	B. Statutes and Regulations	90
	1. Protection of Specified Health Information	90
	a. Freedom of Information Act	90
	b. Confidentiality of Records	90
	c. Medicare/Medicaid Conditions of Participation	91
	2. Protection of Specified Groups	92
	a. Children's Online Privacy Protection Act of 1998	92
	b. Human Subjects in Research	93
	c. Public Health Service Act	93
	3. Protection of Specific Segments of the Health Care Industry	94
	a. Privacy Act of 1974	94
	b. Gramm-Leach-Bliley Act	94
	c. Health Insurance Portability and Accountability Act of 1996—Privacy Regulations	95
	i. Individual Rights	97
	ii. Required and Permitted Uses and Disclosures	101
	iii. "Minimum Necessary" Standard	102
	iv. De-Identified Information and Limited Data Sets	103
	v. Business Associates and Business Associate Contracts	104
	vi. Enforcement	106
	vii. Conflicts With State Law	106

---

*Lisa L. Dahm, J.D., LL.M.-Health, South Texas College of Law, Houston, Texas.

		d.	Health Information Technology for Economic and Clinical Health (HITECH) Act...	107

- d. Health Information Technology for Economic and Clinical Health (HITECH) Act 107
  - i. Summary of Subtitles A, B, and C 107
  - ii. Subtitle D—Amendments to HIPAA's Privacy Rule 110
    - (a) Definitions 110
    - (b) Breach and Notification of Breach 111
    - (c) Business Associates and Business Associate Agreements 113
    - (d) Changes to Individual Rights Granted Under HIPAA's Privacy Rule 115
    - (e) Changes to Marketing and Fundraising Provisions 116
    - (f) Prohibition on the Sale or Marketing of EHRs and PHI 117
    - (g) Improved Enforcement 118
- III. State Privacy Protections 119
  - A. Model Privacy Laws 119
    - 1. Health Information Privacy Model Act 120
    - 2. Uniform Health Care Information Act 120
  - B. State Laws and Regulations 120
    - 1. Common Privacy Protections 121
      - a. Consents and Authorizations 121
      - b. Individual's Right of Access 121
      - c. Individual's Cause of Action for Unauthorized Disclosures 122
    - 2. Common Disclosure Restrictions and Their Effects 122
      - a. What Type of Entity Is Disclosing? 123
      - b. What Type of Health Information Is to Be Disclosed? 123
      - c. Mandatory Versus Permitted Disclosures 124
- IV. Professional Organizations and Groups 125
  - A. Professional Organizations 125
    - 1. American Medical Association 125
    - 2. American Hospital Association 125
    - 3. JCAHO/Joint Commission on Accreditation of Healthcare Organizations 126
  - B. Other Privacy Protection Guidelines 126
- V. Conclusion 126

I. INTRODUCTION

A. Privacy Laws and Standards—Domestic and International

The health care industry has always been an information-intensive one. Decisions are based largely on the information physicians and other health care providers come to know through their encounters and relationships with patients; this foundation is based on the trust patients have in their providers to maintain each patient's confidentiality and to protect the privacy of the information provided.

Today, the United States and Europe[1] have a plethora of privacy laws and standards that protect an individual's health or medical information, but these laws and standards overlap in many areas and frequently vary in their scope and language. In the United States, the proliferation of privacy laws and standards is a relatively recent development. More than 25 years ago, the U.S. Supreme Court recognized a constitutional right to privacy of medical information, and Congress and many state legislatures adopted privacy legislation applicable to governmental agencies.[2] Many states also adopted privacy laws or regulations, and in some cases courts recognized state constitutional or common law rights of privacy.[3] Finally, a number of professional and industry standards that developed established a standard of care for common law purposes, and these standards were often incorporated within contracts.

The U.S. Supreme Court and federal and state legislative and regulatory bodies have applied both general and specific privacy laws in the health care industry. General privacy laws that cross industries have been applied within health care settings, and specific privacy laws have been enacted to regulate all types of matters: who has access to certain types of health information; when a patient's authorization or consent for release is required; what information physicians and other health care providers may disclose; and numerous other aspects of information flow in all manner of health care transactions. Nonetheless, the majority of the existing federal and state laws and regulations are somewhat limited in the scope of their protections.

Some of these laws and standards are of general application, but in the United States, laws are more frequently limited in scope by type of organization or by the type of information that is protected. Most of the health care-oriented laws passed before the late 1990s protect only the written portions of what has been traditionally known as a "medical record."[4] Beginning in the middle to late 1990s, however, legislators and regulators at both the state and federal levels began to expand the scope of protected information, both in terms of information type and protected medium. For example, the Health Insurance Portability and Accountability Act of 1996 (HIPAA)[5] requires health care organizations to protect an individual's health information when it is used for any purpose, including but not limited to medical records, and in any medium, whether written, electronic, or oral.[6] This means, for example, that both HIPAA and state medical

---

[1] This chapter discusses U.S. privacy issues. Chapter 6 (Taylor & Crawford, The European Data Privacy Regime) looks at privacy issues from the European perspective.

[2] *See* JOHN CHRISTIANSEN, AN INTEGRATED STANDARD OF CARE FOR HEALTHCARE INFORMATION SECURITY: RISK MANAGEMENT, HIPAA, AND BEYOND §3.01 (2005) [hereinafter CHRISTIANSEN MONOGRAPH]; Daniel J. Solove, *The Origins and Growth of Information Privacy Law,* 748 PLI/PAT 29 (2003).

[3] *Id.*

[4] Not every document that is generated during a patient's course of treatment is part of that patient's "medical record." *See* LISA L. DAHM, 50-STATE SURVEY ON PATIENT HEALTH CARE RECORD CONFIDENTIALITY 4-5 (1999) [hereinafter DAHM MONOGRAPH]. X-rays and other radiographic films and tracings (such as from fetal monitors, cardiac monitors, and the like) are often stored in other areas and in files outside the patient's traditional "medical record." *See id.* at 5.

[5] Pub. L. No. 104-191, 110 Stat. 1936 (codified at 42 U.S.C. §§1320d *et seq.*).

[6] *See* 45 C.F.R. §160.103 (HIPAA regulatory definition of "protected health information"). *See generally* JOHN A. CHRISTIANSEN, ELECTRONIC HEALTH INFORMATION: PRIVACY AND SECURITY COMPLIANCE UNDER HIPAA §I.C (2000).

records laws apply to hospitals' and physicians' medical records, whether maintained in written, electronic, or hybrid form. Similarly, a health insurance company's use of health information will be regulated by both HIPAA and the Gramm-Leach-Bliley Act (GLBA) implementing statute or regulations adopted by their state.[7]

Failing to comply with an applicable law or standard may have consequences ranging from civil (or, rarely, perhaps criminal) penalties and exclusion or disqualification from participation in governmental programs or industry activities, to breach of contract claims and reputational harm. Identifying and complying with all applicable laws and standards may therefore be burdensome and difficult but is also necessary.

The terms "privacy" and "security" are often used interchangeably when the subject of keeping health information confidential arises. While both terms have an important role in the context of confidentiality, it is the perspective from which confidentiality is viewed that determines which term is appropriate. "Privacy" is used when describing the individual's expectation with regard to his or her information; the individual expects his or her health information to be kept private. "Security," on the other hand, relates to the means and methods used by an entity other than the individual to keep that individual's health information confidential; a hospital stores its patients' medical records in a secure storage area so only those individuals who are authorized to access them can do so.

U.S. privacy issues are discussed in this chapter. For a discussion of European privacy issues, see Chapter 6 (Taylor and Crawford, The European Data Privacy Regime). For a discussion of security, see Chapter 7 (Christiansen, Information Security and Breach Notification).

II. FEDERAL PRIVACY PROTECTIONS

While confidentiality of an individual's health information is the foundation upon which the health care industry is based,[8] there currently exists no single federal or state law that protects the privacy of all such information. Numerous federal laws protect specific portions of that information, and virtually every state has passed legislation designed to ensure the rights of an individual's privacy in some or all of that information, but there is no single state or federal law that protects all of it. An individual's health information is protected by provisions of the U.S. Constitution and those of various states and by specific federal and state laws and regulations. While many of these laws are of longstanding effect, and while many have undergone numerous iterations, they still fall short of protecting all of an individual's health information.

---

[7] *See* CHRISTIANSEN MONOGRAPH at §§1.03, 5.02.

[8] The belief and expectation that an individual's health information is confidential arises from the days of Hippocrates. Physicians, bound by the Hippocratic Oath, are required to protect and keep confidential the information they receive from those within their care. "And whatsoever I shall see or hear in the course of my profession . . . if it be what should not be published abroad, I will never divulge, holding such things to be holy secrets." Quotation from the Hippocratic Oath.

A. U.S. Constitution

Early on, constitutional scholars identified and recognized an individual's right to privacy protection, which was expressed as the right to control "to what extent his thoughts, sentiments, and emotions shall be communicated to others."[9] Since its adoption, the concept of constitutional protection of an individual's right to privacy has been continuously expanded upon and refined by the U.S. Supreme Court.

1. Fourteenth Amendment

In 1965, 75 years after legal scholars began debating the issue of an individual's right to privacy, the U.S. Supreme Court recognized a constitutional right to privacy founded on the concept of personal liberty expressed in the Fourteenth Amendment to the U.S. Constitution.[10] Just eight years later, the Supreme Court recognized that the right of privacy was directly applicable to health care settings for purposes of allowing an individual to interact privately with his or her physician.[11] However, while the Supreme Court has recognized an individual's constitutional right to interact privately with his or her physician, such constitutional protection is generally deemed insufficient to protect the contents of the communications themselves or the specific means of communication used by physicians and patients.[12]

2. Whalen v. Roe

In the first case involving the storage of health-related information in a computer database, the Supreme Court found that the storage of that information did not result in a violation of the right to privacy so long as adequate protections against improper disclosure were in place.[13] In reaching its decision, the Supreme Court explicitly recognized "the threat to privacy implicit in the accumulation of vast amounts of personal information in computerized data banks."[14]

3. Scope of Constitutional Protection

The Supreme Court's rulings would suggest that health information is entitled to limited protection under the Fourteenth Amendment, and that those using or disclosing that information must take steps to ensure that the information is adequately protected against improper disclosure. However, the Supreme Court has yet to expressly define the scope of such privacy protection and has instead considered the issue on a case-by-case basis.

---

[9] Samuel D. Warren & Louis D. Brandeis, *The Right to Privacy*, 4 HARV. L. REV. 193, 198 (1890).
[10] Griswold v. Connecticut, 381 U.S. 479 (1965).
[11] Roe v. Wade, 410 U.S. 113 (1973).
[12] Alissa R. Spielberg, *Online Without a Net: Physician-Patient Communication by Electronic Mail*, 25 AM. J.L. & MED. 267 (1999).
[13] Whalen v. Roe, 429 U.S. 589 (1977).
[14] *Id.* at 605.

Furthermore, the constitutional protections discussed above are extended only to the activities of governmental agencies and organizations and are not applicable to those private business entities that today collect and disseminate the majority of information, including health information, in the United States and throughout the world. Those who use or disclose health information must therefore understand the basic constitutional protections, but should look beyond the U.S. Constitution to the privacy protection imposed by other federal and state laws and regulations, professional codes, and industry guidelines.

B. Statutes and Regulations

As of October 2011, Congress has not enacted federal legislation to uniformly and comprehensively protect the privacy of all health information. The existing federal laws and regulations that relate to privacy of health information are each limited in some way—either they protect only a specific portion of health information (e.g., substance abuse and treatment records), or they protect the health information of only a portion of the population (e.g., children), or they address only information that is handled electronically (e.g., electronic signatures), or they apply to only a particular segment of the health care industry (e.g., "covered entities"). Nonetheless, an understanding of existing federal laws and regulations that regulate the collection, usage, maintenance, and disclosure of some portion of health information in the health care industry, and their respective scopes and limitations, is necessary to those who conduct business in and with the health care industry.

1. *Protection of Specified Health Information*

a. *Freedom of Information Act*

The Freedom of Information Act (FOIA)[15] expressly precludes the disclosure of personnel and medical files by governmental or regulatory entities for purposes of commercial use. However, this general prohibition is only applicable to governmental activities and is subject to numerous exceptions. For example, FOIA would prohibit a business that operates a Web site or electronic communications service for the purpose of collecting public health statistics on behalf of the federal government from disclosing its contact list to advertising or marketing companies.

b. *Confidentiality of Records*

The Confidentiality of Records provisions (CRp)[16] apply only to substance abuse and treatment records, and allow disclosure of such records "only for the purposes and under the circumstances expressly authorized" by that law.[17] The records that the CRp protect are those that are maintained in connection with programs or activities that are directly or indirectly assisted by a governmental

---

[15] 5 U.S.C. §552.
[16] 42 U.S.C. §290dd-2; 42 C.F.R. pt. 2.
[17] 42 U.S.C. §290dd-2(a).

department or authority and that relate to substance abuse education, prevention, training, treatment, rehabilitation, or research.[18]

While the scope of the CRp is relatively limited, the requirements imposed under the statute regarding the privacy and confidentiality protections of the subject records are generally more rigorous and restrictive in nature than the requirements imposed under other state or federal laws. For example, under the CRp, substance abuse and treatment records may be disclosed only with the individual's written consent or pursuant to a court order.[19] Before a court can issue such an order, however, it must conduct a special "show cause" hearing in accordance with very strict and specific regulations.[20]

Compliance with the CRp, therefore, may impose additional or more stringent privacy protection requirements on any business that operates to provide substance abuse services or requires such records to conduct its business. For example, if a business provides online educational or group-discussion sessions for individuals suffering from substance abuse-related illnesses or if it uses information technology in administering an employee assistance program, it may have to implement additional levels of security or encryption to ensure that the records of those sessions are not accessible by anyone except the provider conducting the session and each of the session participants. Further, the business will likely have to obtain a specific written consent from each of the patient participants prior to their participation in the sessions that specifically allows the business to conduct sessions online.

c. Medicare/Medicaid Conditions of Participation

As a condition of participating in the Medicare program, hospitals, long-term care facilities, intermediate care facilities for the mentally retarded, home health agencies, comprehensive outpatient rehabilitation facilities, hospices, and certain other institutional providers must protect the privacy and confidentiality of patient records and must ensure that unauthorized individuals cannot gain access to or alter patient records.[21] Furthermore, under federal laws governing operation of all state Medicaid programs, a state may use the information it has obtained in the process of administering its Medicaid program solely for the program's administration.[22] These requirements apply without regard to whether the provider or state program stores and transmits the data electronically or in paper format.

---

[18] Id.

[19] 42 U.S.C. §290dd-2(b).

[20] 42 U.S.C. §290dd-2(b)(2)(C); 42 C.F.R. §2.64. The hearing must be held in the judge's chambers, and must ensure that no individually identifiable information is disclosed to any person outside the parties to the proceeding. 42 C.F.R. §2.64(c). The court order must limit disclosure to only those parts of the patient's record that are necessary to fulfill the objective of the order, limit the disclosure to only those individuals who have a need to know the information, and include any other protective measures needed to protect the patient, the patient-physician relationship, and the services provided. Id. §2.64(e).

[21] 42 C.F.R. §482.24(b)(3) (hospitals); §483.10(e) (long-term care facilities); §483.410(c) (intermediate care facilities for the mentally retarded); §484.10(d) (home health agencies); §485.60 (comprehensive outpatient rehabilitation facilities); §418.74(b) (hospice).

[22] 42 U.S.C. §1396a(a)(7).

2. Protection of Specified Groups

a. Children's Online Privacy Protection Act of 1998

The Children's Online Privacy Protection Act (COPPA)[23] serves to limit the personal information that Web sites are able to collect from individuals under the age of 13. COPPA mandates the adoption of federal regulations requiring Web sites or online service providers that collect personal information from children to provide notice on their Web sites of:

- the information being collected;
- how the information is used; and
- disclosure practices.

COPPA also requires the organization collecting personal information to obtain verifiable parental consent regarding the collection, use, and disclosure of the collected information, and allows the Federal Trade Commission (FTC) to assess penalties of up to $11,000 per child per violation.

Under COPPA, a business that operates a Web site, such as an online medical-information service provider, will be limited in the information it may collect from individuals under the age of 13, and will be required to comply with the parental notice requirements imposed by the law. Furthermore, if the business intends to collect information from visitors to its Web site, it must develop and implement policies and procedures to verify the age of all visitors and to ensure that the requirements of COPPA are satisfied, as Toysmart.com discovered in its settlement with the FTC.[24]

Although not involving health information, the FTC alleged that Toysmart.com violated its own online privacy policy when it offered to disclose and subsequently sell its customers' personal information to Toysmart.com's busi-

---

[23]Pub. L. No. 105-277, §§1301–08, 112 Stat. 2681–2728 (1998) (codified at 15 U.S.C. §§6501–6506). The day after COPPA was enacted, the American Civil Liberties Union (ACLU) filed an action in the U.S. District Court for the Eastern District of Pennsylvania challenging the statute's constitutionality and asking the court to enjoin its enforcement. The district court rendered 67 separate findings of fact and granted the preliminary injunction on February 1, 1999. According to the district court, once content is posted on the Internet, a provider cannot prevent the content from entering any geographical community. Further, the court found that prohibiting Web publishers from posting material that is "harmful to minors" constitutes a content-based restriction on speech—one that is "both presumptively invalid and subject to strict scrutiny analysis." American Civil Liberties Union v. Reno, 217 F.3d 162, 171 (3d Cir. 2000). Finally, "the District Court held that losing First Amendment freedoms, even if only for a moment, constitutes irreparable harm." Id. at 172. The U.S. Court of Appeals for the Third Circuit affirmed the holding of the district court, basing its determination of COPPA's unconstitutionality almost entirely on the overbreadth of the term "harmful to minors." The Supreme Court granted certiorari on May 21, 2001, in *Ashcroft v. American Civil Liberties Union*, 532 U.S. 1037, 121 S. Ct. 1997 (2001) (petition for certiorari granted), and the Court heard argument on November 28, 2001. On May 13, 2002, the Court vacated the holding and remanded the case to the Third Circuit. Ashcroft v. American Civil Liberties Union, 535 U.S. 564, 122 S. Ct. 1700 (2002). The Court held that COPPA's "reliance on community standards to identify material that is harmful to minors does not *by itself* render the statute substantially overbroad for purposes of the First Amendment." Id. at 587 (emphasis in the original). The Court refused to opine on whether COPPA is overbroad for other reasons, whether it is unconstitutionally vague, or whether it would survive a strict scrutiny analysis. Id.

[24]*In re* Toysmart.com, L.L.C., No. 00-11341-RGS (D. Mass. 2000). Copies of court documents and other information related to this litigation are available at the Federal Trade Commission Web site, *available at* http://www.ftc.gov/opa/2000/07/toysmart2.htm.

ness successor after the company filed for Chapter 11 bankruptcy.[25] In settlement of the litigation, the FTC filed a stipulated consent agreement and final order with the court prohibiting Toysmart.com from making any false or misleading statements about the disclosure of personal information, or from disclosing or selling any customer information, except as provided by the bankruptcy court.[26] The consent agreement also required the immediate deletion or destruction of all information collected by Toysmart.com in violation of COPPA.[27]

b. Human Subjects in Research

The current federal regulations adopted by the Department of Health and Human Services (HHS) and the Food and Drug Administration (FDA) governing the protection of human subjects by health care providers and institutions conducting clinical trials do not impose any substantial restrictions on the disclosure of individually identifiable health information.[28] However, for all clinical trials, the appropriate Institutional Review Board (IRB) must review the adequacy of confidentiality protections in place, and participants in the clinical trial must be informed of the scope (or lack) of confidentiality protection associated with their records prior to participation in the clinical trial. In many cases, the informed consent that an individual signs to participate in the clinical trial informs the individual that the health information generated during the clinical trial will be available to the principal investigator and his or her delegees and to appropriate individuals of the pharmaceutical or device manufacturer.

c. Public Health Service Act

The Public Health Service Act (PHSA)[29] provides for the issuance of certificates of confidentiality upon application to HHS as a means of providing special privacy and confidentiality protections against subpoenas, court orders, and other compelled disclosures in the research area. The operative provision is as follows:

> The Secretary may authorize persons engaged in biomedical, behavioral, clinical, or other research...to protect the privacy of individuals who are the subjects of such research by withholding from all persons not connected with the conducting of the research the names and other identifying characteristics of such individuals.

---

[25] The FTC charged that this action amounted to a deceptive trade practice in violation of §5 of the FTC Act, 15 U.S.C. §459(a). For additional discussion of §5 of the FTC Act, see Chapter 8 (Goldberg & Greene, Enforcement of HIPAA), at VI.A.

[26] In the related bankruptcy case, *In re* Toysmart.com, LLC, No. 00-13995-CJK (Bankr. D. Mass. 2000), the court approved an order prohibiting the sale of Toysmart.com's customer information, except in connection with the sale of the entire Web site to a "qualified buyer," i.e., an entity in a related market that agreed to be Toysmart.com's successor-in-interest with respect to the customer information and to abide by the terms of the Toysmart.com privacy policy. *See* Stipulated Consent Agreement and Final Order, Ex. A, FTC v. Toysmart.com, LLC, No. 00-11341-RGS (D. Mass. 2000).

[27] Stipulated Consent Agreement and Final Order ¶III, FTC v. Toysmart.com, LLC, No. 00-11341-RGS (D. Mass. 2000). (The date for Stipulation and Order Establishing Conditions on Sale of Customer Information (00-13995-CJK) was July 20, 2000.)

[28] 42 C.F.R. pt. 46; 21 C.F.R. pts. 50, 56.

[29] 42 U.S.C. ch. 6A.

Persons so authorized to protect the privacy of such individuals may not be compelled in any Federal, State, or local, civil, criminal, administrative, legislative, or other proceeding to identify such individuals.[30]

Under the PHSA, any business engaged in clinical research may wish to request a certificate of confidentiality as a means of limiting future disclosures of information received during the conducted research.

3. *Protection of Specific Segments of the Health Care Industry*

   a. *Privacy Act of 1974*

The Privacy Act of 1974[31] prohibits federal agencies and organizations (including federal hospitals)—and those agencies and organizations under contract with federal agencies and organizations to perform data-handling activities and services for such agencies and organizations—from disclosing by any means of communication information contained in their systems, including medical records, except in limited circumstances. Pursuant to the requirements of the Privacy Act, all agencies and organizations covered by the Act must comply with "fair information practices" when collecting, using, or disseminating records.

The Privacy Act further provides that whereas the health care provider or facility is the owner of the information contained in the medical record, only the subject individual may authorize the release of such information. The Privacy Act may be applicable if a business operates a national data bank or clearinghouse that electronically stores health information collected by or on behalf of a governmental agency.

   b. *Gramm-Leach-Bliley Act*

The Gramm-Leach-Bliley Act (GLB),[32] signed into law in November 1999, prohibits the disclosure of nonpublic, personal information by financial institutions to third parties who are not affiliated with the disclosing financial institution. Health insurers are specifically included in GLB's definition of "financial institution." GLB further requires all financial institutions to provide notice to the subject individual(s) prior to sharing these individuals' nonpublic, personal information with other unaffiliated entities and to give these individuals an opportunity to opt out of such disclosures.

While neither GLB nor its associated regulations expressly include medical or health information within the definition of protected information, the opt-out provision enables customers of financial institutions to affirmatively assert that any medical or health information held by the institution not be disclosed to any third party. Therefore, if a financial institution possesses an individual's health information, it may not disclose such information to a third party, including a related life insurance company that may be deciding whether to insure

---

[30] 42 U.S.C. §241(d).

[31] 5 U.S.C. §552(a).

[32] 15 U.S.C. §§6801–6809. Also known as the Financial Modernization Act of 1999, the official short title of the Gramm-Leach-Bliley Act is "GLB."

the individual, without first allowing the subject individual to opt out of such disclosure.

c. Health Insurance Portability and Accountability Act of 1996— Privacy Regulations

Within Subtitle F of HIPAA, Congress specifically recognized the absence of and the need for comprehensive privacy legislation to protect the privacy of individually identifiable health information that is transmitted in connection with a HIPAA-defined transaction.[33] Congress imposed a 36-month deadline from the date of HIPAA's enactment for the passage of federal privacy legislation and empowered HHS to promulgate final regulations within 42 months if such legislation was not enacted.[34] On December 28, 2000, HHS published its final privacy regulations in the *Federal Register*[35] somewhat later than required by the law, but the delay was understandable given the more than 50,000 public comments that were submitted in response to the proposed regulations.

When the privacy regulations were finalized, they were to become effective on February 26, 2001.[36] During the transition from the Clinton Administration to the Bush Administration, however, a technical amendment to the final regulations extended the effective date to April 14, 2001.[37] Two days later, HHS Secretary Tommy Thompson solicited comments from the public on the final rule,[38] effectively raising hopes in the industry that the effective date of the regulations would be extended beyond April 14, 2001. Despite receiving thousands of new comments by the March 30, 2001 deadline, the industry's hopes for an extension of the effective date were dashed. A technical amendment to the final privacy regulations issued by HHS delayed the original effective date of February 26, 2001[39] to April 14, 2001.[40] Neither the July 2001 Guidance[41] nor the December 2002 Guidance,[42] both of which were published by the HHS Office for Civil

---

[33] Pub. L. No. 104-191, §264(c)(1).

[34] *Id.*

[35] Standards for Privacy of Individually Identifiable Health Information; Final Rule, 65 Fed. Reg. at 82,462–829 (Dec. 28, 2000) (codified at 45 C.F.R. pts. 160, 164).

[36] *Id.* at 82,829.

[37] Standards for Privacy of Individually Identifiable Health Information; Final Rule, 66 Fed. Reg. at 12,434 (Feb. 26, 2001).

[38] Standards for Privacy of Individually Identifiable Health Information, 66 Fed. Reg. at 12,738 (Feb. 28, 2001).

[39] 65 Fed. Reg. at 82,829.

[40] 66 Fed. Reg. at 12,434.

[41] The Office for Civil Rights, a department within HHS, published answers to common and frequent general and specific questions about the final privacy regulations to provide clarification and guidance to the industry. U.S. DEP'T OF HEALTH & HUMAN SERVS., OFFICE FOR CIVIL RIGHTS, STANDARDS FOR PRIVACY OF INDIVIDUALLY IDENTIFIABLE HEALTH INFORMATION (July 6, 2001).

[42] The Office for Civil Rights published a second Guidance on December 3, 2002, to explain and answer questions about key provisions of the final privacy regulations as amended in August 2002. U.S. DEP'T OF HEALTH & HUMAN SERVS., OFFICE FOR CIVIL RIGHTS, STANDARDS FOR PRIVACY OF INDIVIDUALLY IDENTIFIABLE HEALTH INFORMATION (Dec. 3, 2002).

Rights (OCR), nor the amendments to the final privacy regulations proposed in March 2002[43] and finalized on August 14, 2002,[44] extended the effective date.

Although the privacy regulations (including the preamble and comments discussion) comprise more than 360 pages in the *Federal Register*, HHS admitted that the scope of the regulations is somewhat limited given the limitations inherent within HIPAA.[45] However, the privacy regulations protect *all* individually identifiable health information (IIHI), much more information than that protected under other federal laws and regulations or under various state laws. HIPAA uses the term "health information," which by definition encompasses significantly more information than that found within an individual's "medical record." Health information, as defined in the statute, is:

> any information, whether oral or recorded in any form or medium, that—
>
> (A) is created or received by a health care provider, health plan, public health authority, employer, life insurer, school or university, or health care clearinghouse; and
>
> (B) relates to the past, present, or future physical or mental health condition of an individual, the provision of health care to an individual, or the past, present, or future payment for the provision of health care to an individual.[46]

It is important to recognize that although the privacy regulations establish a standard for dealing with health information, very little health information that is to be protected is in a standardized format. Additionally, the health information that is important to one type of entity varies significantly from that considered important by another type of entity. Even the health information that is maintained within a single entity is likely to vary depending on what part of the entity needs which part of the health information.

For example, health care providers store the majority of an individual's health information within the individual's medical record, but parts of that individual's health information will also be found in records of the business office (patient account information), various ancillary departments (x-rays, histopathology slides, and/or specimens, videotapes, scans, etc.), and support-services departments (special menus, room needs, device invoices, etc.). Most health plans, on the other hand, do not store their members' health information in a central repository organized by individual member. For the most part, any centralized records that do exist contain health information about the policyholder and the policyholder's dependents, and such records are organized first chronologically (most recent health information first) and then by individual. Further, health information at a health plan is typically collected, stored, and maintained by and for the particular function that it serves. For example, an individual's claims information will be stored within the claims processing division, mem-

---

[43] Office of the Secretary; Standards for Privacy of Individually Identifiable Health Information; Proposed Rule, 67 Fed. Reg. at 14,776–815 (Mar. 27, 2002).

[44] Standards for Privacy of Individually Identifiable Health Information; Final Rule, 67 Fed. Reg. at 53,182–273 (Aug. 14, 2002).

[45] 65 Fed. Reg. at 82,471 (Preamble) ("Our approach is also significantly informed by the limited jurisdiction conferred by HIPAA.").

[46] 42 U.S.C. §1320d(4).

bership and enrollment information collected within those divisions will be accessible to individuals within the membership and enrollment divisions, and the history of services rendered to an individual will most likely be located within the case or medical management division.

Also, it is important to recognize that the privacy regulations should not be considered in a vacuum. The regulations must be considered in the context of other existing state laws—wherever such state laws are codified. While some states have passed comprehensive laws and regulations that protect most, if not all of an individual's health information as that term is used in HIPAA, many states have not. Furthermore, the privacy regulations only preempt those state laws that are directly contrary to HIPAA, unless:

- the state law is more stringent than HIPAA;
- the Secretary of HHS determines the state law is necessary to prevent health care fraud and abuse; to ensure appropriate state regulation of insurance and health plans; for mandated state reporting purposes of health care delivery or cost; to serve a compelling public health, safety, or welfare need; or because it involves the regulation of the manufacture, registration, distribution, dispensing, or other control of a controlled substance;
- the state law mandates reporting to the state incidents of abuse, neglect, birth, death, or public health surveillance, investigation, or intervention activities; or
- the state law defines specific reports or information requirements that must be made by a health plan governed by that state's law.[47]

Thus, failing to consider the myriad state laws in effect when accessing, using, or disclosing health information most likely will significantly increase risk and/or exposure to the organization.

In short, the privacy regulations are best understood when they are considered in light of their primary goal: that the individual should have and be able to exercise control over his or her health information—health information that is individually identifiable and therefore "protected health information" or "PHI." With this goal in mind, the key components of the privacy regulations are as follows:

- individual rights;
- required and permitted uses and disclosures;
- the "minimum necessary" standard;
- de-identified information and limited data sets;
- business associates and business associate contracts; and
- conflicts with state law.

i. *Individual Rights*

In drafting the privacy regulations, HHS focused on returning the control of an individual's health information back to the individual. To help to ensure

---

[47] 65 Fed. Reg. at 82,801 (codified at 45 C.F.R. §160.203).

that this goal would be achieved, HHS enumerated several individual rights in the privacy regulations. These rights include the right to:

(1) request restrictions on certain uses or disclosures of the individual's PHI;[48]
(2) receive confidential communications of the individual's PHI;[49]
(3) inspect and copy of the individual's PHI;[50]
(4) request to amend of the individual's PHI and appeal a denial of the individual's requested amendment;[51]
(5) receive an accounting of the disclosures of of the individual's PHI made for purpose other than treatment, payment, or health care operations;[52] and
(6) receive (either electronically or in hard copy) the covered entity's[53] Notice of Privacy Practices.[54]

When the privacy regulations were first proposed, individuals were given the right to restrict uses and disclosures of their health information. In the proposed privacy regulations, there were no boundaries or constraints that applied to this right. For example, an individual could require a hospital to restrict all but one of the individual's treating physicians from accessing the individual's PHI on one day and change that restriction every hour so that a different treating physician was denied access. Not only would tracking and complying with this restriction be administratively burdensome for the hospital, but adherence to such restriction could have an adverse effect on the individual's health. HHS received numerous comments warning that allowing individuals to unilaterally dictate to and by whom and when discrete portions of their health information could be used and/or disclosed would likely result in too onerous a burden for covered entities to manage and control.[55] Fortunately, in the finalized privacy regulations, the individual's right to restrict was modified slightly so that individuals had only the right to *request* a restriction, and the covered entity, in its sole discretion, could either comply with or reject the individual's request.[56]

The individual's right to receive confidential communications of his or her PHI was included to enable those who did not want others to know the details of their condition, treatment, or health to still obtain a copy of their PHI, but to know that others would not be privy to it.[57] A covered entity may require the individual to request a confidential communication in writing, and the in-

---

[48] *Id.* at 82,822 (codified at 45 C.F.R. §164.522(a)(1)).

[49] *Id.* at 82,823 (codified at 45 C.F.R. §164.522(b)(1)).

[50] *Id.* (codified at 45 C.F.R. §164.524(a)(1)).

[51] *Id.* at 82,824 (codified at 45 C.F.R. §164.526).

[52] *Id.* at 82,826 (codified at 45 C.F.R. §164.528(a)(1)).

[53] A "covered entity" is an organization that is subject to HIPAA. There are only three types of organizations that are defined as covered entities under HIPAA: (1) health plans, (2) health care clearinghouses, and (3) health care providers that transmit any health information electronically in connection with a HIPAA transaction. 42 U.S.C. §1320d-1(a).

[54] *Id.* at 82,821 (codified at 45 C.F.R. §164.520(b)(1)(iv)(A)–(F)).

[55] *See id.* at 82,726–30.

[56] *Id.* at 82,822 (codified at 45 C.F.R. §164.522(a)(1)).

[57] *Id.* at 82,823 (codified at 45 C.F.R. §164.522(b)(1)). One of the primary reasons for including a right to receive confidential communications was to protect individuals who might be the subject of domestic abuse if information about them was left in a message at home.

dividual must provide the covered entity with whatever information is needed (e.g., e-mail address, work address rather than home address, etc.) in order for the covered entity to send the individual's PHI confidentially,[58] but the covered entity may not require the individual to provide or justify his or her reason for wanting to keep his or her PHI confidential.[59]

Individuals also have the right to request access to and inspect their PHI.[60] Again, the covered entity may require the individual to submit his or her request in writing[61] and may limit the individual's right to access and inspect his or her PHI only during the covered entity's normal business hours and at a specific location within the covered entity (e.g., in the department in which medical records are stored).[62] If the individual requests a copy of his or her PHI, the covered entity may assess a fee to cover the covered entity's costs of producing that copy and may withhold the requested copy until it receives payment in full for the copy.[63]

More importantly, the individual may access only his or her PHI maintained within a "designated record set."[64] A designated record set is defined as "a group of records maintained by or for a covered entity."[65] The covered entity is the one that determines what comprises a designated record set, but if the covered entity is a health care provider, the individual's designated record set must include both medical records and billing records.[66] If the covered entity is a health plan, the individual's designated record set must include information and records relating to that individual's enrollment, payment, claims adjudication, and case or medical management records.[67] Regardless of the type of covered entity involved, however, all or some part of the designated record set must be used to assist the covered entity to make decisions about the individual who is the subject of the designated record set.[68] The regulations do not require a specific form on which the individual must make his or her request, but the regulations allow covered entities to require the individual to submit the request in writing, so long as the individual has prior notice of such a requirement.[69]

The individual also has the right to request that the covered entity maintaining the individual's PHI amend it.[70] However, whether the PHI is amended is determined solely by the covered entity.[71] If the covered entity agrees to amend

---

[58] *Id.* (codified at 45 C.F.R. §164.522(b)(2)(i)).
[59] *Id.* (codified at 45 C.F.R. §164.522(b)(2)(iii)).
[60] *Id.* (codified at 45 C.F.R. §164.524(a)(1)).
[61] *Id.* (codified at 45 C.F.R. §164.524(b)(1)).
[62] *Id.* at 82,824 (codified at 45 C.F.R. §164.524(c)(3)).
[63] *Id.* (codified at 45 C.F.R. §164.524(c)(4)).
[64] *Id.* at 82,823 (codified at 45 C.F.R. §164.524(b)(1)).
[65] *Id.* at 82,803 (codified at 45 C.F.R. §164.501). In the definition, the term "record" means "any item, collection, or grouping of information that includes protected health information and is maintained, collected, used, or disseminated by or for a covered entity." *Id.*
[66] *Id.* (codified at 45 C.F.R. §164.501(1)(i)).
[67] *Id.* (codified at 45 C.F.R. §164.501(1)(ii)).
[68] *Id.* (codified at 45 C.F.R. §164.501(1)(iii)).
[69] *Id.* at 82,823 (codified at 45 C.F.R. §164.524(b)(1)).
[70] *Id.* at 82,824 (codified at 45 C.F.R. §164.526(a)(1)).
[71] *Id.* at 82,825 (codified at 45 C.F.R. §164.526(a)(2)).

the individual's PHI, it must do so.[72] If the covered entity denies the individual's request, the covered entity must deny the request in writing and grant the individual an opportunity to appeal the denial.[73] The individual's appeal must be provided in writing, and if the covered entity denies the appeal, the individual may draft a statement of disagreement and send it to the covered entity,[74] and the covered entity may draft a rebuttal to the individual's statement of disagreement.[75] From that point on, if the covered entity provides a copy of the individual's PHI, the individual's request, the covered entity's denial, and the individual's statement of disagreement must be included as part of that copy.[76]

An individual has a right to an accounting of the disclosures made of his or her PHI, but only those that are made without his or her authorization or those that are unrelated to treatment, payment, and health care operations—unless the entity disclosing such PHI maintains an electronic health record (EHR).[77] The proposed privacy regulations required an individual's written consent before his or her health information could be used or disclosed. Under the final regulations, however, written consents may still be obtained but are no longer required.

The accounting of disclosures that a covered entity must provide upon the individual's request must include:

(1) the date of the disclosure;
(2) the name and, if known, the address of the entity or person who received the health information;
(3) a brief description of the health information that was disclosed; and
(4) a brief statement of the purpose of the disclosure that reasonably informs the individual of the basis on which the disclosure was made.[78]

The covered entity, therefore, must track and maintain a record of every disclosure made of an individual's health information that is unrelated to treatment, payment, or health care operations, or made without the individual's authorization in order to comply with the requirement to provide the individual an accounting of the disclosures made of the individual's PHI. Some economies of scale can be achieved by centralizing all disclosures through an individual or area within the organization, but assigning new job responsibilities or restructuring the organization to accomplish this objective may disrupt previously routine and smooth workflows at a minimum, and may be impossible to implement without hiring new employees at a maximum.

Initially, the privacy regulations did not require covered entities to maintain an accounting of the disclosures of a patient's PHI if such disclosures were

---

[72]*Id.* (codified at 45 C.F.R. §164.526(c)).
[73]*Id.* (codified at 45 C.F.R. §164.526(d)).
[74]*Id.* (codified at 45 C.F.R. §164.526(d)(2)).
[75]*Id.* (codified at 45 C.F.R. §164.526(d)(3)).
[76]*Id.* (codified at 45 C.F.R. §164.526(d)(5)).

[77]*Id.* at 82,826 (codified at 45 C.F.R. §164.528(a)(1)). If the covered entity maintains PHI electronically, the covered entity must account for all uses and disclosures of the PHI, even those made for purposes of treatment, payment, and health care operations. *See* HIPAA Privacy Rule Accounting of Disclosures Under the Health Information Technology for Economic and Clinical Health Act, Notice of Proposed Rulemaking, 76 Fed. Reg. at 31,432 (May 31, 2011).

[78]65 Fed. Reg. at 82,826 (codified at 45 C.F.R. §164.528(b)(2)).

made for purposes of treatment, payment, or health care operations.[79] However, pursuant to a 2011 proposed rule,[80] covered entities that maintain EHRs *will* have to account for any uses or disclosures of a patient's PHI that are made for purposes of treatment, payment, or health care operations.[81]

The final individual right granted under the privacy regulations is the individual's right to receive a copy of the covered entity's Notice of Privacy Practices. Briefly, the Notice of Privacy Practices is the covered entity's description of what it does with and how it handles the PHI in its possession. In the proposed privacy regulations, the covered entity was required to obtain the individual's signature upon the individual's receipt of the Notice of Privacy Practices. In the final privacy regulations, the covered entity need only "make a good faith effort to obtain an individual's written acknowledgment of receipt of the provider's notice of privacy practices."[82] If the individual refuses to acknowledge receipt, the covered entity must document and maintain a record of such refusal in the Notice of Privacy Practices log. The covered entity must provide an electronic copy of its Notice of Privacy Practices to the individual who requests it.

ii. Required and Permitted Uses and Disclosures

The privacy regulations specify only two instances in which an individual's health information is required to be disclosed: (1) to the individual when requested by the individual; and (2) to HHS for purposes of determining whether the organization disclosing the information is in compliance with the privacy regulations.[83] Fortunately, the amendments proposed in March 2003 and finalized in August 2003 eliminated the need to obtain an individual's consent before using or disclosing that individual's PHI for purposes of treatment, payment, or health care operations.[84] While the consent requirement was eliminated from the finalized amendments, any covered entity may elect to take a more conservative position and implement procedures that require consent.[85] The amendments also specifically authorized one covered entity to disclose an individual's PHI to another covered entity in order for the other covered entity to provide treatment to that individual and for certain of the other covered entity's payment activities and health care operations.[86]

All of the covered entities (health care providers, health plans, and health care clearinghouses) are required to obtain the individual's written authorization in order to use or disclose PHI for purposes other than treatment, payment,

---

[79]*Id.* (codified at 45 C.F.R. §164.528(a)(1)(i)).

[80]76 Fed. Reg. at 31,426.

[81]*Id.* 31,432. "Disclosures to carry out treatment, payment and health care operations as provided in §164.506 would continue to be exempt for paper records." *Id.* For covered entities with EHRs, however, any access or disclosure of an individual's PHI in a designated record set for purposes of treatment, payment, or health care operations must be provided to the individual upon his or her request. *Id.*

[82]67 Fed. Reg. at 53,238.

[83]65 Fed. Reg. at 82,805 (codified at 45 C.F.R. §164.502(a)(2)).

[84]67 Fed. Reg. at 53,268 (codified at 45 C.F.R. §164.506(a)).

[85]*Id.* (codified at 45 C.F.R. §165.506(b)(1)).

[86]*Id.* (codified at 45 C.F.R. §164.506(c)(2), (3), (4)).

or health care operations unless specifically excepted in the regulations.[87] Only in limited instances may PHI be used or disclosed without first obtaining the individual's authorization or giving the individual the opportunity to agree or object to the use or disclosure.[88] The particular instances in which neither is an authorization required nor must the individual be given the opportunity to agree or object to the use or disclosure include:

(1) uses and disclosures required by law;
(2) uses and disclosures for public health activities;
(3) disclosures about victims of abuse, neglect, or domestic violence;
(4) uses and disclosures for health oversight activities;
(5) disclosures for judicial and administrative proceedings;
(6) disclosures for law enforcement purposes;
(7) uses and disclosures about decedents;
(8) uses and disclosures for cadaveric organ, eye, or tissue donation purposes;
(9) uses and disclosures for research purposes;
(10) uses and disclosures to avert a serious threat to health or safety;
(11) uses and disclosures for specialized governmental functions, such as those relating to the military, veterans, or national security and intelligence; and
(12) disclosures for workers' compensation.

While an authorization may not be required for the covered entity to disclose an individual's PHI, such disclosure must be tracked and included on the accounting of disclosures that the covered entity provides to the individual upon his or her request.

iii. "Minimum Necessary" Standard

The privacy regulations require covered entities to release and/or request only the minimum amount of PHI necessary to accomplish the intended purpose of the use, disclosure, or request.[89] However, a covered entity is permitted to rely (if reliance is reasonable under the circumstances) on a request for health information from another covered entity to be one that requests only the minimum amount of information necessary to meet the purpose of the request.[90] For those requests that are routine or for those requests made on a recurring basis, a covered entity is expected to establish criteria designed to limit the PHI that it discloses to that which is reasonably necessary to accomplish the purpose of the request.[91] Each such request must then be scrutinized on an individual basis

---

[87] 65 Fed. Reg. at 82,811 (codified at 45 C.F.R. §164.508(a)(1)).

[88] *Id.* at 82,813 (codified at 45 C.F.R. §164.512).

[89] *Id.* at 82,819 (codified at 45 C.F.R. §164.514(d)(1)).

[90] *Id.* (codified at 45 C.F.R. §164.514(d)(3)(iii)(B)).

[91] *Id.* (codified at 45 C.F.R. §164.514(d)(3)(ii)(A)). HHS restated its concern that "without the minimum necessary standard, covered entities may be tempted to disclose an entire medical record when only a few items of information are necessary, to avoid the administrative step of extracting or redacting the information." 67 Fed. Reg. at 14,786.

to ensure that the information that is disclosed is disclosed in accordance with the established criteria.[92]

Covered entities that request protected health information on a routine or recurring basis must implement policies and procedures to ensure their requests ask for only that which is reasonably necessary to accomplish the purpose of the request.[93] Nonroutine and nonrecurring requests must be individually reviewed to ensure they are properly limited.[94]

iv. De-Identified Information and Limited Data Sets

The privacy regulations protect only that health information that is individually identifiable.[95] If health information is completely or sufficiently de-identified so that the individual who is the subject of the information cannot be identified, disclosure or release of the de-identified health information will not violate the regulations.[96] Thus, prior to disclosing an individual's PHI, the entity must ask:

- whether the information that is shared can be sufficiently de-identified to meet HHS's definition of "de-identified" prior to its use or disclosure; and
- whether disclosure of a limited data set in lieu of completely de-identified data will provide the recipient with sufficient information to meet the recipient's needs.

A limited data set is health information that excludes certain "direct identifiers" such that the health information is not completely de-identified but is still considered to be *not* individually identifiable.[97] A covered entity may use or disclose a limited data set, however, only for purposes of research, public health, or health care operations[98] and only if the covered entity and the recipient of the limited data set enter into a data use agreement.[99] The issues encountered

---

[92] 65 Fed. Reg. at 82,819 (codified at 45 C.F.R. §164.514(d)(3)(ii)(B)).

[93] *Id.* (codified at 45 C.F.R. §164.514(d)(4)(i), (ii)).

[94] *Id.* (codified at 45 C.F.R. §164.514(d)(4)(iii)).

[95] *Id.* at 82,805 (codified at 45 C.F.R. §164.501) (definition of "protected health information"); *see also* 65 Fed. Reg. at 82,818 (codified at 45 C.F.R. §164.514(a)).

[96] *Id.* at 82,818 (codified at 45 C.F.R. §164.514(a)).

[97] 67 Fed. Reg. at 53,270–71 (codified at 45 C.F.R. §164.514(e)(2)). Many of the comments received during the comment period noted that health information that was de-identified to the extent that it contained none of the direct identifiers was virtually useless. *See* Preamble, 67 Fed. Reg. 53,232–38. In response to these comments, HHS allowed use of an individual's birth date, age, sex, city, state, and zip code. *Id.*

[98] 67 Fed. Reg. at 53,271 (codified at 45 C.F.R. §164.514(e)(3)(i)).

[99] *Id.* at 53,270 (codified at 45 C.F.R. §164.514(e)(1)). A data use agreement contains provisions similar to those required in a business associate contract. The agreement must establish that the information in the limited data set will be used only for the purposes of research, public health, or health care operations and must prohibit the limited data set recipient from using or further disclosing the information in a manner that would violate the regulations if done by the covered entity. *Id.* at 53,271 (codified at 45 C.F.R. §164.514(e)(4)(ii)). The agreement must also define who is permitted to use or receive the limited data set and must provide that the limited data set recipient will (1) not use or further disclose the information other than as permitted by the data use agreement or as required by law; (2) use appropriate safeguards to prevent use or disclosure of the information other than as provided for by the data use agreement; (3) report to the covered entity any use or disclosure of the information other than as provided for in the data use agreement

in creating a limited data set are similar to those that arise when attempting to completely de-identify health information; that is, they are operational rather than purely technical.

Problems may arise because recipients are not accustomed to using information in its new, de-identified form. Similarly, limiting the purposes for which the health information may be used and requiring execution of a separate agreement or expanding the scope of a current contract to include additional required language in order for the recipient of the health information to obtain usable data will require additional time and effort on the part of both the creator and the recipient of the limited data set.

v. Business Associates and Business Associate Contracts

The privacy regulations define two categories of "business associates." The first category includes those persons or entities that perform, or assist in the performance of, certain defined functions or activities on behalf of the covered entity (or organized health care arrangement).[100] The second type of business associate includes those persons or entities that provide particular services to or for the covered entity (or organized health care arrangement).[101]

By definition, a business associate cannot be a member of the covered entity's workforce, and the activities performed or services provided by the business associate must involve the use or disclosure of individually identifiable health information.[102] A covered entity may not, however, disclose PHI to a business associate unless the covered entity obtains "satisfactory assurance" that the business associate will appropriately safeguard the information.[103]

Under the privacy regulations, "satisfactory assurance" means a written contract or other written agreement or arrangement with the business associate (a "business associate contract") that incorporates a number of specifically defined provisions.[104] The majority of arrangements in which a covered entity discloses protected health information to a business associate are, most likely, formally documented in a contract between the two parties. The two major challenges raised by the privacy regulations are (1) the impact on the contract

---

of which the recipient becomes aware; (4) ensure that any agents, including subcontractors, to whom the limited data set recipient provides the limited data set agree to the same restrictions and conditions with respect to the limited data set as the limited data set recipient; and (5) not identify the information or contact the individuals who are the subject of the information contained within the limited data set. *Id.*

[100] 65 Fed. Reg. at 82,798 (codified at 45 C.F.R. §160.103). The functions or activities include claims processing, claims administration, data analysis, data processing, data administration, utilization review, quality assurance, billing, benefit management, practice management, repricing, and any other function or activity regulated by the regulations. *Id.*

[101] *Id.* The limited list of services includes legal, actuarial, accounting, consulting, data aggregation, management, administrative, accreditation, and financial services. *Id.*

[102] *Id.* The term "workforce" means "employees, volunteers, trainees, and other persons whose conduct, in the performance of work for a covered entity, is under the direct control of such entity, whether or not they are paid by the covered entity." *Id.*

[103] *Id.* at 82,806 (codified at 45 C.F.R. §164.502(e)(1)(i)).

[104] *Id.* (codified at 45 C.F.R. §164.502(e)(2)). A business associate contract is not required if the disclosures concern the treatment of the individual, if they are disclosures by a group health plan or health insurance insurer or health maintenance organization with respect to a group health plan to the plan sponsor, or if they are disclosures made by a health plan that is a government program providing public benefits. 45 C.F.R. §164.502(e)(2)(ii).

negotiations process and (2) the fact that, in some situations, a covered entity will be a business associate.

Given the specificity and number of required provisions that must be included in the business associate contract,[105] the contract negotiation process is likely to take longer than it has been in the past. In addition, covered entities are likely to require documented proof of the ability of their business associates to meet the requirements of the privacy regulations. For example, a covered entity may require its business associate to provide it with a copy of the business associate's own security and access policies and procedures to determine whether the health information that is provided by the covered entity will be sufficiently limited to those individuals at the business associate who have a business need to access the information. The covered entity may also ask to review the forms and/or systems that the business associate plans to use to obtain and track individual authorizations if it is foreseeable that an individual might request a copy of his or her protected health information from the business associate.

It is conceivable that most covered entities will create a template of the business associate contract that they plan to use with all their business associates.[106] This template will contain the required provisions and expected addenda but will have been created from the covered entity's perspective. In some instances, however, the covered entity will be the business associate in a particular transaction.[107] Thus, when creating a boilerplate template and a set of required addenda, covered entities should remember that they might be asked to sign a business associate contract that was drafted by another covered entity—and that business associate contract will be drafted from that other covered entity's perspective.

---

[105] The business associate contract must establish the permitted and required uses and disclosures of the protected health information that will be disclosed to the business associate and authorize the covered entity to terminate the contract if it determines that the business associate has violated a material term of the contract. 65 Fed. Reg. at 82,808 (codified at 45 C.F.R. §164.504(e)(2)(i), (iii)). More specifically, the business associate must agree that it will (1) not use or further disclose the information other than as permitted or required by the contract or as required by law; (2) use appropriate safeguards to protect the information provided; (3) report any uses or disclosures that are in violation of the contract of which the business associate becomes aware; (4) ensure that the subcontractors and agents of the business associate, if any, to whom protected health information is disclosed agree to be bound by the same provisions as the business associate under the contract; (5) allow an individual to access his or her protected health information in the possession of the business associate; (6) allow the individual to request an amendment of his or her protected health information in the possession of the business associate and incorporate any amendments granted by the covered entity; (7) provide the individual with an accounting of the disclosures of his or her protected health information made by the business associate; (8) make its internal practices, books, and records relating to the use and disclosure of protected health information available to the Secretary of Health and Human Services for purposes of determining the covered entity's compliance with the regulations; and (9) upon termination of the contract, return or destroy, if feasible, all protected health information and any copies of it received from the covered entity or, if such return or destruction is not feasible, extend the protections of the contract beyond the termination date. 45 C.F.R. §164.504(e)(1)(ii).

[106] In the Appendix to the Preamble of the March Notice of Proposed Rule Making, HHS provided model business associate contract provisions in order to help covered entities "more easily comply with the business associate contract requirements of the Privacy Rule." 67 Fed. Reg. at 14,809–10.

[107] 65 Fed. Reg. at 82,799 (codified at 45 C.F.R. §160.103).

vi. Enforcement

Under HIPAA, individuals have no right of action against covered entities that use or disclose their health information inappropriately.[108] The privacy regulations only allow the individual to file a complaint with the covered entity making the unauthorized use or disclosure or with the Secretary of HHS.[109] The Office for Civil Rights has responsibility for investigating and enforcing allegations of general violations of the privacy regulations.[110] The Department of Justice, however, is charged with enforcing the criminal penalties associated with HIPAA, specifically those that relate to the wrongful use or disclosure of individually identifiable health information.

vii. Conflicts With State Law

As a general rule, HIPAA will preempt any contrary provision of state law, including state laws that require medical or health plan records to be maintained or transmitted in written rather than electronic form.[111] There are, however, some limited exceptions to this general rule. A provision of state law will prevail if the Secretary of HHS determines the provision of state law addresses controlled substances, relates to the privacy of individually identifiable health information, or is necessary (1) to prevent fraud and abuse; (2) to ensure appropriate state regulation of insurance and health plans; (3) for state reporting on health care delivery or costs; or (4) for other purposes that serve a compelling need relating to public health, safety, or welfare.[112]

Furthermore, the provision of state law that is contrary to HIPAA will nonetheless prevail if (1) it relates to the privacy of health information and is more stringent than the regulations;[113] (2) it involves the reporting of disease or injury, child abuse, birth, or death; or (3) it is used for the conduct of public health surveillance, investigation, or intervention.[114] Finally, the provision of state law will stand if it requires a health plan to report or to provide access to

---

[108] *See* 42 U.S.C. §§1320d-5 to 1320d-6.

[109] 65 Fed. Reg. at 82,801–02 (codified at 45 C.F.R. §160.306(a)). The regulations specify how and when complaints must be filed and that complainants must file within 180 days of the date the complainant knew or should have known the real or suspected violation occurred. *Id.* (codified at 45 C.F.R. §160.306(b)(3)).

[110] Preamble, 65 Fed. Reg. at 82,472. HHS delegated to OCR the authority to enforce the security standards effective July 29, 2009. *See* Centers for Medicare & Medicaid Servs. Privacy and Security Standards (July 18, 2011), *available at* https://www.cms.gov/hipaageninfo/04_PrivacyandSecurityStandards.asp.

[111] 42 U.S.C. §1320d-7(1).

[112] *Id.* §1320d-7(2).

[113] 65 Fed. Reg. at 82,801 (codified at 45 C.F.R. §160.203(b)). In comparing a provision of state law with the privacy regulations, the provision of state law will be considered "more stringent" if it (1) restricts a use or disclosure that would otherwise be allowed under the privacy regulations; (2) provides the individual with greater access to or amendment of his or her health information; (3) provides more information to the individual; (4) narrows the scope or duration of the consent or authorization, increases the privacy protections afforded, or reduces the coercive effect of obtaining the express legal permission; (5) requires a longer retention of health information or provides more detailed information to the individual relating to an accounting for disclosures; or (6) provides greater privacy protection for the individual. *Id.* at 82,800–801 (codified at 45 C.F.R. §160.202).

[114] *Id.* at 82,801 (codified at 45 C.F.R. §160.203(c)).

information for audits, program monitoring and evaluation, or licensure or certification of individuals or entities.[115] According to the privacy regulations, the term "contrary" means that a covered entity would find it impossible to comply with both the state and federal requirements, or the provision of state law is an obstacle to compliance and enforcement of HIPAA.[116]

d. Health Information Technology for Economic and Clinical Health (HITECH) Act

On February 17, 2009, President Barack Obama signed into law the federal government's stimulus package—the American Recovery and Reinvestment Act of 2009 (ARRA).[117] Two portions of ARRA, specifically Title IV of Division B and Title XIII, are together known as the Health Information Technology for Economic and Clinical Health Act (HITECH Act).[118] One of the primary objectives of the HITECH Act is to increase privacy and security protections for health information and entities that use or access such information.[119] The HITECH Act's new requirements of individuals and entities that use or access health information and its changes to HIPAA and HIPAA's Privacy Rule[120] are discussed below.

i. Summary of Subtitles A, B, and C

Subtitle A, entitled "Promotion of Health Information Technology," comprises two parts: Part 1, entitled "Improving Health Care Quality, Safety, and Efficiency," which is an amendment to the Public Health Service Act;[121] and Part 2, which defines how health information technology (HIT) standards are to be created, certified, and implemented.[122]

Subtitle A of the HITECH Act incorporates several terms used and defined under HIPAA,[123] defines health information technology-related terms such as "Certified EHR Technology,"[124] "Enterprise Integration,"[125] "Health Information

---

[115] *Id.* (codified at 45 C.F.R. §160.203(d)).

[116] *Id.* at 82,800 (codified at 45 C.F.R. §160.202).

[117] Pub. L. No. 111-5, 123 Stat. 115.

[118] HITECH Act (codified at 42 U.S.C. §§201 *et seq.*).

[119] *See* HITECH, §13400 *et seq.* (codified at 42 U.S.C. §§17921 *et seq.*).

[120] Under HIPAA, the Secretary of the Department of Health and Human Services (HHS) was required to promulgate regulations that governed the security and privacy of health information. *See* 42 U.S.C. §1320d-2(d) and 42 U.S.C. §1320d-2 note. On December 28, 2000, the Secretary of HHS published Standards for Privacy of Individually Identifiable Health Information; Final Rule, 65 Fed. Reg. 82,462 (Dec. 28, 2000) (codified at 45 C.F.R. pts. 160 and 164) [hereinafter HIPAA Privacy Rule].

[121] HITECH pt. 1 (codified at 42 U.S.C. §201 *et seq.*).

[122] HITECH pt. 2 (codified at 42 U.S.C. §17901 *et seq.*).

[123] *See* HITECH §3000(3), (4), (6), and (9) (codified at 42 U.S.C. §300jj(3) (Health Care Provider), (4) (Health Information), (6) (Health Plan), and (9) (Individually Identifiable Health Information)).

[124] *Id.* §3000(1) (codified at 42 U.S.C. §300jj(1)). The term "means a qualified electronic health record that is certified" by the Office of the National Coordinator for Health Information Technology (ONCHIT) as meeting standards established by the Secretary of HHS. *Id.*

[125] *Id.* §3000(2) (codified at 42 U.S.C. §300jj(2)). This term means "the electronic linkage of health care providers, health plans, the government, and other interested parties, to enable the electronic exchange and use of health information" throughout the health care industry. *Id.*

Technology,"[126] and "Qualified Electronic Health Record,"[127] and formally establishes and describes the purposes, membership, operations, duties, and goals of the Office of the National Coordinator for Health Information Technology (ONC),[128] the HIT Policy Committee,[129] and the HIT Standards Committee.[130] These committees are responsible for developing and implementing a national health information infrastructure. Subtitle A further provides that HITECH is not to be "construed as having any effect on the authorities of the Secretary [of HHS] under HIPAA privacy and security law"[131] and defines the term "HIPAA

---

[126]*Id.* §3000(5) (codified at 42 U.S.C. §300jj(5)). This term includes all components of a computer system that electronically creates, maintains, accesses, or exchanges health information: "hardware, software, integrated technologies or related licenses, intellectual property, upgrades, or packaged solutions sold as services." *Id.*

[127]*Id.* §3000(13) (codified at 42 U.S.C. §300jj(13)). Under this section of the HITECH Act, this term means an electronic record of health-related information on an individual that:
(A) Includes patient demographic and clinical health information, such as medical history and problem lists; and
(B) has the capacity–
 (i) to provide clinical decision support;
 (ii) to support physician order entry;
 (iii) to capture and query information relevant to health care quality; and
 (iv) to exchange electronic health information with, and integrate such information from other sources.
Id.

What is interesting about the above definition is that it differs fairly substantially from the definition of virtually the identical term located in Section 13400(5) of HITECH. In this later section, an "Electronic Health Record" is "an electronic record of health-related information on an individual that is created, gathered, managed, and consulted by authorized health care clinicians and staff." HITECH§13400(5) (codified at 42 U.S.C. §17921(5)). The fact that the two terms are virtually identical but are defined differently is likely to cause confusion as to what exactly an EHR is. While the headlines of many recent industry articles tout a particular covered entity's acquisition or implementation of an EHR, reading the article itself makes it clear that one health care entity's interpretation of an EHR differs from another's. A "qualified electronic health record" as defined in Subtitle A of HITECH, appears to be more than simply an electronic copy of an individual's medical record, the likely definition most would ascribe to it based on White House comments that began as early as 2004.

On April 27, 2004, then-President George W. Bush signed Executive Order 13335 announcing his commitment to developing and implementing an "interoperable health information technology infrastructure to improve the quality and efficiency of health care." Exec. Order No. 13,335, 69 Fed. Reg. 24,059 (Apr. 30, 2004). On May 27, 2004, at Vanderbilt University Medical Center, he publicly announced the creation of the Office of the National Coordinator for Health Information Technology (ONC), the appointment of David Brailer, M.D., Ph.D. as its Coordinator, and called for creating a system of electronic health records; one for each American citizen by 2014. President George W. Bush, Remarks in a Conversation on Health Care Information Technology at Vanderbilt University Medical Center (May 27, 2004).

In early January 2009, at a speech at George Mason University in Fairfax, Virginia, President Barack Obama also called for an electronic health record for every American by 2014. *See* Dan Childs, Haeree Chang, and Audrey Grayson, *President-Elect Urges Electronic Medical Records in 5 Years*, ABC NEWS MEDICAL UNIT (Jan. 9, 2009), *available at* http://abcnews.go.com/Health/President44/story?id=6606536&page=1.

[128]HITECH §3001 (codified at 42 U.S.C. §300jj–11). The Office of the National Coordinator for Health Information Technology (ONC) was initially established by former President Bush. *See* Exec. Order No. 13,335.

[129]HITECH §3002(a) (codified at 42 U.S.C. §300jj–12(a)).

[130]*Id.* §3003(a)codified at (codified at 42 U.S.C. §300jj–13(a).

[131]*Id.* §3009(a)(1) (codified at 42 U.S.C. §300jj–19(a)(1)).

privacy and security law" to include Part C of Title XI of the Social Security Act, section 264 of [HIPAA] and Subtitle D of title IV of the [HITECH] Act."[132]

In addition, Subtitle A also describes how federal agencies are required to adopt and implement HIT for the direct exchange of health information[133] and when and how each federal agency must coordinate its efforts with private entities.[134] Further, Subtitle A imposes responsibility on the Secretary of HHS to provide numerous reports to congressional committees, including one due in February 2011 on the success of and barriers to a fully electronic national system that allows for the exchange of health information.[135]

Subtitle B, entitled "Testing of Health Information Technology," primarily allocates responsibility for testing HIT to the National Institute of Standards and Technology (NIST),[136] which is also required to consult with the National Science Foundation and other federal agencies to develop grants that will assist in developing and establishing multidisciplinary health care information integration centers across the country.[137]

Subtitle C of the HITECH Act adds another subtitle to Title 30 of the Public Health Service Act.[138] This subtitle describes in some detail the incentives that are available to those entities that support the federal government's efforts to allow for and promote the electronic exchange and use of health information throughout the country. For example, the Secretary of HHS will be provided with immediate funds that can be invested through different federal agencies to support a private and secure nationwide HIT infrastructure;[139] develop and adopt certified EHR for those health care providers that would not otherwise be eligible for government incentives under the Social Security Act if the providers adopted such certified EHRs;[140] conduct training and distribute information on "best practices" for integrating HIT and the provider's delivery of care;[141] develop tools that help promote telemedicine[142] and interoperability of clinical data repositories;[143] enhance privacy and security protections;[144] and foster use of HIT in public health departments.[145] Working through the National Coordinator of ONC, the Secretary of HHS must establish national and regional technical implementation assistance centers,[146] award and monitor state grants to promote HIT,[147] and award grants to assist with a program that will help "facilitate and

---

[132] *Id.* §3009(a)(2) (codified at 42 U.S.C. §300jj–19(a)(2)).
[133] *Id.* §13111(a) (codified at 42 U.S.C. §17901(a)).
[134] *Id.* §13112 (codified at 42 U.S.C. §17902).
[135] *Id.* §13113(a) (codified at 42 U.S.C. §17903(a)).
[136] *Id.* §13201(a) (codified at 42 U.S.C. §17911(a)).
[137] *Id.* §13202(a)(1) (codified at 42 U.S.C. §17912(a)(1)).
[138] *Id.* §13301.
[139] *Id.* §3011(a)(1) (codified at 42 U.S.C. §300jj–31(a)(1)).
[140] *Id.* §3011(a)(2) (codified at 42 U.S.C. §300jj–31(a)(2)).
[141] *Id.* §3011(a)(3) (codified at 42 U.S.C. §300jj–31(a)(3)).
[142] *Id.* §3011(a)(4) (codified at 42 U.S.C. §300jj–31(a)(4)).
[143] *Id.* §3011(a)(5) (codified at 42 U.S.C. §300jj–31(a)(5)).
[144] *Id.* §3011(a)(6) (codified at 42 U.S.C. §300jj–31(a)(6)).
[145] *Id.* §3011(a)(7) (codified at 42 U.S.C. §300jj–31(a)(7)).
[146] *Id.* §3012(a) (codified at 42 U.S.C. §300jj–32(a)).
[147] *Id.* §3013 (codified at 42 U.S.C. §300jj–33).

expand the electronic movement and use of health information among organizations according to nationally recognized standards."[148] The Secretary of HHS, again through the National Coordinator, also has responsibility for ensuring that information technology is integrated into clinical education programs,[149] including those that support higher education of HIT professionals.[150] The National Coordinator has discretionary authority to award grants to establish loans that will help health care providers adopt and implement Certified EHR Technology.[151] Most importantly, Congress appropriated "such sums as may be necessary [to carry out the requirements of the new subtitle] for each of the fiscal years 2009 through 2013."[152]

ii. Subtitle D—Amendments to HIPAA's Privacy Rule

(a) Definitions

Most of the definitions in Subtitle D define terms already familiar to those with a working knowledge of HIPAA's Privacy Rule and Security Regulations. Each of the terms "business associate," "covered entity," "disclose," "health care provider," "health plan," "protected health information," and "use" defined in Subtitle D has the same meaning as that particular term is given in 45 C.F.R. §160.103.[153] Similarly, the definitions of the terms "health care operations," "payment," and "treatment" refer to the respective definitions for each of the same terms found in 45 C.F.R. §164.501,[154] and the meaning of the term "security" is that given the same term found in 45 C.F.R. §164.304.[155] "National Coordinator," "Secretary," and "State" are new terms that are each defined in Subtitle D, although the meaning of each term is somewhat self-explanatory.[156] However, the remaining new terms defined in Subtitle D, "breach," "electronic health record," "personal health record," and "vendor of personal health records,"[157] are critical to understanding the new mandates for covered entities and for business associates as well as how the HITECH Act will impact other entities and improve the privacy and security of protected health information.

---

[148] *Id.* §3013(a) (codified at 42 U.S.C. §§300jj–33(a)).

[149] *Id.* §3015(a) (codified at 42 U.S.C. §300jj–35(a)).

[150] *Id.* §3016(a) (codified at 42 U.S.C. §300jj–36(a)).

[151] *Id.* §3014(a) (codified at 42 U.S.C. §300jj–34(a)).

[152] *Id.* §3018 (codified at 42 U.S.C. §300jj–38).

[153] *See id.* §13400(2), (3), (4), (7), (8), (12), and (17) (codified at 42 U.S.C. §17921(2), (3), (4), (7), (8), (12), and (17)). The provision at 45 C.F.R. §160.103 is the first section common to both HIPAA's Privacy Rule and HIPAA's Security Regulations.

[154] *See* HITECH §13400(6), (10), and (16) (codified at 42 U.S.C. §17921(6), (10), and (16)). The provision at 45 C.F.R. §164.501 is included in HIPAA's Privacy Rule.

[155] *See* HITECH §13400(14) (codified at 42 U.S.C. §17921(14)). The provision at 45 C.F.R. §164.304 is part of HIPAA's Security Regulations.

[156] *See* HITECH §13400(9), (13), and (15) (codified at 42 U.S.C. §17921(9), (13), and (15)). The term "National Coordinator" means the individual in charge of ONC. *See id.* §13400(9). The term "Secretary" means the Secretary of HHS, and the term "State" means "each of the several states, the District of Columbia, Puerto Rico, the Virgin Islands, Guam, American Samoa, and the Northern Mariana Islands." *See id.* §13400(13), (15).

[157] *See id.* §13400(1), (5), (11), and (18) (codified at 42 U.S.C. §17921(1), (5), (11), and (18)).

(b) Breach and Notification of Breach

For covered entities, one of the most significant mandates of the HITECH Act is the requirement that they promptly "notify each individual whose unsecured protected health information has been, or is reasonably believed by the covered entity to have been, accessed, acquired, or disclosed as a result of [a] breach."[158] PHI is considered unsecured when it "is not secured through the use of technology or methodology specified by the Secretary [of HHS]."[159] Specifically, unsecured PHI is PHI "that is not secured by a technology standard that renders protected health information unusable, unreadable, or indecipherable to unauthorized individuals."[160] According to the Guidance published by the Secretary of HHS on April 27, 2009, the only two ways to render PHI unusable, unreadable, or indecipherable to unauthorized individuals are (1) to destroy it or (2) to encrypt it.[161] A breach occurs when unsecured PHI is acquired, accessed, used, or disclosed by an unauthorized individual and the privacy or security of the PHI is or may be compromised.[162]

In order to determine whether the privacy or security of PHI has been compromised, the covered entity must conduct a Risk Assessment to determine whether the unauthorized use or disclosure will result in some harm to the individual.[163] Only if the covered entity determines that the harm posed to the individual is "significant," however, will a breach have occurred.[164] Once a covered

---

[158] *Id.* §13402(a) (codified at 42 U.S.C. §17932(a)); *see also* Breach Notification for Unsecured Protected Health Information; Interim Final Rule, 74 Fed. Reg. 42,740, 42,757 (Aug. 24, 2009) (HHS's acknowledgment in its Impact Statement section of HITECH's specificity with regards to how covered entities are to respond in the event of a breach of unsecured protected health information) [hereinafter Interim Final Rule]. When appropriate, citations to Subtitle D of HITECH will also include a reference to the Interim Final Rule.

[159] HITECH §13402(h)(1)(A) (codified at 42 U.S.C. §17932(h)(1)(A)).

[160] *Id.* §13402(h)(1)(B) (codified at 42 U.S.C. §17932(h)(1)(B)).

[161] Guidance Specifying the Technologies and Methodologies That Render Protected Health Information Unusable, Unreadable, or Indecipherable to Unauthorized Individuals, 74 Fed. Reg. 19,009 (Apr. 27, 2009) [hereinafter April Guidance]. The April Guidance was revised and included in the Interim Final Rule published on August 24, 2009. See Interim Final Rule, 74 Fed. Reg. at 42,741.

[162] *See* HITECH §13400(1)(A) (codified at 42 U.S.C. §17921(1)(A)); *see also* 74 Fed. Reg. at 42,743. Interestingly, the Secretary of HHS concluded, "For an acquisition, access, use, or disclosure of [PHI] to constitute a breach, it must constitute a violation of the [HIPAA] Privacy Rule." 74 Fed. Reg. at 42,744. Such conclusion is based on the fact that only the HIPAA Privacy Rule governs "uses" and "disclosures" of PHI. *See id.*

[163] *Id.* The Secretary of HHS imposed the Risk Assessment requirement in response to commentators' requests to add a harm threshold to the definition of "breach" and to align the Interim Final Rule with many state notification laws. *Id.*

[164] *Id.* The unauthorized use or disclosure must result in a "significant financial, reputational, or other harm to the individual" for it to be considered a trigger for breach notification. *Id.* Otherwise, covered entities could be deluged with questions from individuals whose PHI might have been involved in the unauthorized use or disclosure but who would not be expected to suffer any harm from the breach. *Id.* The Secretary of HHS provided examples of breaches that would technically require notification, but from which the individuals involved would suffer no harm. *See id.* at 42,744–48. For example, if a laptop containing PHI of numerous individuals was stolen but returned and analysis of the laptop revealed that none of the files or data on the laptop had been accessed, a breach would have occurred, but none of the individuals would have suffered

entity discovers that a breach has occurred,[165] the individuals whose PHI is involved must be notified "without unreasonable delay and in no case later than 60 [sixty] calendar days."[166] Notice must be provided in writing and sent via first-class mail to each individual's last known address[167] and must include:

(1) a brief description of what happened, including the date of breach and the date of the discovery of the breach, if known;
(2) a description of the types of unsecured protected health information that were involved in the breach (such as full name, Social Security number, date of birth, home address, account number, or disability code);
(3) the steps individuals should take to protect themselves from potential harm resulting from the breach;
(4) a brief description of what the covered entity involved is doing to investigate the breach, to mitigate losses, and to protect against any further breaches;
(5) contact procedures for individuals to ask questions or learn additional information, which must include a toll-free telephone number, an e-mail address, Web site, or postal address.[168]

If the contact information the covered entity has for one or more individuals whose PHI is involved in the breach is insufficient or out-of-date, the covered entity must provide a substitute form of notice to those individuals.[169] In cases where the contact information of 10 or more individuals is insufficient or out-of-date, the covered entity must conspicuously post the notice on the home page of its Web site for the length of time determined by the Secretary of

---

any harm. *See id*. at 42,745. The Secretary of HHS did provide several factors that a covered entity should consider in determining the level of harm suffered by the individuals as a result of a breach: (1) Who impermissibly used the PHI or to whom was the PHI impermissibly disclosed? (2) What type and amount of PHI was involved? And (3) if the PHI disclosed was disclosed as part of a Limited Data Set, what is the risk that the disclosed PHI could be re-identified? *See id*. at 42,744–46.

[165] A breach is discovered on the first day the breach is known or should reasonably have been known. *See* HITECH §13402(c) (codified at 42 U.S.C. §17932(c)); *see also* Interim Final Rule, 74 Fed. Reg. at 42,768 (to be codified at 45 C.F.R. §164.404(a)(2)).

[166] HITECH §13402(d)(1) (codified at 42 U.S.C. §17932(d)(1)); *see also* 74 Fed. Reg. at 42,768 (to be codified at 45 C.F.R. §164.404(b)).

[167] *See* HITECH §13402(e)(1)(A) (codified at 42 U.S.C. §17932(e)(1)(A)); *see also* 74 Fed. Reg. at 42,768 (to be codified at 45 C.F.R. §164.404(d)(1)(i)). If an individual has specified that he or she prefers to receive notice via electronic mail, the covered entity may send notice to that individual electronically. *See* HITECH, §13402(e)(1)(A) (codified at 42 U.S.C. §17932(e)(1)(A)); *see also* 74 Fed. Reg. at 42,768 (to be codified at 45 C.F.R. §164.404(d)(1)). If the individual whose PHI has been breached is deceased, notice should be sent to the deceased individual's next of kin. *See* HITECH §13402(e)(1)(A) (codified at 42 U.S.C. §17932(e)(1)(A)); *see also* 74 Fed. Reg. at 42,768 (to be codified at 45 C.F.R. §164.404(d)(1)).

[168] HITECH §13402(f) (codified at 42 U.S.C. §17932(f)); *see also* 74 Fed. Reg. at 42,768 (to be codified at 45 C.F.R. §164.404(c)(1)).

[169] *See* HITECH §13402(e)(1)(B) (codified at 42 U.S.C. §17932(e)(1)(B)); *see also* 74 Fed. Reg. at 42,768 (to be codified at 45 C.F.R. §164.404(d)(2)).

HHS.[170] The notice on the covered entity's home page must include a toll-free telephone number an individual can call to determine whether his or her health information might be or is included in the breach.[171]

If the PHI of more than 500 individuals is breached, the covered entity must notify "prominent media outlets serving a State or jurisdiction"[172] and the Secretary of HHS[173] in addition to sending written notice to each individual whose information was involved in the breach. If the PHI of fewer than 500 individuals is breached, the covered entity does not need to notify the Secretary of HHS immediately upon discovery of the breach; the covered entity may document the breach in a log that it must provide to the Secretary of HHS each year.[174]

(c) Business Associates and Business Associate Agreements

While many of the recent articles about the HITECH Act state that business associates must now comply with both HIPAA's Privacy Rule and HIPAA's Security Regulations,[175] the HITECH Act only requires that business associates

---

[170] *See* HITECH §13402(e)(1)(B) (codified at 42 U.S.C. §17932(e)(1)(B)); *see also* 74 Fed. Reg. at 42,768 (to be codified at 45 C.F.R. §164.404(d)(2)(ii)). HITECH fails to address what happens if fewer than 10 individuals whose contact information is insufficient or out-of-date are involved in the breach. However, the Interim Final Rule provides that if fewer than 10 individuals are involved, "substitute notice [to those individuals] may be provided by an alternative form of written notice, telephone, or other means." 74 Fed. Reg. at 42,768 (to be codified at 45 C.F.R. §164.404(d)(2)(i)).

[171] *See* HITECH §13402(e)(1)(B) (codified at 42 U.S.C. §17932(e)(1)(B)); *see also* 74 Fed. Reg. at 42,768 (to be codified at 45 C.F.R. §164.404(d)(2)(ii)(B)).

[172] *See* HITECH §13402(e)(2) (codified at 42 U.S.C. §17932(e)(2)); *see also* 74 Fed. Reg. at 42,768 (to be codified at 45 C.F.R. §164.406).

[173] *See* HITECH §13402 (codified at 42 U.S.C. §17932(e)(3)); *see also* 74 Fed. Reg. at 42,768–69 (to be codified at 45 C.F.R. §164.408). If the PHI of exactly 500 individuals is breached, the covered entity must notify the Secretary of HHS, but the covered entity is not required to notify the media. *See* HITECH §13402 (codified at 42 U.S.C. §17932(e)(3)); *see also* 74 Fed. Reg. at 42,769 (to be codified at 45 C.F.R. §164.408(b)).

[174] *See* HITECH §13402 (codified at 42 U.S.C. §17932(e)(3)); *see also* 74 Fed. Reg. at 42,769 (to be codified at 45 C.F.R. §164.406(c)). According to the Interim Final Rule, the covered entity must provide the log "not later than 60 days after the end of each calendar year." 74 Fed. Reg. at 42,769.

[175] *See, e.g.*, Alston & Bird, LLP, *The HITECH Act: Business Associates Now Directly Covered by HIPAA*, HEALTH CARE ADVISORY 1 (June 26, 2009), *available at* http://www.martindale.com/members/Article_Attachment.aspx?od=293143&id=753318&filename=asr_753320.HITECHAct.pdf ("makes the HIPAA Rules . . . applicable to business associates"); Linn R. Freedman, *The Health Information Technology for Economic and Clinical Health Act (HITECH Act): Implications for the Adoption of Health Information Technology, HIPAA, and Privacy and Security Issues*, HEALTH LAW ALERT 2 (Feb. 2009), *available at* http://www.nixonpeabody.com/linked_media/publications/Health_Law_Alert_02_23_2009.pdf (HITECH Act "requires the application of HIPAA security and privacy provisions and penalties directly to business associates of covered entities"); Laura Jeanne Sanger, *HIPAA Goes HITECH*, HEALTH LAW PERSPECTIVES 1 (Aug. 2009), *available at* http://www.law.uh.edu/healthlaw/perspectives/2009/(LS)%20HITECH.pdf (HITECH Act "increases application of HIPAA privacy standards to business associates of covered entities"); SCHENCK, PRICE, SMITH & KING, LLP, AMERICAN RECOVERY AND REINVESTMENT ACT: HEALTH INFORMATION TECHNOLOGY FOR ECONOMIC AND CLINICAL HEALTH ACT (THE "HITECH ACT") 1, *available at* http://www.spsk.com/Articles/pdf/hitech.pdf ("extending [HIPAA's] provisions directly to business associates").

comply with HIPAA's Security Regulations.[176] A business associate's only "new" responsibility with regards to HIPAA's Privacy Rule is to notify the covered entity if the business associate discovers a breach of unsecured PHI that it "accesses, maintains, retains, modifies, records, stores, destroys, or otherwise holds, uses, or discloses."[177] This requirement, however, is "new" only in the sense that it is now statutory in nature. Under HIPAA's Privacy Rule, one of the required provisions in a Business Associate Agreement (BAA) is that the business associate "[r]eport to the covered entity any use or disclosure of the [PHI] not provided for [in the BAA] of which [the business associate] becomes aware."[178]

A key issue that covered entities will need to address with each of their business associates is how long the business associate has after discovering a breach of PHI in its possession to provide notice of the breach to the covered entity. The HITECH Act requires all required notifications—whether they are made by the covered entity to the individual or by the business associate to the covered entity—to be made "without unreasonable delay and in no case later than 60 calendar days after the discovery of a breach."[179] Breaches are considered "discovered" the first day the covered entity or any agent of the covered entity, or a business associate or any agent of the business associate, as appropriate, knew or should have known about the breach.[180] Since the business associate could be acting as an agent of the covered entity,[181] if this business associate fails to notify the covered entity of a breach discovered by the business associate until the last day of the 60-day period, the covered entity will most likely be unable to notify all affected individuals in time, thus violating the breach notification provisions of the HITECH Act.

---

[176] *See* HITECH §13401(a) (codified at 42 U.S.C. §17931(a)). The HITECH Act also makes business associates who violate HIPAA's Security Regulations subject to the same civil and criminal penalties as may be imposed on covered entities for such violations. *See id.* §13402 (codified at 42 U.S.C. §17931(b)).

[177] *Id.* §13401(a) (codified at 42 U.S.C. §17931(a)); *see also* Interim Final Rule, 74 Fed. Reg. at 42,769 (to be codified at 45 C.F.R. §164.410(a)).

[178] Standards for Privacy of Individually Identifiable Health Information; Final Rule, 65 Fed. Reg. 82,462, 82,808 (Dec. 28, 2000) (codified at 45 C.F.R. §164.504(e)(2)(i)(C)) [hereinafter HIPAA Privacy Rule].

[179] *See* HITECH §13042(d)(1) (codified at 42 U.S.C. §17932(d)(1)); *see also* 74 Fed. Reg. at 42,768 (to be codified at 45 C.F.R. §164.404(b)), and 42,769 (to be codified at 45 C.F.R. §164.410(b)).

[180] *See* HITECH §13402(c) (codified at 42 U.S.C. §17932(c)); *see also* 74 Fed. Reg. at 42,768 (to be codified at 45 C.F.R. §164.404(a)(2)), and 42,769 (to be codified at 45 C.F.R. §164.410(a)(2)).

[181] In its Section-by-Section Description of the Interim Final Rule, the Secretary of HHS highlights the fact that a business associate can be considered either an agent of a covered entity (when the business associate is performing a function or activity for the covered entity) or an independent contractor to the covered entity (when the business associate is performing services on behalf of the covered entity), and determining in what capacity the business associate is performing should be done in accordance with the federal common law of agency. *See* Interim Final Rule, 74 Fed. Reg. at 42,749, 42,754. When acting as an agent of the covered entity, the business associate's discovery of the breach is imputed to the covered entity, which means that the day the breach is discovered by the business associate, and not the day the breach is reported to the covered entity, is the starting day of the 60-day notification period. *See id.* at 42,754.

The HIPAA Privacy Rule mandates that a covered entity that discloses PHI to a business associate, or a covered entity that engages a business associate to create or receive PHI on the covered entity's behalf, must obtain "'satisfactory assurance' that the business associate will appropriately safeguard the information."[182] The HIPAA Privacy Rule further provides that a written contract, the BAA, between the two that includes specific provisions listed in the HIPAA Privacy Rule will be sufficient to meet the "satisfactory assurance" requirement.[183] As the HITECH Act imposes additional requirements on covered entities and on their business associates, covered entities should confirm that their BAAs contain the additional requirements specified in the Act.

(d) Changes to Individual Rights Granted Under HIPAA's Privacy Rule

Under the HIPAA Privacy Rule, an individual has the right to request restrictions on the uses or disclosures of his or her PHI,[184] but the covered entity is not required to agree to the restriction.[185] Under the HITECH Act, if an individual requests that a health care provider *not* disclose the individual's PHI, and the PHI that is the subject of the disclosure pertains to an item or service for which the health care provider is paid out of pocket in full, the covered entity *must* comply with the individual's request.[186]

Also upon the individual's request under the HIPAA Privacy Rule, a covered entity must provide the individual with an accounting of the disclosures of his or her PHI that were made by the covered entity for the six years prior to the date of the individual's request.[187] The HIPAA Privacy Rule excepted certain disclosures from the accounting: (1) disclosures made for the purposes of treatment, payment, or health care operations;[188] (2) those disclosures made to the individual him or herself;[189] (3) disclosures of information used in the covered entity's directory or made to the caregivers providing care to the individual;[190] (4) disclosures made for purposes of national security or intelligence;[191] (5) disclosures to correctional institutions or law enforcement officials;[192] and (6) disclosures that occurred prior to the covered entity's compliance date under the HIPAA Privacy Rule.[193] Under the HITECH Act, a covered entity's disclosures of an individual's PHI that are made for purposes of treatment, payment, and health care operations must be included on the accounting that is provided to

---

[182]HIPAA Privacy Rule, 65 Fed. Reg. at 82,806 (codified at 45 C.F.R. §164.502(e)(1)).
[183]*Id.* (codified at 45 C.F.R. §164.502(e)(2)).
[184]*Id.* at 82,822 (codified at 45 C.F.R. §164.522(a)(1)(i)).
[185]*Id.* (codified at 45 C.F.R. §164.522(a)(1)(ii)).
[186]HITECH §13405(a) (codified at 42 U.S.C. §17935(a)).
[187]HIPAA Privacy Rule, 65 Fed. Reg. at 82,826 (codified at 45 C.F.R. §164.528(a)(1)).
[188]*Id.* (codified at 45 C.F.R. §164.528(a)(1)(i)).
[189]*Id.* (codified at 45 C.F.R. §164.528(a)(1)(ii)).
[190]*Id.* (codified at 45 C.F.R. §164.528(a)(1)(iii)).
[191]*Id.* (codified at 45 C.F.R. §164.528(a)(1)(iv)).
[192]*Id.* (codified at 45 C.F.R. §164.528(a)(1)(v)).
[193]*Id.* (codified at 45 C.F.R. §164.528(a)(1)(vi)).

the individual if the covered entity uses and maintains an EHR system,[194] but the accounting need only include disclosures that are made during the three years prior to the individual's request.[195]

The third individual right under the HIPAA Privacy Rule that was modified by the HITECH Act is the individual's right to access and obtain a copy of the individual's PHI maintained by the covered entity.[196] The HIPAA Privacy Rule limited the PHI the individual could access and/or copy to what the covered entity established as the "designated record set."[197] The individual's right to access, inspect, and/or obtain a copy of his or her PHI under the HITECH Act is somewhat expanded if the covered entity uses or maintains an EHR system. First, the individual has the right to obtain a copy of his or her EHR in an electronic format, and his or her EHR is not limited to the "designated record set" specified under the HIPAA Privacy Rule.[198] Second, the individual has a right to direct the covered entity to transmit the individual's EHR to another entity or person.[199]

(e) Changes to Marketing and Fundraising Provisions

Under the HIPAA Privacy Rule, covered entities were permitted to consider some marketing communications about their services and products "health care operations."[200] Under the HITECH Act, the general rule is that marketing communications are no longer considered a "health care operation"[201] as that term is defined under the HIPAA Privacy Rule, unless the covered entity's or business associate's communication to the individual is "about a product or service and [such communication] encourages recipients of the communication to purchase or use the product or service,"[202] and "the communication is made as described in subparagraph (i), (ii), or (iii) of [the definition of the term 'marketing' in the HIPAA Privacy Rule]."[203] Under the HIPAA Privacy Rule, communications about products and services made by a covered entity are not considered "marketing" if (1) they describe the entities participating in a health care provider network and the products and services those entities provide; (2) they describe products or services necessary for the treatment of the individual; or (3) they facilitate managing the individual's treatment or direct the individual

---

[194]HITECH §13405(c)(1)(A) (codified at 42 U.S.C. §17935(c)(1)(A)). If the covered entity's EHR system was acquired on or prior to January 1, 2009, the accounting provided to the individual must include only those disclosures made on or after January 1, 2014. If the covered entity acquired its EHR system after January 1, 2009, the accounting must include any disclosures made on or after the later of January 1, 2011, or the date the EHR system was acquired.

[195]*Id*. §13405(c)(1)(B) (codified at 42 U.S.C. §17935(c)(1)(B)). See II.B.3.c., above, for the dates governing what must be included on an individual's accounting of disclosures if the covered entity currently has or later acquires an EHR system.

[196]HIPAA Privacy Rule, 65 Fed. Reg. at 82,823 (codified at 45 C.F.R. §164.524(a)(1)).

[197]*Id*.

[198]HITECH §13405(e)(1) (codified at 42 U.S.C. §17935(3)(1)).

[199]*Id*.

[200]*See* HIPAA Privacy Rule, 65 Fed. Reg. at 82,804 (codified at 45 C.F.R. §164.501) (definition of the term "health care operations").

[201]The term "marketing" is specifically included in subsection (v) of the definition of the term "health care operations" in the HIPAA Privacy Rule. *See id*. at 82,803–04.

[202]HITECH §13406(a)(1) (codified at 42 U.S.C. §17936(a)(1)).

[203]*Id*.

to or recommend alternative treatments, health care providers, or health care care settings.[204]

In addition, while the HITECH Act generally exempts "marketing" from "health care operations," it specifically allows a covered entity to receive a reasonable payment for communications that it sends to an individual that describe a drug or biologic currently prescribed for that individual, provided the covered entity had previously obtained from that individual an authorization allowing these types of marketing communications.[205]

Finally, for those fundraising communications that would otherwise be permissible as "health care operations" under the HIPAA Privacy Rule, the HITECH Act mandates that the Secretary of HHS promulgate regulations that clearly describe how covered entities will be required to give individuals to whom such fundraising communications are sent the ability to opt out of any future fundraising communications.[206]

(f) Prohibition on the Sale or Marketing of EHRs and PHI

The HITECH Act specifically prohibits covered entities and business associates from receiving any direct or indirect remuneration for the sale of EHRs or PHI unless one of several exceptions applies and the covered entity or business associate, as appropriate, has obtained from each affected individual a valid authorization that authorizes remuneration for such exchange.[207] The covered entity or business associate can receive remuneration when the purpose of the exchange is (1) for public health activities,[208] (2) for research and the price charged reflects the costs of preparing and transmitting the data,[209] (3) for the individual's treatment,[210] (4) for conducting due diligence with regards to the sale or transfer of assets to another covered entity,[211] (5) for providing an individual with a copy of his or her PHI,[212] and (6) for necessary and appropriate exchanges approved by the Secretary of HHS.[213] A business associate may also receive remuneration from a covered entity for activities that involve exchanges of PHI that the business associate undertakes upon the specific request of the

---

[204] See Standards for Privacy of Individually Identifiable Health Information; Final Rule, 67 Fed. Reg. 53,267 (Aug. 14, 2002) (codified at 45 C.F.R. §164.501) (definition of the term "marketing"). The final HIPAA Privacy Rule was actually published twice—once on December 28, 2000, and again on August 14, 2002—due, in part to the changeover at HHS that occurred when then-President George W. Bush took office. In the August 2002 final Privacy Rule, the definition of "marketing" was revised to include three subsections under Section 1. In the December 2000 final Privacy Rule, there were only two subsections under Section 1 of the definition of "marketing."

[205] See HITECH §13406(a)(2) (codified at 42 U.S.C. §17936(a)(2)). This remuneration exception will also apply to a covered entity's business associate provided the Business Associate Agreement between the covered entity and the business associate includes such a provision. See id. §13406(a)(2)(C) (codified at 42 U.S.C. §17936(a)(2)(C)).

[206] See id. §13406(b) (codified at 42 U.S.C. §17936(b)).
[207] See id. §13405(d)(1) (codified at 42 U.S.C. §17935(d)(1)).
[208] See id. §13405(d)(2)(A) (codified at 42 U.S.C. §17935(d)(2)(A)).
[209] See id. §13405(d)(2)(B) (codified at 42 U.S.C. §17935(d)(2)(B)).
[210] See id. §13405(d)(2)(C) (codified at 42 U.S.C. §17935(d)(2)(C)).
[211] See id. §13405(d)(2)(D) (codified at 42 U.S.C. §17935(d)(2)(D)).
[212] See id. §13405(d)(2)(F) (codified at 42 U.S.C. §17935(d)(2)(F)).
[213] See id. §13405(d)(2)(G) (codified at 42 U.S.C. §17935(d)(2)(G)).

covered entity and on its behalf pursuant to the BAA between the covered entity and the business associate.[214]

(g) Improved Enforcement

The HITECH Act makes HIPAA's civil and criminal penalties applicable to business associates,[215] but covered entities, too, must recognize that there are changes the HITECH Act makes to HIPAA's civil and criminal enforcement provisions that affect them. First, while HIPAA's criminal penalties have long been interpreted to apply only to covered entities,[216] the HITECH Act clarifies that the term "person," as used in the criminal penalties section of HIPAA,[217] now includes employees of and other individuals associated with covered entities and business associates.[218] Second, while individuals still do not have an individual right of action under HIPAA, the HITECH Act does allow state attorneys general to bring a civil action on behalf of the state's residents in a federal district court to enjoin a covered entity from continuing to violate the HITECH Act or to obtain statutory damages on behalf of such residents.[219]

The third major change to HIPAA's civil monetary penalties is that under the HITECH Act, there are now four tiers of civil monetary penalties that may be imposed by the Secretary of HHS against a covered entity or a business associate that violates HIPAA.[220] In the lowest tier, a penalty will be assessed when the covered entity or a business associate fails to comply with HIPAA and it is established that the covered entity or business associate did not know and by exercising reasonable diligence would not have known it was violating HIPAA.[221] The lowest tier penalty starts at an amount of up to $100 per identical violation up to a maximum of $25,000 per calendar year,[222] but can be as high as $50,000 per identical violation up to a maximum of $1,500,000 per calendar

---

[214]*See id.* §13405(d)(2)(E) (codified at 42 U.S.C. §17935(d)(2)(E)).

[215]*See id.* §13404(c) (codified at 42 U.S.C. §17934(c)).

[216]In June 2005, the Department of Justice responded to the Secretary of HHS's request for clarification of the scope of HIPAA's criminal enforcement provision and concluded that only those entities specified in the statute could be prosecuted for violations of the statute. *See* Office of Legal Counsel, Dep't of Justice, Memorandum Op. (June 1, 2005), *available at* http://www.usdoj.gov/olc/hipaa_final.htm.

[217]42 U.S.C. §1320d-6. A "person" who knowingly and wrongfully used or disclosed individually identifiable health information would be subject to criminal penalties ranging from a fine of up to $50,000 and/or imprisonment for up to one year to a fine of up to $250,000 and/or imprisonment for up to 10 years. *See* 42 U.S.C. §1320d-6(b).

[218]*See* HITECH §13409, *amending* 42 U.S.C. §1320d-6(a). The HITECH Act, however, failed to specify whether employees or individuals would be subject to criminal penalties if they committed their criminal acts prior to February 17, 2009 (the enactment of ARRA).

[219]*See id.* §13410(e)(1) (codified at 42 U.S.C. §17939(e)(1)). The total amount of statutory damages imposed is determined by multiplying the number of violations committed by up to $100 and is limited to a maximum of $25,000 during a calendar year. *Id.* §13410(e)(2) (codified at 42 U.S.C. §17939(e)(2)). In addition to damages, a court may award court costs and reasonable attorneys' fees to the state. *Id.* §13410(e)(3) (codified at 42 U.S.C. §17939(e)(3)). Prior to filing its lawsuit, the state attorney general must notify the Secretary of HHS in writing by including in its notice a copy of the state's complaint. *See id.* §13410(e)(4) (codified at 42 U.S.C. §17939(e)(4)).

[220]*See id.* (codified at 42 U.S.C. §17939(a)).

[221]*See id.* (codified at 42 U.S.C. §1320d-5(a)(1)(A)).

[222]*See id.* (codified at 42 U.S.C. §1320d-5(a)(3)(A)).

year.²²³ If the violation by the covered entity or business associate is the result of reasonable cause and not willful neglect, the penalty ranges from an amount of up to $1,000 per identical violation up to a maximum of $100,000 per calendar year, to an amount as high as $50,000 per identical violation up to a maximum of $1,500,000 per calendar year.²²⁴ If the covered entity or business associate commits a violation of HIPAA due to willful neglect, the penalty ranges from an amount of up to $10,000 per identical violation up to a maximum of $250,000 per calendar year, to an amount as high as $50,000 per identical violation up to a maximum of $1,500,000 per calendar year.²²⁵ Finally, if the covered entity or business associate fails to correct the violation it committed due to willful neglect, the Secretary of HHS will impose the maximum penalty of up to $50,000 per identical violation up to a maximum of $1,500,000 per calendar year.²²⁶

III. STATE PRIVACY PROTECTIONS

In the absence of uniform federal privacy legislation that governs the collection, use, and release of health information, individuals and entities must look to state laws to determine the protection afforded such information. Unfortunately, the state laws that currently exist are no different from their myriad federal law companions in that they, too, may be limited as to what they cover and who is subject to them. Further, like the federal laws and regulations associated with privacy and confidentiality, state laws and regulations are numerous, are found in multiple sections of a particular state's code or regulations, are often interpreted differently by the different state courts, and are sometimes inconsistent within a state, not just between states.

Nonetheless, it is important to be as knowledgeable about the applicable state laws as about HIPAA and other federal laws and regulations. While HIPAA essentially establishes the minimum privacy protections for health information, states are free to enact stricter provisions. These stricter state laws, even if they are contrary to HIPAA, will supersede HIPAA and its associated regulations, provided the state laws are more protective of the individual's privacy.²²⁷

The following sections describe the uniform model laws sponsored by various professional associations and the major types of and limitations to the protections provided by the laws and regulations of various states.

A. Model Privacy Laws

There has been some effort by states and associations to develop and present model privacy and security legislation for adoption. As is typical with model legislation, however, each state has the latitude to adopt the model legislation as drafted, revise the model legislation prior to adoption, or completely refuse

---

[223] *See id.* (codified at 42 U.S.C. §1320d-5(a)(1)(A)).
[224] *See id.* (codified at 42 U.S.C. §1320d-5(a)(1)(B)).
[225] *See id.* (codified at 42 U.S.C. §1320d-5(a)(1)(C)(i)).
[226] *See id.* (codified at 42 U.S.C. §1320d-5(a)(1)(C)(ii)).
[227] See II.B.3.c.vii., above.

to adopt it. Changes to model legislation can be minor but often are significant enough that the law, if ultimately passed by a state legislature, no longer resembles the model legislation. Thus, the development of such model legislation is extremely unlikely to lead to the adoption of uniform privacy laws by all states.

1. Health Information Privacy Model Act

The Health Information Privacy Act (HIPA)[228] was promulgated by the National Association of Insurance Commissioners (NAIC) on September 26, 1999. HIPA's stated purpose is to "set standards to protect health information from unauthorized collection, use, and disclosure by requiring insurance carriers to establish procedures for the treatment of all health information." As of 2011, HIPA has not been adopted by any state.

2. Uniform Health Care Information Act

The Uniform Health Care Information Act (UHCIA)[229] was approved for submission to the 50 states, the District of Columbia, Puerto Rico, and the U.S. Virgin Islands by the National Conference of Commissioners on Uniform State Laws (NCCUSL) in 1985. UHCIA serves to govern access to a patient's health care records held by any individual or entity providing patient-care services. UHCIA's applicability, therefore, is limited to health care providers. However, UHCIA applies to all health records, including those that are stored or transmitted electronically. As of October 2011, only Montana and Washington have adopted UHCIA.

B. State Laws and Regulations

Although each of the 50 states and the District of Columbia has adopted some level of privacy protection for health information, the scope of such protections and the legal restrictions on the use and disclosure of health information vary dramatically from state to state.[230] Many state privacy laws were enacted years ago; therefore, they often fail to reflect the dramatic changes in the health care industry and the advances in information technology that have occurred in recent years.[231] Moreover, only a limited number of state laws protect "health information," as that term is defined in HIPAA.[232] Most of the state laws pro-

---

[228] A copy of the final version of HIPA is available from the Web site of the National Association of Insurance Commissioners, at http://www.naic.org.

[229] A copy of the final version of UHCIA is available on NCCUSL's Web site at http://www.nccusl.org.

[230] See LISA L. DAHM, 50-STATE SURVEY ON PATIENT HEALTH CARE RECORD CONFIDENTIALITY (Am. Health Lawyers Ass'n Expert Series, 1999) [hereinafter DAHM MONOGRAPH].

[231] See HEALTH PRIVACY PROJECT, THE STATE OF HEALTH PRIVACY: AN UNEVEN TERRAIN; A COMPREHENSIVE SURVEY OF STATE HEALTH PRIVACY STATUTES (1999), *available at* http://www.healthprivacy.org [hereinafter HEALTH PRIVACY PROJECT].

[232] See DAHM MONOGRAPH, at nn.9–10 and accompanying text. Under HIPAA, "health information" means
    any information, whether oral or recorded in any form or medium, that
    (A) is created or received by a health care provider, health plan, public health authority, employer, life insurer, school or university, or health care clearinghouse; and

tect what has traditionally been considered the individual's "medical record," although Arizona, Maryland, Tennessee, and Virginia use the term "medical record" but have incorporated HIPAA's expanded definition.[233] Despite the lack of uniformity among the state laws, there are some similarities to the protections granted and to the types and effects of restrictions provided.

1. Common Privacy Protections

Many of the state statutes have some commonality, especially as regards specific privacy protections granted. The three most common areas of privacy protection are:

- the requirement to obtain the individual's consent or authorization prior to disclosure or release of health information;
- the individual's right to access his or her own health information; and
- the individual's statutory cause of action against the entity for unauthorized disclosure of the information.

These three common protections are discussed more fully in the paragraphs that follow.

a. Consents and Authorizations

A study conducted by the Institute for Health Care Research and Policy at Georgetown University in Washington, D.C., the Health Privacy Project, revealed that the most common provision in state privacy laws is the requirement that the individual's authorization be obtained prior to the disclosure of his or her health information.[234] However, these state statutes often include broad exceptions, allowing disclosure of the individual's health information without the individual's consent or authorization for treatment and continuing care purposes, in emergency situations, as directory information, to secure payment for health care, and for quality assurance or law enforcement activities.[235] These exceptions also typically vary from state to state.[236] Furthermore, some state statutes mandate the format and content of the required authorization, and many states allow patients to revoke a previously signed authorization.[237]

b. Individual's Right of Access

Individuals are provided some right to access and/or receive a copy of their own health information. However, the state statutes granting such a right vary

---

(B) relates to the past, present, or future physical or mental health or condition of an individual, the provision of health care to an individual, or the past, present, or future payment for the provision of health care to an individual.

Pub. L. No. 104-191, §1171(4) (codified at 42 U.S.C. §1320d(4)).

[233] See DAHM MONOGRAPH, at n.10 and accompanying text.

[234] See HEALTH PRIVACY PROJECT, available at http://www.healthprivacy.org.

[235] See DAHM MONOGRAPH, at nn.16–19, 23–24, 31–32, 37–41, 68–74, and accompanying text. See also HEALTH PRIVACY PROJECT.

[236] See generally DAHM MONOGRAPH; see also HEALTH PRIVACY PROJECT.

[237] See DAHM MONOGRAPH, at nn.23–24 and accompanying text; HEALTH PRIVACY PROJECT.

widely as to how those rights may be granted and/or exercised.[238] The following are examples of the scope-of-access rights granted to patients:

- *No statutory right of access:* Connecticut, Mississippi, Missouri, New Hampshire, North Dakota, and Oklahoma.[239]
- *Statutory right of access to mental health information:* Alabama, Idaho, New Mexico, and District of Columbia.[240]
- *Costs associated with accessing or obtaining a copy of the individual's health information:* ranging from "reasonable fee" to a statutorily defined dollar amount.[241]

State laws granting an individual the right to access his or her health information generally include exceptions, with the most common being the holder's right to refuse access if the holder feels that releasing the records could endanger the life or safety of the subject individual or another person.[242]

c. Individual's Cause of Action for Unauthorized Disclosures

Unlike HIPAA, the majority of states allow an individual a statutory cause of action against the individual or entity that makes an unauthorized release of the individual's protected health information.[243] In some states, the individual must be able to demonstrate actual harm in order to recover damages related to the unauthorized disclosure;[244] in others, an individual may be awarded punitive damages.[245] In Maryland and Rhode Island, the disclosing party may face criminal penalties in addition to civil penalties.[246]

2. Common Disclosure Restrictions and Their Effects

Although the majority of states have enacted laws that prohibit the release of confidential health information without the individual's written authorization or consent, the majority of those statutes and regulations often contain provisions that mandate or allow disclosures depending on certain circumstances or in specific instances.[247] It is important to remember, too, that privacy protections are granted not only within a state's "confidentiality statute" but also in other portions of the state's laws and regulations. For example, numerous states include privacy protection requirements within the statutes and regulations that

---

[238] *See generally* HEALTH PRIVACY PROJECT; *see also* DAHM MONOGRAPH, at nn.22–23 and accompanying text.

[239] *See* DAHM MONOGRAPH, at n.22.

[240] *See* HEALTH PRIVACY PROJECT. See also DAHM MONOGRAPH, at n.30, for a list of the 26 states that have enacted separate statutes protecting mental health information.

[241] *See* DAHM MONOGRAPH, at nn.78–81 and accompanying text; HEALTH PRIVACY PROJECT.

[242] *See* DAHM MONOGRAPH, at n.35; HEALTH PRIVACY PROJECT.

[243] *See* DAHM MONOGRAPH, at nn.50, 52–56, and accompanying text. Under HIPAA, an individual's sole course of action is to report real or suspected noncompliance with the privacy regulations to the Secretary of HHS. HIPAA Privacy Rule, 65 Fed. Reg. at 82,801 (codified at 45 C.F.R. §160.306(a)).

[244] *See* DAHM MONOGRAPH, at nn.50, 54–56.

[245] *See id.* at nn.50, 54.

[246] MD. CODE ANN., HEALTH-GEN. I. §4-309; R.I. GEN. LAWS §5-37.3-9.

[247] *See* DAHM MONOGRAPH; HEALTH PRIVACY PROJECT.

govern an individual or entity's license or certification.[248] Health care providers and entities must comply with these privacy laws to avoid jeopardizing their license to provide health care services. Whether and what a health care provider or health care organization can disclose, and what and how that information can be released, will also be defined in various and numerous state statutes and regulations, not just that state's confidentiality statute.

a. What Type of Entity Is Disclosing?

The application of state privacy protections and disclosure restrictions is often dependent on the type of entity holding the health information. For instance, records held by governmental agencies and officials are often subject to more privacy restrictions than records held by a private entity or individual.[249] Furthermore, some state privacy protections are expressly applicable only to certain types of entities regardless of the entity's governmental status. For example, Arizona law restricts disclosure by insurance entities and utilization review agents.[250] California's revised confidentiality statute, which initially covered only health care providers, now covers managed care organizations and insurance companies.[251] Maine has a broad statute governing disclosure of health information by health care practitioners and facilities such as hospitals and home health providers.[252] Tennessee law creates a statutory right to privacy for care received at a hospital or clinic.[253] Texas and Washington have similar statutes in different sections of their respective codes that apply to health care providers and entities in general[254] and to mental health providers and entities in particular.[255]

b. What Type of Health Information Is to Be Disclosed?

Another common theme of state privacy protections is that the type of health information often determines whether it can be disclosed. For example, the majority of states have passed separate legislation imposing specific restrictions on the use and disclosure of HIV/AIDS test results and related information.[256] At least 18 states have enacted statutes that address the confidentiality of genetic information.[257] More than half of the states have separate laws that protect mental health information, and virtually every state with a confidentiality

---

[248] Such statutes and regulations often mandate disclosure of information to the licensing agency or authority for purposes of enforcement or compliance. Even if not specifically stated, very few individuals or entities will refuse a reasonable request for protected health information if such refusal would jeopardize the individual's or entity's licensure.

[249] See HEALTH PRIVACY PROJECT.

[250] ARIZ. REV. STAT. §§20-2113, 20-2509.

[251] CAL. CIV. CODE §56, *as amended by* S.B. 19.

[252] ME. REV. STAT. ANN. tit. 22, §1711-C 1.

[253] TENN. CODE ANN. §68-11-1502.

[254] TEX. HEALTH & SAFETY CODE ANN. §§241.151 *et seq.*; WASH. REV. CODE §§70 *et seq.*

[255] TEX. HEALTH & SAFETY CODE ANN. §§611.001 *et seq.*; WASH. REV. CODE §§71 *et seq.*

[256] Numerous industry surveys that address particular types of health information such as AIDS/HIV and peer review statutes are available. *See, e.g.*, Robert Ellis Smith, *Compilation of State and Federal Privacy Laws*, PRIVACY J., 1992.

[257] See HEALTH PRIVACY PROJECT.

statute includes a provision within that statute that defers to the federal Confidentiality of Records provisions governing substance abuse and treatment records.[258] Some of these latter laws also include or address specific authorization requirements, disclosure restrictions, and rights of minors.[259]

c. Mandatory Versus Permitted Disclosures

In addition to understanding the extent to which state law protects individuals' health information, businesses also must understand when the information they may be holding will be subject to mandatory disclosure. In contrast to HIPAA, which requires disclosure of protected health information without the individual's consent or authorization in only two instances,[260] some state laws include more than just two mandated disclosures under certain conditions or for specific purposes.[261] For example, several state laws mandate disclosures without first obtaining an individual's authorization in support of law enforcement activities.[262] Moreover, health information may be subject to mandatory disclosure under the subpoena powers of various state instrumentalities.[263] In addition to understanding the extent to which the health information of individuals must be protected under state law, businesses must also understand when the information they may be holding will be subject to mandatory disclosure.

Most state laws, like HIPAA's privacy regulations,[264] do not mandate disclosure of protected health information without the individual's consent or authorization; they simply permit a covered entity to release it.[265] Requests for protected health information should be carefully scrutinized to ensure that no

---

[258] *See* DAHM MONOGRAPH at nn.30–31, 36, and accompanying text; HEALTH PRIVACY PROJECT. For discussion of the Confidentiality of Records provisions, see II.B.1.b, above.

[259] *See generally* DAHM MONOGRAPH; HEALTH PRIVACY PROJECT.

[260] 65 Fed. Reg. at 82,499 (Preamble) ("The final rule retains the provision that requires a covered entity to disclose protected health information only in two instances."); *see also id.* at 82,805 (codified at 45 C.F.R. §164.502(a)(2)). A covered entity must disclose protected health information (1) to the individual when requested under and required by either (a) the individual's right to access and/or inspect his or her health information or (b) the individual's right to receive an accounting of the disclosures made that are unrelated to treatment, payment, and health care operations; and (2) to the Secretary of HHS when required to investigate or determine the covered entity's compliance with the regulations. *Id.*

[261] *See* DAHM MONOGRAPH; HEALTH PRIVACY PROJECT. For example, California requires disclosure of health information if the disclosure is compelled by (1) a court, pursuant to a court order; (2) a board, commission, or agency for purposes of legally authorized adjudication; (3) a party to a court or administrative agency if requested by subpoena, subpoena duces tecum, notice to appear, or an authorized discovery procedure; (4) a board, commission, or administrative agency pursuant to an investigative subpoena; (5) an arbitrator or arbitration panel when arbitration is lawfully requested by either party; (6) a lawfully issued search warrant; or (7) as otherwise authorized by law. CAL. CIV. CODE §56.10, *as amended* by S.B. 19.

[262] *See* DAHM MONOGRAPH, at nn.42–43 and accompanying text.

[263] *See id.* at nn.68–74 and accompanying text.

[264] See II.B.3.c., above.

[265] *See* 65 Fed. Reg. at 82,498 (preamble to 45 C.F.R. §164.502 discussing permitted and required disclosures). See also state laws in California (CAL. CIV. CODE §56), Maine (ME. REV. STAT. ANN. §22-1711), Nevada (NEV. REV. STAT. §629), and Texas (TEXAS HEALTH & SAFETY CODE ANN. §241, and in Senate Bill 11), which all specifically differentiate between mandatory and permissive releases.

unauthorized disclosures are made based on statements from requesters of the information that "releases of the protected health information are required."

IV. Professional Organizations and Groups

A. Professional Organizations

Professional codes of conduct do not have the force of law, but such codes are often recognized by health care providers as binding rules under which they conduct business or provide services. The universal theme of these professional codes is the balancing of the need to maintain and share health information for clinical purposes and the need to protect the confidentiality of an individual's health information.

1. American Medical Association

It is the position of the American Medical Association (AMA) that a physician has an ethical obligation to protect information provided by a patient. This position is expressed in the following statement of the AMA: "The information disclosed to a physician during the course of the relationship between physician and patient is confidential to the greatest possible degree. The physician should not reveal confidential communications or information without the express consent of the patient, unless required to do so by law."[266]

Furthermore, it is the position of the AMA that a physician should use the utmost care to protect computerized medical records; the AMA has developed guidelines to assist physicians in adequately protecting the confidentiality of health information stored in computerized databases.[267] Finally, the AMA has adopted specific guidelines regarding disclosure of information to the media, confidential care for minors, confidentiality of HIV status, disclosure to a patient's attorney, disclosure to data collection companies, and disclosure to insurance company representatives.[268]

2. American Hospital Association

The American Hospital Association has issued a policy and position statement available on its Web site[269] advocating that health care providers take action as necessary to protect their patients' confidential information. The statement further advocates for the adoption of strong uniform federal legislation designed to ensure the implementation of privacy protections.

---

[266] American Med. Ass'n, Ethical Op. 5.05 (2006).
[267] American Med. Ass'n, Ethical Op. 5.07 (1998).
[268] American Med. Ass'n, Ethical Ops. 5.04 (1996), 5.055 (1996), 5.057 (1998), 5.06 (prior to 1977), 5.075 (1998), 5.08 (prior to 1977).
[269] See AMERICAN HOSPITAL ASSOCIATION, http://www.aha.org.

3. JCAHO/Joint Commission on Accreditation of Healthcare Organizations

JCAHO (formerly the Joint Commission on Accreditation of Healthcare Organizations) has developed numerous patient rights and information-management standards regarding confidentiality, privacy, and security of health information.[270] All JCAHO-accredited entities must ensure that they satisfy such standards in order to avoid jeopardizing their accreditation status.

B. Other Privacy Protection Guidelines

In addition to the guidelines for protecting privacy established by the professional organizations discussed in IV.A., above, numerous other guidelines for safeguarding information and protecting privacy have been developed. Organizations that have published such privacy guidelines include, among others, the Organization for Economic Cooperation and Development; National Research Council; American Health Information Management Association; American Medical Informatics Association; Computer-Based Patient Record Institute; the Health Department of New South Wales, Australia; and the Canadian Privacy Commissioner.

Each organization that engages in this debate will likely have some influence on the development of a universal standard for the protection of health information.

V. CONCLUSION

It is perhaps too much to hope that federal and state laws governing privacy of personal health information will ever be reconciled. Even if a single standard is developed and adopted in the U.S., health care organizations might still face the international privacy issues that are discussed in Chapter 6 on the European data privacy regime and that impede doing business on a global scale. Fortunately or unfortunately, privacy of personal health information is an issue that will require significant legal analysis and counsel for a long time to come.

---

[270] See *Information Management Standards*, in JCAHO, ACCREDITATION MANUAL §7.

6

The European Data Privacy Regime*

I.	Introduction	128
	A. European Union Legislation	129
	B. The Importance of National Laws	130
	C. National Regulators and the Article 29 Working Party	131
II.	Key Concepts	132
	A. Personal Data	132
	B. Processing	133
	C. Data Controller and Data Processors	134
III.	Jurisdiction	134
	A. EEA Establishment	134
	B. Non-EEA Established Entities	135
IV.	The European Data Protection Principles	136
	A. Fair and Lawful Processing	136
	B. Particular Conditions for Sensitive Personal Data	137
	C. Valid Consent and Explicit Consent	139
	D. Data Subject Rights	140
	E. Data Security	141
V.	Appointing a Data Processor	142
VI.	Export of Personal Data Outside the EEA	143
	A. Adequate Level of Protection	144
	1. European Commission Findings of Adequacy	144
	2. U.S. Safe Harbor	144
	B. Adequate Safeguards	145
	1. Model Clauses	145
	2. Binding Corporate Rules	146
	C. Exceptions to the General Prohibition	147
	D. Personal Data Export Flow Chart	149
VII.	Administrative Requirements	150
VIII.	The E-Privacy Directive	151
IX.	On the Horizon	153
X.	Consumer Laws and Other Relevant Laws	155

*Amy Taylor and Gail Crawford, Latham & Watkins, LLP, London, England.

I. Introduction

While the United States privacy laws consist of a patchwork of different laws protecting different types of personal data,[1] in the European Union (the EU),[2] data privacy and security are governed by an EU directive that sets out consistent standards across Europe for the use of all categories of personal data (provided the data falls within the definition of "personal data" for purposes of that directive).[3]

This main directive that establishes the data protection regime in the European Economic Area (the EEA)[4] is Data Protection Directive 95/46/EC[5] (the "Data Protection Directive"). In addition, the Privacy and Electronic Communications Directive 2002/58/EC,[6] as amended by the Privacy and Electronic Communications Directive 2009/136/EC[7] (the "E-Privacy Directive"; together with the Data Protection Directive, the "Directives") is an important part of the

---

[1] *See, e.g.*, Children's Online Privacy Protection Act of 1998 (COPPA), Pub. L. No. 105-277 (protecting children's data); Health Information Portability and Accountability Act (HIPAA), Pub. L. No. 104-191 (protecting health information).

[2] The EU is an economic and political partnership of 27 countries (the Member States of the European Union), created following the end of the Second World War with the aim of fostering economic cooperation between the countries of Europe. The EU has since developed into a significant single market and political body, encompassing not only economic matters, but also aid and development, environmental issues, human rights, freedom of trade and people, and many other broad political aims. Since January 1, 2007, when Bulgaria and Romania became the latest countries to join the EU, the list of Member States has stood as follows: Austria, Belgium, Bulgaria, Cyprus, Czech Republic, Denmark, Estonia, Finland, France, Germany, Greece, Hungary, Republic of Ireland, Italy, Latvia, Lithuania, Luxembourg, Malta, the Netherlands, Poland, Portugal, Romania, Slovakia, Slovenia, Spain, Sweden, and the United Kingdom (UK). The following countries are currently candidate states at various application stages to become Member States: Croatia, the Former Yugoslav Republic of Macedonia, Iceland, Montenegro, and Turkey (which has been a candidate state since 1987). The Member States are classified as such as they have each acceded to the EU via a specific accession treaty, acceding the country to the consolidated founding treaties of the EU (which consist of the consolidated versions of the Treaty on European Union, the Treaty on the Functioning of the European Union, and the consolidated version of the Treaty establishing the European Atomic Energy Community).

[3] See II.A., below.

[4] The EEA was created on January 1, 1994, under the Agreement Creating the European Economic Area, to allow three of the four European Free Trade Association (EFTA) states (Iceland, Liechtenstein and Norway, but excluding the fourth state, Switzerland) to participate with the EU Member Sates in the EU internal market, and to bind those EFTA states to relevant EU legislation, adopted following January 1, 1994 (though these EFTA states have no right to vote in the relevant European institutions). Switzerland, the fourth EFTA state, has not signed the Agreement Creating the European Economic Area and is therefore not an EEA Member State; it has, however, entered into a bilateral agreement with the EU (and has subsequently implemented national data privacy laws similar to those elsewhere in Europe).

[5] Directive 95/46/EC of the European Parliament and of the Council of 24 October 1995 on the protection of individuals with regard to the processing of personal data and on the free movement of such data, [1995] OJ L 281/31.

[6] Directive 2002/58/EC of the European Parliament and of the Council of 12 July 2002 concerning the processing of personal data and the protection of privacy in the electronic communications sector, [2002] OJ L 201/37.

[7] Directive 2009/136/EC of the European Parliament and of the Council of 25 November 2009 (amending Directive 2002/22/EC on service and users' rights relating to electronic communications networks and services; Directive 2002/58/EC concerning the processing of personal data and the protection of privacy in the electronic communications sector; and Commission Regulation (EC) 2006/2004 on cooperation between national authorities responsible for the enforcement of consumer protection laws), [2009] OJ L 337/11.

European privacy regime. The E-Privacy Directive governs unsolicited communications, such as direct marketing (spam) by electronic means and the use of cookies and traffic and location data.

The Data Protection Directive establishes the data privacy and security objectives for the EEA in relation to all types of personal data. These objectives have been implemented by all EEA Member States through their national laws. The data protection regime in each Member State is therefore similar in principle, as all are based on the Data Protection Directive and designed to implement its objectives, but national differences have arisen as a result of each Member State's specific interpretation of the Data Protection Directive in its national implementing legislation.

A. European Union Legislation

At an EU level, there are three distinct forms of binding legislation—regulations, directives, and decisions[8]—that are enacted by a combination of the European Parliament, the Council of the European Union, and the European Commission.[9] Decisions deal solely with very specific issues and are applicable only to those organizations or individuals to whom the decision is specifically addressed; they are therefore of less relevance in this area than regulations and directives. Regulations are directly applicable in all EU Member States[10] as soon as they come into force and do not require any further implementation by the Member States. They are therefore more detailed than directives, as they must clearly set out the precise wording of the applicable law. An individual is able to enforce any rights he or she may have under a regulation in his or her national courts from the moment the regulation is in force, and any conflicting national laws are automatically overridden by the regulation. As a result of the direct effect of regulations in each Member State, the rules and enforcement of each regulation are consistent across Europe, as there is no opportunity for the Member States to interpret the regulation.

A directive, on the other hand, is a set of objectives that must be implemented into the national law of each Member State within a certain period of time. Each Member State therefore has a certain degree of flexibility as to exactly how it implements the directive, and an individual cannot enforce his or her rights under a directive until those rights are given effect in the national law of that individual's Member State. As a result of each Member State being

---

[8] Recommendations and opinions may also be issued by the relevant EU institutions, to allow the issuing institution to provide guidance or make a statement on a particular issue, but these are not binding and there is no legal obligation placed on those to whom they are addressed.

[9] These three bodies act together primarily through the co-decision procedure (co-decision is the standard decision-making process, though there are others such as the cooperation, consultation, and assent procedures). In basic terms, the European Commission makes all proposals for new laws, and the European Parliament and the Council of the European Union adopt those laws, with the European Commission then overseeing implementation. The process is designed to prevent either the European Parliament or the Council of the European Union from making legislative decisions unilaterally: both institutions must agree on the wording of a new law before it is adopted (Treaty of the Functioning of the European Union, art. 294, [2010] OJ C 83/47 consolidated version).

[10] The Member States of the European Union are listed in I., above.

required to implement a directive, there are often variances and potential inconsistencies in national laws that result from the implementation process, as each Member State interprets and gives effect to the directive in accordance with its own unique national legal system and values.

While there is inherent flexibility in directive implementation, and conflicting national laws are not automatically overridden by a directive (as they would be in the case of a regulation), that is not to say that Member States have free reign over a directive's objectives and meaning. The various institutions of the European Union[11] have powers to enforce the terms and objectives of directives against Member States that delay in implementing a directive[12] or that fail to implement a directive fully and accurately.[13]

B. The Importance of National Laws

The data protection regime in each Member State is similar in principle, as all are based on the Directives, but significant national differences have arisen as a result of each Member State's specific interpretation of the Directives in its national implementing legislation.[14]

These national differences in implementation of the Directives, and the subsequent need for pan-European organizations to consider each relevant Member State's specific legislation, have created obvious difficulties for such businesses and may ultimately act as an obstacle to efficient data use and transfer within Europe and on a global basis. The effect of this lack of harmonization of data

---

[11] The primary institutions of the European Union are the European Council (which defines the general political direction and priorities of the European Union) and the decision-making institutions: the European Parliament, the Council of the European Union, and the European Commission (discussed above in this section). The Court of Justice and the Court of Auditors also play key roles, upholding European law and auditing the European Union's financial arrangements, respectively.

[12] For example, in July 2011, the European Commission commenced legal action against 20 EEA Member States for failing to meet the implementation deadline for the Privacy and Electronic Communications Directive 2009/136/EC, which passed on May 25, 2011, by sending formal notice of proceedings to those 20 Member States. These Member States (Austria, Belgium, Bulgaria, Cyprus, Czech Republic, France, Germany, Greece, Hungary, Italy, Latvia, Lithuania, Luxembourg, the Netherlands, Poland, Portugal, Romania, Slovakia, Slovenia, and Spain) were given two months in which to reply to the formal notice. If they failed to do so, or if the European Commission was not fully satisfied with the reply, the European Commission could formally request the relevant Member States to implement the legislation. Ultimately, the European Commission can take proceedings against a Member State in the Court of Justice of the European Union if the legislation remains unimplemented. *See* Press Release, European Commission, Digital Agenda: Commission Starts Legal Action Against 20 Member States on Late Implementation of Telecoms Rules (July 19, 2011), *available at* http://europa.eu/rapid/pressReleasesAction.do?reference=IP/11/905&type=HTML.

[13] For example, the Spanish Supreme Court has referred claims from the European Commission and Spanish industry bodies to the European Court of Justice on the grounds that Spain has failed to fully and accurately implement Article 7(f) of the Data Protection Directive (the legitimate interest basis for data processing; see IV.A., below), by qualifying this legitimate interest basis with the requirement that the relevant personal data is contained in public sources (in addition to the requirement that processing is necessary to satisfy a legitimate interest).

[14] For example, as noted in I.A., above, Spain's implementation of the legitimate interests basis for data processing includes an additional requirement that the data must be from a public source in order to satisfy the legitimate interests basis. This additional requirement is not included in the Data Protection Directive wording and has therefore been implemented due to Spain's interpretation of the Data Protection Directive.

privacy laws across Europe (something the Data Protection Directive was in fact intended to relieve) has been thrown into sharp relief with the advancing globalization of organizations and advances in communications and information technology, rendering geographic and physical borders between jurisdictions increasingly irrelevant in our online information society. The pressing nature of these difficulties for organizations is one of the factors behind the wholesale review of the Data Protection Directive and its effectiveness that is currently being carried out by the European Commission.

While the broader principles behind the Directives' wording are common across Europe, the specific wording of national implementing legislation may vary from the wording of the Directives. It is therefore important for each organization, when assessing its European data privacy compliance and putting in place compliance solutions, to seek local law advice for each relevant EEA Member State in order to fully understand the specific implications of each set of national laws for that organization's data privacy practices.

C. National Regulators and the Article 29 Working Party

The Data Protection Directive requires each EEA Member State to establish a public authority as an independent national regulator, responsible for monitoring the implementation and enforcement of the Data Protection Directive by that Member State.[15] These regulators have varying investigative and enforcement powers and different relationships with national governments and judicial bodies, but are all characterized by a specific focus on individual privacy rights and implementation of the Data Protection Directive in their respective jurisdictions.

The national regulators also work together in the form of the European Commission's Article 29 Data Protection Working Party (the "Article 29 Working Party"). This group is made up of representatives of the national data protection regulator from each EU Member State (and therefore does not include the regulators of Iceland, Liechtenstein, or Norway, which are Member States of the EEA but not of the EU).[16] The primary objectives of the Article 29 Working Party include providing formal opinions and advice to the European Commission, providing recommendations to the European Commission and the wider European community, and promoting full and consistent application of the Directives and cooperation of regulators across Europe.[17] The opinions of the Article 29 Working Party are particularly important in practice as, while they are not legally binding on the European Commission, the European Court of Justice, or the Member States, they have a powerful practical impact. The influential impact of the Article 29 Working Party's opinions on the Commission, and the nature of its composition of all EU Member State national regulators, means that national regulators are likely to both follow its guidance and opinions and

---

[15] Data Protection Directive, art. 28.

[16] See explanation of EEA in I., above.

[17] Data Protection Directive, arts. 29 and 20. Rules of Procedure and First Annual Report of the Working Party on the Protection of Individuals with regard to the Processing of Personal Data (XV/5025/97).

to interpret national law in accordance with these standards (though national courts are not legally bound to follow Article 29 Working Party opinions and may rule differently).

II. KEY CONCEPTS

A. Personal Data

The Data Protection Directive and national implementing laws govern the collection and use of "personal data," which the Data Protection Directive defines as

> any information relating to an identified or identifiable natural person ("data subject"); an identifiable person is one who can be identified, directly or indirectly, in particular by reference to an identification number or to one or more factors specific to his physical, physiological, mental, economic, cultural or social identity.[18]

To the extent data does not fall within this definition and is therefore not deemed to be personal data for the purposes of the Data Protection Directive, the European privacy rules will not apply. A number of other laws, described in Section X, below, may still apply but will vary from jurisdiction to jurisdiction.

There is a separate category of personal data under the Data Protection Directive, defined as sensitive personal data, the processing of which is subject to more onerous conditions and stricter restrictions than those imposed by the Data Protection Directive in relation to the use of non-sensitive personal data (as discussed in IV., below). Sensitive personal data is defined in the Data Protection Directive as data relating to a data subject's (1) racial or ethnic origin, (2) political opinions, (3) religious beliefs, (4) trade union membership, (5) physical or mental health, (6) sex life, or (7) actual or alleged criminal offenses.[19] The Article 29 Working Party has indicated that a broad interpretation of "physical or mental health" is required,[20] including not only information relating to specific injuries, illness, or pharmaceutical prescriptions, but also any information linked to the health status of an individual, such as data relating to alcohol and recreational drug use, and any administrative information contained in medical documentation (even where this would not otherwise be considered sensitive, were it not contained in a medical file). As a result, medical and health information are treated as sensitive information across Europe, and therefore the more onerous standards imposed in relation to sensitive personal data in each relevant EEA Member State are applicable when dealing with medical or health data, as discussed in more detail in the remainder of this section.

An individual may be identified either directly by the data (e.g., the individual's full name) or indirectly by some other piece of information, which may not of itself directly identify the individual but may do so when combined with another piece of information that the data controller (see II.C., below) has or

---

[18] Data Protection Directive, art. 2(a).
[19] Data Protection Directive, art. 8(1).
[20] Working Document of the Article 29 Data Protection Working Party on the Processing of Personal Data relating to Health in Electronic Health Records (EHR), 00323/07/EN, WP 131.

has access to. For example, a biological sample may be identified simply by an anonymous patient number identifier; however, the research institute or sponsor may also have in its possession, or have access to, a number of databases through which one could match up the patient number identifier with the names or medical records of the patients to which they relate. In this case, both pieces of information (i.e., the "anonymous" biological sample and the database) are individually classed as personal data (even if the biological sample could not directly identify an individual independently of the database).

The Data Protection Directive applies to all data processed on an automatic or computerized system and also to hardcopy data that forms part of a "personal data filing system."[21] Broadly, such a filing system would need to be sufficiently sophisticated so as to be equivalent (in terms of its indexation) to an automatic or computerized system. Inevitably, given the sophisticated search functions commonly found in electronic databases, a filing system will never be equivalent in terms of speed or ease of searching. However, it may still be a relevant filing system for the purposes of the Data Protection Directive if, when required, specific personal data concerning a particular individual can be readily retrieved from the filing system (notwithstanding that this will be inherently more labor intensive and time consuming than conducting the same search in an automatic or computerized system).

In practice, this is likely to mean that a filing system would need to be arranged by reference to individuals (or to criteria relating to individuals), with sufficient indexing, document identification, subdivision, and so forth to enable the reviewer to readily ascertain that personal data is available in the filing system and in which files that information may be held, and subsequently to apply a standard search process to readily find specific information relating to a particular individual within a file (without searching through every piece of information in the filing system).

B. Processing

Processing is defined broadly in the Data Protection Directive to mean "any operation or set of operations which is performed upon personal data, whether or not by automatic means, such as collection, recording, organization, storage, adaptation or alteration, retrieval, consultation, use, disclosure by transmission, dissemination or otherwise making available, alignment or combination, blocking, erasure or destruction."[22] In practice, processing is interpreted across Europe as essentially referring to anything a person or computerized system could do with data, including, for example, having merely "read-only" access to personal data without the ability to download or save that data, or merely storing personal data despite having no subsequent access to that data.

---

[21] Data Protection Directive, art. 3. "Personal data filing system" is defined in Article 2(c) of the Directive as "any structured set of personal data which are accessible according to specific criteria, whether centralized, decentralized or dispersed on a functional or geographical basis."

[22] Data Protection Directive, art. 2(b).

C. Data Controller and Data Processor

There is a crucial distinction under the Data Protection Directive between the "data controller" and the "data processor."

The data controller is the person or entity "which alone or jointly with others determines the purposes and means of the processing of personal data."[23] The data processor, on the other hand, is the person or entity "which processes personal data on behalf of the controller."[24] Broadly speaking, most of the obligations under the Data Protection Directive (and therefore under national laws) are imposed on the data controller, who then has to ensure compliance by any processors it uses. In practice, distinguishing the data controller from the data processor can be difficult, especially given how data is currently processed: there is often a grey area in which one entity has been appointed by another to process data on the appointing entity's behalf, yet both have a certain level of autonomy over how they handle the data. In these circumstances, it can be helpful to examine who is actually determining the essential, root purposes of the processing.[25]

III. JURISDICTION

The obligation to comply with the relevant national implementing law of a Member State under the Data Protection Directive applies to a data controller that:

(1) is established in that Member State and processes personal data in the context of that establishment;[26] or
(2) is established outside that Member State or the EEA but using equipment in that Member State for processing personal data (excluding for the purposes of transit only).[27]

A. EEA Establishment

An entity will be "established" in an EEA member state if it carries out activities in that Member State in an effective and real manner.[28] For example, such an entity may include one of the following:

(1) an individual ordinarily resident in that Member State;
(2) a body incorporated under, or a partnership or unincorporated corporation formed under, the national law of that Member State; or

---

[23] *Id.* art. 2(d).
[24] *Id.* art. 2(e).
[25] Opinion 1/2010 of the Article 29 Data Protection Working Party on the Concepts of "Controller" and "Processor," 00264/10/EN, WP 169.
[26] Data Protection Directive, arts. 4(1)(a), (b).
[27] *Id.* art. 4(1)(c).
[28] *Id.* recital 19 (as emphasized by the Article 29 Working Party in Opinion 8/2010 of the Article 29 Data Protection Working Party on Applicable Law, 0836-02/10/EN, WP 179 on applicable law).

(3) an entity that maintains an office, branch, or agency or a regular practice in that Member State.

This test therefore deems an entity to be "established" in a Member State if it carries out activities in that Member State (in an effective and real manner), regardless of whether or not the entity is legally formed or located in that Member State in any sense. Further, recent European-level guidance from the Article 29 Working Party[29] has made clear that, where an organization is established in a number of EEA Member States, it must comply with the national laws of each relevant Member State in relation to its operations in each respective jurisdiction.

B. Non-EEA Established Entities

Under the second part of the jurisdiction test (as set out in III., above), the Data Protection Directive's jurisdiction (and that of its national implementing laws) extends to those entities that are not "established" within the EEA but that make use of equipment in an EEA Member State for personal data processing purposes.[30] This is a considerable extension of scope, and in practice it means that even those organizations based (in terms of physical location, employees, consumers, or patient location) exclusively in the U.S. or elsewhere outside the EEA must still consider the applicability of the Data Protection Directive and national laws to their business processes if they use equipment such as servers, back-up servers or data deposits, data processors, or similar facilities within the EEA.

Application of the second part of the jurisdiction test was significantly extended in practice following guidance from the Article 29 Working Party,[31] which makes it clear that the use of cookies by an entity outside the EEA on an end user's personal computer (PC) located within the EEA will constitute the use of equipment (i.e., the end user's PC) in the relevant Member State for data processing purposes, and will therefore bring that non-EEA entity within the scope of the relevant Member State's national privacy laws. Online medical services providers or medical document management providers, for example, based outside the EEA, may therefore find themselves subject to the national privacy laws of each of those EEA Member States in which their end users are physically located (to the extent cookies are placed on each end user's PC, when those end users access the site or online system). Further, data flow strategies aimed at avoiding the application of the Data Protection Directive by locating the relevant personal data and any associated processes outside of the EEA are now technically difficult to maintain, as the relevant national laws will apply to the extent that personal data was collected from an EEA data subject via a cookie on the data subject's PC, regardless of where the data server is located. Equally however, organizations must balance the technical application of the law with

---

[29] Opinion 8/2010 of the Article 29 Data Protection Working Party on Applicable Law, 0836-02/10/EN, WP 179, in relation to Article 4(1)(a) of the Data Protection Directive.

[30] Data Protection Directive, art. 4(1)(c).

[31] Opinion 8/2010 of the Article 29 Data Protection Working Party on Applicable Law, 0836-02/10/EN, WP 179.

the likelihood of enforcement action being taken against non-EEA based businesses, given the relatively limited resources of the national regulators.

Under certain national laws, limited obligations may also be placed directly on a data processor established in or using equipment in a particular EEA Member State. These obligations range from, at the more onerous end, notification to the national regulator, independent responsibility for protecting data subject rights, and more general compliance with relevant national law, to, at the other end of the scale, maintaining minimum security and confidentiality standards and limiting processing to only that instructed by the data controller.

IV. THE EUROPEAN DATA PROTECTION PRINCIPLES

The European regime is based around eight core data protection principles, which provide that data must:

(1) be fairly and lawfully processed;[32]
(2) be collected for specified, explicit, and legitimate purposes and not further processed in a way incompatible with those purposes (data subjects should be notified of all the purposes for which their personal data is being collected at the time it is collected);[33]
(3) be adequate, relevant, and not excessive in relation to the purposes for which they are processed;[34]
(4) be accurate and up to date, and every reasonable step must be taken to ensure that inaccurate or incomplete data (having regard to the purposes for which the data were collected or for which they are further processed) are erased or rectified;[35]
(5) not be kept in a form that permits identification of data subjects for longer than necessary;[36]
(6) be processed in line with the rights of data subjects;[37]
(7) be secure (protecting against unlawful processing and against accidental loss, destruction, or damage to the data);[38] and
(8) not be transferred to countries outside the EEA unless they have an adequate level of protection.[39]

A. Fair and Lawful Processing

In order for processing of non-sensitive personal data to be "fair and lawful" under the first principle listed in IV., above, at least one of the following conditions must be met:

---

[32] Data Protection Directive, art. 6(1)(a).
[33] *Id.* art. 6(1)(b).
[34] *Id.* art. 6(1)(c).
[35] *Id.* art. 6(1)(d).
[36] *Id.* art. 6(1)(e).
[37] *Id.* arts. 12, 14.
[38] *Id.* art. 17.
[39] *Id.* art. 25.

(1) the data subject has unambiguously given his or her consent to the processing;[40]
(2) processing is necessary in relation to a contract to which the data subject is a party, or in order to take steps at the request of the data subject prior to entering into a contract;[41]
(3) processing is necessary for compliance with a legal obligation;[42]
(4) processing is necessary in order to protect the vital interests of the data subject;[43]
(5) processing is necessary in relation to the administration of justice or exercise of a public function;[44] and/or
(6) processing is necessary for the purposes of legitimate interests of the data controller or a third party to whom the data are disclosed, except where unwarranted in any particular case by reason of prejudice to the rights and freedoms or legitimate interests of the data subject.[45]

In practice, many data controllers seek to rely on either obtaining valid consent from the data subject or on the data controller's legitimate interests condition to meet the "fair and lawful" processing requirement. However, issues may arise from such reliance, as consent may be withdrawn by the data subject at any time, or it may be unclear as to whether processing may cause unwarranted prejudice to a data subject in any particular circumstances.

B. Particular Conditions for Sensitive Personal Data

In order to process sensitive personal data such as medical and health information, one or more of a number of stricter conditions must be met. Notably, there is no legitimate interests condition and usually "explicit" consent is needed (as discussed in Section IV.C., below). The potential grounds for processing sensitive personal data are as follows:

(1) the data subject has given his or her explicit consent to the processing of the data;[46] or
(2) processing is necessary for the purposes of carrying out the obligations and specific rights of the controller in the field of employment law in so far as it is authorized by national law providing for adequate safeguards;[47] or
(3) processing is necessary to protect the vital interests of the data subject or of another person where the data subject is physically or legally incapable of giving his or her consent[48] (in a medical context, this

---

[40] *Id.* art. 7(a).
[41] *Id.* art. 7(b).
[42] *Id.* art. 7(c).
[43] *Id.* art. 7(d).
[44] *Id.* art. 7(e).
[45] *Id.* art. 7(f).
[46] *Id.* art. 8(2)(a).
[47] *Id.* art. 8(2)(b).
[48] *Id.* art. 8(2)(c).

relates to processing necessary for a life-saving treatment in a situation where the data subject is not able to express his or her intentions[49]); or

(4) processing is carried out in the course of its legitimate activities with appropriate guarantees by a foundation, association, or any other non-profit-seeking body with a political, philosophical, religious or trade-union aim and on condition that the processing relates solely to the members of the body or to persons who have regular contact with it in connection with its purposes and that the data are not disclosed to a third party without the consent of the data subjects;[50] or

(5) processing relates to data that are manifestly made public by the data subject, or is necessary for the establishment, exercise, or defense of legal claims;[51] or

(6) the data is required for the purposes of preventive medicine, medical diagnosis, the provision of care or treatment, or the management of health-care services, and where those data are processed by a health professional subject under national law or rules established by national competent bodies to the obligation of professional secrecy or by another person also subject to an equivalent obligation of secrecy.[52]

Medical and health data may therefore be collected and handled where strictly required[53] for specific preventative and treatment purposes by health care professionals who are bound by professional obligations of confidence (as imposed under national law or by national health care regulatory authorities) on the specific medical care grounds set out in the Data Protection Directive, provided the other data processing principles are also complied with. Medical data collected and processed for non-prevention or treatment purposes (e.g., for research purposes, or analysis of patient demographics, or health trust general performance) may also be processed according to one of the core data processing grounds set forth above.

In practice, data controllers most commonly rely on the data subject's explicit consent for the processing of medical and health data (for non-treatment purposes). This is most likely due to the fact that, as long as the explicit consent is validly obtained and covers the processing in question, explicit consent provides a relatively reliable processing basis that the data controller can control, proactively manage, and adapt to current and potentially future processing, although the fact that the consent may be withdrawn at any time remains an issue: valid and explicit consent are discussed in further detail in the next section.

---

[49] Working Document of the Article 29 Data Protection Working Party on the Processing of Personal Data relating to Health in Electronic Health Records (EHR), ¶II(5), 00323/07/EN, WP 131.

[50] Data Protection Directive, art. 8(2)(d).

[51] *Id.* art. 8(2)(e).

[52] *Id.* art. 8(3).

[53] Working Document of the Article 29 Data Protection Working Party on the Processing of Personal Data relating to Health in Electronic Health Records (EHR), ¶II(6).

C. Valid Consent and Explicit Consent

In order for a data controller to rely on the data subject's consent as a legitimate ground for processing non-sensitive personal data (e.g., patient or employee names and contact details), the consent must constitute an informed, freely given, and specific indication from the data subject that the subject agrees to his or her data being processed. This requires some sort of affirmative act by the individual in question, for example, clicking an icon or tick box, signing a form, or subscribing for a service involving data processing. An "opt in" consent (i.e., a positive action to indicate consent) rather than an "opt out" consent (i.e., consent is the default and a positive action is required to opt out of that default consent) has long been best practice across Europe and is expressly required in certain Member States, under national case law or legislation.

Guidance from the Article 29 Working Party[54] has reinforced this interpretation of consent and has made clear that it does not consider the right to object to processing, (i.e., an opt out) to be sufficient to constitute valid consent for the purposes of the Data Protection Directive. The Article 29 Working Party also made the following observations in the same Opinion, continuing the theme of a strict view of valid consent:

(1) inaction or silence is unlikely to constitute valid consent;
(2) a widely drafted consent will not be sufficiently specific, as each processing purpose should be specified separately; and
(3) information about processing should be provided directly to the data subject (mere availability of information is insufficient for informed consent).

Explicit consent for the purposes of legitimizing the processing of sensitive personal data[55] is a higher standard than the level of consent required for the processing of non-sensitive data. Explicit consent requires the data controller to ensure that the data subject is absolutely clear on the type of data being processed and the exact nature and extent of the processing (so further detail about the processing activities is needed, compared to that provided when dealing with non-sensitive personal data). Further, the positive consent of the data subject must be absolutely clear: not only is inaction or silence never adequate as valid consent for the processing of sensitive personal data, but consent cannot be inferred from a positive action alone (such as placing a business card in a "contacts" box, or signing up to a "contacts" list with a name and e-mail address).[56] Instead, there must be some affirmative action from the data subject to express consent to the processing of his or her sensitive personal data. As with valid consent for the processing of non-sensitive data, sensitive data processing requires the data subject's consent to be freely given and without any social,

---

[54] Opinion 15/2011 of the Article 29 Working Party on the Definition of Consent, 01197/11/EN, WP 187.

[55] Data Protection Directive, art. 8(2)(a).

[56] Opinion 15/2011 of the Article 29 Working Party on the Definition of Consent, §III.A.1, 01197/11/EN, WP 187.

financial, psychological, or other coercion.[57] Therefore, a data subject's consent that is obtained under a threat that he or she will receive a lower quality of medical treatment or no treatment at all will not be valid consent.[58]

There is no requirement under the Data Protection Directive for the data subject's consent to be recordable. However, from an evidentiary perspective, it is helpful for organizations to keep careful records of consents obtained so that these are accessible for future reference, particularly in the health care sector where the personal data involved is often of a sensitive nature and the processing may be particularly intrusive or especially risky for the data subject (such as the collection, use, and storage of biological and genetic materials). Organizations collecting consents for health data processing online should therefore consider using more reliable consent mechanisms from an evidentiary perspective; digital signatures, for example, would be preferable to functions such as tick boxes or clickable buttons, since these latter mechanisms identify the consenting individual by only an e-mail address.[59]

D. Data Subject Rights

Across the EEA, individuals have various rights of access and correction in relation to personal data about themselves, which they must be able to exercise without excessive delay or expense. The Data Protection Directive requires the national implementing laws of each Member State to provide for rights for the data subject to obtain (from the data controller):

(1) confirmation as to whether or not data relating to them are being processed and information as to the purposes of the processing, the categories of data concerned, and the recipients to whom the data are disclosed;[60]
(2) a copy of their relevant data being processed by the data controller, and any available information as to the source of the data;[61]
(3) knowledge of the logic involved in any automatic processing of data relating to them;[62]

---

[57] Working Document of the Article 29 Data Protection Working Party on the Processing of Personal Data relating to Health in Electronic Health Records (EHR), ¶II(4)(a), 00323/07/EN, WP 131.

[58] Working Document of the Article 29 Data Protection Working Party on the Processing of Personal Data relating to Health in Electronic Health Records (EHR), ¶II(4)(a), 00323/07/EN, WP 131; Opinion 15/2011 of the Article 29 Working Party on the Definition of Consent, §III.A.1, 01197/11/EN, WP 187.

[59] *See generally* Opinion 15/2011 of the Article 29 Working Party on the Definition of Consent, 01197/11/EN, WP 187.

[60] Data Protection Directive, art. 12(a).

[61] *Id.*

[62] *Id.*

(4) as appropriate, the rectification, erasure, or blocking of data the processing of which does not comply with the provisions of the Data Protection Directive;[63] and

(5) notification to third parties to whom the data have been disclosed of any rectification, erasure, or blocking carried out (unless this proves impossible or involves a disproportionate effort).[64]

The majority of EEA Member States have imposed specific time limits for responding to requests from data subjects. A data controller must therefore be aware of these various national-level data subject rights and should design and operate its data processing flows and systems, and establish internal compliance procedures, to ensure it can respond to data subject requests in compliance with such data subject's rights. Where appropriate, this may also extend to ensuring that data processing terms in place with data processors and subprocessors provide for adequate and timely assistance by the processor, to enable the data controller to respond to a data subject request in compliance with the relevant national laws (see V., below).

E. Data Security

The Data Protection Directive's requirements in terms of security measures are broad. They require a data controller to put in place "appropriate technical and organizational measures" to protect personal data from "unlawful destruction or accidental loss, alteration, unauthorized disclosure or access, in particular where the processing involves the transmission of data over a network, and against all other unlawful forms of processing."[65] The data controller must also ensure that this obligation flows through to any data processors processing data on its behalf.[66] What is "appropriate" in each case will depend on the context of the processing and the nature of the personal data itself. The specific provisions of the national law or formal regulatory guidance of the relevant Member State will also impact the security levels required: some jurisdictions, such as Italy, have relatively detailed, prescriptive information security levels that must be put in place. Other jurisdictions, such as the U.K., offer guidelines and best practices, but the exact security measures to be implemented are left for each data controller to determine.

Under the revised E-Privacy Directive,[67] it is mandatory for public communications providers (such as Internet service providers (ISPs) and telecommunications companies) to promptly inform both their customers and the relevant

---

[63] *Id.* art. 12(b).
[64] *Id.* art. 12(c).
[65] *Id.* art. 17(1).
[66] *Id.* arts. 17(2), (3).
[67] See VIII., below. As of July 2011, only the U.K., Denmark, Estonia, Finland, Ireland, Malta, and Sweden have implemented the amended E-Privacy Directive (though the deadline for implementation passed on May 25, 2011).

national regulator of any data security breaches in relation to the personal data they are collecting and processing.[68] While the revised E-Privacy Directive only imposes these mandatory breach notification provisions on public communications providers,[69] certain Member States have implemented breach notification laws that apply more broadly.[70] In any event, the majority of national regulators across Europe would expect other data controllers, including medical services and health care providers, to promptly report serious data security breaches to them. Failure to notify the relevant regulator of major security breaches, which are, in practice, one of the primary triggers of regulator investigations and enforcement action, is likely to result in more severe penalties in the event that sanctions are imposed.

V. Appointing a Data Processor

In the event that a data controller appoints a data processor to process personal data on its behalf, whether that data processor is an entity within the controller's organizational group or a third party, the Data Protection Directive requires a written contract containing specific provisions between the controller and the processor.[71]

The contractual terms governing the data processing must, under the Data Protection Directive, include provisions that oblige the processor to:

(1) act only on the instructions of the data controller, and
(2) establish and maintain data security measures to the same standards as those imposed under the relevant national law on the data controller itself.[72]

These Data Protection Directive requirements are intended to ensure that personal data is protected throughout the data processing chain, by limiting the acts of any subsequent data processors to those authorized by the data controller, who is ultimately responsible for compliance with the relevant national law. Generally, the Data Protection Directive regime imposes statutory obligations on a data controller and then contemplates contractual obligations being imposed by the data controller down the chain on any subsequent data processors (subject to limited direct statutory obligations on processors in some countries).

---

[68] Privacy and Electronic Communications Directive, art. 2(4)(c) (amending Article 4 of the E-Privacy Directive).

[69] *Id.*

[70] Working Document 01/2011, 00683/11/EN, WP 184, of the Article 29 Data Protection Working Party on the current EU personal data breach framework and recommendations for future policy developments notes that Germany and Austria both have national laws in place establishing a mandatory personal data security breach framework across all sectors, not limited to public communications providers.

[71] Data Protection Directive, arts. 17(3) and 17(4).

[72] *Id.* art. 17(3).

In addition to the two provisions required by the Data Protection Directive that are listed above, a data controller may want to impose additional contractual obligations on its processors to enable it to retain sufficient control over the processor's actions with the data, and therefore to ensure it can comply with its primary statutory obligations under national law. For example, the following provisions are commonly included in data processing agreements to protect the data controller (who must ultimately comply with national legislation):

(1) *data subject access*: provisions requiring the processor to notify the data controller of any requests from individual data subjects for access to their personal data and assist the controller's production of such data within certain time periods (as national laws commonly provide for a limited period of time in which a data controller must comply with such requests);

(2) *data processor assistance*: broad provisions requiring the data processor to provide all reasonable assistance to the data controller to enable the controller to comply with its obligations under national law (for example, requiring the data processor to provide access to the personal data at any time, and to correct, delete, or block any personal data on request from the data controller);

(3) *data export*: restrictions on the ability of the data processor to export personal data outside the EEA, commonly other than with the consent of the data controller and with suitable safeguards in place (see VI., below); and

(4) *subprocessors*: restrictions on the ability of the data processor to appoint further subprocessors of the personal data, commonly other than with the consent of the data controller, and a suitable subprocessing agreement in place to ensure the data continues to be protected down the chain.

VI. Export of Personal Data Outside the EEA

The Data Protection Directive contains a general prohibition, subject to certain exceptions, on the transfer of personal data from any country within the EEA to any other country outside the EEA (including, for example, the United States) that lacks data privacy laws that the European Commission has ruled provide adequate protection for the rights and freedoms of data subjects in relation to the processing of their personal data.[73] Therefore, the threshold question for a data controller becomes, "Is it necessary, taking into account the data controller's commercial requirements, to transfer personal data outside the EEA?" If it is necessary, then the data controller will need to consider carefully the various approaches for compliance with the general prohibition, as set out

---

[73] *Id.* art. 25.

in detail below. The following three key considerations illustrate the approach required in practice, which is further detailed in the flow chart in VI.D., below:

(1) Does the third country provide an adequate level of protection (VI.A., below)?
(2) Do the parties have, or can they put into place, adequate safeguards to protect the data (VI.B., below)?[74]
(3) Do any of the exceptions to the general principle apply (VI.C., below)?[75]

A. Adequate Level of Protection

1. European Commission Findings of Adequacy

Transfers within the EEA and transfers from within the EEA to a country that has been deemed by the European Commission to have adequate data privacy laws are not subject to the general prohibition on transfer.[76] As of July 2011, personal data may be transferred to entities located in the following jurisdictions without breaching the general prohibition on data export, as these have all been deemed to have adequate data privacy laws by the European Commission: Andorra, Argentina, Canada, Faroe Islands, Guernsey, Isle of Man, Israel, Jersey, and Switzerland.

2. U.S. Safe Harbor

Transfers can be made to the United States, notwithstanding the general prohibition on transfer under the Data Protection Directive, if the recipient United States organization is self-certified under the U.S. Safe Harbor regime, as such a recipient is deemed to have adequate protection in place.[77] The Safe Harbor rules are a public commitment to data privacy, run by the U.S. Department of Commerce and approved by the European Commission, under which companies self-certify that they are in compliance with the Safe Harbor Principles (which are similar in many respects to the principles of the Data Protection Directive). Organizations in industries that are not under the jurisdiction of the Federal Trade Commission (FTC) cannot avail themselves of the U.S. Safe Harbor rules; notably, financial services providers (including certain insurance activities), telecommunications providers, and non-profit organizations are not regulated by the FTC.

---

[74]*Id.* art. 26(2).

[75]*Id.* art. 26(1).

[76]*Id.* arts. 25(1), (6).

[77]Commission Decision 520/2000/EC of 26 July 2000 pursuant to Directive 95/46/EC of the European Parliament and of the Council on the adequate protection of personal data provided by the Safe Harbour Privacy Principles issued by the U.S. Department of Commerce, [2000] OJ L 215/0007.

Failure to comply with the Safe Harbor Principles may result in the FTC taking enforcement action; however, in the last year or so, there has been significant criticism across Europe of the Safe Harbor program due to the FTC's failure to exercise these enforcement powers in practice. This lack of effective enforcement, coupled with widespread noncompliance with the Safe Harbor principles by certified companies, has led to a more skeptical view in Europe of the real protection conferred by Safe Harbor certification. In Germany, for example, it is clear that German data controllers may not rely solely on a United States data importer's Safe Harbor certification to satisfy German data export requirements, and that additional diligence steps are required to confirm the importer's actual compliance with the Safe Harbor principles: undertaking such diligence should be considered best practice for all European data controllers.

B. Adequate Safeguards

Where an exporting data controller cannot satisfy itself that the third country to which it is exporting provides an adequate level of protection, it may export personal data by putting in place approved adequate safeguards[78]—principally either Model Clauses (as discussed in more detail in VI.B.1., below) or approved binding corporate rules.

1. Model Clauses

A data controller may export personal data to a data recipient outside the EEA by putting in place and complying with European Commission-approved model clauses (the "Model Clauses").[79] The European Commission has approved three sets of Model Clauses, as follows:[80]

(1) *data controller to data controller*: two sets of model clauses that are approved for use between an exporting data controller located within the EEA and an importing data controller located outside the EEA;[81] and

(2) *data controller to data processor*: a third set that has been approved for use between an exporting data controller located within the EEA and an importing data processor located outside the EEA. The previous version of this third set of Model Clauses was replaced by a set with

---

[78] Data Protection Directive, art. 26(2).

[79] *Id.*

[80] The Model Clauses were first introduced in 2001.

[81] The original set is annexed to the Commission Decision of 15 June 2001 on standard contractual clauses for the transfer of personal data to third countries under Directive 95/46/EC (2001/497/EC), and an updated set is annexed to the Commission Decision of 27 December 2004 amending Decision 2001/497/EC as regards the introduction of an alternative set of standard contractual clauses for the transfer of personal data to third countries (2004/915/EC).

effect from May 2010,[82] to take into account the expansion in recent years of business models that involve the international processing of personal data by complex webs of data processors and subprocessors. The 2010 clauses contain specific provisions to allow, under certain conditions, the outsourcing of processing activities to subprocessors while ensuring protection for personal data throughout the processing chain.

2. Binding Corporate Rules

Binding corporate rules are sets of rules and standards put in place throughout multinational organizations (with group entities located outside the EEA) as a mechanism for the compliant transfer of personal data throughout that organization.[83] These internal rules and standards must be binding at all levels throughout the relevant organization and must be approved by the national regulator of each EEA Member State in which the organization is established. This approval process is managed by a lead data protection authority, to which the organization must submit its draft binding corporate rules.[84] Once approved by the lead authority, that authority will liaise with the other relevant EEA data protection authorities to gain their approval (the organization therefore deals solely with the lead authority).[85] Binding corporate rules are becoming more popular, as the process for approval becomes more standardized, and once approved, having these rules in place reduces internal administration for intergroup data transfers. However, to put this popularity into perspective, as of April 2011, only 15 organizations across Europe have had their binding corporate rules approved. The relatively slow take up of binding corporate rules is likely to be due primarily to the long lead time involved before the rules are formally approved (at least one year and commonly longer) and the general lack of familiarity with the rules and process among multinational organizations, particularly those operating in, but based outside of, Europe.

---

[82] The revised set is annexed to the Commission Decision of 5 February 2010 on standard contractual clauses for the transfer of personal data to processors established in third countries under Directive 95/46/EC of the European Parliament and of the Council (2010/87/EU).

[83] See generally the following working documents of the Article 29 Working Party: (1) Working Document on transfers of personal data to third countries: Applying Article 26(2) of the EU Data Protection Directive to Binding Corporate Rules for International Data Transfers, 11639/02/EN, WP 74; and (2) Working Document Establishing a Model Checklist Application for Approval of Binding Corporate Rules, 05/EN, WP 108.

[84] The content of the binding corporate rules will be unique to each organization putting them in place, though all are likely to cover the core requirements such as detail on the data flows, how data subject rights are met, how data subjects are provided with information on the processing of their personal data, a complaint process and regulator cooperation confirmation and process, detail on security practices and other safeguards, together with evidence of the binding nature of the rules at all levels of the organization.

[85] Working Document of the Article 29 Working Party Setting Forth a Co-Operation Procedure for Issuing Common Opinions on Adequate Safeguards Resulting From Binding Corporate Rules, 05/EN, WP 107.

C. Exceptions to the General Prohibition

The Data Protection Directive contains a number of narrowly construed exceptions to the general prohibition on the export of personal data outside the EEA. These exceptions permit a data controller to export data even if no adequate level of protection or adequate safeguards exist.[86] In light of the narrow interpretation of these exceptions across Europe, they should generally be relied upon as a last resort, in the event that adequate safeguards (such as the Model Clauses) cannot be put in place or are not commercially feasible. The Data Protection Directive's exceptions provide for personal data export on the following conditions:

(1) the data subject has given his consent unambiguously to the proposed transfer;[87]
(2) the transfer is necessary for the performance of a contract between the data subject and the controller or the implementation of precontractual measures taken in response to the data subject's request;[88]
(3) the transfer is necessary for the conclusion or performance of a contract concluded in the interest of the data subject between the controller and a third party;[89]
(4) the transfer is necessary or legally required on important public interest grounds or for the establishment, exercise, or defense of legal rights;[90]
(5) the transfer is necessary in order to protect the vital interests of the data subject;[91] or
(6) the transfer is made from a register which according to laws or regulations is intended to provide information to the public and which is open to consultation either by the public in general or by any person who can demonstrate legitimate interest, to the extent that the conditions laid down in law for consultation are fulfilled in the particular case.[92]

As stated above, these exceptions are generally construed narrowly: in particular, the element of "necessity" in a number of these exceptions is interpreted strictly across Europe. For example, where an organization in an EEA Member State collects personal data from its employees, or has research study agreements in place with its research centers or participants in that EEA Member State, and it wishes to export personal data collected from that jurisdiction to its newly consolidated human resources data function or research study data server, as relevant, for efficiency and cost saving purposes, it is unlikely to be

---

[86] Data Protection Directive, art. 26.
[87] *Id.* art. 26(1)(a).
[88] *Id.* art. 26(1)(b).
[89] *Id.* art. 26(1)(c).
[90] *Id.* art. 26(1)(d).
[91] *Id.* art. 26(1)(e).
[92] *Id.* art. 26(1)(f).

able to rely on the "necessary for the performance of a contract" exemptions (in (2) and (3) above). Only true "necessity" will be adequate here (for example, it would be truly necessary for a health care provider in the EEA to transfer medical records to a specialist clinical research organization based in the United States in order to enable the individual to participate in a United States-based clinical research or treatment development program administered via the EEA organization (i.e., on the basis of a contract between the EEA and U.S. organizations, for the benefit of the individual), as the individual could not participate in the program without the export of his or her medical records). On the other hand, any data exports required solely due to the fact that an organization's different functions are organized on a global basis (for example, the central human resources function or payroll function of a global organization is based in the United States, requiring EEA employee personal data to be exported for human resource/payroll processing) or due to the location of an organization's servers or data/function consolidation would not be considered "necessary," as the relevant contract would be capable of performance equally well were the data to remain exclusively within the EEA.

In relation to exemption (4), above, it may be more difficult to rely upon the public interest or legal rights of individuals outside the relevant EEA Member State. That the export of certain personal data from the EEA may be in the interests of the general public of a non-EEA jurisdiction, or may be requested for the purposes of law enforcement authority investigations and proceedings outside the EEA, may not qualify as a legal obligation by virtue of which data export from that EEA Member State would be legitimized.[93]

In such cases, an alternative export solution may be required, such as the data subject's unambiguous consent to the export, or the Model Clauses or binding corporate rules could also be considered where feasible in practice.

---

[93] Working Document 1/2009 of the Article 29 Data Protection Working Party on pre-trial discovery for cross border civil litigation 00339/09/EN, WP 158.

D. Personal Data Export Flow Chart

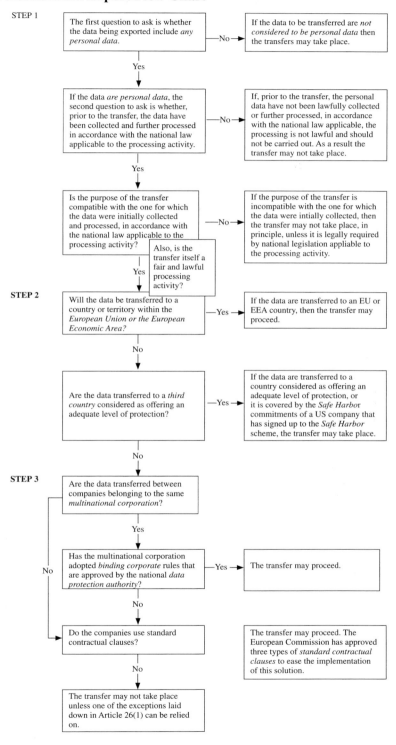

VII. ADMINISTRATIVE REQUIREMENTS

The Data Protection Directive and the national implementing laws across the EEA impose a number of administrative requirements on data controllers.[94] The Data Protection Directive itself requires each Member State to oblige a data controller to notify its national privacy regulator when carrying out any wholly or partly automatic data processing,[95] unless one of the following conditions applies (in which case, the notification process may be simplified or exempted):

(1) notification may be on a simplified basis for processing operations which are unlikely (taking into account the data to be processed) to affect adversely the rights and freedoms of data subjects;[96]
(2) where the data controller appoints a personal data protection officer responsible for independently ensuring the internal application of the national provisions implementing the Directive and who keeps a register of the processing carried out by the controller;[97]
(3) where the sole purpose of the processing is the keeping of a public register;[98] or
(4) where the processing is carried out by a non-profit making organization and relates solely to its members or persons who have regular contact with it.[99]

The Data Protection Directive also requires Member States to implement prior checking procedures for certain high-risk categories of processing (as determined by the Member States themselves) and publication procedures to ensure data subjects can access information provided to the national regulators.

The Data Protection Directive gives considerable flexibility to the Member States as to the practical implementation of these notification and prior checking obligations. As such, there is a wide variety of administrative formalities required of data controllers (and occasionally of data processors), such as notification of processing activities, notification and potentially prior approval of data export outside the EEA, specific notifications when handling or transferring sensitive personal data such as medical and health information, and potential prior approval requirements at various stages of data processing.

For example, in the U.K., data controllers are required to notify (i.e., register with) the national data privacy regulator (the Information Commissioner's Office) prior to processing any personal data, unless the intended processing relates solely to certain exempted purposes (such as processing for the purposes of staff administration, advertising, marketing and public relations, accounts and records, or the maintenance of a public register). This is a notification-only process: no prior approval is required, and no further notification steps are required

---

[94] Data Protection Directive, arts. 18–21.
[95] Id. art. 18(1).
[96] Id. 18(2).
[97] Id.
[98] Id. art. 18(3).
[99] Id. art. 18(4).

in relation to data exports (provided the possibility of data exports and the relevant recipient countries have been included in the initial notification form).

In France, on the other hand, certain processing is subject to the prior approval of the national regulator (the Commission Nationale de l'Informatique et des Libertés (CNIL)), such as the automatic processing of genetic data, unless necessary for medical diagnosis or treatment, or processing of personal data, the purpose or result of which is to exclude an individual from a right, a service, or a contract. The CNIL must be notified of all other automated processing, unless the CNIL issues an exemption. Further, this approval or notification process must be repeated in the event of any subsequent export of personal data outside the EEA (if not already carried out on initial notification), with the data controller required to submit its export solution to the CNIL (for example, a copy of the relevant Model Clauses or U.S. Safe Harbor certification, see VI.A.2. and VI.B.1., above) for the CNIL to check and approve where necessary.

Under the national data privacy laws of Germany, most data controllers have to appoint a data protection officer instead of registering with the competent national data protection authorities. The obligation to appoint a data protection officer usually applies to data controllers who engage more than nine individuals in the automatic processing of personal data. There are some variations on this general rule: under certain circumstances (for example, for the processing of health data), the obligation to appoint a data protection officer applies to data controllers with nine or fewer individuals involved. Further, some types of data controllers (for example, professional data providers or market research companies) are required to register with the data protection authorities, even where they have appointed an internal data protection officer. In very limited circumstances, data controllers are exempt from both the obligation to register and the obligation to appoint a data protection officer.

Data controllers operating throughout the EEA may therefore find it administratively burdensome to ensure compliance with the various filing and notification requirements of each jurisdiction. However onerous this may be, the majority of jurisdictions in the EEA impose financial or other sanctions (such as prohibition on the relevant data processing or transfer) in the event of noncompliance with these requirements.

VIII. THE E-PRIVACY DIRECTIVE

The general rule under the E-Privacy Directive in relation to unsolicited electronic communications (such as automated phone calls, faxes, e-mails, or cell phone SMS (short message service) messages) is that such communications cannot be made to individuals without their prior consent.[100] Further, Member States are required to ensure that unsolicited communications for the purposes of direct marketing are not permitted without the individual's consent or in respect of individuals who do wish to receive such communications[101] (such as

---

[100] Directive 2002/58/EC of the European Parliament and of the Council of 12 July 2002 concerning the processing of personal data and the protection of privacy in the electronic communications sector, art. 13(1), [2002] OJ L 201/0037.

[101] E-Privacy Directive, art. 13(3).

individuals who have signed up to a "do not call" list or similar national database in the relevant Member State, unless such individual has subsequently specifically consented to receive particular communications). There is a commonly relied-upon exemption to this general rule of prior consent, however, that permits unsolicited e-mail and SMS communications to be sent to individuals by an organization if:

(1) the individual's contact details were obtained by that organization in the course of a sale or negotiation for the sale of a product or service;
(2) the direct marketing materials concern "similar products or services"; and
(3) the recipient is clearly and distinctly given the opportunity to object to or opt out of such communications free of charge and in an easy manner.[102]

In all cases of unsolicited communications sent to individuals, whether on the basis of consent or the above exemption, the recipients must be provided with a simple, clear, and effective route to unsubscribe from future communications.

Another area regulated by the E-Privacy Directive is the use of cookies and other similar devices. The latest amendments to the E-Privacy Directive in this area[103] have been significant and controversial. Under the previous wording of the E-Privacy Directive, organizations were permitted to use cookies to collect information from site user's computers on the condition that the site user was provided with "clear and comprehensive information ... inter alia about the purposes of the processing, and [was] offered the right to refuse such processing by the data controller."[104] In light of these rules, common practice throughout Europe has been to rely on the ability of the site user to change its browser settings (i.e., to refuse all or certain cookies), and on a statement in a privacy policy or on the site to explain the site's use of cookies, to satisfy these requirements.

The key change under the amended E-Privacy Directive is the inclusion of a consent condition: using cookies on a site user's computer is only permitted on the condition that the site user "*has given his or her consent*, having been provided with clear and comprehensive information ... inter alia about the purposes of the processing,"[105] unless that cookie is "strictly necessary" for a service explicitly requested by the user.[106] While recital (66) of the revised E-Privacy Directive (which is not a legally binding element of the directive) states that "the user's consent to processing may be expressed by using the appropriate settings of a browser," the Article 29 Working Party's opinion[107] makes clear that, at least in relation to behavioral advertising, the current standard of browser is not adequate to evidence valid consent. There is therefore significant confusion as

---

[102] *Id.* art. 13(2).

[103] As introduced by the 2009 Privacy and Electronic Communications Directive (Directive 2009/136/EC of the European Parliament and of the Council of 25 November 2009). See I., above.

[104] *Id.* art. 5(3).

[105] Privacy and Electronic Communications Directive, art. 2(5), amending Article 5(3) of the E-Privacy Directive (emphasis added).

[106] *Id.*

[107] Opinion 2/2010 of the Article 29 Data Protection Working Party on Online Behavioural Advertising, 00909/10/EN, WP 171.

to how Member States will implement the revised E-Privacy Directive, given the practical implications of the new consent requirement on Internet users' free enjoyment and use of the Internet and online services (as the scope for free online services will be reduced) and the difficult and prohibitive impact for online organizations, Internet commerce businesses, and advertisers.

This controversy and confusion is a key factor in the failure by the majority of Member States to meet the implementation deadline. The deadline for Member States to implement these amendments to the E-Privacy Directive into national law was May 25, 2011. However, as of July 2011, only the U.K., Denmark, Estonia, Finland, Ireland, Malta, and Sweden had implemented the new rules, and the European Commission subsequently commenced legal action against the remaining Member States for their failure to effect national implementation on time.

Member States are therefore, for the most part, delaying implementation and enforcement of these amendments until clear guidance can be made available. They are working with governments, browser manufacturers, and industry groups on the technical solutions available to achieve compliance, such as enhanced browser settings and industry-led solutions. In the meantime, organizations based in, or with online consumers or site users in, Europe should be assessing their use of cookies and considering how they can implement a consent process into their sites and systems. Given that the revised rules came in the form of an amendment to the E-Privacy Directive, each Member State will implement these amendments into their existing national laws, and we have already seen differences in interpretation among those Member States that have already implemented these amendments. Local law advice should be sought by organizations when assessing the relevant national rules that will apply to them and the specific guidance issued by the national legislature and regulator on practical compliance solutions and enforcement.

IX. ON THE HORIZON

The various and rapid advances in technology and the increasingly global nature of many organizations and industries have driven a significant, wholesale review of European privacy rules. This review culminated in a Communication of the European Commission in November 2010,[108] setting out the Commission's proposals for a revised data privacy regime, with a focus on improving the protection of individuals' rights and expanding the responsibility of the data controller.

Some of the European Commission's key objectives are as follows:

(1) increase harmonization between data protection laws of the EEA Member States;
(2) simplify cross-border data transfers and make them less burdensome;

---

[108]Communication from the Commission to the European Parliament, the Council, the Economic and Social Committee and the Committee of the Regions, A comprehensive approach on personal data protection in the European Union, [2010] OJ COM 609/3.

(3) increase effective enforcement by local data protection regulators (potentially including explicit criminal sanctions);
(4) include specific requirements for information that needs to be provided to data subjects in privacy notices and ensure data processing transparency for individuals;
(5) expand the responsibilities of the data controller (potentially mandating the appointment of a company data protection officer, conducting privacy impact assessments, and introducing a general obligation of "accountability," such that the data controller would retain overall responsibility for data processing throughout the chain of data processors and subprocessors and be required to prove that such responsibility has been met in an active, practical manner, in order to be accountable to data subjects); and
(6) clarify the principles governing the scope of the jurisdiction of European privacy laws, which may involve changing to a "country of origin" approach; the applicable law would therefore be that of the one EEA Member State of primary establishment of the data controller, rather than the multiple, and often inconsistent, national laws of the various EEA Member States in which the data controller is handling personal data;[109] however, without a major harmonization exercise, such an approach has the potential to result in confusion for individuals as to their rights, and artificial business restructuring and forum shopping by organizations.

The specific content of a new European data privacy regime will not be clear for some time, and it is likely to be a number of years before the new rules are finalized and ready for implementation by the Member States, but these proposals indicate the broader direction of European law in the future. There is also considerable ongoing debate as to the form the new regime should take: should this be implemented via a revised directive or via a regulation? Many, including the European Data Protection Supervisor, are in favor of a regulation,[110] as it would be directly applicable in each EEA Member State and therefore enforceable without the need for each EEA Member State to implement it into national law (see I.B., above). This direct applicability of a data protection regulation removes the risk of divergence between Member States in interpretation, as compared to a directive, which would require implementation into national law by each Member State, in accordance with its own national interpretation.

However, a data privacy regulation is not the perfect solution: the fact that it is directly applicable in Member States (and automatically overrides any conflicting national laws) effectively means that each Member State must approve the precise wording of the regulation, which is inevitably a very lengthy process. A regulation may be useful if the areas for harmonization are narrowly

---

[109]The Article 29 Working Party has recently published an Opinion (Opinion 8/2010 on Applicable Law (0836-02/10/EN, WP 179)), suggesting a "country of origin" approach.

[110]Opinion of the European Data Protection Supervisor of 14 January 2011 on the Communication from the Commission to the European Parliament, the Council, the Economic and Social Committee and the Committee of the Regions, "A comprehensive approach on personal data protection in the European Union."

defined, but given the broad scope of the core data privacy issues requiring harmonization, there is potential for many years of negotiations between the Member States as to what the uniform European position should be, especially given the current divergent approaches of certain Member States. A revised data protection directive may provide a faster solution to bring Member States in line in core areas, as a directive specifies only the objectives to be reached and leaves implementation at a national level in the hands of each Member State. Directives are consequently approved in much shorter time frames than regulations. The balancing test facing the European Commission is therefore one of timeliness in implementing the required clarifications and revisions against the level of harmonization that is desired and feasible in practice.

X. Consumer Laws and Other Relevant Laws

While the Data Protection Directive governs the collection and processing of all types of personal data across the EEA Member States, there are numerous other laws that may impact the processing of personal and health data across Europe and that vary from country to country. For example, the laws of confidentiality (such as the duty of confidence between a doctor and patient enshrined in the Hippocratic Oath) or the right to privacy protected by common law or constitutional rights may apply, in relevant Member States, to prevent disclosure of personal information. Human rights laws,[111] including the right to respect for private and family life[112] and the right to freedom of expression,[113] may also impact the collection, use, and disclosure of personal data.

Health care sector-specific national laws governing the use of patient health data, biological samples, and genetic data may also be relevant when collecting and processing personal information, particularly in the context of the provision of health care services and in relation to clinical research studies. National laws relating to communications, such as those governing recording, interception, and surveillance and the disclosure and retention of communications data, also regulate the use, storage, and disclosure of personal data in communications data (such as content and traffic data).

European laws on consumer protection are also relevant. The Unfair Commercial Practices Directive,[114] which was due to be implemented into national

---

[111] Individuals may enforce their rights under the European Convention for the Protection of Human Rights and Fundamental Freedoms, [ETS No. 005] (as amended by Protocols 1, 4, 6, 7, 11, 12, 13, and 14), directly in the European Court of Human Rights, against public authorities that breach the Convention. The national laws and constitutions of Member States may also include a variety of basic human rights and/or constitutional rights for individuals, and may impose obligations on organizations other than public authorities, based on the Convention's fundamental freedoms.

[112] European Convention for the Protection of Human Rights and Fundamental Freedoms, art. 8.

[113] *Id.* art. 10.

[114] Directive 2005/29/EC of the European Parliament and of the Council of 11 May 2005 concerning unfair business-to-consumer commercial practices in the internal market and amending Council Directive 84/450/EEC; Directives 97/7/EC, 98/27/EC, and 2002/65/EC of the European Parliament and of the Council and Regulation (EC) No. 2006/2004 of the European Parliament and of the Council, [2005] OJ L 149/22, hereinafter Unfair Commercial Practices Directive.

law by all EEA Member States by June 12, 2007 (though several Member States have not yet fully implemented the directive), establishes a general prohibition on unfair commercial practices[115] that affect consumer decisions (broadly categorized into misleading practices and aggressive practices) and a blacklist of prohibited practices deemed to be inherently unfair (such as pyramid schemes, bait advertising, and false curative health claims). A misleading commercial practice, as prohibited under the Unfair Commercial Practices Directive, could include the collection and use of a consumer's personal data in a misleading manner,[116] such as informing the consumer that his or her information will only be used for a single, limited purpose when that personal data is ultimately used for a range of intrusive purposes (such a sharing that data with third parties or using it for marketing purposes). When collecting and using the personal data of consumers, organizations therefore need to be aware of the Unfair Commercial Practices Directive and avoid using that personal data in a manner that could be misleading.

---

[115]The test for an unfair commercial practice under the Unfair Commercial Practices Directive is (1) the commercial practice is contrary to the requirements of professional diligence; and (2) the practice materially distorts or is likely to materially distort the economic behavior, with regard to the product, of the average consumer whom the practice reaches or to whom it is addressed. Unfair Commercial Practices Directive, art. 5(2).

[116]A commercial practice will be misleading, and will therefore constitute an unfair commercial practice, if it either (1) contains false information and is therefore untruthful (or omits or hides material information that the consumer requires) or (2) in any way deceives or is likely to deceive the average consumer (even if the information is correct) and causes or is likely to cause the average consumer to take a decision that he or she would have not otherwise have taken. Unfair Commercial Practices Directive, art. 6.

7

Information Security and Breach Notification Under HIPAA and HITECH*

I.	Introduction	158
II.	HIPAA Security Requirements	158
	A. Information Security Program Development and Management	162
	1. Confidentiality	164
	2. Integrity and Availability	164
	3. Accountability	164
	4. Balancing the Objectives	165
	B. Implementing HIPAA Security Safeguards	167
	C. HIPAA Security Investigations	167
	D. HIPAA Security Violation Penalty Risks	170
	E. Business Associates and Business Associate Contracts Under the Security Rule	172
III.	HITECH Amendments to HIPAA: Security Implications	174
IV.	HITECH Security Breach Requirements	177
V.	State Security Breach Notification Legislation	179
	A. The Economic Logic of Information Security Breach Disclosure	180
	B. A Brief History of Information Security Breach Notification Laws	181
	C. Analysis of a Representative Information Security Breach Notification Law	183
	1. The Problem of Encryption	184
	2. The Complexities of Notification	185
	3. The Scope of Regulation	187
	D. State Security Breach Notification Laws as of August 2011	189
Appendix 7-A: Sample HITECH/HIPAA Security Gap Analysis Checklist		191

*John R. Christiansen, Christiansen IT Law, Seattle, Washington.

I. Introduction

"Information security," for purposes of this chapter, is the set of legal requirements and standards of care for the protection of digital information in computer systems and networks (collectively, information systems). While there are a number of legal information security regimes applicable for use with different types of information or by different organizations, and some of those regimes may apply to some activities health care organizations engage in, the most important by far is the Health Insurance Portability and Accountability Act of 1996 (HIPAA),[1] its implementing security regulations (the "Security Rule"),[2] and its amendment by the Health Information Technology for Clinical and Economic Health Act (the HITECH Act).[3] The information security requirements of these statutes and regulations will therefore be the focus of this chapter.

As will be discussed, HIPAA provides a "checklist and risk management" framework for information security management by health care providers, health plans, and health care clearinghouses.[4] Failure to implement an information security program that meets these requirements may be the basis for significant civil monetary penalties (CMPs). Perhaps worse, failure to implement an effective information security program may be the cause of a security breach that must be reported, initiating not only a regulatory investigation that may result in CMPs but a cascade of negative publicity, state penalties, and private lawsuits.

II. HIPAA Security Requirements

HIPAA's security mandates are found not only in the Security Rule but also in the Privacy Rule[5] and the legislation itself, both of which require "covered entities" to implement "administrative, physical and technical safeguards" for the protection of protected health information (PHI).[6] The legislative and Privacy Rule requirements apply to PHI in any medium but do not provide specific standards for the safeguards they require.

The Security Rule applies only to PHI that is transmitted or maintained in "electronic media" ("ePHI").[7] It provides standards and attendant implementa-

---

[1] Health Insurance Portability and Accountability Act of 1996 (HIPAA), Pub. L. No. 104-191, 110 Stat. 1936 (codified in scattered sections in U.S.C. tit. 42 and in 42 U.S.C. §§1320d *et seq.*).

[2] 45 C.F.R. Part 164, subpts. A, C (2003).

[3] Health Information Technology for Economic and Clinical Health Act (HITECH), Title XIII of The American Recovery and Reinvestment Act of 2009 (ARRA), H.R. 1, Pub. L. No. 111-5 (Feb. 17, 2009). The sections relevant to this session are in Subtitle D of HITECH Title XIII, entitled "Privacy."

[4] These are HIPAA's "covered entities." *See* 45 C.F.R. §160.103 (2007).

[5] 45 C.F.R. pts. 160, 164. The Privacy Rule is discussed in Chapter 5 (Dahm, Privacy Issues in U.S Health Care). See also Chapter 6 (Taylor & Crawford, The European Data Privacy Regime).

[6] *See* 42 U.S.C. §1320d-d-2(d)(2); Privacy Rule, 45 C.F.R. §164.530(c).

[7] *See* 45 C.F.R. §160.103 (definition of "electronic protected health information"). "Electronic media" is defined at 45 C.F.R. §164.103 as:
 (1) Electronic storage media including memory devices in computers (hard drives) and any removable/transportable digital memory medium, such as magnetic tape or disk, optical disk, or digital memory card; or

tion specifications for "administrative, physical and technical safeguards" for the protection of such information.[8] However, this additional specificity does not drill down into sufficient detail to provide "safe harbor" specifications for any of these safeguards. The Security Rule is intended to be both "scaleable" and "technology-neutral"[9] and therefore requires a security decision-making process rather than specific security results. The result is therefore the delegation of appropriate discretion to the responsible parties.

The basic compliance unit is the "standard," which provides the general rules, conditions, or requirements for performance, operations, procedures, products, systems, or services under the regulation.[10] Each standard is implemented by one or more "specifications," which are "specific requirements or instructions for implementing a standard."[11] Some standards are deemed sufficiently clear that separate specifications are not stated; in those cases, compliance requires following the "instructions" of the standard itself.[12] All other standards are implemented by specifications that are either "required" or "addressable."[13]

The security standards fall into five general categories:

- Administrative safeguards: the policies and procedures required to administer information systems, personnel, and business processes affecting the security of ePHI.
- Physical safeguards: the policies, procedures, and operational requirements for facilities and equipment where ePHI is used or stored.
- Technical safeguards: the policies, procedures and technical solutions used to control electronic access to information systems and devices on which ePHI is stored or processed, or from which it may be obtained.

---

(2) Transmission media used to exchange information already in electronic storage media. Transmission media include, for example, the internet (wide-open), extranet (using internet technology to link a business with information accessible only to collaborating parties), leased lines, dial-up lines, private networks, and the physical movement of removable/transportable electronic storage media. Certain transmissions, including of paper, via facsimile, and of voice, via telephone, are not considered to transmissions via electronic media, because the information did not exist in electronic form before the transmission.

[8] *See* 45 C.F.R. §§164.308 (administrative), 164.310 (physical), and 164.312 (technical). The Security Rule also provides standards for organizational requirements (45 C.F.R. §§164.105, .314) and policies, procedures, and documentation (45 C.F.R. §164.316).

[9] *See* Health Insurance Reform: Security Standards, 68 Fed. Reg. 8334, 8343 (Feb. 20, 2003) (preamble to final Security Rule).

[10] "Standard" is defined as "a rule, condition, or requirement":
(1) Describing the following information for products, systems, services or covered entities:
    (i) Classification of components;
    (ii) Specification of materials, performance, or operations; or
    (iii) Delineation of procedures; or
(2) With respect to the privacy of individually identifiable health information.
45 C.F.R. §160.103. Subsection (2) does not apply to the Security Rule, and because the rule is technology-neutral, Subsections (1)(i) and (1)(ii) as they apply to "materials" generally also should not apply. This definition was adopted in the Privacy Rule and not updated in the Security Rule, and perhaps for that reason is not entirely on point.

[11] *See* 45 C.F.R. §160.103.

[12] *See* 68 Fed. Reg. at 8336.

[13] *See* 45 C.F.R. §164.306(d)(1).

- Organizational requirements: the security provision requirements for business associate contracts and group health plans.
- Documentation requirements: the requirements for development, publication, and retention of policies, procedures, and other safeguard documentation, including risk analyses and incident and breach response reports.

While the organizational and documentation requirements are important, this chapter will focus on the administrative, physical, and technical safeguards requirements.

The Security Rule includes a total of 50 safeguards specifications. Both the specifications stated in a standard and the instructions in a required specification must be followed.[14] The instructions in an addressable specification, by contrast, are presumptive but not mandatory: they need not be followed if the covered entity determines that doing so is not "reasonable and appropriate," given its circumstances and available alternatives, and can properly justify that decision.[15] The analyses used to determine (1) whether to adopt an alternative approach to an addressable specification and (2) precisely how to comply with any specification, required or addressable, are in the end essentially the same.

Both analyses depend upon the results of a risk analysis. Risk analysis and the risk management activities it supports are the crux of Security Rule compliance. Risk analysis and management processes are required implementation specifications under the "security management process" standard,[16] and their results are the required basis for decisions on implementation of all other safeguards.[17]

Under the Security Rule, a "thorough and accurate risk analysis would consider 'all relevant losses' that would be expected if the security measures were not in place. 'Relevant losses' would include losses caused by unauthorized uses and disclosures and loss of data integrity that would be expected to occur absent the security measures."[18]

The results of this risk analysis would then be used to determine the "security measures sufficient to reduce [the identified] risks and vulnerabilities to a reasonable and appropriate level."[19] This is done using a "flexible approach" that considers the following four factors:[20]

- the organization's size, complexity and capabilities;
- the available technical infrastructure, hardware, and software capabilities;

---

[14] *See id.* §164.306(d)(2).

[15] *See id.* §164.306(d)(3). NOTE: the numbering of this regulation as published in 68 Fed. Reg. 8377 identifies this subsection incorrectly as "1," but it follows in sequence after (d)(1) and (d)(2,) so it is presumed the correct designation is (d)(3).

[16] *See* 45 C.F.R. §164.308(a)(1)(i), (ii)(A)–(B).

[17] "Thus, an entity's risk analysis and risk management measures . . . must be designed to lead to the implementation of security measures that will comply with [45 CFR 164.306(a), general requirements for covered entity security.]" 68 Fed. Reg. at 8341.

[18] *Id.* at 8347.

[19] 45 C.F.R. §164.308(a)(1)(ii)(B).

[20] *Id.* §164.306(b).

- the costs of security measures; and
- the probability and criticality[21] of potential risks to ePHI.

Risk analysis findings are also used to support decisions not to adopt addressable specifications and must be documented as required by the rule.[22]

In principle the Security Rule does not require covered entities to totally eliminate risks, only to "take steps, to the best of [their abilities,] to protect [ePHI]."[23] The official interpretation is that Congress intended to set "an exceptionally high goal for the security of electronic protected health information" but "did not mean providing protection, no matter how expensive."[24] While this is certainly better than a requirement of unconditional protection, it leaves unanswered the question, "how much protection is enough?"

An important authority in determining how high to set the bar is federal guidance. In particular, the Centers for Medicare and Medicaid Services (CMS) is the federal agency charged with HIPAA Security Rule enforcement and has issued extensive information security regulatory guidance in its capacity as principal federal health care payments administrator. These authorities are based on general federal information security requirements and well developed, highly credible federal standards and guidance, particularly that provided by the National Institute for Standards and Technology (NIST).

CMS information protection requirements are based on a risk analysis that starts with a ranking of information sensitivity in three categories from "Low" to "High."[25] "Low Sensitivity" information is "virtually in the public domain" and requires "minimal protection"; "Moderate Sensitivity" information is "important" and "must be protected against malicious destruction," but does not pose "significant" disclosure problems (e.g., would cause at most "nonspecific embarrassment" of an individual). Moderate Sensitivity information would include a patient's name, demographic information, and Social Security or other identification number.

---

[21]The term "criticality" is not defined or discussed in the Security Rule, but presumably refers to the degree of harm which could be caused by a security incident affecting ePHI. *See* NATIONAL INSTITUTE OF STANDARDS AND TECHNOLOGY (NIST), NIST SPECIAL PUBLICATION 800-30, RISK MANAGEMENT GUIDE FOR INFORMATION TECHNOLOGY SYSTEMS 21–23 (Oct. 2001) [hereinafter NIST SPECIAL PUBLICATION 800-30] (discussion of "impact analysis"), *cited in* preamble to the Security Rule, 68 Fed. Reg. at 8346.

[22]This follows from the requirement that a decision not to adopt an addressable specification must be based on a determination whether the specified implementation "is a reasonable and appropriate safeguard in its environment, when analyzed with reference to the likely contribution to protecting the entity's electronic protected health information[.]" 45 C.F.R. §164.306(3). In general, the decision "whether a given addressable implementation specification is a reasonable and appropriate security measure . . . will depend on a variety of factors, such as, among others, the entity's risk analysis, risk mitigation strategy, what security measures are already in place, and the cost of implementation." Preamble to Security Rule, 68 Fed. Reg. at 8336; *see also id.* at 8341; 45 C.F.R. §164.306(d)(3).

[23]68 Fed. Reg. at 8346.

[24]*Id.*

[25]This categorization is stated in NIST Federal Information Processing Standard Publication 199, Standards for Security Categorization of Federal Information and Information Systems (Feb. 2004) (FIPS 199), which is required for all federal agencies. *See, e.g.,* Centers for Medicare & Medicaid Servs., Medicare Business Partners Systems Security (CMS Manual System Pub. 100-17, July 17, 2009) at 45.

The most sensitive category is "High Sensitivity" information, which includes any information whose malicious alteration or disclosure could cause an individual medical, psychological, financial, or reputational harm. Clinical and health care payment-related information are categorized as High Sensitivity. Most ePHI probably falls into this category, and risks to ePHI should be weighted accordingly.

The most difficult aspect of this kind of analysis is that the organization's decisions are all too likely to be judged in hindsight, after a security incident or breach has happened, perhaps in the context of a civil or criminal investigation or private litigation. A good record of due diligence in assessing risks and making careful decisions may make all the difference in avoiding serious liability exposures if a serious security event occurs.

A. Information Security Program Development and Management

The need to comply with legal standards that are in turn based principally on risk-based decisions means HIPAA information security should be managed in a hybrid program combining compliance and risk management functions.

"Compliance" functions, for this purpose, are those activities an organization undertakes to identify legal requirements and implement policies and procedures intended to ensure that the organization's personnel, systems, and processes comply with those requirements. Information security is a compliance function simply because a failure to meet legal requirements for information protection can expose a health care organization to significant legal penalties

Information security also includes risk management functions, because it may well be impossible for legislators or regulators to specify detailed information system and business process requirements that can apply to all possible types of organization and information system in any realistic fashion. Risk management is therefore a legal strategy that delegates the security decision-making process to the regulated organizations, subject to some direction as to areas that should be covered and types of protection that should be implemented.

Risk management always begins with risk assessment, in which the organization maps the boundaries and architecture of business processes and information systems that use or are used in connection with protected information.[26] Existing controls and safeguards are identified, as are the material threats[27] to the information and systems and the material vulnerabilities[28] of the system and

---

[26] This discussion of risk management is based on NIST SPECIAL PUBLICATION 800-30, supra.

[27] "A threat is the potential for a particular threat-source to successfully exercise a particular vulnerability." NIST SPECIAL PUBLICATION 800-12, AN INTRODUCTION TO COMPUTER SECURITY: THE NIST HANDBOOK (OCTOBER 1995) at 12 [hereinafter NIST SPECIAL PUBLICATION 800-12]. A "threat-source" is "[e]ither (1) intent and method targeted at the intentional exploitation of a vulnerability or (2) a situation and method that may accidentally trigger a vulnerability." *Id*. In other words, threats include natural events (e.g., fires, floods, and electrical outages); unintentional human activities (e.g., mistaken erasure or transmission of sensitive data); and intentional human activity (e.g., criminal theft of intellectual property or malicious disclosure of personal information).

[28] A "vulnerability" is a "condition or weakness in (or absence of) security procedures, technical controls, physical controls, or other controls that could be exploited by a threat. Vulnerabilities are often analyzed in terms of missing safeguards. Vulnerabilities contribute to risk because they may 'allow' a threat to harm the system." NIST SPECIAL PUBLICATION 800-12, at 62.

processes. This information is then used to estimate the likelihood that various kinds of harmful events will occur, given the identified threats, vulnerabilities, and potential impacts of such events.

The organization then determines a set of strategies to manage the identified risks:

> Risk management is a policy process wherein alternative strategies for dealing with risks are weighed and decisions about acceptable risks are made. The strategies consist of policy options that have varying effects on risk, including the reduction, removal, or reallocation of risk. In the end, an acceptable level of risk is determined and a strategy for achieving that level of risk is adopted. Cost-benefit calculations, assessments of risk tolerance, and quantification of preferences are often involved in this decision-making process.[29]

Based on these risk management decisions, the organization implements a set of policies, procedures, and technical solutions that become the compliance standards adopted by the organization. This set includes both "controls" and "safeguards," considering "controls" as the governance policies, procedures, and organizational structures used to ensure compliance with these standards, and "safeguards" as the policies, procedures, and technical solutions that address specific security issues, threats, and vulnerabilities.[30]

Threats and vulnerabilities in turn are determined based on the objectives of the information security program. The objectives of information security are not entirely settled, but for HIPAA purposes are defined as to "ensure the confidentiality, integrity and availability of all [ePHI] the covered entity creates, receives, maintains, or transmits."[31] This is a typical formulation, sometimes called the "CIA triad."[32]

In health care in particular the CIA goals may not be sufficient, and at least one goal—accountability—may sometimes need to be added.[33] This goal has not been formally recognized in most specifically security-oriented laws, such as the Security Rule, but is implied by the need to ensure that electronic medical record entries, for example, be electronically "signed" using processes that reliably authenticate the professional making the entry.[34]

---

[29] Kevin Soo Hoo, How Much is Enough? A Risk Management Approach to Computer Security, Report of the Consortium for Research on Information Security (Center for Int'l Security & Cooperation June 2009), at 3.

[30] See John Christiansen, An Integrated Standard of Care for Healthcare Information Security: Risk Management, HIPAA, and Beyond (2005) at 32–40. The latter is the sense in which HIPAA uses the term "safeguard."

[31] 45 C.F.R. §164.306(a)(1).

[32] NIST Special Publication 800-12, at 5–7.

[33] See NIST, Special Publication 800-33, Underlying Technical Models for Information Technology Security 2–3 (Dec. 2001) [hereinafter NIST Special Publication 800-33]. The Federal Information Security Management Act of 2002, Title III of the E-Government Act of 2002 (Pub. L. No. 107-347, 116 Stat. 2899), 44 U.S.C.§3532(b)(1), specifies that information security objectives are confidentiality, integrity, availability, and authentication.

[34] See, e.g., Centers for Medicare & Medicaid Servs., Medicare Program Integrity Manual, Chapter 3—Verifying Potential Errors and Taking Corrective Actions (Rev. 383 Aug. 26, 2011) at 3.3.2.4.

The three, sometimes four objectives of information security are therefore confidentiality, integrity, availability, and accountability. These objectives themselves, in turn, require some operational definitions.

1. Confidentiality

"Confidentiality" is the security objective that seems to intersect most transparently with established legal principles, and is defined as a "requirement that private or confidential information is not made available to unauthorized users."[35] The inclusion of "confidential" information within the category of information protected as a matter of "confidentiality" is circular reasoning that explains nothing in itself. A better definition might be the "status accorded to data or information indicating that it is sensitive for some reason, and therefore it needs to be protected against theft, disclosure, or improper use, or both, and must be disseminated only to authorized individuals or organizations with a need to know." [36]

For legal purposes, "confidential information" therefore would be information that is given a legal status that requires the information holder to protect it. The objective of "confidentiality" may be more accurately summarized as the prevention of the use or disclosure of information contrary to law (the source of which may be constitutional, statutory, regulatory, contractual, or common) and/or to organizational policy, including but not limited to external law applicable to the information.

2. Integrity and Availability

The security objective of "integrity" includes both (1) data integrity, meaning that "information and programs [whose functioning may alter data] are changed only in a specified and authorized manner[;]"[37] and (2) system integrity, meaning that the system "performs its intended function in an unimpaired manner, free from deliberate or inadvertent manipulation of the system."[38] "Availability" is a related objective that "systems work promptly and service is not denied to unauthorized individuals."[39]

3. Accountability

"Accountability" may be defined as the ability to know "who has had access to information or resources"[40] or a "requirement that actions of an entity may be traced uniquely to that entity."[41] Accomplishment of this goal therefore

---

[35] NIST SPECIAL PUBLICATION 800-12, at 7; see NIST SPECIAL PUBLICATION 800-30, at 2.

[36] Suzy A. Buckovich et al., *Driving Toward Guiding Principles: A Goal for Privacy, Confidentiality and Security of Health Information*, 6 J. AM. MED. INFORMATICS ASS'N 122, 123 (Mar./Apr. 1999).

[37] NIST SPECIAL PUBLICATION 800-12, at 6.

[38] *Id.*

[39] *Id.* at 7.

[40] Butler Lampson, *Computer Security in the Real World*, in MARSHALL D. ABRAMS INVITED ESSAY PROGRAM (2000) at 3.

[41] NIST SPECIAL PUBLICATION 800-30, at 3.

requires implementation of appropriate "authentication" processes.[42] Accountability, and therefore authentication, is important in settings where the ability to associate some action with an identifiable party has legal consequences, such as medical record signature[43] or authorization execution.

4. Balancing the Objectives

The objectives of information security are not always easy to reconcile. In particular, the goal of information availability seems to oppose the goal of confidentiality, while the goal of system availability (which is necessary to make information available) tends to oppose the goals of accountability and information integrity. Depending on the purposes for which an information system is used, issues involved in any (or all) of these requirements may have legal implications. The balance of these security objectives in a given system may be a judgment call that depends on an informed balancing of the interests served by the system.

The following examples indicate some of the considerations that may enter into risk balancing:

- Systems used to store, process, and transmit High Sensitivity information, disclosure of which could expose subjects, the organization, or others to significant harm (e.g., a database of financial and demographic information about military personnel owned by a health care administrative-services company in conjunction with the Department of Defense) should have a very low tolerance for confidentiality errors. This might be appropriately traded off against availability errors, especially in systems where delayed access to information has relatively low potential for harm (e.g., a delay in processing a claim may be annoying or even cause some financial harm, but would not tend to threaten health or safety).
- Information systems used for services such as claims processing should have a relatively low tolerance for accountability and integrity errors, so that claims are correctly recorded and paid, and that those transactions cannot be repudiated. Again, this might be appropriately traded off against availability errors that might cause delays or inconvenience, as long as those are not so material as to discourage use of the system.
- There should be a low tolerance for availability and integrity errors with respect to clinical record systems used to support real-time diagnosis and treatment, because failure to provide necessary or correct information may cause mistaken diagnoses or care decisions. This might be

---

[42] *Id.*:
To support the principle of individual accountability, the service called user authentication is required. Without reliable identification, there can be no accountability. Thus authentication is a crucial underpinning of information security. Many systems have been penetrated when weak or poorly administered authentication services have been compromised, for example, by guessing poorly chosen passwords.

[43] *Cf.* Roger Schell, *The Internet Rules but the Emperor Has No Clothes*, 12TH ANNUAL COMPUTER SECURITY APPLICATIONS CONFERENCE (Dec. 1996) at 3: "Businesses require accountability at the level of the individual. In an environment such as the Internet that is fraught with malicious users and malicious software, it is vital to ensure that only an authorized individual's decisions are reliably carried out by the software."

appropriately traded off for an increased risk of confidentiality errors, because availability or integrity errors could threaten health or safety, which should be given greater weight than reputational or even financial harms that would typically be the result of confidentiality errors.

One way to analyze balancing these risks would be to distinguish "false positive" from "false negative" security risks. Under this distinction, a false-positive security failure would be one that allowed an unauthorized user to access information (a confidentiality failure), alter information (an integrity failure), or falsely identify himself or herself on access logs or other records (an accountability failure). A false-negative security failure, on the other hand, would be one that denied access to or the ability to alter information to an authorized user (both availability failures).

As a general rule, the implementation of processes and procedures reducing the risk of false-positive failures raises the risk of false negatives and vice versa. As an example, most information systems used to store or process PHI should require access by complex passwords that mix alphanumeric and symbol characters. Because such passwords are hard for third parties to discover, they will tend to reduce the risk of false-positive failures (e.g., breach of confidentiality due to unauthorized third-party access). By the same token, such passwords also tend to reduce the risk of false-positive accountability failures, because unauthorized third parties will not be able to falsely authenticate themselves using the password.

The same characteristics that make strong passwords hard for unauthorized parties to determine also make them hard to remember. A user who is unable to remember his or her password will be unable to access a password-protected system or information, creating a risk of a false-negative security failure and causing lack of availability. Therefore, the same strong-password safeguard (which reduced the risk of "false positive" confidentiality, integrity, and accountability failures) simultaneously increases the risk of false-negative availability failures.

Balancing the risks of false-positive and false-negative security failures will depend primarily on the operational needs of the system and its information support. This might be determined by analyzing the use of passwords in clinical decision-support systems and claims-processing systems.

Strong passwords implemented in a clinical decision-support system may create a risk of avoidable medical errors caused by false-negative denial of access to patient medical information needed for diagnostic or care decisions. For example, in an emergency-room setting, clinical information may be needed on a life-or-death basis, in which case the tolerance for risks that information will not be available must be very low. The hospital operating the emergency room might therefore conclude that the terminals used to provide access to its electronic medical record (EMR) system in the emergency room should not be controlled by strong passwords. Although this does allow for some avoidable false-positive risks to patient confidentiality, it is not inappropriate to conclude that these are outweighed by the reduction in false-negative availability risks that could cause harm to patient health.

The balancing of false-positive risks against false-negative risks is likely to be very different, however, for a claims-processing system. The submission of false health care claims information is a federal criminal offense,[44] which implies that such a system should have a low tolerance for false-positive information integrity and accountability failures. At the same time, financial information does not need to be available with the same urgency applicable to clinical information, a factor that raises the acceptable tolerance for false-negative availability failures. A strong password policy, which would not be appropriate for EMR access in an emergency-room setting, might be very appropriate for access and use of claims-processing systems.

B. Implementing HIPAA Security Safeguards

The first step in implementing a HIPAA information security program is typically a "gap analysis." A gap analysis is simply a review of the current status of an organization's safeguards against the requirements of the Security Rule to identify possible areas in which safeguards are missing or inadequate. A sample gap analysis form is provided as Appendix 7-A to this chapter. But a gap analysis is really a compliance function—a broad but shallow review of the extent to which the organization is likely to be meeting legal requirements—and no substitute for a true risk analysis as the basis for developing and implementing reasonable and appropriate safeguards.

A full Security Rule risk analysis includes review of the entity's written policies, procedures, guidelines, standards or other documentation applicable to each requirement. If documentation is not available, that is noted, as lack of documentation may itself be a material gap. Physical security is assessed by walk-through and observation of relevant facilities, and technical security by review of systems architectures and review and testing of operating systems and applications. Key personnel are interviewed to ensure accurate information about relevant documentation, practices, processes, and systems, but personal knowledge about undocumented practices for compliance with material requirements is not considered sufficient.

The findings of these review processes are then analyzed to determine whether the organization has adequately addressed material risks to ePHI, in the informed judgment of the organization's executive or senior administrative officers, and used as the basis for acceptance of existing safeguards as adequate or development of improved or additional safeguards to reduce risks to an acceptable level. And this process is repeated routinely on a scheduled basis, as well as in response to material changes in information systems, facilities, or operations, and sometimes in case of a material security incident.

C. HIPAA Security Investigations

HIPAA is enforced by the Office of Civil Rights (OCR) of the U.S. Department of Health and Human Services (HHS), which may open an investigation based on a complaint or sua sponte.

The first civil investigative activity under the Security Rule was reported in June 2007, in an audit of Piedmont Hospital in Atlanta, Georgia, by the HHS

---

[44] *See* 18 U.S.C. §1035 (2006).

Office of Inspector General (OIG).[45] The reason for the audit was never officially stated. The consulting firm PricewaterhouseCoopers was retained to conduct Security Rule compliance reviews of 10 to 20 covered entities in 2008,[46] while the 2010 HITECH Act included a mandate for increased auditing.[47] In July 2011, OCR contracted with a different consulting firm, KPMG, to develop and pursue a more comprehensive audit program.[48]

The CMS Office of E-Health Standards and Services (OESS) published guidance in 2008 in the form of a sample checklist of the interviews, documents, and issues that may be requested in a Security Rule compliance interview,[49] as follows:

(1) Personnel that may be interviewed
- President, CEO, or Director
- HIPAA Compliance Officer
- Lead Systems Manager or Director
- Systems Security Officer
- Lead Network Engineer and/or individuals responsible for:
    o Administration of systems that store, transmit, or access electronic protected health information (EPHI)
    o Administration systems networks (wired and wireless)
    o Monitoring of systems which store, transmit, or access EPHI
    o Monitoring systems networks (if different from above)
- Computer Hardware Specialist
- Disaster Recovery Specialist or person in charge of data backup
- Facility Access Control Coordinator (physical security)
- Human Resources Representative
- Director of Training
- Incident Response Team Leader
- Others as identified

(2) Documents and other information that may be requested for investigations/reviews
   (a) Policies and procedures and other evidence that address the following:
     - Prevention, detection, containment, and correction of security violations
     - Employee background checks and confidentiality agreements

---

[45] Jaikumar Vijayan, *HIPAA Audit at Hospital Riles Health Care IT*, COMPUTERWORLD (June 15, 2007), *available at* http://www.computerworld.com/action/article.do?command=viewArticleBasic&articleId=9024921.

[46] Nancy Ferris, *CMS to Check Hospitals for HIPAA Security Compliance*, GOVERNMENT HEALTH IT (Jan. 17, 2008), *available at* http://govhealthit.com/news/cms-check-hospitals-hipaa-security-compliance.

[47] *See* HITECH §13411.

[48] *See* Mary Mosquera, *HHS Taps KPMG to Perform HIPAA Audits*, GOVERNMENT HEALTH IT (July 6, 2011), *available at* http://govhealthit.com/news/hhs-taps-kpmg-perform-hipaa-audits.

[49] U.S. Dep't of Health & Human Servs., Centers for Medicare & Medicaid Servs., Office of E-Health Standards and Servs., Sample—Interview and Document Request for HIPAA Security Onsite Investigations and Compliance Reviews (Feb. 13, 2008), *available at* http://www.training-hipaa.net/compliance/Official-HIPAA-Security-Compliance-Audit-checklist_document-by-DHHS.pdf.

- Establishing user access for new and existing employees
- List of authentication methods used to identify users authorized to access EPHI
- List of individuals and contractors with access to EPHI to include copies of pertinent business associate agreements
- List of software used to manage and control access to the Internet
- Detecting, reporting, and responding to security incidents (if not in the security plan)
- Physical security
- Encryption and decryption of EPHI
- Mechanisms to ensure integrity of data during transmission— including portable media transmission (i.e., laptops, cell phones, blackberries, thumb drives)
- Monitoring systems use—authorized and unauthorized
- Use of wireless networks
- Granting, approving, and monitoring systems access (for example, by level, role, and job function)
- Sanctions for workforce members in violation of policies and procedures governing EPHI access or use
- Termination of systems access
- Session termination policies and procedures for inactive computer systems
- Policies and procedures for emergency access to electronic information systems
- Password management policies and procedures
- Secure workstation use (documentation of specific guidelines for each class of workstation (i.e., on-site, laptop, and home system usage))
- Disposal of media and devices containing EPHI

(b) Other Documents:
- Entity-wide security Plan
- Risk analysis (most recent)
- Risk management plan (addressing risks identified in the risk analysis)
- Security violation monitoring reports
- Vulnerability scanning plans
  o Results from most recent vulnerability scan
- Network penetration testing policy and procedure
  o Results from most recent network penetration test
- List of all user accounts with access to systems that store, transmit, or access EPHI (for active and terminated employees)
- Configuration standards to include patch management for systems that store, transmit, or access EPHI (including workstations)
- Encryption or equivalent measures implemented on systems that store, transmit, or access EPHI

- Organization chart to include staff members responsible for general HIPAA compliance to include the protection of EPHI
- Examples of training courses or communications delivered to staff members to ensure awareness and understanding of EPHI policies and procedures (security awareness training)
- Policies and procedures governing the use of virus protection software
- Data backup procedures
- Disaster recovery plan
- Disaster recovery test plans and results
- Analysis of information systems, applications, and data groups according to their criticality and sensitivity
- Inventory of all information systems to include network diagrams listing hardware and software used to store, transmit, or maintain EPHI
- List of all primary domain controllers (PDC) and servers
- Inventory log recording the owner and movement media and devices that contain EPHI

The KPMG contract terms further indicate that audit teams are expected to consist of three to five individuals (two to three for "small non-complex" organizations) and to include requests for documentation and site visits of two to five days. The discovery of major violations during an audit may be grounds for enforcement action.

D. HIPAA Security Violation Penalty Risks

The principal exposures under HIPAA are to civil penalties assessed by the HHS OCR[50] and criminal penalties administered by the U.S. Department of Justice. HIPAA civil money penalties may be assessed at the rate of no more than $100 per violation, to a maximum annual cap of $25,000 per violation of each "identical requirement or prohibition."[51] In the context of the Security Rule, these "requirements and prohibitions" seem to be the specifications rather than the standards (including those specifications that are inherent in standards). Many of these appear possible only to violate once, though perhaps on a continuing basis.[52] Others might be violated each time a routine, noncompliant activity was conducted, so that the maximum penalty might be reached relatively quickly.[53]

---

[50] *See* 42 U.S.C. §1320d-5(a)(1); Dep't of Health & Human Servs., Civil Money Penalties: Procedures for Investigations, Imposition of Penalties, and Hearings, 68 Fed. Reg. 18,895, 18,897 (Apr. 17, 2003) [hereinafter Civil Penalties Rule].

[51] *See* 42 U.S.C. §1320d-(5)(a)(1).

[52] Such specifications include, for example, those requiring policy development and publication, enforcement roles, and the like. *See, e.g.*, 45 C.F.R. §§164.308(a)(1)(ii)(A)–(C) (risk analysis and management, sanction policy), 164.308(a)(2) (assigned security responsibility), 164.308(7)(ii)(A)–(C) (data backup, disaster recovery, and emergency mode plans).

[53] Routine transmission of unencrypted email including ePHI would violate 45 C.F.R. §164.312(e)(2)(ii) in the absence of proper justification, and many organizations might very quickly exceed the 250 transmissions necessary to reach the annual maximum.

CMPs are administered by OCR. CMPs may be assessed on a "no fault" basis, simply for failing to comply with an applicable rule, but the covered entity may assert defenses that it did not know, and in the exercise of reasonable diligence would not have known, of the noncompliance, or that the noncompliance was "due to reasonable cause and not to willful neglect" and was corrected within 30 days of its discovery or the date on which it would have been discovered in the exercise of "reasonable diligence."[54]

Further, OCR enforcement is intended to be principally through "voluntary compliance" and the provision of "technical assistance" from the OCR.[55] In this context, a good-faith attempt to comply with the Security Rule, even one that the OCR judged insufficient in some respects, should provide a defense against or mitigation of CMPs.

Good-faith security compliance should be an even more effective defense against HIPAA criminal penalties. The criminal penalty provisions are enforced by the U.S. Department of Justice[56] and provide for potential fines and/or imprisonment for a crime that might be characterized as "knowing misuse of PHI."[57]

Criminal penalties are potentially very substantial, including fines of up to $250,000 and 10 years in prison per violation, so that the potential organizational exposure could theoretically be millions of dollars.[58] From an organizational point of view, this risk can be managed by a Security Rule compliance program that follows the Federal Sentencing Guidelines, and is intended to help mitigate potential criminal penalties for organizational violations.[59] This kind of program requires implementation and communication of appropriate policies and procedures, high-level oversight and enforcement, appropriate clearance of responsible individuals, and monitoring and reporting systems—all elements consistent with Security Rule requirements.[60]

As with CMPs, then, a good-faith Security Rule compliance program should provide a good defensive record against potential criminal penalties. It

---

[54] 42 U.S.C. §1320d-5(a)(1). The correction period may be extended at the regulators' discretion. *Id.* §1320d-5(b)(3).

[55] Civil Penalties Rule, 68 Fed. Reg. at 18,897.

[56] *See id.* at 18,896.

[57] *See* John Christiansen, Electronic Health Information: Privacy and Security Compliance Under HIPAA (2000) at 30–40.

[58] The statute provides for three grades of the offense:
- "Simple" violations, punishable by up a fine of up to $50,000 and no more than a one-year prison term.
- Violations committed by "false pretenses," punishable by a fine of up to $100,000 and no more than a five-year prison term.
- Violations committed for "commercial advantage, personal gain, or malicious harm," punishable by a fine of up to $250,000 and no more than a 10-year prison term.

42 U.S.C. §1320d-6(a). The scary part of these penalties is that they may be charged and penalized "per violation," which might allow for pyramiding of hundreds or thousands of charges where, for example, records on hundreds of individuals are wrongfully disclosed in a single electronic transmission. *See* Christiansen, at 29–30.

[59] *See* Christiansen at 40–42, 76–80.

[60] *Compare* Federal Sentencing Guidelines (Nov. 1, 1991) §8A1.2 cmt. 3(k), *with* Security Rule, 45 C.F.R. §§164.308(a)1)((ii)(C) (sanction policy), 164.308(a)(2) (assigned security responsibility), 164.308(a)(3) (workforce security, including clearance), 164.308(a)(5) (security awareness and training), 164.308(a)(6)(ii) (security incident response and reporting), *and* 164.316 (policies. procedures, and documentation).

may still be argued, or a court might even hold, that the program was insufficient in some respect, but the fact that one was established and maintained should mitigate organizational penalties substantially or might even avoid them altogether.[61]

E. Business Associates and Business Associate Contracts Under the Security Rule

The business associate concept was created under the HIPAA regulations as a workaround for jurisdictional limitations under the HIPAA legislation. The HIPAA Administrative Simplification subtitle, the portion of that act that is the basis for the privacy and security regulations now most commonly understood as "HIPAA," was not intended as privacy legislation. Rather, it was intended to require health care payors (insurance companies, health plans, etc.) and health care providers (hospitals, physicians, laboratories, etc.) to transmit and process health claims transactions electronically, in standardized formats and data sets.

Privacy was included in HIPAA only because of the assumption that the public would not trust the expanded use of electronic transactions involving personal information without privacy protections. Security was only included as a standard ancillary to the transactions standards, principally to help ensure the integrity of the transactions. Privacy was even less on point and was provided for only in an uncodified section requiring privacy regulations if Congress failed to enact privacy legislation by August 1999. Congress did not enact such legislation, and HHS had to develop privacy regulations that worked within the jurisdictional limitations of HIPAA's legislative intent.

This is why the HIPAA regulations distinguish covered entities and business associates. Covered entities are the entities subject to HIPAA's jurisdiction because they engage in claims transactions (i.e., health care payors and providers and certain claims processors called health care clearinghouses. Covered entities could be directly required to comply with the Privacy and Security Rules in the protection and use of PHI and penalized if they did not.

However, covered entities frequently need to use other kinds of entities that are not subject to HIPAA jurisdiction to perform a wide range of functions and activities involving the use of PHI. It would be impossible to require covered entities to conduct all such functions and activities themselves, but the PHI protections of the Privacy and Security Rules would be rendered meaningless if they were lost as soon as those functions and activities were performed by noncovered entities.

The Privacy Rule (and later the Security Rule) therefore adopted the concept of the business associate as a legal workaround. While business associates could not be reached by HIPAA directly, they were reached indirectly by regulations that extended protections indirectly by requiring covered entities to have a specific form of contract, the business associate contract, in place before allowing their business associates access to the PHI the covered entities were required to protect. If the business associate violated the contract by doing something improper with the PHI, the covered entity was required to take actions up to and

---

[61] *See* Christiansen at 45.

including contract termination, and the covered entity (but not the business associate) could be penalized for failure to do so.

The rules therefore defined a "business associate"[62] as:

> A person or organization that, on behalf of a covered entity or organized health care arrangement ("OHCA"), but other than in the capacity of a workforce member of such Covered Entity or OHCA:
>
> (i) Performs or assists in the performance of a function or activity involving the use or disclosure of individually identifiable health information or any other function or activity regulated by HIPAA, or
>
> (ii) Provides legal, actuarial, accounting, consulting, data aggregation, management, administrative, accreditation, or financial services to or for such covered entity or arrangement where the provision of the services involves access to individually identifiable health information from such covered entity or arrangement or from another business associate of such covered entity or arrangement.

Under the business associate contract rules, a covered entity may disclose PHI to a business associate or allow a business associate to create or receive PHI on the covered entity's behalf upon "satisfactory assurance" the business associate will "appropriately safeguard" the PHI.[63] A satisfactory assurance is a business associate contract including provisions required in the regulation, or in an equivalent memorandum of understanding if governmental entities are involved, or in plan document provisions if the covered entity is a group health plan.[64] By regulation, a business associate contract must include the following security-related provisions:[65]

- require the business associate to use "appropriate safeguards" to prevent nonpermitted uses/disclosures of all PHI, and implement "administrative, physical and technical safeguards" to protect confidentiality, integrity, and availability of electronic PHI;
- require the business associate to report to the covered entity any security incident of which it becomes aware;[66]
- ensure that business associate agents and subcontractors agree to the same conditions and restrictions as the business associate, and implement "reasonable and appropriate safeguards to protect it";
- make the business associate's "internal practices, books and records" available to HHS for review in determining the covered entity's HIPAA compliance;
- authorize termination of the business associate contract if the covered entity "determines" that the business associate has "violated a material term" of the business associate contract.

---

[62] 45 C.F.R. §160.103.
[63] Privacy Rule, 45 C.F.R. §164.502.
[64] *Id.* §164.504(e).
[65] Security and Privacy Rules, 45 C.F.R. §§164.314(a), 164.504(e).
[66] Health Insurance Reform: Security Standards, 68 Fed. Reg. 8334, 8379 (Feb. 20, 2003) (codified at 45 C.F.R. §164.314(a)(2)(i)(C)).

Covered entities are not liable for unauthorized uses or disclosures of electronic protected health information by their business associate unless the covered entity knows of a pattern of activity or practice in violation of the agreement and fails to take appropriate measures. Only if the covered entity fails to take appropriate measures, which may require termination of the contract or reporting the problem to the Secretary of HHS, will the covered entity be responsible for its business associate's security breach.[67]

III. HITECH AMENDMENTS TO HIPAA: SECURITY IMPLICATIONS

As part of the 2009 stimulus bill, the American Recovery and Reinvestment Act (ARRA), Congress included a set of new privacy and security requirements for health care organizations, including both covered entities and business associates.[68] These provisions, called the Health Information Technology for Clinical and Economic Health (HITECH) Act,[69] extend HHS's regulatory jurisdiction under HIPAA to include new mandates for security compliance by business associates, security provisions in business associate contracts, and security breach notification requirements.

As discussed above, prior to HITECH, business associates were not subject to HHS's jurisdiction under HIPAA. Covered entities were required to implement business associate agreements that imposed privacy and security obligations on business associates,[70] but HIPAA and its implementing regulations did not apply directly to them. Business associates therefore were not subject to regulatory investigation or civil monetary or criminal penalties under HIPAA. HITECH extended regulatory jurisdiction to business associates. In particular, business associates are now directly subject to civil and criminal penalties for violation of the HITECH and HIPAA requirements that apply to them.[71]

Not all HIPAA or HITECH requirements apply to business associates. They are, however, required to comply with the administrative, physical, and technical safeguards and documentation requirements of the security rule.[72] They are also required to comply with the security requirements of HITECH itself,[73] as well as the privacy requirements of the HITECH Act[74] (which are beyond the scope of this section). It is noteworthy that the provisions differentiating "required" from "addressable" safeguard specifications and requiring that safeguards be selected using a "flexible approach" involving analysis of specified factors[75] were not applied to business associates, but it is not clear what that

---

[67] *Id.* (codified at 45 C.F.R. §164.314(a)(1)(ii)).
[68] ARRA, Pub. L. No. 111-5 (Feb. 17, 2009) (H.R. 1).
[69] ARRA tit. XIII [hereinafter HITECH]; *see* ARRA §13001(a).
[70] *See* 45 C.F.R. §164.314.
[71] HITECH §13401.
[72] *Id.*
[73] *Id.*
[74] *Id.* at §13404.
[75] *See* 45 C.F.R. §164.306.

might imply. The HITECH Act requires HHS to provide annual guidance on security safeguards,[76] which may help clarify this issue.

Business associate contracts are still required, however, and in fact will have to include the new HITECH privacy and security compliance requirements.[77] Business associate contracts must also now require business associates to terminate the contract if the covered entity breaches it or to report the breach to HHS if termination or mitigation is not feasible.[78] These appear to be redundant requirements, and the net effect is to increase the potential for penalties if a business associate violates a requirement that is included in both HIPAA and the HITECH Act and in the applicable business associate contract.

The HITECH business associate compliance and business associate contract provisions were effective as of February 17, 2010,[79] and HHS has published interim final regulations that implement the enhanced penalties that the HITECH Act imposed on covered entities and business associates ("HITECH Enforcement IFR")[80] and proposed regulations to implement other HITECH requirements, particularly the business associate regulations ("BA NPRM").[81]

Comments on the BA NPRM were due by September 13, 2010. Unofficially, some HHS representatives have indicated that final regulations in all of these areas, as well as regulations under the HITECH accounting of disclosures requirements and under the Genetic Information Nondiscrimination Act (GINA), will be issued together. At one point it was indicated that these regulations should probably be expected in the first quarter of 2011, but they have not been issued as of the date of this writing.

Many provisions of the BA NPRM would simply update existing HIPAA rules to conform to the HITECH Act. However, important new proposals include the formal extension of regulatory jurisdiction to business associates, the expansion of the definition of business associate to include subcontractors of a business associate (i.e., downstream entities that work at the direction or on behalf of a business associate and have access to PHI but have no direct relationship to a covered entity), and the formal extension of Security Rule compliance obligations to business associates. This latter in particular seems likely to be a surprise—or a shock—to organizations that have been subcontractors not previously subject to HIPAA regulation.

Specifically, the HITECH Act took HIPAA's covered entity and business associate concepts and extended them by incorporating the regulatory definitions of those terms. As noted above, these concepts were not part of the HIPAA legislation, so this was a crucial legislative move, because it extended regulatory jurisdiction related to PHI privacy and security to business associates as well as covered entities.

---

[76] *See* HITECH §13401.

[77] *Id.*

[78] *Id.* at §13404(b).

[79] *Id.* at §13423.

[80] Dep't of Health & Human Servs., HIPAA Administrative Simplification: Enforcement, 74 Fed. Reg. 56,123 (Oct. 30, 2009).

[81] Dep't of Health & Human Servs., Modifications to the HIPAA Privacy, Security, and Enforcement Rules Under the Health Information Technology for Economic and Clinical Health Act, 75 Fed. Reg. 40,868 (proposed July 14, 2010).

What was not apparent to most prior to the BA NPRM is that this extension now makes any party in a chain of relationships that performs a function or activity on behalf of a covered entity a business associate. Not only a business associate in a direct contractual relationship with a covered entity, but also that business associate's subcontractor, and the subcontractor of that subcontractor, and so on as far as the PHI and functions flow—any entity in that chain fits the definition of a business associate.

This application of this logic becomes clear in the revised definition of a business associate and the new definition of "subcontractor" in the BA NPRM. "Subcontractor" is now proposed to be defined as a "person who acts on behalf of a business associate, other than in the capacity of a member of the workforce of such business associate." The definition of business associate is also now proposed to be modified to add subcontractors, even though they do not have a direct relationship to the covered entity. Since a subcontractor is now defined as a business associate, it follows that any person that acts on behalf of such a subcontractor/business associate performing a function or activity involving PHI is also a subcontractor, and therefore a business associate.

The preamble to the BA NPRM gives the following example:

> ...if a business associate, such as a third party administrator, hires a company to handle document and media shredding to securely dispose of paper and electronic protected health information, then the shredding company would be directly required to comply with the applicable requirements of the HIPAA Security Rule ... and the Privacy Rule.[82]

And this business associate status is triggered by the performance of the function or activity involving PHI, whether or not the parties have a contract:

> Even though we use the term "subcontractor," which implies there is a contract in place between the parties, we note that the definition would apply to an agent or other person who acts on behalf of the business associate, even if the business associate has failed to enter into a business associate contract with the person.[83]
>
> ...
>
> The only exception to this proposed rule is for subcontractors which are "conduits," i.e., "data transmission organizations that do not require access to protected health information on a routine basis" and "do not access the information other than on a random or infrequent basis[.]"[84]

It is important for business associates to be aware of their "subcontractor" relationships that require a contract between the entities, because failure to have such an agreement is not only a violation of HIPAA but also subjects the business associate to liability for any of the subcontractors' violations.[85] A business associate can have liability for a subcontractor's violations to the extent that the subcontractor is considered to be an "agent" of the business associate pursuant

---

[82] *Id.* at 40,873.
[83] *Id.*
[84] *Id.*
[85] HHS HIPAA Administrative Simplification: Enforcement, 71 Fed. Reg. 8390 (Feb. 16, 2006).

to the federal common law of agency.[86] And, as with covered entities under the pre-existing HIPAA rules, business associates will be responsible for subcontractors' violations to the extent that the business associate knows of a pattern of noncompliance by the subcontractor that breaches its contract and does not take reasonable steps to cure the breach (see IV., below).

Most of these requirements are likely to continue, with the addition of provisions required by Sections 13401(a) and 13404(a) of the HITECH Act, which state that the Act's privacy and security requirements "shall be incorporated" into business associate contracts.

There is something of a dispute about the interpretation of the term "shall be incorporated" as used in HITECH Sections 13401(a) and 13404(a). One interpretation is that "shall be incorporated" means that the HITECH requirements "are hereby incorporated by law" without further action required by the parties, while another interpretation is that it means that the parties "are hereby directed to incorporate the requirements into their business associate contracts" by amendment or update. There is no clear statement in the BA NPRM, but it does seem to be expected that new business associate contracts will have to be implemented under transitional rules, and this question may be resolved in the final rules. In any case, it seems likely that it will often if not always be desirable to have business associate contract provisions on HITECH "required" issues that clarify and spell out obligations better than the statute and regulations do for the specific contracting arrangement.[87]

What is "incorporated" from the HITECH Act is likely to vary depending on arrangements, but will generally include:

- security breach notification requirements;
- minimum necessary requirements;
- security compliance requirements;
- audit requirements.

IV. HITECH SECURITY BREACH REQUIREMENTS

The HITECH Act also included new security breach notification provisions applicable to covered entities and business associates,[88] as well as comparable requirements for personal health records maintained or used by entities that are not otherwise subject to the HITECH Act and HIPAA;[89] the latter are beyond the scope of this discussion.

Under the new HITECH requirements, any covered entity that maintains "unsecured" PHI and "discovers" a "breach of such information" [sic]

---

[86] HITECH Enforcement IFR, 75 Fed. Reg. at 40,914 (proposed 45 C.F.R. §160.402).

[87] Along with a set of 2002 amendments to the Privacy Rule, HHS published a set of "sample business associate contract" provisions. *See* HHS Standards for Privacy of Individually Identifiable Health Information, 67 Fed. Reg. 53,182, 53264–66 (Aug. 14, 2002). These provisions essentially restate the regulatory requirements for business associate contracts with some additional language, and as a result, they have sometimes proven inappropriate or difficult to interpret or apply in some arrangements.

[88] HITECH §13402.

[89] *See id.* §13407.

is required to notify each individual whose unsecured PHI "has been, or is reasonably believed by the covered entity to have been, accessed, acquired, or disclosed as a result of such breach."[90] Business associates that have protected health information on behalf of a covered entity are in turn required to notify the covered entity of such a breach, including "identification of each [potentially affected] individual."[91]

"Unsecured" PHI is defined as PHI that has not been secured through the use of a technology or methodology identified by HHS by regulations "specifying the technologies and methodologies that render protected health information unusable, unreadable, or indecipherable to unauthorized individuals."[92]

HHS issued draft guidance on April 17, 2009,[93] proposing that PHI would be considered "unusable, unreadable or indecipherable" if (1) it has been encrypted, or (2) the encryption key has not been breached.[94] Encryption for "data at rest" (i.e., in storage) would be required to be consistent with the National Institute of Standards and Technology's (NIST) *Special Publication 800-111*,[95] while "data in transit," (i.e., in transmission) would be required to be encrypted in compliance with Federal Information Processing Standard 140-2.[96] Otherwise, PHI—in either electronic or paper form—is deemed unusable, unreadable, or indecipherable if media on which it is stored or recorded has been destroyed: paper, film, or other hard copy media must be shredded or destroyed so that the information cannot be read or reconstructed, while electronic media must be cleared, purged, or destroyed consistent with NIST *Special Publication 800-88*[97] so that the PHI cannot be retrieved. An Interim Final Rule ("IFR") was published on August 24, 2009, and compliance with the IFR was required September 23, 2009.[98]

A breach is considered "discovered" as of "the first day on which such breach is known" to a covered entity or business associate, "including any person, other than the individual committing the breach, that is an employee, officer, or other agent of such entity or associate" or "should reasonably have

---

[90] *See id.* §13402(a).

[91] *See id.* §13402(b).

[92] *See id.* §13402(h).

[93] HHS Guidance Specifying the Technologies and Methodologies That Render Protected Health Information Unusable, Unreadable, or Indecipherable to Unauthorized Individuals for Purposes of the Breach Notification Requirements Under Section 13402 of Title XIII (Health Information Technology for Economic and Clinical Health Act) of the American Recovery and Reinvestment Act of 2009 (Request for Information), 74 Fed. Reg. 19,006 (Apr. 17, 2009) [hereinafter Draft Breach Guidance].

[94] *Id.* at 19,009.

[95] U.S. DEP'T OF COMMERCE, NATIONAL INSTITUTE FOR STANDARDS AND TECHNOLOGY SPECIAL PUBLICATION 800-111, GUIDE TO STORAGE ENCRYPTION TECHNOLOGIES FOR END USER DEVICES (Nov. 2007).

[96] *See* U.S. DEP'T OF COMMERCE, NATIONAL INSTITUTE FOR STANDARDS AND TECHNOLOGY SPECIAL PUBLICATIONS 800-52, GUIDELINES FOR THE SELECTION AND USE OF TRANSPORT LAYER SECURITY (TLS) IMPLEMENTATIONS (June 2005); 800-77, GUIDE TO IPSEC VPNS (Dec. 2005); 800-113, GUIDE TO SSL VPNS (July 2008).

[97] U.S. DEP'T OF COMMERCE, NATIONAL INSTITUTE FOR STANDARDS AND TECHNOLOGY SPECIAL PUBLICATIONS 800-88, GUIDELINES FOR MEDIA SANITIZATION (Sept. 2006), *available at* http://csrc.nist.gov/publications/nistpubs/800-88/NISTSP800-88_rev1.pdf.

[98] U.S. Dep't of Health and Human Servs., Breach Notification for Unsecured Protected Health Information; Interim Final Rule, 74 Fed. Reg. 74240 (Aug. 24, 2009).

been known to such entity or associate (or person) to have occurred."[99] Once a breach has been discovered, notification must be given "without unreasonable delay and in no case later than 60 calendar days after the discovery of a breach," subject to delay based on law enforcement determination that notification would interfere with investigation or "cause damage to national security."[100] Notification must be given[101]

- by first-class mail, or by e-mail if the individual has specified that as a preference;
- by telephone, if the covered entity deems it urgent "because of possible imminent misuse of unsecured protected health information";
- if 10 or more individuals are involved or contact information is insufficient or out of date, by Web site posting or publication through "major media" in the individuals' residential area; and
- if more than 500 individuals are involved, by publication through a "prominent media outlet" and immediate notice to HHS.

All forms of notice are required to include:[102]

- A brief description of what happened, including the date of the breach and the date of the discovery of the breach, if known.
- A description of the types of unsecured protected health information that were involved in the breach (such as full name, Social Security number, date of birth, home address, account number, or disability code).
- The steps individuals should take to protect themselves from potential harm resulting from the breach.
- A brief description of what the covered entity involved is doing to investigate the breach, to mitigate losses, and to protect against any further breaches.
- Contact procedures for individuals to ask questions or learn additional information, which shall include a toll-free telephone number, an e-mail address, Web site, or postal address.

Covered entities (but not business associates) are required to maintain a log of all breaches and submit them annually to HHS.[103] HHS is required to post an annual list of all Covered Entities that have reported a security breach involving more than 500 individuals.[104]

V. STATE SECURITY BREACH NOTIFICATION LEGISLATION

Information system security breaches—incidents involving unauthorized access to, copying, or altering of data in a computerized information system or

---

[99] 45 C.F.R. §164.404(a)(2).
[100] 45 C.F.R. §164.404(b).
[101] 45 C.F.R. §164.404(d).
[102] 45 C.F.R. §164.404(c).
[103] 45 C.F.R. §164.408(c).
[104] HITECH §13402(e)(4).

network[105]—are an unavoidable, if undesirable, feature of information system usage. Although security breaches cannot be avoided, they can be managed and their harmful effects mitigated, but first they must be acknowledged and described. Until recently, however, organizations experiencing breaches generally had more incentive to conceal them than to acknowledge them and deal with their implications.

These incentives began to shift in 2002, and that shift accelerated in 2005–2006 with a wave of consumer-oriented security breach notification laws. As of October 2010, 46 states, the District of Columbia, Puerto Rico, and the Virgin Islands had all enacted security breach notification laws.[106]

A. The Economic Logic of Information Security Breach Disclosure

Until as recently as 2002, there were few legal requirements and no economic incentives for companies using information systems to acknowledge and publish information about their security breaches. Given the negative effects of security breach revelation on reputation and the potential exposure to regulatory penalties and private claims, it has in fact been "appropriate capitalist behavior" for businesses to try to conceal their security breaches.[107] The same incentive structure holds true for governmental agencies, which may not engage in "capitalist" behavior, but nonetheless probably would prefer not to publicly disclose information that might reflect badly on their competence.

Although this may be appropriate from the perspective of the information-system-using organizations, innocent third parties harmed by such breaches tend to disagree. One response to this kind of tacit shifting of security breach harms to third parties, and to consumers in particular, has been the emergence of "identity theft" as a public policy issue.

"Identity theft" is a variant of fraud that may be defined as the unauthorized procurement and use of information that identifies and authenticates the identity of an individual (e.g., name, Social Security number, driver's license number, etc.), usually to obtain identification documentation or execute commercial or other transactions fraudulently in the individual's name.[108] Although personal

---

[105] This definition is loosely based on the definition of "breach of the security of the system" under Washington's security breach notification law, in §§1(b)(4) and 2(b)(4) of Substitute S.B. 6043, ch. 368, 59th Leg., 2005 Reg. Sess. (Wash. approved May 10, 2005) (WASH. REV. CODE ch. 19.225 and §42.56.590) (S.B. 6043). As discussed in V.C., below, S.B. 6043 in fact applies to only a limited category of information, and therefore only to a limited category of incidents that fit the general definition of "security breach." Compare the definition of "security incident" under the federal security regulations applicable under HIPAA, Pub. L. No. 104-191, 110 Stat. 1936, (codified at 42 U.S.C. §§1230d *et seq.*), the principal federal standards on privacy and security for health care organizations: "Security incident means the attempted or successful unauthorized access, use, disclosure, modification, or destruction of information or interference with system operations in an information system." 45 C.F.R. §164.302.

[106] *See* National Conference of State Legislatures, State Security Breach Notification Laws, *available at* http://www.ncsl.org/default.aspx?tabid=13489.

[107] Emily Frye, *The Tragedy of the Cybercommons: Overcoming Fundamental Vulnerabilities to Critical Infrastructures in a Networked World*, 58 BUS. LAW. 349, 366 (Nov. 2002).

[108] *See, e.g.*, Identity Theft: How It Happens, Its Effect on Victims, and Legislative Solutions, Testimony Before the U.S. Senate Judiciary Subcommittee on Technology, Terrorism, and Government Information (July 12, 2000) (written testimony of Beth Givens, Director, Privacy Rights Clearinghouse):

information useful for identity theft may be contained in any medium, digital media and information systems can store and allow for the copying of personal information much more easily and in much greater quantities than any other.[109]

It is therefore no coincidence that identity theft emerged as a public policy problem with the widespread implementation of information systems serving e-commerce and online financial businesses.[110]

As remedial strategies, prosecution and victim assistance amount to locking the barn door after the horse gets out: the personal information used to facilitate identity theft has already escaped protection. The best that can be done is to try to mitigate ensuing harms, and victims may still find it difficult to get help from law enforcement and other authorities.[111] But neither of these strategies, however limited, may be possible without prompt notice of harmful events, and neither changes incentive structures favoring concealment.

B. A Brief History of Information Security Breach Notification Laws

The incentives began to shift with the passage of security breach notification laws beginning in 2002. The first security breach notification law was enacted in California in 2002 and was effective in 2003.[112] This legislation, most commonly known by its bill number, S.B. 1386, was passed in response to a security incident involving the California State Office of the Controller, which exposed personal information on every employee in the state.[113] S.B. 1386

[W]hat is identity theft? There are numerous variations of this crime. Essentially, it occurs when someone uses bits and pieces of information about an individual—usually the Social Security number—to represent him or herself as that person for fraudulent purposes. Examples are obtaining credit cards and loans in someone else's name and then not paying the bills, opening utility accounts, renting an apartment, getting a cellular phone, purchasing a car or a home, and so on. Another type of identity theft—what I call the worst case scenario—is when the perpetrator commits crimes in the victim's name and gives that person a criminal record.

[109] This is not actually a new problem. Privacy and data misuse concerns first emerged in the late 1960s, as mainframe computers became relatively common in governmental and commercial uses. *See* John Christiansen, Electronic Health Information: Privacy and Security Compliance Under HIPAA (2000) at §§3.01 and 3.02.

[110] Identity theft was perhaps first recognized in law in the federal Identity Theft and Assumption Act of 1998, which provided for criminal penalties and authorized the Federal Trade Commission to implement procedures to educate consumers and receive and refer identity theft complaints for appropriate consumer reporting agency or law enforcement action. *See* Pub. L. No. 105-318, 112 Stat. 3007 (1998) (codified at 18 U.S.C. §1028).

[111] *See, e.g.*, Pamela Scherer McCleod, *Newsmaker Interview: Eric Drew, Victim of First-Ever HIPAA-Convicted [sic] Crime Tells Story & Offers Advice to Laboratories*, XII THE DARK REPORT 9 (Apr. 28, 2005) (interview with Seattle Cancer Care Alliance leukemia patient whose identifying information was used by an Alliance employee to commit tens of thousands of dollars in credit fraud, relating his experiences in tracking down the criminal himself and trying to find an agency willing to take and act on his information and the difficulties he encountered in clearing up the fraudulent accounts).

[112] California S.B. 1386 applies to agencies and businesses by using two separate but almost identical sets of provisions. *See* S.B. 1386, 2001–2002 Sess., ch. 915 (Cal. filed Sept. 26, 2002), *amending and adding to* CAL. CIV. CODE §§1798.29 (agency provisions) *and* 1798.82 (business provisions).

[113] *See* Timothy H. Skinner, *California's Database Breach Notification Security Act: The First State Breach Notification Law Is Not Yet a Suitable Template for National Identity Theft Legislation*, 10 RICHMOND J. L. & TECH. 4, 4–5 (Fall 2003).

applies to both state agencies and any person or business that conducts business in California that "owns or licenses computerized data that includes personal information."[114] S.B. 1386 has been the model for all the other security breach legislation and regulations implemented since.[115]

S.B. 1386 and its progeny are usually described as "security breach notification legislation." This is not entirely accurate, because they in fact only require notification of security incidents involving unencrypted information, and thus they may also be considered "encryption incentive" laws. These laws do not apply to all types of personal information but, consistently with their basis in identity theft control, apply only to categories of information useful for identity theft purposes, which are specified in the statute.

Consistent with their intent to permit individuals to respond to and possibly mitigate the effects of identity theft occurring when their personal information is taken in a security incident, regulated agencies and businesses are to give prompt notice of security breach incidents in writing and/or under some conditions by e-mail, Web site posting, or notification to major public media. Violations of the law may be enjoined, and affected individuals are given a statutory cause of action for damages.

Comparable federal legislation was introduced by California's U.S. Senator Feinstein shortly after S.B. 1386,[116] and S.B. 1386 was the model for incident reporting guidance issued under the Gramm-Leach-Bliley Act[117] for banks and certain other financial institutions. Through 2004, however, there was little security breach notification activity reported.[118] Then, in the early months of 2005, a series of highly publicized incidents brought identity theft and security breach notification laws into the public policy spotlight.

The public policy dam broke with the February 2005 revelation that ChoicePoint, a private credit reporting agency with vast quantities of highly sensitive personal information about consumers, had sold information on almost 145,000 individuals to identity theft criminals fraudulently posing as legitimate customers.[119] Over the following weeks, this announcement was followed by further security incident reports concerning dozens of businesses and governmental agencies and affecting personal information about some 50 million individuals.[120]

---

[114]*See* CAL. CIV. CODE §§1798.29(a) (agency provision), 1798.82(a) (business provision).

[115]Because the state of Washington's law is the principal point of comparison in this section and is analyzed with citations in some detail below, the following generic description of security breach notification laws will not cite any specific statutes.

[116]*See generally* Skinner, *California's Database Breach Notification Security Act*.

[117]*See* U.S. Dep't of the Treasury, Officer of the Controller of the Currency, Board of Governors of the Federal Reserve System, Federal Deposit Insurance Corporation and Office of Thrift Supervision, Interagency Guidance on Response Programs for Unauthorized Access to Customer Information and Customer Notice (Mar. 18, 2005).

[118]*See* Mark Willoughby, *California Privacy Law a Yawner So Far*, COMPUTERWORLD (Mar. 15, 2004), *available at* http://www.computerworld.com/s/article/90860/California_privacy_law_a_yawner_so_far.

[119]Sarah D. Scarlet, *The Five Most Shocking Things About the ChoicePoint Debacle*, CSO MAGAZINE (May 2005), *available at* http://www.csoonline.com/article/220340/the-five-most-shocking-things-about-the-choicepoint-data-security-breach

[120]*See A Chronology of Data Breaches Since the ChoicePoint Incident*, PRIVACY RIGHTS CLEARINGHOUSE (posted Apr. 20, 2005, updated July 11, 2005).

Because only California had a law requiring ChoicePoint to notify affected individuals of the theft, at first ChoicePoint only gave California residents notice.[121] This did not sit well with the citizens of other states the residents of which might have been affected, and under pressure from various state attorneys general, ChoicePoint gave their states' affected residents notice also.[122] Rather than depend on the goodwill of companies in ChoicePoint's position in the future, security breach notification legislation modeled on S.B. 1386 was introduced in at least 28 states and passed in at least 10 by August 2006.[123]

The various state laws, which differ in ways that may be obvious or quite subtle and may or may not be material, already have been a significant problem for some multistate businesses and are likely to become worse in the absence of conscious efforts at harmonization. Existing federal laws, particularly but not only the HITECH breach notification IFR, do not supersede state laws in this area. Health care organizations therefore must work out ways to reconcile or coordinate their obligations under the HITECH breach notification IFR with their state obligations, which for many organizations may well include the laws of several states.

C. Analysis of a Representative Information Security Breach Notification Law

Although there are variations among the state laws, by and large they present common issues. Therefore, it may be useful to identify both common issues and possible points of variation by comparing two of these laws: California S.B. 1386 and Washington S.B. 6043.

Like the California law, Washington S.B. 6043 applies both to governmental agencies and to "persons" and "businesses" that "do business" in the state, in parallel sets of identical provisions.[124] The "doing business" limitation is jurisdictional, and presumably jurisdiction should be determined according to the usual principles for interstate businesses.[125]

S.B. 6043 distinguishes between agencies and "persons or businesses" that "own" and those that "license" regulated information.[126] Regulated information

---

[121] *See* Scarlet, *The Five Most Shocking Things*.

[122] *Id.*

[123] *See* National Conference of State Legislatures, 2005 Breach of Information Legislation, *available at* http://www.ncsl.org/programs/lis/CIP/priv/breach.htm.

[124] *See* S.B. 6043, ch. 368, 59th Leg., 2005 Reg. Sess. (Wash. approved May 10, 2005), at §1 (codified at WASH. REV. CODE ch. 42.17) (agency provisions), *and* §2 (codified at WASH. REV. CODE ch. 19) (business provisions). Compare the description of S.B. 1386 in V.C.3.

[125] This is not necessarily an easy determination, especially for entities doing business online. *See* Raymond T. Nimmer and Holly Towle, THE LAW OF ELECTRONIC COMMERCIAL TRANSACTIONS §7.9 (2003).

[126] *See* S.B. 6043 §§1(1)(a), 2(1). A more useful distinction might be between "data owner" and "data custodian," as suggested by California regulatory guidance on S.B. 1386 compliance, which states, "***Data owner:*** The individual or organization with primary responsibility for determining the purpose and function of a record system. ***Data custodian:*** The individual or organization that has responsibility delegated by the data owner for maintenance and technological management of the record system." Cal. Dep't of Consumer Affairs Office of Privacy Protection, Recommended Practices on Notification of Security Breach Involving Personal Information 8 (Oct. 10, 2003).

is defined as "computerized data which includes personal information."[127] "Computerized data" is not defined, but "personal information" is, as:

- an individual's first name or first initial, plus
- last name, plus
- Social Security number or state identification card number, or
- account, credit, or debit card number in combination with any security code, access code, or password that would permit access to an individual's financial account, but only if
- either the name or the other data elements are not encrypted, and
- the information is not "publicly available information made available to the general public [sic] from federal, state or local government records."[128]

Although this definition does not limit "personal information" to information about Washington residents, notification is only required if the affected data includes information about Washington residents.[129]

1. The Problem of Encryption

The exclusion from the notification requirements of incidents affecting encrypted data is a provision that sounds easier to understand and implement than it really is. Digital data—which is presumably what is meant by "computerized data"—is encrypted using an algorithm (called a "key" in this context) to convert the data from readable form into a form that is not readable unless it is decrypted using the same (or a mathematically related) key.[130] Encryption of computerized data therefore protects personal information included in the data from being read by any party who does not have the decryption key. If only authorized persons can obtain the key needed to decrypt the computerized data, unauthorized individuals are unable to acquire the personal information unless they can break the encryption (i.e., guess or otherwise determine the key).

The use of encryption therefore is generally a good thing for purposes of identity theft prevention, and in fact is even better than notification because it locks the barn door *before* the horse can get out. The use of encryption does impose the burden of key management, which can be substantial if there are many authorized users or if membership in the authorized user group changes frequently. But encryption applications are readily available (and already included in some software), and the public policy behind the statutes is clearly intended to favor the protection of innocent third parties over data owner/licensee convenience in this and other ways.

However, the laws do not specify the strength of the encryption that must be used. There are many different encryption algorithms available, some of which may be readily broken using well-known attacks.[131] But any encryption,

---

[127] S.B. 6043 §§1(1)(a), 2(1).

[128] *Id.* §§1(5), 2(5).

[129] *Id.* §§1(1)(a), 2(1).

[130] This is summarized nicely for a lay reader in BRUCE SCHNEIER, SECRETS AND LIES: DIGITAL SECURITY IN A NETWORKED WORLD 85–119 (2000).

[131] *Id.* at 115–19.

however bad, is enough to get the encrypted data out from under statutory coverage. A better approach might be to require the use of "commercially reasonable" or "industry standard" encryption or the use of encryption based on the recommendations of a qualified security professional. Whatever the statutory requirements, any encryption implementation should be based on expert advice.

2. The Complexities of Notification

Under the Washington and California laws, a reportable incident is any "breach of the security of the system" in which "an unauthorized individual" acquired, or is "reasonably believed to have acquired," personal information.[132] A "breach of the security of the system" is (somewhat redundantly) defined as an "unauthorized acquisition of computerized data that compromises the security, confidentiality or integrity of personal information."[133]

Washington's law varies from California's S.B. 1386 in two important respects. Washington's S.B. 6043 excludes from the definition of a reportable "breach" the good-faith but unauthorized acquisition of computerized data by an employee or agent, for purposes of the employer/principal (as long as the data is not "used or subject to further disclosure").[134] Also unlike S.B. 1386, S.B. 6043 does not require notification of a "technical breach" that "does not seem likely to subject customers [sic] to a risk of criminal activity."[135]

In Washington, notice of reportable incidents must be given to any state resident whose personal information is or is "reasonably believed" to have been affected.[136] If another party owns the computerized data that was affected (e.g., if the security incident occurred at a contract data processing services provider), the data owner must also be notified.[137] Notification to state residents may (but is not required to) be delayed consistent with measures "necessary to determine the scope of the breach and restore the integrity of the system," and to the extent a law enforcement agency determines is necessary for purposes of

---

[132] S.B. 6043 §§1(1)(a), 2(1).

[133] *Id.* §§1(4), 2(4).

[134] *Id.* §§1(1)(a), 2(1).

[135] *Id.* §§1(10)(d), 2(10)(d). It would be worth revising this provision to exclude "incidental acquisition of personal information that does not seem reasonably likely to subject customers [sic; residents?] to a risk of criminal activity" instead. "Technical breach of the security system" is not defined, but appears intended to mean some sort of technical access control failure. In fact, nontechnical, accidental disclosures of information are probably more common, as when an unauthorized individual looks at a computer screen while talking with the operator. Compare the concept of "incidental disclosure" under the HIPAA regulations, which permit:
> incidental uses and disclosures [or protected information] that occur as a by-product of another permissible or required use or disclosure [of that information], as long as the [regulated] entity has applied reasonable safeguards ... with respect to the primary use or disclosure. ... An incidental use or disclosure is a secondary use or disclosure that cannot reasonably be prevented, is limited in nature, and that occurs as a result of another use or disclosure that is permitted [i.e., authorized].

U.S. DEP'T OF HEALTH & HUMAN SERVS., OFFICE OF CIVIL RIGHTS, INCIDENTAL USES AND DISCLOSURES, OCR HIPAA PRIVACY GUIDANCE (Dec. 3, 2002, revised Apr. 3, 2003).

[136] S.B. 6043 §§1(1)(a), 2(1).

[137] *Id.* §§1(1)(2), 2(2).

investigation.[138] Although it is not stated, it appears that notification of a data owner cannot be delayed for these reasons.[139]

Notice, apparently both to residents and data owners, cannot be waived[140] and must be written or electronic unless the conditions for substitute notice are met.[141]

Any electronic notice must be consistent with the federal Electronic Signatures in Global and National Commerce Act (E-SIGN).[142] Under E-SIGN, federal and state laws may not prohibit the use of electronic contracts and transaction records except in contracts and transactions involving consumers.[143] Commercial parties may therefore agree to electronic notice under terms they control. However, E-SIGN compliance for consumer purposes (and in most cases, "residents" will probably be "consumers") may be difficult and onerous, because E-SIGN requires certain prior disclosures and affirmative prior consent that may be withdrawn at any time.[144]

Substitute notice is permitted if the business or agency "demonstrates" (it is not clear to whom) that (1) the cost of written or electronic notice would exceed $250,000; (2) the "affected class of subject persons" exceeds 500,000 individuals; or (3) it does not have sufficient contact information for written or electronic notices.[145] Substitute notice must include all of the following:

- e-mail notice to all subject persons for whom the business or agency has an e-mail address;
- conspicuous posting on the business or agency Web site, if it maintains one; and
- "notification to major statewide media."[146]

One potential difficulty with the notification scheme is that whenever a data licensee experiences a breach, both the data owner and the licensee have a statutory obligation to notify residents. The licensee may well not have any direct relationship to the residents whose personal information is affected, may

---

[138] *Id.* §§1(1)(3), 2(3).

[139] *Id.* §§1(2), 2(2). There is some ambiguity because although §§1(3) and 2(3) state that "notification required by this section may be delayed" upon a law enforcement agency determination, §§1(1)(a) and 2(1) specifically provide that the "disclosure" to residents [sic; presumably notification is intended] must be made "in the most expedient time possible and without unreasonable delay, consistent with the needs of law enforcement." Sections 1(2) and 2(2) do not provide for any delay for any reason, but state that notification must be made "immediately following discovery" of the breach. It is therefore not clear that the permissive delay of §§1(3) and 2(3) relieves a data licensee of the obligation of immediate notification of the data owner under §§1(2) and 2(2).

[140] *Id.* §§1(9), 2(9).

[141] *Id.* §§1(7)(a)–(c), 2(7)(a)–(c).

[142] *Id.* §§1(7)(b), 2(7)(b).

[143] *See* 15 U.S.C. §7001(a)–(b).

[144] *See id.* §7001(c).

[145] S.B. 6043 §§1(7)(c), 2(7)(c). Given the phrasing of the statute, which places the burden on the agency or business to demonstrate that substitute notification is permissible, it is not clear whether this provision implies a positive obligation to give substitute notice to members of an affected class if written or electronic notice is not possible due to insufficient contact information. Presumably, such an obligation would be consistent with the legislative intent.

[146] *Id.* §§1(7)(c)(i)–(iii), 2(7)(c)(i)–(iii).

lack sufficient contact information, and may in fact be prohibited by its contract with the data owner from using the information to contact data subjects. Under the language of the statute, such a licensee is nonetheless required to notify potentially affected residents.[147]

Because the statutory scheme requires "immediate" notification to the data owner,[148] the usual sequence of events should be that notice to the owner precedes notice to residents, so the parties should be able to give notice cooperatively—and ideally will have agreed on procedures in advance. Licensees may wish to insist on at least a joint notification, because licensees have an independent statutory obligation and there is no exception for cases in which another party also gives a notification.

3. The Scope of Regulation

The comparison of S.B. 6043 with its model, S.B. 1386, demonstrates an interpretation problem caused by an inappropriate verbatim copying of one state's laws by another. Washington's S.B. 6043 incorporated the terms "business" and "customer" from S.B. 1386, both of which are defined in California Civil Code Title 1.81, entitled "Customer Records." Title 1.81 amounts to a code of information practices for private "business" entities, equivalent to the code of information practices provided for governmental agencies in Title 1.8.[149] (The agency provisions of S.B. 1386 are codified as part of this latter title.[150])

When S.B. 1386 used the terms "business" and "customer," then, the legislation incorporated the following pre-existing definitions from Title 1.81:

> "Business" means a sole proprietorship, partnership, corporation, association, or other group, however organized and whether or not organized to operate at a profit, including a financial institution organized, chartered, or holding a license or authorization certificate under the law of this state, any other state, the United States, or of any other country, or the parent or the subsidiary of a financial institution. The term includes an entity that destroys records.[151]

> "Customer" means an individual who provides personal information to a business for the purpose of purchasing or leasing a product or obtaining a service from the business.[152]

Neither of these terms, however, has any statutory equivalent in Washington law.[153] This lack of definition, and the phrasing of some of the provisions of S.B. 6043, creates some difficulties in its interpretation.

The term "business" is defined in California's Title 1.81 as essentially any type of nongovernmental entity or association, consistent with its usage in a code of "business" information practices paralleling the code of governmental

---

[147] See id. §2(1).

[148] Id. §2(2).

[149] See CAL. CIV. CODE tit. 1.8 (entitled "Information Practices Act of 1977").

[150] CAL. CIV. CODE §1798.29 (codifying S.B. 1386 §2).

[151] Id. §1798.80(a).

[152] Id. §1798.80(c).

[153] The term "agency," on the other hand, was specifically defined by reference to existing Washington law. See S.B. 6043 §1(b).

information practices. The term "business" in Washington law, on the other hand, appears to be used less as a description of an entity than as an activity.[154] The application of the Washington law to "persons" as well as "businesses"[155] does not really seem to clarify the scope of the statute, although it does appear that the common-law definition of a "business" entity in Washington should have approximately comparable scope to the statutory definition in California.[156] But there are likely to be some marginal cases (nonprofit associations, perhaps?) where resolution will have to be litigated.

The term "customer" is more problematic. This term is used both to limit the obligation to give notice of technical breaches, by providing that notice need not be given of breaches not likely to subject "customers" to a risk of criminal activity,[157] and to define the class of parties authorized to sue for damages for breach of either the business or agency statute.[158] As with the term "business," it is probably true that in many cases the identification of data subjects as "customers" will be noncontroversial—especially if the law is interpreted to incorporate the California definition—but it is certainly a live issue with respect to damages claims against Washington agencies,[159] and as with "businesses" there may be cases at the margin where such identification is not at all clear.

A potentially greater issue than ambiguity at the margins is raised as well, involving owners and licensors of data who do not have a "customer" relationship with the data subjects. For example, a contract processor of health care data could experience a major technical breach affecting personal information about hundreds of thousands of Washington residents and have no obligation to notify anyone because the residents are not its "customers." Likewise, a credit agency could experience a breach that triggered a notification requirement because it involved personal information about Washington residents and fail to give the required notification, and even Washington residents who found themselves victims of serious criminal behavior that they could have avoided if notification had been given could not sue for damages because they were not the agency's "customers." This issue is a difficulty created by the structure of the statute as enacted in California, with its incorporated definition of "customer," so it is not unique to Washington.

---

[154] *See, e.g.*, City of Seattle v. State, 965 P.2d 619 (Wash. 1998) (interpreting city government as engaged in "business" activity, given breadth of definition of that term).

[155] *See* S.B. 6043 §2(1).

[156] *City of Seattle* at 705–06 (dicta indicating nonprofit activity is also "business").

[157] S.B. 6043 §§1(10)(d), 2(10)(d).

[158] *Id.* §§1(10)(a), 2(10)(a).

[159] It is not at all clear that those served by an agency fit the legal definition of "customers." They certainly do not under the California definition. Nor is it clear that such a limitation would be consistent with the policy behind the statute, which otherwise appears intended to protect residents of the state in general, not just those who happen to be agency "customers." By comparison, the "agency" provisions of S.B. 1386 are enforced by existing laws providing for a variety of penalties including but not limited to a suit for damages by any "individual" harmed by the agency's failure to comply. *See* CAL. CIV. CODE §1798.45.

D. State Security Breach Notification Laws as of August 2011

As of August 2011 at least 46 states and territories had adopted security breach legislation based on the California law, as follows:

Alaska	2008 H.B. 65
Arizona	ARIZ. REV. STAT. §44-7501 (2007 S.B. 1042, ch. 23)
Arkansas	ARK. CODE §§4-110-101 et seq.
California	CAL. CIV. CODE §1798.82
Colorado	COLO. REV. STAT. §6-1-716
Connecticut	CONN. GEN. STAT. §36a-701(b)
Delaware	DEL. CODE tit. 6, §§12B-101 et seq.
District of Columbia	D.C. CODE §§28-3851 et seq.
Florida	FLA. STAT. §817.5681
Georgia	GA. CODE §§10-1-910, -911
Hawaii	HAW. REV. STAT. §487N-2
Idaho	IDAHO CODE §§28-51-104 to -107
Illinois	815 ILL. COMP. STAT. §530/1 et seq.
Indiana	IND. CODE §§24-4.9 et seq., 4-1-11 et seq.
Iowa	2008 S.F. 2308
Kansas	KAN. STAT. §§50-7a01, -7a02
Louisiana	LA. REV. STAT. §§51:3071 et seq.
Maine	ME. REV. STAT. tit. 10 §§1347 et seq.
Maryland	MD. CODE, COM. LAW §§14-3501 et seq.
Massachusetts	2007 H.B. 4144, ch. 82
Michigan	MICH. COMP. LAWS §§445.61 et seq.
Minnesota	MINN. STAT. §§325E.61, 325E.64
Montana	MONT. CODE §§30-14-1701 et seq.
Nebraska	NEB. REV. STAT. §§87-801, -802, -803, -804, -805, -806, -807
Nevada	NEV. REV. STAT. §§603A.010 et seq.
New Hampshire	N.H. REV. STAT. §§359-C:19 et seq.
New Jersey	N.J. REV. STAT. §56:8-163
New York	N.Y. GEN. BUS. LAW §899-aa
North Carolina	N.C. GEN. STAT. §75-65
North Dakota	N.D. CENT. CODE §§51-30-01 et seq.
Ohio	OHIO REV. CODE §§1347.12, 1349.19, 1349.191, 1349.192
Oklahoma	OKLA. STAT. §74-3113.1
Oregon	2007 S.B. 583, ch. 759
Pennsylvania	73 PA. STAT. §2303
Puerto Rico	2005 H.B. 1184, Law 111
Rhode Island	R.I. GEN. LAWS §§11-49.2-1 et seq.
South Carolina	2008 S.B. 453, Act 190
Tennessee	TENN. CODE §47-18-2107
Texas	TEX. BUS. & COM. CODE §§48.001 et seq.
Utah	UTAH CODE §§13-44-101, -102, -201, -202, -310

Vermont	VT. STAT. tit. 9, §§2430 et seq.
Virginia	2008 S.B. 307, ch. 566
Washington	WASH. REV. CODE §19.255.010
West Virginia	2008 S.B. 340, ch. 37
Wisconsin	WIS. STAT. §895.507
Wyoming	WYO. STAT. §40-12-501

In addition, California amended its security breach law to expand the definition of "personal information," the potential breach of which would trigger a notification obligation, to include "health information" and "medical information" when combined with the individual's last name and first name or initial.[160] California law defines "health insurance information" as meaning "an individual's health insurance policy number or subscriber identification number, any unique identifier used by a health insurer to identify the individual, or any information in an individual's application and claims history, including any appeals records."[161] "Medical information" is defined as "any information regarding an individual's medical history, mental or physical condition, or medical treatment or diagnosis by a health care professional."[162]

While these definitions focus on information principally created or used by health insurers and health care providers, respectively, the statute applies to any party in possession of such information that experiences a security breach. As of August 2011, no other state or territory appears to have followed California's lead on this point.

---

[160] CAL. CIV. CODE §1798.82(e)(4), (5).
[161] Id. §1798.82(f)(3).
[162] Id. §1798.82(f)(2).

APPENDIX 7-A

SAMPLE HITECH/HIPAA
Security Gap Analysis Checklist
Version 2.1
September 12, 2011

The following tool is intended to provide a Covered Entity or Business Associate with a Security Gap Analysis Checklist against the security risk analysis requirements of HIPAA at 45 C.F.R. Part 164, subpart C (the "Security Rule"), as well as the HITECH requirements.

All covered entities should have completed Security Rule risk analysis and implemented a Security Rule security management process several years ago, maintained and updated as necessary. This analysis and process should cover all information resources and related business processes maintained by the covered entity.

The Checklist should include questions that allow outside reviewers to determine whether or not the covered entity has conducted an appropriate risk analysis by identifying whether or not the kinds of policies, procedures, and technical safeguards that should be its product. An analyst using the Checklist should not expect to be able to make judgments about the adequacy of the safeguards the covered entity has implemented. Rather, the Checklist can be used to help covered entities determine whether the scope of their risk analysis (and mitigation) covers all the Security Rule requirements.

The following tool is therefore intended to indicate gaps in compliance with the Security Rule and HITECH requirements but not to support a risk assessment of the adequacy of the safeguards implemented. In this tool, each row stands for a specific compliance requirement. Each requirement is identified by citation to the HIPAA provision and its title and includes a description of the requirement. The "Safeguard Identification" field for each requirement should be filled in by the individual or team conducting the assessment with information about the safeguards found to be in place, for example, the policy or procedure name and number—or technical application implemented. Upon completion of the gap analysis, the cells should be color coded as follows:

- A gray cell indicates that the requirement is a general one that has compliance specifications in subsequent cells with the actual requirements.
- A green cell indicates that the covered entity has safeguards that appear to cover the scope of the requirement. Comments may nonetheless be provided.
- A yellow cell indicates that the covered entity has safeguards that address the requirement but do not appear to cover its full scope. Comments should be provided about additional items that should be addressed.
- A red cell indicates that the covered entity does not have safeguards that address the requirement.

Citation	Title	Description	Safeguard Questions	Comments
HITECH §13401(a)	Application of Security Provisions and Penalties to Business Associates	"Sections 164.308, 164.310, 164.312, and 164.316 of title 45, Code of Federal Regulations, shall apply to a business associate of a covered entity in the same manner that such sections apply to the covered entity."		
HIPAA 45 C.F.R. §164.308	Administrative Safeguards			
HIPAA 45 C.F.R. §164.308(a)(1)	Security Management Process	"Implement policies and procedures to prevent, detect, contain, and correct security violations."		
HIPAA 45 C.F.R. §164.308(a)(1)(ii)(A)	Risk Analysis (Required)	"Conduct an accurate and thorough assessment of the potential risks and vulnerabilities to the confidentiality, integrity, and availability of EPHI held by the covered entity." This risk analysis should attempt to disclose "all relevant losses" that could be anticipated if security measures were not in place (Preamble, 68 Fed. Reg. at 8347), such as "losses caused by inappropriate uses and disclosures and the loss of data integrity that would occur absent the security measures."		
HIPAA 45 C.F.R. §164.308(a)(1)(ii)(B)	Risk Management (Required)	"Implement security measures sufficient to reduce risks and vulnerabilities to a reasonable and appropriate level to comply with § 164.306(a)."		

App. 7-A.   *Information Security and Breach Notification*   193

Citation	Title	Description	Safeguard Questions	Comments
HIPAA 45 C.F.R. §164.308(a)(1)(ii)(C)	Sanction Policy (Required)	"Apply appropriate sanctions against workforce members who fail to comply with the security policies and procedures of the covered entity." The details of this policy, such as types of sanctions and instances in which they will be applied, are left up to the organization (Preamble, 68 Fed. Reg. at 8348). Sanctions will be based on "the relative severity of the violation" and on the entity's own security policies. *Id.*		
HIPAA 45 C.F.R. §164.308(a)(1)(ii)(D)	Information System Activity Review (Required)	"Implement procedures to regularly review records of information system activity, such as audit logs, access reports, and security incident tracking reports." The Security Rule at 45 C.F.R. §164.304, defines "information systems" as "an interconnected set of information resources under the same direct management control that shares common functionality. A system normally includes hardware, software, information, data, applications, communications, and people."		
HIPAA 45 C.F.R. §164.308(a)(2)	Assigned Security Responsibility (Required)	"Identify the security official who is responsible for the development and implementation of the policies and procedures required by this subpart for the entity."		
HIPAA 45 C.F.R. §164.308(a)(3)(i)	Workforce Security			

Citation	Title	Description	Safeguard Questions	Comments
HIPAA 45 C.F.R. §164.308(a)(3)(ii)(A)	Authorization and/or Supervision (Addressable)	"Implement procedures for the authorization and/or supervision of workforce members who work with EPHI or in locations where EPHI might be accessed."		
HIPAA 45 C.F.R. §164.308(a)(3)(ii)(B)	Workforce Clearance Procedure (Addressable)	"Implement procedures to determine that the access of a workforce member to EPHI is appropriate."		
HIPAA 45 C.F.R. §164.308(a)(3)(ii)(C)	Termination Procedures (Addressable)	"Implement procedures for terminating access to EPHI when the employment of a workforce member ends or as required by determinations made as specified in [workforce clearance procedures]".		
HIPAA 45 C.F.R. §164.308(a)(4)(i)	Information Access Management	"Implement policies and procedures for authorizing access to EPHI that are consistent with the applicable requirements of [the Privacy Rule]."		
HIPAA 45 C.F.R. §164.308(a)(4)(ii)(B)	Access Authorization (Addressable)	"Implement policies and procedures for granting access to EPHI, for example, through access to a workstation, transaction, program, process, or other mechanism."		
HIPAA 45 C.F.R. §164.308(a)(4)(ii)(C)	Access Establishment and Modification (Addressable)	"Implement policies and procedures that, based upon the entity's access authorization policies, establish, document, review, and modify a user's right of access to a workstation, transaction, program, or process."		
HIPAA 45 C.F.R. §164.308(a)(5)(i)	Security Awareness and Training	"Implement a security awareness and training program for all members of its workforce (including management)."		

Citation	Title	Description	Safeguard Questions	Comments
HIPAA 45 C.F.R. §164.308(a)(5)(ii)(A)	Security Reminders (Addressable)	Provide periodic security updates to the workforce.		
HIPAA 45 C.F.R. §164.308(a)(5)(ii)(A)	Protection from Malicious Software (Addressable)	"Implement procedures for guarding against, detecting, and reporting malicious software."		
HIPAA 45 C.F.R. §164.308(a)(5)(ii)(B)	Log-in Monitoring (Addressable)	"Implement procedures for monitoring log-in attempts and reporting discrepancies."		
HIPAA 45 C.F.R. §164.308(a)(5)(ii)(C)	Password Management (Addressable)	"Implement procedures for creating, changing, and safeguarding passwords." Password means confidential authentication information composed of a string of characters. 45 C.F.R. §164.304.		
HIPAA 45 C.F.R. §164.308(a)(6)(i)	Security Incident Procedures	"Implement policies and procedures to address security incidents."[163]		
HIPAA 45 C.F.R. §164.308(a)(6)(ii)(A)	Response and Reporting (Required)	"Identify and respond to suspected or known security incidents; mitigate, to the extent practicable, harmful effects of security incidents that are known to the covered entity; and document security incidents and their outcomes."		
HIPAA 45 C.F.R. §164.308(a)(7)(i)	Contingency Plan	"Establish (and implement as needed) policies and procedures for responding to an emergency or other occurrence (for example, fire, vandalism, system failure, and natural disaster) that damages systems that contain EPHI."		

---

[163]Cross-reference to HITECH §13402, regarding notification of security breaches.

Citation	Title	Description	Safeguard Questions	Comments
HIPAA 45 C.F.R. §164.308(a)(7)(ii)(A)	Data Backup Plan (Required)	"Establish and implement procedures to create and maintain retrievable exact copies of EPHI."		
HIPAA 45 C.F.R. §164.308(a)(7)(ii)(B)	Disaster Recovery Plan (Required)	"Establish (and implement as needed) procedures to restore any loss of data."		
HIPAA 45 C.F.R. §164.308(a)(7)(ii)(C)	Emergency Mode Operation Plan (Required)	"Establish (and implement as needed) procedures to enable continuation of critical business processes for protection of the security of EPHI while operating in emergency mode."		
HIPAA 45 C.F.R. §164.308(a)(7)(ii)(D)	Testing and Revision Procedure (Addressable)	"Implement procedures for periodic testing and revision of contingency plans. Entities will need to determine, based on size, configuration, and security environment, how much of the plan to test and/or revise."		
HIPAA 45 C.F.R. §164.308(a)(7)(ii)(E)	Applications and Data Criticality Analysis (Addressable)	"Assess the relative criticality of specific applications and data in support of other contingency plan components."		
HIPAA 45 C.F.R. §164.308(a)(8)	Evaluation	"Perform a periodic technical and non-technical evaluation, based initially upon the standards implemented under this rule and subsequently, in response to environmental or operational changes affecting the security of EPHI, that establishes the extent to which an entity's security policies and procedures meet the [Security Rule's] requirements."		

Citation	Title	Description	Safeguard Questions	Comments
HIPAA 45 C.F.R. §164.308(b)(1)	Business Associate Contracts[164]	"A covered entity, in accordance with [45 C.F.R. §164.306], may permit a business associate to create, receive, maintain, or transmit [ePHI] on the covered entity's behalf only if the covered entity obtains satisfactory assurances, in accordance with [45 C.F.R. §164.314(a)] that the business associate will appropriately safeguard the information."		
HIPAA 45 C.F.R. §164.310	Physical Safeguards			
HIPAA 45 C.F.R. §164.310(a)(1)	Facility Access Controls	"Implement policies and procedures to limit physical access to its electronic information systems and the facility or facilities in which they are housed, while ensuring that properly authorized access is allowed."		
HIPAA 45 C.F.R. §164.310(a)(2)(i)	Contingency Operations (Addressable)	"Establish (and implement as needed) procedures that allow facility access in support of restoration of lost data under the disaster recovery plan and emergency mode operations plan in the event of an emergency."		
HIPAA 45 C.F.R. §164.310(a)(2)(ii)	Facility Security Plan (Addressable)	"Implement policies and procedures to safeguard the facility and the equipment therein from unauthorized physical access, tampering, and theft."		

---

[164] It is not clear how this requirement should be treated, since HITECH §13401(a) did not refer to 45 C.F.R. §§164.306 and 164.314. If this requirement is applicable to business associates, it appears to mean that the business associate contracts required by 45 C.F.R. §164.314(a)(2), including provisions for business associate safeguards, implementation of safeguards by business associates' subcontractors obtaining PHI, and security incident reporting and termination for business associate breach of the business associate contract, would be applied to subcontractors as if they were business associates within the meaning of the regulation.

Citation	Title	Description	Safeguard Questions	Comments
HIPAA 45 C.F.R. §164.310(a)(2)(iii)	Access Control & Validation Procedure (Addressable)	"Implement procedures to control and validate a person's access to facilities based on their role or function, including visitor control, and control of access to software programs for testing and revision."		
HIPAA 45 C.F.R. §164.310(a)(2)(iv)	Maintenance Records (Addressable)	"Implement policies and procedures to document repairs and modifications to the physical components of a facility which are related to security (for example, hardware, walls, doors, and locks)."		
HIPAA 45 C.F.R. §164.310(b)	Workstation Use (Required)	"Implement policies and procedures that specify the proper functions to be performed, the manner in which those functions are to be performed, and the physical attributes of the surroundings of a specific workstation or class of workstation that can access EPHI."		
HIPAA 45 C.F.R. §164.310(c)	Workstation Security (Required)	"Implement physical safeguards for all workstations that access EPHI, to restrict access to authorized users." Each organization must adopt physical safeguards to restrict access to information available through a workstation, as defined in 45 C.F.R. §164.304.		
HIPAA 45 C.F.R. §164.310(d)(1)	Device and Media Controls	"Implement policies and procedures that govern the receipt and removal of hardware and electronic media that contain EPHI into and out of a facility, and the movement of these items within the facility."		

Citation	Title	Description	Safeguard Questions	Comments
HIPAA 45 C.F.R. §164.310(d)(2)(i)	Disposal (Required)	"Implement policies and procedures to address the final disposition of EPHI, and/or the hardware or electronic media on which it is stored."		
HIPAA 45 C.F.R. §164.310(d)(2)(ii)	Media Re-use (Required)	"Implement procedures for removal of EPHI from electronic media before the media are made available for re-use."		
HIPAA 45 C.F.R. §164.310(d)(2)(iii)	Accountability (Addressable)	"Maintain a record of the movements of hardware and electronic media and any person responsible therefore."		
HIPAA 45 C.F.R. §164.310(d)(2)(iv)	Data Backup and Storage (Addressable)	"Create a retrievable, exact copy of EPHI, when needed, before movement of equipment."		
HIPAA 45 C.F.R. §312	Technical Safeguards			
HIPAA 45 C.F.R. §312(a)(1)	Access Control	"Implement technical policies and procedures for electronic information systems that maintain EPHI to allow access only to those persons or software programs that have been granted access rights as specified in [45 C.F.R.] §164.308(a)(4)."		
HIPAA 45 C.F.R. §312(a)(2)(i)	Unique User Identification (Required)	"Assign a unique name and/or number for identifying and tracking user identity."		
HIPAA 45 C.F.R. §312(a)(2)(ii)	Emergency Access Procedure (Required)	"Establish (and implement as needed) procedures for obtaining necessary EPHI during an emergency."[165]		

---

[165] Cross-reference to contingency planning requirements at 45 C.F.R. §164.308(a)(7)(i).

Citation	Title	Description	Safeguard Questions	Comments
HIPAA 45 C.F.R. §312(a)(2)(iii)	Automatic Logoff (Addressable)	"Implement electronic procedures that terminate an electronic session after a predetermined time of inactivity."		
HIPAA 45 C.F.R. §312(a)(2)(iv)	Encryption and Decryption (Addressable)	"Implement a mechanism to encrypt and decrypt EPHI."[166]		
HIPAA 45 C.F.R. §312(b)	Audit Controls (Required)	"Implement hardware, software, and/or procedural mechanisms that record and examine activity in information systems that contain or use EPHI."		
HIPAA 45 C.F.R. §312(c)(1)	Integrity	"Implement policies and procedures to protect EPHI from improper alteration or destruction."		
HIPAA 45 C.F.R. §312(c)(2)	Mechanism to Authenticate Electronic PHI (Addressable)	"Implement electronic mechanisms to corroborate that EPHI has not been altered or destroyed in an unauthorized manner."		
HIPAA 45 C.F.R. §312(d)	Person or Entity Authentication (Required)	"Implement procedures to verify that a person or entity seeking access to EPHI is the one claimed."		
HIPAA 45 C.F.R. §312(e)(1)	Transmission Security	"Implement technical security measures to guard against unauthorized access to EPHI that is being transmitted over an electronic communications network."		
HIPAA 45 C.F.R. §312(e)(2)(i)	Integrity Controls (Addressable)	"Implement security measures to ensure that electronically transmitted EPHI is not improperly modified without detection until disposed of."		

---

[166]Cross-reference to encryption for HITECH security breach notification purposes, HITECH §13402.

App. 7-A.   *Information Security and Breach Notification*   201

Citation	Title	Description	Safeguard Questions	Comments
HIPAA 45 C.F.R. §312(e)(2)(ii)	Encryption (Addressable)	"Implement a mechanism to encrypt EPHI whenever deemed appropriate."		
HIPAA 45 C.F.R. §164.316	Policies and Procedures and Documentation Requirements			
HIPAA 45 C.F.R. §164.316(a)	Policies and Procedures	"Implement reasonable and appropriate policies and procedures to comply with the . . . the requirements of [the HIPAA security regulations]."		
HIPAA 45 C.F.R. §164.316(b)(1)(i)		"Maintain the policies and procedures implemented to comply with [the HIPAA security regulations] in written (which may be electronic) form."		
HIPAA 45 C.F.R. §164.316(b)(1)(ii)		"If an action, activity, or assessment is required by [the HIPAA security regulations] to be documented, maintain a written (which may be electronic) record of the action, activity, or assessment."[167]		
HIPAA 45 C.F.R. §164.316(b)(2)(i)	Time Limit (Required)	Required documentation to be retained at least six years "from the date of its creation or the date when it was last in effect, whichever is later."		

---

[167]Note need for careful cross-references of documentation requirements, e.g., of user access authorization per HIPAA 45 C.F.R. §164.308(a)(4)(ii)(C), security incident response per HIPAA 45 C.F.R. §164.308(a)(6)(ii), maintenance records per HIPAA 45 C.F.R. §164.310((a)(2(iv), etc. Note also that covered entity HIPAA security safeguards determinations may include documented determinations to implement alternative safeguards for "addressable" specifications under HIPAA 45 C.F.R. §164.306(d)(ii)(3), which HITECH §13401(a) did not reference. It is not clear whether this means business associates cannot implement alternative safeguards for addressable specifications, but in any case where that approach is contemplated, appropriate documentation would be prudent.

Citation	Title	Description	Safeguard Questions	Comments
HIPAA 45 C.F.R. §164.316(b)(2)(ii)	Availability (Required)	"Make documentation available to those persons responsible for implementing the procedures to which the documentation pertains."		
HIPAA 45 C.F.R. §164.316(b)(2)(iii)	Updated (Required)	"Review documentation periodically, and update as needed, in response to environmental or operational changes affecting the security of the [ePHI]."[168]		
HITECH §13401(a)	Application of Security Provisions and Penalties to Business Associates	"The additional requirements of this title [HITECH] that relate to security and that are made applicable with respect to covered entities . . . shall be incorporated into the business associate agreement between the business associate and the covered entity."		
HITECH §13402(b)	Notification in the Case of Breach / Business Associates	"A business associate of a covered entity that accesses, maintains, retains, modifies, records, stores, destroys, or otherwise holds, uses, or discloses unsecured protected health information shall, following the discovery of a breach of such information, notify the covered entity of such breach. Such notice shall include the identification of each individual whose unsecured protected health information has been, or is reasonably believed by the business associate to have been, accessed, acquired, or disclosed during such breach."[169]		

[168]Cross-reference to safeguards evaluation requirement of HIPAA, 45 C.F.R. §164.308(a)(8).
[169]Cross-reference HIPAA Business Associate security incident reporting, 45 C.F.R. §164.308(a)(6)(ii)(A).

Citation	Title	Description	Safeguard Questions	Comments
45 C.F.R. Parts 160 and 164	Breach Notification for Unsecured Protected Health Information; Interim Final Rule			
45 C.F.R. §164.402	Definitions	Breach does not include "use or disclosure of [PHI] that does not include the identifiers listed at [45 C.F.R.] §164.514(e)(2),[170] date of birth, and zip code"		
45 C.F.R. §164.402	Definitions	Breach does not include "use of protected health information by a workforce member or person acting under the authority of a covered entity or a business associate, if such acquisition, access, or use was made in good faith and within the scope of authority and does not result in further use or disclosure in a manner not permitted under [the HIPAA privacy regulations]."[171]		
45 C.F.R. §164.402	Definitions	"Unsecured [PHI] means [PHI] that is not rendered unusable, unreadable, or indecipherable to unauthorized individuals through the use of a technology or methodology specified by the Secretary in the guidance issued under [HITECH §13402(h)(2)]."[172]		

---

[170]Reference is to HIPAA privacy regulation defining acceptable de-identification of PHI.
[171]Cross-reference to HIPAA authorization policies, 45 C.F.R. §164.308(a)(3)(ii)(A), and HITECH/HIPAA minimum necessary policies, HITECH §13405(b) and 45 C.F.R. §164.502(b) .
[172]See references below.

Citation	Title	Description	Safeguard Questions	Comments
45 C.F.R. §164.410	Notification by a Business Associate	"A breach shall be treated as discovered by a business associate as of the first day on which such breach is known to the business associate or, by exercising reasonable diligence, would have been known to the business associate. A business associate shall be deemed to have knowledge of a breach if the breach is known, or by exercising reasonable diligence would have been known, to any person, other than the person committing the breach, who is an employee, officer, or other agent of the business associate (determined in accordance with the federal common law of agency)."[173]		
HITECH §13402(h) Guidance Specifying the Technologies and Methodologies that Render Protected Health Information Unusable, Unreadable, or Indecipherable to Unauthorized Individuals	NIST Special Publication 800–111, Guide to Storage Encryption Technologies for End User Devices	Encryption standards for ePHI at rest.[174]		
HITECH §13402(h) Guidance Specifying the Technologies and Methodologies that Render Protected Health Information Unusable, Unreadable, or Indecipherable to Unauthorized Individuals	NIST Special Publications 800–52, Guidelines for the Selection and Use of Transport Layer Security (TLS) Implementations; 800–77, Guide to IPsec VPNs; or 800–113, Guide to SSL VPNs	Encryption standards for ePHI in transmission.[175]		

---

[173]Cross-reference to HIPAA security incident response, 45 C.F.R. §§164.308(a)(6)(i), 164.308(a)(6)(ii)(A), and business associate reporting, 45 C.F.R. §164.504(e)(2)(ii)(C).

[174]Cross-reference to HIPAA encryption requirement, 45 C.F.R. §164.312(a)(2)(iv).

[175]*Id.* at §164.312(e)(2)(ii).

Citation	Title	Description	Safeguard Questions	Comments
HITECH §13402(h) Guidance Specifying the Technologies and Methodologies that Render Protected Health Information Unusable, Unreadable, or Indecipherable to Unauthorized Individuals	NIST Special Publication 800–88, Guidelines for Media Sanitization	"Electronic media have been cleared, purged, or destroyed" prior to disposal so that ePHI is not recoverable.[176]		
HITECH §13402(h) Guidance Specifying the Technologies and Methodologies that Render Protected Health Information Unusable, Unreadable, or Indecipherable to Unauthorized Individuals	Paper, Other Nonelectronic Media Sanitization	"Paper, film, or other hard copy media have been shredded or destroyed such that the PHI cannot be read or otherwise cannot be reconstructed. Redaction is specifically excluded as a means of data destruction."		

---

[176]Cross-reference to HIPAA disposal requirement, 45 C.F.R. §164.310(d)(2)(ii).

8

Enforcement of the Health Insurance Portability and Accountability Act of 1996*

I. Introduction	208
II. Key HIPAA Features	210
A. Standards and Requirements	210
B. Guidance	214
C. Violations	214
III. Investigations, Breach Reports, and Audits	215
A. Complaint Process and Compliance Reviews	216
B. Breach Reports	217
C. HHS Audits of HIPAA Compliance	218
D. Voluntary Compliance and Resolution Agreements	219
IV. HIPAA Civil Monetary Penalties	220
A. In General	220
B. The Enforcement Rule	222
C. CMP Limitations and Lenience Provisions	222
D. What Is a "Violation"?	224
E. Industry-Wide HIPAA Compliance	226
F. Procedures for Imposition of Civil Monetary Penalties	227
G. Distinctive Features in the Imposition of Civil Monetary Penalties	229
1. Imposition of Penalties	229
2. Public Notice	230
3. Statistical Sampling	230

---

*Alan S. Goldberg, Attorney & Counselor-at-Law, McLean, Virginia, and Adjunct Professor of Health Law, George Mason University School of Law & American University Washington College of Law; Adam H. Greene, Partner, Davis Wright Tremaine LLP, Washington, D.C. The contributions of Daniel H. Orenstein, athenahealth, Inc., Watertown, Massachusetts, in prior versions of this chapter are acknowledged and appreciated.

    4. Liability for Violations by Agents 230
    5. Aggravating and Mitigating Factors 231
  H. Actions by State Attorneys General.. 233
 V. HIPAA Criminal Provisions... 234
  A. In General 234
  B. Intent Standard.. 236
  C. Aiding and Abetting.. 239
  D. Conspiracy 239
  E. Other Potential Theories of Indirect Criminal Liability of
    Business Associates 240
  F. Statute of Limitations 240
 VI. Enforcement Under Other Federal Statutes 241
  A. Federal Trade Commission Act 241
  B. False Claims and False Statements Statutes 242
  C. Mail and Wire Fraud 243
  D. RICO... 244
  E. HIPAA as a Standard of Care 244
 VII. State-Law Preemption... 245
 VIII. Compliance: Establishing a Plan to Avoid Enforcement Actions 247
 IX. Conclusion 249

I. Introduction

The implementation of the Administrative Simplification subtitle of the Health Insurance Portability and Accountability Act of 1996 (HIPAA)[1] has developed in stages, as proposed, final, and amended rules are published and HIPAA is amended or otherwise affected by new legislation and policies.[2] Federal legislative enactments affecting the enforcement of HIPAA have also occurred, such as Title IX of the Public Health Service Act, Section 922, as amended by the Patient Safety and Quality Improvement Act of 2005 (PSQIA),[3]

---

[1] Health Insurance Portability and Accountability Act of 1996 (HIPAA), Pub. L. No. 104-191, 110 Stat. 1936 (1996) (codified as amended at 42 U.S.C. §§1320d to 1320d-9), *available at* http://www.gpo.gov/fdsys/pkg/PLAW-104publ191/pdf/PLAW-104publ191.pdf (not including amendments).

[2] 45 C.F.R. pts. 160 to 164, *available at* http://www.gpoaccess.gov/cfr/; Dep't of Health & Human Servs., Office for Civil Rights, Privacy Rule, *available at* http://www.hhs.gov/ocr/privacy/hipaa/administrative/privacyrule/index.html; Dep't of Health & Human Servs., Office for Civil Rights, Security Rule, *available at* http://www.hhs.gov/ocr/privacy/hipaa/administrative/securityrule/; Dep't of Health & Human Servs., Office for Civil Rights, Breach Notification Rule, *available at* http://www.hhs.gov/ocr/privacy/hipaa/administrative/breachnotificationrule/index.html; Dep't of Health & Human Servs., Office for Civil Rights, HIPAA Enforcement Rule, *available at* http://www.hhs.gov/ocr/privacy/hipaa/administrative/enforcementrule/index.html.

[3] Patient Safety and Quality Improvement Act of 2005, Pub. L. No. 109-41, 119 Stat. 424 (2005), *available at* http://www.gpo.gov/fdsys/pkg/PLAW-109publ41/pdf/PLAW-109publ41.pdf; *see also* Dep't of Health & Human Servs., Office for Civil Rights, Understanding Patient Safety Confidentiality, *available at* http://www.hhs.gov/ocr/privacy/psa/understanding/index.html; *see also* Agency for Healthcare Research and Quality, Patient Safety Organizations Legislation, Regulations, and Guidance, *available at* http://www.pso.ahrq.gov/regulations/regulations.htm.

and the Genetic Information Nondiscrimination Act of 2008.[4] HIPAA was most recently amended by the Health Information Technology for Economic and Clinical Health Act (HITECH Act).[5] The HITECH Act includes provisions that amend and otherwise affect HIPAA and (in a somewhat unusual manner, in effect amend) portions of rules theretofore promulgated under HIPAA. The U.S. Department of Health and Human Services (HHS) published a proposed rule with respect to the HITECH Act in July 2010 (HITECH Act Notice of Proposed Rulemaking (NPRM)), but has not yet finalized the rule as of the date of this publication.[6] When considering enforcement of HIPAA, reference should be made to the HITECH Act and HITECH Act NPRM in addition to HIPAA.

Even before some compliance and enforcement dates occurred,[7] HIPAA's wide-ranging impact affected the entire health care industry and changed how the health care delivery system operates. Now that enforcement dates for many HIPAA rules have occurred and participants in the health care industry realize that HIPAA is here to stay, it is timely to review how HIPAA is enforced and how enforcement affects compliance. Additionally, the status of HIPAA enforcement continues to be very much in flux today, with HHS finalizing regulatory changes to enforcement pursuant to the HITECH Act, a new audit program under development, the recent imposition of the first HIPAA civil money penalty, and HHS entering into an increasing number of formal settlements involving significant settlement amounts and corrective action plans in lieu of imposing civil monetary penalties.

---

[4]Genetic Information Nondiscrimination Act of 2008 (GINA) §105, Pub. L. No. 110-233, 122 Stat. 881 (2008), *available at* http://www.gpo.gov/fdsys/pkg/PLAW-110publ233/pdf/PLAW-110publ233.pdf (codified at 42 U.S.C. §1320d-9).

[5]Health Information Technology for Economic and Clinical Health Act (HITECH Act), div. A, tit. XIII and div. B, tit. IV, Pub. L. No. 111-005, 123 Stat. 115, 226-79, 467-96 (2009), §13301 *et seq.* [hereinafter HITECH Act], *available at* http://www.gpo.gov/fdsys/pkg/PLAW-111publ5/pdf/PLAW-111publ5.pdf.

[6]Modifications to the HIPAA Privacy, Security, and Enforcement Rules Under the Health Information Technology for Economic and Clinical Health Act; Proposed Rule, 75 Fed. Reg. 40,868 (July 14, 2010).

[7]*See* United States v. Sutherland, 143 F. Supp. 2d 609 (W.D. Va. 2001), in which the court looked to HIPAA for guidance, albeit prior to the date on which the Privacy Rule (see II.A., below) was enforceable and without any determination regarding whether the defendant would have been determined to be a HIPAA covered entity had HIPAA been enforceable and applicable to the matter before the court:
> Not only have the courts recognized the importance of the privacy of medical records, but Congress has addressed the issue as well. As part of the Health Insurance Portability and Accountability Act of 1996 (HIPAA), Pub. L. No. 104-191, §§261-264, 110 Stat. 1936 (1996), Congress directed the Secretary of Health and Human Services to promulgate final regulations setting privacy standards for medical records. Pursuant to this directive, the Secretary has recently issued Standards for Privacy of Individually Identifiable Health Information (Standards), 65 Fed. Reg. 82,462 (Dec. 28, 2000) (to be codified at 45 C.F.R. pts. 160 & 164). The rules restrict and define the ability of health plans, heath care clearinghouses, and most health care providers to divulge patient medical records. Although the Standards were effective April 14, 2001, compliance was not required until April 14, 2003. *See* 66 Fed. Reg. 12,434 (Feb. 26, 2001) (to be codified at 45 C.F.R. pts. 160 & 164). Nevertheless, the Standards indicate a strong federal policy to protect the privacy of patient medical records, and they provide guidance to the present case.

Id. at 612.

This chapter will chart the developments in HIPAA enforcement thus far and address several issues that may arise in connection with HIPAA enforcement actions. Before beginning a discussion of HIPAA enforcement, a brief review of the key HIPAA requirements that are subject to enforcement is appropriate.

II. Key HIPAA Features

A. Standards and Requirements

While HIPAA addresses a number of varying areas, including the portability of health insurance, today most references to HIPAA are references to its Administrative Simplification subtitle (Title II, Subtitle F). The core feature of this subtitle is the requirement that HHS adopt national standards and requirements for use with electronic health care transactions. These required standards are set forth in a final rule entitled Standards for Electronic Transactions (Transactions Rule), promulgated on August 17, 2000.[8] The Transactions Rule, as well as the other HIPAA requirements and standards, originally applied directly to three groups within the health care industry[9] that are referred to as "covered entities." The three covered entities, more specifically defined in HIPAA and the HIPAA rules, are health plans, health care clearinghouses, and health care providers that transmit any health information in electronic form in connection with a standard transaction.[10]

---

[8]Health Insurance Reform: Standards for Electronic Transactions; Announcement of Designated Standard Maintenance Organizations; Final Rule and Notice, 65 Fed. Reg. 50,312 (Aug. 17, 2000). Note the distinctions in HIPAA rule making regarding "effective" dates (which are not necessarily dates as of which rules are enforceable) for rules that adopt HIPAA standards, and subsequent "enforcement" dates of standards rules promulgated under HIPAA, including certain delays and extensions by HHS for compliance. Note also that the Enforcement Rule (discussed in IV.B., below), *available at* http://www.hhs.gov/ocr/privacy/hipaa/administrative/enforcementrule/, is not subject to such distinctions:

The Enforcement Rule does not adopt standards, as that term is defined and interpreted under Subtitle F of Title II of HIPAA. Thus, the requirement for industry consultations in section 1172(c) of the Act [HIPAA] does not apply. For the same reason, [HIPAA's] time frames for compliance, set forth in section 1175 of the Act, do not apply to the Enforcement Rule. Accordingly, the Enforcement Rule is effective [and enforceable] on March 16, 2006.

71 Fed. Reg. 8390 (Feb. 16, 2006).

[9]Under the HITECH Act, discussed in I., above, another group, known as HIPAA business associates, was added as being directly subject to enforcement of certain provisions of HIPAA (albeit not thereby classified as covered entities), which greatly expanded the coverage of HIPAA.

[10]HIPAA §262, 42 U.S.C. §1320d-1(a). A "health plan" is defined in the Transactions Rule as "an individual or group plan that provides, or pays the cost of, medical care" (as defined in Section 2791 of the Public Health Service Act, 42 U.S.C. §300gg-91). The term includes certain group health plans, health insurance issuers, health maintenance organizations (HMOs), Medicare, Medicaid, and various other federal health programs, and long-term care policies and employee welfare benefit plans. A "health care provider" is defined as a "provider of services" (as defined in Social Security Act §1861(u), 42 U.S.C. §1395x(u)), a "provider of medical or other health services" (as defined in Section 1861(s), 42 U.S.C. §1395x(s)), and "any other person furnishing health care services or supplies." A "health care clearinghouse" is defined as "a public or private entity that processes or facilitates the processing of nonstandard data elements of health information into standard data elements." 42 U.S.C. §1320d-1. The Medicare Prescription Drug, Improvement, and Modernization Act of 2003 (MMA), Pub. L. No. 108-173 (enacted Dec. 8, 2003), added another covered entity, namely, a prescription drug card plan sponsor, which ceased being relevant when full implementation of the MMA occurred because such sponsors

The Transactions Rule requires covered entities that conduct HIPAA standard transactions electronically to conduct the transactions in the applicable standard formats mandated by the rule.[11] The initial compliance date for the Transactions Rule was October 16, 2002. However, many covered entities took advantage of a one-year statutory compliance extension until October 16, 2003, under the provisions of the Administrative Simplification Compliance Act, commonly known as ASCA.[12]

HIPAA also requires that covered entities have privacy practices and procedures in place to safeguard the privacy of individually identifiable health information[13] and security practices and procedures to protect the security of such information.[14] The final rule implementing the privacy requirements of HIPAA was promulgated on December 28, 2000,[15] and subsequently modified on August 14, 2002[16] (jointly, the Privacy Rule). The purpose of the Privacy Rule is to prevent the improper use and disclosure of certain individually identifiable health information, known as protected health information (PHI), and to provide individuals with certain rights with respect to their PHI.[17] The compliance date for the Privacy Rule for most covered entities was April 14, 2003, with a delayed compliance date of April 14, 2004, for small health plans.[18]

A final security rule (Security Rule) was promulgated on February 20, 2003, with a compliance date for covered entities of April 20, 2005, and a

---

were replaced by sponsors of Part D drug plans (see Part D Plan Sponsor, 42 C.F.R. §423.4 and Part D Plan, 42 C.F.R. §423.4), but obligations imposed upon those classified as such other covered entity continue under HIPAA. An alphabetized glossary of HIPAA-defined terms is provided as Appendix D to this book and on the accompanying CD-ROM.

[11]45 C.F.R. §162.923(a). Note that the Transactions Rule does not require such electronic transactions, although other laws may require certain health care transactions to occur electronically, and in general covered entities that are health plans must accept standard transactions transmitted electronically.

[12]Administrative Simplification Compliance Act, Pub. L. No. 107-105, 115 Stat. 1003 (2001) (*available at* 42 U.S.C. §1320d-4 note).

[13]HIPAA §264 (*available at* 42 U.S.C. §1320d-2 note). The privacy provision of HIPAA at Section 264 did not specifically add new provisions to the consolidated text of the Social Security Act, as did Sections 1171 through 1179 of HIPAA. Instead, the statutory reference "42 U.S.C. §1320d-2 note" commonly is used to cite the portion of HIPAA and the Social Security Act under which the Privacy Rule was promulgated. See Section 105(a) of GINA 2008, 42 U.S.C. §1320d-9, for an example of such citation: "(3) HIPAA PRIVACY REGULATION.—The term 'HIPAA privacy regulation' means the regulations promulgated by the Secretary under this part and section 264 of the Health Insurance Portability and Accountability Act of 1996 (42 U.S.C. 1320d–2 note)."

[14]42 U.S.C. §1320d-2(d).

[15]Standards for Privacy of Individually Identifiable Health Information; Final Rule, 65 Fed. Reg. 82,462 (Dec. 28, 2000).

[16]Standards for Privacy of Individually Identifiable Health Information; Final Rule, 67 Fed. Reg. 53,182 (Aug. 14, 2002). Portions of the Privacy Rule are affected by the HITECH Act, Pub. L. No. 111-05, 123 Stat. 115, 226-79, 467-96 (2009), §13301 *et seq.* See I., above.

[17]Note that the Privacy Rule requires that certain security requirements be met both for PHI that is non-electronic and for PHI that is electronic (some refer to that portion of the Privacy Rule as a "mini-security rule"), as distinguished from the Security Rule, which imposes requirements that have to be met only for electronic PHI. Portions of the Security Rule are affected by the HITECH Act. Note also that under the HITECH Act, business associates will be required to implement certain HIPAA-related practices and procedures.

[18]45 C.F.R. §164.534.

delayed compliance date of April 20, 2006, for small health plans.[19] While the Privacy Rule governs all PHI, the Security Rule is limited to electronic PHI.[20]

HIPAA also requires the development of electronic signature standards and national identifiers for covered individuals, employers, health plans, and health care providers. A rule establishing employer identifier standards was promulgated on May 31, 2002, with an initial compliance date of July 30, 2004, and a delayed compliance date of July 30, 2005, for small health plans.[21] A rule establishing national provider identifier standards (NPI Rule) was promulgated on January 23, 2004, with an initial compliance date of May 23, 2007, and a delayed compliance date of May 23, 2008, for small health plans.[22] The development of other standards and identifiers is pending.

The HITECH Act additionally requires HHS to promulgate regulations requiring covered entities and business associates to report breaches of PHI.[23] HHS promulgated an interim final rule on August 24, 2009 (Breach Notification Rule), which included a compliance date of September 23, 2009.[24] In the event of a breach of unsecured PHI, the Breach Notification Rule requires covered entities to notify the individuals who are the subject of the PHI, to notify the media if the breach involves more than 500 residents of a state or jurisdiction, and to file a breach report with HHS.[25] The Breach Notification Rule also requires business associates to notify covered entities of breaches of unsecured PHI.[26] HHS indicated in the preamble of the Breach Notification Rule that it would not seek enforcement of the new rule for 180 days from the date of publication of the rule (i.e., until February 22, 2010). A noninterim final breach notification rule is expected at the same time that the rule contemplated by the HITECH Act NPRM is promulgated in final form.

The HITECH Act also, for the first time, makes business associates of covered entities directly liable for violations of the HIPAA rules and subject to federal government enforcement under HIPAA.[27] As referenced above, the Breach Notification Rule directly requires a business associate to notify a covered entity of a breach of unsecured PHI.[28] The HITECH Act also provides that business

---

[19]Health Insurance Reform: Security Standards; Final Rule, 68 Fed. Reg. 8334 (Feb. 20, 2003), available at http://www.hhs.gov/ocr/privacy/hipaa/administrative/securityrule/securityrulepdf.pdf.

[20]45 C.F.R. §164.302.

[21]Health Insurance Reform: Standard Unique Employer Identifier, 67 Fed. Reg. 38,009 (May 31, 2002).

[22]HIPAA Administrative Simplification: Standard Unique Health Identifier for Health Care Providers; Final Rule, 69 Fed. Reg. 3434 (Jan. 23, 2004).

[23]HITECH Act §13402 (codified at 42 U.S.C. §17932).

[24]Breach Notification for Unsecured Protected Health Information; Interim Final Rule, 74 Fed. Reg. 42,740 (Aug. 24, 2009).

[25]45 C.F.R. §§164.404, .406, .408. Pursuant to the HITECH Act, the HHS Office for Civil Rights has issued guidance on when PHI is treated as unsecured, available at http://www.hhs.gov/ocr/privacy/hipaa/administrative/breachnotificationrule/brguidance.html.

[26]45 C.F.R. §164.410.

[27]HITECH Act §§13401, 13402, 13404.

[28]45 C.F.R. §164.410.

associates are required to comply with certain provisions of the HIPAA Privacy and Security Rules commencing February 17, 2010.[29]

In the HITECH Act NPRM, HHS proposed to apply all requirements of the Security Rule to business associates.[30] In contrast, the proposal would make business associates subject to only some provisions of the Privacy Rule. Specifically, business associates would be directly liable for impermissible uses and disclosures, failures to facilitate individuals' electronic access to their PHI, and failures to provide HHS with PHI upon request (for purposes of HHS' enforcement of the HIPAA rules).[31] HHS has indicated that it will not seek to hold business associates directly liable for the Security Rule and portions of the Privacy Rule until the amendments to the HIPAA regulations are finalized.[32] HHS' decision to delay enforcement of the Privacy and Security Rules on business associates is not likely to bind other agencies with authority to enforce HIPAA (specifically, the Department of Justice with respect to potential criminal violations and the state attorneys general to whom the HITECH Act granted concurrent civil enforcement authority).

Several lawsuits aimed at invalidating HIPAA, on constitutional and other grounds, have been unsuccessful.[33]

The Privacy, Security, and Breach Notification Rules are administered and enforced by the HHS Office for Civil Rights (OCR).[34] The Security Rule was previously delegated to the Centers for Medicare & Medicaid Services (CMS).[35] The remainder of the HIPAA administrative simplification rules, such as the Transactions Rule, are administered and enforced by CMS (and it is interesting to note that CMS, as a health care component of a covered entity, is subject to OCR's enforcement authority, albeit with such authority apparently never yet exercised).[36]

---

[29] HITECH Act §§13401, 13404.

[30] 75 Fed. Reg. 40,868, 40,917–18 (July 14, 2010).

[31] *Id.* at 40,919.

[32] Dep't of Health & Human Servs., Office for Civil Rights, HITECH Act Rulemaking and Implementation Update, *available at* http://www.hhs.gov/ocr/privacy/hipaa/understanding/coveredentities/hitechblurb.html.

[33] *See, e.g.*, South Carolina Med. Ass'n v. Thompson, 327 F.3d 346 (4th Cir. 2003) (holding that HIPAA did not improperly delegate authority to HHS, that the exercise of regulatory authority was within the scope of authority granted by Congress, and that the statute and regulations are not impermissibly vague); Association of Am. Physicians & Surgeons, Inc. v. Department of Health & Human Servs., 224 F. Supp. 2d 1115 (S.D. Tex. 2002) (holding that HIPAA does not violate the Commerce Clause, that the exercise of regulatory authority by HHS was within the scope of HIPAA, and that the Privacy Rule does not violate the Regulatory Flexibility Act or the Paperwork Reduction Act); *see also* Complaint for Declaratory and Injunctive Relief, Citizens for Health v. Thompson, No. Civ. A. 03-2267, 2004 WL 765356 (E.D. Pa. Apr. 2, 2004) (defendant HHS's motion for summary judgment granted in suit requesting restoration of consent requirement in Privacy Rule removed in modifications to Rule published Aug. 14, 2002), *cert. denied*, 127 S. Ct. 43 (2006).

[34] Office for Civil Rights; Statement of Delegation of Authority, 65 Fed. Reg. 82,381 (Dec. 28, 2000) (delegating to OCR authority with respect to the Privacy Rule); Office for Civil Rights Delegation of Authority, 74 Fed. Reg. 38,630 (Aug. 4, 2009) (delegating to OCR authority with respect to the Security Rule).

[35] Statement of Organization, Functions, and Delegations of Authority, 68 Fed. Reg. 60,694 (Oct. 23, 2003) (delegating to CMS authority with respect to all of the HIPAA administrative simplification rules other than the Privacy Rule).

[36] *Id.*

B. Guidance

In addition to the HIPAA statute and implementing rules, HHS has published guidance documents, answers to "frequently asked questions," and many other educational materials.[37] While these informal releases may be helpful in confirming or rejecting some interpretations of HIPAA requirements and standards, they should not be relied on as legally binding guidance or definitive interpretations.[38] The U.S. Supreme Court has held that informal agency interpretations of statutes and rules are not entitled to judicial deference under the so-called *Chevron* standard, unless Congress delegates the authority to make such interpretations with the intent that they will be legally binding and the procedures for formulating such interpretations are sufficiently formalized and consistent as to have the force of law.[39] The interpretive material published by HHS does not appear to be the type of agency interpretation that would merit judicial deference under the *Chevron* standard as contemplated in the *United States v. Mead Corp.* decision.[40] However, courts may well give deference to interpretations of HIPAA and the HIPAA rules by HHS even absent clear congressional intent. Although these interpretations would not be binding in court proceedings, they could constitute persuasive authority in arguing for a particular interpretation of the HIPAA requirements and standards.

C. Violations

Violations of HIPAA requirements and standards imposed on covered entities, and pursuant to the HITECH Act on business associates, are subject to HHS civil enforcement under the HIPAA civil monetary penalty provisions (HIPAA CMP Provisions). The HITECH Act also provides state attorneys general with authority to enforce the HIPAA CMP Provisions.[41] Certain violations of HIPAA may also be punished under the HIPAA criminal enforcement provisions (HIPAA Criminal Provisions).[42] As discussed below in Section VI., there is also a potential for enforcement of HIPAA violations under other federal statutes.

A multitude of judicial decisions have confirmed that there is no private right of action under HIPAA. In an appeal from the U.S. District Court for the

---

[37] *See* Dep't of Health & Human Servs., Office for Civil Rights, Health Information Privacy, *available at* http://www.hhs.gov/ocr/hipaa/; Dep't of Health & Human Servs., Centers for Medicare & Medicaid Servs., Educational Materials Overview (Dec. 14, 2005), *available at* http://www.cms.gov/EducationMaterials/.

[38] *See, e.g.,* U.S. Food and Drug Administration, Guidances (Aug. 13, 2010), *available at* http://www.fda.gov/RegulatoryInformation/Guidances/default.htm.

[39] United States v. Mead Corp., 533 U.S. 218 (2001). The *Chevron* standard of judicial deference, established in *Chevron U.S.A. Inc. v. Natural Resources Defense Council, Inc.*, 467 U.S. 837 (1984), provides that regulations of a federal agency established pursuant to valid delegated authority are binding in court unless procedurally defective, arbitrary, or capricious in substance or manifestly contrary to the statute.

[40] *Id.*

[41] HITECH Act §13410(e) (codified at 42 U.S.C. §1320d-5(d)).

[42] 42 U.S.C. §§1320d-5, 1320d-6. Portions of the HIPAA CMP Provisions and the HIPAA Criminal Provisions are affected by the HITECH Act, Pub. L. No. 111-005, 123 Stat. 115, 226-79, 467-96 (2009), §13301 *et seq.*

Eastern District of Louisiana, the Fifth Circuit held that "there is no private cause of action under HIPAA and therefore no federal subject matter jurisdiction over [a private party's] asserted claims."[43] Nevertheless, from time to time and incorrectly, the public media and others (including some covered entities) allege or suggest that someone or some entity has "violated HIPAA" without acknowledging that, under applicable law, only the federal government, acting by and through CMS or OCR or the U.S. Department of Justice, and now state attorneys general, can enforce HIPAA. In any event, allegations by governmental authorities and anyone else are just that: allegations, with respect to which alleged violators have many opportunities to mount a defense before any final administrative or judicial determination regarding alleged violations can occur.

To date, HHS has only formally found one covered entity to have violated HIPAA,[44] and only a few individuals have been convicted of, or pleaded guilty to, criminally violating HIPAA.[45]

III. INVESTIGATIONS, BREACH REPORTS, AND AUDITS

HHS announced in 2003 that HHS civil enforcement activities would be subject to two principles: HHS would encourage voluntary compliance as much as possible, and enforcement actions would be complaint-driven.[46] HHS indicated a willingness to seek the cooperation of covered entities to achieve compliance and to provide technical assistance to help covered entities comply.[47] Accordingly, HHS' enforcement actions under HIPAA primarily have been

---

[43] Acara v. Banks, 470 F.3d 569, 572 (5th Cir. 2006).

[44] Press Release, Dep't of Health & Human Servs., *HHS imposes a $4.3 million civil money penalty for violations of the HIPAA Privacy Rule* (Feb. 22, 2011), *available at* http://www.hhs.gov/news/press/2011pres/02/20110222a.html.

[45] *See, e.g.*, Press Release, United States Attorney's Office, W.D. Pa., *Former UPMC Shadyside Hospital Employee Pleads Guilty To HIPAA Violation* (June 30, 2011), *available at* http://www.justice.gov/usao/paw/news/2011/2011_june/2011_06_30_03.html; Press Release, U.S. Attorney's Office, C.D. Cal., *Ex-UCLA Healthcare Employee Sentenced to Federal Prison for Illegally Peeking at Patient Records* (Apr. 27, 2010), *available at* http://www.justice.gov/usao/cac/pressroom/pr2010/079.html.

[46] *See* Dep't of Health & Human Servs., Office for Civil Rights, Protecting the Privacy of Patients' Information (Apr. 14, 2003), *available at* http://www.hhs.gov/ocr/privacy/hipaa/news/2003/privacyfactsapril03.pdf:
   Complaint investigations. Enforcement will be primarily complaint-driven. OCR will investigate complaints and work to make sure that consumers receive the privacy rights and protections required under the new regulations. When appropriate, OCR can impose civil monetary penalties for violations of the privacy rule provisions. Potential criminal violations of the law would be referred to the U.S. Department of Justice for further investigation and appropriate action.

[47] 45 C.F.R. §160.304 sets forth the following:
Principles for achieving compliance.
(a) *Cooperation*. The Secretary will, to the extent practicable, seek the cooperation of covered entities in obtaining compliance with the applicable requirements of this part 160 and the applicable standards, requirements, and implementation specifications of subpart E of part 164 of this subchapter.
(b) *Assistance*. The Secretary may provide technical assistance to covered entities to help them comply voluntarily with the applicable requirements of this part 160 or the applicable standards, requirements, and implementation specifications of subpart E of part 164 of this subchapter.

complaint driven[48] or have been based on the receipt of reports of large breaches of PHI (involving the PHI of 500 or more individuals). However, HHS still has the option of undertaking a HIPAA compliance review at any time.[49] Additionally, there have been several rounds of audits of covered entities regarding Security Rule compliance, and HHS is in the process of preparing a significantly larger round of audits regarding compliance with the Privacy, Security, and possibly Breach Notification Rules. With the enactment of the HITECH Act, and as evidenced by several recent public statements of OCR staff, albeit unofficially, it now appears that HIPAA enforcement efforts are being increased and enhanced.

A. Complaint Process and Compliance Reviews

The HIPAA rules permit any person—whether covered by or protected under HIPAA or otherwise (and likely including illegal aliens, persons located abroad, incarcerated individuals, and minors)—to file a complaint with HHS alleging a violation of the HIPAA requirements, regardless of whether the complainant is or is not in any way involved in the circumstances relating to the complaint.[50] A valid complaint must be filed within 180 days following the date on which the complainant knew or should have known of the alleged HIPAA violation (subject to extension of such period by OCR if "good cause" exists).[51] The complaint also must:

- be filed in writing, either on paper or electronically;
- indicate the name of the alleged violator that is the subject of the complaint;
- describe the acts or omissions that allegedly violate HIPAA requirements; and
- comply with any additional filing procedures imposed by HHS.[52]

HHS may, but is not obligated to, take action on a complaint, including beginning an investigation of the subject covered entity's policies, procedures, or practices and the circumstances surrounding the alleged HIPAA violation.[53]

Investigations are handled by OCR's 10 regional offices and are generally assigned based on the location of the covered entity. If OCR accepts a complaint for investigation, the OCR regional office will notify the person who filed the complaint and the covered entity named in it.[54] Then the complainant and the

---

[48]*See* Dep't of Health & Human Servs., Office for Civil Rights, Enforcement Highlights, *available at* http://www.hhs.gov/ocr/privacy/hipaa/enforcement/highlights/index.html.

[49]45 C.F.R. §160.308; *see* HITECH Act §13411 for new provisions relative to mandatory periodic audits.

[50]45 C.F.R. §160.306; *see also* Dep't of Health & Human Servs., Centers for Medicare & Medicare Servs., Procedures for Non-Privacy Administrative Simplification Complaints Under the Health Insurance Portability and Accountability Act of 1996, 70 Fed. Reg. 15,329 (Mar. 25, 2005).

[51]45 C.F.R. §160.306(b)(3).

[52]*Id.* at §160.306(b) *see also* Dep't of Health & Human Servs., Office for Civil Rights, How to File a Complaint, *available at* http://www.hhs.gov/ocr/privacy/hipaa/complaints/index.html.

[53]45 C.F.R. §160.306(c).

[54]Dep't of Health & Human Servs., Office for Civil Rights, How OCR Enforces the Privacy Rule, *available at* http://www.hhs.gov/ocr/privacy/hipaa/enforcement/process/howocrenforces.html.

covered entity are asked to present information about the incident or problem described in the complaint. OCR may request specific information from each to get an understanding of the facts. Covered entities are required by law to cooperate with complaint investigations.[55] OCR also has the authority to issue administrative subpoenas requiring the attendance and testimony of witnesses and the production of evidence.[56]

As of May 31, 2011, OCR had received 61,333 Privacy Rule complaints, of which OCR had resolved 55,858 (91 percent).[57]

A covered entity that becomes the subject of an investigation must cooperate by permitting HHS access, during normal business hours, to the covered entity's facilities, books, records, accounts, and other sources of information.[58] In extraordinary circumstances, including when HHS has reason to believe that documents have been hidden or destroyed, a covered entity must permit access at any time and without notice.[59] If HHS requires information that is in the exclusive possession of a third-party agency, institution, or person, and the third party refuses to provide the information, the covered entity must certify this fact to HHS and describe the efforts made to obtain the information.[60]

HHS may also initiate a HIPAA compliance review of a covered entity without the necessity of a complaint having been filed.[61] A compliance review may occur when a potential violation of HIPAA comes to HHS's attention, such as through media reports. The compliance review generally follows the same investigative process of a complaint-driven investigation.[62]

The Enforcement Rule provides that a covered entity may not threaten, intimidate, coerce, discriminate against, or take any other retaliatory action against any individual or person for (1) filing a HIPAA complaint; (2) testifying, assisting, or participating in an investigation, compliance review, proceeding, or hearing; or (3) opposing any act or practice prohibited by HIPAA.[63]

B. Breach Reports

Since September 23, 2009, covered entities have been required to report breaches of unsecured PHI to OCR.[64] Covered entities must report breaches involving 500 or more individuals to OCR without unreasonable delay and in

---

[55] 45 C.F.R. §160.310.

[56] 72 Fed. Reg. 18,999 (Apr. 16, 2007).

[57] Dep't of Health & Human Servs., Office for Civil Rights, Enforcement Highlights, *available at* http://www.hhs.gov/ocr/privacy/hipaa/enforcement/highlights/index.html.

[58] 45 C.F.R. §160.310(c)(1). A covered entity's business associate must also agree (most commonly in a business associate agreement) to make the business associate's internal practices, books, and records available to HHS for purposes of determining the covered entity's compliance. *Id.* §164.504(e)(2)(ii)(H).

[59] *Id.* §160.310(c)(1).

[60] *Id.* §160.310(c)(2).

[61] *Id.* §160.308.

[62] *See, e.g., id.* §§160.310, .312, .314.

[63] *See id.* §160.316.

[64] 74 Fed. Reg. 42,740 (Aug. 24, 2009).

no case later than 60 calendar days after discovery of the breach.[65] As required by the HITECH Act, OCR posts information regarding these large breaches on the OCR Web site.[66] Covered entities must also report smaller breaches of unsecured PHI to OCR, but may wait until 60 days after the end of the calendar year before reporting all such smaller breaches,[67] and such breaches are not posted on the OCR Web site.

As of July 2011, OCR has posted 288 large breaches involving over 11 million individuals.[68] The largest cause of reported large breaches was theft (mostly involving laptops), and more reported large breaches involved paper records than any other type of media (although large breaches involving paper records did not tend to affect nearly as many individuals as other types of breaches, such as those involving electronic PHI).[69] Additionally, as of April 2011, OCR has received more than 31,000 reports of breaches affecting fewer than 500 individuals.[70] OCR has indicated that OCR's regions verify and investigate all reported large breaches, while the decision as to whether to investigate smaller breaches is left to each region's discretion.[71]

C. HHS Audits of HIPAA Compliance

HHS has conducted several rounds of audits of covered entities' compliance with HIPAA. The first audits were conducted by the HHS Office of Inspector General (OIG) between 2007 and 2010.[72] OIG audited seven hospitals in order to assess CMS's oversight of the Security Rule. These audits found numerous internal control weaknesses and demonstrated to OIG a need for greater oversight of the Security Rule.[73]

Additionally, CMS conducted two rounds of audits of covered entities' compliance with the Security Rule. The first audit, in 2008, reviewed 10 cov-

---

[65] 45 C.F.R. §164.408(b).

[66] HITECH Act §13402(e)(4) (codified at 42 U.S.C. §17,932(e)(4)).

[67] 45 C.F.R. §164.408(c).

[68] *See* Dep't of Health & Human Servs., Office for Civil Rights, Breaches Affecting 500 or More Individuals, *available at* http://www.hhs.gov/ocr/privacy/hipaa/administrative/breachnotificationrule/breachtool.html.

[69] *Id.*

[70] Sue McAndrew, Deputy Director of Privacy, Dep't of Health & Human Servs., Office for Civil Rights, Presentation at the NIST/OCR HIPAA Security Assurance Conference: Health Information Security Rule Trends in Enforcement (May 11, 2011), *available at* http://csrc.nist.gov/news_events/HIPAA-May2011_workshop/presentations/day2_HIPAA-conference2011-OCR-Enforcement-Activities.pdf.

[71] *See* Dep't of Health & Human Servs., Office for Civil Rights, Fiscal Year 2012 Justification of Estimates for Appropriations Committee 5, *available at* http://www.hhs.gov/about/FY2012budget/ocr_cj_fy2012.pdf.

[72] Dep't of Health & Human Servs., Office of Inspector General, A-04-08-0569, Nationwide Rollup Review of the Centers for Medicare & Medicaid Services Health Insurance Portability and Accountability Act of 1996 Oversight App. A (2011), *available at* http://oig.hhs.gov/oas/reports/region4/40805069.pdf; Dep't of Health & Human Servs., Office of Inspector General, A-04-07-05064, Nationwide Review of the Centers for Medicare & Medicaid Services Health Insurance Portability and Accountability Act of 1996 Oversight, at 5 (2008), *available at* http://oig.hhs.gov/oas/reports/region4/40705064.pdf.

[73] OIG Report A-04-07-05064, at 2.

ered entities that had complaints filed against them, were identified in the media as potentially violating the Security Rule, or were recommended by OCR.[74] In 2009, CMS scheduled a review of an additional six covered entities, this time not limiting CMS's selection to entities with filed complaints.[75]

The HITECH Act requires HHS to conduct periodic audits to ensure that covered entities and business associates comply with the HIPAA rules.[76] These audits are expected to take place in 2012. It is unclear at this time whether the audits will encompass compliance with the Breach Notification Rule in addition to the Privacy and Security Rules. Additionally, while OIG's and CMS's past audits of the Security Rule apparently were used for educational purposes regarding the state of compliance, it is not yet clear whether the privacy and security audits that will be conducted pursuant to the HITECH Act will lead to HHS taking enforcement actions when apparent violations are found.

D. Voluntary Compliance and Resolution Agreements

Following a complaint investigation or compliance review in which HHS finds indications of noncompliance with HIPAA, HHS will attempt to resolve the matter by informal means.[77] Of note, HHS proposes in the HITECH Act NPRM to provide itself with more discretion in this area by proposing that HHS "may," rather than "shall," seek to resolve indications of noncompliance by informal means.[78]

In most cases involving indications of noncompliance with HIPAA (over 13,000 cases as of May 2011), HHS closes the case after a covered entity demonstrates voluntary compliance.[79] In a few cases (six as of July 2011), HHS has settled the case through a more formal resolution agreement.[80]

Resolution agreements neither represent formal findings by HHS of a violation of HIPAA nor represent admissions of liability by the covered entities.[81] Each resolution agreement has involved a payment to the government, ranging from $35,000 to $2.25 million.[82] Resolution agreements also include detailed corrective action plans. Each corrective action plan requires the updating and distribution of policies and procedures, with certain minimum content based on the issues that gave rise to investigation or compliance review, appropriate

---

[74]*Id.* at ii.

[75]*Id.*

[76]HITECH Act §13411 (codified at 42 U.S.C. §17940).

[77]45 C.F.R. §160.312(a).

[78]75 Fed. Reg. 40,914 (July 14, 2010) (proposed 45 C.F.R. §160.312(a)(1)).

[79]Dep't of Health & Human Servs., Office for Civil Rights, Enforcement Highlights (Aug. 31, 2011), *available at* http://www.hhs.gov/ocr/privacy/hipaa/enforcement/highlights/index.html.

[80]Dep't of Health & Human Servs., Office for Civil Rights, Case Examples and Resolution Agreements, *available at* http://www.hhs.gov/ocr/privacy/hipaa/enforcement/examples/index.html.

[81]*See, e.g.*, Dep't of Health & Human Servs., Office for Civil Rights, Resolution Agreement with CVS Pharmacy, Inc., (Jan. 16, 2009), *available at* http://www.hhs.gov/ocr/privacy/hipaa/enforcement/examples/cvsresagrcap.pdf.

[82]*See id.*; Dep't of Health & Human Servs., Office for Civil Rights, Resolution Agreement with Management Services Organization Washington, Inc. (MSO) (Dec. 13, 2010), *available at* http://www.hhs.gov/ocr/privacy/hipaa/enforcement/examples/msoresultionagreement.pdf.

training of members of the workforce, and some level of monitoring.[83] Some corrective action plans require the use of an external monitor, while others permit internal monitoring.[84] Corrective action plans have typically been for a term of three years, although one has a two-year term.[85]

For the first five years that covered entities were required to comply with the Privacy Rule, HHS resolved all indications of noncompliance through voluntary compliance without seeking any financial payment or ongoing corrective action plan. After the HITECH Act, between July 2010 and July 2011, HHS settled four matters with resolution agreements and corrective action plans.[86] Accordingly, it appears that HHS is in the midst of significantly increasing enforcement of the HIPAA rules through an increasing number of cases in which covered entities pay substantial settlement amounts and enter into formal corrective action plans. Nevertheless, HHS continues to close the vast majority of complaint investigations and compliance reviews through voluntary compliance at this time (without a formal resolution agreement).

IV. HIPAA Civil Monetary Penalties

A. In General

When an investigation or compliance review indicates noncompliance with HIPAA and is not informally resolved, HHS may seek to impose a civil monetary penalty. OCR has authority to impose a civil monetary penalty with respect to the Privacy Rule, Breach Notification Rule, and, as of July 2009, the Security Rule provisions, and CMS is responsible for enforcing the Transactions Rule and certain other HIPAA rules.[87] As discussed below, state attorneys general now also have authority civilly to enforce all of the HIPAA rules. Criminal enforcement of HIPAA, in contrast, solely is the responsibility of the U.S. Department of Justice.

HIPAA originally authorized HHS to impose civil monetary penalties of up to $100 per violation for violations of any of the HIPAA requirements, with the total amount imposed with respect to violations of an identical requirement or prohibition in any calendar year not to exceed $25,000. The HITECH Act provides that for violations occurring after February 17, 2009 (the day on which the HITECH Act became law), substantially increased magnitudes of civil

---

[83] *See, e.g.*, Resolution Agreement with CVS Pharmacy, Inc.

[84] *See, e.g.*, Dep't of Health & Human Servs., Office for Civil Rights, Case Examples and Resolution Agreements, *available at* http://www.hhs.gov/ocr/privacy/hipaa/enforcement/examples/index.html.

[85] The corrective action plan with MSO was for two years, while all other corrective action plans have been for three years. Resolution Agreement with Management Services Organization Washington, Inc. (MSO).

[86] *See* Case Examples and Resolution Agreements.

[87] Dep't of Health & Human Servs., Office for Civil Rights, Statement of Delegation of Authority, 65 Fed. Reg. 82,381 (Dec. 28, 2000); Dep't of Health & Human Servs., Office for Civil Rights, Delegation of Authority, 74 Fed. Reg. 38,630 (Aug. 4, 2009); Statement of Organization, Functions, and Delegations of Authority, 68 Fed. Reg. 60,694 (Oct. 23, 2003).

monetary penalties can be imposed, in accordance with new tiered increases in amounts for violations of each of the HIPAA CMP provisions:

(1) in the case of a violation of such provision in which it is established that the person did not know and by exercising reasonable diligence would not have known that such person violated such provision, a penalty for each amount of such violation of an amount that is at least [$100 but not to exceed $50,000] except that the total amount imposed on the person for all such violations of an identical requirement or prohibition during a calendar year may not exceed $25,000;

(2) in the case of a violation of such provision in which it is established that the violation was due to reasonable cause and not to willful neglect, a penalty for each such violation of an amount that is at least [$1,000 but not to exceed $50,000] except that the total amount imposed on the person for all such violations of an identical requirement or prohibition during a calendar year may not exceed $100,000;

(3) in the case of a violation of such provision in which it is established that the violation was due to willful neglect—

(a) if the violation is corrected as described in subsection (b)(3)(A), a penalty in an amount that is least [$10,000 but not to exceed $50,000] except that the total amount imposed on the person for all such violations of an identical requirement or prohibition during a calendar year may not exceed $250,000, and

(b) if the violation is not corrected as described in such subsection, a penalty in the amount at least [$50,000] . . . except that the total amount imposed on the person for all such violations of an identical requirement or prohibition during a calendar year may not exceed $1,500,000.[88]

The above statutory language created some confusion, such as how a single violation under paragraph (A) could be penalized up to $50,000 but multiple violations of an identical violation could not exceed $25,000. HHS clarified this in an interim final rule amending the Enforcement Rule, interpreting the HITECH Act as applying the $1,500,000 calendar year limit on all tiers of violations.[89]

The HITECH Act additionally provides state attorneys general with new authority to enforce HIPAA enforcement provisions as parens patriae who may bring an action in a U.S. district court seeking to enjoin HIPAA violations or to obtain damages.[90] The state attorneys general are limited to obtaining damages of $100 per violation, with the total amount of all violations of an identical requirement or prohibition during a calendar year not to exceed $25,000.[91]

The HITECH Act's substantial changes to the HIPAA CMP provisions, however, suggest that HHS and other government enforcement activities may expand and increase substantially.

---

[88] HITECH Act §13410(d) (codified at 42 U.S.C. §1320d-5(a)(1)).
[89] 74 Fed. Reg. 56,123 (Oct. 30, 2009).
[90] HITECH Act §13410(e) (codified at 42 U.S.C. §1320d-5(d)).
[91] Id. (codified at 42 U.S.C. §1320d-5(d)(2)).

B. The Enforcement Rule

HHS adopted procedures for imposing civil monetary penalties, including rules governing hearing and appeal rights, in a Final Rule adopted on February 16, 2006 (the Enforcement Rule).[92]

The Enforcement Rule applies to complaints and investigations regarding any HIPAA standard or requirement, and not just those contained in the Privacy Rule.[93] This broader scope is reflected in the Enforcement Rule's defined term "administrative simplification provision," which applies to "any requirement or prohibition" contained in the HIPAA law or regulations.[94]

Most HIPAA enforcement activity has been initiated under the HIPAA CMP Provisions administered by HHS, and more particularly, under the Privacy Rule administered by OCR. In this regard, most covered entities facing HIPAA enforcement activity are encouraged to achieve compliance, even during the time of any investigatory proceeding or adjudicatory hearing, rather than being threatened with severe penalties to force compliance. However, neither these generally stated OCR enforcement principles nor the lenience provisions in the HIPAA CMP Provisions, discussed in IV.C., below, apply to the HIPAA Criminal Provisions or to enforcement of violations of HIPAA under provisions of federal laws other than HIPAA. It is uncertain whether or how the lenience provisions or other HIPAA CMP Provisions affect the bringing of actions by state attorneys general under the HITECH Act.[95]

C. CMP Limitations and Lenience Provisions

In enacting the HIPAA CMP provisions, Congress took the unusual approach of including several potentially exonerating provisions for covered entities, making HIPAA compliance less onerous and severe enforcement less likely.[96] More specifically, originally HIPAA did not allow a civil monetary penalty to be imposed on a person if:

---

[92]HIPAA Administrative Simplification: Enforcement; Final Rule, 71 Fed. Reg. 8,390 (Feb. 16, 2006). The term "Enforcement Rule," as used in this chapter, also refers to provisions promulgated in an Interim Final Rule adopted in April 2003. Civil Money Penalties: Procedures for Investigations, Imposition of Penalties, and Hearings, 68 Fed. Reg. 18,895 (Apr. 17, 2003). Note that

> [t]he Enforcement Rule does not adopt standards, as that term is defined and interpreted under Subtitle F of Title II of HIPAA. Thus, the requirement for industry consultations in section 1172(c) of the Act does not apply. For the same reason, the statute's time frames for compliance, set forth in section 1175 of the Act, do not apply to the Enforcement Rule. Accordingly, the Enforcement Rule is effective [that is, enforceable] on March 16, 2006.

71 Fed. Reg. at 8392.

[93]45 C.F.R. §160.300.

[94]*Id.* at §160.302.

[95]HITECH Act §13410(e) (codified at 42 U.S.C. §1320d-5(d)).

[96]Note that in enacting the Genetic Information Nondiscrimination Act of 2008 (GINA), Congress included lenience provisions similar to the original HIPAA lenience provisions. See II.A., above. But such lenience provisions under GINA appear not to be affected by the lenience provisions changes under HIPAA effected by the HITECH Act.

- the act constituted an offense punishable under the HIPAA Criminal provisions;[97]
- the person "did not know, and by exercising reasonable diligence would not have known" of the HIPAA violation;[98] or
- the violation "was due to reasonable cause and not to willful neglect" and the violation "is corrected during the 30-day period beginning on the first date the person liable for the penalty knew, or by exercising reasonable diligence would have known" of the violation.[99]

HIPAA originally further provided that such 30-day time period may be extended if determined appropriate by the Secretary based on the nature and extent of the HIPAA violation; that HHS may provide technical assistance to the covered entity during such period if HHS determines that the covered entity was unable to comply;[100] and that HHS may reduce penalties determined to be excessive if the violations were due to "reasonable cause" and not to "willful neglect" but were not corrected during the above 30-day time period.[101]

When applying these standards in areas of federal law other than HIPAA, federal courts have construed the term "reasonable diligence" to mean a careful examination, not an impracticable or protracted search.[102] "Reasonable cause" has been construed to mean the occurrence of a violation despite the exercise of "ordinary business care and prudence."[103] The term "willful neglect" has been construed to mean a conscious, intentional failure or reckless indifference.[104]

These lenience provisions meant that, unless a violation was knowing or willful, alleged violators would in many instances have ample opportunity to correct mistakes, and in theory, civil penalties could not be imposed (if the violation reasonably were not known to the covered entity or were timely corrected) or would have to be proportionate to the severity of the violations committed (for violations that were due to reasonable cause but not timely corrected).

The HITECH Act removed or limited a number of these lenience provisions. The HITECH Act removed the limitation with respect to violations where the person "did not know, and by exercising reasonable diligence would not have known," of the HIPAA violation.[105] Such violations are now subject to penalties of $100 to $50,000 per violation.[106] The HITECH Act did add a new

---

[97] 42 U.S.C. §1320d-5(a)(1) (prior to the HITECH Act).

[98] Id. §1320d-5(b)(2).

[99] Id. §1320d-5(b)(3)(A).

[100] Id. §1320d-5(b)(3)(B); 45 C.F.R. §160.304(b).

[101] 42 U.S.C. §1320d-5(b)(4). In addition, the Enforcement Rule makes the corresponding cooperation and technical assistance provisions of the Enforcement Rule applicable to all HIPAA standards and requirements and not just those contained in the Privacy Rule. See 45 C.F.R. §§160.300, .304.

[102] See, e.g., Chemetron Corp. v. Jones, 72 F.3d 341 (3d Cir. 1995); In re U.S.H. Corp. of New York, 223 B.R. 654 (Bankr. S.D.N.Y. 1998).

[103] See, e.g., Erickson v. Commissioner, 172 B.R. 900, 910 (Bankr. D. Minn. 1994).

[104] See, e.g., Adams v. Commissioner, 170 F.3d 173 (3d Cir. 1999); Henry v. United States, 73 F. Supp. 2d 1303 (N.D. Fla. 1999); In re McTyre Trucking Co., 223 B.R. 588 (Bankr. M.D. Fla. 1998).

[105] HITECH Act §13410(d)(3)(A) (codified at 42 U.S.C. §17939(d)(3)(A)).

[106] Id. §13410(d)(1) (codified at 42 U.S.C. §1320d-5(a)(1)(A)).

lenience provision with respect to such violations, providing that HHS may resolve such cases with corrective action and without a penalty.[107] As a result, such "unknowing" violations are punishable by a penalty of $100 to $50,000 per violation, but HHS has express authority to resolve such violations through corrective action and without a penalty. This begs the question whether Congress, by singling out these types of violations, expects that HHS will not resolve other types of violations (including those due to reasonable cause but not timely corrected) without imposing a penalty.

Prior to the HITECH Act, civil monetary penalties could not be imposed for violations that were punishable under the HIPAA Criminal Provisions.[108] Under the HITECH Act, civil monetary penalties now may be imposed for violations that are otherwise punishable under the HIPAA Criminal Provisions unless the Department of Justice has actually imposed criminal penalties.[109] Therefore, uncertainty may exist regarding whether civil or criminal penalties ultimately will be imposed for a violation.[110] Certain pre-HIPAA statutory provisions governing civil monetary penalties for health care fraud and abuse apply with respect to the enforcement of the HIPAA CMP Provisions.[111]

Accordingly, as of February 17, 2009 (the date of enactment of the HITECH Act), the following affirmative defenses are available:

- a penalty has been imposed under the HIPAA Criminal Provisions with respect to the act alleged to constitute a violation; or
- the violation is (1) due to reasonable cause and not willful neglect and (2) corrected during either (a) the 30-day period beginning on the date the covered entity liable for the penalty knew, or by exercising reasonable diligence would have known, that the violation occurred, or (b) such additional period as HHS determines to be appropriate based on the nature and extent of the failure to comply.[112]

D. What Is a "Violation"?

The Enforcement Rule leaves the number of HIPAA violations to subjective determination and provides:

> The Secretary will determine the number of violations of an administrative simplification provision based on the nature of the covered entity's obligation to act or not act under the provision that is violated, such as its obligation to act in a certain manner, or within a certain time, or to act or not act with respect to certain persons.[113]

The Enforcement Rule therefore provides some limited guidance as to the factors that the Secretary may use to determine the number of violations, but

---

[107] *Id.* §13410(f) (codified at 42 U.S.C. §1320d-5(e)).
[108] HIPAA §262 (codified at 42 U.S.C. §1320d-5(b)(1)).
[109] HITECH Act §13410(a) (codified at 42 U.S.C. §1320d-5(b)(1)).
[110] *Id.* §13410(a)(1)(A) (codified at 42 U.S.C. §1320d-5(b)(1)).
[111] 42 U.S.C. §1320d-5(a)(2) (referencing 42 U.S.C. §1320a-7a).
[112] *Id.* §1320d-5 (as amended by HITECH Act §13410).
[113] 45 C.F.R. §160.406.

essentially this determination is left to the administrative discretion of HHS. Regarding continuing violations, the Enforcement Rule provides that a separate violation occurs "each day the covered entity is in violation of the provision."[114] This provision expands the circumstances in which multiple violations will occur.

Under the Enforcement Rule, the term "person" includes a natural person as well as any public or private legal entity.[115] The preamble to the proposed Enforcement Rule helpfully notes that persons involved or affected could include:

(1) individuals who are the subject of PHI;
(2) employees for whom the covered entity has an obligation, e.g., the number of employees who took one or more impermissible actions;
(3) persons who receive information in violation of a standard or requirement, e.g., the number of employees who obtain access to PHI improperly; or
(4) other affected persons, e.g., the number of providers affected by a health plan's requirement that providers use codes that violate the Transactions Rule.[116]

If HHS determines that more than one covered entity was responsible for a HIPAA violation, HHS is required to impose a CMP against each covered entity.[117] The Enforcement Rule further provides that a covered entity that is a member of an "affiliated covered entity" as defined in Section 164.105(b) is jointly and severally liable for an imposed CMP.[118]

Although the approach proposed by HHS is flexible, the lack of clarity and specificity may make interpreting the Enforcement Rule more difficult. In addition to the provisions of the Enforcement Rule, further insight into how HHS might determine the number of violations and what HHS might consider a "violation" may be found in judicial interpretations of the federal civil False Claims Act (FCA).[119]

In *United States v. Krizek,* the U.S. District Court for the District of Columbia concluded that each American Medical Association current procedural terminology (CPT) code used to submit the allegedly false claims at issue was a false "claim" under the FCA, even though multiple CPT codes may have appeared on each HCFA-1500 claim form.[120] The number of claims calculated in this manner totaled 8,002. Although the actual damages claimed by the governmental prosecutors amounted to $245,400, additional damages calculated at $10,000 per claim led to a request for damages in the amount of nearly $81 million. The defendants contended that each HCFA-1500 claim form constituted only one claim. On appeal, the D.C. Circuit Court agreed, holding that the

---

[114] *Id.*
[115] *Id.* §160.103.
[116] HIPAA Administrative Simplification; Enforcement; Proposed Rule, 70 Fed. Reg. 20,234 (Apr. 18, 2005).
[117] 45 C.F.R. §160.402(b).
[118] *Id.* §160.402(c).
[119] 31 U.S.C. §§3729–3733.
[120] 909 F. Supp. 32 (D.D.C. 1995), *rev'd*, 111 F.3d 934 (D.C. Cir. 1997).

district court had erroneously treated each CPT code as an individual claim.[121] The court reasoned that the "claim" at issue should relate to a single instance of improper behavior by the defendant.[122] Therefore, each submission of a "request or demand" for payment using the form HCFA-1500, not each individual CPT code, constituted a claim.

In the context of HIPAA, a similar question might arise regarding whether wrongful use or disclosure of a list of 50 patient names that includes PHI constitutes a single violation or 50 violations. Under the theory in *Krizek,* such improper disclosure arguably would constitute only one violation because the disclosure relates to only one action by the user or discloser. Nonetheless, 50 individuals may be injured by the disclosure, so some might argue that 50 separate violations would have occurred; however, the same might be said about a HCFA-1500 form that is submitted with 50 falsely coded claims for services that are paid. If CMS pays incorrectly 50 times, then arguably CMS might assert that there have been 50 violations.

If violations are calculated in a manner similar to that under *Krizek,* the number of violations should be based on the number of incidents of disclosure by the alleged violator and not on the number of disclosures resulting from each incident.

When a potential violation involves an impermissible use or disclosure, HHS may find a variety of related, but distinct, potential violations that led to the impermissible use or disclosure, such as insufficient policies and procedures, training, sanctions, or safeguards. Each of these types of violations may be counted on a daily basis, and each is subject to a separate annual upper limit. Accordingly, after the HITECH Act, potential penalties involving numerous violations can reach tens of millions of dollars per calendar year.

E. Industry-Wide HIPAA Compliance

Due to the complex technical and administrative challenges involved in complying with some of the HIPAA standards and requirements, lack of compliance within the health care industry has been an ongoing issue. An annual survey conducted by the Healthcare Information and Management Systems Society (HIMSS) and Phoenix Health Systems found in their Winter 2006 survey that (1) 80 percent of providers and 86 percent of payors reported that they have met the Privacy Rule requirements; (2) 84 percent of providers and 73 percent of payors reported that they were able to conduct all HIPAA standardized health care transactions, but only 66 percent of providers and 67 percent of payors are actually conducting all such transactions; and (3) 55 percent of providers and 72 percent of payors reported that they are in compliance with the Security Rule.[123]

The top roadblocks to HIPAA compliance cited by provider respondents to the survey included "changes/potential changes in regulations/

---

[121] United States v. Krizek, 111 F.3d 934, 940 (D.C. Cir. 1997).
[122] *Id.* at 940.
[123] HIMSS-Phoenix Healthcare Systems, US Healthcare Industry HIPAA Compliance Survey Results: Winter 2006, *available at* http://www.himss.org/ASP/topics_FocusDynamic.asp?faid=68 (and references to other compliance results reviews).

deadlines," "organizational constraints," and "no anticipated legal consequences for non-compliance."[124]

CMS addressed the prospect of challenges in complying with the Transactions Rule by indicating through various statements and actions that CMS would not seek enforcement against covered entities that were making good-faith steps toward compliance with the Transactions Rule. However, on August 4, 2005, CMS announced that beginning October 1, 2005, CMS would no longer accept or process any noncompliant claims.[125] Industry organizations raised similar concerns about compliance with the NPI Rule.

F. Procedures for Imposition of Civil Monetary Penalties

The procedures adopted in the Enforcement Rule are based on the procedures set forth in the regulations governing the HHS Office of Inspector General's imposition of civil monetary penalties in connection with anti-fraud and abuse enforcement actions.[126] Some notable distinctions from standard federal administrative adjudicatory practice are discussed at Section IV.G., below.

Upon finding indications of noncompliance that cannot be informally resolved, HHS sends a Letter of Opportunity that provides the covered entity an opportunity to submit written evidence of any mitigating factors or affirmative defenses.[127] The covered entity has 30 days to submit any such evidence.[128]

After issuing the Letter of Opportunity and affording an opportunity to respond, if HHS finds that a CMP should be imposed, it then issues a Notice of Proposed Determination.[129] Under the Enforcement Rule, HHS has six years from the date of the act or omission that is the subject of the action to begin an enforcement action to collect civil monetary penalties under the HIPAA CMP Provisions through the issuance of a Notice of Proposed Determination.[130] The Notice of Proposed Determination must include:

---

[124]*Id.* Note that neither HIPAA nor the HITECH Act provides funding resources with respect to covered entity or business association compliance, and HIPAA and the HITECH Act are mostly statutory initiatives containing unfunded federal mandates, albeit with some Medicaid programs receiving HIPAA compliance-related funding, and with the Security Rule providing for some measure of relativity regarding scaling and compliance policies and procedures being proportionate to the size of a covered entity.

[125]Dep't of Health & Human Servs., Centers for Medicare & Medicaid Servs. (CMS), CMS Manual System Pub 100-20 One-Time Notification Transmittal Sheet Transmittal 171, *available at* https://www.cms.gov/transmittals/downloads/R171OTN.pdf.

[126]68 Fed. Reg. 18,897. HHS stated in the preamble to the Interim Final Rule:
There is thus, a significant body of experience with, and understanding of, the OIG procedural rules, both within HHS and in a large part of the regulated universe. Based on this experience, we believe that the [Enforcement Rule] will be workable and promote the efficient resolution of cases where the Secretary's proposed imposition of [civil monetary penalties] is challenged.
No reported decision has been found in which HHS's enforcement determination was appealed to and considered by a federal court.

[127]45 C.F.R. §160.312(a)(3).

[128]*Id.*

[129]*Id.* §160.420.

[130]*Id.* §160.414.

- reference to the statutory basis for the penalty;
- a description of the findings of fact regarding the violation(s) with respect to which the penalty is proposed (if relying on a statistical sampling study, the Secretary must provide a copy of the study);
- the reasons why the violation(s) subject(s) the respondent to a penalty;
- the amount of the proposed penalty;
- any circumstances described in 45 C.F.R. §160.408 that were considered in determining the amount of the proposed penalty; and
- instructions for responding to the notice, including a statement of the respondent's right to a hearing, a statement that failure to request a hearing within 90 days permits the imposition of the proposed penalty without the right to a hearing under §160.504 or a right of appeal under §160.548, and the address to which the hearing request must be sent.[131]

Following receipt of the Notice of Proposed Determination, a respondent has the right to request a hearing before an administrative law judge (ALJ).[132] The hearing request must clearly and directly admit, deny, or explain each of the findings of fact contained in the Notice of Proposed Determination with respect to which the respondent has knowledge.[133] The request for a hearing is a prerequisite to judicial review of a final agency determination with respect to imposition of civil monetary penalties.[134] Therefore, a respondent must request a hearing in order to be able to challenge the imposition of civil monetary penalties or the magnitude of any penalties.

The respondent has the right to appear at a hearing conducted by the ALJ. The respondent has rights typical of those in other federal administrative proceedings, including rights to conduct discovery, present evidence, present and cross-examine witnesses, present oral arguments, and submit written briefs and proposed findings of fact and conclusions of law after the hearing.[135] The Enforcement Rule also sets forth procedures for discovery, presentation of evidence and witnesses, subpoenas, motions, and other procedural matters surrounding the hearing. Consideration must also be given to "sealing" the proceedings with respect to PHI that might be involved.

After the hearing, and following the submission of post-hearing briefs, if any, the ALJ may affirm, increase, or reduce the assessment of civil monetary penalties (presumably to as low as zero).[136] The ALJ's decision is the final decision of HHS,[137] unless the decision is appealed to the HHS Departmental Appeals Board within 60 days following the date of service of the ALJ's decision.[138] The decision of the Board would constitute the final action of HHS,

---

[131] *Id.* §160.420(a).

[132] *Id.* §160.420(b).

[133] *Id.* §160.504(c). "If the respondent has no knowledge of a particular finding of fact and so states, the finding shall be deemed denied." *Id.*

[134] *Id.* §160.422.

[135] *Id.* §160.506.

[136] *Id.* §160.546(b).

[137] *Id.* §160.546(d).

[138] The Enforcement Rule provides that a respondent is bound by a final determination that the respondent violated a HIPAA provision in any other CMP enforcement proceeding. *Id.* §160.532.

from which the respondent may seek judicial review in the U.S. Court of Appeals for the federal circuit in which the respondent resides.[139] Pending such judicial review, the respondent may request a stay of the effective date of any civil monetary penalty.[140]

The respondent has the burden of going forward and the burden of persuasion with respect to (1) affirmative defenses; (2) challenges to the amount or scope of a proposed penalty, including mitigating factors; and (3) any contention that the proposed penalty should be reduced or waived.[141] The Secretary has the burden of going forward and the burden of persuasion on all other issues, including issues of liability and the existence of any aggravating factors.[142] Under the HIPAA Criminal Provisions, proof of the violation beyond a reasonable doubt is required.

HHS has imposed a CMP under HIPAA on one occasion, against Cignet Health in the amount of $4.35 million.[143] Cignet failed to provide 41 individuals with requested copies of their medical records, failed to provide information to OCR (including the medical records at issue) in response to OCR's repeated data requests, and failed to timely respond to OCR's subpoena duces tecum.[144] HHS issued a Notice of Proposed Determination proposing $1.35 million in CMPs attributable to the failure to provide individuals with access to their PHI in accordance with 45 C.F.R. §164.524, and $3.0 million in CMPs attributable to the failure to cooperate with OCR's investigation in accordance with 45 C.F.R. §160.404(b)(2)(iv).[145] Cignet Health did not appeal the Notice of Proposed Determination, and so HHS proceeded with issuing a final determination.[146]

G. Distinctive Features in the Imposition of Civil Monetary Penalties

The Enforcement Rule includes a number of features that are distinct from other federal regulations in terms of how liability is attributed to covered entities, how the amount of civil monetary penalties is calculated, and available defenses to the imposition of civil monetary penalties.

1. Imposition of Penalties

Under the Enforcement Rule, HHS is required to impose a civil monetary penalty upon finding a violation unless the covered entity has established affirmative defenses, which are based on the CMP lenience provisions, discussed

---

[139] 42 U.S.C. §1320a-7a(e).

[140] 45 C.F.R. §160.550(a).

[141] *Id.* §160.534(b)(1).

[142] *Id.* §160.534(b)(2).

[143] Dep't of Health & Human Servs., Office for Civil Rights, Notice of Final Determination regarding Cignet Health (Feb. 4, 2011), *available at* http://www.hhs.gov/ocr/privacy/hipaa/enforcement/examples/cignetpenaltyletter.pdf.

[144] Dep't of Health & Human Servs., Office for Civil Rights, Notice of Proposed Determination regarding Cignet Health, (Oct. 20, 2010), *available at* http://www.hhs.gov/ocr/privacy/hipaa/enforcement/examples/cignetpenaltynotice.pdf.

[145] *Id.*

[146] Notice of Final Determination regarding Cignet Health.

above in Section IV.C.[147] An affirmative defense may be raised at any time during the administrative proceedings.[148] While HHS is required to impose a civil monetary penalty upon finding a violation, it has the enforcement discretion to determine when it will make formal findings of a violation, rather than resolving a complaint investigation or compliance review in an informal manner.

The HITECH Act added that, in cases of willful neglect, HHS is required to impose a civil monetary penalty.[149] In light of the prior requirement for HHS to impose a civil monetary penalty upon any person who violates the HIPAA rules,[150] the legal effect of this additional requirement with respect to willful neglect violations is unclear. The message from Congress appears to be clear, however, which is that HHS should step up enforcement with respect to violations involving willful neglect.

2. Public Notice

The Enforcement Rule includes a provision requiring HHS to notify the following groups and organizations that a civil monetary penalty was imposed: (1) the public at large, (2) state or local medical or professional organizations, (3) state agencies that administer or supervise the administration of state health care programs, (4) utilization and quality control peer review organizations, and/or (5) state or local licensing agencies.[151] The threat of such notice further encourages compliance with HIPAA.

3. Statistical Sampling

The Enforcement Rule authorizes HHS to submit statistical sampling studies detailing the number of violations or setting forth the factors for determining the amount of a civil monetary penalty. A valid study would be considered prima facie evidence of the number of violations or the existence of such factors, and the burden would then shift to the respondent to rebut the evidence contained in such study.[152]

4. Liability for Violations by Agents

The HIPAA CMP Provisions provide that a principal is liable for the actions of its agents acting within the scope of agency.[153] The Enforcement Rule limits this liability, providing that a covered entity is liable for a violation based on the "act or omission" of any agent of the covered entity, including a "workforce member" acting within the scope of his or her agency, unless the agent is

---

[147] 45 C.F.R. §160.410(b).

[148] *Id.* §160.504(c). An affirmative defense may also be raised in connection with an appeal of an ALJ's decision. 45 C.F.R. §160.548(e).

[149] HITECH Act §13410(a)(1)(B) (codified at 42 U.S.C. §1320d-5(c)(1)).

[150] 42 U.S.C. §1320d-5(a)(1).

[151] 45 C.F.R. §160.426. Notably, neither the National Practitioner Data Bank nor the Healthcare Protection and Integrity Data Bank is referenced. *See, e.g.,* Dep't of Health & Human Servs., Health Resources & Servs. Admin., The Data Bank, *available at* http://www.npdb-hipdb.hrsa.gov/.

[152] 45 C.F.R. §160.536.

[153] 42 U.S.C. §1320d-5(a)(2) (incorporating by reference 42 U.S.C. §1320a-7a(l)).

a business associate of the covered entity with a valid business associate agreement and the covered entity (1) did not know of an improper pattern of activity of the business associate, and (2) did not fail to act to terminate the agreement with the business associate or alert HHS of a violation if the agreement could not be terminated.[154] In the HITECH Act NPRM, HHS proposed to remove this exception and make covered entities directly liable for the actions of any agents, including business associates, acting within the scope of agency. If HHS finalizes this change, it will mean that covered entities must be particularly sensitive to whether a business associate may be acting as an agent, which is a fact-specific inquiry that largely rests on the level of control that the covered entity has over the business associate's actions.

5. *Aggravating and Mitigating Factors*

The Enforcement Rule sets forth specific aggravating and mitigating factors that HHS will consider in determining the amount of civil monetary penalties, including the following:

- the nature of the violation, in light of the purpose of the standard or requirement violated;
- the circumstances, including the consequences, of the violation, including but not limited to (1) the time period during which the violation(s) occurred, (2) whether the violation caused physical harm, (3) whether the violation hindered or facilitated an individual's ability to obtain health care, and (4) whether the violation resulted in financial harm;
- the degree of culpability of the covered entity, including but not limited to (1) whether the violation was intentional and (2) whether the violation was beyond the direct control of the covered entity;
- any history of prior offenses of the covered entity, including but not limited to (1) whether the current violation is the same or similar to prior violation(s), (2) whether and to what extent the covered entity has attempted to correct previous violations, (3) how the covered entity has responded to technical assistance from the Secretary provided in the context of a compliance effort, and (4) how the covered entity has responded to prior complaints;
- the financial condition of the covered entity, including but not limited to (1) whether the covered entity had financial difficulties that affected its ability to comply, (2) whether the imposition of a civil money penalty would jeopardize the ability of the covered entity to continue to provide, or to pay for, health care, and (3) the size of the covered entity; and
- such other matters as justice may require.[155]

Consistent with many other provisions of the Enforcement Rule, a range of factors is presented; however, this will not provide much practical information for covered entities until HIPAA CMP Provisions enforcement actions result in Enforcement Rule administrative proceedings.

---

[154] 45 C.F.R. §160.402(c).
[155] *Id.* §160.408.

The HITECH Act NPRM proposed some changes to this list of factors.[156] A purpose of these proposed changes was to reflect the HITECH Act's mandate to base civil monetary penalties on the nature and extent of the violation and the nature and extent of the harm resulting from such violation.[157] HHS also sought to clarify that, while HHS must consider each aggravating and mitigating factor, HHS has discretion with respect to what facts to consider (by stating that consideration of each factor may include, but is not limited to, certain facts). Finally, HHS proposed to replace reference to "violations" with reference to "indications of noncompliance" to allow HHS to consider complaint investigations and compliance reviews in which there were indications of noncompliance, but in which HHS made no formal finding of a violation.

Under the proposal, the following would be aggravating and mitigating factors:

- the nature and extent of the violation, consideration of which may include but is not limited to (1) the number of individuals affected; and (2) the time period during which the violation occurred;
- the nature and extent of the harm resulting from the violation, consideration of which may include but is not limited to (1) whether the violation caused physical harm; (2) whether the violation resulted in financial harm; (3) whether the violation resulted in harm to an individual's reputation; and (4) whether the violation hindered an individual's ability to obtain health care;
- the history of prior compliance with the administrative simplification provisions, including violations, by the covered entity or business associate, consideration of which may include but is not limited to (1) whether the current violation is the same or similar to previous indications of noncompliance; (2) whether and to what extent the covered entity or business associate has attempted to correct previous indications of noncompliance; (3) how the covered entity or business associate has responded to technical assistance from the Secretary provided in the context of a compliance effort; and (4) how the covered entity or business associate has responded to prior complaints;
- the financial condition of the covered entity or business associate, consideration of which may include but is not limited to (1) whether the covered entity or business associate had financial difficulties that affected its ability to comply; (2) whether the imposition of a civil money penalty would jeopardize the ability of the covered entity or business associate to continue to provide, or to pay for, health care; and (3) the size of the covered entity or business associate; and
- such other matters as justice may require.[158]

---

[156] Modifications to the HIPAA Privacy, Security, and Enforcement Rules Under the Health Information Technology for Economic and Clinical Health Act; Proposed Rule, 75 Fed. Reg. 40,868, 40,915 (July 14, 2010).

[157] *Id. at* 40,880.

[158] *Id.*

H. Actions by State Attorneys General

The HITECH Act provides that the attorney general of a state who has reason to believe that an interest of one or more of the state's residents has been or is threatened or adversely affected by a potential HIPAA violation may bring a civil action on behalf of the state's residents in a district court of the United States of appropriate jurisdiction.[159] The civil action may enjoin further violation by the defendant or obtain damages on behalf of residents in the amount of up to $100 per violation (subject to a limit of $25,000 for all violations of an identical requirement or prohibition during a calendar year).[160] The court is also authorized to award reasonable attorneys' fees to the state.[161] While the statute only authorizes suit in U.S. district court, under common law such a suit may also be brought in state court.[162]

The HITECH Act requires a state attorney general to notify HHS before instituting an action.[163] If HHS has "instituted an action" under the HIPAA CMP Provisions, then the state attorney general may not bring an action while HHS's action is pending.[164] The intent of this limitation appears to avoid concurrent actions by HHS and the state attorney general, with HHS provided the first opportunity to bring an action. The statute is unclear, however, as to what constitutes "an action" by HHS, since HHS does not bring actions in court but rather investigates potential violations and issues a Notice of Proposed Determination upon finding a violation, and the covered entity or business associate then has the right to appeal such a notice. Accordingly, the statute might be read as limiting an action by a state attorney general once HHS has initiated an investigation or compliance review, or the statute might be read more narrowly as only limiting a state attorney general's action once HHS has issued a Notice of Proposed Determination.

Whatever reading one takes, the statute does not appear to prohibit the state attorney from proceeding with an action after HHS has concluded HHS's investigation and imposition of a civil monetary penalty, or from HHS beginning an action after a state attorney general has concluded his or her suit. Furthermore, while a state attorney general may not bring an action if HHS has first initiated an action, there is an open question as to whether a state attorney general who brings an action first must cease and hold that action in abeyance if HHS chooses to initiate an action while the attorney general's action is pending.

The first state attorney general enforcement action under the HITECH Act was brought by the Connecticut attorney general in January 2010 and was settled

---

[159] HITECH Act §13410(e) (codified at 42 U.S.C. §1320d-5(d)(1)).

[160] Id. (codified at 42 U.S.C. §1320d-5(d)(1) and (2)).

[161] Id. (codified at 42 U.S.C. §1320d-5(d)(3)).

[162] See Gulf Offshore Co. v. Mobil, 453 U.S. 473, 477-78 (1981) (providing that "state courts may assume subject matter jurisdiction over a federal cause of action absent provision by Congress to the contrary or disabling incompatibility between the federal claim and state court adjudication").

[163] HITECH Act §13410(e) (codified at 42 U.S.C. §1320d-5(d)(4)).

[164] Id. (codified at 42 U.S.C. §1320d-5(d)(7)).

in July 2010.[165] The second such state attorney general enforcement action was brought by the Vermont attorney general and involved the same violation as the Connecticut settlement,[166] clearly demonstrating that a single potential violation of HIPAA may lead to actions by multiple state attorneys general.

OCR conducted a series of training sessions for state attorneys general between April and June 2011 on enforcement of HIPAA to assist the attorneys general with implementing their new enforcement authority under the HITECH Act.[167]

V. HIPAA CRIMINAL PROVISIONS

A. In General

Certain serious violations of HIPAA relating to unique health identifiers and the Privacy Rule are subject to enforcement under the HIPAA Criminal Provisions. The HITECH Act also provides that business associates may be held criminally liable for violating the Security Rule,[168] but it is unclear how a violation of the Security Rule could represent a violation of the HIPAA Criminal Provisions (because the Security Rule addresses required safeguards, rather than the acts of disclosing or obtaining individually identifiable health information). As discussed below, enforcement actions could also be brought under other federal criminal statutes, much in the same way that many criminal actions relating to activities prosecutable under the federal anti-kickback statute[169] have been brought under generally applicable federal criminal statutes, rather than under the criminal enforcement provisions within the anti-kickback statute.

HIPAA provides that a person will face HIPAA criminal penalties if that person (recall that "person" includes individuals and business entities) "knowingly" and in violation of HIPAA:

- uses or causes to be used a unique health identifier;
- obtains individually identifiable health information relating to an individual; or
- discloses individually identifiable health information to another person.[170]

---

[165]Press Release, State of Connecticut, Office of the Attorney General, *Attorney General Announces Health Net Settlement Involving Massive Security Breach Compromising Private Medical and Financial Info* (July 6, 2010), *available at* http://www.ct.gov/ag/cwp/view.asp?Q=462752&A=3869 (announcing a $250,000 settlement for alleged violations of HIPAA and state law).

[166]Press Release, State of Vermont, Office of the Attorney General, *Court Approves Attorney General HIPAA Settlement with Health Insurer* (Jan. 26, 2011), *available at* http://www.atg.state.vt.us/news/court-approves-attorney-general-hipaa-settlement-with-health-insurer.php.

[167]Dep't of Health & Human Servs., Office for Civil Rights, HIPAA Enforcement Training for State Attorneys General (2011), *available at* http://www.hhs.gov/ocr/privacy/hipaa/enforcement/sag/sagmoreinfo.html. Copies of materials provided at such training programs may be available via a federal Freedom of Information Act filing request of OCR.

[168]HITECH Act §13401(b) (codified at 42 U.S.C. §17931).

[169]42 U.S.C. §1320a-7b.

[170]*Id.* §1320d-6(a).

HIPAA criminal penalties increase progressively based on the type of criminal intent of the violator. Penalties generally include:

- a fine of up to $50,000 and/or up to one year of imprisonment;
- a fine of up to $100,000 and/or up to five years of imprisonment if the offense is committed under false pretenses; or
- a fine of up to $250,000 and/or up to 10 years of imprisonment if the offense is committed with intent to sell, transfer, or use individually identifiable health information for commercial advantage, personal gain, or malicious harm.[171]

Among the issues initially debated regarding HIPAA Criminal Provisions was whether a noncovered entity is a "person" subject to criminal prosecution under HIPAA. The first publicly known instance of a noncovered entity so being prosecuted occurred in Seattle, Washington, and was initiated by the U.S. Attorney for the State of Washington.[172] The second such instance occurred in Houston, Texas, and was initiated by the U.S. Attorney for the State of Texas.[173]

Subsequent to the Seattle, Washington, prosecution and after the incarceration of the defendant, an unusual development occurred. In response to an inquiry by the General Counsel of HHS and the Senior Counsel to the Deputy Attorney General, the Office of Legal Counsel (OLC) in the Department of Justice published a Memorandum Opinion[174] addressing "the scope of 42 U.S.C. §1320d-6 (2000)," the criminal enforcement provision of HIPAA. Specifically, the Memorandum addresses

---

[171]*Id.* §1320d-6(b).

[172]United States v. Gibson, No. CR04-0374RSM, 2004 WL 2188280 (W.D. Wash. Aug. 19, 2004). In this case, defendant Gibson, an employee of a cancer center, allegedly used demographic information, consisting of a patient's name, date of birth, and Social Security number—which had been obtained from his employer relating to the payment for and provision of health care services—for his own personal gain to obtain a credit card in the name of the patient. The prosecution determined that Gibson, as a "person" subject to the HIPAA Criminal Provisions, was subject to such prosecution even though he was not a covered entity. Gibson entered into a plea agreement with the prosecutor, and therefore the question whether "person" includes non–covered entity defendants was not adjudicated in this case, because the court accepted the plea agreement and sentenced the defendant to 16 months in prison. The Assistant U.S. Attorney in this case stated:
> This was not a close call, by any means. We felt that Mr. Gibson clearly violated the HIPAA criminal statute. He knew what he was doing; he did what he intended to do; he was caught in the act of improperly disclosing the patient information; and so we prosecuted him under HIPAA. We could also have prosecuted him under other laws, but HIPAA seemed to be the best approach.

Alan S. Goldberg, *Interview of Susan Loitz, AUSA*, 1 ABA HEALTH eSOURCE (No. 2) (Oct. 2004), *available at* http://www.americanbar.org/newsletter/publications/aba_health_esource_home/Volume1_vol1no2_index.html.

[173]The Texas prosecution is summarized in a news release by the Center for Democracy and Technology. *HIPAA Privacy Rule Violation Ends in Guilty Plea* (March 28, 2006), *available at* http://cdt.info/file/hipaa-privacy-rule-violation-prosecution-ends-guilty-plea.

[174]Dep't of Justice, Office of Legal Counsel, Scope of Criminal Enforcement Under 42 U.S.C. §1320d-6, Mem. Op. for General Counsel, U.S. Dep't Health & Human Servs. and Senior Counsel to the Deputy Att'y Gen., Op. O.L.C., (June 1, 2005) [hereinafter Memorandum Opinion], *available at* http://www.usdoj.gov/olc/hipaa_final.htm. The Memorandum Opinion also addresses "whether the 'knowingly' element of the offense set forth in 42 U.S.C. §1320d-6 requires the Government to prove only knowledge of the facts that constitute the offense or whether this element also requires proof that the defendant knew that the act violated the law." *Id.* at 12. See V.B., below, for a discussion of "knowingly."

whether the only persons who may be directly liable under section 1320d-g are those persons to whom the substantive requirements of [HIPAA], as set forth in the regulations promulgated thereunder, apply—i.e., health plans, health care clearinghouses, certain health care providers, and Medicare prescription drug card sponsors—or whether this provision may also render directly liable other persons, particularly those who obtain protected health information in a manner that causes a person to whom the substantive requirements of the subtitle apply to release the information in violation of the law. We conclude that health plans, health care clearinghouses, those health care providers specified in the statute, and Medicare prescription drug card sponsors [the four categories of HIPAA covered entity] may be prosecuted for violations of section 1320d-6. In addition, depending on the facts of a given case, certain directors, officers, and employees of these entities may be liable directly under section 1320d-6, in accordance with the general principles of corporate criminal liability, as these principles are developed in the course of particular prosecutions. *Other persons may not be liable directly under this provision.*[175]

Subsequent to this Memorandum Opinion, federal prosecutors have brought HIPAA criminal enforcement against individuals who are not themselves covered entities through an aiding and abetting or conspiracy theory.[176]

The HITECH Act resolved this matter by revising the HIPAA Criminal Provisions, adding the following:

For purposes of [the HIPAA Criminal Provisions], a person (including an employee or other individual) shall be considered to have obtained or disclosed individually identifiable health information in violation of this part if the information is maintained by a covered entity (as defined in the HIPAA privacy regulation described in section 1180(b)(3)) and the individual obtained or disclosed such information without an authorization.[177]

Accordingly, the Department of Justice now has clear authority criminally to prosecute individuals who are not covered entities without the need to rely on an aiding and abetting or conspiracy theory. This provision applies only to criminal prosecutions; the HIPAA CMP Provisions remain limited to covered entities (and, in accordance with the HITECH Act, business associates).

B. Intent Standard

Enforcement under the HIPAA Criminal Provisions is limited to violations committed "knowingly."[178] This means that a critical element in HIPAA enforcement will be the development of a common understanding of what "knowingly" means under the HIPAA Criminal Provisions. The government and courts have

---

[175] Memorandum Opinion at 1 (emphasis added).

[176] *See, e.g.*, United States v. Jackson, No CR-08-00430 (C.D. Cal. Apr. 9, 2008) (indictment), *available at* https://ecf.cacd.uscourts.gov/ (registration and a fee required) (indictment was brought under 18 U.S.C. §2(b), an aiding and abetting provision); United States v. Ferrer, No. 0:06-cr-60261 (S.D. Fl. Sept. 7, 2006) (indictment), *available at* https://ecf.flsd.uscourts.gov/ (registration and a fee required) (indictment was brought under 18 U.S.C. §2(b), an aiding and abetting provision).

[177] HITECH Act §13409 (codified at 42 U.S.C. §1320d-6(a)).

[178] 42 U.S.C. §1320d-6(a).

interpreted the word "knowingly" differently under different health care statutes, such as under the anti-kickback statute and the FCA. This raises the question whether the "knowingly" standard under the HIPAA Criminal Provisions will be construed by the government and the courts in a manner similar to how "knowingly" is interpreted under the anti-kickback statute or the FCA.[179]

The intent standard under the anti-kickback statute—namely, "knowingly and willfully"[180]—has been construed to require that a defendant must have intended to violate the provisions of the anti-kickback statute or must otherwise have known that commission of the allegedly unlawful act was in violation of the anti-kickback statute.[181] Although the intent requirement for a conviction under the anti-kickback statute is met if only "one purpose" of the arrangement is to violate that statute,[182] the requisite intent must nonetheless be present.

The intent requirement for prosecution under the FCA is different in that the FCA provides that a violation occurs, without regard to whether there is a specific intent to defraud, if the person:

- has actual knowledge of the information;
- acts in deliberate ignorance of the truth or falsity of the information; or
- acts in reckless disregard of the truth or falsity of the information.[183]

Innocent mistake and negligence are defenses to FCA allegations.[184]

A prosecutor might bring a criminal enforcement action attempting to use the FCA intent standard, for example, based on the theory that a violation arose because of disregard of obvious signs of lapses in implementing practices and procedures for safeguarding PHI that resulted in an improper disclosure.

---

[179]*See* Allison Engine Co. v. United States *ex rel*. Sanders, 553 U.S. 662 (2008). This decision implicated a possible change in the likely construction of the terms "knowing" and "knowingly" in the false claims context:
Section 3729(b) provides that the terms "knowing" and "knowingly" "mean that a person, with respect to information—(1) has actual knowledge of the information; (2) acts in deliberate ignorance of the truth or falsity of the information; or (3) acts in reckless disregard of the truth or falsity of the information, and no proof of specific intent to defraud is required." The statutory definition of these terms is easily reconcilable with our holding in this case for two reasons. First, the intent requirement we discern in §3729(a)(2) derives not from the term "knowingly," but rather from the infinitive phrase: "to get." Second, §3729(b) refers to specific intent with regard to the truth or falsity of the "information," while our holding refers to a defendant's purpose in making or using a false record or statement.
Id. at 671 n.2. But thereafter in the Fraud Enforcement and Recovery Act of 2009 (FERA), Pub. L. No. 111-21, 123 Stat. 1617, in Section 4, subsection (a)(1) appears to be intended, via revised 31 U.S.C. 3729(a)(1)(B), specified to "take effect as if enacted on June 7, 2008, and to apply to all claims under the False Claims Act (31 U.S.C. 3729 et seq.) that are pending on or after that date" (that being the date on which the decision in *Allison Engine* was published), to render *Allison Engine* null with respect to the meaning of "knowing" and "knowingly" under Section 3729(b). *But see* U.S. *ex rel*. Sanders v. Allison Engine Co., No. 1:95-cv-970 (S.D. Ohio Oct. 27, 2009).

[180]*See* 42 U.S.C. §1320a-7b(b).

[181]Hanlester Network v. Shalala, 51 F.3d 1390 (9th Cir. 1995); United States v. Jain, 93 F.3d 436 (8th Cir. 1996).

[182]United States v. Greber, 760 F.2d 68 (3d Cir. 1985); United States v. Kats, 871 F.2d 105 (9th Cir. 1989).

[183]31 U.S.C. §3729(b); *see* United States *ex rel*. Quirk v. Madonna Towers, Inc., 278 F.3d 765 (8th Cir. 2002); United States v. Somerstein, 971 F. Supp. 736 (E.D.N.Y. 1997).

[184]*See* United States *ex rel*. Hagood v. Sonoma County Water Agency, 81 F.3d 1465, 1478 (9th Cir. 1996); Hindo v. University of Health Scis., 65 F.3d 608, 613 (7th Cir. 1995).

A prosecutor might also assert that the FCA intent standard applies to a covered entity that engages a "business associate"[185] to provide services. Such liability for the actions of a business associate could be predicated on several cases that have applied a "vicarious liability" theory under the FCA for actions of agents.[186] For instance, if a business associate engaged to print and submit bills on behalf of a covered entity improperly disclosed a list of names, addresses, and health conditions, a prosecutor might try to establish that the covered entity, although aware of a pattern of improper behavior by the business associate, did not try to prevent such behavior and therefore should be punished for deliberately disregarding information that was known to the covered entity and directly led to the improper disclosure of PHI.

In the Memorandum Opinion for the HHS General Counsel and the Senior Counsel to the Deputy Attorney General, discussed above,[187] the Department of Justice OLC addressed "whether the 'knowingly' element of the offense set forth in 42 U.S.C. §1320d-6 requires the Government to prove only knowledge of the facts that constitute the offense or whether this element also requires proof that the defendant knew that the act violated the law."[188] The OLC concluded that

> the 'knowingly' element is best read, consistent with its ordinary meaning, to require only proof of knowledge of the facts that constitute the offense.... A plain reading of [42 U.S.C. §1320d-6(a)] indicates that a person need not know that commission of an act described in subsections (a)(1) to (a)(3) violates the law in order to satisfy the 'knowingly' element of the offense.... Accordingly, to incur criminal liability, a defendant need have knowledge only of those facts that constitute the offense.[189]

The Office of Legal Counsel, after acknowledging the possible absurdity of reading 42 U.S.C. §1320d-6(a) "so as to impose criminal punishment on the basis of a lesser degree of intent than that required for civil sanction," dismissed any such absurdity by noting that 42 U.S.C. §1320d-6 "carves out a limited set [of violations] and subjects them to criminal punishment. Such punishment is reserved for violations involving 'unique health identifiers' and 'individually identifiable health information.'"[190] Oddly, perhaps, the OLC appears to ignore the likelihood that much of HIPAA civil enforcement will relate primarily to wrongful use or disclosure of individually identifiable health information.

---

[185] A "business associate" under HIPAA generally means a person or entity that provides services to a covered entity that involve the use or disclosure of PHI. *See* 45 C.F.R. §160.103.

[186] *See, e.g.*, United States v. O'Connell, 890 F.2d 563 (1st Cir. 1989); Grand Union Co. v. United States, 696 F.2d 888, 891 (11th Cir. 1983); United States v. Hangar One, Inc., 563 F.2d 1155 (5th Cir. 1977).

[187] Dep't of Justice, Office of Legal Counsel, Scope of Criminal Enforcement Under 42 U.S.C. §1320d-6, Mem. Op. for General Counsel, U.S. Dep't Health & Human Servs. and Senior Counsel to the Deputy Att'y Gen., Op. O.L.C., (June 1, 2005) [hereinafter Memorandum Opinion], *available at* http://www.usdoj.gov/olc/hipaa_final.htm. See V.A., above.

[188] Memorandum Opinion at 6, *available at* http://www.usdoj.gov/olc/hipaa_final.htm.

[189] *Id.* at 7. But see V.A., above.

[190] Memorandum Opinion at 7.

C. Aiding and Abetting

A covered entity or business associate or anyone else may be found criminally liable for assisting a person to commit a HIPAA violation.[191] To be convicted of aiding and abetting, a defendant must have assisted in the criminal violation, shared the requisite intent, and taken an affirmative action to make the venture succeed.[192] The use of an aiding and abetting theory is less likely now that, pursuant to the HITECH Act, the government may bring criminal prosecutions directly against individuals who are not covered entities.[193]

D. Conspiracy

Potentially, either a covered entity or a business associate indirectly or anyone else could be liable for a HIPAA violation under a theory of criminal conspiracy. Conviction under a conspiracy theory requires the prosecutor to prove, inter alia, that there was an agreement among two or more persons to commit a crime.[194] In the case of a conspiracy to violate a federal statute, the violation of the federal statute must be an object of the conspiracy.[195] A corporation and the corporation's officers, employees, or agents might be prosecuted as co-conspirators for conspiracy to commit an unlawful act, if the criminal act is directly related to the duties that the officers, employees, or agents had authority to perform.[196]

It is possible to envision a scenario in which a covered entity and a business associate or anyone else could be prosecuted under a conspiracy theory, founded on an intent to violate HIPAA.[197] Only one of the conspirators must have been able, singly, to be convicted of a violation of HIPAA; any conspirator need only have been a part of the conspiracy and need not have been a covered entity. The use of a conspiracy theory is less likely now that, pursuant to the HITECH Act, the government may bring criminal prosecutions directly against individuals that are not covered entities.[198]

---

[191] *See* 18 U.S.C. §2(a); *see, e.g.*, United States v. Anderson, 174 F.3d 515 (5th Cir. 1999); United States v. Ismoila, 100 F.3d 380 (5th Cir. 1996).

[192] *See, e.g., Anderson,* 174 F.3d at 523.

[193] HITECH Act §13409 (codified at 42 U.S.C. §1320d-6(a)).

[194] *See* Blusal Meats, Inc. v. United States, 638 F. Supp. 824 (S.D.N.Y. 1986).

[195] *See* United States v. Johnston, 146 F.3d 785 (10th Cir. 1998); United States v. Lyman, 190 F. 414 (D. Or. 1911).

[196] *See* United States v. Griffin, 401 F. Supp. 1222, 1226 (S.D. Ind. 1975); *see also* United States v. Kemmel, 160 F. Supp. 718, 721 (M.D. Pa. 1958).

[197] An example would be a medical product marketing company with access to a health plan's patient-information databases that works with the health plan to distribute such information to third-party marketing companies without the patients' consents, with the health plan and marketing company agreeing to share the profits from such distributions.

[198] HITECH Act §13409 (codified at 42 U.S.C. §1320d-6(a)).

E. Other Potential Theories of Indirect Criminal Liability of Business Associates

The government might also seek to prosecute a member of the workforce of a covered entity or a business associate or anyone else under other federal statutes, even if the member of the workforce or business associate was not directly involved in the commission of the HIPAA-related offense. For instance, a prosecutor may conduct an investigation in the course of which a member of the workforce or business associate is required to provide information about work-related activities, actions, or omissions of a covered entity. A member of the workforce or business associate who had actual knowledge of a HIPAA violation committed by the covered entity, but failed to notify the government and affirmatively attempted to conceal information about the covered entity's breach, could face charges for misprision of a felony.[199]

A member of the workforce or a business associate or anyone else similarly might be prosecuted for obstructing a federal criminal investigation of a covered entity, by means of bribery, intimidation, or physical force.[200]

In the criminal context, it is important to remember that prosecutors intend to convict alleged violators, and that the HIPAA CMP Provisions for leniency are not applicable to the HIPAA Criminal Provisions. Thus, members of the workforce and business associates will be well advised to obtain separate, competent counsel if they are required to provide information in a criminal investigation of a covered entity for which they provided services.

Those prosecuted under HIPAA or other federal statutes should also be aware of joint representation issues that can arise. If one lawyer or law firm is retained to represent more than one defendant, matters divulged by one jointly represented defendant to the joint legal counsel likely will not be protected from counsel's disclosure of such matters to any other jointly represented defendants because of the consequent absence of attorney-client privilege protections. In addition, if differences arise between or among such defendants, joint counsel might be required to withdraw from such representation. In addition, entering into a joint-defense agreement might also be worthy of consideration.

F. Statute of Limitations

The general federal statute of limitations period applicable to criminal violations, and therefore to violations under the HIPAA Criminal Provisions, is five years from the date of commission of the offense.[201]

---

[199] *See, e.g.*, 18 U.S.C. §4 (prohibits concealing information regarding the commission of a felony).

[200] *See* 18 U.S.C. §§1510, 1512(b).

[201] 18 U.S.C. §3281.

VI. Enforcement Under Other Federal Statutes

Conduct that is an offense under HIPAA may also be a violation of one or more other federal civil or criminal statutes. In much the same way that actions with respect to false claims violations and anti-kickback violations have been brought under generally applicable federal statutes other than the FCA and the anti-kickback statute it may be expected that actions with respect to HIPAA violations will be brought under federal statutes other than HIPAA.

The government may use other statutes for other reasons, including the following:

- the elements of the conduct at issue may more closely approximate a violation of another federal statute than a violation of HIPAA;
- higher penalties or other remedies, such as freezing of assets, may be available under another statute;
- government agencies that do not have authority to enforce HIPAA may seek to penalize acts that violate HIPAA;
- governmental regulators, prosecutors, or judges may be more familiar with other federal statutes; or
- there may be existing case law or procedural requirements relating to another federal statute that are more favorable to the government.

A. Federal Trade Commission Act

Section 5 of the Federal Trade Commission Act prohibits unfair or deceptive acts or practices in or affecting commerce.[202] The Federal Trade Commission (FTC) has argued that a covered entity's failure to adhere to its notice of privacy practices, including implementing reasonable and appropriate measures to protect information against unauthorized access, represents an unfair act or practice under the FTC Act.[203] The FTC has enforced this theory through joint investigations with OCR, resulting in joint resolutions in which parties entered into resolution agreements (involving financial settlements) and three-year corrective plans with HHS and 20-year consent orders with the FTC.[204] When the FTC has reason to believe that Section 5 has been violated, the FTC issues a complaint setting forth its charges.[205] The entity may settle the charges by signing a consent agreement (without admitting liability), which often remains in

---

[202] 15 U.S.C. §45(a)(1).

[203] In the Matter of CVS Caremark Corporation Complaint, FTC (Docket No. C-4259), *available at* http://www.ftc.gov/os/caselist/0723119/090623cvscmpt.pdf; In the Matter of Rite Aid Corporation Complaint, FTC (Docket No. C-4308), *available at* http://www.ftc.gov/os/caselist/0723121/101122riteaidcmpt.pdf.

[204] Press Release, Dep't of Health & Human Servs., Office for Civil Rights, *CVS Pays $2.25 Million and Toughens Practices to Settle HIPAA Privacy Case* (Feb. 18, 2009), *available at* http://www.hhs.gov/news/press/2009pres/02/20090218a.html; Press Release, Dep't of Health & Human Servs., Office for Civil Rights, *Rite Aid Agrees to Pay $1 Million to Settle HIPAA Privacy Case* (July 27, 2010), *available at* http://www.hhs.gov/news/press/2010pres/07/20100727a.html.

[205] Federal Trade Commission, *A Brief Overview of the Federal Trade Commission's Investigative and Law Enforcement Authority* (July 2008), *available at* http://www.ftc.gov/ogc/brfovrvw.shtm.

place for 20 years.[206] Alternatively, the entity can dispute the charges before an administrative law judge, with appeal rights to the full Commission and then an appropriate U.S. Circuit Court of Appeals.[207]

B. False Claims and False Statements Statutes

Prosecutors have at their disposal numerous civil and criminal false claims and false statements statutes. The FCA is the most extensively used. The FCA imposes civil penalties on any person who, among other things

- knowingly presents, or causes to be presented, to the federal government a false and fraudulent claim for payment or approval; or
- knowingly makes, uses, or causes to be made a false record or statement to get a false or fraudulent claim paid or approved by the federal government.[208]

The FCA is a particular favorite among federal prosecutors because of the flexible intent standard and the high level of monetary damages—treble damages and up to $10,000 per claim.

Another available false claims statute is the Program Fraud Civil Remedies Act of 1986. This statute provides in part that any person who makes, presents, or submits to the federal government a claim that the person "knows or has reason to know" is false, fictitious, or fraudulent, or who includes a statement that is false, fictitious, or fraudulent, is subject to civil money penalties of up to $5,000 per false claim or statement and up to twice the amount claimed in lieu of damages.[209]

The Medicare program and Medicaid program civil monetary penalties statute imposes civil penalties on any person who knowingly presents, or causes to be presented, to the federal government a claim that misrepresents the medical items or services provided, or with respect to which there was an underlying violation of certain Medicare program or Medicaid program obligations. A violation is punishable by a civil monetary penalty of up to $10,000 for each item or service, plus up to treble damages.[210]

Another commonly used federal criminal statute prohibits the making of "false statements" to the government, including to a federal health program such as the Medicare program. The statute is violated if a person dealing with a federal government agency "knowingly and willfully":

- falsifies, conceals, or covers up by any trick, scheme, or device a material fact;
- makes any materially false, fictitious, or fraudulent statement or representation; or

---

[206]*Id.*

[207]*Id.*

[208]*See* 31 U.S.C. §3729(a). See Fraud Enforcement and Recovery Act of 2009, Pub. L. No. 111-21, 123 Stat. 1617 (2009), for amendments affecting the FCA, discussed above in V.B.

[209]31 U.S.C. §3802.

[210]42 U.S.C. §1320a-7a.

- makes or uses any false writing or document knowing the same to contain any materially false, fictitious, or fraudulent statement or entry.[211]

Violations of this statute are punishable by a fine, up to five years of imprisonment, or both.

A portion of HIPAA other than the Administrative Simplification Subtitle also added a false statements provision specific to health care benefit programs. Under that provision, a person may be subject to a fine, up to five years of imprisonment, or both, if such person "knowingly and willfully":

- falsifies, conceals, or covers up by any trick, scheme, or device a material fact; or
- makes any materially false, fictitious, or fraudulent statements or representations, or makes or uses any materially false writing or document knowing the same to contain any materially false, fictitious, or fraudulent statement or entry.[212]

It is possible that any of these statutes could be used, however inappropriately, to prosecute those who might otherwise be punished for HIPAA violations, if a covered entity submitted a claim for services with respect to which there was a HIPAA violation, under the theory that a claim so submitted was false because the claim related to services rendered in connection with which there was an underlying violation of federal law.[213] In this regard, strategies in which covered entities aimed to reduce risk by shifting billing and other responsibilities to business associates might be limited, because a prosecutor might consider prosecuting a covered entity for submitting false claims if the covered entity were alleged to have been involved in, or aware of, the conduct resulting in the submission of false claims for payment.[214] But thus far, no such prosecutorial initiatives appear to have been undertaken.

C. Mail and Wire Fraud

The federal mail and wire fraud statute is available as a prosecutorial tool in cases that involve sending fraudulent items through the U.S. mail or via commercial courier or electronic means. The statute, in relevant part, prohibits the use of the mail for the purpose of executing "any scheme or artifice to defraud, or for obtaining money or property by means of false or fraudulent

---

[211] 18 U.S.C. §1001; *see, e.g.*, United States v. Greber, 760 F.2d 68 (3d Cir. 1985) (claims forms representing that health monitors were operated for longer than actually operated was a false statement under 18 U.S.C. §1001).

[212] 18 U.S.C. §1035.

[213] Prosecutors have brought successful actions under the FCA when the alleged "falsity" of the claim was an underlying anti-kickback statute violation. *See* United States *ex rel*. Thompson v. Columbia/HCA Healthcare, 20 F. Supp. 2d 1017 (S.D. Tex. 1998); United States *ex rel*. Pogue v. American Healthcorp., 914 F. Supp. 1507 (M.D. Tenn. 1996); United States *ex rel*. Roy v. Anthony, 914 F. Supp. 1504 (S.D. Ohio 1994).

[214] *See, e.g.*, United States v. Teeven, 862 F. Supp. 1200 (D. Del. 1992); United States *ex rel*. Marcus v. Hess, 317 U.S. 537, 63 S. Ct. 379 (1943) (federal government obtained FCA recoveries based on causation as opposed to direct presentment of claims). But see IV.A., above.

pretenses, representations, or promises."[215] In addition, persons are prohibited from transmitting any communication by means of wire, radio, or television for the purpose of executing "any scheme or artifice to defraud, or for obtaining money or property by means of false or fraudulent pretenses, representations, or promises."[216] Mail and wire fraud violations are punishable by fines and up to five years of imprisonment for each violation, or both. The federal mail and wire fraud statute may be used in circumstances where protected health information, such as a health insurance number, is impermissibly disclosed through the mail for a fraudulent purpose, such as through the submission of a false claim for payment.

D. RICO

The Racketeer Influenced and Corrupt Organizations Act (RICO) has been used to prosecute a wide variety of crimes that are not necessarily related to organized criminal ventures, including many prosecutions of health care organizations. Among other proscribed activities, RICO prohibits a person from receiving any income, directly or indirectly, from a pattern of "racketeering activity," which means committing a prohibited act, such as mail or wire fraud, at least twice within 10 years.[217] A prosecutor must prove each of the following elements to succeed in convicting on a RICO claim: the existence of an enterprise, which is defined as "any individual, partnership, corporation, association or other legal entity, and any union or group of individuals associated in fact although not a legal entity"; that the enterprise affected interstate commerce; that the defendant was employed by or associated with the enterprise; that the defendant participated, either directly or indirectly, in the conduct or affairs of the enterprise; and that the defendant engaged in a pattern of racketeering activity.[218] A RICO violation is punishable by a fine, up to 20 years imprisonment, or both.[219]

RICO might potentially be used by the federal government in a criminal prosecution against a covered entity as well as members of the workforce and business associates who allegedly are participating in the same criminal scheme with the covered entity. But thus far, no such prosecutorial initiatives appear to have been undertaken.

E. HIPAA as a Standard of Care

Industry observers have long speculated that, although there is no private right of action under HIPAA, the HIPAA standards might be applied by courts as a standard of care in civil negligence cases. A North Carolina Court of Appeals decision applied the Privacy Rule nondisclosure requirements as a

---

[215] 18 U.S.C. §1341.
[216] *Id.* §1343.
[217] *Id.* §§1961, 1962.
[218] United States v. Kopituk, 690 F.2d 1289 (11th Cir. 1982).
[219] 18 U.S.C. §1963.

standard of care for medical practitioners.[220] This decision is also notable for the fact that the pleading of the standard of care only made a general reference to HIPAA, which the court deemed sufficient, so as not to "defeat the purpose of simple notice pleadings."[221] In addition, the court did not require that the claim for damages was substantiated by an expert opinion and found that the claim of negligent infliction of emotional distress alone was sufficient to allow the case to go forward.[222]

Similarly, the U.S. District Court for the Eastern District of Missouri held that a state claim for negligence per se can be premised solely on an alleged violation of HIPAA, despite the lack of a private right of action under HIPAA.[223]

VII. STATE-LAW PREEMPTION

The application of HIPAA state-law preemption principles will determine whether federal HIPAA or a state law that covers the same subject matter will be enforceable and, therefore, under which law enforcement can be founded. The general HIPAA rule on preemption, which is subject to several exceptions, is that a HIPAA standard or requirement will supersede a contrary state law.[224] The most significant exception is that, in the context of the HIPAA privacy requirements, a contrary but more stringent (i.e., more protective)[225] state health-privacy law will not be superseded and therefore will remain enforceable under state law.[226]

Further, a state law is not superseded if HHS determines under 45 C.F.R. §160.204 that the provision of state law is necessary:

- to prevent fraud and abuse related to the provision of or payment for health care;
- to ensure appropriate state regulation of insurance and health plans to the extent expressly authorized by statute or regulation;
- for state reporting on health care delivery or costs; or
- for purposes of serving a compelling need related to public health, safety, or welfare, and if a standard, requirement, or implementation specification under HIPAA is at issue, if HHS determines that the intrusion into privacy is warranted when balanced against the need being served.

---

[220] Acosta v. Byrum, 638 S.E.2d 246 (N.C. Ct. App. 2006).

[221] *Id.* at 251.

[222] *See id.* at 252.

[223] I.S. v. Washington Univ., No. 4:11CV235SNLJ, 2011 WL 2433585 (E.D. Mo. June 14, 2011).

[224] 42 U.S.C. §1320d-7(a); 45 C.F.R. §160.203; United States *ex rel.* Stewart v. Louisiana Clinic, No. Civ. A. 99-1767, 2002 WL 31819130 (E.D. La. Dec. 12, 2002) (holding that HIPAA preempts noncontrary state provider/patient privilege law); *see also* State v. Downs, 923 So. 2d 726 (La. Ct. App. 2005) (finding no preemption when HIPAA and LA. REV. STAT. §13:3715.1(B)(1) are not "contrary" to one another in connection with subpoenaed information).

[225] The law is deemed to be more protective of privacy if the law prohibits uses and disclosures of PHI that would be permitted under the Privacy Rule, or in the case of patient access, provides greater patient access rights than the Privacy Rule. *See* 45 C.F.R. §160.202.

[226] *Id.* §160.203(b).

A state law also is not superseded if HHS determines that the principal purpose of the state law is to regulate the manufacture, registration, distribution, dispensing, or other control of any controlled substance (as defined in 21 U.S.C. §802 or as deemed by state law).[227]

Also exempt from being superseded are state laws that:

- provide for the reporting of disease or injury, child abuse, birth, or death, or for the conduct of public health surveillance, investigation, or intervention; or
- require a health plan to report, or provide access to, information for the purpose of management audits, financial audits, program monitoring and evaluation, or the licensure or certification of facilities or individuals.[228]

Because of the potential for the enforcement of state laws that are not superseded, HIPAA compliance should include compliance with applicable state law unless a relevant HIPAA standard or requirement completely supersedes the state law. In most cases, state law will not be preempted because it is possible to comply both with HIPAA and the state law.

For example, a state law may require a hospital to disclose the medical record of a patient when a subpoena is presented and the patient is a named party in the case, whereas such disclosure is prohibited under the Privacy Rule unless the hospital takes certain steps to ensure that the patient is notified or a protective order is obtained with respect to the patient's PHI. There generally is no preemption in this situation because a covered entity likely can comply with both laws: the covered entity either discloses in compliance with the subpoena and also takes any necessary steps under the Privacy Rule (such as seeking a qualified protective order), or the patient is not a named party and the covered entity therefore does not disclose the medical record (thereby complying with both laws). A conflict in this situation would only occur in the unlikely event that the state law required disclosure but prohibited the covered entity from taking any necessary actions under the Privacy Rule, in which case the Privacy Rule would preempt the state law (since the state law was not more stringent, i.e., it was not more protective of the patient).

The Supreme Court of Georgia held in 2007 that HIPAA preempted a Georgia statute requiring that a plaintiff in a medical malpractice case provide a broad authorization for release of the plaintiff's medical records.[229] The court based this holding in part on the court's view that (1) the Georgia statute did not give the plaintiff notice of the right to revoke the authorization; and (2) the Georgia statute did not otherwise satisfy the requirements of a valid HIPAA authorization, in particular, the Georgia statute's "failure to require a specific and meaningful identification of the information to be disclosed and failure to provide for an expiration date or a sufficient expiration event."[230] The court also

---

[227] 42 U.S.C. §1320d-7(a)(2), (b); 45 C.F.R. §160.203(a).
[228] 42 U.S.C. §1320d-7(b), (c); 45 C.F.R. §160.203(c) and (d).
[229] Allen v. Wright, No. S06G2018 (Ga. May 14, 2007).
[230] *Id.* at 6–7.

noted that the holding was consistent with a recent Georgia Court of Appeals' decision interpreting the same statutory release requirement.[231]

VIII. COMPLIANCE: ESTABLISHING A PLAN TO AVOID ENFORCEMENT ACTIONS

As with other regulatory requirements in health care, compliance should be enhanced by establishing and implementing compliance policies and procedures designed to reduce the likelihood of a HIPAA violation and to provide for appropriate responses and remedial action if a violation occurs. Covered entities and business associates that already have compliance plans in place should consider supplementing them to include policies and procedures for compliance with HIPAA requirements including those arising under the HITECH Act and analogous state laws. Those that do not yet have a compliance plan should consider implementing a plan that includes addressing HIPAA and a broader range of regulatory concerns as well as HIPAA.

A HIPAA compliance plan, whether standing alone or integrated into a broader compliance plan, may be structured to satisfy each of the seven required elements of the U.S. Sentencing Commission Guidelines for the Sentencing of Organizations:[232]

- development and distribution of written standards of conduct and written policies and procedures;
- designation of a compliance officer and/or compliance committee that oversees the compliance effort and reports directly to the highest level officer and governing body of the organization;
- regular, effective education and training of employees;
- reporting mechanism for employees to report compliance issues to the compliance officer, including procedures to protect the anonymity of reporters and to protect them from retaliation;
- periodic auditing and evaluation of compliance efforts;
- disciplinary mechanisms to enforce compliance standards; and
- policies and procedures to respond to detected compliance violations, to take corrective action, and to prevent future similar violations.

Although detailed treatment of each of these requirements is beyond the scope of this chapter, further guidance on developing effective compliance

---

[231] *Id.* (citing Northlake Med. Center, LLC v. Queen, 634 S.E.2d 486 (Ga. Ct. App. 2006)).

[232] *See* U.S. SENTENCING COMMISSION , 2010 FEDERAL SENTENCING GUIDELINES MANUAL, 8B2.1, *available at* http://www.ussc.gov/Guidelines/2010_guidelines/Manual_HTML/8b2_1.htm ("(D) Apply §8C2.5 (Culpability Score) to determine the culpability score. To determine whether the organization had an effective compliance and ethics program for purposes of §8C2.5(f), apply §8B2.1 (Effective Compliance and Ethics Program")). Note that the HHS OIG has not indicated that the ongoing litigation relating to these Guidelines should in any way derogate from the advisability of those in the health care industry continuing to implement corporate compliance plans. *See* Douglas E. Motzenbecker, *Supreme Court Further Undercuts Sentencing Guidelines*, LITIGATION NEWS (Mar. 2008), *available at* http://www.abanet.org/litigation/litigationnews/2008/march/0308_article_guidelines.html; *see also* American Bar Association, The New Federal Sentencing Guidelines for Organizations: Great for Prosecutors, Tough on Organizations, Deadly for the Privilege (Mar. 2005).

programs can be found in industry-specific guidance documents published by the HHS OIG.[233] There are also many organizations, consultants, and lawyers available to provide guidance on developing a compliance program that meets the Sentencing Commission sentencing guidelines' requirements and is consistent with applicable OIG guidance.

To integrate the HIPAA requirements into existing compliance plans, covered entities and business associates should make sure that the written standards incorporate current and future HIPAA requirements and that the policies and procedures that are developed incorporate mechanisms for responding to HIPAA concerns including allegations of violations.

Careful thought will be needed in developing policies and procedures regarding various aspects of HIPAA implementation. For instance, compliance with the standard transaction requirements under the Transactions Rule will require policies for handling the receipt of nonstandard transactions and for converting information that exists in nonstandard format, whether kept in paper files or in an electronic database, into standard electronic format. In the Privacy Rule context, policies will have to be developed to address areas that include:

- implementing Privacy Rule patient access rights—that is, patients' rights to obtain access to PHI, amend PHI, and obtain an accounting of certain disclosures of PHI; issues to be addressed in developing these polices may include determining who will be responsible for processing access requests, the method for accessing the appropriate information from databases and filing systems, and the format of the response to patient access requests;
- implementing procedures and systems that ensure compliance with restrictions on uses and disclosures of PHI; issues to be addressed include ensuring that authorizations or other permissions are obtained when required, that restrictions requested by individuals on the disclosure of PHI are complied with, that unless permitted under HIPAA only minimally necessary disclosures are made, and that disclosures for which an accounting is required (including pursuant to the HITECH Act's new accounting for disclosures of electronic PHI in electronic health record requirements[234]) are appropriately tracked so that an accounting of disclosures may be provided to an individual as required upon request;
- documenting written acknowledgments of the organization's Notice of Privacy Practices or good-faith attempts to obtain such written acknowledgment.[235]

---

[233] Dep't of Health & Human Servs., Office of Inspector General, Compliance Guidance, *available at* http://oig.hhs.gov/fraud/complianceguidance.asp.

[234] HITECH Act §13405(c) (codified at 42 U.S.C. §17935(c)).

[235] *See* 45 C.F.R. §164.520(c) for implementing specifications under the Privacy Rule for provision of a Notice of Privacy Practices; *see also* OCR references regarding the Notice of Privacy Practices, including:

> Covered Direct Treatment Providers must also: Provide the notice to the individual no later than the date of first service delivery (after the April 14, 2003 compliance date of the Privacy Rule) and, except in an emergency treatment situation, make a good faith effort to obtain the individual's written acknowledgment of receipt of the notice. If an acknowledgment cannot be obtained, the provider must document his or her efforts to obtain the acknowledgment and the reason why it was not obtained.

IX. Conclusion

The scope and complexity of HIPAA causes anxiety in the health care industry. The possibility that the enactment of the HITECH Act will lead to increased enforcement has raised this level of anxiety. Some hope that HHS will continue to promote and assure compliance through education and cooperative efforts rather than the imposition of harsh penalties. While it is likely that most enforcement actions will continue to be resolved through voluntary corrective action, it also is likely that HHS will resolve a small but growing number of matters through penalties or settlement amounts.

Criminal prosecution under the HIPAA Criminal Provisions will require that the violator "knowingly" committed the offense[236] and that the prosecutor can meet the higher standard of proof for criminal actions (that is, beyond a reasonable doubt). Serious HIPAA offenses also may be prosecuted under other federal civil and criminal statutes that apply to the specific conduct at issue.

As with other areas of health regulation, among the best HIPAA defenses is a corporate compliance program.[237] It will be most efficient for those entities that have already adopted corporate compliance programs to update them to incorporate compliance with HIPAA requirements and standards. Those that have not yet adopted corporate compliance programs, including law firms and other professional firms that provide services as a business associate to covered entities, should consider doing so now. In developing a compliance strategy, however designed, health care and other entities should be sure to address compliance with state laws that are not superseded by HIPAA or that only are partially superseded by HIPAA. But first, a careful reading of the HIPAA enforcement provisions enacted by Congress and the implementing rules is recommended. Also of critical importance is a continuing education component for corporate compliance programs. Continuing education can provide current knowledge to all who are involved in any way in compliance, including in particular those newly or temporarily hired, while recollections of others are refreshed and new developments are addressed and taken into account in administering HIPAA implementation and compliance.

Dep't of Health & Human Servs., Office for Civil Rights, Notice of Privacy Practices for Protected Health Information (published Dec. 3, 2002, and revised Apr. 3, 2003), *available at* http://www.hhs.gov/ocr/privacy/hipaa/understanding/coveredentities/notice.html. There is no requirement under the Security Rule for tendering a notice of security practices (or in the Privacy Rule mandating inclusion of Security Rule policies and procedures as a part of the Privacy Rule Notice of Privacy Practices), although having such a document available for use might be helpful both for workforce educational purposes and for patients.

[236] See discussion of the Fraud Enforcement and Recovery Act of 2009, Pub. L. No. 111-21, in VI.B., above.

[237] See VIII., above.

9

E-Health Liability*

I.	Introduction	252
II.	Professional Licensure and Credentialing	254
	A. Licensure Generally	254
	B. Penalties for Violating Licensure Laws	257
	C. Pharmacogenetics	259
	D. Public Health Emergencies	260
	E. Practice of Telemedicine Without Full Licensure	261
	1. The Consultation Exception	261
	2. Endorsement	262
	3. Reciprocity	262
	4. Special License	263
	5. Telehealth Networks	263
	F. Credentialing	264
III.	Initiatives Regarding Regulation of Telemedicine	264
	A. Joint Working Group on Telemedicine	265
	B. Federation of State Medical Boards	266
	C. Nurse Licensure Compact	267
IV.	Malpractice	268
	A. Existence of Physician-Patient Relationship	268
	B. What Is the Legal Duty?	271
	C. Informed Consent and the Duty to Disclose	272
	D. Vicarious Liability	274
	E. Patient Abandonment	275
	F. Availability of Insurance for Telemedicine Encounters	276
	1. Malpractice Insurance and Gaps in Coverage	276
	2. Disclaimers of Liability	277
	3. What Malpractice Does Cover	277
	a. "Specified-Risk" or "Specified-Perils" Coverage	277
	b. "All-Risk" or "Open-Perils" Coverage	277
	c. Recommendation	278

---

*Daphne D. Walker, Tenet Healthcare Corporation, Dallas Texas, formerly of Fulbright & Jaworski L.L.P. The author thanks J.A. (Tony) Patterson, Jr., who authored earlier versions of this chapter, previously titled "Professional Licensure and Liability Issues."

V.	International Practice of Medicine	278
	A. Telemedicine	278
	B. Medical Tourism	278
	C. Medicaid and Medicare Reimbursement	279
	D. International Legal and Licensing Issues	280
VI.	Electronic Health Information	281
	A. Physician-Patient Relationship	282
	B. Standard of Care	283
	C. Certifications	283
	D. Liability	284
VII.	Conclusion	286

I. Introduction

Health care professionals, including physicians, nurses, pharmacists, and other licensed health care providers, are highly regulated. Regulation of health care professionals has traditionally been the province of the states. The "omnipresence" of the Internet and rapid advances in medical technologies place new challenges on the states, and the federal government, to ensure that the interests of the public—and individual patients—are protected. Regulators are issuing new regulatory positions under existing laws, and legislators are enacting new laws in an attempt to address the industry changes being brought about through e-health.[1]

This chapter addresses the regulation of health care professionals, principally physicians, engaged in e-health. The reader may use this chapter to help identify issues, identify some of the existing state or federal laws that address the issues, and use these aids to look to applicable law in the jurisdiction or jurisdictions implicated in his or her particular facts and circumstances.

A series of examples helps set the stage for the chapter.

Example 1: A cardiologist with a specialty physician group in Cleveland, Ohio, is asked to review an echocardiogram of a hospital patient who resides in Archer City, Texas, and the echocardiogram is transmitted electronically by another cardiologist in Wichita Falls, Texas.

Example 2: A Minnesota-based group of oncologists sets up a Web site that provides information on cancer, including treatment options and side effects, and includes a certain feature that permits a Web site visitor to "ask the doctor" questions about cancer.

Example 3: A physician at a teaching hospital in Baltimore, Maryland, examines via an interactive television system a patient located in an examining room in New Castle, Pennsylvania, with the help of a local Pennsylvania physician.

---

[1]This Introduction will focus on telemedicine or "cyber" medicine, which broadly defined means the use of electronic technologies to provide health care at a distance, often across state lines. This chapter will examine issues pertinent to physicians except as otherwise noted.

Example 4: A group of psychiatrists in New York City offers "online" psychotherapy to enrollees of a health benefit plan who are located throughout the United States.

In the first example above, is the physician located in Ohio legally practicing medicine in Texas, where the patient is located? Must he or she first obtain licensure in Texas? In the third example, is the consulting physician in Baltimore considered to be practicing across state lines? In the second and fourth examples, are the Minnesota- and New York-based physicians practicing medicine legally in the various jurisdictions where the Web users are physically located? In all of these examples, is there a physician-patient relationship? If so, is there an obligation to obtain the informed consent of the patient for the physician services provided, and if so, who has that obligation? Fact patterns such as these will become increasingly prevalent in the Internet era. The questions posed are currently difficult to answer, and the answers will differ among the states.

During the 1980s, the practice of medicine rarely involved practice across state lines, because the technology facilitating this kind of practice had not yet been developed. Consequently, it was relatively straightforward, for example, for a state medical practice board to determine whether a particular physician was under its jurisdiction.

With the spectacular advances in technology, including its application to the diagnosis of disease and treatment of patients, however, the practice of medicine across state lines, through the use of technology, has become increasingly common. All indications are that interstate practice by telemedicine will become standard in the future. Regrettably, state licensure laws and regulations have not kept pace with the advances in the application of electronic technology to health care. It is important, but remains difficult, for interstate telemedicine practitioners and state authorities alike to determine whether and under what circumstances telemedicine services constitute the practice of medicine, and whether a particular physician is in fact providing medical services in a given jurisdiction.

States are addressing these issues with the enactment of new statutes and the promulgation of new regulations. But different states have addressed the issues in very different ways, leading to dramatic inconsistencies in the way licensure statutes—especially as they apply to the interstate practice of telemedicine—are applied. Despite these inconsistencies, the increasing level of legislative activity is a clear indication that the states are beginning to recognize the inevitability of the growth of telemedicine. It is anticipated that, over time, experience and familiarity with the practice of telemedicine will lead to a relatively consistent set of state licensure statutes and regulations that will facilitate the practice of medicine across state lines. However, as discussed in II., below, that is not currently the case. As of 2011, the states have not developed a consistent set of statutes and regulations governing the practice of telemedicine. Whether consistency can be accomplished without federal intervention is open to question, especially given the American Medical Association's current opposition to national licensure approaches for telemedicine.[2]

---

[2] *See* Am. Med. Ass'n, Physician Licensure: An Update of Trends, *available at* http://www.ama-assn.org/ama/pub/about-ama/our-people/member-groups-sections/young-physicians-section/advocacy-resources/physician-licensure-an-update-trends.page.

Indeed, as a consequence of the variability in state licensure laws, there is a growing call by telemedicine advocates for the federal government to play an increased role in the licensure of health professionals. Of course, this approach would contravene the history of professional licensure as a matter falling within the sole purview of the states.

The resolution of these licensure issues is a critical first step in unlocking telemedicine's vast potential. Telemedicine advocates rightly claim that its widespread practice will revolutionize the practice of medicine. Those advocates believe it will dramatically increase the access of patients to high quality health care, given that the locations of the physician and patient are generally irrelevant: clearly, the physician and patient need not be in the same place for health services to be provided.

Government policymakers generally agree with the telemedicine advocates, expecting telemedicine to improve greatly the overall quality and accessibility of health care, especially in rural and underserved areas.[3] However, strong cautionary voices cite the potential dangers to patients who will be subject to vital care decisions made by someone they have never seen and by whom they have never been examined. Will the kinds of fraud increasingly being perpetrated on the Internet find their way into the practice of telemedicine? Who will police the system to protect the public? None of the advantages of telemedicine will be fully realized, however, if laws applicable to the practice of interstate telemedicine do not keep pace with the advances in technology.

Federal and state health care program reimbursement for services using telemedicine is a strong factor in the growth and acceptance of telehealth services. From the federal perspective, the *Medicare Carriers Manual* is regularly updated to provide for the coverage, payment, and claims procedures applicable to Medicare reimbursement for telehealth services.[4]

The practice of medicine by interstate and international sources via telemedicine and other means is becoming more popular over time. Advanced technology and lower costs for health care services overseas make diagnosis or treatment by international providers advantageous. However, licensing, reimbursement, and liability issues remain challenging for these new methods of accessing health care.

II. PROFESSIONAL LICENSURE AND CREDENTIALING

A. Licensure Generally

States have traditionally regulated the practice of medicine through their police power. The courts, both federal and state, have long upheld on constitutional grounds the right of states to establish standards regulating the health care

---

[3]FED. COMMC'NS COMM'N, TELECOMMUNICATIONS & HEALTH CARE ADVISORY COMM., FINDINGS AND RECOMMENDATIONS (submitted Oct. 15, 1996).

[4]These procedures are found in the Medicare Internet-Only Manuals (IOMs), Publication 100-2, MEDICARE BENEFIT POLICY MANUAL, ch. 15, §270, *available at* http://www.cms.gov/Manuals/IOM/list.asp.

professions as a means for states to protect the public health and safety of their citizens.[5]

All states and the District of Columbia require a physician to be licensed in the state in which he or she practices medicine. Generally, the requirements a physician must satisfy to be licensed in a state include:

- graduation from an accredited medical school;
- successful completion of licensure examination;
- certification as being of good character; and
- completion of an accredited residency program.[6]

The "practice of medicine" is defined by each state. Texas, for example, defines the practice of medicine as:

> The diagnosis, treatment, or offer to treat a mental or physical disease or disorder or a physical deformity or injury by any system or method, or the attempt to effect cures of those conditions, by a person who:
>
> A. publicly professes to be a physician or surgeon; or
>
> B. directly or indirectly charges money or other compensation for those services.[7]

This definition is consistent with the definition in many other state licensure statutes. Whether the practice of telemedicine fits into this general definition remains unclear in many jurisdictions. A number of progressive states, such as Texas, South Dakota, and Montana, have specifically addressed the problem and included in their licensure statutes provisions that specifically declare that activities related to telemedicine constitute the practice of medicine.

A person who is physically located in another jurisdiction but who, through the use of any medium, including an electronic medium, performs an act that is part of a patient care service initiated in a particular state, including the taking of an x-ray examination or the preparation of pathological material for examination, and that would affect the diagnosis or treatment of the patient, could be considered to be engaged in the practice of medicine and thus subject to appropriate regulation by the applicable state's board.[8]

Thus, in the first example in the Introduction,[9] the Ohio physician may clearly be viewed by the Texas Medical Board as practicing medicine in Texas and be subject to regulation by the state board. On the other hand, in those states that have not followed this example—for example, New York (relevant in

---

[5]U.S. CONST. amend. X; Collins v. Texas, 223 U.S. 288 (1912); Dent v. West Va., 129 U.S. 114 (1889).

[6]See, e.g., 49 PA. CODE §17.1.

[7]TEX. OCC. CODE ANN. §151.002(13).

[8]See, e.g., TEX. OCC. CODE ANN. §151.056(a); see also ALA. CODE §§34-24-500 to -508; ARIZ. REV. STAT. ANN. §§36-3601 to -3603 (addressing providers such as podiatrists, psychologists, and physician assistants in addition to physicians); CAL. BUS. & PROF. CODE §§2052.5, 2290.5; CAL. HEALTH & SAFETY CODE §1374.13; GA. CODE ANN. §43-34-31.1; HAW. REV. STAT. §453-2; ILL. COMP. STAT. 60/49-5; MD. CODE ANN., HEALTH OCC. §14-302(4); MISS. CODE ANN. §73-25-34; MO. ANN. STAT. §334.010; MONT. CODE ANN. §§37-3-341 to -349; NEB. REV. STAT. §71-7614; NEV. REV. STAT. §630.020; N.C. GEN. STAT. §90-18; OKLA. STAT. tit. 36, §§6801 to 6804; tit. 59, §492(c)(2)(b); tit. 63, §1-2701; S.D. CODIFIED LAWS §36-4-41; and TENN. CODE ANN. §63-6-209.

[9]See I., above.

the fourth example above)—it is unclear whether the practice of *telemedicine* constitutes the practice of *medicine*. In some states, the subject of telemedicine is not addressed in detail, but practice across state lines in the case of an emergency or the occasional, infrequent, or irregular practice across state lines is exempted from regulation.[10] State medical boards are likely to conclude that telemedicine does constitute the practice of medicine in their state, primarily because the physician still engages in diagnosis and treatment—albeit using a different medium than is conventionally the case,[11] and because states have constitutional authority to protect the health and safety of their citizens.

State laws are the principal regulatory scheme for professional licensure. They normally address telemedicine directly with specific provisions defining and regulating telemedicine. States also use indirect ways to regulate telemedicine, such as by including various terms for telemedicine ("electronic means" is a term used often) in the definition of what will constitute the practice of medicine. These statutes or rules generally require an out-of-state physician to become licensed in the applicable state where the treatment is given (fully or specially, if so permitted) or to meet an exception.[12] Various states grant either exemptions or "special licenses,"[13] such as "restrictive licenses," to those physicians whose out-of-state practices meet certain requirements or "limited licenses" in which a state grants an out-of-state physician limited practicing rights.[14] In those states that do not recognize out-of-state licenses, the common practice still is to require full registration within the state.[15] In most states, physicians risk loss of licensure in their "home state," civil liability, and criminal prosecution if they are not licensed in the state in which they practice medicine.[16]

---

[10]*See, e.g.*, VT. STAT. ANN. tit. 26, §1313(b); VA. CODE ANN. §54.1-2901.

[11]U.S. DEP'T OF COMMERCE, TELEMEDICINE REPORT TO CONGRESS, 47–48 (1997).

[12]*See, e.g.*, ALASKA STAT. §08.64.370 (an exception exists for a nonresident who is asked by a state resident licensee to assist in diagnosis or treatment); ARK. CODE ANN. §§17-95-203, -206, -207 (physicians physically located outside the state who perform patient care through electronic mediums are engaged in the practice of medicine with some exceptions); IND. CODE §25-22.5-1-1.1 (the practice of medicine includes the diagnosis or treatment of a person in Indiana when the services are transmitted through electronic communication if done on a regular, routine, or nonepisodic basis); KY. REV. STAT. ANN. §§311.560, 311.5975 (although it is not the practice of medicine to engage in infrequent contacts when a medical professional is called in by a licensed practitioner for consultation or assistance, the statutes contain specific rules related to telehealth); MINN. STAT. §147.032 (specific provisions address the interstate practice of telemedicine, including annual registration and certain exceptions); MO. REV. STAT. §334.010 (making it unlawful to practice medicine across state lines); NEV. REV. STAT. §§630.020, .047, .049, .261(e) (a special license may be issued to allow the practice of medicine using equipment transferring information concerning medical conditions electronically, telephonically, or by fiber optics); OR. REV. STAT. §§677.135, .137, .139 (contain provisions establishing a special license, exceptions for mere consultations, responsibilities, prohibited practices, and confidentiality requirements); *see also* U.S. GEN. ACCOUNTING OFFICE, INTERNET PHARMACIES: ADDING DISCLOSURE REQUIREMENTS WOULD AID STATE AND FEDERAL OVERSIGHT, No. GAO-01-69 (Oct. 2000), *available at* http://www.gao.gov/cgi-bin/getrpt?GAO-01-69.

[13]Benedict Stanberry, *Legal and Ethical Aspects of Telemedicine,* 12(4) J. TELEMED. & TELECARE 166 (June 1, 2006).

[14]Glenn W. Wachter, *Interstate Licensure of Telemedicine Practitioners,* TELEMEDICINE INFORMATION EXCHANGE (Mar. 10, 2000).

[15]Stanberry, 12 J. TELEMED. & TELECARE at 166.

[16]Sarah E. Born, *Telemedicine in Massachusetts: A Better Way to Regulate,* 42 NEW ENG. L. REV. 195, 198 (Fall 2007).

Likewise, a host of licensure issues has developed from the expansion of wellness programs and disease management services provided via telephone and the Internet to individuals located across the country. Are the individuals who remotely provide health care recommendations and nutrition advice required to be licensed health care professionals (e.g., nurses, physicians, pharmacists, physical therapists, or dieticians)? The answer depends upon whether or not the services provided by these wellness program professionals or disease management consultants constitute a professional practice that is licensed by the state where the individual receiving the service is located. Careful attention to the nature of the services being provided and the definitions of what constitutes the practice of a professional service requiring licensure or certification is necessary in each jurisdiction where a "patient" is located.

Likewise, many states have enacted statutes or rules making it a violation of pharmacy and pharmacist licensing laws to dispense a prescription in an Internet-based transaction without there being a valid physician-patient relationship.[17] In an effort to help consumers identify legitimate Internet pharmacies, the National Association of Boards of Pharmacy has developed a certification program for pharmacies called the Verified Internet Pharmacy Practice Sites (VIPPS).[18]

B. Penalties for Violating Licensure Laws

Violation of state licensure statutes and regulations, commonly referred to as the "unauthorized practice of medicine," usually occurs in one of three ways:

1. an unlicensed person engages in activities that constitute the practice of medicine;

2. the activities of a licensed individual fall outside the scope of the license; and

3. an individual holds himself/herself out as a physician without having a valid license.[19]

A corollary of the "unauthorized practice of medicine" prohibition is the "corporate practice of medicine" or fee-splitting prohibition, which may also have application in the telemedicine setting, if an effect of the telemedicine arrangement is that a lay corporation is practicing medicine in another jurisdiction through a licensed physician and/or obtaining profits from the provision of a physician's professional services.[20] On a finding of a violation of the corporate

---

[17]*See, e.g.*, FLA. STAT. ch. 465 (requires Internet pharmacies, whether inside or outside of Florida, to be registered; imposes discipline on pharmacists dispensing when it is known or done with reason to know the purported prescription is not based on a valid practitioner-patient relationship; and makes it a second-degree felony to distribute a medicinal drug without a permit by an Internet pharmacy); *see also* TEX. OCC. CODE §562.056.

[18]Information on the VIPPS program is found at the Programs link at the Association's Web site at http://www.nabp.net.

[19]See, Alison M. Sulentic, *Crossing Borders: The Licensure of Interstate Telemedicine Practitioners*, 25 J. LEGIS. 1, 9 (1999).

[20]A majority of states recognize some form of this doctrine. *See* John Wiorlek, *The Corporate Practice of Medicine: An Outmoded Theory in Need of Modification*, 8 J. LEGAL MED. 465 (1987) (analyzing all 50 states' views regarding the corporate practice of medicine).

practice of medicine or fee-splitting prohibition, a state licensing board may take a variety of actions, including injunctive relief and revoking the license of the physician facilitating the corporate practice of medicine or fee splitting.[21]

The penalties for practicing without a license vary from state to state. In California, for example, one who engages in the unlicensed practice of medicine in a manner that creates the risk of great bodily harm is subject to "imprisonment in the state prison or in the county jail for not exceeding one year."[22] Persons who engage in the unlicensed practice of medicine in Massachusetts "shall be punished by a fine of not less than one hundred nor more than one thousand dollars or by imprisonment for not less than one month or more than one year, or both."[23] In Rhode Island, violators

> shall be imprisoned not more than three (3) years or fined not more than one thousand dollars ($1,000) or shall suffer both fine and imprisonment; and in no case when any provision of this chapter has been violated shall the person violating these provisions be entitled to receive compensation for services rendered.[24]

In the examples set out in the Introduction,[25] unless appropriate licensure were obtained or an exemption for infrequent practice were available, the Ohio physician would be subject to sanction in Texas; the Minnesota and New York "online" physicians would be subject to sanction in any jurisdiction where a "patient" is physically located; and the Maryland physician would be subject to sanction in Pennsylvania.

As the use of the Internet and technological advances has expanded, so have violations of state law. These violations have been most prevalent in the practice of prescribing drugs on Internet Web sites. Criminal penalties,[26] as well as civil remedies,[27] have been sought for these violations of law. The principal regulatory concerns include the absence of a proper examination and medical

---

[21] *See, e.g.*, TEX. OCC. CODE ANN. §§164.052, 165.155.

[22] CAL. BUS. & PROF. CODE §2052.

[23] MASS. ANN. LAWS ch. 112, §6.

[24] R.I. GEN. LAWS §5-37-12; *see also* N.C. GEN. STAT. §90-18; OKLA. STAT. tit. 59, §2067; OR. REV. STAT. §677.325.

[25] See I., above.

[26] A federal jury in Texas convicted two Texas pharmacists (and three physicians also pleaded guilty) for operating a Web-based pharmacy that dispensed controlled substances without engaging in proper medical practices of creating a medical history, conducting a mental or physical examination of the patient, using proper testing for establishing or confirming proper diagnosis, or establishing a process for monitoring the patient's response to the medications. United States v. Fuchs, No. 3:02CR0369P (N.D. Tex. Feb. 23, 2005), *aff'd*, 467 F.3d 889 (5th Cir. 2006). The Tenth Circuit upheld the conviction of a physician for conspiracy to distribute controlled prescription drugs outside the usual course of professional practice (21 U.S.C. §1956(h)), based, in part, on facts developed at the trial court that the defendant physician approved 90 to 95 percent of all prescription drug requests without ever examining the purported patient. United States v. Nelson, D.C. No. CR-01-142R (10th Cir. Sept. 20, 2004).

[27] A Kansas court assessed monetary penalties under the state's consumer protection act against a physician who prescribed Viagra over the Internet to a female agent in the Kansas Attorney General's Office (Kansas *ex rel.* Stovall v. Alivio, 61 P.3d 687 (Kan. 2003)). The California Medical Board assessed more than $48 million in fines against out-of-state physicians for prescribing drugs over the Internet to California residents in violation of the provisions of the California Business and Professions Code requiring a good-faith medical examination of the patient before prescribing. The Oregon Attorney General filed suit against two Oregon doctors for violating consumer protection laws in the sale of drugs over the Internet. Press Release, Dep't of

history review of the patient.[28] The physician should also ensure that the patient is well informed of the nature of the physician-patient relationship through informed consent.[29]

C. Pharmacogenetics

Personalized medicine, or pharmacogenetics, is based on the principle that therapy focused on the genetic makeup of each individual results in improved therapeutic responses and a reduction in adverse drug reactions.[30] Targeted patient therapies result in myriad legal issues, in addition to licensure requirements, including FDA regulatory matters, intellectual property, and product liability concerns.[31] For example, how is FDA approval of these drugs and the marketing of these drugs handled?[32] There may be intellectual property rights and licensing agreements that are specific to each genetic-specific drug.[33] The manufacturers of patient-specific medication may be liable for adverse reactions.[34]

However, pharmaceutical companies may use pharmacogenomics (which is a term often used interchangeably with pharmacogenetics but refers more generally to the study of all the many different genes that determine drug behavior) in an attempt to avoid products liability claims.[35] For instance, in order for a plaintiff to recover on a defective-design theory, the plaintiff must show that the drug's foreseeable risks were "so great compared to the therapeutic benefits that no reasonable physician would prescribe the drug for any class of patients."[36] A

Justice, *Attorney General Files Lawsuit Against Two Oregon Medical Doctors* (Oct. 23, 2003), *available at* http://www.doj.state.or.us/releases/2003/rel102303.shtml.

[28]In addition to the developments described in Section II.B., the Texas Attorney General has issued an opinion that a physician must conduct an "in person" examination of a patient as required prior to an inpatient mental health facility commitment, which thereby precludes an examination via audiovisual telecommunication. Texas Att'y Gen. Op. No. GA-0066 (Apr. 28, 2003). The Texas Medical Board had earlier adopted a policy outlining unprofessional conduct in Internet prescribing. The Medical Board of California has issued an information release for physicians called Drugs on the Information Highway at http://www.mbc.ca.gov/licensee/internet_prescribing.html, as has the New York Board for Professional Medical Conduct's Special Committee on Telemedicine, at http://www.health.state.ny.us/nysdoh/opmc/telemedicine.htm. As noted in II.A., above, Florida requires Internet pharmacies, whether inside or outside of Florida, to be registered, imposes discipline on pharmacists dispensing with knowledge or with reason to know the purported prescription is not based on a valid practitioner-patient relationship, and makes it a second-degree felony for an Internet pharmacy to distribute a medicinal drug without a permit. The physician-patient relationship in "cybermedicine" and the resulting exposure to medical malpractice liability is presented in Ruth Ellen Smalley, *Comment: Will a Lawsuit a Day Keep the Cyberdocs Away? Modern Theories of Medical Malpractice as Applied to Cybermedicine*, 7 RICH. J.L. & TECH. 29 (Winter 2001).

[29]*See, e.g.*, KY. REV. STAT. ANN. §311.5975 (requiring that informed consent be given before services are provided); TEX. OCC. CODE §111.002.

[30]Teresa Kelton, Esq., *Pharmacogenomics: The Re-discovery of the Concept of the Tailored Drug Therapy and Personalized Medicine*, 19 No. 3 HEALTH LAWYER 1, 3 (2007).

[31]*Id.* at 7.

[32]*Id.*

[33]*Id.* at 8.

[34]*Id.*

[35]Scott Sasjack, *Demanding Individually Safe Drugs Today: Overcoming the Cross-labeling Legal Hurdle to Pharmacogenomics*, 34 AM. J.L. & MED. 7, 14 (2008).

[36]*Id.* at 14–15.

pharmacogenomic test revealing therapeutic benefits of a particular drug could help defeat a defective-design theory.[37] However, the failure to make appropriate disclosure of the drug's risks by an advising physician qualified to provide that disclosure, or disclosure by someone not holding any or an appropriate license, opens the way for claims against that physician for professional negligence even if the products liability claim fails.

D. Public Health Emergencies

Recent catastrophic events including terrorism, natural disasters, and contagious diseases have resulted in public health emergencies on a state and national basis, creating a need for states to coordinate their legal preparedness efforts.[38] The Emergency Management Assistant Compact (EMAC) is the principal agreement for facilitating mutual aid among the states to address key issues such as licensing and liability.[39] States need to have well organized and structured policies and procedures in place to handle public health emergencies in order to facilitate the availability of health care professionals from outside the state who can provide care in emergency situations without fear of becoming liable for unauthorized practice. Coordination of efforts to address all manner of public health issues via electronic means is central to this material aid.

EMAC has developed model EMAC legislation for states to adopt, so they may join the interstate agreement or "compact" as a "party state."[40] This model legislation promotes mutual assistance among the states during emergencies or disasters.[41] Through the compact, health care professionals and other licensed individuals have reciprocal rights to practice their professions during emergency circumstances in party states. For example, a nurse licensed in State A, but not in State B, would have the ability to practice nursing in State B if State B had an emergency hurricane situation and requested the nurse's assistance in State B.[42]

In addition, the model EMAC legislation provides for governmental immunity and protections from tort liability for the employees of a party state that is rendering aid.[43] Likewise, through EMAC, social distancing measures (e.g., isolation, quarantine, closure, and cancellation of schools and public events) and other well-organized responses to national emergencies can take place across multiple state-wide disciplines, sectors, and jurisdictions, which is necessary for

---

[37] *See id.* at 15.

[38] Cheryl H. Bullard, Rick D. Hogam, Matthew S. Penn, Honorable Janet Ferris, Honorable John Cleland, Daniel Stier, Ronald M. Davis, Susan Allan, Leticia Van de Putte, Virginia Caine, Richard E. Besser, and Steven Gravely, *The National Action Agenda for Public Health Legal Preparedness: Improving Cross-sectoral and Cross-jurisdictional Coordination for Public Health Emergency Legal Preparedness,* 36 J.L. MED & ETHICS 57, 57–58 (Spring 2008).

[39] *See id.* at 60.

[40] *See* Emergency Management Assistant Compact, *Model Intrastate Legislation, available at* http://www.emacweb.org.

[41] *Id.*

[42] *See id.*

[43] *Id.*

achieving full preparedness and avoiding certain liability claims during national public health hazards.[44]

E. Practice of Telemedicine Without Full Licensure

There are some existing mechanisms available to telemedicine practitioners—lawfully licensed in one state—who practice in more than one state and do not want to undergo the process of being fully licensed in those states. The effectiveness of these mechanisms varies, but generally, the mechanisms fall short of solving all the complex licensure issues that limit the ability of practitioners to provide telemedical services in more than one state. Thus, being lawfully permitted to practice via telemedicine in a state is just the starting point for compliance with the laws of the various jurisdictions in which a physician engages in the practice of medicine across state lines.

1. The Consultation Exception

The so-called "consultation exception" generally allows an out-of-state physician to consult without licensure with a local lawfully licensed physician regarding a patient in that state. The extent of the consultation exception varies by state. Pennsylvania, for example, has a broad exception: "A person authorized to practice medicine or surgery or osteopathy without restriction by any other state, may, upon request by a medical doctor, provide consultation to the medical doctor regarding the treatment of a patient under the care of the medical doctor."[45] Ohio allows the practice of medicine to include "[a] physician or surgeon residing in another state or territory who is a legal practitioner of medicine or surgery therein, when in consultation with a regular practitioner of this state."[46]

Many states restrict the consultation exception by limiting the frequency of contact a consulting physician may have with local physicians.[47] Some states also place restrictions on the ability of an out-of-state telemedicine practitioner to solicit patients or receive calls in the state.[48]

The consultation exception is primarily suited to the telemedicine practitioner who provides occasional telemedicine services across state lines. The practitioner who provides consultations from time to time in one or more other states will be able to take advantage of this exception. This exception, however, is unlikely to be of great use to the out-of-state physician who has regular contact with a patient or patients in another state or who regularly consults with local physicians in another state. Thus, in the third example set forth in the

---

[44]Bullard, et al., 36 J.L. MED & ETHICS at 61–62.

[45]Section 16, Pennsylvania Medical Practice Act. *See also* Mo. REV. STAT. §334.010.3 ("A physician located outside of this state shall not be required to obtain a license when: (1) In consultation with a physician licensed to practice medicine in this state; and (2) the physician licensed in this state retains ultimate authority and responsibility for the diagnosis or diagnoses and treatment in the care of a patient located within this state").

[46]OHIO REV. CODE ANN. §4731.36(A).

[47]*See, e.g.*, IOWA CODE ANN. §148.2.

[48]MD. CODE ANN., HEALTH OCC. §14-302(4).

Introduction,[49] the Maryland physician may fall within the consultation exception, thereby not needing to seek a license of any sort from the Pennsylvania medical board, if his or her contact with Pennsylvania patients is requested by a local physician.

In the second example,[50] if the "online" Minnesota physician is providing medical advice to an Ohio resident, the physician may qualify for the consultation exception, if his or her contacts are both initiated by a licensed Ohio physician and are irregular. The difficulty with an "open" Web-based site is that the contacts are unlikely to be initiated by a local physician and the contact—or solicitation—is recurring. Careful attention must be given to the frequency of consultation allowed by a particular statute, state administrative regulation, or board of medicine.

2. *Endorsement*

Some states allow a physician licensed in one state to gain permission to practice in a second state by requesting review and endorsement of his or her credentials.[51] As a general rule, an applicant seeking endorsement must be in good standing in his/her own state and meet all requirements for licensure in that second state.[52] There are, however, several drawbacks to the endorsement procedure:

- The process is usually lengthy, cumbersome, and costly.
- A candidate licensed in a state with less stringent licensure requirements will not usually qualify for endorsement in a state with stricter licensure requirements.
- Endorsement is not valuable for a telemedicine practitioner whose practice involves several states.[53]

Endorsement may be of great value for practitioners who regularly practice in a second state and whose home states' requirements are consistent with those of the second state. Beyond these circumstances, however, the endorsement procedure is unlikely to be of great use to most telemedicine practitioners.

3. *Reciprocity*

A practitioner may obtain a license from any state with which his or her home state has entered into a reciprocity agreement. In Missouri, for example, the medical board may grant a license to an out-of-state licensee from a state that has substantially equivalent licensure standards, so long as that state provides reciprocal privileges to physicians licensed in Missouri.[54] This license usually

---

[49] See I., above.
[50] See I., above.
[51] *See, e.g.*, 49 PA. CODE §17.2 (endorsement); §17.4 (extraterritorial, for physicians residing or practicing near the state's boundary line).
[52] *Id.*
[53] Alison M. Sulentic, *Crossing Borders: The Licensure of Interstate Telemedicine Practitioners*, 25 J. LEGIS. 1, 21–22 (1999).
[54] MO. ANN. STAT. §334.043.

authorizes the physician "to practice in the same manner and to the same extent as physicians and surgeons are authorized to practice [under Missouri law]."[55]

Some advantages of reciprocity are obvious. First, reciprocity allows states to enter into arrangements with other states that have licensure requirements consistent with their own in order to foster "cross licensure." Second, reciprocity helps foster relationships between providers in "sister" states. Notwithstanding these advantages, obtaining a reciprocal license can be costly and time consuming.

In addition, reciprocity provisions do not reconcile differences between state laws regarding the regulation of the practice of medicine. Moreover, reciprocity agreements are usually entered into by two states only. Agreements implicating such a small number of states likely will not facilitate greatly the interstate practice of telemedicine.

4. Special License

A small number of states require out-of-state physicians who wish to provide telemedical services to obtain a special license.[56] Alabama law, for instance, provides:

> [a] special purpose license issued by the commission to practice medicine or osteopathy across state lines limits the licensee solely to the practice of medicine or osteopathy across state lines as defined herein. The special purpose license in this state is valid for a period of three years, shall expire on a renewal date established by the commission in its regulations in the third calendar year after its issuance, and may be renewed upon receipt of a renewal fee as established by the commission in its regulations.[57]

An advantage of special licensure statutes is that the statutory definition of the practice of medicine usually includes telemedicine. These statutes also tend to specify the type of services an out-of-state physician may provide under the license. This specification removes some of the uncertainty regarding the types and scope of services that may be rendered by out-of-state physicians that is inherent in the consultation and endorsement exceptions.

Because special-purpose licenses are created by one state without the cooperation of other states, obtaining a special-purpose license may be as cumbersome as obtaining a full license, especially if the state chooses to use its own entry-to-practice standards. In addition, this type of license does little to resolve the issues that arise when a telemedicine practitioner wants to provide services to several states.

5. Telehealth Networks

On February 18, 2010, the Federal Communications Commission (FCC) announced the funding for the build-out of an additional 16 broadband telehealth networks that will link hundreds of hospitals in the states of Iowa, Louisiana,

---

[55]*Id.*
[56]*See, e.g.*, ALA. CODE §34-24-502; 225 ILL. COMP. STAT. 60/49-5; 22 TEX. ADMIN. CODE §§174.1–.15.
[57]ALA. CODE §34-24-502.

Maine, Michigan, Minnesota, Missouri, Montana, Nebraska, New Hampshire, New York, Ohio, Oregon, Pennsylvania, South Dakota, Vermont, Virginia, West Virginia, and Wisconsin.[58] This funding was in addition to six projects that had been previously announced on April 16, 2009. The FCC established this Rural Health Care Pilot Program (RHCPP) to increase patient access to care via telemedicine and support the transfer of electronic medical records, which will improve the quality of care for patients.[59] To ensure the success of the networks in the RHCPP, the FCC also extended the key project deadline for vendor selection to June 30, 2011.[60] However, state medical licensing laws could be an impediment to the full effectiveness of such networks. Some states, such as Wyoming, are modifying state licensing procedures to allow an exemption for certain out-of-state telemedicine consultations.[61]

F. Credentialing

Recognizing the burden placed on hospitals in credentialing physicians and other practitioners performing telemedicine services, the Centers for Medicare & Medicaid Services (CMS) published its final rule governing the hospital credentialing requirements for these professionals on May 5, 2011.[62] In accordance with those rules, a hospital's governing body, through agreement with a distant-site telemedicine entity, may grant privileges to physicians and practitioners employed by the distant-site telemedicine entity based on the hospital's medical staff recommendations and such staff recommendations may rely on information provided by the distant-site telemedicine entity.[63] The final rule is a convergence from the proposed rule, which would have required the hospital allowing the telemedicine services to verify, directly or through a third-party credentialing verification organization, the credentials of practitioners applying for telemedicine privileges.

III. Initiatives Regarding Regulation of Telemedicine

There are several proposed initiatives that could go a long way in resolving some of the licensure issues implicated by the interstate practice of telemedicine. Despite these efforts, interstate practitioners will continue to face serious licensure hurdles given that many states appear unwilling to cede any part of their authority to regulate the licensure of health care professionals within their respective jurisdictions.

---

[58]News Release, Federal Communications Commission, *FCC Update on Rural Health Care Pilot Program Initiative, Rural Telemedicine Program Funds 16 More Broadband Telehealth Networks* (Feb. 18, 2010), *available at* http://www.fcc.gov/cgb/rural/rhcp.html.

[59]*Id.*

[60]*Id.*

[61]Kathy Method, *Wyoming Seeks to Expand Its Telehealth Network,* Med. Econ. (Apr. 24, 2009), *available at* http://medicaleconomics.modernmedicine.com/memag/Modern+ Medicine+ News/Wyoming-seeks-to-expand-its-telehealth-network/ArticleStandard/ Article/detail/593965.

[62]*See* 76 Fed. Reg. 25,550 (May 5, 2011).

[63]42 C.F.R. §482.12(a)(9).

A. Joint Working Group on Telemedicine

In a 1997 report to Congress, the Joint Working Group on Telemedicine[64] proposed seven models to resolve the licensure issues related to the interstate practice of telemedicine:

(1) Use of the consultation exceptions that exist in many jurisdictions for the out-of-state physician who occasionally consults with in-state colleagues.
(2) Endorsement of a practitioner licensed in states with equivalent standards.
(3) Registration by licensed out-of-state practitioners who wish to practice in the state on a part-time or intermittent basis.[65]
(4) Mutual recognition by states of the policies of the state from which the practitioner is licensed.
(5) Reciprocity agreements in which states would permit out-of-state licensees to practice in a reciprocal state without creating common standards for licensure or individualized review of license application.
(6) Limited licensure that would require an out-of-state practitioner to apply for a license that would allow him or her to provide only a narrow, defined range of health services.
(7) A national licensure system in which the federal government would establish a standardized and uniform criteria for practice nationwide (and that would preempt existing state licensure laws).

These proposals reflect three different approaches in attempting to resolve the concerns presented by the interstate practice of telemedicine. First, a state may independently make efforts to regulate telemedicine using a variety of methods, including consultation exceptions and endorsement. Second, a state may join forces with other states to regulate telemedicine practitioners by entering into reciprocal agreements to recognize the licenses of practitioners who have satisfied the license requirements in their home states. Third, entities may work toward the creation of a federal system of licensure establishing threshold standards.[66]

It appears, at least for the foreseeable future, that the first two approaches—in which states independently regulate telemedicine practitioners or, in the alternative, join forces via reciprocal agreements—will be the preferred method of regulation. State legislatures are not likely to willingly surrender power to the federal government in what historically and constitutionally has been a province of the states. On the other hand, it is not clear that the current licensure statutes are adequate to meet the demands of a technologically sophisticated and rapidly

---

[64]The Joint Working Group was formed in 1995 to assist the Secretary of HHS draft and submit a report regarding telemedicine to the vice president.

[65]In 1996, California passed the Telemedicine Development Act of 1996, which, among other things, required the board of medicine to propose guidelines that would permit a physician licensed in his or her home state to register with the board to provide direct telemedicine services in California rather than being a mere consultant. CAL. BUS. & PROF. CODE §2052.5.

[66]Alison M. Sulentic, *Crossing Borders: The Licensure of Interstate Telemedicine Practitioners,* 25 J. LEGIS. 1, 18 (1999).

changing health care delivery system. As a result, the federal government may have an increased role in the regulation of interstate telemedicine unless the states themselves fashion a workable alternative.

B. Federation of State Medical Boards

State legislators and regulators are aware of the difficulties caused by licensure systems that do not consider the impact of telemedicine, and they recognize that flaws in the system may be limiting access to health care for some of the neediest citizens. As noted earlier, however, states generally do not want federal government involvement in what has been, and continues to be, an area of virtually exclusive state regulation.

One result of the quandary has been the Model Act of the Federation of State Medical Boards (FSMB), which proposes the creation of special or limited licenses "to practice telemedicine across state lines upon application for the same from a person holding a full and unrestricted license to practice medicine in any and all states ... in which such individual is licensed, provided there has not been previous disciplinary or other action against the applicant by the state or jurisdiction."[67] The special-purpose license is required only for "those physicians who 'regularly or frequently' engage in the practice of medicine across state lines."[68]

The FSMB approach accomplishes two things. First, it unambiguously declares that the practice of telemedicine does indeed constitute the practice of medicine. Second, the Model Act provides an opportunity for the states to create uniform nationwide licensure standards without the involvement of the federal government. Importantly, states will still have the authority to establish their own entry-to-practice requirements.

Critics, however, contend that the Model Act is only a limited solution. It still requires the obtaining of a license, a time-consuming and sometimes cumbersome process.[69] Harsher critics argue that the Act merely consolidates what is already taking place in some states, doing little or nothing to address the fundamental licensure problems associated with interstate telemedicine practice. These criticisms notwithstanding, some legislatures have passed legislation mirroring the major provisions of the Model Act.[70]

---

[67]FEDERATION OF STATE MEDICAL BOARDS OF THE UNITED STATES, A MODEL ACT TO REGULATE THE PRACTICE OF MEDICINE ACROSS STATE LINES (1996), *available at* http://www.fsmb.org/pdf/1996_grpol_Telemedicine.pdf.

[68]*Id.*

[69]Center for Telemedicine Law, *Telemedicine and Interstate Licensure: Findings and Recommendations of the CTL Licensure Task Force,* 73 N.D. L. REV. 109, 121 (1997).

[70]*See, e.g.*, TENN. CODE ANN. §231; ALA. CODE §34-24-500.

C. Nurse Licensure Compact

Nurses, like physicians, are subject to state licensure and are likewise involved in multistate delivery of care. Perhaps the best model for the interstate licensure of telemedicine practitioners can be found in the Nurse Licensure Compact drafted by the National Council of State Boards of Nursing.[71] The council has been successful in getting several states to participate in an interstate compact that will provide mutual recognition of participating state nursing licenses.

Under the compact, a registered nurse or licensed practical nurse who holds a license in his or her home state will be recognized as holding a multistate license that will permit the nurse to practice in any state that has adopted the compact, so long as he or she follows the rules of the state in which the patient is located. This approach—compact states agreeing to waive their entry-to-practice standards for nurses licensed by other compact states but continuing to enforce the individual state standards with respect to applicants for their initial licensure with the state—may have important advantages over the FSMB's Model Act approach. The nurse-licensure-compact approach ensures greater uniformity in regulation and would permit full multistate scope of practice in states other than the physician's home state.

A national database, the so-called Coordinated Licensure System, compiles the licensure history (including disciplinary history) of nurses nationwide.[72] Note, however, that the disciplinary authority of the "remote" or "other state" does not extend beyond its borders.[73] The state of original license maintains that authority.

The compact is very much like the system in place for state licensing drivers of motor vehicles: a driver licensed in one state may drive in another without obtaining a license so long as he or she complies with that state's driving laws and does not intend to permanently change state residency. Likewise, the compact allows nurses to engage in the practice of nursing in another state without being required to obtain a license in that state. Fewer than half of the states are currently participating in the compact, meaning that for those states not participating, the same licensure stumbling blocks (discussed above) still prevail. Nevertheless, the compact goes a long way in providing a viable model that could be applied to multistate licensure of physicians in order to provide a uniform set of licensure standards, thereby facilitating the interstate practice of medicine.[74]

---

[71] To review the compact and related materials, see https://www.ncsbn.org/nlc.htm. The final version of the compact was adopted on November 6, 1998.

[72] *Id.*

[73] *Id.*

[74] Ross D. Silverman, *The Changing Face of Law and Medicine in the New Millennium*, 26 AM. J.L. & MED. 255, 269 (2000).

IV. Malpractice

A. Existence of Physician-Patient Relationship

For liability of any kind to arise in a telemedicine setting, there must first exist a physician-patient relationship.[75] The physician-patient relationship arises out of a consensual relationship between the patient and the physician, necessarily requiring that the patient consent to be treated by the physician and that the physician consent to treat the patient.[76]

The nature of a telemedicine patient encounter or consult, however, adds other factors to the creation of a physician-patient relationship.[77] Traditionally, a primary care physician would refer the patient to the specialist at the remote location. The patient would make an appointment with the specialist and be seen physically by the specialist. In this context, there is little question about the existence of a physician-patient relationship and the fact that the relationship with the primary care physician may have terminated with respect to that particular treatment.[78]

In the telemedicine setting, however, the existence or *non*existence of a physician-patient relationship is not so clear cut. In the examples set forth in the Introduction,[79] is there a physician-patient relationship between the Texas resident and the Ohio physician? Is there such a relationship between the Pennsylvania patient and the Maryland physician? Or the New York psychiatrist and a

---

[75] *See, e.g.*, St. John v. Pope, 901 S.W.2d 420, 423 (Tex. 1995) (holding that "a physician cannot be liable for malpractice unless the physician breaches a duty flowing from a physician-patient relationship") (citation omitted); Dominguez v. Kelly, 786 S.W.2d 749, 751 (Tex. App. El Paso 1990, writ denied) ("It is a well established principle of law that a physician is liable for malpractice or negligence *only* where there is a physician-patient relationship as a result of a contract, express or implied, that the doctor will treat the patient with proper professional skill and there is a breach of professional duty to the patient.") (emphasis supplied; citation omitted). (The analyses in this portion of the chapter are based upon, and the citations are made to, Texas law. The reader may use these principles and citations as the starting point for researching the law in other jurisdictions.)

The implications of finding a valid physician-patient relationship go well beyond the issue of physician liability. For example, the Texas State Board of Pharmacy has adopted rules related to the professional responsibility of pharmacists in dispensing Internet-based prescriptions. The rules require the pharmacist to determine that a prescription was issued under a valid patient-practitioner relationship. "A pharmacist may not dispense a prescription drug if the pharmacist knows or should have known that the prescription was issued on the basis of an Internet-based or telephonic consultation without a valid patient-practitioner relationship." *See* 22 Tex. Admin. Code §291.34(b)(1)(B). Minimum criteria for determining a valid relationship may be based on rules established by the Texas Medical Board.

[76] *See* Ortiz v. Shah, 905 S.W.2d 609, 611 (Tex. App. Houston [14th Dist.] 1995, writ denied) (The physician-patient relationship "is a consensual one and, when no prior relationship exists, the physician must take some action to treat the patient before the relationship can be established.") (citation omitted); *St. John* at 423 ("It is only with a physician's consent, whether express or implied, that the doctor-patient relationship comes into being.").

[77] *See e.g.*, LTC Charles M. Lott, MSC USA (Ret.), *Legal Interfaces in Telemedicine Technology*, 161 Mil. Med. 280, 282 (1996) (discussing physician-patient telemedicine relationships); Phyllis F. Granade, J.D., *Malpractice Issues in the Practice of Telemedicine*, 1 Telemed. J. 87 (1995) (same); Jim Reid, PA-C, *Obstacles to Telemedicine Development, in* A Telemedicine Primer: Understanding the Issues 67, 76–79 (1996) (same).

[78] Note that the laws of some states specifically provide that the physician-patient relationship of the local physician continues. *See, e.g.*, Mo. Rev. Stat. §334.010.3.

[79] See I., above.

"patient" in Rhode Island? How does one characterize the relationship between the Minnesota oncologist who answers an "ask the doctor" question and the questioner?

Fundamentally, in the telemedicine setting, will the existence of a patient-physician relationship be determined by the standards of a traditional medical setting? In the examples in the Introduction, the Texas and Pennsylvania physicians still "refer" the patient to the remote physician, but the patient and the remote physician may not meet face to face. This is particularly true where the local physician is using store-and-forward technology[80] to carry out the telemedicine session. In addition, the oncologist and/or psychiatrist may communicate with the patient via electronic mail.

Finally, the patient may access a Web site sponsored by the oncologists and obtain medical information from the site. Any of these situations raises the question of whether a physician-patient relationship has been created and whether the remote physician has "examined" the patient with or without obtaining the traditional consent to treat the patient.

There is not yet sufficient precedent on the existence of a physician-patient relationship in the telemedicine setting to articulate a general rule. However, analogous authority from telephone consults is illustrative of the approaches courts might take in this context. For example, in *Bienz v. Central Suffolk Hospital*,[81] a court denied a motion for summary judgment on the basis that there existed a question of material fact: whether a telephone call to a physician's office for purposes of initiating treatment created a physician-patient relationship sufficient to support a medical malpractice cause of action. In *Tsoukas v. Lapid*,[82] the court held that a telephone call to a physician listed by the patient's health maintenance organization (HMO) in an attempt to schedule an appointment did not establish a physician-patient relationship when the caller did not have an ongoing physician-patient relationship with the caregiver.[83]

Generally, a referring physician is not liable for the acts of the specialist.[84] Additionally, the absence of face-to-face interaction between the remote

---

[80]This application of telemedicine involves recording the patient interaction with the local physician or a technician and forwarding the recording to the remote physician for review at a later time. Telemedicine sessions may also be conducted in real time. Real time is the "capture, processing and presentation of data, audio, and/or video signals at the time that data are originated on one end and received on the other end at a rate of 30 frames per second." *Glossary, in* TELEMEDICINE THEORY & PRACTICE 407, 416 (Rashid L. Bashshur, et al., eds., 1997).

[81]557 N.Y.S.2d 139 (A.D. 2 Dep't 1990).

[82]733 N.E.2d 823 (Ill. App. 1 Dist. 2000).

[83]*See also* Clanton v. Von Haam, 340 S.E.2d 627 (Ga. Ct. App. 1990) (the fact that a physician had treated a patient for an unrelated condition, and that he returned her call and listened to her symptoms after she telephoned his office and complained of back pains, did not itself create a physician-patient relationship); Miller v. Sullivan, 625 N.Y.S.2d 102 (A.D. 3d Dep't 1995) (a telephone call affirmatively advising a prospective patient as to a course of treatment can constitute a professional service for the purpose of creating a physician-patient relationship only when the advice, if incorrect, would be actionable).

[84]*See, e.g.*, Johnson v. Whitehurst, 652 S.W.2d 441, 445 (Tex. App. Houston [1st Dist.] 1983, writ ref'd n.r.e.) (stating "the referring doctor cannot be liable for the negligence of the doctor to whom he referred the patient, unless the referring doctor was negligent in recommending the second physician") (citing Moore v. Lee, 109 Tex. 391, 211 S.W. 214 (1919)); Ross v. Sher, 483 S.W.2d 297, 301 (Tex. Civ. App. Houston [14th Dist.] 1972, writ ref'd. n.r.e.) ("[T]he referring doctor . . . cannot be liable for the negligence of [the specialist] unless the evidence shows that [the

physician and the patient does not necessarily negate the existence of a physician-patient relationship.[85]

In another situation analogous to a telemedicine session, courts have found that a physician-patient relationship existed between the patient and a consulting physician when the consulting physician had a contractual relationship with the treating physician to conduct the laboratory analysis of the patient.[86] The treating physician, a pathologist, contracted with another pathologist to perform certain laboratory analyses on behalf of his patients.[87] A patient brought an action against the treating physician and the consulting physician for a misdiagnosis in the pathology report prepared by the consulting physician.[88] The consulting physician argued that because he did not see the patient and had not "personally selected" the patient, no physician-patient relationship existed.[89]

The court concluded that because the diagnostic services were performed on behalf of the patient (i.e., an affirmative action had been taken by the physician), a physician-patient relationship had been formed.[90] In the examples set out in the Introduction,[91] it would not be difficult to ascertain the creation of a physician-patient relationship in the Texas patient, the Pennsylvania patient, and the New York psychotherapy examples.[92] However, determining the existence of a physician-patient relationship in the context of the oncology Web site would be harder to assess.

Similar issues are raised in a store-and-forward telemedicine setting. Suppose that in our Texas example, the Texas physician records the echocardiogram

---

referring doctor] failed to exercise reasonable care in recommending the second physician."). *See generally* King v. Flamm, 442 S.W.2d 679, 681 (Tex. 1969) (a general practitioner is not required to consult with a specialist on every conceivable complication that may arise in his practice; "If he exercises the care and skill of other physicians similarly situated, he is not responsible for error of judgment even though a specialist would not have make the same mistake.") (citation omitted). A general practitioner does have a duty to seek consultation with a specialist when he knows, or in the exercise of reasonable care should know, that the services of a specialist are needed. *Id.* Generally, a specialist is expected to possess a higher degree of skill and learning than a general practitioner. Burks v. Meredith, 546 S.W.2d 366, 370 (Tex. Civ. App. Waco 1977, writ ref'd n.r.e.).

[85]St. John v. Pope, 901 S.W.2d 420, 424 (Tex. 1995) ("The fact that a physician does not deal directly with a patient does not necessarily preclude the existence of a physician-patient relationship."). The plaintiff in *St. John* was attempting to hold the on-call physician who was consulted by the emergency room physician over the telephone liable for resulting injuries from his treatment in the hospital on the basis that by talking with the treating physician over the phone about the treatment of the patient, the on-call physician had formed a physician-patient relationship. *Id.* at 420–22. The Texas Supreme Court found that a physician-patient relationship did not exist because the on-call physician declined to treat the patient because he felt the patient's condition was beyond his ability to treat. *Id.* at 423–24.

[86]Dougherty v. Gifford, 826 S.W.2d 668, 674 (Tex. App. Texarkana 1992, no writ).

[87]*Id.* at 668–69.

[88]*Id.* at 669.

[89]*Id.* at 674.

[90]*Id.* at 674–75 ("Where . . . healthcare services are rendered on behalf of the patient and are done for the patient's benefit, a consensual physician-patient relationship exists for the purposes of medical malpractice.") (quoting Walters v. Rinker, 520 N.E.2d 468, 472 (Ind. Ct. App. 1988)); *see also* Peterson v. St. Cloud Hosp., 460 N.W.2d 635 (Minn. Ct. App. 1990) (holding as a matter of law that a physician-patient relationship existed between a pathologist and a patient notwithstanding the lack of direct contact with the patient).

[91]See I., above.

[92]In fact, under Texas law, it is clearly stated that the consulting physician is considered to be engaged in the practice of medicine in Texas.

and forwards it to the Ohio specialist for his or her review and diagnosis. The Ohio physician reviews the examination and misdiagnoses the patient's condition, which results in injury to the patient. Who is liable: the Ohio physician, the Texas physician, or both? Like the consulting pathologist in *Dougherty v. Gifford*,[93] the Ohio physician did not "personally select" the patient, nor was the patient necessarily aware that the Ohio physician would be diagnosing his condition.

Nevertheless, the Ohio physician has intentionally rendered health services on behalf of the patient, and under the reasoning of *Dougherty* and the authority cited therein, the Ohio physician may be deemed to have created a physician-patient relationship. The fact that the patient may not have given "consent" to the examination also raises issues of liability for failure to obtain informed consent.

B. What Is the Legal Duty?

In general, a physician owes a duty to a patient to exercise ordinary medical care. Ordinary care is that degree of care that a reasonably prudent physician would have exercised under the same or similar circumstances. In an action for medical malpractice, generally, a patient has the burden to prove that (1) the physician owed a duty to the patient; (2) the physician breached such duty; (3) the physician's breach of duty caused the patient's injury; and (4) the patient indeed suffered an injury.[94] Whether a physician's actions are negligent is determined by judging whether the physician met the applicable standard of care.[95]

Some commentators argue that there are distinct differences between traditional medicine and telemedicine that necessitate a legal duty and standard of

---

[93] 826 S.W.2d 668 (Tex. App. Texarkana 1992, no writ).

[94] Ortiz v. Shah, 905 S.W.2d 609, 610 (Tex. App. Houston [14th Dist.] 1995, writ denied) (citations omitted); *see also* Stolle v. Baylor College of Med., 981 S.W.2d 709, 712 (Tex. App. Houston [1st Dist.] 1998, rev. denied) ("The elements of a medical negligence claim are (1) a duty to conform to a certain standard of care; (2) a failure to conform to the required standard; (3) actual injury; and (4) a reasonably close causal connection between the conduct and the injury."). Additionally, the Texas Medical Liability and Insurance Improvement Act provides that a plaintiff must send notice to the defendant physician at least 60 days before the filing of an action. Tex. Rev. Civ. Stat. Ann. art. 4590i, §4.01(a). A two-year statute of limitations applies to all health care liability claims. Tex. Rev. Civ. Stat. Ann. art. 4590i, §10.01; MacGregor Med. Ass'n v. Campbell, 985 S.W.2d 38, 41 (Tex. 1999). A "health care liability claim" is "a cause of action against a health care provider or physician for treatment, lack of treatment, or other claimed departure from accepted standards of medical care or health care or safety which proximately results in injury or death of the patient." Tex. Rev. Civ. Stat. Ann. art. 4590i, §1.03(a)(4). Proper pre-suit notice within the two-year period tolls the limitations period for 75 days. Tex. Rev. Civ. Stat. Ann. art. 4590i, §4.01(c); Thompson v. Community Health Inv. Corp., 923 S.W.2d 569, 571 (Tex. 1996) (same).

[95] *See* LeNotre v. Cohen, 979 S.W.2d 723, 727 (Tex. App. Houston [1st Dist.] 1998, no pet. h.) (citation omitted) ("The general negligence standard of care for a physician is to undertake a mode or form of treatment which a reasonable and prudent member of the medical profession would undertake under the same or similar circumstances.") (citing Hood v. Phillips, 554 S.W.2d 160, 165 (Tex. 1977)). The plaintiff must establish that the physician failed to meet the standard of care by medical expert testimony. *See* Hart v. Van Zandt, 399 S.W.2d 791, 792 (Tex. 1965); Hall v. Tomball Nursing Ctr., Inc., 926 S.W.2d 617, 620 (Tex. App. Houston [14th Dist.] 1996, no writ) (citations omitted) *see also* Park Place Hosp. v. Estate of Milo, 909 S.W.2d 508, 511 (Tex. 1995) ("In a medical malpractice case, plaintiffs are required to show evidence of a 'reasonable medical probability' or 'reasonable probability' that their injuries were proximately caused by the negligence of one or more of the defendants.") (citations omitted).

practice that is unique to telemedicine.[96] While the standards for the underlying medical services rendered do not differ, the method and manner in which those services are rendered will necessarily differ.

For example, because the physician and patient are not in the same physical location, the parameters of the physician-patient relationship, discussed earlier,[97] must be adapted to account for the manner in which the remote physician interacts with the patient. Also, the heavy reliance on technology and other third-party intermediaries may alter the concept of the typical physician-patient interaction. Thus, the telemedicine community must determine whether the differences warrant seeking a telemedicine-specific standard of practice through legislation, rather than working for an evolution of principles through case law.

C. Informed Consent and the Duty to Disclose

Another duty that arises in any physician-patient relationship is the duty of the physician to disclose the risks involved in the particular treatment being administered by the physician and obtain the patient's consent on that basis. Generally, physicians have a duty to make reasonable disclosure to a patient of the risks that are incident to the medical diagnosis and treatment rendered by such physician.[98] This duty derives from the patient's right to have information adequate to exercise an informed consent to or refusal of a procedure.[99]

The nature and extent of the disclosure depends on the medical problem and the patient's ability to appreciate the information disclosed.[100] There are some instances in which a disclosure may so disturb the patient that such disclosure acts as a hindrance to the treatment required.[101]

To show that an injury has resulted from a physician's failure to disclose, a patient must generally show (1) the existence of an unrevealed risk that should have been made known; (2) that the unrevealed risk was harmful to the patient; and (3) that a disclosure of significant risks incidental to treatment would have resulted in the patient's decision to forego the treatment.[102] A patient may recover for damages even where the physician showed the "utmost care" in

---

[96] *See* Phyllis F. Granade, J.D., *Malpractice Issues in the Practice of Telemedicine,* 1 TELEMED. J. 87, 89 (1995) ("Telemedicine must act to set its own standards of practice: accepted methodology, standard requirements for involved technology, standard system specifications, etc.").

[97] See IV.A., above.

[98] Wilson v. Scott, 412 S.W.2d 299, 301 (Tex. 1967) (citation omitted).

[99] *Id.* at 301 (citation omitted). Inadequate informed consent encompasses the "failure of the physician or health care provider to disclose or to adequately disclose the risks and hazards involved in the medical care or surgical procedure rendered by the physician or healthcare provider." TEX. REV. CIV. STAT. ANN. art. 4590i, §6.02.

[100] *Wilson,* 412 S.W.2d at 301 (citation omitted).

[101] *Id.*

[102] Karp v. Cooley, 493 F.2d. 408, 422 (5th Cir.), *cert. denied,* 419 U.S. 845 (1974) (footnotes omitted); TEX. REV. CIV. STAT. ANN. art. 4590i, §6.02.

the delivery of the medical services for which inadequate or no disclosure was made.[103]

State statutes governing telemedicine licensure may address the question of obtaining consent.[104] Additionally, even if the statute is silent, the state's administrative regulations may address the issue.[105]

Absent a statutory or regulatory requirement, generally a referring physician has no duty to obtain the patient's informed consent to a procedure to be performed by another physician.[106] The law only requires that the physician obtain consent for any procedures that he or she personally performs. Similarly, courts have found that a health care facility has no duty to secure the informed consent of the patient.[107] Thus, in the example of an Ohio cardiologist being asked to review an echocardiogram transmitted by a Texas cardiologist[108] from a risk management standpoint, the local (Texas) physician should consider obtaining patient consent for the procedures performed by the remote physician if the remote (Ohio) physician chooses not to do so.

Given the liability risks attendant to an informed consent, the consulting local physician should normally ensure that the remote physician obtains the needed consent. However, in instances when the patient does not know that the remote physician is reviewing the examination and when the local physician merely passes on the diagnosis given by the remote physician without divulging the remote physician's participation, whether consent should be obtained becomes unclear and the lines dividing those who may or may not be responsible for obtaining consent are blurred.

The same difficulty in distinguishing responsibility may also exist where the physician is an employee of the health care institution. Although the facility may not be responsible for obtaining a patient's consent, it may nevertheless be vicariously liable for its physician employee's failure to obtain such consent. However, in instances when consent is not required, the consulting and

---

[103]Luna v. Nering, 426 F.2d 95, 98 (5th Cir. 1970) (citing *Wilson*, 412 S.W.2d 299). However, a claim based on a doctor's failure to fully disclose is governed by the Medical Liability and Insurance Improvement Act of Texas. Galvan v. Downey, 933 S.W.2d 316, 318 (Tex. App. Houston [14th Dist.] 1996, writ denied). And, disclosure of the risk in compliance with the Medical Liability and Insurance Improvement Act of Texas creates a rebuttable presumption that the physician was not negligent in failing to disclose the risk. TEX. REV. CIV. STAT. ANN. art. 4590i, §6.07(a)(1); *Galvan,* 933 S.W.2d at 318.

[104]*See, e.g.*, CAL. HEALTH & SAFETY CODE §2290.5(c).

[105]See, for example, 22 TEX. ADMIN. CODE §174.10, which requires written informed consent to be obtained from the patient by the consulting physician, or, if not obtained, then by the physician consulted when electronic consultation occurs other than by fax or telephone. Included in the patient's consent must be an acknowledgment that the confidentiality of medical information may be compromised by electronic transmission.

[106]*See* Edwards v. Garcia-Gregory, 866 S.W.2d 780, 783–84 (Tex. App. Houston [14th Dist.] 1993, writ denied) (citation omitted); Johnson v. Whitehurst, 652 S.W.2d 441, 445 (Tex. App. Houston [1st Dist.] 1983, writ ref'd n.r.e.).

[107]*See, e.g.*, Nevauex v. Park Place Hosp., Inc., 656 S.W.2d 923, 925 (Tex. App. Beaumont 1983, writ ref'd n.r.e.) (finding that the duty of securing the patient's informed consent rests on the doctor treating the physician and that no such duty was owed by the hospital).

[108]See I., above.

consultant physicians would be well advised to obtain consent appropriate to the nature of the consultation.

The best practice may be to ensure that the patient's written consent is obtained by a physician. This consent should acknowledge the following:

- the consultation,
- the use of electronic means to diagnose or treat, and
- the risk of compromise of confidentiality of medical information by electronic transmission.

D. Vicarious Liability

The risk of vicarious liability in a telemedicine setting is no different than in a traditional medical setting. The ways in which it manifests will differ according to the unique relationships that occur in telemedicine. Although the greater share of liability for the delivery of telemedicine services will lie with the participating physicians, a health care institution cannot escape liability for the actions of the physicians entirely.

A health care institution faces the risk of being vicariously liable for the actions of the physicians who provide health care services for the telemedicine systems implemented by the health care institution.[109] Generally, under the doctrine of respondeat superior, a health care institution is vicariously liable for the negligence of an agent or employee acting within the scope of his or her agency or employment, even where the health care institution has not personally committed a wrong.[110] The justification for this seemingly harsh rule is that the health care institution has the "right to control" the means and methods of such agent's or employee's work and, thus, should be responsible for any resulting actions.[111]

Because the "right to control" creates the risk of vicarious liability, the health care institution should carefully consider the relationship between the institution and the physicians providing health care services in the telemedicine system. The risk of vicarious liability for the transmitting institution will be higher if the telemedicine services are offered through a physician[112] employed by the transmitting institution or an affiliate, due to the strong presumption that the transmitting institution has the right, and duty, to control its employees. When the right to control is significantly diminished, the health care institution generally is not vicariously liable for the tort or negligence of the independent contractor.[113] Thus, the use of independent contractors to provide telemedicine

---

[109] *See generally* Baptist Mem'l Hosp. Sys. v. Sampson, 969 S.W.2d 945 (Tex. 1998).

[110] *Id.* at 947 (citation omitted).

[111] *Id.* (citation omitted).

[112] The Texas Medical Practice Act (TMPA) permits a nonprofit health corporation organized pursuant to §162.001 to contract with or employ physicians when the entity meets certain criteria (set forth in 22 Tex. Admin. Code, ch. 177). Tex. Occ. Code §§162.001–.003. A hospital may be a member of a nonprofit health corporation.

[113] *Sampson*, 969 S.W.2d at 947 (citation omitted).

services lessens the risk of vicarious liability because an independent contractor has sole control over the means and methods of his or her work.[114]

Providing telemedicine services through independent contractors will not necessarily eliminate the risk of vicarious liability, however. If the transmitting institution offers telemedicine services, but uses the employed physicians of an affiliated entity to provide the health care services, liability arising out of ostensible agency[115] likely still exists. Liability for the ostensible agency of an independent contractor, regardless of the supposed absence of the right to control, is based on the notion that a representation by the health care institution caused the patient to rely justifiably on the appearance of the existence of an agency.[116]

Consequently, although a health care institution ordinarily is not liable for the negligence of a physician who is an independent contractor, it may be vicariously liable for the medical malpractice of an independent contractor physician when a patient can establish the elements of ostensible agency.[117] To avoid liability for the ostensible agency of an independent contractor, a health care institution must make sure that the relationship between the institution and the physician is made clear to patients receiving telemedicine services.

The health care institution's risk does not stop with vicarious liability concerns, however. In addition to considering the acts for which a health care institution may risk vicarious liability, the health care institution must also consider those actions for which the institution may be directly liable. In some instances, the patient may have a cause of action against the individual physician, and the patient may retain a direct cause of action against the hospital when the hospital was negligent in the performance of a duty owed directly to the patient.[118] For example, if the equipment used by the transmitting institution malfunctions, the patient may have a cause of action against the transmitting institution.

E. Patient Abandonment

A patient may have a cause of action for abandonment when, without reasonable notice to the patient, a physician unilaterally discontinues treatment at a time when continued medical treatment is necessary. From a telemedicine perspective, a predicate for patient abandonment is the existence of a physician-patient relationship. To avoid a claim of patient abandonment, a physician should, before withdrawing from a physician-patient relationship, provide the patient with reasonable notice of his or her withdrawal and provide adequate alternative medical care. The Texas State Board of Medical Examiners, for example,

---

[114] *Id.* (citation omitted).

[115] *Id.* at 947 ("Liability may be imposed ... under the doctrine of ostensible agency in circumstances when the principal's conduct should equitably prevent it from denying the existence of an agency.") (citation omitted).

[116] *Id.* at 947–48 (citations omitted).

[117] *Id.* at 948 (citations omitted). The elements of ostensible agency are "(1) the principal, by its conduct, (2) caused [the patient] to reasonably believe that the putative agent was an employee or agent of the principal, and (3) that [the patient] justifiably relied on the appearance of agency." *Id.* (citing RESTATEMENT (SECOND) OF AGENCY §267 (1958)).

[118] *Id.* at 949 (citations omitted).

requires a physician who prescribes over the Internet to ensure that follow-up physician care is provided.[119]

F. Availability of Insurance for Telemedicine Encounters

Issues relating to medical malpractice insurance arise in connection with telemedicine encounters.[120]

1. Malpractice Insurance and Gaps in Coverage

In any setting, a consequence of a physician-patient relationship is the potential for a claim for malpractice. Physicians customarily carry malpractice liability insurance to guard against such claims. In the telemedicine setting, however, once the physician-patient relationship is established, the physician's medical malpractice insurance may not protect the physician from related malpractice claims because most policies include either a condition or an exclusion that expressly states that there is no coverage in the event a physician does not have a valid license in the jurisdiction in which he or she is practicing medicine.

Thus, depending on the jurisdiction in which the claim is brought, the physician may be left without malpractice insurance coverage. Accordingly, a physician considering engaging in telemedicine should either:

- be appropriately licensed in all jurisdictions in which he or she may be perceived as practicing medicine; or
- seek to have his or her malpractice liability insurance policy endorsed to provide coverage in any jurisdiction where the physician may be perceived to be practicing medicine, despite the fact that the physician is licensed only in the jurisdiction where his or her primary medical practice is located.

In the examples set out in the Introduction,[121] the following courses of action would be prudent:

- The Maryland physician should be appropriately licensed in Pennsylvania, given that his or her contacts with Pennsylvania patients may be regular and continuous.
- The Ohio physician should obtain a Texas special-purpose license.
- The New York physicians should seek to have their malpractice liability policies endorsed to provide coverage in any jurisdiction where they may be perceived to be practicing medicine.

---

[119]TEXAS STATE BOARD OF MEDICAL EXAMINERS, INTERNET PRESCRIBING POLICY, *available at* http://www.texmed.org/Template.aspx?id=3508.

[120]This section is adapted with permission from Susan Huntington, P.A., J.D., Vice President, Chubb Executive Risk, *Emerging Professional Liability Exposures for Physicians on the Web*, Address at the American Bar Association Health Law Section seminar on electronic health care law issues (Oct. 6, 2000).

[121]See I., above.

2. Disclaimers of Liability

The availability of insurance to guard against claims stemming from information posted on an Internet Web site and communication between physicians and third parties in the electronic mail setting is similarly problematic. In the Internet Web site context, health care Web sites typically include disclaimers to the effect that no physician-patient relationship is established and that information posted on a Web site is for information only. By the same token, a physician responding to inquiries from third parties via electronic mail may include disclaimers to the effect that a physician-patient relationship does not arise by virtue of the limited interaction. Although there is not authority on this point, such disclaimers are not likely to be dispositive of risk.

In addition, characterizing patient interactions as merely informational (i.e., there is no physician-patient relationship) may have an unanticipated adverse consequence from an insurance standpoint. In brief, there may be no medical malpractice insurance available to the Minnesota oncologists who were merely providing information to a third party, because the physicians were not rendering medical care. Yet, do the physicians still have a duty under the traditional tort theory to those who access their Web site that may result in a liability claim (for detrimental reliance, for example)?

3. What Malpractice Does Cover

a. "Specified-Risk" or "Specified-Perils" Coverage

Medical malpractice insurance is intended to cover medical incidents (i.e., acts, errors, or omissions in the rendering of or failure to render medical care) that arise from a physician-patient encounter. Most medical malpractice policies are known as "specified-risk" or "specified-perils" insurance coverage. This type of policy covers liability incurred by an insured but only if it arises from one of the specific causes listed in the policy. Language in a typical medical malpractice policy concerning covered specified risks might include the following:

> "medical services" means health care, medical care, or treatment provided to any individual including, without limitation, any of the following: medical, surgical, dental, psychiatric, mental health, chiropractic, osteopathic, nursing or other professional health care ... or the furnishing or dispensing of medications, drugs, blood, blood products, or medical, surgical, or dental supplies.

Specified-risk policies are commonly used to address well known and predictable risk exposures.

b. "All-Risk" or "Open-Perils" Coverage

The other type of coverage is known as "all-risk" or "open-perils" insurance. This type of insurance covers liability arising from any cause whatsoever subject to specific exclusions or conditions due to the evolving nature of Internet legal exposures. Many of the Internet insurance policies now on the market are the "all risk" type. What follows is an example of all-risk–covered "Internet activities":

"Internet Activities" means (1) dissemination or other use of printed, verbal, numerical, audio, or visual expression, or any other expression, regardless of the medium upon which such expression is fixed; and (2) transaction of business on an Internet site.

c. *Recommendation*

Given the uncertainty of the legal rules governing the Internet and the types of claims that will be generated by online activities, an insurance policy that is limited to specific named perils is likely to be inadequate. All-risk policies typically exclude any claims alleging bodily injury. This exclusion creates a huge gap in coverage for online physicians like the Minnesota oncologists described in the Introduction to this chapter.[122] The probable legal exposure for a physician's Internet activities is an alleged patient injury resulting from reliance on Web site information, online advice from the physician, or the physician's failure to respond in a timely matter. A single policy that addresses both alleged patient injuries and the liability exposure does not exist as of early 2011. Thus, to obtain adequate protection from liability, physicians are forced to attempt to piece together several policies that may or may not provide "seamless" coverage for the "online" physician.

V. INTERNATIONAL PRACTICE OF MEDICINE

A. Telemedicine

American companies increasingly outsource a variety of services to lower-cost international service providers in order to save money. In addition to blue-collar manufacturing jobs, such as machine operator and equipment maintenance technician, and white-collar service jobs, such as accountant and engineer, there is a trend toward outsourcing medical services and medical information services to foreign countries.[123] Foreign health care providers may be the next wave of professionals whose services are less expensive than their U.S. counterparts' and, as a result, whose services are provided offshore. However, it remains unsettled how these providers will be reimbursed and how their services will ultimately be regulated. Based on current law, as presented elsewhere in this topic, there are serious risks in delivering medical and other health care services via telemedicine from overseas.

B. Medical Tourism

Medical tourism has become increasingly popular. Medical tourism is travel planned in advance to obtain treatment or surgery outside the patient's

---

[122] See I., above.

[123] *See* Thomas R. McLean, *The Offshoring of American Medicine: Scope, Economic Issues and Legal Liabilities,* 14 ANN. HEALTH L. 205 (2005).

usual country of residence.[124] In the past, medical tourism was primarily the traveling of patients from less-developed countries to industrialized countries in order to obtain better health care services.[125] Recently, though, individuals are traveling from industrialized countries to less-developed nations to obtain treatment at lower costs or to obtain alternative treatments that are not available in their home countries.[126] In addition, medical tourism takes place to avoid certain legal regulations pertaining to health care treatment (such as unregulated embryo gender identification or assisted suicide).[127]

Like international telemedicine, international medical tourism is essentially unregulated. However, to some extent, existing domestic laws, such as privacy protection, licensing regulations, and health and safety laws, may address some of these issues now and will certainly do so even more in the future.[128] In addition, these services are, for the most part, paid for out of pocket versus being covered by private and government payors.

C. Medicaid and Medicare Reimbursement

Medicaid does not distinguish between telemedicine and face-to-face care; currently, many states specifically allow Medicaid reimbursement for services using telemedicine. Medicaid reimbursement for telemedicine services is furnished at the state's option and is viewed as a cost-effective alternative to the more traditional face-to-face way of providing medical care. However, various states limit the services that may be covered by a government payor when the service is provided via interactive video teleconferencing. Thus, it appears that Medicaid covers the type of service, not necessarily the means by which the service is provided. For example, citizens who are reimbursed for a particular covered service received in their home state would likely be reimbursed for that service if received via interactive video teleconferencing from a provider located in another state or a foreign country.

Medicare is more stringent than Medicaid in its treatment of the beneficiary's location while receiving care. Effective October 1, 2001, Section 223 of the Medicare, Medicaid and SCHIP Benefits Improvement and Protection Act of 2000 (BIPA) provides for coverage and payment of Medicare telehealth services, including consultation, office visits, individual psychotherapy, and pharmacologic management delivered via telecommunications systems.[129] Under BIPA, Medicare beneficiaries are eligible for telehealth services only if those services are presented from an originating site located in either a rural Health Practice Shortage Area, a county outside of a metropolitan statistical area, or a location that is part of a federal telemedicine demonstration project as

---

[124]Nicolas P. Terry, *Under-regulated Health Care Phenomena in a Flat World: Medical Tourism and Outsourcing,* 29 W. NEW ENG. L. REV. 421, 422 (2007).

[125]*Id.*

[126]*Id.* at 423.

[127]*Id.* at 431–432.

[128]*Id.* at 421.

[129]MEDICARE BENEFIT POLICY MANUAL, ch. 15, §270, *available at* http://www.cms.gov/Manuals/IOM/list.asp.

of December 31, 2000.[130] Thus, Medicare, to date, does not reimburse telehealth provided to patients from overseas.

D. International Legal and Licensing Issues

The interstate licensing and standard-of-care issues discussed in this chapter should apply to international telemedicine and medical tourism services as well.[131] However, the licensing laws leave open myriad unanswered questions and concerns. For example, is a foreign telemedicine physician required to hold an appropriate visa before examining a U.S. patient?[132] What state and federal laws apply to foreign telemedicine or foreign medical tourism consultations? Are international telemedicine or medical tourism providers required to comply with Health Insurance Portability and Accountability Act of 1996 (HIPAA) requirements? How do federal trade regulations impact these foreign services? Are these foreign telemedicine services reimbursable under U.S. private and government health plans? What country has jurisdiction over litigation cases involving foreign health care services?

Even absent definitive answers to these questions, it is clear that efforts will continue for the exportation of medical services as telemedicine gains in popularity[133] due to expansive worldwide access to the Internet, the ability to transmit digital images, widespread dissemination of medical information, and increased access to medical knowledge by allied health care professionals as well as lay people.[134] Similarly, the Internet allows international health care providers to easily market their services at what would likely be a lower cost than American health care services.[135]

A variety of health care services are already provided on an international basis. Medical transcription and billing services are regularly outsourced to international companies,[136] which may result in increased liability concerns. For example, in 2003, a transcriptionist in Pakistan threatened to release patient information on the Internet if the University of California, San Francisco Medical Center did not pay her wages.[137]

Telemedicine technology gives physicians the ability to prescribe medication to, diagnose, and treat patients from remote international locations, but the same licensing issues that pertain to interstate health care provided via telemedi-

---

[130] *Id.*

[131] *See* Thomas R. McLean, *The Future of Telemedicine & Its Faustian Reliance on Regulatory Trade Barrier for Protection*, 16 HEALTH MATRIX 443, 461–469 (2006); Carmen E. Lewis, *My Computer, My Doctor: A Constitutional Call for Federal Regulation of Cybermedicine*, 32 AM. J.L. & MED. 585 (2006); Katherine J. Herrmann, *Cybersurgery: The Cutting Edge*, 32 RUTGERS COMPUTER & TECH. L.J. 297, 317–318, 320–322 (2006).

[132] McLean, 16 HEALTH MATRIX at 459.

[133] Thomas R. McLean, *The Offshoring of American Medicine: Scope, Economic Issues and Legal Liabilities*, 14 ANN. HEALTH L. 215 (2005).

[134] *See id.* at 221–25.

[135] *Id.* at 226–27.

[136] *Id.* at 215.

[137] D. A. Lazarus, *A Tough Lesson on Medical Privacy: Pakistani Transcriber Threatens UCSF Over Back Pay*, S.F. CHRON., Oct. 22, 2003.

cine apply to these international services.[138] For example, when an American radiologist practices international teleradiology within the United Kingdom (UK), the UK Department of Health requires the American radiologist to be licensed in the UK. Likewise, licensing requirements in the United States have prevented British radiologists from interpreting images obtained in the United States.[139] Some argue that, from an international perspective, geographically based jurisdictions, accreditation, and licensing schemes make less sense as telemedicine grows more prevalent.[140]

Although some health care services can be provided by international health care providers via telemedicine, it remains to be seen how these services are or will be regulated effectively by law. As a consequence, the United Nations has launched efforts to update the licensing arena for greater professional services portability, allowing the medical community full use of the changing technological environment.[141] In order to determine which country's law applies to a particular health care transaction or service presently, the traditional approach is taken: a transaction is localized within the jurisdiction with which it is deemed to have the closest relationship, and that jurisdiction exerts legal authority over the transaction.[142] Future international laws and treaties will be crucial in determining the impact of telemedicine in years to come.[143] Negotiating these laws and treaties will require coordination among many countries and may result in permitting foreign telemedicine health care providers to enter into each country's respective health care market through cyberspace, which may or may not be a welcome visit for local practitioners.

In addition, electronic health information, which is discussed in more detail below in Section VI., is increasingly being serviced internationally. As a result, problems and regulatory schemes to address these problems are growing on a worldwide basis.[144]

VI. ELECTRONIC HEALTH INFORMATION

Electronic health information, electronic medical records, or electronic health records (EHR), as well as other terms, describe a collection in electronic

---

[138]McLean, 14 ANN. HEALTH at 243.

[139]Seong K. Mun, *Teleradiology and Emerging Business Models*, 11 J. TELEMED. & TELECARE 271 (Jan. 1, 2005).

[140]Michael A. Goldberg, *E-health and the Universitas 21 Organization: 4. Professional Portability*, 11 J. TELEMED. & TELECARE 230 (Jan. 1, 2005).

[141]*Id.*

[142]Benedict Stanberry, *Legal and Ethical Aspects of Telemedicine,* 12(4) J. TELEMEDICINE & TELECARE 166 (June 1, 2006).

[143]Thomas R. McLean, *International Law, Telemedicine & Health Insurance: China as a Case Study*, 32 AM. J.L. & MED. 7, 34 (2006).

[144]*See* Karin Retzer, *Article 29 WP Working Document: E-Health Records*, 8 No. 6, PRIVACY & INFO. L. REP. 5 (2007). The "Working Document on the processing of personal data relating to health in electronic health records" was prepared by the Article 29 Data Protection Working Party to harmonize the rights of patients in regard to health records across the European Union and provides recommendations on appropriate standards. *Id.*

format of health information about individual patients and populations.[145] EHR also includes the software products and services used to create and manage health information in electronic format.[146] Intertwined with EHRs are electronic prescribing, which is defined by the Agency for Healthcare Research and Quality as the use of computing devices to communicate drug prescriptions.[147] EHR is a mechanism for incorporating health information in both paper and electronic format into a digital collection for the purpose of improving the efficiency and effectiveness of the health care system in the United States.[148]

Currently, there are a variety of forces, governmental and private, pushing for wide-spread implementation of EHR by physicians, health care facilities, and other providers. The Office of Inspector General (OIG) of the Department of Health and Human Services (HHS) and CMS have published respectively the anti-kickback statute safe harbors and Stark law exceptions for electronic prescribing and EHR in order to allow various entities to make these resources available to physicians.[149]

Many states' governors have issued executive orders calling for health information technology and health information exchange to improve health care. These states are developing working plans to adopt and exchange EHR.[150]

On a federal level, the American Recovery and Reinvestment Act of 2009 (ARRA) provides for the Secretary of HHS to use federal money to promote the electronic exchange and use of health information in the United States and to carry out health information technology activities.[151] ARRA provides for (i) approximately $1.5 billion in grants to go, in part, toward the acquisition of health information technology systems, for health centers including health center controlled networks;[152] and (ii) $300 million to support regional or sub-national efforts toward health information exchange.[153] As these efforts spur the implementation and broader use of EHR and telemedicine, the risk of acting in violation of one or more state's laws is much greater.

A. Physician-Patient Relationship

The interoperability of EHR is necessary for its success. "Interoperable" is defined by the Institute of Electrical and Electronics Engineers as "the ability

---

[145]Karoline Kreuser, *The Adoption of Electronic Health Records: Benefits and Challenges,* 16 ANN. HEALTH L. 317, 318 (2007).

[146]David C. Kibbe, Shana Campbell Jones, & Joseph McMenamin, *The Interoperable Electronic Health Records: Preserving Its Promise by Recognizing and Limiting Physician Liability,* 63 FOOD & DRUG L.J. 75, 75 (2008).

[147]*Id.* at 75–76.

[148]Kreuser, 16 ANN. HEALTH L. at 318.

[149]Alice G. Gosfield, *Medicare and Medicaid Fraud and Abuse Current Through the July 2007 Update,* MEDFRAUD §2:56 (2007).

[150]Catherine M. Boerner, *Health and Quality of Care: Two Areas Every Compliance Officer Should Know About,* 9 No. 3 J. HEALTH CARE COMPLIANCE 33, 34 (May–June 2007).

[151]American Recovery and Reinvestment Act, Pub. L. No. 111-5, 123 Stat. 115 (Feb. 17, 2009) (H.R. 1), 132–133, *available at* http://frwebgate.access.gpo.gov/cgi-bin/getdoc.cgi?dbname=111_cong_bills&docid=f:h1enr.pdf.

[152]H.R. 1 at 61.

[153]H.R. 1 at 65.

of two or more systems or components to exchange information and to use the information that has been exchanged."[154] A "web" of physicians who all have electronic access to a patient's health information may have a physician-patient relationship with the patient.[155] Once a patient's EHR is updated, each of the patient's doctors could be automatically notified of this change.[156]

Interoperability presents an opportunity to drastically improve health care efficiencies and expand the physician-patient relationship. However, with efficiencies and increased access to information come questions regarding the physician-patient relationship. Does each physician who reviews a patient's electronic health information have a physician-patient relationship with the patient? If so, when does such relationship begin and end?

An implied physician-patient relationship may arise by virtue of a telephone communication between the patient and the physician. As a result, the same could be said for an electronic communication, leading to a more loosely defined physician-patient relationship and potentially leading to an implied duty of care for physicians.[157]

B. Standard of Care

The standard of care for a provider is based on the degree of skill and care ordinarily practiced by a reasonably prudent practitioner in the same practice and, depending upon the jurisdiction, in a similar community.[158] With the widespread implementation of EHR, the definition and interpretation of the standard of care will likely change and become more global. Providers may be required to adopt EHR in order to meet the standard of care. In addition, physicians may be required to meet the standards in each jurisdiction in which a patient is located, if the physician has reviewed or had access to that patient's EHR.

In the future, the physician licensure requirements will likely include standards for use and transmission of EHR, which may vary depending upon the state. As providers transmit this information across state lines, providers will need to comply with the licensure and certification requirements of those states.

C. Certifications

The development of EHR has resulted in a flurry of certification programs for software vendors and professionals working with EHR. In some instances, certification programs and policies have replaced or supplemented licensing requirements. Likewise, Surescripts, which operates the largest e-prescribing

---

[154] David C. Kibbe, Shana Campbell Jones, & Joseph McMenamin, *The Interoperable Electronic Health Records: Preserving Its Promise by Recognizing and Limiting Physician Liability*, 63 FOOD & DRUG L.J. 75, 79 (2008).

[155] *Id.* at 79. EHR leads to not only increased access by health care providers to health information, but increased access by the patient to his or her own health information, which may include information that should be shielded from the patient for psychological and emotional stability reasons. *Id.* at 80.

[156] *Id.* at 79.

[157] *Id.* at 80.

[158] *Id.* at 80–81.

network in the United States, provides an e-prescribing network that is composed of the prescriber, pharmacy, and payor, who must use the Surescripts software and complete the Surescripts certification process in order to participate in the Surescripts network.[159] In order to meet the interoperability requirement for the e-prescribing and EHR safe harbors and the corresponding exceptions for the Stark law, certification by the Certification Commission for Health Information technology is necessary.[160]

D. Liability

The increased accessibility of medical records by health care providers increases the duty of care and ultimate responsibility and potential liability for such providers. The potential for causes of action relating to products liability, fraud, malpractice, and privacy and security concerns will be increased by the electronic transmission of health information.

In particular, patients have a higher level of concern about the preservation of their privacy when their health information is included in electronic medical records.[161] Electronic record systems will obviously result in additional risks of accuracy problems and fraud by unauthorized individuals accessing, and tampering with, patient records.[162]

Electronic personal health records allow patients to keep their health records in one place and share them with their health care providers. These electronic medical record systems provide efficient access to health information and are becoming more and more popular, but not without risks. Google Health is one of the leaders in providing these personal health record tools.[163] Google Health draws its information from a variety of sources, such as its partner hospitals, pharmacies, and laboratories.[164] Such information often includes claims data that, according to some health technology experts, is notoriously inaccurate and incomplete.[165]

For example, a 59-year-old kidney cancer survivor, when he transferred his medical records from Beth Israel Deaconess Medical Center to Google Health, was inaccurately told by Google Health that his cancer had spread to either his brain or spine.[166] In cases such as these, Google Health and other similar per-

---

[159] *Health Information Technology Report Finds Significant Uptick in E-Prescribing*, 16 AM. HEALTH LAW. ASS'N NEWS, Apr. 24, 2009.

[160] *See generally* CERTIFICATION COMM'N FOR HEALTH INFORMATION TECH., http://www.cchit.org.

[161] Leslie P. Francis and Nicolas P. Terry, *Ensuring the Privacy and Confidentiality of Electronic Health Records*, 2007 U. ILL. L. REV. 681, 696.

[162] *Id.* at 704. Federal laws such as HIPAA protect the privacy and security of health information. *See id.* at 713.

[163] *See* Lisa Wangsness, *Electronic Health Records Raise Doubt: Google Service's Inaccuracies May Hold Wide Lesson*, THE BOSTON GLOBE BOSTON.COM (Apr. 13, 2009), http://www.boston.com/news/nation/washington/articles/2009/04/13/electronic_health_records_raise_doubt/.

[164] *Id.*

[165] *Id.* (citing Dr. David Kibbe, Senior Technology Advisor to the American Academy of Family Physicians).

[166] *Id.*

sonal health records companies may be liable for breach of contract, negligence, defamation, or a host of other claims based on such inaccurate information.

On a national basis, the National Practitioner Data Bank was established to improve the quality of health care by encouraging physicians, dentists, and other health care practitioners to identify and ultimately discipline those who engage in unprofessional conduct and to prevent them from moving from state to state without disclosure of such conduct.[167] The information reported to the Data Bank is available to state licensing boards, hospitals, and other health care entities and is treated as confidential.[168] Civil money penalties of up to $10,000 are imposed by the HHS OIG on those who violate confidentiality provisions.[169]

Not only is there concern for preserving the confidentiality of disciplinary actions against health care providers, but there is obviously concern for protecting the confidentiality, privacy, and security of health information in general. The ARRA Health Information Technology for Economic and Clinical Health (HITECH) Act was signed into law by President Barack Obama on February 17, 2009.[170] It includes language that expands significantly the scope of the HIPAA privacy and security standards.[171] Prior to the HITECH Act, only health care providers, health plans, and health care clearinghouses (covered entities) were subject to government enforcement for violations of HIPAA. Due to the passage of the HITECH Act, as of February 17, 2010, the federal government may assess criminal fines and penalties against vendors and contractors of covered entities (business associates) that disclose protected health information in violation of a business associate agreement.[172] This Act also obligates these business associates to comply with the administrative, physical, and technical safeguards, and the policies, procedures, and documentation requirements reflected in the HIPAA security rules.[173]

Covered entities also will be required to notify a patient if his or her personal health information is disclosed unlawfully no later than 60 days after the covered entity learns of that disclosure.[174] The HITECH Act's more stringent privacy and security requirements expose health care providers and their consultants to greater risk for liability, especially since these professionals are ultimately required to disclose their own violations. Any violation of HIPAA as provided in the HITECH Act may result in disciplinary action by the applicable licensing board and even civil liability by state attorneys general, who have the authority under the Act to seek injunctions and to file civil actions for damages in federal courts in connection with HIPAA violations.[175]

---

[167]Brian E. Appel, *National Practitioner Data Bank: Fact Sheets*, in ALI-ABA COURSE OF STUDY MATERIALS (Feb. 2008).

[168]*Id.*

[169]*Id.*

[170]American Recovery and Reinvestment Act, Pub. L. No. 111-5, 123 Stat. 115, tit. XIII (Feb. 17, 2009).

[171]*See* H.R.1, 112, *available at* http://frwebgate.access.gpo.gov/cgi-bin/getdoc.cgi?dbname=111_cong_bills&docid=f:h1enr.pdf.

[172]*Id.* at 150.

[173]*Id.* at 146.

[174]*Id.* at 147.

[175]*Id.* at 160.

With the duty to prevent and disclose security and privacy breaches, should there be a duty for physicians and other health care providers to disclose their medical errors to their patients and their licensing boards? In general, the medical field's culture discourages disclosure to avoid medical malpractice actions.[176] Nevertheless, studies reflect that patients often file suit due to their belief that their physicians failed to be honest with them. Consequently, if physicians disclose medical errors to their patients, then perhaps lawsuits and disciplinary action can be avoided.[177] However, long-distance medicine may complicate the opportunity of a physician to make an effective disclosure or to create the kind of physician-patient interpersonal relationship that may avoid liability exposure.

VII. Conclusion

The failure of existing law to keep up with technology in many substantive areas is apparent throughout this volume. The entrepreneurial nature of the e-health industry creates momentum in the direction of pushing activities to their legal limits, and when this momentum pushes against the legal uncertainties in the area of professional practice—for which the price of mistakes may be measured in health and in lives—choices carry more weight and more risk. It is crucial that lawyers keep current with legal developments in this area to allow e-health businesses to effectively manage the risks of moving forward with a technology that promises to make health care more accessible and more predictable.

---

[176] Richard W. Bourne, *Medical Malpractice: Should Courts Force Doctors to Confess Their Own Negligence to Their Patients?* 61 Ark. L. Rev. 621, 627 (2009).

[177] *See id.* at 627.

10

FDA Regulation of E-Health Technology and Services[*]

I.	Introduction	288
II.	FDA Regulation of Online Activities	289
	A. Internet Drug Sales	289
	1. FDA Enforcement Activities	290
	2. Consumer Education	290
	B. Online Direct-to-Consumer Advertising	291
	1. Sponsored Links	291
	2. DTC Promotion of Genetic Testing Services	292
III.	FDA and Electronic Health Records	293
	A. FDA Authority to Regulate EHR	293
	B. ONC Regulation of EHR	294
	C. Increased Scrutiny and Oversight of EHR Systems	294
	1. FDA Working Group	294
	2. Legislative Inquiries	295
	D. FDA and ONC Collaboration	295
	1. HIT Policy Committee Recommendation	296
	2. Concerns	296
	3. Future Collaboration	296
IV.	FDA Regulation of Telemedicine	297
	A. What Is Telemedicine?	297
	B. mHealth Technologies	298
	C. FDA Regulation of Mobile Medical Devices	299
	1. Overview	299
	2. "Intended Use" of Mobile Medical Devices	299
	a. "Accessory" and "Component" Devices	300
	b. Regulatory Class	300
	D. Why Regulate Telemedicine?	301
	1. Safety Concerns	301
	2. Legislative Interest	301
	3. Industry Growth	302

---

[*]J. Benneville Haas and Eric C. Greig, Latham & Watkins, LLP, Washington, D.C.

		E.	The FDA and Telemedicine in the Early 2000s	302
			1. Early Guidance	303
			2. Further Guidance Documents	303
		F.	Recent Developments in FDA Telemedicine Regulation	304
		G.	FDA Final Rule on Medical Device Data Systems	304
			1. Exclusion of EHR	305
			2. Uncertain Applications	305
		H.	Draft Guidance: Mobile Medical Applications	306
			1. Scope	306
			2. Classification of Mobile Platforms and Applications	306
			3. Definition of Mobile Application "Manufacturer"	307
		I.	Future Direction of Telemedicine Regulation	307
		J.	Possible Collaboration with the Federal Communications Commission	309
	V.	The Sentinel Initiative		309
		A.	Structure and Objective of the Initiative	310
		B.	Current Status and Future Plans	311
		C.	Privacy and Security Concerns	312

I. INTRODUCTION

The U.S. Department of Health and Human Services (HHS), Food and Drug Administration (FDA) has jurisdiction over the regulation of food, drugs, medical devices, and cosmetics throughout the United States.[1] As former FDA Commissioner Andrew C. von Eschenbach explained, "FDA is responsible for ensuring the safety and high quality of more than a trillion dollars worth of products that are critical for the survival and well-being of all Americans."[2] Its mission includes ensuring that foods are safe, wholesome, sanitary and properly labeled; protecting the public from electronic product radiation; advancing the public health by helping to speed product innovations; and helping the public get the accurate science-based information they need, as well as regulating tobacco products, human and veterinary drugs, vaccines, and other biological products.[3]

The agency's authority comes primarily from the federal Food, Drug, and Cosmetic Act of 1938 (FDCA),[4] which the FDA has the responsibility to administer and enforce. The FDCA imposes significant conditions and restrictions on regulated-product labeling, establishes premarket clearance and approval requirements, and regulates the manufacture, storage, distribution, promotion, and advertising of products within the purview of the FDA.[5]

---

[1] Dep't of Health & Human Servs., Food & Drug Admin., What We Do (Nov. 18, 2010), *available at* http://www.fda.gov/AboutFDA/WhatWeDo/default.htm.

[2] Dep't of Health & Human Servs., Food & Drug Admin., Overview of FDA Mission (July 6, 2009), *available at* http://www.fda.gov/NewsEvents/Testimony/ucm154019.htm.

[3] Dep't of Health & Human Servs., Food & Drug Admin., What Does FDA Do? (Dec. 17, 2010), *available at* http://www.fda.gov/AboutFDA/Transparency/Basics/ucm194877.htm.

[4] 21 U.S.C. §301 *et seq.*

[5] Dep't of Health & Human Servs., Food & Drug Admin., FDA History, Part II (June 18, 2009), *available at* http://www.fda.gov/AboutFDA/WhatWeDo/History/Origin/ucm054826.htm.

Although the FDA's mission centers primarily on the safety and efficacy of the products it regulates, this chapter examines FDA involvement in electronic health ("e-health") regulation, with an emphasis on those activities relating to privacy and security concerns. The chapter begins with an overview of the FDA's e-health regulation, which spans such topics as Internet pharmacies and online drug promotion. The chapter continues with a more detailed discussion of three particular areas of regulation: (1) the FDA's possible involvement in electronic health record (EHR) certification through collaboration with the Office of the National Coordinator for Health Information Technology (ONC); (2) the FDA's emerging regulation of telemedicine, particularly mobile health devices and applications; and (3) the FDA's implementation of an active adverse event surveillance system known as the Sentinel Initiative.

II. FDA Regulation of Online Activities

The FDCA authorizes the FDA to regulate the sale, importation, distribution, and promotion of drugs in the United States, and that authority extends to online activities. Initially, the FDA focused its oversight and enforcement activities on illegitimate drug sales facilitated by Internet pharmacies. The FDA can trace its Internet enforcement actions back to 1994, and in 1999 the agency released an Internet Drug Sales Action Plan to address increasing online drug sales.[6] The agency later targeted direct-to-consumer (DTC) advertising and on-line drug promotion, and has recently directed its attention towards social media and online genetic testing services. In addition to its enforcement activities, the FDA issues notices informing the public of the general risks of online drug and device sales, as well as specific schemes that could endanger public health.[7] The ever-changing online landscape provides new and unique challenges to the FDA's oversight, and the agency continues to develop policies and regulations to address these emerging issues.

A. Internet Drug Sales

The development of the "Internet pharmacy" created a marketplace in which consumers could obtain FDA-approved drugs from a licensed pharmacist in a convenient and private manner. The global, impersonal nature of the Internet, however, also facilitated activities prohibited by the FDA, including the marketing and sale of unapproved or fraudulent drugs that may pose serious health risks to unaware consumers.

---

[6] Dep't of Health & Human Servs., Food & Drug Admin., Drug Sales Over the Internet (Aug. 6, 2009), *available at* http://www.fda.gov/NewsEvents/Testimony/ucm115047.htm.

[7] Dep't of Health & Human Servs., Food & Drug Admin., Buying Medicines Over the Internet (Feb. 8, 2011), *available at* http://www.fda.gov/drugs/resourcesforyou/consumers/buyingusingmedicinesafely/buyingmedicinesovertheinternet/default.htm.

1. FDA Enforcement Activities

Two offices within the FDA are primarily responsible for regulating online drug sales: the Office of Regulatory Affairs (ORA) and the Office of Compliance in the Center for Drug Evaluation and Research (CDER). In response to complaints from consumers, industry, health officials, and government authorities, these offices review the Web sites of companies regulated by the FDA to determine their compliance with FDA regulations. Prior to 1999, the FDA initiated at least 60 enforcement actions related to suspected illegal Internet drug sales.[8] Beginning in 2004, the FDA's Center for Food Safety and Applied Nutrition (CFSAN) and the CDER Division of Information Disclosure Policy began issuing "cyber" letters"—electronic versions of the agency's written warning letters—to Web site operators promoting and selling unapproved products that claim to diagnose, mitigate, treat, cure, or prevent a specific disease.[9] Through the issuance of cyber letters and warning letters, and in coordination with the Drug Enforcement Administration (DEA), Federal Bureau of Investigation (FBI), Office of National Drug Control and Policy (ONDCP), and numerous state agencies, the FDA continues to investigate and prosecute Web sites that engage in illegal Internet drug sales.[10]

2. Consumer Education

To educate consumers regarding the risks of unlicensed online pharmacies, the FDA maintains a public database that contains recommendations and warnings regarding general and specific improper practices related to online drug sales.[11] The FDA provides consumers with a link to the National Association of Boards of Pharmacy (NABP), an organization that accredits online pharmacies through its Verified Internet Pharmacy Practice Sites (VIPPS) program. The agency's public education materials include summaries of FDA's past enforcement activities against online schemes—such as selling fake cancer "cures"—and a list of drugs that should never be purchased over the Internet or from foreign sources due to serious known risks.[12] Through enforcement activities against violative practices, coordination with state and federal agencies, and the provision of consumer education materials, the FDA seeks to minimize the public health risks associated with Internet drug sales while maintaining the benefits of increased access, convenience, and privacy.

---

[8] FDA, *Drug Sales Over the Internet*.

[9] Dep't of Health & Human Servs., Food & Drug Admin., Cyber Letters 2004 (June 18, 2009), *available at* http://www.fda.gov/Drugs/GuidanceComplianceRegulatoryInformation/EnforcementActivitiesbyFDA/CyberLetters/ucm054719.htm.

[10] A Prescription for Safety: Hearing on H.R. 3880, the Internet Pharmacy Consumer Protection Act Before the H. Comm. On Government Reform, 108th Cong. 29 (2004) (statement of William K. Hubbard, Associate Commissioner for Policy and Planning, HHS).

[11] FDA, *Buying Medicines Over the Internet*.

[12] Dep't of Health & Human Servs., Food & Drug Admin., FDA Consumer Safety Alert: Don't Buy These Drugs Over the Internet or From Foreign Sources (Mar. 9, 2010), *available at* http://www.fda.gov/Drugs/ResourcesForYou/Consumers/BuyingUsingMedicineSafely/BuyingMedicinesOvertheInternet/ucm202893.htm.

B. Online Direct-to-Consumer Advertising

In addition to facilitating legitimate and illegitimate pharmaceutical sales, the Internet represents an entirely new form of media by which drug and device companies may advertise their products directly to consumers. The FDA has issued specific guidance relating to DTC advertising that identifies the risk information that advertisers must include in DTC advertisements published in print and broadcast media.[13] The FDA's Division of Drug Marketing, Advertising, and Communications (DDMAC) regulates DTC advertising by reviewing promotional and advertising materials to ensure the information presented is "truthful, balanced and accurately communicated."[14] Drugs and medical devices are "misbranded" under the FDCA if they are advertised in a false or misleading manner,[15] or if the product's advertisements do not present a "fair balance" between information related to risks and benefits.[16] The FDCA prohibits the misbranding of any pharmaceutical or medical device in interstate commerce,[17] and the FDA may initiate an enforcement action against such a product.

1. Sponsored Links

The FDA recently focused its enforcement efforts on DTC Internet advertising by drug manufacturers. In a high-profile enforcement action in March 2009, DDMAC sent warning letters to 14 pharmaceutical companies after reviewing the advertising materials found in "sponsored links" purchased by those companies on major Internet search engines.[18] Generally, sponsored links, such as those provided by Google Adwords, contain only short headlines and descriptions (often fewer than 25 characters), followed by a hyperlink to a Web site containing more information. Due to the abbreviated nature of the advertisements, the companies targeted by DDMAC failed to include required information related to the risks or approved indications for the subject drugs, which would have ensured the sponsored links presented a "fair balance" of risks and benefits. The companies were instructed to immediately cease dissemination of the violative material and to submit a written response to the FDA.[19]

In light of the continued interest and regulatory uncertainty regarding Internet advertising, the FDA held public meetings in November 2009 to solicit public input on the promotion of FDA-regulated products using the Internet

---

[13] Dep't of Health & Human Servs., Food & Drug Admin., et al., Guidance for Industry: Consumer-Directed Broadcast Advertisements, *available at* http://www.fda.gov/downloads/Drugs/GuidanceComplianceRegulatoryInformation/Guidances/UCM070065.pdf.

[14] Dep't of Health & Human Servs., Food & Drug Admin., Division of Drug Marketing, Advertising, and Communications (DDMAC) (July 25, 2011), *available at* http://www.fda.gov/AboutFDA/CentersOffices/CDER/ucm090142.htm.

[15] 21 U.S.C. §352(a).

[16] 21 C.F.R. §202.1(e)(5)(iii).

[17] 21 U.S.C. §331(b).

[18] *See* Dep't of Health & Human Servs., Food & Drug Admin., FDA Warning Letter re. Eli Lilly & Co. (Mar. 26, 2009), *available at* http://www.fda.gov/downloads/Drugs/GuidanceComplianceRegulatoryInformation/EnforcementActivitiesbyFDA/WarningLettersandNoticeofViolationLetterstoPharmaceuticalCompanies/UCM143536.pdf.

[19] *See id.*

and social media tools.[20] The FDA has not yet issued proposed rules or guidance specific to online DTC advertising for drugs and medical devices, and the agency continues to investigate the effects of Internet promotion to inform future guidance or rulemaking.[21]

2. DTC Promotion of Genetic Testing Services

Although retail genetic testing represents a relatively new development in the medical device universe, DTC advertising for genetic testing services has already drawn the attention of the FDA. On May 10, 2010, the FDA issued an "untitled" letter—a letter citing violations that do not meet the threshold that would justify a warning letter—to Pathway Genomics Corporation (PGC), which was prepared to commercialize a home-use saliva collection kit for genetic testing.[22] The letter notified PGC that the company's product appeared to be a medical device requiring premarket clearance or approval before commercial launch, and that the agency would like to discuss with PGC whether its product was subject to FDA regulation.[23] On June 10, 2010, and July 19, 2010, the FDA sent letters to 15 other device manufacturers that marketed genetic tests directly to consumers.[24] As explained by the director of the FDA's Center for Devices and Radiological Health (CDRH), Dr. Jeff Shuren, the FDA issued the letters due to the "escalation in risk and aggressive marketing" of genetic tests, which could lead patients to make medical decisions based on data from genetic tests that have not received independent premarket review or been proven safe, effective, or accurate.[25] The FDA scheduled public meetings in March 2011 to discuss the risks and benefits of DTC genetic testing services, but as of July 2011, the FDA had not issued a proposed rule or guidance on the subject.[26]

---

[20]Promotion of Food and Drug Administration-Regulated Medical Products Using the Internet and Social Media Tools; Notice of Public Hearing, 74 Fed. Reg. 48,083 (Sept. 21, 2009), *available at* http://edocket.access.gpo.gov/2009/pdf/E9-22618.pdf.

[21]76 Fed. Reg. 23821 (Apr. 28, 2011).

[22]Dep't of Health & Human Servs., Food & Drug Admin., Letter from James Woods, Ctr. for Device & Radiological Health, FDA to James Plante, Founder and CEO, Pathway Genomics Corp. (May 10, 2010), *available at* http://www.fda.gov/downloads/MedicalDevices/Resources forYou/ Industry/UCM211875.pdf.

[23]*Id.*

[24]*See, e.g.*, Dep't of Health & Human Servs., Food & Drug Admin., Letter from Alberto Gutierrez, Ctr. for Device & Radiological Health, FDA to Anne Wojcicki, Pres., 23andMe, Inc. (June 10, 2010), *available at* http://www.fda.gov/downloads/MedicalDevices/ResourcesforYou/Industry/UCM215240.pdf; Dep't of Health & Human Servs., Food & Drug Admin., Letter from James Woods, Ctr. for Device & Radiological Health, FDA to Andrew Alexander, Founder and Dir., easyDNA (July 19, 2010), *available at* http://www.fda.gov/downloads/MedicalDevices/ProductsandMedicalProcedures/InVitroDiagnostics/UCM219601.pdf.

[25]Direct-to-Consumer Genetic Testing and the Consequences to the Public: Hearing before the Subcomm. on Oversight and Investigations (2010) (statement of Jeffrey Shuren, MD, Director, Center for Devices and Radiological Health), *available at* http://www.fda.gov/NewsEvents/Testimony/ucm219925.htm.

[26]76 Fed. Reg. 6623 (Feb. 7, 2011).

III. FDA AND ELECTRONIC HEALTH RECORDS

A. FDA Authority to Regulate EHR

As the FDA continues to evaluate new risks associated with changes in health technology, areas in which the agency previously practiced a hands-off approach are gaining a more prominent place in its plans for future regulation. The regulatory history of EHR provides such an example. Generally, EHR may be defined as longitudinal electronic records of patient health information generated by one or more encounters in any care delivery setting.[27] The FDA has authority to regulate computer-based and software-based products if they meet the definition of a "device" found at 21 U.S.C. §321(h), but it has been the FDA's long-standing practice not to regulate such technology unless it interfaces directly with a medical device in some way.[28] The FDA's practice of enforcement discretion was limited by the Draft Software Policy issued in 1989, which explained that the FDA's oversight of software should depend primarily on the risk to the patient should the software fail to perform in accordance with its specifications, although that Policy was withdrawn in 2005.[29]

The increased use of health information technology (HIT) and EHR by health care providers has led to increased risk to patients and corresponding regulatory oversight by the FDA. In testimony to the HIT Policy Committee on February 25, 2010, Dr. Shuren stated that in the previous two years, the FDA had received 260 voluntary reports of HIT-related malfunctions that had the potential to cause patient harm.[30] In light of the identified risk to patients, the FDA confirmed that HIT software is a medical device subject to FDA regulation and determined that FDA oversight of HIT is necessary.[31] The agency is considering a number of approaches to ensure the safety and effectiveness of HIT. These include:

(1) Focus on postmarket safety by requiring HIT vendors and providers to electronically register and submit medical device reports (MDRs) to the FDA containing reports of all adverse events associated with the technology;

(2) Focus on both manufacturing quality and postmarket safety by requiring all HIT systems to comply with the postmarket requirements listed in Item 1 and adhere to the FDA's Quality Systems Regulations, which require manufacturers to meet minimum guidelines to ensure the quality and consistency of products on the market; or

---

[27] National Institutes of Health, National Center for Research Resources, Electronic Health Records Overview (Apr. 2006), *available at* http://www.ncrr.nih.gov/publications/informatics/ehr.pdf.

[28] *Id.*

[29] Dep't of Health & Human Servs., Food & Drug Admin., FDA Policy for the Regulation of Computer Products (Nov. 13, 1989), *withdrawn by* 70 Fed. Reg. 824, 890 (Jan. 5, 2005).

[30] Jeffrey Shuren, Director, FDA Center for Devices and Radiological Health, Address at Health Information Technology Policy Committee (Feb. 25, 2010), *available at* http://integracon.files.wordpress.com/2011/07/hitpolicycommitteemeeting021510jeffshurentestimony.pdf.

[31] *Id.*

(3) Apply the traditional regulatory framework that the FDA applies to other medical devices to HIT, such as requiring risk-based premarket review; establishing device-specific requirements for selected products, and requiring the implementation of postmarket studies or product labeling.[32]

B. ONC Regulation of EHR

FDA's foray into HIT makes it the second federal agency tasked with regulating EHR technology. The American Recovery and Reinvestment Act of 2009 (ARRA) included the Health Information Technology for Economic and Clinical Health (HITECH) Act, which legislatively established the ONC.[33] The HITECH Act authorized and charged the ONC with the "coordination of nationwide efforts to implement and use the most advanced health information technology and the electronic exchange of health information."[34] The HITECH Act established two committees responsible for advising the ONC on aspects of technological standards, implementation specifications, and certification criteria: (1) the HIT Policy Committee, which establishes the priorities for developing, recognizing, and implementing specifications and certification criteria; and (2) the HIT Standards Committee, which develops the standards, specifications, and criteria to be enacted by the ONC.[35] Both committees have spent considerable time and effort developing policies and standards related to the certification and adoption of HIT, including requirements related to the functionality, privacy, and security of HIT systems.[36]

C. Increased Scrutiny and Oversight of EHR Systems

1. FDA Working Group

In addition to authorizing the ONC to enact regulations and policies to facilitate the adoption and development of a nationwide HIT infrastructure, the ARRA provided $19 billion to motivate health care providers to transition from traditional paper records to EHR. The designation of $19 billion towards EHR adoption increased legislative and executive scrutiny of existing EHR programs and entities. For example, shortly after passage of the ARRA, the FDA established a working group composed of representatives from CDRH, the Office of Device Evaluation (ODE), the Office of Science and Engineering Laboratories (OSEL), and the Office of Surveillance and Biometrics (OSB) to examine how and whether the FDA should regulate EHR. The specific task of the working

---

[32]*Id.*

[33]American Recovery and Reinvestment Act of 2009, Pub. L. No. 111-5, 123 Stat. 115.

[34]The Office of the National Coordinator for Health Information Technology (ONC), About ONC (Dec. 8, 2010), *available at* http://healthit.hhs.gov/portal/server.pt/community/healthit_hhs_gov__onc/1200.

[35]76 Fed. Reg. 1263.

[36]Office of the National Coordinator for Health Information Technology, Regulations & Guidance (Aug. 5, 2011), *available at* http://healthit.hhs.gov/portal/server.pt/community/healthit_hhs_gov__regulations_and_guidance/1496.

group was to develop recommendations for the FDA's role in EHR regulation in relation to potential risks to patients created by the rapid increase in the number of providers reliant on EHR technology. CDRH held hearings in February 2010 to receive public comment on FDA's proposed regulation of EHR. Dr. Shuren's February 25, 2010, statement indicates that FDA has determined that it has the authority to regulate EHR and plans to exercise that authority.

2. Legislative Inquiries

Scrutiny into the practices and safety of existing EHR systems also extended to the legislative branch. In October 2009 and January 2010, Senator Charles Grassley of Iowa, the ranking Republican on the Senate Committee on Finance, sent letters to EHR vendors and health care providers to inquire into their practices and experience with EHR systems.[37] Sen. Grassley focused his questions to vendors on "gag order" clauses vendors have included in their contracts to prevent parties from publicly releasing information regarding faults or errors with HIT operating systems. Sen. Grassley also requested that HIT vendors submit any policies related to voluntary reporting of adverse events that could lead to patient care or safety issues. The letters to hospitals and other providers requested information about those hospitals' experiences with EHR vendors, including any quality and safety concerns and the financial incentives EHR vendors could offer hospitals to purchase certain technology or programs. After learning of the lack of mandatory reporting of adverse events stemming from HIT malfunctions, Sen. Grassley publicly wondered whether "it is time to revisit FDA's responsibilities in regulating HIT products being used in clinical care."[38]

D. FDA and ONC Collaboration

The FDA has stated that it has the authority and expertise to regulate HIT, including EHR, as medical devices. However, the distinct role of the FDA in relation to ONC regulation of HIT has not yet been determined. Generally, the FDA would direct its attention to reducing the patient risk associated with these systems, while the ONC would work towards the development of specific HIT standards and requirements to foster adoption, increase interoperability across systems, and protect the privacy and confidential information of patients. Although the two agencies have different goals for HIT regulation, their overlapping jurisdiction may create uncertainty and confusion that could add expense and delay to the nationwide adoption of HIT systems encouraged by the HITECH Act.

---

[37] Press Release, Sen. Chuck Grassley of Iowa, *Grassley Asks Hospitals About Experiences With Federal Health Information Technology Program* (Jan. 20, 2010), *available at* http://finance.senate.gov/newsroom/ranking/release/?id=82d23510-4ca0-4e17-a7ef-53e9e3e7f750.

[38] Press Release, U.S. Senate Committee of Finance, *Grassley Asks HHS to Describe Steps to Ensure Patient Safety When Implementing Health Information Technologies* (Feb. 24, 2010), *available at* http://finance.senate.gov/newsroom/ranking/release/?id=82d23510-4ca0-4e17-a7ef-53e9e3e7f750.

1. HIT Policy Committee Recommendation

To avoid the possibility that the FDA and ONC would regulate HIT in different and irreconcilable manners, the HIT Policy Committee recommended in April 2010 that the ONC and the FDA collaborate on areas of HIT that implicate patient safety.[39] While the ONC expressed its "concerns" related to FDA involvement in HIT, the agency recognized that the FDA has "valuable experience that could help the ONC accomplish its goals."[40] For instance, the ONC sought the FDA's assistance in developing certification programs that improve patient safety, and solicited the FDA's input on noncertified software that may create safety risks, such as the programs used by retail pharmacies that do not process electronic order cancellations, resulting in the over-medication of patients.[41]

2. Concerns

Concerns regarding the FDA's involvement in EHR include a variety of different issues. First, the FDA's focus on the safety of specific, individual "devices" or software does not account for the complex socio-technical universe in which HIT operates.[42] The FDA's focus on individual devices could result in reporting requirements that do not address common HIT issues that could implicate patient safety, such as incompatible work processes across different HIT systems. Additionally, HIT stakeholders believe the application of the FDA's Quality System Regulations to EHR could harm innovation and increase vendor and product costs, creating a substantial barrier to entry for smaller vendors.[43] Finally, FDA reporting requirements must address the patient confidentiality and data integrity issues paramount to the HIT arena. If the FDA reporting system requires certain confidential information to be sent to the agency, the FDA can also require specific IT system designs to adequately protect that data during the transfer. However, this type of regulation—covering the specific technological standards of HIT systems—would normally fall squarely within the purview of the ONC, thereby creating the potential for inconsistent standards.

3. Future Collaboration

As more organizations study the implications of FDA and ONC regulation of EHR, new proposals recommending FDA and ONC collaboration have begun to emerge. On July 29, 2011, the National Research Council's *Report on Home Health Technology* recommended that the FDA and ONC collaborate to regulate, certify, and monitor health care applications that integrate medical devices

---

[39] Letter from Paul Egerman and Marc Probst, Co-Chairs, Adoption Certification Workgroup, HIT Policy Committee, to David Blumenthal, National Coordinator for Health Information Technology, HHS (Apr. 22, 2010), *available at* http://healthit.hhs.gov/portal/server.pt/gateway/PTARGS_0_11673_911847_0_0_18/AdoptionCertificationletterHITSafetyFINAL508.pdf.

[40] *Id.*

[41] *Id.*

[42] *Id.*

[43] Bradley Merrill Thompson, FDA Regulation of Mobile Health: MobiHealthNews 2010 Report (June 2010), *available at* http://mobihealthnews.com/wp-content/pdf/FDA_Regulation_of_Mobile_Health.pdf.

and HIT.[44] Although the report echoed the HIT Policy Committee's prior recommendation regarding collaboration between the FDA and ONC, it did not provide further specifics of that collaboration.

The disparate missions, authority, and constituencies of the FDA and ONC must be reconciled or delineated prior to any successful collaboration on the subject of EHR regulation. The EHR adoption program funded by the HITECH Act continues to accelerate towards nationwide launch, yet the respective regulatory roles of the FDA and ONC for HIT and EHR remain undefined.

IV. FDA REGULATION OF TELEMEDICINE

In his State of the Union address on January 25, 2011, President Barack Obama declared:

> [W]ithin the next five years, we will make it possible for business to deploy the next generation of high-speed wireless coverage to 98% of all Americans. This isn't just about a faster Internet and fewer dropped calls. It's about ... a patient who can have face-to-face video chats with her doctor.[45]

The President's words alluded to a rapidly growing "telemedicine" trend in the health care arena, which actually extends far beyond the mere merger of video conferencing technologies with medical practice.

A. What is Telemedicine?

"Telemedicine," according to the American Telemedicine Association, is "the use of medical information exchanged from one site to another via electronic communications to improve patients' health status."[46] Though closely associated with HIT, which encompasses EHR and associated IT systems, telemedicine includes the storage and transmission of diagnostic images, remote monitoring of patient data (such as vital signs), and live, remote consults with medical specialists.[47] Juniper Research predicts that the global market in wireless patient monitoring services *alone* will reach $1.9 billion by 2014,[48] and if a 2010 report by a mobile market research and consulting company is correct, "the long-expected mobile revolution in healthcare is set to happen."[49]

---

[44] NATIONAL ACADEMY OF SCIENCE ET AL., NATIONAL RESEARCH COUNCIL COMMITTEE ON THE ROLE OF HUMAN FACTORS IN HOME HEALTH CARE, HEALTH CARE COMES HOME: THE HUMAN FACTORS (July 2011), *available at* http://www7.nationalacademies.org/dbasse/Report_Brief_Health_Care_Comes_Home_The_Human_Factors.pdf.

[45] President Barack Obama, State of the Union Address (Jan. 25, 2011), *available at* http://www.npr.org/2011/01/26/133224933/transcript-obamas-state-of-union-address.

[46] American Telemedicine Ass'n, Telemedicine Defined, *available at* http://www.americantelemed.org/i4a/pages/index.cfm?pageid=3333.

[47] *Id.*

[48] Brian Dolan, *mHealth predictions: $1.9B, $4.4B, $4.6B*, MOBIHEALTHNEWS (Apr. 14, 2010), *available at* http://mobihealthnews.com/7270/mhealth-predictions-1-9b-4-4b-4-6b/.

[49] Jenara Nerenberg, *500 Million People to Use Mobile Health Apps by 2015: mHealth Study*, FAST COMPANY (Nov. 11, 2010), *available at* http://www.fastcompany.com/1701769/mhealth-summit-wraps-reveals-booming-industry.

According to the report, by 2015, half a billion people will be using mobile health applications.[50]

B. mHealth Technologies

The use of mobile communication technologies for health care purposes, also known as "mHealth," has recently received particular attention within the telemedicine field.[51] The mHealth Regulatory Coalition, a private-sector group composed of mHealth companies and trade associations, explains that the objective of mHealth technologies is "to extend the boundary of care delivery beyond the four walls of a provider's facility through existing mobile and wireless networked technologies."[52] The realization of such a change in care delivery models could improve both the quality of patients' lives (by eliminating the need for doctors' visits and other health care-associated hassles) and the overall state of patient health (for example, by detecting and warning of dangerous health conditions). The Coalition proposes that mHealth be defined to include two main categories of products: (1) "technology architecture," which includes software technologies and three categories of hardware (medical device technologies, communications technologies, and network infrastructure); and (2) "software platforms and interfaces," which are hardware-software combinations that provide "the fundamental structure on which other hardware and/or software function," ranging from devices such as iPhones to broader platforms such as the Internet.[53]

Telemedicine in general, including mHealth, is subject to federal government involvement in four primary areas: (1) reimbursement for telemedicine services by federal health insurance programs; (2) the direct provision of telemedicine services by federal health care program providers; (3) federal grants and contracts for telemedicine projects; and (4) regulation of the telemedicine services and devices themselves. It is this final category that involves the FDA.[54] The mHealth Regulatory Coalition predicts that "the FDA's regulation of [mHealth] products is going to be a major factor in determining how the growth and benefits of these technologies play out."[55] Yet, as recently as July 2011, observers have concluded that "most mobile software hasn't been clearly designated into the different [FDA regulatory classifications], making it difficult for developers and users alike to know which technologies require FDA

---

[50] *Id.*

[51] McKinsey & Co., mHealth: A New Vision for Healthcare (2010), *available at* http://gsmworld.com/documents/mHealth_report.pdf.

[52] mHealth Regulatory Coalition, A Call for Clarity: Open Questions on the Scope of FDA Regulation of mHealth (Dec. 22, 2010), *available at* http://mhealthregulatorycoalition.org/wp-content/uploads/2010/12/mrcwhitefinal122210.pdf.

[53] *Id.*

[54] American Telemedicine Ass'n, Joint Federal Agency Coordination on Telemedicine, *available at* http://www.americantelemed.org/files/public/policy/SixFixes_JointFederalAgencyCoordination.pdf.

[55] mHealth Regulatory Coalition, A Call for Clarity.

approval."⁵⁶ Though the FDA has since released draft guidance regarding mobile medical applications, the regulation of telemedicine continues to be marked by considerable uncertainty. The following sections provide a brief introduction to FDA medical device regulation, followed by an examination of the rationales for (and difficulties with) telemedicine regulation, a description of the current state of FDA telemedicine regulation, and a look at the future steps that the FDA is expected to take.

C. FDA Regulation of Mobile Medical Devices

1. Overview

Section 201(h) of the FDCA defines a medical device as:

> an instrument, apparatus, implement, machine, contrivance, implant, in vitro reagent, or other similar or related article, including any component, part, or accessory, which is ... intended [either] for use in the diagnosis of disease or other conditions, or in the cure, mitigation, treatment, or prevention of disease ... [or] to affect the structure or any function of the body of man or other animals ....⁵⁷

Thus, as noted in the statute, the determination of whether a product is a medical device subject to FDA regulation hinges on the product's intended use.

The intended use of a product is the use that is intended by the product's manufacturer or, more specifically, by the "persons legally responsible for the labeling of devices."⁵⁸ Although a product may be used for multiple purposes, its intended use is primarily determined by the manner in which the product is promoted, including statements made in the product's advertising, claims made in the product's labeling, and comments made by sales representatives. The use of a product by consumers in a manner for which the product is not advertised or labeled may be considered in determining a product's "intended use" if the manufacturer is aware of and encourages the consumer practice.⁵⁹ A product intended only to improve "wellness" is not a medical device subject to FDA regulation,⁶⁰ although distinguishing between products that are wellness-oriented and those that are medically oriented is not always straightforward.⁶¹

2. "Intended Use" of Mobile Medical Devices

As a result of the critical role that "intended use" plays in the identification of medical devices, even products that are seldom considered medical devices

---

⁵⁶*Classification for mHealth devices could simplify FDA regulation*, FIERCE MOBILE HEALTHCARE (July 7, 2011), *available at* http://www.fiercemobilehealthcare.com/story/mhealth-coalition-creates-new-classification-system-fdas-mhealth-regs/2011-07-07.

⁵⁷21 U.S.C. §321(h)

⁵⁸21 C.F.R. §801.4

⁵⁹*Id.*

⁶⁰Dep't of Health & Human Servs., Food & Drug Admin. et al., Draft Guidance for Industry and Food and Drug Administration Staff: Mobile Medical Applications (July 21, 2011), *available at* http://www.fda.gov/downloads/MedicalDevices/DeviceRegulationandGuidance/GuidanceDocuments/UCM263366.pdf.

⁶¹mHEALTH REGULATORY COALITION, A CALL FOR CLARITY.

in a colloquial context—including mobile products such as smart phones or iPads—may fall within the FDA's purview if advertised with reference to a medical function. Industry tallies of mobile medical applications ("apps") estimate that "there are 17,000 plus increasingly sophisticated wireless health applications in the market and thousands applications more in active development."[62] The definition of a medical device provided by the FDCA allows for the possibility that "an iPhone or Blackberry loaded with the proper apps or enabling a key medical service [could become] a FDA-regulated device. That is an industry with over five billion previously unregulated potential medical devices."[63]

a. "Accessory" and "Component" Devices

The extent to which an iPhone, Blackberry, or other mHealth- or telemedicine-related product may be subject to FDA regulation also depends on whether the product may be described as an "accessory" or a "component" of a medical device: "A product that supports (i.e., is connected to) another medical device could be either a medical device in its own right, a component of the medical device, or an accessory of the medical device."[64] The distinction between accessories and components lies in the purchaser of the product: end-users purchase accessories, while device manufacturers purchase components.[65] Again, this analysis is colored by intended use: an accessory is "a finished device that is 'distributed separately but intended to be attached to or used in conjunction with another finished device,' often called the parent device," while a component is "something that is 'intended to be included as part of the finished, packaged, and labeled device.'"[66] The regulatory requirements for accessories and components differ considerably. Accessories must satisfy FDA requirements because they are destined for distribution directly to the consumer. In contrast, FDA regulatory requirements generally do not apply to components, for which the responsibility for complying with FDA regulations falls on the manufacturer of the finished product.[67]

b. Regulatory Class

The range of requirements with which an FDA-regulated product must comply is determined by the amount of risk associated with the product. The FDA stratifies medical devices into three different classes, with Class I encompassing products that present the least amount of risk and Class III comprising products with the greatest risk profiles. The number and stringency of require-

---

[62]Triple Tree Research, *When Should 'Blackberry', 'iPhone' and 'FDA' Be Used in the Same Sentence?*, UNCOMMON CLARITY RESEARCH BLOG (Apr. 11, 2011), http://blog.triple-tree.com/2011/04/11/when-should-%E2%80%98blackberry%E2%80%99-%E2%80%98iphone%E2%80%99-and-%E2%80%98fda%E2%80%99-be-used-in-the-same-sentence/.

[63]*Id.*

[64]Dep't of Health & Human Servs., Food & Drug Admin., Guidance, Content of a 510(k), http://www.fda.gov/MedicalDevices/DeviceRegulationandGuidance/HowtoMarketYourDevice/PremarketSubmissions/PremarketNotification510k/ucm142651.htm.

[65]*See* 21 C.F.R. §820.3(c); §801.20(a)(5).

[66]21 C.F.R. §820.3(c).

[67]*See* 21 C.F.R. §820.1(a).

ments that the device must satisfy increase in accordance with the device's designated class.[68] If a device is deemed an accessory, the FDA may assign it to its own regulatory classification; absent such a designation, the accessory will be regulated in the same class as the parent device and held to the same requirements. If more than one parent device exists, the accessory will be regulated at the level of the highest classified parent.[69]

In addition, the FDA regulates medical devices in accordance with "guidance documents" that set specific standards for particular technologies. If the FDA has issued a guidance document that pertains to a particular product, that document will typically offer guidelines for determining the class to which the product will be assigned and will articulate particular requirements that must be satisfied before the device receives FDA approval or clearance.

D. Why Regulate Telemedicine?

1. Safety Concerns

Although videoconferencing technologies, mobile software applications, tablets, smart phones, and other burgeoning communications devices may fit within the FDCA's definition of medical devices, FDA regulation is not inevitable. The agency could choose to exercise its enforcement discretion and refrain from regulating these products. However, in addition to the FDA's recently-issued guidance document outlining the likely future regulation of mobile medical software applications, multiple factors point toward considerable agency involvement in telemedicine and mHealth regulation. As noted above, in February 2010 Dr. Shuren testified that the FDA would soon depart from its practice of generally abstaining from regulating HIT devices, citing over two hundred reports of potentially harm-causing malfunctions in health information technologies.[70] While HIT falls outside of the telemedicine umbrella, harm-causing malfunctions are just as possible among telemedicine devices, and some observers are concerned that "it is a short hop [from looking at HIT] to looking at the hardware and software that typifies mHealth applications."[71]

2. Legislative Interest

Political pressures may also contribute to an FDA interest in telemedicine regulation. In addition the letters sent to EHR vendors and hospitals, Senator Grassley sent a letter to Kathleen Sebelius, Secretary of Health and Human Services (HHS), inquiring into HHS's strategy for regulating EHR. Senator Grassley further suggested that the FDA reassess its regulatory responsibilities

---

[68]Dep't of Health & Human Servs., Food & Drug Admin., Overview of Medical Device Regulation: Device Classification http://www.fda.gov/MedicalDevices/DeviceRegulationandGuidance/Overview/ClassifyYourDevice/default.htm.

[69]FDA, *Content of a 510(k)*.

[70]Jeffrey Shuren, Director, FDA Center for Devices and Radiological Health, Address at Health Information Technology Policy Committee (Feb. 25, 2010), *available at* http://integracon.files.wordpress.com/2011/07/hitpolicycommitteemeeting021510jeffshurentestimony.pdf.

[71]THOMPSON, FDA REGULATION OF MOBILE HEALTH.

regarding HIT.[72] The Senator's attention comes at a time of heightened political focus on health care in general following the passage and continued controversy of the Patient Protection and Affordable Care Act (PPACA).[73]

3. Industry Growth

Finally, as previously noted, the mHealth industry expects to see tremendous growth in the next few years. Consulting firm CSMG estimates that in the U.S., revenues for mobile health services will exceed $4.6 billion by 2014.[74] As telemedicine assumes a larger role in the delivery of health care, the extent of the FDA's involvement may similarly increase.

Despite these drivers towards greater FDA regulation, the regulation of telemedicine, and mHealth in particular, poses a considerable array of problems. One of these is the difficulty of distinguishing those mHealth products with a "medical" intended use from those that feature only a "wellness" intended use. For instance, does an app that allows the user to track caloric intake or weight loss have a wellness-themed intended use, even when used to combat obesity? Other areas of complexity include the appropriate characterization of products as either accessories or components, and concerns over the interconnectivity and flexibility of mHealth devices. In addition, "mHealth products marketed by several different entities often are merged together in many different ways by different manufacturers or by consumers, for a variety of uses," complicating both the task of regulation and the act of assessing a product's risk.[75]

E. The FDA and Telemedicine in the Early 2000s

Until 2011, the FDA's approach to telemedicine regulation was primarily shaped by a series of guidance documents addressing related topics. One of the oldest was issued in 1999 under the title *Guidance for Industry, FDA Reviewers and Compliance on Off-the-Shelf Software Use in Medical Devices*.[76] Off-the-shelf (OTS) software refers to commercially available software components that a manufacturer incorporates into a medical device. Manufacturers that utilize OTS software have no control over the software's "life cycle," yet retain responsibility for the ultimate safety and efficacy of their medical devices. The FDA's guidance addressed the premarket submission requirements associated with OTS software use, establishing a tiered "level of concern" system under which differing degrees of documentation and hazard mitigation are required.

---

[72] Letter from Charles E. Grassley, Ranking Member, Senate Committee on Finance, to Hospitals (Jan. 19, 2010), *available at* http://www.grassley.senate.gov/news/Article.cfm?customel_dataPageID_1502=24867.

[73] Pub. L. No. 111-148, 124 Stat. 119 (2010).

[74] Brian Dolan, *mHealth predictions: $1.9B, $4.4B, $4.6B*, MOBIHEALTHNEWS (Apr. 14, 2010), *available at* http://mobihealthnews.com/7270/mhealth-predictions-1-9b-4-4b-4-6b/.

[75] MHEALTH REGULATORY COALITION, A CALL FOR CLARITY.

[76] Dep't of Health & Human Servs., Food & Drug Admin., et al., Guidance for Industry, FDA Reviewers and Compliance on Off-The-Shelf Software Use in Medical Devices (Sept. 9, 1999), *available at* http://www.fda.gov/downloads/MedicalDevices/DeviceRegulationandGuidance/GuidanceDocuments/ucm073779.pdf.

1. Early Guidance

Three additional guidance documents impacting telemedicine devices emerged between 2000 and 2002. The first of these, *Guidance for the Submission of Premarket Notifications for Medical Image Management Devices*,[77] clarified that "medical image storage devices" and "medical image communications devices" are Class I devices that are exempt from FDA premarket notification requirements, while "picture archiving and communications systems," which provide "one or more capabilities relating to the acceptance, transfer, display, storage, and digital processing of medical images," are Class II devices subject to premarket notification requirements. The second document, entitled *Guidance for Industry: Wireless Medical Telemetry Risks and Recommendations*,[78] directed manufacturers of wireless medical telemetry systems to use bands associated with a Wireless Medical Telemetry Service created by the Federal Communications Commission (FCC) to avoid electromagnetic interference from other radiofrequency sources in the same band. Finally, the document entitled *General Principles of Software Validation: Final Guidance for Industry and FDA Staff* articulated policies pertaining to the validation of medical device software, explained the difference between software validation and software verification, and detailed the application of Quality System Regulation to medical software.[79]

2. Further Guidance Documents

Other significant guidance documents include *Guidance for the Content of Premarket Submissions for Software Contained in Medical Devices* and *Cybersecurity for Networked Medical Devices Containing Off-the-Shelf (OTS) Software*, both of which were released in 2005. The first of these documents described the information that the FDA suggested including in the premarket submissions of "software devices, including stand-alone software applications and hardware-based devices that incorporate software."[80] The second warned manufacturers that use OTS software that they remain responsible for their devices' cybersecurity, including in regards to such threats as "viruses and worms." It

---

[77]Dep't of Health & Human Servs., Food & Drug Admin., et al., Guidance for Industry: Guidance for the Submission of Premarket Notifications for Medical Image Management Devices (July 27, 2000), *available at* http://www.fda.gov/downloads/MedicalDevices/DeviceRegulationandGuidance/GuidanceDocuments/ucm073721.pdf.

[78]Dep't of Health & Human Servs., Food & Drug Admin., et al., Guidance for Industry: Wireless Medical Telemetry Risks and Recommendations (Sept. 27, 2000), *available at* http://www.fda.gov/downloads/MedicalDevices/DeviceRegulationandGuidance/GuidanceDocuments/ucm070921.pdf.

[79]Dep't of Health & Human Servs., Food & Drug Admin., et al., General Principles of Software Validation; Final Guidance for Industry and FDA Staff (Jan. 11, 2002), *available at* http://www.fda.gov/downloads/MedicalDevices/DeviceRegulationandGuidance/GuidanceDocuments/ucm085371.pdf.

[80]Dep't of Health & Human Servs., Food & Drug Admin., et al., Guidance for the Content of Premarket Submissions for Software Contained in Medical Devices (May 11, 2005), *available at* http://www.fda.gov/downloads/MedicalDevices/DeviceRegulationandGuidance/GuidanceDocuments/ucm089593.pdf.

also addressed the FDA review and reporting requirements associated with implementation of a "cybersecurity patch."[81]

F. Recent Developments in FDA Telemedicine Regulation

By 2008, the FDA had granted approval to a small but rapidly growing number of mHealth devices. CardioSen'CTM, "the world's first personal cellular-digital 12-lead ECG transmitter used for the purpose of remote real-time diagnosis of arrhythmia, ischemia, and myocardial infarction," successfully completed the FDA's premarket review process on August 4, 2008.[82] At least three other "first" mHealth devices received FDA approval in the first seven months of 2011. The first medical iPhone app (Mobile MIM), which allows doctors to receive CT, MRI, and PET images for purposes of making diagnoses, was approved in February 2011.[83] The first smart phone-connected ultrasound device (Mobisante) was approved that same month.[84] And the first "iPhone connected blood pressure monitor with online monitoring and measurement storage" received approval in June 2011.[85]

In addition to the recent increase in FDA-approved mHealth devices, the state of telemedicine regulation has been significantly affected by the release in 2011 of two highly anticipated FDA documents: the *FDA Final Rule on Medical Device Data Systems* and the *Draft Guidance for Industry and Food and Drug Administration Staff: Mobile Medical Applications.*[86]

G. FDA Final Rule on Medical Device Data Systems

On February 9, 2011, the FDA revised its classification of medical device data systems (MDDS) from the highest risk (Class III), which requires premarket approval, to the lowest risk (Class I), which requires compliance only

---

[81] Dep't of Health & Human Servs., Food & Drug Admin., et al., Cybersecurity for Networked Medical Devices Containing Off-the-Shelf (OTS) Software (Jan. 14, 2005), *available at* http://www.fda.gov/downloads/MedicalDevices/DeviceRegulationandGuidance/GuidanceDocuments/ucm077823.pdf.

[82] Press Release, SHL Telemedicine, *CardioSen'CTM Receives FDA Clearance* (Aug. 4, 2008), *available at* http://www.shl-telemedicine.com/press-release/Cardiosenc/.

[83] News Release, Dep't of Health & Human Servs., Food & Drug Admin., *FDA Clears First Diagnostic Radiology Application for Mobile Devices* (Feb. 4, 2011), *available at* http://www.fda.gov/NewsEvents/Newsroom/PressAnnouncements/ucm242295.htm.

[84] *FDA Approves Two Firsts: Mobisante, Mobile MIM*, TELECARE AWARE (Feb. 4, 2011), *available at* http://www.telecareaware.com/index.php/fda-approves-two-firsts-mobisante-mobile-mim.html.

[85] Al Fresco, *Withings Launches World's First iPhone Connected Blood Pressure Monitor With Online Monitoring and Measurement Storage,* BIKE WORLD NEWS (Jan. 5, 2011), *available at* http://www.bikeworldnews.com/2011/01/05/withings-launches-worlds-first-iphone-connected-blood-pressure-monitor-online-monitoring-measurement-storage/; *see also mHealth: iPhones to Provide Mobile Means for Monitoring Blood Pressure*, MOBILE MARKETING WATCH (June 21, 2011), *available at* http://www.mobilemarketingwatch.com/mhealth-iphones-to-provide-mobile-means-for-monitoring-blood-pressure-16425/.

[86] *See* 76 Fed. Reg. 8638 (Feb. 15, 2011); Dep't of Health & Human Servs., Food & Drug Admin., et al., Draft Guidance for Industry and Food and Drug Administration Staff: Mobile Medical Applications (July 21, 2011), *available at* http://www.fda.gov/downloads/MedicalDevices/DeviceRegulationandGuidance/GuidanceDocuments/UCM263366.pdf.

with "general controls" such as good manufacturing practice requirements, adverse event reporting, and registration requirements.[87] The rule clarifies that an MDDS is "a device that is intended to transfer, store, convert from one format to another according to preset specifications, or display medical device data. ... An MDDS does not modify the data or modify the display of the data."

1. Exclusion of EHR

Electronic medical records and electronic prescribing systems are explicitly excluded from the down-classification under the February 2011 final rule. In addition, the FDA warned that any device "intended to be used in connection with active patient monitoring" does not constitute an MDDS and thus may be subject to regulatory requirements exceeding those applicable to Class I devices, because the speed of MDDS operation is not covered by the regulations, and the active monitoring of patients "depends on the timeliness of the data transmission."[88] Such active monitoring devices excluded from Class I include those with alarms or alert functions, although a Class I MDDS may store or display "as part of a historical record" alarm-related data, such as that produced by a connected device, which the MDDS itself does not analyze.[89]

2. Uncertain Applications

The final rule came with the FDA's acknowledgment that malfunctioning MDDS devices may cause problems involving data transfer, storage, conversion, or display that result in mistaken treatments or diagnoses. However, the FDA reasoned that "the risks associated with MDDSs are generally from inadequate software quality and incorrect functioning of the device itself," and "general controls will provide a reasonable assurance of safety and effectiveness."[90] Following the rule's release, some analysts and news reports highlighted the FDA's flexibility and commitment to reducing regulatory burdens; others noted that the rule leaves quite a bit unclear, as the implication for those devices not included as MDDSs could be either that they belong to a "higher" regulatory class or, precisely the opposite, that they might not be subject to FDA regulation at all.[91] A more specific question of whether the MDDS category includes mobile medical applications that similarly offer only data storage, display, or transmittal functions was answered five months later, in July 2011, when the FDA released its draft guidance on mobile medical applications.

---

[87] *See* Final Rule, Medical Device Data Systems, 76 Fed. Reg. 8638.
[88] *Id.* at 8644.
[89] *Id.*
[90] *Id.* at 8639.
[91] *FDA Finalizes Regulation for Certain Software, Hardware Used with Medical Devices*, SYS-CON MEDIA (Feb. 14, 2011), *available at* http://www.sys-con.com/node/1715367; *see also* Brian Dolan, *Understanding FDA's new MDDS Rule*, MOBIHEALTHNEWS (Feb. 15, 2011), *available at* http://mobihealthnews.com/10234/understanding-fdas-new-mdds-rule/.

H. Draft Guidance: Mobile Medical Applications

Though distributed only "for comment purposes" and not yet intended for implementation, the FDA's draft guidance document of July 19, 2011, provided a first look at how the FDA plans to regulate "select software applications intended for use on mobile platforms," known as "mobile medical apps."[92] Pursuant to the draft guidance, a mobile medical app is a mobile app—a "software application that can be executed (run) on a mobile platform, or a web-based software application that is tailored to a mobile platform but is executed on a server"—that satisfies the FDCA's definition of a medical device and either (1) is used as an accessory to a regulated medical device, or (2) transforms a mobile platform into a regulated medical device.[93]

1. Scope

As a preliminary matter, it is important to understand the types of applications that are not covered by the FDA's proposed guidance.[94] Mobile apps that perform administrative or office operations such as tracking billable hours or determining billing codes are not considered mobile medical apps, nor are mobile apps that serve as health record systems. Mobile apps that "log, record, track, evaluate or make decisions or suggestions" regarding general health and wellness, such as "dietary tracking logs," "appointment reminders," and apps providing "posture suggestions" also are not included.[95] Mobile apps that provide electronic versions of reference materials and textbooks also are not included, though apps that use both patient data and reference material to provide automatic diagnoses are considered to be mobile medical apps.[96]

In addition, the determination that a mobile medical app must itself be a medical device implicates the "intended use" considerations described earlier. Thus, statements made as part of the app's labeling and marketing become relevant. The draft guidance clarifies that if an app is intended to provide a function generally not considered a medical purpose—for example, if the app merely causes a device to shine a bright light—the app will not be deemed a medical device even if used for medical activities such as patient examinations unless the manufacturer promoted this medical usage.[97]

2. Classification of Mobile Platforms and Applications

Addressing concerns regarding the classification of mobile platforms themselves (smart phones, tablet computers, etc.), the FDA emphasized in its July 2011 draft guidance that "if it is possible to run mobile medical apps on

---

[92] Dep't of Health & Human Servs., Food & Drug Admin. et al., Draft Guidance for Industry and Food and Drug Administration Staff: Mobile Medical Applications (July 21, 2011), *available at* http://www.fda.gov/downloads/MedicalDevices/DeviceRegulationandGuidance/GuidanceDocuments/UCM263366.pdf.
[93] *Id.*
[94] *See id.*
[95] *Id.*
[96] *Id.*
[97] *Id.*

BrandNamePhone but BrandNamePhone is not marketed by BrandNameCompany with a medical device intended use, then BrandNameCompany would not be a medical device manufacturer."[98]

The draft guidance also specifies classifications for certain types of mobile medical apps. Apps that serve MDDS functions are subject to the same requirements as MDDSs and fall in Class I. Apps that control "the intended use, function, modes, or energy source of the connected medical device" are considered accessories subject to the same regulatory requirements as the connected device. Likewise, an app that analyzes data from another medical device and produces an alarm, a recommendation, or new data must satisfy the classification requirements of the other medical device. Finally, apps that convert a mobile platform into a regulated device are held to the same regulatory requirements as those typically associated with that device. For example, if an app converts an iPhone into an electronic stethoscope, the classification applicable to electronic stethoscopes becomes the classification applicable to that mobile medical app.[99]

For apps that do not serve these particular functions, the FDA reports that the standard expectation "that the manufacturer of an accessory would meet the requirements associated with the classification of the connected device … may not be well-suited for mobile medical apps … because of the wide variety of functions mobile medical apps can potentially perform." The agency has thus requested comments regarding an appropriate approach.[100]

3. Definition of Mobile Application "Manufacturer"

An additional key provision included in the draft guidance is the definition of a "mobile medical app manufacturer." The FDA proposed that the term exclude "entities that exclusively distribute mobile medical apps, without engaging in manufacturing functions; examples of such distributors may include owners and operators of 'android market,' 'iTunes store,' and 'BlackBerry App World.'" However, anyone who "initiates specifications, designs, labels, or creates a software system or application in whole or from multiple software components" may be a mobile medical device manufacturer, including entities that use commercial off-the-shelf (COTS) software. If a "developer" is used to produce an app, the "author" who dictates the specifications nonetheless remains the manufacturer unless manufacturing and distribution responsibilities rest entirely with another entity.[101]

I. Future Direction of Telemedicine Regulation

In addition to providing guidance, the FDA's *Mobile Medical Applications* draft guidance identified a range of issues that the FDA has not yet addressed but intends to examine in the future. These include "wireless safety considerations, classification and submission requirements related to clinical decision

---

[98] *Id.*
[99] *Id.*
[100] *Id.*
[101] *Id.*

support software, [and] the application of quality systems to software."[102] The FDA also expressed its intention to continue monitoring other mobile apps not covered by the draft guidance, and stated that mobile medical apps designed to "analyze, process, or interpret medical device data" from multiple medical devices would be separately addressed in future guidance.[103]

Of course, mobile applications represent only one part of the mHealth universe. When asked in June 2011 how close he believed the FDA to be in providing "concrete guidance for mobile healthcare devices and applications," Robert McCray, President and CEO of the Wireless-Life Science Alliance, replied, "I expect we're going to be in this area of uncertainty for quite some time."[104] He added that "[b]ased on history, I don't know that anyone expects that there will be a clear set of 'do these five things objectively and you're good to go.'"[105]

Whenever it arrives, increased FDA regulation in the telemedicine arena will have significant effects on this emerging industry. The potential benefits stemming from FDA regulation could reach beyond the protection of patient safety and device efficacy. By imposing barriers of entry to the health markets, federal regulations may ensure that only those entities willing to make the requisite investments will be able to bring their products to market; as one article puts it, "FDA law means don't enter this business unless you're willing to do it right."[106] At the same time, greater barriers of entry allow for less competition and thereby offer innovators greater security in the exclusivity (and thus profitability) of their devices. In addition, by ensuring that telemedicine technologies remain safe, FDA regulation may "help[] protect the image of an industry and the confidence of its customers."[107]

On the other hand, greater FDA regulation may also carry potential disadvantages. Perhaps most obvious are the costs imposed on businesses. FDA regulation might necessitate more costly marketing, more extensive and expensive testing, and more elaborate postmarket reporting and monitoring mechanisms. Erecting strict regulatory requirements may also reduce the freedom with which manufacturers are able to innovate and, by adding more steps in the path to market, may further delay the realization of key technologies.[108] Finally, the FDA's own process of certifying regulatory compliance might further impede technological progress, as the glacial pace of bureaucratic activity may prove incompatible with the quick pace of a rapidly evolving industry.[109]

---

[102] *Id.*

[103] *Id.*

[104] Dan Bowman, *Mobile Healthcare's 'Amazon' Moment on the Horizon*, FIERCEMOBILE HEALTHCARE (June 1, 2011), *available at* http://www.fiercemobilehealthcare.com/story/mobile-healthcares-amazon-moment-horizon/2011-06-01.

[105] *Id.*

[106] BRADLEY MERRILL THOMPSON, FDA REGULATION OF MOBILE HEALTH: MOBI HEALTHNEWS 2010 REPORT (June 2010), *available at* http://mobihealthnews.com/wp-content/pdf/FDA_Regulation_of_Mobile_Health.pdf.

[107] *Id.*

[108] *Id.*

[109] Steven Overly, *For Health IT Firms, Regulatory Questions Abound*, WASHINGTON POST (May 22, 2011), *available at* http://www.washingtonpost.com/business/capitalbusiness/for-health-it-firms-regulatory-questions-abound/2011/05/19/AFWMWF9G_story.html.

J. Possible Collaboration with the Federal Communications Commission

One development currently looming in the field of telemedicine regulation involves a possible collaboration between the FDA's CDRH and the Federal Communications Commission (FCC). The FCC is an independent federal entity with responsibilities that include "governing radio devices so as to provide for effective operation and communication."[110] Wireless telemedicine devices thus fall within the intersection of the FDA's and the FCC's areas of expertise. In July 2010, the two regulatory bodies held a joint public meeting to address ways by which they could cooperatively work to ensure mHealth device efficacy and safety.[111]

Subsequent to the meeting, the FDA and FCC released a Memorandum of Understanding (MOU) in which they agreed to collaborate to "promote initiatives related to the review and use of FDA-regulated medical devices...that utilize radiofrequency emissions or otherwise fall under the jurisdiction of the FCC." The MOU was designed to facilitate the agencies' exchange of information and expertise, and articulated the parties' intent to harmonize and clarify the array of regulatory requirements that apply to wireless and broadband mHealth devices.[112]

While the FDA-FCC collaboration has yet to take shape, its eventual emergence will likely mark a pivotal step in the regulation of telemedicine in the United States.

V. THE SENTINEL INITIATIVE

On September 27, 2007, President George W. Bush signed into law the Food and Drug Administration Amendments Act of 2007 (FDAAA).[113] Section 905 of the FDAAA, titled "Active Postmarket Risk Identification and Analysis," requires the Secretary of Health and Human Services to work with private, academic, and other public entities to "develop validated methods for the establishment of a postmarket risk identification and analysis system to link and analyze safety data from multiple sources." It further requires the Secretary to "establish and maintain procedures for risk identification and analysis based on electronic health data" in compliance with the Health Insurance Portability and Accountability Act (HIPAA), and to "establish and maintain procedures to provide for active adverse event surveillance" based on federal health-related

---

[110] Memorandum of Understanding Between the Federal Communications Commission and the Food and Drug Administration Center for Devices and Radiologic Health (2010), *available at* http://transition.fcc.gov/Daily_Releases/Daily_Business/2010/db0726/DOC-300200A2.pdf [hereinafter FCC/FDA MOU].

[111] Press Release, FCC, *FCC/FDA Joint Meeting Scheduled to Streamline Review Process for Life-saving Wireless Medical Technology* (June 15, 2010), *available at* hraunfoss.fcc.gov/edocs_public/attachmatch/DOC-298805A1.pdf; Press Release, FCC, *FCC, FDA Take Steps to Promote Innovation and Investment in Wireless-enabled Medical Devices* (July 26, 2010), *available at* hraunfoss.fcc.gov/edocs_public/attachmatch/DOC-300226A1.pdf

[112] FCC/FDA MOU.

[113] Pub. L. No. 110-85 (2007).

electronic data, private sector health-related electronic data, and other data that the Secretary "deems necessary to create a robust system."[114]

Although the FDAAA provides the Secretary with a significant amount of discretion regarding the data sources, data collection measures, and "complimentary approaches" that may be used to meet the statute's requirements, Section 905 also articulates specific deadlines and numerical targets that the Secretary's system must satisfy. The Secretary must report to Congress the way in which the system has been used "to identify specific drug safety signals and to better understand the outcomes associated with drugs marketed in the United States" by no later than four years following the law's enactment.[115] Moreover, by July 1, 2010, the Secretary must have established validated methods for dealing with the data of at least 25 million patients; as of July 1, 2012, that number rises to 100 million patients.[116]

In response to the FDAAA Section 905 mandate, Health and Human Services Secretary Mike Leavitt announced FDA's launch of the Sentinel Initiative in May 2008.[117]

A. Structure and Objective of the Initiative

The FDA described the Sentinel Initiative in August 2011 as "a national electronic system that will transform the FDA's ability to track the safety of drugs, biologics, medical devices—and ultimately all FDA-regulated products once they reach the market."[118] The system that the Sentinel Initiative seeks to design would "actively query diverse automated healthcare data holders," including insurance and administrative claims databases and EHR systems, in order to enhance the agency's tracking of adverse events related to the medical products that it regulates. The system is intended to serve as a complement to FDA's other adverse-event tracking mechanisms in a proactive, quick, and secure manner.[119]

Under the structure envisioned, individual owners and managers of data who participate in the Sentinel Initiative will retain control over their health information when responding to inquiries made by the FDA. Information reported to FDA will summarize results determined pursuant to the data holders' own analysis.[120] The FDA will actively monitor the data by requesting responses to specific, targeted questions.[121] Although the FDA has queried insurance-claims records and administrative databases in past adverse-event tracking activities,

---

[114]*Id.*

[115]*Id.*

[116]*Id.*

[117]Dep't of Health & Human Servs., Food & Drug Admin., FDA's Sentinel Initiative (Aug. 22, 2011), *available at* http://www.fda.gov/Safety/FDAsSentinelInitiative/ucm2007250.htm.

[118]*Id.*

[119]*Id.*

[120]*Id.*

[121]Rachel E. Behrman, MD, MPH, et al., *Developing the Sentinel System—A National System for Evidence Development*, 364 NEW ENG. J. MED. 498–499 (2011), *available at* http://www.fnih.org/sites/all/files/documents/New%20England%20Journal%20of%20Medicine-%20Developing%20the%20Sentinel%20System.ashx_.pdf [hereinafter Behrman, *Developing the Sentinel System*].

the agency explained the difference between those activities and the Sentinel Initiative:

> [Before, the FDA] only worked with one particular healthcare system at a time to evaluate a given safety issue. Its goal now is to create a linked, sustainable system... that will draw on existing automated healthcare data from multiple sources to actively monitor the safety of medical products continuously and in real-time.[122]

This approach is considered "active" in contrast to FDA's past "passive" methods, and will equip the FDA to implement its own safety evaluations rather than relying on other parties to voluntarily report suspected adverse reactions.[123]

Though coordinated by the FDA, the Sentinel Initiative features the involvement of nonprofit organizations and the private sector.[124] The eHealth Initiative (eHI), which represents stakeholders spanning the health care industry and seeks to promote the use of information and technology to improve health care quality and efficiency,[125] announced in May 2008 that it will assist the government in designing a legal framework and assessing a data-collection strategy. eHI's role is specifically geared towards "developing legal guidance documents and model agreements to support responsible handling of electronic information" and "test[ing] and evaluat[ing] the feasibility and value of using electronic health information... to support post-market surveillance."[126] In addition, Harvard Pilgrim received a year-long FDA contract in 2009 to advance the program's development. Renewable for a possible four additional years, the contract assigns Harvard Pilgrim responsibility for establishing a "coordinating center" as part of a small-scale model of the Sentinel Initiative, serving to "identify appropriate databases, develop a scientific framework for obtaining real-time data, and ensure data quality."[127] Other collaborative components of the Sentinel Initiative include a grant awarded to the Brookings Institution to host conferences addressing issues associated with medical product surveillance.[128]

B. Current Status and Future Plans

FDA reports that the Sentinel Initiative will be "developed and implemented in stages."[129] Among noteworthy recent developments has been the

---

[122]Dep't of Health & Human Servs., Food & Drug Admin., FDA's Sentinel Initiative: Background (Jan. 19, 2010), *available at* http://www.fda.gov/Safety/FDAsSentinelInitiative/ucm149340.htm.

[123]DEP'T OF HEALTH & HUMAN SERVICES, FOOD & DRUG ADMIN., ET AL., THE SENTINEL INITIATIVE: ACCESS TO ELECTRONIC HEALTHCARE DATA FOR MORE THAN 25 MILLION LIVES (July 2010), *available at* http://www.fda.gov/downloads/Safety/FDAsSentinelInitiative/UCM233360.pdf [hereinafter FDA, THE SENTINEL INITIATIVE].

[124]*eHealth Initiative's Drug Safety Collaboration to Partner with FDA on Sentinel Initiative*, DRUGS.COM (May 2008), *available at* http://www.drugs.com/news/ehealth-initiative-s-safety-collaboration-partner-fda-sentinel-initiative-8226.html.

[125]eHealth Initiative, About Us, *available at* http://www.ehealthinitiative.org/about-us.html.

[126]Drugs.com, *eHealth Initiative's Drug Safety Collaboration*.

[127]News Release, Dep't of Health & Human Servs., Food & Drug Admin., *FDA Awards Contract to Harvard Pilgrim to Develop Pilot for Safety Monitoring system* (Jan. 8, 2010), *available at* http://www.fda.gov/NewsEvents/Newsroom/PressAnnouncements/ucm196968.htm.

[128]*Id.*

[129]Dep't of Health & Human Servs., Food & Drug Admin., FDA's Sentinel Initiative (Aug. 22, 2011), *available at* http://www.fda.gov/Safety/FDAsSentinelInitiative/ucm2007250.htm.

initiation of a pilot program known as Mini-Sentinel, which, as of January 2011, included 27 institutions and approximately 200 epidemiologists, data analysts, and other scientific and technical experts. Mini-Sentinel's objectives are to enable a small-scale assessment of safety and privacy complications as well as to serve as a laboratory for studying possible Sentinel Initiative data collection and analysis mechanisms.[130] Participating data holders provide access to the electronic health information of over 60 million Americans and analyze their own data using software distributed by Harvard Pilgrim's coordinating center, which integrates the contributions of the various partners. This arrangement is known as a "distributed" model because it relies on a distributed data network instead of a centralized database.[131] Mini-Sentinel's data currently comes from "administrative claims environments with pharmacy dispensing data," though information from outpatient and inpatient EHR and registries will be added subsequently.[132] An article in the *New England Journal of Medicine* further explains that "source data reside behind the data partners' institutional firewalls," while the FDA receives information in the aggregate, such as "the number of new users of a product who experience a particular outcome, grouped according to age, sex, other treatments, and health status."[133] It is hoped that the lessons learned from Mini-Sentinel will contribute to an efficient and reliable long-term and broad-scale Sentinel program;

Now in its second year, the Mini-Sentinel program plans to begin its first active surveillance evaluation, monitoring acute myocardial infarction occurrences among patients taking oral hypoglycemic agents. Other short-term plans include expanding the data sources covered by the pilot program.[134]

The FDA reported that it satisfied the FDAAA's deadline for accessing data from 25 million people by July 2010[135] and is "working towards" meeting the statute's July 2012 target of 100 million people.[136]

C. Privacy and Security Concerns

Section 905 of the FDAAA explicitly addresses privacy concerns relating to the analysis of drug safety data and contracts with other entities in connection with the FDA's active postmarket risk identification system.[137] The Act provides that the FDA "shall not disclose individually identifiable health information when presenting such drug safety signals and trends or when responding to

---

[130] Mini-Sentinel, Background (2010–2011), *available at* http://mini-sentinel.org/about_us/.
[131] Behrman, *Developing the Sentinel System*, 364 NEW ENG. J. MED. 498–99.
[132] Mini-Sentinel, *Background*.
[133] Behrman, *Developing the Sentinel System*, 364 NEW ENG. J. MED. at 498.
[134] ENGELBERG CENTER FOR HEALTH CARE REFORM AT BROOKINGS, MEETING SUMMARY: SENTINEL INITIATIVE PUBLIC WORKSHOP (Jan. 2011), *available at* http://www.brookings.edu/~/media/Files/events/2011/0112_sentinel_workshop/FINAL%20Sentinel%20Public%20Workshop%20Summary%20031411.pdf.
[135] FDA, THE SENTINEL INITIATIVE at 1.
[136] *Id.*
[137] Food and Drug Administration Amendments Act of 2007, Pub. L. No. 110-85.

inquiries regarding such drug safety signals and trends." In contracting with the FDA, the FDAAA requires that the contracted entity not violate HIPAA regulations, not violate Sections 552 or 552a of Title 5 of the United States Code regarding "the privacy of individually-identifiable beneficiary health information," and—echoing the restriction placed on the FDA itself—not reveal "individually identifiable health information when presenting drug safety signals and trends or when responding to inquiries regarding drug safety signals and trends." Furthermore, the final clause of Section 905 states that "[n]ot later than 18 months after the date of the enactment of this Act, the Comptroller General of the United States shall evaluate data privacy, confidentiality, and security issues relating to accessing, transmitting, and maintaining data for the active postmarket risk identification and analysis system." The Government Accountability Office (GAO) must report on its findings to the House of Representatives Committee on Energy and Commerce and the Senate Committee on Health, Education, Labor and Pensions.

The GAO delivered its required congressional briefing in March 2009. Three months later, the Office summarized its conclusions in a report entitled *Privacy and Security: Food and Drug Administration Faces Challenges in Establishing Protections for Its Postmarket Risk Analysis System*. Despite acknowledging in its very first sentence that implementation of the Sentinel Initiative is just beginning, the GAO report highlighted the fact that the FDA had yet to devise a plan or designate milestones for addressing the privacy and security issues implicated by the Sentinel Initiative. As noted, "[b]ecause the Sentinel system will rely on sensitive electronic health data, FDA will likely be faced with several significant privacy and security challenges." These challenges include (i) securing public involvement and notifying the public of how health data are used, (ii) establishing appropriate legal mechanisms for privacy protection, (iii) ensuring that data is de-identified, (iv) erecting oversight and enforcement mechanisms, (v) defining a clear purpose for the system, and (vi) seeing to it that health data are used only for that specified purpose. The report did not recommend that Congress take any legislative action at the current time; rather, it recommended that "the Commissioner of FDA develop a plan, including milestones, for developing the Sentinel system and for addressing the privacy and security challenges."[138]

Various nongovernmental organizations have also focused on the Sentinel Initiative's privacy and security implications. The Electronic Privacy Information Center (EPIC) has warned that the personal information excised from de-identified data can often be "matched back to true identities" by what is known as "re-identification."[139] EPIC further warned that the FDA's contracts with private entities such as Harvard Pilgrim shift the responsibility for maintaining data privacy and security onto private actors, a process that EPIC characterizes as the "FDA's hands-off approach to privacy issues."[140] EPIC is not alone in its

---

[138] U.S. GOV'T. ACCOUNTABILITY OFFICE, PRIVACY AND SECURITY: FOOD AND DRUG ADMINISTRATION FACES CHALLENGES IN ESTABLISHING PROTECTIONS FOR ITS POSTMARKET RISK ANALYSIS SYSTEM, GAO 09-355 (2009), *available at* http://www.gao.gov/new.items/d09355.pdf.

[139] Epic.org, FDA's Sentinel Initiative, *available at* http://epic.org/privacy/medical/sentinel/default.html.

[140] *Id.*

concerns. At a workshop focusing on the impact of the Sentinel Initiative held in January 2011, "one theme that came through loud and clear was the tension or the balance... between protecting patients' privacy and data mining as much meaningful data as possible."[141] A particular concern was that data used in the system could become a "goldmine" for plaintiffs' attorneys, directing them towards promising areas of products liability litigation.[142]

The FDA is cognizant of such concerns. It agreed with the GAO's recommendation that it design a privacy and security plan featuring specific milestones, and a "Privacy" section on the Mini-Sentinel Web site states that:

> [t]he Mini-Sentinel pilot places high priority on ensuring the privacy of individual health information. Direct identifiers, such as name, date of birth, and address, are removed before information is sent to the Operations Center or the FDA. The FDA, the [Mini-Sentinel Coordinating Center], and Collaborators adhere to federal and state privacy-related laws and regulations."[143]

Dr. Rachel Behrman's 2011 article in the *New England Journal of Medicine* added that "[d]ata privacy and security are top priorities that were key considerations in the decision to build Mini-Sentinel as a system that uses a distributed data system and distributed analysis whenever possible."[144] In addition to those safeguards stemming from the use of a distributed model, the FDA is actively investigating methods by which to ensure that in situations where more than de-identified data is required, "only the minimum amount of directly identifiable information necessary" is delivered by the data holder.[145] In addition, pursuant to the Federal Information Security Management Act (FISMA) of 2002, the FDA Certification and Accreditation process will include a full assessment of the Sentinel system before it becomes operational.[146]

---

[141] Sherrie Conroy, *FDA's Sentinel System: Privacy, Product Liability... and Property and Casualty Insurance*, MEDICAL DESIGN (Jan. 14, 2011), *available at* http://blog.medicaldesign.com/perspectives/2011/01/14/fdas-sentinel-system-privacy-product-liability-and-property-and-casualty-insurance/.

[142] *Id.*

[143] GAO-09-355; Mini-Sentinel, Background (2010–2011), *available at* http://mini-sentinel.org/about_us/default.aspx.

[144] Behrman, *Developing the Sentinel System*, 364 NEW ENG. J. MED. at 498–99.

[145] FDA, THE SENTINEL INITIATIVE.

[146] *Id.*

11

Obligations in Response to a Health Care Data Security Breach*

I.	Introduction	316
II.	Breach Defined	318
III.	Risk Assessment	320
	A. Nature of Breach	321
	B. Identity of Any Known Recipient	323
	C. Mitigating Actions	323
	D. Covered Entity Obligations When Risk of Individual Harm is Small	324
IV.	Exceptions to the Definition of Breach	325
	A. Good-Faith Disclosures Within the Scope of Employment	325
	B. Inadvertent Disclosures by Otherwise Authorized Individuals	326
	C. Information Disclosed Not Reasonably Retained	328
	D. Disclosures of the Limited Data Set Excluding Certain Identifiers	329
V.	Identity of Breaching Party	330
	A. Obligations for Covered Entities When Multiple Entities Transfer PHI and/or Breach Security Requirements	330
	B. Business Associate Requirements	331
VI.	Notification Requirements	335
	A. Timing Requirements	335
	B. Method of Providing Notice	336
	C. Contents of Notice	338
VII.	Potential Liabilities Created by the HITECH Act	339
	A. Civil Penalties	340
	B. Criminal Penalties	341
VIII.	Conclusion	342

---

*Mark Faccenda, Fulbright & Jaworski L.L.P., Washington, D.C.

I. Introduction

The Health Information Portability and Accountability Act of 1996 (HIPAA) continues to evolve; recent changes require health care providers subject to HIPAA to notify patients in the event that their protected data has been impermissibly disclosed, potentially subjecting those patients to harm. The U.S. Department of Health and Human Services (HHS) has clarified under the Health Information Technology for Economic and Clinical Health Act (HITECH Act) that health care providers are obliged to maintain the confidentiality of patient health information, and has set forth their obligations in the event of a failure to do so.[1] In the interest of transparency, recent amendments to the HIPAA Privacy Rule require that covered entities disclose to patients the fact that their protected health information (PHI) has been disclosed in violation of the HIPAA Privacy Rule. In the event of a suspected breach of unsecured protected health information, covered entities need to conduct a three-part analysis of the facts related to the potential breach in order to determine whether an actual breach of patient data has occurred. To the extent that such analysis results in a determination that a breach has occurred, HIPAA requires the breaching entity to notify patients that their data has been impermissibly disclosed.[2] This chapter will address the steps that a covered entity (or a business associate of a covered entity) must take

---

[1] See Modifications to the HIPAA Privacy, Security, and Enforcement Rules Under the Health Information Technology for Economic and Clinical Health Act, 75 Fed. Reg. 40,868 (proposed July 14, 2010) (to be codified at 45 C.F.R. pts. 160, 164), in which HHS stated:
> The Standards for Privacy of Individually Identifiable Health Information, known as the "Privacy Rule," were issued on December 28, 2000, and amended on August 14, 2002. See 65 [Fed. Reg.] 82462, as amended at 67 [Fed. Reg.] 53182. The Security Standards for the Protection of Electronic Protected Health Information, known as the "Security Rule," were issued on February 20, 2003. See 68 [Fed. Reg.] 8334. The Compliance and Investigations, Imposition of Civil Money Penalties, and Procedures for Hearings regulations, collectively known as the "Enforcement Rule," were issued as an interim final rule on April 17, 2003 (68 [Fed. Reg.] 18895), and revised and issued as a final rule, following rulemaking, on February 16, 2006 (71 [Fed. Reg.] 8390).

Id.
The HITECH Act was adopted as part of the American Recovery and Reinvestment Act of 2009, Pub. L. 111-5, div. A, tit. XIII & div. B, tit. IV; *see also* 75 Fed. Reg. at 40,869. As HHS has explained,
> [t]he HITECH Act, enacted on February 17, 2009, is designed to promote the widespread adoption and standardization of health information technology. Subtitle D of title XIII, entitled "Privacy," supports this goal by adopting amendments designed to strengthen the privacy and security protections of health information established by HIPAA. These provisions include extending the applicability of certain of the Privacy and Security Rules' requirements to the business associates of covered entities; requiring HIPAA covered entities and business associates to provide for notification of breaches of "unsecured protected health information"; establishing new limitations on the use and disclosure of protected health information for marketing and fundraising purposes; prohibiting the sale of protected health information; requiring the consideration of a limited data set as the minimum necessary amount of information; and expanding individuals' rights to access and receive an accounting of disclosures of their protected health information, and to obtain restrictions on certain disclosures of protected health information to health plans. In addition, subtitle D adopts provisions designed to strengthen and expand HIPAA's enforcement provisions.

75 Fed. Reg. at 40,869.

[2] *See* 42 U.S.C. §17932; Breach Notification for Unsecured Protected Health Information, 74 Fed. Reg. 42,740 (interim final rule issued Aug. 24, 2009) (to be codified at 45 C.F.R. pts. 160, 164).

when discovering the disclosure of patient information, potentially in violation of HIPAA Privacy Rule requirements.[3]

Going forward, HITECH Act breach detection and notification requires that HIPAA covered entities

> provide notification to affected individuals and to the Secretary of HHS following the discovery of a breach of unsecured protected health information. In addition, in some cases, the [HITECH Act] requires covered entities to provide notification to the media of breaches. In the case of a breach of unsecured protected health information at or by a business associate of a covered entity, the [HITECH Act] requires the business associate to notify the covered entity of the breach. Finally, the Act requires the Secretary to post on an HHS Web site a list of covered entities that experience breaches of unsecured protected health information involving more than 500 individuals.[4]

The HITECH Act and regulations promulgated thereunder create a three-step process under which a covered entity may determine any potential obligation to provide notice in the event of a protected health information breach. First, a covered entity must determine whether there has been an impermissible disclosure of unsecured protected health information under the HIPAA Privacy Rule.[5] "HIPAA Rules define 'protected health information' as the individually identifiable health information held or transmitted in any form or medium by... HIPAA covered entities and business associates, subject to certain limited exceptions."[6] "The Privacy Rule protects individuals' health information by regulating the circumstances under which covered entities may use and disclose protected health information and by requiring covered entities to have safeguards in place to protect the privacy of the information."[7]

Second, the covered entity must determine, and document, whether the impermissible disclosure compromises the security or privacy of that protected

---

[3] *See* 45 C.F.R. §160.103. The HIPAA Privacy Rule applies to entities including: "(1) A health plan. (2) A health care clearinghouse. (3) A health care provider who transmits any health information in electronic form in connection with a transaction covered by [HIPAA regulations]." While the HIPAA Privacy Rule applies directly to these "covered entities," HIPAA rules may also apply to entities serving as a "business associate" of the covered entity, a term generally applying to any person who

> performs, or assists in the performance of:... [a] function or activity involving the use or disclosure of individually identifiable health information, including claims processing or administration, data analysis, processing or administration, utilization review, quality assurance, billing, benefit management, practice management, and repricing; or... provides, other than in the capacity of a member of the workforce of such covered entity, legal, actuarial, accounting, consulting, data aggregation..., management, administrative, accreditation, or financial services to or for such covered entity.

As further discussed in V.B., below, HIPAA privacy requirements apply equally to covered entities and their business associates; however, for purposes of simplicity, the breach notification rule will be described herein as it would apply to covered entities, unless stated otherwise.

[4] 74 Fed. Reg. at 42,740.

[5] *Id.* at 42,741.

[6] *Id.* at 42,740. See also 75 Fed. Reg. at 40,869 and 45 C.F.R. §160.103, the latter defining protected health information, certain exceptions aside, as "individually identifiable health information...that is...transmitted by electronic media;...maintained in electronic media; or...transmitted or maintained in any other form or medium."

[7] 75 Fed. Reg. at 40,869.

health information.[8] This occurs when there is a significant risk of financial, reputational, or other harm to the individual. However, not all breaches require that the covered entity provide notice. In the event that a covered entity determines that a potential breach is accompanied by little risk of such harm, or in the event that it determines that mitigating steps taken have eliminated the potential for such harm, the covered entity may avoid disclosure requirements.

Third, the covered entity must ascertain whether the incident falls under one of the exceptions to the definition of "breach" set forth under the HITECH Act and regulations promulgated thereunder.[9] The HITECH Act provides for three such exceptions; each is discussed in detail in IV., below.

In circumstances involving disclosures among covered entities, or involving a business associate acting as an agent on behalf of one or more covered entities, the covered entity must conduct an additional analytical step in order to determine which particular covered entity, business associate, or combination thereof would be subject to any potential breach notification requirements.[10]

Failure to comply with HIPAA Privacy Rule requirements, including those governing a covered entity's potential disclosure obligations, is accompanied with increased risk as a result of the HITECH Act. Legislative amendments to the HIPAA Enforcement Rule have created new and higher levels of potential liability for failure to adhere to HIPAA provisions. Covered entities may now be liable for civil monetary penalties in cases where they were unaware that a violation had even occurred. In addition, penalties may now reach into the millions of dollars in connection with a HIPAA violation.[11] In this regard, it behooves the covered entity to be diligent in maintaining the privacy of its patients' protected health information in the first place, and to remain diligent in detecting and disclosing any potential failures to maintain patient privacies. Because not all disclosures of patient protected health information rise to the level of a prohibited breach, the first step is to be aware of the circumstances that may result in liability.

II. BREACH DEFINED

The HITECH Act defines breach to mean any "unauthorized acquisition, access, use or disclosure of [protected health information] which compromises the security or privacy of such information, except where an unauthorized person to whom such information is disclosed would not reasonably have been able to retain such information."[12] "Disclosure" is defined in HIPAA regulations as "the release, transfer, provision of, access to, or divulging in any other manner of information outside the entity holding the information."[13] The regulatory definition of the term "breach" also states that impermissible disclosures must

---

[8] 74 Fed. Reg. at 42,744.
[9] 74 *Id*. at 42,746–47.
[10] 74 *Id*. at 42,753–55.
[11] *See* HIPAA Administrative Simplification: Enforcement, 74 Fed. Reg. 56,123, 56,125 (interim final rule issued Oct. 30, 2009) (to be codified at 45 C.F.R. pt. 160).
[12] HITECH Act §13400(1)(A) (codified at 42 U.S.C. §17921(1)(A)).
[13] *Id*. §13400(4), 45 C.F.R. §160.103.

"[compromise] the security or privacy of the protected health information. For purposes of this definition, compromises the security or privacy of the protected health information means poses a significant risk of financial, reputational, or other harm to the individual."[14] Thus, a breach of protected health information for purposes of the HITECH Act means, generally, an unauthorized acquisition, access, use, or disclosure of protected health information where a covered entity cannot ensure that such acquisition, access, use, or disclosure does not present a risk to the subject of that information. Such risk may include the potential for financial risk, public embarrassment, or discrimination.

However, not all circumstances where a potentially unauthorized acquisition, access, use, or disclosure has been made is considered a "breach" under the HIPAA Privacy Rule. The HITECH Act makes the distinction between disclosures of protected health information and disclosures of *unsecured* protected health information; only the latter results in a violation of the HIPAA Privacy Rule. The HITECH Act "defines 'unsecured protected health information' as 'protected health information that is not secured through the use of a technology or methodology specified by [HHS] in guidance.'"[15] The use of HHS-specified "technologies and methodologies that render protected health information unusable, unreadable, or indecipherable to unauthorized individuals" can safeguard otherwise impermissible disclosures.[16]

To the extent that a covered entity employs such technologies and methodologies, it may be excused from obligations to provide notice of any potential breach. "Covered entities and business associates that implement the specified technologies and methodologies with respect to protected health information are not required to provide notifications in the event of a breach of such information—that is, the information is not considered 'unsecured' in such cases."[17]

Thus, the first obligation that a covered entity must assume is an analysis of its data protection technologies and methodologies *prior to* any potential breach. By ensuring its use of mechanisms compliant with HHS specifications, a covered entity may prevent further analysis during the post-breach period. As will be discussed in VI.A., regarding a covered entity's timing requirements for providing notice, this step may be of great importance to the covered entity attempting to satisfy deadlines for providing notice in the event of a breach. HHS further clarifies that, even though a covered entity may be using encryption technology to safeguard its patients' protected health information, the use

---

[14] 45 C.F.R. §164.402(1)(i).

[15] 74 Fed. Reg. at 42,741; *see also* HITECH Act §13402(h).

[16] 74 Fed. Reg. at 42,741. See also *id.* at 42,742, which describes the technologies and methodologies rendering protected health information unusable, unreadable, or indecipherable. It states, in part, that electronic protected health information is
> rendered unusable, unreadable, or indecipherable to unauthorized individuals if ... [it] has been encrypted ... by "the use of an algorithmic process to transform data into a form in which there is a low probability of assigning meaning without use of a confidential process or key" ... and such confidential process or key that might enable decryption has not been breached." HIPAA Privacy Rule compliant encryption processes must be "tested by the National Institute of Standards and Technology (NIST) and judged to meet this standard."

[17] *Id.* at 42,741.

of technology not deemed by HHS to be compliant will not protect the covered entity from the notice requirement:

> If a covered entity chooses to encrypt protected health information to comply with the Security Rule, does so pursuant to this guidance, and subsequently discovers a breach of that encrypted information, the covered entity will not be required to provide breach notification because the information is not considered "unsecured protected health information" as it has been rendered unusable, unreadable, or indecipherable to unauthorized individuals. *On the other hand, if a covered entity has decided to use a method other than encryption or an encryption algorithm that is not specified in this guidance to safeguard protected health information, then although that covered entity may be in compliance with the Security Rule, following a breach of this information, the covered entity would have to provide breach notification to affected individuals.*[18]

To the extent that a covered entity has not performed such analysis prior to any breach potentially creating a notice requirement, the covered entity may seek to verify whether the encryption technologies employed meet HHS standards. In the event that such attempted verification does not result in a determination of compliance, it remains possible that a disclosure will not require that notice be provided, to the extent that a second level of analysis results in a determination that the breach did not pose a significant risk of harm to the subject of the unsecured protected health information. The next section addresses the covered entity's obligation to perform and document a risk assessment supporting any determination not to notify affected individuals due to a lack of potential harm as a result of a breach of unsecured protected health information.

III. Risk Assessment

The definition of "breach" has limits:

> The [HITECH] Act and regulation next limit the definition of "breach" to a use or disclosure that "compromises the security or privacy" of the protected health information. Accordingly, once it is established that a use or disclosure violates the Privacy Rule, the covered entity must determine whether the violation compromises the security or privacy of the protected health information.[19]

In response to stakeholder comments suggesting that this language would inherently require the subject of any data breach to be harmed, HHS adopted an interpretation of the statutory requirement clarifying this point. "We agree that the statutory language encompasses a harm threshold and have clarified ... that 'compromises the security or privacy of the protected health information' means 'poses a significant risk of financial, reputational, or other harm to the

---

[18] *Id.* at 42,741–42 (emphasis added). See also *id.* at 42,744, which further clarifies that:
a violation of the Security Rule does not *itself* constitute a potential breach under [45 C.F.R. Part 164 Subpart D], although such a violation may lead to a use or disclosure of protected health information that is not permitted under the Privacy Rule and thus, may potentially be a breach under this subpart.
(emphasis added).

[19] 74 Fed. Reg. at 42,744.

individual.'"[20] A covered entity may avoid any potential disclosure requirement in the event of a breach of unsecured protected health information where it makes a good-faith determination that the subject of a breach would not be harmed as a result. To avoid disclosure, the covered entity must document the facts and circumstances giving rise to a potential disclosure requirement along with its conclusion that patients involved are not likely to be harmed.

"To determine if an impermissible use or disclosure of protected health information constitutes a breach, covered entities and business associates will need to perform a risk assessment to determine if there is a significant risk of harm to the individual as a result of the impermissible use or disclosure."[21] HHS suggests a number of considerations that may indicate whether or not a potential breach creates a level of risk for the patient. Included among the factors that the covered entity may wish to consider, given the circumstances of the disclosure in question, are the type and amount of data disclosed, to whom it was disclosed, and what actions, if any, were taken in light of the disclosure.[22]

Once the following factors are analyzed, the covered entity must document the conclusions drawn from the totality of circumstances. This documentation may serve to protect the covered entity if the decision to not disclose a breach of unsecured protected health information is ultimately called into question.

A. Nature of Breach

"In performing a risk assessment, covered entities and business associates should ... consider the type and amount of protected health information involved in the impermissible use or disclosure."[23] "If the nature of the protected health information does not pose a significant risk of financial, reputational, or other harm, then the violation is not a breach."[24] HHS recognizes that some types of protected health information carry greater weight than others. While a patient's Social Security number and zip code are each protected by the HIPAA Privacy Rule, the potential for risk is much greater should the former fall into the wrong hands. HHS provides further examples:

> [I]f a covered entity improperly discloses protected health information that merely included the name of an individual and the fact that he received services from a

---

[20] *Id.*

[21] *Id.*

[22] *See id.* HHS also indicates that factors considered in Office of Management and Budget Memorandum M-07-16 (May 22, 2007) may provide additional guidance with respect to the factors that a covered entity may wish to consider when performing a risk analysis. It states, in part, that
> agencies should consider a number of possible harms associated with the loss or compromise of information. Such harms may include the effect of a breach of confidentiality or fiduciary responsibility, the potential for blackmail, the disclosure of private facts, mental pain and emotional distress, the disclosure of address information for victims of abuse, the potential for secondary uses of the information which could result in fear or uncertainty, or the unwarranted exposure leading to humiliation or loss of self-esteem.

Office of Management and Budget, Memorandum M-07-16, *Safeguarding Against and Responding to the Breach of Personally Identifiable Information* (May 22, 2007), at 15.

[23] 74 Fed. Reg. at 42,745.

[24] *Id.*

hospital, then this would constitute a violation of the Privacy Rule, but it may not constitute a significant risk of financial or reputational harm to the individual.[25]

HHS contrasts the above example with a hypothetical disclosure of more sensitive information, potentially tipping the balance toward a notification requirement:

> If the information indicates the type of services that the individual received (such as oncology services), that the individual received services from a specialized facility (such as a substance abuse treatment program), or if the protected health information includes information that increases the risk of identity theft (such as a social security number, account number, or mother's maiden name), then there is a higher likelihood that the impermissible use or disclosure compromised the security and privacy of the information.[26]

HHS cautions, however, that such obvious examples are not the only such instances of impermissible disclosure giving rise to cause for notice. Rather, each occasion of disclosure should be analyzed on a case-by-case basis, for even seemingly innocuous disclosures may create the potential for harm:

> The risk assessment should be fact specific, and the covered entity or business associate should keep in mind that many forms of health information, not just information about sexually transmitted diseases or mental health, should be considered sensitive for purposes of the risk of reputational harm—especially in light of fears about employment discrimination.[27]

Equally important to a covered entity's analysis is the scope of the impermissible disclosure. A disclosure involving the accidental delivery of a single patient's information to the wrong party is limited in the potential risk it may bring. As noted above, even a disclosure of one person's information may require that the covered entity provide notice, to the extent that such disclosure is particularly sensitive. Compare this, however, with a breach involving the theft of several unsecured laptops. Because the latter example may potentially expose many patients to risk, this type of disclosure may be considered more likely to require that the covered entity provide notice. The latter example also illustrates the second factor to be considered in any risk assessment—the identity of the recipient of impermissibly disclosed patient data. As discussed below, a party purposefully misappropriating hospital technology is not likely to protect patient privacy and may even be considered *likely* to abuse such information.[28]

---

[25] *Id.*

[26] *Id.*

[27] *Id.*

[28] *Id.* As further discussed in relation to mitigating circumstances, even obviously hazardous breaches may be tempered by further circumstances:
> For example, if a laptop is lost or stolen and then recovered, and a forensic analysis of the computer shows that its information was not opened, altered, transferred, or otherwise compromised, such a breach may not pose a significant risk of harm to the individuals whose information was on the laptop.

Id. HHS cautions, however, that "we do not consider it reasonable to delay breach notification based on the hope that the computer will be recovered." *Id.*

B. Identity of Any Known Recipient

HHS recognizes that some unintended recipients may do a better job of protecting unsecured protected health information than others, either due to their familiarity with HIPAA Privacy Rule requirements, or, more importantly, their *own* obligations to maintain patient confidentiality. HHS guidance discusses the potential for harm when an inadvertent disclosure is made to another covered entity:

> If, for example, protected health information is impermissibly disclosed to another entity governed by the HIPAA Privacy and Security Rules..., there may be less risk of harm to the individual, since the recipient entity is obligated to protect the privacy and security of the information it received in the same or similar manner as the entity that disclosed the information.[29]

It is the recipient's own potential liability in this case that may permit a covered entity to recognize that the risk of further disclosure is slight. Presumably, other covered entities, or employees thereof, would recognize their obligation to return or destroy protected health information impermissibly disclosed.

"In contrast, if protected health information is impermissibly disclosed to any entity or person that does not have similar obligations to maintain the privacy and security of the information, the risk of harm to the individual is much greater."[30] In this case, disclosures to the general public, or to employees or agents of the covered entity not trained in HIPAA Privacy Rule requirements, would not be accompanied with the same level of assurance that the initially disclosed information would not be further disclosed.

C. Mitigating Actions

HHS recognizes that, in certain circumstances, an initial disclosure may be met with an immediate mitigating response; often, this action will permit a covered entity to avoid a notice obligation. Again, however, HHS cautions that mitigating responses should be considered on a case-by-case basis, as not all mitigating activities are likely to provide the same level of assurance that a patient has not been subjected to risk of harm.

"Where a covered entity takes immediate steps to mitigate an impermissible use or disclosure, such as by obtaining the recipient's satisfactory assurances that the information will not be further used or disclosed (through a confidentiality agreement or similar means) or will be destroyed," the covered entity may conclude that such use or disclosure does not require a subsequent provision of notice.[31] "If such steps eliminate or reduce the risk of harm to the individual to a less than 'significant risk,' then [HHS interprets] that the security and privacy of the information has not been compromised and, therefore, no breach has

---

[29]*Id.* at 42,744. HHS also indicates that disclosures to federal agencies bound by the Privacy Act of 1974 (codified at 5 U.S.C. §552a) and the Federal Information Security Management Act of 2002 (codified at 44 U.S.C. §3541 *et seq.*) may be considered similarly protected. *Id.*

[30]74 Fed. Reg. at 42,744.

[31]*Id.*

occurred."[32] As discussed above, mitigating factors such as the return of errant correspondence or an agreement to delete an misdirected email, combined with the recipient's assurance that the protected health information has not been reviewed, may give the covered entity a high level of assurance that the risk to patients under such circumstances is low, thereby obviating the need to provide notice.

Once the circumstances described above have been determined, the covered entity must combine the totality of those circumstances in a report supporting its conclusion that the totality of circumstances does not create a significant level of risk sufficient to warrant provision of notice to patients. Where the totality of circumstances indicates otherwise, notification may be required.

D. Covered Entity Obligations When Risk of Individual Harm Is Small

"Through a risk assessment, a covered entity or business associate may determine that the risk of identifying a particular individual is so small that the use or disclosure poses no significant risk of harm to any individuals."[33] HHS illustrates this point by analyzing a disclosure of patient zip codes. It indicates that such a disclosure may not "create a significant risk that a particular individual can be identified. Therefore, there would be no significant risk of harm to the individual."[34]

> If there is no significant risk of harm to the individual, then no breach has occurred and no notification is required. If, however, the covered entity or business associate determines that the individual can be identified based on the information disclosed, and there is otherwise a significant risk of harm to the individual, then breach notification is required.[35]

"Covered entities and business associates must document their risk assessments, so that they can demonstrate, if necessary, that no breach notification was required following an impermissible use or disclosure of protected health information."[36] HHS notes that the covered entity ultimately "bears the burden of demonstrating that no breach occurred."[37] Thus, the covered entity's performance of risk analysis becomes an important tool in justifying the decision not to provide notice in the event that further investigation, federal or otherwise, ensues. In this regard, the covered entity has incentive to perform its risk analysis and document as thoroughly as possible to protect against any potential future liability.

It should also be noted that even in the event a covered entity determines that a breach did not occur, due to the disclosure's satisfaction of breach exception requirements negating the need to report under the Notification Rule, the covered entity may still have a future obligation to report the disclosure as part

---

[32] *Id.* at 42,744–45.
[33] *Id.* at 42,746.
[34] *Id.*
[35] *Id.*
[36] *Id.*
[37] *Id.*

of a proposed routine notification requirement. HHS has published a proposed rule that would create a right to an accounting of disclosures of protected health information, including disclosures otherwise permissible under the HIPAA Privacy Rule.[38] For this reason, hospitals having conducted a risk analysis as described above may be ultimately required to provide notification of a disclosure not rising to the level of breach.

IV. Exceptions to the Definition of Breach

Covered entities having performed a risk analysis have made a determination as to the potential for personal harm to patients as a result of a potentially impermissible disclosure of unsecured protected health information. The HITECH Act, however, permits three exceptions to those disclosures considered to be a breach. Additionally, certain disclosures not involving specified direct identifiers are not considered to be a breach. In the event that a covered entity recognizes that the disclosure in question has the potential to create a significant amount of risk to the patients involved, it may still avoid Breach Notification Rule obligations to the extent that it meets one of the four sets of circumstances described below.

A. Good-Faith Disclosures Within the Scope of Employment

The first exception to the HIPAA Breach Notification Rule permits a covered entity to avoid the patient notification process where an otherwise impermissible breach is made in good faith in the course of workplace events. "Any unintentional acquisition, access, or use of protected health information by an

---

[38]*See* HIPAA Privacy Rule Accounting of Disclosures Under the Health Information Technology for Economic and Clinical Health Act, 76 Fed. Reg. 31,426, 31,431 (proposed May 31, 2011) (to be codified at 45 C.F.R. pt. 164). HHS has proposed that

> covered entities will continue to be required to account for disclosures that are impermissible under the Privacy Rule. While individuals will learn of most impermissible disclosures through the Breach Notification Rule at [45 C.F.R.] §164.404, we expect that some individuals will be interested in learning of impermissible disclosures that did not rise to the level of a breach (*e.g.*, because the disclosure did not compromise the security or privacy of the protected health information). This ensures that covered entities and business associates maintain full transparency with respect to any impermissible disclosures by allowing a means (either through receipt of a breach notice or by requesting an accounting) for individuals to learn of all ways in which their designated record set information has been disclosed in a manner not permitted by the Privacy Rule. We propose to exempt from the accounting requirement impermissible disclosures in which the covered entity (directly or through a business associate) has provided breach notice. We do not believe it is necessary to require the covered entity or its business associates to account for such disclosures since the covered entity has already made the individual aware of the impermissible disclosure through the notification letter required by the Breach Notification Rule. The breach notification requirement serves the same purpose as the accounting requirement, but it is much more rigorous in that it is an affirmative duty on the covered entity to notify the individual of an impermissible disclosure in a more timely and detailed manner than the accounting for disclosures. Nonetheless, covered entities are free to also include in the accounting disclosures for which breach notification has already been provided to the individual if they choose to do so. We request comment on the burdens on covered entities and benefits to individuals associated with also receiving an accounting of disclosures that includes information provided in accordance with the breach notification requirement.

Id.

employee or individual acting under the authority of a covered entity or business associate" will not be considered to be a breach

> if such acquisition, access, or use was made in good faith and within the course and scope of the employment or other professional relationship of such employee or individual, respectively, with the covered entity or business associate; [and] such information is not further acquired, accessed, used, or disclosed by any person.[39]

HHS guidance clarifies the statutory exception, indicating that disclosures of this nature may be excused if made by any member of a covered entity's workforce; that is, the exception is not limited to employees proper.[40]

While disclosures need not be made by employees in order to be excepted under this provision, the "direct control" requirement found in the definition of workforce members would likely, but not necessarily, exclude disclosures made by business associates acting on behalf of covered entities. Disclosures made by covered entities are more likely to be covered under the second exception to the Breach Notification Rule, if at all.

B. Inadvertent Disclosures by Otherwise Authorized Individuals

The second exception to the Breach Notification Rule permits certain disclosures by persons acting not under the direct control of the covered entity but on the covered entity's behalf. "Any inadvertent disclosure from an individual who is otherwise authorized to access protected health information at a facility operated by a covered entity or business associate to another similarly situated individual at [the] same facility" will not be considered to be a breach requiring notice.[41]

This exception may be particularly applicable across the health care sector, rather than to health care providers *per se*, and provides potentially greater flexibility. Business associates and other covered entities with whom a covered entity teams to provide health care services may not be under the control of the responsible covered entity, but certainly may perform services *on behalf* of that covered entity:

> A person is acting under the authority of a covered entity or business associate if he or she is acting on its behalf. This may include a workforce member of a covered entity, an employee of a business associate, or even a business associate of a covered entity. Similarly, to determine whether the access, acquisition, or use was made "within the scope of authority," the covered entity or business associate should consider whether the person was acting on its behalf at the time of the inadvertent acquisition, access, or use.[42]

Physician-hospital relationships are another arrangement to which this exception may apply. If a physician breaches unsecured protected health in-

---

[39] HITECH Act §13400(1)(B)(i).

[40] 74 Fed. Reg. at 42,747. "Workforce member is a defined term in 45 C.F.R. 160.103 and means 'employees, volunteers, trainees, and other persons whose conduct, in the performance of work for a covered entity, is under the direct control of such entity, whether or not they are paid by the covered entity.'"

[41] HITECH Act §13400(1)(B)(ii).

[42] 74 Fed. Reg. at 42,747.

formation as a result of his or her treatment of hospital inpatients, and if that disclosure is an inadvertent breach occurring within the hospital to, for example, another health care provider, the breach will not require that the hospital provide notice to patients.

Although the statutory language creating this exception does not explicitly include the requirement that the breached data not be further acquired, accessed, used, or disclosed, as provided for in the good-faith disclosures exception, HHS interprets this exception to implicitly require the same:

> While the statutory language provides that this exception applies where the recipient does not further use or disclose the information, we have interpreted this exception as encompassing circumstances where the recipient does not further use or disclose the information in a manner not permitted under the Privacy Rule. In circumstances where any further use or disclosure of the information is permissible under the Privacy Rule, we interpret that there is no breach.[43]

HHS makes the distinction between entities otherwise authorized to access protected health information and those without authorization. While those persons without authorization to access protected health information more obviously include parties with no association to the covered entity, including those outside the covered entity's workforce, it also includes workforce members not authorized to access protected health information as part of their job responsibilities with respect to a covered entity and those employees acting outside the scope of their authorization to access protected health information. The first example—workforce members not authorized to access protected health information—may include hospital employees who require no access to patient information for the performance of their duties on behalf of the hospital. The second example—employees acting outside the scope of their authorization—includes employees otherwise permitted to access protected health information but who access such information for reasons other than the performance of their duties.[44] Those who access protected health information out of personal curiosity are an example.[45] Neither of these types of individuals is considered to be authorized

---

[43]*Id*. HHS illustrates this exception:
A billing employee receives and opens an e-mail containing protected health information about a patient which a nurse mistakenly sent to the billing employee. The billing employee notices that he is not the intended recipient, alerts the nurse of the misdirected e-mail, and then deletes it. The billing employee unintentionally accessed protected health information to which he was not authorized to have access. However, the billing employee's use of the information was done in good faith and within the scope of authority, and therefore, would not constitute a breach and notification would not be required, provided the employee did not further use or disclose the information accessed in a manner not permitted by the Privacy Rule.
Id.

[44]*Id*.

[45]*See id*. HHS provides an example:
[A] receptionist at a covered entity who is not authorized to access protected health information [who] decides to look through patient files in order to learn of a friend's treatment. In this case, the impermissible access to protected health information would not fall within this exception to breach because such access was neither unintentional, done in good faith, nor within the scope of authority.
Id.

to access protected health information sufficient to permit an exception to the Breach Notification Rule.

The HITECH Act excepts the disclosure of unsecured protected health information from the Breach Notification Rule to the extent that "any such information received as a result of such disclosure is not further acquired, accessed, used, or disclosed without authorization by any person."[46] HHS has interpreted this statutory provision to mean "information ... not further used or disclosed in a manner not permitted by the Privacy Rule."[47]

C. Information Disclosed Not Reasonably Retained

HHS interpreted the HITECH Act definition of "breach," which does not include circumstances where a recipient of information "would not reasonably have been able to retain the information," to recognize a third exception to the Breach Notification Rule.[48] HHS "slightly modified [the statutory] language to except from 'breach' situations where a covered entity or business associate has a *good faith belief* that the unauthorized person to whom the disclosure of protected health information was made would not reasonably have been able to retain the information."[49]

HHS provides multiple examples of situations potentially permitting a good-faith belief that an errant disclosure of unsecured protected health information is not likely to have been retained by the recipient. HHS contemplates the return of unopened correspondence marked as undeliverable as one such circumstance.[50] To the extent that a returned envelope appears to have remained intact, a reasonable person could reach a good-faith conclusion that persons having possession of the envelope prior to its return would be unable to have retained the contents thereof.[51] The conclusion that a hypothetical recipient in this example could not have retained the protected health information in question seems natural; in this situation, it is reasonable to conclude that the information was never viewed in the first place.

In comparison, HHS provides another example, one where a patient is erroneously handed the wrong record, which is immediately collected by the nurse making the error.[52] This example presents a closer judgment call; at the very least, the potential exists for the receiving patient to have looked at another person's protected health information. However, "if the nurse can reasonably conclude that the patient could not have read or otherwise retained the information, then this would not constitute a breach."[53] Factors that the covered entity may wish to consider include the amount of time that the record was in the patient's possession and the volume of information present in the record.

---

[46] HITECH Act §13400(1)(B).
[47] 74 Fed. Reg. at 42,748.
[48] HITECH Act §13400(1)(A); 74 Fed. Reg. at 42,741, 42,748.
[49] 74 Fed. Reg. at 42,748 (emphasis added).
[50] *Id.*
[51] *Id.*
[52] *See id.*
[53] *Id.*

HHS reiterates that, much like the burden borne by the covered entity opting not to provide notice pursuant to a risk analysis as described above, "with respect to any of the three exceptions discussed above, a covered entity or business associate has the burden of proof... for showing why breach notification was not required."[54] Similar to the covered entity's obligation in performing a risk analysis, HHS anticipates that covered entities relying on one of the aforementioned exceptions will document the circumstances and conclusions drawn therefrom justifying a decision to not provide notice under the Breach Notification Rule.[55]

D. Disclosures of the Limited Data Set Excluding Certain Identifiers

HHS also provides for a "narrow, explicit exception" to the Breach Notification Rule where the data disclosed is not likely to identify the subject of that disclosure.[56] The direct identifiers listed in 45 C.F.R. § 164.514(e)(2) are deemed to be those most likely to identify the subject thereof in the event of a breach.[57] HHS indicates that disclosures not containing any of those 16 identifiers, as well as dates of birth and zip codes, will not be considered to be a breach. HHS "deem[s] an impermissible use or disclosure of [information excluding the 18 cited data types] to not compromise the security or privacy of the protected health information, because we believe that impermissible uses or disclosures of this information—if subjected to the type of risk assessment described above—would pose a low level of risk."[58]

However, HHS reiterates that this is a narrow exception, and "if, for example, the information does not contain birth dates but does contain zip code information or contains both birth dates and zip code information, then this narrow exception would not apply."[59] Any disclosures of the 18 data points, apparently even *de minimis* disclosures, would then require the covered entity to conduct a risk assessment in order to "determine if the risk of re-identification poses a significant risk of harm to the individual."[60]

---

[54] *Id.*
[55] *Id.*
[56] *Id.* at 42,746.
[57] 45 C.F.R. §164.514(e)(2) lists the following 16 identifiers:
(i) names; (ii) postal address information, other than town or city, State, and zip code; (iii) telephone numbers; (iv) fax numbers; (v) electronic mail addresses; (vi) Social Security numbers; (vii) medical record numbers; (viii) health plan beneficiary numbers; (ix) account numbers; (x) certificate/license numbers; (xi) vehicle identifiers and serial numbers, including license plate numbers; (xii) device identifiers and serial numbers; (xiii) Web Universal Resource Locators (URLs); (xiv) Internet Protocol (IP) address numbers; (xv) biometric identifiers, including finger and voice prints; and (xvi) full face photographic images and any comparable images.
[58] 74 Fed. Reg. at 42,746.
[59] *Id.*
[60] *Id.*

V. IDENTITY OF BREACHING PARTY

In the process of providing health care services to its patients, a covered entity might find itself transferring protected health information among a variety of parties, each performing a service necessary towards the provision of care. Parties in the data transfer continuum may include other covered entities, business associates, and subcontractors of one, the other, or both. Each transaction of patient information brings with it the potential that unsecured protected health information may be impermissibly disclosed in the process. When a covered entity makes a prohibited disclosure within its own facility, it is clear who is responsible for any potential Breach Notification Rule requirements. When an impermissible disclosure is made as a result of a transaction among covered entities, business associates, and subcontractors, however, all parties involved must determine their specific obligations under the Breach Notification Rule.

HHS notes "that a covered entity or business associate is not responsible for a breach by a third party to whom it permissibly disclosed protected health information, including limited data sets, unless the third party received the information in its role as an agent of the covered entity or business associate."[61] In light of this guidance, it becomes necessary to determine precisely who has potentially breached a patient's unsecured protected health information and in what capacity. Without an element of agency between a covered entity and a third party, the covered entity does not assume any obligation to provide notice under the Breach Notification Rule. To the extent, however, that a third party has potentially breached patient information in the furtherance of its duties with respect to an arrangement between the third party and a covered entity, that covered entity will ultimately be responsible for providing any notice required.

A. Obligations for Covered Entities When Multiple Entities Transfer PHI and/or Breach Security Requirements

As discussed above, it is a business associate's or subcontractor's responsibilities on behalf of a covered entity that create an obligation to adhere to the HIPAA Privacy Rule. While the HITECH Act makes clear that HIPAA rules apply equally to covered entities and business associates alike, it is the latter's association with the former that creates this obligation. Without an obligation to a covered entity, the business associate has no obligation under HIPAA.[62]

---

[61] *Id.*

[62] *See* 75 Fed. Reg. at 40,869. HHS has explained that Section 13404 of the HITECH Act makes business associates of covered entities civilly and criminally liable under the Privacy Rule for making uses and disclosures of protected health information that do not comply with the terms of their business associate contracts. The [HITECH] Act also provides that the additional privacy and security requirements of subtitle D of the [HITECH] Act are applicable to business associates and that such requirements shall be incorporated into business associate contracts.

Id. However, see also 75 Fed. Reg. at 40,887:

[T]he Privacy Rule currently does not directly govern business associates. However, the provisions of the HITECH Act make specific requirements of the Privacy Rule applicable to business associates, and create direct liability for noncompliance by business associates with regard to those Privacy Rule requirements. In particular, section 13404 of the HITECH Act,

Conversely, it is the agency relationship between the business associate and the covered entity that creates a responsibility on the part of the covered entity. While the business associate has an obligation to disclose potential breaches for which it is responsible to the covered entity, the covered entity is ultimately required to provide any notice to patients under the Breach Notification Rule.[63]

However, where protected health information is transferred among multiple covered entities, and where the recipient covered entity also impermissibly discloses that information, it is the disclosing covered entity's responsibility to provide notice under the Breach Notification Rule. "To the extent that a third party recipient of the information is itself a covered entity, and the information is breached while at the third party... then the third party will be responsible for complying" with the requirements of the Breach Notification Rule.[64]

The following examples illustrate the obligations between covered entities and business associates in the event of a protected health information breach. Where a physician received protected health information from a hospital and subsequently violated the Privacy Rule, it is the physician who would be required to provide notice to patients under the Breach Notification Rule.[65] A consultant acting as a business associate of the hospital making the same violation of the Privacy Rule would create an obligation on the part of the hospital under the Breach Notification Rule.[66] Further, note that the same physician described above, this time acting in a business associate capacity with respect to the hospital, would create a notice obligation on the part of the hospital under the Breach Notification Rule in the event that the physician violated the confidentiality of protected health information.[67] These examples illustrate the importance of accurately identifying the relationship between parties sharing patient protected health information for Breach Notification Rule compliance purposes.

B. Business Associate Requirements

"Following the discovery of a breach of unsecured protected health information, a business associate is required to notify the covered entity of the breach so that the covered entity can notify affected individuals."[68] While business associates are now responsible for the same obligations under the HIPAA Privacy Rule as their covered entity counterparts, this rule is a departure from the equality that covered entities and business associates now share under the Privacy

---

which became effective February 18, 2010, addresses the application of the provisions of the HIPAA Privacy Rule to business associates of covered entities.
While the HITECH Act's incorporation of business associates may not yet be codified as part of the HIPAA regulatory Privacy Rule, HHS makes clear that the obligation to ultimately make that incorporation is mandated by statute and as a function of the covered entity's obligation.

[63] *See* 74 Fed. Reg. at 42,753.
[64] *Id.* at 42,746.
[65] *See id.*
[66] *Id.* at 42,753.
[67] *Id.*
[68] *Id.*

Rule.[69] This is likely due, in part, to the business associate's role in providing assistance to the covered entity. HHS has stated that

> even though the business associate is not directly liable under the HIPAA Rules for failure to provide the notice, the covered entity remains directly liable for failure to provide the individuals with its notice of privacy practices because it is the covered entity's ultimate responsibility to do so, despite its having hired a business associate to perform the function.[70]

A business associate is an entity that performs a function or activity involving the use or disclosure of individually identifiable health information on behalf of a covered entity, such activities including, but not limited to, claims processing, data processing, utilization review, quality assurance, billing, benefit management, practice management, and other specified services involving the disclosure of protected health information, including consulting, legal, administrative, and management.[71] If a business associate has breached the unsecured protected health information of an individual during the performance of its services on behalf of a covered entity, the same notice provisions apply as would apply were the covered entity the breaching party.[72]

In the interest of clarity to the notice recipient, HHS anticipates that the covered entity would ordinarily provide notice to its patients that their protected health information has been breached.[73] However, HHS acknowledges that the business associate may be a more appropriate party to provide notice where doing so would be sensible given the totality of circumstances.[74] HHS "encourage[s] the parties to consider which entity is in the best position to provide notice to the individual, which may depend on circumstances, such as the functions the business associate performs on behalf of the covered entity and which entity has the relationship with the individual."[75]

Regardless of the party providing notice to patients—covered entity or business associate—HHS instructs the two to work together to provide a straightforward message to the patient whose protected health information has been breached. "We ... encourage the parties to ensure [that] the individual does not receive notifications from both the covered entity and the business associate about the same breach, which may be confusing to the individual."[76] Given the

---

[69] *See* 75 Fed. Reg. at 40,869.

[70] *Id.* at 40,889.

[71] 74 Fed. Reg. at 42,753; *see also* 45 C.F.R. §160.103. Note that the definition excludes members of a covered entity's workforce from those persons eligible for consideration as a business associate.

[72] 74 Fed. Reg. at 42,753. See also 75 Fed. Reg. at 40,869, which states that "Section 13402 of the [HITECH] Act sets forth the breach notification provisions, requiring covered entities and business associates to provide notification following discovery of a breach of unsecured protected health information."

[73] 74 Fed. Reg. at 42,753.

[74] *Id.* at 42,755. See also *id.* at 42,752, where HHS anticipates that in cases where a business associate breaches the unsecured protected health information and "the entities involved are unable to determine which entity's protected health information was involved, the covered entities may consider having the business associate provide the notification to the media on behalf of all of the covered entities."

[75] *Id.* at 42,755.

[76] *Id.*

potential for covered entities and business associates alike to be liable under the HIPAA Enforcement Rule and the obligation that both work together to detect data breaches of and subsequently provide notice when warranted, it is incumbent upon the two parties to anticipate the respective roles of each in the event of a breach.

This issue is compounded by the fact that obligations for both are created not only under the HIPAA Privacy Rule and the Breach Notification Rule but also by the business associate agreements between the parties. HHS recognizes that "HIPAA Rules already require a business associate contract to provide that the business associate report to the covered entity uses or disclosures not provided by the contract as well as security incidents of which the business associate becomes aware."[77] However, because agreements may have been executed prior to the adoption of the HITECH Act, the business associate's reporting obligations under the business associate agreement may not reflect statutorily mandated notification deadlines.

While HHS has stated its belief that "it is appropriate to leave it up to covered entities and business associates to determine how the required reporting should be implemented," as a matter of practice, it is advisable that such business associate agreements clearly state the obligations of the business associate and the covered entity in the event of a data breach.[78] Such agreements should clearly state the time frame in which the business associate is to report to the covered entity any discovered breach and what information is to be provided to the covered entity.[79] While, ultimately, the covered entity and business associate are free to establish a breach discovery and notice arrangement that suits their needs, each party should understand its respective obligations under the business associate agreement to ensure it provides that the requirements of the Breach Notification Rule are met.[80]

HHS has stated:

> Section 13404 of the HITECH Act provides that a business associate may use and disclose protected health information only if such use or disclosure is in compliance with each applicable requirement of [45 C.F.R.] §164.504(e), and also applies the provisions of [45 C.F.R.] §164.504(e)(1)(ii), which outline the actions that

---

[77]*Id.* at 42,754 (citing 45 C.F.R. §§164.314(a)(2)(i)(C), 504(e)(2)(ii)(C)).

[78]*Id.*

[79]See *id.*, which states:
[I]n addition to the identification of affected individuals, [45 C.F.R.] §164.410(c)(2) requires a business associate to provide the covered entity with any other available information that the covered entity is required to include in the notification to the individual under [45 C.F.R.] §164.404(c), either at the time it provides notice to the covered entity of the breach or promptly thereafter as information becomes available.

[80]*See id.* at 42,754–55. HHS provides that it
[does] not intend...to interfere with the current relationship between covered entities and their business associates. Business associates and covered entities will continue to have the flexibility to set forth specific obligations for each party, such as who will provide notice to individuals and when the notification from the business associate to the covered entity will be required, following a breach of unsecured protected health information, so long as all required notifications are provided and the other requirements of the [Breach Notification Rule] are met.
Id.

must be taken if the business associate has knowledge of a breach of the contract, to business associates.[81]

Further, HHS proposed to revise 45 C.F.R. §164.504(e)(2)(ii)(C) to require that "business associates report breaches of unsecured protected health information to covered entities, as required by [45 C.F.R.] §164.410."[82] This proposed revision is intended to "align the requirements for the business associate contract with the requirements in the HITECH Act and elsewhere within the HIPAA Rules."[83]

The HITECH Act further provides that subcontractors of business associates are obligated to adhere to the same privacy requirements as apply to covered entities and business associates.[84] The intent behind this inclusion is to "avoid having privacy and security protections for protected health information lapse merely because a function is performed by an entity that is a subcontractor rather than an entity with a direct relationship with a covered entity."[85] The potential effect could mean that, as protected health information is passed from covered entity to business associate to subcontractor (and their subcontractors, and so on), each party is obligated to be aware of their responsibilities to maintain data privacy and provide notice in the event of a failure to do so. Failure to adhere to Privacy Rule requirements on the part of a subcontractor could bring the same potential for liability under HIPAA's Enforcement Rule.[86]

---

[81] 75 Fed. Reg. at 40,888.

[82] *Id.* at 40,889.

[83] *Id.*

[84] *See, e.g., id.* at 40,873, where HHS addressed a proposed amendment to the definition of business associate to include those parties acting as a subcontractor to the business associate:

We propose to add language in paragraph (3)(iii) of the definition of "business associate" to provide that subcontractors of a covered entity—i.e., those persons that perform functions for or provide services to a business associate, other than in the capacity as a member of the business associate's workforce, are also business associates to the extent that they require access to protected health information. We also propose to include a definition of "subcontractor" in [45 C.F.R.] §160.103 to make clear that a subcontractor is a person who acts on behalf of a business associate, other than in the capacity of a member of the workforce of such business associate. Even though we use the term "subcontractor," which implies there is a contract in place between the parties, we note that the definition would apply to an agent or other person who acts on behalf of the business associate, even if the business associate has failed to enter into a business associate contract with the person.... The proposed modifications are similar in structure and effect to the Privacy Rule's initial extension of privacy protections from covered entities to business associates through contract requirements to protect downstream protected health information.

[85] 75 Fed. Reg. at 40,873.

[86] *See id.*:

[T]he proposed definition of "subcontractor" also is consistent with Congress' overall concern that the privacy and security protections of the HIPAA Rules extend beyond covered entities to those entities that create or receive protected health information in order for the covered entity to perform its health care functions. For example,... [HITECH Act] section 13408 makes explicit that certain types of entities providing services to covered entities—*e.g.,* vendors of personal health records—shall be considered business associates. Therefore, consistent with Congress' intent in [HITECH Act] sections 13401 and 13404... as well as its overall concern that the HIPAA Rules extend beyond covered entities to those entities that create or receive protected health information, [HHS has proposed] that downstream entities that work at the direction of or on behalf of a business associate and handle protected health information would also be required to comply with the applicable Privacy and Security Rule provisions in the same manner as the primary business associate, and likewise would incur liability for acts of noncompliance.

VI. Notification Requirements

The HITECH Act establishes that covered entities are now required to provide notice to patients in the event that their protected health information has been breached. The statute requires that:

> [A] covered entity that accesses, maintains, retains, modifies, records, stores, destroys, or otherwise holds, uses, or discloses unsecured protected health information... shall, in the case of a breach of such information that is discovered by the covered entity, notify each individual whose unsecured protected health information has been, or is reasonably believed by the covered entity to have been, accessed, acquired, or disclosed as a result of such breach.[87]

A. Timing Requirements

The HITECH Act requires that covered entities provide notice to patients "without unreasonable delay and in no case later than 60 calendar days after the discovery of a breach by the covered entity involved."[88] A breach is considered to have been "discovered" by a covered entity as of the first day on which the covered entity knows or reasonably should have known of the breach.[89] This means that, under certain circumstances, even breaches not having been discovered in fact may be subject to breach notification requirements if the breach "would have been known, to any person, other than the person committing the breach, who is a workforce member or agent of the covered entity," by exercising reasonable diligence.[90] This requirement illustrates the importance of covered entities establishing proactive HIPAA compliance programs with guidance demonstrating when data has been breached and how breaches should be internally reported. Because HHS guidance makes clear that the 60-day requirement "begins when the incident is first known, not when the investigation of the incident is complete, even if it is initially unclear whether the incident constitutes a breach," it is important to begin preparation for any potential notice requirement immediately once a breach has been suspected.[91]

HHS also indicates that the identity of the discoverer plays a role in establishing the commencement of the 60-day window for notification. As discussed above, the HITECH Act excludes the individual committing the breach from persons having "discovered" that breach. To that extent, the 60-day notice

---

[87] HITECH Act §13402(a). See also 45 C.F.R. §164.404(a)(1), which requires that "a covered entity shall, following the discovery of a breach of unsecured protected health information, notify each individual whose unsecured protected health information has been, or is reasonably believed by the covered entity to have been, accessed, acquired, used, or disclosed as a result of such breach."

[88] HITECH Act §13402(d)(1). See also 74 Fed. Reg. at 42,749, which notes that 45 C.F.R. §164.404(b)
> mirrors the statutory requirement in section 13402(d) of the [HITECH] Act and requires that, except when law enforcement requests a delay in accordance with [45 C.F.R.] §164.412... a covered entity shall send the required notification without unreasonable delay and in no case later than 60 calendar days after the date the breach was discovered by the covered entity.

[89] 45 C.F.R. §164.404(a)(2).

[90] Id.

[91] 74 Fed. Reg. at 42,749.

period does not commence until the breach is known (or reasonably should have been known) to *someone else* at the covered entity.[92] Further, to the extent that a breach is discovered by a business associate, the role of the business associate with respect to the covered entity will determine whether the 60-day notice period has begun. "If a business associate is acting as an *agent* of a covered entity, then... the business associate's discovery of the breach will be imputed to the covered entity... *based on the time the business associate discovers* the breach."[93] "In contrast, if the business associate is an *independent contractor* of the covered entity (*i.e.*, not an agent), then the covered entity must provide notification *based on the time the business associate notifies the covered entity* of the breach."[94] In this regard, the business associate agreement may seek to clarify the relationship between the parties so that each may be aware of its respective timing requirements.

Perhaps most importantly, HHS warns that the 60-day notice period is an "outer limit" and that the true timing requirement with respect to a covered entity's provision of notice is the "without unreasonable delay" language contained in 45 C.F.R. §164.404(b).[95] HHS indicates that it may deem notice provided within 60 days of discovery to have been unreasonably delayed if, for example, "a covered entity has compiled the information necessary to provide notification to individuals on day 10 but waits until day 60 to send the notifications."[96] Such delayed notice "would constitute an unreasonable delay despite the fact that the covered entity has provided notification within 60 days."[97] This guidance illustrates the importance of beginning the steps addressed in this chapter without delay once a covered entity has discovered a potential breach of unsecured protected health information.

B. Method of Providing Notice

Notification must be made in writing and delivered by first-class mail at the last known address for the individual who has been the subject of a unsecured protected health information breach.[98] Alternatively, "if the covered entity knows the individual is deceased and has the address of the next of kin or personal representative of the individual," written notice may be provided in the same manner as above to either the next of kin or personal representative.[99] "Consistent with the [HITECH Act], the [Breach Notification Rule] also

---

[92] HITECH Act §13402(c).
[93] 74 Fed. Reg. at 42,754 (emphasis added) (citing 45 C.F.R. §164.404(a)(2)).
[94] *Id.* (emphasis added).
[95] *See id.* at 42,749.
[96] *Id.*
[97] *Id.*
[98] *See* 45 C.F.R. §164.404(d)(1)(i).
[99] 45 C.F.R. §164.404(d)(1)(ii). See also 74 Fed. Reg. at 42,750, where HHS indicates that "under 45 C.F.R. §164.502(g), a 'personal representative' of a deceased individual is a person who has authority to act on behalf of the decedent or the decedent's estate." HHS further notes that "where the individual affected by a breach is a minor or otherwise lacks legal capacity due to a physical or mental condition, notice to the parent or other person who is the personal representative of the individual will satisfy" the Breach Notification Rule. 74 Fed. Reg. at 42,750.

Ch. 11.VI.B.   *Obligations in Response to a Health Care Data Security Breach*   337

provides that written notice may be in the form of electronic mail, provided the individual agrees to receive electronic notice and such agreement has not been withdrawn."[100]

HHS contemplates that a number of alternative methods of providing notice may be necessary when the individual's address, or in some cases, the individual's identity, is not known. "In the case in which there is insufficient or out-of-date contact information that precludes written notification to the individual... a substitute form of notice reasonably calculated to reach the individual shall be provided."[101] When a covered entity has inadequate contact information for fewer than 10 individuals, "substitute notice may be provided by an alternative form of written notice, telephone, or other means."[102] HHS suggests that a covered entity "may provide substitute notice by e-mail even if the patient has not agreed to electronic notice" as one means of substitute notice in the event that a patient's home address is not known.[103] While HHS has provided several examples of substitute notice compliant with the Breach Notification Rule, the overarching guideline in considering forms of substitute notice states that such notice must merely be "reasonably calculated to reach the individuals for whom it is being provided."[104]

In the event that a covered entity cannot provide written notice in the manner described above and the covered entity lacks contact information for 10 or more individuals, notice must "be in the form of either a conspicuous posting for a period of 90 days on the home page of the Web site of the covered entity involved, or conspicuous notice in major print or broadcast media in geographic areas where the individuals affected by the breach likely reside."[105] Media or Internet notifications must include a toll-free telephone number through which members of the public may determine whether their unsecured protected health information was breached.[106] HHS gives one other circumstance that may require a substitute form of notice be provided: where urgency may be a factor, notice may be provided by telephone or other means.[107]

Similar to the substitute notice contemplated above, which involves notice to individuals through print or broadcast mass media, the HITECH Act provides for notification "to" the mass media when a breach of unsecured protected health information involves more than 500 residents of any particular state or jurisdiction.[108] Notice must be provided "to prominent media outlets serving a state or jurisdiction, following the discovery of a breach if the unsecured protected health information of more than 500 residents of such State or jurisdiction is,

---

[100] 74 Fed. Reg. at 42,750; *see also* HITECH Act §13402(e)(1)(A); 45 C.F.R. §164.404(d)(1).
[101] 45 C.F.R. §164.404(d)(2).
[102] *Id.* §164.404(d)(2)(i).
[103] 74 Fed. Reg. at 42,751.
[104] 45 C.F.R. §164.404(d)(2).
[105] *Id.* §164.404(d)(2)(ii)(A); *see also* HITECH Act §13402(e)(1)(B).
[106] 45 C.F.R. §164.404(d)(2)(ii)(B); *see also* HITECH Act §13402(e)(1)(B).
[107] 45 C.F.R. §164.404(d)(3).
[108] 45 C.F.R. §164.406. See also 74 Fed. Reg. at 42,752, in which HHS differentiates between media notice and the substitute notice through mass media under 45 C.F.R. §164.404(d)(2)(ii)(A) "in that [the former] is directed 'to' the media and is intended to supplement, but not substitute for, individual notice."

or is reasonably believed to have been, accessed, acquired, or disclosed during such breach."[109] HHS clarifies that this requirement is governed along jurisdictional lines: although a breach of patient data involving 600 patients (300 in State A and 300 in State B) would seemingly exceed the more-than-500-person requirement, since the breach does not involve more than 500 residents in any one jurisdiction, then supplemental mass media notification is not required.[110]

In the event that a covered entity breaches the unsecured protected health information of 500 or more individuals *overall*, the covered entity must provide additional notice to HHS.[111] The HITECH Act requires that notice be provided immediately; HHS clarified in the interim final rule implementing the regulatory requirement that it interprets this timing requirement consistently with the Breach Notification Rule deadline, in other words, "without unreasonable delay but in no case later than 60 calendar days following discovery of a breach."[112] Breaches involving fewer than 500 individuals also require that the covered entity provide notice to HHS; in this circumstance, the covered entity may keep a record during the course of the year and submit a report to HHS within 60 days from the end of the calendar year.[113]

C. Contents of Notice

Notifications provided to individuals must include the following five elements, to the extent possible. The covered entity must provide a brief description of what happened, including the date of both the breach and discovery.[114] The covered entity must provide a description of the types of unsecured protected health information involved.[115] The covered entity must provide a description of any steps that the subjects of data breaches should take to protect themselves from potential harm resulting from the breach.[116] The covered entity must provide a brief description of investigative and mitigating actions taken since the breach.[117] Finally, the covered entity must provide contact information

---

[109] 74 Fed. Reg. at 42,752; *see also* HITECH Act §13402(e)(2); 45 C.F.R. §164.406.

[110] *See* 74 Fed. Reg. at 42,752. Note that, in this example, supplemental mass media notice is not required even though the relevant broadcast media may serve both State A and State B.

[111] 45 C.F.R. §164.408; HITECH Act §13402(e)(3). Note that the HHS notice requirement does not contain the same jurisdictional nexus. Also note that the threshold codified in 45 C.F.R. §164.406 requires notice to the media in the event of a breach involving "*more than 500* residents," whereas the threshold codified in 45 C.F.R. §164.408 requires notice to HHS in the event of a breach involving "*500 or more* individuals." 45 C.F.R. §§164.406(a), 408(b) (emphasis added).

[112] 74 Fed. Reg. at 42,753.

[113] *Id.*

[114] 45 C.F.R. §164.404(c)(1)(A).

[115] *Id.* §164.404(c)(1)(B). HHS has "emphasize[d] that this provision requires covered entities to describe only the *types* of information involved. Thus, covered entities should not include a listing of the *actual* protected health information that was breached." 74 Fed. Reg. at 42,750 (emphasis added).

[116] 45 C.F.R. §164.404(c)(1)(C).

[117] *Id.* §164.404(c)(1)(D).

for individuals to ask questions or learn additional information, including a toll-free phone number, postal address, or e-mail address.[118]

HHS requires that notices provided to patients under the Breach Notification Rule be written in plain language, so as to permit maximum understanding on the part of the recipient.[119] "To satisfy this requirement, the covered entity should write the notice at an appropriate reading level, using clear language and syntax, and not include any extraneous material that might diminish the message it is trying to convey."[120]

VII. POTENTIAL LIABILITIES CREATED BY THE HITECH ACT

In addition to implementing the Breach Notification Rule, the HITECH Act also created stiffer civil monetary penalties for HIPAA violations.[121] The HITECH Act created a series of tiered penalties, each a significant increase over prior penalty limits.[122] As a result of the HITECH Act, covered entities violating the HIPAA Privacy Rule or the Breach Notification Rule may be assessed penalties up to $1.5 million for each violation of an identical HIPAA provision over the course of a calendar year.[123]

Also notable is the HITECH Act's imposition of civil monetary penalties upon covered entities under circumstances "in which it is established that the [covered entity] did not know (and by exercising reasonable diligence would not have known)" that the covered entity violated a HIPAA provision.[124] Prior to the adoption of the HITECH Act, lack of knowledge was a viable affirmative defense to HIPAA liability.[125]

However, the HITECH Act also created a 30-day cure period that permits covered entities to avoid civil monetary penalty liabilities to the extent that they

---

[118] HITECH Act §13402(f); 45 C.F.R. §164.404(c)(1)(E).

[119] 45 C.F.R. §164.404(c)(2).

[120] 74 Fed. Reg. at 42,750.

[121] 75 Fed. Reg. at 40,869 states:
The Enforcement Rule establishes rules governing the compliance responsibilities of covered entities with respect to cooperation in the enforcement process. It also provides rules governing the investigation by [HHS] of compliance by covered entities, both through the investigation of complaints and the conduct of compliance reviews. It establishes rules governing the process and grounds for establishing the amount of a civil money penalty where [HHS] has determined a covered entity has violated a requirement of a HIPAA Rule.

[122] See HIPAA Administrative Simplification: Enforcement, 74 Fed. Reg. 56,123 (interim final rule issued Oct. 30, 2009) (to be codified at 45 C.F.R. pt. 160), which amends 45 C.F.R. pt. 160, subpts. A and D, to reflect new requirements created by HITECH Act §13410(d). See also 74 Fed. Reg. at 56,124 (indicating that, prior to the adoption of the HITECH Act, HIPAA civil monetary penalties were "not more than $100 for each...[and] the total amount imposed...for all violations of an identical requirement...during a calendar year may not exceed $25,000").

[123] See HITECH Act §13410(d)(2) (codified at 42 U.S.C. §1320d–5(a)(3)(D)); see also 45 C.F.R. §160.404(b)(2).

[124] HITECH Act §13410(d)(1) (codified at 42 U.S.C. §1320d–5(a)(1)(A)).

[125] See 74 Fed. Reg. at 56,128 (HITECH Act §13410(d) "revises [42 U.S.C. 1320d–5(b)] to...[s]trike the limitation on imposing a penalty when a covered entity establishes, to the [HHS] Secretary's satisfaction, that it 'did not know, and by exercising reasonable diligence would not have known' of the violation").

cure most alleged HIPAA violations within that time frame.[126] HIPAA violations where the covered entity did not know and by exercising reasonable diligence would not have known of the violation, and HIPAA violations due to reasonable cause, may be cured within 30 days without liability.[127] HIPAA violations due to a covered entity's willful neglect may be penalized at a lower rate than that imposed if the violation were not cured, but the covered entity may not avoid liability altogether.[128]

A. Civil Penalties

The HITECH Act, which "establishes categories of violations that reflect increasing levels of culpability, requires that a penalty determination be based on the nature and extent of the violation and the nature and extent of the harm resulting from the violation, and establishes tiers of increasing penalty amounts."[129] The civil monetary penalty structure revised by the HITECH Act "differs significantly from its predecessor by its establishment of several categories of violations that reflect increasing levels of culpability."[130] "The revised penalty scheme also differs significantly from its predecessor in its establishment of the range of available penalty amounts for each category of violation by reference to tiers of penalty amounts."[131]

When a covered entity did not know, or by exercising reasonable diligence would not have known, that it was violating a HIPAA provision, it may be penalized between $100 and $50,000 for each violation.[132] When a covered entity's HIPAA violation was due to reasonable cause, it may be penalized between $1,000 and $50,000 for each violation.[133] When a covered entity's HIPAA violation was due to its willful neglect, it may be penalized between $10,000 and $50,000 if it cures the violation within 30 days as described above; where such violation is not cured, the covered entity may be penalized up to $50,000 for each violation.[134] HHS may impose cumulative penalties for all violations "of

---

[126] *See* 74 Fed. Reg. at 56,128. HITECH Act §13410(d) extend[ed] the affirmative defense for violations that are timely corrected, which was previously limited to violations due to "reasonable cause and not to willful neglect," to all violations not due to willful neglect.... Violations due to willful neglect are ... not eligible for extension, nor will their timely correction be an affirmative defense. Timely correction will, however, determine which tier of penalty amounts will be applicable to violations due to willful neglect.

[127] 45 C.F.R. §164.410(b)(2).

[128] *Id.* §§164.410(b)(2), 164.404(b)(2)(iii).

[129] 74 Fed. Reg. at 56,124; *see also* HITECH Act §13410(d).

[130] 74 Fed. Reg. at 56,127.

[131] *Id.*

[132] 45 C.F.R. §164.404(b)(2)(i)(A); *see also* 74 Fed. Reg. at 56,125.

[133] 45 C.F.R. §164.404(b)(2)(ii)(A); *see also* 74 Fed. Reg. at 56,125. The regulation at 45 C.F.R. §160.401 defines reasonable cause to include "circumstances that would make it unreasonable for the covered entity, despite the exercise of ordinary business care and prudence, to comply with the administrative simplification provision violated."

[134] 45 C.F.R. §§164.404(b)(2)(iii)(A), 404(b)(2)(iv)(A); *see also* 74 Fed. Reg. at 56,125.

an identical requirement or prohibition during a calendar year" up to the amount of $1.5 million.[135]

Despite the increased civil monetary penalties imposed by the HITECH Act, HHS maintains some flexibility to grant lenient penalties when warranted. HHS may opt to waive penalties under the reasonable cause provision "to the extent that the payment of such penalty would be excessive relative to the compliance failure involved."[136] Further, HHS has indicated its intent to refrain from imposing "the maximum penalty amount in all cases. Rather...HHS penalty determinations will be based on the nature and extent of the violation, the nature and extent of the resulting harm, as well as the other factors...such as the covered entity's history of prior compliance or financial condition."[137]

B. Criminal Penalties

Criminal penalties under the HIPAA Enforcement Rule are available to the extent that a covered entity has knowingly "use[d] or cause[d] to be used a unique health identifier; obtain[ed] individually identifiable health information relating to an individual; or disclose[d] individually identifiable health information to another person."[138] It is the last of these provisions—the knowing disclosure of individually identifiable health information to another person—that is most directly related to a covered entity's obligations under the Breach Notification Rule. "A person (including an employee or other individual) shall be considered to have obtained or disclosed individually identifiable health information in violation of this part if the information is maintained by a covered entity...and the individual obtained or disclosed such information without authorization."[139]

Criminal penalties for covered entities violating HIPAA provisions as described above start with fines of $50,000 and/or imprisonment for not more than one year.[140] "If the offense is committed under false pretenses," a covered entity may be "fined not more than $100,000, imprisoned not more than 5 years, or both."[141] Finally, for violations where the covered entity had "intent to sell, transfer, or use individually identifiable health information for commercial advantage, personal gain, or malicious harm," a covered entity may be penalized "not more than $250,000," and the covered entity may be "imprisoned not more than 10 years, or both."[142]

---

[135]45 C.F.R. §164.404(b)(2).
[136]HITECH Act §13410(d) (codified at 42 U.S.C. §1320d–5(b)(3)); *see* 74 Fed. Reg. at 56,125.
[137]74 Fed. Reg. at 56,128; *see also* 45 C.F.R. §160.408.
[138]42 U.S.C. §1320d–6(a).
[139]*Id.* §1320d–6(a)(3).
[140]*Id.* §1320d–6(b)(1).
[141]*Id.* §1320d–6(b)(2).
[142]*Id.* §1320d–6(b)(3).

VIII. Conclusion

As set forth above, HHS "envision[s] that covered entities and business associates will need to do the following to determine whether a breach occurred" and take action to provide notice to patients when warranted.[143] "First, the covered entity or business associate must determine whether there has been an impermissible use or disclosure of protected health information under the Privacy Rule."[144] "Second, the covered entity or business associate must determine, and document, whether the impermissible use or disclosure compromises the security or privacy of the protected health information. This occurs when there is a significant risk of financial, reputational, or other harm to the individual."[145] "Lastly, the covered entity or business associate may need to determine whether the incident falls under one of the exceptions" to the definition of breach.[146]

To the extent that it determines that a breach of unsecured protected health information has occurred, the covered entity may need to provide notice to the patients involved, to HHS, and to local mass media, depending on the circumstances. Because the HITECH Act has increased the regulatory obligations for covered entities under the Breach Notification Rule, as well as the penalties for failure to abide by those regulations, covered entities must be diligent in determining whether an impermissible breach of patient data has taken place and to act promptly towards the satisfaction of its obligations under the Breach Notification Rule.

---

[143] 74 Fed. Reg. at 42,748.
[144] *Id.*
[145] *Id.*
[146] *Id.*

12

Due Diligence in E-Health Transactions*

I.	Introduction	344
II.	The Nature of Due Diligence and Its Purposes	345
III.	Standard for Due Diligence Review	347
IV.	Composition of the Due Diligence Team	348
V.	Procedure for the Due Diligence Review	349
	A. Planning	349
	B. Confidentiality Agreements	350
	C. Checklists	350
	D. Location	351
	E. Reporting the Results	352
VI.	Contents of the Due Diligence Review	353
	A. Disclosure Controls	354
	B. Internal Controls	354
	C. Audit Committee Activities	355
	D. Code of Ethics	356
	E. Off-Balance-Sheet Transactions	356
	F. Implications of Sarbanes-Oxley for the Due Diligence Review	356
	G. Certification of EHR Products	357
	H. Data Security and Privacy	357
VII.	Focus of the Due Diligence Review	358
	A. Assets	359
	B. Liability	360
	C. Agreements	363
	D. Capabilities and Liabilities	364
	E. Interviews	364
VIII.	Common Pitfalls in Due Diligence	365
IX.	Understanding Health Care Entities and Operations	366
	A. Tax-Exempt Status	367

---

*L. Robert Guenthner III, SNR Denton US LLP, Chicago, Illinois; Arthur G. House, Paley Rothman Goldstein Rosenberg Eig & Cooper, Chartered, Bethesda, Maryland.

B.	Accreditation and Certification Issues	368
C.	Protected Health Care Information	368
D.	Health Planning Approvals	369
E.	Conditions for Reimbursement	370
F.	Research or Grant Considerations	370
G.	Obligations to Provide Notice	370
X.	Laws and Regulations Specific to the Health Care Industry	370
XI.	Conclusion	376

I. INTRODUCTION

The e-health industry remains a rapidly developing and constantly changing environment. The development of certification criteria, meaningful use standards, and other similar regulations has dramatically increased the importance of understanding the regulatory environment and the compliance, or lack thereof, with applicable laws and regulations of industry participants. The industry depends on transactions such as supplier-and-vendor relationships, Web site development and hosting relationships, joint ventures, and strategic partnerships. As the regulatory scheme matures and the industry comes to grips with the economic impact of such regulations, extremely close scrutiny of proposed relationships and transactions should be expected. Due diligence is the means by which that scrutiny is applied to such transactions. This chapter discusses the general principles of the due diligence process and how they apply to typical e-health transactions.

Developments in corporate governance generally, coupled with highly publicized instances of corporate fraud and data and security breaches, have affected all industries, including the e-health industry. As a result, due diligence of proposed transactions, including data and privacy security, continues to be a topic of extreme importance.

Regulatory activities at the federal level, including the American Recovery and Reinvestment Act of 2009 (ARRA)[1] and provisions in the Patient Protection and Affordable Care Act of 2010 (PPACA)[2] have continued to spur the rapid development of the e-health or health information technology (HIT) industry. In an effort to spur the development and, more importantly, the adoption and use of HIT on a nationwide basis, Congress passed substantial subsidies as part of ARRA and the Health Information Technology for Economic and Clinical Health Act (HITECH Act).[3] The legislation provides approximately $19.2 billion of incentives over five years for hospitals and physicians to "meaningfully use" certified electronic health record (EHR) systems. In addition, funds are being provided to the states for low-interest loans to help providers finance health care information technology and for grants to regional health information exchanges to unite local providers.

---

[1] Pub. L. No. 111-05, 123 Stat. 115 (Feb. 17, 2009).
[2] Pub. L. No. 111-148, 124 Stat. 119 (Mar. 23, 2010).
[3] ARRA, Pub. L. No. 111-05, 123 Stat. 115, HITECH Act, ARRA §§3001 *et seq.*

ARRA offers incentives for those providers deemed to be "meaningful users of EHR technology." In January 2010, the Department of Health and Human Services (HHS), Centers for Medicare and Medicaid Services (CMS) issued an interim final rule defining the requirements for "meaningful use"[4] and subsequently issued the final "meaningful use" rules in July of 2010.[5] Those rules also were expected to contain procedures for applying for incentives. Generally speaking, however, the market has experienced considerable confusion with regard to the application of these rules. The changing rules and regulations and the relative newness of their application and enforcement continues to cause some level of uncertainty in the marketplace and emphasizes the need for careful and thorough due diligence in any transaction.

Along with the availability of stimulus money has come a renewed program of certification of EHR. Control over the certification is passing to the federal government. HHS and the Office of the National Coordinator for Health Information Technology (ONCHIT) have established rules for criteria that support "meaningful use" of EHR,[6] while the Commerce Department's National Institute of Standards and Technology (NIST) has developed version 1.0 and 1.1 testing procedures.[7] The process is complex and will continue to evolve.

Additionally, the increased use of "cloud computing," both within health care and in other industries, as a means of outsourcing traditional information technology (IT) facilities has focused attention on the need for a thorough due diligence process and an active vendor management relationship with "cloud providers." Cloud computing can take many forms, including private clouds, public clouds, and hybrid clouds. The level of customization and protection can vary greatly from form to form and also from provider to provider. For companies in the health care industry, obviously data security and privacy is crucial in establishing a cloud computing relationship. Only through thorough due diligence prior to entering into such a relationship can companies feel comfortable that such protections are in place and are adequate for their data.

II. THE NATURE OF DUE DILIGENCE AND ITS PURPOSES

While frequently considered a tedious task assigned to junior attorneys and businesspeople, due diligence is actually a critical component of most business transactions. It is through due diligence that the parties to a commercial transaction understand what they are undertaking and the risks involved. Due diligence is the source of commercial intelligence concerning a transaction, from economic feasibility to operational practicality, that will be used to make critical determinations about the transaction.

The specific purposes of due diligence vary with the nature and scope of the transaction, but will usually include one or more of the following:

---

[4] 75 Fed. Reg. 1844 (Jan. 13, 2010).
[5] 75 Fed. Reg. 44314 (July 28, 2010).
[6] *Id.*; *see also* http://healthit.hhs.gov/.
[7] The approved testing procedures are available at http://healthcare.nist.gov/use_testing/finalized_requirements.html.

(1) *To understand the business being acquired or the parties with whom one is contracting.* A client must have a complete understanding of the business and parties involved in order to analyze properly and completely the risks and the benefits associated with a transaction. Similarly, for an attorney to advise the client properly and efficiently and to prepare effective transaction documents, particularly in complex transactions, the attorney must have a thorough understanding of the business and parties involved.

(2) *To understand and evaluate the information contained in the agreements, disclosure schedules, exhibits, and so on.* The parties must be in a position to judge whether the disclosures being made in connection with the contemplated transaction are complete, correct, and appropriate. This becomes particularly important in transactions involving a securities offering, bond financing, or similar capital development that is subject to the disclosure provisions of federal securities law.

(3) *To identify legal and other impediments to consummating the proposed transaction.* It is important for clients to know what obstacles stand between them and the desired outcome of a transaction. Thorough due diligence often uncovers legal, financial, and other business obstacles that may cause a client to rethink a transaction. It is far better for a client to decide not to proceed with a transaction at the due diligence stage than later in the process when it has invested additional resources and is subject to increasing momentum toward the closing or, worse, to learn after closing that the fundamentals of the transaction were flawed.

(4) *To limit professional responsibility and provide a basis for opinions.* Attorneys and other professionals increasingly are expected to provide opinions in connection with proposed transactions. Without developing through due diligence the knowledge and background support necessary to render such opinions competently, their opinions will expose them to the risk of substantial professional liability.

In light of the potentially serious implications in the health care industry of entering into any sort of commercial transaction with parties who commit or are accused of committing fraud, and the increased scrutiny and legal requirements imposed by courts and regulators in recent fraud cases, due diligence has taken on a new purpose: to ensure that a party with whom a client is engaging in a transaction maintains adequate safeguards to avoid claims of fraud—financial or otherwise. Failure to establish these safeguards is particularly troublesome for publicly traded entities but can have serious implications for privately held businesses as well.

In light of the ever changing and increasingly regulated e-health or HIT industry, it is important that any transaction participant fully understand the concept of "meaningful use" and how a transaction partner's systems may or may not qualify under that standard. Additionally, prior to entering into any material transaction, it is essential that the parties to that transaction obtain an understanding of their proposed partner's ability to implement, monitor, and manage a data security and privacy program.

Medical data breaches, such as the one that affected Health Net Inc.'s computerized records and exposed personal information related to approximately 1.9 million people, are becoming more frequent. Nine of Health Net's computer drives were reported missing, exposing the personal records of nearly two million policyholders, including addresses, Social Security numbers, financial data, and other information about customers, employees, and health care providers.[8]

Because the regulatory and financial consequences of such breaches can be far reaching, it is advisable to determine whether a potential business partner has an acceptable data breach preparedness plan in place. The structure and design of such a plan is beyond the scope of this chapter, but at a minimum, in the due diligence process, the diligence team should confirm that the plan meets the following minimum standards:

- Establishes an incident response team. Such a team might include in-house IT personnel, legal counsel, compliance and security personnel, and public relations personnel, as well as outside experts with data breach experience.
- Federal and state data breach laws and regulations change frequently. The organization should have a mechanism to keep abreast of privacy laws and regulations and notification mandates on an ongoing basis.
- Establishes a data breach protocol so that the organization's response is outlined and responsibilities assigned in advance of a breach.

III. Standard for Due Diligence Review

How the review is organized and implemented is dependent on the facts and circumstances of the particular transaction. As a practical matter, because it is impossible to review every piece of information potentially relevant to a transaction, it is prudent to establish a "materiality standard" to limit the scope of review to matters and documents that are most likely to be material to the parties' consideration of the transaction.

Materiality is an imprecise concept, however. A $1 million risk in a multi-billion-dollar transaction may be immaterial, while a $50,000 risk in a $1 million transaction may be critical. Similarly, a small dollar risk that could trigger media scrutiny may be material to a client that wishes to avoid publicity, but completely immaterial to a client for whom public scrutiny is irrelevant.

In addition, the appropriate materiality standard may vary in different parts of the due diligence review. For instance, a legal compliance issue of a particular dollar threshold may be material, while a simple contractual liability of the same dollar amount would be immaterial, depending on the circumstances of the deal. Likewise, the potential for an adverse judgment in a governmental investigation may be material, where the potential for an adverse judgment in a civil lawsuit of the same amount would be immaterial.

What the reviewer should consider material, therefore, depends substantially upon the type and size of the transaction, the particular risks that the

---

[8] *Regulators Investigate Health Net Security Lapse Involving Personal Information of 1.9 Million People*, Los Angeles Times, March 14, 2011, at Business.

transaction may present, and the sensitivities of one or more of the parties. Materiality should be set on a case-by-case basis by the transaction team, including the client, after careful consideration and discussion of the facts and circumstances regarding the transaction.

As with materiality, no clear standard exists for determining whether one has performed "enough" due diligence. Theoretically, due diligence could continue until every piece of potentially relevant information has been thoroughly reviewed. The practical limitations placed on a commercial transaction team typically prohibit the expenditure of resources such a comprehensive review would require. Given the importance of due diligence to the client's ability to evaluate the transaction, however, the due diligence team should do as thorough a job in its review as it can.

The challenge for the due diligence team is to establish with the client a balance between conducting a review sufficient to permit the client to make informed judgments about the proposed undertaking but not so comprehensive as to obstruct the client's desire to complete the transaction. Achieving this balance requires early and ongoing communication with the client, the exercise of judgment as to whether all relevant information has been discovered, and consideration of whether further investigation will produce new information.

One approach to these issues is to structure the due diligence review initially to cover broad areas for review and to pursue a more detailed review to the extent the initial examination reveals a material problem. Depending upon the seriousness of the issue discovered, the more detailed review may be limited to the particular area involved or may encompass the subject company's entire operations.

For example, finding a problem in the initial review that suggested the existence of a pattern of serious corporate compliance deficiencies would likely trigger a more comprehensive examination of the party's entire operations. An isolated but serious problem in the area of Medicare billing, however, might require a more thorough review of just the party's billing procedures. Using this layered approach necessarily requires the client to assume some risk as the price of obtaining the advantage of balancing the degree of thoroughness of due diligence with the speed and efficiency of the process.

IV. COMPOSITION OF THE DUE DILIGENCE TEAM

Given the importance of due diligence to the transaction and the speed with which most clients want it completed, it is important to provide adequate staffing for the due diligence review from the outset. The team usually consists of attorneys and businesspeople from various specialty areas.

The larger the transaction, the more likely the client is to expect a multidisciplinary team. In smaller transactions, however, clients may anticipate a small due diligence team. Depending upon the complexity of the transaction, therefore, it is incumbent upon the attorney to educate the client that failing to deploy the right expertise in the team to save costs may ultimately lead to higher costs if the due diligence team fails to identify substantial risks.

Attorneys should play a leading role on the due diligence team and in structuring the due diligence process. The senior attorney representing a party usually takes responsibility for defining with the client the scope and depth of the due diligence review, and the results of his or her planning are often negotiated with the other parties to the transaction to arrive at a mutually-agreed-upon diligence effort. The transaction agreement may describe the due diligence the parties will undertake.

A due diligence team may include any number of attorneys, who may have varying levels of experience. Corporate attorneys, often with some expertise in the particular industry, typically lead the due diligence team, and depending upon the nature of the transaction, the team will include attorneys from the areas of antitrust, environmental, employee benefits, tax, intellectual property, financing (especially if tax-exempt financing is involved), and other areas of law. Once the senior attorney has designed the overall review, a senior associate will often have the operational responsibility to supervise the actual review being conducted by more junior attorneys.

The due diligence team frequently includes other professionals such as accountants, investment bankers, other outside consultants, line managers, human resources personnel, internal auditors, information systems professionals, and management personnel. These professionals bring valuable expertise and experience to the team that can substantially enhance the team's effectiveness.

Line managers, for instance, usually are concerned about the practical application and effect of a transaction on the client's operations. They know where to look for potential problems in a party's operations or structure and frequently can identify problems the attorneys or other professionals on the team would miss. The nonlegal professionals should function as an integral part of the team under the overall supervision of the attorneys and be organized to assist the attorneys in advising the client concerning the transactions.

A note of caution: to the extent the team is reviewing its own client's operations in preparation for due diligence review by another party, the attorneys should make a great effort to engage the assistance of these personnel in a manner that will protect their work under the attorney-client or attorney work-product privileges.

V. Procedure for the Due Diligence Review

A. Planning

To be effective and cost efficient, due diligence requires consummate planning and organization, as discussed in the previous section. Taking the time to organize the effort at the outset will save time and money and will enable the team to conduct its review as systematically as possible. The responsible attorney should establish a realistic due diligence schedule with the parties, identify what is to be reviewed, prepare a due diligence list that describes the documents to be collected and reviewed, and assign responsibility for gathering and organizing materials.

B. Confidentiality Agreements

Before beginning the due diligence review, the parties should enter into a confidentiality agreement prohibiting the improper use or disclosure of information obtained during the review. Much of the reviewed material may be highly confidential and proprietary and require confidentiality protection. This is particularly important in acquisitions where the other party is a competitor and the consummation of the transaction is contingent upon the satisfactory completion of the due diligence review. If the transaction does not close, the confidentiality agreement should prevent the reviewing party from using that information for its own benefit.

A due diligence review often includes proprietary information that can have significant legal and business implications. It is important, both for business reasons and to ensure that the review does not violate antitrust law or regulations, that the transaction team consider the competitive issues arising from a due diligence review. Techniques for dealing with some of the competitive issues raised by having competitors review each other's files include:

- redaction of sensitive material;
- providing only summaries rather than actual documents;
- limiting review to outside consultants and advisors who are bound by confidentiality agreements; and
- limiting review to areas in which the disclosing and reviewing parties do not compete.

C. Checklists

In many cases, the due diligence process will be initiated by the reviewing party delivering to the other party a due diligence request or due diligence checklist, which is simply a list of items the reviewing party desires to examine during the review. It may also include a list of physical assets that the due diligence team would like to inspect and personnel who the team would like to interview during the review.

While there are many standard due diligence lists that may be useful in a transaction, each party should review proposed lists carefully before the due diligence review begins to ensure that:

- the requested material is relevant to the contemplated transaction;
- the requested material can be provided without a breach of any other person's or entity's privacy rights or breach of any agreement to which the disclosing party is bound;
- the disclosure of the requested material would not be improper from an antitrust perspective; and
- the task of assembling the requested material is not unduly burdensome given the nature and size of the contemplated transaction.

It is much more efficient and less likely to cause a confrontation if the parties agree on the scope of the due diligence review in advance.

Most e-health transactions will require due diligence review of unusual issues and materials. It is often helpful to include these in the due diligence checklist for the transaction. Following are a number of examples:

(1) provide uniform resource locators (URLs) and identification and password access to all Web sites maintained by the company;
(2) provide copies of all data privacy and all internal and external security policies and procedures;
(3) provide copies of all Health Insurance Portability and Accountability Act of 1996 (HIPAA)[9] and other compliance plans and all related notices, correspondence, and other materials;
(4) provide printed copies of all click-wrap licenses[10] employed by the company;
(5) provide any documents or correspondence related to Food and Drug Administration (FDA) certifications or jurisdictional disputes with the FDA;
(6) provide a list of all third parties with links to or from any Web site maintained by the company and copies of all linking agreements;
(7) provide copies of all policies and procedures regarding Web site usage and content;
(8) provide copies of all online contracts and agreements, including application service provider and service license agreements, to which the company is a party;
(9) provide descriptions of all source code used in software developed by or for the company, proof of ownership or right to use the software, and copies of all source code escrow agreements; and
(10) provide copies of all advertising and sponsorship policies and procedures.

D. Location

The due diligence review may be conducted at one or more offices of a party or at the offices of one of the team members or both. In large transactions involving facilities at multiple locations, due diligence teams usually travel to each location at which relevant documents are stored and review the documents there.

In some transactions, it may be easier and most efficient to ship copies of documents to a central location, such as one of the parties' offices, the offices of their counsel, or some other mutually agreeable location. Confidentiality requirements for the transaction will often dictate where and how due diligence is conducted. Having a due diligence team in one's office is not likely to go unnoticed and may create substantial anxiety and disruption among employees.

A due diligence review will proceed most smoothly if all of the documents to be reviewed are collected in a central location, or data room, and organized

---

[9] Pub. L. No. 104-191, 110 Stat. 1936 (1996).
[10] Click-wrap licenses are software licenses whose terms are set forth on a Web site or displayed at the time the software is downloaded by a user. The license is accepted or rejected by means of a "mouse click."

in accordance with the due diligence document list. This will allow the team to find documents easily and to review them systematically.

In today's business environment, with the increasing uses of technology and less reliance on paper documents, it is becoming more common for due diligence materials to be sent to the team for review rather than sending the team to the documents. This is particularly true in smaller transactions where substantial travel costs for the due diligence team may be unacceptable to the client.

Sending the appropriate documents to a central location for review allows for a multidisciplinary review without the cost of transporting a large due diligence team to various sites. This approach also reduces the risk of a loss of confidentiality and avoids the disruptions that may be caused by on-site review.

E. Reporting the Results

Wherever the team conducts its review, it should be prepared to record its findings as it examines documents or property. Having chart forms available for recording information from contracts and other documents will save time and improve the team's ability to retrieve information later in the transaction. As the review progresses, the team should prepare comprehensive, legible notes on the materials reviewed, all organized according to the master due diligence list.

In addition, the team should have its specialists prepare due diligence memoranda (sometimes referred to as "first-layer memoranda") concerning their findings, which can be used to prepare the final due diligence report to the client. The notes and memoranda should describe what was reviewed, what was found in the review, and any questions or issues that arose during the review. If the review includes interviews of individuals, the team's notes should include a detailed summary of each interview. The team should treat all notes, interview summaries, and first-layer memoranda as confidential.

The results of a due diligence review must be conveyed to the client in a clear, concise manner that takes into consideration the nature of the findings, the special interests of the client, and the need for confidentiality. The due diligence report should give the client the information it needs to make informed decisions concerning whether it should proceed with the proposed transaction.

While the exact contents of the report will vary depending on the transaction and the client, a due diligence report should have the following characteristics:

- The due diligence report should summarize the due diligence results, but detailed supporting information should be readily available.
- The report should be organized to present the findings in priority order, with those most important to the client presented first.
- A report on large or complex due diligence reviews should contain an executive summary.
- The due diligence results should be presented in a manner easily understood by the client's management and directors.
- The report should contain recommended solutions to problems identified in the review and recommendations for additional action where further review or reconsideration of the business terms would be appropriate.

- The report should clearly identify who will be responsible for any recommended follow-up action.
- Whether the report is a memorandum, a letter, or PowerPoint slides, the report should be prepared by legal counsel and should be marked "Confidential and subject to attorney-client privilege."

The due diligence report should be based on the due diligence team's notes, interview summaries, and first-layer memoranda. These provide the support for the findings reported to the client in more summary fashion. At the conclusion of the due diligence review, all of these materials should be organized to facilitate retrieval so that the team can quickly provide the client with details concerning a particular issue. Often, it is advisable to assign the task of organizing these materials to one person on the team, who will also be responsible for informing the team as to how the documents are categorized and for retrieving materials that may be needed later in the transaction.

A note of caution: it is not always desirable for the due diligence team to prepare a written document. This is true where the information is particularly confidential or where the size or nature of the transaction makes the preparation of such a written report prohibitive. In such cases, the due diligence team may not produce a memorandum but instead will report orally on its findings.

VI. Contents of the Due Diligence Review

A new area of inquiry is rapidly developing in the due diligence process, particularly with respect to mergers and acquisitions diligence, where one or both parties are publicly held entities. The Sarbanes-Oxley Act of 2002[11] has dramatically altered the landscape for these organizations. Although Sarbanes-Oxley does not, today, get the media attention it did when first enacted, transaction participants are well advised to remember that it is alive and well. Sarbanes-Oxley was adopted as a method of promoting corporate responsibility and good corporate governance at publicly traded companies. Among other things, Sarbanes-Oxley mandates substantial reforms in corporate governance, public disclosure, independence of auditors, and the role of independent directors, particularly those on a company's audit committee. Sarbanes-Oxley also exposes companies and their officers to significant criminal and civil sanctions and penalties.

While Sarbanes-Oxley does not apply directly to not-for-profit corporations, many state attorneys general, using their statutory powers of oversight with respect to not-for-profit entities, are imposing requirements on these entities similar to those established by Sarbanes-Oxley for public companies. Sarbanes-Oxley increasingly is seen as establishing the standard for best practices in all corporations. Due diligence involving a not-for-profit corporation, therefore, should include a consideration of whether the target entity is

---

[11] Pub. L. No. 107-204, 116 Stat. 745 (2002).

complying with the particular governance practices and requirements imposed on it by state regulators.

A. Disclosure Controls

Among other things, Sarbanes-Oxley has imposed on reporting companies an obligation to develop and maintain adequate "disclosure controls and procedures," which are defined by the Securities and Exchange Commission (SEC) as the procedures necessary to ensure that the information the company is required to disclose in periodic reports is processed and disclosed properly and in a timely fashion.[12]

Any company considering an acquisition of or other substantial partnering transaction with a reporting company will want to evaluate that company's disclosure controls to determine how those controls work, how formal they are, how closely they are followed in practice, and how often they are evaluated for efficacy.

Similarly, reporting companies considering transactions with nonreporting companies will want to review and understand the controls and procedures of the nonreporting company to determine how they will need to be modified or supplemented as part of a reporting company.

Due diligence items in this area will include review and evaluation of the written description of these controls, meetings with the responsible representatives, and review and evaluation of any monitoring or other evaluation materials.

B. Internal Controls

As directed by Section 401 of Sarbanes-Oxley, the SEC has adopted rules requiring reporting companies, subject to certain limited exceptions, to include in their annual reports a report of management on the company's internal control over financial reporting. The internal control report must include:

- a statement of management's responsibility for establishing and maintaining adequate internal control over financial reporting for the company;
- management's assessment of the effectiveness of the company's internal control over financial reporting as of the end of the company's most recent fiscal year;
- a statement identifying the framework used by management to evaluate the effectiveness of the company's internal control over financial reporting; and
- a statement that the registered public accounting firm that audited the company's financial statements included in the annual report has issued an attestation report on management's assessment of the company's internal control over financial reporting.

---

[12]Certification of Disclosure in Companies' Quarterly and Annual Reports, Securities Act Release No. 33-8124 (Sept. 9, 2002), *available at* http://www.sec.gov/rules/final/33-8124.htm.

Under the SEC rules, a company is required to file the registered public accounting firm's attestation report as part of the annual report.[13]

As with the disclosure controls, attorneys involved in any transaction involving a reporting company will need to understand how each party operates with regard to these internal controls, to examine these controls, and to understand how they fit within the requirements of Sarbanes-Oxley. Gaining a firm grasp on the controls will be a necessary part of any due diligence review.

C. Audit Committee Activities

Sarbanes-Oxley has also placed increased emphasis on the role of the audit committee in corporate governance and the reporting and monitoring process. Under the new rules, the audit committee must be composed of independent directors and must adopt and follow an audit committee charter. Additionally, the new rules require a company to disclose that its board has determined that the company either:

- has at least one "audit committee financial expert" serving on its audit committee; or
- does not have an audit committee financial expert serving on its audit committee.

The rules define an audit committee financial expert as a person who has *all* of the following attributes:

- an understanding of generally accepted accounting principles (GAAP) and financial statements;
- the ability to assess the general application of GAAP in connection with the accounting for estimates, accruals, and reserves (but not necessarily experience in applying these principles);
- experience preparing, auditing, analyzing, or evaluating financial statements that present a breadth and level of complexity of accounting issues that are *generally comparable* to the breadth and complexity of issues that can reasonably be expected to be raised by the company's financial statements, or experience in *actively supervising* one or more persons engaged in such activities;
- an understanding of internal controls and procedures for financial reporting; and
- an understanding of audit committee functions.

Here again, in light of these new rules, any company engaging in a significant transaction with a reporting company, particularly an acquisition or merger, will need to understand the audit committee process, the composition of the audit committee, and whether the committee includes a financial expert.

---

[13]Final Rule: Management's Reports on Internal Control Over Financial Reporting and Certification of Disclosure in Exchange Act Periodic Reports, Securities Act Release No. 33-8238 (June 6, 2003), *available at* http://www.sec.gov/rules/final/33-8238.htm.

Diligence procedures in this area should include a review of the audit committee charter, composition, and minutes, as well as interviews with key audit committee members, such as the chair and the financial expert, if any.

D. Code of Ethics

Section 406(a) of Sarbanes-Oxley directs the SEC to issue rules requiring each reporting company to disclose immediately whether it has adopted a code of ethics for its senior financial officers and to disclose any change in or waiver of the provisions of its code of ethics. The SEC, in turn, requires the disclosure to be included in annual reports on Forms 10-K and 10-KSB (pursuant to new Item 406 of Regulations S-K and S-B) and in annual reports on Forms 20-F and 40-F (pursuant to amendments to those forms).

Determining the existence and the contents of this code of ethics will be an important part of the due diligence process going forward.[14]

E. Off-Balance-Sheet Transactions

Section 401(a) of Sarbanes-Oxley concerns the disclosure of off-balance-sheet arrangements, contractual obligations, and contingent liabilities. These rules require disclosure of off-balance-sheet arrangements that have, or are reasonably likely to have, a current or future effect that is material to investors on a company's financial condition, changes in financial condition, revenues or expenses, results of operations, liquidity, capital expenditures, or capital resources. The rules also require public companies (excluding small business issuers) to provide an overview of certain known contractual obligations in a tabular format in their management discussion and analysis (MD&A) disclosures.

Increasingly, directors and officers are requiring greater justification for the amounts paid for, and valuations placed on, intellectual property (IP) assets. While the determination of value of IP remains perhaps as much an art as a science, what previously tended to be a somewhat relaxed acceptance of the expert valuation report is being replaced by a more wary and skeptical approach.

Due diligence process, therefore, will require an examination of all off-balance-sheet activity, not only to alert the client to the company's practices but to ensure its compliance with the new rules. In addition, the due diligence review should include an investigation into any special-purpose-entity transactions and transactions with insiders.[15]

F. Implications of Sarbanes-Oxley for the Due Diligence Review

As discussed above, the disclosure and other requirements imposed by Sarbanes-Oxley will necessitate a more thorough investigation of the controls,

---

[14] Disclosure Required by Sections 406 and 407 of the Sarbanes-Oxley Act of 2002, Securities Act Release No. 33-8177, *available at* http://www.sec.gov/rules/final/33-8177.htm (for correction to final rule, see http://www.sec.gov/rules/final/33-8177a.htm).

[15] Final Rule: Disclosure in Management's Discussion and Analysis about Off-Balance Sheet Arrangements and Aggregate Contractual Obligations, Securities Act Release No. 33-8182, *available at* http://www.sec.gov/rules/final/33-8182.htm.

procedures, and operations of transaction partners than may have previously been the standard. Simply reviewing and relying on the audited financial statements will no longer suffice for adequate financial due diligence.

In light of the requirements of Sarbanes-Oxley, due diligence investigations should now include:

- more thorough analysis of corporate accounting and related disclosures;
- a detailed investigation of off-balance-sheet transactions;
- a complete analysis of all special-purpose entities and related-party transactions;
- review of internal controls and procedures; and
- review of all audit committee and other board committee charters, composition, minutes, and related materials.

G. Certification of EHR Products

As the HIT and e-health industry becomes standardized under government regulation, the value of a potential partner will depend, in no small part, on whether the products and services provided by that partner will meet the highest level of certification and accreditation. As of October 2010, perhaps the most significant issue in this context is the question of whether HIT or e-health products satisfy the definition of "meaningful use" as provided for in ARRA. In addition, it is important to determine the ability of products and services to meet other certification or accreditation criteria that are important in the marketplace. For example, the Certification Commission for Health Information Technology (CCHIT) provides certification against its own internally developed and published criteria. This certification can have a meaningful impact on the marketplace's willingness to accept and adopt a product or technology.

As a result, it is incumbent upon companies engaging in any sort of transaction with a company involved in the EHR space to determine, as a component of its overall diligence, whether or not the EHR products are certified or, in the case of the ARRA requirements, are positioned to meet the requirements when they are finalized. This analysis requires a thorough understanding of the relevant legally required certification criteria as well as those criteria or certifications that, while not legally mandated, may be important to the purchasers of EHR products and services.

H. Data Security and Privacy

As discussed in I. and II. above and in other parts of this book,[16] the importance of robust data security and privacy policies whether in a contracting partner or a potential acquisition target simply cannot be overstated. All companies today, but particularly those that deal in and maintain sensitive protected

---

[16]See Chapter 5 (Dahm, Privacy Issues in U.S. Health Care), Chapter 6 (Taylor & Crawford, The European Data Privacy Regime), Chapter 7 (Christiansen, Information Security and Security Breach Notification Under HIPAA and HITECH), Chapter 8 (Goldberg & Greene, Enforcement of the Health Insurance Portability and Accountability Act of 1996), and Chapter 11 (Faccenda, Obligations in Response to a Health Care Data Security Breach).

information such as protected health information (PHI), have serious privacy and security concerns. The cost of a security breach is real, and is often very substantial. Furthermore, compliance with an ever-changing web of local, federal, and foreign laws and regulations can be daunting to even the most diligent of companies. As a result, it is imperative that, prior to entering into any transaction, the parties understand to what degree their proposed partner has had issues with security or privacy breaches and, even if there is no such negative history, to understand the means by which the proposed partner has protected their data from such intrusions or inadvertent disclosure. This can include everything from actual data security and privacy policies to things as mundane as hardware protection (i.e., password usage and levels of strength) and management of access to data.

VII. Focus of the Due Diligence Review

Initially, the fundamental determination is made that the subject company is duly qualified to conduct business in the appropriate jurisdictions. In addition, attention should be paid to the propriety of its underlying corporate documents. Counsel should assemble and review the articles or certificates of incorporation or organization, as amended, and the bylaws, as amended, to assure that they were properly adopted or ratified. Attention also should be paid to the organizational records of the company, including the initial meetings of the incorporators, stockholders, and directors. If the company has not maintained formal minutes of all meetings, the corporate minutes should be brought up to date properly. If meeting notes are available, management should prepare minutes for board and board committee meetings or should have the company's board ratify the past actions of the board and its committees. If the company's governing documents are incomplete or have not been properly amended, its board should adopt restated governing documents and ratify past board actions.

Is the stock ledger up to date and accurate? If not, the record of ownership should be promptly clarified and certified as accurate by the appropriate corporate officer, usually the corporation's secretary. Extraordinary actions—for example, entering into real estate or large equipment leases or purchases, adoption of employee stock ownership plans (ESOPs) or bonus plans, selection of corporate legal counsel or auditors, establishment of executive compensation, acceptance of organized labor contracts, hiring or termination of key personnel—should occur only with board authorization. If such authorization is not evident in the corporate records, ratification of those actions should be required during the due diligence process.

The specific content of the review will depend largely upon the nature of the transaction, the characteristics of parties, and the potential risks associated with the transaction. While a thorough due diligence may involve examination of a multiplicity of issues, most due diligence efforts in the health care industry focus on several key areas of the target company's operations: its assets, its liabilities, its contracts, and its compliance with unique health industry regulations.

A. Assets

A key component of any due diligence is an asset-related due diligence review. The primary questions in this review are as follows:

- What sorts of assets are involved in the transaction?
- What risks and liabilities are tied to those assets?
- Are the assets adequately protected?

When examining e-commerce companies, the due diligence team must pay particular attention to the company's intellectual property assets on which it will depend for its existence. For e-health businesses, trademarks and copyrights have particular relevance, while patents tend to be less common.

The first step in conducting asset-related due diligence is to conduct an audit of intellectual property protected. In addition to reviewing the copyright and trademark documentation, the due diligence team should examine software and hardware license and maintenance agreements granted to third parties, government contracts, and distribution, integration, and value added reseller (VAR) agreements granted to third parties. It should also review company documentation of software source and object code as well as specifications, design documents, laboratory notebooks, and correspondence relating to any novel intellectual property.

Particularly important to e-health businesses will be a review of the pendency or possibility of business-method patents. While patents tend to be less common for e-health enterprises, they can be quite important, and the due diligence team should review them, including the file wrapper histories for issued patents and any patents that have been applied for but may not yet have been issued.

Given the importance of trademarks and other intellectual property to e-health businesses, the due diligence team should have a thorough understanding of the intellectual property assets owned by the target enterprise and document what steps the company has taken to protect them. The team should identify all registrations and applications associated with the target company, gather the prosecution histories (consisting of the entire history of an application, including all communications between the applicant and the government pertaining to the application and all government office actions taken with respect to the application) for review by intellectual property counsel, and verify the claimed date of first use in interstate commerce.

Additionally, the due diligence team should conduct a search to determine title to claimed marks, domestic and foreign. If the marks were acquired from a third party, the due diligence review should include an examination of the underlying acquisition documents to confirm their validity and to ensure that proper assignments have been recorded and that the target company actually acquired the rights it purports to own.

Once it is determined that the company has properly acquired title to the marks through registration or acquisition, the team should verify that the marks remain valid. It should be determined, for example, that no transfers or assignments of the marks have occurred, that all registration and renewal fees have been timely paid, and that all Section 8[17] and Section 15[18] affidavit filings have been properly made with the U.S. Patent and Trademark Office.

The team should also determine whether any opposition, cancellation, or other proceedings are pending with regard to the marks. It is often useful to review the target company's product advertising or promotional literature to see how the trademarks are used in actual practice and to check the company's Web site to understand how the company and others that may be linked to the site use the company's name and marks.

In addition, the team should examine carefully the terms of agreements dealing with trademarks, such as consent letters, mutual-use agreements, licenses, and opposition settlement agreements (e.g., are they transferable? are consents necessary? are the agreements for a limited term? do the agreements carry terms or conditions that could restrict the buyer's intended use of the marks?). The team should also consider whether the marks are encumbered in any way (e.g., have any security interests been filed against the marks or have they been pledged as collateral?).

It is important to verify the continued use and enforcement of the marks. The due diligence team should determine whether any of the marks have gone unused for any period and understand clearly how the marks have been enforced in the past. Finally, the team should determine whether the company conducts trademark clearance and should obtain and review all correspondence and court documentation pertaining to the company's marks.

Copyright assets must also be reviewed carefully as part of the due diligence. After identifying all copyrighted material associated with the business, the due diligence team should check title and renewal-fee status and should determine whether the company has procedures to identify copyrightable material and to use and protect copyrighted works. The due diligence team should determine whether the company has followed work-for-hire practices to assure ownership of materials created by third parties and whether the company has obtained copyright assignments where required.

Other questions related to copyrights include: How has the seller marked its copyrighted materials? Has the company given or taken assignments of copyrights? And have those assignments been recorded? As with trademarks, the team should obtain and review all agreements pertaining to the copyrights in which the company has taken or given a license. Are such licenses for a limited term? Must action be taken to renew the licenses? Is there a revenue stream associated with the licenses? If so, are royalties being properly paid or collected? The investigation should also look for other third-party rights in the copyrights (i.e., are the copyrights pledged as collateral or subject to a security interest?).

B. Liabilities

A review of the target organization's liabilities requires an investigation into whether it has taken reasonable and adequate steps to protect its legal status

---

[17] 15 U.S.C. §1058 (duration of registration).
[18] 15 U.S.C. §1065 (incontestability of right to use mark under certain conditions).

and protect itself against loss. Liability arises from a wide array of sources, both internal and external, and for e-commerce businesses, special concerns exist.

Perhaps the most serious potential liability for an e-commerce enterprise arises from system security. The review must consider the target's system security from all perspectives and determine whether the company has established a layered approach to security, whether the system perimeter is secure, who has and is able to obtain access to the system, whether the system software and operating system is secure, and whether a contingency plan has been developed for recovery of both system and public information. A thorough investigation of the target's information system, including hardware, software, policies, and procedures is necessary to answer these questions in anticipation of a corporate transaction in which the party or parties may view these systems as a key component of the business involved.

The due diligence team will also need to determine whether the company has the necessary licenses and copyrights for its operations. Thorny business and legal problems obviously abound for a business that has built its operations on technology that infringes on intellectual property belonging to others. Thus, the review should confirm that the target possesses and maintains appropriate software and hardware licenses, that its company's advertising and marketing programs and plans do not infringe protected rights, and that its other areas of operations do not unduly expose the company to the substantial financial and public relations risks associated with intellectual property rights infringement.

The target's Web site also presents a multitude of possible risks and should be part of the team's review. Numerous agreements support an e-commerce Web site, such as those for Web development, hosting, and content licensing. The due diligence team should obtain and review these and other records to determine that the target has appropriate documentation to permit the continued use of its Web site. This review should include work-made-for-hire forms, software licenses, Web site use forms, and picture and name release forms. As the target's interactive Web site will be a principal medium of advertising for the e-commerce business and a fundamental part of its business operations, the team must determine that the Web site does not infringe on anyone's intellectual property rights.

The due diligence team should also understand and measure the Web site's performance. While the number of hits (i.e., the number of point-and-clicks on the target company's site) provides a crude measure of Web site performance, it provides little useful information, and the team may consider alternative methods of measurement, such as registered users, audience reach, page-view traffic, and revenue.[19]

For e-health enterprises, the privacy requirements of state and federal law are a major source of potential liability. Consequently, the due diligence team must examine the target company's privacy policy and compliance program to determine whether they are well drafted, given priority by the organization's management, well implemented, and effective. The team should review the policy itself, the infrastructure the company has in place to implement the policy,

---

[19] Jonathan Bick, *Due Diligence for "Dot-Com" Deals*, N.Y.L.J. 221 (1999).

and the corrective actions the company has taken to protect against the improper disclosure of customer or patient data.

If the target company is an enterprise covered by HIPAA, the team should investigate the extent to which the target's compliance program has responded to recent privacy regulations promulgated by HHS as required by HIPAA.[20] The team also should ascertain whether the company has implemented procedures to bring it into compliance by the regulation's effective date, both with respect to its own use and transmission of protected health information and to its relationship with any entities that qualify as business associates under the regulations.

Effective December 1, 2006, the Federal Rules of Civil Procedure governing the discovery of electronically stored information (ESI) were changed.[21] Under the new rules, noncompliance with discovery requirements during litigation can result in court-imposed sanctions.[22] As a result, businesses now must determine how to store and maintain electronic records for possible retrieval in the event of litigation. The amended rules make the identification, classification, content, and storage of ESI a new area of inquiry by counsel conducting due diligence on a potential merger or acquisition target.

A detailed discussion of the impact of the new rules is beyond the scope of this chapter, but briefly, amended Rule 26(f)(3) requires a conference of the parties to discuss ESI during the discovery-planning conference at the beginning of litigation. The rule requires that counsel discuss the preservation, disclosure, and discovery of ESI. Such ESI could include, for example:

- files on servers and business computers;
- files on back-up storage, USB drives, DVD, and compact disc storage, etc.;
- business files contained on employee laptops, regardless of whether such files exist on the company server;
- business files on personal digital assistants (PDAs);
- voice mail files;
- business files on employee cell phones, digital cameras, and other recording devices; and
- files stored on company systems that are no longer in use.[23]

Amended Rule 26(b)(2)(B) provides that parties are not required to provide discovery of ESI from sources that the party identifies as not reasonably accessible "because of undue burden or cost"; however, courts may order the production of difficult-to-access ESI in cases in which "good cause" exists.[24]

Amended Rule 37(f) provides a so-called "safe harbor," which provides protection where a party fails to provide ESI "lost as a result of the routine, good-faith operation of an electronic information system."[25]

---

[20] For discussion of the HHS privacy regulations, see Chapter 5 (Dahm, Privacy Issues in U.S. Health Care), at II.B.3.c.
[21] FED. R. CIV. P. 26(f)(3).
[22] FED. R. CIV. P. 26(c).
[23] FED. R. CIV. P. 26(f)(3).
[24] FED. R. CIV. P. 26(b)(2)(B).
[25] FED. R. CIV. P. 37(f).

Counsel should be aware that recent cases have resulted in substantial damages awards to parties who were able to show that their ability to pursue a civil action was impaired by another party's failure to produce ESI. Some commentators have suggested that the damages awarded may have exceeded the damages that could have resulted from the case in chief. Thus, corporations that are unprepared to respond to discovery of ESI may be more vulnerable to litigation.

Counsel engaged in due diligence will want to review the nature and organization of ESI at the company to be acquired in order to determine whether the acquisition target can reasonably respond to discovery requirements contained in Rule 26 in the event of litigation. For example, inquiry might be directed to:

- The identity of storage points of electronically stored information:
  ° Where are the storage repositories located?
  ° Are they fixed or mobile, e.g., servers or laptops, voice mail systems, or text and messages on mobile telephones?
  ° What is the nature of the material stored?
  ° What is the format of the electronic files and will any special technology be required to retrieve the files?
- The nature of any document retention plan employed by the company:
  ° How long are certain types of ESI to be maintained?
  ° Has the plan been reviewed to assure that it meets both the business and litigation needs of the company?
  ° Does the company have in place a requirement to preserve ESI once litigation is anticipated?
  ° Does the preservation requirement override the company's normal document retention plan?
  ° Is there a mechanism in place to alert employees to preserve e-mails, instant messages, voice mails, and other ESI?

C. Agreements

The target company's business arrangements will show the due diligence team what obligations the target has made to others and what commitments others have made to it, many of which could be material to the client's evaluation of the target and the transaction. The due diligence team must review and understand all of the material agreements to which the target is a party.

Before beginning its contract review, the team should consider whether the target's activities subject it to multistate obligations and, if so, determine whether the company is in good standing in the appropriate jurisdictions. If the company is not properly qualified and in good standing, it does not have the capacity to enter into contracts in those jurisdictions.

For e-commerce businesses, this is not always an easy thing to determine. Unlike traditional hospital or manufacturing businesses, the location of an e-commerce enterprise may be unclear. In most jurisdictions, where an e-health business must be qualified and in good standing will depend on the location at which the firm owns or operates communications equipment or servers, where the firm engages in ongoing or repetitive transactions, where the company has a physical presence (e.g., offices, employees, patient records, inventory), where its patient transactions take place, and where orders are taken and filled.

The due diligence team should also determine the tax status in, and obtain tax status certificates from, all relevant jurisdictions. Internet taxation is an unclear and evolving area and varies from jurisdiction to jurisdiction. The problem is compounded for an e-commerce business because the use of the Internet enables it to engage in business and product sales and services around the globe. The team, therefore, examines the tax law and regulations of not only the various federal and state governments but also pertinent foreign jurisdictions.

What specific agreements the team should consider will depend on the scope of the target company's business and the nature of the transaction. Most substantial transactions, however, will require an extensive contract review. For example, the team will likely need to review channel agreements, partnership and joint-venture agreements, affiliation documents (i.e., research and development agreements), impression guarantees (i.e., agreements authorizing a link to third-party controlled Web sites or a presence on those sites), customer and supply agreements, stock-option agreements, stockholder agreements, proxy agreements, pledge and security agreements, buy-sell agreements, noncompetition agreements, voting trusts, and employment agreements. In addition, the due diligence team should carefully review all Web site resident agreements, including related registration forms, click-wrap licenses, privacy policy, customer and vendor agreements, and warranties and disclaimers.

D. Capabilities and Protections

Particularly in instances of due diligence for the purposes of evaluating a potential contracting partner, it is absolutely essential that the due diligence team fully investigate the capabilities of, and the protections afforded by, that contracting partner. As an example, as discussed above, cloud computing is becoming increasingly common, both in the health care industry and in other industries. Before entering into any cloud computing arrangement, the company engaging such service will want to thoroughly understand the cloud provider's data security and privacy policies and capabilities, the performance statistics that can be expected from the cloud provider, any service limitations imposed (by contract or by practice) by the cloud provider, the level of data segregation provided, the access to data pursuant to government authority or litigation, and intellectual property protections. Although all of this should be laid out in the cloud service agreement, it is important for a potential cloud customer to look into the background and resources of its proposed provider, speak to other customers, and generally undertake a thorough due diligence process before committing itself and turning over control of data, particularly highly sensitive data such as protected health information.

E. Interviews

Often of equal or greater importance to the document review are the due diligence interviews of key managers of the target company. These interviews should be conducted with management staff, operational personnel, and other employees who may have information concerning matters within the scope of the due diligence review. The team should conduct these interviews separately and later compare the responses from the various employees for inconsistencies or information that would suggest the need for further inquiry.

Frequently, the interview will take the form of an informal conversation between the interviewee and one or more members of the due diligence team. It is often prudent to conduct the interviews after the inspection of documents, property, plants, equipment, and other relevant assets so that the team can pursue questions raised by the inspection. It is important for the team to remember that the interview is a voluntary interview, not testimony, a deposition, or other court-ordered action. Nonetheless, complete and accurate representations by interviewees will further the effort to close the transaction and can reduce their employer's exposure to future liability under the transaction agreements.

VIII. COMMON PITFALLS IN DUE DILIGENCE

The most immediate result of poor due diligence is a failure to identify issues and problems that would be material to the client's evaluation of the transaction and that may have prevented substantial financial harm to the client. Inadequate or ineffective due diligence can also constitute a breach of the directors' fiduciary obligations to the company and shareholders to make informed judgments based on complete knowledge of the circumstances surrounding a proposed transaction. In addition, faulty due diligence can result in professional liability for the due diligence team and destroy client relationships.

Common mistakes made during due diligence include:

(1) *Failure to consider due diligence as an important part of the transaction.* It is a serious mistake for any management team to view due diligence as merely a necessary evil that requires little attention. If the chief executive officer treats it as an afterthought, his or her entire team will not take the effort seriously.

(2) *Reducing the scope of due diligence to save transaction costs.* A due diligence review is expensive, especially when complex or novel business operations are involved. While it is the client's prerogative to assume risk, the attorney should be certain he or she does so with as complete an understanding of the potential risk as possible. Cutting corners on due diligence is a real gamble because few attorneys can predict with any reasonable certainty what damages actually exist in a particular enterprise.

(3) *Failure to take adequate notes during the review.* In the effort to review large amounts of material in a short period, reviewers who fail to maintain adequate notes on their work will have great difficulty providing their client with a thorough analysis and due diligence report.

(4) *Failure to train the due diligence team properly.* Due diligence work is often assigned to junior associates, so it is important that the team be properly trained in due diligence generally and in the particular review it will be conducting. The team should also be briefed on the issues it will likely encounter or the questions of particular interest to the client.

(5) *Failure to give the team a good understanding of the entire transaction.* As so much of the due diligence effort depends on the facts and circumstances of the particular transaction, the due diligence team must have a good understanding of the entire transaction. With this understanding, team members will be less likely to miss problems that will be material to the client's ultimate decision on the transaction. The team should receive, therefore, a thorough briefing on the transaction at the outset of the due diligence review and whenever the transaction changes materially during the review.
(6) *Fear or intimidation.* The due diligence team should not be afraid to probe issues and really investigate or to ask questions of interviewees or superiors for fear of appearing uninformed, naïve, or just plain stupid. It is often that "dumb question" that uncovers a critical issue.
(7) *Loss of focus.* Due diligence work can be deadly dull and mind-numbingly tedious. It is easy to lose interest and lose attention to detail, which can undermine the review.
(8) *Loss of objectivity.* A due diligence team is not serving its client's interest if the team just wants to complete the transaction or to find others' mistakes. The team must maintain a clear, objective focus on the purpose of its review and the details of its work to serve the client effectively.

IX. UNDERSTANDING HEALTH CARE ENTITIES AND OPERATIONS

Conducting due diligence in the health care industry requires knowledge of the target organization's business and the laws and regulations applicable to it. To appreciate the implications of an institutional health care provider as a party to the transaction, the due diligence team must understand the provider's key constituencies and how they relate to each other.

If the transaction involves an entity that provides services to a hospital and its medical staff, for example, the team should learn the status of hospital-staff relations in the hospital and review medical staff bylaws and rules that may affect the provision of those services. If the target institution in an acquisition is a hospital sponsored by a religious organization, the team should understand the sponsor's authority over the institution and any issues of particular concern to the sponsor (e.g., the provision of reproductive health services in a Catholic hospital).

In many ways, organizations in the health care industry are similar to business organizations in other industries. They usually have complex labor and employment structures, organizational maintenance requirements, real estate operations, and varied contractual relationships and are subject to local, state, and federal regulations applicable to most businesses.

Some might argue that Sarbanes-Oxley is unlikely to apply to the bulk of health care entities because the majority of health care entities are not reporting companies. Such a view would be shortsighted. While, by its terms, Sarbanes-Oxley applies only to reporting companies, its effects are actually much broader.

In fact, Sarbanes-Oxley has implications on all for-profit entities, whether publicly or privately held, as well as for nonprofit organizations.

Understanding and complying with the provisions of Sarbanes-Oxley is critical for privately held entities where the exit strategy involves a public offering or an acquisition by a publicly held company. Thus, due diligence efforts should demonstrate that a private company is aware of and ready for, if not in compliance with, the provisions of Sarbanes-Oxley. Moreover, potential investors, partners, employees, and other constituents will likely look to Sarbanes-Oxley as a scorecard against which to measure companies that they are investigating.

In the nonprofit context, many leading commentators have suggested that state attorneys general and other regulators will look to Sarbanes-Oxley for guidelines by which to measure the corporate governance of nonprofit entities and their directors.[26] Thus, when partnering with a nonprofit, it will be equally important to investigate the topics covered by Sarbanes-Oxley.

A. Tax-Exempt Status

Notwithstanding their similarities to other types of organizations, health care organizations are unique in many respects. As discussed in X., below, they are subject to laws and regulations designed specifically for health care providers. These organizations also operate a unique business, many in a tax-exempt context. Due diligence team members must understand the unique character of the business of the health care entity the team is examining so that the members can recognize the implications to the transaction of what they observe. Thus, creating a due diligence team that included no experienced health care lawyers to review a hospital or other complex health care provider would invite serious problems.

Depending on the nature of its business, an e-health enterprise may be subject to the same level of government regulation as a traditional health care provider. For example, if one or both of the parties to the transaction are tax exempt under Section 501(c)(3) of the Internal Revenue Code, due diligence must examine the unique requirements applicable to tax-exempt entities to make certain that the transaction will not jeopardize an exemption and that an entity's failure to operate in a manner consistent with the requirements of its exemption will not jeopardize the transaction.

If one party is tax exempt and the other is taxable, the team must exercise special care in due diligence to determine that the structure of the transaction and the relationship between the parties will meet tax-law requirements and avoid loss of exemptions or the imposition of intermediate sanctions. If one or both of the parties to the transaction have issued tax-exempt debt, due diligence

---

[26]*See, e.g.*, Jeff Jones, *N.Y.'s Attorney General Seeking to Apply Sarbanes-Oxley Act*, NON-PROFIT TIMES, Mar. 1, 2003; Richard Larkin, *Sarbanes-Oxley and Nonprofits*, NONPROFIT ALERT (BDO Seidman, LLP), *available at* http://www.bdo.com/about/publications/industry/np_apr_03/article1.asp; OFFICE OF INSPECTOR GEN., U.S. DEP'T OF HEALTH AND HUMAN SERVS., AMERICAN HEALTH LAWYERS ASS'N, CORPORATE RESPONSIBILITY AND CORPORATE COMPLIANCE: A RESOURCE FOR HEALTH CARE BOARDS OF DIRECTORS, *available at* http://www.healthlawyers.org/hiresources/PI/InfoSeries/Documents/OIG_CorpRespCorpCompliance.pdf.

must determine whether the structure of the transaction is consistent with the party's debt documents and the private-use restrictions of the Internal Revenue Code.

B. Accreditation and Certification Issues

If one of the parties to the transaction is an institutional health care provider, its accreditation by the Joint Commission (formerly the Joint Commission on Accreditation of Healthcare Organizations) or another less well known body may be a prerequisite to its participation in the transaction. Due diligence should determine the party's accreditation status. In transactions involving medical education facilities, it is important to consider both health care and educational accreditations. The target company's current and past accreditation status and accrediting body reports will tell the due diligence team a great deal about the target's operations and its ability to meet accreditation standards.

In addition, e-health companies, particularly those involved in the development and sale of EHR products, may be required to be certified under the process developed by ONCHIT and other regulators. Moreover, as the EHR and other HIT markets mature, there may well be other market driven certifications and accreditations. A company's experience with these certifications and accreditations will highlight both the product's value in the marketplace as well as the relevant company's sophistication with the legal and business environment in which it operates.

C. Protected Health Care Information

If a transaction will require access to protected health care information,[27] the due diligence team must determine whether it will need to review some or all of the information, whether applicable law and privacy provisions of HIPAA[28] and the HITECH Act (created under ARRA)[29] will permit the team to access it, and whether the party with custody of such information is equipped to provide it in a form required by the transaction.

The HITECH Act includes, among other things, several amendments to HIPAA's privacy and security provisions. For example, the HITECH Act extends certain HIPAA provisions and penalties to business associates of covered entities. The HITECH Act also includes various security breach notification requirements, such as a requirement that if the unsecured protected health information of more than 500 residents of a state or jurisdiction is, or is reasonably believed to have been, accessed, acquired, or disclosed during a breach, the covered entity must provide notice of such breach to prominent media outlets serv-

---

[27]See generally Chapter 4 (Shapiro & Tector, Privacy, PHRs, and Social Media), Chapter 5 (Dahm, Privacy Issues in U.S. Health Care), Chapter 6 (Taylor & Crawford, The European Data Privacy Regime), and Chapter 8 (Goldberg & Greene, Enforcement of the Health Insurance Portability and Accountability Act of 1996).
[28]Pub. L. No. 104-191, 110 Stat. 1936 (Aug. 21, 1996).
[29]Pub. L. No. 111-05, 123 Stat. 115 (Feb. 17, 2009), §§13001 *et seq.*

ing the state or jurisdiction.[30] Other provisions of the HITECH Act address the minimum necessary standard, accounting for disclosures, the sale of protected health information, marketing, fundraising, electronic health records, personal health records, and HIPAA enforcement.[31] It is important to remember that this is a rapidly changing area of law that should be carefully considered. For example, despite having been adopted over two years earlier, as of October 2011, the breach notification rules remained an interim final rule and there was no clear consensus of when the final rule will be published or precisely what form it will take

Additionally, the states have become increasingly active in data security and notification laws. A number of jurisdictions have begun to enforce the HI-TECH Act. Mississippi became the 46th state (plus D.C., Puerto Rico, and the Virgin Islands) to adopt a breach notification law.[32] As of October 2011, only Alabama, Kentucky, New Mexico, and South Dakota lack such a law.[33]

Massachusetts enacted into law in 2010 a set of comprehensive data security standards.[34] These standards require any entity that maintains information on a Massachusetts resident to implement a written information security program. Given the potentially broad scope of coverage of the Massachusetts law, it requires counsel to determine whether the transaction participants maintain information on Massachusetts residents.

It is recommended that inquiry be made as to whether any material business partner has cyber-risk insurance that covers the cost of a data breach.

D. Health-Planning Approvals

In many states, certain capital expenditures by a health care provider in excess of statutory thresholds will require a permit from the state health-planning agency. If the transaction involves such a capital expenditure, the due diligence review should determine whether the provider has obtained or will be able to obtain the required permit in a timely fashion. Failure to make this determination early in the due diligence process can substantially delay the transaction, because the process for obtaining health-planning approvals in many states can be quite lengthy.

---

[30] ARRA/HITECH, Pub. L. No. 111-05, 123 Stat. 115 (Feb. 17, 2009), §13402; interim final rule, 74 Fed. Reg. 42,740 (Aug. 24, 2009) (codified at 45 C.F.R. pt. 164, subpt. D).

[31] *Id.*

[32] Beasely Allen, *Mississippi Joins Ranks of States With Data Breach Law*, JERE BEASELY REPORT (May 21, 2010), *available at* http://www.jerebeasleyreport.com/2010/05/mississippi-joins-ranks-of-states-with-data-breach-law/.

[33] Kristen J. Matthews, *HHS and FTC Announce New Breach Notification Rules for Unsecured Protected Health Information*, PROSKAUER PRIVACY LAW BLOG (Sept. 29, 2009), *available at* http://privacylaw.proskauer.com/2011/08/articles/security-breach-notification-l/breach-notification-obligations-in-all-50-states/#more; *see also* National Conference of State Legislatures, State Security Breach Notification Laws, *available at* http://www.ncsl.org/IssuesResearch/TelecommunicationsInformationTechnology/SecurityBreachNotificationLaws/tabid/13489/Default.aspx.

[34] McDonald Hopkins LLC, New Massachusetts Data Security Laws Go Into Effect March 1, 2010, *available at* http://www.mcdonaldhopkins.com/alerts/alert.aspx?id=IZDsDSmLskmRQc5bbncFBg.

E. Conditions for Reimbursement

If the transaction will affect a party's Medicare or Medicaid reimbursement, or if a party's reimbursement will affect its ability to participate in the transaction, the due diligence review should determine whether the party's past reimbursement is subject to future adjustment or offset and whether the structure of the transaction will be consistent with applicable reimbursement law.

F. Research or Grant Considerations

If the transaction involves a party that engages in medical research and/or an entity that intends to provide a good or service related to that research, the review should include an examination of the party's research administration to determine, among other things, whether it complies with applicable federal regulations governing research with human subjects and research grant administration.

If one party to the transaction is a Hill-Burton grant recipient and if use of facilities funded by such grants is relevant to the transaction, the review should determine whether the terms of the party's grants permit the intended future use and whether the party has complied with its grants, so as to avoid the often cumbersome involvement of the U.S. Department of Housing and Urban Development.

G. Obligations to Provide Notice

Health care providers must give notice to a variety of regulatory and other organizations in connection with changes to their operations and the ownership of their assets. The due diligence team should determine what notices will be required of any provider party in the transaction and include appropriate covenants in the transaction agreements.

X. LAWS AND REGULATIONS SPECIFIC TO THE HEALTH CARE INDUSTRY

Clearly, conducting due diligence in the health care industry requires knowledge of the laws and regulations applicable to the target health care organization. The health care industry is one of the country's most heavily regulated industries. Given this regulatory scheme, the due diligence team will simply be unable to conduct meaningful due diligence unless it has the expertise necessary to understand how the regulatory environment will affect the parties to the transaction. Again, trying to conduct due diligence without attorneys and other professionals experienced in the health care industry will create substantial risk that the effort will fail to identify issues of major importance to the client in the transaction.

The regulatory environment in which health industry organizations operate is extremely fluid. The rules change regularly and often in ways that defy logic. It is critical, therefore, that the due diligence team be experienced and current. Moreover, depending on the nature of the organization and its business, one set of regulations may be more important than another. For example, the regulations governing Medicare billing will be a major due diligence consideration for a company that provides billing services for a hospital, whereas the state professional licensure law may be more important in an acquisition of a nurse-midwifery practice. For almost all health industry organizations, however, the following regulatory issues will be important:

(1) *Medicare fraud and abuse law.* Any transaction that involves a flow of referrals for health care goods or services paid for by state or federal health care reimbursement programs may put the entity at risk of sanctions provided by statute and regulation.

(2) *Stark self-referral restrictions.* Any transaction that involves an ownership interest by a physician in a business that provides a health care service covered by the Stark law[35] and its attendant regulations may create risk of sanctions.

(3) *HIPAA.* The Health Insurance Portability and Accountability Act of 1996[36] is a sweeping regulatory scheme, the administrative simplification requirements of which affect any protected health information transmitted electronically by an entity covered by the law. Failure to comply with these requirements will subject an entity to sanctions.

(4) *Licensure.* Most health care providers are required to have a license to operate. Many state licensure laws affect the extent to which hospitals, physicians, and other health care practitioners may engage in the practice of their profession or the provision of health care that requires the use of telecommunications to send information across state lines. If the transaction involves telemedicine, due diligence should determine whether the parties will be properly licensed to proceed with the operations as proposed.

(5) *Tax law.* Most institutional health care providers are exempt from federal income taxation under Section 501(c)(3) of the Internal Revenue Code, and as such are subject to comprehensive, complex regulations, compliance with which is closely scrutinized by the Internal Revenue Service. These regulations govern virtually every relationship a tax-exempt organization has with any person or other taxable entity.

In most other areas of regulation commonly found in business enterprises, provisions exist that are uniquely applicable to the health care industry. For example, due diligence for a hospital in the environmental law area would require an understanding of the regulations governing disposal of medical waste.

---

[35]42 U.S.C §1395nn.
[36]Pub. L. No. 104-191, 110 Stat. 1936 (1996).

The HITECH Act is discussed in more detail in other areas of this book.[37] For purposes of due diligence, however, it is important for the due diligence team to be aware of the increased scope and enforcement authority and penalties under HIPAA resulting from the HITECH Act. For example, many of a company's HIPAA privacy and security policies and procedures may need to be amended to reflect the new HITECH Act requirements.

Companies also need to adopt policies with respect to detecting breaches of unsecured PHI, conducting a risk assessment regarding such breaches, including potential liability exposure for past and future breaches and breach notification obligations to individuals, the Secretary of HHS, and the media. Covered entities should update their business associate agreements and take steps to ensure that their business associates are in compliance with the HIPAA Privacy and Security Rules.

The health care industry is rapidly converting from paper medical records to electronic health records (EHR). Several local, state, and federal government and privately sponsored EHR and other e-health projects are currently under way, including the formation of community health records and health data networks designed to provide a single record for each citizen in the community that can be accessed electronically by the patient and any authorized health care provider. With the growth of EHR systems and networks has come an increased need to focus on the security and privacy of individually identifiable health information used in e-health-related enterprises.

The due diligence investigation with regard to HIPAA compliance should be given more than a cursory examination. While the HHS Office of Civil Rights—the HIPAA enforcement agency—has taken a benign approach to enforcement, it is inevitable that the government in time will become more aggressive in its imposition of civil money penalties and criminal sanctions as its expectations for compliance and internal pressures to generate revenues increase. It is important, therefore, for any e-health industry participant to understand fully the processes and procedures used by the target or partner entity to ensure compliance with the privacy and security requirements. Questions that must be answered include:

- Is the entity in question a covered entity?
- If a covered entity, has it complied with the Privacy Rule, the Security Rule, the Provider Identifier Rule, and the Transactions and Code Set Rule?
- If a covered entity, does it have business associates with appropriate agreements in place?
- If not a covered entity, is the entity in question a business associate to a covered entity?
- If not a covered entity, has it complied with applicable state privacy and security laws?

---

[37] See generally Chapter 7 (Christiansen, Information Security and Security Breach Notification Under HIPAA and HITECH); Chapter 8 (Goldberg & Greene, Enforcement of the Health Insurance Portability and Accountability Act of 1996).

The definition and defining characteristics of a covered entity are discussed elsewhere in this book.[38] In performing due diligence on a covered entity, however, the investigator should look, at a minimum, for the following:

- designation of a privacy officer and a security officer;
- notice of privacy practices, and distribution of and acknowledgment of receipt of such notice;
- policies and procedures addressing use and/or disclosure of protected health information in the following circumstances, if applicable:
  ○ permitted uses and disclosures of health information;
  ○ uses and disclosures of health information requiring an authorization;
  ○ uses and disclosures of health information for marketing;
  ○ uses and disclosures of health information for fundraising;
  ○ disclosures of health information for certain public health activities;
  ○ disclosures of health information for certain health oversight activities;
  ○ disclosures of health information required by law;
  ○ disclosures of health information for law enforcement purposes;
  ○ disclosures of health information pursuant to legal proceedings;
  ○ disclosures of health information where there is a serious threat to health or safety;
  ○ disclosures of health information for workers' compensation purposes;
  ○ disclosures of health information for military or national security purposes;
  ○ disclosures of health information to family, friends, and personal representatives;
  ○ availability of health information in a disaster;
  ○ reasonable safeguards to protect the confidentiality of health information;
  ○ disclosure of health information minimally necessary to accomplish the purpose of the disclosure;
  ○ business associates;
  ○ limited data sets and data use agreements;
  ○ rights of patients to access health information;
  ○ rights of patients to request amendments to health information;
  ○ rights of patients to an accounting of disclosures;
  ○ rights of patients to request restrictions on uses and disclosures of their health information;
  ○ rights of patients to alternative communications;
  ○ maintenance of HIPAA-required documentation;
  ○ workforce training;
  ○ internal enforcement of privacy requirements;
  ○ privacy violations committed by business associates;
  ○ government enforcement; and
  ○ privacy complaints; and

---

[38] See Appendix D, HIPAA Glossary.

- participation in an affiliated covered entity or an organized health care arrangement with appropriate documentation and coordinated policies and procedures.

Covered entities must do the following:

- Conduct health information security assessments as needed to determine the risks to the privacy and security of protected health information.
- Ensure the confidentiality, integrity, and availability of all electronic protected health information (ePHI) the covered entity creates, receives, maintains, or transmits.
- Protect against any reasonably anticipated threats or hazards to the security or integrity of ePHI.
- Protect against any reasonably anticipated uses or disclosures of ePHI that are not permitted or required.
- Adopt policies and procedures addressing implementation of the following administrative, physical, and technical safeguards:
  - prevent, detect, contain, and correct security violations;
  - ensure that all members of its workforce have appropriate access to ePHI, and prevent those workforce members who do not have appropriate access from obtaining access to ePHI;
  - authorize access to ePHI;
  - security awareness and training program for all members of its workforce (including management);
  - address security incidents;
  - response to an emergency or other occurrence (e.g., fire, vandalism, system failure, and natural disaster) that damages systems that contain ePHI;
  - periodic technical and nontechnical evaluation, based initially upon the standards implemented under this rule and subsequently in response to environmental or operational changes affecting the security of ePHI, that establishes the extent to which an entity's security policies and procedures are effective;
  - require a business associate who creates, receives, maintains, or transmits ePHI on the covered entity's behalf to do so only if the covered entity obtains satisfactory assurances that the business associate will appropriately safeguard the information;
  - limit physical access to its electronic information systems and the facility or facilities in which they are housed, while ensuring that properly authorized access is allowed;
  - specify the proper functions to be performed, the manner in which those functions are to be performed, and the physical attributes of the surroundings of a specific workstation or class of workstation that can access ePHI;
  - govern the receipt and removal of hardware and electronic media that contain ePHI into and out of a facility, and the movement of these items within the facility;

- for electronic information systems that maintain ePHI, allow access only to those persons or software programs that have been granted access rights;
- implement hardware, software, and/or procedural mechanisms that record and examine activity in information systems that contain or use ePHI;
- protect ePHI from improper alteration or destruction; and
- guard against unauthorized access to ePHI that is being transmitted over an electronic communications network.

If the target organization participates in a health data network, the due diligence inquiry should include a determination of the importance to the target's enterprise of its participation in the network. It should also include a review of the contracts between the network participants to determine, among other things:

- what rights and obligations the target has with respect to health information critical to the target's business;
- whether the target has responsibility for the operation of the network;
- who the other network participants are and what rights they have to the health information in the network;
- what cross licenses, if any, are in place for the intellectual property used by the network, particularly if the target has contributed intellectual property to the network;
- how the network is governed and managed day to day;
- what items of service the target provides and to whom;
- the role of vendors in the network;
- how existing network participants are removed from and new participants are added to the network;
- whether appropriate business associate agreements are in place, if needed; and
- what warranties, limitations on liability, and disclaimers are in place to protect the target.

The specific terms of the network participation and vendor agreements supporting a health data network or community EHR system will depend upon the type of network involved.

Due diligence should also include consideration of whether the network has dealt appropriately with applicable regulatory issues, such as the anti-kickback provisions of the Social Security Act, the Stark law anti-self-referral requirements, antitrust concerns for participating competitors, and the requirements of the Internal Revenue Code for tax-exempt organizations. How the network has prepared for possible professional liability actions will be an important inquiry if the target is a health care or services provider.

The level of importance of the network to the target's business should dictate the extent to which due diligence investigators focus on the network's infrastructure and operation.

XI. Conclusion

E-health businesses combine components found in a triad of commercial enterprises—traditional business models, specialized health industry operations, and e-commerce Web-based endeavors. Adequate due diligence in the financing, merger, or acquisition of an e-health business requires, on a fundamental level, the same disciplined, systematic approach required in traditional business transactions. It also requires new areas of inquiry unique to the e-health industry. E-health businesses require a more thorough and detailed understanding of the aspects unique to the health care community, such as privacy and security requirements, that may not be a factor in a typical commercial transaction. In addition, many e-health businesses are for-profit entities whose investors have an ultimate exit strategy that involves becoming, or combining with, a public reporting company. In these contexts, diligence on compliance with Sarbanes-Oxley may be as critical as any other area of investigation. Where a reporting company is not involved or likely to become involved in the future, e-health companies and their due diligence investigators should expect that outsiders will still judge the target company against the standards of Sarbanes-Oxley.

Identifying these areas and including individuals who are familiar with them on the due diligence team will enable that team to gain a full understanding of the target business and improve the client's ability to make informed and effective decisions concerning its willingness to complete the transaction. That process, in turn, can also lead to more efficient and effective documentation of the transaction.

13

Contracts in the Digital Age: Adapting to Changing Times*

I.	Introduction	378
II.	Jurisdiction	380
III.	The Relevant Statutes and Principles of Contract Law	385
	A. Electronic Signatures in Global and National Commerce Act (E-SIGN)	386
	B. Uniform Electronic Transactions Act (UETA)	389
	C. Uniform Computer Information Transactions Act (UCITA)	394
IV.	Litigation: Courts Coping With a New Means of Contracting	398
	A. Browse Wrap Agreements	400
	B. Click Wrap Agreements	403
	C. Shrink Wrap Agreements	405
	D. Common Principles	408
V.	HIPAA/HITECH Business Associate Agreements	408
	A. Introduction	408
	B. Statutory and Regulatory Requirements	410
	1. Business Associate	410
	2. HITECH Mandated Changes to Privacy Rule	413
	a. Minimum Necessary	414
	b. Logging and Auditing	415
	c. Restricted Disclosures	415
	d. Fundraising and Marketing	416
	e. Access to Patient Record	418
	f. Role of State Law	418
	3. HITECH Mandated Changes to Security Rule	418
	a. Administrative Safeguards	419
	b. Physical Safeguards	419
	c. Technical Safeguards	419

---

*Arthur E. Peabody, Jr., Lead Medicare Counsel, Blue Cross Blue Shield Association, Washington, D.C.

d.	Breach Reporting Requirement	420
e.	Additional Responsibilities	423
f.	Monetary Penalties	423
VI. Conclusion		424

I. Introduction

It is estimated that 79 percent of all adult Americans—or 239.2 million citizens—use the Internet daily.[1] The sale of all kinds of personal computers continues to soar, notwithstanding the economic downturn. In the first quarter of 2010 alone, Intel, the world's largest chip maker for personal computers, reported $10.3 billion in sales.[2] Sales of software rose to $244 billion in 2010.[3] Of the many millions of people surfing the Internet daily, 79 percent have purchased a product online.[4] The United States Census Bureau's statistics reflect that there were $65.8 billion in drugs, health aids, and beauty-related products purchased in 2008; nearly nine percent of these purchases occurred over the Internet or through "e-commerce."[5] In other recent statistics, it is estimated that at least 18.3 million adults have purchased a health-related item online.[6] It is expected that the Internet sale of health-related products will continue to grow as Americans continue to use the Internet as a source for medical information, their own health records, and health-related products.[7]

The health care insurance industry has also expanded its marketing and other activities to the Internet, and applicants for health insurance can now apply online. Increasingly, health plans use the Internet to enable prospective enrollees to obtain "quotes" for health insurance coverage and, once enrolled, to reach out to patients directly with tips for staying healthy and keeping costs down. Additionally, health plans help health care providers acquire technol-

---

[1] PLUNKETT'S E-COMMERCE & INTERNET BUSINESS ALMANAC 2011: E-COMMERCE & INTERNET BUSINESS INDUSTRY MARKET RESEARCH, STATISTICS, TRENDS & LEADING COMPANIES (Feb. 2, 2011), *available at* http://www.plunkettresearch.com (report available for purchase).

[2] A. Vance, *PC Sales Are on Course for Big Increase in 2010*, NEW YORK TIMES, April 14, 2010, at B3.

[3] GARTNER, 2010 REVENUE AND MARKET SHARE STATISTICS, *cited in* K. Finley, *Enterprise Software Sales Rebounded in 2010*, READWRITEWEB (May 6, 2011), *available at* http://www.readwriteweb.com/enterprise/2011/05/enterprise-software-sales-rebo.php.

[4] *Id.*

[5] U.S. CENSUS BUREAU, STATISTICAL ABSTRACT OF THE UNITED STATES: 2011, Table 1055.

[6] K. Peters, *Health Care e-Commerce is Nothing to Sneeze At*, INTERNET RETAILER (Feb. 28, 2007), *available at* http://www.internetretailer.com/2007/02/28/health-care-e-commerce-is-nothing-to-sneeze-at.

[7] The e-commerce market for health care encompasses a large range of products: pharmaceuticals, vitamins, vision care, beauty items, and medical supplies, including durable medical equipment. For example, Drugstore.com reported earnings of $224.8 million for the period ending June 2009. To capture individuals with varied interests, it has established six new "niche" Web sites, ranging from sites offering advice and medications for allergies to "AtHisBest.com." In the words of Tracy Wright, chief financial officer, "[w]e want to be everywhere they want to be." *See* B. Briggs, *Drugstore.com Looks to Niche Sites for Growth*, INTERNET RETAILER (Sept. 22, 2010), *available at* http://www.internetretailer.com/2010/09/22/drugstorecoms-growth-plan-includes-more-microsites.

ogy and use information collected by that technology to afford better care to patients. President Obama has repeatedly enunciated a national goal that all Americans have an electronic medical record by 2014. The federal government is implementing a massive program costing many millions of dollars, including incentives to hospitals and physicians for the adoption of electronic medical records, to bring our nation's medical care delivery system into the twenty-first century. A national health information exchange is in the offing. Likewise, an insurance exchange is planned for those citizens unable to obtain health insurance otherwise. In these and many other ways, contracts will be implicated, whether they are made between entities represented by persons in face-to-face encounters, between a person and a computer, or just between machines without the involvement of any human being.

Our legal institutions have had to respond to changes brought about by the ever-increasing use of the Internet to do business, including the making of contracts. More specifically, the law of contracts has had to be made compatible with the digital age where contracts can ostensibly be made by pushing a button on a computer, exchanging e-mails, or simply engaging in conduct that suggests the parties have had a meeting of the minds—even when there is no formally executed, signed, and dated document labeled as a contract.

Finally, contracts that may or may not be entered into over the Internet remain of significance to all entities engaged in the health care industry. As technology continues to grow and the use of electronic means of exchanging the health care information of individual citizens becomes more commonplace, means of protecting the security of this information—and the privacy of patients—can only become more critical to the success of using technology to improve care and reduce burgeoning health care costs. In this vein, business associate agreements required of health entities supporting health care providers and others possessing individual health care information in electronic media are essential to meeting the requirements of the Health Information Technology for Economic and Clinical Health Act (HITECH Act)[8] and the mandates of the Health Insurance Portability and Accountability Act (HIPAA).[9]

In sum, this chapter addresses the evolving law of contracts as we enter the digital age, including associated common law doctrines, jurisdiction, the relevant federal statutes, and developments in the decisional law that aid in understanding the changes in traditional contract law that both the legislative and judicial branches of government have made to accommodate the use of the Internet as a daily instrument of commerce. In addition, it examines the topic of business associate contracts in light of the recent regulatory changes made to HIPAA to meet the ranging mandates of the HITECH Act, all intended to protect the privacy of users as personal identifiable information enters cyberspace at an ever-increasing rate.

---

[8] Pub. L. No. 111-5, §§13001-424, 123 Stat. 226 (2009).
[9] Pub. L. No. 104-191, 110 Stat. 1936 (1996).

II. JURISDICTION

The power of a court to assert authority over a business entity has changed with the changing times. In departing from traditional principles, the Supreme Court[10] has reflected that "it is an inescapable fact of modern commercial life that a substantial amount of commercial business is transacted solely by mail and wire communications across state lines, thus obviating the need for physical presence within a State in which business is conducted." As the use of the Internet has changed the ability of businesses to provide information and products to consumers and other business entities, the law of personal jurisdiction based on Internet use has grown and developed, with courts struggling to identify a uniform approach.[11] Personal jurisdiction is not easy to discern in the context of the Internet. Most courts have found traditional notions of personal jurisdiction unsatisfactory; others have found that traditional concepts fit neatly into cyberspace. Most lawyers remember first-year procedure when jurisdictional concepts are explored, including state long-arm statutes that allow courts to exercise jurisdiction over "out of state" defendants where the defendant has maintained "minimum contacts" with the state such that the minimal requirements of due process can be satisfied.[12]

The cases and commentators generally agree that "the likelihood that personal jurisdiction can be constitutionally exercised is directly proportionate to the nature and quality of commercial activity that an entity conducts over the Internet."[13] Most courts have utilized a "sliding scale" to evaluate the commercial activity the entity engages in over the Internet.[14] In *Zippo Manufacturing Co. v. Zippo Dot Com, Inc.*,[15] a federal district court first developed the sliding scale analysis, and the case continues to be widely cited for the enunciated proposition. In developing its analysis, the *Zippo* court relied heavily on an earlier Sixth Circuit case, *CompuServe v. Patterson*,[16] extending the doctrine that where an entity intentionally reaches beyond its boundaries to conduct business with foreign residents over the Internet, jurisdiction ensues. The sliding scale of *Zippo*, however, is not without its critics. Some courts have found more traditional notions of personal jurisdiction to be more than satisfactory to address the issue of personal jurisdiction in the context of e-commerce.

---

[10] Zippo Mfg. Co. v. Zippo Dot Com, Inc., 952 F. Supp. 1119 (W.D. Pa. 1997) (quoting Burger King Corp. v. Rudzewicz, 471 U.S. 462, 476 (1985)).

[11] Personal jurisdiction can be either general or specific. General jurisdiction exists when a nonresident defendant engages in "systematic and continuous" activities in the forum state, whether or not those activities are related to the particular cause of action. Specific jurisdiction exists when a defendant engages in purposeful activity with the forum, and the claims asserted in the litigation arise from these activities. See Helicopteros Nacionales de Colombia v. Hall, 466 U.S. 408, 414–16 (1984); Burger King v. Rudzewicz, 471 U.S. 462, 472–73 (1985). It is generally accepted that general jurisdiction over "out of state" defendants is more difficult to establish than specific jurisdiction.

[12] International Shoe Co. v. Washington, 326 U.S. 310, 316 (1945).

[13] *Zippo*, 952 F. Supp. at 1124.

[14] *Id.*

[15] *Id.*

[16] 89 F.3d 1257 at 1260 (6th Cir. 1996); *Zippo*, 952 F. Supp. at 1126.

Some circuits have embraced the sliding scale analysis initially announced in *Zippo*.[17] Other circuits have adopted the sliding scale of interactivity as one factor among others to define the more traditional "purposeful availment"[18] factor.[19]

Where the *Zippo* model has not been expressly adopted, some circuits, including the Federal Circuit, nevertheless have used the distinction between active, passive, and interactive Web sites as one factor, among others, to determine the appropriateness of personal jurisdiction over a defendant.[20] While many circuits have adhered to the sliding scale analysis, some have opted for

---

[17] *See* Toys "R" Us v. Step Two, 318 F.3d 446, 452 (3d Cir. 2003) (recognizing the *Zippo* case as a "seminal authority regarding personal jurisdiction based upon the operation of an Internet web site"); Mink v. AAAA Dev., 190 F.3d 333, 336 (5th Cir.1999) (adopting the sliding scale analysis to assess *general* jurisdiction, even though the Fifth Circuit later recognized that the *Zippo* analysis is not always "well adapted to the general jurisdiction inquiry"); Revell v. Lidov, 317 F.3d 467, 471 (5th Cir. 2002); Cybersell, Inc. v. Cybersell, 130 F.3d 414, 419 (9th Cir. 1997) (finding that "the common thread, well stated by the district court in *Zippo,* is that 'the likelihood that personal jurisdiction can be constitutionally exercised is directly proportionate to the nature and quality of commercial activity that an entity conducts over the Internet'").

[18] "Availment" is commonly defined in terms of benefiting from the laws of the forum. "The purposeful availment inquiry ... focuses on the defendant's intentionality. This prong is only satisfied when the defendant purposefully and voluntarily directs his activities toward the forum so that he should expect, by virtue of the benefit he receives, to be subject to the court's jurisdiction based on [contacts with the forum]." United States v. Swiss Am. Bank, 274 F.3d 610, 623–24 (1st Cir. 2001).

[19] *See* ALS Scan. v. Digital Serv. Consultants, 293 F.3d 707, 714 (4th Cir. 2002) (adopting and adapting the sliding scale analysis); Neogen v. Neo Gen Screening, 282 F.3d 883, 890 (6th Cir. 2002); Lakin v. Prudential Sec., 348 F.3d 704, 711 (8th Cir. 2003) (holding that the "*Zippo* model is an appropriate approach in cases of specific jurisdiction"); *see also* Oldfield v. Pueblo De Bahia Lora, 558 F.3d 1210, 1220 (11th Cir. 2009) (critical of the *Zippo* case; the court declined to express any firm opinion as to its applicability); Roblor Mktg. Group v. GPS Indus., 645 F. Supp. 2d 1130 (S.D. Fla. 2009) (finding the sliding scale a useful guidepost but not dispositive and adopting the "purposeful availment requirement under a more traditional approach").

[20] *See* Cossaboon v. Maine Med. Ctr., 600 F.3d 25 (1st Cir. 2010) (although it has these interactive features, MMC's Web site does not sell or render services online; instead, the site is primarily informational and discusses the health care services provided at MMC's facility in Maine); McBee v. Delica Co., 417 F.3d 107, 124 (1st Cir. 2005) ("[T]he mere existence of a website that is visible in a forum and that gives information about a company and its products is not enough, by itself, to subject a defendant to personal jurisdiction in that forum.... Something more is necessary, such as interactive features which allow the successful online ordering of the defendant's products."); Jennings v. AC Hydraulic, 383 F.3d 546, 549–50 (7th Cir. 2004) (holding that "[p]remising personal jurisdiction on the maintenance of a website, without requiring some level of 'interactivity' between the defendant and consumers in the forum state, would create almost universal personal jurisdiction because of the virtually unlimited accessibility of websites across the country"); Soma Med. Intern. v. Standard Chartered Bank, 196 F.3d 1292, 1296 (10th Cir. 1999) (drawing the distinction between active, passive, and interactive Web sites to assess general jurisdiction); Trintec Indus. v. Pedre Promotional Prods., 395 F.3d 1275, 1281 (Fed. Cir. 2005) ("Although [plaintiff] has shown that [defendant]'s Web sites contain some interactive features aimed at transacting business, it is unclear how frequently those features are utilized or, indeed, whether any District residents have ever actually used [defendant]'s Web site to transact business").

a more restrictive reading of the *Zippo* case.[21] Finally, several circuits disfavor the use of the sliding scale analysis altogether to assess personal jurisdiction.[22]

When a Web site is interactive, the exercise of jurisdiction is determined by examining (1) "the level of interactivity" and (2) "the commercial nature of the exchange of information that occurs on the Web site."[23] It is a fact-bound analysis. The "sliding scale" has generally been defined by its opposites. In *Zippo*, the court found the sliding scale consistent with what it perceived as "well developed personal jurisdiction principles."[24]

> At one end of the spectrum are situations where a defendant clearly does business over the Internet. If a defendant enters into contracts with residents of the foreign jurisdiction that involve the knowing and repeated transmission of computer files over the Internet, personal jurisdiction is proper. At the opposite end are situations where a defendant has simply posted information on the Internet Web Site which is accessible to users in foreign jurisdictions. A passive Web site that does little more than make information available to those interested in it is not grounds for the exercise of personal jurisdiction.... The middle ground is occupied by interactive web sites where the user can exchange information with the host computer. In these cases, the exercise of jurisdiction is determined by examining the level of interactivity and commercial nature of the exchange of information that occurs on the Web site.[25]

A passive Web site that does little more than make information available to those interested in its subject matter is not the proper basis for the exercise of personal jurisdiction.[26] For example, the simple placement of advertising on a Web site is generally insufficient to establish jurisdiction over a nonresident.[27]

---

[21] *See* Best Van Lines v. Walker, 490 F.3d 239, 252 (2d Cir. 2007) (holding that while the sliding scale analysis may "help frame the jurisdictional inquiry in some cases ... 'it does not amount to a separate framework for analyzing internet-based jurisdiction.' ... Instead, 'traditional statutory and constitutional principles remain the touchstone of the inquiry' ... As the *Zippo* court itself noted, personal jurisdiction analysis applies traditional principles to new situations.").

[22] *See* State of Illinois v. Hemi Group, 622 F.3d 754, 759 (7th Cir. 2010) ("We reach the same conclusion here. *Zippo*'s sliding scale was always just short-hand for determining whether a defendant had established sufficient minimum contacts with a forum to justify exercising personal jurisdiction over him in the forum state. But we think that the traditional due process inquiry described earlier is not so difficult to apply to cases involving Internet contacts that courts need some sort of easier-to-apply categorical test."); Gorman v. Ameritrade Holding Corp., 293 F.3d 506, 510–511 (D.C. Cir. 2002) (opting for the traditional notions of personal jurisdiction when assessing general jurisdiction on the ground that "'Cyberspace' ... is not some mystical incantation capable of warding off the jurisdiction of courts built from bricks and mortar. Just as our traditional notions of personal jurisdiction have proven adaptable to other changes in the national economy, so too are they adaptable to the transformations wrought by the Internet"); *Trintec*, 395 F.3d 1275 (briefly discussing but not adopting *Zippo* standard).

[23] Zippo Mfg. Co. v. Zippo Dot Com, Inc., 952 F. Supp. 1119, 1124–25 (W.D. Pa. 1997).

[24] *Id.*

[25] *Id.* at 1123.

[26] *Id.* at 1124–25; CareFirst of Md. v. CareFirst Pregnancy Ctrs., 334 F.3d 390 (4th Cir. 2004).

[27] High Country Investor v. McAdams, 221 F. Supp. 2d 99 (D. Mass. 2002); Weinstein v. Todd Marine Enterprises, Inc., 115 F. Supp. 2d 668 (E.D. Va. 2000) (no jurisdiction based on placement of Internet classified advertisements that were not interactive); Desktop Technologies, Inc. v. Colorworks Reproduction & Design, Inc., 1999 WL 98572 (E.D. Pa. 1999); Mid City Bowling Lanes & Sports Palace, Inc. v. Invercrest, Inc., 35 F. Supp. 2d 507 (E.D. La. 1999); Patriot Systems, Inc. v. C-Cubed Corp., 21 F. Supp. 2d 1318 (D. Utah 1998); SF Hotel Company v. Energy Investments, 985 F. Supp. 1032 (D. Kan. 1997); Weber v. Jolly Hotels, 977 F. Supp. 327 (D.N.J. 1997); Bensusan Restaurant Corp. v. King, 937 F. Supp. 295 (S.D.N.Y. 1996).

The creation or maintenance of a Web site does not confer jurisdiction.[28] Courts often cite the failure of the Web site to offer items for sale, provide files or programs for downloading, afford links to other Web sites, and the failure of the Web site to have interactive features or to aim marketing activities to a particular jurisdiction as factors militating against exercise of personal jurisdiction over a nonresident.[29]

In the middle of the scale are situations where a defendant operates an interactive Web site, allowing a user to exchange information with the host computer. In such a case, the exercise of jurisdiction is determined by examining the level of interactivity and the commercial nature of the exchange of information that occurs on the site.[30] Courts have reached differing conclusions with respect to those cases falling into the middle "interactive" category. Some courts have declined to assert personal jurisdiction over the defendant based solely on the defendant's interactive Web site.[31] However, some courts have found that an interactive Web site alone is sufficient to establish minimum contacts.[32] Others have found minimum contacts through additional non-Internet activity in the forum, regardless of whether the activity is related to the underlying claim.[33] Finally, some courts have required additional conduct in the forum that is related to the plaintiff's cause of action.[34]

While many courts have utilized the *Zippo* test in one form or another, the approach is not without its critics.[35] Some see a trend back to the application of more traditional personal jurisdiction analysis. As the Eleventh Circuit noted in *Oldfield v. Pueblo De Bahia Lora*,[36] *Zippo*'s interactivity litmus test is inconsistent with traditional due process analysis because it excludes all "passive" Web sites from supporting personal jurisdiction, even though the level of interactivity

---

[28]Hearst v. Goldberger, 1997 WL 97097 (S.D.N.Y. 1997); *In re* Magnetic Audiotape Antitrust Litigation, 171 F. Supp. 2d 179 (S.D.N.Y. 2001) (foreign parent's noninteractive Web site was insufficient basis for personal jurisdiction); CEM v. Personal Chemistry AB, 192 F. Supp. 2d 438 (W.D.N.C. 2002); Bird v. Parsons, 289 F.3d 865 (6th Cir. 2002); Haas v. Four Seasons Campground, 952 A.2d 688 (Pa. Super. 2008).

[29]American Homecare Fed'n v. Paragon Scientific, 27 F. Supp. 2d 109 (D. Conn. 1998); K.C.P.L. v. Nash, 1998 WL 823657 (S.D.N.Y. 1998); Hinners v. Robery, 336 S.W.3d 891 (Ky. 2011).

[30]Hitachi v. Cain, 106 S.W.3d 776 (Tex. App. 2003); Fenn v. Mleads Enters., 137 P.3d 706 (Utah 2006).

[31]Edberg v. Neogen, 17 F. Supp. 2d 104 (D. Conn. 1998).

[32]GTE New Media Servs. v. Ameritech, 21 F. Supp. 2d 27 (D.D.C. 1998); Caldwell v. Cheapcaribbean.com, 2010 U.S. Dist. LEXIS 93200 (E.D. Mich. Sept. 8, 2010).

[33]Mieczkowski v. Masco, 997 F. Supp. 782 (E.D. Tex. 1998); *see also* Neogen v. Neo Gen Screening, 282 F.3d 883 (6th Cir. 2002); McCluskey v. Bedford High Sch., 2010 WL 5525153 (E.D. Mich. Dec. 30, 2010).

[34]Parks Inns Int'l v. Pacific Plaza Hotels, 5 F. Supp. 2d 762 (D. Ariz. 1998); Tadayon v. Saucon Indus., 2011 WL 1770172 (D. Md. May 9, 2011); State of Ill. v. Hemi Group, 622 F.3d 754 (7th Cir. 2010); Roser v. Jackson & Perkins, 2010 WL 4823074 (N.D. Ill. Nov. 15, 2010); VGM Fin. Servs. v. Singh, 708 F. Supp. 2d 822 (N.D. Iowa 2010); Henning v. Suarez, 713 F. Supp. 2d 459 (E.D. Pa. 2010); JDA Health Sys. v. Chapin Revenue Cycle Mgmt., 2011 WL 2518938 (N.D. Ill. June 23, 2011).

[35]P. Mehrotra, *Back to the Basics: Why Traditional Principles of Personal Jurisdiction are Effective Today and Why Zippo Needs to Go*, 12 N.C. J. L. & TECH. 229 (2010); C. Rhoades, *Rethinking Personal Jurisdiction over the World Wide Web*, 52 THE ADVOC. (TEX.) 53 (2010).

[36]558 F.3d 1210, 1220 (11th Cir. 2009).

is of minimal significance with respect to whether a defendant has directed the Web site toward the forum.

Rather than utilizing such an artificial approach, at least one commentator has suggested that courts should simply apply traditional analysis, looking to whether (1) the defendant directed the Internet activity into the state, (2) the Internet contact gave rise to the cause of action, and (3) the exercise of jurisdiction is constitutionally reasonable.[37] Another commentator, although arguing that the traditional personal jurisdiction approach should yield in the Internet context, has noted that *Zippo*'s interactivity model is somewhat unpredictable and should be modified to preserve the constitutionally required "foreseeability" and "fairness" principles.[38] Under this approach, a finding that the Web site was highly interactive for purposes of *Zippo* would only give rise to a presumption of purposeful availment, allowing a defendant to proffer evidence that it was not purposefully targeting the forum, thereby defeating personal jurisdiction sought by the plaintiff over the nonresident.

More recently, some courts have applied a test that captures both the concepts articulated in *Zippo* and those by the Supreme Court in *Calder v. Jones*,[39] establishing an "effect test standard" in the non-Internet area, a notion approximating that advocated by the commentators referenced above. These courts have analyzed whether the Web site through its operation targeted individuals or companies outside its own jurisdiction. If so, some courts have utilized this ground as a basis for asserting personal jurisdiction over nonresident parties in the targeted state—or to deny jurisdiction where the Web site was engaged in business but did not target the particular jurisdiction where jurisdiction is sought.

In *Henning v. Suarez*,[40] the court examined in detail all the contacts the defendant had in Pennsylvania: 1.5 percent of total sales in five years; sales not central to defendant's business; small percentage of advertising dollars; little use of distributors; Web site did not "target" Pennsylvania for sales. Following this analysis of the facts, the court found that the defendant entity had insufficient continuous contacts to justify general jurisdiction, because none of its activities were specifically calculated to attract Pennsylvania customers. Likewise, in *Annie Oakley Enterprises v. Sunset Tan Corporate and Consulting*,[41] the federal district court in Indiana failed to exercise jurisdiction due to the small number of sales in Indiana and its finding that the Web site did not target Indiana residents.

---

[37] *Id.* (citing B. Spencer, *Jurisdiction and the Internet: Returning to Traditional Principles to Analyze Network-Mediated Contacts,* 2006 U. ILL. L. REV. 71, 86–103 (2006)).

[38] *See id.* (discussion of commentators).

[39] 465 U.S. 783 (1984). Under the effects test enunciated by the Court, specific jurisdiction may be established by showing the defendants "purposeful availment" of the benefits of the laws of the forum and harm to the individual within the forum where the harm is both intentional and aimed at the forum. Watchdog v. Schweiss, 2009 WL 276856 at *4 (S.D. Ind. Feb. 5, 2009) (citing *Calder*).

[40] 713 F. Supp. 2d 459 (E.D. Pa. 2010*); see also* Cossaboon v. Maine Med. Ctr., 600 F.3d 25 (1st Cir. 2010) (finding no jurisdiction where Web site was not "purposefully directed" to the nonresident jurisdiction).

[41] 703 F. Supp. 2d 881 (N.D. Ind. 2010).

Finally, other courts have sought to evaluate the "quality and nature" of the defendants' contacts with the forum where jurisdiction is sought.[42] This approach requires an analysis of whether the contacts with the forum constitute the "bread and butter of the defendants' daily business."[43] This analysis consists of an evaluation of such factors[44] as whether the defendants conduct daily business in the forum, percentage of total sales in the jurisdiction, taxes assessed and paid, use of the forum's resources, and whether the Web site advertised and solicited business there.[45]

In sum, while some courts have followed *Zippo* and its sliding scale analysis, other courts have either explicitly rejected it or used it only as a general guide. Although the body of law in this area is growing, there is presently no consensus on when personal jurisdiction may be asserted as a result of interactions over the Internet.

III. THE RELEVANT STATUTES AND PRINCIPLES OF CONTRACT LAW

There are three statutes that have a significant impact on electronic contracting: the Electronic Signature in Global and National Commerce Act (E-SIGN);[46] the Uniform Electronic Transactions Act (UETA),[47] which has been adopted in all but three jurisdictions; and the Uniform Computer Information Transactions Act (UCITA),[48] which has been enacted in only two jurisdictions, and which in four jurisdictions had led to the enactment of "anti-UCITA" statutes rebuking its mandates.[49] As a result, E-SIGN and UETA are the most significant of the three federal statutes.

---

[42] Manning v. Flannery, 2010 WL 55295 (E.D. Pa. Jan. 6, 2010).

[43] *In re* Chocolate, 641 F. Supp. 2d 367, 384 (E.D. Pa. 2009).

[44] The Supreme Court has noted, "So long as [business activity] creates a 'substantial connection' with the forum, even a single act can support jurisdiction." McGee v. International Life Ins. Co., 355 U.S. 220, 223 (1957). The Court has further noted, however, that "some single or occasional acts" related to the forum may not be sufficient to establish jurisdiction if "their nature and quality and the circumstances of their commission" create only an "attenuated" affiliation with the forum. International Shoe Co. v. Washington, 326 U.S. 310, 318 (1945); World-Wide Volkswagen Corp. v. Woodson, 444 U.S. 286, 299 (1980); Burger King Corp. v. Rudzewicz, 471 U.S. 462, 476 (1985).

[45] Manning v. Flannery, 2010 WL 55295 at *6–7 (E.D. Pa. Jan. 6, 2010); *see also* Molnlycke Health Care v. Dumex Med. Surgical Prods., 64 F. Supp. 2d 448 (E.D. Pa. 1999).

[46] Pub. L. No. 106-229, 114 Stat. 464 (2000), codified at 15 U.S.C. §§7001 *et seq.*

[47] Uniform Electronic Transactions Act, Uniform Laws Annotated (1999). Illinois, New York, and Washington have not enacted UETA but have their own electronic transaction statutes. ILL. COMP. STAT. 5-175/1-101 *et. seq.*; N.Y.S. TECH. LAW §§301–309, 401–402; WASH. REV. CODE §§19.34.010 *et seq.*

[48] NATIONAL CONFERENCE OF COMMISSIONERS ON UNIFORM LAWS, *Uniform Computer Information Transaction Act* (Aug. 2, 2002), *available at* http://www.law.upenn.edu/bll/archives/ulc/ucita/2002final.htm.

[49] Maryland and Virginia have enacted UCITA. MD. CODE ANN., COM. LAW §§22-101 *et seq.* (2007); VA. CODE ANN. §§59.1-501.1 *et seq.* (2007). Iowa, North Carolina, Vermont, and West Virginia have enacted "anti-UCITA" statutes that bar the application of the model statute in those states. *See* IOWA CODE §554D.104(4); N.C. CODE §66.329; W.VA. CODE §55-8-15.

A. Electronic Signatures in Global and National Commerce Act (E-SIGN)

E-SIGN,[50] a federal statute grounded in the commerce clause, provides:

Notwithstanding any statute, regulation, or other rule of law [other than E-SIGN] ...

(1) A signature, contract, or other record relating to such transaction may not be denied legal effect, validity, or enforceability solely because it is in electronic form; and

(2) A contract relating to such transaction may not be denied legal effect, validity, or enforceability solely because an electronic signature or electronic record was used in its formation.[51]

In brief, that statute brings some clarity to the legality and enforceability of the increasing number of contacts that are being consummated on the Internet where the traditional indicia of a contract are lacking.

Significantly, the statute is viewed as primarily procedural in nature. It does not change any substantive contract law, i.e., it does not alter, limit, or otherwise affect other requirements of any other law except to the extent the other law requires contracts or other records to be written, signed, or in nonelectronic form.[52] Likewise, it does not require anyone to agree to the use or acceptance of electronic records or signatures.[53] If the circumstances suggest that the parties have used electronic media to make a contract, whether a contract is enforceable under E-SIGN is determined by using substantive contract law; the contract simply cannot be denied enforceability because it is in electronic form[54] and signed with an electronic signature.[55]

The ability of states to modify or limit the provisions of E-SIGN is severely limited.[56] The states may adopt UETA, but any exception to UETA enacted by any state that is inconsistent with E-SIGN is preempted, and any alternatives must be consistent with E-SIGN and must reference E-SIGN when enacted. It is clear that E-SIGN preempts the ability of states to modify or reject E-SIGN's core tenets—namely, that no contract may be deemed unenforceable because it is in electronic form and bears an electronic signature.

---

[50]Pub. L. No. 106-229, 14 Stat. 464 (June 30, 2000) (codified at 15 U.S.C. §§7001 *et seq.*).

[51]15 U.S.C. §7001(a)(1) and (2).

[52]*Id.* §7001(b)(1).

[53]*Id.* §7001(b)(2).

[54]An electronic record is "a contract or other record created, generated, sent, communicated, received, or stored by electronic means." *Id.* §7006(4).

[55]An electronic signature is an "electronic sound, symbol, or process, attached to or logically associated with a contract or other record and executed or adopted by a person with the intent to sign the record. *Id.* §7006(5). Generally, electronic signatures are defined as an electronic sound (e.g., audio of a person's voice), symbol (e.g., a graphic representation of a person in a file), or process. A subcategory of electronic signature consists of a digitalized image of a handwritten signature; not generally considered a secure form of signature because a document may have been changed following placement of the digital signature on the document. Electronic signatures based on an industry standard called Public Key Infrastructure (PKI) utilize encryption technologies that preclude copying, tampering, and any alteration. For a description, see Symantec Managed PKI Services, available at http://www.symantec.com/business/verisign/managed-pki-services.

[56]15 U.S.C. §7002(a).

The impact of the statute is far reaching. In Section 7001(h), the statute provides, "A contract or other record ... may not be denied legal effect ... solely because its formation, creation, or delivery involved the action of one or more electronic agents so long as the action of any such electronic agent is legally attributable to the person to be bound." Section 7006(3) defines an electronic agent as a "computer program or an electronic or other automated means used independently to initiate an action or response to electronic records or performance in whole or in part without review by an individual at the time of action or response."

Thus, under the provisions of E-SIGN, contracts in electronic form[57] and contract requirements mandating written signatures cannot be denied validity because they are in electronic form.[58] Indeed, computers that communicate with each other absent the involvement of human beings—after the machine has been set up or programmed, of course—may engage in contracting. Those contracts will be given effect so long as the person authorizing the contracting is legally responsible for initiating the programming that enables the computer to make the contract. The purchase of items over the Internet is the most common example. The buyer places an order by filling in the order form on the Web site of the seller. Generally, once the order is placed, it is accepted by the seller's "computer" absent intervention of any person. The operation of the Web site eBay, commonly known to millions of Americans, is another good example of this principle. Sellers offer items for sale, and prospective bidders place bids, including at their option their highest bid. As new bids are initiated by other buyers, the computer places additional bids for earlier bidders up to their highest bids. At the end of the time frame allocated for bidding for a particular item, it is not unusual for the computers to be placing and registering the bids of multiple prospective buyers—all in a few seconds. Each of these bids, initially programmed by an individual, represents a contract—even though additional bids are placed by and accepted by a computer absent human intervention.

Notwithstanding the statutes blessing most computerized transactions as contracts, there are exceptions, apparently reflecting the view of the drafters of the statute that some transactions are simply too important to rely on computers to make. For example, wills, codicils, testamentary trusts, adoptions, divorces, "other matters of family law," and subjects covered by the provisions of the Uniform Code except Sections 1-107 and 1-206 and Articles 2 and 2A

---

[57] *See* Sawyer v. Mills, 295 S.W.2d 79 (Ky. 2009) (tape recording of oral agreement is an electronic record).

[58] *See* Campbell v. General Dynamics, 407 F.3d 546 (1st Cir. 2005) ("By its plain terms, the E-SIGN Act prohibits any interpretation of the [Act's] 'written provision' requirement that would preclude giving legal effect to an agreement solely on the basis that it was in electronic form."); Specht v. Netscape Commc'ns Corp., 306 F.3d 17, 18 (2d Cir. 2002) (under E-SIGN, an agreement required to be in writing cannot be denied legal effect solely because it is "provided to users in a downloadable electronic form."); Prudential Ins. Co. of Am. v. Dukoff, 674 F. Supp. 2d 401, 412 (E.D.N.Y. 2009) (accepting electronic signature on insurance application); Day v. Persels, 2011 WL 1770300 (M.D. Fla. May 9, 2011) (accepting electronic signature on credit counseling enrollment form requiring mandatory arbitration in the event of a dispute); Seagate v. CIGNA, 2006 WL 1071881 (N.D. Cal. Apr. 21, 2006) (written notice includes electronic notice); *In re* Cafeteria Operators, 299 B.R. 411 (N.D. Tex. 2003) (e-mails are writings); Naldi v. Grunberg, 80 A.D.3d 1 (N.Y. App. Div. 2010) (New York has adopted E-SIGN's substantive provisions into New York state law, including recognition that e-mails constitute writings that satisfy the statute of frauds).

are exempted.[59] In addition, there is an exception for court orders and other legal documents as well as notices for the termination of utilities, eviction, foreclosures, cancellation of health and life insurance, recall of defective products, and documents accompanying the transportation or instructions for handling dangerous materials, e.g., pesticides.[60]

Moreover, E-SIGN qualifies its general rule of validity for electronic contracts that involve consumer transactions to a significant degree. When another statute, regulation, or other rule of law requires information to be provided or made available in writing, E-SIGN provides that the electronic record will satisfy the writing requirement only if the consumer consents.[61]

In this regard, E-SIGN is very specific. The following requirements must be met:

(1) The consumer must affirmatively consent to receive an electronic record and must not have withdrawn the consent.
(2) The consumer must be provided, prior to consenting, with a "clear and conspicuous" statement informing the consumer of the following:
   a. The right or option of the consumer to have the record provided or made available on paper;
   b. The right of the consumer to withdraw the consent to electronic records and of any conditions, consequences (which may include termination of the parties' relationships), or fees in the event of withdrawal;
   c. Whether the consent applies only to the particular transaction or to the identified categories of records;
   d. The procedures the consumer must use to withdraw consent and to update information;
   e. How, after consent, the consumer may obtain a paper copy of an electronic record and whether a fee will be charged for the copy.
(3) Prior to consenting, the consumer must be provided with a statement of the hardware and software requirements for access to the electronic records.[62]

Affirmative consent also requires a reasonable demonstration that the consumer will be able to access the electronic records to which the consent applies.[63] A consumer may, for example, confirm electronically or in writing that he or she can access electronic records. The parties also have the option of showing that the consumer actually accessed the record. Consent must be reacquired if there is a change in hardware or software, because the statute seeks to ensure that the consumer can access and retain the record.[64] Finally, the failure to secure or confirm consumer consent with the statute's provisions permits the consumer to

---

[59] 15 U.S.C. §7003(a).
[60] *Id.* §700 (b) and (c).
[61] *Id.* §7001(c)(1); *see also* Prudential Ins. Co. of Am. v. Prusky, 413 F. Supp. 2d 489 (E.D. Pa. 2005) (parties must agree to use electronic means of contracting; they are not obligated to do so by E-SIGN).
[62] 15 U.S.C. §7001(c)(1).
[63] *Id.* §7001(c)(1)(C)(ii).
[64] *Id.* §7001(c)(1)(D).

raise the issue of whether the electronic record is adequate evidence of the transaction. However, the absence of consent does not, per se, void the contract.[65]

In sum, consistent with the core theme of most consumer protection statutes, E-SIGN affords strict procedural requirements to ensure that consumers consent to the use of electronic records and affords protections to ensure that they can read them and, as a result, can take whatever steps may be necessary to protect their rights.

Moreover, Congress explicitly stated its intention that E-SIGN apply to the business of insurance.[66] In that vein, certain protections are afforded to brokers and agents, i.e., an electronic contract will be honored even if there is some "deficiency in electronic procedures" so long as the agent is not negligent, did not develop the procedures, and did not deviate from the procedures.[67]

In sum, by federal statute Congress has acted to ensure that contracts cannot be denied legal effect because they are electronic in form or contain an electronic signature. In general, the statute is one of process. Beyond the core mandate relating to electronic form and signatures, traditional contract law applies, including the specific contract laws of each of the several states and territories. In the United States, with some exceptions, basic contract law is reflected in the Uniform Commercial Code as enacted by the states. Of note to practitioners of health care law is the provision applying the statute's provisions to the business of insurance.

B. Uniform Electronic Transactions Act (UETA)

The Uniform Electronic Transactions Act (UETA) was adopted by the National Conference of Commissioners on Uniform State Laws (NCCUSL) in July 1999 in response to questions regarding the ability of parties to form enforceable agreements by electronic means. UETA duplicates the essential provisions of E-SIGN and provides some definition of its requirements. As a "uniform law" designed by the Uniform Law Commission, it is not a federal statute; it has been offered to the individual states and territories as a "recommendation" of how to address myriad issues that have been raised regarding the use of electronic means to enter into contracts. UETA enjoys almost universal acceptance by the states; all but three of the states have adopted its provisions. The states, within the constraints of E-SIGN, are free to adopt amendments to UETA, and many have done so.[68]

UETA makes clear that its purpose is to facilitate and broaden electronic transactions based on reasonable, professionally acceptable means consistent with traditional contract principles and to make the law of electronic transactions uniform among the states. The Act's objective is:

> To make sure that transactions in the electronic marketplace are as enforceable as transactions memorialized on paper and with manual signatures, but without

---

[65] *Id.* §7001(c)(3).
[66] *Id.* §7001(i).
[67] *Id.* §7001(j).
[68] This chapter addresses only the uniform law proposed by the Commission; for state amendments, the reader should consult the relevant state statutes.

changing any of the substantive rules of law that apply. This is a very limited objective—that an electronic record of a transaction is the equivalent of a paper record, and that an electronic signature will be given the same legal effect, whatever that might be, as a manual signature. The basic rules in UETA serve this single purpose.[69]

UETA validates electronic transactions and electronic signatures. It provides that a record or signature cannot be denied legal effect or enforceability because of its electronic form.[70] As mandated likewise by E-SIGN, a contract is not to be denied legality simply because it is in electronic form.[71] In addition, when a law requires a signature, an electronic record or signature is fully acceptable and cannot be used to deny the contract.[72] Whether the electronic record or signature has legal effect depends on other applicable law, including traditional contract principles.[73]

UETA does not mandate the use of electronic records and makes clear that electronic means must be agreed to by the parties to the transaction.[74] Importantly, the uniform law provides some definition to the issue of whether the parties have agreed to the use of electronic means to enter into a contract. Whether one party agreed to consent to conduct a transaction electronically is to be made by viewing all the surrounding circumstances, including the context and conduct of the parties.[75] Consent for one transaction does not carry over to another;

---

[69] State statutes enacted on the basis of the Uniform Electronic Transactions Act, collected by the National Conference of State Legislatures, are available at http://www.ncsl.org/Default.aspx?TabID=13484.

[70] Blake v. Murphy, 2010 WL 3717245 (N.D. Miss. Sept. 14, 2010); Jefferson v. Best Buy, 2010 WL 1533107 (M.D. Ala. Mar. 18, 2010); Alliance Laundry Sys. v. Thyssenkrupp Materials, 570 F. Supp. 2d 1061 (E.D. Wis. 2008); Borjas v. Indiana, 946 N.E.2d 1230 (Ind. 2011) (electronic signatures have the same force and effect as written signatures); Weiss v. Weiss, 239 P.3d 123 (Mont. 2010) (upholding electronic transfer of funds); Alpha Capital Anstalt v. Qtrax, 2010 WL 841364 (N.Y. Sup. Ct. Feb. 1, 2010).

[71] UETA §7(a), (b).

[72] UETA §7(c), (d); see EPCO Carbon Dioxide Prods. v. JP Morgan Chase Bank, 467 F.3d 466 (5th Cir. 2006) (Louisiana's UETA allows an electronic signature to satisfy the signature requirement for most legal documents); Barwick v. Geico, 2011 WL 1198830 (Ark. Mar. 31, 2011) (electronic signature satisfied writing requirement citing Arkansas' adoption of UETA); Anderson v. Bell, 234 P.3d 1147 (Utah 2010) (electronic signature satisfies applicable signature requirement); see also Ni v. Slocum, 127 Cal. Rptr. 3d 620 (2011) (statutes authorizing electronic signatures do not apply to initiative petitions).

[73] UETA §5(e). In addition, Section 8 of UETA is a "savings" provision. If the parties have agreed to an electronic transaction and a law requires one of them to send the other information, that transmission may be done electronically so long as this can be accomplished in a manner that permits the receiving party to retain the electronic information on receipt.

[74] UETA §5(a), (b); see International Casings Group v. Premium Standard Farms, 358 F. Supp. 2d. 863 (W.D. Mo. 2005) (Missouri's version of UETA is only relevant where the parties have both agreed to perform transactions electronically); New York v. Hernandez, 915 N.Y.S.2d 824 (N.Y. City Ct. 2011) (rejected use of breath tests in DWI proceeding because defendant had not "consented" to the use of an electronic signature on the test certification form); Powell v. Newton, 703 S.E.2d 723 (N.C. 2010) (no contract in electronic form because parties agreed to paper document with signatures); Unique Staff Licensing v. Onder, 2010 WL 5621289 (Tex. App. Dec. 9, 2010) (court recognized that the parties had agreed to proceed electronically; contract evidenced by the exchange of e-mails and conduct of the parties in following terms of disputed contract for two years).

[75] UETA §5(b).

a party may decline to conduct other transactions electronically, a power that cannot be waived or varied by agreement.[76]

The uniform law provides guidance on the issue of whether and when an electronic record or signature can be attributable to a person.[77] First, it states boldly that an electronic record or signature is attributable to the person if it was that person's act. This fact can be established "in any manner," including the use of security procedures to show the person to which the record or signature is attributable. For example, simple security procedures may be employed, as in the case of a computer owned by a specific person (not a public computer) who accessed the computer in question by using his or her own password, used a personal identification number, or employed another security code.[78] While mere ownership of the computer may prove inadequate, its private use requiring the management of various security devices would be relevant evidence. Moreover, the law of agency can be employed to bind companies to the acts of its managing agents.[79] The broad standard might even permit the use of a facsimile of letterhead with relevant information that could be appropriately attributed to the sender—irrespective of whether the document contained a traditional signature.[80] Of course, evidence of fraud would be highly relevant to attributing a transaction to a specific person.[81] In any event, the section appears to endorse a broad standard to authenticating whether the record or signature is attributable to a certain individual.

Once a record or signature can be attributed to a certain individual, the validity of the "contract" will be determined in the same manner as a traditional paper contract. UETA does not change substantive contract law.[82]

In the context of electronic transactions, there is no more important legal issue than offer and acceptance—especially where there is interaction solely among machines, with no human interaction, or transactions where only part of the transaction is initiated by a human being. Like E-SIGN, UETA provides that a contract may be formed solely by the interaction of computers, without any need, beyond the initial programming of the computer or other machine, for any human interaction.[83] Indeed, no person may even be initially aware that a contract has been consummated—until notified by their computer.

With the use of computers, the kind and amount of interactions is variable, ranging from no interactions to those involving at least one or more human beings, to individuals acting as agents, to individuals engaging in acts that any

---

[76] *Id.* §5(c).

[77] *See* Kerr v. Dillard Store Servs., 2009 WL 385863 (D. Kan. Feb. 17, 2009) (store lacked security procedures; unable to determine whether electronic signatures genuine); Fractional Villas v. Tahoe Clubhouse, 2009 WL 465997 (S.D. Cal. Feb. 25, 2009) (failure to show agent visited Web site).

[78] *See* UETA §9(a).

[79] UETA §9(a) & cmts.

[80] Kaminiski v. Land Tech, 2011 WL 1035533 (Cal. Ct. App. Mar. 23, 2011) (court noted that documents prepared with unsigned signature blocks did not constitute a contract even if viewed as an electronic document).

[81] *See* Neuson v. Macy's, 249 P.3d 1054 (Wash. Ct. App. 2011) (questioning authenticity of electronic signature).

[82] UETA §9(a) cmt. 6.

[83] *Id.* §2(2) (defining automatic transaction).

person would be free to refrain from or actively choose to engage in, including acts that any reasonable person would know would result in an agreement. As the comments to the model law explain, such an affirmative act exhibiting a degree of intent to enter into a commitment is the simple act of clinking on a "button" marked, "I agree." While UETA can assist by analyzing the many facets of electronic transactions, the ultimate question of whether there is an enforceable contract will be answered by the application of substantive law of contracts, which will be based on the subject matter of the transaction and the surrounding circumstances. These circumstances will most assuredly include the interaction of machines and or the presence of human intervention. Nonetheless, Section 14(c) of the model law makes clear—again—that the substantive law of contracts that would apply to a paper contract will apply no differently when the transaction is electronic.[84] Nonetheless, UETA recognizes, like E-SIGN, that contracts can be entered into by machines—absent human interaction.

Section 15 of UETA addresses another set of issues germane to electronic transactions, when has an electronic record been sent or received, and where has it been sent from and received? An electronic record is deemed sent in the following circumstances:

(1) the record has to be properly addressed to an information processing system used by the recipient for the receipt of electronic records of the kind the sender has sent and to a system from which the recipient can retrieve the record;
(2) the record must be in a form that the system can process; and
(3) the record must have entered a region of the system used by the intended recipient where the sender has lost control of the transmission.[85]

In sum, a sending is complete when the transmission/document has been properly addressed, sent outside the sender's control, and sent in a form that the recipient's system can process, i.e., read and retain. Again, UETA is concerned with process here and has set forth criteria by which a "proper sending" can be judged; thereafter, substantive contract law operates to provide any further analysis.

Pursuant to UETA, a record is received when it enters the information system that the intended recipient customarily uses for the receipt of similar electronic records and from which the recipient is able to gain access or retrieve the record.[86] In addition, the record must have been sent to a recipient's "system" where it can be "processed." The emphasis here is on the receipt of the document by the recipient in a system designated for use or customarily utilized for such a purpose where the recipient can gain access to the document. The comment to this section of UETA notes that many individuals have different e-mail addresses, namely, one used for business purposes and another for personal use.

---

[84] *Id.* §14(3) & cmt. 1; *see also* 15 U.S.C §7001, Prefatory Note, UETA; UETA §3 & cmts. 6, 7; §5(a), (d) & cmts.; §6 & cmts.; §8 & cmts. 1–3.

[85] UETA §15(a) & cmts. 1, 2. The "test" is not retrieval. Internal e-mails sent within an entity may be retrieved; the electronic document may enter a recipient's mailbox and be "received," yet be capable of being retrieved before the recipient opens it—it nonetheless has been received. *See id.* §15(a) cmt. 2.

[86] *Id.* §15(b).

Some individuals have yet additional e-mail addresses for specialized purposes. The thrust of the comment suggests that for a business record to be received within the meaning of the model statute, it must have been sent to the business e-mail address of the recipient. If not, the document may be deemed "not received."[87]

Although the commentary states that like other provisions of UETA, the substantive law of contracts is maintained, the concept of receipt may have some legal consequence, since e-mail includes the feature of issuing a receipt for the e-mail when received.[88] If the substantive statute involved provides for acceptance on receipt, the issuance of a receipt for the e-mail/document when it is received could be used to prove when the document was received by the recipient. However, a receipt will only prove that a document was received; it will not be adequate to show what the mail or document stated or provided for.[89] As to the place of receipt, the commentary makes clear that it is the location of the recipient where the information is received, i.e., not where the information is located, processed, or accessed—apparently a recognition that a the processing system can be located in a different physical location from that of the recipient, change from time to time, or remain unknown.[90] Under UETA, it makes no difference whether the recipient knows that the information has been received; the important factor is whether the document has entered the recipient's information system.[91] Finally, disputes as to whether mail or a document was actually sent or received when there is evidence that the material was either not sent or not received is to be addressed by other law.[92]

In sum, a sending is complete when the transmission/document has been properly addressed, sent outside the sender's control, and sent in a form that the recipient's system can process, i.e., read and retain. When the record enters the system of the recipient customarily used to the receipt of similar messages or documents and the recipient can access the material, the document is deemed received.

UETA provides for "transferable records" in Section 16. Notes under Article 3 and documents under Article 7 of the Uniform Commercial Code (UCC) are transferable records when in electronic form. Such notes and documents are negotiable instruments. The negotiation of these instruments relies upon these notes and documents as the single, unique "token"[93] of the obligations and rights contained in the note or document. Maintaining that quality as a unique token for electronic records is the subject of Section 16.

A transferable record exists when there is a single authoritative copy of that record in unalterable form in the "control" of a person. A person in control is a holder for the purposes of transferring or negotiating that record under the

---

[87] *Id.* §15(b) cmt. 3.

[88] *See* United States Ins. Co. v. Wilson, 18 A.3d 110 (Md. Ct. Spec. App. 2011) (court references UETA and UCITA as recognizing that state law will govern matters of offer and acceptance).

[89] UETA §15(f).

[90] *Id.* §15(d).

[91] *Id.* §16(e).

[92] *Id.* §15(g).

[93] *Id.* §16 cmt. 1.

Uniform Commercial Code. Section 16 acts a substitute provision for a revised UCC provision addressing negotiable instruments in electronic form; covers only the equivalent of paper promissory notes and paper documents of title (excluding UCC Articles 3 and 4); requires agreement of the parties that the electronic record is to be considered a transferable record; and excludes issues related to enforceability against intermediate transferees and transferors, i.e., endorser liability under a paper note, warranty liability that would attach in a paper note, and issues of the effect of taking a transferable note on the underlying obligation.[94]

Sections 17, 18, and 19 of UETA are "optional provisions" to be considered for adoption by states. These provisions seek to eliminate barriers that exist in the use of electronic media by states.

Finally, courts have frequently cited UETA as adopted by the various states as the basis for enforcing contracts that are in electronic form, including contracts entered into by electronic mail.[95]

C. Uniform Computer Information Transactions Act (UCITA)

UCITA, a joint project of the NCCUSL and the American Law Institute (ALI), began as an amendment to Article 2 of the UCC. The NCCUSL and the ALI share responsibility for keeping the Uniform Commercial Code up to date to meet the evolving needs of the American and global economies. While UCITA was originally submitted in 1999 as a proposed uniform law and modification to the UCC, it was withdrawn in 2002 after the ALI did not grant its assent. In the absence of approval by the ALI, the NCCUSL renamed the proposed uniform law as UCITA and approved it as a separate proposed model law.

Although UCITA was adopted in Maryland[96] and Virginia,[97] it is not expected to be adopted by any other states. At least four states—Iowa, North Carolina, West Virginia, and Vermont—have enacted UCITA "bomb shelter" legislation, statutes that specifically prohibit UCITA from applying to the citizens of those states.

UCITA suffered a substantial blow in 2003 when it failed to gain the endorsement of the American Bar Association (ABA). This lack of support ultimately led the NCCUSL to discharge the UCITA Drafting Committee and to conclude that no further resources should be expended to promote the Act. Because UCITA has been adopted by Virginia and Maryland and has been cited by various courts in their decisions regarding electronic contracts, however,

---

[94] *Id.* §16 cmts. 2, 4.

[95] *See* Campbell v. General Dynamics Gov't Sys., 407 F.3d 546 (1st Cir. 2005) (upholding electronic contract clause mandating arbitration entered into by e-mail); Jefferson v. Best Buy, 2010 WL 1533107 (M.D. Ala. Mar. 18, 2010) (contract by e-mail); Blake v. Murphy Oil USA, 2010 WL 3717245 (N.D. Miss. Sept. 14, 2010) (electronic signature); Loparex v. MPI Release Techs., 2011 WL 1326274 (S.D. Ind. Mar. 25, 2011) (accepting electronic signature); Turner v. U-Haul of Fla., 2008 WL 709107 (M.D. Fla. Mar. 14, 2005) (denying contract but acknowledging validity of electronic contracts. *Cf.* McMunigal v. Bloch, 2010 WL 5399219 (N.D. Cal. Dec. 23, 2010).

[96] MD. CODE ANN. §§21-101 *et seq.*

[97] VA. CODE ANN. §§59.1-501 *et seq.*

the model law may have some limited applicability to health care transactions involving electronic information.[98]

UCITA states that it applies exclusively to "computer information transactions,"[99] which are defined as agreements that deal with the creation, modification, access to, license, or distribution of computer information.[100] "Computer information" is defined as information that is transmitted in a form directly capable of being processed by, or obtained from, a computer, together with any copy, associated documentation, or packaging.[101] Generally, computer information means any digital information. If a particular transaction involves both computer information and other subject matter, UCITA ordinarily applies only to aspects of the transaction involving computer information.[102]

Based on the definition of computer information transactions, UCITA applies to, among other things, contracts for the development, licensing, or purchase of computer programs, contracts for the creation or distribution of multimedia works, contracts for access to the Internet or online information, contracts to distribute information on the Internet, and data processing contracts.[103] Transactions that fall outside the scope of UCITA include the following: sales or leases of goods; casual exchanges of information; employment contracts; contracts where computer information is insignificant; financial services transactions; insurance services transactions; contracts for books, magazines, or newspapers; and contracts for sound recordings or motion pictures.[104]

The Prefatory Note to UCITA explains that the Act was drafted in response to the fundamental economic changes caused by the growth in information products and services and the accompanying need for a uniform body of contract law to govern information transactions:

> The need for a coherent, uniform body of law has never been greater. Revolutions in telecommunications and computer technology have made geography increasingly irrelevant to modern commerce.... Even as online systems have altered how many information transactions are performed...fundamental issues associated with contracting online remain unanswered.... The liberating promise of technology cannot be fully realized unless there is a predictability in the legal rules that govern such transactions. This is the need that UCITA addresses. It clarifies and sets forth uniform legal principles applicable to computer information transactions. UCITA is a statute for our time.[105]

While UCITA sanctions contracts in electronic form, it seeks to bring the same uniformity and certainty to the substantive rules that apply to information technology transactions that the UCC does to the sale of goods. UCITA is

---

[98] See UCITA, History of UCITA, *available at* http://www.UCITA.com/What_History.html.
[99] UCITA §103(a).
[100] *Id.* §102(a)(11).
[101] *Id.* §102(a)(10).
[102] *Id.* §103(a)(1). The parties can agree to apply or preclude the application of UCITA to the entire transaction if the subject matter of the agreement is not goods and computer information is a material part of the transaction. *Id.* §104.
[103] *Id.* §103 cmt. 2.
[104] *Id.* §103(d) & cmt. 3.
[105] UCITA, Prefatory Note.

modeled after the UCC and its contract formation provisions borrow heavily from the provisions of Article 2.

Parties may form a contract based on computer information in any manner sufficient to show agreement, ranging from an offer and acceptance consistent with traditional contract notions to conduct by the parties or their electronic agents that shows agreement.[106] Absent conduct or performance to the contrary, the Act provides that there can be no contract if there is a material disagreement on a material term.[107] Any disagreement must exist at the time the contract was ostensibly formed; it cannot consist of a later dispute as to the terms of the agreement. Interestingly, the proposed uniform law permits the parties to leave terms open for agreement at a later time.[108] If later the parties cannot agree, there is no contract, and the parties must restore each other to the status quo ante, including the destruction of any information each received from the other.[109] UCITA borrows from Article 2 with respect to rules governing offers, nonconforming acceptances as counteroffers, and the like.[110]

Like E-SIGN and UETA, UCITA makes provisions for electronic agreements or contracts.[111] Part 2, Subpart B, is largely devoted to these rules. If an offer is made via electronic message and evokes an electronic message of acceptance, a contract is formed when the electronic acceptance is received.[112] It is likewise possible for a contract to be formed by the interaction of a human being with a computer.[113] Contracts formed with the interaction of machines or electronic agents will be found to exist if the circumstances indicate the acceptance of an offer—absent fraud, electronic mistake, or some other invalidating factor such as a faulty machine.[114]

A signature or its electronic equivalent is the basic means of authentication under UCITA. A party relying upon that authentication has the burden of establishing attribution that can be shown in any manner, including evidence of the efficacy of any "attribution procedure" used in the communication. An "attribution procedure" is any procedure that provides greater assurance than a simple transmission of information that the "authentication" is that of the party to which it is attributed.

Attribution procedures may have an impact on message content in an electronic communication. Similar to UETA, under UCITA, if a procedure is in place to detect errors or changes in the message communicated, a party that conforms to the procedure is not bound by an error or change that results because the other party does not conform to the procedure. There is a special rule for consumers. Consumers who make errors while entering automated transactions

---

[106] UCITA §112(d).
[107] Id. §202(d).
[108] Id. §202(c), (e).
[109] Id. §202(e).
[110] Id. §§203–205.
[111] Id. §107 & pt. 2, subpt. B §§208–215.
[112] Id. §206. If the electronic response consists of beginning performance, performing or affording access to available information, the contract is formed when the performance is received or access is enabled or the materials sought are received.
[113] Id.
[114] Id. cmt. 3.

are not bound by the unintended erroneous message, so long as the consumer notifies the other party of the error promptly after it is identified, properly returns the computer information received, and has not obtained value or benefit from using the information.[115]

UCITA provides a comprehensive set of rules for licensing computer information, including computer software and other clearly identified forms of computer information. UCITA acts as a set of contract rules together with intellectual property law to control unauthorized copying.[116]

A licensing contract or license involves the transfer of computer information, i.e., from a vendor (a licensor) to a recipient (the individual or entity who wishes to use the vendor's software in its computers). A license may also contain informational rights, including rights flowing from patents or copyrights, and rights that restrict the use of the information by other persons. A licensing contract contains restrictions on the use and transfer of the computer information by the licensee or recipient of the computer information during the entire term of the licensing contract. If the licensee breaches a condition or restriction, the licensor may have a remedy as specified in the contract or licensing agreement.[117]

Licensing of computer information constitutes the standard of the computer information industry. UCITA seeks to establish certainty with respect to the law in this area by establishing basic rules for licensing activity. Largely default rules, these rules can be waived or modified by the parties to the licensing agreement. Rules relating to fairness and the contract process cannot be waived. The obligations of good faith, diligence, and reasonableness, limitations on enforcement imposed by the principle of unconscionability, and any standard imposed by UCITA cannot be waived by agreement of the parties.[118]

UCITA provides for "mass market licenses." Both "shrink wrap" and "click wrap" licenses are mass market licenses.[119] These mass market licenses are provided with the product in the store as part of the transfer of the computer information. UCITA recognizes the new means of contracting. Terms must be readily available to the licensee with an appropriate time for review. This means that any terms must be made readily available in either paper or electronic form that the licensee can print and store easily. If, following review, the licensee does not wish to agree to the terms for the use of the electronic information, the licensee can return the software or other information to the vendor.[120] This right of return cannot be waived.

UCITA's rules for licensing contracts for computer information and informational rights cover formation through final agreement, including rules for remedies in the event of a breach, warranties, and rules pertaining to the risk of loss in a computer information transaction. Most rules are grounded in the law

---

[115] UCITA §213.
[116] Id. §209.
[117] Id.
[118] Id.
[119] Id.
[120] Id.

of sales and common law principles of contract.[121] As such, licensing contacts are essentially commercial contracts. Unlike commercial law, UCITA grants an express power to a court to deny enforceability of a licensing contract if the contract violates fundamental public policy.[122] This significant feature of UCITA is not contained elsewhere.

While only two states have enacted UCITA, it has had some impact, describing acceptable practices for shrink wrap and click wrap licenses and reflecting standards for generally acceptable practices in other areas. Courts have found that UCITA's provisions offer assistance with respect to many issues raised in electronic contracting. For example, in *Specht v. Netscape*,[123] the Second Circuit found that its provisions offer insight into the "evolving circumstances" that place Internet users on notice of licensing terms to which they must comply to avail themselves of offered services.[124] Courts have referred to UCITA in reported opinions dealing with licensing issues even where UCITA does not directly apply.[125] Commentators have found that the model law "maintains the contextual, balanced approach to standard terms that can be found in the paper world."[126]

Health care transactions are not exempted from E-SIGN, UETA, or UCITA. This means that health care transactions affecting interstate commerce can be validated by electronic means, including electronic signatures.[127] Health insurance and health plans can accept applications completed online but cannot cancel policies electronically.

IV. LITIGATION: COURTS COPING WITH A NEW MEANS OF CONTRACTING

The use of the Internet to purchase goods and services is widespread and reflects mass market consumer transactions. Millions of Americans and retailers enter into contracts by a variety of nontraditional electronic means—by telephone, e-mail, or over the Internet—with almost no thought whatsoever. Such practices have become customary. Few, if any, read "terms and conditions" provisions, including terms set forth on the Web site itself, printed on the boxes of software or other products they buy, "wrapping" the CDs they use in their computers, accompanying the invoices they receive after purchase, or con-

---

[121] UCITA §§201 *et seq.* (formation of contract), §§301 *et seq.* (construction), §§401 *et seq.* (warranties), §§501 *et seq.* (transfer of interests and rights), §§601 *et seq.* (performance), §§701 *et seq.* (breach of contract), and §§801 (remedies).

[122] *Id.* §209(a)(1).

[123] 306 F.3d 17 (2d Cir. 2002).

[124] *Id.* at 34.

[125] *See, e.g., id.*; Rhone Poulenc Agro v. Dekalb Genetics, 284 F.3d 1323 (Fed. Cir. 2002); ProCD v. Zeidenberg, 86 F.3d 1447 (7th Cir. 1996); iLAN Sys. v. Netscout Serv. Level Corp., 183 F. Supp. 2d 328 (D. Mass. 2002).

[126] R. Hillman and J. Rachlinski, *Standard Form Contracting in the Electronic Age*, 77 N.Y.U. L. REV. 429, 491 (2002).

[127] Almost all health transactions will fall within the meaning of "interstate commerce." However, could a patient electronically sign an advance directive before entering the hospital or during hospitalization? What about medical decisions requiring informed consent?

tained in the privacy notices posted on most retail Web sites. Consumers may use electronic media in such a way as to enter implied contracts manifested by their conduct, e.g., through telephone conversations or using e-mail exchanges to manifest the intent to purchase a particular item or service. These "contracts" will be honored by courts so long as the elementary features of a contact can be identified, i.e., (1) an offer and acceptance, (2) some legally sufficient consideration, (3) for a legitimate purpose, and (4) by parties with legal capacity to enter a contract. Generally, these contracts will be recognized by courts—notwithstanding the absence of the traditional paper agreement and signature demonstrating agreement. The intent of the parties, however manifested, is a guiding principle. Electronic contracts and electronic signatures are "regularly honored."[128]

Many goods and services offered for purchase on the internet or in the electronic context come accompanied with "terms and conditions." These conditions, especially those pertaining to the "purchase" of software, seek to limit or otherwise regulate the conduct of the purchaser. For example, these terms may designate the law of a particular state to control any future dispute, mandate arbitration as the sole means for the resolution of any dispute, limit or disclaim warranties, prohibit the sale of the item or software to another person or entity, or otherwise regulate the purchaser's use of the product or service. The courts have had to address whether these terms or conditions are enforceable in a variety of contexts, including agreements that have been characterized as "browse wrap," "click wrap, or "shrink wrap" agreements. While some commentators have suggested that "[t]he Internet is turning the process of contracting on its head," there is an evolving body of contract law that seeks to accommodate traditional contracting principles to the twenty-first century, including Internet transactions on the mass consumer market.[129]

This section sets forth the holdings of these courts and provides some commentary with respect to the current state of the law with respect to browse wrap, click wrap, and shrink wrap agreements.[130] In many respects, the law is well established and the different approaches to the issues well identified. While the law surrounding contract formation when the Internet is employed has matured, commentators continue to analyze various aspects of the issue.[131] Since notice of the terms and conditions has played such a prominent role in the analysis of browse wrap, click wrap, and shrink wrap agreements, that topic has received particular attention.[132]

---

[128]Magyar v. St. Joseph Regional Med. Ctr., 544 F.3d 766 (7th Cir. 2008) (citing Electronic Signatures in Global and National Commerce Act, 15 U.S.C. §7001, Uniform Electronic Transactions Act, and Indiana's Electronic Signature Act, IND. CODE ANN. §5-24-3-1).

[129]Hillman and Rachlinski, 77 N.Y.U. L. REV. at 491.

[130]This discussion is limited to basic principles; a full discourse on contract law and the Uniform Commercial Code is beyond the scope of this chapter.

[131]P. Morror, *Cyberlaw: The Unconscionability/Unenforceability of Contracts (Shrink-Wrap, Clickwrap, and Browse-Wrap) on the Internet: A Multijurisdictional Analysis Showing the Need for Oversight*, 11 U. PITT. J. TECH. L. & POLICY 7 (2011) (critical review).

[132]*See, e.g.*, S. Han, *Predicting the Enforceability of Browse-Wrap Agreements in Ohio*, 36 OHIO N.U. L. REV. 31 (2010).

A. Browse Wrap Agreements

Browse wrap agreements typically appear as a hyperlink at the bottom or top of a Web page and may be labeled as terms of use, legal terms, or some other description of the Web site's entity's intent to impose conditions on the use of the Web site or the material made available to the user. The precise terms or conditions do not appear on the initial Web page, and some action must be taken to gain access to them on another page of the Web site. The hyperlinks may be highlighted in a different color or have some distinguishing feature from the background of the initial Web page or the Web site wallpaper. If the user does not act to locate the terms, the use of the Web site or the transaction at issue may take place without any notice to the user of the precise terms attendant to the transaction.[133]

In *Specht v. Netscape*,[134] a leading and oft cited case, the U.S. Court of Appeals for the Second Circuit held that the plaintiff was not bound by an arbitration clause found in the Web site's license terms because the plaintiff could not have learned of the terms unless, prior to executing the download of material, he had scrolled down the Web page to a screen located below the download button. Here, notice of the terms and conditions lacked conspicuousness and failed to give the buyer adequate notice of the contested arbitration clause. The users could download the software without any indication that there were legal terms to follow.

More specifically, the court concluded that when a consumer is invited to download free software "at the immediate click of a button," reference to terms and conditions on a "submerged screen" is not sufficient to place individuals on notice of these terms.[135] The court explicitly rejected the defendants' argument that the consumer had "as much time as they need" to review the terms because there was no reason to believe that consumers would scroll down and search for the subsequent screens to find the terms.[136] The court cited the testimony of plaintiffs that they saw no need to scroll down to find terms that they were unaware of.[137]

The Second Circuit reiterated the holding in *Specht* as recently as 2010 when in *Hines v. Overstock.com*,[138] the court ruled that no contract was formed online where no constructive notice was afforded. The user had to scroll to the end of the page to see reference to terms. Review of the terms was not necessary to make purchases. Specifically, the court noted, "Very little is required to form a contract nowadays—but this alone does not suffice."[139]

---

[133] *See* Register.com v. Verio, 356 F.3d 393, 403 (2d Cir. 2004); Ticketmaster v. Tickets.com, 2003 WL 21406289 (C.D. Cal. Mar. 7, 2003); Pollstar v. Gigmania, 170 F. Supp. 2d 974, 981 (E.D. Cal. 2000).

[134] 306 F.3d 17 (2d Cir. 2002).

[135] *Id.* at 32.

[136] *Id.*

[137] *Id.*

[138] 2010 WL 2203030 (2d Cir. June 3, 2010).

[139] Hines v. Overstock.com, Inc., 668 F. Supp. 2d 362, 367 (E.D.N.Y. 2009).

Likewise, in *Motise v. America Online*,[140] the court declined to bind a nonmember America Online (AOL) user to the terms of a license agreement when the nonmember used the account of an AOL member; the nonmember user had not received any notice of the terms and conditions of use, including the choice of forum clause at issue. In addition, in *Softman Products v. Adone Systems*,[141] the court held that a reseller of software packages was not bound by an end-user license agreement because it had never installed the software and, as a result, had no opportunity to view or accept the terms of the license, terms that were not contained in the packaging but presented only when a user installed the software. Here, the defendant had not assented to the terms of the license—and had had no opportunity to do so.

In *Sotelo v. DirectRevenue*,[142] the court failed to validate a notice advising individuals downloading free software that the software would be accompanied by "spyware" that would track their computer browsing behavior in order to develop targeted advertising. The court found that users were not afforded any notice of the terms and conditions that ostensibly afforded notice of the spyware prior to the installation of the free software. The court observed that the spyware "begins consuming computer resources when it is installed," and it is difficult to remove.[143]

On the other hand, other courts have found contracts to have been made when the terms had to be accessed by a hyperlink or cited factors they viewed as evidence of consent to the licensor's terms and conditions of use. In *Net-2Phone v. Superior Court*, a consumer group challenged Net2Phone's practice of "rounding up" charges to the nearest minute irrespective of the actual time used. The appellate court rejected the argument that no notice had been afforded to consumers to this practice when the terms had to be accessed by a hyperlink.[144] In *Hubbert v. Dell*,[145] the plaintiff alleged that Dell had engaged in false advertising of one of its products. Dell responded, in part, by asserting that the arbitration clause contained in its terms and conditions compelled arbitration of any dispute. The court found the clause to be enforceable, finding that a contract existed even when the terms had to be located through the use of a hyperlink, because the hyperlinked terms appeared on multiple pages in the order process. Three different pages that plaintiffs had to go through contained the notice, "All sales are subject to Dell's Terms and Conditions."

Other courts have found consent implied by the user's conduct, In *Register. com v. Verio*,[146] the court criticized the notice on the Web site presented to the defendant concurrently with the information sought but bound the defendants due to its awareness of its terms from continuous usage. In *Pollstar v. Gigmania*,

---

[140] 346 F. Supp. 2d 563, 565 (S.D.N.Y. 2004). The court did, however, bind the nonmember as a sublicensee of the member. The court held that the nonmember could have no greater rights than the AOL member who had agreed to the terms. *Id.* at 566; *accord* CoStar Realty Info., Inc. v. Field, 612 F. Supp. 2d 660, 677 (D. Md. 2009).
[141] 171 F. Supp. 2d 1075 (C.D. Cal. 2001).
[142] 384 F. Supp. 2d 1219 (N.D. Ill. 2005).
[143] *Id.* at 1228.
[144] 135 Cal. Rptr. 2d 149, 152–53 (2003).
[145] 835 N.E.2d 113 (Ill. App. Ct. 2005).
[146] 356 F.3d 393 (2d Cir. 2004).

the court directly observed that "people sometimes enter into a contract by using a service without first seeing the terms."[147]

In finding a forum selection clause enforceable, the court in *Cairo v. Crossmedia Services* reasoned that Cairo had notice and that its subsequent use of the Web site was adequate to impute knowledge of the terms and conditions of use.[148] In *Southwest Airlines v. BoardFirst, LLC*[149] the court noted the evolution of commercial transactions in enforcing a browse wrap agreement, recognizing that "browse wraps have become more prevalent in today's increasingly e-driven commercial landscape."[150] The court identified the key factor as "whether a Web site user has actual or constructive notice of a site's terms and conditions prior to using the Web site."[151] Here, there was no dispute that the defendant had actual knowledge.

In *Hotmail Corp. v. Van Money Pie*,[152] the court found that the defendants had entered into a contract by obtaining a number of Hotmail mailboxes and therefore were bound by a "Terms of Service Agreement" that they had allegedly breached by using Hotmail's services to send spam and other illicit material. In *America Online v. Booker*,[153] a Florida court upheld a forum selection clause in a "freely negotiated agreement" contained in the online terms of service. In *Mortensen v. Timberline Software*, the court found that the buyer assented to the software terms by installing and using the software.[154]

The Supreme Court of Oklahoma ruled in *Rogers v. Dell Computer Corp.*,[155] where the parties entered into a contract to sell and buy a computer, that the plaintiff's acceptance and failure to return the computer was not necessarily consistent with the buyer's willingness to agree to any subsequent terms. Indeed, the court found that the acceptance of the computer was consistent with a contract being formed at the time the order was placed. The court noted that the statement of terms and conditions lacked any statement that acceptance was based on the willingness of the buyer to agree to the additional terms set forth in a "Terms and Conditions of Sale." Since the court was looking for evidence as to the circumstances that existed between the parties when the contract was entered into, and the record failed to reflect such evidence, the court remanded the case. Nonetheless, discussion in the case indicates hostility to the notion that acceptance of the item accompanied with terms and conditions of sale and the failure to return the item, here a computer, indicates acceptance of subsequent terms and conditions.[156]

---

[147] 170 F. Supp. 2d 974, 981 (E.D. Cal. 2000).

[148] 2005 WL 756610 (N.D. Cal. Apr. 1, 2005); *see also* Major v. McCakkister, 302 S.W.3d 227 (Mo. Ct. App. 2009) (immediately visible notice on the Web site, "By submitting you agree to the Terms of Use" placed by a hyperlink to the terms that appears on every other Web page).

[149] 2007 WL 4823761 (N.D. Tex. Sept. 12, 2007).

[150] *Id.* at *5.

[151] *Id.*; *see also* Snap-On Business Solutions v. O'Neil, 708 F. Supp. 2d 669, 683 (N.D. Ohio 2010) (actual or constructive knowledge).

[152] 1998 WL 388389 (N.D. Cal. Apr. 16, 1998).

[153] 781 So. 2d 423, 425 (Fla. Dist. Ct. App. 2001).

[154] 998 P.2d 305 (Wash. 2000).

[155] 138 P.3d 826 (Mont. 2005).

[156] *Id.* at 832–33.

The issue arises in other contexts. For example, in *Schafer v. AT&T Wireless Services*,[157] the court held an arbitration clause to be enforceable because the purchaser of cellular phone service, including a free phone, had notice on the box in which the phone was received that there were terms and conditions and that use of the phone constituted acceptance of those conditions.[158]

Finally, demonstrating the broad sweep of the concept, in *Corbis Corp. v. Integrity Wealth Management*,[159] the court denied the defendants' motion to dismiss finding that an allegation that "by using Corbis images obtained from the www.corbis.com website, the defendant and its agents agreed to be bound by the terms of the Corbis Content License Agreement."

These cases suggest that browse wrap licensing agreements may be upheld by the courts based on the specific facts of each case when the court can reasonably conclude that the buyer had notice of the terms and conditions or acted in a manner sufficient to manifest assent. The courts focus on how notice was provided, e.g., on several pages leading to the conclusion of the transaction as opposed to being located far below the buy or download button, and how consent was given, e.g., through multiple uses of the Web site where consent may be reasonably implied. A notice of terms and conditions that is not in some fashion conspicuously displayed or is difficult to locate, and to which consent cannot be reasonably inferred by the conduct of the buyer, will be the most difficult to sustain if challenged in court. Other courts have also focused on the buyer's use of the product and failure to return it within a reasonable period of time, an act which the courts find as a method for the buyer to ultimately reject the terms and conditions of use.[160] Finally, those states that have enacted UETA have for the most part endorsed browse wrap agreements by virtue of enactment of the model law.[161]

B. Click Wrap Agreements

Click wrap agreements require users to assent affirmatively to terms before downloading or using a service or product. Online buyers indicate their assent by clicking on icons or buttons, e.g., "I Agree," or "I Disagree," or "Yes" or "No." By clicking on the appropriate icon, the purchaser affirmatively registers agreement with the applicable terms or conditions or otherwise signals the intent to buy and/or use the product. Such action creates a binding contract.[162]

---

[157] 2005 WL 850459 (S.D. Ill. Apr. 1, 2005).

[158] *Id.* (citing Hill v. Gateway, 105 F.3d 1147 (7th Cir. 1997), and ProCD v. Zeidenberg, 86 F.3d 1447 (7th Cir. 1996)).

[159] 2009 WL 3835976 (W.D. Wash. Nov. 16, 2009).

[160] Fiser v. Dell, 165 P.3d 328 (N.M. Ct. App. 2007).

[161] *See, e.g.*, OHIO REV. CODE ANN. ch. 1306(B), (G), (H), and (M). Viewed most broadly, these provisions suggest that so long as the owner of the Web site can show that the terms and conditions of use were prominently or conspicuously displayed on the site, almost any action by the user on the Web site may be deemed an acceptance of the terms of the browse wrap agreement.

[162] *See* R. Dickens, *Finding Common Ground in the World of Electronic Contracts*, 11 MARQ. INTELL. PROP. L. REV. 379 (2007).

Courts have routinely validated clip wrap agreements, including forum selection and mandatory arbitration clauses. In *Lieschke v. Realworks*,[163] the court enforced an arbitration clause presented on the Web by a click wrap agreement, staying court proceedings in Illinois pending the completion of arbitration in the State of Washington. In *Forrest v. Verizon Communications*,[164] the court enforced a forum selection clause because the user had the opportunity to review the terms. Likewise, in *Caspi v. Microsoft Network*,[165] the court enforced a click wrap agreement relating to a forum selection clause. In *Moore v. Microsoft Corp.*,[166] the software user was found by the court to be bound to terms that were prominently displayed on the computer screen before software could be installed and where the user was required to indicate assent by clicking, "I agree."[167] In *Smallwood v. NCsoft Corp.*,[168] the court validated a click wrap agreement of the customary type, *i.e.*, the user was presented with a message on his computer screen requesting him to indicate his agreement with the terms and conditions of use by clicking on an icon. Courts have simply looked to determine if the user had reasonable notice of the terms and conditions and manifested assent.[169] It is not even necessary for the user to scroll down through the agreement and read it.[170] In sum, the courts have ruled that click wrap agreements "are enforceable contracts."[171]

In *i.LAN Systems v. Netscout Service Level Corp.*,[172] the court, in liberally construing the UCC, adopted the view that the purpose underlying the model statute was to continue "expansion of commercial practices through custom, usage, and agreement of the parties."[173] The court found that the purchaser explicitly accepted the click wrap license agreement when it clicked on the box stating, "I agree." Reasoning that if shrink wrap agreements where assent is implicit create an enforceable licensing agreement, it must also be correct to enforce a click wrap agreement where the agreement is explicit.[174] In *RealPage*

---

[163] 2000 WL 198424 (N.D. Ill. Feb. 11, 2000).

[164] 805 A.2d 1007 (D.C. 2002).

[165] 732 A.2d 528, 533 (N.J. Super. Ct. App. Div. 1999).

[166] 293 A.D.2d 587 (N.Y. App. Div. 2002).

[167] A.V. v. iParadigms, 544 F. Supp. 2d 473 (E.D. Va. 2008).

[168] 2010 WL 3064474 (D. Haw. Aug. 4, 2010).

[169] Jallali v. National Bd. of Osteopathic Med. Exam'rs, 2009 WL 1818380 (Ind. Ct. App. May 28, 2010).

[170] RealPage v. EPS, 560 F. Supp. 2d 539 (E.D. Tex. 2007); *see also* Feldman v. Google, 513 F. Supp. 2d 229 (E.D. Pa. 2007) (click wrap agreement enforceable notwithstanding absence of a definite price term); Forsyth v. First Trenton Indemnity, 2010 WL 2195996 (N.J. Super. Ct. App. Div. May 28, 2010) (employee agreed to arbitrate employment disputes by clicking on the button, "I certify"); Barnett v. Network Solutions, 38 S.W.3d 200 (Tex. App. 2001) (click wrap agreement valid where the user was required to scroll down through the terms of the agreement before accepting and proceeding to make purchase; no requirement to read the contract); *accord* Groff v. America Online, 1998 WL 307001 (R.I. Super. Ct. May 27, 1998).

[171] Recursion Software v. Interactive Intelligence, 425 F. Supp. 2d 756 (N.D. Tex. 2006). However, violation of the terms and conditions contained in a Web site to which a user has agreed may not result in a violation of the criminal law because normally breaches of contract are not subject to criminal prosecution. United States v. Drew, 259 F.R.D. 449 (C.D. Cal. 2009).

[172] 183 F. Supp. 2d 328 (D. Mass. 2002).

[173] *Id.* at 338 (quoting UCC §1-102).

[174] Davidson & Assocs. v. Jung, 422 F.3d 630, 642 (8th Cir. 2005) (recognizing a click wrap agreement).

v. EPS, the court accepted a click wrap agreement where the user clicked on a box, "I accept the terms of the licensing agreement," but found the agreement unenforceable due to vagueness or "indefiniteness."[175]

In a 2011 case, *Schnabel v. Trilegiant*,[176] the court rejected the terms of a click wrap agreement where the users had allegedly entered a password and city of birth to enroll in a "Great Fun program" for a monthly fee. The court declined to find a contract because the users were not given adequate notice of the eventual receipt of additional terms by e-mail and were not given the opportunity to reject the e-mail and its proffered terms, including an alleged arbitration clause.[177]

In sum, click wrap agreements have enjoyed general acceptance in the courts, with some exceptions. Assent has been found by clicking on the "button" marked, "I agree."

C. Shrink Wrap Agreements

Shrink wrap licensing agreements have produced two lines of cases. Shrink wrap contracts are license agreements or other terms and conditions of a contractual nature that can be read by the consumer only after opening the product. The term derives from the shrink wrap used to cover CDs and software packages.

In *ProCD v. Zeidenberg*, the Seventh Circuit found that where an individual purchased software in a box containing licensing terms which were displayed on the computer screen every time the user utilized the software, the user's repeated notice and failure to return the software resulted in an enforceable contact.[178] More specifically, in *ProCD*, the court held that shrink wrap licenses accompanying off-the-shelf computer software are enforceable unless their terms are objectionable under general contract law.[179]

The defendant purchased ProCD software at a retail outlet and made the database information therein available on the World Wide Web at a lower cost than what ProCD charged consumers. The district court had refused to enforce the license agreement that came with the software because the purchaser did not agree to "hidden terms," i.e., those inside the box—even though a printed notice on the outside of the box referred to the license terms inside. The Seventh Circuit reversed. The court, by the noted Judge Easterbrook, opined, "Notice on the outside, terms on the inside, and a right to return the software for a refund if the terms are unacceptable (a right that the license expressly extends) may be a means of doing business valuable to buyers and sellers alike."[180] The court discussed several examples of "money now, terms later" transactions, e.g., the purchase of insurance, airline tickets, electronic goods containing warranties

---

[175] 560 F. Supp. 2d 539, 546 (E.D. Tex. 2007).
[176] 2011 WL 797505 (D. Conn. Feb. 24, 2011).
[177] *Id.*
[178] 86 F.3d 1447, 1451 (7th Cir. 1996); *see also* Bowers v. Baystate Techs., 320 F.3d 1317 (Fed. Cir. 2003) (upholding shrink wrap contract).
[179] 86 F.3d at 1449.
[180] *Id.* at 1451 (citing E. Allen Farnsworth, 1 FARNSWORTH ON CONTRACTS §4.26 (1990) and RESTATEMENT (SECOND) OF CONTRACTS §211 (1981)).

inside the box, and drugs with inserts describing interactions and contraindications. Turning to the software industry, the court noted that software is often ordered over the phone and the Internet and that increasingly the delivery is also over the Internet.

The Seventh Circuit again upheld license terms in a pay-now-terms-later transaction with an accept-or-return provision in *Hill v. Gateway 2000*.[181] In *Hill*, the customer ordered a computer over the phone, paying with a credit card, and received the computer in the mail accompanied by a list of terms to govern if the customer did not return the computer within 30 days.[182] The court posed this question: "Are these terms effective as the parties' contract, or is the contract term-free because the order-taker did not read any terms over the phone and elicit the customer's assent?"[183] Relying in part on *ProCD*, the court held that the terms were effective, stating: "Practical considerations support allowing vendors to enclose the full legal terms with their products."[184] The terms of the licensing agreement were upheld.

The Third Circuit addressed shrink wrap agreements in *Step-Saver Data Systems v. Wyse Technology*.[185] A company seeking to resell the software for installation on a customer's multiuser computer system telephoned a software manufacturer and asked for a shipment of software, which the manufacturer verbally agreed to provide. The reseller then sent a written purchase order specifying quantity, price, and shipping and payment information. The manufacturer then shipped the software along with an invoice matching the purchase order. On the box containing the software, however, was a shrink wrap license agreement that contained a provision limiting the manufacturer's liability to the price paid for the shipment. The court held that the limitation of liability was not enforceable because it was merely a proposed agreement under UCC Section 2-207 to which the reseller never agreed. The court refused to find implied assent because the limitation of liability was material,[186] and UCC Section 2-207(2)(b) does not allow material terms to be added by implication.[187] This holding was fully adopted in a later case against the same software manufacturer, *Arizona Retail Systems v. Software Link*.[188]

Other courts have rejected the notion of a shrink wrap licensee. In a copyright and patent infringement case where the seller of software argued that it retained ownership of the software and that the shrink wrap license contained with each copy was binding, giving to the buyer only a license to use the soft-

---

[181] 105 F.3d 1147, 1150 (7th Cir.), *cert. denied*, 522 U.S. 808 (1997).

[182] *Id.* at 1148.

[183] *Id.*

[184] *Id.* at 1149.

[185] 939 F.2d 91 (3d Cir. 1991).

[186] The court was also troubled by the fact that the parties had agreed that some provisions of the "shrink wrap" agreement did not apply to the buyer, i.e., a limitation on selling the software to others. The court wondered how the purchaser could know which terms of the shrink wrap agreement were essential to the seller and which ones were not when the seller continued to sell software to the buyer. *Id.* at 103.

[187] *Id.* at 105.

[188] 831 F. Supp. 759, 766 (D. Ariz. 1993); *see* Illinois Wholesale Cash Register v. PCG Trading, 2008 WL 4924817 at *7 (N.D. Ill. Nov. 13, 2008).

ware, in stark, critical language, the court stated that shrink wrap licenses are not simply "invalid" but "contracts of adhesion, unconscionable, and/or unacceptable under the UCC."[189] In this case, the court found that the purchaser became an owner by way of sale, noting in a footnote that courts are "loathe to rule that such end-users should lose the benefits of ownership they had originally bargained for."[190] In *Wachter Management v. Dexter & Chaney*,[191] the Supreme Court of Kansas held that when a buyer and seller enter into a written contract for the purchase and sale of software, shrink wrap licensing terms accompanying the delivery of the software are only proposed modifications or amendments to the written contract and must be accepted in order to become part of the contract.

The holding of *ProCD* is best summarized by the court in *Hill v. Gateway*: "terms inside a box of software bind consumers who use the software after an opportunity to read the terms and to reject them by returning the product."[192] *ProCD* did not apply UCC Section 2-207; it applied only UCC Section 2-204 and concluded that the absence of a timely rejection was sufficient to show assent.

The analytical difference between *Step-Saver* and *ProCD* is whether "money now, terms later" forms a contract (1) at the time of the purchase order or (2) when the purchaser receives the box of software, sees the license agreement, and does not return the software.[193] If the purchase order is the contract, UCC Section 2-207 applies[194] and material terms cannot be added to the contract without explicit assent. If the contract is not formed until after the purchaser sees the shrink wrap license agreement, UCC Section 2-204 applies and the act of keeping the software implicitly shows assent.[195]

As such, there are two lines of precedent developing: (1) those courts endorsing the validity of "shrink wrap" agreements based the view that the contract is finalized on receipt of the software with accompanying terms that the buyer has an opportunity to accept or reject by returning the software, and (2) those courts taking the view that the receipt of the "additional terms" on the box containing the software constitutes a request for modification of the original terms of the contract—terms that must be accepted to become part of the contract and enforceable. The federal circuits are split.[196] The federal district courts

---

[189] Novell v. Network Trade Ctr., 25 F. Supp. 2d 1218 (D. Utah 1997).

[190] *Id.* at 1230.

[191] 144 P.3d 747 (Kan. 2006).

[192] 105 F.3d 1147, 1148 (7th Cir. 1997).

[193] In *Step-Saver Data Systems v. Wyse Technology*, 939 F.2d 91, 104 (3d Cir. 1991), the court rejected the "failure to return" analysis on the basis that no course of conduct between the parties could be established because the sale of the software, notwithstanding repeated orders, constituted the parties' initial commercial experience.

[194] The Third Circuit opinion in *Step-Saver* by Judge John Minor Wisdom (sitting by designation) includes a full scholarly discussion of the applicable UCC provisions. *Id.*

[195] *See, e.g.*, Klocek v. Gateway, 104 F. Supp. 2d 1332, 1338–39 (D. Kan. 2000) (noting distinction and rejecting *ProCD*); M.A. Mortenson. v. Timberline Software, 998 P.2d 305, 312–14 (Wash. 2000) (en banc) (noting distinction and embracing *ProCD*).

[196] The Sixth, Ninth, Eleventh, and Federal Circuits appear to follow the Seventh Circuit's decision in *ProCD v. Zeidenberg*, 86 F.3d 1447, 1451 (7th Cir. 1996). The Fifth Circuit appears to share the position of the Third Circuit's decision in *Step-Saver Data Systems v. Wyse Technology*,

outside those circuits that have addressed the question and the state courts are likewise split based on their reading of the applicable UCC provisions along with any modifications enacted by the respective states. Notwithstanding the courts' two divergent approaches to determining the validity of shrink wrap agreements, the cases are fact specific and evaluate the specific circumstances of the dealings between the parties.

As the years have passed, shrink wrap agreements have come to enjoy general acceptance. In *TracFone Wireless v. SND Cellular*, the court simply stated, "In Florida and the federal circuits, shrink wrap ... agreements are valid and enforceable contracts."[197] Perhaps a better statement might have included the modifier, "generally," but the point is that shrink wrap agreements are in widespread use and are generally accepted as enforceable contracts.

D. Common Principles

Several principles can be gleamed from all the browse wrap, click wrap, and shrink wrap cases. Assent remains critical but can be manifested in numerous ways. Assent can include conduct, words, signatures, e-mails, or other means that indicate agreement. Assent must occur after the party has had the opportunity to review the terms of the agreement. However, the party need not have read the agreement or understood its terms. Only an opportunity is required. Assent must include some manner in which the party can decline to assent. If assent is declined, the contract fails and the party can retain no benefit from the ostensive transaction—i.e., the software or computer must be returned.

V. HIPAA/HITECH BUSINESS ASSOCIATE AGREEMENTS

A. Introduction

The last two years have seen the most dramatic increase in federal regulation of patient privacy since the enactment of HIPAA in 1996.[198] The HITECH Act,[199] part of President Obama's "stimulus package," was primarily intended to bring the health care industry into the twenty-first century by providing incentives to encourage the widespread adoption of electronic health records (EHR).

---

939 F.2d 91 (3d. Cir. 1991); *see also* Wall Data v. Los Angeles Cnty. Sheriff's Dep't, 447 F.3d 769 (9th Cir. 2006); Lexmark Int'l v. Static Control Components, 387 F.3d 522 (6th Cir. 2004); Bowers v. Baystate Techs., 320 F.3d 1317 (Fed. Cir. 2003); Greenberg v. National Geographic Soc'y, 244 F.3d 1267 (11th Cir. 2001) (all cases acknowledging shrink wrap agreements).

[197]715 F. Supp. 2d 1246, 1259 (S.D. Fla. 2010).

[198]Health Insurance Portability and Accessibility Act, Pub. L. No. 104-191, 110 Stat. 1936 (1996). The Privacy Rule has not been amended since 2002, the Security Rule not since 2003. While the Enforcement Rule was amended in the October 30, 2009, interim final rule to incorporate the enforcement-related HITECH statutory changes, it had not been otherwise amended since 2006. Modifications to the HIPAA Privacy, Security, and Enforcement Rules Under the Health Information Technology for Economic and Clinical Health Act, 75 Fed. Reg. 40,868, 40,871 (proposed July 14, 2010) (to be codified at 45 C.F.R. pts. 160 & 164).

[199]Pub. L. No. 111-5, §§13001-424, 123 Stat. 226 (2009).

Since there is general recognition that this effort could not be successful without ensuring adequacy of privacy protections for the protected health information (PHI) of individual citizens, the HITECH Act also introduced substantial changes to HIPAA and its implementing regulations—imposing limitations on the ability of health and health-related businesses and covered entities to disclose such information and mandating stronger safeguards for the protection of PHI.[200]

The HITECH Act impacts providers of health care or covered entities and their contractual and other relationships with their "business associates," including any subcontractors of the business associate. Although HIPAA and its implementing regulations had provided for "a business associate agreement" to ensure that these entities complied with various HIPAA requirements, the HITECH Act provides that business associates are to be held directly responsible for the statute's requirements as well as compliance with its business associate agreements with covered entities. Business associates now need to comply with HIPAA's security and privacy requirements directly and can be held accountable by the federal government for violating HIPAA or a business associate agreement; the failure to do so can result in the imposition of civil and criminal penalties.[201] In addition, the statute imposes more stringent privacy and security requirements.

Covered entities include health care providers that transmit any health care information in electronic form, health plans, and health clearinghouses. The HITECH Act expands the list of entities that may be business associates to include organizations that provide data transmission of PHI to covered entities or business associates and that require access to PHI on a routine basis. These entities may include regional health information exchanges, e-prescribing gateways, and any vendor with contracts with a covered entity that offers personal health care records to patients.[202] Interestingly, attorneys who act as "business associates" for providers and other covered entities and obtain PHI in the act of representing these entities will need to comply with all of HIPAA's requirements. "Business associates" can be described generally as those who provide or render service to a covered entity and that service involves access to PHI. The subcontractors of business associates are also required to enter into business associate agreements with their business associates.[203]

---

[200]Press Statement, Blumenthal and Verdugo, Statement on Privacy and Security—Building Trust in Health Information Exchange (July 8, 2010).

[201]Under the HITECH Act, a business associate must comply with §§164.308, 164.310, 164.312, and 164.316 of the HIPAA Security Rule at Title 45 C.F.R. *See* HITECH §13401(a) (codified at 42 U.S.C. §17931). As to the Privacy Rule, by regulation, the agency did not add references to business associates because "we found such changes to be unnecessary, since a business associate generally may only use or disclose protected health information in the same manner as a covered entity (therefore any Privacy Rule limitation on how a covered entity may use or disclose protected health information automatically extends to business associates)." 75 Fed. Reg. at 40,888. It appears for all practical purposes, business associates need to comply with all of the substantive provisions of both the Security and Privacy Rules.

[202]HITECH §13400(2) (codified at 42 U.S.C. §17931) (referencing 45 C.F.R. §160.103(3)).

[203]75 Fed. Reg. at 40,912; 45 C.F.R. §160.103(3)(iii).

This section focuses on the fundamental considerations both covered entities and their business associates need to take into account when entering into a business associate agreement or contract.[204] While some provisions for inclusion in a business associate agreement are suggested,[205] any business associate agreement should be tailored to the specific circumstances of both the covered entity or provider and the business associate—and the business associate and any of its subcontractors.[206]

B. Statutory and Regulatory Requirements

The enactment of the HITECH Act dramatically changed and increased the burdens on business associates to comply with HIPAA's Security and Privacy Rules.[207] Covered entities may have one or more business associates. Many have dozens of organizations assisting their efforts to deliver and/or administer the delivery of health care to patients, and as such, these organizations possess some PHI, including PHI that is transmitted electronically. HHS sought to afford protections to PHI by extending the reach of HIPAA "downstream from a covered entity to its business associates and, then, to the subcontractors of each business associate."[208] To do so, the proposed regulation makes clear that a business associate is not permitted "to use or disclose protected health information in a manner that would violate the requirements of the Privacy Rule, if done by the covered entity."[209] A subcontractor of the business associate is likewise bound.[210]

1. Business Associate

HIPAA defines "business associate" at 45 C.F.R. §160.103 as:

---

[204] HITECH states that most of its requirements apply directly to business associates—irrespective of any agreement or contract—and can, as such, be directly enforced by federal authorities. Business associate agreements are nonetheless required and are important, since the agreements will, at a minimum, specify the respective roles of the covered entities and business associates in assuring compliance with HIPAA requirements.

[205] HHS published a "sample" business associate agreement to implement the original HIPAA requirements. *See* Standards for Privacy of Individually Identifiable Health Information, 67 Fed. Reg. 53,182, 53,264 (final rule issued Aug. 14, 2002) (to be codified at 45 C.F.R. pts. 160 & 164). The document remains significant because it emphasizes the need for all contracts to reflect the precise "business arrangements between the covered entity and the business associate." There are other "generic" sample business associate agreements available on the Web.

[206] Since vendors are not subject to HIPAA, the HITECH Act provides the Federal Trade Commission with new powers to authorize its use of its "unfair and deceptive trade practice" enforcement provisions against vendors that violate privacy and security mandates. HITECH §13407 (codified at 42 U.S.C. §17937). Implementing regulations impose similar requirements.

[207] The changes to the HIPAA Security and Privacy Rules implement statutory requirements that became effective on February 18, 2010. Covered entities were provided 180 days "beyond the effective date of the final rule" to come into compliance with the rule's provisions. 75 Fed. Reg. at 40,871. In general, covered entities and business associates were afforded one year to negotiate contracts that complied with statutory requirements. *Id.* at 40,889.

[208] *See, e.g., id.* at 40,833 (explaining how business entities and their subcontractors would comply with proposed 45 C.F.R. §164.314(a)(2)(i)(C) in the event of a breach of PHI).

[209] *Id.* at 40,887; 45 C.F.R. §164.502(a).

[210] 75 Fed. Reg. at 40,883; 45 C.F.R. §164.308(b).

[A] person who:

(i) on behalf of such covered entity or of an organized health care arrangement... in which the covered entity participates, but other than in the capacity of a member of the workforce of such covered entity or arrangement, performs, or assists in the performance of:

> (A) a function or activity involving the use or disclosure of individually identifiable health information, including claims processing or administration, data analysis, processing or administration, utilization review, quality assurance, patient safety activities... billing, benefit management, practice management, and repricing; or
>
> (B) Any other function or activity regulated by this subchapter; or

(ii) Provides, other than in the capacity of a member of the workforce of such covered entity, legal, actuarial, accounting, consulting, data aggregation (as defined in §164.501 of this subchapter), management, administrative, accreditation, or financial services to or for such covered entity, or to or for an organized health care arrangement in which the covered entity participates, where the provision of the service involves the disclosure of individually identifiable health information from such covered entity or arrangement, or from another business associate of such covered entity or arrangement, to the person.

In sum, the definition of "business associate" is broad and includes all those entities having some affiliation with covered entities in the delivery of health care or the support of health care services afforded by the covered entity and having some use of or contact with protected health information.

Before the enactment of the HITECH Act, HIPAA security and privacy requirements applied only indirectly to business associates. There were no regulatory requirements for business entities to comply with the HIPAA Security and Privacy Rules. Before HITECH, any security and privacy rules were made applicable to business entities through a business associate agreement or a contract between the covered entity and the business associate. In this circumstance, the only remedy available for noncompliance with the contract by the business associate was a potential breach of contract action by the covered entity.

With the direct requirement imposed by statute and regulation that business entities comply with many of HIPAA's security and privacy requirements, business entities that fail to comply, including those subject to breaches of PHI, face potential civil monetary penalties and other enforcement actions by HHS. Under the Act, business associates are subject to the same civil and criminal penalties as covered entities. The requirements also extend to the subcontractors of business associates. Notwithstanding the direct statutory requirement for business associates with comply with HIPAA's security and privacy requirements, HITECH mandates that the security and privacy requirements applicable to business associates "shall be incorporated into the business associate agreement between the business associate and the covered entity."[211] The goal is to

---

[211]HITECH §§13401(a), 13404(a) (codified at 42 U.S.C. §§17931, 17934). Initially, there was some "push back" from covered entities and commentators questioning the need to amend all business associate agreements to include all new requirements. Some simply asked why a contract

improve overall security for the protection of health care information—and the privacy—of individuals.

With the enhanced responsibility imposed on business associates, entities should determine whether they meet the statutory definition of business associate. In many cases, it will be readily ascertainable. In other cases, more precise analysis may be required. No entity should assume the responsibilities and liabilities attendant to entering into a business associate agreement before undertaking a comprehensive analysis to determine whether the entity meets the definition of "business associate." Moreover, if the entity determines that it falls within the definition, each business associate should negotiate a contract or agreement with each covered entity that is specific to its functions and delineates its responsibilities pursuant to HITECH's privacy and security mandates. The agreements should define the parties' legal relationship and express clear representations and warranties of compliance, as well as other requirements and responsibilities suggested by the discussion of HIECH Act mandated changes to the HIPAA Security and Privacy Rules set forth below. Specific provisions in business associate agreements may serve to reduce the strain in the parties' business relationship in the event of a breach of unsecured PHI.

Pursuant to the pre-HITECH rules, business entities were obligated to afford basic security and privacy protections by entering into agreements with covered entities in order to lawfully create, receive, maintain, or transmit electronic PHI on the covered entity's behalf. [212]

With the passage of the HITECH Act, these obligations are clarified, and others are applied directly to business associates. Section 13404 of the HITECH Act expressly requires that a business associate comply with the Privacy Rule at 45 C.F.R. §164.504(e) if the business associate desires to use or disclose protected health information that the business associate obtains or creates pursuant to a business associate agreement. Section 164.504(e) contains various requirements imposed on business associates as follows:

- The business associate is not authorized to use or further disclose protected health information in a manner that would violate the requirements of the Privacy Rule if done by the covered entity, except for the business associate's use and disclosure of protected health information for the proper management and administration of the business associate and the business associate's provision of data aggregation services relating to the health care operations of the covered entity.
- The business associate must (a) not use or further disclose the protected health information except as permitted or required by the business associate agreement or as required by law; (b) use appropriate safeguards to prevent the use or disclosure of the information; (c) report to the covered entity any use or disclosure of the information of which it becomes aware; (d) ensure that any agents, including subcontractors to whom the

---

was necessary in light of the statutory requirements; others argued that it was not required as a matter of law. In light of the passage of time, these criticisms have become muted; it appears that there has been sufficient time for all covered entities and their business associates to digest the requirements and modify and/or execute new agreements.

[212] 45 C.F.R. §164.308(b).

business associate provides protected health information, agrees to the same restrictions and conditions that apply to the business associate with respect to the protected health information; (e) make available protected health information in accordance with appropriate access requirements; (f) make available protected health information for amendment; (g) incorporate any amendments to protected health information in accordance with applicable rules; (h) make available the information required to provide an accounting of disclosures; (i) make its internal practices, books, and records available to the HHS Secretary for purposes of determining compliance; and (j) return or destroy all protected health information at the termination of the business associate agreement.

Section 13404 of the HITECH Act also states that such requirements "shall be incorporated into the business associate agreement between the business associate and the covered entity."[213]

Finally, subcontractors are included within the scope of coverage of the HITECH Act. Those persons who perform functions for or provide services to a business associate, other than in the capacity of a member of the business associate's workforce, are also business associates to the extent that they require access to PHI. Such a provision avoids a lapse in protecting PHI because a function is being handled by an entity that is a subcontractor rather than an entity with a direct relationship with the covered entity.[214] In implementing what HHS believed to be Congress's "concern that the privacy and security protections of HIPAA Rules extend beyond covered entities to those entities that create or receive protected health information in order for the covered entity to perform its health care functions," HIPAA protections have been extended to "downstream entities" that handle PHI.[215]

2. HITECH Mandated Changes to Privacy Rule

Pursuant to the HITECH Act, there are significant changes to the HIPAA Privacy Rule that directly impact the obligations of a business associate and need to be addressed in the business associate agreement. Business associates and covered entities will have to decide how to address these requirements in a business associate agreement based on their specific circumstances.

---

[213] The applicable section states, "[A] business associate may use or disclose such protected health information only if such use or disclosure ... is in compliance with the requirements of [45] CFR 164.504(e). The additional requirements of this subtitle that relate to privacy and that are made applicable with respect to covered entities shall also be applicable to such a business associate and shall be incorporated into the business agreement." HITECH §13404 (codified at 42 U.S.C. §17934). Section 13404(a) discusses the application of contract requirements to business associates; paragraph (b) applies the provision of 45 C.F.R. §164.504(e)(1)(ii) regarding knowledge of a pattern of activity that constitutes a material breach or violation of a contract to business associates; and paragraph (c) applies to HIPAA civil and criminal penalties. Some covered entities are requiring business associates to protect PHI even if the vendor does not presently obtain possession of PHI—in the event that their services in the future require some use or possession of PHI. For example, a software company may write a program for a health care purpose without the need for any PHI; however, the program may be tested with or eventually utilize PHI.

[214] 75 Fed. Reg. at 40,873, 40,883.

[215] Id. at 40,883. Covered entities have no obligation to enter into contracts with its business associate's subcontractors; that is the responsibility of the business associates.

a. Minimum Necessary

First, the HITECH Act clarifies the "minimum necessary rule."[216] Under the previous HIPAA rule, covered entities who were requested to disclose protected health information (PHI) when disclosure was permissible were required to disclose only the minimum amount of information needed to meet the party's request. Under the HITECH Act, compliance with security and privacy requirements can be demonstrated by limiting disclosures to a "limited data set" defined in 45 C.F.R. §164.514(e)(2), or by limiting disclosure to the "minimum necessary to accomplish the intended purpose of such use, disclosure, or request."[217] A limited data set can be identified by a qualified statistician or reflect the removal of specific information from any request, i.e., name, address, telephone and fax number, e-mail address, Social Security number, medical record numbers, and nine other identifiers.[218]

Until new guidance is issued, a covered entity and its business associates may limit disclosures to a limited data set or the minimum necessary as they may determine.[219] HITECH directs HHS to issue guidance as to what constitutes "minimum necessary." This guidance will replace the interim requirements. To date, such guidance has not been issued. Covered entities and business associates need to evaluate the wisdom of including an "automatic amendment" clause to the business associate agreement where the business entity agrees to comply with any additional federal regulatory requirements that may arise during the contract period. As to the specific issue, the parties may wish to negotiate their own definition of "minimum necessary," determine the minimum necessary on a case-by-case basis, or agree to disclose a limited data set as it is presently defined.

In addition, the business associate agreement may contain limitations on the collection of data, i.e., the converse of minimum necessary. The entity should be limited to collecting only that PHI that is reasonably necessary to permit it to perform its substantive contractual or other obligations. In the context of protecting patient privacy, information that has not been collected cannot be breached. In addition, the contract may limit access to the data to only those individuals in need of it in order to perform their assigned tasks. Further, since most breaches of PHI have to date involved lost or stolen computers,[220] covered entities should consider imposing rules regulating the use of computers by the employees of their business associates. Limiting the use of computers, including unnecessary downloading, printing, or e-mailing PHI, may serve to limit breaches of PHI. Moreover, provisions that require the destruction of old, stale data likewise limit the amount of data retained and the possibility of breaches.

---

[216] HITECH §13405(b)(1) (codified at 42 U.S.C. §17935(b)(1)).

[217] *Id.*

[218] *Id.*; 45 C.F.R. §164.514(a), (b).

[219] 75 Fed. Reg. at 40,896; *see also id.* at 40,887–88.

[220] In a recent incident, *The Boston Globe* reported on August 6, 2011 that "a doctor who works at Brigham and Women's and Faulkner hospitals lost an external hard drive in June, and the computer device may have contained medical information for 638 patients." The data covers inpatient hospital stays at the hospitals from July 2009 to January 28, 2011. Brigham hospital "has sent letters to those [affected] patients describing the problem."

Finally, any termination clause should include a provision for the return or destruction of all PHI in the business associate's possession.

b. Logging and Auditing

As originally enacted, HIPAA only required covered entities to keep a log of limited information disclosed to third parties.[221] On request, the entity was required to provide an "accounting" to the patient of the disclosures. Most "routine" disclosures, for example, except for disclosures to "carry out treatment, payment and health care operations," were excluded from the requirement.[222] The HITECH Act changes this rule for all health providers that utilize electronic health records (EHR).[223] This change eliminates the primary exception so that all disclosures will have to be logged and accounted for. A proposed rule, issued on May 21, 2011, has generated substantial controversy.[224] The proposed rule creates a "right" for patients to access a report to be created by covered entities and/or business associates sufficient to permit individuals to learn about individuals who have accessed their PHI through an electronic record.[225] Since many covered entities have many business associates, the business associate agreement should specify how these required logs will be addressed when requested by a patient.

c. Restricted Disclosures

Providers must agree to any request made by a patient to restrict disclosure of PHI to an insurance company if the patient paid for the service in cash.[226] Under the old rules, a provider could refuse to agree to a patient's request to restrict routine disclosures of PHI.[227] The agency commentary in the Federal Register raises a number of issues that covered entities and business associates should address in business associate agreements. For example, how will a

---

[221] 45 C.F.R. §164.528(a)(1)(i). Section 13405(c) of the HITECH Act provides that an individual has a right to receive an accounting of such disclosures made during the three years prior to the request. With respect to disclosures by business associates through an EHR to carry out treatment, payment, and health care operations on behalf of the covered entity, §13405(c) requires the covered entity to provide either an accounting of the business associates' disclosures, or a list and contact information of all business associates (enabling the individual to contact each business associate for an accounting of the business associate's disclosures). HIPAA Privacy Rule Accounting of Disclosures Under the Health Information Technology for Economic and Clinical Health Act, 76 Fed. Reg. 31,426 (rule proposed May 31, 2011) (to be codified at 45 C.F.R. pt. 164).

[222] Id.

[223] Id.

[224] 76 Fed. Reg. 31,426. Critical comments were filed by many health care and health care related organizations, including the American Medical Association, College of Healthcare Information Management Executives (CHIME), Healthcare Billing and Management Association, Federation of American Hospitals, Association of American Medical Colleges, American Hospital Association, and American Health Information Management Association (AHIMA).

[225] Nahra, *The HIPAA Accounting NPRM and the Future of Health Care Privacy*, 3 HEALTH IT LAW & INDUSTRY (BNA) (July 4, 2011).

[226] HITECH §13405(a) (codified at 42 U.S.C. §17935).

[227] 45 C.F.R. §164.522(a); Modifications to the HIPAA Privacy, Security, and Enforcement Rules Under the Health Information Technology for Economic and Clinical Health Act, 75 Fed. Reg. 40,868, 40,900 (proposed July 14, 2010) (to be codified at 45 C.F.R. pts. 160 & 164).

restriction sought by a patient be implemented if a prescription is sent to a pharmacy electronically? When the patient arrives at the pharmacy, the pharmacy may have already sent the information to a health plan for payment.[228] Could appropriate contractual provisions facilitate the notification of providers "downstream" that an individual intends to pay out of pocket for a prescription or other health services and will be invoking the restriction set forth in the statute? Does the HITECH Act impose any such obligation?[229]

The HITECH Act adds a new provision prohibiting providers from receiving payment in exchange for disclosing PHI to third parties—unless a patient signs a release.[230] There are various exceptions—generally relating to the care of the patient, "public health activities," and research—as defined in the appropriate regulation.[231] In addition, releases of PHI in a limited data set do not require an authorization.[232] The commentary makes clear that an entity may charge a patient for any data the individual may request.[233] The covered entity and its business associates may address these issues by contract.

d. Fundraising and Marketing

The HITECH Act imposed additional restrictions on the ability of covered entities and business associates to use PHI for fundraising[234] to benefit their institutions and marketing communications [235] to potential buyers and users of their products. Entities engaged in marketing and fundraising will need to pay particular attention to these issues.

The restrictions imposed by the HITECH Act on marketing appear to be intended to curtail a covered entity's ability to use the exceptions to the definitions of marketing in the Privacy Rule to send communications motivated by financial gain to individuals, including former patients. Covered entities need to review the requirements of these regulations carefully when proposing marketing activities to any entity that might fall within the definition of business associate to ensure that the requirements are met. The requirements narrow prior exceptions and focus on whether the marketing activity is undertaken for remuneration.

---

[228] 75 Fed. Reg. at 40,899.

[229] *Id.* HHS invited comments on these and other issues, including whether technologies exist that would facilitate notification among providers of restrictions sought by individuals paying for services in cash when the information sought to be restricted moves "downstream" to other providers.

[230] HITECH §13405(d)(1) (codified at 42 U.S.C. §17935(1)). Under the applicable regulation, the release or authorization must state "whether remuneration will be received by the covered entity with respect to the subject to the authorization. Otherwise the individual would not be put on notice that the disclosure involves remuneration and thus, would not be making an informed decision as to whether to sign the authorization." 75 Fed. Reg. at 40,890; 45 C.F.R. §164.508(a)(4).

[231] HITECH §13405(d)(2) (codified at 42 U.S.C. §17935); *see* 75 Fed. Reg. at 40,890 (containing a fuller description of the exceptions).

[232] 75 Fed. Reg. at 40,891.

[233] *Id.*

[234] HITECH §13406(b) (codified at 42 U.S.C. §17936); *see also* 75 Fed. Reg. at 40,869.

[235] *Id.*

Carefully drawn contractual provisions are necessary to enable business associates to do limited amounts of marketing for covered entities absent compliance with requirements for authorization, notice, and an opportunity to opt out.[236] For example, covered entities and business associates alike can make communications promoting general health, the importance of maintaining a healthy diet, or getting an annual checkup; these practices are not defined as marketing. [237] Absent remuneration, business entities can send communications regarding an individual's treatment or prescription refill reminders; describe health-related products or services included in a plan of benefits; and contact individuals regarding treatment alternatives.

If remuneration is afforded by the covered entity to the business associate—which will almost always be the case—more stringent requirements are imposed. When communicating to an individual regarding a health-related product or service when remuneration has been afforded, the communication falls outside the regulatory definition of marketing only if the covered entity or business associate has advised the patient in a privacy notice of the individual's ability to "opt out" of receiving any such communications and discloses that the health care provider is receiving payment for making the communication.[238] Communications of prescription refill reminders are exempt only if the remuneration received for making the communication "is reasonably related to the... cost of making the communications."[239] Face-to-face communications do not invoke these requirements.[240] These business arrangements should be evaluated on a case-by-case basis in light of the regulatory changes.

When a business associate enters into an arrangement with a covered entity—in exchange for remuneration—to sell it own products or services, such a situation is now defined as a sale of PHI and invokes the requirement that the individual consent by signing a release. In sum, the business associate agreement should specify with particularity the kind and dimension of the services to be afforded to its covered entity and any remuneration to be afforded. The parties may also benefit from a recitation of the steps the business entity will take, e.g., issuing an appropriate privacy notice, when engaging in any marketing activities for a covered entity.[241]

The rules for fundraising have also been tightened.[242] The new proposed regulation would strengthen the opt-out provision of the current regulation by requiring all fundraising materials to contain a clear opt-out provision as well as treat the individual's decision to opt out as a revocation of authorization within the meaning of 45 C.F.R. §164.508 of the Privacy Rule.[243] The intent of the regulation is to ensure that the individual's decision to opt out is honored; a

---

[236]The commentary in the Federal Register recognizes that business associates conduct "marketing" for covered entities in accordance with their contract. 75 Fed. Reg. at 40,886. The regulatory approach taken here is to narrow the definition of marketing.

[237]*Id.* at 40,886–87.

[238]*Id.* at 40,886.

[239]*Id.* at 40,885.

[240]*Id.*

[241]*Id.*

[242]HITECH §13406(b) (codified at 42 U.S.C. §17936).

[243]75 Fed. Reg. at 40,896–97.

"reasonable effort" standard has been repealed. Business associate agreements need to reflect these requirements in some manner if fundraising is one of the business associate's responsibilities. Lawyers should review and redraft, as necessary, privacy notices, including the necessary opt-out provisions.[244]

e. Access to Patient Record

The HITECH Act requires that if a provider maintains PHI in electronic form, the provider must afford this information in electronic form to the patient if the patient so requests.[245] While the former rule limited the right of patient access to whether "the form or format, is readily producible," covered entities and their business associates that maintain such information in electronic form would be required under these proposed modifications to provide some type of electronic copy if requested by an individual."[246]

f. Role of State Law

Finally, it should be noted that state law plays a role in business associate contracts. The proposed rule modifying HIPAA's requirements in light of the HITECH Act makes clear that HIPAA preempts state law that is contrary to HIPAA—except to the extent state privacy requirements are stricter, in which case the stricter standard applies.[247] This concept must be kept in mind when a business associate is negotiating an agreement with a covered entity in a different jurisdiction.

In sum, in addition to imposing the requirements of the Privacy Rules on business associates, the HITECH Act imposes additional burdens that may properly be addressed in business associate agreements.

3. HITECH Mandated Changes to Security Rule

Significant changes to HIPAA's security rules were mandated by the HITECH Act. Under the HITECH Act, business associates will be directly subject to the administrative, physical, and technical safeguard requirements of the Security Rule, as well as the requirements to maintain policies, procedures, and documentation of security activities "in the same manner that such sections apply to the covered entity."[248] Accordingly, business associates must implement reasonable and appropriate policies and procedures to incorporate the requirements described in the following subsections.

---

[244]HHS requested comment on any number of issues relating to fundraising, including whether an opt-out provision should apply to all future fundraising activities or just the particular fundraising campaign at hand. Providers are also seeking to utilize additional information to support their fundraising efforts, e.g., in addition to demographic information and dates of hospitalization, treatment outcomes and the patient's department of service are sought. *Id*. at 40,897. These requests and others for comment indicate that the proposed regulation may change; therefore, careful attention to a final rule will be required. No new regulations had issued through Oct. 2011.

[245]*Id*. at 40,901; HITECH §13405(e) (codified at 42 U.S.C. §17934).

[246]See 75 Fed. Reg. 40,869 for a general description of provisions.

[247]HITECH §13421 (codified at 42 U.S.C. §17951).

[248]HITECH §13401(a) (codified at 42 U.S.C. §17931); *see* 75 Fed. Reg. at 40,882–83.

a. Administrative Safeguards

In accordance with 45 C.F.R. §164.308, business associates must implement, identify, establish, or perform

(1) policies and procedures to prevent, detect, contain, and correct security violations;
(2) the security official who is responsible for the development and implementation of the policies and procedures required by the Security Rule for the business associate;
(3) policies and procedures to ensure that all members of its workforce have appropriate access to electronic PHI, and to prevent those workforce members who do not have access from obtaining access to electronic protected health information;
(4) policies and procedures for authorizing access to electronic PHI that are consistent with the applicable requirements of the Privacy Rule;
(5) a security awareness and training program for all members of its workforce (including management);
(6) policies and procedures to address security incidents;
(7) policies and procedures for responding to an emergency or other occurrence (for example, fire, vandalism, system failure, or natural disaster) that damages systems that contain electronic PHI; and
(8) a periodic technical and nontechnical evaluation in response to environmental or operational changes affecting the security of electronic PHI that establishes the extent to which an entity's security policies and procedures meet the requirements of the Security Rule.

b. Physical Safeguards

In accordance with 45 C.F.R. §164.310, business associates must implement

(1) policies and procedures to limit physical access to its electronic information systems and the facility or facilities in which they are housed, while ensuring that properly authorized access is allowed;
(2) policies and procedures that specify the proper functions to be performed, the manner in which those functions are to be performed, and the physical attributes of the surroundings of a specific workstation or class of workstation that can access electronic PHI;
(3) physical safeguards for all workstations that access electronic protected health information, to restrict access to authorized users; and
(4) policies and procedures that govern the receipt and removal of hardware and electronic media that contain electronic protected health information into and out of a facility, and the movement of these items within the facility.

c. Technical Safeguards

In accordance with 45 C.F.R. §164.312, business associates must implement

(1) technical policies and procedures for electronic information systems that maintain electronic PHI to allow access only to those persons or software programs that have been granted access rights;
(2) hardware, software, and/or procedural mechanisms that record and examine activity in information systems that contain or use electronic PHI;
(3) policies and procedures to protect electronic PHI from improper alteration or destruction;
(4) procedures to verify that a person or entity seeking access to electronic PHI is the one claimed; and
(5) technical security measures to guard against unauthorized access to electronic PHI that is being transmitted over an electronic communications network.

As a result of the direct imposition of these requirements on business associates, business entities need to ensure that they are in compliance with HIPAA's security rules to comply with the HITECH Act. Business associates must address certain administrative, physical, and technical safeguards in the same manner as a covered entity.

All business entities will need a secure and professionally based and supported comprehensive information system. In addition, any information system would include appropriate security measures, policies, procedures, and documentation to demonstrate compliance.[249] The security standards require, inter alia, a business entity to conduct a risk analysis to assess potential risks and vulnerabilities to electronic PHI, implement reasonable risk management measures, ensure appropriate staff and training programs, and implement procedures to identify and address breaches. To further these requirements, a business entity should assess current security risks and gaps, develop an implementation plan, document all decisions, and reassess compliance periodically and modify its implementation plan, as necessary.[250] These requirements impose on covered entities and business associates a heightened need to ensure compliance. Provisions in the business associate agreement covering each of these areas in some manner should be considered mandatory.

d. Breach Reporting Requirement

Additionally, a new breach reporting requirement has been added.[251] The HITECH Act creates a breach notification requirement[252] that requires covered entities, their business associates, and subcontractors of their business associates

---

[249] *See* 45 C.F.R. §164.306(b) (flexible requirements).

[250] *See* Dep't of Health & Human Servs., Center for Medicare & Medicaid Servs., HIPAA Security and Privacy Rules, Privacy and Security Standards, *available at* http://www.cms.gov/HIPAAGenInfo/04_PrivacyandSecurityStandards.asp.

[251] *See* DATA BREACH ENCRYPTION HANDBOOK, ABA SCIENCE AND TECHNOLOGY LAW SECTION (L. Thomson, ed., 2011) (full discussion of data breach notification requirements and major data breaches to date).

[252] HITECH §13402(a) (codified at 42 U.S.C. §17932). See discussion of applicable regulations, Breach Notification for Unsecured Protected Health Information, 74 Fed. Reg. 42,740 (interim final rule with request for comments, Aug. 24, 2009) (to be codified at 45 C.F.R. pts. 160 & 164).

to notify patients of any unauthorized access[253] to their unsecured PHI.[254] It is critical to note that the notification rule only applies to PHI that is "unsecured" within the meaning of the HITECH Act. In general, this means that covered entities need not notify patients if the PHI is encrypted or has been destroyed. In addition, there are other standards and requirements that mandate the analysis of each breach to determine if notification is required. As such, the relevant regulations mandate the conduct of a risk assessment where the covered entity and the relevant business associate can assess these issues.

Business associates are required to notify their covered entities whenever they discover a breach of unsecured PHI.[255] Business associate agreements should specify this obligation and set forth requirements for policies and procedures to both identify breaches of unsecured PHI and respond to any breach should it occur.[256] Consideration should be given to explicitly setting forth the need to encrypt PHI. Encryption of PHI—rendering the PHI "unusable, unreadable, or indecipherable"—provides a "safe harbor" where no notifications in the event of a breach are required.[257] Although the HITECH Act would permit other means to ostensibly protect PHI, only by encrypting data can a covered entity or business associate qualify for the safe harbor the regulations provide for when PHI is protected by encryption.[258]

All business associate agreements should emphasize means to prevent breaches of PHI—not merely steps to follow should a breach occur. Encryption of PHI together with a professionally developed and maintained computerized information system is the best protection against breaches of PHI. In addition to a requirement for a response plan and a team to address any breach that may occur, training requirements for staff should be set forth in business associate agreements as a means not merely of responding to breaches but of preventing them.

Moreover, the current regulation specifies a "harm standard" by which a breach of unsecured PHI is to be defined. In other words, a breach of unsecured PHI that violates the HIPAA Privacy Rule is nonetheless not a breach within the meaning of the regulation unless it "poses a significant risk of financial, reputational, or other harm to the individual."[259] In order to determine "harm," a

---

[253] The HITECH Act defines a breach as the unauthorized acquisition, access, use, or disclosure of PHI that compromises the security or privacy of such information. HITECH §13400 (codified at 42 U.S.C. §17921).

[254] HITECH §13407 (codified at 42 U.S.C. §17937) applies similar breach notification provisions to vendors of personal health records and their third party service providers. 74 Fed. Reg. 42,962 (Aug. 29, 2009).

[255] A breach is the "acquisition, access, use, or disclosure of protected health information in a manner not permitted under Subpart E of this part [HIPAA Privacy Rule] which compromises the security or privacy of the protected health information." 45 C.F.R. §164.402.

[256] Such policies may include procedures governing breach discovery, internal reporting, and notification; requirements for training employees; a complaint procedure; sanctions for personnel misusing PHI; documentation requirements; and a statement of patients' rights.

[257] See 74 Fed. Reg. at 42,742–43 (encryption standards).

[258] See id. at 42,742 (discussion of encryption).

[259] See id. at 42,744.

risk assessment must be performed.[260] The business associate agreement should require a risk assessment for every breach and specify how and by whom this risk assessment is to be performed.[261] Since the covered entity will ultimately bear the responsibility for any breach, a business associate agreement might well contain a provision requiring the business associate to notify the covered entity of all potential breaches. The covered entity may not agree with the business associate's "risk assessment."

The HITECH Act contains strict time frames for notifications required to individuals and governmental entities. The regulations provide that the covered entity has 60 days from the time the party discovered the breach, or should have known of the breach, to notify the individual. The covered entity is dependent on notification of a breach by the business entity in order to meet this requirement in a timely manner. The covered entity may wish to negotiate a provision that the business associate notify the covered entity immediately of the discovery of a breach so the covered entity can meet the statutory imposed time frame for mandated notifications. In light of the serious nature of breaches, a covered entity should consider requiring business entities to advise it of any potential breach as soon as the business associate has reason to believe a breach may have occurred. Some covered entities are requiring "immediate notice" or notice within one business day of learning of a potential breach or circumstances that may suggest a breach has occurred.

The absence of specific provisions governing which party will provide the required notifications, investigate the breach, and coordinate their efforts could result in noncompliance and substantial exposure to civil monetary penalties by HHS. Whatever procedures are negotiated, they should be specific and fully take into account the covered entities' and business associates' respective responsibilities, including specific provisions for notification of the covered entity of a breach and a delineation of the process that the business associate will follow to ensure that the covered entity can comply with HITECH requirements.

In light of the breach notification requirement, many covered entities have sought to require business associates to enhance their information systems to afford greater security to PHI and privacy to individuals. It is not clear that all business associates have welcomed these overtures. Enhanced security, including the establishment of separate servers to address the needs of particular covered entities, can be an expensive proposition. Some business entities that have

---

[260] *See id.* at 42,744–45; *see also* OMB Memorandum M-07-16, *available at* http://www.whitehouse.gov/OMB/memoranda/fy2007/m07-16.pdf.

[261] In addition, there are other exceptions delineated in the regulation that may negate the requirement to provide the requisite notification in event of a breach, e.g., unauthorized disclosure of information in the form of a limited data set, "good faith" and inadvertent disclosures to and among members of an entity's workforce, and disclosures where the entity holds a good-faith belief that the person to whom the disclosure has been made could not have been able to retain the information. These factors emphasize both the need for and the complexity of the required risk assessment and the factors that must be considered when determining whether a breach within the meaning of the current HITECH regulations has taken place. HHS has withdrawn these regulations for OMB prior to their issuance as "final" final. In the meantime, the Final Interim Regulations remain in effect. *See* http://www.hhs.gov/ocr/privacy/hipaa/administrative/breachnotificationrule/index.html.

different relationships with various covered entities have found that the requirements for security are not alike in the eyes of different covered entities.

Covered entities are now required to notify individuals of breaches of PHI, but business associates are only required to notify their covered entities of a breach when it is discovered. As such, this imposes on the covered entity all of the costs, burden, and public exposure associated with sending notifications and responding to queries from patients and others. While a business associate agreement should contain a provision for notification of the covered entity by the business associate when any breach is discovered, the covered entity may desire to specify in the business associate agreement the identify of who is responsible for notifying patients when unsecured PHI was improperly used or disclosed by the business associate. In light of the increased responsibilities placed on business associates—including increased liability—the procedures and responsibilities of the respective parties in the event of a breach should be clearly addressed in a business associate agreement.

In light of the costs and exposure to liability in the event of a breach, a covered entity should consider adding indemnification provisions to agreements with their business associates for protection in the event an associate violates applicable privacy and security standards. Covered entities should be mindful not to limit such indemnification to any cap that may be set forth in any other contract with the business associate and be aware of any implications for their insurance coverage.[262] In addition, covered entities may wish to incorporate a provision into agreements with their business associates that the associates will report their own disclosures of PHI to patients, thus removing the burden of doing so from the covered entities.

e. Additional Responsibilities

Additional responsibilities are placed on business associates regarding misuse of PHI that may be addressed in the business associate agreement, including termination should their covered entities violate privacy and security protections afforded by the statute and implementing regulations. For example, if a business associate ascertains a "pattern of activity or practice" by a covered entity that breaches its business associate contract, the business associate must address the breach, terminate the contract, or report the noncompliance to HHS.[263]

f. Monetary Penalties

Finally, monetary penalties have been increased. HITECH creates a tiered system of "civil monetary penalties" that can be imposed on covered entities

---

[262]Entities should consider the implications of indemnification clauses and review all insurance policies to determine whether their insurance policies preclude coverage of costs or damages associated with an indemnification obligation of an insured.

[263]The HITECH Act §13404(b) (codified at 42 U.S.C. §17934), expressly applies the so-called "snitch provision" of HIPAA, found in §164.504(e)(1)(ii) of the Privacy Rule, to a business associate in the same manner that such provision applies to a covered entity. Consequently, the business associate is under an affirmative duty to either take reasonable steps to cure the breach or other violation of the covered entity or terminate the business associate agreement, if feasible. If termination is not feasible, the business associate must report the breach or violation to the HHS Secretary.

that violate HIPAA's protections.[264] These penalties range from a minimum of $100 per day up to a maximum of $1.5 million.[265] If federal authorities find that the violation resulted from willful neglect, a fine must be imposed. In addition, the HITECH Act authorized state attorneys general to enforce HIPAA; previously enforcement authority was limited to HHS.[266] HHS was also afforded additional authority to audit health care providers to determine their compliance with HIPAA.[267] These measures are designed to prevent and/or minimize the incidence of breaches.

VI. Conclusion

The digital revolution in health care is reflected in a host of ways, ranging from the multitude of contracts entered into every day over the Internet for health and health-related products to the need for business associate agreements to protect the security of PHI and the privacy of patients. Professors, commentators, and the courts have been challenged to fit traditional contract principles into a world where more and more commercial transactions of all types are being conducted by electronic means. This chapter serves as an introduction to emerging issues in contract law—one facet of the digital revolution in health care—and the need for all those entities handling personal health information to maintain its security and, as a result, the privacy of patients. As the future evolves, we will see how our legal and health institutions adapt to an ever-changing environment where computers "conduct business" and where their use holds out the promise of helping to reduce health care costs but risks wholesale invasions of privacy. Enforceability of electronic contracts and the privacy of patients will remain challenges for the foreseeable future.

---

[264]Modifications to the HIPAA Privacy, Security, and Enforcement Rules Under the Health Information Technology for Economic and Clinical Health Act, 75 Fed. Reg. 40,868, 40,877–81 (proposed July 14, 2010) (to be codified at 45 C.F.R. pts. 160 & 164).

[265]45 C.F.R. §160.404.

[266]HITECH §13410 (codified at 42 U.S.C. §17939).

[267]HITECH §13411 (codified at 42 U.S.C. §17940).

14

Evaluating Antitrust Concerns in the Electronic Marketplace*

I.	Introduction	426
	A. Electronic Marketplaces	426
	B. Overview of Antitrust Law	426
	C. Antitrust Issues in the E-Commerce Setting	429
II.	Collaborations With Competitors	430
	A. Guidance	430
	B. Market Definition	431
	C. Facilitating Collusion	432
	1. Inherent Risks of Sharing Information	432
	2. Controlling the Risks	433
	3. Heightened Standard for Circumstantial Evidence	436
	D. Group Boycott	436
	E. Group Purchasing and Sales	437
	1. Traditional Analysis	437
	2. New Issues Created by the Electronic Marketplace	438
III.	Legal Analysis of Vertical Integration Issues	439
	A. Competitor Control of Vertically Related Entity	439
	B. Practical Limitations of the Theory	441
IV.	Exclusionary Practices	443
	A. Network Effects	443
	B. Exclusive Use Requirements	444
	C. Most-Favored-Nation Requirements	445
V.	Standards and Certification	447
	A. Significance to Electronic Health Care	447
	B. Historical Analysis	448
	C. Health Care Experience With Private Standard-Setting	450
VI.	Conclusion	452

*Patricia Wagner, Epstein Becker Green, P.C., Washington, D.C.

I. Introduction

A. Electronic Marketplaces

Electronic marketplaces typically are classified as connecting either businesses to consumers (B2C) or businesses to other businesses (B2B). Where a business is connected with consumers, electronically or otherwise, few antitrust issues are suggested. Where businesses seek to connect with each other, the same cannot be said. In fact, the rapid development of B2B electronic marketplaces raised sufficient antitrust concerns to cause the Federal Trade Commission (FTC) to hold a public workshop on the subject, resulting in a 35-page staff report entitled *Competition Policy in the World of B2B Electronic Marketplaces (FTC Staff Report).*[1]

For the sake of convenience, this chapter uses the FTC definition of B2B electronic marketplaces: "B2B electronic marketplaces . . . are a 'distinct system of suppliers, distributors, commerce service providers, infrastructure providers and customers that use the Internet for communications and transactions.'"[2]

The *FTC Staff Report* concludes that traditional antitrust principles apply to the electronic marketplace and proceeds to describe this application to issues raised in the workshop, with substantial reliance on the FTC's own *Antitrust Guidelines for Collaborations Among Competitors (Competitor Collaboration Guidelines).*[3] The legal analysis attendant to these B2B issues is not different from the traditional analysis of joint ventures. The principal issues generally can be classified within three categories:

- *Market structure:* Will the creation of the electronic marketplace itself be likely to substantially lessen competition, create an unreasonable restraint of trade, or constitute monopolization?
- *Collateral contractual restraints:* Do the contractual requirements imposed by the operators of the marketplace on either the participants or the operators themselves constitute unreasonable restraints of trade?
- *Facilitating collusion:* Will the operation of the marketplace be likely to facilitate collusion among the participants or the operators, impacting on collateral activities that otherwise would be competitive?

B. Overview of Antitrust Law

Because traditional antitrust analysis will apply in the e-health context, a brief introduction to the most applicable antitrust laws may be in order. The federal statutes are subject to both criminal and civil enforcement. The U.S. Department of Justice (DOJ) has jurisdiction to enforce all of the federal antitrust

---

[1] FEDERAL TRADE COMM'N STAFF, ENTERING THE 21ST CENTURY: COMPETITION POLICY IN THE WORLD OF B2B ELECTRONIC MARKETPLACES (2000) [hereinafter FTC STAFF REPORT], *available at* http://www.ftc.gov/os/2000/10/b2breport.pdf.

[2] *Id.* pt. 1, at 1B2.

[3] FEDERAL TRADE COMM'N & U.S. DEP'T OF JUSTICE, ANTITRUST GUIDELINES FOR COLLABORATIONS AMONG COMPETITORS (2000) [hereinafter COMPETITOR COLLABORATION GUIDELINES], *available at* http://www.ftc.gov/os/2000/04/ftcdojguidelines.pdf.

laws, and the FTC has jurisdiction to enforce its own Federal Trade Commission Act,[4] as well as certain other federal antitrust statutes. In addition, private plaintiffs can bring civil claims under the federal antitrust laws and, if successful in the litigation, are automatically entitled to treble damages, as well as an award of attorney fees.[5]

Sections 1 and 2 of the Sherman Act[6] and Section 7 of the Clayton Act[7] will probably be the most applicable to issues arising in e-health arrangements. Section 1 of the Sherman Act declares illegal "every contract, combination... or conspiracy in restraint of trade or commerce."[8] Despite its sweeping language, Section 1 has been interpreted to prohibit only unreasonable restraints on competition, as every contract or combination arguably restricts trade or commerce by binding the parties involved.[9] A violation of Section 1 of the Sherman Act requires concerted activity and, as a result, requires conduct that is occurring between two or more separate economic entities.

Under Section 1, conduct can be evaluated under the "per se" standard or under the "rule of reason" standard. Per se violations are the most serious antitrust offenses, and are the ones for which entities and individuals may be criminally indicted. A per se analysis does not require an analysis of the affected market or of anti-competitive effects of the conduct. Rather, per se offenses involve activities that because of their "pernicious effects on competition and lack of any redeeming virtue are conclusively presumed to be unreasonable and therefore illegal without elaborate inquiry as to the precise harm they have caused or the business excuse for their use."[10] Per se offenses include price-fixing, bid rigging, and division of product or geographic markets among competitors. In addition, tying and horizontal group boycotts can be evaluated under the per se standard, although the U.S. Supreme Court has noted that these two offenses (unlike the other per se offenses) require a threshold showing of market power possessed by the defendants.[11]

Under the rule of reason analysis, the conduct is evaluated for its likely, or actual, anti-competitive effects. Conduct that would likely be evaluated under a rule of reason analysis includes dealing on an exclusive basis when the arrangement forecloses competitors from the market, engaging in group boycott activities, entering into most-favored-nation contracts, and agreeing to use market power (defined as the ability to raise prices or exclude competitors) to exclude or disadvantage a competitor.

Resale price maintenance (sometimes referred to as vertical price-fixing) is also a Section 1 offense but is no longer considered a per se violation under

---

[4] 15 U.S.C. §§41–58, as amended.
[5] 15 U.S.C. §15.
[6] 15 U.S.C. §§1, 2.
[7] 15 U.S.C. §18.
[8] 15 U.S.C. §1.
[9] Business Elecs. Corp. v. Sharp Elecs. Corp., 485 U.S. 717, 723 (1988).
[10] Northern Pac. Ry. Co. v. United States, 356 U.S. 1, 5 (1958).
[11] FTC v. Indiana Fed'n of Dentists, 476 U.S. 447, 106 S. Ct. 2009 (1986); Jefferson Parish Hosp. Dist. No. 2 v. Hyde, 466 U.S. 2, 104 S. Ct. 1551 (1984); Northern Pac. Ry. Co. v. United States, 356 U.S. 1, 78 S. Ct. 514 (1958); Standard Oil Co. v. United States, 221 U.S. 1, 31 S. Ct. 502 (1911).

federal law.[12] In *Leegin Creative Leather Products v. PSKS, Inc.*,[13] the U.S. Supreme Court overruled nearly a century of antitrust jurisprudence and held that minimum resale price maintenance, or vertical price-fixing, is no longer per se illegal. Prior to *Leegin*, in *State Oil Co. v. Khan*,[14] the Court had held that vertical price-fixing arrangements that set a maximum resale price were no longer per se illegal. In *Leegin*, the Court extended the analysis to hold that even minimum resale price maintenance would be evaluated under the rule of reason, rather than treated as per se illegal. Nevertheless, in response to the Court's opinion in *Leegin*, some states have adopted statutes that make minimum resale price maintenance illegal. For example, in Maryland, "a contract, combination, or conspiracy that establishes a minimum price below which a retailer, wholesaler, or distributor may not sell . . . is an unreasonable restraint of trade."[15] Variation among the states on the approach to resale price maintenance can be challenging, particularly for entities operating in e-commerce.

Section 2 of the Sherman Act[16] addresses monopolization (and variations thereof) and can be violated by a single actor. In general, this statute prohibits a firm that has a strong market position from engaging in exclusionary practices such as offering services below variable cost, engaging in price discrimination without a legitimate business justification, or taking action that would be unprofitable except for its exclusionary effect. The determination of illegal monopolization generally depends on three elements:

(1) the defendant's possession of monopoly power within a relevant market;
(2) the defendant's acquisition or maintenance of this power for exclusionary or anti-competitive means or the use of the power for exclusionary or anti-competitive purposes; and
(3) injury to the plaintiff as a result of the monopoly power and exclusionary or anti-competitive conduct.[17]

Finally, the other federal antitrust statute most likely to become an issue in certain e-health activities is Section 7 of the Clayton Act.[18] Section 7 generally prohibits mergers and acquisitions that threaten to substantially lessen competition in any line of commerce, in any section of the country. Section 7 also applies to the formation of joint ventures that threaten anti-competitive results.

In addition to the federal statutes, most states have antitrust statutes that generally track federal law. Nevertheless, state attorneys general may also enforce federal law as parens patriae for their citizens.

---

[12] Leegin Creative Leather Products v. PSKS, Inc., 551 U.S. 877 (2007).
[13] *Id.*
[14] 522 U.S. 3 (1997).
[15] MD. CODE ANN., COM. LAW §11-204(b).
[16] 15 U.S.C. §2.
[17] *See, e.g.*, United States v. Aluminum Corp. of Am., 148 F.2d 416 (2d Cir. 1945).
[18] 15 U.S.C. §18.

C. Antitrust Issues in the E-Commerce Setting

The types of activities related to e-health (and other e-commerce) that may be most likely to create antitrust issues include the following:

- business-to-business (B2B) exchanges (which, in turn, typically include joint purchasing or joint sales arrangements, as well as other information-sharing activities);
- partial or complete vertical integration;
- standard-setting by competitors; and
- the misuse of intellectual property.

The creation of health care provider networks to facilitate (and sometimes allegedly to inhibit) managed care contracting historically has raised concerns over the impact of any given network on the ability of others to form competing networks, as well as concerns over the impact of network operations on the prices of health care services sold through that network. Similar concerns have been expressed about the effect of electronic networks. Where the size and rules of engagement for a given network make it unlikely that others can compete or even enter into the market, Section 7 of the Clayton Act[19] (substantial lessening of competition as a result of merger, acquisition, or formation of a joint venture) as well as Section 2 of the Sherman Act[20] (monopolization) may be implicated. As always, Section 1 of the Sherman Act[21] (conspiracy and other agreements constituting unreasonable restraint of trade) casts a shadow over any anti-competitive arrangement among competitors.

These issues can arise in a variety of contexts, whether through the use of health information exchanges to evaluate efficiency and effectiveness of health care treatment, through implementation of accountable care organizations (ACOs) or other clinical integration arrangements where providers share information on patients, or in the vertical integration of health care entities. With the advent of health reform legislation,[22] the resulting ACOs, as well as the focus on development of health information exchanges (HIEs) and electronic medical records, the development of new and, perhaps, innovative provider networks is likely to be coupled with electronic exchanges of information.

While antitrust issues of all varieties may be expected to emerge over time in the e-commerce context, this chapter focuses on the issues listed above as the most likely to draw scrutiny in the near term. While this proliferation of horizontal cooperation and vertical cross-ownership may not create new antitrust issues, it certainly exacerbates the old ones.

---

[19] 15 U.S.C. §18.
[20] 15 U.S.C. §2.
[21] 15 U.S.C. §1.
[22] See Patient Protection and Affordable Care Act, Pub. L. No. 111-148, 124 Stat. 119 (2010).

II. Collaborations with Competitors

A. Guidance

In 1996, the FTC and DOJ issued the *Statements of Antitrust Enforcement Policy in Health Care* (*Enforcement Statements*) to provide health care entities guidance on collaborative agreements that take place in a health care context.[23] One area addressed in the *Enforcement Statements* is physician network joint ventures, defined as physician-controlled joint ventures "in which the physician participants collectively agree on prices or price related terms and jointly market their services."[24] The *Enforcement Statements* offer an antitrust safety zone if the physicians in the network share substantial financial risk and the network includes no more than 30 percent of the physicians in each specialty, so long as network membership is nonexclusive, i.e., the physicians can participate in multiple networks. Where participation requires exclusivity, the safety zone is reduced to apply only to those networks that have financial risk sharing and that include no more than 20 percent of physicians in each specialty. While the *Enforcement Statements* introduced a concept of clinical integration for physician networks (networks where physicians exchange clinical information in order to increase the quality of care to patients), such networks do not meet safety zone requirements and are subject to the rule of reason analysis.[25]

Because ACOs operate on the premise that significant information will be exchanged between otherwise unaffiliated providers, the FTC and DOJ issued a "Statement of Antitrust Enforcement Policy Regarding Accountable Care Organizations Participating in the Medicare Shared Savings Program," outlining how these provider collaborations could avoid antitrust scrutiny.[26] Like the *Enforcement Statements*, the Statement also establishes a safety zone for certain ACOs in the Medicare Shared Savings Program. To qualify for the ACO safety zone, providers must meet the requirements of the Medicare Shared Savings Program. The FTC and DOJ noted that compliance with that program will demonstrate that the providers have developed significant clinical integration (through the sharing of medical information and focus on quality of care) to avoid per se scrutiny that might otherwise apply to competitors sharing information. The ACO safety zone, like that in the *Enforcement Statements*, applies to the ACO only if two or more independent providers who are providing shared services collectively have 30 percent or less of the market share for that shared service. In addition:

---

[23]Federal Trade Comm'n & U.S. Dep't of Justice, Statements of Antitrust Enforcement Policy in Health Care (1996) [hereinafter Enforcement Statements], *available at* http://www.ftc.gov/bc/healthcare/industryguide/policy/index.htm.

[24]*Id.* at 62.

[25]*Id.* at 80.

[26]Statement of Antitrust Enforcement Policy Regarding Accountable Care Organizations Participating in the Medicare Shared Savings Program (Oct. 20, 2011), *available at* http://www.ftc.gov/opa/2011/10/aco.shtm.

- any hospital or ambulatory surgery center in the ACO is nonexclusive—e.g., allowed to contract or affiliate with other ACOs or commercial payors; and
- any dominant provider of any service that no other ACO participant is providing in the same market (greater than a 50 percent market share) is nonexclusive.[27]

A similar theme is present in the more general *Competitor Collaboration Guidelines,* which also offer a structural safety zone for "general" competitor collaborations (generally synonymous with joint ventures among competitors), as follows: "Absent extraordinary circumstances, the Agencies do not challenge a Competitor Collaboration where the market shares of the collaboration and its participants collectively account for no more than 20 percent of each relevant market in which competition may be affected."[28] However, the *Competitor Collaboration Guidelines* go on to state that "[t]he safety zone, however, does not apply to agreements that are per se illegal, or that would be challenged without a detailed market analysis, or to competitor collaborations to which a merger analysis is applied."[29]

B. Market Definition

Numerous efforts to electronically interconnect health care providers and health information systems have occurred around the nation. State-level health information exchange initiatives have been and are being pursued, bringing the Internet "network of networks" concept more directly to health care information. Indeed, current legislation has provided incentives for health information exchanges, including establishing an Office of the National Coordinator for Health Information Technology, which among other things oversees the development of state HIEs.[30] In addition, current legislation encourages providers not only to utilize electronic medical records (EMRs)[31] but to ensure those EMRs are "interoperable" so that information exchanges can occur among different unaffiliated providers. The legal issues raised by these new initiatives include issues raised by joint ventures involving multiple competitors and proposals to share information among competitors, including what is the relevant market for these types of arrangements.

One potentially significant development regarding these issues occurred in 2002 with the settlement of the FTC's prosecution of the Hearst Trust, relating to its acquisition of First Data Bank, Inc., and the related action brought by the DOJ. Both of the companies involved in these actions were providers of electronic databases containing clinical, pricing, and other information on prescription and nonprescription pharmaceuticals. Each company sold a so-called

---

[27]*Id.* at 21,895. The Statement of Antitrust Enforcement Policy Regarding Accountable Care Organizations Participating in the Medicare Shared Savings Program provides a safety zone for certain rural providers as well.

[28]COMPETITOR COLLABORATION GUIDELINES at 20.

[29]*Id.*

[30]American Recovery and Reinvestment Act, Pub. L. No. 111-5, §3001.

[31]*Id.* §4101.

"integratable drug data file," which allows pharmacists to conveniently track both the prices and the clinical aspects of pharmaceuticals. The complaint in this action related primarily to contentions that the parties had not complied with certain aspects of the Hart-Scott-Rodino premerger notification requirements in connection with the acquisition of First Data Bank by the Hearst Trust, and to additional allegations that the acquisition was itself illegal under the standards of Section 7 of the Clayton Act.[32]

Most interesting for electronic health care issues is the allegation in the complaint that electronic integratable drug information databases constitute a separate product market from identical information kept and used manually. As the FTC complaint alleges, "[d]rug information in other [nonelectronic] forms is not an adequate substitute for the provision of such information through integratable drug data files."[33] Because the case was settled through a consent judgment,[34] the issue of whether electronic health care information constitutes a separate product market distinct from manual or hard copy versions of the same information was never fully developed. If the allegation is true, however, it may portend future antitrust litigation made more serious by allegations of high market concentration when that market is limited to electronic health care activities, taken separately from legacy activities.

C. Facilitating Collusion

1. Inherent Risks of Sharing Information

Issues certainly can be predicted where health care exchanges propose to sell provider services or any combination of products or services that are dominated by a limited number of competitors. As discussed below, electronic marketplaces that are operated or ultimately controlled by a group of horizontally aligned companies (competitors) are destined to raise the most sensitive antitrust issues. One of the reasons for this sensitivity is that any rules of participation adopted by these competitors, which ultimately work to exclude other competitors, are at risk of being characterized as a horizontal group boycott, or the sharing of information could be seen as facilitating collusion and be deemed a per se violation of Section 1 of the Sherman Act.

The electronic marketplace can make information available in quantities and at speeds that were, until recently, unimaginable. Acquiring information about market conditions, competitors, and customers once required painstaking processes at substantial expense, often returning information that was likely to be stale and too anecdotal to be reliable. The electronic marketplace can make this information available instantly, inexpensively, and globally. For antitrust purposes, this is both a virtue and a vice.

---

[32]Federal Trade Comm'n v. Hearst Trust, Civil No. 1:01CV00734 (D.D.C. complaint filed Apr. 4, 2001), *available at* http://www.ftc.gov/os/2001/04/hearstcmp.htm.
[33]*Id.*
[34]*See* Federal Trade Comm'n v. Hearst Trust, Civil No. 1:01CV00734 (D.D.C. final judgment filed Dec. 14, 2001), *available at* http://www2.ftc.gov/os/2001/12/hearst finalorder.pdf; United States v. Hearst Trust, Civil No. 1:01CV02119 (D.D.C. motion for entry of final judgment filed Oct. 10, 2001), *available at* http://www.usdoj.gov/atr/cases/f9200/9291.pdf.

Antitrust law has long regarded the sharing of information about recent market conditions as an important part of facilitating competition, and the sharing of detailed information about competitive plans among competitors as an important part of facilitating collusion. Where the information shared, in substance and in timeliness, permits competitors to glean the intimate inner workings of each other's situations, coordination based on this information may be too predictable to ignore.

The opportunities for mischief created by the ways in which information can be shared over even the most ordinary workings of the electronic marketplace have been a principal focus of recent commentary from enforcement agents and agencies. Commissioner Swindel of the FTC, for example, has warned: "[W]hile a B2B exchange can be very pro-competitive, such an arrangement can also give rise to anti-competitive information sharing among actual or potential competitors. This can increase the likelihood of collusion on price, output, or other competitive variables, to the detriment of competition and consumers."[35]

When the subject turns to the use of an electronic marketplace to facilitate price-fixing or other forms of collusion, the first precedent cited is invariably the consent judgment reached in *United States v. Airline Tariff Publishing Co.*[36] While predating the Internet-based exchanges currently under scrutiny, this case offers a glimpse of similar issues, employing similar technology, leading to what the agencies are likely to describe as the result of human nature allowed to run its course through cyberspace.

The defendants in *Airline Tariff* were six airlines and their jointly owned and operated electronic service, which collected and disseminated data on airfares. The government charged that the carriers had used a complex set of conventions regarding pricing plans as a way of communicating future pricing intentions and coordinating fares. Because the defendants agreed to entry of an injunction prohibiting the types of conduct believed to facilitate this price coordination, no record was created to explain all of the details.

2. Controlling the Risks

The concept that a little information is a good thing, but a lot of information may not be, has been telegraphed to health care providers for years through the *Enforcement Statements*. Three of the nine *Enforcement Statements* deal with the collection and dissemination of information. The most pertinent here, Statement 6, addresses provider participation in exchanges of price and cost information. Statement 6 offers an antitrust "safety zone" for exchanges of price and cost information among providers only under the following circumstances:

- the survey is managed by a third party (e.g., a purchaser, government agency, health care consultant, academic institution, or trade association);

---

[35]Comm'r Orsen Swindle, Antitrust in the Emergent B2B Marketplace, Speech delivered at the Princeton Club, New York City (July 19, 2000). For an index of speeches on the FTC Web site, see www.ftc.gov/speeches/speech1.htm. *See also* FTC STAFF REPORT, pt. 3, at 4–6.

[36]Civil Action No. 92-2854 (D.D.C. final consent judgment entered Nov. 2, 1993), *available at* http://www.justice.gov/atr/cases/dir23.htm.

- the information provided by survey participants is based on data more than three months old; and
- there are at least five providers reporting data on which each disseminated statistic is based, no individual provider's data represents more than 25 percent on a weighted basis, and any information disseminated is sufficiently aggregated that recipients cannot identify the prices charged or compensation paid by any particular provider.[37]

Similarly, the 2011 Statement of the FTC and DOJ signals that providers participating in ACOs that have market power should adopt certain procedural safeguards to ensure that information exchanged among ACO members is not inappropriately used.[38] For example, the Statement suggests that those ACOs that include two or more independent providers with collectively "high" market shares should adopt procedural safeguards that ensure that, among other things, the members of the ACO don't share information on pricing or engage in conduct that might restrict a payor's ability to establish alternative networks or network designs.[39]

The information sharing safety zone of the *Enforcement Statements*, as with the case law on which the statements are loosely based, reflects an effort to balance the need to know what is going on in the market in order to make sensible competitive decisions against the presumed (and sometimes proven) human tendency to use this information collusively and for anti-competitive gains. The Supreme Court itself has historically struggled with this balance, focusing ultimately on characteristics of the information and the industry in question in order to predict the effect of any given information sharing program.

The case most often described as coming close to establishing a rule of per se illegality for the exchange of price information among competitors is *United States v. Container Corp. of America*.[40] This case involved a civil price-fixing complaint that was brought by the United States and dismissed by the trial court. The Supreme Court reversed the dismissal of the complaint, explaining that, as charged, the exchange of price information among competitors seemed to have the effect of keeping prices within a fairly narrow ambit. Knowledge of a competitor's price usually meant matching that price. The court focused on the fact that the industry was dominated by a few sellers, the product in question was fungible, competition for sales was based solely on price, and market-wide demand for the product was inelastic. Consequently, the exchange of price data tended to lead to price uniformity, as sellers recognized that a lower price would not mean a larger share of the available business but only a sharing of the existing business at a lower return.

Subsequently, other courts have read *Container Corp.* as suggesting that a violation of the Sherman Act may be found where the market structure and nature of competition indicate that an information exchange program will lead

---

[37] ENFORCEMENT STATEMENTS at 50.

[38] Statement of Antitrust Enforcement Policy Regarding Accountable Care Organizations Participating in the Medicare Shared Savings Program (Oct. 20, 2011), *available at* http://www.ftc.gov/opa/2011/10/aco.shtm.

[39] *Id.*

[40] 393 U.S. 333 (1969).

to price stabilization and a reduction in price competition. Particularly harsh language is found in *Flav-O-Rich, Inc. v. North Carolina Milk Commission*.[41] In *Flav-O-Rich,* the North Carolina Milk Commission disseminated information to its members regarding prices and costs of certain wholesale products. One milk processor-distributor sued, claiming that this was a price-fixing violation. The federal district court ultimately found that the conduct in question was mandated by the state of North Carolina and therefore was exempt from Sherman Act scrutiny. The court noted, however, that if there were no state action exemption, the conduct would be a violation of the Sherman Act and explained that the following facts led to this conclusion: there were a small number of sellers and a large number of buyers of milk in the state; there were few perceptible differences between brands of milk; the primary means of competition was pricing; and the demand for the product as a whole was inelastic, such that competition through price was only significant to the extent that an individual seller could increase its share of the market by taking customers away from its competitors. The court stated: "Under these circumstances, the court agrees with plaintiff that price exchanges would result in price stability in violation of *United States v. Container Corp.*"[42]

Other courts, including the U.S. Supreme Court, have held that the mere exchange of price-related information or dissemination of that information by a third party is not unlawful in and of itself but requires an additional showing of an anti-competitive effect.[43]

Both the FTC and the Antitrust Division of the DOJ have been asked to review proposed data dissemination services. Most of the review letters have related to dissemination services that provided only aggregated or average cost or price information. Some, however, have proposed services that would provide product-specific and seller-specific information. Government review letters typically have emphasized that a program disseminating information, even specific prices of products identified by seller, is not inherently illegal, but that a number of factors, including most prominently the structure of the industry and the nature of the information exchanged, must be considered to determine whether the program is likely to lead to anti-competitive effect.[44]

Because the electronic marketplace tends to make information about individual competitors available more quickly and more completely than ever before, these issues are likely to become both more common and more sensitive with increased information exchanges being encouraged. The result may be a more competitive market. If the opportunity to act collectively on this information is just too tempting to pass up, however, the result may be less competition.

---

[41] 593 F. Supp. 13 (D.N.C. 1983), *aff'd*, 734 F.2d 11 (4th Cir. 1984) (unpublished table decision), *cert. denied*, 469 U.S. 853, 105 S. Ct. 176 (1984).

[42] *Id.* at 15.

[43] *See, e.g.*, United States v. United States Gypsum Co., 438 U.S. 422, 443 (1978); United States v. Citizens & S. Nat'l Bank, 422 U.S. 86 (1975); Rosefielde v. Falcon Jet Corp., 701 F. Supp. 1053, 1061–62 (D.N.J. 1988).

[44] *See, e.g.*, FTC Adv. Op. (Feb. 8, 1985); DOJ Bus. Rev. Ltr. (June 12, 1992); DOJ Bus. Rev. Ltr. (Sept. 8, 1988); DOJ Bus. Rev. Ltr. (Mar. 24, 1988); DOJ Bus. Rev. Ltr. (June 20, 1986).

3. Heightened Standard for Circumstantial Evidence

The litigation exposure related to information exchanges may have been mitigated by the U.S. Supreme Court decisions in *Bell Atlantic Corp. v. Twombly*[45] and *Ashcroft v. Iqbal*.[46] In those cases, the Court emphasized that a complaint must state a claim that is plausible in order to survive a motion to dismiss. In *Twombly*, the Court emphasized that pleading conclusory statements of a conspiracy does not justify the cost imposed in pursuing discovery to determine whether such a conspiracy occurred. The Court explained that merely pleading parallel conduct together with conclusions of a conspiracy mirrors the ambiguity of the behavior itself, consistent with conspiracy, but also consistent with rational competitive business strategies unilaterally prompted by common perceptions of the market. Pleading facts that are also consistent with unilateral conduct does not support an inference of conspiracy, even at the pleading stage.

D. Group Boycott

While the risk of a per se violation remains a valid concern with respect to price-fixing and exchanges of information, the Supreme Court has severely limited the application of the group boycott label. In *Northwest Wholesale Stationers v. Pacific Stationery & Printing Co.*,[47] the Supreme Court held that expulsion of one competitor from a purchasing cooperative controlled by other competitors would be per se illegal only where the cooperative in question possessed market power or unique access to a business element necessary for effective competition. Otherwise, the expulsion is tested under the rule of reason.

Much like a competitor-controlled B2B, *Northwest Wholesale Stationers* involved a purchasing cooperative made up of approximately 100 office supply retailers within a certain geographic region. The cooperative acted as the primary wholesaler for those retailers. Retailers who were not members of the cooperative were permitted to purchase wholesale supplies from the cooperative at the same price as members. At the end of each year, however, the cooperative distributed its profits to members in the form of a percentage rebate on purchases. Effectively, therefore, members purchased supplies at a price significantly lower than did nonmembers. The plaintiff in the action was a former member that was expelled from the cooperative after deciding to maintain its own wholesale operation as well as participating in the cooperative. This basis for the expulsion, however, was never formally given to the plaintiff, and the expulsion was viewed as having been effectuated without explanation or a procedural opportunity to be heard or to challenge the decision. The Supreme Court explained that some concerted refusals to deal, or group boycotts, historically have been found so likely to restrict competition without offsetting efficiency gains that they should be condemned as per se violations of Section 1 of the Sherman Act. The Court also explained that the types of boycotts historically viewed as per se illegal generally involve joint efforts by firms to disadvantage competitors either

---
[45] 550 U.S. 544 (2007).
[46] 129 S. Ct. 1937 (2009).
[47] 472 U.S. 284, 297–98 (1985).

by directly denying, or persuading or coercing suppliers or customers to deny, relationships that the competitors need. Such boycotts typically cut off access to a supply, facility, or market necessary to enable the boycotted firm to compete and typically were perpetrated by firms possessing market power.

The *Northwest Wholesale Stationers* Court distinguished purchasing cooperatives from other forms of concerted activity more likely to result in anti-competitive effects. Purchasing cooperatives (as with B2B exchanges in general) have the potential to increase economic efficiency and render markets more competitive on balance. The cooperative may permit economies of scale to be achieved in both purchasing and storing supplies and also may help ensure ready access to goods when needed. The cooperative approach also may enable smaller retailers to reduce prices and maintain retail stocks in a way that allows them to compete more effectively with larger retailers. The Court also recognized that a cooperative must have rules for participation in order to function effectively. The Court explained that determining the likelihood of anti-competitive effects would require a detailed factual picture of market structure, including some showing that the cooperative possessed market power or unique access to business elements necessary for effective competition. The Court specifically stated: "Unless the cooperative possesses market power or exclusive access to an element essential to effective competition, the conclusion that expulsion is virtually always likely to have an anti-competitive effect is not warranted."[48] Here, the plaintiff made no showing that it met any of the tests for per se illegality. Rather than demonstrating market power or essential business elements, the plaintiff had emphasized a lack of procedural safeguards in membership termination. The lack of procedural safeguards, however, was viewed as inconsequential by the Court.

E. Group Purchasing and Sales

1. Traditional Analysis

Perhaps the most frequently described activity of the electronic marketplace is serving as a forum for the purchase and sale of goods and services. Group purchasing arrangements have a long and relatively trouble-free history within the health care industry. These arrangements are, in fact, so well recognized and accepted within this industry that they are the focus of one of the nine *Enforcement Statements* of antitrust enforcement policy.[49]

As explained in Statement 7 of the *Enforcement Statements:* "Through such joint purchasing arrangements, the participants frequently can obtain volume discounts, reduce transaction costs, and have access to consulting advice that may not be available to each participant on its own." In effect, joint purchasing arrangements are given substantial latitude because of the presumption that they have the potential to create purchasing efficiencies through demand aggregation, benefitting both buyers and sellers. Statement 7 explains that antitrust concerns are unlikely to be raised in connection with joint purchasing,

---

[48] 472 U.S. at 296.
[49] ENFORCEMENT STATEMENTS at 53.

unless the arrangement accounts for so large a portion of the purchases of a given product or service that the arrangement effectively creates market power (described there as the power to drive the price of goods and services purchased below competitive levels), or the products being purchased jointly account for so large a portion of the total costs of the products or services being sold by the participants that the joint purchasing arrangement may facilitate price-fixing or otherwise reduce competition. Statement 7 further offers an "antitrust safety zone" for joint purchasing arrangements among health care providers, so long as the following conditions are met:

- the purchases being effected jointly account for less than 35 percent of the total sales of the product or service in the relevant market; and
- the cost of the products and services purchased jointly accounts for less than 20 percent of the total revenues from all products or services sold by each competing participant in a joint purchasing arrangement.

Where the joint purchasing arrangement does not fall within the safety zone, Statement 7 explains, antitrust risks can be reduced by permitting members of the joint purchasing arrangement to purchase products and services outside the joint purchasing arrangement; using an independent agent to conduct negotiations on behalf of the joint purchasing arrangement; or maintaining confidentiality of communications between the purchasing group and each individual participant such that other participants are not privy to these communications.

Where purchasers of health care services, e.g., employers, have sought to aggregate their purchases from health care providers through business coalitions, similar deference has been afforded to these purchaser coalitions, again with an apparent assumption that efficiencies in purchasing and sales are thereby made possible. For example, in early 1994, the DOJ's Antitrust Division issued two business review letters to coalitions of purchasers of health care services.[50] Each of these letters concludes that the formation of coalitions to purchase health care services from providers has the potential to create efficiencies in the delivery of services that could help to lower health care costs.

2. New Issues Created by the Electronic Marketplace

One of the challenges for group purchasing arrangements arranged through B2B electronic marketplaces may well be to substantiate the concept that collaborative purchasing decisions offer efficiencies beyond those created by the electronic marketplace itself. A frequently discussed benefit of electronic marketplaces has been the automated aggregation of both demand and supply and the dramatic reduction of transaction costs. Where the marketplace itself creates the efficiencies previously presumed to be achieved through collaborative purchasing decisions, will future collaborative decisions be justifiable? The answer to this question may be particularly difficult where the electronic marketplace also facilitates separate delivery directly to the ultimate customer, even as the order itself comes from the group purchasing organization.

---

[50] See U.S. DOJ Rev. Ltr., Houston Healthcare Coalition (Mar. 23, 1994); U.S. DOJ Rev. Ltr., Bay Area Business Group on Health (Feb. 18, 1994).

III. LEGAL ANALYSIS OF VERTICAL INTEGRATION ISSUES

A. Competitor Control of Vertically Related Entity

The structural analysis of a joint venture, B2B or otherwise, begins with Section 7 of the Clayton Act, which prohibits acquisitions that may "lessen substantially competition." As stated by one court:

> [I]t is no longer questioned that Section 7 applies to the acquisition of newly formed companies, such as this joint venture, as well as to the acquisition of companies already engaged in commerce.... Thus the only question is whether the *probable effect* of the joint venture is substantially to lessen competition.[51]

In highly concentrated markets, a joint venture involving potential entrants may support a conclusion that the probable effect is substantially to lessen competition.[52] In *Yamaha v. FTC*,[53] the U.S. Court of Appeals for the Eighth Circuit described one of the most aggressive approaches to this potential entrant doctrine, stating:

> [T]he doctrine, under the circumstances of this case, would bar under §7 acquisitions by a large firm in an oligopolistic market, if the acquisition eliminated the acquired firm as a potential competitor, and if the acquired firm would otherwise have been expected to enter the relevant market de novo. To put the question in terms applicable to the present case, would Yamaha, absent the joint venture, probably have entered the U.S. outboard motor market independently, and would this new entry probably have increased competition more than the joint venture?[54]

The *Enforcement Statements* and the case law dealing with market structure are written primarily from the perspective of joint ventures involving horizontal competitors. Typically, market concentration issues are raised directly when the horizontally aligned venturers create a venture that also is horizontally aligned with its parents. The myriad of relationships unique to health care, however, make this industry more sensitive than most when vertical relationships, joint-ventured or not, are created.

A structural approach to a vertical joint venture was used by the FTC in a successful prosecution (to the extent success is measured by achieving a consent decree without actually litigating the issue) in the *Home Oxygen* cases, arising in Northern California.[55] In the *Home Oxygen* cases, physicians who were the referral source for purchasers of ancillary products owned the ancillary product resellers, thus raising a concern that competing resellers would be foreclosed from sources of patient referrals.

---

[51] Northern Natural Gas Co. v. Federal Power Comm'n, 399 F.2d 953, 962 (D.C. Cir. 1968) (emphasis added) (citation omitted).

[52] United States v. Penn-Olin Chem. Co., 378 U.S. 158, 168–172 (1964).

[53] 657 F.2d 971, 977 (8th Cir. 1981).

[54] *Id.* at 977.

[55] *In re* Home Oxygen & Med. Equip. Co., FTC Nos. 901-0109 & 901-0020 (1994). See the FTC Web site, www.ftc.gov/ftc/antitrust.htm, for public documents, information on policies, highlights, and case filings on matters of antitrust/competition.

The complaint in the *Home Oxygen* cases alleged that 60 percent of the pulmonologists practicing within the relevant geographic market purchased interests in two home oxygen companies, and that pulmonologists had the ability to influence the choice of oxygen systems purchased by their patients. The subsequent consent decree required that not more than 25 percent of the referral sources in any relevant area be owners of the same home oxygen company.

Perhaps most interesting in the scenario of the *Home Oxygen* cases was the fact that ultimately the consent decree was modified to allow all of the participating pulmonologists to retain their investment interests in the subject company, once that company was sold to a large publicly traded company. As a result, ultimately 60 percent of the pulmonologists in the area still owned shares in the same home oxygen company, but their ability to influence its profitability was diluted. The implicit conclusion appears to be that if the percentage of ownership is sufficiently small, to the point that physicians' own referral of patients will not have a noticeable impact on company profits, then human nature will not cause the physicians to send their patients to the company in which they have invested. However, a tension still lingers as to whether ownership alone is sufficient to create liability or whether there must, in fact, be some sort of agreement to exclusively use the self-owned vendor.

The presumption that vertically related firms with any material level of cross-ownership will be reluctant to do business with competitors of the equity holders is the foundation of the case law analyzing vertical acquisitions. Nevertheless, it is a very difficult concept on which to prevail in court.

One of the earliest vertical equity cases was the United States' challenge to DuPont Co.'s acquisition of 23 percent of the stock of General Motors (GM), which reached the Supreme Court in 1957.[56] This acquisition was perceived as vertical in nature because GM was a large purchaser of paint and other automotive finishes from DuPont. The Supreme Court held the acquisition to be unlawful and required divestiture of the stock. The Court determined that automotive finishes and fabrics were a separate product market, and that DuPont's ownership of 23 percent of the stock of a large customer had the effect of foreclosing this customer to competing sellers of finishes and fabrics. The evidence showed that after the acquisition of the stock, GM purchases of DuPont products increased dramatically. There also was anecdotal evidence showing that one of the reasons for acquiring the stock was to obtain influence over GM's purchasing decisions. In fact, DuPont's annual reports at the time mentioned the common interest in GM's purchase of DuPont products, helping the Supreme Court to conclude that DuPont's acquisition of a 23 percent interest was not a mere passive investment.

In a subsequent case, the Supreme Court described the negative aspects of a vertical relationship as follows:

> The primary vice of a vertical merger or other arrangement tying a customer to a supplier is that, by foreclosing the competitors of either party from a segment of the market otherwise opened to them, the arrangement may act as a "clog on competition" which deprives . . . rivals of a fair opportunity to compete.[57]

---

[56] United States v. E.I. DuPont de Nemours & Co., 353 U.S. 586 (1957).
[57] Brown Shoe Co. v. United States, 370 U.S. 294 (1962) (citations omitted).

The reason it is so difficult to win in vertical integration cases is illustrated by the language of the Second Circuit in *Fruehauf Corp. v. FTC*,[58] explaining:

> But we are unwilling to assume that any vertical foreclosure lessens competition. Absent very high market concentration or some other factor threatening a tangible anticompetitive effect, a vertical merger may simply realign sales patterns, for insofar as the merger forecloses some of the market from the merging firms' competitors, it may simply free up that much of the market, in which the merging firm's competitors and the merged firm formerly transacted, for new transactions between the merged firm's competitors and the merging firm's competitors.[59]

Despite this difficulty, in recent years the FTC has taken an interest in vertical mergers and integrations in the health care space. The FTC has entered consent decrees that ensure that the flow of sensitive competitor information is protected, by requiring segregation of business lines and creation of "firewalls."

For example, in 1995, the FTC investigated the acquisition of a pharmacy benefit manager (PBM) by Eli Lilly. In order for the transaction to be completed, Eli Lilly entered into a consent agreement with the FTC to address the FTC's concerns that the acquisition would inappropriately limit the access of other pharmaceutical companies to the PBM's formulary, thereby restricting competition. Under the consent agreement, Eli Lilly had to create a firewall to segregate the two business lines, the PBM had to maintain an open formulary, and Lilly had to appoint an independent committee to administer the open formulary.[60] Similarly, 1999, the FTC reviewed a transaction after the acquisition of Medco by Merck had taken place. As was true in the Eli Lilly matter, the FTC's concern was that the acquisition (i) would lead to the foreclosure of other pharmaceuticals; (ii) would lead to "reciprocal dealing, coordinated interaction, interdependent conduct and tacit collusion among Merck and other vertically integrated pharmaceutical companies"; (iii) had eliminated an independent negotiator from the market; (iv) would decrease incentives for innovation by other manufacturers; and (v) would lead to an increase in prices and decrease in quality of pharmaceuticals. Similar to the Lilly consent order, the Merck-Medco consent agreement required the creation of a firewall to segregate the two business lines, maintenance by Medco of an open formulary, and appointment of an independent committee to administer the open formulary.[61]

B. Practical Limitations of the Theory

The problem with a purely structural approach to the analysis of competitor-controlled B2Bs and other vertical relationships is illustrated by the FTC's recent termination of the investigation relating to the formation of Covisint. Covisint was a nascent B2B exchange owned by five automotive manufacturers, which together constitute approximately one-half of worldwide automotive

---

[58]603 F.2d 345 (2d Cir. 1979).
[59]*Id.* at 352 n.9.
[60]120 F.T.C. 243 (1995).
[61]News Release, Federal Trade Comm'n, *Merck Settles FTC Charges that Its Acquisition of Medco Could Cause Higher Prices and Reduced Quality for Prescription Drugs* (Aug. 27, 1998), *available at* http://www.ftc.gov/opa/1998/08/merck.shtm.

production. The formation of Covisint received significant attention both from the FTC and the press, at least in part because of its stated purpose of creating a consolidated electronic marketplace by which the five founders, and presumably other auto manufacturers that later joined the marketplace, could purchase all of their input materials. Consequently, tens of thousands of automotive suppliers would be required to use this marketplace to make all of their sales to the exchange operators. While the closing letters from the FTC emphasized that it was making no determination that violations may not occur as this marketplace operates, the mere formation of the exchange, with no bylaws, operating rules, or other terms of engagement yet in place, would not be impeded by government action.

The clear signal from the FTC's action with respect to Covisint,[62] and the likely actions with respect to other nonoperational marketplaces, is that conduct and contract issues, not mere size, will to this point be determinative. It is too early yet to apply a purely structural analysis to these methods of doing business. As winners and losers in these markets appear, however, this likely will cease to be true. *Choiceparts v. General Motors*,[63] took up where the Covisint investigation left off and illustrates the risks attendant to vertical control of a B2B exchange. The complaint in *Choiceparts* alleged, in substance, that the three leading U.S. automakers, all co-founders of Covisint, created a joint venture B2B to perform as an advanced automotive parts locator. The plaintiff was the owner and operator of a competing online service. The plaintiff alleged that the defendant co-founders conspired to withhold automotive parts data the plaintiff needed, and that the defendants did so in order to prevent the plaintiff from developing its own Internet-based parts locator service. The joint venture B2B only dealt in parts of the joint venture owners. The plaintiff alleged an unlawful restraint of trade in violation of Section 1 of the Sherman Act as well as a conspiracy to monopolize the advanced parts locator market in violation of Section 2 of the Sherman Act. The plaintiff's allegations withstood defendants' motion for summary judgment, and the parties ultimately settled the matter.[64]

Interestingly, the parties' final settlement in *Choiceparts* occurred after the decision in *Verizon Communications v. Trinko*.[65] There, the U.S. Supreme Court in 2004 clarified and emphasized the proposition that there is no duty to aid competitors. The *Trinko* case arose in the context of relations among telecommunications providers. The plaintiff, a lawyer, proposed to represent a class of consumers allegedly injured by the alleged failure of Verizon to provide adequate service to local exchange carriers that competed with Verizon in the resale of the services in question. The Supreme Court held that the complaint failed to state a cause of action, as it was based upon a presumption that Verizon had a duty to work cooperatively with competitors who needed to purchase these wholesale services in order to compete in the resale thereof. The Court clarified

---

[62] For Covisint closing information, see http://www.ftc.gov/opa/2000/09/covisint.htm.

[63] No. 01-cv-0067 (N.D. Ill. filed Jan. 4, 2001) (see opinion on summary judgment at 2005 WL 736021).

[64] *Id.*

[65] 540 U.S. 398 (2004).

that no such duty existed, other than in very extraordinary circumstances that did not exist here.

In 2009, the U.S. Supreme Court extended the reasoning of the *Trinko* case in *Pacific Bell Telephone Co. v. LinkLine Communications, Inc.*[66] In *LinkLine*, the Court extended the *Trinko* "no duty to deal with a competitor" philosophy to hold that a complaint failed to state a cause of action under Section 2 of the Sherman Act where it alleged that the defendant had engaged in a price squeeze by charging high prices for interconnection services to competitors and low prices for the final product to consumers. This "price squeeze" allegedly left competitors unable to effectively compete in the resale of the services. The Supreme Court explained that the "nub of the complaint" in both *Trinko* and *LinkLine* is identical, i.e., that the defendants had abused their power in the wholesale market in order to prevent rival firms from competing effectively in a retail market. With respect to the price squeeze alleged in *LinkLine*, the Court held that the defendant was not required to price its various services in a manner calculated to preserve its rivals' profit margins.

IV. Exclusionary Practices

A. Network Effects

In *Northwest Medical Laboratories v. Blue Cross and Blue Shield*,[67] an Oregon state court of appeals perhaps anticipated the day when network effects will mean that competitors will all require access to a single network in order to compete, or even survive. While holding that a provider excluded from a network that lacked market power could not demonstrate the antitrust injury necessary to sustain a cause of action, the court stated in dicta, "[i]f participation in the joint venture confers a 'significant competitive advantage' and the venture holds a substantial market position, it may be required to allow competitors to participate or obtain the advantages of membership on a reasonable and nondiscriminatory basis."[68] This type of rule typically is applied to anything deemed an "essential facility," i.e., those who lack access cannot compete. While essential facilities rarely have been identified in the past, a world of overwhelming network effects could change that situation dramatically.

The conclusion that network effects ultimately will dictate that all participants in an industry be members of the same exchange may, however, be premature. The *FTC Staff Report*[69] suggests that exchange "interoperability" is an important consideration in determining the likely anti-competitive effects of any given exchange. This refers to the ability of one exchange to allow its participants to transact business within another exchange. If interoperability, in fact, becomes commonplace, then the network effects of any given exchange may be nullified as the members of one exchange can do business through others, so

---

[66] 555 U.S. 438 (2009).
[67] 775 P.2d 863 (Or. Ct. App. 1989), *aff'd*, 310 Or. 72 (1990).
[68] *Id.* at 871.
[69] FTC Staff Report pt. 1, C8.

B. Exclusive Use Requirements

As EMRs proliferate, the lack of interoperability of medical records could create antitrust concerns. Anti-competitive effects could occur in a market where a dominant hospital or hospital system provides EMR equipment and/or technology to physicians and either (1) provides technology that has no interoperability and/or (2) requires the physicians only to use the technology for information sharing with the hospital, or both. This conduct could induce the physicians to use only the hospital providing the software, and could prevent, implicitly or explicitly, other hospitals from accessing those physicians (e.g., from gaining admissions from those physicians). The ability to control physicians relates to the ability of a hospital to maintain and/or enhance its market power. As a result, that conduct could preclude or exclude the hospitals from competing effectively in the marketplace. Of course, to the extent the physicians might agree (or "conspire") with a hospital or hospitals to limit the use of EMR software, the joint conduct might be reviewed under a Section 1 standard.[70]

Although not addressing the specific issues related to EMRs, the *FTC Staff Report* summarizes the concerns over exclusivity, stating:

> Exclusivity practices—and ownership interests giving rise to *de facto* exclusivity—affect the extent to which participants in a B2B are able to support or patronize a rival B2B or other alternative trading system. Tying the participants to a single B2B may undermine the ability of alternatives to compete, effectively increasing the B2B's market power. Indeed, adding exclusivity to a setting already characterized by substantial network effects could "tip" the market in favor to a given B2B and impede development of alternatives.[71]

The issues here are not dramatically different from issues historically presented by various forms of health care provider networks. Where a physician network, for example, requires that participants not sell services through other networks, other networks may find it impossible to compete if they cannot obtain access to a sufficient number of participants. Similarly, where a health maintenance organization (HMO) provides a financial incentive to physicians if they choose to deal exclusively with that HMO's physician network, typically by offering a higher rate of reimbursement to those who select exclusivity, significant barriers to entry may be presented to competing HMOs.

Issues such as these have been discussed at length in connection with rules of operation of electronic marketplaces. Where the participants in the exchange also are the owners of the exchange, this in itself may be enough of an incentive to create de facto exclusivity.[72]

---

[70] *See, e.g.*, Toys "R" Us, Inc. v. Fed. Trade Comm'n, 221 F.3d 928 (7th Cir. 2000).
[71] FTC STAFF REPORT pt. 3, at 29.
[72] *Id.*

Despite the relatively restrictive safety zone of the *Enforcement Statements*[73] and the many consent decrees dealing with acceptable levels of participation in provider networks, the case law addressing exclusive dealing requirements in health care networks remains limited. The classic case on this subject is *U.S. Healthcare, Inc. v. Healthsource, Inc.*[74] The defendant HMO in *U.S. Healthcare* employed contracts with its participating physicians that offered them higher capitation payments in exchange for an agreement not to participate with any other HMO. This clause was challenged by a competing HMO, which contended that it constituted both a per se unlawful group boycott and an unlawful exclusive dealing arrangement. The court ruled, however, that the arrangement was purely vertical (between each physician and the HMO) and therefore was not a horizontal agreement that could be characterized as a boycott. Consequently, the arrangement was not per se unlawful. The exclusive dealing arrangement also was found not to violate the rule of reason because it did not foreclose other HMOs from a substantial part of the market for physician participants, and there was no evidence of any adverse effect on the ability of other HMOs to operate.

The *U.S. Healthcare* case illustrates the significance of having a pro-competitive purpose for each restraint adopted by a network. The court suggested that the exclusive dealing provision was adopted by the defendant HMO in order to improve its operations and not specifically to harm any third party. Had there been evidence of an intent to prevent other HMOs from entering the market, the court suggested, the outcome could have been different.

These issues may be among the first to be tested in the context of electronic markets used by health care providers. Where competitors and other participants are closely linked to a particular network, agreements with that network that restrict competitive decisions, e.g., pricing of individual products or services, may be especially sensitive.

C. Most-Favored-Nation Requirements

A most-favored-nation (MFN) clause is a covenant by which one contracting party agrees to give its best price to the other contracting party. In the context of electronic marketplaces, this typically might take the form of an agreement by which a vendor agrees not to sell at a lower price through another marketplace. Such an MFN clause certainly is not unique to electronic arrangements.

MFN clauses typically are tested under the rule of reason to determine whether they have an unreasonable anti-competitive impact by raising or stabilizing prices. However, MFN clauses potentially are subject to the per se rule applicable to horizontal price-fixing when they are imposed by a group of competitors upon themselves as a thinly veiled price-fixing agreement. Despite this possible price-fixing analysis, the *FTC Staff Report* classified the MFN clause reviewed in a health care matter as a form of implicit exclusivity, subject to the

---

[73] *See* ENFORCEMENT STATEMENTS.
[74] 986 F.2d 589 (1st Cir. 1993).

rule of reason.[75] According to the *FTC Staff Report*, the effect of the MFN clause utilized by RxCare of Tennessee, that state's leading pharmacy network, effectively penalized members for participating in competing discount networks. The MFN clause in question required that members who accepted lower reimbursement rates outside the network then must reduce their rates within the network. Because the network represented such a large portion of its members' business, the rule allegedly made participation in other networks unacceptable and inhibited the establishment or expansion of competing networks. The network in question agreed to a consent order with the FTC, prohibiting further use of an MFN clause.

In *Blue Cross and Blue Shield of Ohio v. Bingamin*,[76] the federal district court discussed the possibility that an MFN clause might violate the Sherman Act and the circumstances under which that would occur. The court considered whether a Civil Investigative Demand (CID)[77] investigating an MFN clause used by a large health insurer should be set aside. The court explained that, because the MFN clause had the potential to violate the Sherman Act if it had an anti-competitive effect, the CID was valid.

The DOJ brought an MFN action against Blue Cross Blue Shield of Michigan in 2010.[78] The DOJ alleges violations of both Section 1 and Section 2 of the Sherman Act, stating that:

> Blue Cross' use of MFNs has reduced competition in the sale of health insurance in markets throughout Michigan by inhibiting hospitals from negotiating competitive contracts with Blue Cross' competitors. The MFNs have harmed competition by (1) reducing the ability of other health insurers to compete with Blue Cross, or actually excluding Blue Cross' competitors in certain markets, and (2) raising prices paid by Blue Cross' competitors and by self-insured employers. By reducing competition in this manner, the MFNs are likely raising prices for health insurance in Michigan. The MFNs unreasonably restrain trade in violation of Section 1 of the Sherman Act, 15 U.S.C. §1, and Section 2 of the Michigan Antitrust Reform Act, MCL 445.772.[79]

Government agencies have succeeded in extracting a string of consent decrees from large organizations imposing MFN clauses.[80] This is in spite of the fact that demonstrating the anti-competitive effect of an MFN clause is difficult (witness the lack of success for plaintiffs in these actions in court). Nevertheless, the current case in Michigan and the fact that the DOJ has broadened its

---

[75] FTC STAFF REPORT pt. 3, at 27 (discussing *In re* RxCare of Tenn., Inc., 121 F.T.C. 762 (1996)).

[76] 1996-2 Trade Cas. (CCH) ¶71,600 (N.D. Ohio 1996).

[77] A CID is a discovery tool used by the DOJ. *See* 15 U.S.C. §1312.

[78] Civil Action No. 2:10-cv-15155-DPH-MKM, *available at* http://www.justice.gov/atr/cases/f263200/263235.htm.

[79] *Id.*

[80] *See, e.g.*, United States v. Vision Servs. Plan, 1996-1 Trade Cas. (CCH) ¶71,404 (D.D.C. 1996); United States v. Delta Dental Plan, 1995-1 Trade Cas. (CCH) ¶71,048 (D. Ariz. 1995).

MFN investigation across multiple states suggest that the DOJ is undeterred by this difficulty and currently active in this area.[81]

V. Standards and Certification

A. Significance to Electronic Health Care

Transacting business over the Internet (or other electronic networks) requires standardization of both protocols and terminology, if only to simplify transactions and assure that the parties to a transaction have a common understanding of what is being bought, sold, or communicated. The need for uniformity is obvious in this context, and the participants will need to go out of their way to create antitrust violations, though some surely will.

As electronic markets in health care proliferate, the process of sorting winners from losers undoubtedly will involve efforts by participants to differentiate themselves, and some of this differentiation inevitably will involve the adoption of standards that determine who may participate and how they distinguish one seller's product or service from another. This is not a new concept to health care providers. Individual providers historically have differentiated themselves based on such criteria as board certification, standards for medical staff membership, medical society membership criteria, and various forms of private accreditation. Products also are differentiated based on certification by private associations.

Private standards and certification in health care also have been adopted as criteria for participation in or payment by other organizations. Board certification or medical society membership may be necessary for hospital staff privileges. Accreditation may be a criterion for reimbursement. Professional society acceptance of products or procedures may be relied on by insurers for coverage determinations.

With the advent of EMRs and the requirement that providers be able to demonstrate "meaningful use" with EMRs, the importance of standards and certifications will increase. Indeed, currently vendors can receive certification that their electronic software is "interoperable" with other electronic health records. For example, an EMR vendor can be certified by the Certification Commission for Health Information Technology, and such certification requires the review of the software's security and general function (among other things).[82] With this increased emphasis on standards and certification will come increased controversy by those who feel excluded or disadvantaged by the process or who feel the process is stifling innovation in software.

---

[81]Thomas Catan and Avery Johnson, *Justice Widens Blue Cross Probe Across Several States*, WALL ST. J. (Mar. 26, 2011), *available at* http://online.wsj.com/article/SB10001424052748704474804576222804064289720.html?mod=go.

[82]*See, e.g.*, Office of the National Coordinator for Health Information Technology, Regulations and Guidance (Aug. 5, 2011), *available at* http://healthit.hhs.gov/portal/server.pt/community/healthit_hhs_gov__regulations_and_guidance/1496.

B. Historical Analysis

Private standard-setting typically involves the exercise of judgment regarding the adoption of rules and criteria that may give some competitors an advantage, real or perceived, over others. The need for standards in the e-health industry is in its infancy, at least compared to the long history of disputes in health care and other industries over the adoption and application of standards and the related issue of certification.

These private standard-setting activities generally increase the efficiency with which businesses function and are typically pro-competitive. Private standard-setting also has proven to offer the occasional irresistible temptation for those in control of the process to seize the opportunity to create an unfair advantage over competitors, sometimes with costly results.

Private standard-setting, as an element of industry self-regulation, has been a frequent battleground for antitrust litigants and has been both applauded for its pro-competitive benefits and criticized for its anti-competitive potential. For example, in a recent advisory opinion relating to proposed certification activity, the FTC staff stated:

> In general, private standard-setting and certification or accreditation programs have the potential to promote competition by providing useful information to consumers. Such programs can make it easier for consumers to obtain useful information and to select among providers of a product or service. By providing information about quality and performance of products or services, standard-setting programs may facilitate quality competition and price/quality comparisons, increase consumer confidence in product quality and thereby increase demand, and facilitate entry by new sellers.[83]

Those who applaud the pro-competitive potential of private standard-setting activities often have an equally noteworthy tendency to mention in the next breath the potential for anti-competitive harm posed by these activities. For example, in the 1997 Advisory Opinion quoted above, the FTC staff continued:

> In some circumstances, standard-setting programs can have anti-competitive effects that require an analysis of the reasonableness of the underlying standards. For example, some aspects of an accreditation or certification program may directly impose an unreasonable restraint on competition among the participants in the program. In addition, adherence to a standard-setting program may in effect be an agreement not to sell nonaccredited products or services. In other circumstances, competitors may abuse or distort the standard-setting process for the purpose of reducing competition, thus imposing significant harm to market competition while not providing the pro-competitive benefits that can flow from standard-setting programs. In instances where a product cannot succeed in the market without meeting certain product standards, standards that lack a reasonable basis may restrain competition unreasonably.
>
> Further, a standard may have a direct exclusionary effect when market participants agree not to deal with uncertified entities. Concerted effort to enforce product

---

[83]FTC Staff Advisory Op., Apr. 17, 1997, *available at* http://http://www.ftc.gov/bc/adops/fahctlet.shtm (Foundation for the Accreditation of Hematopoietic Cell Therapy). The FTC's health care antitrust advisory opinions are generally available on the agency's Web site, http://www.ftc.gov/bc/advisory.htm.

standards can warrant more rigorous antitrust scrutiny than does the establishment of standards.[84]

Some federal court decisions reflect a certain reluctance to find unlawful conduct based on standard-setting activities. For example, in *Consolidated Metal Products v. American Petroleum Institute*,[85] a trade association allegedly had delayed certification for a certain manufacturer's product. Because there was no showing that the trade association had attempted to coerce third persons to follow its recommendations, or that consumers could not buy the product in question, the court found no antitrust violation, based either on a per se or rule of reason standard.

Similarly, in *Zavaletta v. American Bar Ass'n*,[86] the ABA's refusal to grant accreditation to a particular law school was described by the court as the mere expression of an opinion. The fact that many states allowed only graduates of ABA-accredited law schools to sit for the bar examination or practice law was not sufficient to show a restraint of trade. The court explained: "An organization's towering representation does not reduce its freedom to speak out."[87]

More recently, in *McDaniel v. Appraisal Institute*,[88] a real estate appraiser who had been denied certification by a private standard-setting body was found to have shown no injury to competition because he was still free to compete in the marketplace. The association's certification program was described as enhancing competition and efficiency by reducing search costs and mistakes for consumers. Only the plaintiff was injured by reducing his ability to compete; the market was not harmed.

The most recent Supreme Court case addressing private standard-setting activities is *Allied Tube & Conduit Corp. v. Indian Head, Inc.*[89] The private standard-setting body involved in *Allied Tube* was known as the National Fire Protection Association (NFPA), a private, voluntary organization with members representing labor, academia, insurers, organized medicine, firefighters, and government. The NFPA published, among other things, product standards and codes relating to fire protection through a process known as "consensus standard making." One of the codes involved was the National Electrical Code, which established product and performance requirements for the design and installation of electrical wiring systems. Numerous state and local governments routinely adopted the Code into law. Private certification laboratories often refused to list or label an electrical product that did not need the standards of the Code. Some underwriters refused to insure structures not built in conformity with the Code.

One of the products covered by the Code was electrical conduit. Electrical conduit historically had been made only of steel, so the Code applied only to steel conduit. The plaintiff introduced a plastic conduit product, which apparently had certain technical benefits. The plaintiff submitted its product for approval under the Code, and a vote on the submission was scheduled at the

---

[84] *Id.*
[85] 846 F.2d 284 (5th Cir. 1988).
[86] 721 F. Supp. 96 (E.D. Va. 1989).
[87] *Id.* at 98.
[88] 117 F.3d 421 (9th Cir. 1997), *cert. denied*, 523 U.S. 1022 (1998).
[89] 486 U.S. 492 (1988).

annual meeting of the NFPA. The largest producer of steel conduit, along with other members of the association, successfully worked to pack the meeting in order to control the vote and keep the plastic conduit from receiving approval.

At trial, the jury found that the defendant had conspired unlawfully with other persons to exclude plaintiff's product from the Code. However, the district court entered judgment notwithstanding the verdict, on the basis that the defendant's conduct was protected by the First Amendment. The court of appeals subsequently reversed the trial court's decision, and the Supreme Court affirmed, holding that the standard-setting process of a private association such as the defendant was not entitled to First Amendment immunity from antitrust liability.

The First Amendment defense considered by the Supreme Court in *Allied Tube* was based on a doctrine known as *Noerr-Pennington* (so named for two cases that first articulated the concept).[90] The *Noerr-Pennington* doctrine has been a particularly important defense in several private standard-setting cases. This may be predictable because the actual harm to the plaintiff in these cases often is caused by the adoption of a private standard by government entities. In *Allied Tube*, however, the Supreme Court narrowed the apparent scope of the defense by explaining that where the context is the standard-setting process of a private association, rather than an open political arena, economically interested parties may not abuse their decision-making authority, only to then hide behind *Noerr-Pennington*.[91] In contrast, where the standard-setting forum is a true political arena, such as a legislature, the Court noted, even unethical and deceptive practices would be immune.[92]

C. Health Care Experience With Private Standard-Setting

Not surprisingly, certification and standard-setting activities have been frequent subjects of litigation in matters involving the health care industry, and the courts have acknowledged some unique issues. The potential for special treatment of health care certification and accreditation cases is illustrated by the Seventh Circuit's decision in *Wilk v. American Medical Ass'n*.[93] The *Wilk* case raised the most common substantive antitrust issue emanating from standard-setting activities and certification, i.e., whether the private standard-setting procedure is being used to effectuate a boycott of persons deemed not to meet the standards in question. The Seventh Circuit acknowledged a very narrow quality of care defense for accreditation standards that might be available, under limited circumstances, to the defendants.

In the health care setting, a disadvantaged party cannot succeed simply by showing that standards set privately are unreasonably high but must show anti-competitive intent. The practical futility of arguing for lower accreditation standards without a showing of anti-competitive intent is illustrated by the find-

---

[90]*See* Mine Workers v. Pennington, 381 U.S. 657 (1965); Eastern R.R. Presidents Conference v. Noerr Motor Freight, Inc., 365 U.S. 127 (1961).
[91]486 U.S. at 501.
[92]*Id.* at 499.
[93]719 F.2d 207 (7th Cir. 1983).

ings and conclusions entered by the trial court in *Sherman College of Straight Chiropractic v. American Chiropractic Ass'n.*[94] The plaintiffs in *Sherman* were a chiropractic college, a chiropractic academic standards association, and certain practitioners who contended that the defendant association set accreditation standards that were too high, thereby impairing plaintiffs' ability to compete. To meet the defendant's accreditation standards, chiropractors were required to make diagnoses in the nature of primary caregivers, while the plaintiffs were practitioners of nondiagnostic chiropractic services. Most state licensing boards had adopted the defendant's pro-diagnostic standard in determining whether to license chiropractic applicants. Consequently, enrollment at the plaintiff's chiropractic college was stagnant, as its graduates were eligible to become licensed chiropractors in only 11 states. The defendant contended that any harm to the plaintiffs was a result of the independent actions of state legislative or administrative bodies, and that the defendant's actions were legitimate measures intended to better educate the chiropractic profession and promote better health care for patients.

The court first concluded that a rule of reason standard was appropriate to evaluate cases involving the impact of professional educational standards on the consuming public. The court then stated: "While a profession certainly could undertake a regulatory measure which would disserve the public interest, the general presumption is that the public interest is served by the promotion of enhanced education and training requirements."[95] The court went on to explain that it would be reluctant to presume that higher educational standards would have an adverse effect on the consuming public. There was no direct evidence here that the public interest was prejudiced or that competition had been diminished.

Health care providers are well acquainted with various court-imposed procedural requirements for determining who is and is not eligible for new or continued membership in various organizations. The typical medical staff, for example, is unlikely to constitute a monopoly within any given geographic market (with some rural exceptions). However, because of the importance of medical staff membership to the ability to practice,[96] courts typically have imposed procedural due process requirements on medical staff decision-making.[97]

When a competitor alleges that he or she has been harmed by the standard-setting decisions of a private body that includes competitors of the plaintiff, the outcome may be difficult to predict. In *Daniel v. American Board of Emergency Medicine*,[98] the defendants closed the "practice track" method of achieving eligibility to take the board certification exam, reverting solely to an educational standard. As a result, the plaintiff-physician, and presumably others like him, became ineligible for certification. Ruling on the defendant's motion to dismiss,

---

[94]654 F. Supp. 716 (N.D. Ga. 1986), *aff'd*, 813 F.2d 349 (11th Cir. 1987), *cert. denied*, 484 U.S. 854 (1987).

[95]*Id.* at 722.

[96]For example, courts have considered medical staff privileges a right deserving of due process protections. *See, e.g.*, Patrick v. Burget, 486 U.S. 94 (1988).

[97]*Id.*

[98]802 F. Supp. 912 (W.D.N.Y. 1982).

the *Daniel* court accepted as true the plaintiff's allegations that there was a separate market for board-certified emergency physicians, and that the defendants, therefore, comprised the entire market. The court then departed from the approach of some other cases and concluded that the antitrust laws are intended to protect even one competitor's right to enter and compete in a relevant market. As the court stated,

> there is no question that Defendants certify emergency medicine physicians throughout the United States and, in so doing, are engaged in and affect interstate commerce. Any limitation on the number of Board-certified emergency room physicians conceivably resulting from the Board's present certification practices would certainly have an impact on hospital services throughout the country.[99]

A contrasting view of market power may be found in *Sanjuan v. American Board of Psychiatry & Neurology*.[100] Like the plaintiff in the *Daniel* case, the plaintiff-psychiatrists in *Sanjuan* were denied certification by the defendant board. In this case, however, the court dismissed the case on the pleadings, explaining that the lack of board certification did not remove the plaintiffs from the market. The court explained: "It is hard to see how these activities could amount to an exercise of market power, which entails cutting back output in the market and driving up prices to consumers."[101] Although the court speculated that the plaintiffs might have been able to devise a theory that consumers were being prevented from shopping intelligently for psychiatric services, this was not a theory advanced in the pleadings.

Perhaps in recognition of the need for updated guidance, the FTC will be holding a public forum to discuss competition issues in standard-setting.[102] Specifically, the forum is intended to "examine the legal and policy issues surrounding the competition problem of 'hold-up' when patented technologies are included in collaborative standards,"[103] although it is likely that entities will be able to glean broader standard-setting guidance.

VI. CONCLUSION

The electronic marketplace, though in its infancy, is rapidly being adapted to the direct sale of health care services and products, as well as serving as a forum for the collection and dissemination of information. In some ways, these marketplaces now serve as a sort of permanent meeting, during which competitors can learn all there is to know about each others' prices, plans, and possibilities. While this information may be used to facilitate competition for the benefit

---

[99] *Id.* at 923.

[100] 40 F.3d 247 (7th Cir. 1994), *cert. denied*, 516 U.S. 1159 (1996).

[101] *Id.* at 251.

[102] *See* News Release, Federal Trade Comm'n, *FTC to Host Public Forum on Competition Issues in Standard-Setting* (May 9, 2011), *available at* http://www.ftc.gov/opa/2011/05/standard-setting.shtm.

[103] *Id.*

of consumers, history and human nature suggest other outcomes are also possible. The enforcers certainly intend to be vigilant in assuring that the permanent meeting of the electronic marketplace does not become just another opportunity for mischief. Providers must do the same.

15

The Intersection of Health Law and Intellectual Property Law*

I.	Introduction	458
II.	Federal Acts and Agencies	459
	A. HIPAA	459
	1. Background	459
	2. Privacy and Security Rules	460
	3. Identifier Standards	460
	4. TCS Standards	460
	5. Enforcement Rule	461
	B. HITECH Act	461
	1. Background	461
	2. Health Information Technology Standards	462
	3. Incentive Payments	462
	4. Strengthened Privacy Rules and Breach Notification	463
	5. Strengthened Penalties	463
	C. Standards for Privacy of Individually Identifiable Health Information	464
	1. Background	464
	2. What Is Protected	464
	3. Who Is Subject to the Privacy Rule	465
	4. Disclosures of PHI	466
	a. Required Disclosures	466
	b. Permissible Disclosures for Public Health, Law Enforcement, and Oversight Purposes	467

---

*Authored and edited by Paul Roberts, Foley and Lardner of Washington, D.C. Mr. Roberts thanks the following contributing authors for their work in preparing the following sections to this chapter: Section II: Natalie Morris, Hogan Lovells (summer intern), Washington, D.C.; Section III: Sharra Brockman, Verv Law, Pittsburg, PA; Sections IV & V: Charles Davis, Hogan Lovells (summer intern), Washington, D.C.; Section VI: Elizabeth Hage, Ritter Law Firm, LLC, Birmingham, Alabama; Section VIII: Brady Kriss, Law Office of Brady Kriss, Esq., Cambridge, Massachusetts; Section IX: Hogan Lovells (summer intern),Washington, D.C.; and Section X: Meghan Overgaard, Hogan Lovells, Washington, D.C.

			c.	Disclosures for Research Purposes..................................	467
			d.	Disclosures for Marketing Purposes.............................	468
			e.	Minimum Necessary Requirement.................................	468
		5.		Administrative Safeguards of the Privacy Rule......................	469
	D.	The Hatch-Waxman Act..			469
		1.		Introduction	469
		2.		Abbreviated New Drug Application	470
		3.		Generic Drugs and Patent Infringement	471
		4.		Safe Harbor..	472
		5.		Patent Term Extension and Market Exclusivity for Pioneer Drug Companies...	472
III.	Copyrights and Health Law				473
	A.	What Is a Copyright?..			473
	B.	Exclusive Rights of Copyright Ownership			474
	C.	Derivative Works and Substantial Similarity			474
	D.	Obtaining a Copyright			475
	E.	Duration of Copyrights			475
	F.	Berne Convention			476
	G.	Section 117 of the Copyright Act: Computer Programs............			476
	H.	Medical Materials and Copyright Law			476
		1.		Protection for Medical Documents and Images	477
		2.		European and U.S. Database Protection................................	477
	I.	Proprietary Databases and Copyright			478
IV.	Impact of Computer-Related Legislation on Medical Record Privacy..				478
	A.	Computer Privacy Acts			478
	B.	Health Insurance Portability and Accountability Act			479
	C.	Computer Fraud and Abuse Act...			480
	D.	Digital Millennium Copyright Act...			482
	E.	Other Relevant Computer Privacy Acts			485
		1.		Electronic Communications Privacy Act................................	485
		2.		Semiconductor Chip Protection Act	485
		3.		Children's Online Privacy Protection Act...............................	486
V.	Medical Codes and How They Affect Privacy				486
	A.	HCPCS/CPT			487
	B.	ICD-9-CM...			489
	C.	DRG...			490
	D.	Medical Codes and the Re-identification Problem.........................			491
VI.	Trademark—Protecting Indicia of Ownership..................................				493
	A.	Trademarks in General and Identification With a Source of Goods			493
		1.		What Can Be Trademarked?...	494
		2.		Trademark Remedies...	495
		3.		Trademark Laws	496
		4.		Dilution...	496
	B.	How Trademarks Are Used?..			499
		1.		Purple Gloves	499
		2.		How Trademarks Can Protect a Surgical Product or Medicine	500
		3.		The Aspirin Story	500
	C.	Domain Names			501

		1.	Protect Domain Name	501
		2.	Secure Domain Name	501
VII.	Patents and Patent Law for the Health Attorney			502
	A.	Patent Drafting, Patent Prosecution, and Patent Rights and Enforcement		503
		1.	The Parts of a Patent Application	503
		2.	Patent Prosecution	506
		3.	Patent Rights and Enforcement	506
	B.	The Patent Statutes in Detail and Some Commonly Misunderstood Concepts of Patent Law		507
		1.	The Four Requirements for Obtaining a Patent: "Idea" Versus "Invention"	507
		2.	Section 112, First Paragraph: Written Description and Enablement	507
		3.	Section 101: Statutory Class of the Invention	508
		4.	Section 102: Novelty Versus Originality	509
		5.	Unobviousness and Invalidity	510
	C.	Bringing a Product to Market		512
		1.	Freedom to Operate	512
		2.	Filing and Acquiring Patents	514
	D.	Nuances in the Medical Field		516
		1.	Enablement Requirements for Claiming Multiple Configurations of Drugs and Materials	516
		2.	HIPAA Regulations and Patent Claim Strategy	519
VIII.	Trade Secrets—Protecting Essential Information			521
	A.	Sources of Trade Secret Law		522
	B.	Uniform Trade Secrets Act		522
	C.	Establishing Ownership of a Trade Secret		523
		1.	The Nature of the Information	523
		2.	Preserving Secrecy	523
		3.	Proper and Improper Means of Acquisition of a Trade Secret	524
IX.	Preliminary Transactional Agreements and Proprietary Rights			524
	A.	Modern Applications in the Health Care Industry		524
		1.	Protected Health Information and Electronic Health Records	525
			a. Health Services Contracting	525
			i. Software Vendors	527
			ii. Warranties in Technology Transfers	528
			iii. Regulatory Compliance Covenants	528
			iv. Foreign Contractors	529
			b. Health Research	529
			c. Health Information Exchange and State Practices	530
			d. ACOs and Data Sharing	531
		2.	Proprietary Rights in Product Development	531
			a. Collaboration Agreements	531
			b. Trade Secrets	532
	B.	Suggested Drafting Provisions for the Creation of Effective Nondisclosure Agreements		533
		1.	Access to Confidential Information	533
		2.	Restricted Use of Confidential Information	534
		3.	Nondisclosure of Confidential Information	534

		4.	Nonsolicitation of Customers and Employees.........................	534
		5.	Reservation of Proprietary Rights	534
X.	Managing Exposure to Intellectual Property Litigation.........................			534
	A.	Due Diligence		535
		1.	Identifying Potential Rights Holders	535
		2.	Identifying the Scope of Existing Rights................................	536
		3.	Determining How to Proceed: Licenses, Workarounds, and Declaratory Relief	536
	B.	Strategic Intellectual Property Acquisitions		538
		1.	Strategic Intellectual Property Filings	538
		2.	Cross-Licensing Agreements and Patent Pools	539
	C.	Corporate Policies and Employee Education..................................		540
		1.	Policies for Existing Employees and Independent Contractors	540
		2.	Policies Addressing Concerns Relating to Nonemployees......	542
		3.	Ensuring Policies Are Properly Implemented	543
	D.	Minimizing Exposure to Unavoidable Intellectual Property Litigation...		543
		1.	Insurance...	544
		2.	Industry and Government Outreach	544
		3.	Alternative Dispute Resolution...	545
	E.	Conclusion		546

I. INTRODUCTION

The goal of this chapter is to provide a comprehensive overview of the main areas of intellectual property (IP) law that an attorney or medical professional working with a medical software company, drug, or device company, diagnostic company, or health-related government agency can turn to when confronted with IP-related issues. Conversely, this chapter also provides the intellectual property law attorney with a background in health law to more efficiently conduct his or her practice. In its treatment of issues involving both health law and IP law, the chapter explains the foundations of the Health Insurance Portability and Accountability Act (HIPAA), the Hatch-Waxman Act, and the Health Information Technology for Economic and Clinical Health (HITECH) Act, assuming little to no preexisting familiarity with these laws. Next, the chapter discusses copyright law and its relation to health law, as well as closely related aspects of computer law and the medical health codes. The trademark law section details aspects of trademark law in the health field and also provides a foundation in domain name law. The patent law section discusses the requirements for obtaining a patent, explains the components of a patent, steps through the patent prosecution process, and explains the fundamentals of patent rights, licensing, and enforcement. The patent section also explains some basic patent considerations of bringing a new drug or device to market, touches upon some of nuances to patent law in the biotech field, and explains what to consider with regard to HIPAA when preparing or enforcing patent claims. The trade secret section provides basic information about trade secrets, discussing the Uniform Trade Secrets Act. The next section provides an in-depth look at how to draft and enforce nondisclosure agreements (NDAs), closely tied to trade-secret law. And the last section discusses how to manage IP-related risks at a health company and what to consider when responding to IP-related threats.

II. Federal Acts and Agencies

This section begins with a brief overview of two significant federal health care privacy laws: HIPAA, administered by the U.S. Department of Health and Human Services (HHS),[1] and the HITECH Act, administered by HHS and the Federal Trade Commission (FTC).[2] This section also contains a discussion of the Hatch-Waxman Act and its potential effects on developing a patent.

A. HIPAA

1. Background

In 1996, Congress passed HIPAA, which prohibits certain restrictions on access to group health insurance and requires the Secretary of HHS (Secretary) to implement rules to protect the privacy of health information.[3] Title I of HIPAA limits the ability of employers to charge higher rates or refuse coverage to employees, their spouses, or their dependents due to current health status or a preexisting medical condition. Title I also requires the employer to allow employee enrollment in a group health plan outside of the enrollment period on the occurrence of certain "life events" such as divorce, marriage, or the birth or adoption of a child.

---

[1] HHS is a cabinet-level department tasked with protecting the health of Americans and providing human and social services. HHS administers approximately 300 programs relating to disease prevention, medical research, food and drug regulation, and health and social assistance for children, families, the disabled, and the elderly. The United States Public Health Service (PHS) forms the largest division within HHS and includes all of its 11 agency divisions. In addition to its public health and research functions, HHS is responsible for promulgating rules relating to privacy, security, and enforcement under HIPAA's Administrative Simplification Provisions through the Office for Civil Rights. In 2009, the passage of the HITECH Act further strengthened HHS's enforcement powers under HIPAA. It also granted HHS's Office of the National Coordinator for Health Information Technology authority to promulgate uniform technical standards to improve the quality and increase the utilization of health information technology, including electronic health records.

[2] The FTC is an independent agency comprising the Bureau of Consumer Protection, the Bureau of Competition, and the Bureau of Economics. The Bureau of Consumer Protection has the authority to enforce federal laws and FTC regulations that protect consumers against fraud, false advertising, deception, unfair business practices, and identity theft. The Bureau of Competition enforces antitrust laws, administers the premerger notification provisions of the Hart-Scott-Rodino Act, and reviews proposed mergers to ensure that a merger will not violate antitrust laws. The Bureau of Economics supplies economic analysis to the Bureaus of Fair Trade and Consumer Protection and studies the economic effects of proposed legislation. Since 2009, the FTC has had enforcement authority over the HITECH Act's breach notification requirements for vendors of personal health information and other non-HIPAA entities that may nonetheless have access to health information. Certain non-HIPAA entities who fail to report a breach of unsecured health information to the FTC and to the affected individuals will be treated as having committed an unfair and deceptive act under the Federal Trade Commission Act.

[3] HIPAA, Pub. L. No. 104-191 (1996) (codified as amended in scattered sections of 42 U.S.C.).

Title II of HIPAA includes the Administrative Simplification Provisions, which require the Secretary to promulgate rules to improve the efficiency of the health care system and to protect the privacy of health information. HHS has issued six rules under the Administrative Simplification Provisions: the Privacy Rule, the Security Rule, the TCS Standards, the Employer Identifier Standard, the National Provider Identifier Standard, and the Enforcement Rule. A brief description of each of these rules follows.

2. Privacy and Security Rules

The HIPAA Privacy Rule regulates how covered entities, which include medical providers who transmit medical information electronically, health plans, and health care clearinghouses, use and disclose health information that identifies a person by name or by other identifying information.[4] This rule is discussed in more detail later in this section. The Security Rule requires covered entities to establish administrative, technical, and physical safeguards to guarantee the confidentiality of protected health information in electronic form.[5] Among other security requirements, covered entities are required to perform risk analysis for potential breaches of their security systems, establish workstation security and access controls to prevent unauthorized access to protected information, and establish transmission security measures to ensure the integrity and safety of data as it is being transferred.[6]

3. Identifier Standards

Under the National Provider Identifier Standard established by the Centers for Medicare and Medicaid Services (CMS),[7] all covered entities must use a unique 10-digit code assigned to all health care providers when engaging in most electronic transactions.[8] Since the implementation of the Employer Identifier Standard in 2004, covered entities have also been required to use a unique employer identification number when engaging in a transaction where any employer information is communicated electronically.[9]

---

[4] 45 C.F.R. pts. 160, 164 subparts A, E (2010).

[5] 45 C.F.R. pts. 160, 164 subparts A, C.

[6] *Id.*

[7] CMS is an agency within HHS that administers the Medicare program and monitors and manages state-run Medicaid and Children's Health Insurance Programs. Together these programs insure approximately 102 million, or almost one in three, Americans. CMS is also responsible for promulgating rules establishing "unique health identifiers" as mandated by the HIPAA Administrative Simplification Provisions. CMS also has rulemaking and enforcement authority over the Transaction and Code Set (TCS) Standards required by HIPAA. In order to facilitate communication of protected health information by covered entities, these rules establish uniform standards for transmitting health-related information electronically and uniform codes to describe medical procedures, drugs and devices.

[8] 45 C.F.R. pt. 162, subpart D.

[9] *Id.*, subpart F.

4. TCS Standards

The transactions and code set (TCS) standards also require the use of standardized codes to describe medical and administrative activities associated with the transaction.[10] For example, covered entities must use the Healthcare Common Procedure Coding System when describing health care procedures in electronic transactions. The TCS rule also requires covered entities to utilize the standard form and content requirements established for a particular type of transaction, such as communications between covered entities regarding enrollment in a health plan, claims status, and the like.[11]

5. Enforcement Rule

Finally, the Enforcement Rule establishes enforcement procedures and civil and criminal penalties for covered entities that violate an Administrative Simplification Provision.[12] The Office for Civil Rights (OCR) within HHS enforces the Administrative Simplification Provisions by investigating complaints filed by individuals and conducting compliance reviews.[13] The Secretary has the authority to impose a civil fine of up to $50,000 per violation of a provision in cases where the violation resulted from willful neglect and was not corrected within 30 days of the day the entity knew or should have known about the violation.[14] However, in cases where the covered entity proves that the violation was not due to willful neglect and was corrected within 30 days, the Secretary cannot impose civil fines at all.[15] A covered entity can request a hearing before an administrative law judge to challenge the imposition of civil fines.[16]

A person who knowingly obtains or discloses protected health information in violation of the Privacy Rule is subject to a criminal fine of $50,000 and faces prison time of one year; if the violator obtained the information with "intent to sell, transfer, or use individually identifiable health information for commercial advantage, personal gain, or malicious harm," the penalty is a fine of up to $250,000 and jail time of up to 10 years.[17]

B. HITECH Act

1. Background

In February 2009, Congress passed the HITECH Act as part of the American Recovery and Reinvestment Act of 2009 (ARRA).[18] In passing the HITECH Act, Congress expressed a desire to improve the health information technology infrastructure in order to improve health care quality and reduce costs, while at

---

[10] *Id.*
[11] *Id.*
[12] 45 C.F.R. pt. 160, subparts C, D, E.
[13] *Id.* §§160.306–.308.
[14] *Id.* §160.404.
[15] *Id.* §160.410.
[16] *Id.* §160.504.
[17] HIPAA tit. II §1177, 42 U.S.C. §1320d-6.
[18] Pub. L. No. 111-5, 123 Stat. 115 (2009).

the same time strengthening and expanding HIPAA's privacy provisions. The Congressional Budget Office estimated that the HITECH Act would save the health system approximately $60 billion at a cost of approximately $20 billion.[19]

2. Health Information Technology Standards

The HITECH Act officially mandated the creation of the Office of the National Coordinator for Health Information Technology (ONC), which had previously been established by executive order, in order to centralize government efforts to increase the use of and establish standards for electronic health records (EHR) and other health information technologies (HIT).[20] The ONC is required to develop, update, and make available an EHR technology for use by health care providers at a reasonable cost, unless the Secretary determines that such technology is being adequately developed in the marketplace.[21] The HITECH Act also required the ONC to review the HIT Standards Committee's recommendations for HIT "standards, implementation specifications, and certification criteria."[22] Upon ONC endorsement of these standards, the Secretary is then required to determine whether to adopt them in the form of a regulation; technologies conforming to these standards are considered "certified."[23] As they upgrade and purchase new HIT, federal agencies are required to use certified technologies and must also include requirements to conform to the standards in any contracts with health plans, providers, or insurers.[24]

3. Incentive Payments

In order to encourage private-sector use of certified HIT, the HITECH Act includes an incentive-payment system for Medicare and Medicaid participating providers. In order to qualify for the incentive, the provider must demonstrate "meaningful use" of certified EHR technology.[25] CMS has defined "meaningful use" to include the electronic coding of health information, tracking of health conditions, and communication of health information.[26] Eligible providers can receive up to $44,000 for using EHR from 2011 to 2014, but from 2015 forward they will be subject to reductions in Medicare and Medicaid reimbursement if they do not use EHR. Participating hospitals receive an incentive payment of at least $2 million for meaningful use of EHR, and also will receive payment adjustments if they do not meaningfully use EHR from 2015 forward.[27]

---

[19]Letter from Robert Sunshine, Acting Director of the Congressional Budget Office, to Sen. Charles Rangel (Jan. 21, 2009), *available at* http://www.cbo.gov/ftpdocs/99xx/doc9966/HITECHRangelLtr.pdf.
[20]HITECH, Pub. L. No. 111-5 §3001 (2009); Exec. Order No. 13,335, 69 Fed. Reg. 2823 (Jan. 20, 2004).
[21]HITECH §3007.
[22]*Id.* §3001.
[23]*Id.* §§3000, 3004.
[24]*Id.* §§13111, 13112.
[25]*Id.* §4101.
[26]42 C.F.R. pts. 412, 413, 422, and 495 (2010).
[27]HITECH §§4101, 4102.

4. Strengthened Privacy Rules and Breach Notification

Many provisions in the HITECH Act reflect congressional concern with the privacy and security of health information as the digital exchange of such information becomes more common. One of the most significant changes to HIPAA imposed by the HITECH Act was to make most provisions of the HIPAA Security Rule directly applicable to business associates of covered entities; such business associates are now subject to HIPAA enforcement penalties for violations of the policy documentation requirements and the physical, technical, and administrative safeguards required by the Security Rule.[28] Another major provision in HITECH relates to notification of breaches of health information not secured by encryption technology, i.e. "unsecured protected health information."[29] The HITECH breach rules require HIPAA covered entities to report breaches of unsecured health information to the individual involved, and in certain cases to the Secretary, within 60 days of the discovery of the breach. Business associates of covered entities must report breaches of unsecured health information to the covered entity, and certain vendors of health records, which include entities that offer or maintain personal health records, must also report breaches to the FTC and the affected individuals even though they are not subject to HIPAA.[30] Because the other privacy provisions in the HITECH Act strengthen and expand the HIPAA Privacy Rule, these provisions are discussed in II.C., below, on the Privacy Rule.

5. Strengthened Penalties

Finally, the HITECH Act increased the penalties for violations of the Administrative Simplification Provisions of HIPAA. The HITECH Act clarified that criminal penalties can apply to individuals who violate HIPAA and not just the covered entity as an organization.[31] The HITECH Act also requires the Secretary to formally investigate complaints alleging that a violator acted with willful neglect.[32] The HITECH Act also increased the civil penalties that can be imposed for a HIPAA violation. Previously, the Secretary could only impose fines of up to $100 per violation with an annual maximum penalty of $25,000; the Act increased the per-violation maximum fine to $50,000 and the annual maximum fine to $1.5 million.[33] Finally, the HITECH Act authorized state attorneys general to enforce HIPAA in federal courts.[34]

---

[28] *Id.* §13401.
[29] *Id.* §13402.
[30] *Id.* §13407.
[31] *Id.* §13409.
[32] *Id.* §13410(a).
[33] *Id.* §13410(d).
[34] *Id.* §13410(e).

C. Standards for Privacy of Individually Identifiable Health Information

1. Background

This section provides more detail on the requirements of the HIPAA Privacy Rule and the strengthened privacy provisions imposed by the HITECH Act. HIPAA originally included provisions requiring the Secretary to promulgate rules to ensure the confidentiality of individually identifiable health information.[35] In 2000, HHS published the final Privacy Rule and in 2002 published modifications to the Privacy Rule.[36] On April 13, 2003, covered entity compliance with the rule became mandatory.[37]

The HITECH Act included a number of provisions modifying the HIPAA Privacy Rule, including strengthened disclosure accounting requirements, a tightened "minimum necessary" disclosure standard, and further limitations on the disclosure of protected health information for marketing purposes. However, the Secretary has yet to incorporate the HITECH requirements into the Privacy Rule. Therefore, this discussion focuses on the Privacy Rule as it is currently in force and mentions changes imposed by the HITECH Act where appropriate.

2. What Is Protected

HIPAA covers only "protected health information" (PHI), which is information created or received by a covered entity that identifies a particular individual by name or by any manner from which the identity of the individual could reasonably be ascertained.[38] PHI for the purposes of the Privacy Rule includes not only information regarding an individual's physical or mental health condition but any information about the receipt of and payment for medical services.[39] PHI can exist in any media form and includes oral communications.

De-identified health information is not covered by the Privacy Rule.[40] De-identified health information does not identify the patient by name or by any other means from which the patient could be identified.[41] In order to ensure that health data qualifies as de-identified health information, a covered entity must either have a qualified statistician determine that a person's identity cannot be ascertained by the data or must remove 18 identifiers from the data set, including ZIP codes, birthdays, and telephone numbers.[42]

---

[35] HIPAA tit. II.
[36] 65 Fed. Reg. 82,462 (Dec. 28, 2000), *and* 67 Fed. Reg. 53,181 (Aug. 14, 2002) (codified at 45 C.F.R. §§164.101 *et seq.*).
[37] 45 C.F.R. §164.534 (2010).
[38] *Id.* §160.103.
[39] *Id.* §160.103.
[40] *Id.* §164.502(d)(2).
[41] *Id.* §164.514(a).
[42] *Id.* §164.514(b).

3. Who Is Subject to the Privacy Rule

The Privacy Rule applies to health plans, health care clearinghouses, and any health care provider who transmits health care information in electronic form.[43] A health plan is defined as any individual or group plan that pays for medical care, and includes group health plans, HMOs, Medicare, and Medicaid, and state Children's Health Insurance Programs.[44] Health care clearinghouses are public or private entities, including billing services and repricing companies, that process health information received in a nonstandard format and place it into a standard format or vice versa.[45] Finally, the HIPAA Privacy Rules define "health care provider" as a person or organization "who furnishes, bills, or is paid for health care in the normal course of business."[46]

A covered entity is permitted to disclose PHI to business associates, provided that the covered entity receives "satisfactory assurances" that the business associate will protect the health information it receives in the course of its business.[47] When a covered entity hires another organization to perform certain administrative tasks that require the disclosure of protected health information, such as claims processing, data analysis, data aggregation, or billing and financial services, the covered entity is required to enter a business associate agreement with the organization.[48] Such an agreement must establish in writing the allowable uses and disclosures of PHI by the business associate and must include measures that the business associate must take to ensure the security of PHI.[49] A covered entity will be considered not in compliance with the business associate requirements of the Privacy Rule if it does not take reasonable steps to correct breaches of the agreement by the business associate.[50]

Business associates generally cannot make any disclosures of PHI that the covered entity could not make itself.[51] However, there is an exception for data aggregation services; under the Privacy Rule, a business associate performs data aggregation services when it combines PHI from different covered entities in order to permit data analysis regarding the health care operations of those covered entities.[52] Therefore, even though data aggregation involves an otherwise impermissible disclosure of PHI to a third party, these services are permitted under HIPAA subject to the previously discussed requirements placed on business associates generally.

Prior to the HITECH Act, business associate violations of the Privacy Rule did not result in HIPAA enforcement penalties for the business associate. The HITECH Act makes a breach of the business associate agreement a violation of the Privacy Rule itself and subjects the business associate to civil and criminal

---

[43] *Id.* §160.102.
[44] *Id.* §160.103.
[45] *Id.*
[46] *Id.*
[47] *Id.* §164.502(e)(1)(i).
[48] *Id.* §164.502(e)(2), 164.504(e).
[49] *Id.* §164.504(e)(1)(ii).
[50] *Id.* §164.504(e).
[51] *Id.* §164.504(e)(2)(A).
[52] *Id.* §§164.504(e)(2)(B), .501.

penalties under HIPAA. Furthermore, additional privacy requirements added by the HITECH Act are also directly applicable to business associates even when they are not mentioned in the business associate agreement. Finally, business associates are now in violation of HIPAA if they know of a pattern of activity of a covered entity that violates HIPAA and fail to takes steps to end the violation, terminate the contract, or report the covered entity to HHS.[53]

The HITECH Act also clarifies that entities involved in data transmission of protected health information that requires routine access to protected health information fall under the definition of a business associate.[54] HITECH specifically requires organizations such as health information exchange organizations, regional health information organizations, and e-prescribing gateways to enter business associate agreements.[55]

4. Disclosures of PHI

a. Required Disclosures

Unless the covered entity has received permission in writing from the patient or the disclosure is permitted under an exception to the Privacy Rule, a covered entity cannot disclose PHI to any third party other than a business associate.[56] However, in some circumstances disclosure may be required; for example, if an individual requests access to his or her own PHI or requests an accounting of the disclosures of that PHI, a covered entity generally must provide it.[57] Furthermore, a covered entity may be required to disclose PHI during an investigation by HHS regarding compliance with the Privacy Rule.[58]

The HITECH Act strengthens an individual's right to receive information about disclosures of PHI and to limit disclosures of PHI. The Act requires covered entities that use EHR and their business associates to provide information for all disclosures of PHI made over the past three years, including disclosures for treatment, payment, and health care operations, upon request of an individual.[59] Additionally, covered entities using EHR must provide a copy of the EHR upon request and can only charge a fee that covers the cost of the request.[60] Previously, entities had to provide health records in the form requested only if "readily producible" in that format; covered entities also did not have to account for disclosures for treatment, health care operations, or payment purposes.[61]

---

[53] HITECH §13404.
[54] *Id.* §13408.
[55] *Id.*
[56] 45 C.F.R. §164.508(a).
[57] *Id.* §164.502(a)(2).
[58] *Id.*
[59] HITECH §13405(c).
[60] *Id.* §13405(e).
[61] 45 C.F.R. §§164.522, .528.

b. Permissible Disclosures for Public Health, Law Enforcement, and Oversight Purposes

Disclosure of PHI without patient permission is permitted, but not required, in a number of limited circumstances.[62] Covered entities may disclose PHI to the extent needed to perform treatment, payment, and health care operations.[63] Health care operations include quality assessment, audits, business planning, underwriting activities of health insurance companies, customer service, and creating de-identified health information or limited data sets.[64] Covered entities are also permitted to disclose PHI when they are required to do so by law, regulation, or court order.[65] Permitted disclosures also include reporting cases of certain diseases that are tracked by federal agencies, reporting child abuse or neglect, reporting adverse reactions to drugs regulated by the FDA, notifying individuals who may have been exposed to a disease when notification is required by law, and reporting information to employers regarding a work-related illness or injury.[66] If a covered entity believes that an adult patient is a victim of domestic violence, the entity can report the abuse to a government agency to the extent authorized by law, provided that it finds that reporting is necessary to protect the patient or another person from serious harm.[67]

Furthermore, health oversight agencies may request and covered entities may disclose PHI for the purpose of enabling the oversight agencies to perform their auditing and investigatory functions.[68] Covered entities may also disclose PHI to help law enforcement locate a suspect, witness, or missing person and gather information regarding a victim of a crime or a suspicious death.[69]

c. Disclosures for Research Purposes

Under the Privacy Rule, a covered entity can use or disclose PHI for research purposes without obtaining authorization of the individual only if (1) an Institutional Review Board approves the waiver of the authorization requirement, (2) the researcher maintains that the PHI will be used only for research purposes and that the PHI requested is required for the research, or (3) if the research pertains to a deceased person, the researcher assures that the PHI is necessary for and will be used only for research purposes and provides documentation of the death of the individual.[70] For purposes of the Privacy Rule, research includes any "systematic investigation...designed to develop or contribute to generalizable knowledge."[71] Therefore, studies undertaken by a business associate or the covered entity itself that did not result in "generalizable knowledge,"

---

[62]See id. §164.512 for a full list of disclosures permitted without authorization from the individual.
[63]Id. §164.506.
[64]Id. §164.501.
[65]Id. §164.512(a).
[66]Id. §164.512(b).
[67]Id. §164.512 (a), (c).
[68]Id. §164.512(d).
[69]Id. §164.512(f).
[70]Id. §164.512(i).
[71]Id. §164.501.

e.g., quality assessments or development of best practices for the organization, would be considered a health care operation and would not be subject to the restrictions that apply to PHI disclosures for research purposes.

d. Disclosures for Marketing Purposes

Except for face-to-face communications between a covered entity and an individual, patient authorization is required before a covered entity can use or disclose PHI for marketing purposes.[72] However, the definition of marketing under the Privacy Rules does not include communications made for treatment purposes or communications by covered entities regarding availability and insurance coverage of health care products and services.[73] Furthermore, health plans can advertise changes and updates to their plans as well as what providers are in their network.[74]

The HITECH Act places further limitations on the ability of covered entities to disclose PHI for marketing purposes. Under the HITECH Act, even if the communication falls into one of the exceptions mentioned previously, if the covered entity is paid for making the communication, it must receive prior authorization from the patient. However, the Act includes a number of exceptions to this requirement: communications about a drug currently used by the patient and communications by a business associate made on behalf of the covered entity do not require prior authorization.[75] Furthermore, the HITECH Act prohibits the sale of PHI except for public health, research, health care operation, payment, or treatment purposes.[76]

e. Minimum Necessary Requirement

Even if permitted by the Privacy Rule, nearly all disclosures are nevertheless subject to the "minimum necessary" constraint, which requires that covered entities disclose only the amount of information required to achieve the purpose of the request for PHI.[77] When a covered entity discloses PHI on a routine basis, it must establish procedures to ensure that the disclosure is limited to the minimum amount of information necessary to meet the purpose of the disclosure.[78] For nonroutine requests for PHI, the covered entity must establish criteria to ensure that the request complies with the minimum necessary requirement.[79] However, if a public official, a business associate, another covered entity, or a researcher makes a request for PHI that appears reasonable under the circumstances, the covered entity may assume that the request meets the minimum necessary standard.[80]

---

[72] *Id.* §164.508(a)(3).
[73] *Id.* §164.501.
[74] *Id.*
[75] HITECH §13406.
[76] *Id.* §13405(d).
[77] 45 C.F.R. §§164.502(b), .514(d).
[78] *Id.* §164.514(d)(3).
[79] *Id.*
[80] *Id.*

The HITECH Act strengthens the minimum necessary requirement by stating that covered entities will be in compliance only if the covered entity limits the disclosure to a "limited data set," which requires the removal of a number of individual identifiers but not enough to render the data de-identified.[81] If the limited data set will not satisfy the purpose of the request, the covered entity can then disclose the minimum amount of PHI necessary to meet the requestor's needs. The Act also requires a case-by-case analysis of each request to determine if it satisfies the minimum necessary requirement.[82]

5. Administrative Safeguards of the Privacy Rule

The Privacy Rule requires covered entities to establish policies and procedures designed to safeguard PHI, to train their workforce on these policies, to create reasonable "administrative, technical, and physical safeguards" to secure PHI from involuntary disclosures, and to provide a process for individuals to complain about potential breaches of the Privacy Rule or about the entity's HIPAA policies and procedures.[83] Unlike the Security Rule, these provisions apply to PHI in electronic and nonelectronic form.[84] When a covered entity learns of a breach of its privacy policies, it must take steps to alleviate any harm that results from the unpermitted disclosure.[85]

D. The Hatch-Waxman Act

1. Introduction

This section discusses the Drug Price Competition and Patent Term Restoration Act of 1984, also known as the Hatch-Waxman Act,[86] which resulted from a compromise between the manufacturers of generic pharmaceutical drugs, the manufacturers of new pharmaceutical drugs ("pioneer" drug companies), and customers of these products. The section begins with a discussion of changes made to the Food and Drug Administration (FDA)[87] approval process and the patent laws, benefiting generic drug manufacturers, followed by a discussion of patent term extensions and other benefits granted to pioneer drug companies to encourage innovation and investment.

---

[81]HITECH §13405; 45 C.F.R. §164.514(e)(2).
[82]HITECH §13405.
[83]45 C.F.R. §164.530.
[84]*Id.*
[85]*Id.* §164.530(f).
[86]Pub. L. No. 98-417, 98 Stat. 1585 (1984) (codified as amended in scattered sections of 15, 21, 28, and 35 U.S.C.).

[87]The FDA is an agency within HHS responsible for ensuring the safety of food, medical devices, prescription and over-the-counter drugs and supplements, tobacco products, vaccines, and cosmetics. Before drugs and medical devices may legally be sold in the United States, a manufacturer must obtain FDA approval and perform preclinical testing and a series of clinical trials. In some cases, a patent dispute may prevent the FDA from approving the distribution of a drug. The FDA is also responsible for monitoring clinical trials and ensuring the safety and privacy of human subjects participating in studies involving FDA-regulated products. The rules protecting human research subjects act in conjunction with HIPAA, and depending on the nature of the study, both privacy regimes may apply to health information a researcher obtains from study participants.

Prior to the enactment of the Hatch-Waxman Act, the FDA generally required generic drug manufacturers to file a New Drug Application (NDA), which requires costly clinical studies, before marketing generic drugs, even though such studies had already been performed on the identical pioneer drug. Furthermore, in order to avoid potential patent infringement, the generic manufacturer had to wait until the expiration of the pioneer drug company's patent before it could even begin the studies, further impeding the entry of generics into the market.[88] By the 1980s, concerns over increasing prices of pharmaceuticals and the lack of competition in the drug market led to the passage of the Hatch-Waxman Act in 1984.[89]

However, Congress also recognized the need for protecting the intellectual property rights of pioneer drug companies in order to encourage the development of new drugs. Generic drug manufacturers received substantial benefits in the form of an accelerated regulatory review process called the Abbreviated New Drug Application (ADNA) in exchange for lengthened patent terms for the pioneer drug, exclusive nonpatent marketing rights, and the ability of the pioneer to challenge FDA approval of potentially patent-infringing generic drugs before those drugs enter the market. Generic drug manufacturers also received a "safe harbor" from patent infringement suits when they perform otherwise infringing activities that are "reasonably related" to the development of information necessary under a federal law regulating medical products.[90] Therefore, generic drug manufacturers can perform bioequivalence studies prior to the expiration of the pioneer drug patent.

2. Abbreviated New Drug Application

Instead of having to perform clinical trials to prove the safety of their products, under the Hatch-Waxman ADNA regime, generic drug manufacturers only have to prove that their products are the same as a brand-name drug that has received prior NDA approval.[91] For a generic drug manufacturer to utilize the ADNA process, it must prove that its product has the same pharmaceutical characteristics and is bioequivalent to a pioneer drug with an approved New Drug Application.[92] In order to satisfy the condition that the drugs be pharmaceutically equal, the generic drug must have the same labeling, active ingredient, route of administration, dosage form, and strength as the pioneer drug.[93] In order to meet the bioequivalence condition, the applicant must show that the absorption of the active ingredient "[does] not show a significant difference from the rate and extent of absorption of the [pioneer] drug."[94] Finally, the applicant must supply information on the chemistry, manufacturing, and controls of its drug.[95]

---

[88] Eli Lilly & Co. v. Medtronic, Inc. 496 U.S. 661, 669–71 (1990).
[89] Elizabeth S. Weiswasser & Scott Danzis, *The Hatch-Waxman Act: History, Structure, and Legacy*, 71 ANTITRUST L.J. 585 (2003).
[90] 35 U.S.C. §271(e)(1).
[91] 21 U.S.C. §355(j).
[92] *Id.* §355(j)(2)(A).
[93] *Id.*
[94] *Id.*
[95] *Id.*

However, it need not supply any information on the safety or effectiveness of the drug.

3. Generic Drugs and Patent Infringement

When submitting an NDA, pioneer drug companies must provide the FDA with patent information for "any patent which claims the drug for which the [NDA] applicant submitted the application or which claims a method of using such drug and with respect to which a claim of patent infringement could reasonably be asserted if a person not licensed by the owner engaged in the manufacture, use, or sale of the drug."[96] The FDA then publishes this patent information in the *Approved Drug Products With Therapeutic Equivalence Evaluations*, or the *"Orange Book."* When a generic drug manufacturer submits an ANDA, it must make one of four certifications for patents listed in the *Orange Book* for the drugs it is replicating: (1) there are no patents listed for that drug, (2) the patents have expired, (3) the patents will be expired by the time the ADNA is approved, or (4) the patents are invalid or will not be infringed.[97] When the first two types of certifications occur, the FDA can approve the ADNA immediately, and in the third case, the FDA can approve the ADNA effective on the date of the patent expiration.[98] Under the last type certification, known as a "Paragraph IV" certification, the applicant must notify the patent holder of the Paragraph IV filing and provide a statement of the factual and legal reasons why the applicant believes the patent is invalid or will not be infringed.[99] If the patent holder has not responded within 45 days, the FDA can approve the ADNA immediately; however, if the patent holder sues for patent infringement within 45 days, the FDA cannot approve the ADNA application for 30 months, the date of patent expiration, or the date on which a court declares the patent invalid or not infringed, whichever is shorter.[100] These provisions essentially ensure that the patent holder will be able to prevent the marketing of a generic before patent disputes have been fully resolved.

The Hatch-Waxman Act encourages potential generic drug manufacturers to make Paragraph IV certifications by granting the first ADNA applicant to make such a certification a 180-day period of time when the FDA cannot approve other ADNAs containing Paragraph IV certifications.[101] The 180-day exclusivity period begins running as soon as the manufacturer markets the drug and can be forfeited if the manufacturer fails to market the drug within a certain period of time.[102]

---

[96] *Id.* §355(b)(1).
[97] *Id.* §355(j)(2)(A).
[98] *Id.* §355(j)(5)(B)(i), (ii).
[99] *Id.* §355(j)(2)(A)(iv).
[100] *Id.* §355(j)(5)(B)(iii).
[101] *Id.* §355(j)(5)(B)(iv).
[102] *Id.* §355(j)(5)(B)(iv)(I), (D)(i)(I).

4. Safe Harbor

In order to promote faster entry of generic drugs into the market, the Hatch-Waxman Act included a provision that reversed a federal court of appeals decision in which the court had held that uses of patented drugs for purposes related to regulatory approval requirements constitute patent infringement.[103] The Act states:

> It shall not be an act of infringement to make, use, offer to sell, or sell within the United States or import into the United States a patented invention...solely for uses reasonably related to the development and submission of information under a Federal law which regulates the manufacture, use, or sale of drugs or veterinary biological products.[104]

The U.S. Supreme Court has read this safe harbor to include protection for testing of any "patented invention," including medical devices, and not just the testing of patented drugs.[105] Furthermore, the Court has held that a use of patented invention need not necessarily lead to information that is actually submitted to a federal agency in order to qualify for the safe harbor; the drug maker need only have a "reasonable basis for believing that [the results from research using the patented compound] would be appropriate to include in a submission to the FDA."[106]

5. Patent Term Extension and Market Exclusivity for Pioneer Drug Companies

In exchange for the provisions easing the ability for generic drug manufacturers to market and perform studies on their products, the Hatch-Waxman Act includes a number of provisions that lengthen the time of the patent owned by the pioneer drug company as well as the time before the FDA can approve the marketing of certain similar drugs. These latter provisions grant the pioneer drug maker a period of market exclusivity outside of the patent regime.

Pioneer drug patent owners often expend much of the time of their patent in periods of testing and regulatory review, during which they receive little or no profit from their invention. The Hatch-Waxman Act recovered some of this lost patent protection by lengthening the patent term by an amount of time based on the length of the "regulatory review period."[107] Hatch-Waxman defines this period as the time between the acceptance of the Investigational New Drug Application (INDA), i.e., the application permitting clinical trials, and the time that an NDA is submitted, plus the time it takes the FDA to approve the NDA.[108] Only half of the time between the INDA and the submission of the NDA can be applied toward the patent term extension, and the total amount of patent term

---

[103] Roche Prods. v. Bolar Pharm. Co., 733 F.2d 858 (Fed. Cir. 1984).
[104] 35 U.S.C. §271(e)(1).
[105] Eli Lilly & Co. v. Medtronic, Inc., 496 U.S. 661 (1990).
[106] Merck KGaA v. Integra Lifesciences I, Ltd., 545 U.S. 193, 207 (2005).
[107] 35 U.S.C. §156(c).
[108] *Id.* §156(g).

extension cannot exceed 5 years or 14 years after the NDA submission, whichever is shorter.[109]

Hatch-Waxman also includes a number of provisions to encourage the development of new drugs by providing for periods of market exclusivity for certain classes of drugs. In these cases, the FDA cannot accept an ADNA for a certain period of time after the acceptance of a pioneer's NDA. For example, when a pioneer submits an NDA for a drug that contains a new chemical entity, which the FDA defines as "the molecule...responsible for the physiological or pharmacological action of the drug substance," the FDA cannot accept an ANDA for a copy of that drug for five years.[110] Similar provisions granting market exclusivity exist for new dosages or uses for existing approved drugs when the pioneer has engaged in new clinical studies showing the safety and effectiveness of the drug at that new dose or for that new purpose.[111]

III. COPYRIGHTS AND HEALTH LAW

Copyright law interacts more and more with the medical field as digitization of records and electronic transfers of information become standard. This section first covers copyright basics, including rights given to copyright owners and limits on those rights, derivative works, obtaining copyright protection and its duration, and international treaties. It then examines how copyright law applies to medical materials and databases.

A. What Is a Copyright?

The Copyright Act of 1976 protects an original work of authorship fixed in a tangible medium of expression.[112] Practically, this means a work eligible for copyright protection first must contain a minimum spark of creativity[113] to satisfy the originality requirement, and second, it must be recorded in a medium that is "sufficiently permanent or stable to permit it to be perceived, reproduced, or otherwise communicated for a period of more than transitory duration."[114]

Unlike patent law, copyright's originality requirement does not require that the work be completely novel or unique, but simply that the work was created through independent and creative efforts.[115] Patent and copyright law, though, are similar in their approach to the protection of ideas. Ideas themselves are not the proper subject matter for either patents or copyrights;[116] however, patent law

---

[109] *Id.* §156(c), (g).

[110] 21 U.S.C. §355(c)(3)(E)(ii).

[111] *Id.* §355(c)(3)(E)(iii).

[112] 17 U.S.C. §102.

[113] Feist Publ'ns, Inc. v. Rural Tel. Serv. Co., Inc., 499 U.S. 340, 111 S. Ct. 1282, 18 USPQ2d (BNA) 1275 (1991).

[114] 17 U.S.C. §101.

[115] *Feist Publ'ns*, 499 U.S. 340, 18 USPQ2d (BNA) 1275.

[116] 35 U.S.C. §101; 17 U.S.C. §102(b); *see* Harper & Row Publishers, Inc. v. Nation Enter., 471 U.S. 539, 556, 105 S. Ct. 2218 (1985); Diamond v. Chakrabarty, 447 U.S. 303 (1980); Parker v. Flook, 437 U.S. 584 (1978).

may protect the practical way that an idea is implemented, and copyright may protect the unique way that an idea is expressed or described.

B. Exclusive Rights of Copyright Ownership

The Copyright Act expressly recognizes six exclusive rights of copyright ownership: (1) reproduction; (2) preparation of derivative works; (3) public distribution; (4) public performance; (5) public display; and (6) public digital performance of a sound recording.[117] The scope of each of these rights is defined by the Copyright Act.

The exclusive right of reproduction applies to "copies," which are defined by the Copyright Act as "material objects, other than phonorecords, in which a work is fixed by any method now known or later developed, and from which the work can be perceived, reproduced, or otherwise communicated, either directly or with the aid of a machine or device."[118] Similarly, the exclusive right of public distribution is the right to distribute those copies to the public, either by selling, renting, or lending.[119]

A copyright owner may choose to license to others some of these individual rights while retaining others. For example, the author of a book may license or assign to a publishing company the rights to reproduce and distribute his book. If the publishing company then also prepares a derivative work, it has infringed that exclusive right retained by the author.

C. Derivative Works and Substantial Similarity

As noted above in II.C., above, one of the exclusive rights granted to copyright owners is the right to prepare derivative works. A derivative work is an original work of authorship derived from an existing work.[120] Examples may include a documentary film with archival footage, a drawing based on a photograph, or a translation of a foreign-language novel. Copyright protection for derivative works extends only to new material added to the existing work, and does not broaden or otherwise impact any copyright protection in the preexisting material.[121] Because a derivative does not impact copyright protection in the preexisting material, the author of a derivative work must have permission to use any preexisting material that is not in the public domain, or the use will be an unauthorized infringement.

A fine line exists between a derivative work and a work that is merely a substantially similar copy of a protected work. One way to understand the difference is to view a copy for what it is, essentially a reproduction, and a derivative as a new work, one that uses artistic creativity to recast the existing material. In fact, for such a work to be protectable in itself, this recasting must result in

---

[117] *Id.* §106.
[118] *Id.* §101.
[119] *Id.* §106(3).
[120] *Id.* §101.
[121] *Id.* §103(b).

a derivative that is significantly different from the original copyrighted work.[122] There are two reasons for this requirement: first, it avoids the confusion that would result from two virtually identical works being copyrighted; second, it prevents the owner of a copyrighted work from extending the duration of his or her copyright by creating such an identical work and applying for its copyright protection as a derivative.[123]

D. Obtaining a Copyright

A copyright vests in an original work of authorship when it is fixed in a tangible medium of expression.[124] After the United States adopted the Berne Convention, discussed in III.F., below, in 1988, certain U.S. formalities were done away with, such as the requirement that a copyright notice ("© 2011 John Doe") be affixed to works to secure protection. The language of the current Copyright Act indicates that notice "may" be used.[125]

Although no formalities are required, registration does yield benefits. For example, e-filing a copyright application and obtaining a registration is not only affordable but also allows a copyright owner to file an infringement suit[126] and recover statutory damages and attorneys' fees.[127]

E. Duration of Copyrights

The duration of copyright protection depends on when the work first became protected under federal copyright law. If the work was created on or after January 1, 1978 (the effective date of the 1976 Copyright Act), then copyright protection continues from the moment of creation to December 31 of the year that is 70 years after the death of the author, or the last surviving author in the case of joint works.[128] If the work was created prior to January 1, 1978, then different duration rules apply. In general terms, copyright protection for works that remained unpublished as of January 1, 1978, is the same duration as copyright protection for works created on or after January 1, 1978, except that the protection will extend to at least December 31, 2002, and if the work was published on or before December 31, 2002, then the term does not expire before December 31, 2047.[129]

---

[122] Gaiman v. McFarlane, 360 F.3d 644 (7th Cir. 2004).

[123] *Id.*

[124] 17 U.S.C. §102(a).

[125] *Id.* §401(a).

[126] *Id.* §411(a).

[127] *Id.* §§504(c), 505.

[128] *Id.* §302. For anonymous and pseudonymous works and works made for hire, the duration of copyright protection extends from the date of creation to the end of the year that is the earlier of 95 years after publication or 120 years after creation.

[129] 17 U.S.C. §§302(a), 303(a), 304 & 305.

F. Berne Convention

The Berne Convention for the Protection of Literary and Artistic Works is the principal international copyright convention and affords authors of member countries (or works published in member countries) "national treatment." Under the Convention, a covered work will enjoy at least the same level of protection in a member country as is provided to the works of its own nationals, and strong minimum protections are provided to ensure a level of equality among member countries. Furthermore, as discussed above, covered authors need not comply with any formalities (such as notices or registrations) to benefit from the Convention's protections.[130] The United States and approximately 163 other countries have joined the Convention.[131]

G. Section 117 of the Copyright Act: Computer Programs

The Copyright Act not only grants exclusive rights to copyright owners, it also limits those rights by creating certain exemptions. One such exemption is found in 17 U.S.C. §117, which allows copying of computer programs in certain situations. Under Section 117, copying of original computer programs is permitted if three requirements are met. First, the copy must be made or obtained by the owner of a lawful copy of the original computer program. Second, the additional copy must be made for backup (or archival) purposes only. Finally, if the original program copy is given away or sold, the backup copy must be destroyed or transferred with the original.[132]

Note that Section 117 does not provide for copies of other digital items or programs, such as music or movie files. Section 117 also does not permit an individual to sell or purchase backup copies of computer programs alone, but only in conjunction with the sale or purchase of the original program.

H. Medical Materials and Copyright Law

Copyright law may be especially instructive within a medical context, where patient information, database, and privacy issues all blur traditional lines of intellectual property ownership and protection. In general, medicine is based on data: gathering and processing information is often the crux of a health care provider's role. What, if any, of this information may be protected by copyright law?

---

[130] Berne Convention, art. 5(2).

[131] The United States enacted legislation in 1988 to implement the revised Convention, amending 17 U.S.C. §101. Pub. L. No. 100-568, 102 Stat. 2853 (1998) (codified at 17 U.S.C. §101). For current notifications and further information about the Convention, see http://www.wipo.int/treaties/en/ip/berne.

[132] 17 U.S.C. §117(a).

1. Protection for Medical Documents and Images

Just as ideas are not protectable under copyright law, neither is information such as facts and data.[133] Therefore, to the extent that medical materials like patient lists or patient notes merely recite data in alphabetical or otherwise standard formats, they are ineligible for copyright protection because they fall short under the originality requirement.[134] However, often materials like medical records also contain conclusions and treatment plans. These items will likely constitute original expression because they go beyond a mere recital of information and present an interpretation of it.

Images present an even more complicated issue. Certain types of medical images, like X rays or CT scans, merely capture a basic image and require little creative input on the part of the radiology technician. Other types of images, however, require a level of skill and originality that may elevate the results from a collection of information to a copyrightable work. Ultrasound studies, for example, may fall into this category. Because every patient is different, ultrasound technicians must be well trained and exercise a good deal of professional judgment in the positioning of the probe, in deciding when the image accurately captures the area of interest, and in choosing what portions of the ultrasound to record to video. In fact, achieving a good ultrasound video is so important that sometimes hospitals will have their own technicians re-perform ultrasounds on patients with records from other providers to ensure that the best images have been captured.

Although it may be possible for medical documents and images to contain originality beyond the mere recitation of facts and data, whether these materials would be subject to copyright protection and, if so, who would own them has not yet been addressed by the courts.

2. European and U.S. Database Protection

Just as the conclusion section of a patient's file may be protectable under copyright law because it contains interpretations of data, similarly, unique selections and arrangements of data may also be protected under database or compilation laws.

In 1998, the European Union's executive body, the European Commission, sought to harmonize the scope of copyright protection for information databases by requiring member states to implement its new database law, Directive 96/9/EC.[135]

Prior to the issuance of the Directive, European nations were split on the level of originality required for the protection of a database. The Directive created a new, uniform standard of originality and also listed certain exclusive rights and limitations on database protection.

---

[133]Feist Publ'ns, Inc. v. Rural Tel. Serv. Co., Inc., 499 U.S. 340, 111 S. Ct. 1282, 18 USPQ2d (BNA) 1275 (1991).

[134]*Id.*

[135]Directive 96/9/EC of the European Parliament and of the Council of the European Union, 1996 O.J. (L 77/20) (Mar. 11, 1996) (on the legal protection of databases).

Notably, the Directive requires that the database "constitute the author's own intellectual creation" in the way its contents have been selected and arranged.[136] Protection under the Directive does not extend to the contents of the database, nor does it impact any existing rights in those contents.[137] It is also not limited to electronic databases but encompasses physical ones as well.[138]

In many ways, this approach mirrors the U.S. model for compilations under 17 U.S.C. §101, which provides that a compilation is "a work formed by the collection and assembling of preexisting materials or of data that are selected, coordinated, or arranged in such a way that the resulting work as a whole constitutes an original work of authorship." The Copyright Act further notes in 17 U.S.C. §103(b) that copyright in a compilation "extends only to the material contributed by the author of such work, as distinguished from the preexisting material employed in the work, and does not imply any exclusive right in the preexisting material." As discussed above, U.S. law does not protect information itself but can protect how that information is chosen and arranged within a compilation or database.[139]

I. Proprietary Databases and Copyright

Database laws have created new ways for health care companies to both protect patient privacy and further secure their own intellectual property. By designing proprietary database formats, medical software and resource companies like Epic and Cerner are able to preclude unauthorized users from accessing saved data with other programs. If the data within a protected system are exposed, these companies may have remedies in copyright law, among other areas, for the illegal reproduction of their software.

IV. IMPACT OF COMPUTER-RELATED LEGISLATION ON MEDICAL RECORD PRIVACY

A. Computer Privacy Acts

Health information, including medical reports and communications among doctors and health care providers, is increasingly becoming digitized. Medical services providers are using electronic storage of patient information in order to improve patient services, streamline access to information for doctors or nurses, simplify the sharing of medical records between service providers, increase efficiency of billing for insurers, and lower costs. Further, the 2010 Patient Protection and Affordable Care Act contains multiple provisions promoting electronic medical records.[140] This new emphasis on electronic recordkeeping and communication holds great promise for streamlining the health care industry.

---

[136] *Id.* art. 3(1).
[137] *Id.* art. 3(2).
[138] *Id.* recital 14.
[139] Feist Publ'ns, Inc. v. Rural Tel. Serv. Co., Inc., 499 U.S. 340, 111 S. Ct. 1282, 18 USPQ2d (BNA) 1275 (1991).
[140] Pub. L. No. 111-148, 124 Stat. 119 (2010).

However, this new-found emphasis on electronic recordkeeping and communication creates novel dangers for sensitive health information. For many medical service providers, data is stored on large central servers that can be accessed from a multitude of terminal or wireless devices. While this central storage model strongly promotes efficient access to information, it also creates a central location where one act of unauthorized access can lead to a wealth of private information. Such unauthorized access can occur both from within the health care company, such as doctors, nurses, or other employees, or from an outside attack, such as third-party hackers or even patients attempting to access information to which they are not provided access. Thus, it is necessary for those within the health care industry to understand the laws that protect sensitive and private electronic information.

B. Health Insurance Portability and Accountability Act

The Health Insurance Portability and Accountability Act[141] created a series of regulations affecting how health care providers handle sensitive medical data. A generalized and thorough description of HIPAA provisions is provided in II.A., above. In particular, the Security Rule[142] promulgated under HIPAA requires health care clearinghouses, health plans, and health care providers to employ specific technological safeguards to ensure the confidentiality and security of electronic records. These technological safeguards oblige large-scale medical data storage systems to assign a unique name or number to each patient or user of the system.[143] Further addressable safeguards, such as automatic log-off for users after a set time of inactivity and encryption of sensitive data, substantially increase the difficulty of both obtaining unauthorized access and using sensitive data even if a server is inappropriately accessed.[144]

Along with the technological safeguards required by the Security Rule, administrative safeguards promote security for confidential patient records.[145] All covered health care providers must implement procedures regulating user access to medical electronic data, including procedures that provide initial access to such data, limiting access to only a specific subset of data, and terminating access to data when necessary.[146] Required scanning of systems for malicious software, log-in monitoring, and specific username/password procedures for accessing highly sensitive data form some of the minimum safety standards required for sensitive medical data.[147] The administrative safeguards also necessitate contingency plans, such as required data backups and emergency recovery plans, to protect data from system failures or third-party destruction of data.[148]

---

[141]Pub. L. No. 104-191, 110 Stat. 1936 (1996).
[142]45 C.F.R. §164.312 (2011).
[143]*Id*. §164.312(a)(2).
[144]*Id*.
[145]*Id*. §164.308.
[146]*Id*. §164.308(a)(3).
[147]*Id*. §164.308(a)(5).
[148]*Id*. §164.308(a)(7).

Further, the HITECH Act,[149] enacted as a portion of the American Recovery and Reinvestment Act of 2009,[150] expanded the safeguards originally provided by HIPAA. A full description of HITECH provisions is provided in II.B., above. The HITECH Act enlarges the coverage of privacy provisions of HIPAA regarding confidential medical information to include private entities working with health care providers.[151] HITECH also requires that any health care provider covered by HIPAA must inform any patient of a breach of confidential medical information.[152] Finally, HITECH restricts disclosure of patient information to only when required for payment by an insurer, and requires that the health care provider maintain a full accounting of all disclosures of electronic medical information.[153]

Between HIPAA and HITECH, substantial regulations exist that require medical providers to create some form of minimum electronic protections for sensitive patient data. Further, HIPAA allows for civil penalties to be levied by the Department of Health and Human Services against health care providers for unlawful disclosure of sensitive electronic medical information.[154] However, HIPAA does not create a private right of action, and enforcement is only through HHS.[155] While HIPAA and HITECH and their accompanying regulations do create minimum standards for protection of sensitive electronic information, HIPAA does not provide any sort of recourse for a health care provider against either an employee or an external party for unauthorized access.

C. Computer Fraud and Abuse Act

The Computer Fraud and Abuse Act[156] (CFAA) provides broad protection for a health care provider against unauthorized access to centralized medical data. The CFAA states that anyone who "intentionally accesses a computer without authorization or exceeds authorized access, and thereby obtains...information from any protected computer," violates the Act.[157] The CFAA defines a protected computer as any computer "which is used in or affecting interstate or foreign commerce or communication."[158] Courts have interpreted "protected computer" to be any computer connected to the Internet, which would include large servers that might house important medical data.[159] Thus, a third party who is unaffiliated with a health care provider, such as a hacker, who remotely

---

[149] Pub. L. No. 111-5, div. A, tit. XIII, 123 Stat. 115, 226–77 (2009).
[150] Pub. L. No. 111-5, 123 Stat. 115 (2009).
[151] 42 U.S.C §17902 (West 2010).
[152] *Id.* §17932(b).
[153] *Id.* §17935.
[154] 42 U.S.C. §1320(d)-5 (2006).
[155] Logan v. Dep't of Veterans Affairs, 357 F. Supp. 2d 149, 155 (D.D.C. 2004).
[156] 18 U.S.C. §1030 (2006).
[157] *Id.* §1030(a)(2)(c).
[158] *Id.* §1030(e)(2)(b).
[159] Continental Grp., Inc. v. KW Prop. Mgmt., L.L.C., 622 F. Supp. 2d 1357, 1370 (S.D. Fla. 2009).

accesses a health care server that stores medical records violates Section 1030(a)(2)(c) of the CFAA.[160]

However, the question of violation of the CFAA through unauthorized access by a current employee of a health care provider is a more complex question. When a third party with no affiliation to the health care provider accesses a corporate server without authorization, there is no question the party is without access and in violation of the CFAA. When a current employee accesses information to sell to a competitor or to view medical files of another doctor's patient, the law is not as clear. The federal courts of appeal are split on the interpretation of the "without access or exceeds authorized access" language of the CFAA. The Seventh Circuit followed the tenants of agency law and held that authorized access ceases when an employee breaches his or her duty of loyalty to the employer.[161] Under this interpretation, an employee accessing a health care company's corporate records or medical records to provide information to a competitor would be acting "without access," because access was automatically terminated when the employee acted outside the interests of the employer. The Ninth Circuit, on the other hand, applied a stricter interpretation of "exceeds authorized access." Under the Ninth Circuit interpretation, an employee remains authorized to use a computer, even if that employee circumvents limitations placed on his or her access, until that access is explicitly terminated.[162] In jurisdictions following the Ninth Circuit interpretation of the CFAA, an employee accessing corporate records or medical records beyond the limitations of approved access would likely not be held in violation of the CFAA, unless the employee was acting after that access had been explicitly revoked. As of October 2011 there had been no U.S. Supreme Court decision clarifying the interpretation of the CFAA. There are also other provisions of the CFAA that may apply to protection of medical records, such as Section 1030(a)(5)(A), which bans the use of programs that steal information from or cause damage to protected computers, but the vast majority of civil litigation under the CFAA has involved violations of Section 1030(a)(2)(c).

The CFAA was initially enacted as a criminal statute that imposed either fines or imprisonment for violation of its terms.[163] However, the CFAA was amended to provide for civil action between private parties for violations of the CFAA, allowing recovery of compensatory damages and possible injunctive relief.[164] It has been difficult for parties to maintain a civil cause of action under the CFAA, because Section 1030(g) requires that the alleged conduct in question violate one of the enumerated subsections of Section 1030(c)(4)(A)(i). For most violations of the CFAA, the only reasonable subsection allowing for a civil action is Section 1030(c)(4)(A)(i)(I), which permits a cause of action if economic damages exceed $5,000. It is tricky to prove the value of electronic

---

[160]*See, e.g.*, United States v. Phillips, 477 F.3d 215, 218–19 (5th Cir. 2007).
[161]*See* International Airport Ctrs., L.L.C. v. Citrin, 440 F.3d 418, 420–21 (7th Cir. 2006).
[162]*See* LVRC Holdings, L.L.C. v. Brekka, 581 F.3d 1127, 1133 (9th Cir. 2009).
[163]18 U.S.C. §1030(c).
[164]*Id.* §1030(g).

information[165], and courts have struggled with valid claims for information theft under the CFAA that must be dismissed for inability to meet the $5,000 jurisdictional limit.[166] However, for medical records, Section 1030(c)(4)(A)(i)(II) of the CFAA provides a civil cause of action for any violation of Section 1030(a) that modifies or impairs the medical treatment of an individual, independent of the extent of economic damage. Thus, any prohibited action affecting medical records or medical communication within a health care facility would allow for a cause of action without the difficulty of proving pecuniary losses. The inclusion of this provision within the 1996 amendments to the CFAA, as well as comments during debate on the amendment,[167] demonstrate that the CFAA has been specifically adapted to protect sensitive medical information.

The CFAA, due to its strong protections against unauthorized access to protected information and direct cause of action, has previously been applied to the data of health care providers. For example, in *Doe v. Dartmouth-Hitchcock Medical Center*,[168] a mentally ill patient sued a medical center when one of the doctors employed at the center accessed the plaintiff's medical history solely out of curiosity, as the plaintiff was not assigned to that doctor. While the court held that the employer hospital could not be held liable for the actions of the employee doctor through vicarious liability, the parties and the court agreed that the CFAA is applicable to electronic medical records, and the doctor could have been liable if included as a party to the suit.[169] Based on interpretation of the statute and the *Dartmouth-Hitchcock* case, the CFAA provides both strong deterrence and a considerable avenue for recovery of damages for health care providers that store sensitive, confidential records and communications on a centralized server.

D. Digital Millennium Copyright Act

The Digital Millennium Copyright Act[170] (DMCA), enacted in 1998, amended the U.S. copyright law to provide added protections to digital works protected under copyright. The DMCA contains two provisions that could apply to health care providers: (1) a safe harbor provision for Internet service providers (ISPs) and (2) an explicit ban on programs that circumvent copyright protection and management systems.[171]

The safe harbor provision of the DMCA states that a service provider is not liable for copyright infringement if the provider either (1) transmits material automatically at the request of the user through a system or network controlled by the service provider, (2) caches copyrighted information on a system or net-

---

[165] *See, e.g.*, Charlotte Decker, *Cyber Crime 2.0: An Argument to Update the United States Criminal Code to Reflect the Changing Nature of Cyber Crime*, 81 S. Cal. L. Rev. 959, 982–84 (2008).

[166] *See* Continental Grp., Inc. v. KW Prop. Mgmt., L.L.C., 622 F. Supp. 2d 1357, 1370–71 (S.D. Fla. 2009).

[167] 142 Cong. Rec. S10886-01 (statement of Sen. John Kyl).

[168] No. CIV. 00-1000-M, 2001 WL 873063, at *1–2 (D.N.H. July 19, 2001).

[169] *Id.* at *5–6.

[170] Pub. L. No. 105-304, 112 Stat. 2860 (1998).

[171] *Id.*

work controlled by the service provider, (3) stores copyrighted information at the direction of a user on a system or network controlled by the service provider, or (4) provides information location tools that allow a user to access copyrighted information.[172] Each of these four categorical safe harbor protections has specific statutory guidelines and limitations that must be met in order for a service provider to have a valid defense against a copyright infringement suit for the service provider's actions.[173] A service provider[174] is generally any provider of online services or network access, which would include ISPs and essentially any large network, such as a large internal network for a health care provider. In general, in order to qualify under the safe harbor provisions of the DMCA, the service provider must (1) not have actual knowledge of specific copyright infringements, (2) promptly remove the infringing material when provided notice, (3) restore the material if given counter notice by the infringer proving no infringement, and (4) inform account holders of these policies.[175] Thus, when a service provider automatically, at the request of a user, places copyrighted information on a network and complies with all requirements under the DMCA, then the service provider has a defense against suit for copyright protection.

While Congress initially enacted the safe harbor provision in part to protect large ISPs from suit due to users posting copyrighted pictures, music, or movies to the Internet without the ISP's knowledge,[176] the safe harbor provision could be applied to health care records. While there is no current case law on the DMCA applied to medical software, records, or databases, situations in which safe harbor protections were extended to ISPs sued for the posting of copyrighted electronic media online could be extended to a health care context.[177] For example, if a third party, such as an employee at a health care provider, posted online a copyrighted program or computer code written specifically to analyze medical records, the ISP would be immune from suit if the elements of the safe harbor provision were met. More importantly, the owner of the copyright, such as a hospital or large medical provider that commissioned the writing of the code, would have a nonlegal method to oblige that the code be removed from public view. One requirement to qualify for safe harbor protection, as mentioned previously, is that the service provider must promptly remove infringing material when provided notice.[178] Thus, the copyright owner can request that the ISP remove the posting and the ISP must comply, or the DMCA safe harbor protections are no longer available. Because the copyright holder can simply request that the ISP remove the code from public view instead of having to engage in the arduous and expensive procedure of filing a lawsuit, the safe harbor provision creates a much more efficient method of protecting copyrighted material.

---

[172] 17 U.S.C. §512(c) (2006).
[173] *Id.*
[174] *Id.* §512(k)(1)(B).
[175] *Id.* §512(a)–(d). *See* Viacom Int'l Inc. v. YouTube, Inc., 718 F. Supp. 2d 514, 523–24 (S.D.N.Y. 2010).
[176] ALEXANDER LINDEY AND MICHAEL LANDAU, LINDEY ON ENTERTAINMENT, PUBLISHING AND THE ARTS §1:50.50 (3d ed. 2011).
[177] *See, e.g., Viacom*, 718 F. Supp. 2d at 526.
[178] 17 U.S.C. §512(a)–(d).

Aside from software, the safe harbor provision could protect ISPs who have medical databases or medical images stored on an ISP's server. The DMCA could also apply to cloud computing. In cloud computing, an ISP or other large networked server stores information that can be accessed anywhere an Internet connection exists. The information is commonly password protected, but it is highly accessible anywhere in the world. Placing medical information in a cloud computing system would allow a physician to access records or prescribe medicine to a patient from anywhere, which would be helpful if the physician were at a conference or on vacation. ISPs are even beginning to offer this service on a limited basis as technology develops.[179] Currently, the DMCA has been applied in limited situations to protect ISPs in a cloud computing environment, but no case has yet touched on protected health information inappropriately shared on a cloud computing server.[180] Thus, if medical information shared on a cloud computing service is copyrightable, the DMCA may protect an ISP under the safe harbor provisions of the DMCA against actions of a health care employee in inappropriately placing protected medical information on the ISP's cloud server.

Along with the safe harbor provision of the DMCA, the anti-circumvention[181] provision of the DMCA may apply to the health care industry. Under Section 1201, it is illegal for a party to circumvent a technological measure that protects copyrighted material or to create and traffic programs that allow for circumvention of such technological measures. Congress enacted Section 1201 to protect digital rights management technology employed by the entertainment industry to protect music and movies from illegal distribution. However, the anti-circumvention provision might have use in protecting medical databases. HIPAA requires technological and administrative safeguards to protect confidential patient information. Further, courts have previously held that a password system is within the statutory definition of a technological safeguard under the DMCA.[182] Thus, safeguards, such as encryption or password protection, could be viewed as a copyright protection measure if copyrighted databases resided on the server or if medical records or images on the server had copyright protection. If a party attempted to directly circumvent these measures, it is likely that the party would violate the anti-circumvention provisions of the DMCA. One limitation[183] to this theory of protection under the DMCA for copyrighted material on a health provider's server is that copyright infringement would not occur if an unauthorized third party entered a valid username/password combination. While password protection is a technological safeguard, the intent of the DMCA's anti-circumvention provision is to prevent against a technological circumvention more akin to hacking instead of unauthorized use of a valid user-

---

[179] Verizon.com, Leverage the Power of a Health Information Exchange, *available at* http://www.verizonbusiness.com/solutions/healthcare/info/hie.xml.

[180] *See, e.g.*, Marc A. Melzer, *Copyright Enforcement in the Cloud*, 21 FORDHAM INTELL. PROP. MEDIA & ENT. L.J. 403, 424–28 (2011).

[181] 17 U.S.C. §1201 (2006).

[182] *See* I.M.S. Inquiry Mgmt. Sys., LTD v. Berkshire Info. Sys., Inc., 307 F. Supp. 2d 521, 531–32 (S.D.N.Y. 2004).

[183] *See* Egilman v. Keller & Heckman, L.L.P., 401 F. Supp. 2d 105, 112 (D.D.C. 2005).

name and password.[184] In such cases, courts have held that the Computer Fraud and Abuse Act is the more appropriate statute for protection against unauthorized input of a valid third-party password.[185]

E. Other Relevant Computer Privacy Acts

1. Electronic Communications Privacy Act

While not as expansive as the CFAA or DMCA for privacy protection, the Electronic Communications Privacy Act[186] (ECPA) provides protections against public disclosure of electronic communications. The ECPA has two major subsections, known as the Wiretap Act[187] and the Stored Communications Act.[188] The Wiretap Act prevents a party from intercepting or procuring any electronic communication, which would include e-mail.[189] The Stored Communications Act prevents a service provider from divulging to the public the contents of any electronic communication stored by that service provider.[190] Both the Wiretap Act and the Stored Communications Act provide for civil causes of action by an aggrieved party directly against a service provider that divulged protected electronic communications.[191] For a health care provider that maintains its own e-mail server, the Stored Communications Act prevents the provider from disclosing any e-mails stored on the provider's server to the public. Thus, under the ECPA, a health care provider may not disclose the electronic communications of its employees to the public without permission. Because of the strong privacy protection against public e-mail disclosure created by the ECPA, doctors or nurses can be candid about patient treatment in their internal communications without worrying about potential ramifications if the e-mails become public knowledge.

2. Semiconductor Chip Protection Act

Medical devices depend on significant computing power to accomplish the intricate tasks such devices are built to perform. At the heart of this computing power is the central processing unit, which consists predominately of a semiconductor chip. Prior to 1984, semiconductor designs were not protected by copyright laws, so chip designs were easily imitated with essentially no recourse for the inventor of a new semiconductor design, outside of a potential patent infringement suit.[192] Congress enacted the Semiconductor Chip Protection Act[193] (SCPA) of 1984 in order to provide protections for novel designs

---

[184]See I.M.S., 307 F. Supp. 2d at 532.
[185]See Egilman, 401 F. Supp. 2d at 112.
[186]Pub. L. No. 99-508, 100 Stat. 1848 (1986).
[187]18 U.S.C. §§2510–2521 (2006).
[188]Id. §§2701–2711.
[189]Id. §2511.
[190]Id. §2702.
[191]See id. §§2520, 2707.
[192]Brooktree Corp. v. Advanced Micro Devices, Inc., 977 F.2d 1555, 1561–62 (Fed. Cir. 1992).
[193]Pub. L. No. 98-620, §302, 98 Stat 3335, 3347 (1984).

of semiconductor chips. Under this Act, the owner of a mask work, which is a topological creation embodied in a chip, may apply to the Register of Copyrights for registration of the mask.[194] If recognition is granted, the owner of the mask has exclusive rights to reproduce the mask, which prevents rival chip manufacturers from copying the chip design directly.[195] However, an exception to the wide-ranging protections of the SCPA allows a party to reverse engineer a protected mask and use information gained from the mask design to create an original work, as long as the initial mask does not include an end-user licensing agreement or reverse-engineering clause prohibiting reverse engineering.[196] Thus, if a medical device manufacturer created a new processor design for a device, that processor mask would be protected under the SCPA if it were appropriately registered. Further, if a medical device manufacturer reverse engineered a protected mask to create a new processor for a device, that processor would not violate the SCPA if the new processor were original.[197]

3. Children's Online Privacy Protection Act

In response to concerns over the widespread use of the Internet by children, Congress passed the Children's Online Privacy Protection Act[198] (COPPA) to protect children from disclosing private information. Under COPPA, an operator of a Web site directed to children may not collect personal information from a person under the age of 13.[199] However, COPPA does allow a Web site operator to collect such information if the operator obtains parental consent and provides notice of what information could be collected from the child.[200]

Due to the increased technological sophistication of children and their widespread use of the Internet from a young age, interactive Web sites promoting children's health may be a method for health care providers to educate children about the dangers of conditions such as obesity and diabetes. If a health care provider created a Web site to teach children about nutrition at a young age, for example, COPPA would prohibit the Web site from requesting personal information, such as age or sex for statistical purposes, without parental consent. As childhood obesity continues to grow as an epidemic and health care providers are forced to reach out to children at a young age, regulation under COPPA will become of more substantial concern in the health care industry.

V. MEDICAL CODES AND HOW THEY AFFECT PRIVACY

Medical codes are alphanumeric values that are assigned to diseases, diagnoses, procedures, pharmaceuticals, and devices that are used by doctors or nurses in the treatment of a patient. By using short representative codes instead

---

[194] 17 U.S.C. §908 (2006).
[195] *Id.* §905.
[196] *Id.* §906; *see Brooktree*, 977 F.2d at 1565–66.
[197] 17 U.S.C. §906.
[198] 15 U.S.C. §§6501–6506.
[199] *Id.* §6502.
[200] *Id.*

of long-form descriptions, doctors can share information efficiently using a uniform language. Further, information can be sent to insurance providers in a standardized format that will promote prompt payment for services rendered by the health care provider. Medical codes are also designed to decrease transcription error at all stages of the treatment process. Instead of having to transcribe long-form instructions, an employee only has to transcribe a simple code that can be relayed to an insurer, treatment facility, or doctor at a different hospital or office. Finally, these codes are not facially tied to a particular patient but are general for all patients. Thus, transmission of the codes does not violate any of the privacy provisions of HIPAA or the HITECH Act, as evidenced by omission of medical codes from the enumerated list of personal health information redacted to create de-identified health information under HIPAA guidelines.[201] As the codes are inherently nonpersonal, use of medical codes encourages release of de-identified medical data for statistical analysis.

Medical coding initially failed to promote uniformity and efficiency in medical recordkeeping and billing due to the vast array of codes that were developed. However, Congress removed this inefficiency of medical code diversity through provisions of HIPAA. In HIPAA, Congress instructed the Secretary of HHS to choose preferred code sets in order to standardize the industry,[202] and HHS has updated the list over time as codes have evolved.[203] Of the current lists of available codes, the most widely used include the International Classification of Diseases, ninth edition, Clinical Modification (ICD-9-CM), and the combination of Current Procedural Terminology (CPT) codes with the Health Care Financing Administration Common Procedure Coding System (HCPCS). While other codes are available for use under HIPAA for coding drugs, biologics, and dental work, the vast majority of medical coding falls under the purview of ICD-9-CM or HCPCS/CPT.

A. HCPCS/CPT

HCPCS/CPT codes are procedure codes created by the CMS as the approved method for coding medical procedures. Further, the Secretary of HHS adopted HCPCS/CPT specifically for coding of physician services, including general physician services, physical/occupational therapy, radiologic procedures, and clinical laboratory tests.[204] Between HHS's adoption of HCPCS/CPT as an approved medical coding system and CMS's adoption of HCPCS/CPT as the approved method of billing a procedure under Medicare/Medicaid, HCPCS/CPT is the predominant procedure code used in the health care industry.

The HCPCS/CPT codes include three levels of identifiers. The first level is the CPT code, which is maintained and developed by the American Medical Association. CPT is a five-digit numeric code that identifies a procedure or

---

[201] 42 C.F.R. §164.514 (2011).
[202] 42 U.S.C. §§1320d-2(c), -3(a) (2006).
[203] 42 C.F.R. §162.1002.
[204] *Id.*

service performed for a patient.[205] The CPT codes are grouped into six major subsections: Anesthesiology (00100–01999), Surgery (10040–69990), Radiology (70010–79999), Pathology (800049–89399), Medicine (90281–99199) and Evaluation and Management (99201–99499).[206] For example, a left heart cardiac catheterization is given CPT code 93510.[207] These five-digit codes can then be modified for a more thorough description of the procedure. The modifier "-50" at the end of a five-digit code, for example, means the procedure was a bilateral procedure.[208] Between the five-digit code and modifiers, the CPT code can specifically describe exactly what procedure was performed on the patient. Levels two and three of the HCPCS/CPT codes describe procedures not included in the CPT. Level two codes are five-digit codes that consist of a letter followed by four numbers.[209] The level two HCPCS codes are maintained by CMS and describe items or services such as drugs, devices and medical supplies, including the amount of a drug administered. For example, code J3120 describes an injection of up to 100 mg of testosterone.[210] Level three HCPCS codes are assigned locally by specific Medicare carriers for new and emerging technologies.[211] Between the three levels of HCPCS/CPT codes, a procedure can be defined with exceptional certainty in an easily identifiable number that is consistent among health care providers.

The use of CPT codes as mandated by the CMS and recommended by HHS creates concerns with regard to intellectual property. Beginning in the 1960s, the American Medical Association (AMA) developed CPT and has maintained CPT under copyright protection.[212] In 1977, Congress required the Health Care Financing Administration (HCFA) to establish a uniform code for physicians' services billed to Medicare or Medicaid, and HCFA decided to adopt the CPT as the preferred code.[213] In order to use the CPT code, HCFA agreed to not use any other medical coding system in exchange for a free license for use.[214] However, a medical book publisher then sued the AMA seeking a declaratory judgment that the copyright on the CPT should be invalidated because the AMA misused its copyright in the license agreement with HCFA.[215] The U.S. Court of Appeals for the Ninth Circuit first held that the requirement of Congress and HCFA requirement that Medicare/Medicaid billing use CPT codes did not force the AMA to lose its copyright.[216] However, the court then held that the AMA did misuse its copyright in forbidding HCFA from using any other medical codes

---

[205] D. Bergeson, *Coding Basics for Heath Care Attorneys*, AHLA-PAPERS P02060308, Feb. 6, 2003.
[206] *Id.*
[207] *Id.*
[208] *Id.*
[209] *Id.*
[210] *Id.*
[211] *Id.*
[212] *See* Practice Mgmt. Info. Corp. v. Am. Med. Ass'n, 121 F.3d 516, 517 (9th Cir. 1997).
[213] *Id.*
[214] *Id.* at 517–18.
[215] *Id.* at 518.
[216] *Id.* at 519–20.

outside of the CPT as a condition for the grant of the license.[217] The court held that it was not the decision of HCFA to use CPT exclusively that embodied the copyright misuse, but the language of the license requiring exclusive use that overstepped the rights that were granted to the copyright holder.[218] Thus, the AMA still maintains a copyright on the CPT codes, but the AMA cannot require those using the CPT codes to use CPT exclusively. Because the copyright on the CPT codes remains valid, the AMA can still require any party that intends to use or republish the CPT to first receive a license from the AMA. The AMA will grant licenses for republication of the CPT, but parties intending to reprint the CPT in a commercial product must obtain a distribution license from the AMA and pay the attendant licensing fees.[219] Thus, transmission of CPT codes should not violate provisions of the DMCA or other copyright protection measures as long as all parties involved have received the necessary license for use of CPT codes from the AMA.

B. ICD-9-CM

ICD-9-CM codes are diagnosis codes maintained by the United States National Center for Health Statistics and CMS.[220] Because the codes were initially created and modified from the World Health Organization's International Classification of Diseases and are maintained by public entities, there are no copyright issues with use of ICD-9-CM codes. The ICD-9-CM codes are used to describe a patient's diagnosis or condition, unlike the CPT codes, which describe the treatment the patient received.[221] For this reason, ICD-9-CM codes are integral for insurance billing and payment, as they are a common source for determining the medical necessity of a treatment.

ICD-9-CM codes can be broken into three components. The main component is known as the diagnosis code, which describes the patient's symptoms with a number. The diagnosis code differs somewhat from the CPT codes in that the number of digits in the code is not fixed, but the number of digits increases with the specificity of the diagnosis.[222] For example, as explained by Bergeson,[223] a patient with a diagnosis of a burn on the abdominal area would be given a code of 942. Further specificity regarding the diagnosis would then be given after a decimal point. If the person had a third-degree burn, then the diagnosis code would become 942.3. Finally, if the diagnosis required a more precise location of the injury, a second digit after the decimal would be added.

---

[217] *Id.* at 520–22.

[218] *Id.* at 521.

[219] American Medical Association, CPT Frequently Asked Questions, *available at* http://www.ama-assn.org/ama/pub/physician-resources/solutions-managing-your-practice/coding-billing-insurance/cpt/frequently-asked-questions.page.

[220] D. Bergeson, *Coding Basics for Heath Care Attorneys*, AHLA-PAPERS P02060308 n.5, Feb. 6, 2003.

[221] *Id.*

[222] *Id.*

[223] *Id.*; *see also* DEPARTMENT OF HEALTH AND HUMAN SERVICES, INTERNATIONAL CLASSIFICATION OF DISEASES, NINTH REVISION, CLINICAL MODIFICATION (ICD-9-CM) [hereinafter HHS CLINICAL MODIFICATION], *available at* ftp://ftp.cdc.gov/pub/Health_Statistics/NCHS/Publications/ICD9-CM/2010/.

For a third-degree burn victim with the burn on a breast, the diagnosis code would become 942.33. By combining the severity digit with the detailed location digit, a general diagnosis can become highly specified.[224]

The other two major components of the ICD-9-CM codes, the V-Codes and E-Codes, provide supplementary information for the diagnosis.[225] The V-Codes describe factors that help to explain why the person sought medical attention. These codes begin with the letter "V" and contain two to four numeric digits. For example, the code V15.6 describes a person admitted for poisoning.[226] The E-Codes describe the causes of a condition or incident and consist of the letter "E" followed by three or four numeric digits. For example, the code E-906.0 describes an injury caused by a dog bite.[227] Between the diagnosis code, the V-Code, and the E-Code, a very clear description of a patient's diagnosis and cause of injury can be presented through a simple alpha numeric code. In combination with the HCPCS/PCT codes, a complete description of a patient's interaction with a doctor, from cause of injury to diagnosis to full treatment, can be simplified to three or four medical codes.

Of note, the ICD-9-CM code standard will no longer be supported under HIPAA as of Oct. 1, 2013, and the new ICD-10-CM code standard will be adopted.[228] The adoption of the ICD-10-CM standard has led to some concern in the medical community as the ICD-10-CM standard contains more than five times the number of codes of the ICD-9-CM system.[229] However, CMS has reassured health care providers that the new ICD-10-CM standard will not affect HCPCS/CPT codes and will not be any more difficult to use than the prior ICD-9-CM system.[230]

C. DRG

The ICD-9-CM and HCPCS/CPT codes are used by physicians for patient billing. However, hospitals use a different set of codes, known as Diagnosis Related Groupings (DRG), for billing Medicare or Medicaid for the average cost of inpatient treatment for a specific diagnosis.[231] These DRG codes are tied directly to a diagnosis based on the ICD-9-CM code. For example, a diagnosis of a patient with gram-negative pneumonia, ICD-9-CM 482.83, would have a related DRG code of 79.[232] While doctors are told not to code probable or suspected diagnoses under ICD-9-CM (but only code symptoms), hospitals

---

[224]Bergeson at n.5.

[225]*Id.*

[226]HHS CLINICAL MODIFICATION.

[227]*Id.*

[228]42 C.F.R. §162.1002 (2011).

[229]*See* Rita A. Scichilone, *Are We There Yet? Compliance-Ready Computer-Assisted Coding New Technologies Help Organizations Work Smarter Towards Compliance-Ready Systems*, 11 J. HEALTH CARE COMPLIANCE 55, 55–56 (2009).

[230]Dep't of Health & Human Servs., Centers for Medicare & Medicaid Servs., ICD-10-CM/PCS: Myths & Facts (Apr. 2010), *available at* http://www.cms.gov/ICD10/Downloads/ICD-10MythsandFacts.pdf.

[231]D. Bergeson, *Coding Basics for Heath Care Attorneys*, AHLA-PAPERS P02060308 n.5 (Feb. 6, 2003).

[232]*Id.*

can code probable or suspected diagnoses under DRG because reimbursement from Medicare or Medicaid is based on the average patient with a given diagnosis.[233] Each DRG code corresponds to a specific reimbursement from Medicare or Medicaid for the treatment provided for a specific diagnosis. Because DRG codes are so specific for a diagnosis, two very similar diagnoses (such as gram-negative pneumonia and non-gram-negative pneumonia) can have different DRG codes and different reimbursements, leading to concern about "DRG creep."[234] DRG creep refers to the practice of hospitals assigning the DRG code with the higher reimbursement for similar diagnoses, leading to inappropriately high payments from Medicare or Medicaid. Outside of concerns with DRG creep, however, DRG coding by hospitals is very similar to the ICD-9-CM coding performed by physicians.

D. Medical Codes and the Re-identification Problem

While medical codes provide an efficient and effective method to transmit patient medical treatment and billing information between, for example, health care providers and insurers, these medical codes do carry inherent privacy risks. HIPAA classifies medical records depending on the extent of information contained within the records. Full medical records and personally identifying information are protected to the full extent of HIPAA's power.[235] However, HIPAA creates an exception for what is termed de-identified health information, which is considered outside HIPAA's strict protections.[236] HIPAA's guidelines for creating de-identified health information are exacting.[237] For a more detailed description of the removal of personal identifiers under HIPAA guidelines to create de-identified data, see VII.D.2., below. These removed identifiers include information such as names, geographical locations or ZIP codes, telephone numbers, dates, Social Security numbers, and medical record numbers.[238] The goal behind the de-identification exception is to promote sharing of depersonalized medical data for use in large-scale statistical studies to improve treatment plans or target funding for training in specific areas. Because this data has been theoretically stripped of all information that could be tied back to an original patient, there would be no need to expand the stringent privacy protections of HIPAA to cover de-identified health information. However, the de-identification of medical records as required by HIPAA is not complete. Techniques exist that can re-identify these bare bones records and can connect a patient to a specific line of medical data within a database, potentially revealing that patient's full medical record for an interested party. Aside from just basic criminal interests such as blackmail, re-identification of medical data could be of substantial value to a variety of commercial parties, such as for pharmaceutical suppliers or medi-

---

[233] *Id.*
[234] *Id.*
[235] 42 C.F.R. §164.502 (2011).
[236] *Id.* §164.502(d).
[237] *Id.* §164.514.
[238] *Id.*

cal device manufacturers, for directed marketing purposes.[239] Re-identification of both medical and nonmedical databases has recently become a popular topic, as three high-profile situations have demonstrated how tenuous the privacy afforded by de-identified data can appear.[240]

First, in the mid-1990s, researchers determined that 87.1 percent of Americans could be uniquely identified by their five-digit ZIP code, birth date, and sex.[241] To demonstrate the power of these specific identifiers for re-identification, researchers analyzed a de-identified data set, created for health care research by a Massachusetts government agency, which included information summarizing every state employee's hospital visits.[242] The de-identified health information had name, address, and Social Security numbers removed for all patients included in the study database, but the fields of ZIP code, birthdate, and sex remained in the database. By use of these three identifiers, in combination with complete public voter rolls from cities in Massachusetts, the researchers were able to access the Massachusetts governor's full medical history through the de-identified information.[243]

Next, in 2006, America Online (AOL) released 20 million search queries for 650,000 users and attempted to create anonymity by replacing information such as AOL username and IP addresses with unique identification numbers.[244] The project was originally hailed as a landmark for data set analysis, but bloggers were able to connect specific searches to specific unique identification numbers. With a small amount of research, reporters at the *New York Times* were able to connect one of the unique identification numbers to a specific person, destroying the anonymity of the de-identified data.[245]

Finally, the most public demonstration of the power of re-identification came from the "Netflix Prize" data set.[246] Netflix offered the first team that could significantly improve Netflix's movie recommendation algorithm a $1 million prize.[247] In order to provide data for the prize research, Netflix released over 100 million records revealing how 500,000 users rated movies between the years 1999 and 2005. Netflix removed personally identifying information such as user names, but each user was assigned a unique identifier to preserve continuity

---

[239] Brief for Electronic Privacy Information Center as Amicus Curiae Supporting Appellee, IMS Health Inc. v. Sorrell, 630 F.3d 263 (2d Cir. 2010); *see also* Milt Freudenheim, *And You Thought a Prescription Was Private*, N.Y. TIMES, Aug. 8, 2009, *available at* http://www.nytimes.com/2009/08/09/business/09privacy.html.

[240] Paul Ohm, *Broken Promises of Privacy: Responding to the Surprising Failure of Anonymization*, 57 UCLA L. REV. 1701, 1717 (2010).

[241] *Id.* at 1719.

[242] *Id.* at 1719–20.

[243] *Id.* at 1720.

[244] *Id.* at 1717–18.

[245] Michael Barbaro & Tom Zeller, *A Face is Exposed for AOL Searcher No. 4417749*, N.Y. TIMES, Aug. 9, 2006, at A1.

[246] Paul Ohm, *Broken Promises of Privacy: Responding to the Surprising Failure of Anonymization*, 57 UCLA L. REV. 1701, 1721–22 (2010); *see also* Arvind Narayanan & Vitaly Shmatikov, *Robust De-Anonymization of Large Sparse Datasets*, *in* PROCEEDINGS OF THE 2008 IEEE SYMPOSIUM ON SECURITY AND PRIVACY 111, 121 (2008).

[247] Ohm at 1721–22.

between ratings by that same user.²⁴⁸ Researchers showed that, based on the precise ratings of only six obscure movies, the researchers could identify a user 84 percent of the time.²⁴⁹ Thus despite anonymization efforts, researchers were still able to link users with the Netflix published ratings with a high degree of certainty. Even further, knowing the precise rating of two movies and the date the rating was assigned allowed researchers to identify 68 percent of users.²⁵⁰ Finally, by comparison of the de-identified Netflix user ratings with Internet Movie Database (IMDb) user ratings, which publically include user names, two users out of 50 in a small IMDb sample could be identified with statistical certainty.²⁵¹ This public disclosure of potentially embarrassing information regarding movie preferences led Netflix customers to file a class action lawsuit, which Netflix settled once the Federal Trade Commission became involved.²⁵²

These three examples show how seemingly de-identified data can be utilized, in concert with freely available public data, to obtain private information. While HIPAA does require that the ZIP code be removed from medical records, a person's age (as determined from year of birth) or sex are still valid identifiers that can remain on medical records.²⁵³ Removal of address or location information makes re-identification more difficult, but the combination of medical information, such as medical codes, with some personally identifying information, such as age or sex, raises the risk of re-identifying de-identified data using advanced re-identification techniques.²⁵⁴ Because of these concerns with re-identification, health care providers must be prudent in their public disclosure of data for research purposes so that patient confidentiality concerns are protected to the greatest extent possible.

VI. Trademark—Protecting Indicia of Ownership

A. Trademarks in General and Identification With a Source of Goods

A trademark is a word, symbol, or phrase used to identify a particular manufacturer's or seller's products and distinguish them from the products of another.²⁵⁵ For example, the trademark "Johnson's" identifies the baby products (and other products) sold by Johnson & Johnson, Inc. When such marks are used to identify services rather than products, they are called service marks, although they are generally treated just the same as trademarks.

Under some circumstances, trademark protection can extend beyond words, symbols, and phrases to include other aspects of a product, such as its color or packaging. For example, the purple color of Nexium or the unique shape of a pill bottle might serve as a trademark. Such features fall generally under the

---
²⁴⁸*Id.*
²⁴⁹*Id.*
²⁵⁰*Id.*
²⁵¹*Id.* at 1722.
²⁵²*Id.*
²⁵³42 C.F.R. §164.514 (2011).
²⁵⁴Ohm at 1711–16.
²⁵⁵15 U.S.C. §1127.

term "trade dress," and they may be protected if consumers associate them with a particular manufacturer rather than the product in general. However, such features will not be protected if they confer any sort of functional or competitive advantage. For example, a manufacturer cannot lock up the use of a particular unique bottle shape if that shape confers some sort of functional advantage (e.g., is easier to stack or easier to grip).[256]

Trademarks make it easier for consumers to quickly identify the source of goods or services. Instead of reading the fine print on a product, consumers can look for the name or logo of the company. By making goods easier to identify, trademarks also give manufacturers an incentive to invest in the quality of their goods. After all, if a consumer tries a product and finds the quality lacking, it will be easy for the consumer to avoid that product in the future and instead buy another brand. Trademark law furthers these goals by regulating the proper use of trademarks.

1. What Can Be Trademarked?

A trademark is generally thought of as a word, name, or logo. The Trademark Act of 1946 (known as the "Lanham Act") states that trademarks and service marks include "words, names, symbols, devices, or a combination of the same.[257]" Case law has expanded the definition of what may serve as a trademark to color,[258] trade dress,[259] and groups of letters[260] to name a few.

In order to serve as a trademark, a mark must be distinctive, or capable of identifying a particular good or service. In determining whether a mark is distinctive, the U.S. Supreme Court has noted five basic categories of trademarks: (1) fanciful, (2) arbitrary, (3) suggestive, (4) descriptive, and (5) generic.[261] Trademarks that are fanciful, arbitrary, or suggestive are deemed to be inherently distinctive, because they perform the limited function of identifying the source of a product or service. Trademarks that are not fanciful, arbitrary, or suggestive, or that are merely descriptive, still may be considered distinctive and therefore entitled to protection under the doctrine of secondary meaning. A trademark may acquire secondary meaning if the primary significance of the mark in the minds of consumers is the association with the source of goods or services.[262]

By definition, a generic term is the name of the product or service.[263] Generic names are not registrable on either the Principal or the Supplemental

---

[256] Qualitex Co. v. Jacobson Prods. Co., Inc., 115 S. Ct. 1300 (1995).
[257] 15 U.S.C. §1127.
[258] *Qualitex*, 115 S. Ct. 1300.
[259] Samara Bros. v. Wal-Mart Stores, Inc., 529 U.S. 205 (2000).
[260] Arrow Fastener Co. v. Stanley Works, 35 USPQ2d 1449 (2d Cir. 1995).
[261] Two Pesos, Inc. v. Taco Cabana, Inc., 505 U.S. 763, 112 S. Ct. 2753 (1992).
[262] *Id.*
[263] 15 U.S.C. §1052.

Register.²⁶⁴ A trademark that is generic is not protectable under the Lanham Act. The rationale behind this is that generic words do not identify the source of the goods but instead describe the product itself, and therefore should be available to all who wish to use the words. For example, the U.S. Court of Appeals for the Fourth Circuit has held that the phrase "You Have Mail" is generic or commonly used without secondary meaning, and that the phrase therefore could not be protected by America Online, Inc.²⁶⁵ In the health care industry, Lanolin and Aspirin are two examples of former trademarks that have become generic terms.

Section 32(1) of the Lanham Act protects federally registered marks by prohibiting the use in commerce of any reproduction, counterfeit, copy, or colorable imitation of that mark in connection with the sale, offering for sale, distribution, or advertising of any goods or services that is likely to cause confusion, or to cause mistake, or to deceive.²⁶⁶

Section 43(a) of the Lanham Act applies to trademarks that are not federally registered. For these unregistered marks, Section 43(a) prohibits the use in commerce of any mark that is likely to cause confusion as to the source, sponsorship, or affiliation of goods or services, as well as any false or misleading statement in commercial advertising that misrepresents the nature, characteristics, qualities, or geographic origin of the advertised or competitive goods or services.²⁶⁷

2. Trademark Remedies

Successful trademark plaintiffs are entitled to a wide range of remedies under federal law. Such plaintiffs are routinely awarded injunctions prohibiting the defendant from further infringing or diluting use of the trademark.²⁶⁸ In trademark infringement suits, monetary relief may also be available, including (1) defendant's profits, (2) damages sustained by the plaintiff, and (3) the costs of the action.²⁶⁹ Damages may be trebled upon showing of bad faith. In trademark dilution suits, however, damages are available only if the defendant willfully traded on the plaintiff's goodwill in using the mark. Otherwise, plaintiffs in dilution actions are limited to injunctive relief.²⁷⁰

---

²⁶⁴The Lanham Act sets up two registers, the Principle Register and the Supplemental Register. Inherently distinctive marks can be registered in the Principle Register, and descriptive marks (i.e., not inherently distinctive) can be registered in the Supplemental Register. In order to move a descriptive mark from the Supplemental Register to the Principle Register, the trademark owner must prove secondary meaning. A mark on the Supplemental Register does not imbue the owner with the exclusive use rights otherwise afforded to owners of marks on the Principle Register.

²⁶⁵America Online, Inc. v. AT&T Corp., 243 F.3d 812 (4th Cir. 2001), *cert. dismissed*, 534 U.S. 946 (2001).

²⁶⁶15 U.S.C. §1114(1).

²⁶⁷*Id.* §1125(a).

²⁶⁸*Id.* §1116(a).

²⁶⁹*Id.* §1117(a).

²⁷⁰*Id.* §1125(c).

3. Trademark Laws

The Lanham Act is found in Title 15 of the United States Code and contains the federal statutes governing trademark law in the United States. The protection afforded by states to trademark owners will likely be coextensive with or no greater than the federal protections. However, some states go through the "clearance" process (checking for availability) as thoroughly as do the examiners in the U.S. Patent and Trademark Office (USPTO), the federal office that reviews inventions and trademark applications to determine whether they satisfy the requirements for obtaining a patent. Courts in those states are therefore more willing to impose harsh penalties on infringers. In other states that merely ensure that no direct competitor matches before approving a state trademark registration, the courts are less willing to impose the full extent of the remedial benefits that otherwise would be available under some state statutes. Nonetheless, it is advisable to register marks locally or regionally so as to discourage local infringing activities.

As of November 2003, the United States joined the Madrid Protocol, an international treaty that facilitates trademark protection in approximately 60 countries, including most of the world's major economies.[271] U.S. trademark owners may now file a single international application with the USPTO, make a single payment in U.S. currency, and simultaneously apply to register their mark in any Madrid Protocol countries where they are doing, or intend to do, business. It is no longer necessary to pursue multiple applications with national trademark offices or to hire foreign counsel or other agents, such as translators, at the application stage. Each national trademark office to which the international application is forwarded must review the application on an accelerated basis, as if the applicant had filed directly with that office, and may refuse protection for the mark in its territory. Ultimately, an International Registration will be effective only in those countries in which the application is not refused or successfully opposed, but issues raised in one jurisdiction will not affect the fate of designations in other jurisdictions. The most serious disadvantage of an International Registration is its dependency on the validity of the home country application or registration during the first five years after the International Registration is issued. Many U.S. trademark owners will find, however, that the Madrid Protocol system is more flexible and cost-effective than country-by-country trademark registrations.

4. Dilution

Effective in January 1996, Congress passed the Federal Trademark Dilution Act of 1995 (the Dilution Act).[272] The Dilution Act amended Section 43 of the Lanham Act to offer protection against the dilution of certain famous

---

[271]*Id.* §§1141 *et seq.*; 37 C.F.R. §§7.1–7.41; *see also* Common Regulations Under the Madrid Agreement Concerning the International Registration of Marks and the Protocol Relating to That Agreement (Common Regulations) (in force April 2004), *available at* http://www.wipo.int/madrid/en/legal_texts/common_regulations.htm. On October 1, 2004, the European Community joined the Madrid Protocol, allowing companies to pursue Community Trade Marks via the Madrid Protocol system.

[272]Pub. L. No. 104-98, 109 Stat. 985 (1996).

marks without the necessity of showing any likelihood of consumer confusion.[273] Under the Dilution Act, the owner of a famous mark is entitled, subject to principles of equity, to enjoin any unauthorized commercial use of the mark if the use begins after the mark has become famous and causes dilution of the distinctive quality of the mark.[274]

The statute lists a number of factors that a court may consider in determining whether a mark is distinctive and famous, including:

- degree of inherent distinctiveness;
- duration and extent of prior use of the mark;
- duration and extent of advertising and publicity of the mark;
- geographical extent of use of the mark;
- industry or trade within which the mark is used; and
- degree of recognition of the mark within the industry or trade.[275]

Under the Dilution Act, dilution is defined to mean "the lessening of the capacity of a famous mark to identify and distinguish goods or services, regardless of the presence or absence of (1) competition between the owner of the famous mark and other parties, or (2) likelihood of confusion, mistake, or deception."[276] A court is not required to rely on traditional definitions of dilution, such as blurring or tarnishment.

The protection afforded by the Dilution Act applies only to a commercial use of the trademark. However, the mere registration of a domain name using a famous mark also could constitute dilution under the Dilution Act. In the case of *Panavision International L.P. v Toeppen*,[277] the U.S. Court of Appeals for the Ninth Circuit upheld a district court ruling that the registration of the domain names "panavision.com" and "panaflex.com" constituted dilution by diminishing the capacity of Panavision to identify and distinguish its goods and services on the Internet. The defendant in that case had also registered domain names using the famous marks of other companies, including Delta Airlines, Neiman Marcus, Eddie Bauer, Lufthansa, and over 100 others.

Nonetheless, many offending but noncommercial uses of a trademark may not fall within the parameters of the Dilution Act. For example, many celebrities are the subjects of Web sites that have been created and are maintained by their fans. If the owner of the Web site does not charge for use of the site or otherwise engage in commercial activity using the site in such a way that use of trademarked mark is enhanced by the famous name or trademark, then the use of the famous name or mark on the site may not be actionable under the Dilution Act.

Prior to 2003, the courts had split on whether owners of famous marks had to provide actual dilution or merely likelihood of dilution. The U.S. Supreme Court resolved the split in *Moseley v. V Secret Catalogue, Inc.* by holding that a plaintiff must show that its trademark has suffered actual dilution.[278] This

---

[273] 15 U.S.C. §§1125(c), 1127.
[274] *Id.*
[275] 15 U.S.C. §1125(c).
[276] *Id.* §1127.
[277] 141 F.3d 1316 (9th Cir. 1998).
[278] 537 U.S. 418 (2003).

requirement does not, however, extend to showing the economic consequences of dilution, such as lost sales or profits.[279] The concern for trademark practitioners then became how to reliably prove actual dilution.

In response to the Court's decision in *Moseley*, Congress passed legislation that provides stronger trademark dilution protection for "famous" marks. Rather than having to prove actual dilution, as required by *Moseley*, the Trademark Dilution Revision Act of 2006[280] (TDRA) allows the owner of a famous mark to prevent the use of another mark if such other mark "is likely to cause dilution by blurring or dilution by tarnishment of the famous mark, regardless of the presence or absence of actual or likely confusion, of competition, or of actual economic injury."[281] "Dilution by blurring" is defined to include an association arising from the similarity between a famous mark and another mark that impairs the distinctiveness of the famous mark. "Dilution by tarnishment" is defined to include an association arising from the similarity between a famous mark and another mark that harms the reputation of the famous mark.[282]

Enactment of the TDRA was meant to make things simpler for the owners of famous marks. A review of recent cases reveals, however, that decisions in this area of the law remain inconsistent. For example, in *Perfumebay, Inc. v. eBay, Inc.*, the well-known auction site claimed that Perfumebay diluted the eBay trademark. The Ninth Circuit noted that Perfumebay totally incorporates eBay. Additionally, the court reasoned that the textual nature of the Internet limited the number of ways a junior mark could distinguish itself from the senior mark and textual similarity should be given more weight in this case. The court also held that the eBay mark is so highly distinctive that consumers would be likely to see the Perfumebay mark as essentially the same as eBay's mark despite their notable differences.

In *Starbucks Corp. v. Wolfe's Bourough Coffee, Inc.*,[283] the Second Circuit affirmed the district court's determination that Starbucks failed to establish dilution by tarnishment but vacated and remanded the district court finding that Starbucks failed to prove dilution by blurring. Courts consider six nonexclusive factors in determining whether there is dilution by blurring:

(1) the degree of similarity between the allegedly infringing mark and the famous mark;
(2) the degree of inherent or acquired distinctiveness of the famous mark;
(3) the extent to which the owner of the famous mark is engaging in substantially exclusive use of the mark;
(4) the degree of recognition of the famous mark;
(5) whether the user of the allegedly infringing mark intended to create an association with the famous mark; and
(6) any actual association between the mark or trade name and the famous mark.

---

[279]*Id.* at 433.
[280]Pub. L. No. 109-312 (codified at 15 U.S.C. §1125(c)).
[281]15 U.S.C. §1125(c)(1).
[282]*Id.* §1125(c)(2).
[283]588 F.3d 97 (2d Cir. 2009).

In deciding to remand the case, the Second Circuit held that a plaintiff is not required to prove substantial similarity between plaintiff's and defendant's marks.[284] The *Starbucks* decision is significant because it underscores how significant the TDRA can be for owners of famous marks. No longer must a mark owner prove that the marks are "very" or "substantially" similar. Additionally, the mark holder does not have to present evidence of "bad faith" intent by the alleged infringer to associate its mark with the famous mark. Thus, companies with strong and well-known marks should consider pursuing dilution claims against similar marks instead of conventional infringement claims.

When comparing the two cases, the reasoning of the court seems inconsistent. Most probably consider the marks in the *Starbucks* case to be more similar than those in the *Perfumebay* case. Additionally, the term "Charbucks" could evoke the picture in someone's mind of burnt coffee, thereby tarnishing the brand of Starbucks. What is clear is that the case law on the subject of dilution is still developing.

B. How Are Trademarks Used?

1. Purple Gloves

Kimberly-Clark Worldwide, Inc. has a global brand that owns well-known brands such as Kleenex, Scott, Huggies, Pull-Ups, and Depends, to name a few. Kimberly-Clark is also known in the health care industry for providing their signature high-quality purple nitrile exam gloves.

In 1999, Kimberly-Clark filed a trademark for the color purple for "protective gloves for industrial use, and disposable nitrile gloves for use in laboratories and cleanroom environments" and "gloves for medical and surgical uses." This trademark was registered on the Principal Register on July 23, 2002.

In 2003, Kimberly-Clark filed a second registration for the color purple for "disposable nitrile gloves for general use." This trademark was registered on the Principal Register on June 6, 2006. Kimberly-Clark filed the second registration to broaden the scope of the company's trademark rights. "For general use" can cover many different potential uses of the product.

In December 2005, Innovative Healthcare Corp. filed an action with the U.S. Trademark and Trial Appeal Board to cancel Kimberly-Clark's trademark registration for the color purple for protective gloves. Kimberly-Clark subsequently filed a lawsuit in federal court against Innovative Healthcare, alleging trademark infringement of Kimberly-Clark's federally registered color purple trademark. The cancellation action was put on hold as a result. The parties reached an agreement to resolve the cancellation action and the federal lawsuit in August of 2007. As provided in the agreement, the federal court entered a consent judgment in which Innovative Healthcare would cease selling, distributing, and importing purple- and lavender-colored protective gloves. The cancellation action was dismissed with prejudice.

---

[284]*Id.* at 107.

2. How Trademarks Can Protect a Surgical Product or Medicine

Trademarks can protect the name and logo of a surgical product or medicine. Additionally, in certain instances, a trademark may also protect the product or medicine's color or shape. Registering these things will prevent other companies from producing products that are confusingly similar to the registered brand. Unlike patents, trademarks have an advantage in that they can last forever. Companies in the health care industry should make the most of the rights provided by trademark registration.

Health care companies should take a strategic approach to developing new brands to maximize competitive advantage. One example of this is AstraZeneca's migration from Prilosec to Nexium. AstraZeneca undertook one of the most expensive marketing campaigns in the history of the drug industry with ads appearing everywhere proclaiming, "Today's purple pill is Nexium, from the makers of Prilosec." As a result, the introduction and promotion of Nexium allowed AstraZeneca to prevent the revenue loss it would have experienced with competition from the introduction of generic versions that would be priced significantly lower.

Many companies choose to use a global brand. Take Johnson and Johnson, for example. The company has built a vast array of product lines under its brand, including but not limited to Band-Aid Brand, Johnson's baby products, Neutrogena, and Tylenol. Many of these products have been around for many years, and because the customers who use these products trust them, they often use other Johnson products as well. Other companies, such as Unilever, have decided to reduce the number of their brands to a more manageable number and thereby have the ability to focus more on building up and protecting the brands they own.

3. The Aspirin Story

Generic "marks" are incapable of functioning as trademarks. The rationale for creating the category of generic marks is that no manufacturer or service provider should be given exclusive right to use words that generically identify a product. Often such marks are rejected by the USPTO when registered. At times, however, a valid trademark becomes generic if the trademark owner and/or the consuming public misuse the mark sufficiently so that it becomes the generic name for the product. Two prime examples of former trademarks that became the generic name for a product are "cellophane" and "aspirin."

The term "Aspirin" was trademarked by Bayer Company in 1899. Bayer's trademark was registered worldwide for Bayer's brand of acetylsalicylic acid. Thereafter, competitors began to refer to their own medicine as aspirin. Additionally, Bayer began a widespread advertising campaign for the product featuring the slogan "Bayer—Tablets of Aspirin." The Aspirin trademark was officially canceled in the United States in 1921 when the Southern District of New York held that aspirin referred to the class of medicines and not uniquely the Bayer product.[285] Today, when you ask someone for aspirin in the United States, you are likely to be offered an assortment of Advil, Tylenol, or Bayer

---

[285]Bayer Co. v. United Drug Co., 272 F. 505 (S.D.N.Y. 1921).

products. (In more than 80 other countries, however, Aspirin remains a registered trademark of Bayer.)

Trademarks and service marks are frequently just words. It is the usage of the words that can often destroy trademark rights. Some of the strongest marks are the most fragile in this respect. For example, "aspirin," "escalator" and "thermos" are words that once signified the source of a particular brand of painkiller, moving staircase, and insulated food container, respectively. Now they are common terms for these products and are available for use by anyone. The respective companies did not properly use and adequately protect their marks, and thus each of these marks has become generic. If the marks had been used properly, then their owners would have had a tremendously valuable trademark today. Instead, competitors are free to use the words to describe their own products.

The following are some basic rules that are important in protecting trademarks and service marks:

(1) Use marks as adjectives and not as nouns or verbs.
(2) Use marks on or in connection with their approved product or service.
(3) Use the trademark notice.
(4) Use marks exactly as they were registered.

C. Domain Names

1. Protect Domain Name

Many attorneys and in-house counsel maintain that filing a domain name[286] with a registry service is the only step required to protect a domain name. However, an applicant should begin by registering its trademark with the USPTO, because an applicant that has obtained a unique domain name but has not obtained a federal registration for it with the USPTO may find itself the defendant in an action for infringement. For example, the holder of a mark in the real world may notify the applicant that its domain name has the potential of confusing the public as to the origin of the applicant's Web site and creates an implication that the mark's holder is somehow involved in or with applicant's site.

A mark composed of a domain name may be registered with the U.S. Patent and Trademark Office as a trademark or service mark. However, just like any other mark, the domain name is registrable only if it functions to identify the particular source of goods or services offered. In other words, it must be distinctive so as to be capable of distinguishing the applicant's goods or services from those of others.

2. Secure Domain Name

Securing a domain name involves registering the name the applicant wants with the Internet Corporation for Assigned Names and Numbers (ICANN)

---

[286] A domain name is part of a URL that is the whole address one places in the address bar of a browser. For example, the following URL is in italics and the domain name is bold: *http://horses.**about.com**/example/pony*.

through a domain name registrar. An applicant should register its domain name so that the applicant does not lose it to a competitor later. The applicant goes to a registrar and pays a registration fee for the domain name. Registration gives the applicant the right to the name for a year, and the applicant will have to renew it annually.

Here are some tips for registering the domain name with the registrar:

- The registration should be in the name of the company or the company's top-level management. Often an employee will put it in his or her name, but this can cause a problem for the company when the employee resigns or is terminated.
- The company may wish to purchase variations of its domain name to prevent cybersquatting.
- All registrars must follow the Uniform Domain Name Dispute Resolution Policy (UDRP).[287] Under the policy, most types of trademark-based domain-name disputes must be resolved by agreement, court action, or arbitration before a registrar will cancel, suspend, or transfer a domain name. Disputes alleged to arise from abusive registrations of domain names may be addressed by expedited administrative proceedings that the holder of trademark rights initiates by filing a complaint with an approved dispute-resolution service provider. In order to prevail, the trademark owner must show:
    o that the trademark owner owns a trademark (either registered or unregistered) that is the same or confusingly similar to the registered second-level domain name;
    o that the party that registered the domain name has no legitimate right or interest in the domain name; and
    o that the domain name was registered and used in bad faith.

VII. PATENTS AND PATENT LAW FOR THE HEALTH ATTORNEY

This section informs the medical professional or manager about some of the fundamental concepts of patents and patent law so that he or she can make informed decisions in all areas of patent law, but with an emphasis on medical patents and products. Section VII.A. provides a basic overview of the patent application process as well as patent enforcement. It is intended mostly to introduce basic patent vocabulary and step the reader through the patent process from start to finish.

All the sections that follow build on this framework. Section VII.B. explains some of the more commonly misunderstood concepts of patent law, including originality and invalidity. This section also explains the four main requirements of patents in more detail, and also provides information regarding clarity and the duty of disclosure. Section VII.C. provides an overview of how to bring a

---

[287]Internet Corporation for Assigned Names and Numbers, Uniform Domain Name Dispute Resolution Policy (Oct. 24, 1999), *available at* http://www.icann.org/en/udrp/udrp-policy-24oct99.htm.

product to market, focusing on updating freedom to operate opinions, deciding when and how often to file patent applications, and how to set policies at companies and universities to generate inventions. Section VII.D. explains some of the nuances associated with patents in the medical field, including enablement requirements for claiming multiple configurations of drugs and materials, and how medical software and computer systems need to be claimed so that they cover HIPAA-compliant systems.

A. Patent Drafting, Patent Prosecution, and Patent Rights and Enforcement

The following subsection introduces the parts of a patent application and also provides an overview of patent prosecution, i.e., the process of amending the application and responding to the Patent Office's arguments that the application as filed does not meet the requirements for obtaining a patent. Details concerning the nature of rights are explained, as are the concepts of patent licensing and patent litigation.

1. The Parts of a Patent Application

American patents are issued by the U.S. Patent and Trademark Office (USPTO). A patent application contains nine main parts: title, background, summary, brief description of the drawings, detailed description of the drawings, claims, figures or drawings, a declaration, and an abstract. All applications filed in the USPTO (and indeed nearly every other country) must include these nine parts. The "specification" includes the background, summary, brief description of the drawings, detailed description of the drawings, and abstract, while the disclosure includes the specification plus the claims.

The title of the patent application is simply that, a title. It is generally written to encompass the broadest understanding of the invention, but "the purpose of the title is not to demarcate the precise boundaries of the claimed invention but rather to provide a useful reference tool for future classification purposes."[288]

The background part of the application explains the previously researched and invented technology upon which the current invention seeks to improve. Occasionally, an invention may be the first in its field, but even then there is still related information that the "pioneering" invention builds upon. "Prior art" refers to the body of information in the field of the invention that existed before the patent application in question was filed. Generally, attorneys drafting the background section of a patent application will use this section to explain the fundamental concepts of the technology and the problem that the invention is designed to resolve.

The summary part provides a succinct explanation of the solution to the problem that the inventor found. Because courts sometimes interpret statements made in the summary to limit the scope of terms in the claims, care should be taken when making statements that set forth what the invention requires or what it cannot contain. To avoid unintentionally limiting the scope of a patent's

---

[288] Pitney Bowes, Inc. v. Hewlett-Packard Co., 182 F. 3d 1298, 1312 (Fed. Cir. 1999).

claims, attorneys often use open language such as "the invention may contain part A and part B," or "in some configurations of the invention, part A connects to part B." The summary of the invention, along with the figures and detailed description, are designed to provide an explanation for what the terms of the claims mean and how to make and use the invention. The claims provide the outer limits of the property right the patentee obtains when the patent is granted, but the meaning of the terms in the claims are controlled by various doctrines. Because the ultimate amount of the scope the applicant can claim is often unknown when the patent if filed, the Patent Law (particularly 37 C.F.R. §1.181) allows the applicant to amend the claims during prosecution of the patent, and therefore the summary and detailed description should be written with the understanding that the applicant may need to narrow the scope of the claims if the patent office locates prior art of which the applicant is unaware.

The figures or drawings are illustrations of embodiments of the invention. The figures can be schematics, photographs of prototypes, flow charts, box diagrams, or other illustrations that show what the invention might look like or how it may be practiced. The USPTO prefers India ink line drawings as the format for the drawings, and requires the applicant to show certain requirements should the invention need to be illustrated in other ways.[289]

The brief description of the figures or drawing provides a cheat sheet of sorts as to what they represent. Often a person reviewing a patent for the first time might struggle to understand what the figures show. By using the brief description of the invention, the reviewer can obtain a bird's-eye view of the figures that aids in understanding the disclosure as a whole.

The detailed description of the invention is the meat and potatoes of the invention. This is the section of the application that explains all the different ways the invention may be designed, built, and used. It includes references to the figures or drawings, and these references usually appear as numbers with arrows to elements in the figures. With some narrow exceptions, if this section does not describe a particular configuration that the applicant wishes to claim after the application is filed, the applicant will be prevented from claiming it later (with the exception that the summary, abstract, and figures can also provide this disclosure.) A belt-and-suspenders approach to drafting patent applications involves making sure that every conceivable way the invention could be practiced is presented in the detailed description in order to provide flexibility with amending the claims during prosecution should the patent office locate especially relevant prior art.

Claims come in two chief varieties: independent and dependent. An independent claim is self-contained and reads like a long paragraph, reciting all the features of a particular embodiment of an invention. Dependent claims "depend" from an independent claim or another dependent claim and incorporate all the features of the claim from which they depend. Writing claims in dependent form makes it easier for the examiner or reader to see what the differences are between similar claims. They are also much cheaper to file in most countries

---

[289] USPTO, MANUAL OF PATENT EXAMINATION AND PROCEDURE §608.02 (8th ed. July 2010 rev.) [hereinafter MPEP].

(many countries charge for claims in excess of a certain number, and sometimes independent claims cost more to file).

The claims of the patent application are the single most important piece of the application for determining what the invention is and what it is not. This delineation of what is covered by the claims is what patent attorneys refer to as "claim scope." An ideal claim set includes every conceivable variation of the invention that is patent eligible,[290] described in the specification,[291] enabled by the specification,[292] novel in view of the prior art,[293] and unobvious in view of the prior art.[294] Since the entire breadth of the prior art is rarely known by the attorney when drafting the claims, the attorney uses his or her best judgment as to how broad to make the claims when filing for the patent application. After the application is filed, the patent office will search for publications and patents that disclose all the features in the claims and reject the claims that it believes do not satisfy one or more these requirements. Performing a literature search or prior art search before the patent application is filed can therefore aid the attorney in dialing in the claims so that they only include novel and unobvious subject matter. Still, since no prior art search is ever exhaustive (one must consider, for example, the myriad languages and difficult-to-obtain publications involved), a prior art search represents only a sampling of the prior art that the patent office may uncover.

The declaration and abstract are the two final major pieces of a patent application. The declaration provides basic information about the inventors, requires the inventor swear to certain statements, and provides priority information (description of related patents and patent application invented by the inventor). The abstract provides a one-paragraph explanation of the invention and appears on the front cover of the application. Both the declaration and abstract are required, but they can be submitted after the application is filed for an additional fee.

Once the attorney finishes preparing all nine sections, the inventor signs the declaration, and the attorney files the application. Once the application is received by the USPTO, the office will check these nine parts for compliance with a host of statutes and regulations, the four most important being the requirements of patent subject matter eligibility (35 U.S.C. §101), novelty (35 U.S.C. §102), obviousness (35 U.S.C. §103), and disclosure sufficiency (35 U.S.C. §112, first paragraph). Because of a backlog of patent applications, most patent offices around the world have a pendancy time of several years before a substantive review of the application takes place. However, formalities such as checking to see if any parts are missing, checking fees, and the like usually takes place within a month or two. In addition to the four main requirements, other requirements such as clarity of the claims[295] are very significant and together with the four main requirements account for the majority of the type of rejections an applicant can expect to see. But unlike applications rejected based on

---

[290] 35 U.S.C. §101.
[291] *Id.* §112.
[292] *Id.*
[293] *Id.* §102.
[294] *Id.* §103.
[295] *Id.* §112 ¶2.

the clarity of the claims, patent applications rejected on the basis of the first four requirements may never be allowed, because if the application does not contain patent-eligible subject matter, novel subject matter, unobvious subject matter, or an enabling disclosure, the invention is not patentable. Other common but less frequent bases for rejection include obvious double patenting,[296] missing or incomplete declaration,[297] blurry or incorrectly labeled figures,[298] and description formalities, such as page numbering and font size.[299] The entire process of preparing an application so that it meets these requirements is called patent drafting.

2. Patent Prosecution

Once an application is finalized and filed at the patent office, the application will be checked for compliance with the above requirements, and in most cases, the patent office (particularly a patent examiner) will reject the application for failure to comply with one of the statutory provisions cited in VI.A.1., above. The applicant is typically given up to six months to respond, which usually involves amending the claims so that they are not anticipated by or rendered obvious by some prior art. A response also includes remarks explaining why the claims as presented are patent eligible, novel, and unobvious. The patent examiner will examine the amendments and remarks and issue a subsequent office action. The subsequent office action can maintain the previous grounds of rejection, issue new grounds of rejection, or allow the application. This process (commonly referred to as "patent prosecution") continues until the patent office convinces the applicant that the invention described in the application is not patentable, or the applicant convinces the patent office that all the requirements are satisfied. In the event of a deadlock between the patent examiner and the application, there are several avenues of appeal.

3. Patent Rights and Enforcement

Once a patent application is issued (i.e., given an official patent number), the owner of the patent (the assignee) is granted several rights, including the rights to prevent others from making, using, selling, offering to sell, or importing (collectively "practicing") the claimed invention. It is important to note that a patent does not permit the owner to practice the invention described in his or her patent. Rather, a patent only permits the assignee to prevent others from practicing the claimed invention.

If the assignee of a patented invention believes another entity is practicing that invention, the assignee can request the entity to pay royalties for using the invention. The negotiation and formalization of terms of use and amount of royalties is called patent licensing. Sometimes agreement cannot be reached, and in such cases the patent owner may be left with the decision whether to file a suit for patent infringement. In a patent infringement suit, the owner of the

---

[296] *In re* Goodman, 11 F.3d 1046, 29 USPQ2d 2010 (Fed. Cir. 1993) (judicial doctrine).
[297] 37 C.F.R. §1.63.
[298] MPEP §608.02.
[299] *See id.* §608.01.

B. The Patent Statutes in Detail and Some Commonly Misunderstood Concepts of Patent Law

The following section explains the basic requirements of obtaining a patent in more detail. Patent applications are often rejected in view of these requirements, so it is advantageous to understand what they mean. This section also explains the duty of disclosure and why it is advantageous to research and disclose known publications and patents. Finally, this section explains some commonly misunderstood concepts in detail, including the difference between originality and novelty and the difference between invalidity and obviousness.

1. The Four Requirements for Obtaining a Patent: "Idea" Versus "Invention"

Before deciding whether to file for a patent application, it is important to understand the patentability requirements the patent office will apply before it will grant a patent. One can consider this to be the difference between a "good idea" and a "patentable invention." A "good idea" is simply a solution to a vexing problem. A "patentable invention" is not only a solution to a vexing problem but also a sufficiently described solution[300] that no one else came up with before,[301] that was not obvious at the time of the invention,[302] and that applies to one of the four statutory classes of invention.[303] The invention must also be claimed using sufficiently clear and distinct language,[304] and the inventor and all of its agents must disclose to the patent office all known material relevant to the patentability of the invention.[305]

2. Section 112, First Paragraph: Written Description and Enablement

The requirement that a patent application must be sufficiently described to be patentable really includes two requirements: written description and enablement. The written description requirement provides that the patent specification and figures must disclose the invention set forth in the claims. To use a simple example, if one amended the claims of a patent application so that it claimed a protein for use in treating disease X, and the specification only described treating disease Y, the USPTO would reject a claim under 35 U.S.C. §112 because it did not describe a protein for treating disease Y.

The enablement requirement provides that the applicant must set forth a description of the invention in enough detail that a person having ordinary skill

---

[300] 35 U.S.C. §112 ¶1.
[301] Id. §102.
[302] Id. §103.
[303] Id. §101.
[304] Id. §112 ¶2.
[305] 37 C.F.R. §1.56.

in the art can make and use the claimed invention. This person of "ordinary skill" is a hypothetical person of ordinary creativity having specialized knowledge in the field of the invention. If this person of ordinary skill can make and use the claimed invention without undue experimentation or research, the invention is described in sufficient detail to pass the enablement requirement.

3. Section 101: Statutory Class of the Invention

It is a fundamental principle of patent law that many brilliant ideas are not patentable, solely because the idea exists in a field that is not susceptible to patent protection. *Romeo and Juliet* is a brilliant idea, but would it have been patentable? No. $E=mc^2$—brilliant? Yes. Patentable? No. To be patent eligible, a patent application must claim the invention as a process, machine, manufacture, or composition of matter, or a new and useful improvement thereof.[306] A machine is simply an object that performs a useful function. A manufacture is a product made by a specific machine and/or process. Compositions of matter are man-made compounds such as genetically modified animals, man-made foods, and textiles. Processes are methods of performing a task, but mental processes, natural phenomena, and abstract ideas are judicially excluded under the policy that these concepts should remain free for everyone to use as the building blocks for future inventions.[307]

Patent-eligible subject matter differs by country, particularly in the process area. Lately, there has been a shift in patent eligibility case law requiring processes to be drawn to tangible processes, so processes such as manipulating an electronic signal and business processes are generally held to be patent ineligible.[308] However, methods of treating individuals or diagnosing physical conditions are patentable in the U.S.[309] In other countries, such as in Europe, some inventions drawn to surgical procedures are not patentable under Article 52(4) EPC (European Patent Convention) since that provision excludes from patentability any method of treating humans or animals by surgery or therapy and diagnostic methods practiced on humans or animals. The policy behind the exclusion of such methods is grounded in the interest of public health to ensure that those who practice such methods in connection with the medical treatment of humans or the veterinary treatment of animals are not hindered by patents.[310]

Many varieties of surgical methods and living compounds have been considered for patentability in Europe, and the result has varied depending on the category. Examples include therapeutic methods (not patentable under T 789/96),[311] diagnostic methods (sometimes patent eligible under T 385/86,8),[312] surgical methods (not patentable under *Enlarged Board of Appeal Decision*

---

[306] 35 U.S.C. §101.
[307] Bilski v. Kappos, 130 S. Ct. 3218, 177 L. Ed. 2d 792 (2010).
[308] *In re* Nujten, 500 F.3d 1346 (Fed. Cir. 2007); *Kappos*, 130 S. Ct. 3218.
[309] Prometheus Labs. v. Mayo Collaboratives, 581 F.3d 1336 (Fed. Cir. 2009).
[310] *See* T 116/85.
[311] T 0789/96 (Therapeutic method/ELA MEDICAL) of 23.8.2001. The text of patent appeal decisions at the EPC can be reviewed at http://www.epo.org/law-practice/case-law-appeals.html.
[312] T 0385/86 (Non-invasive measurement) of 25.9.1987; T 0385/88 () of 23.8.1990.

G 5/83,11), DNA and protein sequences (patentable under Rule 23e(2) EPC),[313] and embryonic stem cells (not patentable under Rule 23d EPC). However, techniques such as using disclaimers to exclude patent-ineligible subject matter are generally allowed in Europe, provided there is a clear and unambiguous disclosure of the subject matter remaining in the claim after considering what subject matter has been removed by the disclaimer.[314] Both in the U.S. and in Europe, patent eligibility can turn on how the application is originally written, so when considering patent applications on processes in the U.S. or medical or surgical processes in Europe, it is highly recommended to have an attorney review the application before an initial patent filing. It is also worth noting that in the U.S., one cannot generally sue doctors for performing patented surgical methods, but equipment makers and third-party suppliers are not immune from suit.[315]

4. Section 102: Novelty Versus Originality

Simply stated, an invention must be novel to be patentable. But what does "novel" mean? In the U.S., it means that the inventor must conceive of the invention first. In patent law, as opposed to copyright law, an invention must be new (i.e., not publicly known by others before the inventor came up with the idea). It does not matter whether the inventor came up with the idea on his or her own or how hard the inventor worked at arriving at the invention. The emphasis in the U.S. is on who came up with the invention first, whereas in Europe and elsewhere it is who filed the application on the invention first that controls.

Receiving a rejection in a patent application under 35 U.S.C. §102 is the way the Patent Office tells the applicant that the current invention as claimed is not new (novel). There are two ways to respond to such a rejection. The applicant may either argue that the prior art patent or publication is different from what the applicant is claiming or change the claim (assuming the disclosure provides sufficient support) so that the claim includes elements not in the prior art.

When working with a patent attorney to explain why an invention is different from whatever prior art the patent office cites, the client should look at the claims and find an element in the claims that is not disclosed in the prior art. A patent claim may specify components A through D, and the prior art may specify components A through E. It is not enough to say your invention does not require E (in most cases); what is needed is to specify which component of A through D is lacking in the prior art. For example, if your element B in the claim is different from the element B in the prior art, the applicant should tell the attorney why the claimed element B is different. To do so, the client should review the paragraph or page that the Patent Office specifies discloses element B and consider whether it is the same as the claimed element B. If it is not the same, the attorney should be informed of the difference.

Sometimes, after review of the portions of the prior art reference, it may become clear that the currently pending claim is the same as the prior art disclosure (i.e., the claimed elements match the disclosed components of the prior

---

[313] See http://www.epo.org/law-practice/legal-texts/html/epc/2010/e/ma1.html for the full text of the European Patent Convention Law.
[314] T 1107/06.
[315] 35 U.S.C. §287(c).

art) and the two component Bs are the same. At this point, one would seek to amend the claim to include a new feature that the prior art reference does not contain, or modify how one of the elements is claimed so that it is different from the disclosed component. This new feature needs to be illustrated in the figures and described in the specification in order to be claimed (although it may be possible to add the feature to the existing figures or specification, provided the needed feature appears somewhere in the original disclosure). A patent attorney will often provide suggestions as to which elements to claim to overcome the rejection. However, the client should provide the attorney suggestions as to what appears to be lacking in the prior art to focus the attorney's review. This can improve the quality, and decrease the cost, of filing an amendment or formulating a response.

5. Unobviousness and Invalidity

Often when a patent examiner cannot find all the features of a claim in a single reference, he or she will combine two or more references by modifying or substituting a feature from the first or primary prior art reference with a feature from a secondary or teaching reference. The examiner will then explain why he or she believes making the modification would have been obvious to one having ordinary skill in the art.

But what does obviousness mean in the patent context? An invention is said to be "obvious" when a person having ordinary skill in the art at the time the invention was made and having read all the relevant prior art in the field would have arrived at the same solution being proposed by the applicant. In the U.S., the burden is on the examiner to form a prima facie determination of obviousness.[316] This involves mentally stepping backward in time and into the shoes worn by the hypothetical "person of ordinary skill in the art" when the invention was unknown and just before it was made. The examiner must consider in view of all factual information and prior art, whether the claimed invention "as a whole" would have been obvious at that time to that person. Knowledge of an applicant's disclosure must be put aside in reaching this determination, yet kept in mind in order to determine the "differences," conduct the search, and evaluate the "subject matter as a whole" of the invention.[317] In considering the burden of proof the examiner must present to form the prima facie determination of obviousness, the Supreme Court in *KSR International Co. v. Teleflex Inc.*[318] held that the analysis supporting a rejection under 35 U.S.C. §103 should be made explicit, and that "rejections on obviousness cannot be sustained with mere conclusory statements; instead, there must be some articulated reasoning with some rational underpinning to support the legal conclusion of obviousness."

The Supreme Court's explanation may make sense to patent attorneys, but in the author's experience, the ordinary meaning of the word "obvious" will dominate an inventor's mind when considering this question. As a result, it can be challenging for a patent attorney to obtain assistance from an inventor as

---

[316]MPEP §2142.
[317]*Id.*
[318]550 U.S. 398, 127 S. Ct. 1727, 82 USPQ2d 1385 (2007).

to whether an invention would have been obvious for patent law purposes, but here is a suggested approach. Step 1, the attorney should reinforce to the inventor that the question is whether the invention would have been obvious to one having *ordinary* skill in the invention. It does not matter whether the invention would have been obvious to the *inventor* if he or she had access to the most relevant prior art. Step 2, does the examiner propose a combination, i.e., does the examiner explain what must be changed in the first or primary reference so that combination discloses all the features of the claim? Step 3, does the secondary reference disclose the feature the examiner is asserting would be obvious to change? Step 4, does the examiner provide a logical rationale (it need not be in the references) as to why making the modification or substitution would have been obvious? Step 5, does the combination disclose all the features of the claim? By stepping through this process for every claim rejected under Section 103, the applicant can check to see whether the examiner has met his or her burden to provide a prima facie case of obviousness.

Typically, inventors are predisposed to believe their invention is not obvious, because it most likely was not obvious to them when they started working on the solution or even moments before they arrived at the solution. In contrast, when faced with a patent infringement claim, engineers and scientists are very quick to conclude (even without any documentation) that the asserted claims are obvious, and therefore the patent is invalid. Patent invalidity is a defense to patent infringement, but a hard one to establish because of the heavy burden of proof: the defendant must prove by clear and convincing evidence that the claimed invention is obvious.[319]

In contrast, it is the plaintiff's burden to prove patent infringement. When managing or supervising engineers or scientists from the context of patent litigation defense work, it is very important to reinforce the concept that all patents are presumed valid, and despite what the scientist or engineer might think, the asserted patent has the benefit of such a presumption. Generally, a manager wants to focus the engineer's or scientist's time on explaining what features of the accused product do not appear in the claims (or at least what is arguable), because it is often difficult for outside counsel to gain a complete understanding of the accused product without assistance from those who designed the product. One way to respond to a stubborn engineer or scientist who is having trouble focusing on finding these differences because of his or her opinion that the patented claim is clearly obvious, is to ask the engineer or scientist to find and produce documents published before the filing date of the patent that disclose all the features of the patent or otherwise render them obvious in view of a second reference. Typically, the scientist or engineer initially will have trouble recognizing that what was obvious 10 years ago (or whenever the asserted patent was originally filed) is very different from what might be obvious now. But by asking the engineer or scientist to find documents published before the filing date of the patent, one forces the engineer or scientist to consider obviousness at the time of the invention of the patent as opposed to the time of the lawsuit. This small pushback on the engineer or scientist may be what is needed to keep him or her on the track of finding differences between the claims and the product.

---

[319] Microsoft Corp. v. i4i Ltd. P'ship, 131 S. Ct. 647 (2010).

Moreover, documents related to prior published commercial products of the company can be very helpful in supporting an invalidity defense, so it makes sense to have the scientist or engineer look for them.

C. Bringing a Product to Market

From a patentability standpoint, bringing a new product to market involves many things, including performing and updating freedom to operate analyses, setting and enforcing policies to generate new inventions, filing and updating patent applications, acquiring and licensing new patents, and designing the product around identified patents.

1. Freedom to Operate

When developing a product, there are several concerns a cautious company will have:

(1) Can I get a patent on my product?
(2) Can I stop others from building knock-offs of my product?
(3) Can I build my product without infringing someone else's product?

Questions (1) and (2) are highly related, but Question (3) is not. The answer to Question (1) depends in part on whether the company filed an application on its product *before* it started marketing that product. (In the U.S., there is a one-year grace period for filing a patent application, but most other countries have no grace period.) Whether the company can get a patent also depends on whether its patent application satisfies the conditions for patentability discussed in VII.B., above.

The answer to Question (2) depends on whether the application discloses all the meaningful alternatives to a particular invention. For example, perhaps Company A makes sunglasses and it wishes to patent a new type of sunglasses in which the jaw (i.e., the bottom of the frame) can disengage from the nose piece to allow the user to swap the lenses. The jaw is mounted on a hinge connected to the frame and can snap into the nose piece with a pressure tab. Such an invention could be patentable if it were new, and claim to this invention might appear as follows:

1. A pair of sunglasses comprising:
   a. a frame for holding lenses,
   b. a nose piece for supporting the sunglasses on a user's nose,
   c. a jaw connected on a first side to the frame with a hinge and connected on a second side to the nose piece with a pressure tab, said jaw capable of rotating from a first position to a second position, wherein in the first position the jaw keeps the lens securely in place, and in the second position, the lens is removable from the sunglasses.

At a first glance, this looks like a pretty broad claim, and indeed it would cover a lot of products, but would it prevent other companies from making knock-off products? Probably not, because the claim does not cover a number of alternate embodiments. For example, the hinge could be placed on the nose piece and the pressure tab placed on the frame. Or perhaps the top of the frame could contain a movable arm, and the jaw could be fixed, so that when the arm was separated the user could remove the lens by lifting the lens upward. Or perhaps the jaw could utilize a pressure tab on each side so that it was completely removable. All of these alternate configurations would be outside the scope of the above claim, and present viable design-around options for a competitor.

A good way to prepare a patent application so it can contain claims to all the commercially significant alternatives is to write the disclosure so that it discloses all the variations the inventor can think of for building the invention. The more variations the inventor can disclose, the more claims the attorney can write to try to increase the coverage of a patent. While this practice is good in theory, it creates certain additional costs and complications. Often, each alternate configuration must be claimed in a separate application called a divisional application. Each divisional application has separate filing fees and prosecution costs. Each additional configuration must be illustrated and described in the specification, which increases the cost to prepare the application. Generally, the more valuable it is for a company to extend its coverage of an invention, the more configurations it will attempt to disclose and claim. Budget restrictions, however, will typically limit the disclosure in a patent application only to commercially significant alternatives. In the example above, perhaps having the hinges at the nose piece would be aesthetically undesirable, and if so, the company would likely opt not to disclose and claim that configuration, because even if competitors chose to build sunglasses in this configuration, they would not sell well.

So now that the company has obtained a patent on its desired commercial implementation, and perhaps two or three of the most likely alternate embodiments, can the company go ahead and begin marketing and selling the new sunglasses without fear of patent infringement? No.

Owning a patent covering a product or even several patents thereon does not provide the owner rights to build the product, but rather it provides the owner rights to prevent others from making, using, selling, offering for sale, or importing the product. It is entirely possible that the patent office has issued another patent covering the same product, even though it granted a patent on the company's claim. This is possible because the second patent could cover different features of the sunglasses, such as the lenses, or a different combination of the product's features. Or perhaps the second patent was filed earlier but was not published as an application. Regardless of the mechanism (and there are several others not mentioned here), it is possible that one or more other patents cover the intended product even though a patent was issued on the product.

In order to determine whether another patent exists, a "freedom to operate" search should be performed. In such a search, an attorney will locate (sometimes with the help of a search company) all the patents he or she can find that are relevant to the new product. Often these searches will be focused based on competitors (all sunglasses patents owned by Oakley, Revo, Smith, etc.), but often will include searches on particular areas of the technology to reduce the chances of missing relevant prior art.

Suppose Company B wants to develop a new ultrasonic flosser that utilizes ultrasonic toothbrush technology, but instead of a brush, the flosser uses a Y-shaped fork that has floss connected to each side of the Y. Company B has been making ultrasonic toothbrushes for a while, but with the constant increase in competition, it needs a new product to increase sales. The company comes to its attorney and says research is underway, but they want to lock up the technology with a "blocking patent" so no one else can build the flosser, and they want clearance that no one will sue them. For a manager, an inventor, or in-house counsel, the goals are pretty much the same: acquire as much protection as possible for the least cost while simultaneously minimizing the company's exposure for developing the new product. Assuming that backdrop, the company may contact its outside counsel and ask them for their assistance.

Suppose a call to outside counsel includes the CEO of the company, its in-house counsel, one of the inventors, and a partner and an associate from the outside law firm. The conversation will typically start with an explanation of the company, the product, and perhaps the inventors. The description of the product will often be very confusing to the attorneys, since the inventors will attempt to explain the product by comparing it to products the attorneys have not seen and will often use specialized vocabulary not familiar to the attorneys. In most cases, the product is still in development, and some of technical details are still being ironed out. Patentability of the invention will often lie in the resolution of these technical details, so taking rigorous notes as these problems are identified and resolved will greatly aid the attorney in acquiring patent protection. As a manager, it is important to ask product developers what problems they are working on and what solutions they are considering. What might seem obvious to a very skilled engineer as since-applied engineering principles might be unobvious to one having ordinary skill in the art and therefore deserving of patent protection.

On the initial call, it is important for the company representatives to describe the product to the attorneys at a level that an entry-level engineer would understand, preferably one straight out of college. One thing that often is not discussed but should be is whether the company or these inventors have filed any patents before. Any related prior art patents and patent applications should be sent to the attorneys so that they can review them during the call. Since prior patents and patent applications might be prior art, it is a good idea to disclose this information to the attorneys as soon as possible, because the prior application may make it more difficult to obtain protection.

During the call, there are two chief questions the company should have in mind: (1) How do I create barriers to entry for my competitors? and (2) How do I reduce the exposure of the company to patent infringement? The answer to Question (1) is to file and acquire as many patents as possible on the technology. The answer to Question (2) is to perform frequent freedom to operate searches and acquire defensive patents.

2. *Filing and Acquiring Patents*

There are chiefly two ways to obtain patent protection on an invention. Either the company develops the protection on its own by filing a patent application, or it purchases patents or licenses them. Most patent applications are written on beta level or first-generation devices or methods, because most companies realize they should file for a patent before the product is released on the market. While that is true, it is not the whole story. The most effective way to file a patent application is on a schedule as design details are worked out. Expanding on the example in VII.C.1., above, perhaps a special ultrasonic motor needs to be developed, because the original intended motor for the toothbrush is too weak. So a new motor is developed, and a patent application describing how to build this new motor should be prepared. Perhaps this new motor requires a different power supply, and changing the power supply affects the implementation of the docking system to recharge the ultrasonic flosser. Indeed, as each new problem is encountered and solved, a separate patent application should be considered. But whether a patent application should be filed turns on whether the invention as it currently stands is patentable over known prior art.

It is very common for inventors and owners of a company to believe an invention is patentable over all competing products—that is why they came to the attorney in the first place. It is very likely that our exemplary company, Company B, attends trade shows, knows the products of all the competitors, reads all the toothbrush periodicals, and so forth. As a company, the inventors are an expert on ultrasonic dental technology, they "know" their flosser is revolutionary, and they are sure no one has thought about it before—or have they?

Unfortunately, in nearly every case, the answer is yes, there is a patent application on a similar product either filed or in the process of being filed. The reason for this is that most products are evolutionary, not revolutionary. And while it may be true that the company that came up with this great brand-new idea on its own, it could also be the case that other individuals have also been thinking about this idea for the past three years and filing applications on the product since then. "Impossible," says the company. "If such a product existed, we would have seen it." True, but perhaps the reason the company has not seen it is that no one could develop a light enough motor and a power supply that was inexpensive enough to make such a product marketable. Or perhaps (as future research from the company will show) a Y-shaped flosser only works for the front teeth, and what is really needed is a bendable Y-shaped flosser for the molars. Or maybe if the Y-shaped flosser was H-shaped instead, the user could bite down on the floss, making it easier and faster to floss. So maybe the Y-shaped flosser isn't such a good idea compared to the H-shaped flosser after all.

As one continues along this development cycle, refinements and modifications are made to the original "raw" idea. The refinement and modifications are generally what is patentable. Normally, the raw idea is not patentable, because it tends to be obvious in view of the components already available. Indeed, if one having ordinary skill in the art looked at a manual for an ultrasonic toothbrush and a flosser, he or she might conclude that combining the two is obvious. And if a patent application were filed on such a combination without further disclosure, a patent examiner would likely conclude the invention was obvious.

So when does the company file on the invention—in the beginning, in the middle, or at the end of product development? The answer is potentially "all three." However, filing multiple applications can get expensive, so to offset that cost, patentability searches can be performed to see if there is prior art describing the modifications. If there is not, then the company would likely elect to file on the invention. If there is prior art, then the company might want to keep refining the invention so that it differs from the prior art. However, once development yields a patentable invention, the process does not stop at filing an application. As future updates and revisions are accomplished, the patent application should be updated through improvement patent (called "continuation in part") applications. (Many countries have improvement patents, but when to file them depends on the particular country's laws.) This refinement and filing process continues until a final product is made.

During this filing and refinement process, a freedom to operate analysis should also be performed. While the filing process concentrates on finding patentable subject matter, the freedom to operate process focuses on whether the future product will infringe any issued patents. See the discussion in VII.C.1., above. While it is true that modifications to the product may alter whether making the product will infringe a patent, waiting until the product is finished is not a good idea because modifying the product when it is finished can be very expensive. However, modifying the product while it is in development could be more cost efficient. To move back to our flosser example, maybe a company already has a patent on an H-shaped head for an ultrasonic flosser. What then?

There are really three options: obtain a license for the H-shaped head patent, determine whether a strong enough argument regarding invalidity can be made, or design around the claimed invention. Maybe instead of two sets of floss, the top part of the head can have floss, while the bottom part has a rubber bite plate so that the user can use his or her lower jaw to push the floss on the top part of the head into the top teeth, and vice versa.

Typically, freedom to operate searches are performed in a similar way to patentability searches. In a patentability search, one focuses on whether the invention contains features not in the disclosure of the prior art. In a freedom to operate search, one focuses on whether the product has all the features recited in one of the claims of a pending patent. The analyses are different, but the searches often have a lot of overlap. To be compliant with the duty of disclosure described previously, all patents identified in patentability and freedom to operate searches should be catalogued and eventually submitted to the patent office, so that the patentability of the invention over the prior art will be considered.

D. Nuances in the Medical Field

Sections VII.A. through C., above, discuss the parts of a patent application, some of the requirements for obtaining a patent, what rights are afforded to the owner of a patent, what to do to obtain a patent, and when to request a freedom to operate opinion. Many of these principles are the same regardless if one is selling proteins for treating illnesses, sunglasses, or toothbrushes, but there are several nuances in patent law that only apply to the medical field. These nuances include enablement requirements for claiming multiple configurations of drugs and materials, and how medical software and computer systems need to be claimed so that they encompass HIPAA-compliant systems.

1. *Enablement Requirements for Claiming Multiple Configurations of Drugs and Materials*

Enablement (one of the requirements of 35 U.S.C. §112) requires that the applicant explain the invention so that one having ordinary skill in the art can make and use the invention without undue experimentation. A problem arises when a very specific implementation is described (typically one that is new or pioneering in the field), but the claims cover a number of alternate configurations that are not described in the application. The general rule regarding claim scope is that one is allowed to write claims as broad as possible until the breadth of the claims bumps up against the prior art.[320] The first paragraph of 35 U.S.C. §112 adds a separate requirement: one can only obtain claims as broad as the disclosure enables. The enablement requirement considers the skill and creativity of the ordinary person.

To take a simple example, imagine a patent application for a coffee mug. The application discloses how to form and mold the ceramic mug, but it does not disclose anything about the handle. Later, during prosecution, it is determined that adding a handle is necessary to overcome prior art based on a flower pot. Can the attorney add a handle to the claim? No, because the "written description" requirement of Section 112, first paragraph, will prevent the attorney from claiming subject matter not disclosed. But what if the application disclosed a passing remark that coffee mugs can be made with handles? To add the claim now would require the drawings to illustrate a handle attached to the cup, so adding the subject matter regarding the handle would be difficult. Perhaps a block diagram of a cup and handle could be added to satisfy the written description requirement. But how is the handle attached? How is it connected? How can you build a coffee mug with a handle if the attachment mechanism is not known? If this were the first application on coffee mugs, then at the time of the invention it would have been at least debatable whether the disclosure for a coffee mug with a handle was enabled.

Still not convinced? Does enablement sound very similar to written description? In the previous example it was, but consider an extension of the example that makes enablement a lot clearer. Imagine the application discloses that the coffee mug can be made with a revolving handle made of gelatin. How in the world can you build a coffee mug with a revolving handle made of gelatin? How it would it work? In this example, although the written description requirement is clearly satisfied (i.e., it disclosed that the coffee cup could have a revolving handle made of gelatin), the enablement requirement is clearly not satisfied.

So how does the concept of enablement fit into the drug and pharmaceutical context? There are two chief examples. In one, the applicant discloses a very specific protein, provides thorough proof that it will treat a certain disease, then tries to claim a very broad version of the protein to lock up all the variants (this is called a "genus claim" in patent lingo). In the other example, the applicant tries to claim that a particular drug can cure all forms of a disease, or can cure multiple diseases, when evidence of its effectiveness and a treatment protocol for treating one disease is disclosed.

Courts tend to regard drugs and proteins as having a high degree of unpredictability. The amount of guidance or direction needed to enable the invention is inversely related to the amount of knowledge in the state of the art as well as the predictability in the art.[321] The "predictability or lack thereof" in the art

---

[320] 35 U.S.C. §§102, 103.
[321] *In re* Fisher, 427 F.2d 833, 839 (C.C.P.A. 1970).

refers to the ability of one skilled in the art to extrapolate the disclosed or known results to the claimed invention.[322] When one skilled in the art can readily determine the effect of a change to disclosure without undue experimentation, then there is predictability in the art, whereas if one skilled in the art cannot readily anticipate the effect of a change, then there is lack of predictability in the art.[323] In the chemical context,

> there may be times when the well-known unpredictability of chemical reactions will alone be enough to create a reasonable doubt as to the accuracy of a particular broad statement put forward as enabling support for a claim. This will especially be the case where the statement is, on its face, contrary to generally accepted scientific principles. Most often, additional factors, such as the teachings in pertinent references, will be available to substantiate any doubts that the asserted scope of objective enablement is in fact commensurate with the scope of protection sought and to support any demands based thereon for proof.[324]

Although, as noted above, "[t]he scope of the required enablement varies inversely with the degree of predictability involved, ... even in unpredictable arts, a disclosure of every operable species is not required."[325] In some cases, a single embodiment may provide sufficient disclosure to obtain broad genus claims, whereas in other cases it may not.[326] Generally, courts tend to find the electrical and mechanical fields to be more predictable than the chemical and physiological fields.[327] In a 2010 decision, *Ariad Pharmaceuticals, Inc. v. Eli Lilly and Co.*,[328] the U.S. Court of Appeals for the Federal Circuit held that the written description inquiry is fact specific, and the details of the analysis will vary from case to case "depending on the nature and scope of the claims and on the complexity and predictability of the relevant technology." Therefore, the court could not provide any bright-line rules such as how many species (specific examples) must be disclosed to support a genus claim. In the chemical arts, one or two is probably not enough.

The take-home lesson is to make sure that at least some of the claims cover the specific embodiment disclosed. One can attempt to obtain broader genus claims, and argue that the specific disclosure enables the broader genus claim, but a safer approach is to disclose as many specific embodiments as possible. How many are necessary to entitle the applicant to claim a genus will depend upon the predictability of technology as well as the skill of the hypothetical person. Generally, one or two specific embodiments is not sufficient to claim the genus.

---

[322] MPEP §2164.03.

[323] *Id.*

[324] *In re* Marzocchi, 439 F.2d 220, 223–24, (C.C.P.A. 1971).

[325] MPEP §2164.03.

[326] *Compare In re* Cook, 439 F.2d 730, 734, 169 USPQ 298, 301 (C.C.P.A. 1971), *with* Ariad Pharms., Inc. v. Eli Lilly and Co., 598 F.3d 1336 (Fed. Cir. 2010).

[327] *See In re* Fisher, 427 F.2d 833, 839, 166 USPQ 18, 24 (C.C.P.A. 1970); *In re* Wright, 999 F.2d 1557, 1562, 27 USPQ2d 1510, 1513 (Fed. Cir. 1993); *In re* Vaeck, 947 F.2d 488, 496, 20 USPQ2d 1438, 1445 (Fed. Cir. 1991).

[328] 598 F.3d 1336 (Fed. Cir. 2010).

2. HIPAA Regulations and Patent Claim Strategy

When drafting claims for a patent application or seeking to enforce a patent against a potential infringer, consideration of HIPAA's regulations is important. As explained in II.A., above, HIPAA requires covered entities such as insurance companies, doctors, and health care clearinghouses to protect individually identifiable health information. Although rarely considered by a patent prosecutor, HIPAA's laws may have a substantial effect on whether an entity will or would be likely to infringe some types of patents. HIPAA regulations impact how and when medical data can be transferred, so it is possible to draft claims to a medical system, for example, that would not likely be used, because if it were, the system would violate HIPAA.

Of course, HIPAA sets out in intricate detail what sorts of information can be considered individually identifiable health information, but generally such information relates to a patient's condition, treatment, or billing. The regulations define individually identifiable information as information that provides a reasonable basis for believing the information can identify the individual.[329]

The regulations also provide that this same information may be transferred so long as it de-identified.[330] Information is said to be de-identified when a statistician confirms the information is de-identified or when all of the identifiers relating to the individual and the individual's relatives, household members, and employers are removed. The covered entity also cannot have actual knowledge that the remaining information could be used to identify the individual. The regulations provide a safe harbor for de-identifying data, i.e., if all the certain types of information is removed, then the covered entity may transfer the data.

HIPAA permits the transfer of individually identifiable health information, for certain types of uses, including treatment, payment for medical services, public health reasons like flu outbreaks, and police reports concerning incidents such as gunshots. The HIPAA Privacy Rule addresses the use and disclosure of individuals' protected health information by "covered entities." Subject to the Privacy Rule, covered entities must make reasonable efforts to use, disclose, and request only the minimum amount of protected health information needed to accomplish the intended purpose of the use, disclosure, or request. This means the covered entities should only request the minimum amount of information they need for the purpose they need it. Thus, for example, if one prepared a claim that involved requesting the transfer of or access to more than the minimum amount of information needed, the claim would not likely be practiced. Similarly, if one asserted a patent requiring the transfer of individually identifiable health information that was not in an exempted category, the claim would not likely be infringed. HIPAA's regulations also apply to internal software that can distribute information within an organization. They require the implementation of software that restricts access and uses of protected health information based on the specific roles of the members of an organization's workforce. So if claimed software required medical information be available to all users, the patent in question would not likely be infringed. It is all too easy to write a

---

[329] 45 C.F.R. §160.103.
[330] *Id.* §164.514(b).

claim that sounds fine on paper, but would not be infringed, because a company would not commercialize the system because it violates HIPAA. A claim to a non-HIPAA compliant embodiment probably does not provide much value to the patentee, because it is unlikely that it will be infringed.

Overall, HIPAA provides some very specific scalable guidelines on how to ensure the confidentiality, integrity, and availability of all electronic personal health information a covered entity creates, receives, maintains, or transmits, and these guidelines should be considered when drafting or enforcing patent claims. Confidentiality means that electronic personal health information is not available or disclosed to unauthorized persons. Integrity means that electronic personal health information is not altered or destroyed in an unauthorized manner. Availability means that electronic personal health information is accessible and usable on demand by an authorized person.

Looking at the HIPAA regulations at a more granular level, they contain a number of very specific administrative[331] and technical[332] software requirements. Since HIPAA provides a scalable architecture depending on covered entity resources and size, however, some "requirements" are actually "required" while others are merely "addressable." "Required" requirements must be implemented, while "addressable" requirements call for the entity to (1) assess whether the specification is a reasonable and appropriate safeguard in its environment and is likely to contribute to protecting the entity's electronic protected health information, and (2) implement the specification or document why it would not be reasonable and appropriate and implement an equivalent alternative measure if reasonable and appropriate.

These requirements (where required or addressable) are important to keep in mind. If one, for example, were to claim a system that did not use any encryption, or could not be backed up, or did not have user name access or even unique user names, it would be unlikely that computer software designed for transferring or manipulating patient records would infringe the claims of the patent, because such a system probably would not comply with HIPAA (and thus probably would not be built by a competitor). The rules at 45 C.F.R. §§164.308 and 164.312, cited above, provide the full text of the following requirements, highlights of which are provided here:

- For software systems designed to be deployed using a clearinghouse, it is important to disclose and claim that the clearinghouse has a computer system that is separate from the controlling organization and can restrict access to the larger organization (required feature).
- Software programs should be explained and claimed so that they contemplate user level access from a work station (addressable feature).
- Software programs should be explained and claimed so that they contemplate monitoring and logging user access (addressable).
- Security updates in programs should be updatable (addressable).
- Software should contemplate it will be used with antivirus software (addressable).

---

[331] *Id.* §164.308.
[332] *Id.* §164.312.

- Software implementation should contemplate remote monitoring of log-in attempts (addressable).
- Password access and forced updating of passwords should be contemplated in the patent application (addressable).
- Software should contemplate intrusion detection, prevention, and lockdown procedures to minimize data loss (required).
- Databases should be backed up on remote systems, and plans for accessing information afterwards in the event of natural disasters should be documented in the application (required).
- Establish and implement procedures to create and maintain retrievable exact copies of electronic protected health information (required).
- Unique usernames for access are required.
- Emergency access procedures to information are required.
- Automatic log-off procedures based on time should be described (addressable).
- Hardware and software audit controls should be described (addressable).
- Software should describe routines for verifying information integrity so as to detect and prevent improper alteration or destruction (addressable feature).
- Software should be able to verify that a user attempting to access records is the same person presenting who is presenting the credentials. This is often called user authentication, and an RSA token[333] is a commercial example (addressable feature).
- Software should have security measures to ensure that information is not improperly changed when it is being transmitted (addressable feature).
- Software should have security measures to provide encryption of transmissions (addressable feature).

VIII. TRADE SECRETS—PROTECTING ESSENTIAL INFORMATION

Trade secrets can be a valuable and effective way to protect an organization's informational and process assets that may not be protectable under other forms of intellectual property. An organization with a valuable invention, process, or formula may be able to protect that asset through trade secret law instead of via a patent where a patent is not available, not economical, or otherwise not preferable. Certain assets that fall outside of copyright law may also be protected with trade secret law, including data sets and patient information.

This section provides a quick overview of the important aspects of trade secret law to help in the determination of when protecting an asset as a trade secret is a good option.

A trade secret is business information that is both valuable because it is secret and subject to efforts to maintain secrecy. Trade secret law has its origins in the common law of torts and in unfair competition law. Unlike patent law, trade secret law does not grant the owner an exclusive right to use or exploit the trade

---

[333] *See* http://www.rsa.com/.

secret. Instead, trade secret law prohibits the use of improper means to acquire a valuable business secret.

A. Sources of Trade Secret Law

Trade secret law exists primarily as state statutory and common law, though there is some federal law addressing issues related to trade secrets. The most widely adopted source for trade secret law is the Uniform Trade Secrets Act (UTSA). Forty-six states, the District of Columbia, the U.S. Virgin Islands, and Puerto Rico have adopted the UTSA. The states that have not adopted the Act (Massachusetts, New Jersey, New York, and Texas) apply similar principles to define the scope of protection for trade secrets or rely on common law for trade secret protection.[334]

In addition to the federal and state statutes that protect trade secrets, common law principles—such as principles of equity governing special relationships—and contract principles also may be used to define rights in trade secrets. Although common law rights usually will exist independently of statutory protections, those rights also may be preempted or superseded by federal or state patent, trademark, or copyright law. State common law treatment of trade secrets is outlined in the *Restatement of Unfair Competition*.[335]

The Economic Espionage Act of 1996 is a federal statute that incorporates a definition of trade secrets that is similar to the UTSA's definition (discussed in VII.B., below), and establishes some federal trade secret protection.[336]

B. Uniform Trade Secrets Act

Under the UTSA, a trade secret is defined as

> information, including a formula, pattern, compilation, program, device, method, technique, or process, that: (i) derives independent economic value, actual or potential, from not being generally known to, and not being readily ascertainable by proper means by, other persons who can obtain economic value from its disclosure or use, and (ii) is the subject of efforts that are reasonable under the circumstances to maintain its secrecy.[337]

Each of these requirements applies independently, but both depend on maintaining the overall secrecy of the information.

Information may have the requisite independent economic value if the development of the information required considerable time, effort, or expense (in certain cases, even if the information was compiled or derived from public

---

[334]Information on states' adoption of the Uniform Trade Secrets Act can be found at http://nccusl.org/Act.aspx?title=Trade%20Secrets%20Act. UTSA legislation is pending in Massachusetts and New Jersey. *See, e.g.*, H.2846, 2010–2011 Leg. Session (Mass.); A.921, 2010–2011 Leg. Session (N.J.); S.2456, 2010–2011 Leg. Session (N.J.).

[335]RESTATEMENT (THIRD) OF UNFAIR COMPETITION (1995).

[336]18 U.S.C. §§1831–1839. Both the Economic Espionage Act and the UTSA provide protection for material (1) that derives independent value from its not being known to the public, and (2) is the subject of reasonable efforts to maintain its secrecy. Unlike the UTSA, however, the Economic Espionage Act contains a detailed list of material that could be protected.

[337]UTSA §1.

sources) or if the information conveys a competitive advantage to the owner. In order to meet the second requirement of the UTSA definition of a trade secret, the owner of the information must exert reasonable efforts to maintain the secrecy of the information. This requires that the owner take continuous and affirmative steps to prevent others from accessing or using the information.

C. Establishing Ownership of a Trade Secret

1. The Nature of the Information

In order to qualify for protection as a trade secret, under either the UTSA or common law, information must be valuable to the company and must derive its value at least in part from the fact that the information is secret. Similar criteria exist under common law, where a trade secret is "any information that can be used in the operation of a business or other enterprise and that is sufficiently valuable and secret to afford an actual or potential advantage over others."[338] Trade secret law does not have the stringent novelty requirement of patent law. However, a certain degree of novelty is implied in the requirement that the trade secret be secret and not generally known.[339] Additionally, it is not required that a trade secret be exclusive to one owner for it to be valuable by virtue of its secrecy. It is sufficient that the trade secret be not generally known and thereby afford an advantage to the competitors who possess it over those who do not.[340]

2. Preserving Secrecy

Once valuable proprietary information has been created, it is necessary for the possessor of that information to take reasonable steps to ensure the secrecy of the information in order for it to be treated as a trade secret under common law or the UTSA. Trade secret owners need only take reasonable steps to ensure secrecy, not all conceivable steps, but they must make some active efforts to ensure secrecy.[341] Measures taken to preserve the secrecy of trade secrets fall into two general categories: physical measures and contractual measures. Physical measures include limiting physical access to trade secrets by unauthorized persons (e.g., locking filing cabinets, requiring key-card access to offices or research areas). Contractual measures to protect the secrecy of trade secrets allow for the use of the trade secret by employees and for the licensing of trade secrets to third parties. Contractual measures may be implemented in nondisclosure agreements, employment agreements, noncompetition agreements, employee manuals, and licensing agreements. Disclosure of the secret to those who have an obligation to maintain secrecy does not destroy the trade secret.[342] It is important, however, that companies with trade secrets make it clear to employees

---

[338] RESTATEMENT (THIRD) OF UNFAIR COMPETITION §39.

[339] "Novelty is only required of a trade secret to the extent necessary to show that the alleged trade secret is not a matter of public knowledge." SI Handling Sys., Inc. v. Heisley, 753 F.2d 1244, 1255 (3d Cir. 1985).

[340] See Kewanee Oil Co. v. Bicron Corp., 416 U.S. 470 (1974).

[341] See Motorola, Inc. v. Fairchild Camera & Instrument Corp., 366 F. Supp. 1173 (D. Ariz. 1973); see also Surgidev Corp. v. ETI Inc., 828 F.2d 452 (8th Cir. 1987).

[342] Metallurgical Indus., Inc. v. Fourtek, Inc., 790 F.2d 1195 (5th Cir. 1986).

what information is being protected as a trade secret, and that the employees have an obligation to keep that information secret.

3. Proper and Improper Means of Acquisition of a Trade Secret

Trade secret law does not impart to the possessor of a trade secret a right of exclusive use of the secret. If ownership of a trade secret is established, then the UTSA prohibits the improper acquisition, disclosure, or use of that trade secret by another. Such improper activity is generally referred to as "misappropriation" and is discussed in greater detail in IX.C., below.

There are, however, proper means to obtain a trade secret. These include:

- independent discovery or invention via parallel or coincidental research;
- discovery via reverse engineering;
- discovery by observation of a product that is publicly available, in use, or on display;
- discovery through analysis of publicly available information, data, or manuals.

IX. Preliminary Transactional Agreements and Proprietary Rights

This section focuses on identifying some of the key issues associated with transactions involving proprietary rights in technology and information. In an uncertain economy that must continually adjust to accelerating innovation and radical changes in technology, many businesses routinely use preliminary agreements to explore the feasibility and negotiate the material terms of potential business transactions. Agreements that are typically used in a preliminary capacity include the letter of intent (LOI) or memorandum of understanding (MOU), the request for proposal (RFP), and the nondisclosure agreement (NDA). Using these types of agreements effectively requires the parties to balance two inherently conflicting objectives: creating binding obligations in certain areas while leaving the parties free to disengage from any permanent relationship.

In the context of the health care industry, NDAs (sometimes referred to as confidentiality agreements or secrecy agreements) have been used to protect proprietary rights related to product development and protected health information. This section presents a brief overview of some of the most significant modern applications of preliminary agreements, especially NDAs, in the health care industry and provides several suggested drafting provisions to aid in the creation of effective agreements.

A. Modern Applications in the Health Care Industry

Health care companies that generate individually identifiable health information, to which a variety of proprietary obligations and rights attach, often engage other companies to provide support services and technology. These relationships involve three different kinds of confidential information: (1) information related to the proprietary rights of one party, such as patent, copyright, trademark, and trade secrets, (2) administrative data generated in conjunction with the use of licensed technology, and (3) patients' individually identifiable protected health information (PHI). Each of these categories of information requires different kinds of secrecy measures. Accordingly, preliminary agreements related to transactions involving health care companies often contain multiple separate confidentiality provisions addressing PHI and other proprietary rights such as those related to product development.

1. Protected Health Information and Electronic Health Records

In addition to terms requiring each party to maintain the confidentiality of the other's proprietary information, preliminary agreements involving health care companies generally contain separate provisions addressing the protection of patients' individually identifiable PHI, the possession of which incurs a variety of confidentiality obligations under federal law. Such provisions have become increasingly important as the health care industry has adopted systems for maintaining electronic health records (EHR). Although estimates vary, recent data from the National Ambulatory Medical Care Survey (NAMCS), conducted by the CDC National Center for Health Statistics, indicates that 34.8 percent of office-based physicians reported using EHR in 2007, representing a 91.2 percent increase since 2001. Projecting from the same baseline data, the study estimates that from 53.6 percent to 64.5 percent of office-based physicians were using EHR technology by 2010.[343] The number of doctors using EHR is expected to continue increasing over the next decade as the infusion of formerly uninsured patients into the health care market, the presence of HITECH incentive funds, and innovations and declining prices in the EHR market compel providers to invest more substantially in electronic records technologies. In a world of increasingly digitized health information, nondisclosure agreements will continue to be particularly helpful to patient data protection efforts in the arenas of health care services contracting, health research, health information exchange, and accountable care organizations (ACOs).

a. Health Services Contracting

As providers responsible for protecting confidential patient data under HIPAA have outsourced more aspects of daily health care practice—particularly those related to EHR, including billing, transcription, and record keeping—the importance of implementing NDAs with health service contractors has grown, and a variety of recent cases have underscored the con-

---

[343] *See* Hing E. & Hsiao, C.J., *Electronic Medical Record Use by Office-Based Physicians and Their Practices: United States, 2007*, *in* U.S. DEPARTMENT OF HEALTH AND HUMAN SERVICES, CENTERS FOR DISEASE CONTROL AND PREVENTION, NATIONAL CENTER FOR HEALTH STATISTICS, NATIONAL HEALTH STATISTICS REPORTS, No. 23 (Mar. 31, 2010).

sequences of failing to do so.[344] Broadly, HIPAA requires covered entities to maintain privacy agreements with all "business associates,"[345] including all indirectly employed providers of legal, actuarial, accounting, consulting, data aggregation, management, administrative, accreditation, or financial services for the covered entities.[346] These business associate agreements may not authorize business associates to use or disclose protected information except as necessary in the course of their business duties to the covered entities.[347] Alternatively, if a covered entity chooses to provide limited data sets rather than PHI, it can use a limited data set agreement instead of a business associate agreement to establish nondisclosure expectations.[348]

The U.S. Department of Health and Human Services provides a sample business associate agreement, which provides the following suggested specific use and disclosure provisions regarding PHI:[349]

a. Except as otherwise limited in this Agreement, Business Associate may use Protected Health Information for the proper management and administration of the Business Associate or to carry out the legal responsibilities of the Business Associate.

b. Except as otherwise limited in this Agreement, Business Associate may disclose Protected Health Information for the proper management and administration of the Business Associate, provided that disclosures are Required By Law, or Business Associate obtains reasonable assurances from the person to whom the information is disclosed that it will remain confidential and used or further disclosed only as Required By Law or for the purpose for which it was disclosed to the person, and the person notifies the Business Associate of any instances of which it is aware in which the confidentiality of the information has been breached.

c. Except as otherwise limited in this Agreement, Business Associate may use Protected Health Information to provide Data Aggregation services to Covered Entity as permitted by 45 CFR §164.504(e)(2)(i)(B).

d. Business Associate may use Protected Health Information to report violations of law to appropriate Federal and State authorities, consistent with § 164.502(j)(1).

Among those groups that do not need to execute business associate agreements with covered entities are affiliates that have designated themselves as

---

[344] *See, e.g.*, U.S. Dep't of Health & Human Servs., Resolution Agreement with Management Services Organization Washington, Inc. (Dec. 13, 2010), *available at* http://www.hhs.gov/ocr/privacy/hipaa/enforcement/examples/msoresagr.html (obligating health care company to pay $35,000 to the U.S. Department of Health and Human Services and to formulate a detailed Corrective Action Plan where it was shown that the company intentionally failed to employ appropriate privacy safeguards and disclosed electronic patient data to a corporate affiliate that used the data for marketing purposes).

[345] *See* 45 C.F.R. §164.504(e) (2010).

[346] *See id.* §160.013.

[347] *See id.* §160.504(e)(2)–(4).

[348] *See* 67 Fed. Reg. 53,247, 53,252 (Aug. 14, 2001); *see also* 45 C.F.R. §164.524(e).

[349] U.S. Dep't of Health and Human Servs., Sample Business Associate Contract Provisions (June 12, 2006), *available at* http://www.hhs.gov/ocr/privacy/hipaa/understanding/coveredentities/ contractprov.html.

part of a single, combined covered entity[350] and medical device manufacturers to the extent they are "health care providers."[351] Special guidelines regarding software vendors, warranties in technology transactions, regulatory compliance covenants, and foreign contractors are discussed below.

i. Software Vendors

Software vendors do not require business associate agreements if they are engaged only in the "mere provision" of software to covered entities without the data management or processing services typically provided by other business associates.[352] Arguably, this CMS interpretation of the HIPAA Privacy Rule, discussed in II.A. and C., above, could apply to all software vendors, even if the software is "hosted" by the licensor on a remote computer (server) and is accessible to the licensee only remotely via the Internet. This kind of software license is referred to as an application service provider (ASP) relationship.

However, many health care attorneys representing covered entities under HIPAA have taken the position that a software vendor's ability to access protected health information during the course of performing software maintenance or repair, and nothing more, makes the software vendor a business associate for purposes of the Privacy Rule. This interpretation in most cases misreads the Privacy Rule and causes vendors of software with health care applications to incur enormous costs in negotiating the hundreds, if not the thousands, of separate business associate agreements that will be received from its software licensees.

The analysis of whether a software provider qualifies as a business associate can become particularly complex under many online business arrangements involving some input of, or access to, PHI that resides on a system maintained by the vendor. Accordingly, before determining whether or not a business associate relationship exists, the parties should carefully analyze the flow of protected information and the vendor's ability to access it. If a business associate relationship is determined to exist, the covered entity and the software vendor or ASP should enter into a business associate agreement that complies with HIPAA privacy standards.[353]

In order to avoid becoming contractually obligated to maintain the confidentiality of PHI, for example, a technology transferor (such as a vendor of software used to support electronic medical records storage or medication barcoding dispensers) may want to include a provision similar to the following in a contract with a technology transferee (health care provider):

> Each party shall be separately and independently obligated to maintain the confidentiality of any patient identifiable medical information that is within the possession of such party, consistent with the requirements of such federal and state laws and regulations that are applicable to such party and that obligate it independently of this Agreement to maintain the confidentiality of such information. Nothing in this Agreement is intended or shall be construed to limit or otherwise reduce, or to cause Licensor to assume, comply with, guarantee or indemnify, any of Licensee's

---

[350] 65 Fed. Reg. 82,643 (Dec. 28, 2000).
[351] *Id.*
[352] 45 C.F.R. §160.103; *see also* 65 Fed. Reg. 82,643.
[353] *See* 45 C.F.R. §164.504(e)(2) (listing requirements for business associate agreements).

obligations as a provider of medical care or services, including, but not limited to, any obligation of Licensee regarding licensing, accreditation, certification, standards of medical practice, or confidentiality of medical information.

ii. Warranties in Technology Transfers

Over the years, it has become customary for technology transfers not to include much in the way of warranties. The only warranty that transferors generally will offer to transferees is the warranty of noninfringement (sometimes referred to as the warranty of title). In such warranties, most technology transferors will warrant to the transferee that the technology or information that is transferred under the agreement will not infringe on the proprietary rights of any other person or entity. Accordingly, the licensor typically agrees to indemnify and defend the transferee for breach of such warranty. Beyond a warranty of noninfringement, and depending upon the nature of the technology and the relative bargaining power of the parties, the transferee may be able to obtain additional warranties, such as a warranty of performance according to agreed specifications like processing speed and capacity.

In addition, many health care industry transferees seek warranties from the transferor that the technology complies with federal, state, and local laws and regulations relating to its use, including warranties of compliance with HIPAA and particularly the security and privacy regulations promulgated thereunder by CMS. Some transferors have been willing to offer such broad HIPAA compliance warranties, even though they allocate substantial risk to the transferor for liabilities associated with instances of noncompliance over which the transferor has no control.

In fact, it would seem illogical, if not altogether impossible, for a transferor to warrant that its technology "complies" with the CMS Privacy Rule. The Privacy Rule applies more to procedures than it does to systems, although the rule does require a covered entity to implement reasonable safeguards to ensure the security of protected information.[354] Stated in other terms, the transferor may warrant that the licensed technology has the capacity to be adapted so as to permit overall system compliance with the requirements of the CMS security rule. However, transferors should be careful about assuming regulatory compliance obligations through systems or technical warranties.

iii. Regulatory Compliance Covenants

Due to the ever-increasing burden of and risks associated with compliance with federal and state regulatory mandates for the health care industry, many contractors, particularly technology transferors, include in their agreements specific covenants, representations, and warranties regarding regulatory compliance on the part of the transferees, especially if the transferees are licensed health care providers. An example of such a provision is as follows:

> Licensee agrees to assume sole and complete responsibility for ensuring that the Software and its use by Licensee and any End User, and Licensee's performance of its obligations under this Agreement, and all Licensee policies and procedures

---

[354] *See* 45 C.F.R. §164.530(c).

relating to the foregoing, are at all times during the term of this Agreement, in compliance with: (i) all applicable federal laws and regulations relating to the participation by Licensee in the Medicare program or state Medicaid program, and state laws and regulations applicable to participation by Licensee in any state Medicaid program; (ii) all applicable state laws and regulations requiring Licensee to obtain any license, authorization or other permit to use the Software or perform its obligations under this Agreement, or to provide or arrange for the provision of health care and related services as contemplated herein; (iii) all applicable standards and requirements, if any, for accreditation by JCAHO (the Joint Commission on Accreditation of Healthcare Organizations); (iv) all governing instruments of Licensee, as such may be amended from time to time; and (v) all other federal, state, and local laws and regulations applicable to the provision of health care services or payment for such services, including in particular, but without limitation, laws relating to licensure and regulation of physicians, other medical professionals, clinical laboratories, hospitals, and health care facilities, confidentiality of patient-related information, and laws governing billing and collecting payments from payors and arrangements between providers and sources of referrals of patients, medical services, or supplies (collectively "Applicable Laws"). Without limiting the foregoing, Licensee acknowledges and agrees that Applicable Laws means and includes the electronic data transmission, security, and privacy provisions of the federal Health Insurance Portability and Accountability Act of 1996 (HIPAA), and such regulations as may be lawfully promulgated thereunder by the Department of Health and Human Services (HHS), as such laws and regulations may be amended or replaced from time to time. Licensee further agrees independently to take any and all actions that may be necessary or appropriate in order to evaluate and assess Licensee's compliance with Applicable Laws, including but not limited to, seeking expert advice or an opinion of legal counsel. Licensor has no obligation under this Agreement or otherwise, and nothing in this Agreement is intended or shall be construed, to advise or counsel Licensee or render legal any opinion, representation, or warranty regarding compliance of the Software or any use thereof by Licensee with any Applicable Laws.

iv. Foreign Contractors

Additional precautions may always be included in NDAs with contractors performing services involving PHI, and special nondisclosure provisions are particularly important in contracts with vendors or consultants located outside the U.S. and beyond the reach of its laws. An effective NDA with a foreign contractor should specify what law will govern disputes over compliance and address technology safeguards, subcontracting arrangements with other vendors, employee training regarding PHI and HIPAA, the employees who will have access to PHI, the length of time PHI is to be retained in the course of the contractual relationship, and indemnity for the covered entity in case of disclosures by the contractor or its employees.

b. Health Research

Patient data has taken on even greater importance in health research since HIPAA's passage, particularly due to the availability of health records in electronic form and the growing role of retrospective medical studies that make use of existing data. For example, major research databases now exist to aid in the study of cancer, circulation support, failing organ systems, and organ transplants.[355] However, federal regulations still substantially limit the circumstances under which researchers can obtain patient data. Providers of PHI and entities engaged in medical research must therefore take steps to comply with HIPAA's confidentiality requirements in any transactions involving the provision or use of patient data.

As amended in 2002 and 2009, HIPAA prohibits covered entities from using PHI without patient authorization for most purposes, including research, other than treatment or payment.[356] HHS regulations allow PHI to be used for research only if one of three conditions is met: (1) the PHI is completely de-identified, (2) researchers obtain explicit written consent from the data subject, or (3) an Institutional Review Board or Privacy Board provides consent.[357] If a consent agreement with a data subject is pursued, the authorization must be "study-specific" and cannot simply agree to "unspecified future research."[358] Alternatively, if researchers seek Privacy Board or Institutional Review Board approval, the HIPAA Privacy Rule permits the waiver of individual authorization only if three additional conditions are met: (1) the use or disclosure of PHI involves only "minimal risk" to individuals' privacy, (2) the research "could not practicably be conducted" without the waiver, and (3) the research "could not practicably be conducted without access to and use of" the PHI.[359] Providers and users of PHI for health research must therefore be extremely cautious in any data transactions under the current Privacy Rule and should execute careful written agreements regarding data protection in conformance with the study-specific and minimal-risk standards when identifiable patient information is involved.

c. Health Information Exchange and State Practices

In addition to the HIPAA Privacy Rule, many health care organizations are encouraged to comply with regional practices embraced by various state initiatives and health information technology networks with regard to electronic health information exchange and patient consent. Four general approaches have evolved, largely by state: (1) a "must-all" approach requiring patient consent to any exchange of PHI, (2) an "opt-in" approach forbidding exchange of PHI unless a patient authorizes it, (3) an "opt-out" approach permitting exchange of PHI unless a patient chooses not to authorize it, and (4) a "no-opt" approach permitting exchange of PHI and declining to give patients the ability to opt out.[360] Additional approaches have included the development of standardized consent forms, comprehensive consent management bodies, and electronic au-

---

[355] *See* INSTITUTE OF HEALTH MEDICINE, BEYOND THE HIPAA PRIVACY RULE: ENHANCING PRIVACY, IMPROVING HEALTH THROUGH RESEARCH 116–18 (2009), *available at* http://books.nap.edu/openbook.php?record_id=12458.

[356] 45 C.F.R. §164.508(a).

[357] *See id.* §§164.508(a)(1), .512(i), .514(a).

[358] 67 Fed. Reg. 53,181, 53,226 (Aug. 14, 2002).

[359] *See* 45 C.F.R. §164.512(i)(iii)(2)(ii).

[360] *See* John R. Christiansen, *Legal Speed Bumps on the Road to Health Information Exchange*, 1 J. HEALTH & LIFE SCI. L. 1, 42 (2008).

thorization mechanisms.³⁶¹ Health care organizations seeking to revise contractual NDA provisions regarding patient information exchange are encouraged to consult the best practices recommendations of local organizations and health information technology vendors involved in health information exchange.

d. ACOs and Data Sharing

CMS's recent Proposed Rule for Accountable Care Organizations (ACOs)³⁶² under the Affordable Care Act envisions an expansive role in health care reform for ACOs, in which groups of health care providers and suppliers would qualify to receive shared savings in Medicare payments by meeting various criteria. Under the proposed rule, ACOs are also subject to slightly different requirements regarding confidentiality and the storage of patient data.

To receive shared savings under the proposed rule, at least 50 percent of an ACO's physicians must be "meaningful" EHR users by the start of the second performance year.³⁶³ Development of electronic patient data systems is therefore crucial to success for ACOs. In regard to the use of patient information, the proposed rule also envisions an expanded ability for CMS to share aggregate data and Medicare Parts A, B, and D claims information with ACOs, including basic patient identifiers such as name, date of birth, gender, and health insurance claim number, as long as participating ACOs take appropriate steps in requesting such information and enter Data Use Agreements with CMS.³⁶⁴ However, the proposed rule also suggests an opt-out system that would require ACOs to notify patients of their data-sharing practices and offer them the choice not to have their PHI shared.³⁶⁵ In light of these extensive proposals for new data sharing rules for ACOs, health care organizations wishing to participate in ACOs and transactions involving PHI should continue to monitor development of the proposed regulation before drastically changing patient data handling practices.

2. Proprietary Rights in Product Development

a. Collaboration Agreements

Pharmaceutical and biotechnology companies have externalized significant portions of drug discovery and development in recent years by strategically entering collaborations with smaller companies focused on discovery and early stage clinical development.³⁶⁶ Because the goal of such a collaboration is the development of intellectual property to which all involved parties may have some claim, a collaboration agreement that protects the parties' confidential information and proprietary rights is crucial from the beginning of the endeavor.

---

³⁶¹ *Id.*
³⁶² 76 Fed. Reg. 19,528 (Apr. 7, 2011) (to be codified at 41 C.F.R. pt. 425).
³⁶³ *Id.* at 19,648.
³⁶⁴ *Id.* at 19,554–59.
³⁶⁵ *Id.* at 19,559–60.
³⁶⁶ *See* Patrick McGee, *Pharma, Biotech Allies Replenish Pipeline*, PHARMAASIA, Dec. 1, 2006, *available at* http://www.pharmaasia.com/article-5917-pharmabiotechalliesreplenish pipeline-Asia.html.

Any preexisting intellectual property engaged by the parties in the course of the collaboration should be addressed through nondisclosure and licensure provisions allowing the other party temporary license to use the intellectual property only during the collaboration and consistent with its aims. Preexisting trade secrets disclosed in the context of the collaboration should also be addressed in nondisclosure provisions.

Each party is also likely to have intellectual property rights in the product created through the collaboration, which may be contractually approached through licensure, joint ownership, or practical alternatives to joint ownership such as allocation of ownership by field. While both parties are likely to share in some degree of ownership of the intellectual property jointly created, nondisclosure provisions may still be important in governing the types of publications and disclosures the parties consider appropriate following product development, especially where patents are involved. Parties may consider drafting NDAs that allow for each party's review or preapproval of the other's publications before they are disclosed. Additional helpful confidentiality provisions may address expectations for the protection of proprietary information after the collaboration ends and indemnification for the parties in case of patient data exposure.

b. Trade Secrets

Certain intellectual property involved in the health care industry and health research, including production processes, chemical formulas, software algorithms, and source code, can be protected from disclosure under state trade secrets laws as well as under contractual restrictions.[367] All states recognize trade secrets protection in some form, and almost all have adopted at least part of the Uniform Trade Secrets Act.[368] Broadly, the UTSA requires that (1) the trade secret is not generally known outside of the owner's organization, (2) the trade secret provides economic value or business advantage to the owner through its exclusive use, and (3) the owner undertakes reasonable steps to preserve the secrecy of the trade secret.[369] However, state laws regarding trade secrets vary substantially in terms of their particular requirements and protections. In particular, state trade secrets laws disagree as to the types of information to which protected status may attach, types of relief granted, the incorporation of statutory, UTSA, or common law rules, trade secrets definitions, fundamental policy considerations, evidentiary requirements, and justifications for denying trade secret protections.[370]

Given this variance in state trade secrets protections, health care entities, particularly those involved in product development, are well advised to include contractual terms expressly prohibiting the disclosure of proprietary information or at least limiting the number of people with whom and the conditions

---

[367] *See* PLC LAW DEPARTMENT 7-501-7068, Confidentiality and Nondisclosure Agreements (subscription), *available at* http://usld.practicallaw.com/7-501-7068?q=nondisclosure%20agreement.

[368] *See id.*

[369] *See id.*

[370] *See generally* BRIAN M. MALSBERGER, TRADE SECRETS: A STATE-BY-STATE SURVEY (3d ed. 2006).

under which it may be shared in the contexts of employment agreements, collaboration agreements, service contracts, or other transactions. These contractual provisions may be especially important given the unique challenges, such as reliance on health information technology vendors, collaborative health research, and mixed paper and electronic records,[371] faced by health care companies in undertaking "reasonable steps" to preserve the secrecy of their trade secrets as required for protection under the UTSA.

B. Suggested Drafting Provisions for the Creation of Effective Nondisclosure Agreements

1. Access to Confidential Information

Almost every company has its own form of NDA. Consequently, notwithstanding conventional wisdom, no standard form of NDA exists. In fact, many NDAs are drafted strategically to give the recipient of confidential information an advantage in the event of litigation. For example, many NDAs define confidential information to include only those written materials that are clearly marked as confidential prior to their disclosure to the recipient. Moreover, most NDAs require the disclosing party to grant broad rights of access to all of its books of account and business records, without excluding particular classes of information, such as trade secrets, software source codes, price lists and cost data (so as to avoid potential antitrust issues), attorney-client privileged communications, and similar types of information that should not necessarily be disclosed in conjunction with preliminary agreements.

In order to ensure that an NDA serves the best interests of both parties in a situation involving proprietary rights, the NDA should be narrowly drafted to apply to specific *included* categories of information by listing the included categories on an attached schedule, with all other information automatically excluded. It should also grant only limited access rights that are tailored to the needs of the proposed relationship. Alternatively, but less desirably, the NDA may exclude access to certain categories of information, such as attorney-client privileged communications, price lists and cost data, software source codes, and secret business plans and ideas, with the presumption of access to all other information.

Access rights granted in conjunction with a joint venture for the development of a software application should be different from those granted in conjunction with a possible acquisition. Even in the latter case, if the potential acquiring company is a competitor of the selling company, even greater consideration should be given to drafting an NDA that affords only limited access to specific categories of nonproprietary information.

---

[371] *Cf.* Nationwide Mutual Ins. Co. v. Mortensen, 606 F.3d 22 (2d Cir. 2010) (holding that an insurance company's client data and internal information regarding client needs and purchasing histories were not protected as trade secrets against former employee appropriation where the data at issue was available in inadequately protected paper files in agent offices as well as in the company's secure computer system).

2. Restricted Use of Confidential Information

The NDA or other preliminary agreement should expressly state the limited purpose for which the recipient may use confidential information. In most circumstances, the agreement should restrict the permitted use of confidential information to a single purpose: the evaluation by the recipient of whether or not to proceed with the proposed transaction. All other uses should be expressly prohibited. Moreover, if the information disclosed under the agreement includes copies of software programs in object code or other inventions or prototypes, then the agreement also should include specific prohibitions on copying, preparation of derivative works, display, reverse engineering, and similar uses.

3. Nondisclosure of Confidential Information

In addition to restrictions and prohibitions on the use of confidential information, the NDA or other preliminary agreement also should expressly identify the classes of individual persons to whom such information may be disclosed and by whom the information may be used for the permitted purpose under the agreement. Disclosure to any other persons or entities other than those listed should be expressly prohibited.

4. Nonsolicitation of Customers and Employees

In some cases, particularly in preliminary agreements between competitors, it may be appropriate to include provisions that prohibit the solicitation of customers or employees. Depending on the circumstances, customer lists and even the identities of key employees may constitute protectable trade secrets. Of course, the best protection is to avoid any obligation to disclose this type of information in conjunction with a preliminary agreement.

5. Reservation of Proprietary Rights

All preliminary agreements should routinely include confirmation that the parties to the agreement do not intend the agreement to constitute a sale, assignment, lease, license, or other transfer of any proprietary rights or other interests in any of the disclosed information. This confirmation should be combined with an express reservation by the disclosing party of any and all rights that it may have in and to the information disclosed, including but not limited to any and all patent, copyright, trademark, trade name, trade secret, and other intangible rights therein.

X. MANAGING EXPOSURE TO INTELLECTUAL PROPERTY LITIGATION

The cost of intellectual property litigation can be high. For example, the cost of litigating a typical patent infringement lawsuit is reportedly between

$2 million to $10 million,[372] excluding any potential award of damages against the defendant. Nonetheless, there are mechanisms available to companies in the health industry that are commonly used to manage exposure to intellectual property litigation. In particular, companies in the health industry should consider how due diligence, strategic intellectual property acquisitions, and the implementation of appropriate corporate policies can help reduce the likelihood of intellectual property litigation. In addition, since the risk of intellectual property litigation can never be entirely eliminated, companies in the health industry should also consider whether insurance coverage, industry and government outreach, and litigation alternatives such as mediation and alternative dispute resolution can be beneficial to them.

A. Due Diligence

One of the most common mechanisms companies use to reduce their exposure to intellectual property litigation is due diligence. By engaging in due diligence, a company can ensure that it has made efforts to identify the particular rights holders and the respective scope of each holder's rights in an area. After a company has knowledge of a rights holder and the scope of that entity's rights, it can then make an informed decision about how to proceed.

1. Identifying Potential Rights Holders

Public records frequently provide information about potential rights holders. As these records can often be searched for free, they can provide a preliminary sense of what rights others may have already claimed in a particular area.[373] However, these databases are of limited value. The search functionality is typically limited. In addition, there are many sources of rights that may not be included in these databases. For example, public databases will not provide information about trade secrets, which by definition are not publicly known.[374] Likewise, even when the existence of the rights might be publicly known, the information simply may not be in the particular database. Thus, even though ownership of a trademark can be publicly known, a search of the Patent and Trademark Office's database would not reveal the ownership of common law trademark rights

---

[372] *See* S. Hsieh, *More Patent Cases are Being Taken on Contingency Fee Basis*, LAWYERS USA, Aug. 14, 2006, *available at* http://www.allbusiness.com/primary-metal-manufacturing/foundries-nonferrous-foundaries/4076833-1.html; T. Riordan, *Patents: Licensing Boutiques Help Inventors with Patent Claims Against Big Companies*, N.Y. TIMES, June 10, 2002, *available at* http://www.nytimes.com/2002/06/10/technology/10PATE.html.

[373] For example, both the Patent and Trademark Office and the Register of Copyrights maintain free searchable databases online. *See Search Copyright Records*, U.S. COPYRIGHT OFFICE (2010), *available at* http://www.copyright.gov/records/; *Search for Patents*, UNITED STATES PATENT AND TRADEMARK OFFICE (Jan. 12, 2011), *available at* http://www.uspto.gov/patents/process/search/.

[374] *See* MILGRIM ON TRADE SECRETS §1.01 (2011). As a result, companies must generally rely on other mechanisms to reduce the risk of trade secrets liability.

for an entity that is ineligible for federal trademark rights.[375] Similarly, because the Copyright Act does not require registration,[376] a copyrighted work will not necessarily show up in a search of the Register of Copyrights' database.

In short, while a search of public records can provide useful background, it is unlikely to provide the extensive information about rights holders in the area that is necessary to properly minimize exposure to intellectual property litigation. In order to get this more extensive information, a company in the health industry may want to consider hiring in-house employees who are experienced in performing these initial searches. Alternatively, the searches can be outsourced to one of the many search firms that perform extensive searches. Either way, the identification of as many potential rights holders in an area as possible is important for minimizing risk, as the risk of litigation involving an existing rights holder can only be managed if that rights holder is identified. Ultimately, a health company will have to balance the cost of such searches with the cost of the risk of potential litigation.

2. Identifying the Scope of Existing Rights

Once a rights holder is identified, the next step is to determine the scope of those rights. The most common way of accomplishing this is to seek an opinion from a qualified attorney, often called a patent infringement opinion, a trademark infringement opinion, or a copyright infringement opinion, as to the validity of the existing rights and whether the company's proposed project would infringe upon those rights. In addition to providing the company useful information about the potential scope of the existing rights, an opinion of invalidity or noninfringement from an attorney who is an expert in the area may help the company should litigation later arise.[377]

3. Determining How to Proceed: Licenses, Workarounds, and Declaratory Relief

After an existing rights holder has been identified and the scope of those rights has been analyzed, the company must then determine how to proceed with the project. If the health company has succeeded in obtaining an opinion

---

[375] In order to be eligible for federal trademark protection, a mark must be used in interstate or foreign commerce. *See* McCarthy on Trademarks and Unfair Competition §19:117 (4th ed. 2011). Thus, marks may be eligible for state protection only. *See id.* §22:1. While many states provide a system for trademark registration, these systems often provide only procedural benefits. *See id.* As a result, the likelihood that a mark is registered, and thus can be discovered during a search, is reduced. *See id.*

[376] *See* 17 U.S.C. §408(a).

[377] For example, in trademark cases, one of the eight "*Polaroid* factors" used to determine whether there is a likelihood of confusion between the plaintiff's mark and the defendant's mark is the defendant's good faith in adopting its mark. *Polaroid Corp. v. Polarad Elecs. Corp.*, 287 F.2d 492 (2d Cir. 1961). *See* W.W.W. Pharm. Co. v. Gillette Co., 984 F.2d 567, 572 (1993). "Good faith can be found if a defendant has selected a mark which reflects the product's characteristics, *has requested a trademark search or has relied on the advice of counsel.*" *Id.* at 575 (emphasis added). Likewise, in a patent infringement case, reliance on the opinion of counsel may preclude a finding of willful infringement. *See, e.g.*, Radio Steel & Mfg. Co. v. MTD Prods., Inc., 788 F.2d 1554, 1559 (Fed. Cir. 1986) (noting that in order to determine whether the defendant relied in good faith on an opinion of counsel that the patent was not infringed, the fact finder must consider the "totality of the circumstances").

of invalidity or noninfringement from a qualified expert attorney, the company may determine that the risk of exposure to intellectual property litigation by the existing rights holder is low enough that the project should proceed as is. If, however, the attorney was unwilling to provide an opinion of invalidity or noninfringement, the opinion stated that the project would not infringe only if certain modifications were made, or the company wants to further lower the risk of exposure to intellectual property litigation, the company can do so by (1) seeking a license from the existing rights holder, (2) attempting to work around the existing rights, or (3) seeking declaratory relief that the existing rights are invalid or not infringed.

Seeking a license may be a reasonable business decision where the company is comfortable approaching the rights holder for a license and the rights holder is willing to license the rights for a price that the company is willing to pay. Unfortunately, these conditions will not always be met. For example, if the rights holder is a competitor, the health company may not feel comfortable seeking a license, especially where such negotiations may result in the disclosure of confidential information. Alternatively, the rights holder may set the price so high that it is no longer strategically desirable to acquire the licensed rights. Furthermore, the rights holder may simply decide not to offer the license—as it is fully within its rights to do.[378]

When acquiring a license is not a reasonable option, another alternative available to companies in the health industry is attempting to design the project to avoid the existing rights. For example, the company may choose a new trademark or slogan that is more unique and less likely to infringe on existing rights than perhaps the preferred trademark or slogan is. Similarly, if an existing patent is involved, the company may attempt to design the product or method in order to avoid the existing patent claims. Once again, an opinion by qualified counsel may be useful in determining whether a workaround is possible. Yet workarounds may still result in the risk of intellectual property litigation, because the rights holder may still believe that the workaround infringes its rights. This is because the outer bounds of the scope of intellectual property rights can be unclear. Copyrights, for example, protect more than just direct rote copying; they also cover works with "a 'substantial similarity' of copyrightable expression."[379] Whether "substantial similarity" exists can often be a difficult

---

[378] This is due to the fact that one of the key rights granted with intellectual property rights is the right to exclude. *See* Sean Flynn, *Using Competition Law to Promote Access to Knowledge*, ACCESS TO KNOWLEDGE IN THE AGE OF INTELLECTUAL PROPERTY (2010), *available at* http://www.wcl.american.edu/pijip/documents/flynn08122008.pdf ("Intellectual property rights grant rights to exclude competition with the right holder to create incentives and rewards for innovation...."). Indeed, the Patent Act explicitly protects the right of the patent owner to refuse to grant licenses. *See* 28 U.S.C. §271(d) ("No patent owner otherwise entitled to relief for infringement or contributory infringement of a patent shall be denied relief or deemed guilty of misuse or illegal extension of the patent right by reason of his having ... refused to license or use any rights to the patent.").

[379] *See* Hoehling v. Universal City Studios, Inc., 618 F.2d 972, 977 (2d Cir. 1980).

determination to make.[380] Likewise, the precise bounds of patent claims can be unclear until they are construed by the court.[381]

Finally, in some cases, it may make sense for companies in the health industry to seek a declaratory judgment from a court of competent jurisdiction that either the existing rights are invalid or the proposed use does not infringe.[382] While seeking a declaratory judgment does not avoid litigation, it may resolve the dispute at an earlier stage in the project's development, when changes are easier to make. In order to seek such a judgment in federal court, the company must first prove there is an actual controversy.[383] The U.S. Supreme Court has explained that this requirement asks "whether the facts alleged, under all the circumstances, show that there is a substantial controversy, between parties having adverse legal interests, of sufficient immediacy and reality to warrant the issuance of a declaratory judgment."[384] Thus, seeking a declaratory judgment will only be an option once there is a dispute; it will not act as a mechanism for essentially getting a "noninfringement opinion" from the courts.[385]

B. Strategic Intellectual Property Acquisitions

Another mechanism that companies in the health industry may consider in order to reduce exposure to intellectual property litigation is the strategic acquisition of intellectual rights. This can help the company by (1) improving its negotiating power with other companies in the industry, (2) potentially minimizing the scope of rights that others can acquire, and (3) improving the scope of rights that the company itself has, thus potentially lowering the risk that the company infringes upon another's rights. Two of the most common methods used to acquire strategic intellectual property rights are strategic intellectual property filings and cross-licensing agreements.

1. Strategic Intellectual Property Filings

In some instances, the strategic filing of intellectual property applications, such as patent applications and trademark and copyright registrations, may help a company limit its exposure to intellectual property litigation. These filings may cover intellectual property rights that the company does not necessarily see as rights that will be actively enforced, but which will remain useful for defen-

---

[380] *See id.* ("Because substantial similarity is customarily an extremely close question of fact, summary judgment has traditionally been frowned upon in copyright litigation." (citations omitted)).

[381] *See* K. Osenga, *Linguistics and Patent Claim Construction*, 38 RUTGERS L.J. 61, 63–65, 68–69 (2006).

[382] *See generally, e.g.*, Arrowhead Indus. Water, Inc. v. Ecolochem, Inc., 846 F.2d 731 (Fed. Cir. 1988) (permitting a declaratory judgment action where the patent owner had sent threatening letters to the plaintiff and one of its customers).

[383] *See* 28 U.S.C. §2201. The Supreme Court has interpreted this language to require the presence of an actual case or controversy under Article III of the U.S. Constitution. *See* MedImmune, Inc. v. Genentech, Inc., 549 U.S. 118, 126–27 (2007).

[384] *See id.* at 127 (quoting Maryland Casualty Co. v. Pacific Coal & Oil Co., 312 U.S. 270, 273 (1941)).

[385] *See Arrowhead*, 846 F.2d at 736.

sive purposes. These strategic rights can be useful in improving a company's negotiating power and in precluding others from obtaining rights.

Strategic intellectual property rights can improve a party's negotiating power when a company in the health industry negotiates for another's rights, either through a license or a settlement. These strategic rights can provide the company with bargaining power, because they may include rights that the other side wants, such as when a cross-licensing agreement, discussed in further detail in IX.B.2., below, is being negotiated. Alternatively, they may provide a company with bargaining power during settlement negotiations where litigation has already been filed by providing the company with rights that it may be able to exert against the plaintiff through an infringement counterclaim.[386]

Additionally, strategic rights may work to minimize the intellectual property rights that others are able to acquire. For example, in the United States, strategic intellectual property filings may also act to firm up a health company's trademark rights. Once a federal trademark is registered, that mark is given precedence throughout the country.[387] In contrast, common law rights lack this additional protection,[388] and thus the rights are typically only obtained in the jurisdictions where there is actual use or secondary meaning.[389] In other words, where common law rights are relied upon, another company is free to use the same mark in another jurisdiction—indeed, if another company does so, it may be able to exclude the health company from using the mark in that jurisdiction.[390] A strategic federal trademark registration could avoid this result. Likewise, strategic patents may also act as prior art that prevents another entity from obtaining a patent due to obviousness[391] or that may provide a defense that the patent claims are invalid due to obviousness if litigation does occur.[392] Thus, strategic intellectual property filings can both provide a company with negotiation power and limit the rights that others can acquire.

2. *Cross-Licensing Agreements and Patent Pools*

A company in the health industry can also strategically acquire intellectual property rights by entering into cross-licensing agreements or patent pools. With cross-licensing agreements, a company enters into an agreement with another entity to license some or all of their intellectual property rights to one

---

[386]This potential benefit will only apply, however, when the party on the other side of the table is also involved in the industry. It will not apply where the other party is a nonpracticing entity, sometimes referred to as a troll, since the nonpracticing entity exists solely to license and enforce intellectual property. *See* M. Jones, *Permanent Injunction, A Remedy by Any Other Name is Patently Not the Same: How* eBay v. MercExchange *Affects the Patent Right of Non-Practicing Entities*, 14 Geo. Mason L. Rev. 1035, 1036 (2006).

[387]*See* McCarthy on Trademarks and Unfair Competition §26:31 (4th ed. 2011). However, certain statutory defenses or a defect in the registration will overcome this right. *See id.*

[388]Indeed, state trademark registrations also typically do not convey this benefit. *See id.* §22:1.

[389]*See id.* §§22:1, 26:27.

[390]*See id.* §§26:1–:3, :25, :31.

[391]*See generally* Harmon on Patents: Black-Letter Law and Commentary 444–504 (2007) (explaining the nonobviousness requirement for patentability).

[392]*See id.* at 777 (failure to meet the nonobvious requirement for patentability is an invalidity defense to a patent infringement suit).

another.[393] These agreements are commonly used where two companies each have patents that may apply to the other's products or processes.[394] In addition to including existing intellectual property rights, those patents may also include those rights an entity acquires during the period of the agreement.[395] By entering into a cross-licensing agreement, each party can take advantage of the rights licensed by the other party without risking litigation. Additionally, because multiple rights are licensed at one time, it lowers the transaction costs for both the licensors and the licensees.

Patent pools are similar to licensing agreements. However, instead of licensing the rights to each other, the companies agree to offer a package license to the patents involved to other entities.[396] This arrangement is beneficial where the companies have manufacturers that may not hold intellectual property rights to cross-license.[397] Like cross-licensing agreements, patent pools can reduce both the risk of intellectual property litigation and the transaction costs for the licensing parties.

C. Corporate Policies and Employee Education

Yet another method by which companies in the health industry may consider reducing exposure to intellectual property litigation is implementing appropriate corporate policies to reduce the likelihood of infringing upon another's intellectual property rights. These policies generally should address the conduct of employees and independent contractors, but they should also address the proper procedures for screening prospective employees and ideas submitted by nonemployees. Once appropriate policies are instituted, companies should also take steps to train employees to follow the policies.

1. Policies for Existing Employees and Independent Contractors

With existing employees and independent contractors, three major issues that a health company should consider when developing internal policies are ensuring that (1) the employees' and independent contractors' work products are original creations that the company will own, (2) the company and its employees are aware of the limitations of any rights to use others' intellectual property that the company may have, and (3) the health company's information remains secure. As the specifics of the policy that a company enacts will reflect the particular needs of that company, these issues are discussed in a general manner here.

First, companies in the health industry should consider whether they have policies in place to verify that employees and independent contractors create original work products. Companies should also make efforts to make sure that

---

[393] *See* C. Shapiro, *Navigating the Patent Thicket: Cross Licenses, Patent Pools, and Standard Setting*, 1 INNOVATION POLICY AND THE ECONOMY 119, 127 (2001) (A.B. Jaffe, J. Lerner & S. Stern, eds.), *available at* http://www.nber.org/chapters/c10778.pdf.
[394] *See id.*
[395] *See id.*
[396] *See id.*
[397] *See id.*

proper records are maintained about the development of trademarks, such as slogans and other marketing materials, inventions, and any other type of intellectual property that the company creates. These records may be important later on in order to show that the work was independently created,[398] that a trademark was adopted in good faith,[399] that the company's invention was created before another's similar invention,[400] or that infringement was not willful.[401] Thus, while these records may be most useful once intellectual property litigation occurs, they may also be useful tools during early negotiations with potential plaintiffs that emphasize the weakness of the potential plaintiffs' position.

In addition to enacting policies that ensure that proper records are retained, companies in the health industry should also consider taking steps to educate employees about the legal consequences of those records. For example, the company may want to stress the importance that the records are accurate. The importance of accuracy is twofold: first, the evidentiary value of positive records will likely be discounted if they were sloppily created or maintained, and second, sloppy statements may later be held against the company if litigation occurs. Also, the company should consider explaining its need for the records, so that employees do not feel like the request is unduly burdensome.

In addition to ensuring that there are record retention policies, companies in the health industry should also consider implementing an appropriate legal review process (either by in-house counsel or outside counsel) for works that involve intellectual property. This review process should include the creation of (or the review of existing) contractual provisions for both employees and independent contractors that require the employees and independent contractors to verify in writing that their work both is original and does not infringe others' intellectual property rights. In addition, the contractual provisions should also address the ownership of works created by employees and independent contractors in order to make certain that the company owns the works created.

Second, company policies should be put into place to ensure that the company and its employees are well aware of the limitations of any rights to others' intellectual property that the company may have. Whenever the company is using another's intellectual property, such as software, pursuant to a license or other agreement, legal counsel should review the scope of the agreement and implement policies that help guide employees in their use of the intellectual property.

Third, a company in the health industry should consider implementing policies that aim to protect the company's information and keep it secure. In short, just as a company wants to ensure that it is not using improperly gained information from a competitor, the company also should make reasonable efforts to guarantee that its competitors do not improperly gain information from the company. Even though there are legal mechanisms that the health company

---

[398] See NIMMER ON COPYRIGHT §13.01(B) (2011).

[399] See W.W.W. Pharm. Co. v. Gillette Co., 984 F.2d 567, 572 (1993).

[400] See HARMON ON PATENTS: BLACK-LETTER LAW AND COMMENTARY §§16.52-.56, 29.5 (2007).

[401] Even when intent is not relevant to the issue of liability, it can affect the damages awarded. See, e.g., HARMON ON PATENTS §§11.5-.11; McCARTHY ON TRADEMARKS AND UNFAIR COMPETITION §23:112 (4th ed. 2011); NIMMER ON COPYRIGHT §14.04(B).

can use to prevent the competitor from using ill-gotten information,[402] it can be risky and costly to rely on those mechanisms solely. Indeed, in the case of trade secrets, inadequately protecting the confidential information alone can be sufficient for the company to lose all trade secret protection.[403] Thus, it is much easier, inexpensive, and less risky to address information security up front.

As with other policies, the particular information security policy will depend on a particular company's needs. However, factors a company may consider include:

- Who needs access to the information?
- Is there any reason for the information to ever leave the company's premises?
- If the information can be taken off premises, what restrictions (such as requiring the use of encrypted storage devices or secure transfer mechanisms) should be put in place to protect the information once it leaves the premises?
- How will the policy be enforced?

The answers to these questions will help craft the ultimate information security policy. In addition, companies should consider entering into nondisclosure agreements before they reveal confidential information to independent contractors. This again will help protect the secrecy of the company's information.

2. Policies Addressing Concerns Relating to Nonemployees

Generally, there are three types of nonemployees that a company in the health industry should consider having policies in place to address. The first is prospective employees, who may be coming from a competitor. The second is nonemployees who submit an idea to the health company, such as a research proposal that could lead to a new medical invention. The third is ex-employees, who have left or are in the process of leaving a company.

With prospective employees, companies in the health industry may want to implement policies and procedures in order to properly screen the prospective employee. These policies should address, for example, the issue of whether the potential employee is subject to a noncompete agreement or other agreement that prohibits the potential employee from working for the company or possibly puts the company at risk if the employee begins working there.[404] Additionally, the policies should set forth a clear statement about the proper treatment of trade secrets and other confidential information the potential employee may have learned while working for his or her prior employer, particularly where the prior employer is a competitor or where the prospective employee had a special relationship, such as a fiduciary relationship, with the prior employer. This policy should emphasize the importance of confidentiality and make it absolutely clear

---

[402] For example, the company may be able to bring an action for misappropriation of trade secrets. *See* MILGRIM ON TRADE SECRETS §1.01 (2011).

[403] *See* MILGRIM ON TRADE SECRETS §§1.03-.04.

[404] *See, e.g.*, MILGRIM ON TRADE SECRETS §4.01 (describing common contractual agreements that companies used to protect trade secret information).

that previously learned confidential information is not to be disclosed to the company or other employees.

The concerns with nonemployees who may submit an idea to the health company are different. Rather than a concern about how the individual's prior employment may affect the health company, the concern with nonemployees is about the information itself. Thus, before a health company even considers an idea submitted by a nonemployee, it should require that a contract is in place that governs the discussions. This contract should be written in order to avoid allegations of idea misappropriation if the company is working on related projects that may not be publicly known.[405] Additionally, if the discussions contemplate the exchange of confidential information by the health company, the contract should also address the nondisclosure of that information by the nonemployee.

As for ex-employees, the rights of the company to contractually limit an ex-employee's right to compete and/or use trade secrets varies dramatically by state. In addition, factors such as whether the employee developed the secret, whether the secret is company-specific or industry-specific, the length of time at the company, the reason for termination, etc., are taken into account.[406]

3. Ensuring Policies Are Properly Implemented

While having appropriate policies is a good first step, companies should also implement the policies by educating employees so that they are aware of the policies and the policies' requirements. While training will necessarily address the company's particular policy, key areas will include:

- the importance of keeping the company's information confidential;
- the need to maintain proper records about the creation of anything that includes intellectual property, such as trademarks or inventions, and the implications of these records; and
- the importance of obtaining written permission and the appropriate rights where another's work or other intellectual property will be used.

D. Minimizing Exposure to Unavoidable Intellectual Property Litigation

Unfortunately, there is no way to eliminate a company's exposure to all intellectual property litigation. Yet there are some mechanisms for managing the remaining risk. One possible solution is to purchase insurance that covers intellectual property litigation to minimize the cost risk involved in such litigation. Additionally, where health companies are subject to identified ongoing risks, industry and government outreach may help minimize exposure to intellectual property litigation. Finally, when a dispute is unavoidable, a company in the health industry may want to consider whether the intellectual property dispute

---

[405] For a more detailed discussion of the concept of idea misappropriation, *see generally* NIMMER ON COPYRIGHT §19D.02(A)(3).

[406] For more information on this topic, see, for example, PASCALE LAGESSE & MARIANN NORRBOM, RESTRICTIVE COVENANTS IN EMPLOYMENT CONTRACTS AND OTHER MECHANISMS FOR PROTECTION OF CORPORATE CONFIDENTIAL INFORMATION (2006).

can be resolved using alternative dispute resolution methods, such as mediation or arbitration.

1. Insurance

Since intellectual property litigation can be so expensive, insurance is one way to limit a company's exposure to large, unanticipated costs. As companies in the health industry may have some insurance coverage through the company's comprehensive general business liability policy, the company should first check its general business liability policy to determine precisely what intellectual property litigation exposure, if anything, is covered.

If the comprehensive general liability policy provides inadequate protection from intellectual property litigation, the company should consider purchasing intellectual property–specific insurance.[407] While these policies will vary in both cost and coverage, one particular type of policy that may be of interest to health companies is patent insurance. These policies typically cover the costs of defending a patent infringement lawsuit, including attorneys' fees and other defense expenses, damages awards, and settlement costs.[408] Thus, these policies may enable a company to limit its exposure to unanticipated and expensive patent litigation.

Yet despite the fact that insurance policies can be a useful way of minimizing a company's exposure to large, unanticipated costs, they are certainly not a panacea. First, insurance policies frequently do not cover willful infringement of another's intellectual property rights.[409] Second, like all other insurance policies, intellectual property–specific insurance policies can be discoverable.[410] As these policies often ask very specific questions about a company's legal compliance programs in place to avoid intellectual property infringement and other activities, a company may walk a thin line between full disclosure to the insurance company and providing information that an adversary can use against the company in later litigation.[411] Finally, intellectual property insurance policies can be quite costly.[412] As a result, these policies may not be a viable solution for all companies in the health industry.

2. Industry and Government Outreach

If a company in the health industry faces continuous intellectual property exposure from a particularly vexatious source, it may be appropriate to con-

---

[407] For a summary of the types of these policies, *see generally* M. Simensky & E.C. Osterberg, *The Insurance and Management of Intellectual Property Risks*, 17 CARDOZO ARTS & ENT. L.J. 321, 325–43 (1999).

[408] *See id.* at 329–31.

[409] *See id.* at 328–29.

[410] *See id.* at 328.

[411] *See id.* at 328, 330, 336, 338–39.

[412] *See, e.g., id.* at 330 (citing the cost of patent insurance as around $3,000 annually per patent, but noting that costs can greatly vary).

sider industry or government outreach. This, however, will not protect the company from any one particular source of exposure. Rather, such outreach aims to minimize the risk posed by the vexatious source. For example, if other industry members face the same exposure, they may be able to work together to minimize the industry's exposure, e.g., by the use of cross-licensing agreements and patent pools, discussed in IX.B.2., above.

Government outreach, on the other hand, may work to minimize the intellectual property rights available to sources of vexatious litigation. While government outreach can be particularly important whenever government is considering changing the scope of intellectual property rights,[413] it may also be useful in persuading legislators to introduce limited legislation aimed to solve a particular problem facing health care companies. However, since such limitations will minimize rights globally, health care companies should ensure that any changes passed will not limit their own rights in an undesirable manner. Government outreach thus can be a useful mechanism for minimizing long-term exposure to intellectual property litigation where health care companies face liability but do not exert their own rights.

3. Alternative Dispute Resolution

Another method that a health company may use to minimize the cost of intellectual property litigation is to seek to resolve an existing dispute using alternative dispute resolution mechanisms. Both mediation and arbitration may be able to resolve the dispute in a faster manner for a smaller cost than traditional litigation.[414] In addition, alternative dispute resolution procedures may provide other benefits, such as reducing the burden of discovery, providing for confidentiality of the proceedings, avoiding the uncertainty of the appeals process, and providing the flexibility for creative solutions to resolve the dispute.[415] However, since it is unlikely that the parties entered into a prior contract with each other mandating the use of such mechanisms, the availability of such mechanisms will likely depend on the opposing parties' willingness to use them. Where a rights holder is seeking to squeeze a large payment out of a health company based on the threat of expensive litigation rather than the strength of the party's rights, the rights holder is unlikely to agree to such mechanisms.

---

[413] For example, a large number of companies engaged Congress with regard to the most recent patent reform efforts. *See* A. Becker, *Patent Reform Measure Ignited Fierce Lobbying Effort*, WASH. POST, Mar. 27, 2011, *available at* http://www.washingtonpost.com/capital_business/patent-reform-measure-ignited-fierce-lobbying-effort/2011/03/25/AFzD9VkB_story.html.

[414] *See* M. Smith, *Mediation as an Alternative to Litigation in Patent Infringement Disputes*, 11 ADR BULLETIN 113, 115 (2009), *available at* http://epublications.bond.edu.au/cgi/viewcontent.cgi?article=1481&context=adr.

[415] *See id.* at 115–16.

E. Conclusion

Any comprehensive risk management plan must be based on the particular circumstances of the company. Nonetheless, due diligence, strategic intellectual property acquisitions, and the implementation of appropriate corporate policies are mechanisms that can help reduce the risks associated with intellectual property litigation. Moreover, insurance coverage, industry and government outreach, and litigation alternatives such as mediation and alternative dispute resolution can help manage the remaining risks. Thus, these are all key mechanisms that a company in the health industry should consider when developing a comprehensive risk management plan.

16

Allocation and Mitigation of Liability*

I.	Introduction	548
II.	Category-Based Risks	549
	A. E-Content Providers	549
	1. Consumer-Oriented E-Content Providers	549
	a. Unauthorized Use of Copyrighted Material	550
	b. Unauthorized Use of a Trademark or Service Mark	553
	c. Liability for Erroneous Information/Defamation	557
	d. Unlicensed/Unauthorized Practice of Medicine	562
	2. Provider-Oriented E-Content Providers	563
	B. E-Product Providers	564
	1. Consumer-Oriented E-Product Providers	564
	a. E-Prescribing Risks	565
	b. Privacy and Data Security Issues—Excluding HIPAA	568
	i. State Data Breach Notification Statutes	569
	ii. PCI Data Security Standard	569
	iii. Federal Trade Commission Section 5 Actions	570
	iv. The Red Flags Rule	572
	2. Provider/Business-Oriented E-Product Providers	573
	a. Employee Access to Health Insurance Accounts	573
	b. Provider Publication Tools	574
	C. E-Connection Providers	574
	1. Unauthorized Use of Copyrighted Material	574
	2. Unauthorized Use of Trademark/Service Mark	575
	3. Infringement of Proprietary Rights in Technology	575
	4. Privacy and Data Security	576
	5. Liability for Erroneous Information/Defamation	576
	D. E-Care Providers	577
	1. Unlicensed/Unauthorized Practice of Medicine	577
	2. Malpractice	578
	3. Technology Performance Issues	578
	4. Privacy and Data Security	579

---

*Brian R. Balow, Dickinson Wright PLLC, Troy, Michigan.

		5. FDA Regulation of Telemedicine	579
	E.	EHR System Providers	580
		1. Privacy and Data Security—HIPAA and HITECH	580
		2. Medicare and Medicaid Incentive Programs and Achievement of Meaningful Use	582
		3. Allocation of Rights and Obligations Among HIE Participants	583
III.	Allocation and Mitigation of Risk		585
	A.	The Risk: Unauthorized Use of Copyrighted Material....................	585
		1. Before a Claim Occurs—Mitigation..	585
		2. Before a Claim Occurs—Allocation	586
		3. When a Claim Occurs—Mitigation...	587
	B.	The Risk: Unauthorized Use of a Trademark or Service Mark	588
		1. Before a Claim Occurs—Mitigation..	588
		2. Before a Claim Occurs—Allocation	588
		3. After a Claim Occurs—Mitigation...	589
	C.	The Risk: Publication of Erroneous or Defamatory Information	590
		1. Before a Claim Occurs—Mitigation..	590
		2. Before a Claim Occurs—Allocation	590
		3. When a Claim Occurs—Mitigation...	590
	D.	The Risk: Unlicensed or Unauthorized Practice of Medicine	591
		1. Before a Claim Occurs—Mitigation..	591
		2. Before a Claim Occurs—Allocation	592
	E.	The Risk: E-Prescribing and Malpractice......................................	592
		1. Before a Claim Occurs—Mitigation..	592
		2. Before a Claim Occurs—Allocation	593
	F.	The Risk: Privacy and Data Security Compliance.........................	593
		1. Before a Claim Occurs—Mitigation..	593
		2. Before a Claim Occurs—Allocation	594
		3. When a Claim Occurs—Mitigation...	595

I. Introduction

It is now abundantly clear that every type of e-health provider faces real and substantial legal and regulatory risks associated with its business. These providers fall into several categories: e-content, e-product, e-connection, e-care, and electronic health record (EHR) system providers.[1] The first step in managing the risks these providers face is knowledge of their existence, which is the primary focus of this book. Once known, the objective is to minimize, and if possible eliminate, the risks and consequently their attendant liabilities.

This chapter (1) generally identifies the risks applicable to each e-health provider category and explains why those risks apply to the category, (2) provides a detailed summary of the penalties and liabilities potentially deriving

---

[1] See Chapter 2 (Healey, E-Health Industry Overview) at I.

from those risks, and (3) offers recommendations and techniques for the allocation and mitigation of those risks.

Recently, health information technology (HIT) issues have taken center stage in the e-health regulatory environment. Whether in conjunction with compliance under the Health Information Technology for Economic and Clinical Health Act (HITECH Act),[2] achievement of "meaningful use" criteria under the Medicare Shared Savings Program,[3] or the developing rules for accountable care organizations under the Patient Protection and Affordable Care Act (PPACA),[4] e-health providers now more than ever must understand and comply with the myriad laws and regulations governing HIT. The Department of Health and Human Services (HHS), through its Office of Civil Rights (OCR), has begun aggressive enforcement action against alleged violations under the Health Information Portability and Accountability Act (HIPAA)[5] and the HITECH Act involving unauthorized dissemination of protected health information (PHI). Combined with the strong public and private sector push for the adoption of EHR, this has created fertile ground for risk. Consequently, a substantial portion of this chapter is devoted to privacy and data security issues and methods for properly addressing those issues.

II. CATEGORY-BASED RISKS

A. E-Content Providers

E-content providers occupy various roles in the health care industry, and one e-content provider may fill multiple roles. Some of these roles are consumer directed (i.e., consumer-oriented e-content providers), and the assessment of such providers' potential legal and regulatory risk depends in part on the motivation underlying their behavior. Profit-driven content is, for example, likely to draw greater scrutiny from the Federal Trade Commission (FTC) than would mission-driven content delivered by a nonprofit charitable organization. Provider-oriented e-content providers, whose clientele are health care professionals, perhaps face lessened risks because of their audience's status. The degree of this risk, however, will depend in substantial part upon the terms under which content is delivered to the professional.

1. Consumer-Oriented E-Content Providers

Consumer-oriented e-content providers generally provide members of the public with access to health news and information, usually over the Internet and more recently through smart phone applications ("apps").[6] These e-content

---

[2] 42 U.S.C. §§17932 *et seq.* (2010).
[3] 75 Fed. Reg. 44,314 (July 28, 2010) (to be codified at 42 C.F.R. pts 412, 413, 422, and 495).
[4] Pub. L. No. 111-148, 124 Stat. 119 (2010).
[5] Pub. L. No. 104-191, 110 Stat. 1936 (enacted Aug. 21, 1996).
[6] According to a *New York Times* report, as of November 2010, there existed more than 17,000 health care–related apps available for the iPhone and Android markets. Sonia Kolesnikov-Jessop, *Do-it-Yourself Health Care with Smartphones*, N.Y. TIMES (Feb. 28, 2011), *available at* http://www.nytimes.com/2011/03/01/technology/01iht-srhealth01.html?_r=1.

providers may either "push" information to their audience or have their audience "pull" information from them (e.g., from their Web domains); they do not, however, solicit or otherwise intentionally obtain information from consumers. These content providers may also act as portals, connecting the consumer to other sites with specialized information on diseases, drugs, insurance, or other health-related topics, or they may provide information directly on a narrow or wide range of topics. Examples of this type of consumer-oriented e-content provider include WebMD, the Mayo Clinic, and eHealthInsurance.

Consumer-oriented e-content providers also include companies that provide consumers with the ability to communicate with others who have similar health problems, interests, or concerns. Examples of this type of consumer e-content provider include Patients Like Me, DailyStrength, and Cancer Hope Network.

Most consumer-oriented e-content providers do not charge for access to the content. In some cases, the Web site is provided as a public service, a community outreach initiative, an effort to promote policy positions, or advertising for products and services. In other cases, the site generates revenue by selling advertisements that are often displayed to match the information sought by the user, or by selling detailed listings in health care provider directories that facilitate contact between site users and the subscribing providers.

Regardless of whether they reap direct compensation from their intended audience, consumer-oriented e-content providers should reasonably expect that consumers will rely on the completeness and the accuracy of the provided content. As a result, such e-content providers may face the following legal and regulatory risks associated with content creation, publication, and dissemination.

a. Unauthorized Use of Copyrighted Material

Inadequate editorial control, a misunderstanding of the copyright law (and in particular the "fair use" defense), a general inattention to detail, or a combination of these factors can result in content publication or use that infringes on a third party's copyright. With the ready availability of written materials on the Internet and the ability to easily link to other content, the risk of improper copying and publication is ever present for e-content providers.

A prima facie claim of copyright infringement requires only that the plaintiff show (1) ownership of the copyright, (2) that the alleged infringer had access to the infringed material, and (3) actual copying. It is not necessary to prove that the defendant had any knowledge, motive, or intent to infringe on the plaintiff's copyright. A defendant may be liable for copyright infringement even for action that is taken innocently or with a good-faith belief that it did not constitute infringement. While the oft-cited "fair use" defense may be available to a consumer-oriented e-content provider, it is usually much narrower than imagined, and therefore should not be relied on without properly studying its application to the particular circumstances. In elementary terms, if the e-content provider makes "transformative use" of copyrighted material,[7] such action may

---

[7] The most common forms of fair use are comment and criticism, and parody. *See generally* http://fairuse.stanford.edu/Copyright_and_Fair_Use_Overview/chapter9/.

qualify as fair use under the federal Copyright Act. The point here is simply to avoid an unexplored conclusion that a particular copying of material must be fair use: the issue should be properly analyzed by a competent professional prior to publication.

Databases may be protectable under the Copyright Act as a type of compilation, but only if the selection, coordination, and arrangement of the compilation are protectable apart from the copyrights, if any, of the individual elements of the compilation.[8] The U.S. Supreme Court first addressed the protection of compilations of data (where each piece of data individually lacked copyrightability) in *Feist Publications, Inc. v. Rural Telephone Service Co.*,[9] holding that the plaintiff's selection of the name, town, and telephone number as the only information to include in the compilation was not copyrightable. However, federal courts do tend to afford copyright protection if the compiler exercised recognizable industry and subjective judgment in the selection and arrangement of factual data.

Compilations of information continue to be protectable under the Copyright Act if the defendant has exercised creativity in selecting and arranging a group of facts.[10] Where there are, however, so few ways of expressing an idea that protection of the expression would effectively accord protection to the idea itself, then a compilation of such information is not protectable under copyright law.[11]

The issue of copyright protection for compilations of facts was explored in 2009 in *Health Grades, Inc. v. Robert Wood Johnson University Hospital, Inc.*[12] Health Grades developed and distributed objective ratings of hospitals, physicians, and other health care providers in a "1-3-5 Star" format. The ratings were developed by analyzing information from a variety of sources using proprietary methods. Health Grades made these ratings available on its Web site under a limited license to individuals to make only one copy for that person's noncommercial use. Health Grades alleged that Robert Wood Johnson Hospital (RWJ) used the ratings from Health Grades' Web site in press releases and articles promoting its hospital and services. Health Grades sued the hospital for copyright and trademark infringement. Considering RWJ's motion to dismiss the complaint, the district court held that Health Grades' ratings were not merely unprotected facts, but were creations based on the selection, weighing, and arrangement of facts discovered by Health Grades, thus meeting the "originality" requirement for copyright protection[13] and sufficient to state a claim for copyright infringement. Significantly, the court did not address the possible affirmative defense of fair use that might be available to RWJ.[14] Nevertheless, this case makes clear that consumer-oriented e-content providers must consider

---

[8] 17 U.S.C. §101.

[9] 499 U.S. 340, 111 S. Ct. 1282, 18 USPQ2d (BNA) 1275 (1991).

[10] F.A. Davis Co. v. Wolters Kluwer Health, Inc., 413 F. Supp. 2d 507 (E.D. Pa. 2005); CDN Inc. v. Kapes, 197 F.3d 1256 (9th Cir. 1999).

[11] N.Y. Mercantile Exch., Inc. v. Intercontinental Exchange, Inc., 497 F.3d 109 (2d Cir. 2007).

[12] 634 F. Supp. 2d 1226 (D. Colo. 2009).

[13] *Id.* at 1234.

[14] *Id.* at 1238.

potential risks associated with publishing compiled information developed by third parties.

Liability for copyright infringement can be direct, contributory, or vicarious, depending upon the conduct of the defendant in relation to the infringing activity. Contributory liability may be imposed on someone who knowingly or with reason to know of the infringing activity of another induces, causes, or materially contributes to the infringing conduct.[15] Thus, if an e-content provider has reason to know that it is linking to content that is improperly published on a third party's Web site, the e-content provider could be liable for contributory infringement. Vicarious liability may be imposed on someone who receives a direct financial benefit from the infringement and who has the right and ability to supervise the allegedly infringing activity.[16] Knowledge of the activity as infringement is not required to impose vicarious liability, and personal liability may extend to officers and directors who meet the required elements.[17]

The Copyright Act authorizes specific injunctive and monetary relief for copyright infringement. These remedial provisions are set forth in Sections 502, 503, 504, 505, and 509 of the Copyright Act. Injunctive relief may be granted to prevent or restrain copyright infringement or to take possession of or compel destruction of infringing copies. Monetary damages also may be recovered, and the plaintiff may elect either actual damages or statutory damages. Statutory damages are currently set at $750 to $30,000 for any one work infringed, and the court may adjust the amount awarded, depending upon the circumstances of the case.

If the infringement is willful, the court may increase the award of statutory damages up to $150,000 for any one work infringed. In contrast, if the infringement is innocent (the defendant was not aware and had no reason to believe that the acts constituted copyright infringement), the court in its discretion may reduce an award of statutory damages to a minimum of $200 for any one work infringed.[18] In addition, a prevailing party (plaintiff or defendant) also may recover costs and attorneys' fees.[19]

Finally, it is worth noting that Section 506 of the Copyright Act makes four activities criminally actionable: willful infringement for profit, fraudulent use of a copyright notice, fraudulent removal of a notice, and false representation in connection with a copyright application. For purposes of this section, "willful infringement for profit" includes copying for purposes of commercial advantage or private financial gain. Thus, a for-profit e-content provider that knowingly and without permission published a third party's copyrighted material could face criminal liability under the Copyright Act. Penalties for criminal copyright infringement include fines and imprisonment up to one year, or, up to five years imprisonment if the violation involves 10 or more copies of one or more copy-

---

[15]*See, e.g.*, Apple Computer, Inc. v. Microsoft Corp., 821 F. Supp. 616 (N.D. Cal. 1993), *aff'd*, 35 F.3d 1435 (9th Cir. 1994), *cert denied*, 513 U.S. 1184 (1995).

[16]Fonovisa, Inc. v. Cherry Auction, Inc., 76 F.3d 259, 262 (9th Cir. 1996); Polygram Int'l Publ'g, Inc. v Nevada/TIG, Inc., 855 F. Supp. 1314, 1325–26 (D. Mass. 1994).

[17]*See, e.g.*, Fermata Int'l Melodies, Inc. v. Champions Golf Club, Inc., 712 F. Supp. 1257 (S.D. Tex. 1989), *aff'd*, 915 F.2d 1567 (5th Cir. 1990).

[18]17 U.S.C. §504.

[19]*Id.* §505; *see also* Fogerty v. Fantasy, Inc., 510 U.S. 517, 114 S. Ct. 1023 (1994).

righted works that have a total retail value of more than $2,500. The second of two such violations could carry a penalty of up to 10 years imprisonment.[20]

b. Unauthorized Use of a Trademark or Service Mark

Similarly, an e-content provider at times may either "create" and use a trademark, service mark, or logo, or publish third-party trademarks, service marks, or logos in conjunction with content delivery, without considering its right (or lack thereof) to do so. As with copyright infringement, unfamiliarity with the law or poor editorial control, or both, can result in a trademark infringement claim under federal or state law or a trademark dilution claim for a famous mark under the Federal Trademark Dilution Act.

The principal source of substantive rights protecting trademarks is the federal Trademark Act of 1946, substantially revised in 1989 and commonly referred to as the Lanham Act.[21] The Lanham Act protects against unauthorized or confusing use of trademarks, but the availability of trademark protection will vary with the strength of the mark.

The U.S. Supreme Court has identified five basic categories of trademarks: (1) fanciful, (2) arbitrary, (3) suggestive, (4) descriptive, and (5) generic.[22] Trademarks that are fanciful, arbitrary, or suggestive are deemed to be inherently distinctive, because they perform the limited function of identifying the source of a product or service. Trademarks that are not fanciful, arbitrary, or suggestive, or that are merely descriptive, still may be considered distinctive and therefore entitled to protection under the doctrine of secondary meaning. A trademark may acquire secondary meaning if the primary significance of the mark in the minds of consumers is the association with the source of goods or services.[23] A trademark that is generic is not protectable under the Lanham Act. For example, the U.S. Court of Appeals for the Fourth Circuit has held that the phrase "You Have Mail" is generic or commonly used without secondary meaning and that the phrase therefore could not be protected by America Online, Inc.[24]

Section 32(1) of the Lanham Act protects federally registered marks by prohibiting the use in commerce of any reproduction, counterfeit, copy, or colorable imitation of that mark in connection with the sale, offering for sale, distribution, or advertising of any goods or services that is likely to cause confusion, to cause mistake, or to deceive.[25] Section 43(a) of the Lanham Act applies to trademarks that are not federally registered. For these unregistered marks, Section 43(a) prohibits the use in commerce of any mark that is likely to cause confusion as to the source, sponsorship, or affiliation of goods or services, as well as any false or misleading statement in commercial advertising that misrepresents

---

[20] 18 U.S.C. §2319.

[21] 15 U.S.C. §§1501 *et seq.*

[22] Two Pesos, Inc. v. Taco Cabana, Inc., 505 U.S. 763, 112 S. Ct. 2753 (1992).

[23] *Id.*

[24] America Online, Inc. v. AT&T Corp., 243 F.3d 812 (4th Cir. 2001), *cert. denied*, 534 U.S. 946 (2001).

[25] 15 U.S.C. §1114(1) (2006).

the nature, characteristics, qualities, or geographic origin of the advertised or competitive goods or services.[26]

Thus, federally registered marks are entitled to Lanham Act protection under both Sections 32(1) and 43(a), while unregistered marks are entitled to protection only under Section 43(a). In both cases, the touchstone of infringement is the likelihood of consumer confusion in the market. Under either Section 32 or Section 43(a), to successfully pursue a cause of action for infringement, a plaintiff must plead and prove the following four basic elements: (1) standing to sue under the Lanham Act; (2) personal jurisdiction; (3) the likelihood of confusion; and (4) secondary meaning, or distinctiveness, of the mark.[27] It is not necessary to allege or prove intent to infringe.[28]

E-content providers adopting trademarks must principally be cognizant of "likelihood of confusion" potentially created through their use of a mark. Whether a likelihood of confusion exists between the plaintiff's and the defendant's marks will depend upon an analysis of the specific facts of each case, including factors such as the similarity of the two marks, the similarity of the two products or services, actual consumer confusion, the strength of the plaintiff's mark, and the defendant's good faith.

A likelihood of confusion may arise for e-content providers in many ways. The provider may simply adopt a trademark without undertaking any due diligence, in the form of a proper search, to determine whether others in the health care industry may be using the same or similar marks. The provider may use a famous or distinctive mark as a domain name, resulting in a likelihood of consumer confusion.[29] Similarly, the use of a famous or distinctive mark as a "metatag" by someone other than the owner of that mark is likely to cause consumer confusion, because the use of the mark will direct people to a Web site that is not related to the owner of the mark.[30]

In 1995, Congress passed the Federal Trademark Dilution Act of 1995 (the Dilution Act),[31] which became effective January 16, 1996.[32] The Dilution Act amended Section 43 of the Lanham Act to offer protection against the dilution of certain famous marks without the necessity of showing any likelihood of consumer confusion.[33] Under the Dilution Act, the owner of a famous mark is entitled, subject to principles of equity, to enjoin any unauthorized commercial use of the mark if the use begins after the mark has become famous and causes dilution of the distinctive quality of the mark.[34] The statute lists a number of fac-

---

[26] *Id.* §1125(a).

[27] *See, e.g.*, Quabaug Rubber Co. v. Fabiano Shoe Co., 567 F.2d 154 (1st Cir. 1977).

[28] However, if the facts of the case support an allegation of fraud, intent to infringe may aid in the proof of likelihood of confusion and could provide grounds for an award of attorneys' fees under Section 35(a).

[29] See discussion in this section, below, regarding the Anticybersquatting Consumer Protection Act.

[30] For a definition and discussion of metatags in the context of infringement, see II.A.1.b., below.

[31] Pub. L. No. 104-98, 109 Stat. 985 (1996).

[32] Amended by the Trademark Dilution Revision Act of 2006, 15 U.S.C. §1125(c).

[33] 15 U.S.C. §§1125(c), 1127.

[34] *Id.*

tors that a court may consider in determining whether a mark is distinctive and famous, including:

- degree of inherent distinctiveness;
- duration and extent of prior use of the mark;
- duration and extent of advertising and publicity of the mark;
- geographical extent of use of the mark;
- industry or trade within which the mark is used; and
- degree of recognition of the mark within the industry or trade.[35]

Under the Dilution Act, dilution is defined to mean "the lessening of the capacity of a famous mark to identify and distinguish goods or services, regardless of the presence or absence of (1) competition between the owner of the famous mark and other parties, or (2) likelihood of confusion, mistake, or deception."[36] A court is not required to rely on traditional definitions of dilution such as blurring or tarnishment.

Importantly for consumer-oriented e-content providers, the protection afforded by the Dilution Act applies only to a commercial use of the trademark. Many otherwise offending but noncommercial uses of a trademark may therefore not fall within the parameters of the Dilution Act. For example, many celebrities are the subjects of Web sites that have been created and are maintained by their fans. If the Web site does not charge for use of the site or otherwise engage in commercial activity on the site that is enhanced by the famous name or trademark, then the use of the famous name or mark on the site may not be actionable under the Dilution Act. However, other causes of action may arise, such as violation of the Anticybersquatting Consumer Protection Act (discussed below in this section), the right to privacy, the right of publicity, and other state laws.

Under Section 34(a) of the Lanham Act, the court has the power to grant injunctions, according to the principles of equity and upon such terms as the court may deem reasonable, to prevent infringement of a registered trademark or a violation under Section 43(a).[37] In most cases, principles of equity will require the plaintiff to demonstrate the possibility of irreparable harm, a likelihood of success on the merits, and that in the balance of hardships, the potential injury to the plaintiff from denying injunctive relief will exceed the potential injury to the defendant if the relief is granted.

In some cases, demonstrating a likelihood of consumer confusion will create a presumption that the plaintiff will suffer irreparable harm and has no adequate remedy at law. However, injunctive relief may not be imposed against the publisher "of a newspaper, magazine, or other similar periodical or an electronic communication containing infringing matter or violating matter" if the injunction "would delay the delivery of such issue or transmission of such electronic communication after the regular time for such delivery or transmission."[38] This exception may become more important as periodical publishing goes online.

---

[35]*Id.* §1125(c).
[36]*Id.* §1127.
[37]*Id.* §1116(a).
[38]*Id.* §1114(2)(c).

Under Section 35 of the Lanham Act, a successful plaintiff is entitled to recover compensatory damages, profits, the costs of the action, and, in exceptional cases, treble damages and attorneys' fees.[39] The statute expressly provides that the court may assess profits and damages, and in assessing profits the plaintiff is required to prove defendant's sales only, while the defendant must prove all of the elements of cost or deductions claimed.

In assessing damages, the court may enter judgment, according to the circumstances of the case, for any sum in excess of the amount found as actual damages, but not exceeding three times such amount. Since the scope of the statute is very broad, courts have adopted different approaches to computing damages awards and awarding profits. The statute does, however, provide that only in exceptional cases may the court award attorneys' fees, and most courts typically require evidence of the defendant's bad faith to find the requisite exceptional circumstances.

The Anticybersquatting Consumer Protection Act (ACPA) offers additional protection to the owner of a famous or distinctive mark when that mark is used in conjunction with a domain name.[40] In the early days of the domain name "gold rush," people would stake a claim by registering the domain names of famous marks in order to sell them to the proper owner of the mark. Under the ACPA, the owner of a known trade name is entitled to protection against the bad-faith registration or use of a domain name that is identical to, or confusingly similar to, the owner's mark.[41]

Prior to the ACPA, some courts had held that trademark infringement or dilution under the Lanham Act did not include the mere registration of a domain name, because mere registration did not constitute the use of a trade name in commerce.[42] The ACPA, however, makes actionable the registration, trafficking, or use of a domain name that is either identical to or confusingly similar to a trademark that was distinctive or famous at the time the domain name was registered, provided that the defendant has a bad-faith intent to profit from the mark.

The ACPA lists a number of factors that a court may consider in determining whether a "renegade" registrant acted in bad faith, including:

- trademark or rights of the registrant to the domain name;
- use of the domain name by the registrant;
- registrant's intent to divert consumers;
- any offer to sell the domain name; and
- whether the registrant has registered or acquired other domain names incorporating famous or distinctive trademarks.[43]

Federal courts have independent jurisdiction under the ACPA to determine whether a domain name registrant acted in bad faith, even if the registrant previously lost in an arbitration conducted as part of the Uniform Domain Name

---

[39] *Id.* §1117(a). Attorneys' fees may be available in exceptional cases.
[40] *Id.* §1125(d).
[41] *Id.*
[42] *See, e.g.*, Lockheed Martin Corp. v. Network Solutions, Inc., 194 F.3d 980 (9th Cir. 1999); Juno Online Services, L.P. v. June Lighting, Inc., 979 F. Supp. 684 (N.D. Ill. 1997).
[43] 15 U.S.C. §1125(d).

Dispute Resolution of ICANN (the Internet Corporation for Assigned Names and Numbers).[44]

Under the ACPA, the owner of the famous mark can file a civil action in rem against the domain name itself, if the owner is unable to obtain personal jurisdiction over the registrant of the domain name or the registrant cannot be located after the exercise of due diligence.[45] The ACPA authorizes awards of both damages and injunctive relief. Damages may be awarded only for domain names registered after the effective date of the ACPA (November 29, 1999), and damages include, at the election of the plaintiff, either actual damages (including costs and attorneys' fees) or statutory damages of up to $100,000 per domain name. Injunctive relief includes the forfeiture, cancellation, or transfer of the domain name. Finally, the ACPA also provides that the domain name registry may not be held liable for damages or injunctive relief, unless the registry acted in bad faith or with reckless disregard, which includes the willful failure to comply with a court order.[46]

The courts have enforced the ACPA[47] against cybersquatters. One court awarded statutory damages of $50,000 per domain name plus attorneys' fees and costs.[48] Another court refused to dismiss a complaint seeking statutory damages, although the plaintiff failed to allege any actual damages incurred because of the defendant's activities.[49] The lesson here for e-content providers is to avoid the use of a domain name that incorporates another's famous mark, particularly if the provider operates its Web site for profit and the provider intends through the registration and use of the offending domain name to divert consumers to the Web site.

c. Liability for Erroneous Information/Defamation

Unlike pure e-connection providers, which merely offer a conduit for access to content, e-content providers are clearly exposed to potential claims for erroneous information or defamation if they act as the authors or editors of their content. While governed by state law and therefore subject to some variation, the general elements of defamation include (1) a false and defamatory statement, (2) unprivileged publication to a third party, (3) fault on the part of the publisher, and (4) actionability of the statement irrespective of special harm or the existence of special harm caused by the publication.[50] Additionally, numerous lawsuits have been brought against e-content providers pertaining solely to the accuracy of information delivered on the Internet, with varying degrees of success.

Numerous Web sites geared to health topics contain content written by independent authors not employed by the e-content provider. This circumstance

---

[44]Sallen v. Corinthians Licenciamentos LTDA, 273 F.3d 14 (1st Cir. 2001).

[45]Id.

[46]Id.

[47]15 U.S.C. §1125(d).

[48]Pinehurst, Inc. v. Wick, 256 F. Supp. 2d 424 (M.D.N.C. 2003).

[49]FieldTurf, Inc. v. Triexe Mgmt. Group, Inc., 2003 U.S. Dist. LEXIS 22280 (N.D. Ill. Dec. 10, 2003).

[50]Floyd v. WBTW, 2007 U.S. Dist. LEXIS 92482 (S.D. Cal. Dec. 17, 2007).

creates an issue of who, if anyone, is liable if someone reads or makes use of erroneous or incomplete information about a particular health condition on a Web site and is harmed as a result. Cases involving allegedly erroneous medical information published in books and newspapers are especially useful when analyzing potential liability for inaccuracies in content found on an e-content provider's Web site. In these cases, courts generally focus on one of two issues: (1) whether the defendant had a duty to the injured party, or (2) whether the First Amendment shields the defendant from liability.

Generally, publishers will not be held liable for merely disseminating erroneous information, absent malice or bad faith.[51] In a 1981 New York case, the court considered whether a misstatement in a pamphlet on birth control could result in liability for the pamphlet's publisher.[52] In that case, the plaintiff, while considering a tubal ligation, read a booklet published by Planned Parenthood. The booklet stated that contraceptives need not be used after tubal ligation. The plaintiff subsequently became pregnant and sued Planned Parenthood and other defendants. The court recognized that a defendant could be liable where it is "bound by some relational duty arising out of a public calling, contract, or other."[53] The court additionally found, however, that "[o]ne who publishes a text cannot be said to assume liability for all 'misstatements,' said or unsaid, to a potentially unlimited public for a potentially unlimited period."[54] Under the circumstances of the case, the court held that, although the harm suffered by the plaintiff may have been reasonably foreseeable, the defendant owed no duty to the plaintiff that could support a cause of action for negligence.[55]

A 1998 case decided by the U.S. District Court for the District of Maryland considered whether a medical textbook publisher could be held liable in negligence for injuries suffered by a nursing student.[56] The student became ill and treated herself after consulting a medical textbook published by the defendant. She was injured and sued the defendant for negligence, contending that the recommended treatment was in error and that the book contained no warning of the risks or potential consequences.[57] The court found in favor of the defendant, holding that a publisher has no liability for erroneous content, absent evidence that the publisher took responsibility for creation of the content.[58]

Several other courts have been unwilling to extend liability to publishers based on allegedly erroneous content, including, for example, information regarding securities investments,[59] travel conditions,[60] and an attorney's qualifica-

---

[51] *See, e.g.*, Lunney v. Prodigy Servs. Co., 723 N.E.2d 539, 542 (N.Y. 1999).
[52] Roman v. New York City, 442 N.Y.S.2d 945 (N.Y. App. Div. 1981).
[53] *Id.* at 947.
[54] *Id.* at 948.
[55] *Id.* at 947–48.
[56] Jones v. J. B. Lippincott Co., 694 F. Supp. 1216 (D. Md. 1988).
[57] *Id.* at 1216.
[58] *Id.* at 1216–17.
[59] Gutter v. Dow Jones, Inc., 490 N.E.2d 898, 900 (Ohio 1986).
[60] Birmingham v. Fodor's Travel Publ'ns, Inc., 833 P.2d 70 (Hawaii 1992).

tions.[61] In each of these cases, the absence of an owed duty from the publisher to the reader resulted in a finding of no liability.

Courts may not protect a publisher from liability where the publisher undertakes a specific duty to provide a service that is necessary for the protection of a specific person or thing.[62] For example, in a 1994 California case, the court found a nonprofit corporation liable when it published a directory of approved plumbing products, and the plaintiff was damaged by defective pipes that were listed in the directory as approved.[63] The court held that, because the defendant undertook a duty to enforce uniform standards for pipes by delisting or withdrawing certification for nonconforming pipes, the defendant was liable to purchasers injured by the nonconforming pipe.[64]

In defamation cases, the standards for publisher and distributor liability differ from those involving erroneous information.[65] Generally, one who repeats or republishes a libel is subject to liability as if he or she had published the statement originally.[66] In defamation cases, courts use various terms, including "vendors," "publishers," "re-publishers," and "distributors," to describe the entities that transmit defamatory statements. The terms most commonly used are "publishers" and "distributors." A publisher is an entity, such as a newspaper or book publisher, that is responsible for creating or editing content in a publication.[67] Distributors include entities, such as libraries or booksellers, that make publications available to the general public.[68] A plaintiff bringing a defamation suit against a distributor must prove that the defendant was aware of the content of the specific statement that is the subject of the lawsuit.[69] If the defendant is a publisher, the defendant is presumed to have some degree of control over the content of the publication, and the plaintiff need not prove that the publisher was specifically aware of the defamatory utterance.[70] Clearly, an e-content provider acting as a publisher must exercise prudence in reviewing the content it intends to publish, regardless of the source. On the other hand, if the e-content provider is merely acting as a distributor of content created by third parties (e.g., by simply linking to other sites), and exercises no editorial control over such distributed content, the potential for liability for a defamation claim is substantially lessened.

---

[61] Barden v. HarperCollins Publ'ns, Inc., 863 F. Supp. 41, 43–45 (D. Mass. 1994).

[62] Cf. RESTATEMENT (SECOND) OF TORTS §324A (1965):
One who undertakes, gratuitously or for consideration, to render services to another which he should recognize as necessary for the protection of a third person or his things, is subject to liability if his failure to exercise reasonable care increases the risk of harm, if he has undertaken to perform a duty owed by the other to the third person, or if the harm is caused by reliance of the other person upon the undertaking.

[63] FNS Mortg. Serv. Corp. v. Pacific Gen. Group, Inc., 29 Cal. Rptr. 2d 916 (Cal. Ct. App. 1994).

[64] Id. at 916–17.

[65] See II.A., above.

[66] See, e.g., Cianci v. New Times Publ'g Co., 639 F.2d 54, 61 (2d Cir. 1980).

[67] See David R. Sheridan, Zeran v. AOL and the Effect of Section 230 of the Communications Decency Act Upon Liability for Defamation on the Internet, 61 ALB. L. REV. 147 (1997).

[68] Id. at 150.

[69] Id.

[70] Id. at 150, 153.

In *Cubby, Inc. v. CompuServe, Inc.*,[71] a federal district court in New York examined alleged defamatory statements made in a publication carried on CompuServe's computer information service. CompuServe's database included several electronic "bulletin board" forums. One of these contained a daily newsletter, *Rumorville USA* (*Rumorville*), covering topics relating to journalism. The plaintiff, Cubby, Inc., started a competing electronic newsletter called *Skuttlebut*. The plaintiffs claimed that *Rumorville* contained defamatory statements about *Skuttlebut* and sued CompuServe and others for libel, business disparagement, and unfair competition.[72] CompuServe argued that it acted as a distributor, rather than a publisher, of the statements and should not be held liable for statements disseminated without its knowledge.[73] CompuServe asserted that it neither knew nor had reason to know of the statements.[74]

According to the court, interactive computer services and other distributors of information in e-commerce, such as CompuServe,[75] may be compared to libraries, bookstores, and newsstands, which have no editorial control over the content of the materials on their shelves. The court also observed that it is not feasible for such distributors to examine every publication they list.[76] Based on these factors, the court concluded that "[g]iven the relevant First Amendment considerations, the appropriate standard of liability to be applied to CompuServe is whether it knew or had reason to know of the allegedly defamatory Rumorville statements."[77]

For e-content providers that establish a forum for the exchange of information among users, such as support groups for sufferers of particular medical conditions, immunity from liability associated with the users' posted content may be afforded through the Communications Decency Act (CDA).[78] Under the CDA, "[n]o provider or user of an interactive computer service shall be treated as the publisher or speaker of any information provided by another information content provider."[79] Thus, assuming the e-content provider does not edit the information provided by its Web site users, the provider should not face publisher liability.

In *Delfino v. Agilent Technologies, Inc.*,[80] the California Court of Appeal in 2006 affirmed a trial court's decision that the liability protection afforded republishers under the CDA extends protection to employers that provide employees with Internet access against liability for unauthorized statements by employees or others using those computer systems, unless the defendant engaged in cul-

---

[71] 776 F. Supp. 135 (S.D.N.Y. 1991).

[72] *Id.* at 138.

[73] *Id.*

[74] *Id.* at 139.

[75] *Id.* at 140.

[76] *See id.* (CompuServe had "no more editorial control over such a publication than does a public library, book store, or newsstand, and it would be no more feasible for CompuServe to examine every publication it carries for potentially defamatory statements than it would be for a distributor to do so").

[77] *Id.* at 140–41.

[78] 47 U.S.C. §230.

[79] *Id.* §230(c)(1).

[80] 145 Cal. App. 4th 790 (Cal. Ct. App. 2006).

pable conduct with respect to the creation of the misleading or otherwise actionable communication. The court ruled that employers in such circumstances are among the class of parties potentially immune as a provider or user of an interactive computer service and therefore the defendant employer had no liability for intentional infliction of emotional distress and related torts arising from an employee's use of the employer's computer system to send threatening messages over the Internet to the plaintiffs, where the employer did not discover that its system had been used to send the threatening messages until the following year, the employer promptly terminated the employee when it made that discovery, and the content was provided by the employee, not the employer. The court also held that the plaintiffs had failed to make a prima facie showing on their tort claims.

In contrast, however, courts have ruled that republisher immunity does not apply where the publisher is the provider of the defamatory content. While finding an employer protected by republication immunity in *Delfino*, for instance, the California court acknowledged that the employer could have been held vicariously liable for threats made by an employee using the company's e-mail and other communication systems, if the employer knew or should have known he was using its computer to accomplish his cyberthreats and failed to take appropriate measures to prevent and redress the wrongful actions. In this instance, however, the court found no vicarious liability as (1) the court found no business relationship to support the finding that the employer owed a duty to the plaintiffs or that the employee's cyberthreats directed toward the plaintiffs arose out of, or were in any way connected with, his employment; (2) there was no evidence the employer breached any duty of care with respect to the supervision or retention of the employee where it had no knowledge of the content of any of the employee's threatening e-mails or postings before receiving the arrest affidavit; and (3) there was no evidence that the employee in fact used the employer's system after the employer learned of his prior misconduct.[81]

Some courts have held that the First Amendment to the U.S. Constitution protects defendant publishers and authors from negligence claims. Even though the defendants in these cases are private entities, they are able to invoke the First Amendment because suits based on state common law or statutes constitute state action and are therefore subject to free speech limitations.[82] The availability of a First Amendment defense in this context also relies on the rule that constitutional protections extend to speech that is purely commercial in nature.[83]

In a 1991 decision, the U.S. Court of Appeals for the Ninth Circuit concluded that a book publisher had no negligence liability to mushroom enthusiasts who relied on the book and became extremely ill (to the extent that they needed liver transplants) after eating mushrooms that the book had indicated were safe.[84] In support of its decision, the court stated that the First Amendment

---

[81]*Id.*

[82]*See, e.g.*, New York Times v. Sullivan, 376 U.S. 254, 265 (1964).

[83]*See, e.g.*, Lorillard Tobacco Co. v. Reilly, 533 U.S. 525, 121 S. Ct. 2404, 2421 (2001); Virginia State Bd. of Pharmacy v. Virginia Consumer Council, 425 U.S. 748, 761–64 (1976); *see also* South Carolina State Ports Auth. v. Booz-Allen & Hamilton, Inc., 676 F. Supp. 346, 349 (D.D.C. 1987).

[84]Winter v. G.P. Putnam's Sons, 938 F.2d 1033 (9th Cir. 1991).

prevented the extension of liability "to the ideas and expressions contained in a book."[85]

In a 1977 case from the Eastern District of New York, the court held that the publisher of an encyclopedia of chemicals and drugs was not liable in damages for negligently misrepresenting the toxicity of a component of the plaintiff's product.[86] To begin with, the court concluded that the publisher owed no duty to the plaintiff.[87] In addition, the court opined that the publisher's "right to publish free of fear of liability is guaranteed by the First Amendment."[88]

Despite the success of First Amendment and other defenses in protecting e-content providers from liability for erroneous or defamatory information, such providers should nevertheless at all times be cognizant of the status they occupy vis-à-vis the content offered and the manner in which it is delivered. Any time an entity disseminates, or allows the dissemination of, substantial amounts of information, the potential will exist for tort claims based upon that information, and no defense is absolute.

d. Unlicensed/Unauthorized Practice of Medicine

Depending upon the substance and the method of delivery of content, a consumer-oriented e-content provider could be deemed (1) to be engaged in the practice of medicine, (2) to be practicing medicine in multiple jurisdictions, (3) to be establishing a physician-patient relationship with visitors to its Web site, or (4) a combination of (1) through (3). The first two instances pose the risk of practicing medicine without a license or without a valid licensing exception, and the third poses the risk of committing medical malpractice, failing to obtain informed consent, or both.

Chapter 9 outlines in great detail the overall risks to e-health providers arising from the use of telemedicine.[89] The application of these risks to consumer-oriented e-content providers is illustrated through two of the four telemedicine examples used throughout that chapter:

> *Example 2:* A Minnesota-based group of oncologists sets up a Web site that provides information on cancer, including treatment options and side-effects, and a certain feature that permits a Web site visitor to "ask the doctor" questions about cancer.
>
> *Example 4:* A group of psychiatrists in New York City offers "online" psychotherapy to enrollees of a health benefit plan located throughout the United States.

In particular, consumer-oriented e-content providers must discern whether their content delivery constitutes, or could constitute, the practice of medicine.[90]

---

[85] *Id.* at 1036.
[86] Demuth Dev. Corp. v. Merck & Co., 432 F. Supp. 990, 992 (E.D.N.Y. 1977).
[87] *Id.*
[88] *Id.* at 993.
[89] See Chapter 9 (Walker, E-Health Liability). "Telemedicine" is defined therein as "the use of electronic technologies to provide health care at a distance, often across state lines."
[90] In Texas, the "practice of medicine" is defined as
 [t]he diagnosis, treatment, or offer to treat a mental or physical disease or disorder, or a physical deformity or injury by and system or method or the attempt to effect cures of those

This is likely a multijurisdictional inquiry, potentially involving all 50 states as well as international laws and regulations, unless the e-content provider has devised some mechanism that limits content access to visitors from only specified jurisdictions. If it is clear that the content itself or its delivery does not involve the practice of medicine, the provider need not further consider licensing, malpractice, or related issues.

If, on the other hand, there exists a possibility that the e-content provider's offering involves the practice of medicine, then the provider must consider licensing requirements in all jurisdictions in which prospective patients reside. Due to the nascency of the interjurisdictional use of telemedicine techniques, there is an absence of coordination of licensing requirements, and consequently for the time being there is no "safe harbor" method for practicing telemedicine across state lines or international boundaries. Penalties for the unauthorized practice of medicine vary from state to state, but typically include both fines and imprisonment.[91]

If an e-content provider is deemed to be practicing medicine, in addition to licensing requirements, the provider must be conscious of whether its offerings or techniques are such that they create an actual physician-patient relationship with persons accessing the content. The physician-patient relationship arises out of a consensual relationship between the patient and the physician, necessarily requiring that the patient consent to be treated by the physician and that the physician consent to treat the patient. Whether such relationship exists is a fact-specific inquiry. Under the strict definition of consumer-oriented e-content provider used here, wherein the provider avoids direct interaction with content users, the opportunity for establishing a physician-patient relationship seems remote. Nonetheless, because this is an evolving area of law, e-content providers should be cognizant of the potential for the establishment of a physician-patient relationship through their activities. If such a relationship is deemed to exist, an e-content provider may then be subject to a treating professional's duty of care to the patient, as well as the duty to obtain informed consent for any "treatment" delivered through the content.

2. *Provider-Oriented E-Content Providers*

Provider-oriented e-content providers seek to deliver information to health care providers rather than individual consumers. Such businesses offer health care professionals access to up-to-date information on health plan formularies or requirements, drug interaction data, medical research, reference material, and other data. Examples of provider-oriented e-content providers include Modern-

---

conditions by a person who: A. publicly professes to be a physician or surgeon; or B. directly or indirectly, charges money or other compensation for those services.
TEX. OCC. CODE ANN. §151.002(13). In Michigan, it is defined as
the diagnosis, treatment, prevention, cure, or relieving of a human disease, ailment, defect, complaint, or other physical or mental condition, by attendance, advice, device, diagnostic test, or other means, or offering, undertaking, attempting to do, or holding oneself out as able to do, any of these acts.
MICH. COMP. LAWS ANN. §333.17001(1)(f).

[91] In Michigan, the unauthorized practice of law is a felony. MICH. COMP. LAWS ANN. §333.16294.

Healthcare.com, the American Medical Association (AMA), the *New England Journal of Medicine*, the *Journal of Medical Internet Research*, various drugstore and pharmacy chains offering drug interaction information, and iHealthBeat. Additionally, numerous social media sites and smart phone apps have been and continue to be developed by provider-oriented e-content providers.[92] This definition expressly and intentionally excludes individuals or entities transmitting, processing, and storing personally identifiable information, including protected health information; such activities are conducted through individuals or entities belonging to the e-connection, e-care, and electronic health system categories discussed below in II.C., D., and E.

Provider-oriented e-content providers are potentially subject to the risks described in II.A.1.a.–c. above, for the reasons described there. Additionally, these e-content providers may be subject to commercial liability depending upon the terms and conditions under which the content is delivered to the professionals. Chapter 13 on contracting principles provides a detailed examination of e-health contracting issues and related risks.[93] Because of their intended audience, however, provider-oriented e-content providers should not generally face licensure and related malpractice/informed consent issues.

B. E-Product Providers

E-product providers serve not only consumers (as consumer-oriented e-product providers) but also health care providers (e.g., physicians, hospitals, labs, and other care facilities) and businesses that provide their employees with medical benefits (as, collectively, provider/business-oriented e-product providers). The characteristics of the products being sold by e-product providers, the status of the intended customer, and the means by which the products are sold are all relevant and important considerations in understanding and managing the risks applicable to these providers and in the underlying transactions.

1. Consumer-Oriented E-Product Providers

Online or Internet pharmacies are now commonplace, and are often affiliated with well known "bricks-and-mortar" national drugstore and megastore chains.[94] These pharmacies account for a large segment of consumer-oriented e-product providers. Consumer-oriented e-product providers also include online sellers of health and beauty aids and online sellers of unregulated medical supplies.[95]

---

[92] See Medical Smartphones, http://www.medicalsmartphones.com, for a list of apps directed to health care professionals.

[93] See Chapter 13 (Peabody, Contracts in the Digital Age: Adapting to Changing Times).

[94] WalMart, CVS, Walgreens, and SavOn Drugs are among the traditional drugstore chains that operate Internet pharmacies.

[95] Examples include OnlineMedicalSupply.com, U.S. Medical Supplies, and Vitality Medical.

a. E-Prescribing Risks

Although the use of online pharmacies has reached public acceptance and is often an insurance company's preferred method for covering prescription medications, some online pharmacies attempt to use the anonymity of the Internet to elude Food and Drug Administration (FDA) jurisdiction. The Drug Enforcement Administration (DEA) recognizes online pharmacies as a major contributing factor to the high level of prescription drug abuse occurring in the United States.[96] Through online companies engaging in unlawful practices, consumers have purchased prescription drugs without prescriptions, unapproved new drugs, and products labeled with fraudulent health claims. The FDA administers and enforces the federal Food, Drug, and Cosmetic Act (FDCA) and has initiated civil and criminal enforcement actions against Internet pharmacies and other persons based on sales of unapproved new drugs, the dispensing of prescription drugs without a valid prescription, and other online drug sales and marketing activities that violate the FDCA. Other federal laws and regulations governing Internet pharmacy operations are the Controlled Substances Act, the Federal Trade Commission Act, and U.S. Postal Service regulations.[97]

The principal types of unlawful conduct involving Internet drug sales that the FDA has identified are as follows:

- the importation, sale, or distribution of an adulterated or misbranded drug;
- the importation, sale, or distribution of an unapproved new drug;
- illegal promotion of a drug;
- the sale or dispensing of a prescription drug without a valid prescription; and
- counterfeit drugs.[98]

The FDA has focused its online drug sales–related enforcement activities on unapproved new drugs, health fraud, and prescription drugs sold without a valid prescription, particularly where there is a significant public health risk.[99] A "significant public health risk" generally exists, in the FDA's view, when a consumer is at risk for harm from the use of the product as the result of not taking approved drugs for a specific disease or condition or of delaying medical treatment recognized as safe and effective for a specific disease or condition.[100] Purchasing prescription drugs on the Internet from unscrupulous sellers who bypass the prescription drug regulatory system often creates a public health risk.

The FDA also is concerned about the use of online questionnaires by nontraditional Internet pharmacies:

---

[96] Implementation of the Ryan Haight Online Pharmacy Consumer Protection Act of 2008; Final Rule, 74 Fed. Reg. 15,597 (Apr. 6, 2009).

[97] See Chapter 10 (Haas & Greig, FDA Regulation of E-Health Technology and Services), at IV., for a detailed discussion of federal regulation of telemedicine.

[98] Testimony of former FDA Commissioner Dr. Jane Henney before the Senate Committee on Health, Education, Labor, and Pensions (Mar. 2000), *available at* http://www.fda.gov/News-Events/Testimony/ucm114957.htm.

[99] *Id.*

[100] *Id.*

FDA believes that the selection of prescription drug products or treatment regimens for a particular patient should be made with the advice of a licensed health care practitioner familiar with the patient's current health status and past medical history. In situations where a customary physician-patient relationship does not exist, the patient is essentially practicing self-diagnosis. Consequently, the risk of negative outcomes such as harmful drug interactions, contraindications, allergic reactions or improper dosing is greatly magnified.[101]

The FDA's enforcement activity against Internet pharmacies, online drug sales sites, and affiliated persons has ranged from consumer education efforts to criminal convictions.[102] Judicial enforcement actions are filed at the FDA's recommendation by the Department of Justice. Federal district courts have jurisdiction to enjoin activities that violate the FDCA's prohibitions on misbranding, adulteration, or counterfeiting,[103] and any drug that is misbranded or adulterated is subject to seizure.[104] Activities such as misbranding, adulteration, or counterfeiting also can result in civil and criminal penalties.[105]

A form of strict liability applies to criminal violations of the FDCA. Under the so-called *Park* doctrine, an individual can be criminally liable for violations of the FDCA without having actual knowledge of the violation and without having an intent to violate the law.[106] Specifically, an individual who has a responsible relationship to the violations—such as an officer of a corporation—may be prosecuted for failure to detect, prevent, or correct the violations.[107]

On August 24, 2011, the FDA announced that it had reached a $500 million settlement with Google in conjunction with a criminal investigation associated with Google's receipt of advertising revenue from online Canadian pharmacies.[108] Commenting on the settlement, the acting head of the FDA's Office of Criminal Investigations stated that "[t]oday's agreement demonstrates the commitment of the Food and Drug Administration to protect the US consumer and hold all contributing parties accountable for conduct that results in vast profits at the expense of the public health."[109]

The National Association of Boards of Pharmacy (NABP) has developed the Verified Internet Pharmacy Practice Sites (VIPPS) program to certify online pharmacies that have complied with the licensing and inspection requirements of their states and the states to which they dispense pharmaceuticals. In addition, pharmacies displaying the VIPPS seal have demonstrated to NABP their compliance with VIPPS criteria, including patient rights to privacy, authentica-

---

[101] *Id.*

[102] See generally the FDA Web site, http://www.fda.gov, for information regarding enforcement activities. Information on criminal investigations is available at http://www.fda.gov/ICECI/CriminalInvestigations/default.htm.

[103] 21 U.S.C. §332(a) (2006).

[104] *Id.* §334.

[105] *Id.* §333.

[106] PETER BARTON HUTT ET AL., FOOD AND DRUG LAW 307–308 (Foundation Press 3d ed. 2007). The doctrine of strict liability under the FDCA originated in *United States v. Dotterweich*, 320 U.S. 277 (1943), and was reaffirmed in *United States v. Park*, 421 U.S. 658 (1975).

[107] *See* FOOD AND DRUG LAW, at 308 (discussing *Dotterweich* and *Park* cases).

[108] *See* http://www.fda.gov/ICECI/CriminalInvestigations/ucm271207.htm.

[109] *Id.*

tion, and security of prescription orders; adherence to a recognized quality assurance policy; and provision of meaningful consultation between patients and pharmacists.[110]

An Internet pharmacy, like any other type of pharmacy, must also comply with state pharmacy laws, including licensure and registration requirements. Every state has a board of pharmacy or equivalent state board or agency that regulates the practice of pharmacy in the state. The board of pharmacy administers and enforces the state pharmacy law and, in some states, the state controlled substances act and related laws.[111] Pharmacies and pharmacists must comply with their state's regulations governing the issuance, dispensing, and refilling of prescriptions in addition to complying with federal regulations.

Pharmacists who violate state licensure laws or controlled substances laws are subject to discipline through license revocation proceedings.[112] Violations of the pharmacist licensure requirement and other provisions of state pharmacy law by any person typically are punishable as criminal offenses.[113]

Each state requires a person to be licensed by the state board of pharmacy to operate or "conduct" a pharmacy in the state.[114] In many states, a "pharmacy" is defined as a physical location, not a business or activity. For example, the California Pharmacy Act provides:

> "Pharmacy" means an area, place, or premises licensed by the board in which the profession of pharmacy is practiced and where prescriptions are compounded. "Pharmacy" includes, but is not limited to, any area, place, or premises described in a license issued by the board wherein controlled substances, dangerous drugs, or dangerous devices are stored, possessed, prepared, manufactured, derived, compounded, or repackaged, and from which the controlled substances, dangerous drugs, or dangerous devices are furnished, sold, or dispensed at retail.[115]

Most states already have an answer to the question of where an Internet pharmacy must be licensed or registered. Long before states faced the problems of regulating Internet pharmacies, they had to address the phenomenon of out-of-state mail-order pharmacies. As a result, the pharmacy laws in most states expressly require nonresident, or out-of-state, pharmacies to be licensed or registered with the state into which drugs are being dispensed, and in most of these states, there is a separate licensure category for this type of pharmacy. Michigan law prohibits a pharmacist from dispensing a prescription by mail

---

[110]Dep't of Health & Human Servs., Food & Drug Admin., Buying Prescription Medicine Online: A Consumer Safety Guide (Mar. 30, 2010), *available at* http://www.fda.gov/Drugs/ResourcesForYou/ucm080588.htm; National Association of Boards of Pharmacy, VIPPS, *available at* http://www.nabp.net/vipps/intro.asp.

[111]*See* NATIONAL ASS'N OF BDS. OF PHARMACY, 2011 SURVEY OF PHARMACY LAW (2011), *available for purchase at* http://www.nabp.net/index.asp [hereinafter NABP SURVEY] (listing names of designated pharmacy board or agency in each state); *see also, e.g.*, CAL. BUS. & PROF. CODE §4001 (West 1990) (creating Cal. Bd. of Pharmacy within Dep't of Consumer Affairs); CAL. BUS. & PROF. CODE §4011 (authorizing Bd. of Pharmacy to administer and enforce the California Pharmacy Law and Uniform Controlled Substances Act).

[112]NABP SURVEY at 32–33.

[113]*See, e.g.*, CAL. BUS. & PROF. CODE §§4320–4344 (establishing civil and criminal penalties for violations of state pharmacy law).

[114]*See, e.g., id.* §4110(a).

[115]*Id.* §4037(a).

when the original prescription was received by mail.[116] Pharmacies and other persons involved in Internet drug sales that ship drugs into a state without a license have been the subject of state enforcement actions for violations of state pharmacy laws.[117]

Many states, along with the AMA and the Federation of State Medical Boards (FSMB), have taken the position that a physician who issues a prescription without conducting a physical examination of the patient is, in most instances, committing unprofessional conduct and violating state medical practice laws.[118] The AMA Guidelines provide as follows:

> Physicians who prescribe medications via the Internet shall establish, or have established, a valid patient-physician relationship, including, but not limited to, the following components. The physician shall: (i) obtain a reliable medical history and perform a physical examination of the patient, adequate to establish the diagnosis for which the drug is being prescribed and to identify underlying conditions and/or contraindications to the treatment recommended/provided; (ii) have sufficient dialogue with the patient regarding treatment options and the risks and benefits of treatment(s); (iii) as appropriate, follow up with the patient to assess the therapeutic outcome; (iv) maintain a contemporaneous medical record that is readily available to the patient and, subject to the patient's consent, to his or her other health care professionals; and (v) include the electronic prescription information as part of the patient medical record. Exceptions to the above criteria exist in the following specific instances: treatment provided in consultation with another physician who has an ongoing professional relationship with the patient, and who has agreed to supervise the patient's treatment, including use of any prescribed medications; and on-call or cross-coverage situations.[119]

The prescribing authority of physicians and other health care providers is governed by state law, not federal law. The source of prescribing authority for physicians typically is the state medical practice act. The medical practice act generally is enforced by a state medical board, which has the authority to license physicians and grant prescribing privileges. State medical boards generally have the power to investigate complaints against physicians and other licensees and to impose sanctions for violations of the state medical practice laws.

Finally, an Internet pharmacy operator could potentially face negligence or other state law tort claims in the event of an error in delivery of the type or quantity of prescribed medication.

b. Privacy and Data Security Issues—Excluding HIPAA

Like all vendors of goods over the Internet, consumer-oriented e-product providers have risks associated with the information obtained in conjunction with each transaction. While the HIPAA Privacy Rule and Security Rule, which

---

[116]*See id.* at 45, 47.

[117]*See State Boards of Pharmacy Take Action to Stop Licensees Involved in Unlawful Internet Drug Outlet Schemes,* NABP NEWSLETTER (Dec. 10, 2010), *available at* http://www.nabp.net/news/state-boards-of-pharmacy-take-action-to-stop-licensees-involved-in-unlawful-internet-drug-outlet-sch/.

[118]FSMB, Model Guidelines for the Appropriate Use of the Internet in Medical Practice (Apr. 2002); AMA Policy H-120.949, Guidance for Physicians on Internet Prescribing (2003).

[119]*Guidance for Physicians on Internet Prescribing.*

are discussed in II.E.1., below, and covered in detail in Chapters 5, 7, and 8, may also apply to such transactions, the discussion here is limited to other privacy and data security laws potentially applicable to consumer-oriented e-product providers.

Assuming an e-product provider accepts credit card payments and billing information, that provider will necessarily be collecting "personally identifiable information" (PII)[120] of its customers. This, in turn, implicates the application of more than 40 states' data breach notification statutes,[121] the Payment Card Industry Data Security Standard (PCI DSS),[122] and Federal Trade Commission oversight under Section 5 of the FTC Act[123] and the recently effective Red Flags Rule.[124] There is no existing federal law generally covering consumer data breach notification requirements, although many bills have been introduced on this topic over the last several years.

i. State Data Breach Notification Statutes

The various state data breach notification laws pose significant compliance problems for businesses receiving PII from multiple jurisdictions. Although there are significant commonalities among these laws, there also exist some material distinctions respecting notification requirements.[125] Consequently, an affected e-product provider may not adopt a "one-size-fits-all" strategy for responding to a covered data breach. For example, several states mandate notification to their attorneys general (AGs) *prior to* notifying affected individuals.[126] Thus, if a breach involves PII from individuals in 10 different states, and any one of them requires prior notice to an AG's office, the e-product provider must tailor its response strategy to ensure that this requirement is met. The risks deriving from noncompliance with the various breach notification statutes include civil penalties[127] and private actions brought by affected individuals.[128]

ii. PCI Data Security Standard

The Payment Card Industry Data Security Standard is a private standard established by the PCI Security Standards Council (PCI Council). According to their Web site:

---

[120] Depending on the statute, PII is sometimes called "individually identifiable information." Generally, PII consists of a person's last name, first name or initial, and any of the following additional information: (1) Social Security number, (2) driver's license or identification card number, or (3) financial institution information (e.g., credit card number).

[121] As of 2011, 46 states have enacted data breach notification statutes.

[122] *See* PCI SECURITY STANDARDS COUNCIL, www.pcisecuritystandards.org.

[123] 15 U.S.C. §§41–58.

[124] 16 C.F.R. §681.1.

[125] Chapter 11 of this book provides a detailed analysis of the various state data breach notification laws.

[126] *See, e.g.*, MD. CODE ANN. COM. LAW §14-3504(h) ("Prior to giving the notification required under subsection (b) of this section and subject to subsection (d) of this section, a business shall provide notice of a breach of the security of a system to the Office of the Attorney General.").

[127] *See, e.g.*, MICH. COMP. LAWS ANN. §445.72 ($250 per failure to notify, maximum $750,000); OHIO REV. CODE §1349.19 ($1,000 to $10,000 per day following expiration of 45-day notice period).

[128] *See, e.g.*, CAL. CIV. CODE §1798.82.

The PCI Council is an open global forum, launched in 2006, that is responsible for the development, management, education, and awareness of the PCI Security Standards, including the Data Security Standard (PCI DSS), Payment Application Data Security Standard (PA-DSS), and PIN Transaction Security (PTS) requirements.

The Council's five founding global payment brands—American Express, Discover Financial Services, JCB International, MasterCard Worldwide, and Visa Inc.—have agreed to incorporate the PCI DSS as the technical requirements of each of their data security compliance programs. Each founding member also recognizes the QSAs, PA-QSAs and ASVs certified by the PCI Security Standards Council.

All five payment brands share equally in the Council's governance, have equal input into the PCI Security Standards Council and share responsibility for carrying out the work of the organization. Other industry stakeholders are encouraged to join the Council as Participating Organizations and review proposed additions or modifications to the standards.[129]

An e-commerce vendor's compliance obligation under PCI DSS is contractual, arising through merchant agreements entered into with banks authorized to process transactions under the referenced payment brands. Thus, a consumer-oriented e-product provider must be cognizant of its obligations under these agreements, including the requirements for achieving and maintaining PCI DSS compliance and the penalties and liabilities that may arise from breaching the contractual obligations. The risk of PCI DSS noncompliance is at least in part derivative of the payment brands' right, at their discretion, to fine an acquiring bank $5,000 to $100,000 per month for PCI DSS compliance violations. Merchant agreements typically pass this fine on to the merchant, in this case the e-product provider. Additionally, the bank may elect to either increase its transaction fees or terminate the merchant agreement in the event of PCI DSS noncompliance.

iii. Federal Trade Commission Section 5 Actions

The Federal Trade Commission (FTC) is the federal agency charged with protecting consumers. The FTC's mission is to promote the efficient functioning of the marketplace by protecting consumers from unfair or deceptive acts or practices and to increase consumer choice by promoting vigorous competition.[130] The FTC's primary authority over the collection, use, and disclosure of personal data collected online is derived from the FTC Act[131] and the Children's Online Privacy Protection Act of 1998 (COPPA).[132]

Under Section 5 of the FTC Act, the FTC has the authority to prevent unfair or deceptive acts or practices in or affecting commerce.[133] With the exception of certain industries and activities, the FTC Act gives the FTC broad

---

[129] *See* http://www.pcisecuritystandards.org/organization_info/index.php.

[130] Online Profiling: Benefits and Concerns: Before the Senate Committee on Commerce, Science, and Transportation, 106th Cong. (2000) (statement of Jodie Bernstein, Director, Bureau of Consumer Protection, Federal Trade Comm'n), *available at* http://www.ftc.gov/os/2000/06/onlineprofile.htm.

[131] 15 U.S.C. §§41 *et seq.*

[132] *Id.* §§6501 *et seq.*

[133] *Id.* §45(a)(2).

investigative and law enforcement authority over entities engaged in or whose business affects commerce, including commerce on the Internet.[134] Such authority, however, does not include criminal law enforcement authority.

In an online setting, the FTC Act has been interpreted to prohibit violations of privacy policies and policies that are deceptive, such as those that purport to offer more protection than they actually provide. The FTC Act does not require entities to establish privacy policies or to take any action to protect consumers; rather, it punishes entities that choose to establish such policies and then do not follow them, as well as those entities that have policies containing deceptive information. In addition, the FTC has indicated that Web site operators may also be liable for the actions of operators of other Web sites to which they provide a hyperlink.[135]

The FTC's first Internet-privacy case involved GeoCities, a virtual community of consumer home pages where computer users in different locations could interact online. The FTC alleged that GeoCities violated the FTC Act by misrepresenting the purposes for which it was collecting personal identifying information through its online membership application form and registration forms. GeoCities stated that it would not disclose membership information without member consent when, in fact, it marketed and sold such information.[136]

The FTC and GeoCities entered into a consent order in February 1999 that settled the case. Although GeoCities does not admit to or agree with the FTC's allegations, the consent order contains a number of guidelines providing insight into the FTC's evaluation of online privacy practices under the FTC Act.[137] Since its settlement with GeoCities, the FTC has acted against a number of other Web site operators, focusing on alleged misrepresentations regarding data collection and use policies or other unfair trade practices.[138]

The FTC has also used Section 5 to pursue actions related to unauthorized access to credit card data. In perhaps the best-known data security breach case, the FTC brought proceedings against TJX Companies, Inc., a holding company that owns many retailing companies (including T.J. Maxx and Marshalls), in connection with the theft of tens of millions of credit and debit payment card numbers used at TJX's stores, as well as the personal information of approximately 455,000 consumers who returned merchandise to the stores. TJX also faced lawsuits from a group of state attorneys general, Visa and MasterCard,

---

[134]Certain air carriers, banks, savings and loan associations, credit unions, and common carriers, as well as entities in the business of insurance, are wholly or partially exempt from FTC jurisdiction. 15 U.S.C. §§45(a)(2), 46(a), 1012(b).

[135]*Five Agencies Zoom In On Web Healthcare,* JENKS HEALTHCARE BUS. REP. ¶19 (Apr. 9, 2000), *available at* http://hin.largo.apdi.net/_largomain/largomain.asp (site requires password).

[136]*In re* GeoCities, No. C-3849, 1999 FTC LEXIS 17 (FTC Feb. 5, 1999) (consent order), *available at* http://www.ftc.gov/os/1999/9902/9823015.do.htm.

[137]*Id.*

[138]*In re* Liberty Fin. Cos., Inc., No. C-3891 (FTC Aug. 12, 1999) (consent order), *available at* http://www.ftc.gov/os/1999/9905/lbtyord.htm (alleging that the Web site falsely represented that personal information collected from children, including information about family finances, would be maintained anonymously); FTC v. ReverseAuction.com, Inc., No. 000032 (D.D.C. Jan 6, 2000) (stipulated consent order), *available at* http://www.ftc.gov/os/2000/01/reverseconsent. htm (alleging that the Web site violated consumers' privacy by obtaining consumers' personal information from a competitor's site and then sending deceptive spam to those consumers soliciting their business).

and a class action brought by banks claiming that tens of millions of dollars in fraudulent charges had been made on the affected cards, and that millions of cards had been canceled and reissued.

In 2009, TJX settled virtually all of the pending matters. The FTC entered into a consent order obligating TJX to establish and maintain a comprehensive security program reasonably designed to protect the security, confidentiality, and integrity of personal information it collects from or about consumers. The program must contain administrative, technical, and physical safeguards appropriate to each TJX company's size, the nature of its activities, and the sensitivity of the personal information it collects, and TJX must retain independent, third-party security auditors to assess their security programs on a biennial basis for the next 20 years. The settlement also contains bookkeeping and record-keeping provisions to allow the FTC to monitor compliance with the order.

On perhaps the more painful side, TJX paid Visa $40.9 million, MasterCard $24 million, the state attorneys general $9.75 million, and the banks in the class action approximately $500,000 to settle all claims. In the end, the case represented a $75 million lesson in the importance of maintaining data security.

iv. The Red Flags Rule

In November of 2007 the FTC and five other federal agencies jointly issued final regulations under the Fair and Accurate Credit Transactions Act (FACTA).[139] These regulations, known collectively as the "Red Flags Rule," impose requirements for the identification of patterns, practices, and specific forms of activity that indicate the possible existence of identity theft. The Red Flags Rule mandates the adoption of a written program that identifies relevant warning signs—"red flags"—of identity theft. Examples include unusual account activity, fraud alerts on a consumer report, or attempted use of suspicious account-related documents. The FTC began enforcing the Red Flags Rule on January 1, 2011.

The rule covers financial institutions and creditors that offer or maintain covered accounts. The term "account" is defined in the Red Flags Rule as "a continuing relationship established by a person with a financial institution or creditor to obtain a product or service for personal, family, household, or business purposes."[140] The definition of "covered account" is divided into two parts. The first part refers to "an account that a financial institution or creditor offers or maintains, primarily for personal, family, or household purposes that involves or is designed to permit multiple payments or transactions."[141] An account that meets this part of the definition is always a covered account. A "creditor" is defined as someone who regularly, and in the ordinary course of business, meets one of three general criteria. They must:

---

[139] Identity Theft Red Flags and Address Discrepancies Under the Fair and Accurate Credit Transactions Act of 2003, 72 Fed. Reg. 63,718 (Nov. 9, 2007) (to be codified at 12 C.F.R. pts. 41, 222, 334, 364, 571, 681 and 16 C.F.R. pt. 681).

[140] 16 C.F.R. §681.1(b)(1).

[141] 16 C.F.R. §681.1(b)(3).

- obtain or use consumer reports in connection with a credit transaction;
- furnish information to consumer reporting agencies in connection with a credit transaction; or
- advance funds to—or on behalf of—someone, except for funds for expenses incidental to a service provided by the creditor to that person.[142]

Through an amendment to the Fair Credit Reporting Act adopted in December of 2010, Congress made clear that the Red Flags Rule does not apply to service providers, including health care providers.[143] Depending on the mechanics of their business, however, consumer-oriented e-product providers may be covered by the Red Flags Rule through an ongoing business relationship with their customers, involving the extension of credit by the provider to their customers. This may have particular application to medical equipment vendors.

A Red Flags program must also set forth response mechanisms to mitigate damage in the event that fraudulent activity is uncovered and a process for improving internal controls to prevent recurrence of such activity. Finally, a compliance program must be managed by the entity's board of directors or senior management, must include appropriate staff training, and must provide for appropriate oversight of third-party service providers.

Noncompliance can result in civil money penalties up to $3,500 per violation, injunctions, regulatory enforcement actions, and, frankly, bad publicity.[144]

2. Provider/Business-Oriented E-Product Providers

a. Employee Access to Health Insurance Accounts

Some health benefits providers offer their customers (i.e., employers that provide health insurance and related benefits to their employees) an e-product that enables the employee beneficiary to directly access his or her health benefits account. Depending on the structure of the product (and especially any data capture from the accessing employee), the e-product provider may be exposed to privacy and data security risks associated with the employee data residing in the account. These risks include those described in II.B.1.b.i. and II.B.1.b.iii., above (state data breach notification laws and FTC Section 5 enforcement actions), as well as those associated with HIPAA and the HITECH Act, discussed in II.E.1., below.

---

[142] 16 C.F.R. §681.1(b)(4).

[143] Red Flag Program Clarification Act of 2010, Pub. L. No. 111-319, 124 Stat. 3457 (to be codified at 15 U.S.C. §1681m(e)(4)).

[144] 16 C.F.R. §1.98(m). The FTC has posted information about the Red Flags Rule:
The FTC can seek both monetary civil penalties and injunctive relief for violations of the Red Flags Rule. Where the complaint seeks civil penalties, the U.S. Department of Justice typically files the lawsuit in federal court, on behalf of the FTC. Currently, the law sets $3,500 as the maximum civil penalty per violation. Each instance in which the company has violated the Rule is a separate violation. Injunctive relief in cases like this often requires the parties being sued to comply with the law in the future, as well as provide reports, retain documents, and take other steps to ensure compliance with both the Rule and the court order. Failure to comply with the court order could subject the parties to further penalties and injunctive relief.
Federal Trade Comm'n, Red Flags Rule Compliance and Enforcement, *available at* http://www.ftc.gov/bcp/edu/microsites/redflagsrule/faqs.shtm#E.

b. Provider Publication Tools

Certain e-products enable medical professionals to electronically disseminate information about their practices and to generate online forms for completion prior to a patient visit. While the use of these tools poses certain risks to the e-care provider (discussed in II.C., below), the e-product provider must understand risks associated with the performance of the tool (contract and warranty claims, principally), including outcomes from the use of the tool, and mitigate such risks.

C. E-Connection Providers

Many, if not most, e-connection providers act as mere conduits for the businesses of e-content, e-product, e-care, and EHR system providers. Paradoxically, however, this seemingly passive status makes it feasible for an e-connection provider to face nearly all of the risks faced by each of the other e-provider categories—after all, the business conducted by the e-providers relies entirely on the availability of the e-connection. Of course, this analysis is definitionally dependent: the more "involved" an e-connection provider becomes in its support of another provider (e.g., through manipulation of data or information), the closer it moves from being a "pure" e-connection provider to becoming an e-product provider or an EHR system provider. For purposes of this discussion, then, an e-connection provider simply offers the means of communication and does not provide any other service associated with or otherwise ancillary to that means of communication.[145] The present risks to such e-connection providers are therefore limited to *how* information is transmitted and do not concern *what* information is transmitted.

1. Unauthorized Use of Copyrighted Material

Generally, through the application of the Online Copyright Infringement Liability Limitation Act (OCILLA),[146] e-connection providers are not liable for unauthorized use of published material that is distributed via their connection.[147] Because, however, this is a dynamic area of the law, e-connection providers must use vigilance in keeping attuned to new developments in this area. Moreover, OCILLA's provisions are somewhat complex and require proper application in order to attain the safe harbors provided under the law.

Under OCILLA, an e-connection provider cannot be found liable for copyright infringement by reason of the storage at the direction of a user of material that resides on a system or network controlled or operated by or for the service provider, if the provider:

---

[145] The definition of "service provider" from OCILLA, discussed in II.C.1., immediately below, is instructive: "an entity offering the transmission, routing, or providing of connections for digital online communications, between or among points specified by a user, of material of the user's choosing, without modification to the content of the material as sent or received."

[146] 17 U.S.C. §512.

[147] *Id.*

(A) (i) does not have actual knowledge that the material or an activity using the material on the system or network is infringing;
   (ii) in the absence of such actual knowledge, is not aware of facts or circumstances from which infringing activity is apparent; or
   (iii) upon obtaining such knowledge or awareness, acts expeditiously to remove, or disable access to, the material;
(B) does not receive a financial benefit directly attributable to the infringing activity, in a case in which the service provider has the right and ability to control such activity; and
(C) upon notification of claimed infringement as described in paragraph (3), responds expeditiously to remove, or disable access to, the material that is claimed to be infringing or to be the subject of infringing activity.[148]

Additionally, and subject to similar conditions as those pertaining to storage of material described above, an e-connection provider is not liable for copyright infringement due to "transmitting, routing, or providing connections for, material through a system or network controlled or operated by or for the service provider, or by reason of the intermediate and transient storage of that material in the course of such transmitting, routing, or providing connections"[149] or "the intermediate and temporary storage of material on a system or network controlled or operated by or for the service provider."[150] Thus, an e-connection provider may cache content without facing infringement liability, provided that it meets the conditions set forth in OCILLA.

This immunity from liability does not mean that e-connection providers have no duty respecting the transmission or storage of copyrighted material through their service. In addition to the express conditions for immunity, OCILLA imposes affirmation obligations on e-connection providers respecting the removal of infringing material identified as accessible through their service. These "take-down" procedures are discussed in III.A.3., below.

2. Unauthorized Use of Trademark/Service Mark

As with e-content providers, an e-connection provider may publish third-party trademarks, service marks, or logos in conjunction with its provision of services and without considering its right (or lack thereof) to do so. Again, unfamiliarity with the law or poor editorial control, or both, can result in a trademark infringement claim under federal or state law or a trademark dilution claim for a famous mark under the Federal Trademark Dilution Act. See detailed discussion in II.A.1.b., above.

3. Infringement of Proprietary Rights in Technology

Given the limited scope of an e-connection provider's services, the risk of infringing a third party's proprietary rights in technology is limited. There is a possibility that an e-connection provider's services, and particularly its method of operation or the business method underlying the service, might infringe a

---

[148] 17 U.S.C. §512(c).
[149] Id. §512(a).
[150] Id. §512(b).

third party's patent rights. This is discussed in detail in II.E., below, respecting EHR system providers, where the risk is more evident.

4. Privacy and Data Security

As defined in this discussion, an e-connection provider would not undertake actions that would expose it to responsibility or liability under the various privacy and data security laws and regulations. The state data breach notification laws discussed in II.B.1.b.i., above, generally apply to an individual or entity who "owns or licenses data that are included in a database," which is not the case with entities engaged solely in the transmission, routing, or providing of connections for users of the Internet. Additionally, such providers do not meet the definition of "covered entity" or "business associate" germane to HIPAA/HITECH, discussed in II.E.1., below, and in particular are not equivalent to a health information exchange.

It is worth noting that proposed federal legislation would require e-connection providers to retain electronic data, specifically "the temporarily assigned network addresses the service assigns to each account," for a minimum of 18 months.[151] The proposed legislation does not contain mandates regarding the protection of such data, merely stating that "[i]t is the sense of Congress that records retained pursuant to section 2703(h) of title 18, United States Code, should be stored securely to protect customer privacy and prevent against breaches of the records."[152]

5. Liability for Erroneous Information/Defamation

Section 230(c)(1) of the Communications Decency Act[153] confers broad immunity to interactive computer service providers, providing that "no provider or user of an interactive computer service shall be treated as the publisher or speaker of any information provided by another information content provider." There are three essential elements that a defendant must establish in order to claim Section 230 immunity: (1) the defendant is a provider or user of an interactive computer service, (2) the cause of action treats the defendant as a publisher or speaker of information, and (3) the information at issue is provided by another information content provider.

Courts have ruled that Section 230 bars claims against Internet service providers for republication in a wide range of contexts. In *Carafano v. Metrosplash.com*,[154] the U.S. Court of Appeals for the Ninth Circuit upheld immunity for an Internet dating service provider from liability stemming from a third party's submission of a false profile. The plaintiff, Carafano, claimed the false profile defamed her, but because the content was created by a third party, the court held the Web site was immune, even though it had provided multiple choice selections to aid profile creation.

---

[151] Protecting Children From Internet Pornographers Act of 2011, H.R. 1981, 112th Cong. (2011).
[152] *Id.*
[153] 47 U.S.C. §230(c)(1).
[154] 339 F.3d 1119 (9th Cir. 2003).

In another 2003 case, *Batzel v. Smith*,[155] the Ninth Circuit upheld immunity for a Web site operator for distributing an e-mail to a listserv where the plaintiff claimed the e-mail was defamatory. Though there was a question as to whether the information provider intended to send the e-mail to the listserv, the court decided that for determining the liability of the service provider, "the focus should be not on the information provider's intentions or knowledge when transmitting content but, instead, on the service provider's or user's reasonable perception of those intentions or knowledge." The court found immunity proper "under circumstances in which a reasonable person in the position of the service provider or user would conclude that the information was provided for publication on the Internet or other 'interactive computer service.'"

In *Green v. AOL*,[156] the Third Circuit court of appeals upheld immunity for AOL against allegations of negligence. Green claimed AOL failed to adequately police its services and allowed third parties to defame him and inflict intentional emotional distress. The court rejected these arguments, because holding AOL negligent in promulgating harmful content would be equivalent to holding AOL "liable for decisions relating to the monitoring, screening, and deletion of content from its network—actions quintessentially related to a publisher's role."

D. E-Care Providers

E-care providers deliver electronic means for health care professionals to provide care to their patients. Telemedicine, in which a physician or other health care professional uses electronic means to interact with a patient or to review data or images, allows the professional to remotely monitor a patient or make a diagnosis or treatment decision. With the expansion of communication capabilities built into medical devices, coupled with the increase in wireless networks, telemedicine has become a mainstream issue rather than a hypothetical exercise.

E-care providers face several risks and must recognize (1) privileging and credentialing issues posed to adopters of telemedicine technology, (2) potential for malpractice claims being brought as a result of a telemedicine-based consultation, (3) potential responsibility and liability associated with the performance of the telemedicine technology itself, (4) issues pertaining to the security of the information and data transmitted through the use of telemedicine devices, and (5) FDA regulation of telemedicine devices.

1. Unlicensed/Unauthorized Practice of Medicine

While the discussion in II.A.1.d. is germane to e-care providers, the principal concern raised by the use of telemedicine devices is jurisdictional, and centers on privileging and credentialing issues. Suffice it to say that e-care providers must have a thorough knowledge of the various state laws and regulations

---

[155] 333 F.3d 1018 (9th Cir. 2003).
[156] 318 F.3d 465 (3d Cir. 2003).

pertaining to the practice of telemedicine or assume the risk of being charged with practicing medicine without a license.[157]

On May 5, 2011, CMS released a final rule easing certain requirements for telemedicine credentialing (the "Final Rule").[158] The Final Rule became effective on July 4, 2011. The Final Rule permits hospitals and critical access hospitals to implement proxy credentialing with Medicare-certified hospitals as well as other telemedicine entities regardless of whether they are a Medicare-certified hospital.

2. Malpractice

The risks to e-care providers include the potential establishment of a physician-patient relationship between the patient and the remote consulting physician. The more direct the contact between the e-care provider and the patient, the more likely under the various state laws that a physician-patient relationship may be established, together with a concomitant duty of care to the patient.[159]

E-care providers should note that malpractice insurance coverage for telemedicine encounters involving direct care of patients may not exist if the claim is brought where the patient resides. Most medical malpractice insurance covers only "face to face" encounters within the state in which the doctor practices and is licensed. Consequently, doctors who provide telemedicine services to patients outside of the state in which they are licensed can be exposed to uninsured claims if state law requires the physician to be licensed in the state where the test results are delivered. Some states, however, protect e-care providers by requiring insurers to cover claims against the providers involving an out-of-state patient. Obligations of malpractice insurance carriers must be examined on a state-by-state basis. Insurance underwriters are also offering separate policies for clinicians who provide interpretive telemedicine services, such as teleradiology.

3. Technology Performance Issues

E-care providers that supply telemedicine technology must, like any equipment or software provider, be aware of the commercial and tort-based risks associated with the sale and use of such products. E-care providers of telemedicine technology should be particularly sensitive to the intended use of the device or service, recognizing that depending on the circumstances, a failure of the device could result not only in claims for money damages but also in personal injury or wrongful death claims. This in turn raises issues concerning product liability insurance coverage for the e-care provider and the relevant device. A

---

[157] See Chapter 9 (Walker, E-Health Liability) at III for a detailed discussion of telemedicine privileging and credentialing issues.

[158] Medicare and Medicaid Programs: Changes Affecting Hospital and Critical Access Hospital Conditions of Participation: Telemedicine Credentialing and Privileging, 76 Fed. Reg. 25,550 (May 5, 2011) (codified at 42 C.F.R. pts. 482, 485).

[159] A lawyer speaking at the University of Maryland School of Law stated that "[t]o date, very few telemedicine malpractice cases [exist] (of those cases, most relate to internet prescribing rather than negligent care administered through telemedicine)." Virginia Rawthorn, J.D., Legal Impediments to the Practice of Medicine (2011), *available at* www.dhmh.state.md.us/mhqcc/pdf/2011/UMD-8-23-telemedicinepresentation.

full survey of the law in this area is beyond the scope of this chapter, but myriad resources exist discussing product liability law.

4. Privacy and Data Security

See the discussion in II.B.1.b.i regarding state data breach notification laws, as well as the discussion concerning HIPAA, the HITECH Act, and protected health information in II.E.1, below. Whether these issues and obligations will attach to an e-care provider depends on what information is delivered to the e-care provider, how it is delivered, and what is done with the information following delivery (e.g., under HIPAA/HITECH, whether the e-care provider is a covered entity or a business associate).[160] These issues are front of mind in the telemedicine industry, as evidenced by the following comment from the American Telemedicine Association:

> For telehealth patients and providers, there are technical and legal concerns about the privacy and security of common internet-based communications and HIPAA compliance. Atta's Standards and Guidelines Committee is preparing to study the area of real-time communications using general purpose networks (texting, instant messaging, Skype, VoIP, web-based, etc.). Since patients may choose less private and secure methods, one of the issues will be how telehealth providers can assure that the patient is informed about and consents to their choice of communications method.[161]

5. FDA Regulation of Telemedicine

In July 2011, a division of the health care management news source Fierce Healthcare reported that "to date, most mobile software hasn't been clearly designated into the different [FDA regulatory classifications], making it difficult for developers and users alike to know which technologies require FDA approval."[162] Though the FDA has since released draft guidance regarding mobile medical applications, the regulation of telemedicine continues to be marked by considerable uncertainties.

The point for e-care providers is to remain attuned to further FDA regulatory developments affecting telemedicine. As noted, there exist at least three drivers for increased FDA regulation of telemedicine: (1) safety concerns, (2) legislative interest, and (3) industry growth. The FDA's recent proposed guidance in the area of mobile medical applications reflects its continuing and growing interest in this area and tips its hand respecting issues it deems important: "wireless safety considerations, classification and submission requirements related to clinical decision support software, [and] the application of quality systems to software." A failure to keep abreast of regulatory developments could result in fines and penalties associated with the sale of an unapproved device,

---

[160] See Chapter 7 (Christiansen, Information Security and Breach Notification Under HIPAA and HITECH) Appendix 7-A: Sample HITECH/HIPAA Security Gap Analysis Checklist.

[161] American Telemedicine Association, Business and Finance SIG HIPAA/HITECH Resources Work Group (Apr. 2011).

[162] Sara Jackson, *Classification for mHealth Devices Could Simplify FDA Regulation*, FIERCE MOBILE HEALTHCARE (July 7, 2011), *available at* http://www.fiercemobilehealthcare.com/story/mhealth-coalition-creates-new-classification-system-fdas-mhealth-regs/2011-07-07.

and perhaps more importantly, loss of substantial investment in telemedicine technology that cannot be approved under FDA regulatory requirements.

E. EHR System Providers

Many providers of integrated electronic health records technology (EHR systems providers) combine e-content, e-product, e-connection, and e-care business models. These systems typically provide a medical record program, clinical support tools, real-time access to patient records across providers within a system, the capability for patients to interface with the physician to request services or information, and often integration with the facility's billing and administrative staff. The United States government has supported the development of health information technology and the related implementation of EHR systems as a way to improve the quality of health care and realize certain efficiencies in delivery.[163] This discussion concerns the application of the following legal issues to EHR systems providers and EHR systems users: (1) privacy and data security under HIPAA and HITECH, (2) Medicare and Medicaid Incentive Programs and achievement of meaningful use, and (3) allocation of rights and obligations among health information exchange (HIE) participants.

1. Privacy and Data Security—HIPAA and HITECH

Suffice it to say that EHR systems vendors and users falling within the "covered entity" and "business associate" definitions under HIPAA must be fully versed in the privacy and data security requirements imposed under these laws and their implementing regulations. HHS, through its Office for Civil Rights, has recently responded aggressively to violations involving protected health information, levying fines in the millions of dollars.[164] Furthermore, the data breach notification provisions of the HITECH Act, with their potential for significant negative publicity, merit assessment of the implementation of data encryption methods described in published guidance under the HITECH Interim Final Rule.[165]

The HITECH Act makes HIPAA's civil and criminal penalties applicable to business associates,[166] but covered entities too must recognize that there are changes the HITECH Act makes to HIPAA's civil and criminal enforcement provisions that affect them. First, while HIPAA's criminal penalties have long

---

[163]The underpinnings of these initiatives, as well as their myriad legal and regulatory mandates, are addressed in Chapters 3, 4, 5, and 7.

[164]*See HIPAA Enforcement Escalates—What Does This Mean for the Healthcare Industry?*, ABA HEALTH eSOURCE, Vol. 7, No. 8 (Apr. 2011).

[165]Guidance Specifying the Technologies and Methodologies That Render Protected Health Information Unusable, Unreadable, or Indecipherable to Unauthorized Individuals, 74 Fed. Reg. 19,009 (Apr. 27, 2009) [hereinafter April Guidance]. The April Guidance was revised and included in the Interim Final Rule published on August 24, 2009. *See* Breach Notification for Unsecured Protected Health Information; Interim Final Rule, 74 Fed. Reg. 42,740, 42,757 (Aug. 24, 2009) (to be codified at 45 C.F.R. 160, 164).

[166]*See* HITECH §13404(c) (codified at 42 U.S.C. §17934(c)).

been interpreted to apply only to covered entities,[167] the HITECH Act clarifies that the term "person," as used in the criminal penalties section of HIPAA,[168] now includes employees of and other individuals associated with covered entities and business associates.[169] Second, while individuals still do not have an individual right of action under HIPAA, the HITECH Act does allow state attorneys general to bring a civil action on behalf of the state's residents in a federal district court to enjoin a covered entity from continuing to violate the Act or to obtain statutory damages on behalf of such residents.[170]

Under the HITECH Act, there are now four tiers of civil monetary penalties that may be imposed by the Secretary of HHS against a covered entity or a business associate that violates HIPAA.[171] In the lowest tier, a penalty will be assessed when the covered entity or a business associate fails to comply with HIPAA and it is established that the covered entity or business associate did not know and by exercising reasonable diligence would not have known it was violating HIPAA.[172] The lowest tier penalty starts at an amount of up to $100 per identical violation up to a maximum of $25,000 per calendar year,[173] but can be as high as $50,000 per identical violation up to a maximum of $1,500,000 per calendar year.[174] If the violation by the covered entity or business associate was the result of reasonable cause and not willful neglect, the penalty ranges from an amount of up to $1,000 per identical violation up to a maximum of $100,000 per calendar year to an amount as high as $50,000 per identical violation up to a maximum of $1,500,000 per calendar year.[175] If the covered entity or business associate commits a violation of HIPAA due to willful neglect, the penalty ranges from an amount of up to $10,000 (per identical violation) up to a maximum of $250,000 per calendar year to an amount as high as $50,000 per identical violation up to a maximum of $1,500,000 per calendar year.[176] Finally, if the covered entity or business associate fails to correct the violation it committed

---

[167] In June 2005, the Department of Justice responded to the Secretary of HHS's request for clarification of the scope of HIPAA's criminal enforcement provision and concluded that only those entities specified in the statute could be prosecuted for violations of the statute. See Op. O.L.C. (June 1, 2005), available at http://www.usdoj.gov/olc/hipaa_final.htm.

[168] 42 U.S.C. §1320d-6 (2006). A "person" who knowingly and wrongfully used or disclosed individually identifiable health information would be subject to criminal penalties ranging from a fine of up to $50,000 and/or imprisonment for up to one year to a fine of up to $250,000 and/or imprisonment for up to 10 years. Id.

[169] See HITECH §13409, amending 42 U.S.C. §1320d-6(a). HITECH, however, failed to specify whether employees or individuals would be subject to criminal penalties if they committed their criminal acts prior to February 17, 2009 (the enactment of the ARRA).

[170] See id. §13410(e)(1) (codified at 42 U.S.C. §17939(e)(1)). The total amount of statutory damages imposed is determined by multiplying the number of violations committed by up to $100 and is limited to a maximum of $25,000 during a calendar year. Id. §14310(e)(2) (codified at 42 U.S.C. §17939(e)(2)). In addition to damages, a court may award court costs and reasonable attorneys' fees to the state. Id. §14310(e)(3) (codified at 42 U.S.C. §17939(e)(3)). Prior to filing its lawsuit, the state attorney general must notify the Secretary of HHS in writing by including in its notice a copy of the state's complaint. See id. §14310(e)(4) (codified at 42 U.S.C. §17939(e)(4)).

[171] See HITECH §13410(a) (codified at 42 U.S.C. §17939(a)).
[172] See id. §13410(d) (codified at 42 U.S.C. §1320d-5(a)(1)(A)).
[173] See id. §13410(d) (codified at 42 U.S.C. §1320d-5(a)(3)(A)).
[174] See id. §13410(d) (codified at 42 U.S.C. §1320d-5(a)(1)(A)).
[175] See id. §13410(d) (codified at 42 U.S.C. §1320d-5(a)(1)(B)).
[176] See id. §13410(d) (codified at 42 U.S.C. §1320d-5(a)(1)(C)(i)).

due to willful neglect, the Secretary of HHS will impose the maximum penalty of up to $50,000 per identical violation up to a maximum of $1,500,000 per calendar year.[177]

2. Medicare and Medicaid Incentive Programs and Achievement of Meaningful Use

To promote the adoption of EHR systems, the HITECH Act provides for incentive payments under Medicare and Medicaid to eligible professionals implementing an EHR system and achieving "meaningful use" of electronic information through the use of that system. This is the "carrot." The "stick" is that eligible professionals in the Medicare program who fail to meet the meaningful use criteria face reimbursement reductions that start at 1 percent and increase each year that meaningful use is not achieved, up to a maximum reduction of 5 percent (such reductions do not apply to eligible professionals opting into the Medicaid program).

Per the CMS Web site,

> [f]or the purposes of the Medicare and Medicaid Incentive Programs, eligible professionals, eligible hospitals and critical access hospitals (CAHs) must use certified EHR technology. Certified EHR technology gives assurance to purchasers and other users that an EHR system or module offers the necessary technological capability, functionality, and security to help them meet the meaningful use criteria. Certification also helps providers and patients be confident that the electronic health IT products and systems they use are secure, can maintain data confidentially, and can work with other systems to share information.

Thus, if an EHR system is intended for use by an eligible professional, the EHR system user must ensure that the EHR system vendor is certified.[178] The Stage 1 meaningful use criteria center on electronically capturing health information in a structured format, using that information to track key clinical conditions, and communicating that information for care coordination purposes (whether that information is structured or unstructured but in structured format whenever feasible), implementing clinical decision support tools to facilitate disease and medication management, using EHRs to engage patients and families, and reporting clinical quality measures and public health information. Stage 1 is therefore keyed to requiring functionalities in certified EHR technology that will achieve these identified criteria.

EHR system users must assess the degree of responsibility for achieving meaningful use they expect of the certified EHR system vendor. At a minimum, the EHR system vendor must maintain certification throughout the period of intended use of the system. The extent of the EHR system user's reliance on the system to meet Stage 1 meaningful use criteria will drive additional requirements from the EHR system vendor. An EHR system is a substantial investment, not only in terms of actual money spent for the software, consulting services, and ongoing maintenance and support for the system, but also in terms of the potential financial liability in the event the system impedes the EHR system

---

[177] *See id*. §13410(d) (codified at 42 U.S.C. §1320d-5(a)(1)(C)(ii)).

[178] HHS maintains a listing of certified EHR vendors at HealthIT.HHS.gov.

user's ability to achieve meaningful use. This is an issue of contract law and consequently requires the careful attention of the EHR system user at the time the user evaluates EHR system provider options.

3. Allocation of Rights and Obligations Among HIE Participants

The structural, financial, and technical complexities facing health information exchanges reflect the numerous legal issues that impact such entities. This discussion focuses on issues faced by Regional Health Information Organizations (RHIOs). RHIOs are health information exchange (HIE) initiatives that employ "open" systems to support the exchange of health information among independent entities within a defined geographic region.

A survey of RHIOs conducted in 2007 identified 138 organizations that promoted clinical data exchange, of which approximately one quarter were determined to be defunct.[179] Of the 83 respondents to the survey, 32 reported facilitating health information exchange among independent entities and 3 reported facilitating health information exchange among physicians and hospitals that were part of the same integrated network as of Jan 1, 2007. Forty-five of the RHIOs were still in the planning stages.[180]

Despite these somewhat sobering statistics, RHIOs continue to form and to operate. Laws and regulations that impact RHIOs include:[181]

- *Privacy and confidentiality laws.* Federal, state, and common law create minimum protections regarding the privacy and confidentiality of identifiable health and personal information in electronic, written, verbal, and any other form. Those principally applicable to RHIOs include HIPAA, the HITECH Act, and various state health codes and regulations.[182]
- *Security laws.* Federal data security regulations under HIPAA and the HITECH Act, although technology neutral, require implementation of appropriate security safeguards to protect certain electronic health care information that may be at risk while permitting appropriate access, availability, integrity, and use of that information. The technological "neutrality" means that specific security measures adopted by clinical service providers may comply with the security regulations yet impede interoperability and health information exchange. When participating in a RHIO, covered entities must conduct an assessment of the potential risks and vulnerabilities to the confidentiality, integrity, and availability of electronic protected health information held by the entity. Also, they must implement sufficient administrative, physical, and technical safeguards (considering their size, funding, and ability) to protect

---

[179]Julia Adler-Milstein, *The State of Regional Health Information Organizations: Current Activities and Financing*, 27 HEALTH AFFAIRS (2008), *available at* http://content.healthaffairs.org/content/27/1/w60.full?sid=21336488-e04f-498e-a851-8a17abd51347.

[180]*Id.*

[181]Much of this information was culled from MICHIGAN HEALTH INFORMATION NETWORK, CONDUIT TO CARE: MICHIGAN'S e-HEALTH INITIATIVE (Dec. 2006), available at http://www.michigan.gov/documents/mihin/MiHIN_Report_Compress_v2_180321_7.pdf.

[182]*See, e.g.*, MICH. PUBLIC HEALTH CODE, MICH. COMP. LAWS ANN. §333.20175(1).

information that the covered entity creates, receives, maintains, or transmits through participation in the RHIO.
- *Health care fraud and abuse laws.* These laws are intended to prevent fraud and abuse by regulating the relationships between physicians and other health care entities. The federal Stark law prohibits a physician from making referrals for certain "designated health services" (DHS) payable by Medicare to an entity with which the physician has a financial relationship, unless an exception applies. The law also prohibits the entity from submitting claims to Medicare or anyone else for Medicare DHS that are furnished as a result of a prohibited referral. The Stark law is enforced by the Centers for Medicare and Medicaid Services. Violations of the statute are punishable by denial of payment for all DHS claims, refund of amounts collected for DHS claims, and civil monetary penalties for knowing violations of the prohibition. The federal anti-kickback statute provides criminal penalties for individuals or entities that knowingly and willfully offer, pay, solicit, or receive remuneration in order to induce or reward the referral of business reimbursable under any of the federal health care programs. Remuneration may be direct or indirect. Prohibited conduct includes not only the payment of remuneration intended to induce or reward referrals of patients, but also the payment of remuneration intended to induce or reward the purchasing, leasing, or ordering of, or arranging for or recommending the purchasing, leasing, or ordering of, any good, facility, service, or item reimbursable by any federal health care program. Violations of the anti-kickback statute may also result in the imposition of civil money penalties, exclusion from federal health programs, and liability under the False Claims Act.

On August 8, 2006, the Centers for Medicare and Medicaid Services and the Office of the Inspector General for HHS published final rules to facilitate certain e-prescribing and electronic health records efforts under the federal Stark law, and the federal anti-kickback law.[183] These rules create exceptions to the Stark and anti-kickback laws for efforts aimed at increasing use of e-prescribing and electronic health records. These rules are complex, and should be carefully reviewed and carefully implemented if relying on any of their safe harbor provisions.

- *Federal tax laws.* Parties that join together to form an HIE may include one or more tax-exempt entities. Tax-exempt organizations are prohibited from providing improper financial or other benefits to a private individual or entity. Since HIE contemplates the interchange of information between tax-exempt entities and private or for-profit entities, these laws must be addressed in structuring an HIE and defining terms of participation.
- *Intellectual property.* Legal concerns will need to be addressed in developing an HIE including the ownership of the system that electronically transmits health information and its components. Software licensing and ownership issues will need to be resolved regarding each element and

---

[183] 71 Fed. Reg. 45,110 (Aug. 8, 2006) (to be codified at 42 C.F.R. pt. 1001).

process that makes up the HIE (e.g., data formats, data layouts, interfaces, security measures, process to standardize data, creation of an aggregate health record, record locator system, etc.). Additionally, in connecting to the HIE and building interoperability with their current systems, clinical service providers may encounter legal issues related to current software licensing agreements.
- *E-prescribing.* See the discussion in II.B.1.a. The issues described there will apply to the use of an HIE for prescribing medication via electronic means.

These issues make clear that RHIO organizers and participants must take extreme care when structuring, forming, and operating the exchange. The rights and obligations of the participants must be clearly set forth in organizational documents, and the exchange must be operated in accordance with those documents in order to minimize disputes among the participants, and to also lessen the risk to the entity and its constituents of noncompliance with applicable state and federal laws.

III. Allocation and Mitigation of Risk

Knowledge of the risks and attendant liabilities identified in II., above, is the first step in their allocation, mitigation, or both. Affected e-providers should become familiar with these risks and how they apply to and impact the conduct of their business. Once this is established, e-providers can assess their options for allocation and mitigation of the known and applicable risks.

The ensuing discussion and analysis identifies the risks, the affected e-provider categories, and the allocation and mitigation techniques available to those affected e-providers. "Allocation" speaks to the spreading of risk among affected parties. "Mitigation" speaks to the lessening of the risk itself. Allocation techniques are typically applied before the risk manifests; mitigation techniques can be generally applied prior to or after the risk manifests.

A. The Risk: Unauthorized Use of Copyrighted Material

The risk pertaining to unauthorized use of copyrighted materials is discussed in II.A.1., above. This risk applies to e-content providers and e-connection providers.

1. Before a Claim Occurs—Mitigation

E-content providers actively involved in content publication decisions must have a strong working knowledge of the copyright laws.[184] This in turn should translate into the development of a process for clearing content prior to publication.[185] The use of such a process should serve to mitigate the risk of a

---

[184] Stanford University's Fair Use and Copyright Web site, at http://www.fairuse.stanford.edu, contains abundant materials addressing copyright law and its application in various scenarios.

[185] Sample clearance materials can be found at http://www.copyright.cornell.edu and at http://www.readwritethink.org/files/resources/lesson_images/lesson1085/CanIUseIt.pdf.

copyright infringement claim by ensuring that copyrighted material is properly published. Furthermore, in the event that a claim arises despite adopting and properly implementing a rational process, the potential for a willful infringement claim is substantially lessened, if not eliminated.[186]

E-connection providers, on the other hand, should have complete familiarity with OCILLA and the requirements for application of its immunity provisions to the e-connection provider's activities.[187] In particular, an e-connection provider must designate an agent to receive notification of copyright infringement involving its service, as follows:

> Designated agent.—The limitations on liability established in this subsection apply to a service provider only if the service provider has designated an agent to receive notifications of claimed infringement described in paragraph (3), by making available through its service, including on its website in a location accessible to the public, and by providing to the Copyright Office, substantially the following information:
>
> (A) the name, address, phone number, and electronic mail address of the agent.
>
> (B) other contact information which the Register of Copyrights may deem appropriate.[188]

2. Before a Claim Occurs—Allocation

E-connection providers can and should include appropriate disclaimers and hold harmless provisions in their terms of use regarding the content that is published and accessed through the use of the e-connection service. For example, Google's 2011 Terms of Service include the following:

> 8. Content in the Services
>
> 8.1 You understand that all information (such as data files, written text, computer software, music, audio files or other sounds, photographs, videos or other images) which you may have access to as part of, or through your use of, the Services are the sole responsibility of the person from which such content originated. All such information is referred to below as the "Content."
>
> 8.2 You should be aware that Content presented to you as part of the Services, including but not limited to advertisements in the Services and sponsored Content within the Services[,] may be protected by intellectual property rights which are owned by the sponsors or advertisers who provide that Content to Google (or by other persons or companies on their behalf). You may not modify, rent, lease, loan, sell, distribute or create derivative works based on this Content (either in whole or in part) unless you have been specifically

---

[186]*Compare* Island Software & Computer Serv., Inc. v. Microsoft Corp., 413 F.3d 257, 264 (2d Cir. 2005) (expressing majority view of willfulness as objective recklessness), *with* Dolman v. Agee, 157 F.3d 708, 715 (9th Cir. 1998) (expressing minority view of willfulness requiring knowledge that actions constitute infringement); *see also* Robert Aloysius Hyde, *A Reckless Disregard of the Ordinary Infringer?: Moving Toward a Balanced and Uniform Standard for Willful Copyright Infringement*, 35 U. TOL. L. REV. 377, 383–87 (2003) (surveying requirements of federal appellate courts for willful copyright infringement).

[187]See II.C.1., above.

[188]17 U.S.C. §512(c)(2) (2006).

told that you may do so by Google or by the owners of that Content, in a separate agreement.

8.3 Google reserves the right (but shall have no obligation) to pre-screen, review, flag, filter, modify, refuse or remove any or all Content from any Service. For some of the Services, Google may provide tools to filter out explicit sexual content. These tools include the SafeSearch preference settings (see http://www.google.com/help/customize.html#safe). In addition, there are commercially available services and software to limit access to material that you may find objectionable.

8.4 You understand that by using the Services you may be exposed to Content that you may find offensive, indecent or objectionable and that, in this respect, you use the Services at your own risk.

8.5 You agree that you are solely responsible for (and that Google has no responsibility to you or to any third party for) any Content that you create, transmit or display while using the Services and for the consequences of your actions (including any loss or damage which Google may suffer) by doing so.

Again, it is important for risk management purposes that a true e-connection provider undertake steps to ensure that such status is maintained. Undertaking activities that extend beyond simply providing a means of communication can result in the additional duties and resultant risks imposed on e-content and e-product providers.

3. *When a Claim Occurs—Mitigation*

An e-connection provider must follow the "take-down" procedures set forth in OCILLA in order to enjoy the immunity from copyright infringement liability provided under that statute:

(1) In general.— A service provider shall not be liable for monetary relief, or, except as provided in subsection (j), for injunctive or other equitable relief, for infringement of copyright by reason of the storage at the direction of a user of material that resides on a system or network controlled or operated by or for the service provider, if the service provider—

(A) (i) does not have actual knowledge that the material or an activity using the material on the system or network is infringing;

(ii) in the absence of such actual knowledge, is not aware of facts or circumstances from which infringing activity is apparent; or

(iii) upon obtaining such knowledge or awareness, acts expeditiously to remove, or disable access to, the material;

(B) does not receive a financial benefit directly attributable to the infringing activity, in a case in which the service provider has the right and ability to control such activity; and

(C) upon notification of claimed infringement as described in paragraph (3), responds expeditiously to remove, or disable access to, the material that is claimed to be infringing or to be the subject of infringing activity.[189]

---

[189] *Id.* §512(c)(1)(C).

OCILLA provides e-connection providers with a safe harbor in the event that content is removed improperly but in good faith—i.e., if the request for removal is delivered by someone other than the copyright holder.[190] Thus, assuming that the take-down request contains the elements required under OCILLA,[191] it is likely better to err on the side of adherence than to question a take-down request.

An e-content provider should promptly investigate all copyright infringement claims. If the content at issue is of marginal importance to the e-content provider, the prudent course of action may be to remove the content in exchange for the purported owner's written agreement not to pursue further claims. Otherwise, the e-content provider should consult with counsel to fully understand the nature of the claim, the available defenses, and the magnitude of the potential liability if infringement exists.

B. The Risk: Unauthorized Use of a Trademark or Service Mark

The risk of unauthorized use of a trademark or service mark applies to e-content and e-connection providers.

1. Before a Claim Occurs—Mitigation

An e-content provider should adopt and implement trademark clearance policies and procedures prior to use of a mark in conjunction with its own goods and services, including the registration of any domain names that include the mark. At a minimum, the procedures must include a search of United States Patent and Trademark Office (USPTO) records for registrations of the same or similar marks and a search of other general databases to uncover possible uses of the same or a similar unregistered mark. In some cases, depending on the importance of the mark to the e-content provider and the market or industry in which it is used, the e-content provider might obtain a clearance opinion from legal counsel. As with a properly adopted and implemented copyright clearance procedure, the adoption and implementation of a trademark clearance procedure can, at a minimum, avoid liability for willful infringement of another's mark.

2. Before a Claim Occurs—Allocation

If an e-content provider publishes third party content, including trademarks and logos, it should have a binding agreement with the third party that authorizes the e-content provider to publish the trademarks and logos and contains representations, warranties, and indemnification from the third party respecting its rights in the trademarks and logos. Of course, the value of even a well crafted indemnity depends on the collectability of the indemnitor. Consequently, an e-content provider should additionally consider requiring that third-party content providers maintain advertising liability insurance, and that the third party deliver a certificate of coverage naming the e-content provider as an additional insured prior to publication of the trademark or logo.

---

[190] *Id.* §512(g).
[191] *Id.* §512(c)(3).

Similarly, an e-connection provider should include provisions in its terms of use spelling out that users have sole responsibility and liability associated with their publication of trademarks and logos through the use of the e-connection service. For example, Yahoo!'s Terms of Service state that its users agree not to "upload, post, email, transmit or otherwise make available any Content that infringes any patent, trademark, trade secret, copyright or other proprietary rights ('Rights') of any party," and further provide:

> You agree to indemnify and hold Yahoo! and its subsidiaries, affiliates, officers, agents, employees, partners and licensors harmless from any claim or demand, including reasonable attorneys' fees, made by any third party due to or arising out of Content you submit, post, transmit, modify or otherwise make available through the Yahoo! Services, your use of the Yahoo! Services, your connection to the Yahoo! Services, your violation of the TOS, or your violation of any rights of another.

3. After a Claim Occurs—Mitigation

As with copyright infringement claims, e-content and e-connection providers should promptly and thoroughly investigate trademark infringement or dilution claims (often in the form of "cease and desist" letters). If the trademark at issue is important to the provider's business and therefore worth defending, the provider should consult counsel to determine a proper response to the claim. Otherwise, the provider should consider stopping its use or publication of the mark in exchange for a written waiver of claims from the claiming party.

If the dispute involves a domain name, and retention of the domain name is material to the provider's business, the provider should submit the dispute under the ICAAN Uniform Domain Name Dispute Resolution Policy (UDRP).[192] All ICAAN-accredited registrars of top-level domains must adopt the policy. The UDRP is a policy between a registrar and its customer and is included in registration agreements for all ICANN-accredited registrars. The rules promulgated under the UDRP provide for a form of speedy arbitration between the domain-name registrant and the party claiming trademark rights in the domain name.[193] The arbitration panel will either reject the challenge or accept it and order the domain name registration transferred to the trademark claimant. To succeed on the merits, the complainant must specify the trademark or trademarks on which the complaint is based and the goods and services with which the mark is used, the manner in which the domain name is identical or confusingly similar to a trademark or service mark in which the complainant has rights, why the domain-name holder should be considered as having no rights or legitimate interests with respect to the domain name that is the subject of the complaint, and why the domain name should be considered as having been registered and being used in bad faith.[194]

---

[192]The UDRP policies and rules are collected at http://www.icann.org/udrp/.

[193]*See Rules for Uniform Domain Name Dispute Resolution Policy*, INTERNET CORPORATION FOR ASSIGNED NAMES AND NUMBERS (Oct. 30, 2009), http://www.icann.org/dndr/udrp/uniform-rules.htm.

[194]*Id.* ¶3.

C. The Risk: Publication of Erroneous or Defamatory Information

The risk of publishing erroneous or defamatory information is potentially applicable to both e-content and e-connection providers.

1. Before a Claim Occurs—Mitigation

The e-provider's actual function is fundamental to risk mitigation respecting both erroneous and defamatory information claims. The less editorial control exercised over third-party content, the less the risk of liability arising from that content. Thus, in determining its risk profile, an e-content provider must decide whether it will "filter" third-party content that it publishes or allows to be published on its Web site. If it elects not to filter the content, the e-content provider should publish a clear disclaimer in its terms of service, stating that it undertakes no editorial control over third party content and therefore undertakes no responsibility or liability associated with such content, including its completeness or accuracy.

As to its own original content, and also if it affirmatively elects to filter and edit third-party content, an e-content provider must establish and fully implement an editorial process designed to verify the accuracy of content and also to vet the content for potentially defamatory material. Since the definition of defamation differs among jurisdictions, the e-content provider should consult with counsel if the potentially defamatory nature of content is in doubt. As in other cases, though, it is better to err on the side of caution and not publish statements that might be viewed as defamatory.

An e-connection provider must ensure that its service offerings and delivery remain narrow enough to fall within the protections afforded under the Communications Decency Act.[195] Specifically, in order to maintain the immunity granted under the CDA, e-connection providers should not undertake any function that would render them a publisher of content.

2. Before a Claim Occurs—Allocation

If an e-content provider engages third parties to provide content, it should have a written agreement whereby the third party assumes all legal responsibility for the delivered content, including representations and warranties as to the originality, completeness, and accuracy of the content, and indemnifies the e-content provider against claims associated with the content. The value of the indemnity will, of course, depend on the financial condition of the third party, and the e-content provider might therefore require the third-party content provider to carry insurance covering the indemnified risks.

3. When a Claim Occurs—Mitigation

If content is alleged to be defamatory, and unless a compelling reason exists for continuing to publish such content, e-content providers should likely remove the offending content, conditioning such removal on an understanding

---

[195] See the discussion in II.C.5., above.

that the removal is not an admission of liability. Continued publication after receipt of a defamation allegation can potentially increase the publisher's monetary liability if the claim succeeds.[196] If a third party is responsible for the offending content, the e-content provider should deliver written notice to the third party of the claim and, depending on the contractual relationship between the e-content provider and the third party, seek indemnity for the defamation claim.

D. The Risk: Unlicensed or Unauthorized Practice of Medicine

The risk of being charged with the unlicensed or unauthorized practice of medicine applies to e-content and e-care providers.

1. *Before a Claim Occurs—Mitigation*

The key issue for e-content providers is avoiding crossing the line beyond which their publication and delivery of content is deemed to involve the practice of medicine. Once that line is crossed, the e-content provider is faced with the licensure and duty-of-care issues discussed in II.A.1.d, above. A general rule of thumb for mitigating this risk is the less interactive the Web site, the better; the corollary being, the more general the content, the better. The statutory definitions of practicing medicine, e.g. "the diagnosis, treatment, prevention, cure, or relieving of a human disease, ailment, defect, complaint, or other physical or mental condition, by attendance, advice, device, diagnostic test, or other means, or offering, undertaking, attempting to do, or holding oneself out as able to do, any of these acts,"[197] suggest that e-content providers should take affirmative steps to ensure that the information published cannot be construed as meeting any of those statutory criteria.

Along similar lines, e-content providers should consider adopting terms of use that include very clear disclaimers regarding the intent and use of the content—i.e., that it does not constitute medical advice. The WebMD Web site contains the following language:

> The contents of the WebMD Site, such as text, graphics, images, information obtained from WebMD's licensors, and other material contained on the WebMD Site ("Content") are for informational purposes only. The Content is not intended to be a substitute for professional medical advice, diagnosis, or treatment. Always seek the advice of your physician or other qualified health provider with any questions you may have regarding a medical condition. Never disregard professional medical advice or delay in seeking it because of something you have read on the WebMD Site!
>
> If you think you may have a medical emergency, call your doctor or 911 immediately. WebMD does not recommend or endorse any specific tests, physicians,

---

[196]The vast majority of states continue to allow punitive damages claims in tort actions, including defamation actions. A refusal to remove claimed defamatory material is potentially evidence of malice, a customary basis for a punitive damage claim. *See, e.g.,* Betts v. Allstate Ins. Co., 154 Cal. App. 3d 688, 709, 201 Cal. Rptr. 528 (1984); *criticized in* Gagnon v. Continental Casualty Co., 211 Cal. App. 3d 1598, 1603 260 Cal. Rptr. 305 (1989) ("There must be substantial evidence of: (a) an intent to vex, annoy and injure; or (b) a conscious disregard of the plaintiff's rights, before punitive damages may be awarded").

[197]MICH. COMP. LAWS ANN. §333.17001(1)(f).

products, procedures, opinions, or other information that may be mentioned on the Site. Reliance on any information provided by WebMD, WebMD employees, others appearing on the Site at the invitation of WebMD, or other visitors to the Site is solely at your own risk.[198]

E-care providers, on the other hand, may in fact be engaged in the practice of medicine. In this case, risk mitigation should focus on knowledge of and adherence to the licensure and credentialing requirements in each jurisdiction in which the e-care provider's services are delivered and received.

2. Before a Claim Occurs—Allocation

E-content providers that publish third-party content and that wish to avoid being deemed as practicing medicine should obtain indemnities from third-party content providers covering claims that the third-party providers' content constitutes the practice of medicine.

E. The Risk: E-Prescribing and Malpractice

Risks associated with e-prescribing and malpractice apply to e-product and e-care providers.

1. Before a Claim Occurs—Mitigation

Perhaps the surest mitigation technique for e-product providers engaged in e-prescribing is through VIPPS certification. The certification process requires that the e-product provider demonstrate compliance with licensing and inspection requirements of the state in which they reside as well as those into which they dispense pharmaceuticals. The VIPPS Web site states:[199]

> To be VIPPS accredited, a pharmacy must comply with the licensing and inspection requirements of their state and each state to which they dispense pharmaceuticals. In addition, pharmacies displaying the VIPPS seal have demonstrated to NABP compliance with VIPPS criteria including patient rights to privacy, authentication and security of prescription orders, adherence to a recognized quality assurance policy, and provision of meaningful consultation between patients and pharmacists.

Absent VIPPS certification, e-product providers engaged in e-prescribing must learn and comply with the various state licensing requirements for dispensing pharmaceutical drugs and operating a pharmacy. Additionally, such e-product providers must be cognizant of FDA and other federal regulatory enforcement activities targeted at online pharmacies. In particular, these e-product providers should adopt methods to ensure that they are receiving and processing valid prescriptions and to validate patient identity and information, and also to

---

[198] WebMD Terms and Conditions of Use found at http://www.webmd.com/about-webmd-policies/about-terms-and-conditions-of-use?ss=ftr.
[199] National Association of Boards of Pharmacy, VIPPPS, *available at* http://vipps.nabp.net.

ensure that they are not purchasing counterfeit drugs for resale.[200] The VIPPS acceditation criteria. If followed, the VIPPS accreditation criteria should substantially mitigate the risks of e-prescribing;[201] additionally, the National Association of Boards of Pharmacy publishes substantial and useful information concerning the establishment and operation of Internet pharmacies.

E-care providers practicing telemedicine should consider whether and if so under what circumstances they are willing to establish a physician-patient relationship with the ultimate recipient of their consultation. There may exist competing concerns—the ability to obtain payor reimbursement for the services if no such relationship exists and the risk attendant to the duty of care established through a physician-patient relationship. If reimbursement is not an issue, the e-care provider might opt to forego direct communication with the patient and work only with the referring physician. Doing so can reduce the possibility of the creation of a physician-patient relationship, thus mitigating the risk of a malpractice claim.

2. Before a Claim Occurs—Allocation

E-care providers utilizing telemedicine technology should review the terms and conditions under which the technology is sold or otherwise provided to the e-care provider. If the technology is relatively new, the e-care provider may have some leverage to require the technology vendor to indemnify the e-care provider against any claims that arise from defects in the technology.

F. The Risk: Privacy and Data Security Compliance

Risks associated with compliance with data privacy and security laws and regulations apply to e-product providers, e-care providers, and EHR system providers and users.

1. Before a Claim Occurs—Mitigation

Every entity that will handle personally identifiable information under state law or electronic protected health information (EPHI) under HIPAA must adopt policies and procedures for the proper protection and security of that information. The policy must be formally approved by the entity's senior management. Personnel having access to the PII or EPHI, or the systems storing or processing PII or EPHI, must be trained periodically on the policies and procedures. Violations of the policies and procedures must result in actual consequences to the offender.

---

[200] The FDA has published *Standards for Securing the Drug Supply Chain—Standardized Numerical Identification for Prescription Drug Packages*. While these standards have no legal effect, e-care providers engaged in e-prescribing should remain abreast of further FDA and pharmaceutical industry developments.

[201] The VIPPS accreditation criteria are available at http://www.nabp.net/programs/accreditation/vipps/vipps-criteria.

The Guidance on Risk Analysis Requirements Under the HIPAA Security Rule from the HHS Office of Civil Rights[202] is instructive in developing a comprehensive policy and related procedures for the protection of EPHI. A well crafted policy should capture not only HIPAA requirements but any more stringent applicable state law requirements and the requirements under the FTC's Red Flags Rule (if applicable), discussed in II.B.1.b.iv., above.

Covered entities and business associates under HIPAA should consider adopting encryption techniques for EPHI in order to avoid the data breach notification requirements under the HITECH Act.

E-product providers should review their merchant agreements to determine their compliance obligations respecting the PCI Data Security Standard, and if they determine that the Standard applies, they should undertake the actions required to become compliant.

2. *Before a Claim Occurs—Allocation*

This issue is particularly germane to RHIOs, discussed in II.E.3., above, but it is also relevant in the selection and implementation of any EHR system. A RHIO's operative documents should set forth each participant's responsibility respecting the security of EPHI. The common platform for this allocation of risk is a Data Use and Reciprocal Support Agreement (DURSA). The Nationwide Health Information Network (NHIN) Cooperative DURSA Work Group developed a draft DURSA.[203] In most cases, each participant in a RHIO agrees to adhere to the data privacy and security laws and regulations applicable to that participant (i.e., in its capacity as a covered entity or business associate under HIPAA). The allocation of risk, might, however, depend in part on the technical structure of the RHIO and the flow of EPHI within that structure.[204] Decentralized, peer-to-peer systems generally warrant the risk profile reflected in the NHIN draft DURSA, in which each participant expressly assumes responsibility for the EPHI in its possession. If, however, the RHIO provides that the EPHI is centrally managed, and the "governing authority" is not a governmental entity, the operative documents may obligate the governing authority to assume the risk of unauthorized EPHI disclosure and indemnify the participants against that risk.

EHR system users should explore an EHR system vendor's willingness, or lack thereof, to assume at least some of the risk associated with unauthorized access to EPHI. The risk shifting can be in the form of specific performance warranties from the EHR system vendor as well as indemnities covering third-

---

[202]Dep't of Health & Human Servs., Office of Civil Rights, Guidance on Risk Analysis Requirements under the HIPAA Security Rule (July 14, 2010), *available at* http://www.hhs.gov/ocr/privacy/hipaa/administrative/securityrule/rafinalguidancepdf.pdf, also provided as Appendix F-2 on the CD accompanying this volume.

[203]Nationwide Health Information Network Cooperative DURSA Work Group, Data Use and Reciprocal Support Agreement (DURSA), *available at* http://healthit.hhs.gov/portal/server.pt/gateway/PTARGS_0_10731_849891_0_0_18/DRAFT%20NHIN%20Trial%20Implementations%20Production%20DURSA-3.pdf

[204]*See, e.g.*, Current and Emerging Models of Health Information Exchange, Potential Privacy, Security and Legal Issues, *available at* http://www.health.state.mn.us/e-health/mpsp/legwg/potlegissues071106.pdf.

party claims arising from the breach of those performance warranties. This issue should be surfaced early in the acquisition process, and the EHR system user should consider developing standard warranty and indemnity language and include it as a requirement in any request for proposal or request for quote.

3. When a Claim Occurs—Mitigation

If a data security breach involves PII, the affected e-provider must promptly investigate the circumstances surrounding the breach and ascertain the identity of the affected individuals and where they reside.[205] The response period differs from state to state, as does the required content of the notification, the method of delivery, and the need to advise any law enforcement or other governmental entity of the breach. The National Conference of State Legislatures maintains a current listing of state data breach notification laws,[206] which should be consulted once the residences of affected individuals are determined.

If the data security breach involves credit card data, the affected e-provider must follow the notification procedures established by VISA, American Express, Discover, and MasterCard.[207] Failure to cooperate could lead to increased fines and revocation of the e-provider's right to process credit card transactions. Moreover, each of these card issuers possesses substantial resources to assist in mitigating the effects of a data security breach.

---

[205] See Chapter 11 (Faccenda, Obligations in Response to a Health Care Data Security Breach), at III.C., for a discussion of risk mitigation in the event of an unauthorized disclosure of EPHI.

[206] National Conference of State Legislatures, State Security Breach Notification Laws (Oct. 12, 2010), *available at* http://www.ncsl.org/default.aspx?tabid=13489.

[207] *See, e.g.*, Visa, Responding to a Data Breach: Communications Guidelines for Merchants, *available at* http://usa.visa.com/download/merchants/cisp_responding_to_a_data_breach.pdf.

17

Discovery and Admission of Electronic Information as Evidence*

I. Introduction	597
II. Background of the Development of Rules and Standards for Electronic Evidence	598
III. Technology Implications for Electronic Evidence: An Electronic Medical Record Information Ecosystem	601
IV. The 2006 Amendments to the Federal Rules of Civil Procedure	604
A. Spoliation and the Obligation to Preserve ESI	606
B. Production of ESI	608
C. Inadvertent Disclosure of Privileged or Protected Health Information	610
V. Admission of ESI	611
VI. Special Problems	614
A. Electronic Signatures and Electronic Medical Records	614
B. Electronic Health Records and Health Information Exchange	618

I. Introduction

    The term "paradigm shift" is something of a cliché in technology discussions and has often been badly misused.[1] Still, sometimes changes in technology make existing concepts and practices (paradigms) unworkable and obsolete, and there is no choice but to develop and shift to new concepts and practices.

    This is what has happened to the rules for the discovery and courtroom introduction of evidence over the past decade or so. The existing rules of evidence, and the practices developed around them, proved inappropriate for dealing with

---

    *John R. Christiansen, Christiansen IT Law, Seattle, Washington.
    [1]The term "paradigm shift" was originally coined by Thomas Kuhn to refer to changes in scientific theories and practices, such as the shift from the classical Newtonian approach to Einsteinian relativity in physics. *See* THOMAS S. KUHN, THE STRUCTURE OF SCIENTIFIC REVOLUTIONS (1962). The overuse of this term for technology marketing purposes in particular has made it something of an annoying cliché, but sometimes even a cliché has real meaning.

evidence produced from computers, electronic media, and information systems,[2] because of the ways these new technologies interact with information.

The rules for managing information and information systems in order to deal with these new concepts and practices are still in development. It appears logical and prudent to use or leverage existing information security compliance requirements to implement a coordinated if not integrated program,[3] but this approach is not yet common.

II. Background of the Development of Rules and Standards for Electronic Evidence

All evidence is a form of information. The information may be presented in the form of verbal testimony from a witness, the visible status of a physical object, or written statements on paper. The judge or jury hears, sees, or reads this evidence and then uses it to decide issues in the case. This process is so fundamental it seems odd even to bring it up, but starting with fundamentals may help one understand how electronic information challenges existing concepts and practices. A good example is medical records, which have traditionally been paper but are increasingly becoming electronic, and perform an essential function as the official record of diagnosis and treatment.

A paper record is physically stable: it comes into existence at a readily identifiable point in time that can be recorded, and it can be stored, used, and managed throughout its life cycle in ways that protect its integrity. This is why, for example, health information management standards and professional practices call for record signatures, file room checkout logs, and the like. And it is very difficult to alter a paper record without leaving traces of the alteration, the presence of which will at least bring the integrity of the document into question.[4]

Paper medical records are therefore easy to locate for purposes of production and straightforward to authenticate as documentation, the source and accuracy of which can be determined. As long as the secondary information about their management provides assurances of the paper records' integrity, the

---

[2]For purposes of this chapter, "information system," an important term for electronic evidence analysis, will be defined as "an interconnected set of information resources under the same direct management control that shares common functionality. A system normally includes hardware, software, information, data, applications, communications and people." This definition is from the Health Insurance Portability and Accountability Act of 1996 (HIPAA) Security Rule, 45 C.F.R. §164.301. While HIPAA and its implementing regulations (collectively, "HIPAA") do not specifically apply to evidentiary matters, this is a fair general description, and using it may help with the integration of compliance and evidentiary response policy. *See also* FED. R. CIV. P. 37(f) (referring to operations of "electronic information system").

[3]*See, e.g.*, Mira Weiss, *Providers v. Health Insurers: Pro-Provider Reforms and the Growth of the Compliance Imperative*, 10 HMOs AND HEALTH PLANS 1 (Winter 2007).

[4]KEVIN BRADY ET AL., THE SEDONA CONFERENCE COMMENTARY ON ESI EVIDENCE & ADMISSIBILITY 4 (Mar. 2008) [hereinafter SEDONA ADMISSIBILITY COMMENTARY]. The Sedona Conference is a conference series that has been producing highly influential, often authoritative, works on electronic evidence issues for several years. *See* THE SEDONA PRINCIPLES ADDRESSING ELECTRONIC DOCUMENT PRODUCTION iv–vi, 5–9 (Richard Braman ed., 2d ed. 2007) [hereinafter SEDONA BEST PRACTICES]. Many if not all of these publications are available through the Sedona Conference Web site, http://www.thesedonaconference.org/.

information stored in paper medical records is deemed reliable for admission and use in court.[5]

Electronic information does not fit this model. "Electronic information is not stored by altering matter. Information is stored in a more abstract way by means of machines utilizing flows of information, with records stored and processed in multi-layered systems with interacting components."[6] As a result, much, much more information can be created and stored,[7] while the same information can be transmitted, altered, and copied, either automatically or intentionally and, under some conditions, undetectably.[8] The concept of an "original document" may no longer be meaningful,[9] and the same information, or more or less altered versions of it, may be stored in a wide range of devices and media—some of which may also be difficult or impossible to identify.[10]

For evidentiary purposes, then, the crucial differences between paper-based and electronic information are the difficulties posed by (1) locating it all and (2) authenticating it—that is, obtaining sufficient assurance that the information is what it purports to be and not a false or altered version—once it has been located. The former issues involve discovery, while the latter involve the admissibility and credibility of electronic evidence.

These are the issues that have emerged from the wholesale and accelerating transition from paper-based to electronic processes throughout the economy. Attempts to adapt discovery and evidentiary rules to electronic information began in the 1970s with the addition of the term "data compilation," meaning "any means of storing information other than the conventional words and figures in written or documentary form [including but] by no means limited to, electronic computer storage."[11]

The courts generally adapted the rules to the emerging issues[12] and, in 1999, the federal Electronic Signatures in Global and National Commerce Act (E-SIGN) and its state counterpart, the Uniform Electronic Transactions Act (UETA), expressly clarified that "electronic records" and "electronic signatures" may not be denied legal effect simply because they are in electronic form.[13] By the early years of the twenty-first century, however, the widespread implementation of highly complex "information ecosystems"[14] forced a genuine break with precedent.

---

[5] *See* WILLIAM ROACH ET AL., MEDICAL RECORDS AND THE LAW 383–86 (4th ed. 2006).

[6] GEORGE PAUL & BRUCE NEARON, THE DISCOVERY REVOLUTION: E-DISCOVERY AMENDMENTS TO THE FEDERAL RULES OF CIVIL PROCEDURE 4 (2006) [hereinafter DISCOVERY REVOLUTION].

[7] *Id.* at 4–6.

[8] *See, e.g.*, Steven W. Teppler, *Spoliation of Digital Evidence: A Challenging Approach to Challenges and Sanctions*, 4 THE SCITECH LAWYER 20 (Fall 2007); *see also* DOROTHY E. DENNING, INFORMATION WARFARE AND SECURITY 241–57 (1999).

[9] DISCOVERY REVOLUTION at 7.

[10] *Id.* at 5.

[11] Notes of Advisory Committee on Rule 803, FED. R. EVID. 803.

[12] *See, e.g.*, Orin S. Kerr, *Computer Records and the Federal Rules of Evidence*, U.S. ATTORNEYS BULLETIN (Mar. 2001).

[13] *See* CHRISTIANSEN, AN INTEGRATED STANDARD OF CARE FOR HEALTHCARE INFORMATION SECURITY §5.03(A) (2005).

[14] *See* DISCOVERY REVOLUTION at 8 & n.13.

At the federal level, this break came with the 2006 amendments to the Federal Rules of Civil Procedure (2006 Amendments). The 2006 Amendments represent a complete conceptual shift away from the paper-based model, and instead deal with electronic evidence of all kinds under the category of "electronically stored information" (ESI).[15] The amended rules include:

- FED. R. CIV. P. 16(b)(5) (ESI discovery terms may be included in scheduling order);
- FED. R. CIV. P. 26(a)(1) (disclosure of information at outset of case);
- FED. R. CIV. P. 26(b)(2) (pertaining to costs of production of ESI);
- FED. R. CIV. P. 26(f)(3) (ESI production issues to be addressed at discovery planning conference);
- FED. R. CIV. P. 33(d) (option to provide ESI as business record as interrogatory response);
- FED. R. CIV. P. 34(b) (option to specify format for production of ESI); and
- FED. R. CIV. P. 37(f) (safe harbor for ESI lost due to routine, good faith information system operations).

The rules do not provide a definition of ESI; the closest they come to a definition is a description of the kinds of information that may be subject to production:

> Any party may serve on any other party a request...to produce and permit the party making the request, or someone acting on the requestor's behalf, to inspect, copy, test, or sample any designated documents or electronically stored information—including writings, drawings, graphs, charts, photographs, sound recordings, images, and other data or data compilations stored in any medium from which information can be obtained.[16]

In order to deal with the complexities of effective discovery of ESI from highly complicated information systems, the 2006 Amendments essentially force parties to cooperate in developing and executing a discovery strategy that is intended to accommodate the costs and burdens of production.[17]

Just because ESI can be produced does not make it admissible in court, of course. The key issue for this purpose is the authenticity of the information, a question that has been argued in terms of both general evidentiary authentication principles and hearsay.[18] Generally, the courts have tended to be fairly

---

[15] *See* FED. R. CIV. P. 26(a)(1)(B) (providing that parties ordinarily must make prediscovery disclosure of "a copy of, or a description by category and location of, all documents, electronically stored information, and tangible things that are in the possession, custody, or control of the party and that the disclosing party may use to support its claims or defenses, unless solely for impeachment").

[16] FED. R. CIV. P. 34(a). *Compare* THE SEDONA GLOSSARY: FOR E-DISCOVERY AND DIGITAL INFORMATION MANAGEMENT 20 (Conor Crowley & Sherry Harris eds., 2d ed. 2007) [hereinafter SEDONA GLOSSARY] ("ESI: Electronically stored information, regardless of the media or whether it is in the original format in which it was created, as opposed to stored in hard copy (i.e. on paper).").

[17] *See* DISCOVERY REVOLUTION at 9.

[18] *See* Orin S. Kerr, *Computer Records and the Federal Rules of Evidence*, U.S. ATTORNEYS BULLETIN (Mar. 2001).

liberal about the admission of ESI,[19] but a few courts have taken a more critical view and sometimes excluded ESI.[20]

The precise issues presented for the production and admission of ESI will always depend crucially upon the architecture[21] of the information system(s) involved. The next section analyzes some of the evidentiary implications of a sample electronic medical record (EMR) system.[22]

III. TECHNOLOGY IMPLICATIONS FOR ELECTRONIC EVIDENCE: AN ELECTRONIC MEDICAL RECORD INFORMATION ECOSYSTEM

The "information ecosystem" of even a relatively small organization can be a complex mix of computers and software applications. Workstation computers may be of different brands, running applications ranging from word processing and spreadsheets to e-mail, also provided by different vendors. Computers may communicate through a local area network (LAN),[23] an intranet,[24] a wireless network, specialized communications channels for certain kinds of transactions,[25] the Internet, or all of these. Remote access[26] may be permitted, and laptops may be allowed on the network(s), and if not allowed may be used anyway. One or many servers[27] may provide data and applications, and data may

---

[19]*Id.*

[20]*See* Cooper Offenbecher, *Admitting Computer Record Evidence after In Re Vinhnee: A Stricter Standard for the Future?*, 4 SHIDLER J. L. COM. & TECH. 6 (Oct. 17, 2007), *available at* http://www.lctjournal.washington.edu/Vol4/a06Offenbecher.html.

[21]"Architecture: The term architecture refers to the hardware, software or combination of hardware and software comprising a computer system or network." SEDONA GLOSSARY at 3.

[22]Terminology in this field is currently somewhat confusing, in particular with respect to the EMR and the closely related electronic health record (EHR). Both the EMR and EHR may be defined as an "electronic record of health-related information on an individual that can be created, gathered, managed, and consulted by authorized clinicians and staff," with the distinction that the EMR is used "within a single organization" (e.g., a hospital), while an EHR is used "across more than one health care organization." *See* NATIONAL ALLIANCE FOR HEALTH INFORMATION TECHNOLOGY, REPORT TO THE OFFICE OF THE NATIONAL COORDINATOR FOR HEALTH INFORMATION TECHNOLOGY ON DEFINING KEY HEALTH INFORMATION TECHNOLOGY TERMS (Apr. 28, 2008). For simplicity's sake, this analysis focuses on the single-organization EMR.

[23]"LAN (Local Area Network): A group of computers at a single location (usually an office or home) that are connected by phone lines, coaxial cable or wireless transmission." SEDONA GLOSSARY at 30.

[24]"Intranet: A private network that uses Internet-related technologies to provide services within an organization or defined infrastructure." *Id.* at 28.

[25]For example, electronic data interchange (EDI) for health claims transmission. *Cf.* Alan Smith, *Accountability in EDI Systems to Prevent Employee Fraud*, 22 INFORMATION SYS. MGMT. 30 (Spring 2005).

[26]"Remote Access: The ability to access and use digital information from a location off-site from where the information is physically located. For example, to use a computer, modem, and some remote access software to connect to a network from a distant location." SEDONA GLOSSARY at 44.

[27]"Server: Any central computer on a network that contains ESI or applications shared by multiple users of the network on their client PCs. A computer that provides information to client machines. For example, there are web servers that send out web pages, mail servers that deliver email, list servers that administer mailing lists, FTP servers that hold FTP sites and deliver ESI to requesting users, and name servers that provide information about Internet host names." *Id.* at 47.

be stored in dedicated database servers, backup or archive media,[28] workstation or laptop hard drives,[29] portable devices such as "personal digital assistants" or "smart phones," any or all of the above, and more.

The information present in this kind of system may be in many forms. At perhaps the simplest presentation level, electronic text documents produced by word processing applications, financial documents produced by spreadsheet applications, and e-mail messages store human-readable information in readily identifiable files. Unless electronically protected, these electronic documents may be duplicated or altered with great flexibility within the scope of the application. Electronic documents may be embedded in or attached to other electronic documents, especially e-mail. Each of these electronic documents in turn has associated metadata that describes key aspects of the document's creation and life cycle.[30]

Information may also be stored in one or more databases separate from workstations and other computers, and provide it on demand by the user or an application. This information may be used to create or update an electronic document, or may be presented to the user as an ephemeral display.

The information system also creates information about transactions and events that occur in it. Individual users are—or should be—associated with unique identifiers[31] as well as authentication data such as a password.[32] User transaction and related data may be included in electronic documents as metadata and may also be recorded in audit logs or trails.[33] Peripheral equipment such as copiers may also create and store such information,[34] as do some medical devices.[35]

---

[28] "Media: An object or device, such as a disc, tape, or other device, on which data is stored." *Id.* at 33.

[29] The HIPAA Security Rule does not distinguish desktop and laptop computers, including both in the definition of "workstations." *See* 45 C.F.R. §164.304.

[30] "Metadata: Data typically stored electronically that describes characteristics of ESI, found in different places in different forms. Can be supplied by applications, users or the file system. [*sic*] Metadata can describe how, when and by whom ESI was collected, created, accessed, modified and how it is formatted. Can be altered intentionally or inadvertently. [*sic*] Certain metadata can be extracted when native files are processed for litigation. Some metadata, such as file dates and sizes, can easily be seen by users; other metadata can be hidden or embedded and unavailable to computer users who are not technically adept. Metadata is generally not reproduced in full form when a document is printed to paper or electronic image." SEDONA GLOSSARY at 33.

[31] This is required by the HIPAA Security Rule at 45 C.F.R. §164.312(a)(2)(i).

[32] Some form of authentication is required by the HIPAA Security Rule, at 45 C.F.R. §164.312(d).

[33] "Audit Log or Audit Trail: In computer security systems, a chronological record of when users logged in, how long they were engaged in various activities, what they were doing, and whether any actual or attempted security violations occurred. An audit trail is an automated or manual set of chronological records of system activities that may enable the reconstruction and examination of a sequence of events and/or changes in an event." SEDONA GLOSSARY at 4. Audit controls, such as logs or audit trails, are required under the HIPAA Security Rule, at 45 C.F.R. §164.312(b).

[34] *See* EUROPEAN UNION NETWORK AND INFORMATION SECURITY AGENCY, SECURE PRINTING (Apr. 2008).

[35] *Cf.* U.S. FOOD AND DRUG ADMIN., GUIDANCE FOR INDUSTRY—CYBERSECURITY FOR NETWORKED MEDICAL DEVICES CONTAINING OFF-THE-SHELF (OTS) SOFTWARE (Jan. 14, 2005).

The implications of this "smearing around" of information throughout an information system[36] may be better appreciated graphically. Figure 15-1 provides a simplified schematic of an EMR and part of its associated information ecosystem.[37]

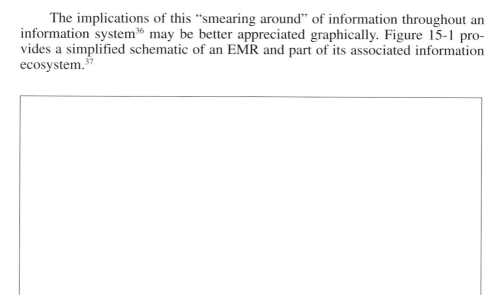

In Figure 15-1, the central application is the EMR software hosted in the EMR server at the center of the diagram. An individual user such as a physician might use the workstation labeled "Chart" to access the records on an individual patient through the EMR. He or she would log on to "Chart" using user authentication information that the system administrator (SysAdmin) had previously loaded onto the User ID Server. The EMR server software would then search the Chart Entries and Patient Info databases and transfer the relevant information to the Chart workstation.

The user would then have an ephemeral view of patient information, including but not limited to previous medical record entries.[38] Based on this view, the user might then make treatment decisions, including prescription of a drug. The choice of drugs might be based in part on information from a drug interactions

---

[36]*See* GEORGE PAUL & BRUCE NEARON, THE DISCOVERY REVOLUTION: E-DISCOVERY AMENDMENTS TO THE FEDERAL RULES OF CIVIL PROCEDURE 5 (2006) [hereinafter DISCOVERY REVOLUTION].

[37]This schematic is not intended to and probably does not accurately represent the architecture of any actual EMR or information system. It is provided solely for purposes of a representative analysis of the kinds of evidentiary issues presented by such systems, and does not even begin to address such complexities as outsourcing and virtualization.

[38]This ephemeral view might also, for example, include decision-support tools such as reminders and alerts:
  Alerts, reminders, pop-ups, and similar tools are used as aides in the clinical decision-making process. The tools themselves are not considered part of the legal health record; however, associated documentation is considered a component. For example, a provider is alerted to perform a diabetic foot exam on a diabetic patient. The initial alert that prompts the provider is not part of the legal health record, but the subsequent action taken by the provider, including the condition acted upon and the associated note detailing the exam, is considered part of the record.
AHIMA e-HIM Work Group on the Legal Health Record, *Update: Guidelines for Defining the Legal Health Record for Disclosure Purposes*, 76 JOURNAL OF AHIMA 8, 64A-G (Sept. 2005).

database hosted by an external information services provider, and the prescription would be generated automatically over an electronic prescribing network linked to an external pharmacy. The user might then generate a draft chart entry but decide to finish it at home and e-mail it to her home e-mail account via the Internet (or download it into her personal USB drive), and also print a hard copy to review over lunch.

The EMR server would store the draft entry in the Chart Entries database and perhaps place other patient encounter information in the Patient Info database, and once the entry was completed, the draft would be updated. User and device information about most—but probably not all—of these transactions would be logged in the Audit Trails database.

Note that different types of information may be subject to different (sometimes overlapping) legal characterizations. The Chart Entries and at least some Patient Info data will be part of the patient's legal EHR,[39] some of it serving the functions of a traditional medical record and some of it serving as a "designated record set" for HIPAA purposes.[40] Audit Trail information does not directly serve either of these functions, though it may be necessary to authenticate medical record information for admissibility purposes or relevant to HIPAA compliance.[41] Most—probably not all—of the different types of information in the system are backed up, perhaps off site, and probably on different schedules and for different retention periods.[42]

As this example shows, depending on the specific configuration of an information system, the transactions that are permitted, and the details of information creation and tracking, ESI that is potentially relevant to a patient encounter and care decision may be present almost anywhere in the system.

IV. THE 2006 AMENDMENTS TO THE FEDERAL RULES OF CIVIL PROCEDURE

The production of all discoverable ESI from an information system (or ecosystem) like the one described in III., above, in a case where, for example, a

---

[39] "The legal health record is generated at or for a healthcare organization as its business record and is the record that will be disclosed upon request." *Id.*

[40] The "designated record set" is the "group of records maintained by or for" a health care organization about an individual, including medical and billing records, and other records used "to make decisions about individuals." 45 C.F.R. §164.501. "Record" includes "any item, collection or grouping of information." *Id.* The designated record set is the set of records a HIPAA covered entity is required to permit the subject individual to review, copy, and request be amended.

[41] For example, covered entities are required to provide individuals with an accounting of unauthorized disclosures of information from their designated record sets for a period of six years before the date of the request for the accounting. 45 C.F.R. §164.528. System logs generally provide the principal evidence as to the identity of users accessing, and therefore disclosing, information.

[42] For example, patient information relevant to HIPAA compliance would need to be retained for at least six years, see 45 C.F.R. §164.530(j)(2); medical record information, probably would need to be retained for at least 10 and maybe many more years, see WILLIAM ROACH ET AL., MEDICAL RECORDS AND THE LAW 40–44 (4th ed. 2006); and audit trails information might be kept for a much shorter period of time, see John R. Christiansen, *Managing HIPAA Security Compliance: Organizational Governance and Risk Acceptance*, 24 NEW PERSPECTIVES IN HEALTHCARE AUDITING 6 (Spring 2005).

medical error occurred could be difficult and burdensome under the best of conditions.[43] Under the highly adversarial conditions characteristic of much litigation, it might become nearly impossible. The 2006 Amendments therefore more or less force the parties to cooperate in identifying and resolving possible ESI discovery issues. They do so on the one hand by requiring the party that controls the ESI to try in good faith to preserve it, and on the other by requiring the parties to confer and try to resolve the burdens and costs of production.

The foundations for actual production of ESI are the required initial disclosure (by copies or description) of all ESI "in the possession, custody or control of [each] party ... that the disclosing party may use to support its claims or defenses, unless solely for impeachment"[44] and the discovery conference and discovery plan provisions providing a vehicle for resolving "issues relating to disclosure or discovery of [ESI]."[45] In particular, parties may have problematic issues with respect to the scope and format[46] of ESI to be produced, the costs of production, and protection in case of erroneous disclosure of privileged information.

Effective preservation and production of ESI requires significant, in some organizations perhaps unprecedented, cooperation among attorneys and information technology staff, and, in many health care organizations, health information management staff. While legal counsel is the interface with the court and adverse parties, identification and preservation of ESI is likely to require detailed knowledge of information system architecture and functions that only

---

[43]Under FED. R. CIV. P. 26(b)(1), discoverable evidence includes not only admissible evidence but also information that "appears reasonably calculated to lead to the discovery of admissible evidence." For discovery purposes, then, relevance is broadly construed and not limited to the precise issues set out in the pleadings or the merits of the case. Oppenheimer Fund, Inc. v. Sanders, 437 U.S. 340, 351 (1978). Discovery requests may be deemed relevant if there is any possibility that the information may be relevant to the general subject matter of the action. *Id.*

In a medical error case involving, for example, a dispute about the accuracy of an entry into an EMR, discoverable evidence might well include all administrative and system information bearing upon the integrity of that record—including transaction logs, user identifier and authentication data issuance and management, secondary patient information, alternate and draft versions of the entry, etc. *Compare* AMERICAN BAR ASSOCIATION INFORMATION SECURITY COMMITTEE, PKI ASSESSMENT GUIDELINES 45–53 (2003) [hereinafter PKI ASSESSMENT GUIDELINES], *with* Thomas J. Smedinghoff & Ruth Hill Bro, *Moving with Change: Electronic Signature Legislation as a Vehicle for Advancing E-Commerce*, XVII JOHN MARSHALL J. COMPUTER AND INF. LAW 721 (Spring 1999) at 731, 744–52 (discussing evidentiary principles applicable to use of electronic signatures to authenticate electronic records and transactions).

[44]FED. R. CIV. P. 26(a)(1)(B).

[45]FED. R. CIV. P. 26(f).

[46]"Format (noun): The internal structure of a file, which defines the way it is stored and used. Specific applications may define unique formats for their data (e.g., 'MSWord document file format'). Many files may only be viewed or printed using their originating application or an application designed to work with compatible formats. There are several common email formats, such as Outlook and Lotus Notes. Computer storage systems commonly identify files by a naming convention that denotes the format (and therefore the probable originating application). For example, 'DOC' for Microsoft Word document files; 'XLS' for Microsoft Excel spreadsheet files; 'TXT' for text files; 'HTM' for Hypertext Markup Language (HTML) files such as web pages; 'PPT' for Microsoft Powerpoint files; 'TIF' for tiff images; 'PDF' for Adobe images; etc. Users may choose alternate naming conventions, but this will likely affect how the files are treated by applications." SEDONA GLOSSARY at 23.

the information technology staff will have.[47] Searching ESI prior to disclosure to try to winnow out nondiscoverable privileged or confidential information, and searching it upon receipt to identify information that is actually useful, may require specialized skills and tools.[48] Discovery planning, motions to compel or limit discovery, and requests or motions to allocate discovery costs will all usually depend on both technical information and legal argument.

A. Spoliation and the Obligation to Preserve ESI

Given the malleability of ESI and the ways that both intentional and automatic information system processes can alter or destroy it, prompt preservation when it might be needed in litigation is essential.[49] While the 2006 Amendments do not address this specifically, the provisions for ESI disclosure and sanctions for failure to properly disclose, along with related case law, create a clear obligation to preserve ESI on notice of litigation, balanced by a recognition that sometimes even good-faith efforts cannot prevent spoliation[50] by routine activities.

Penalties for spoliation can be draconian. In one of the seminal cases on ESI spoliation, where the defendant provided an inadequate explanation for the loss of backup tapes containing potentially crucial e-mails, the court instructed the jury that there was an adverse inference that the e-mails would have supported the plaintiff, and the jury awarded $9.2 million in compensatory and $20 million in punitive damages.[51]

While not provided for in the 2006 Amendments, a number of federal courts have found that there is a "federal common law of spoliation" that gives rise to a duty to avoid spoliation of relevant evidence for use at trial.[52] Duties to preserve evidence may also arise out of statutory or regulatory record-keep-

---

[47] *See* GEORGE PAUL & BRUCE NEARON, THE DISCOVERY REVOLUTION: E-DISCOVERY AMENDMENTS TO THE FEDERAL RULES OF CIVIL PROCEDURE 72–82 (2006) [hereinafter DISCOVERY REVOLUTION].

[48] *See generally* Jason R. Baron, ed., *The Sedona Conference Best Practices Commentary on the Use of Search and Information Retrieval Methods in E-Discovery*, 8 THE SEDONA CONFERENCE J. (Fall 2007).

[49] *See, e.g.*, Steven W. Teppler, *Spoliation of Digital Evidence: A Challenging Approach to Challenges and Sanctions*, 4 THE SCITECH LAWYER 20, 23 (Fall 2007):
A compelling argument may be made to the effect that the presence of "control" [over evidence] takes on even greater significance as it relates to the generation of digital evidence. This increased importance is the direct consequence of (1) computer-generated information's inherent ephemerality, and (2) the ease with which alterations or deletions of computer-generated information may be made undetectable, nor nearly impossible to detect.

[50] "Spoliation refers to the destruction or material alteration of evidence or to the failure to preserve property for another's use as evidence in pending or reasonably foreseeable litigation." Silvestri v. General Motors, 271 F.3d 583, 588 (4th Cir. 2001).

[51] Zubulake v. UBS Warburg LLC, No. 1:02-CV-01243-SAS (S.D.N.Y. Mar. 16, 2005). *See also* Coleman (Parent) Holdings, Inc. v. Morgan Stanley & Co., Inc., No. 03 CA 5045 (Fla. S.D. Cir. Ct. Mar. 2005), *damages award reversed on other grounds*, Morgan Stanley & Co. Inc. v. Coleman (Parent) Holdings Inc., No. 4D05-2606 (Fla. Dist. Ct. App. Mar. 12, 2007), where the court gave an adverse inference instruction based on the defendant's destruction of e-mails and failure to produce other electronic records, and the jury awarded plaintiff $1.45 billion.

[52] *See, e.g., Silvestri*, 271 F.3d 583; *see also* DISCOVERY REVOLUTION at 43–44.

ing obligations,[53] a point perhaps of particular concern in the heavily regulated health care sector.

The trigger for a litigation hold is generally said to be when a party is "aware of likely litigation"[54] or litigation is "reasonably anticipated."[55] Precisely when this occurs depends very much on the facts of the situation; one way of framing the issue is that it occurs "when an organization is on notice of a credible threat it will become involved in litigation or anticipates taking action to initiate litigation."[56] Certainly this occurs upon receipt of a summons; it may also occur on notice of a regulatory action, and receipt of a demand letter; whether it occurs upon receipt of other communications or other information depends on the facts and circumstances.[57] In health care, for example, the occurrence of a "never event" might be considered a circumstance under which the organization reasonably anticipates litigation.[58]

The actual implementation of a litigation hold may be a complex process requiring coordination across different offices and areas of expertise including technical staff, legal counsel, and (in health care) health information management staff.[59] Implementation requires that the destruction or alteration of relevant ESI be stopped, which requires identification of all sites where it is stored, notification of all personnel with control over its processing, and identification and suspension of all automatic processes that might affect it.[60] The hold may need to be maintained until the litigation is concluded and should be documented to defend against claims of spoliation.[61]

Complicating implementation of a litigation hold is the fact that many applications in the information system may automatically overwrite information for valid reasons, such as updating and storage management.[62] For this reason, a spoliation "safe harbor" was added in the 2006 Amendments,[63] providing that,

---

[53]*See* Byrnie v. Town of Cromwell Bd. of Ed., 243 F.3d 93, 108–09 (2d Cir. 2001).

[54]DISCOVERY REVOLUTION at 43 (citing *Zubulake*, No. 1:02-CV-01243-SAS).

[55]CONOR CROWLEY ET AL., EDS., THE SEDONA COMMENTARY ON LEGAL HOLDS: THE TRIGGER AND THE PROCESS (Aug. 2007 Public Comment Version) [hereinafter SEDONA HOLDS COMMENTARY].

[56]*Id.* at 5.

[57]*Id.* at 5–7.

[58]*See* U.S. Dep't of Health & Human Servs., Centers for Medicare & Medicaid Servs., *Eliminating Serious, Preventable, and Costly Medical Errors* (May 18, 2006):
According to the National Quality Forum ("NQF"), "never events" are errors in medical care that are clearly identifiable, preventable, and serious in their consequences for patients, and that indicate a real problem in the safety and credibility of a health care facility. . . . Examples of "never events" include surgery on the wrong body part; foreign body left in a patient after surgery; mismatched blood transfusion; major medication error; severe "pressure ulcer" acquired in the hospital; and preventable post-operative deaths.
Given typical litigation patterns, a hospital that experienced an event in which a patient was seriously harmed due to a clearly identifiable, preventable error that indicated problems in the hospital's safety and credibility probably ought to anticipate litigation as soon as the patient or family can locate a lawyer.

[59]DISCOVERY REVOLUTION at 45; *see* AHIMA e-HIM Work Group on e-Discovery, *New Electronic Discovery Civil Rule*, 77 JOURNAL OF AHIMA 8, 68 A-H (Sept. 2006).

[60]*See* SEDONA HOLDS COMMENTARY at 11–16.

[61]*Id.* at 15–17.

[62]DISCOVERY REVOLUTION at 45.

[63]*See* FED. R. CIV. P. 37(f), Committee Note.

"[a]bsent exceptional circumstances, a court may not impose sanctions under these rules on a party for failing to provide electronically stored information lost as a result of the routine, good-faith operation of an electronic information system."[64]

The "good faith" standard does not protect negligence, and the provision "applies only to information lost due to the routine operation of an electronic information system—the ways in which such systems are generally designed, programmed, and implemented to meet the party's technical and business needs."[65] For example, reinstalling software after a computer crash, which deleted discoverable ESI after proceedings were commenced (and a temporary restraining order and document request were served) did not qualify for the safe harbor.[66]

Generally, "in order to take advantage of the good-faith exception, a party needs to act affirmatively to prevent the system from destroying or altering information, even if such destruction would occur in the regular course of business."[67] If a party acting in good faith inadvertently fails to preserve ESI that can be restored, it may be ordered to do so at its own expense.[68]

B. Production of ESI

Actual production of ESI, especially where large quantities from a complex information system are concerned, can raise serious issues of accessibility and costs of identification and production. The receiving party may not have hardware capable of reading some kinds of media[69] or software capable of reading ESI created by a different application.[70]

Generally, under established law, the disclosing party should be responsible for the costs of making ESI accessible. "[I]f a party chooses an electronic storage method, the necessity for a retrieval program or method is an ordinary and foreseeable risk."[71] At the same time, identification and production of ESI,

---

[64] FED. R. CIV. P. 37(f).

[65] Id.

[66] United States v. Krause, 367 B.R. 740 (D. Kan. June 4, 2007).

[67] Doe v. Norwalk Cmty. Coll., No. 3:04-cv-1976, 2007 WL 2066496, at *4 (D. Conn. July 16, 2007). *But see* Columbia Pictures Indus. v. Bunnell, 2007 WL 2080419 (C.D. Cal. May 29, 2007) (requiring party to preserve ephemeral Internet Protocol addresses stored in random access memory (RAM), which would ordinarily be overwritten almost immediately, under specific circumstances of case).

[68] *See* Advanced Micro Devices Inc. v. Intel Corp., No. 1:05-cv-00441-JJF, MDL No. 05-1717-JJF (D. Del. Sept. 25, 2007) (party required to spend over $20 million to restore mistakenly deleted e-mail).

[69] *See, e.g.*, Sattar v. Motorola, Inc., 138 F.3d 1164, 1171 (7th Cir. 1998) (party produced e-mails in four-inch tapes inaccessible to the requesting party, which lacked the equipment and software to read them).

[70] *See, e.g.*, Scotts Co. LLC v. Liberty Mut. Ins. Co., No. 2:06-CV-899, 2007 WL 1723509 (S.D. Ohio June 12, 2007), *and* Butler v. Kmart Corp., No. 2:05-CV-257-P-A, 2007 WL 2406982 (N.D. Miss. Aug. 20, 2007).

[71] *In re* Brand Name Prescription Drugs Antitrust Litig., 94 C 897, MDL 997, 1995 WL 360526, at *2 (N.D. Ill. June 15, 1995); *see also Sattar*, 138 F.3d 1164.

perhaps in "non-native" format,[72] may be very expensive and burdensome.[73] A receiving party facing format accessibility issues, or a disclosing party facing cost and burden issues, may therefore use the discovery planning process to try to resolve these problems. If not, or if insufficient information is disclosed to enable appropriate framing of discovery, motion practice is of course available.[74]

Rule 34(b), Federal Rules of Civil Procedure, allows a party to "specify the form or forms in which [ESI] is to be produced." If the responding party objects, or the requesting party fails to specify, the responding party is required to respond, stating the form or forms it will use, and the requesting party may move to compel.[75] Unless the parties agree or there is a court order, ESI must be produced in the "form or forms in which it is ordinarily maintained[76] or in a form or forms that are reasonably usable."[77]

These provisions raise at least two potentially important issues: (1) Is there any reason to request ESI in any particular format? And (2) what about ESI that is in a particularly difficult-to-access form, such as "legacy" data in archives or older components of the system?[78]

There are a number of reasons for a requesting party to specify format. On the one hand, it may help make ESI readable, as with the conversion of database files (which ordinarily function only within their native application) into text or image files.[79] Metadata may also enhance ESI searchability[80] or include information about the editing or creation of a record,[81] which might in some cases lead to other relevant evidence or affect the authenticity (and therefore admissibility) of the ESI. On the other hand, for the disclosing party, a format conversion that eliminates metadata may help eliminate privileged or confidential information and control production more efficiently.[82]

---

[72] "Native Format: Electronic documents have an associated file structure defined by the original creating application. This file structure is referred to as the 'native format' of the document. Because viewing or searching documents in the native format may require the original application (for example, viewing a Microsoft Word document may require the Microsoft Word application), documents may be converted to a neutral format as part of the record acquisition or archive process." SEDONA GLOSSARY at 35.

[73] *See* Jason R. Baron, ed., *The Sedona Conference Best Practices Commentary on the Use of Search and Information Retrieval Methods in E-Discovery*, 8 THE SEDONA CONFERENCE J. 192 (Fall 2007).

[74] *Cf.* GEORGE PAUL & BRUCE NEARON, THE DISCOVERY REVOLUTION: E-DISCOVERY AMENDMENTS TO THE FEDERAL RULES OF CIVIL PROCEDURE 73 (2006) [hereinafter DISCOVERY REVOLUTION] ("Beware: Lack of Information Will Foster Motion Practice.").

[75] FED. R. CIV. P. 34(b).

[76] That is, in native format. DISCOVERY REVOLUTION at 88.

[77] FED. R. CIV. P. 34(b).

[78] "Legacy Data, Legacy System: Legacy Data is ESI in which an organization may have invested significant resources, but has been created or stored by the use of software and/or hardware that has become obsolete or replaced ('legacy systems')." SEDONA GLOSSARY at 30.

[79] *See* DISCOVERY REVOLUTION at 86.

[80] *Cf. In re* Payment Card Interchange Fee and Merchant Discount Antitrust Litig., MD 05-1720 (JG) (JO), 2007 WL 121426 (E.D.N.Y. Jan. 12, 2007) (removal of metadata contrary to intent that data searchability should not be degraded).

[81] *Id.*

[82] *Id.*

So far the courts appear split on whether or not metadata is required to be disclosed.[83] A party seeking electronic records including metadata over objection should probably be ready to demonstrate its possible relevance.[84]

In order to deal with the problem that not all formats are readily accessible, and ESI in older formats in particular may be difficult to access with current software and hardware, Rule 26(b)(2) of the Federal Rules of Civil Procedure creates a "two-tier approach" that distinguishes ESI in general from ESI "from sources that [a] party identifies as not reasonably accessible because of undue burden or cost." If the party objecting to production can make this showing, the court may order the requesting party to bear some of the costs (or, of course, the parties might agree on this question).[85]

The burden of proof is on the objecting party. "Cost shifting does not even become a possibility unless there is first a showing of inaccessibility. [*sic*] Thus it cannot be argued that a party should ever be relieved of its obligation to produce accessible data merely because it may take time and effort to find what is necessary."[86]

Some situations may raise the question whether the requesting party should be able to directly access the responding party's information system to ascertain whether assertions about accessibility are valid.[87] Generally, however, "open access" to another party's information system for discovery purposes will not be considered appropriate, absent perhaps egregious misconduct in discovery by that party.[88]

C. Inadvertent Disclosure of Privileged or Protected Health Information

In cases involving large quantities of ESI, it may not be reasonably possible to identify and remove all privileged information prior to disclosure.[89] For this reason, the amendments to Rule 26(b)(5), Federal Rules of Civil Procedure, include a provision permitting a party that has inadvertently disclosed privileged ESI to move to retrieve it by notifying the receiving party. The receiving party must then "return, sequester or destroy" the ESI and any copies and may not use or disclose it until the claim of privilege has been resolved.[90]

---

[83]*Compare* Williams v. Sprint/United Mgmt. Co., 230 F.R.D. 640 (D. Kan. Sept. 29, 2005) (metadata to be disclosed), *with* Kentucky Speedway, LLC v. National Ass'n of Stock Car Auto Racing, No. 05-138-WOB, 2006 WL 5097354 (E.D. Ky. Dec. 18, 2006) (metadata usually not relevant and so not ordinarily required to be produced).

[84]*See Kentucky Speedway, LLC*, 2006 WL 5097354.

[85]FED. R. CIV. P. 26(b), Advisory Committee Note. *See generally* DISCOVERY REVOLUTION at 124–31.

[86]Peskoff v. Faber, 240 F.R.D. 26, 31 (D.D.C. 2007).

[87]FED. R. CIV. P. 26(f), Advisory Committee Note; DISCOVERY REVOLUTION at 13

[88]*See, e.g.*, Butler v. Kmart Corp., No. 2:05-CV-257-P-A, 2007 WL 2406982 (N.D. Miss. Aug. 20, 2007).

[89]FED. R. CIV. P. 26, Advisory Committee Note; *see* THE SEDONA PRINCIPLES ADDRESSING ELECTRONIC DOCUMENT PRODUCTION 8–9 (Richard Braman ed., 2d ed. 2007) [SEDONA BEST PRACTICES].

[90]FED. R. CIV. P. 26(b)(5)(B).

The rule amendment is not intended to change existing law on waiver of the attorney-client privilege by inadvertent discovery disclosure.[91] Precedent in this area recognizes a range of results, from a "strict" standard that disclosure waives the privilege, through a case-by-case determination whether it is reasonable to find waiver, to a "lenient" standard under which inadvertency is a complete defense.[92]

The same principles also apply to health care information protected by the physician-patient privilege. This privilege is usually waived with respect to health information about an individual who has filed a lawsuit placing his health into issue,[93] but will otherwise be presented whenever medical record information, physician-patient communications, and certain other categories of privileged patient information are present in litigation where a plaintiff's health is not an issue or nonplaintiff health information is sought.[94]

Apart from the possible waiver or loss of privilege, the inadvertent disclosure of ESI, including protected health information (PHI) protected by HIPAA, would violate the HIPAA Privacy Rule. Under the Privacy Rule, a covered entity may disclose PHI in discovery only (1) in response to a court order; (2) after giving potentially affected individuals notice and an opportunity to intervene; (3) upon a subpoena or discovery request and written assurances from the requesting party that it has made a good-faith effort to notify potentially affected individuals and give them an opportunity to intervene; or (4) upon a subpoena or discovery request accompanied by a protective order compliant with the regulations that has been issued or is being sought by the requesting party.[95]

Ideally, these issues should be identified before commencement of discovery and dealt with in the scheduling order.[96]

V. ADMISSION OF ESI

As a general rule, to date the courts have been quite lenient in the admission of ESI.[97] Some have shown a greater willingness to require a foundational showing for its admission,[98] and one opinion in particular has provided a detailed review of the issues presented.[99] Attacks on the validity of computer-generated breathalyzer and voting machine data may indicate a more aggressive approach on the part of litigators as well, which may lead to this becoming a more contentious area.

---

[91] DISCOVERY REVOLUTION at 147.
[92] Id. at 147–48.
[93] See WILLIAM ROACH ET AL., MEDICAL RECORDS AND THE LAW 378–79 (4th ed. 2006).
[94] Id. at 376–81.
[95] See 45 C.F.R. §164.512(e).
[96] See SEDONA BEST PRACTICES at 16.
[97] See Orin S. Kerr, Computer Records and the Federal Rules of Evidence, U.S. ATTORNEYS BULLETIN (Mar. 2001).
[98] See In re Vinhnee, 336 B.R. 437 (B.A.P. 9th Cir. 2005).
[99] Lorraine v. Markel Am. Ins. Co., No. PWG-06-1893, 241 F.R.D. 534 (D. Md. 2007).

Different types of ESI necessarily require different foundations,[100] and admission of ESI "is determined by a collection of evidence rules that present themselves like a series of hurdles to be cleared by the proponent of the evidence."[101] One fundamental and important distinction is between ESI that is human generated but computer stored and ESI that is both computer generated and computer stored.[102] Human-generated ESI may constitute hearsay and so needs to be analyzed for admission accordingly,[103] while computer-generated records (including metadata) are not hearsay.[104]

The authenticity of all types of ESI may be challenged and require a judicial determination of authenticity.[105] ESI should be admissible on a prima facie showing that it is the evidence the proponent claims it to be.[106]

> The degree of foundation required to authenticate computer-based evidence depends on the quality and completeness of the data input, the complexity of the computer processing, the routineness of the computer operation, and the ability to test and verify results of the computer processing. Determining what degree of foundation is appropriate in any given case is in the judgment of the court. The required foundation will vary not only with the particular circumstances but also with the individual judge.[107]

This foundation may be established through secondary evidence such as the testimony of witnesses familiar with the information or systems and evidence of the reliability of the processes used.[108] For these purposes,

> [t]he logical questions extend beyond the identification of the particular computer equipment and programs used. The entity's policies and procedures for the use of the equipment, database, and programs are important. How access to the pertinent database is controlled and, separately, how access to the specific program is controlled are important questions. How changes in the database are logged or

---

[100] *See id.* (distinguishing e-mail, Internet Web site postings, text messages and chat room content, computer animations and simulations, and digital photos), *and* KEVIN BRADY ET AL., THE SEDONA CONFERENCE COMMENTARY ON ESI EVIDENCE & ADMISSIBILITY 4 (Mar. 2008) [hereinafter SEDONA ADMISSIBILITY COMMENTARY] (distinguishing e-mail; Web postings, text messages and chat room content; and computer-stored records and databases).

[101] *Lorraine*, 241 F.R.D. at 538.

[102] *See* People v. Holowko, 486 N.E.2d 877–79 (Ill. 1985); *cf. Lorraine*, 241 F.R.D. 534.

[103] This issue is discussed at length in *Lorraine*, 241 F.R.D. at 562–577

[104] *See id.* at 564; *compare* United States v. Hamilton, 413 F. 3d 1138 (10th Cir. 2005):
[T]he header information that accompanied each pornographic image is not hearsay. Of primary importance to this rule is the uncontroverted fact that the header information was automatically generated by the computer hosting the newsgroup each time Hamilton uploaded a pornographic image to the newsgroup. In other words, the header information was generated instantaneously by the computer without the assistance or input of a person. As concluded by the district court, this uncontroverted fact clearly places the header information outside of Rule 801(c)'s definition of "hearsay." In particular, there was neither a "statement" nor a "declarant" involved here within the meaning of Rule 801.
413 F.3d at 1142.

[105] *Lorraine*, 241 F.R.D. at 537–38.

[106] *Id.* at 542.

[107] *Id.* at 544 (quoting WEINSTEIN ON EVIDENCE §900.06[3]).

[108] *Id.* at 543.

recorded, as well as the structure and implementation of backup systems and audit procedures for assuring the continuing integrity of the database, are pertinent to the question of whether records have been changed since their creation.[109]

At its most rigorous, the required foundation may have up to 11 elements, including evidence showing the following:

1. The business uses a computer.
2. The computer is reliable.
3. The business has developed a procedure for inserting data into the computer.
4. The procedure has built-in safeguards to ensure accuracy and identify errors.
5. The business keeps the computer in a good state of repair.
6. The witness had the computer create a readout of certain data.
7. The witness used the proper procedures to obtain the readout.
8. The computer was in working order at the time the witness obtained the readout.
9. The witness recognizes the exhibit as the readout.
10. The witness explains how he or she recognizes the readout.
11. If the readout contains strange symbols or terms, the witness explains the meaning of the symbols or terms for the trier of fact.[110]

In addition, it may also be essential to demonstrate the security of ESI in storage.[111]

While most of these elements should usually be readily demonstrable, the element of reliability may turn out to be problematic if challenged, particularly where complex systems are involved.[112]

Cases in which there is reason to doubt the reliable functioning of material elements of the information system may present even greater problems. If the reliability of ESI may be affected by possible software or system defects, it might be appropriate to have an independent analysis of application source code

---

[109] *Id.* at 558 (quoting *In re* Vinhnee, 336 B.R. 437, 445 (B.A.P. 9th Cir. 2005)).

[110] *Vinhnee*, 336 B.R. at 446–47 (*citing* EDWARD IMWINKELREID, EVIDENTIARY FOUNDATIONS §4.03[2] (5th ed. 2002)). Note that this standard is not generally accepted in the courts, most of which use "more relaxed" standards. *Lorraine*, 241 F.R.D. at 573–74.

[111] *Vinhnee*, 336 B.R. at 444.

[112] *See* SEDONA ADMISSIBILITY COMMENTARY at 7–8 (footnote omitted):
Indeed, a networked computer may be considered by computer and network security experts to be inherently un-trustworthy, requiring enhancement or upgrading to be considered both trustworthy and reliable. Accordingly, it could be argued that the trustworthiness of a computer should not be presumed, but must be demonstrated by the proponent of ESI.

or an independent information system assessment.[113] And the reliability of the software used to retrieve data may itself be subject to challenge.[114]

In summary, then, when the admission of ESI is challenged the proponent should be prepared to show the following:

- the human or automatic processes that caused the ESI to be created;
- the processes (administrative and technical) that provide assurance that the ESI that was created is what it purports to be;
- the processes that provide assurance that the ESI was not altered (or was not altered without an accurate record) during storage; and
- the processes that provide assurance that the ESI was not altered as produced.

In other words, the foundation for the authentication of ESI for admission is likely to include evidence of the reliability of the organization's processes for the creation, transmission, processing, storage, and production of the ESI. Such foundational evidence may itself therefore be discoverable evidence—including ESI such as system data and metadata.

VI. Special Problems

Given the diversity and complexity of the information systems and information processing arrangements that have been and are being implemented, there are a number of potential special problem areas, many of which may arise in only a few cases, or perhaps never. Two types of problems are likely to arise for a number of health care organizations, however: (1) electronic signatures and electronic medical records and (2) electronic health information exchange. Both raise significant potential evidentiary issues that perhaps have not been adequately considered in many organizations working with such systems.

A. Electronic Signatures and Electronic Medical Records

The transition from paper records to EMRs is not, in most systems, a simple transfer from paper records to electronic records whose native format is materially the same as paper. Even text documents, such as word processing files, cannot be "signed" (and therefore authenticated) in ways that are materially equivalent to paper record signatures, while more complex systems may present complicated issues the term "signature" serves only to confuse.

---

[113] *See* William Head and Thomas Workman, *An Analysis of 'Source Code' Litigation in the United States: What Challenges Have Been Asserted, and Where is this Litigation Heading?*, in INTERNATIONAL COUNCIL ON ALCOHOL, DRUGS AND TRAFFIC SAFETY (Aug. 30, 2007) (challenges to breathalyzer software accuracy); RABA TECHNOLOGIES LLC, TRUSTED AGENT REPORT DIEBOLD ACCUVOTE-TS VOTING SYSTEM (Jan. 24, 2004) (challenging reliability of voting machine software). *Cf.* Cobell v. Kempthorne (formerly Cobell v. Norton), No. 96-1285 (D.D.C. Jan. 30, 2008) (finding, after 11 years of litigation, including independent system testing under special master oversight, that United States Indian trust asset-related information systems and related processes were so badly secured and badly managed that reliable evidence was not available to supporting legal remedy of accounting for trust asset mismanagement).

[114] *See* van Buskirk and Liu, *Digital Evidence: Challenging the Presumption of Reliability*, 1 J. DIGITAL FORENSIC PRACTICE 19 (2006).

The long-established rule is that medical records are required to be signed, contemporaneously with their creation or promptly thereafter, by the responsible medical professional who creates them.[115] The traditional requirement was, of course, handwritten (or sometimes rubber stamp) signature of paper records, and some states had "quill pen" laws that specifically required them.[116] This requirement is intended to ensure the authenticity of the record;[117] that is, the signature is itself secondary information authenticating the record, like a user name and password in electronic document metadata.

All laws requiring handwritten signatures and paper records have been preempted by federal and state electronic signatures legislation. The principal federal law on point is the Electronic Signatures in Global and National Commerce Act (E-SIGN),[118] which was enacted in 1999 to promote electronic commerce and preempts almost all federal and state laws that prohibit or limit the use of electronic signatures and records. E-SIGN does not establish any required technology or process for electronic signatures, but instead allows parties to implement electronic signatures using mutually agreed-upon or accepted processes and indicators.[119]

E-SIGN specifically does not preempt its state counterpart, UETA, a model law promoted by the National Conference of Commissioners on Uniform State Laws. Like E-SIGN, UETA preempts almost all state law requirements for "quill pen" or "wet" signatures and paper records without specifying any required technologies or processes for electronic signatures. UETA has been enacted in almost all states,[120] and between them these statutes enable EMRs and electronic signatures in all states without specific additional legislation.

A few states have enacted legislation that gives favorable evidentiary presumptions to digital signatures created based upon a state-licensed or state-certified certification authority in a public key infrastructure (PKI).[121] Digital signatures are a form of electronic signature in which an encryption process based on encryption "keys" is applied to electronic records. Application of this process makes it impossible to modify the electronic record without detection,

---

[115]*See* E-HIM Work Group on Implementing Electronic Signatures, *Implementing Electronic Signatures, in* AHIMA PRACTICE BRIEF (Oct. 2003) (including Appendix e, State-by-State Review of Regulations Pertaining to Electronic Signature).

[116]Note that rubber stamps, while often permitted, are considered much less reliable than an actual signature. WILLIAM ROACH ET AL., MEDICAL RECORDS AND THE LAW 64–65 (4th ed. 2006).

[117]*Id.* at 62.

[118]Electronic Signatures in Global and National Commerce Act, Pub. L. No. 106-229 (2000) (codified at 15 U.S.C. §§7001 *et seq.*). See generally Chapter 7 in this book on contracting principles for e-health transactions.

[119]An electronic signature, for all purposes relevant to this discussion, including E-SIGN and UETA, is any symbol or process attached to or logically associated with an electronic record that was created by the author with the intent to sign the record.

[120]*See* National Conference of State Legislatures, Uniform Electronic Transactions Act, *available at* http://www.ncsl.org/default.aspx?tabid=13484.

[121]*See* AMERICAN BAR ASSOCIATION INFORMATION SECURITY COMMITTEE, PKI ASSESSMENT GUIDELINES 30–31 (2003) [hereinafter PKI ASSESSMENT GUIDELINES].

and when encryption keys are distributed to users and managed securely they create "nonrepudiable" electronic signatures.[122]

It is not clear whether E-SIGN preempts digital signatures statutes—the "broad" interpretation of E-SIGN holds that it does, while the "narrow" interpretation holds it does not[123]—and there is no case law on point. The Notice of Proposed Rule Making for the HIPAA Security Rule published in 1998 proposed requiring that any electronic signatures used by HIPAA covered entities be digital signatures.[124] The subsequent passage of E-SIGN raised questions about the validity of this requirement, and it was not included in the final rule.[125]

There is therefore no legal requirement that electronic signatures take any particular form or be based upon any particular technology or process. The reliability of the technology and processes used to authenticate ESI is, however, potentially crucial to its admissibility. The information that constitutes any electronic signature must be reliably associated with the person whose signature it is supposed to be. The more reliable the processes used to generate and protect the password, biometric data, or encryption key used to create the signature, the more difficult it will be for the signer to repudiate. Conversely, if the processes used to generate or protect the information are not sufficiently reliable, the electronic signature may not even be admissible in litigation, or if admissible, may be found not credible.

ESI should therefore be authenticated using processes whose reliability is proportionate to its sensitivity, as provided in the authentication guidance issued by the Centers for Medicare and Medicaid Services (CMS). While this guidance is directly applicable only to CMS and its contractors, it is based on general federal information security requirements and well developed, highly regarded federal standards.[126]

---

[122]"Nonrepudiation" means that there is
[s]trong and substantial evidence of the identity of the signer of a message [or other electronic record] and of message integrity, sufficient to prevent a party from successfully denying the origin, submission or delivery of the message and the integrity of its contents.... In a legal context, sufficient evidence to persuade the ultimate authority (judge, jury or arbiter) as to such origin, submission, delivery and integrity, despite an attempted denial by the purported sender.
PKI ASSESSMENT GUIDELINES at 283.

[123]*Id.* at 53–54.

[124]*See* U.S. Dep't of Health & Human Servs., Security and Electronic Signature Standards, 63 Fed. Reg. 43,241 (proposed Aug. 12, 1998).

[125]Even "broad" preemption would only affect the evidentiary presumptions provided in the laws, not the evidentiary value of the electronic signature processes themselves. Compared to other electronic signature processes, "PKI technology offers inherently strong factual inferences in support of attribution, which can take the place of a purely legal presumption." PKI ASSESSMENT GUIDELINES at 54. Whether digital signature statutes are preempted or not, digital signatures are in any case permitted under E-SIGN and UETA if accepted by the parties, and PKI is a valid "security procedure" for the validation of the integrity of electronic records and attribution of electronic signatures under UETA. *Id* at 54–55.

[126]The CMS Guidance is based on standards from the National Institutes of Standards and Technology (NIST) that as a statutory matter apply only to federal agencies. However, NIST influenced the drafting of the HIPAA Security Rule. *See, e.g.*, U.S. Dep't of Health & Human Servs., Health Insurance Reform: Security Standards; Final Rule, 68 Fed. Reg. 8334, 8346 (Feb. 20, 2003) (preamble). Federal regulators review federal agency HIPAA Security Rule compliance against NIST standards. *See* U.S. DEP'T OF HEALTH & HUMAN SERVS. OFFICE OF INSPECTOR GENERAL, FISCAL 2006 WORK PLAN 35–37 (2005). NIST has also provided a crosswalk of refer-

CMS information protection requirements use a risk analysis that ranks information sensitivity in three categories from "Low" to "High."[127]

- "Low Sensitivity" information is "virtually in the public domain" and requires "minimal protection."
- "Moderate Sensitivity" information is "important" and "must be protected against malicious destruction," but does not pose "significant" disclosure problems (e.g., would cause at most "nonspecific embarrassment" of an individual). "Moderate Sensitivity" information would include a patient's name, demographic information, and Social Security or other identification number.
- "High Sensitivity" information includes any information whose malicious alteration or disclosure could cause an individual medical, psychological, financial, or reputational harm, including clinical and health care payment-related information.

Medical record information would therefore be High Sensitivity, while all other PHI would be either High or Moderate Sensitivity.

Appropriate authentication is determined by matching the sensitivity level of the information against four "Assurance Levels" based on the potential consequences of authentication errors.[128] High Sensitivity information accessed from a secure internal workstation requires Level 3 assurance, while remote access (e.g., from a laptop while traveling) requires Level 4 assurance.[129] The distinction between Level 3 and Level 4 is based not upon a difference in information sensitivity levels but on the security of the access sites and computer used for remote access. Under these standards, an acceptable EMR electronic signature—i.e., one that provided assurances of protection of the medical record against inappropriate alteration or destruction—would require "two factor" authentication using both a password (or PIN) and a "soft" or "hard" cryptographic token.[130]

At this point, none of these requirements have the force of law outside the federal government and its contractors. While the determination of the adequacy

---

ences to federal guidance applicable to implementation of the HIPAA Security Rule. *See* U.S. DEP'T OF COMMERCE, NATIONAL INST. OF STANDARDS & TECH., AN INTRODUCTORY RESOURCE GUIDE FOR IMPLEMENTING THE HEALTH INSURANCE PORTABILITY AND ACCOUNTABILITY ACT (HIPAA) SECURITY RULE, NIST Special Publication 800-66 (Mar. 2005).

[127]*See* CMS INFORMATION SYSTEMS SECURITY POLICY, STANDARDS AND GUIDELINES HANDBOOK, VERSION 1.2, at 43–44 (July 19, 2004). Federal authentication requirements were established by the U.S. EXECUTIVE OFFICE OF THE PRESIDENT, OFFICE OF MANAGEMENT AND BUDGET, E-AUTHENTICATION GUIDANCE FOR FEDERAL AGENCIES (OMB 04-04 Dec. 16, 2003) [hereinafter E-AUTHENTICATION GUIDANCE FOR FEDERAL AGENCIES]. These requirements are implemented by the U.S. DEP'T OF COMMERCE, NATIONAL INST. OF STANDARDS & TECH., ELECTRONIC AUTHENTICATION GUIDE, (NIST Special Publication 800-63, Sept. 2004) [hereinafter NIST ELECTRONIC AUTHENTICATION GUIDE]. This follows standard federal practice and agency requirements. Federal sensitivity categorization in fact includes a fourth category, "High Sensitivity and National Security Interest," which CMS has concluded does not apply to any information under its control, and which by the same token should generally not apply to other health care organizations.

[128]E-AUTHENTICATION GUIDANCE FOR FEDERAL AGENCIES at 5.
[129]E-AUTHENTICATION GUIDANCE FOR FEDERAL AGENCIES at 9–11.
[130]NIST ELECTRONIC AUTHENTICATION GUIDE at 35–36, 38, 40.

of the electronic signature/authentication processes an organization implements is up to the discretion of the organization, this determination should take into account the risk that ESI authenticated by a low-reliability electronic signature may not be as credible as desired (or potentially might not even be admissible), if the purported signer could not recall making or even tried to repudiate the signature.

B. Electronic Health Records and Health Information Exchange

One of the major, bipartisan public policy goals in health care is the implementation of health information exchange (HIE) on a large, ultimately national scale.[131] HIE is often used as both a noun and a verb, referring to either the communications networks or organizations that use the communications networks or the information exchange activities that take place across them.[132] These groups of organizations—usually contractual associations—are usually called regional health information organizations (RHIOs) or "subnetwork organizations."[133]

The foundational component for most HIE projects is the EHR. As noted above, the EHR is distinguished from the EMR (at the public policy level) by serving as a clinical record for a group of clinical organizations, where the EMR serves a single organization.[134] From an evidentiary standpoint, then, the EMR assumes the functions of the traditional paper medical record maintained and used by a single provider, while an EHR draws information from—and provides it to—multiple organizations and includes but is not limited to traditional medical record information.[135]

Whatever the term, the key issue is that clinical data is made available from the EMR or EHR to other organizations participating in HIE.

> More specifically, we conceptualize the [national health information infrastructure] as a cluster of nodes. We define a node as a physical healthcare environment with the requisite health information management technology to collect, store, display and transmit patient-identifiable, structured, clinical data in an electronic format. Therefore, a sole practitioner in private practice using a simple, electronic health record (EHR) system who has access to the Internet could function as a node. On the other hand, we would also consider a large, academic medical center's inpatient facility as a single node, as well.[136]

---

[131] *See* Christiansen, *Legal Speed Bumps on the Road to Health Information Exchange*, 1 J. HEALTH & LIFE SCIENCES LAW 1, 4–14 (2008).

[132] *Id.* at 8.

[133] *Id.* at 12–13.

[134] *See* NATIONAL ALLIANCE FOR HEALTH INFORMATION TECHNOLOGY, REPORT TO THE OFFICE OF THE NATIONAL COORDINATOR FOR HEALTH INFORMATION TECHNOLOGY ON DEFINING KEY HEALTH INFORMATION TECHNOLOGY TERMS (Apr. 28, 2008).

[135] *See, e.g.*, DAVE GARETS & MIKE DAVIS, HIMSS ANALYTICS, LLC, ELECTRONIC MEDICAL RECORDS VS. ELECTRONIC HEALTH RECORDS: YES, THERE IS A DIFFERENCE (HIMSS Analytics, LLC 2006), *available at* http://www.himssanalytics.org/docs/WP_EMR_EHR.pdf.

[136] *See* Dean F. Sittig et al., *A Draft Framework for Measuring Progress Towards the Development of a National Health Information Infrastructure*, in BMC MED. INFO & DECISION MAKING 1, 6 (2005).

Ch. 17.VI.B.   *Discovery and Admission of Electronic Information as Evidence*   619

In any HIE, different entities are likely to own different elements of the network,[137] different types of users and different organizations may have different rights to use or access information or portions of the network,[138] and there may be many sites where workstations are vulnerable to unauthorized use.[139] The ESI created, stored, and transmitted throughout the network is therefore at risk of alteration or loss to the extent that users fail to prevent unauthorized use or access.[140]

This raises potentially very problematic issues of the production—and perhaps at least as significantly, the authentication—of ESI. Depending on how information has been flowing around the network, a wide range of participants may have potentially relevant ESI. For example, system data created as part of network transactions is very likely to be relevant to issues about when and how a given record was created, transmitted, and received, and perhaps what other parties may have had access to it.

An EHR record created by the collection of information from a variety of different organizations may need to be authenticated with reference to the systems, transaction data, and user data of all those organizations. To the extent that any organization participating in HIE is a custodian of systems in which PHI is stored or transmitted, that organization will have to vouch for the reliability of those processes. At the same time, the integrity of the content of ESI—medical record entries, for example—will have to be demonstrated by the custodians of the systems that created it.

Beyond production difficulties, this kind of arrangement may lead to significant admissibility or credibility issues. For example, where a patient is harmed due to a decision based on medical record ESI obtained from another clinician through an EHR, the clinician who provided the information may have a good reason to deny providing that information, to avoid liability for the harm. The receiving clinician may be unable to authenticate the information without foundational evidence from the providing clinician.

While such information may be obtained from an uncooperative entity by subpoena or court order (or by making the providing clinician a party), the same ESI preservation obligations may not apply (especially to metadata), and additional cost issues will certainly arise.[141]

In order to avoid such disputes and the metastasis of evidentiary motion practice into adversarial litigation between HIE participants, HIE conditions of participation (whether in RHIO bylaws, contracts among the parties, or

---

[137] *See* THE QUEST FOR INTEROPERABLE HEALTH RECORDS: A GUIDE TO LEGAL ISSUES IN ESTABLISHING HEALTH INFORMATION NETWORKS (Kristen Rosati & Marilyn Lamar eds., 2005); John R. Christiansen, *When Networks Collide: Managing the Risks Arising from the Interaction of Healthcare and Information Systems*, 11 THE HEALTH LAWYER 10, 12–13 (1998).

[138] *See* SARAH ROSENBAUM ET AL., CHARTING THE LEGAL ENVIRONMENT OF HEALTH INFORMATION 8–9 (2005).

[139] *See, e.g.*, A GUIDE TO HIPAA SECURITY AND THE LAW 64–65 (Stephen S. Wu ed., 2007).

[140] *See, e.g.*, Christiansen, *When Networks Collide*.

[141] *See generally* ALAN BLAKELY ET AL., THE SEDONA CONFERENCE COMMENTARY ON NON-PARTY PRODUCTION AND RULE 45 SUBPOENAS (2008).

otherwise) should specify the obligations of participants to provide relevant information in discovery and in support of its admission (and perhaps its credibility). This may be difficult to negotiate, particularly where different participants use different processes for authentication.[142]

---

[142] For example, an organization that permits remote EMR access only upon two-factor authentication may consider medical record information provided by an organization that permits it upon user name and simple password (or shared access) less reliable than the information it generates itself. At the same time, the latter organization may not consider the costs and burdens of two-factor authentication something it wants to assume. In the absence of legal standards, however, if two such parties wish to engage in HIE, they will have to develop a way of allocating legal risks and liabilities—or fight about it if and when the issue arises in litigation.

18

Legal Ethics and E-Health*

I. Introduction	623
II. Use of Technology in the Practice of Health Law	623
A. Attorney E-Competence in Managing Technology	623
1. Confidentiality and Privacy of Electronic Information	624
a. Misdirected Facsimiles or E-Mail	624
b. Managing Compliance with HIPAA and the HITECH Act	624
2. Security of Electronic Information	625
a. Back Up	625
b. Viruses	625
c. Internet E-Mail and Encryption	625
i. Duty of Confidentiality	626
ii. Waiver of Attorney-Client Privilege	626
iii. Malpractice Liability	627
iv. HITECH Act Violations	627
d. Hardware Risks	627
i. Hard Drive or Remote Disk Drive Use	627
ii. Deleting Data	628
e. E-Mailed Documents	628
f. Other Issues	628
3. E-Discovery	628
a. Scope of Discovery	629
b. Ethical Requirements	629
c. Social Media and Professional Communications	629
i. Ethical Considerations	630
ii. Admissibility	630
iii. Special Issues	630
4. Electronic Filings	630

---

*Sheryl Tatar Dacso, J.D., Ph.D., Houston, Texas; Kari Loeser, J.D., San Francisco, California. The authors thank William Freivogal, who authorized an earlier version of this chapter.

			a	Affecting the Practice of Law..	630
			b.	Affecting Health Care Laws...	630
		5.	\multicolumn{2}{l	}{Use of Cellular Phones, PDAs, and Other Devices.................}	631
		6.	\multicolumn{2}{l	}{Cloud Computing ....}	631
	B.	\multicolumn{3}{l	}{Ethical Issues with Technology Use ....}	631
		1.	\multicolumn{2}{l	}{Web Sites. ....}	631
		2.	\multicolumn{2}{l	}{Social Media...}	632
			a.	Blogs..	632
			b.	Wiki Pages...	633
			c.	Facebook	633
			d.	Myspace and LinkedIn	634
			e.	Twitter	634
			f.	Use of Social Media by Attorneys—Use Caution............	635
		3.	\multicolumn{2}{l	}{Corporate Family Conflict Issues ....}	635
	C.	\multicolumn{3}{l	}{Other Ethical Considerations ....}	635
		1.	\multicolumn{2}{l	}{Solicitation of Business. ....}	635
		2.	\multicolumn{2}{l	}{Researching Potential Jurors or Witnesses ....}	636
		3.	\multicolumn{2}{l	}{Ex Parte Communications ....}	637
III.	\multicolumn{4}{l	}{Knowledge of Client Misconduct ....}	637
	A.	\multicolumn{3}{l	}{Attorney-Client Privilege..}	639
	B.	\multicolumn{3}{l	}{Ethics Rules on Confidentiality ....}	640
		1.	\multicolumn{2}{l	}{Confidentiality. ....}	640
		2.	\multicolumn{2}{l	}{Assisting a Client's Crime or Fraud ....}	640
		3.	\multicolumn{2}{l	}{Audits and Investigations ....}	641
			a.	Hiring Consultants...	642
			b.	Crime/Fraud Exception to the Attorney-Client Privilege...	642
		4.	\multicolumn{2}{l	}{Representing the Organization ....}	642
			a.	"Climbing the Corporate Ladder"	642
			b.	Preventing Misunderstandings About Who Represents Whom...	643
			c.	Causing a Constituent to Be Fired...................................	643
IV.	\multicolumn{4}{l	}{Conflicts of Interest..}	643
	A.	\multicolumn{3}{l	}{Joint Representation...}	644
		1.	\multicolumn{2}{l	}{Model Rule 2.2 ....}	644
		2.	\multicolumn{2}{l	}{Model Rule 2.2 and the Ethics 2000 Commission ....}	644
		3.	\multicolumn{2}{l	}{Restatement ....}	645
		4.	\multicolumn{2}{l	}{Joint Confidences and the Ethics 2000 Commission..............}	645
		5.	\multicolumn{2}{l	}{Recommendation ....}	645
		6.	\multicolumn{2}{l	}{Joint Representation in Commercial Negotiations ....}	646
		7.	\multicolumn{2}{l	}{"Unintentional" Joint Representation.........................}	647
		8.	\multicolumn{2}{l	}{Litigation and Joint Representation.............................}	648
	B.	\multicolumn{3}{l	}{Close Corporations ....}	649
	C.	\multicolumn{3}{l	}{Partnerships and Limited Partnerships ....}	651
		1.	\multicolumn{2}{l	}{General Partnerships..}	651
		2.	\multicolumn{2}{l	}{Limited Partnerships..}	652
	D.	\multicolumn{3}{l	}{Conflicts and Malpractice Liability ....}	653

I. Introduction

The Internet, combined with growing technology capabilities, offers unprecedented access to information, products, and services. At the same time, it makes possible forms of communication and practices that raise ethical and legal concerns. Relationships between attorneys and their clients as well as entire transactions can occur without a face-to-face encounter. The availability of social media presents opportunities for marketing but heightens liability exposure for inadvertent disclosures and implied attorney-client relationships.

The pervasiveness of information technology raises complex and new approaches to the analysis of an attorney's legal duty and ethical responsibility. This chapter first discusses the use of information technology by health care lawyers and the effect of such technology on the attorney's ethical responsibilities and legal duties to his or her client. It next addresses new areas of liability, as the expanding use of technology intersects with legal ethics rules with respect to matters of attorney competence in its use and deployment in practice, as well as heightened compliance obligations with respect to client information privacy and confidentiality. This includes issues related to the use and storage of information that may be subject to civil and criminal investigations or client misconduct and e-discovery issues. The last part of the chapter considers several complex and difficult conflict-of-interest issues that may confront the health care practitioner who, on one hand, maintains a privileged attorney-client relationship with his or her client but, on the other hand, because of that relationship assumes separate legal duties for maintaining the privacy and security of protected health information and complying with federal and state laws, rules, and regulations.

Since the legal system and ethical guidelines often lag behind technology, attorneys who work with clients that use health information technology and who use such technology themselves must constantly stay informed of both ethical and legal duties. While the list of issues is not exhaustive, those discussed in this chapter are the ones currently posing important concerns for the conscientious lawyer.

II. Use of Technology in the Practice of Health Law

A. Attorney E-Competence in Managing Technology

The first rule in legal ethics, as expressed in the Model Rules of Professional Conduct of the American Bar Association (ABA), is that a lawyer must be competent.[1] Lawyers must understand their ethical and legal responsibilities when using technology that involves access to and use and storage of client information, particularly if that information contains sensitive identifiable patient

---

[1] *See* ABA Model Rules of Prof'l Conduct R. 1.1 (1983) ("A lawyer shall provide competent representation to a client.").

health information protected under federal and state laws.[2] Failure of a lawyer to use technology properly can lead to client harm and result in a claim that the lawyer has acted incompetently. The integrity of the lawyer's computer system is important to avoid unauthorized access. A simple stroke of a key can send confidential information to persons who are not the intended recipients. For these reasons and others, attorneys who rely on electronic data and Internet communications should adopt systems and processes that incorporate privacy and security standards necessary to protect their clients.

1. Confidentiality and Privacy of Electronic Information

a. Misdirected Facsimiles or E-Mail

It is, of course, possible to send a fax or an e-mail to the wrong person, thereby disclosing client confidences to someone who should not have them. Speed dialing and the ability to send documents to multiple locations with the press of one or two buttons only increase the danger. Of course, the same is true for e-mail communications involving one's client.[3] The ABA in 2011 issued Formal Opinion 11-459, entitled *Duty to Protect the Confidentiality of E-Mail Communications with One's Client*, concluding that a lawyer sending or receiving substantive communications with a client via e-mail must warn the client about the risk of sending or receiving an electronic communication using a computer or other device when there is a significant risk that a third party may gain access to that communication.[4] This opinion has implications with respect to attorneys communicating with clients where such communications are at risk for access by third parties such as employers or others based on the setting (e.g., an Internet café or hotel).

b. Managing Compliance with HIPAA and the HITECH Act

As more health care lawyers assume responsibility for assisting their clients' regulatory compliance efforts and responses to the various agencies that audit health care entities, medical record information may be shared electronically between the attorney and client. Many attorneys do not realize that using or accessing personal health information (PHI) in the course of representing a client can make them subject to the same compliance requirements as a business associate of a covered entity under the Health Insurance Portability and

---

[2] Protected Health Information is defined under federal HIPAA laws as any information about health status, provision of health care, or payment for health care that can be linked to a specific individual. It is also referred to as "individually identifiable health information." *See* Health Information Portability and Accountability Act (HIPAA) and the Privacy Rule, 42 C.F.R. §§164.501 *et seq.*

[3] ABA Comm. on Ethics & Prof'l Responsibility, Formal Op. 368 (1992), discusses when the recipient of an inadvertently-transmitted document containing the opposing party's confidences may use the information. While both misdirected faxes and e-mails are mentioned in passing, the focus of the opinion is on whether the attorney-client privilege was waived, not whether Rule 1.6 or DR 4-101 was violated.

[4] ABA Comm. on Ethics & Prof'l Responsibility, Formal Op. 11-459 (2011) (based on the ABA Model Rules of Professional Conduct, as amended by the ABA House of Delegates through August 2011).

Accountability Act (HIPAA).[5] Attorneys must now understand not only their clients' duties as business associates but also their own obligations as attorneys under the Health Information Technology for Economic and Clinical Health Act (HITECH Act) who may find themselves in conflict with their clients.[6] This is discussed further in II.A.2., below.

2. Security of Electronic Information

The principal provision requiring lawyers to protect client information is ABA Model Rule 1.6. The ways in which a lawyer can violate his or her duties of confidentiality to a client through the misuse of technology are virtually endless. The following discussion lists the most prominent of those.

a. Back Up

Crucial client data can be lost through failure to back up a computer system. On the other hand, in some instances a lawyer would have preferred to destroy data—in situations, of course, where destruction would have been perfectly legal—but the lawyer did not know how the firm's back-up system worked and later discovered to his or her chagrin that the data remained on a tape in a warehouse. Moreover, the HITECH Act imposes on attorneys' obligations regarding the security of PHI, including systems for storage, retrieval, and recovery.[7]

b. Viruses

Failure of a lawyer to use standard antivirus software can cause the loss of crucial client data. New computer viruses appear on a routine basis and can invade computer operating systems and render the host system vulnerable to external access of all data. Antivirus software has become essential to the ethical attorney's practice of law.

c. Internet E-Mail and Encryption

A debate persists about whether lawyers should communicate with or about clients using Internet e-mail without encryption. Encryption is a way to render outgoing e-mail content unreadable except to the intended recipient. Four issues emerge in the debate over communicating with or about clients via unencrypted e-mail:

---

[5] 45 C.F.R. §§164.502(e), 164.504(e), 164.532(d) and (e).

[6] American Recovery and Reinvestment Act of 2009, Health Information Technology for Economic and Clinical Health Act (HITECH Act), §§13001 *et seq.,* Pub. L. No. 111-05, 123 Stat. 115 (Feb. 17, 2009) (codified at 42 U.S.C. §§201 *et seq.*). Under the HITECH Act, all business associates, as defined in the Act, have a statutory obligation to comply with both HIPAA and the HITECH Act, violations of which may subject them to statutory penalties for failure to comply with HIPAA's Privacy, Security, or Breach Notification Rules. *See* 45 C.F.R. pts. 160, 164 & subpts. C (Security), D (Breach Notification) & E (Privacy).

[7] For detailed discussions of security issues in the e-health context, see Chapter 7 (Christiansen, Information Security and Breach Notification Under HIPAA and HITECH) and Chapter 11 (Faccenda, Obligations in Response to a Health Care Data Security Breach).

- Is it a violation of ethics rules on confidentiality?
- Could it cause a waiver of the attorney-client privilege?
- Does it expose the lawyer to a malpractice claim?
- Does it create exposure for violating the HITECH Act rules?

Several factors are germane to all four issues. First, the increased ability of outside persons to "hack" into e-mail communications has made such communications subject to heightened security concerns. Similar to tapping a landline telephone, these cyber attacks or intrusions are both felonies under the same federal law.[8] Second, the unauthorized access by outside third parties to client information is a crime. An attorney who consciously disregards establishing minimal security or policies regarding unauthorized access may have compromised his or her client's interests, subjected the client to potential liability for violating federal and state laws, and become subject to the financial consequences of federal or state enforcement actions as a business associate. The inadvertent disclosure of confidential information via e-mail raises several ethical issues.[9]

i. Duty of Confidentiality

The ABA and all of the major states' ethics committees have opined that communicating with or about clients using unencrypted e-mail is appropriate except in the most extreme circumstances.[10] Such circumstances would include those where the communications relate to information subject to HIPAA and the HITECH Act.

ii. Waiver of Attorney-Client Privilege

The federal Electronic Communications Privacy Act (ECPA) provides as follows: "No otherwise privileged wire, oral, or electronic communication intercepted in accordance with, or in violation of, the provisions of this chapter shall lose its privileged character."[11] That certainly takes care of federal courts. At least one state court has now taken the position that sending a message via e-mail (presumably unencrypted) does not waive the attorney-client privilege.[12]

---

[8] *See* Electronic Communications Privacy Act, 18 U.S.C. §§2510 *et seq.*

[9] An excellent summary of these issues appears at David Hricik, *E-Mail and Client Confidentiality: Lawyers Worry Too Much about Transmitting Client Confidences by Internet E-Mail*, 11 GEO. J. LEGAL ETHICS 459 (1999). The author of this chapter for this book's first edition wrote one of the early articles advancing the view that communicating on the Internet without encryption should not raise ethical issues. *See* William Freivogel, *Internet Communications, Part II, A Larger Perspective*, 8 ALAS LOSS PREVENTION 2 (Jan. 1997), *available at* http://www.legalethics.com/?page_id=410.

[10] ABA Comm. on Ethics and Prof'l Responsibility, Formal Op. 413 (1999); D.C. Legal Ethics Comm. Op. 281 (1998); Ill. Adv. Op. 96-10 (1997); Mass. Comm. on Prof'l Ethics Op. 00-1 (2000); N.Y. Comm. on Prof'l Ethics Op. 809 (1998). Encryption proponents, on the other hand, cited *The T.J. Hooper*, 60 F.2d 737, 740 (2d Cir. 1932), in which a failure to have a radio (available but uncommon at the time) rendered a tugboat not seaworthy, to support arguments for encryption ("a whole calling may have unduly lagged in the adoption of new and available devices").

[11] 18 U.S.C. §2517. However, more recent cases have found a waiver of privilege where data was not adequately scrubbed. *See* Victor Stanley, Inc. v. Creative Pipe, Inc., 250 F.R.D. 251 (D. Md. 2008), *and* Mount Hawley Ins. Co. v. Felman Prod., Inc., 271 F.R.D. 125 (S.D. W. Va. 2010).

[12] City of Reno v. Reno Police Protective Ass'n, 59 P.3d 1212 (Nev. 2002), *modified on denial of reh'g*, 2003 Nev. LEXIS 25 (Nev. May 14, 2003).

That being said, where an attorney is involved in representing a client in a health care investigation subject to federal fraud and abuse laws, and where preserving the attorney-client privilege is critical to managing the case and client data, such a violation could cost the defendant client the right to claim attorney-client privilege where the information has been disclosed outside of the protected attorney-client communication.

iii. Malpractice Liability

The Attorneys' Liability Assurance Society (ALAS) found there were no reports of a malpractice claim against a lawyer resulting from the theft of information transmitted via the Internet or any other medium.[13]

iv. HITECH Act Violations

The HITECH Act not only expands enforcement of HIPAA violations against covered entities such as providers, insurers, and clearinghouses, but also extends to business associates (including attorneys) who fail to comply with the HIPAA rules.[14] This poses both an ethical and a legal dilemma, since a health care attorney's violation of HIPAA has consequences for both the attorney and the health care client. Attorneys who use agents and subcontractors will have to address these new requirements for their own obligations for HIPAA compliance.

d. Hardware Risks

i. Hard Drive or Remote Disk Drive Use

Lawyers increasingly send documents as e-mail attachments. However, some use compact disks (CDs) or small external memory drives (sometimes referred to as "flash" or "thumb" drives) that have a lot of storage capacity and are portable. Re-use of these drives or CDs could result in a breach of client confidentiality. For example, it may be possible for the recipient to detect earlier drafts of the subject document, or the CD or external drive could contain confidential information of other clients. Data that have been "deleted" from a flash drive may remain there, hidden. Lawyers should ensure that they know how to erase all such hidden data if they are going to give a client access to a flash drive.

When hardware is scrapped, traded in, or sold, steps should be taken to ensure that it is scrubbed of all underlying data. Likewise, hardware that is rented or leased should be checked for client information before being returned to its owner.

Lawyers should be very careful not to allow other client information to remain on such media.

---

[13] *See* William Freivogel, *Legal Ethics & E-Health, in* E-HEALTH BUSINESS & TRANSACTIONAL LAW at 484 (1st ed. 2005).

[14] HITECH Act, §13001 (enacted as part of the American Recovery and Reinvestment Act of 2009 (ARRA), Pub. L. No. 111-5, tit. XII (2009)). As of February 17, 2010, the HITECH Act empowered the federal government to impose civil and criminal penalties directed at business associates.

ii. Deleting Data

Most lawyers now know that hitting the delete button does not remove the document from a computer's hard drive. The document remains retrievable until it is "written over." Even overwritten documents sometimes can be recovered if the expertise and software are available. This is how federal regulators recover data from hard drives when the owner has attempted deletion of certain files. Thus, the lawyer who thinks that client data has been eliminated may be mistaken.

e. E-Mailed Documents

Some word processing software will allow recipients of e-mailed documents to see "metadata," hidden data that reveals, for example, who authored the document and when. In many cases, the recipient can also see what changes have been made to the document. There are ways to scrub documents of this information. Lawyers sending documents should learn how to do this and ensure that it is done before the documents are sent to the other side or, perhaps just as bad, to the client. For those lawyers who search other parties' documents for hidden data, caution is advised. Various state ethics committees have taken divergent views on the propriety of doing so.[15]

f. Other Issues

Health care clients are subject to a myriad of federal and state laws and regulations on the control of patient information, not the least of which are those that relate to privacy.[16] Information technology affects the availability of information in many ways, and health care lawyers claiming to be competent must understand and be able to advise clients on such technical concepts as encryption, cookies, Web beacons, and so forth.

3. E-Discovery

Enhanced information and computer technology have advanced the use of electronic discovery by the courts and among legal counsel. The use of e-discovery is no longer optional for litigation counsel.[17] The use of social media has

---

[15] For state ethics committees that have concluded that the search for metadata is unethical, see Ala. State Bar Office of Gen. Counsel, Op. 2007-02 (Mar. 14, 2007); Ariz. Op. 07-03 (Nov. 2007); D.C. Op. 341 (Sept. 2007); Fla. Bar Prof'l Ethics Comm., Op. 06-02 (Sept. 15, 2006); N.H. Op. 2008-2009/4 (2009); Me. Op. 196 (Oct. 2008); and N.Y. State Bar Ass'n Comm. on Prof'l Ethics, Op. No. 749 (Dec. 14, 2001) & 782 (2004). For ethics committees concluding such searches are not unethical, see ABA Comm. on Ethics & Prof'l Responsibility, Formal Op. 06-442 (Aug. 5, 2006), and Md. State Bar Ethics Comm., Op. 2007-09 (Oct. 16, 2006). *See also* Col. Op 119 (2008) (taking a middle ground); Pa. Op. 2007-500 (2008) (saying "it depends"); David Hricik, *Mining for Embedded Data: Is it Ethical to Take Intentional Advantage of Other People's Failures?* 8 N.C. J. L. & TECH. 231 (2007).

[16] For detailed discussions of privacy issues in the e-health context, see Chapter 5 (Dahm, Privacy Issues in U.S. Health Care) and Chapter 6 (Taylor & Crawford, The European Data Privacy Regime).

[17] Courts have begun to sanction attorneys who refuse to use e-discovery. *See* Univ. of Montreal Pension Comm. v. Banc of Am. Secs., 685 F. Supp. 2d 456 (S.D.N.Y. 2010); Rimkus Consulting Group v. Cammarata, 688 F. Supp. 2d 598 (S.D. Tex. 2010).

affected the application of discovery, as there is no privacy for social network posts, and although most social media sites have disclaimers, their operators cannot assert any privacy or privileged protection for information maintained on their sites. Also, because the rules of e-discovery are in development, the evaluation of electronic information should not be left to inexperienced persons or associate attorneys. Ethical dilemmas often arise with the use of search terms and whether they should be shared with opposing counsel. Much valuable information resides on the hard drives of the parties to litigation. A client whose lawyer does not know how to discover that information is at a distinct disadvantage.[18] The use of e-discovery is beyond the scope of this chapter, but the following basic information is relevant to e-health and ethics.

a. Scope of Discovery

A party may serve on any other party a request for information that is (1) nonprivileged; (2) in the responding parties "possession, custody or control"; (3) reasonably calculated to lead to the discovery of admissible evidence; (4) stored in any medium from which information can be obtained either directly or, if necessary, after translation by the responding party into a reasonably usable form; (5) including, without limitation, writings, drawings, graphs, charts, photographs, sound recordings, images, and other data or data compilations.[19]

b. Ethical Requirements

The exchange of information through e-discovery is subject to both ethical and legal requirements. These include the following:

- MODEL RULES OF PROF'L CONDUCT R. 1.1—Competence
- MODEL RULES OF PROF'L CONDUCT R. 3.2—Expediting Litigation
- MODEL RULES OF PROF'L CONDUCT R. 3.4—Fairness to Opposing Counsel
- FED. R. CIV. P. 1—Speedy and Inexpensive Resolution
- FED. R. CIV. P. 26(g)—Discovery Certifications

c. Social Media and Professional Communications

Taking legal positions in online communications could undermine the position a lawyer is taking, or may have to take, on behalf of a client. In the context of a law firm, one partner or associate may undermine the position being taken by another. For example, in one instance a lawyer posted on the Internet opinions that were highly critical of another firm that was representing a tobacco company. It turned out that the lawyer's firm was co-counsel with the law firm being criticized.

---

[18] For a good discussion of electronic discovery, see Douglas A. Cawley, *Deleted but Not Removed*, LEGAL TIMES, July 21, 1997, at S34. Electronic discovery is also discussed in Chapter 17 (Christiansen, Discovery and Admission of Electronic Information as Evidence).

[19] *See* FED. R. CIV. P. 26(b)(1), 34(a).

i. Ethical Considerations

So long as an attorney does not "friend" a party when seeking discovery of information that may be posted on sites such as MySpace and Facebook, accessing discoverable information from such sites does not violate ethics rules.[20]

ii. Admissibility

In one case, the standard of admissibility of information obtained "legally" from electronic sources and social media was that the party offering the evidence need only make a "prima facie showing that it is what he or she claims it to be."[21]

iii. Special Issues

To date, most cases using social media have arisen in the context of employment law, tort, and insurance cases and in connection with the impeachment of evidence. However, special issues arise related to the First and Fourth Amendments to the U.S. Constitution, setting forth protections as to free speech and privacy, respectively.

4. Electronic Filings

a. Affecting the Practice of Law

Some tribunals and government agencies require electronic filing;[22] some prohibit electronic filing.[23] Failure to know the difference can cause harm to a client.

b. Affecting Health Care Laws

Health care laws and regulations affect whether or not certain kinds of health care business can be conducted electronically. Some laws and regulations—for example, those applying to prescriptions—require the presence of a hard copy trail. Insurance laws, too, sometimes have specific requirements regarding the maintenance of paper and digital files. Again, to satisfy the ethical duty of competence, lawyers advising health care clients must be able to give them guidance on these requirements.

---

[20] *See* N.Y. St. Bar Ass'n Ethics Op. 843 (Sept. 10, 2010).

[21] *See* Lorraine v. Markel Am. Ins. Co., 241 F.R.D. 534, 542 (D. Md. 2007). In *Lorraine*, the judge tried to provide a starting place for understanding the requirements for the admissibility of electronic evidence.

[22] For example, the U.S. Securities and Exchange Commission requires public companies to file registration statements, periodic reports, and other forms electronically through its Electronic Data Gathering, Analysis, and Retrieval (EDGAR) system. *See* 17 C.F.R. pt. 230 *et seq.*

[23] *See, e.g.*, Georgia Dep't of Transp. v. Norris, 474 S.E.2d 216 (Ga. Ct. App. 1996), *rev'd on other grounds*, 486 S.E.2d 826 (Ga. 1997) (lawyer's filing was deemed late because he had used a fax machine to transmit a crucial filing on the last day it was due; the Georgia Supreme Court reversed because the lawyer had put the document in the mail the day before it was due).

5. Use of Cellular Phones, PDAs, and Other Devices

We live in a wireless world of iPhones, iPads, BlackBerrys, and numerous other hand-held devices that make communications easier and ethical risks greater for the health care attorney. For all the reasons discussed earlier in this chapter, attorneys must use caution when e-mailing or texting client information.

Use of portable phones should not raise privilege or confidentiality issues. This is because unauthorized interception and use of portable phone conversations violates ECPA, the same federal law that prohibits unauthorized interception of e-mail messages.[24] Caution is advised, however. There have been a number of ethics opinions and court decisions to the effect that there is no reasonable expectation of privacy on cellular or cordless phones.[25]

6. Cloud Computing

Wikipedia defines cloud computing as the delivery of computing as a service rather than a product, whereby shared resources, software, and information are provided to computers and other devices as a utility over a network rather than being housed in a fixed location on site. For attorneys, cloud computing poses some risk, since the applications and some of the data used in managing one's electronic information system are not under one's direct control.

B. Ethical Issues with Technology Use

1. Web Sites

Many law firm Web sites contain instructions to viewers on how to contact the firm. At times, these instructions even include an e-mail template that enables viewers to insert their name and address and append a message. While seemingly innocuous, there is reason for caution with this practice related to solicitation and possible disclosures in other client information. Examples of issues that may arise with law firm Web sites include:

- A stranger to a law firm e-mails confidential information to the firm, and the firm subsequently discovers that it represented the party against which the stranger wanted to bring an action. Receipt of the confidences of the other side under these circumstances presents a very real danger that the receiving firm will be conflicted out of the matter.
- A client interested in the law firm submits an unsolicited e-mail with links to public, third-party Web sites or corporate intranet sites. By clicking through, the attorney or law firm may also be inadvertently violating confidences of an existing client.

---

[24] 18 U.S.C. §2517(4).

[25] *See* Albert Gidari, Jr., *Proprietary Rights: Privilege and Confidentiality in Cyberspace*, THE COMPUTER LAW., Feb. 1996 at 1; David Hricik, *Confidentiality and Privilege in High-Tech Communications*, THE PROF. LAW., Feb. 1997, at 1; Peter R. Jarvis & Bradley F. Tellam, *High-Tech Ethics and Malpractice Issues*, THE PROF. LAW., 1996 Symposium, at 51; *see also* ABA/BNA LAW. MANUAL ON PROF. CONDUCT at 55:01–55:424 (Oct. 30, 1996).

To address these types of scenarios, any invitation for a viewer to contact the firm should contain language similar to the following: "We will not have an attorney-client relationship with you until you have spoken to a lawyer in the firm and have been sent an engagement letter. Do not put any confidential information in a message to us until a lawyer in the firm asks you for it."

It also would be advisable to assign one staff member to review all such incoming e-mails and complete a conflict-of-interest check. If the matter appears to present a conflict, the staff member would notify the sender immediately that the firm cannot be involved. The staff member then would delete the sender's message and not reveal its contents to anyone else in the firm. This procedure should be put in writing and made part of the firm's office manual. Although no published cases or opinions exist to approve such a screening procedure, by having it and following it, the firm would have an arguable basis for avoiding disqualification.

2. Social Media

A new form of Internet communications now exists through tools known collectively as "social media." These tools include blogs, wiki pages, and social networking sites such as Facebook.com, Myspace.com, LinkedIn.com, and Twitter.com.[26] Potential ethical issues surrounding conflicts of interest may arise as a result of a client, or potential client, disclosing or posting various information on these Web sites, which in turn imposes additional due diligence requirements for the attorney or law firm. The following is a brief discussion of key considerations for such Internet communications.

a. Blogs

Blogs are generally known as the shorthand for "Web log"—simply put, an online journal or diary that is maintained by the owner/user.[27] Blogs are so commonly known that government agencies often "lurk" and read the open access information posted on blogs to facilitate and provide insight into ongoing investigations.[28] As such, many companies are now banning or prohibiting employees from accessing such blogs using company computers or corporate Internet capabilities.[29] Attorneys and law firms may wish to consider a similar internal policy or impose specific restrictions to avoid inappropriate disclosures and breaches of confidentiality and also to mitigate conflicts of interest.

---

[26] A wealth of social networking and communication Web sites may exist. These are only given as representative examples of the more commonly-utilized ones as of 2011.

[27] Blogs proliferate on the Internet. Simply go to http://www.google.com and type "blog" or go to http://www.blogger.com to create your "own" blog.

[28] For example, anecdotally, when reading certain blog content, it becomes very conceivable that agencies such as the U.S. Department of Justice might review past blog posts on http://www.cafepharma.com when investigating pharmaceutical or life science companies for fraud, kickbacks, and other criminal investigations. *See generally* CafePharma, *available at* http://www.cafepharma.com.

[29] *See generally* Ed Silverman, *Glaxo Blocks Employee Access to CafePharma*, PHARMALOT, *available at* http://www.pharmalot.com/2010/05/glaxo-blocks-employee-access-to-cafepharma/.

b. Wiki Pages

Wiki pages are known as Web encyclopedias, with content freely shared, contributed by, and posted by self-identified experts on public domain Web sites such as Wikipedia.com.[30] Even some professional associations, such as the American Health Lawyers Association, have initiated a Wiki page.[31] The implications for attorneys practicing in health law typically include the inadvertent or intentional disclosure of sensitive and proprietary information by one client to another client (or opposing party) through a Wiki page and the free sharing of information. Another ethical issue arises due to lack of oversight in identifying and mitigating conflicts of interest. No attorney discipline cases to date have been based on Wiki page information, but given the high likelihood of inaccurate or misleading information, attorneys should give close consideration to counseling clients and themselves as to the potential problems associated with online Wiki encyclopedias.

The potential invasion of privacy and First Amendment issues associated with Internet social media are not explored here. Attorneys should note the 2011 events associated with the "WikiLeaks" episode—the criminal investigation of WikiLeaks founder Julian Assange and many others for disclosing sensitive and classified information on their anti-secrecy Web site.[32] This investigation is still underway, and the criminal trial is pending, but the Web site cablegate.wikileaks.com is currently inoperable and indicates hosting, or posting on, Wiki pages may be subject to regulation.[33]

c. Facebook

Facebook is a booming Internet Web site due to its popularity, ease of use, and pervasive influence. At last count, Facebook has an estimated 500 million users[34] and continues growing. Given the ease of access and the type and frequency of postings by users, individuals (such as clients or potential clients) may post on Facebook personal, confidential, and/or sensitive information. It would be reasonable for attorneys or firms to create a mock Facebook account to use as part of a standard conflict-of-interest check, as well as to monitor the use and disclosure of information being shared by colleagues, members of the firm, or other law firm employees. It is also recommended that firms create an Internet use policy that explicitly identifies by whom, when, how, or if the use of Facebook will be permitted. The same recommendations might apply when counseling health care clients.

---

[30] Ironically, when conducting research, the authors discovered a Wiki page on blogs. *See* Wikipedia, Blog, *available at* http://en.wikipedia.org/wiki/Blog.

[31] *See generally* American Health Lawyers Association, Health Law Wiki, *available at* http://www.healthlawyers.org/Resources/Health%20Law%20Wiki/Home.aspx.

[32] *See* Glenn Kessler, *WikiLeak's Unveiling of Secret State Department Cables Exposes U.S. Diplomacy*, WASHINGTON POST (Nov. 28, 2010), *available at* http://www.washingtonpost.com/wp-dyn/content/article/2010/11/28/AR2010112802395.html.

[33] *Id.*

[34] Facebook, Facebook Statistics, *available at* http://www.facebook.com/press/info.php?statistics.

In a cautionary tale for practicing attorneys, an attorney requested a continuance from a judge based on the death of a family member and then posted a string of Facebook pictures that showed her drinking and partying.[35] Similarly, consider the case of an assistant public defender in Illinois who posted information about her clients on Facebook using their first names, a derivative of their first names, or their jail identification numbers.[36] The Illinois Disciplinary Commission found her in violation for revealing private and confidential client information and "defeating the administration of justice or bring[ing] the legal system into disrepute," and she received a 60-day suspension.[37]

A complaint filed several years ago involved a celebrity whose confidential health information was compromised. The complainant alleged that an unknown employee of the health facility identified and shared intimate details with the news media for profit and personal gain. Appropriate corrective action and investigation of the facility occurred, but this same type of scenario could more quickly and instantly happen now through the use of Facebook.[38]

d. Myspace and LinkedIn

Myspace[39] and LinkedIn[40] are two other social networking Web sites that have become common avenues for attorney advertising and client referrals. Many law firm recruiters and potential corporate employers will review candidates' Facebook, Myspace, and LinkedIn profiles as a preliminary background check,[41] in addition to the standard background and criminal history check. Lawyers and law firms would be well advised to consider incorporating the same proactive steps when investigating new hires, as well as when reviewing conflict-of-interest checks on current and potential clients.

e. Twitter

Twitter[42] is a Web site that allows users to "tweet"—i.e., make comments, remarks, or check in on their current location. The site allows users to "follow" certain individuals and to interact or converse with other followers or users in a

---

[35] *See* Molly McDonough, *Facebooking Judge Catches Lawyer in Lie*, ABA JOURNAL LAW NEWS NOW (July 31, 2009), *available at* http://www.abajournal.com/news/article/facebooking_judge_catches_lawyers_in_lies_crossing_ethical_lines_abachicago/.

[36] *See In re* Kristine Ann Peshek, Illinois Attorney and Disciplinary Committee Proceeding 09-CH-89 (Aug. 25, 2009).

[37] *See id.*

[38] UCLA Health Center settled allegations in 2011 that staff had accessed electronic protected health information of celebrity patients in violation of HIPAA and put in place a corrective plan to better safeguard patient information. *See* Press Release, Dep't of Health & Human Servs., *University of California settles HIPAA Privacy and Security case involving UCLA Health System facilities* (July 7, 2011), *available at* http://www.hhs.gov/news/press/2011pres/07/20110707a.html.

[39] Myspace, *available at* http://www.myspace.com.

[40] LinkedIn, *available at* http://www.linkedin.com.

[41] Of note, depending on the individual's privacy settings, it may be entirely possible that a potential employer could see all of one's family photos, college activities, and current activities/associations.

[42] Twitter, *available at* http://www.twitter.com.

real-time, synchronous manner. Twitter may be utilized by attorneys for advertising, client communications, or other communication purposes. As with the other social media discussed above, the need for a specific law firm policy and clear guidelines on appropriate usage is indicated. When advising health care clients that may use Twitter, take special note of the federal and state laws and regulations governing patient privacy and confidentiality.[43]

f. Use of Social Media by Attorneys—Use Caution

One of the best ways for an attorney to avoid violations of client confidentiality, inadvertent advertising in violation of state bar rules, or other inappropriate communications is to create a policy setting forth evaluative and procedural rules for considering and disseminating information via social networking. These policies should include how to address inadvertent or wrongful disclosures by means of social networking that could cause not only violations of ethical responsibility but also professional liability.

3. Corporate Family Conflict Issues

All lawyers and law firms recognize the need to do conflict-of-interest checks at the outset of any new matter. This might be done by computer, but it need not be. Common practice may include manual conflict-check procedures using file-room cards and/or accounting records that are quite satisfactory. One area that is neglected by most firms, however, is a check of corporate affiliations. A lawyer who wants to take on a matter adverse to a corporation needs to know whether his or her firm already represents the corporation's parent, subsidiary, or other affiliate.[44]

Large law firms check corporate relationships with each new matter. They use computers to do conflicts checks and include in those checks data on corporate relationships of the new client as well as other parties to the matter. This data is available online and on CD-ROMs. Some law firms use books, but the results of such searches should be entered into the firm's conflicts database. A good law or business librarian can help identify the easiest-to-use and most economical sources of corporate family information.

C. Other Ethical Considerations

1. Solicitation of Business

Another consideration implicated with e-health matters is the solicitation of business, given the availability of various social media. Attorneys must be aware of, and heed, the ethical and professional rules of conduct in terms of communications about a lawyer's services, advertising, direct contact with prospective

---

[43] *See, e.g.*, HIPAA Privacy Rule, 42 C.F.R. §164.
[44] Such a relationship may, or may not, create a conflict of interest. A thorough discussion of this issue appears in the online guide *Freivogel on Conflicts*, at http://www.freivogelonconflicts.com (go to the Table of Contents and click on "Corporate Families").

clients, communications, and use of firm name and letterhead.[45] Pursuant to ABA Model Rule 7.1, if an attorney wished to solicit clients through a medium such as Facebook, such advertisement must not be false or misleading, and the lawyer should review whether a qualified legal referral system applies to Facebook referrals.

2. Researching Potential Jurors or Witnesses

It is also important to consider the permissible boundaries and uses of social media such as Facebook when researching potential jurors or witnesses for a pending matter.

In March 2009, the Philadelphia Bar Association provided guidance on whether an attorney may utilize an agent (not recognized by the witness) to go to Facebook and Myspace pages, contact the witness, "friend" her, and obtain access to information on the pages. The bar committee opined that several Pennsylvania Rules of Conduct were implicated, namely Rule 5.3 (Responsibilities Regarding Nonlawyer Assistants) and Rule 8.4 (Misconduct). The committee advised that such conduct would constitute misconduct and the making of a false statement of material fact to a witness.[46]

In 2010, the New York City Bar determined that a lawyer may use his or her real name and profile to send a "friend request" to obtain information from an unrepresented person's social networking Web site without disclosing the reasons for the request.[47] However, the attorney must use truthful information, subject to compliance with all other ethical requirements.[48]

In May 2011, the San Diego County Bar Legal Ethics Committee reached a similar conclusion by specifically prohibiting attorneys from gaining access to information via social networking by seeking information or entry to a restricted social media Web page without the consent of that party's attorney.[49] In California and New York, an attorney is free to view and access social media pages of an adverse party (to obtain information about the lawsuit) so long as the lawyer does not "friend" the party and relies on public pages that are open and accessible.[50] It is also clear that obtaining information about a party that is contained in a social media Web site (Facebook, MySpace, and the like) but that is also publically available in online or print media or a subscription research service, such as Nexis or Factiva, is permitted.[51]

---

[45] *See generally* MODEL RULES OF PROF'L CONDUCT R. 7.1 (Communications Concerning a Lawyer's Services), R. 7.2 (Advertising), R. 7.3 (Direct Contact with Prospective Clients), R. 7.4 (Communication of Fields of Practice and Specialization), & R. 7.5 (Firm Names and Letterhead) (2000).

[46] *See* Philadelphia Bar Association, Professional Guidance Committee, Op. 2009-2 (Mar. 2009). Note, however, that the PBA Guidance is advisory only and is not binding upon the Disciplinary Board of the Supreme Court of Pennsylvania or any other court.

[47] *See* New York City Bar, Committee on Professional Ethics Formal Op. 2010-2 (Sept. 2010) (Obtaining Evidence from Social Networking Websites).

[48] *Id.*

[49] *See* San Diego County Bar Legal Ethics Committee Op. 2011-2 (May 24, 2011).

[50] *Id.*

[51] *Id.*; *see also* New York State Bar Association Ethics Op. 843 (2010).

3. Ex Parte Communications

Communications on the Internet via an adversary's Web site are considered ethically prohibited. In 2005, the Oregon State Bar noted that written communications via the Internet (Web, e-mail, Facebook) are analogous to written communications via traditional mail or messenger and are prohibited pursuant to ex parte contact rules.[52] If a lawyer knows that the person with whom he or she is communicating is a represented person, the Internet communication is prohibited.

In summary, the above discussion highlights various ethical obligations, considerations, and advisory guidelines for electronic communications and social media interactions with clients and others in represented matters.

III. KNOWLEDGE OF CLIENT MISCONDUCT

Enforcement activities against health care providers by the Office of the Inspector General (OIG) of the U.S. Department of Health and Human Services (HHS), the Department of Justice (DOJ), and state agencies continue unabated. Recoveries of civil and criminal penalties over the past several years have amounted to billions of dollars. There is significant enforcement activity and penalties now being imposed. Convicted health care providers have been going to prison.[53] In-house counsel and attorneys who advise health care clients should be acutely aware of the implications for violating health care–specific laws and regulations, including but not limited to the anti-kickback laws,[54] laws and regulations governing Medicare/Medicaid billing,[55] and the HIPAA Privacy Rule. Of note, the HHS Office for Civil Rights (OCR) has increased enforcement and punitive fines over the past years. As of September 2011, OCR imposed $7.16 million in fines for the impermissible disclosure or mishandling of personal health information pursuant to the federal Privacy Rule. The chart below provides a sample of OCR enforcement activities related to violations of the HIPAA Privacy Rule or the HITECH Act and regulations. Counsel who represent health care clients have an ethical and legal obligation to ensure appropriate identification, mitigation, and corrective actions are taken by clients to avoid such large penalties.

---

[52] *See generally* Oregon State Bar Formal Op. No. 2005-164 (2005).

[53] For a flavor of the enforcement trends by HHS and OIG, peruse the OIG Web site on Enforcement Trends at http://oig.hhs.gov/fraud/enforcement/criminal/.

[54] 42 U.S.C. §1320a-7b (last amended 1987).

[55] The primary basis is the False Claims Act, 31 U.S.C. §§3729–3733. Subsequent amendments and other legislation also outline the parameters for Medicare and Medicaid billing, including Social Security Act §1909, 42 U.S.C. §1396h; the Fraud Enforcement and Recovery Act of 2009 (FERA), Pub. L. No. 111-21, 123 Stat. 1617 (May 20, 2009); the Patient Protection and Affordable Care Act (ACA), Pub. L. No. 111-148, 124 Stat. 119 (Mar. 23, 2010); and the Dodd-Frank Wall Street Reform and Consumer Protection Act (the Dodd-Frank Act), Pub. L. No. 111-203 (July 21, 2010).

Date	Entity	Fine	Basis
July 2010	Rite Aid Pharmacy	$1 million	Failure to safeguard patients' PHI[56]
February 2011	Cignet Health	$4.3 million	HITECH, denial of patient access to records[57]
February 2011	Massachusetts General Hospital	$1 million	Failure to safeguard patients' PHI and impermissible disclosures[58]
July 2011	UCLA Health System	$865,500	Impermissible disclosure of patients' PHI[59]

The climate for health care lawyers is indeed challenging. In 1999, two Kansas City lawyers were tried in federal court for crimes arising out of their clients' involvement in a kickback scheme. The trial judge acquitted the lawyers at the close of the prosecution's case, although all of their clients were convicted.[60] During 2000, the general counsel of a large health care provider in Pennsylvania was indicted and sued civilly for millions of dollars in a case arising out of alleged misconduct of the provider's management.[61] Regulators and prosecutors have an impressive variety of theories for implicating lawyers in the client's activities, including obstruction of justice,[62] aiding and abetting,[63] conspiracy,[64] and misprision of a felony.[65]

---

[56] *See* Press Release, Dep't of Health & Human Servs., *Rite Aid Agrees to Pay $1 Million to Settle HIPAA Privacy Case* (July 27, 2010), *available at* http://www.hhs.gov/news/press/2010pres/07/20100727a.html.

[57] *See* Press Release, Dep't of Health & Human Servs., *HHS Imposes a $4.3 Million Civil Money Penalty for Violations of the HIPAA Privacy Rule* (Feb. 22, 2011), *available at* http://www.hhs.gov/news/press/2011pres/02/20110222a.html.

[58] *See* Press Release, Dep't of Health & Human Servs., *Massachusetts General Hospital Settles Potential HIPAA Violations* (Feb. 24, 2011), *available at* http://www.hhs.gov/news/press/2011pres/02/201102224b.html.

[59] *See* News Release, Dep't of Health & Human Servs., Office for Civil Rights, *UCLA Health System Settles Potential HIPAA Privacy and Security Violations* (July 26, 2011), *available at* http://www.hhs.gov/ocr/privacy/hipaa/news/uclahs.html.

[60] *Federal Jury Convicts Four in Medicare Kickback Case,* KAN. CITY TIMES (Apr. 5, 1999). *See also* United States v. LaHue, Case No. 97-20031-01-JWL (D. Kan. Indictment filed June 11, 1997); United States v. Anderson, Case No. 98-20030-JWL (D. Kan. Superceding Indictment filed July 15, 1998); *In re* Grand Jury Subpoenas, 144 F.3d 653 (10th Cir. May 15, 1998).

[61] *Ex-AHERF General Counsel Arraigned,* PITTSBURGH POST-GAZETTE, Mar. 21, 2000; *State Sues AHERF Officers,* PITTSBURGH POST-GAZETTE, Feb. 24, 2000.

[62] See 18 U.S.C. §1510 and comparable state laws.

[63] See 18 U.S.C. §2 and comparable state laws.

[64] See 18 U.S.C. §371 and comparable state laws.

[65] See 18 U.S.C. §4 and comparable state laws.

For attorneys who represent or work with pharmaceutical manufacturers, the case of *United States v. Stevens*[66] is another cautionary tale. Stevens, counsel for GlaxoSmithKline, was indicted on one count of criminal obstruction of justice, one count of concealing and falsifying documents, and four counts of making false statements to the U.S. Food and Drug Administration (FDA). The criminal indictment arose from her handling of and reliance on outside counsel advice in an off-label promotion investigation.[67] The court ultimately dismissed all charges against Stevens on the basis that she responded to the FDA "in the course of bona fide legal representation of a client [GlaxoSmithKline] and in good faith reliance on both external and internal lawyers for GlaxoSmithKline."[68] The court emphasized that the client did not seek assistance in committing a crime or perpetrating fraud, but sought assistance in responding to the FDA, and thus concluded that the safe harbor of the crime/fraud exception was an absolute bar to indictment.[69]

Despite its positive outcome, the *Stevens* case reinforces the need for health care attorneys to ensure they document, investigate, and meet all ethical obligations individually, in addition to relying on advice of outside counsel.

Ethics rules play a major role in these situations, in particular the rules relating to client crimes or fraud and those relating to client confidences. Client confidentiality rules are discussed in III.B., below, following a brief outline of the closely-related issue of attorney-client privilege.

A. Attorney-Client Privilege

This summary of the attorney-client privilege is not exhaustive but is designed to enable the reader to compare its application with the ethics rules on confidentiality.[70]

The purpose of the attorney-client privilege is to encourage clients to be candid with their lawyers.[71] It clearly applies to what the client tells the lawyer. Ordinarily, it also applies to what the lawyer tells the client, particularly when what the lawyer says reflects what the client has said to the lawyer.[72]

---

[66] No. RWT-10-694 (D. Md. May 10, 2011) (transcript of record), *available at* http://lawprofessors.typepad.com/files/110510stevens.pdf.

[67] *See* Press Release, Dep't of Justice, *Pharmaceutical Company Lawyer Charged with Obstruction and Making False Statements* (June 30, 2011), *available at* http://www.justice.gov/opa/pr/2010/November/10-civ-1266.html.

[68] *Stevens*, RWT-10-694 (D. Md. May 10, 2011).

[69] *Id.* Judge Titus specifically noted:
[A] lawyer should never fear prosecution because of advice that he or she has given to a client who consults him or her, and a client should never fear that its confidences will be divulged unless its purpose in consulting the lawyer was for the purpose of committing a crime or fraud.
Id., slip op. at 9.

[70] Because the principles described here are not controversial, most citations are to leading treatises rather than specific cases. The main sources are JOHN H. WIGMORE, A TREATISE ON EVIDENCE (J. McNaughton, ed., rev. 1961) [hereinafter WIGMORE], and RESTATEMENT (THIRD) OF THE LAW GOVERNING LAWYERS (2000) [hereinafter RESTATEMENT].

[71] RESTATEMENT §68 cmt. c.

[72] RESTATEMENT §§68, 70 (all communications from the lawyer to the client are protected).

The attorney-client privilege applies only in the context of a proceeding. Privilege rules govern attempts by a party to discover attorney-client communications or to elicit evidence of attorney-client communications at a hearing. One writer refers to the privilege as one "against testimonial compulsion."[73] Although there is no occasion to apply the attorney-client privilege rules absent a proceeding, the rules are implicated for communications that occur prior to the commencement of a proceeding as well as communications that take place during the proceeding. Because the attorney-client privilege can be waived,[74] one must be careful not to do so even though no proceeding has yet been brought.

B. Ethics Rules on Confidentiality

1. Confidentiality

The core rules on confidentiality are found in Rule 1.6 of the ABA Model Rules of Professional Conduct. The model confidentiality rules contain certain exceptions. For example, consistent with the rules of most states, since 2003, Model Rule 1.6 has permitted a lawyer to disclose future or past client fraud where the lawyer's services have been, or are being, used by the client.[75]

State complements of Model Rule 1.6 provide a variety of exceptions not included in the ABA version. Thus, for example, while some states permit a lawyer to reveal a proposed client crime if substantial financial injury[76] is threatened, in other states, confidentiality rules permit a lawyer to reveal a client's intention to commit a crime only where there is a threat of bodily injury.[77] In still other states, lawyers may reveal confidential information to rectify past client conduct. In some states, disclosure not only is permitted but is mandated.[78]

Differences among states' confidentiality rules[79] are too complex for the average good health care lawyer to deal with on his or her own. There are experts on these rules, and lawyers should get their help in the face of proposed— or past—client criminal or fraudulent conduct.

2. Assisting a Client's Crime or Fraud

Rule 1.2(d) of the ABA's Model Rules of Professional Conduct prohibits lawyers from assisting a client's crime or fraud. The language of Model Rule 1.2(d) is as follows:

---

[73]EDNA SELAN EPSTEIN, THE ATTORNEY-CLIENT PRIVILEGE AND THE WORK-PRODUCT DOCTRINE 3 (3d ed. 1997).

[74]WIGMORE §2327.

[75]MODEL RULES OF PROF'L CONDUCT R. 1.6(b). At the American Bar Association's annual meeting in August 2003, the ABA House of Delegates voted to change Rule 1.6 of the Model Rules of Professional Conduct to its current form. As discussed below in III.B.4.a., the House of Delegates also changed Model Rule 1.13 on disclosure issues.

[76]*See, e.g.*, Georgia Rule of Professional Conduct 1.6, Texas Rule 1.6, New Hampshire Rule 1.6, Massachusetts Professional Conduct Rule 1.6, Pennsylvania Rule 1.6.

[77]*See, e.g.*, California Rules of Professional Conduct 3-100, Florida Rule 1.6, Washington Rule 1.6.

[78]*See, e.g.*, Wisconsin Supreme Court Rules 20:1:6.

[79]For a chart showing how the states differ, see THOMAS MORGAN & RONALD ROTUNDA, SELECTED STANDARDS ON PROFESSIONAL RESPONSIBILITY 135–53 (2000).

> A lawyer shall not counsel a client to engage, or assist a client, in conduct that the lawyer knows is criminal or fraudulent, but a lawyer may discuss the legal consequences of any proposed course of conduct with a client and may counsel or assist a client to make a good faith effort to determine the validity, scope, meaning or application of the law.

The ethics rules of every state contain the same, or a similar, prohibition.

What is "assistance," in the context of Rule 1.2(d)? A 1992 ABA Opinion put it this way:

> We do not believe that knowledge of a client's ongoing fraud necessarily requires the lawyer's withdrawal from representation wholly unrelated to the fraud, even if the fraud involves the lawyer's past services or work product. On the other hand, complete severance may be the preferred course in these circumstances, in order to avoid any possibility of the lawyer's continued association with the client's fraud. We would simply point out, however, that withdrawal from matters totally unrelated to the fraud is more likely to be permissive, and governed by Rule 1.16(b), than mandatory under Rule 1.16(a)(1).[80]

Model Rule 1.16 governs when a lawyer may or must withdraw from representation. The rule provides that withdrawal is required where continued representation would cause the lawyer to violate Rule 1.2(d).

3. Audits and Investigations

Information technology has added additional layers of complexity to the task of auditing or investigating health care provider operations. Just one example is the need to determine compliance with HIPAA[81] when many of the provider's activities are conducted online.

Many health care providers—and not a few lawyers—believe that by having a law firm conduct an audit or investigation, the provider stands a better chance of preventing disclosure of the findings. That perception may be false. For example, lawyers may interview employees and review documents and find evidence of over-billing. When the lawyer tells the client about the over-billing and advises that it must be reported, the client may refuse, perhaps because it means having to disgorge large sums of money or it may cause the OIG or the DOJ to dig for more. Because the failure to report may itself be a crime or fraud, these circumstances may require the law firm to withdraw from representation. In addition, depending on the jurisdiction, the law firm may have to reveal the client's conduct to regulators.[82]

While conversations between lawyers and client personnel may be subject to ethics rules on confidentiality and the attorney-client privilege, the business records reviewed by lawyers are not. Moreover, neither the ethics rules nor the attorney-client privilege will prevent regulators from calling the client's

---

[80] ABA Comm. on Ethics and Prof'l Responsibility, Formal Op. 366 (1992).

[81] *See* 42 U.S.C. §§1320d *et seq*. HIPAA is also discussed in Chapter 5 (Dahm, Privacy Issues in U.S. Health Care); Chapter 7 (Christiansen, Information Security and Breach Notification Under HIPAA and HITECH); and Chapter 8 (Goldberg & Greene, Enforcement of the Health Insurance Portability and Accountability Act of 1996).

[82] See III.B.1. and III.B.2., above.

personnel to testify about their knowledge and day-to-day activities. The fact that they discussed these matters with lawyers would not make any difference.

a. Hiring Consultants

Suppose a decision is made to hire a consultant to conduct an audit. Does it make any difference whether the lawyer or the client does the hiring? If the lawyer hires the consultant, then arguably the consultant's report to the lawyer is not discoverable. Nevertheless, the knowledge of the provider's employees and the business records forming the basis of the report are still discoverable and admissible in a hearing. In addition, once the lawyer receives the report, he or she still is subject to the ethics rules on assisting client crimes or fraud and to possible exceptions to the confidentiality rules.

b. Crime/Fraud Exception to the Attorney-Client Privilege

Suppose the lawyer discovers a kickback scheme or over-billing during or as the result of a compliance audit. Suppose further that the client shows no sign of bringing its activities into compliance. Under these circumstances, the client could trigger an exception to the attorney-client privilege. As a general rule, courts hold that if a lawyer-client communication is in furtherance of a crime or fraud, the privilege does not protect the communication from discovery or use during a hearing.[83]

4. Representing the Organization

a. "Climbing the Corporate Ladder"

Rule 1.13 of the Model Rules of Professional Conduct deals with the obligation of the lawyer when he or she is representing a corporation or other organization. The rule provides that the lawyer's obligation is to the organization rather than to any individual or group of individuals. When an organizational constituent refuses to follow the law, and the lawyer believes that the result could harm the organization, the lawyer must go over the constituent's head to see that the correct action is taken.[84]

The U.S. Securities and Exchange Commission (SEC) regulations[85] adopted pursuant to requirements in the Sarbanes-Oxley Act of 2002 mandate "climbing the ladder" where public companies are involved.[86] The SEC was considering whether to amend the regulations to require a lawyer to notify the SEC if the lawyer resigns for "professional reasons"; that is, if the lawyer is required to withdraw because "going up the ladder" did not do any good. An alternative under consideration is to require the company to note the resignation in an SEC Form 8-K[87] or similar filing.

---

[83] JOHN H. WIGMORE, A TREATISE ON EVIDENCE §2298 (J. McNaughton, ed., rev. 1961).
[84] Rule 1.13(b) of the Model Rules of Professional Conduct is explicit about this.
[85] 17 C.F.R. pt. 205.
[86] Sarbanes-Oxley Act of 2002, Pub. L. No. 107-204, 116 Stat. 745 (enacted July 30, 2002).
[87] Form 8-K is the "current report" used to report material events or corporate changes not previously reported by a company in a quarterly report (Form 10-Q) or annual report (Form 10-K).

In August 2003 the ABA House of Delegates amended Model Rule 1.13 to make clear that in certain circumstances a lawyer *must* "climb the ladder." The House also added a provision allowing a lawyer to go outside the organization to disclose fraud when "climbing the ladder" did not work.

b. Preventing Misunderstandings About Who Represents Whom

Model Rule 1.13(d) provides: "In dealing with an organization's directors, officers, employees, members, shareholders or other constituents, a lawyer shall explain the identity of the client when it is apparent that the organization's interests are adverse to those of the constituents with whom the lawyer is dealing."

One of the most dangerous things that a business lawyer can do is not be precise about who is, and who is not, the lawyer's client in a multi-party context. Otherwise, when things go bad for some of the participants, they will point the finger at the organization's lawyer and claim that he or she should have protected them.[88]

c. Causing a Constituent to Be Fired

An audit or investigation can result in the lawyer for the organization recommending that an executive or other employee be fired. There is reason for caution here. First, "whistleblowers" are given a cause of action for unlawful discharge by the federal False Claims Act and by similar state statutes.[89] Another risk surfaced in a case in the U.S. District Court for the District of New Jersey, *Mruz v. Caring, Inc.*[90] In *Mruz*, the court held that several terminated executives could sue the employer's law firm under federal and state Racketeer Influenced and Corrupt Organizations (RICO) laws based on a claim that the law firm assisted other executives in a cover-up of health care fraud. Any time a law firm suspects that an assignment may result in termination or other discipline against a client's employee, it should involve experienced labor counsel.

IV. CONFLICTS OF INTEREST

The core conflict-of-interest provisions are Rules 1.7 through 1.13 of the Model Rules of Professional Conduct. The various types of issues that arise under these rules number in the dozens.[91] The discussion in this section concentrates on three areas that health care lawyers are likely to encounter on a fairly regular basis:

---

[88] An example of this is a case in which a jury returned a $59 million verdict against a law firm where there was a dispute about whether the law firm represented just the organization or, in addition, represented one of its owners. *See* Automated Marine Propulsion Sys., Inc. v. Sverdlin, No. 97-02103 (Tex. Dist. Ct. Oct. 27, 1998).

[89] *See* 31 U.S.C. §3730(h). *See also* New York State False Claims Act, N.Y. STATE FINANCE LAW §§187–194.

[90] 991 F. Supp. 701 (D.N.J. 1998).

[91] See FREIVOGEL ON CONFLICTS, an online guide to conflicts of interest, at http://www.freivogelonconflicts.com. The table of contents contains 34 categories of issues.

- joint representation;
- close corporations; and
- partnerships.

The last part of the discussion outlines the ways in which lawyer insensitivity to the conflict-of-interest rules can result in malpractice exposure.

A. Joint Representation

Joint representation issues arise when two persons come to a lawyer and ask him or her to represent them both. In most circumstances, the lawyer may legally and ethically do this. Frequently, a request for joint representation will require the lawyer to obtain the consent of both parties under the state equivalent of Model Rule 1.7. However, even with consent, difficult situations may arise when the parties have conflicting interests, for example, buyer and seller.[92]

The single most troublesome issue in joint representation situations has to do with confidences. What is the lawyer to do when he or she learns something from one client that would be valuable to the other? This is a serious problem when the first client does not want the other client to have the information. The lawyer is torn between the duty of confidentiality under Rule 1.6 and the duty to keep all clients informed under Rule 1.4.

1. Model Rule 2.2

Model Rule 2.2, which has the clumsy title "Intermediary," is the rule that was supposed to deal with joint representation. Most states adopted Rule 2.2 when they adopted their own versions of the Model Rules. With respect to confidences, Comment 6 to Rule 2.2 merely states that there is a delicate balance between keeping each client informed (Rule 1.4) and maintaining confidentiality (Rule 1.6). Comment 6 goes on to say that when the balance cannot be maintained, the lawyer must withdraw. This is not particularly helpful.

2. Model Rule 2.2 and the Ethics 2000 Commission

When read closely, Model Rule 2.2 adds only one concept not covered by the other conflict-of-interest rules. Virtually everyone agrees that when a lawyer finds that joint clients' interests are adverse, the lawyer must withdraw from representing all of them. What Rule 2.2 adds is that the lawyer may not continue on behalf of fewer than all of them, even with consent. Courts rarely have cited Rule 2.2. In fact, the rule is so questionable that the ABA Commission on the Evaluation of the Rules of Professional Conduct (Ethics 2000 Commission) has, to date, taken the position that it should be eliminated. In Rule 2.2's stead, the Ethics 2000 Commission has proposed the addition of comments to Rule 1.7 designed to address some of these issues.[93]

---

[92] See IV.A.6., below.
[93] See ETHICS 2000 COMM'N, PROPOSED RULE 1.7 (AUGUST 2000 REPORT TO HOUSE OF DELEGATES), *available at* http://www.abanet.org/cpr/e2k-rule17.html.

The ABA House of Delegates adopted the Ethics 2000 Commission's recommendation to abolish Model Rule 2.2 in 2002. It remains to be seen how many states will follow suit.

3. Restatement

The American Law Institute's *Restatement (Third) of the Law Governing Lawyers* deals with joint representation in a nonlitigation setting at Section 130, which states that consent may allow a lawyer to continue on behalf of fewer than all the clients if a conflict develops. The issue of confidentiality is not addressed in Section 130. However, Comment *l* to Section 60 provides that if the lawyer believes that the client without the information needs to know it, then the lawyer has discretion to reveal it.[94]

A recent case that discusses this issue in detail is *A. v. B.*,[95] decided by the New Jersey Supreme Court in 1999. In that case, a law firm was representing a husband and wife in estate planning. The firm discovered that the husband was a defendant in a paternity suit and believed that the wife did not know about the suit. The law firm wanted to tell the wife, but the husband would not allow it. Litigation ensued, and the New Jersey Supreme Court, in a comprehensive analysis, held that the firm had discretion to tell the wife. The court specifically adopted the analysis of Comment *l* to Section 60 of the *Restatement*.[96]

4. Joint Confidences and the Ethics 2000 Commission

The Ethics 2000 Commission attempts to deal with confidentiality in Comment 30 to its proposed Rule 1.7.[97] The Commission recognizes the difference between the attorney-client privilege and confidentiality under the ethics rules. As to the latter, the Commission seems to be saying that, absent agreement, when lawyers find themselves in the *A. v. B.* situation, they must not reveal the information and must withdraw. State and local ethics opinions concur with the position of the Ethics 2000 Commission.[98]

5. Recommendation

At the outset of any joint representation situation, an engagement letter or other written waiver should state what the lawyer will do in an *A. v. B.*–type situation. Following is an example:

> If we learn something from one of you that we believe the other needs to know in connection with the representation, our obligation will be to reveal the information.

---

[94] *See* RESTATEMENT (THIRD) OF THE LAW GOVERNING LAWYERS (2000) §60, cmt. *l*, illus. 2, 3.

[95] 726 A.2d 924 (N.J. 1999).

[96] The court also relied, in part, on New Jersey's version of Model Rule 1.6, which is pro-disclosure in cases of potential client fraud. The court noted that ethics committees in New York and Florida would have prohibited the disclosure. *See id.* at 931 (citing N.Y. Comm. on Prof'l Ethics Op. 555 (1984), and Fla. Op. 95-4 (1997)).

[97] *See* ETHICS 2000 COMM'N, PROPOSED RULE 1.7.

[98] *See* D.C. Legal Ethics Comm. Op. 296 (2000); Fla. Op. 95-4 (1997); N.Y. Comm. on Prof'l Ethics Op. 555 (1984); N.Y. City Comm. on Prof'l and Judicial Ethics Formal Ops. 1999-07 (1999), 1994-10 (1994).

You agree that in the event of a disagreement over this disclosure, we may continue to represent one or both of you. Notwithstanding this agreement, our ethical or legal obligation may be to stop representing both of you.

6. *Joint Representation in Commercial Negotiations*

Most joint representation situations involve clients who are basically on the same side of things—multiple purchasers, for example. Very little helpful guidance exists on joint representation where the parties are across the table from each other, such as a buyer and seller or a lender and borrower.

Comment 12 to existing Model Rule 1.7 provides, in part, that "a lawyer may not represent multiple parties to a negotiation whose interests are fundamentally antagonistic to each other, but common representation is permissible where the clients are generally aligned in interest even though there is some difference of interest among them."

This comment is not particularly helpful, and the comments to the Ethics 2000 Commission's proposed version of Rule 1.7, dealing with multiple representation in nonlitigation contexts, do not provide much additional guidance.

A few jurisdictions have provided slightly more specific instruction. For example, in *Baldasarre v. Butler*,[99] the New Jersey Supreme Court held that the same lawyer may not represent the purchaser and seller of commercial real estate if the transaction is "complex"—even with consent. *Baldasarre* involved a lawyer who had done that very thing.

The Massachusetts Bar Association (MBA) has offered guidance for a lawyer who wants to represent a lender and borrower in the same real estate transaction.[100] A 1990 opinion by the MBA's Committee on Professional Ethics states that a lawyer may not represent such parties jointly, even with consent, unless the transaction involves a single-family residence where the essential terms have already been agreed to. The opinion further provides that the lawyer must explain that if the lawyer learns something from one party that would be relevant to the other, the lawyer will make the disclosure.

To illustrate the multiple representation issue in the context of an e-health negotiation, consider the scenario in which a lawyer has represented a health maintenance organization (HMO) as well as a local Internet service provider (ISP) for several years. Although the HMO's chairman and the ISP's owner are acquainted, they have had no business dealings with one another until recently. At a golf outing, the HMO chairman mentions to the ISP chairman that he is interested in retaining the ISP to assist the HMO in developing an Internet strategy. They know they have the same lawyer, and they ask the lawyer to meet with them. May the lawyer represent both parties in these discussions and in concluding a deal?

The short answer to this question is "maybe." To begin with, the lawyer must be diligent in explaining to the clients the potential for conflicts and about

---

[99] 625 A.2d 458 (N.J. 1993). In *Baldasarre,* one of the parties sued the lawyer and his law firm and was awarded a judgment of almost $2 million. The whole sad story is told in the appellate court's opinion. *See* Baldasarre v. Butler, 604 A.2d 112 (N.J. Super. Ct. App. Div. 1992).

[100] Mass. Comm. on Prof'l Ethics Op. 1990-3 (1990).

dealing with confidences. The lawyer also must take a realistic view about the application of Model Rule 1.7, which requires that the lawyer must "realistically believe" that "the representation will not be adversely affected" and that the client must consent "after consultation." If the lawyer does all these things and is honest, the chances for professional discipline are slight.

Discipline is only part of the story, however. Whenever a lawyer represents more than one party in a transaction, he or she is in substantial danger of a malpractice claim. No matter how careful and diligent the lawyer has been, a disadvantaged client will have a potent claim for a jury. Usually these situations are not laid out in published cases; they almost always are settled because they are so dangerous.

7. "Unintentional" Joint Representation

Unintentional joint representation occurs when a law firm believes it is representing one or more specific clients, only to learn that others involved in the matter at issue claim that the law firm also was representing them. Unintentional joint representation has become a very dangerous conflict-of-interest phenomenon, and law firms and their malpractice carriers are paying millions of dollars in settlements in these situations.

Exemplifying the risks of unintentional joint representation is the case of *Automated Marine Propulsion Systems, Inc. v. Sverdlin*,[101] from Harris County, Texas. In this case, the plaintiff, Anatoly Sverdlin, owned a marine repair and manufacturing company. Sverdlin needed money to expand and brought in venture capitalists. The company hired a law firm to represent it in dealing with the venture capitalists, and the law firm wrote a letter to Sverdlin saying that it was representing the company. As a result of the restructuring and disputes among the parties, the venture capitalists wound up in control of the company. Sverdlin sued everyone, including the law firm. He claimed that the law firm represented him and caused him to lose his company. The law firm produced the letter it had written regarding representation, but Sverdlin denied seeing it. In October 1998, the jury returned a verdict against all defendants totaling in excess of $1 billion. The amount assessed against the law firm was approximately $50 million. That might have included significant overlapping amounts and duplication, but the law firm, according to the press, promptly settled its part of the case for $20 million.

In *Rallis v. Cassady*,[102] a California appellate court outlined the factors that may create in an employee's mind the notion that a lawyer for a corporation also is representing the employee: the lawyer has represented the individual in the past over a long period of time or in several matters; the lawyer had repeated contacts with the individual while representing the corporation; the individual had a particular personal interest in the matter but did not have independent counsel; the corporation gave the individual advice while representing

---

[101] No. 97-02103 (Tex. Dist. Ct. Oct. 27, 1998). The description of *Sverdlin* is taken from two articles in *Texas Lawyer*: see *Judge Cuts Top 1988 Jury Award by Billion to $300 Million,* TEX. LAW. (Jan. 31, 1999); Brenda S. Jeffreys, *Irate Jury Slams Gardere*, TEX. LAW. (Nov. 9, 1998).

[102] 100 Cal. Rptr. 2d 763 (Cal. Ct. App. 2000).

the corporation; the individual disclosed confidential information to the lawyer; and/or the individual paid part of the lawyer's fees.

To minimize the risks of an unintentional joint representation, any lawyer who is involved in a multi-party transaction must write a letter to everyone involved saying who is and who is not the client. As demonstrated by the *Sverdlin* case, the safest course is to have this letter signed and returned to the lawyer by all parties to the transaction.

8. Litigation and Joint Representation

In most respects, the considerations in representing multiple parties in litigation are similar to those discussed in the preceding sections. In litigation, the lawyer asked to represent more than one party must do an analysis to ensure that the joint parties' interests are not adverse. This process involves the usual analysis of the relevant state equivalent of Model Rule 1.7. On this point, the Ethics 2000 Commission's proposed Rule 1.7 is largely unchanged and specifically recognizes the acceptability of representing more than one party in civil litigation, if the appropriate conflicts analysis is done at the outset.[103]

Section 128 of the *Restatement*, "Representing Parties with Conflicting Interests in Civil Litigation," does not purport to be different from the Model Rule. It provides as follows:

> Unless all affected clients consent to the representation under the limitations and conditions provided in §122, a lawyer in civil litigation may not:
>
> (1) represent two or more clients in a matter if there is substantial risk that the lawyer's representation of one of the clients would be materially and adversely affected by the lawyer's duties to another client in the matter; or
>
> (2) represent one client in asserting or defending a claim against another client currently represented by the lawyer, even if the matters are not related.

Even where the parties appear to have common interests, an attorney who undertakes joint representation in a civil litigation matter should obtain a written agreement or engagement letter stating what the lawyer's obligations and rights are if a conflict arises during the litigation. An interesting case that shows the value of such an agreement is the California appellate court's decision in *Zador Corp. v. Kwan*.[104] There, the law firm obtained from both parties an agreement that if a conflict developed, the law firm could continue on behalf of Zador Corp. A conflict did develop, and the court held that the agreement was effective in allowing the law firm to continue on behalf of the corporation. The court cited, seemingly with approval, a California State Bar ethics committee opinion that a law firm can enforce such an agreement even if it means using confidences from the former client against the former client.[105]

While a joint representation agreement may assist a lawyer in avoiding disqualification or a charge of unethical conduct, a court will not necessarily

---

[103] *See* ETHICS 2000 COMM'N, PROPOSED RULE 1.7.

[104] 37 Cal. Rptr. 2d 754 (Cal. Ct. App. 1995).

[105] *See id.* at 763 (citing Cal. Comm. on Prof'l Responsibility and Conduct, Formal Op. 1989-115).

enforce it. The court may find, for example, that a nonconsentable conflict existed at the outset, or that one or more parties lacked the sophistication to understand the consequences of the agreement.

B. Close Corporations

The issue that arises most frequently in connection with close corporations is whether the lawyer for a close corporation is ipso facto the lawyer for the shareholders. This issue is apt to come up when the lawyer takes on a matter directly adverse to one of the shareholders and the shareholder moves to disqualify the lawyer. It also comes up when one of the shareholders attempts to sue the lawyer for malpractice. In most situations, the shareholder cannot sustain the action unless the shareholder can establish that he or she was a client of the lawyer.

Most jurisdictions hold the view that representation of a closely held corporate entity does not make the lawyer counsel for the owners or officers. Typically, the issue is whether the lawyer should be disqualified or whether one of the owners has privity for purposes of suing the lawyer for malpractice.[106]

Jesse v. Danforth,[107] from the Wisconsin Supreme Court, is a unique case. In the *Jesse* case, a law firm had represented several doctors in setting up a corporation. After the corporation was formed, the firm represented only the corporation. Later the firm brought a medical malpractice action against two of the incorporators. They moved to disqualify the firm, based on the earlier representation. The court ruled that the firm should not be disqualified. As to the earlier representation of the incorporators, the court said:

> [W]here (1) a person retains a lawyer for the purpose of organizing an entity and (2) the lawyer's involvement with that person is directly related to that incorporation and (3) such entity is eventually incorporated, the entity rule applies retroactively such that the lawyer's pre-incorporation involvement with the person is deemed to be representation of the entity, not the person.[108]

Other cases have held that the lawyer for the corporate entity did have some sort of duty to one or more constituents. In only a small handful of those cases did the court rule that a lawyer for a close corporation was ipso facto the

---

[106]*See, e.g.*, SEC v. Credit Bancorp, LTD, 96 F. Supp. 2d 357 (S.D.N.Y. 2000) (involving application of attorney-client privilege); In re Manshul Constr. Corp. (Geron v. Schulman), 228 B.R. 532 (Bankr. S.D.N.Y. 1999) (only one shareholder; no disqualification); In re Berger McGill, Inc., 242 B.R. 413 (Bankr. S.D. Ohio 1999) (motion to employ counsel granted; court rejected per se approach); Silver Dunes Condo. v. Beggs & Lane, 763 So. 2d 1274 (Fla. Dist. Ct. App. 2000) (no liability); Salit v. Ruden, McClosky, Smith, Schuster & Russell, P.A., 742 So. 2d 381 (Fla. Dist. Ct. App. 1999) (no liability). For a much more complete collection of cases, see FREIVOGEL ON CONFLICTS, at http://www.freivogelonconflicts.com (click on "Corporations" in the Table of Contents).

[107] 169 Wis. 2d 229, 485 N.W.2d 63 (1992).

[108]*Id.* at 241, 485 N.W.2d 67.

lawyer for the shareholders.[109] There is a split among the handful of state ethics committees that have considered the issue.[110]

An Oregon Supreme Court decision, *Granewich v. Harding*,[111] deserves separate mention. In *Granewich,* a law firm represented a close corporation, and a minority shareholder sued the law firm for "aiding and assisting" the majority shareholder in breaching his fiduciary duty to the minority shareholder. The court held that the complaint stated a cause of action.

To illustrate the issue of representation in the context of a closely held e-health business, suppose that a lawyer has represented a successful businessman for some years. The businessman-client expresses an interest in starting a Web-based business, the focus of which will be to provide an online decision support system for cardiac surgeons. The businessman brings in a surgeon to help. The surgeon attends all the meetings and ultimately plans to be the chief operating officer of the entity they will form. The businessman will own 80 percent of the common stock, and the surgeon will own 20 percent. One of the first things the lawyer needs to do in this situation is to have an express written understanding about who (and what) is, and who (and what) is not, the lawyer's client. Absent such a writing, confusion and liability may be quick to follow, especially if the business fails.

Joining the Wisconsin Supreme Court's ruling in *Jesse v. Danforth*[112] is Arizona Ethics Opinion 02-06,[113] which provides that a lawyer may structure a start-up in a way that avoids representation of the organizing individuals, even though the entity does not exist for a period of time at the start. A later opinion consistent with *Jesse* and the Arizona ethics opinion is *Manion v. Nagin*.[114]

---

[109] *See, e.g.,* Rosman v. Shapiro, 653 F. Supp. 1441 (S.D.N.Y. 1987) (just two 50 percent shareholders enough to distinguish above cases); Woods v. Superior Ct., 197 Cal. Rptr. 185 (Cal. Ct. App. 1983) (lawyer could not handle dispute between shareholders); Opdyke v. Kent Liquor Mart, Inc., 181 A.2d 579 (Del. Ch. 1962) (lawyer had acquired interest adverse to client); Schaeffer v. Cohen, Rosenthal, Price, Mirkin, Jennings & Berg, P.C., 541 N.E.2d 997 (Mass. 1989) (lawyer may have fiduciary duty to shareholders of close corporation); In re Brownstein, 602 P.2d 655 (Or. 1979), *and In re* Banks, 584 P.2d 284 (Or. 1978) (both held discipline appropriate where relationships so close); Committee on Legal Ethics v. Frame, 433 S.E.2d 579 (W. Va. 1993) (lawyer disciplined for being adverse to a person who was the majority shareholder of a close corporation client). For additional cases holding that the corporation's lawyer may owe duties to constituents, see FREIVOGEL ON CONFLICTS, Corporations, at http://www.freivogelonconflicts.com. An article critical of the entity rule as applied to close corporations is Lawrence E. Mitchell, *Professional Responsibility and the Close Corporation: Toward a Realistic Ethic*, 74 CORNELL L. REV. 467 (1989).

[110] *Compare* Cal. Comm. on Prof'l Responsibility and Conduct, Formal Op. 1999-153 (lawyer for close corporation may represent it and shareholder against another shareholder); D.C. Legal Ethics Comm. Op. 216 (1991) (where bank seized the shares of one of two 50 percent shareholders of corporation to collect debt, lawyer for corporation could represent corporation against bank); *and* Va. Legal Ethics Comm. Op. 1517 (1993) (lawyer for close corporation can represent one shareholder in litigation against the other, so long as lawyer has not obtained confidences from the other), *with* R.I. Ethics Adv. Panel Op. 93-58 (lawyer for close corporation may not represent one of two shareholders against the other without the other's consent).

[111] 329 Or. 47, 985 P.2d 788 (1999).

[112] 169 Wis. 2d 229.

[113] Ariz. Comm. on Rules of Prof'l Conduct Op. 02-06 (2002), *available at* http://www.myazbar.org/Ethics/pdf/02-06.pdf.

[114] No. Civ. 00-238, 2004 WL 234402 (D. Minn. Feb. 5, 2004) (unreported).

C. Partnerships and Limited Partnerships

1. General Partnerships

Does the lawyer for a general partnership also represent the individual partners for conflict-of-interest purposes? In a well reasoned and comprehensive 1991 opinion, the ABA Ethics Committee said no.[115] The syllabus of the opinion states, in part, "A partnership is an organization within the meaning of Rule 1.13. Generally, a lawyer who represents a partnership represents the entity rather than the individual partners."

This ABA opinion goes on to caution that the lawyer may wind up having duties to individual partners. For example, the lawyer may have to protect confidences gained from individual partners where there is an expectation of confidentiality. The lawyer also may have duties to individual partners under circumstances leading the partners to believe that they are clients.

A substantial majority of cases follow the ABA approach both in the disqualification context, and in the context of whether the individual partner was a client for purposes of bringing a malpractice action against the partnership's lawyer.[116] State and local ethics opinions are to the same effect.[117]

In *Collins v. Collins*,[118] a Connecticut superior court ruled that a lawyer who represented both partners when they created the partnership could not represent one against the other. The partner whom the lawyer sought to oppose was a former client, and the court said that the new matter was substantially related to the creation of the partnership. This position also was the thrust of a Connecticut State Bar ethics opinion.[119]

In *Cacciola v. Nellhaus*,[120] a Massachusetts appellate court opinion, a lawyer represented a four-person partnership. Unbeknownst to one of the partners, the lawyer represented a second partner to buy out a third. After the first partner died, his estate sued the lawyer. The court agreed that the lawyer did not have a lawyer-client relationship with the deceased partner. However, the court held that the plaintiff had stated several causes of action. One was breach of fiduciary duty to the deceased partner for failing to keep him advised of the buyout. Another was for aiding and abetting the acquiring partner in breaching his fiduciary duty to the deceased partner. The last was for intentionally interfering with the contractual relations of the deceased partner, based on the fact that the lawyer knew the deceased partner also was interested in buying out his partners.

---

[115] ABA Comm. on Ethics and Prof'l Responsibility, Formal Op. 361 (1991).

[116] *See, e.g.*, Hopper v. Frank, 16 F.3d 92 (5th Cir. 1994) (no malpractice action); Responsible Citizens v. Superior Ct., 20 Cal. Rptr. 2d 756 (Cal. Ct. App. 1993) (no disqualification); Griva v. Davison, 637 A.2d 830 (D.C. 1994) (court held malpractice action possible, depending upon facts); Rice v. Strunk, 670 N.E.2d 1280 (Ind. 1996) (no malpractice action); Security Bank v. Klicker, 418 N.W.2d 27 (Wis. Ct. App. 1987) (no malpractice action).

[117] *See* Cal. Comm. on Prof'l Responsibility and Conduct, Formal Op. 1994-37; NY. City Comm. on Prof'l and Judicial Ethics, Formal Op. 1994-10; Va. Legal Ethics Comm. Op. 1458 (1992).

[118] No. 424017, 1999 Conn. Super. LEXIS 1803 (Conn. Super. Ct. July 12, 1999).

[119] *See* Conn. Op. 13 (1993).

[120] 733 N.E.2d 133 (Mass. App. Ct. 2000).

Al-Yusr Townsend & Bottum Co. v. United Mid East Co.,[121] a Pennsylvania federal district court case, involved a joint venture. The *Al-Yusr* court held that given the special nature of joint ventures, the lawyer for the joint venture also was the lawyer for the individual members of the joint venture. The court did not compare partnerships to joint ventures, but rather relied on a series of Pennsylvania cases holding that the lawyer for an unincorporated association is ipso facto lawyer for its members.

In *Greate Bay Hotel & Casino, Inc. v. City of Atlantic City*,[122] the court held that a lawyer for a business trust could take a position directly adverse to one of the trust's owners. The court did not compare business trusts with partnerships. It relied on cases holding that business trusts are free-standing entities.

2. Limited Partnerships

The ABA ethics opinion addressing conflicts of interest in the general partnership context basically does not take a position on limited partnerships.[123] In a footnote, the opinion states as follows:

> It should be noted that because the structural organization of limited partnerships, in which only the general partners have managerial responsibility and limited partners are usually passive investors, differs from that of general partnerships, the application of the Model Rules to the two forms of partnership may not be the same in all circumstances. Judicial decisions dealing with the responsibility of an attorney who represents a limited partnership, or its general partner, to the limited partners have not been wholly consistent.[124]

While a majority of courts hold that representing a limited partnership does not make the limited partners clients,[125] courts have found ways to impose duties on the partnership's lawyer toward the limited partners.[126]

---

[121] Civil Action No. 95-1168, 1995 U.S. Dist. LEXIS 14622 (E.D. Pa. 1995).

[122] 624 A.2d 102 (N.J. Super. Ct. Law Div. 1993).

[123] See IV.C.1., above.

[124] ABA Comm. on Ethics and Prof'l Responsibility, Formal Op. 361, at n. 1 (1991).

[125] Following is a sampling of cases in which courts took the position that a lawyer for a limited partnership was not, without more, a lawyer for the limited partners. Usually the issue was whether one or more limited partners could sue the lawyer for the limited partnership for malpractice or under the securities laws. Rhode Island Depositors Econ. Prot. Corp. v. Hayes, 64 F.3d 22 (1st Cir. 1995); Fortson v. Winstead, McGuire, Sechrest & Minick, 961 F.2d 469 (4th Cir. 1992); Richter v. Van Amberg, 97 F. Supp. 2d 1255 (D.N.M. 2000); Quintel Corp., N.V. v. Citibank, N.A., 589 F. Supp. 1235 (S.D.N.Y. 1984); Morin v. Trupin, 711 F. Supp. 97 (S.D.N.Y. 1989). More such cases can be found at FREIVOGEL ON CONFLICTS, *at* http://www.freivogelon-conflicts.com (click on "Partnerships" in the Table of Contents). *See also* Md. Op. 95-54 (1995); N.Y. City Comm. on Prof'l and Judicial Ethics Formal Op. 1994-10.

[126] *See, e.g.*, Ferguson v. Lurie, 139 F.R.D. 362 (N.D. Ill. 1991) (limited partners allowed to see documents otherwise protected by attorney-client privilege); Pucci v. Santi, 711 F. Supp. 916 (N.D. Ill. 1989) (lawyer for limited partnership is lawyer for the limited partners); Roberts v. Heim, 123 F.R.D. 614 (N.D. Cal. 1988) (limited partners are clients insofar as the attorney-client privilege is concerned); Johnson v. Superior Ct., 45 Cal. Rptr. 2d 312 (Cal. Ct. App. 1995) (duty of loyalty owed to all partners). For more such cases, see FREIVOGEL ON CONFLICTS, *at* http://www.freivogelonconflicts.com (click on "Partnerships" in the Table of Contents). *See also* James M. Fischer, *Representing Partnerships: Who Is/Are the Client?*, 26 PAC. L.J. 961 (1995); Michael R. H. Post, *Representing a Tax Matters Partner: Who is the Client?*, 6 GEO. J. LEGAL ETHICS 527 (1993).

D. Conflicts and Malpractice Liability

A lawyer's lack of sensitivity to the nuances of the conflict of interest rules can be incredibly costly to good law firms. For example, in 1994, the U.S. Court of Appeals for the Second Circuit upheld a $2 million verdict against a large, prestigious New York City firm.[127] The firm allegedly had dropped one client and then represented another in purchasing property that the first client had tried to purchase. In Louisiana, a lawyer who had represented both sides in an acquisition was hit with a $5 million malpractice verdict, which held up on appeal.[128] A prominent Chicago firm recently paid $21 million to settle a malpractice claim by Mike Tyson, who claimed that the firm had favored another client to his disadvantage.[129] A Philadelphia firm settled a conflicts case several years ago for $3 million.[130] In 1992, in the largest lawyer liability verdict rendered to that time, an Oklahoma jury awarded $120 million against a lawyer who allegedly changed sides in an oil field development dispute.[131] Many more such cases get no publicity and settle quietly, oftentimes for millions of dollars.

---

[127] Milbank, Tweed, Hadley & McCloy v. Boon, 13 F.3d 537 (2d Cir. 1994).

[128] Schlesinger v. Herzog, 672 So. 2d 701 (La. Ct. App. 1996).

[129] *See* Scott Domer, *Uncivil Litigation in Tyson Case*, LAW.COM (May 23, 2000).

[130] *See Legal Beat: Pepper, Hamilton, & Scheetz Settles for $3 Million*, WALL ST. J., Nov. 17, 1992, at B16.

[131] *See* Edward Felsenthal, *State Jury Awards Record $120 Million in Damages in Lawyer Malpractice Suit*, WALL ST. J., Oct. 29, 1992, at A3.

Appendix Table of Contents

Appendix A:	**Internet Health Sites**..	657
Appendix B:	**Government Agencies**	681
Appendix C:	**E-Health Glossary**	695
Appendix D:	**Health Insurance Portability and Accountability Act (HIPAA) Glossary**	717
Appendix E:	**Documenting the Deal [Forms]**.................................	767

E-1 HIPAA Business Associate Agreement Forms............................ 769

    E-1.1 Business Associate Agreement [HIPAA Administrative Simplification Subtitle]: General Form 769

    E-1.2 Business Associate Agreement [HIPAA Administrative Simplification Subtitle]: Addendum 779

E-2 Resolution Agreement... 783

    E-2.1 Example of Resolution Agreement and Corrective Action Plan (Without External Monitoring)... 787

    E-2.2 Example of Resolution Agreement and Corrective Action Plan (With External Monitoring)... 803

Appendix F: Selected HIPAA Materials 827

F-1 HHS, Security and Electronic Signature Standards; Proposed Rule, 63 Fed. Reg. 43,242 (Aug. 12, 1998) .... (on CD only)

F-2 HHS, Office of Civil Rights, Guidance on Risk Analysis Requirements Under the HIPAA Security Rule (July 14, 2010) .... (on CD only)

F-3 HHS, Educational Materials for State Attorney General Educational Event on Enforcement of Health Privacy Laws, etc. (2011)... (on CD only)

Appendix A

Internet Health Sites*

Source: Amy Jurevic Sokol, Tulsa, Oklahoma.

Table of Contents
I. Web Sites 658
    - Alternative Medicine 658
    - Ambulatory Care Center Directories 659
    - Benchmarks 659
    - Bioethics 660
    - Clinical Tools 660
    - Clinical Trials 660
    - Clinics 661
    - Continuing Education 661
    - Directories 661
    - Disease/Health Information 662
    - Drug Information 662
    - Drug Manufacturers 663
    - E-Health—General 663
    - E-Health—Regulatory Guidance 664
    - Federal Courts 665
    - Glossaries 666
    - Health Care Providers 666
    - Health Information and E-Commerce Associations/
      Commissions 666
    - Health Information Exchanges 667
    - Health Plans 669
    - HIPAA—Administrative Simplification: Government Sites 669

---

*This appendix document is also available on the CD-ROM accompanying this volume.
  Web sites and documents on the Internet are subject to change with little or no notice. Web sites are provided in this appendix for research; readers may check an organization's main page for changes, updates, and further information on topics of interest. If a specific link does not work, the Search feature on an organization's main page may be useful in locating a document or page. An Internet Search Engine may also be used to locate the item.

- HIPAA—Administrative Simplification: Not-for-Profit Organizations 670
- HIPAA—HITECH 670
- HIPAA—Standard Transactions 670
- Homes for the Aging 670
- Hospices 670
- Hospital Directories 671
- Interoperability 671
- Legal Directories/Resources 671
- Legal Professional Organizations 672
- Medical Advice/Patient Diagnostic Tools 672
- Medical Journals 673
- Medical Libraries 674
- Medical Schools 674
- Medicare/Medicaid 674
- National Practitioner Databank/Healthcare Integrity and Protection Databank 674
- News 675
- Nursing 675
- Outcomes Data 675
- Pandemic Planning 675
- Patient Education Materials 676
- Patient Eldercare Education and Services 676
- Patient Health Information (General) 676
- Personal Health Records 676
- Pharmacies 677
- Pharmacy Boards 677
- Physician Assistants 677
- Portals 677
- Privacy/Security 677
- Professional Associations 678
- Telemedicine/Interstate Licensure 680
- Vendors 680

I. WEB SITES (TOPICS ARRANGED ALPHABETICALLY)

- **Alternative Medicine**
  - National Center for Complementary and Alternative Medicine (http://nccam.nih.gov/)
  - Medline Plus Web page on Complementary and Alternative Medicine (http://www.nlm.nih.gov/medlineplus/complementaryandalternativemedicine.html)
  - The Office of Cancer Complementary and Alternative Medicine (OCCAM) (http://www.cancer.gov/cam/)
  - WHO guidelines on developing consumer information on proper use of traditional, complementary, and alternative medicines (http://apps.who.int/medicinedocs/en/d/Js5525e/)

- WEIL (http://www.drweil.com). This site includes eating plans and recipe suggestions for 50 ailments and conditions; daily question-and-answer; information on herbs, vitamins, and therapies and techniques; "eight weeks to optimum health" program; and message boards.

- **Ambulatory Care Center Directories**
  - Pennsylvania Department of Health, Health Care Facility Directory (http://www.portal.state.pa.us/portal/server.pt/community/outpatient_facilities/14151/health_facility_locator/558512)
  - Wisconsin Department of Health Directory of Health Care Providers (http://dhs.wisconsin.gov/provider/index.htm)
  - Joint Commission Directory of Accredited Organizations (http://www.qualitycheck.org/consumer/searchQCR.aspx). The Joint Commission on Accreditation of Healthcare Organizations site includes information about ambulatory care, behavioral care, health care networks, home health, hospitals, laboratory, long-term care, and long-term care pharmacy. The information on the site includes the latest survey, the next scheduled survey, the accreditation status, and the latest accreditation decision.

- **Benchmarks**
  - Centers for Disease Control and Prevention, National Center for Health Statistics (http://www.cdc.gov/nchs/fastats/)
  - Centers for Disease Control and Prevention; National Center for Injury Prevention and Control; Scientific Data, Statistics, and Surveillance (http://www.cdc.gov/injury/wisqars/dataandstats.html)
  - Centers for Medicare & Medicaid Services, Information for Researchers (http://www.cms.hhs.gov/home/rsds.asp)
  - National Institute of Mental Health, Statistics (http://www.nimh.nih.gov/statistics/index.shtml)
  - U.S. Census Bureau, Health Insurance Data (http://www.census.gov/hhes/www/hlthins/hlthins.html)
  - U.S. Department of Health & Human Services, Administration on Aging, Statistical Information on Older Persons (http://www.aoa.gov/AoARoot/Aging_Statistics/index.aspx)
  - U.S. Department of Health & Human Services, Administration for Children and Families Statistics (http://www.acf.hhs.gov/programs/ccb/data/index.htm)
  - U.S. Department of Health & Human Services, Health Resources and Services Administration. This site includes Data on HPSAs (http://datawarehouse.hrsa.gov/)
  - U.S. Department of Health & Human Services, Substance Abuse and Mental Health Services Administration, National Mental Health Information Center (http://www.samhsa.gov/dataoutcomes/urs/)
  - U.S. Department of Labor, Bureau of Labor Statistics (http://www.bls.gov/iif/)

- **Bioethics**
  - Center for Practical Bioethics (http://practicalbioethics.org/)
  - Public Responsibility in Medicine and Research (http://www.primr.org)
  - The National Catholic Bioethics Center (http://www.ncbcenter.org/NetCommunity/)
  - The President's Council on Bioethics (http://www.bioethics.gov/)
  - Center for the Study of Bioethics, Medical College of Wisconsin (http://www.mcw.edu/bioethicsandmedhumanities.htm)
  - The National Institutes of Health-Bioethics Resources on the Web (http://bioethics.od.nih.gov/)
  - University of Pennsylvania Center for Bioethics (http://www.bioethics.upenn.edu/)
  - Georgetown University Medical Center, Center for Clinical Bioethics (http://clinicalbioethics.georgetown.edu/)
  - The Society for Medical Decision Making (http://www.smdm.org/)
  - American Society for Bioethics and Humanities (http://www.asbh.org)

- **Clinical Tools**
  - The Medical Algorithms Project (http://www.medal.org/visitor/login.aspx). This site contains over 13,500 Scales, Tools, Assessments, Scoring Systems, and other Algorithms intended for Medical Education and for Biomedical Research.
  - National Center for Emergency Medicine Informatics (http://www.ncemi.org/). This site includes calculators and algorithms applicable to emergency medicine.
  - National Guideline Clearinghouse (http://www.guideline.gov)
  - Agency for Healthcare Research and Quality, Clinical Parameters (http://www.ahcpr.gov)
  - American Academy of Pediatrics Current Clinical Practice Guidelines (http://aappolicy.aappublications.org/endorsed_practice_guidelines/index.dtl)
  - National Heart, Lung, and Blood Institute (http://www.nhlbi.nih.gov/health/indexpro.htm). Provides clinical guidelines for asthma, cholesterol, COPD, hypertension, and obesity.

- **Clinical Trials**
  - Food and Drug Administration, IRB Information Sheets (http://www.fda.gov/ScienceResearch/SpecialTopics/RunningClinicalTrials/default.htm)
  - ClinicalTrials.gov is a registry of federally and privately supported clinical trials conducted in the United States and around the world. It provides information about a trial's purpose, who may participate, locations, and phone numbers for more details. (http://www.clinicaltrials.gov/)
  - Department of Health and Human Services Office for Human Research protections (http://www.hhs.gov/ohrp/)

- Department of Health and Human Services Health Information Privacy and Research (http://www.hhs.gov/ocr/privacy/hipaa/understanding/special/research/index.html)
- Center Watch (http://www.centerwatch.com/) provides a listing of clinical trials, notification of clinical trials by e-mail, drugs in clinical trials, recently approved drugs, and news about clinical trials.
- National Cancer Institute Clinical Trials (http://www.cancer.gov/CLINICALTRIALS)
- National Institute of Mental Health Clinical Trials (http://www.nimh.nih.gov/health/trials/index.shtml)

- **Clinics**
  - Substance Abuse and Mental Health Services Administration, Treatment Locator (http://dasis3.samhsa.gov/). The locator includes more than 11,000 residential treatment centers, inpatient drug treatment and alcohol treatment programs, and outpatient treatment programs for drug abuse and addiction and alcoholism. Listings include treatment programs for marijuana, cocaine, and heroin addiction, as well as drug and alcohol treatment programs for teenagers, adolescents, and adults.
  - Health Resources and Services Administration Health Center Locator (http://findahealthcenter.hrsa.gov/Search_HCC.aspx) has a locator for federally funded health centers.
  - American Lung Association Flu Clinic Locator (http://www.lungusa.org/lung-disease/influenza/flu-vaccine-finder/). Provides the date, times, address, and phone number of the Clinics offering flu shots and a map showing where the Clinic is located.

- **Continuing Education**
  - Medscape (http://cme.medscape.com/)
  - CMEweb.com (http://www.cmeweb.com/gindex.php)
  - Accreditation Council for Continuing Medical Education (http://www.accme.org)
  - American Medical Informatics Association (http://www.amia.org/education)
  - American Academy of Family Physicians (https://nf.aafp.org/Cme/CmeCenter/Default.aspx)
  - American College of Physicians–American Society of Internal Medicine (http://www.acponline.org/education_recertification/cme/)
  - Care2learn.com (http://www.care2learn.com/)

- **Directories**
  - Yahoo Health (http://health.yahoo.net/)
  - The University of Iowa Hardin MD Directory (http://hardinmd.lib.uiowa.edu/)
  - Martindale's Health Science Guideline 2009 (http://www.martindalecenter.com/HSGuide.html) is a large directory of information that contains 141,100 Medical Cases & Grand Rounds; 1,625 Courses/

Textbooks; 67,900 Teaching Modules and Files, 550 Journals; 4,800 Databases, Atlases & Image Databases and 1,000's of Videos/Movies.
- Martindale's Desk Reference (http://www.martindalecenter.com/)
- Medline Plus Directories (http://www.nlm.nih.gov/medlineplus/directories.html)
- Health Links (http://www.healthlinks.net/)

- **Disease/Health Information**
  - Centers for Disease Control and Prevention (CDC) (http://www.cdc.gov/)
  - National Institutes of Health (NIH) (http://www.nih.gov)
  - U.S. National Library of Medicine (NLM) (http://www.nlm.nih.gov)
  - MEDLINE Plus Health Topics (http://www.nlm.nih.gov/medlineplus/healthtopics.html)
  - MEDLINE Plus Medical Encyclopedia (http://www.nlm.nih.gov/medlineplus/encyclopedia.html)
  - MEDLINE Plus Consumer Health Libraries (http://www.nlm.nih.gov/medlineplus/libraries.html)
  - Merck Manual of Diagnosis and Therapy (http://www.merckmanuals.com/professional/index.html)
  - Merck Manual-Home Edition (http://www.merck.com/mmhe/index.html)
  - Morbidity and Mortality Weekly Published by the Centers for Disease Control (http://www.cdc.gov/mmwr/)
  - Web Health MD (http://www.webmd.com)
  - Medscape (http://medscape.com)
  - Mayo Health Oasis (http://www.mayoclinic.com/health/medical/HomePage)
  - Health Finder (http://www.healthfinder.gov)
  - The Neuroscience Center (http://www.neuroscience.cnter.com/)

- **Drug Information**
  - Drug Index (http://www.rxlist.com/script/main/hp.asp). This site has a searchable database of 4,000 drugs with interaction information and a list of the top 200 drugs.
  - MEDLINE Plus (http://www.nlm.nih.gov/medlineplus/druginformation.html). This site is a guide to more than 9,000 prescription and over-the-counter medications, provided by the United States Pharmacopoeia.
  - Physicians Desk Reference (http://www.pdr.net/)
  - Illness and Medication Information (http://www.rxmed.com)
  - Food and Drug Administration, New Drug Approvals List (http://www.fda.gov/Drugs/NewsEvents/ucm130961.htm)
  - Pharmacy Times (http://www.pharmacytimes.com/)
  - Journal of Oncology Pharmacy Practice (http://www.oncologypharmacypractice.com/)
  - Pharmacy Online (http://www.priory.com/pharmol.htm)
  - United States Pharmacopoeia (http://www.usp.org)

- American Society of Health-System Pharmacists (http://www.ashp.org)
- American Pharmacists Association (http://www.pharmacist.com/)
- American Society of Consultant Pharmacists (http://www.ascp.com/)
- National Association of Chain Drug Stores U.S. Pharmacist List of National and State Pharmacy Associations (http://www.nacds.org/wmspage.cfm?parm1=615)
- Virtual Library: Pharmacy Association Links (http://www.pharmacy.org/association.html)
- American College of Clinical Pharmacy Position Papers (http://www.accp.com/govt/positionPapers.aspx)
- Institute for Safe Medication Practices (http://www.ismp.org/)
- Pharmaceutical Research Manufacturers Association (http://www.phrma.org). This site includes information about drugs in development and industry statistics.
- National Council for Prescription Drug Program (http://www.ncpdp.org)

- **Drug Manufacturers**
  - Abbott (http://www.abbott.com/index2.htm)
  - Boehringer Ingelheim (http://www.boehringer-ingelheim.com/)
  - Bristol-Myers Squibb (http://www.bms.com/pages/default.aspx)
  - Eli Lilly (http://www.lilly.com/Pages/home.aspx)
  - Genentech (http://www.gene.com/gene/index.jsp)
  - GlaxoSmithKline (http://www.gsk.com/index.htm)
  - Johnson & Johnson (http://www.jnj.com/connect/)
  - Merck (http://www.merck.com/index.html)
  - Novartis (http://novartis.com)
  - Pfizer (http://www.pfizer.com/home/)
  - Sanofi Aventis (http://en.sanofi.com/index.asp)

- **E-Health—General**
  - AMA "Guidelines for Medical and Health Information Sites on the Internet" (http://jama.ama-assn.org/cgi/content/full/283/12/1600?maxtoshow=&HITS=10&hits=10&RESULTFORMAT=&titleabstract=guidelines+for+information+sites+web&searchid=1057001235367_3724&stored_search=&FIRSTINDEX=0&journalcode=jama)
  - AMA "Guidelines for Physician-Patient Electronic Communications" (http://www.ama-assn.org/ama/pub/about-ama/our-people/member-groups-sections/young-physicians-section/advocacy-resources/guidelines-physician-patient-electronic-communications.page)
  - AMA Ethics Opinion 5.026: The Use of Electronic Mail (http://www.ama-assn.org/ama/pub/physician-resources/medical-ethics/code-medical-ethics/opinion5026.page)
  - Health on the Net Foundation Code of Conduct (http://www.hon.ch)
  - Health Management Technology (http://www.healthmgttech.com/). This site provides coverage of health care information technology solutions.

- E-health Initiative (http://www.ehealthinitiative.org/) is a not-for-profit organization devoted to drive improvement in the quality, safety, and efficiency of health care through the use of information and information technology.
- University of Toronto Centre for Global E-Health Innovation (http://www.ehealthinnovation.org/)
- European E-Health News Portal (http://www.ehealthnews.eu/)
- World Health Organization Regional Office for Europe E-Health Page (http://www.emro.who.int/index.asp)
- National eHealth Collaborative (http://www.nationalehealth.org/)
- The Rockefeller Foundation eHealth Connection (http://ehealth-connection.org/)
- CTeL Center for Telehealth and e-Health Law (http://www.ctel.org/)
- ISfTeH Internal Society for Telemedicine & eHealth (http://www.isft.net/cms/index.php?id=1)
- National Governors Association Center for Best Practices Health (http://www.nga.org/cms/render/live/center/health)
- National Institutes of Health Gallery of Mobile Apps and Sites (http://www.nlm.nih.gov/mobile/)
- National Institutes of Health Mobile Health Information and Resources (http://www.fic.nih.gov/ResearchTopics/Pages/MobileHealth.aspx)
- California Health & Human Services eHealth Initiative (http://demo2.symsoftsolutions.com/ehealth/Home.aspx)
- California Telemedicine and eHealth Center (http://www.cteconline.org/)
- World Health Organization Global Observatory for eHealth (http://www.who.int/kms/initiatives/ehealth/en/)
- New York eHealth Collaborative (NYeC) (http://www.nyehealth.org/)
- Pennsylvania eHealth Initiative (http://www.paehi.org/)
- Health Information Security & Privacy Provider Education Toolkit (http://www.secure4health.org/)

- **E-Health- Regulatory Guidance**
  - CMS Office of E-Health Standards and Services (https://www.cms.gov/CMSLeadership/14_Office_OESS.asp)
  - FDA Draft Guidance for the Industry and FDA Staff Regarding Mobile Medical Applications (http://www.fda.gov/MedicalDevices/DeviceRegulationandGuidance/GuidanceDocuments/ucm263280.htm)
  - FDA Final Guidance for the industry and FDA Staff Regarding Software Validation (http://www.fda.gov/MedicalDevices/DeviceRegulationandGuidance/GuidanceDocuments/ucm085281.htm)
  - FDA Guidance for the Industry Regarding Cybersecurity for Networked Medical Devices Containing Off-the-Shelf (OTS) Software (http://www.fda.gov/MedicalDevices/DeviceRegulationandGuidance/GuidanceDocuments/ucm077812)

- FDA Device Advice: Comprehensive Regulatory Assistance (http://www.fda.gov/MedicalDevices/DeviceRegulationandGuidance/default.htm)
- FDA Sentinel Initiative (http://www.fda.gov/Safety/FDAsSentinelInitiative/ucm2007250.htm)
- FTC Health Breach Notification Rule (http://business.ftc.gov/privacy-and-security/health-privacy/health-breach-notification-rule)
- FTC Children's Online Privacy (COPPA) (http://business.ftc.gov/privacy-and-security/children%E2%80%99s-online-privacy)
- HHS HITECH Act Enforcement Rule (http://www.hhs.gov/ocr/privacy/hipaa/administrative/enforcementrule/hitechenforcementifr.html)
- The Office of the National Coordinator for Health Information Technology Fact Sheets (http://healthit.hhs.gov/portal/server.pt/community/healthit_hhs_gov__fact_sheets/1238)
- The Office of the National Coordinator for Health Information Technology Regulations and Guidance (http://healthit.hhs.gov/portal/server.pt/community/healthit_hhs_gov__regulations_and_guidance/1496)
- The Office of the National Coordinator for Health Information Technology Initiatives (http://healthit.hhs.gov/portal/server.pt/community/healthit_hhs_gov__onc_initiatives/1497)
- The Office of the National Coordinator for Health Information Technology Certification Programs (http://healthit.hhs.gov/portal/server.pt/community/healthit_hhs_gov__certification_program/2884)
- The Office of the National Coordinator for Health Information Authorized Testing and Certification Bodies (http://healthit.hhs.gov/portal/server.pt/community/healthit_hhs_gov__onc-authorized_testing_and_certification_bodies/3120)
- Federal Trade Commission Information on Online Privacy (http://www.ftc.gov/reports/privacy3/)

- **Federal Courts**
  - U.S. Supreme Court Decisions (http://www.findlaw.com/casecode/supreme.html). Cases from 1893 to the present.
  - U.S. Federal Courts (http://www.uscourts.gov/Home.aspx)
  - U.S. Sentencing Guidelines (http://www.ussc.gov/)
  - U.S. Court of Appeals First Circuit (http://www.ca1.uscourts.gov/)
  - U.S. Court of Appeals Second Circuit (http://www.ca2.uscourts.gov/)
  - U.S. Court of Appeals Third Circuit (http://www.ca3.uscourts.gov/)
  - U.S. Court of Appeals Fourth Circuit (http://www.ca4.uscourts.gov/)
  - U.S. Court of Appeals Fifth Circuit (http://www.ca5.uscourts.gov/)
  - U.S. Court of Appeals Sixth Circuit (http://www.ca6.uscourts.gov/internet/default.html)
  - U.S. Court of Appeals Seventh Circuit (http://www.ca7.uscourts.gov/)
  - U.S. Court of Appeals Eighth Circuit (http://www.ca8.uscourts.gov/)
  - U.S. Court of Appeals Ninth Circuit (http://www.ca9.uscourts.gov/)
  - U.S. Court of Appeals Tenth Circuit (http://www.ca10.uscourts.gov/)

- U.S. Court of Appeals Eleventh Circuit
  (http://www.ca11.uscourts.gov/)
- U.S. Court of Appeals for the District of Columbia
  (http://www.cadc.uscourts.gov/internet/home.nsf)

- **Glossaries**
  - Minnesota Department of Health Glossary of e-Health Terms
    (http://www.health.state.mn.us/e-health/glossary.html)
  - eClinical eHealth Glossary (http://www.eclinicalforum.org/eClinicaleHealthGlossary/tabid/144/Default.aspx)
  - Whatis.com (http://whatis.techtarget.com/). IT-specific encyclopedia.

- **Health Care Providers**
  - American Dental Association, Find a Dentist
    (http://www.ada.org/professional.aspx)
  - American Medical Association, Online Doctor Finder
    (https://extapps.ama-assn.org/doctorfinder/recaptcha.jsp)
  - MedlinePlus—Directories of Physicians, Health Care Professionals, and Facilities (http://www.nlm.nih.gov/medlineplus/directories.html)
  - American Chiropractic Association Find a Doctor of Chiropractic
    (http://www.acatoday.org/search/memsearch.cfm)
  - Administrators in Medicine, Docfinder Searches
    (http://www.docboard.org/aim/)
  - American Psychological Association—Find a Psychologist
    (http://locator.apa.org/)
  - American Osteopathic Association: Find a D.O.(http://www.osteopathic.org/osteopathic-health/find-a-do/Pages/default.aspx)
  - Health Grades (http://www.healthgrades.com). This site provides ratings for 650,000 physicians, 5,000 hospitals, and 400 health plans; searchable by name, geography, and specialty.
  - NCQA HMO Quality Report Cards (http://www.ncqa.org)
  - Find A Doc (http://www.findadoc.com)

- **Health Information and E-Commerce Associations/Commissions**
  - American Health Lawyers Association (AHLA)
    (http://www.healthlawyers.org/Pages/Default.aspx)
  - American Medical Informatics Association (AMIA) (http://www.amia.org/). This site includes publications such as the *Journal of the AMIA* and *Guidelines for the Clinical Use of Electronic Mail with Patients* as well as position papers.
  - American Health Information Management Association (AHIMA) (http://www.ahima.org). This site provides information on hot topics in health information management, a resource center for patients and consumers, federal regulatory and legislative updates, and publications.
  - College of Healthcare Information Management Executives (CHIME)
    (http://www.cio-chime.org/)

App. A.   *Internet Health Sites*   667

- Electronic Healthcare Network Accreditation Commission (EHNAC) (http://www.ehnac.org)
- Healthcare Information Management Systems Society (HIMSS) (http://www.himss.org/ASP/index.asp)
- Data Interchange Standards Association (DISA) (http://www.disa.org)
- MIS Training Institute (http://www.misti.com)
- Workgroup for Electronic Data Interchange (http://www.wedi.org)

- **Health Information Exchanges**
  - Adirondack Regional Community Health Information Exchange (http://www.archiehealthexchange.org/)
  - Alaska eHealth Network (http://www.ak-ehealth.org/)
  - Arizona Governor's Office of Health Information Exchange (http://azgovernor.gov/hie/)
  - Bayou Tech Community Health Network (BYNET) (http://www.bynet-la.org/)
  - Bronx RHIO (http://www.bronxrhio.org/)
  - Cal eConnect (http://www.caleconnect.org/)
  - Chesapeake Regional Information System for Our Patients (CRISP) (http://www.crisphealth.org/)
  - Colorado Regional Health Information Organization (CORHIO) (http://www.corhio.org/)
  - Community Health Information Collaborative (http://www.medinfosystems.org/)
  - Delaware Health Information Network (http://www.dhin.org/)
  - East Kern County Integrated Technology Association (EKCITA) (http://www.ekcita.org/)
  - eHealth Connecticut Health information Exchange (http://www.ehealthconnecticut.org/HIE.aspx)
  - e-Health Network of Long Island (http://ehealthnetworkli.org/)
  - Florida RHIO Finder (http://www.floridarhios.com/findarhio.html)
  - Hawaii Health Information Exchange (http://www.hawaiihie.org/)
  - Health Bridge (http://www.healthbridge.org/)
  - Health Information Network of Arizona (http://www.ehealthnetworkaz.org/)
  - HealthInfoNet (http://www.hinfonet.org/)
  - Health Information Partnership for Tennessee (http://www.hiptn.org/)
  - Health Information Technology Oversight Council (HTOC) (http://www.oregon.gov/OHA/OHPR/HITOC/)
  - Health Monitoring Systems (http://www.hmsinc.com/)
  - HealthShare Montana (http://www.healthsharemontana.org/)
  - Georgia Health Information Exchange (http://www.georgia.gov/00/channel_title/0,2094,31446711_154959664,00.html)
  - Idaho Health Data Exchange (http://www.idahohde.org/dsite/)
  - Illinois Health Information Exchange (http://www.hie.illinois.gov/)
  - Indiana Health Information Technology (IHIT) (http://www.indianahealthit.com/)
  - Indiana Health Information Exchange (http://www.ihie.org/)

- Iowa eHealth (http://www.iowaehealth.org/)
- Kansas Health Information Technology Initiative (KanHIT) (http://www.kanhit.org/)
- Kentucky Health Information Exchange (http://khie.ky.gov/Pages/index.aspx)
- Long Island Patient Information Exchange (http://www.lipix.org/)
- Louisiana Rural Health information Exchange (http://www.larhix.org/)
- Medical Information Network (http://min-ns.org/)
- MedVirginia (http://www.medvirginia.net/)
- Michigan Health Information Exchange (http://www.mhin.com/)
- Michigan Health information Network (http://www.michigan.gov/mihin)
- MidSouth eHealth Alliance (http://www.midsoutheha.org/)
- Missouri Health Information Network (http://www.ms-hin.ms.gov/hin/MS-HIN.nsf/)
- Missouri Health Connection- Health Information Exchange (http://healthinformationexchanges.org/missouri-health-connection-health-information-exchange/)
- Nebraska Health Information Initiative (http://www.nehii.org/)
- New England Health Exchange Network (http://www.nehen.org/)
- New Mexico Health Information Collaborative (https://www.nmhic.org/)
- New York eHealth Collaborative (NTeC) (http://www.nyehealth.org/)
- New York RHIO (Southern Tier Health Link) (http://www.sthlny.com/)
- North Carolina Healthcare Exchange (http://www.nchex.net/)
- North Carolina Health Information Exchange Council (http://www.nchica.org/GetInvolved/NCHIE/intro.htm)
- North Dakota Health Information Technology (http://www.healthit.nd.gov/)
- Northern Virginia RHIO (http://www.novarhio.org/)
- Ohio Health Information Partnership (http://www.clinisync.org/)
- Oklahoma Health Information Exchange Trust (http://www.ohiet.org/default.aspx)
- One Health Port (http://www.onehealthport.com/HIE/index.php)
- One Health Record (Alabama) (http://onehealthrecord.alabama.gov/)
- Open Source Health Records Exchange (OpenHRE) (http://www.openhre.org/)
- Pennsylvania eHealth Initiative (http://www.paehi.org/)
- Redwood MedNet (http://www.redwoodmednet.org/index.html)
- Rochester RHIO (http://www.grrhio.org/)
- Texas Health Services Authority (http://www.thsa.org/)
- South Carolina Health Information Exchange (SCHIEx) (http://www.schiex.org/)
- South Dakota eHealth Collaborative (http://www.ehealth.dsu.edu/Default.aspx)
- State Health Alliance for Records Exchange (http://ohit.arkansas.gov/share/Pages/default.aspx)
- Sushoo Health Information Exchange (http://www.sushoo.com/)

- Utah Health Information Network (http://www.uhin.org/pages/home.php)
- Vermont Information Technology Leaders (http://www.vitl.net/)
- Western Health Information Network (http://whinit.org/)
- West Virginia Health Information Network (http://www.wvhin.org/Pages/default.aspx)
- Wisconsin Health Information Exchange (http://www.whie.org/)
- Wisconsin Statewide Health Information Exchange (Wisconsin Statewide Health Information Network (WISHIN)
- Wyoming Health Information Technology (http://www.wyominghit.org/wyoming-partners/e-health-partnership/)

- **Health Plans**
  - Aetna U.S. Healthcare (http://www.aetna.com/index.htm)
  - Anthem Blue Cross (http://www.anthem.com/ca/health-insurance/home/overview)
  - Blue Cross and Blue Shield (http://www.bluecares.com)
  - CIGNA (http://www.cigna.com)
  - Coventry Health Care (http://www.coventryhealthcare.com/index.htm)
  - Humana (http://www.humana.com)
  - Kaiser Permanente (https://www.kaiserpermanente.org/)
  - Prudential (http://www.prudential.com/view/page/public)
  - UnitedHealthcare (http://www.uhc.com)
  - WellPoint (http://www.wellpoint.com)

- **HIPAA—Administrative Simplification: Government Sites**
  - Administrative Simplification Home Page (http://aspe.hhs.gov/ADMNSIMP/). This U.S. Department of Health and Human Services Web site includes the Administrative Simplification provisions of HIPAA, the proposed and final regulations associated with it, and frequently asked questions about HIPAA.
  - Department of Health and Human Services: Office for Civil Rights—Privacy of Health Records (http://www.hhs.gov/ocr/privacy/index.html)
  - HHS Health information Technology (http://www.hhs.gov/healthit/privacy/).This Web site provides resources on a privacy and security framework, HIPAA and Health IT, state resources, model personal health record privacy notice, medical identity theft, and Federal laws and regulations.
  - HHS Office for Civil Rights (http://www.hhs.gov/ocr/office/about/rgn-hqaddresses.html). This link provides a list of regional privacy officers.
  - HIPAA—Combined Regulation Text (http://www.hhs.gov/ocr/privacy/hipaa/administrative/combined/index.html)
  - HHS Centers for Medicare & Medicaid Services (CMS), HIPAA Page (http://www.hhs.gov/ocr/privacy/)
  - Medicare Electronic Data Interchange (EDI) (http://www.cms.gov/ElectronicBillingEDITrans/)

- **HIPAA—Administrative Simplification: Not-for-Profit Organizations**
  - Workgroup for Electronic Data Interchange (WEDI) (http://www.wedi.org). This site includes a list of conferences and educational seminars, list of related Web sites, HIPAA legislation, HIPAA glossary, industry technical reports, committees, and advisory groups.
  - Electronic Healthcare Network Accreditation Commission (EHNAC) (http://www.ehnac.org)
  - American Hospital Association HIPAA resources (http://www.aha.org/aha_app/issues/HIPAA/index.jsp)

- **HIPAA—HITECH**
  - HITECH Breach Notification Interim Final Rule (http://www.hhs.gov/ocr/privacy/hipaa/understanding/coveredentities/breachnotificationifr.html)
  - HITECH Enforcement Rule (http://www.hhs.gov/ocr/privacy/hipaa/administrative/enforcementrule/index.html)
  - HHS HIT Extensions Centers Program (http://healthit.hhs.gov/portal/server.pt?open=512&objID=1335&mode=2&cached=true)
  - HHS Meaningful Use (http://healthit.hhs.gov/portal/server.pt?open=512&objID=2996&mode=2)

- **HIPAA—Standard Transactions**
  - Washington Publishing Company (http://www.wpc-edi.com). This site includes all of the implementation guides, data conditions, and the data dictionary for the X12N standard implementations being proposed for adoption; health claims and equivalent encounter information (professional, institutional, and dental); coordination of benefits; enrollment and disenrollment in a health plan; eligibility for a health plan; health care payment and remittance advice; health plan premium payments; first report of injury; health claim status; and referral certification and authorization.
  - National Uniform Claim Committee (http://www.nucc.org)
  - ASCX12 The Accredited Standards Committee (http://www.x12.org)
  - National Council for Prescription Drug Programs (http://www.ncpdp.org). This site provides all information regarding ordering the implementation guides and other necessary documentation for the proposed retail drug claim standard.

- **Homes for the Aging**
  - Centers for Medicare & Medicaid Services, Nursing Home Compare (http://www.medicare.gov/default.aspx)

- **Hospices**
  - Directory of Hospices Provided by the National Hospice and Palliative Care Organization (http://iweb.nhpco.org/iweb/Membership/MemberDirectorySearch.aspx)

- **Hospital Directories**
  - American Hospital Directory (http://www.ahd.com/)
  - Hospital Link (http://www.hospitallink.com/)
  - JCAHO/Joint Commission on Accreditation of Healthcare Organization Directory of Accredited Organizations (http://www.qualitycheck.org/consumer/searchQCR.aspx). This site includes accreditation information on ambulatory care, behavioral care, health care networks, home health, hospitals, laboratory, long-term care, and long-term-care pharmacy. The Joint Commission page provides information about the latest survey, the next scheduled survey, the accreditation status, and the latest accreditation decision.

- **Interoperability**
  - HITSP (http://www.hitsp.org/). The Healthcare Information Technology Standards Panel is a partnership between the public and private sectors with the goal of integrating standards that enable the sharing of information among organizations and systems.
  - National Institute of Standards and Technology (NIST) IT portal (http://www.nist.gov/health-it-portal.cfm).
  - Certification Commission for Health Information Technology (CCHIT) (http://www.cchit.org/)
  - Health Level Seven International (http://www.hl7.org/). Health Level Seven is an international organization with 55 member countries with the goal of creating global standards for the interoperability of health information technology.

- **Legal Directories/Resources**
  - Google Scholar (http://scholar.google.com/). Google scholar is a search engine intended for research that includes articles, theses, books, abstracts, and court opinions, from academic publishers, professional societies, online repositories, universities, and other Web sites. It also includes a method for listing other cases and articles that cite and are related to the article or case cited.
  - Findlaw (Legal Site) (http://lp.findlaw.com/). This site is a search engine for all types of legal resources, including federal and state law
  - American Law Sources On-Line (http://www.lawsource.com/also). This site provides a compilation of links to online sources of the laws of the United States, Canada, and Mexico.
  - GPO FDsys Federal Digital System (http://www.gpo.gov/fdsys/). This site is a gateway for federal information.
  - USAGov (http://www.usa.gov/index.shtml). The U.S. Government's Web portal.
  - National Association of Secretaries of States (NASS) (http://www.nass.org/). This Web site provides contact information for all of the Secretaries of State and links to all of the Secretary of State's Web sites.
  - THOMAS (http://thomas.loc.gov/home/thomas.php). Federal legislative information.

- U.S. Code (http://uscode.house.gov/lawrevisioncounsel.shtml). Published by the Law Revision Counsel.
- U.S. Executive Branch Web sites (http://www.loc.gov/rr/news/fedgov.html). Includes the Executive Office of the President, Executive Agencies, Independent Agencies, Quasi-Official Agencies, and Boards, Commissions, and Committees.
- The White House (http://www.whitehouse.gov/)
- Law Library of Congress, Guide to Law Online (http://www.loc.gov/law/help/guide.php)
- Law Library of Congress, the Federal Judiciary (http://www.loc.gov/law/help/guide/federal/usjudic.php)
- Law Library of Congress, U.S. States and Territories (http://www.loc.gov/law/help/guide/states.php)
- WashLaw (http://www.washlaw.edu/). Legal research resources on the Internet.

- **Legal Professional Organizations**
  - American Bar Association (http://www.americanbar.org/aba.html)
  - American Bar Association, Health Law Section (http://www.americanbar.org/groups/health_law.html)
  - American Health Lawyers Association (http://www.healthlawyers.org/Pages/Default.aspx)
  - Association of Corporate Counsel (http://www.acc.com/)

- **Medical Advice/Patient Diagnostic Tools**
  - eCleveland Clinic (http://www.eclevelandclinic.org/eCCHome.jsp) provides online second opinions.
  - RADIIA (http://radiia.com/radiology-services.php?gclid=CPX3koDd_qkCFZBT7AodGVoUxw /) provides online radiology second opinions.
  - Canceropinions.com (http://www.canceropinions.com/Home.aspx) provides online second opinions for cancer.
  - Partners Online Specialty Consultations (https://econsults.partners.org/v2/%28v5jyo2j0a5kopj55yrptaf45%29/Default.aspx) provides online second opinions.
  - John Hopkins Remote Second Opinion for Gastroenterology and Hepatology (http://www.hopkins-gi.org/CMS/CMS_Page.aspx?SS=&CurrentUDV=31&CMS_Page_ID=A2FC95A8-3B00-4BA7-AAF4-D55591E271DB /) and for neurology and neurosurgery (http://www.hopkinsmedicine.org/second_opinion/neuro/services/neuroimmunology-forms/); Johns Hopkins Medicine International Second Opinions (http://www.hopkinsmedicine.org/international/patients/second_opinions.html)
  - AmIhealthy.com (http://www.amihealthy.com)
  - WebMD Symptom Checker (http://symptoms.webmd.com/default.htm)
  - Healthline Symptom Checker (http://www.healthline.com/symptomsearch? subtractterm=all)

- Mayo Clinic Symptom Checker (http://www.mayoclinic.com/health/symptoms/SymptomIndex)

- **Medical Journals**
  - Journal of the American Medical Association (JAMA) (http://jama.ama-assn.org/)
  - New England Journal of Medicine (http://www.nejm.org/). Published by the Massachusetts Medical Society.
  - American Family Physician (http://www.aafp.org/online/en/home.html). Published by the American Academy of Family Physicians.
  - The Lancet (http://www.thelancet.com/)
  - National Library of Medicine Pub Med (http://www.ncbi.nlm.nih.gov/PubMed/)
  - Chest Journal (http://chestjournal.chestpubs.org/). Published by the American College of Chest Physicians.
  - Brain Pathology (http://www.wiley.com/bw/journal.asp?ref=1015-6305). Published by the International Society of Neuropathology.
  - British Medical Journal (http://www.bmj.com/)
  - Annals of Internal Medicine (http://www.annals.org/content/current). Published by the American College of Physicians–American Society of Internal Medicine.
  - American Family Physician (http://www.aafp.org/online/en/home/publications/journals/afp.html). Published by the American Academy of Family Physicians.
  - Archives of Family Medicine (http://archfami.ama-assn.org/). Published by the American Medical Association.
  - Annals of Thoracic Surgery (http://ats.ctsnetjournals.org/). Published by the Society of Thoracic Surgeons and the Southern Thoracic Surgical Association.
  - Archives of Internal Medicine (http://archinte.ama-assn.org/). Published by the American Medical Association.
  - American Psychologist (http://www.apa.org/pubs/journals/amp/index.aspx). Published by the American Psychological Association.
  - Archives of Surgery (http://archsurg.ama-assn.org/). Published by the American Medical Association.
  - Archives of Pediatric and Adolescent Medicine (http://archpedi.ama-assn.org/). Published by the American Medical Association.
  - Arteriosclerosis, Thrombosis, and Vascular Biology, Journal of the American Heart Association (http://atvb.ahajournals.org/)
  - Annals of Emergency Medicine (http://www.annemergmed.com/). Published by the American College of Emergency Physicians.
  - Academic Emergency Medicine, the Journal of the Society of Academic Emergency Medicine (http://www.wiley.com/bw/journal.asp?ref=1069-6563)
  - Lippincott's Nursing Center Nursing Journals (http://www.nursingcenter.com/library/index.asp). Provides links to nursing journals.

- Priory Medical Journals Online (http://www.priory.co.uk/)
- Genome Research (http://genome.cshlp.org/)
- Infectious Diseases in Children (http://www.pediatricsupersite.com/)
- Human Reproduction Abstracts (http://humrep.oxfordjournals.org/)
- Journal of Clinical Pediatric Dentistry (http://pediatricdentistry.metapress.com/home/main.mpx)
- Journal of AIDS/HIV (http://www.ccspublishing.com/j_aids.htm). Published by The National Medical Society.
- Journal of Arthritis and Rheumatism (http://www.rheumatology.org/publications/ar/). Published by the American College of Rheumatology.
- Journal of Emergency Nursing (http://www.ena.org/publications/jen/Pages/Default.aspx). Published by the Emergency Nurses Association.
- Medscape (http://www.medscape.com)
- Physical Therapy Journal (http://ptjournal.apta.org/). Published by the American Physical Therapy Association.
- World Wide Wounds, The Electronic Journal of Wound Practice Management (http://www.worldwidewounds.com/)

- **Medical Libraries**
  - Hardin Library for the Health Sciences, University of Iowa (http://www.lib.uiowa.edu/hardin/)

- **Medical Schools**
  - The Association of American Medical Colleges (http://www.aamc.org/medicalschools.htm). This site provides an alphabetical list of US and Canadian medical schools.

- **Medicare/Medicaid**
  - Centers for Medicare & Medicaid Services (CMS) Home Page (http://www.cms.gov/default.asp)
  - U.S. Department of Health and Human Services (http://www.hhs.gov/)
  - HHS Office of Inspector General (http://oig.hhs.gov/)
  - Office of Inspector General—Fraud Alerts (http://oig.hhs.gov/fraud/fraudalerts.asp)
  - HHS Office of Inspector General, Safe Harbor Regulations (http://oig.hhs.gov/fraud/safeharborregulations.asp)
  - HHS Office of Inspector General, Compliance Guidance and Press Releases (http://oig.hhs.gov/fraud/complianceguidance.asp)

- **National Practitioner Databank/Healthcare Integrity and Protection Databank**
  - National Practitioner Data Bank and Healthcare Integrity and Protection Databank (http://www.npdb-hipdb.com)
  - National Practitioner Data Bank and Healthcare Integrity and Protection Databank Guidebook (http://www.npdb-hipdb.com/npdbguidebook.html)

- **News**
  - The National Women's Health Information Center Daily News (http://www.womenshealth.gov/)
  - Science Daily Health and Medicine News (http://www.sciencedaily.com/news/health_medicine/)
  - Health Finder (http://www.healthfinder.gov/news/)
  - New York Times Health Section (http://www.nytimes.com/pages/health/index.html)
  - CNN Interactive Health (http://www.cnn.com/HEALTH/index.html)
  - American Hospital Association News (http://www.ahanews.com/ahanews_app/index.jsp)

- **Nursing**
  - American Academy of Nurse Practitioners (http://www.aanp.org/AANPCMS2)
  - American Association of Managed Care Nurses (http://www.aamcn.org)
  - American Nurses Association (http://www.nursingworld.org)
  - American Organization of Nurse Executives (http://www.aone.org)
  - National Student Nurses Association (http://www.nsna.org)
  - Nursing Center.com (http://www.nursingcenter.com/home/index.asp)

- **Outcomes Data**
  - National Cancer Institute Surveillance Epidemiology and End Results (http://seer.cancer.gov/)
  - Life Expectancy Rates Table by the CDC (http://www.cdc.gov/nchs/fastats/lifexpec.htm)
  - United States Decennial Life Tables (http://www.cdc.gov/nchs/products/life_tables.htm)
  - Data Ferret (Federal Electronic Research and Review Extraction Tool) (http://dataferrett.census.gov/). A tool developed by the Bureau of Census and Bureau of Labor Statistics that allows searches of national census and statistical data by keyword.

- **Pandemic Planning**
  - Avian Influenza (http://www.cdc.gov/flu/avian/)
  - Emergency Preparedness and Response (http://www.bt.cdc.gov/)
  - HHS Pandemic Influenza Plan (http://www.hhs.gov/pandemicflu/plan/)
  - National Vaccine Program Office (http://www.hhs.gov/nvpo/immunizations/activities/index.html)
  - National Wildlife Health Center Avian Influenza (http://www.nwhc.usgs.gov/disease_information/avian_influenza/index.jsp)
  - Pandemic Flu (http://www.flu.gov/)
  - United States Department of Agriculture Avian Influenza (http://www.usda.gov/wps/portal/usdahome?navtype=SU&navid=AVIAN_INFLUENZA)

- World Health Organization Epidemic and Pandemic Alert and Response (http://www.who.int/csr/en/)

- **Patient Education Materials**
  - MD Consult (fee) (http://www.mdconsult.com/das/patient/body/200437203-2/33/toc?tab=cond)
  - U-Write It (some free resources) (http://www.u-write.com). Provides resources for writing your own patient handouts.
  - Pritchett & Hull Associates Inc. (some free resources) (http://www.p-h.com)
  - Channing Bete Company (fee) (http://www.channing-bete.com/)
  - Immunization Action Coalition (free) (http://www.immunize.org). Free patient education materials on immunizations.
  - Medline Plus Interactive Health Tutorials (http://www.nlm.nih.gov/medlineplus/tutorials.html)

- **Patient Eldercare Education and Services**
  - The Care Guide (http://www.thecareguide.com/home.aspx). Guide to options for senior care
  - The Senior Care Guide (http://www.theseniorcareguide.com/). Guide to licensed senior care options
  - Elder Web (http://www.elderweb.com/). Information on elder care topics.

- **Patient Health Information (General)**
  - Real Age (http://www.realage.com/)
  - Web MD (http://www.webmd.com/)
  - Aetna Intelihealth (http://www.intelihealth.com/IH/ihtIH/WSIHW000/408/408.html)
  - The University of Iowa Hardin MD (http://hardinmd.lib.uiowa.edu/)
  - The Mayo Clinic (http://www.mayoclinic.com/)
  - The Cleveland Clinic Health Information Center (http://my.clevelandclinic.org/health/default.aspx)
  - Med Help (http://www.medhelp.org/)
  - U.S. Department of Health and Human Services Health Finder (http://www.healthfinder.gov/)
  - MedicineNet.Com (http://www.medicinenet.com/script/main/hp.asp)
  - Medline Plus (http://medlineplus.gov/)
  - New York Online Access to Health (http://www.noah-health.org/)

- **Personal Health Records (PHR)**
  - Health Vault (http://www.microsoft.com/en-us/healthvault/)
  - My Personal Health Record (http://www.myphr.com/)
  - CMS—Overview of PHRs (http://www.cms.gov/perhealthrecords/)
  - Mayo Clinic Health Manager (https://healthmanager.mayoclinic.com/)
  - Dossia (http://www.dossia.org/)
  - World Medical Card (http://www.wmc-card.com/index.php)
  - myMediConnect (http://www.mymediconnect.net/)

- WebMD PHR (http://www.webmd.com/phr)
- PHR for Veterans (http://www.myhealth.va.gov/)
- Search for PHRs (http://www.myphr.com/resources/choose.aspx)

- **Pharmacies**
  - Caremark Inc. (https://www.caremark.com/wps/portal)
  - CVS/Pharmacy (http://www.cvs.com/CVSApp/user/home/home.jsp)
  - drugstore.com (http://www.drugstore.com)
  - familymeds.com (http://www.familymeds.com/user-home/home.aspx)
  - Merck-Medco Managed Care L.L.C. (http://www.medcohealth.com/medco/corporate/home.jsp)
  - Rx.com Pharmacy (http://www.rx.com)
  - Super Valu Pharmacies (http://www.supervalu-pharmacies.com/landing/LandingAction.action)
  - CIGNA Tel-Drug, Inc. (https://teldrug.healthcare.cigna.com/healthcare/teldrug/app/public/welcome.do)
  - Walgreens (http://www.walgreens.com)

- **Pharmacy Boards**
  - National Association of Boards of Pharmacy listing of all state pharmacy boards (http://www.nabp.net/)

- **Physician Assistants**
  - American Academy of Physician Assistants (http://www.aapa.org)

- **Portals**
  - Discovery Health Channel (http://health.discovery.com/)
  - Web Medicine (http://www.webmed.com)
  - MSN Health (http://health.msn.com)
  - InteliHealth (http://www.intelihealth.com/IH/ihtIH/WSIHW000/408/408.html)

- **Privacy/Security**
  - Patient Safety Act-Confidentiality (http://www.hhs.gov/ocr/privacy/psa/understanding/index.html)
  - Patient Safety Organizations Home Page (http://www.pso.ahrq.gov/index.html)
  - Data Loss DB-Data Base Breach Notification Letters (http://datalossdb.org/primary_sources/)
    Summary of the Health Information Technology for Economic and Clinical Health (HITECH) Act as part of the American Recovery and Reinvestment Act of 2009 (http://opencrs.com/document/R40161). The full text of the American Recovery and Reinvestment Act is available here (http://www.opencongress.org/bill/111-h1/text)
  - Online Privacy Alliance Guidelines for Online Privacy Policies (http://www.privacyalliance.org/resources/ppguidelines.shtml)
  - The state of Texas Health Services Web site provides links to other state HIPAA Web sites (http://www.dshs.state.tx.us/hipaa/links.shtm)

- Privacy: Report on the Privacy Policies and Practices of Health Web Sites by the California Healthcare Foundation (http://www.chcf.org/publications/2000/01/report-on-the-privacy-policies-and-practices-of-health-web-sites)
- AMA Guidelines for Medical and Health Information Sites on the Internet (http://jama.ama-assn.org/cgi/content/full/283/12/1600)
- The Federal Trade Commission's Report to Congress on Privacy Online (http://www.ftc.gov/reports/privacy3/)
- Model State Privacy Act (http://www.publichealthlaw.net/ModelLaws/MSPHPA.php)
- Electronic Privacy Information Center Privacy Laws by State (http://epic.org/privacy/consumer/states.html)
- Electronic Privacy Information Center Medical Record Privacy (http://epic.org/privacy/medical/)
- Center for Democracy and Technology (http://www.cdt.org/)
- For the Record (http://www.nap.edu/catalog.php?record_id=5595)

- **Professional Associations**
  - Accreditation Council for Continuing Medical Education (http://www.accme.org)
  - American Academy of Family Physicians (http://www.aafp.org/online/en/home.html)
  - American Academy of Clinical Endocrinology (http://www.aace.com)
  - American Academy of Dermatology (http://www.aad.org)
  - American Academy of Medical Administrators (http://www.aameda.org)
  - American Academy of Neurology (http://www.aan.com)
  - American Academy of Nurse Practitioners (http://www.aanp.org/AANPCMS2)
  - American Academy of Nursing (http://www.aannet.org/i4a/pages/index.cfm?pageid=1)
  - American Academy of Ophthalmology (http://www.aao.org)
  - American Academy of Otolaryngologists (http://www.entnet.org)
  - American Academy of Orthopaedic Surgeons (http://www.aaos.org)
  - American Academy of Pediatrics (http://www.aap.org)
  - Association for Healthcare Documentation Integrity (http://www.ahdionline.org/)
  - America's Health Insurance Plans (http://www.ahip.org)
  - American Association of Managed Care Nurses (http://www.aamcn.org)
  - American Association of Medical Assistants (http://www.aama-ntl.org)
  - American Cancer Society (http://www.cancer.org/index)
  - American College of Physician Executives (http://www.acpe.org/)
  - American College of Cardiology (http://www.cardiosource.org/acc)
  - American College of Emergency Physicians (http://www.acep.org/)
  - American College of Healthcare Executives (http://www.ache.org)

- American College of Medical Practice Executives (http://www.mgma.com/)
- American College of Nurse Midwives (http://www.acnm.org)
- American College of Obstetricians & Gynecologists (http://www.acog.org/)
- American College of Occupational and Environmental Medicine (http://www.acoem.org/)
- American College of Physicians (http://www.acponline.org)
- American College of Radiology (http://www.acr.org/)
- American College of Rheumatology (http://www.rheumatology.org/)
- American College of Surgeons (http://www.facs.org/)
- American Diabetes Association (http://www.diabetes.org)
- American Gastroenterological Association (http://www.gastro.org/)
- American Geriatrics Association (http://www.americangeriatrics.org/)
- American Heart Association (http://www.heart.org/HEARTORG/)
- American Hospital Association (http://www.aha.org/aha_app/index.jsp)
- American Medical Association (http://www.ama-assn.org)
- American Medical Informatics Association (http://www.amia.org)
- American Medical Women's Association (http://www.amwa-doc.org/)
- American Nurses Association (http://www.nursingworld.org)
- American Organization of Nurse Executives (http://www.aone.org)
- American Physical Therapy Association (http://www.apta.org/)
- American Psychiatric Association (http://www.psych.org)
- American Society of Anesthesiologists (http://www.asahq.org/)
- American Society of Plastic and Reconstructive Surgeons (http://www.plasticsurgery.org/)
- American Society for Reproductive Medicine (http://www.asrm.org/)
- American Urological Association (http://www.auanet.org/content/homepage/homepage.cfm)
- Association of State Medical and Osteopathic Board Executive Directors (http://www.docboard.org/aim/)
- Federation of State Medical Boards (http://www.fsmb.org)
- Massachusetts Health Data Consortium (http://www.mahealthdata.org/)
- Medical Group Management Association (http://www.mgma.com)
- National Association of Boards of Pharmacy (http://www.nabp.net/)
- National Student Nurses Association (http://www.nsna.org)
- Professional Association of Health Care Office Management (http://www.pahcom.com)
- National Health Care Anti-Fraud Association (http://www.nhcaa.org/eweb/StartPage.aspx)
- Health Care Compliance Association (http://www.hcca-info.org//AM/Template.cfm?%20Section=Home)
- Health Care Financial Management Association (http://www.hfma.org)
- American Institute of Certified Public Accountants (http://www.aicpa.org/Pages/Default.aspx)

- Association of Certified Fraud Examiners (http://www.acfe.com/)
- American Society for Healthcare Risk Management (http://www.ashrm.org/)

- **Telemedicine/Interstate Licensure**
  - Office for the Advancement of Telehealth (http://www.hrsa.gov/ruralhealth/about/telehealth/). This government site includes publications such as the Telehealth Technology Guidelines, Reimbursement/Legislative Update, and Privacy Update. This site also includes a list of grants for telemedicine programs.
  - National Council of State Boards of Nursing (https://www.ncsbn.org/nlc.htm). This site provides information on the status of the Interstate Nurse Licensure Compact.
  - Telemedicine Report to Congress, dated January 31, 1997 (http://www.ntia.doc.gov/reports/telemed/execsum.htm)

- **Vendors**
  - Allscripts (http://www.allscripts.com/)
  - BlueWare Inc. (http://blueware.us/)
  - Cerner (http://www.cerner.com/)
  - Comchart (http://www.comchart.com)
  - encounterPro (http://www.encounterpro.com/pediatric-emr-home.html)
  - Epic Systems Corporation (http://www.epic.com/)
  - Medigrate Corporation (http://www.medigrate.com)
  - Medical Information Technology, Inc. (http://www.meditech.com)
  - McKesson (http://www.mckesson.com/en_us/McKesson.com/)
  - Purkinje Inc. (http://www.purkinje.com/en/)
  - Sage (http://www.sagehealth.com/)
  - Spacelabs Medical Inc. (http://www.spacelabshealthcare.com/)
  - Softmedical Inc. (http://www.softmedical.com/)
  - TeleResults Corporation (http://www.teleresults.com)
  - 3M Health Information Systems (http://solutions.3m.com/wps/portal/3M/en_US/3M_Health_Information_Systems/HIS/)

Appendix B

Government Agencies*

Source: Amy Jurevic Sokol, Tulsa, Oklahoma

DEPARTMENT OF HEALTH AND HUMAN SERVICES

Web site: http://www.dhhs.gov
e-mail: hhsmail@os.dhhs.gov
Address: 200 Independence Ave., S.W.
                Washington, DC 20201
Telephone: 1-877-696-6775

Employee Directory: http://directory.psc.gov/employee.htm
Contacting HHS: http://www.hhs.gov/ContactUs.html
HHS Information Resource Directory: http://www.hhs.gov/about/referlst.html

Administration for Children and Families

Web site: http://www.acf.hhs.gov/
Contacts: http://www.acf.hhs.gov/acf_contact_us.html
Address: 370 L'Enfant Promenade, S.W.
                Washington, DC 20447
Telephone: (202) 619-0724

Administration on Aging

Web site: http://www.aoa.gov/
Contacts: http://www.aoa.gov/AoARoot/About/Contact_Us/Index.aspx
e-mail: aoainfo@aoa.hhs.gov
Address: Administration on Aging
                Washington, DC 20201
Telephone: (202) 401-4634

---

*This appendix document is also available on the CD-ROM accompanying this volume. Web sites and e-mail addresses are subject to change with little or no notice.

Agency for Healthcare Research and Quality

Web site: http://www.ahcpr.gov
e-mail: info@ahrq.gov
Address: Office of Communications and Knowledge Transfer
               540 Gaither Road, Suite 2000
               Rockville, MD 20850
Telephone: (301) 427-1364

Frequently Asked Questions: http://info.ahrq.gov/cgi-bin/ahrq.cfg/php/enduser/std_alp.php

Agency for Toxic Substances and Disease Registry (ATSDR)

Web site: http://www.atsdr.cdc.gov
e-mail: cdcinfo@cdc.gov
Address: Agency for Toxic Substances and Disease Registry
               4770 Buford Hwy NE
               Atlanta, GA 30341
Telephone: (800) 232-4636

Centers for Disease Control and Prevention

Web site: http://www.cdc.gov
e-mail: cdcinfo@cdc.gov
Address: Centers for Disease Control and Prevention
               1600 Clifton Rd.
               Atlanta, GA 30333
Telephone: (800) 232-4636

A to Z Index: http://www.cdc.gov/az/a.html

Centers for Medicare and Medicaid Services (CMS)

Web site: http://www.cms.gov/
Address: 7500 Security Boulevard
               Baltimore, MD 21244-1850
Medicare Service Center: 800-MEDICARE (800-633-4227)
Medicare Service Center TTY: 877-486-2048
Report Medicare Fraud & Abuse: 800-HHS-TIPS (1-800-447-8477)
Contacts Database: http://www.cms.gov/apps/contacts/
Regional Office Overview: http://www.cms.gov/RegionalOffices/

CMS Regional Offices

Region I: Boston

Address: John F. Kennedy Federal Building, Suite 2325
                Boston, MA 02203-0003
Telephone: (617) 565-1188
States served: Connecticut

Maine
Massachusetts
New Hampshire
Rhode Island
Vermont

Region II: New York

Address: 26 Federal Plaza, Room 3811
New York, NY 10278-0063
Telephone: 212-616-2205
States & territories served:
New Jersey
New York
Puerto Rico
Virgin Islands

Region III: Philadelphia

Address: The Public Ledger Building, Suite 216
150 South Independence Mall West
Philadelphia, PA 19106
Telephone: (215) 861-4140
States & territories served:
Delaware
District of Columbia
Maryland
Pennsylvania
Virginia
West Virginia

Region IV: Atlanta

Address: Atlanta Federal Center
61 Forsyth Street, S.W., Suite 4T20
Atlanta, GA 30303-8909
Telephone: (404) 562-7150
States served: Alabama
Florida
Georgia
Kentucky
Mississippi
North Carolina
South Carolina
Tennessee

Region V: Chicago

Address: 233 North Michigan Avenue, Suite 600
Chicago, IL 60601
Telephone: (312) 886-6432
States served: Illinois

Indiana
Michigan
Minnesota
Ohio
Wisconsin

Region VI: Dallas

Address: 1301 Young Street, Suite 714
Dallas, TX 75202
Telephone: (214) 767-6427
States served: Arkansas
Louisiana
New Mexico
Oklahoma
Texas

Region VII: Kansas City

Address: 601 East 12th Street, Room 235
Kansas City, MO 64106
Telephone: (816) 426-5233
States served: Iowa
Kansas
Missouri
Nebraska

Region VIII: Denver

Address: 1600 Broadway, Suite 700
Denver, CO 80202
Telephone: (303) 844-2111
States served: Colorado
Montana
North Dakota
South Dakota
Utah
Wyoming

Region IX: San Francisco

Address: 90–7th Street, Suite 5-300
San Francisco, CA 94103-6706
Telephone: (415) 744-3501
States & territories served:
American Samoa
Arizona
California
Guam
Hawaii
Nevada
Northern Mariana Islands

Region X: Seattle

Address: 2201 6th Ave, Suite 801
Seattle, WA 98121
Telephone: (206) 615-2306
States served: Alaska
Idaho
Oregon
Washington

Food and Drug Administration

Web site: http://www.fda.gov
FDA Pubic Affairs Specialists: http://www.fda.gov/AboutFDA/ContactFDA/FindanOfficeorStaffMember/FDAPublicAffairsSpecialists/default.htm
Address: 10903 New Hampshire Ave.
Silver Spring, MD 20903
Telephone: 1-888-463-6332

A to Z Index: http://www.fda.gov/SiteIndex/default.htm

Health Resources and Service Administration (HRSA)

cWeb site: http://www.hrsa.gov/index.html
Contacts: http://www.hrsa.gov/about/contact/index.html
e-mail: ask@hrsa.gov
Address: 5600 Fishers Lane
Rockville, MD 20857
Telephone: 1-888-275-4772

A to Z Index: http://www.hrsa.gov/az/index.html

Indian Health Service

Web site: http://www.ihs.gov
e-mail: feedback@ihs.gov
Address: 801 Thompson Avenue, Ste. 400
Rockville, MD 20852
Telephone: (301) 443-1083

Area Offices: http://www.ihs.gov/PhoneDirectory/index.cfm?module=home&ci=2
Telephone Directory: http://www.ihs.gov/PhoneDirectory/

National Institutes of Health (NIH)

Web site: http://www.nih.gov
e-mail: NIHinfo@od.nih.gov
Address: 9000 Rockville Pike
Bethesda, MD 20892
Telephone: (301) 496-4000
Directory: https://ned.nih.gov/search/

Publications List: http://nihpublications.od.nih.gov/search.aspx

Office for Civil Rights (OCR)

Web site: http://www.hhs.gov/ocr/
e-mail: ocr@os.dhhs.gov
Address: Office for Civil Rights
U.S. Department of Health and Human Services
200 Independence Avenue, S.W.
Room 509F, HHH Building
Washington, DC 20201

OCR Regional Offices

Region I: Boston

Address: J. F. Kennedy Federal Building, Room 1875
Boston, MA 02203
Telephone: (617) 565-1340
States served: Connecticut
Maine
Massachusetts
New Hampshire
Rhode Island
Vermont

Region II: New York

Address: Jacob Javits Federal Building
26 Federal Plaza, Suite 3312
New York, NY 10278
Telephone: (212) 264-3313
States & territories served:
New Jersey
New York
Puerto Rico
Virgin Islands

Region III: Philadelphia

Address: Public Ledger Building
150 S. Independence Mall West, Suite 372
Philadelphia, PA 19106-9111
Telephone: (215) 861-4441
Hotline: 1-800-368-1019
States & territories served:
Delaware
District of Columbia
Maryland
Pennsylvania
Virginia
West Virginia

Region IV: Atlanta

Address: Atlanta Federal Center, Suite 3B70
61 Forsyth Street, S.W.
Atlanta, GA 30303-8909
Telephone: (404) 562-7886
States served: Alabama
Florida
Georgia
Kentucky
Mississippi
North Carolina
South Carolina
Tennessee

Region V: Chicago

Address: 233 N. Michigan Ave., Suite 240
Chicago, IL 60601
Telephone: (312) 886-2359
States served: Illinois
Indiana
Michigan
Minnesota
Ohio
Wisconsin

Region VI: Dallas

Address: 1301 Young Street, Suite 1169
Dallas, TX 75202
Telephone: (214) 767-4056
States served: Arkansas
Louisiana
New Mexico
Oklahoma
Texas

Region VII: Kansas City

Address: 601 East 12th Street, Room 248
Kansas City, MO 64106
Telephone: (816) 426-7278
States served: Iowa
Kansas
Missouri
Nebraska

Region VIII: Denver

Address: 999 18th Street, Suite 417
Denver, CO 80202
Telephone: (303) 844-2024
States served: Colorado
Montana
North Dakota
South Dakota
Utah
Wyoming

Region IX: San Francisco

Address: 90 7th Street, Suite 4-100
San Francisco, CA 94103
Telephone: (415) 437-8310
States & territories served:
American Samoa
Arizona
California
Guam
Hawaii
Nevada

Region X: Seattle

Address: 2201 Sixth Avenue, M/S:RX-11
Seattle, WA 98121-1831
Telephone: (206) 615-2287
States served: Alaska
Idaho
Oregon
Washington

Office of Inspector General

Web site: http://www.oig.hhs.gov
Address: Office of Inspector General
Office of Public Affairs
330 Independence Ave., S.W.
Room 5541
Washington, DC 20201
Telephone: (202) 619-1343
Contacts: http://www.oig.hhs.gov/contact-us/
Hotline: 1-800-447-8477

Advisory opinions: http://www.oig.hhs.gov/fraud/advisoryopinions.asp

Office of the Surgeon General

Web site: http://www.surgeongeneral.gov/
Address: Office of the Surgeon General
5600 Fishers Lane
Room 18-66
Rockville, MD 20857
Telephone: (301) 443-4000

Substance Abuse & Mental Health Services Administration (SAMHSA)

Web site: http://www.samhsa.gov
e-mail: samhsainfo@samhsa.hhs.gov
Address: P.O. Box 2345
Rockville, MD 20847-2345
Telephone: (240)-276-2000
Contacts: http://www.samhsa.gov/about/contactUs.aspx

DEPARTMENT OF JUSTICE

Web site: http://www.usdoj.gov
e-mail: Ask DOJ@usdoj.gov
Address: 950 Pennsylvania Ave., N.W.
Washington, DC 20530
Telephone: (202) 514-2000

Antitrust Division

Web site: http://www.usdoj.gov/atr/
e-mail: antitrust.atr@usdoj.gov
Address: Antitrust Division
Department of Justice
950 Pennsylvania Avenue, NW
Washington, DC 20530

Telephone directory: http://www.justice.gov/atr/contact/phoneworks.htm
United States Attorneys' Manual: http://www.usdoj.gov/usao/eousa/foia_reading_room/usam

Antitrust Library
450 Fifth Street, NW
Washington, DC 20530
(202) 514-5870

Appellate Section
950 Pennsylvania Avenue, NW
Washington, DC 20530
(202) 514-2413

Competition Policy Section
450 Fifth Street, NW
Washington, DC 20530
(202) 307-6665

Economic Litigation Section
450 Fifth Street, NW
Washington, DC 20530
(202) 307-6323

Economic Regulatory Section
450 Fifth Street, NW
Washington, DC 20530
(202) 307-6591

Executive Office
450 Fifth Street, NW
Washington, DC 20530
(202) 514-4005

Foreign Commerce Section
450 Fifth Street, NW
Washington, DC 20530
(202) 514-2464

Legal Policy Section
450 Fifth Street, NW
Washington, DC 20530
(202) 514-2512

Litigation I Section
1401 H Street, NW
Washington, DC 20530
(202) 307-6694

Litigation II Section
1401 H Street, N.W.
Washington, DC 20530
(202) 307-0924

Litigation III Section
450 Fifth Street, NW
Washington, DC 20530
(202) 616-5935

Networks and Technology Section
450 Fifth Street, NW
Washington, DC 20530
(202) 616-0944

Telecommunications and Media Section
450 Fifth Street, NW
Washington, DC 20530
(202) 514-5621

Transportation, Energy, and Agriculture Section
450 Fifth Street, NW
Washington, DC 20530
(202) 307-6351

DEPARTMENT OF LABOR

Occupational Safety and Health Administration

Web site:	http://www.osha.gov
Address:	200 Constitution Avenue, N.W.
	Washington, DC 20210
Telephone:	1-800-321-6742
Contacts:	http://www.osha.gov/html/Feed_Back.html

List of Regional Offices: http://www.osha.gov/html/RAmap.html

DEPARTMENT OF THE TREASURY

Internal Revenue Service

Web site:	http://www.irs.gov
Address:	1111 Constitution Avenue, N.W.
	Washington, DC 20224
Contacts:	http://www.irs.gov/contact/index.html?navmenu=menu3

Local IRS Offices: http://www.irs.gov/localcontacts/index.html
List of Phone Numbers: http://www.irs.gov/help/article/0,,id=96730,00.html

DEPARTMENT OF VETERANS AFFAIRS

Web site:	http://www.va.gov
Address:	810 Vermont Ave., N.W.
	Washington, DC 20420

Phone Numbers: https://iris.custhelp.com/app/answers/detail/a_id/1703
Facilities directory: http://www.va.gov/landing2_locations.htm

COMMISSION ON CIVIL RIGHTS

Web site:	http://www.usccr.gov
Address:	624 Ninth Street, N.W.
	Washington, DC 20425
Telephone:	(202) 376-7700

Contacts: http://www.usccr.gov/contact/contndx.htm

Regional Offices

Eastern Regional Office

Address: 624 Ninth Street, N.W., Suite 500
Washington, DC 20425
Telephone: (202) 376-7533
States & territories served:
Connecticut
Delaware
District of Columbia
Maine
Maryland
Massachusetts
New Hampshire
New Jersey
New York
Pennsylvania
Rhode Island
Vermont
Virginia
West Virginia

Southern Regional Office

Address: 61 Forsyth Street, S.W.
Suite 1840 T
Atlanta, GA 30303
Telephone: (404) 562-7000
States served: Florida
Georgia
Kentucky
North Carolina
South Carolina
Tennessee

Mid-Western Regional Office

Address: 55 West Monroe Street, Suite 410
Chicago, IL 60603
Telephone: (312) 353-8311
States served: Illinois
Indiana
Michigan
Minnesota
Ohio
Wisconsin

Central Regional Office

Address: 400 State Avenue, Suite 908
Kansas City, KS 66101
Telephone: (913) 551-1400
States served: Alabama
Arkansas
Iowa
Kansas
Louisiana
Mississippi
Missouri
Nebraska
Oklahoma

Rocky Mountain Regional Office

Address: 999 18th Street, Suite 1380 South
Denver, Colorado 80202
Telephone: (303) 866-1040
States served: Colorado
Montana
North Dakota
South Dakota
Utah
Wyoming

Western Regional Office

Address: 300 North Los Angeles Street, Suite 2010
Los Angeles, California 90012
Telephone: (213) 894-3437
States served: Alaska
Arizona
California
Hawaii
Idaho
Nevada
New Mexico
Oregon
Texas
Washington

GOVERNMENT PRINTING OFFICE

Web site:	http://www.gpo.gov
e-mail:	ContactCenter@gpo.gov
Address:	Superintendent of Documents U.S. Government Printing Office 732 North Capital Street, N.W. Washington, DC 20401
Telephone:	(202) 512-1800
Contacts:	http://www.gpo.gov/contact.htm

NATIONAL LABOR RELATIONS BOARD

Web site:	http://www.nlrb.gov
Address:	1099 14th Street Washington, DC 20570-0001
Telephone:	1-866-667-6572
Contacts:	http://www.nlrb.gov/contact-us

Office Locator: http://www.nlrb.gov/who-we-are/regional-offices

SOCIAL SECURITY ADMINISTRATION

Web site:	http://www.ssa.gov
Address:	6401 Security Blvd. Baltimore, MD 21235
Telephone:	(800) 772-1213
Contacts:	http://www.ssa.gov/pgm/reach.htm

Office Locator: https://secure.ssa.gov/apps6z/FOLO/fo001.jsp

Appendix C

E-Health Glossary*

Source: Amy Jurevic Sokol, Tulsa, Oklahoma

802.11:

    The IEEE standard group for wireless local area networks, whether connecting station-to-station or station-to-access point. The physical layer covers diffused infrared, direct sequence, and frequency-hopping spread-spectrum transmissions. For security and privacy, 802.11 accommodates the use of Wired Equivalent Privacy (WEP), a wireless authentication protocol based on I.D. keys and bit encryption.

802.3:

    A group of standards recognized by the IEEE defining the characteristics of Ethernet networks. The network traffic from workstations and peripherals is distributed using a Carrier Sense Multiple Access With Collision Detection (CSMA/CD) access protocol.

A

ActiveX:

    A standard for the creation of reusable software components compatible with Microsoft's Component Object (COM) architecture. ActiveX is used in Windows Applications and Web sites.

American National Standards Institute (ANSI):

    A nonprofit organization that works to establish acceptance of electronic data standards.

---

*This appendix document is also available on the CD-ROM accompanying this volume.

American Standard Code for Information Interchange (ASCII):

This coding standard represents each character into a numeric form readable by any computer. This "universal" language allows otherwise incompatible systems to exchange information. A later standard (called Unicode) allows for the inclusion of multibyte character sets.

Analog Transmission:

A method of information transfer that transforms varying frequencies and volumes of sound into electric impulses. Home telephones still use this format, but other communication forms are quickly converting to digital modes.

Application Service Provider (ASP):

An entity that allows clients to tap into and use applications hosted on an off-site server, usually on a subscription or per-member, per-month basis. An ASP allows the client to control processing and workflow, while eliminating the need to purchase and maintain application software.

Assembler:

A computer program that translates source code written in assembly language into machine language.

Assembly Language:

A low-level programming language that is composed of processor-level instructions.

B

Back End, Front End:

The "back end" system is the server or host computer, and the "front end" is the client or user interface, such as a graphical screen or a Web site. For online systems, the front end is what the user sees and interacts; the back end is the Web server and its corresponding host computers.

Backbone:

A high-bandwidth communication line that connects several lower-bandwidth communication lines.

Bandwidth:

A measurement describing how much information can be transmitted at once through a communications medium such as analog transmission, radio frequency, or digital transmission. The capacity of information increases relative to a higher megahertz (cycles per second) in an analog transmission and in megabits/second (Mbps) for digital transmission.

Baseline:

A level of performance that is considered normal, average, or typical over a period of time used to compare current performance to identify trends in performance and service delivery.

Bioinformatics:

The use of information technology to acquire, store, manage, and analyze biological data.

Biometrics:

Electronic capture and analysis of biological characteristics, such as fingerprints, facial structure, or patterns in the eye.

Biosense:

The Biosense Program was mandated in the Public Health Security and Bioterrorism Preparedness and Response Act of 2002 and was launched in 2003 to establish an integrated national public health surveillance system for early detection and rapid assessment of potential bioterrorism-related illness.

Biosurveillance:

The automated monitoring of data intended to detect an emerging epidemic, either as a result of natural origin or bioterrorism.

Browser:

Software that allows a user to navigate the Internet.

Buffer:

A storage area or memory used to temporarily store data to compensate for different rates of flow of data, timing of events, or amounts of data that can be handled by devices or processes involved in the transfer or use of data.

Bug:

A fault in a program that causes the program to perform in an unintended or unanticipated manner.

C

Cable Modem:

A modem that communicates over television cable instead of telephone lines. It can allow a continuously "live" connection to the Internet and transfer rates of about 1.5 Mbps.

Caching:

The Internet practice of storing partial or complete copies of materials from frequently accessed Internet sites.

Capacity:

The volume that an element or media can hold.

Call Center:

A central hub for receiving calls and routing callers to the appropriate resources. In health care, call centers (staffed, automated, outsourced, or in-house) can be used to offload non-emergency callers, link consumers to educational messages, or route them to physician scheduling systems.

Case-Based Reasoning:

A form of artificial intelligence often used by expert systems that bases decision making on prior case experience instead of a predefined rule set. Each new problem is compared with all similar cases the system has encountered.

Centers for Medicare and Medicaid Services (CMS):

Previously called the Health Care Financing Administration (HCFA).

Certificate Authority (CA):

An independent licensing agency that vouches for a person's identity in encrypted electronic communication. Acting as a type of electronic notary public, a CA verifies and stores a sender's public and private encryption keys and issues a digital certificate or "seal of authenticity" to the recipient.

Clinical Messaging:

The electronic transmission of clinical information between health care providers or health care provider(s) and patient(s).

Clinical Guideline Prompts:

Reminders to health care providers to consider certain actions at a particular point in time, for instance, vaccinations when clinically indicated.

Cloud Computing:

A method of increasing IT capacity or to add capabilities without investing in additional infrastructure, training, or licensing by utilizing subscription-based or pay-per-use service in real time over the Internet.

Code-Division Multiple Access (CDMA):

A wireless communication method that uses digital spread-spectrum technology rather than time division. Each transmission is identified by a unique code, allowing multiple calls to use the same frequency spread. Voice and data can be transmitted simultaneously during the same call.

Coder/Decoder (CODEC):

Uses hardware and/or software to translate analog signals into digital signals and to compress the signals. A CODEC improves the efficiency of transmitted data because it allows images and sounds to be sent using a lower bandwidth.

Community Health Information Network (CHIN):

A system of communication created for common use by health professionals, patients, and the community. This system combines hospital information systems (HIS) with medical databases, community health information, and online computer services.

Compiler:

A computer program that translates high-level language programs into machine language or object code.

Component Object Model (COM):

Microsoft's framework for object-oriented programming and the basis for ActiveX. Objects created using COM can be accessed by any other COM-compliant application.

Computer-Based Patient Record (CPR):

A computer-based patient record (CPR) provides access to all resources on a patient's health history and insurance information. A CPR is a linking system rather than an independent database and is more a process than a product. An integrated CPR will link to separate sources detailing medical history and images, laboratory results, and drug allergies.

Computerized Provider Order Entry (CPOE):

A computer application that allows a health care provider to electronically enter an order for treatment or diagnosis.

Connectivity:

The ability of programs to connect to and communicate with other elements of the computer system.

Cookie:

A piece of information passed from a Web server to the user's Web browser. If the browser accepts the cookie, its data, accessible only by the server/domain that sent it, are stored on the user's hard drive and retrieved automatically whenever the server's page is visited. Cookies are used to store passwords, ordering information, preferences, and bookmarks. Some cookies expire the same day, others last several years.

Cost-Per-Click:

A rate model for Web-site advertising, where the advertiser's charges are based on the number of users who click on the ad.

D

Data Mining:

The comparison and study of large databases to discover new data relationships. Mining a clinical database may produce new insights on outcomes, alternate treatments, or effects of treatment on different races and genders.

Data Repository:

A database acting as an information storage facility. Although often used synonymously with *data warehouse*, a repository does not have the analysis or querying functionality of a warehouse.

Data Warehouse:

A database that stores information like a data repository but also allows users to access data to perform research-oriented analyses.

Database:

An aggregation of records or other data that is updatable. Databases manage and archive large amounts of information.

Database Management System (DBMS):

A program such as Microsoft SQL Server, Oracle, or Sybase for creating and accessing one or more databases.

Decision Support System:

Software that taps into database resources to assist users in making decisions on care options. A clinical decision support system gives physicians structured (rules-based) information on diagnoses and treatments.

Digital Certificate:

Also called a digital ID. An official electronic identity document based on public/private key encryption and obtained through a certificate authority. Includes a user's name and registered serial number as well as the user's public key and its expiration date. Most certificates conform to the International Telecommunication Union's X.509 standard, but not all are compatible across all Web browsers.

Digital Imaging and Communications in Medicine (DICOM):

A standard developed by the American College of Radiology and the National Equipment Manufacturers Association to define the connectivity and communication protocols of medical imaging devices.

Digital Signature:

Also called an electronic signature. An encrypted digital tag added to electronic communication to verify the identity of the sender. The primary market force behind such signatures has been electronic commerce, but new uses are appearing in the health care industry, including electronic prescriptions and doctor-patient communications.

Digital Subscriber Line (DSL):

A wide area network technology that utilizes copper wires to provide a dedicated high-bandwidth connection.

Documentation:

Manuals or instructions provided to aid in understanding the structure and the intended uses of an information system or its components.

Domain Name:

The registered name that represents a specific administrative unit (domain) on the Internet.

Driver:

A program that links a peripheral device or internal function to the operating system and activates all device functions.

E

E-business/E-commerce:

An overarching term for service, sales, and collaborative business conducted over the Internet, either business-to-consumer or business-to-business. Some define e-commerce as a monetary transaction segment of e-business, but in most cases, the terms are synonymous.

E-care:

An umbrella term referring to the automation of all aspects of the care delivery process across administrative, clinical, and departmental boundaries throughout the health care delivery system. The beneficiary of the convergence of multiple technologies such as object-oriented and adaptive applications that leverage the Web to link disparate systems and enable automated, real-time responses to inquiries and clinical alerts. It also can incorporate disease management, workflow automation, and supply chain management.

E-health:

Both a concept and a business strategy, e-health empowers users by bringing health information, products and services online. Portals and niche sites can include everything from consumer health content, health plan descriptions, and insurance quotes to ask-a-doctor messaging. Some sites, such as online pharmacies, cross over into e-business/e-commerce.

Electronic Data Interchange (EDI):

Standardized electronic format for business transactions sent from one computer to another. EDI consists of strings of data in a format prearranged and accepted by both sending and receiving computer systems. Much business-to-business (B2B) e-commerce is based on EDI. Health care EDI includes electronic claims submission, electronic remittance notices, and electronic eligibility checks. HIPAA mandates standardized EDI transaction sets to be ANSI ASC X-12 code sets developed and authorized by the standard setting entity.

Electronic File Transfer:

The movement of one or more computer files from one location to another location over the Internet or Intranet.

Electronic Prescribing:

The electronic transmission of prescription information from a health care provider's computer to a pharmacy's computer.

Embedded Computer:

A computer that comprises a portion of some industrial application. Generally embedded computers lack many of the peripheral devices commonly included in general purpose home or office computers.

Embedded Software:

Software that runs on an embedded computer.

Encryption:

E-coding data with the intent to keep the information secure from anyone but the addressee. Encryption can include a password, public and private keys, or a complex combination of all.

E-risk:

The malpractice, civil, criminal, and licensure risks a health care provider faces when conducting e-health activities.

Evidence Based Practice:

The conscientious and explicit use of current best evidence in making decisions about the care of individual patients.

Expert System:

A topic-specific software program designed to imitate human decision-making using detailed knowledge of a particular subject and rules for applying the facts to a scenario.

Extensible Markup Language (XML):

A new version of SGML developed by the World Wide Web Consortium (W3C). XML mainly deals with data elements and uses HTML for display. XML is being promoted as an EDI tool optimized for Internet-based transactions. Instead of forcing the Web programmer to use proprietary building blocks based on the specific browser, XML will allow customizable element tags and multiple destinations within a single link.

Extranet:

Works like an intranet but allows access by outside individuals who have a valid password or encrypted equivalent. By customizing various levels of content access, an extranet can interact with outsiders without losing all of its private nature.

F

Fault Tolerance:

The ability of device or network to prevent downtime due to system failure usually achieved through redundancy.

Firewall:

A security protection system that includes software and hardware and often a router, which is situated between a private network and outside networks. It screens user names, source addresses, destination addresses, and all other information that is entering or leaving the private network. The firewall system allows, denies, or limits the access to the private network, depending on the system rules.

Framing:

The inclusion of content from one Web site by another Web site. The content is displayed in a "frame" making it difficult to tell that the content is not part of the original site.

G

Gap Analysis:

Traditionally, this is an assessment of what a given population needs versus the facilities, services, and expertise available to serve those needs.

Gateway:

A computer used to provide translations between different types of standards. Generally refers to computers that translate complex protocol suites; for example, different e-mail messaging systems. Currently, it has been used to describe a "door" from a private data network to the Internet.

Genomics:

The study of the genome—an organism's biological blueprint of DNA, chromosomes, and genes.

Graphical User Interface (GUI):

An interface that allows a person to operate a software program through visual images (called icons), drop-down menu choices, and button or tool bars instead of complex keystrokes. The most common manipulating device is a mouse. The GUI is what makes "point and click" capabilities possible.

H

Handheld Device:

A portable computer that is small enough to hold in a person's hand. Examples of handheld devices are personal data assistants and bar code scanners.

Health Alert Network (HAN):

The communication system used by the CDC to exchange disease information with state and local health departments.

Health Care Interoperability:

The ability of diverse computer systems to work together, usually through interfaces.

Health Informatics

The use of computer technology in health care to store, share, transmit and analyze clinical knowledge and data.

Health Information Exchange (HIE):

A system where clinical information is transferred electronically between disparate computer systems while maintaining the meaning of the information being exchanged.

Health Information Organization (HIO):

An organization that oversees, governs, and facilitates the exchange of clinical information among organizations (HIEs) according to recognized standards.

Health Insurance Portability and Accountability Act (HIPAA):

See generally Appendix D: Health Insurance Portability and Accountability Act (HIPAA) Glossary.

Health Level 7 (HL-7):

HL-7 is an interface standard for exchanging and transferring health data between computer systems. It is also the name of a nonprofit ANSI-accredited organization. ANSI approves all national standards. The ANSI X-12 committee handles health care related standards, including claims and remittance, mandated by HIPAA. HL-7 controls demographics and other messaging standards. The newest HL-7 version—3.0—incorporates XML technology.

Hypertext Link (Link):

This visual aid, usually signified by highlighting, underlining, or graphics, instructs the computer to display a specific Web document. This system permits users to move easily within a Web site or across Web sites residing on different computers.

Hypertext Mark-up Language (HTML):

A computer language used to format content for the World Wide Web.

Hypertext Transfer Protocol (HTTP):

An application protocol that defines the set of rules for exchanging files on the Web.

I

Input/Output (I/O):

Any operation, program, or device that transfers data to or from a computer.

Institute of Electrical and Electronic Engineers (IEEE):

An organization involved in the development and promulgation of standards. The IEEE Standards represent the formalization of current norms of professional practice through the process of obtaining the consensus of practicing professionals.

Institutional Review Board (IRB):

An appropriately constituted group that has been formally designated to review and monitor biomedical research involving human subjects.

Intelligent Agent:

Also called an Internet agent. A miniprogram designed to retrieve specific information automatically. Agents rely on cookies to keep track of the user's preferences, store bookmarks, and deliver news through push technology.

Interactive Voice Response (IVR):

An automated call handler. Most IVR systems can be configured to deliver appointment reminders and lab results, provide information-on-demand via menu choices and keep a log of callers. "Voice response" refers to the system's ability to "speak" the menu choices and data results to the caller. IVR is one form of computer telephony integration.

Interface:

The point of interaction between two computer components or computer systems that allows the exchange of data between the systems or components.

Internet:

An international network of computers that operates on a backbone system without a true central host computer. Today's Internet links thousands of universities, government institutions, and companies, but when it was created in the 1960s, the Internet linked just four computers. Technically, the Internet and the World Wide Web are not interchangeable terms; the Web is an integral child of the Internet whose ease of use has made it much more popular than its less graphical parent.

Internet Protocol (IP):

The method or protocol by which packets of information are sent across the Internet.

Internet Service Provider (ISP):

A company that provides modem or network users with access to the Internet and the World Wide Web. Some charge by the hour, but most offer monthly or yearly flat rates. Recently, some telephone companies have become ISPs, offering Internet access combined with local telephone service.

Intranet:

A member-only network that looks and acts like the World Wide Web. Intranets allow companies to take advantage of Web-based technologies and create a private means of exchanging images and text among networked users.

Intrusion Detection:

System tools designed to recognize unauthorized and malicious entry into a network or host, including monitoring for suspicious packet traffic, tracking intruders, and identifying where the security hole is. Many intrusion detection tools can also detect a variety of misuse originating from inside the network.

L

Latency:

A measure of delay, often network delay.

Legacy System:

An old method, computer system, technology, or application that continues to be used.

Local Area Network (LAN):

A network of computers and peripherals in close proximity, usually in the same building. A LAN can facilitate high-speed exchange of text, audio, and video data among hundreds of terminals.

M

Master Patient Index (MPI):

A software database program that collects a patient's various hospital identification numbers, perhaps from the laboratory, radiology, admissions, and so on, and keeps them under a single, enterprise-wide identification number.

Meaningful Use:

A list of criteria for electronic health records to be met for Medicare and Medicaid incentive payments. Failure to meet the required criteria by 2015 will result in reduced Medicare and Medicaid payments.

Medication Reconciliation:

Alerts to health care providers in real time of potential administration errors such as wrong patient, wrong drug, wrong dose, wrong route, and wrong time in support of medication administration or pharmacy dispense/supply management and workflow.

Metatag:

An HTML marker tag not visible to users that are used by search engines to determine which Internet sites correspond to the search terms entered by the user.

N

Network:

A system that connects several remotely located computers either by cable or using wireless technology.

Network Time:

The time spent establishing network connections to complete a transaction.

O

Object Code:

Machine-readable code that is made up of a series of binary numbers.

Object Oriented Programming:

A technology for writing programs that are composed of self-sufficient modules that contain all of the needed information to manipulate a data structure.

Open Source Software

The recipient of Open Source Software has the freedom to:
* run the program, for any purpose
* study how the program works, and adapt it to his or her needs
* redistribute copies so he or she can help his or her neighbor
* improve the program, and release his or her improvements to the public, so that the whole community benefits

Open Standards

Standards for information exchange that are freely available without restriction on access to or use of the standard.

Operating System:

Software that controls the execution of programs.

Optical Character Reader (OCR):

A scanner that translates text from a printed page into electronic text, eliminating keyboard input. The accuracy of the translation can depend on the typeface on the paper original.

Optical Networking:

A technology that uses fiber optics to transmit voice and data.

P

Packet:

A "package" of digitally transmitted information. Packets are coded with an address that allows network devices called routers to forward them to their destination.

Packet Switching:

A routing method where data are broken down into small blocks called packets and sent to users on a network. Each packet has ordering instructions so the receiving system can reassemble the blocks in the proper order. Transmitting data as packets greatly improves the efficiency and reliability of a network.

Peripheral Device:

Equipment that is directly connected to a computer. It can be used either to input or output data.

Personal Digital Assistant (PDA):

A handheld computer that provides access to notes, phone lists, schedules, and, with additional connectivity, paging systems. PDAs have no hard drive and most lack keyboards. Input is predominantly pen-based, although speech recognition may become more prevalent.

Picture Archiving and Communication System (PACS):

The acquisition, archival, and retrieval of digital images over a computer network for diagnosis and review at dedicated workstations.

Ping:

An internet echo message used to confirm the reachability of a network device.

Planned Downtime:

Any time period during which an element in a network is shut down for system maintenance, upgrades, or moves.

Port:

A connection point through which a computer sends or receives data. It may connect a computer to a printer, a modem, or a vast network.

Portal:

A Web site that acts as a doorway to a variety of other sites and services. Health care portals can guide high volumes of users to search engines, drug databases, consumer content, online prescription services, medical supplies, and physician continuing medical education; thus, companies and health systems took quick notice of the advertising/investment potentials.

Proxy Server:

A server that acts as a gateway between a company's intranet and the outside Internet. They are used in combination with, or as the next checkpoint after, a firewall. Proxy servers also are useful as temporary storage devices, allowing quick access to information that is used heavily for a short period of time.

Public Key Infrastructure (PKI):

Also called public key cryptography, PKI uses complex mathematical formulas to transform messages into seemingly unintelligible forms and back again. PKI employs an algorithm using two different but mathematically related "keys"—one for creating a digital signature or transforming data into a seemingly unintelligible form, and another key for verifying a digital signature or returning the message to its original form. Computer equipment and software utilizing two such keys are often collectively termed an "asymmetric cryptosystem" and two complementary keys have to match to verify the authenticity of signer.

R

Record Locator Service (RLS):

An electronic index of patient identifying information that directs providers in a health information exchange to the location of patient health records held by providers and group purchasers.

Regional Health Information Organization (RHIO):

A local or regional entity composed of multiple enterprises or organizations that create a local secure network and infrastructure for health care organizations and consumers in that region.

S

Scalability:

Scalability is the ability to add users and increase the capabilities of an application without having to making significant changes to the application software or the system on which it runs.

Seamless Integration:

A system with the flexibility to accept new devices and programs without disrupting other functions or requiring extensive installation tasks.

Search Engine:

A tool for finding information quickly from a variety of sources on the Internet or the World Wide Web. Users can enter keywords or narrow their search using boolean language, and the search engine will list as many relevant sources as it can find. Not all engines are designed the same way; some gather information by keyword registry; others use a "bot"—a robot program that wanders the Web and scans the first few hundred words of each Web site it encounters.

Secure Electronic Transaction (SET):

An encryption/authentication protocol designed for financial transactions over the Internet. Using digital signatures and a digital certificate among buyer, financial institution, and seller, SET allows users to make Internet purchases by credit card without letting the merchant see the actual credit card number. This system runs on SSL and S-HTTP, and resembles public key infrastructure in concept.

Secure Hypertext Transfer Protocol (S-HTTP):

An encrypted version of HTTP for transmitting messages or data packets securely over a standard Web site. This technique encrypts the data but not the connection.

Secure Sockets Layer (SSL):

SSL is an encryption protocol (40-bit or 128-bit) that establishes a secure transmission connection between a user and a host. E-commerce health sites may offer an SSL site address that begins with "https://."

Security Incident:

Any real or suspected adverse event in relation to the security of computer systems or networks. A security incident is the act of violating or the violation of an explicit or implied security policy.

Smart Card:

A portable, updatable card that can be used to store personal identification, medical history, and insurance information. Because it has its own microprocessing chip, a smart card can store thousands more bits of information than a magnetic stripe card, although it requires a special card-reading device.

Source Code:

Human readable code written in a "high level" programming language.

Spam:

Unsolicited e-mail usually containing advertising content.

Standard Generalized Mark-up Language (SGML):

The parent language for HTML. SGML is a more complex and syntactically complete language that is, arguably, capable of formatting any type of content.

T

Tablet Computer:

A flat-panel laptop that uses a stylus pen or touch-screen, rather than a keyboard, for entry of data and commands.

Telecommunications:

The use of wire, radio, visual, or other electromagnetic channels to transmit or receive signals for voice, data, and video communications.

Teleconferencing:

Interactive electronic communication between multiple users at two or more sites, which facilitates voice, video, and/or data transmission systems: audio, audiographics, computer, and video systems.

Teleconsultation:

A consultation between multiple providers where the providers are in different locations.

Telediagnosis:

The detection of a disease as a result of evaluating data transmitted to a receiving station from instruments monitoring a remote patient.

Telehealth:

A broad term describing the combined efforts of health telecommunication, information technology, and health education to improve the efficiency and quality of health care.

Telematics:

The use of information processing based on a computer in telecommunications and the use of telecommunications to permit computers to transfer programs and data to one another.

Telemedicine:

The utilization of telecommunications for the delivery of health care services.

Telementoring:

The use of audio, video, and other telecommunications and electronic information-processing technologies to provide individual guidance or direction.

Telemetry:

The science and technology of automatic measurement and transmission of data via wires, radios, or another medium from stations based in remote locations to receiving stations for recording and analysis.

Telemonitoring:

The process of using audio, video, and other telecommunications and electronic information-processing technologies to monitor the health status of a patient from a distance.

Telepresence:

The method of using robotic and other instruments that permit a clinician to perform a procedure at a remote location by manipulating devices and receiving feedback or sensory information that contributes to a sense of being present at the remote site and allows a satisfactory degree of technical achievement.

Teletext:

A broadcasting service utilizing several otherwise unused scanning lines (vertical blanking intervals) between frames of television pictures to send data from a central database to receiving television sets.

Teleradiology:

Conducting radiology image exchange and/or image interpretations electronically.

Telnet:

A protocol standard and associated application program that permits users to log on to other computers using a character-based (text) interface. Telnet is commonly used to provide access to Unix, Linux, and Mainframe computers.

Traffic:

The data that travels over a network. Nodes create network traffic when they send data to one or more recipients.

Transmission Control Protocol/Internet Protocol:

A set of communications protocols developed for the Defense Advanced Research Projects Agency to internetwork dissimilar systems.

V

Voice Over IP (VOIP):

Voice delivered using the Internet Protocol. VOIP is a term used in IP Telephony for a set of facilities for managing the delivery of voice information using the Internet Protocol.

Virtual Local Area Network (VCAN):

A logical grouping of two or more nodes that are not necessarily on the same physical network segment but which share the same IP network number.

Virtual Private Network (VPN):

A concept often used to create extranets and to provide remote access to private systems, VPNs make use of various encryption mechanisms to relay private traffic across public networks (often the Internet).

Voice Over the Internet Protocol (VOIP):

The ability of a machine or program to recognize and carryout voice commands or take dictation.

W

Web-Enabled:

Software applications that can be used directly through the Web.

Wide Area Network (WAN):

A network that links computers over a distance, sometimes across hundreds of miles, using digital telecommunications technology.

Appendix D

Health Insurance Portability and Accountability Act (HIPAA)* Glossary‡

Compiled: Amy Jurevic Sokol, Tulsa, Oklahoma
Source: See individual entries for source information.

A

Ability to Add Attributes:

> One possible capability of a digital signature technology, for example, the ability to add a time stamp as part of a digital signature. Part of digital signature on the matrix.
>
> 63 Fed. Reg. 43,242, 43,271 (Aug. 12, 1998)

Access:

> The ability or the means necessary to read, write, modify, or communicate data/information or otherwise make use of any system resource.
>
> 45 C.F.R. §164.304

Access Authorization:

> Information-use policies/procedures that establish the rules for granting and/or restricting access to a user, terminal, transaction, program, or process. Part of information access control on the matrix.
>
> 63 Fed. Reg. 43,242, 43,271 (Aug. 12, 1998)

---

*Health Insurance Portability and Accountability Act of 1996, Pub. L. No. 104-191, 110 Stat. 1936 (Aug. 21, 1996).
‡This appendix document is also available on the CD-ROM accompanying this volume..

Access Control:

A method of restricting access to resources, allowing only privileged entities access. (PGP, Inc.) Types of access control include, among others, mandatory access control, discretionary access control, time-of-day, classification, and subject-object separation. Part of Media Controls on the matrix. Part of technical security services to control and monitor access to information on the matrix.

63 Fed. Reg. 43,242, 43,271 (Aug. 12, 1998)

Access Controls:

The protection of sensitive communications transmissions over open or private networks so that they cannot be easily intercepted and interpreted by parties other than the intended recipient. Part of mechanisms to prevent unauthorized access to data that is transmitted over a communications network on the matrix.

63 Fed. Reg. 43,242, 43,271 (Aug. 12, 1998)

Access Establishment:

The security policies, and the rules established therein, that determine an entity's initial right of access to a terminal, transaction, program, or process. Part of information access control on the matrix.

63 Fed. Reg. 43,242, 43,271 (Aug. 12, 1998)

Access Level:

A level associated with an individual who may be accessing information (for example, a clearance level) or with the information that may be accessed (for example, a classification level).

63 Fed. Reg. 43,242, 43,271 (Aug. 12, 1998)

Access Modification:

The security policies, and the rules established therein, that determine types of, and reasons for, modification to an entity's established right of access to a terminal, transaction, program, or process. Part of information access control on the matrix.

63 Fed. Reg. 43,242, 43,271 (Aug. 12, 1998)

Accountability:

The property that ensures that the actions of an entity can be traced uniquely to that entity. Part of media controls on the matrix.

63 Fed. Reg. 43,242, 43,271 (Aug. 12, 1998)
45 C.F.R. §160.103

Act:

The Social Security Act.

45 C.F.R. §160.163

Administrative Procedures to Guard Data Integrity, Confidentiality, and Availability:

Documented, formal practices to manage (1) the selection and execution of security measures to protect data, and (2) the conduct of personnel in relation to the protection of data. A section of the matrix.

63 Fed. Reg. 43,242, 43,272 (Aug. 12, 1998)

Administrative Safeguards:

Administrative actions, and policies and procedures, to manage the selection, development, implementation, and maintenance of security measures to protect electronic protected health information and to manage the conduct of the covered entity's workforce in relation to the protection of that information.

45 C.F.R. §164.304

Administrative Simplification Provision:

Any requirement or prohibition established by:

(1) 42 U.S.C. 1320d–1320d-4, 1320d-7, and 1320d-8;

(2) Section 264 of Pub. L. 104–191; or

(3) This subchapter [Subchapter C—Administrative Data Standards and Related Requirements].

45 C.F.R. §160.302

Alarm:

In communication systems, any device that can sense an abnormal condition within the system and provide, either locally or remotely, a signal indicating the presence of the abnormality. Part of mechanisms to prevent unauthorized access to data that is transmitted over a communications network on the matrix.

63 Fed. Reg. 43,242, 43,272 (Aug. 12, 1998)

ALJ:

Administrative Law Judge.

45 C.F.R. §160.302

ANSI:

The American National Standards Institute.

45 C.F.R. §160.163

Applications and Data Criticality Analysis:

An entity's formal assessment of the sensitivity, vulnerabilities, and security of its programs and information it receives, manipulates, stores, and/or transmits. Part of contingency plan on the matrix.

63 Fed. Reg. 43,242, 43,272 (Aug. 12, 1998)

Assigned Security Responsibility:

Practices put in place by management to manage and supervise (1) the execution and use of security measures to protect data, and (2) the conduct of personnel in relation to the protection of data. Part of Physical safeguards to guard data integrity, confidentiality, and availability on the matrix.

63 Fed. Reg. 43,242, 43,272 (Aug. 12, 1998)

Assure Supervision of Maintenance Personnel by Authorized, Knowledgeable Person:

Documented formal procedures/instruction for the oversight of maintenance personnel when such personnel are in the vicinity of health information pertaining to an individual. Part of personnel security on the matrix.

63 Fed. Reg. 43,242, 43,272 (Aug. 12, 1998)

Asymmetric Encryption:

Encryption and decryption performed using two different keys, one of which is referred to as the public key and one of which is referred to as the private key. Also known as public-key encryption.

63 Fed. Reg. 43,242, 43,272 (Aug. 12, 1998)

Asymmetric Key:

One half of a key pair used in an asymmetric ("public key") encryption system. Asymmetric encryption systems have two important properties: (1) the key used for encryption is different from the one used for decryption; and (2) neither key can feasibly be derived from the other.

63 Fed. Reg. 43,242, 43,272 (Aug. 12, 1998)

Audit Controls:

The mechanisms employed to record and examine system activity. Part of technical security services to control and monitor access to information on the matrix.

63 Fed. Reg. 43,242, 43,272 (Aug. 12, 1998)

Audit Trail:

Data collected and potentially used to facilitate a security audit. Part of mechanisms to prevent unauthorized access to data that is transmitted over a communications network on the matrix.

63 Fed. Reg. 43,242, 43,272 (Aug. 12, 1998)

Authentication:

The corroboration that a person is the one claimed.

45 C.F.R. §164.304

Authorization Control:

The mechanism for obtaining consent for the use and disclosure of health information. Part of technical security services to control and monitor access to information on the matrix.

63 Fed. Reg. 43,242, 43,272 (Aug. 12, 1998)

Automatic Logoff:

After a pre-determined time of inactivity (for example, 15 minutes), an electronic session is terminated. Part of entity authentication on the matrix.

63 Fed. Reg. 43,242, 43,272 (Aug. 12, 1998)

Availability:

The property that data or information is accessible and useable upon demand by an authorized entity.

45 C.F.R. §164.304

Awareness Training for All Personnel (Including Management):

All personnel in an organization should undergo security awareness training, including, but not limited to, password maintenance, incident reporting, and an education concerning viruses and other forms of malicious software. Part of Training on the matrix.

63 Fed. Reg. 43,242, 43,272 (Aug. 12, 1998)

B

Biometric:

A biometric identification system identifies a human from a measurement of a physical feature or repeatable action of the individual (for example, hand geometry, retinal scan, iris scan, fingerprint patterns, facial characteristics, DNA sequence characteristics, voice prints, and handwritten signature).

63 Fed. Reg. 43,242, 43,272 (Aug. 12, 1998)

Board:

The members of the HHS Departmental Appeals Board, in the Office of the Secretary, who issue decisions in panels of three.

45 C.F.R. §160.502

Breach:

The unauthorized acquisition, access, use, or disclosure of protected health information which compromises the security or privacy of such information.

(1)(i) For purposes of this definition, *compromises the security or privacy of the protected health information* means poses a significant risk of financial, reputational, or other harm to the individual.

(ii) A use or disclosure of protected information that does not include the identifiers listed in 45 C.F.R. §164.514(e)(2), date of birth, and zip code does not compromise the security or privacy of the protected heath information.

(2) Breach excludes:

(i) Any unintentional acquisition, access, or use of protected health information by a workforce member or person acting under the authority of a covered entity or a business associate, if such acquisition, access, or use was made in good faith and within the scope of authority and such information is not further acquired, accessed, used, or disclosed in an unauthorized manner or by an unauthorized person.

(ii) Any inadvertent disclosure by a person who is authorized to access protected health information at a covered entity or business associate to another person authorized to access protected health information at the same covered entity or business associate, or organized health care arrangement in which the covered entity participates, and the information received as a result of such disclosure is not further used or disclosed in a manner not permitted.

(iii) A disclosure of protected health information where a covered entity or business associate has a good faith belief that an unauthorized person to whom the disclosure was made would not reasonably have been able to retain such information.

45 C.F.R. §164.402

Breach of Security:

With respect to unsecured PHR identifiable health information of an individual in a personal health record, the acquisition of such information without the authorization of the individual.

American Recovery and Reinvestment Act of 2009, Pub. L. No. 111-5 §13407 (f) (1)

Business Associate:

(1) Except as provided in paragraph (2) of this definition, *business associate* means, with respect to a covered entity, a person who:

    (i) On behalf of such covered entity or of an organized health care arrangement (as defined in §164.501 of this subchapter) in which the covered entity participates, but other than in the capacity of a member of the workforce of such covered entity or arrangement, performs, or assists in the performance of:

        (A) A function or activity involving the use or disclosure of individually identifiable health information, including claims processing or administration, data analysis, processing or administration, utilization review, quality assurance, billing, benefit management, practice management, and repricing; or

        (B) Any other function or activity regulated by this subchapter; or

    (ii) Provides, other than in the capacity of a member of the workforce of such covered entity, legal, actuarial, accounting, consulting, data aggregation (as defined in §164.501 of this subchapter), management, administrative, accreditation, or financial services to or for such covered entity, or to or for an organized health care arrangement in which the covered entity participates, where the provision of the service involves the disclosure of individually identifiable health information from such covered entity or arrangement, or from another business associate of such covered entity or arrangement, to the person.

(2) A covered entity participating in an organized health care arrangement that performs a function or activity as described by paragraph (1)(i) of this definition for or on behalf of such organized health care arrangement, or that provides a service as described in paragraph (1)(ii) of this definition to or for such organized health care arrangement, does not, simply through the performance of such function or activity or the provision of such service, become a business associate of other covered entities participating in such organized health care arrangement.

(3) A covered entity may be a business associate of another covered entity.

45 C.F.R. §160.103

C

Certification:

The technical evaluation performed as part of, and in support of, the accreditation process that establishes the extent to which a particular computer system or network design and implementation meet a pre-specified set of security requirements. This evaluation may be performed internally or by an external accrediting agency. Part of administrative procedures to guard data integrity, confidentiality, and availability.

63 Fed. Reg. 43,242, 43,272 (Aug. 12, 1998)

Certification Criteria:

Criteria:

(1) To establish that health information technology meets applicable standards and implementation specifications established by the Secretary; or

(2) That are used to test and certify that health information technology includes required capabilities.

45 C.F.R. § 170.102.

Certified EHR Technology:

A complete EHR or combination of EHR Modules, each of which:

(1) Meets the requirements included in the definition of a Qualified EHR; and

(2) Has been tested and certified in accordance with the certification program established by the National Coordinator as having met all applicable certification criteria adopted by the Secretary.

45 C.F.R. § 170.102

Chain of Trust Partner Agreement:

Contract entered into by two business partners in which it is agreed to exchange data and that the first party will transmit information to the second party, where the data transmitted is agreed to be protected between the partners. The sender and receiver depend upon each other to maintain the integrity and confidentiality of the transmitted information. Multiple such two-party contracts may be involved in moving information from the originator to the ultimate recipient, for example, a provider may contract with a clearing house to transmit claims to the clearing house; the clearing house, in turn, may contract with another clearing house or with a payer for the further transmittal of those same claims. Part of administrative procedures to guard data integrity, confidentiality and availability on the matrix.

63 Fed. Reg. 43,242, 43,272 (Aug. 12, 1998)

Civil Monetary Penalty or Penalty:

The amount determined under 45 C.F.R. §160.404 and includes the plural of these terms.

45 C.F.R. § 160.302

Classification:

Protection of data from unauthorized access by the designation of multiple levels of access authorization clearances to be required for access, dependent upon the sensitivity of the information. A type of access control on the matrix.

63 Fed. Reg. 43,242, 43,272 (Aug. 12, 1998)

Clearinghouse:

A public or private entity that processes or facilitates the processing of nonstandard data elements of health information into standard data elements.

HIPAA, Subtitle F, Section 262(a), SSA Act Section 1171(2), and 63 Fed. Reg. 43,242, 43,272 (Aug. 12, 1998)

Code Set:

Any set of codes used for encoding data elements, such as tables of terms, medical concepts, medical diagnostic codes, or medical procedure codes.

HIPAA, Pub. L. No. 104-191, §262(a).

Code Set Maintaining Organization:

An organization that creates and maintains the code sets adopted by the Secretary for use in the transactions for which standards are adopted in this part.

45 C.F.R. §162.103

Combination Locks Changed:

Documented procedure for changing combinations of locking mechanisms, both on a recurring basis and when personnel knowledgeable of combinations no longer have a need to know or a requirement for access to the protected facility/system. Part of termination procedures on the matrix.

63 Fed. Reg. 43,242, 43,272 (Aug. 12, 1998)

Common Control:

Exists if an entity has the power, directly or indirectly, significantly to influence or direct the actions or policies of another entity.

45 C.F.R. §164.103

Common Ownership:

Exists if an entity or entities possess an ownership or equity interest of 5 percent or more in another entity.

45 C.F.R. §164.103

Complete EHR:

EHR technology that has been developed to meet all of the applicable certification criteria adopted by the Secretary.

45 C.F.R. § 170.102

Compliance Date:

The date by which a covered entity must comply with a standard, implementation specification, requirement, or modification adopted under this subchapter.

45 C.F.R. §160.103

Confidentiality:

The property that data or information is not made available or disclosed to unauthorized individuals.

45 C.F.R. §164.304

Context-Based Access:

An access control based on the context of a transaction (as opposed to being based on attributes of the initiator or target). The "external" factors might include time of day, location of the user, strength of user authentication, etc. Part of access control on the matrix.

63 Fed. Reg. 43,242, 43,272 (Aug. 12, 1998)

Contingency Plan:

A plan for responding to a system emergency. The plan includes performing backups, preparing critical facilities that can be used to facilitate continuity of operations in the event of an emergency, and recovering from a disaster. Contingency plans should be updated routinely. Part of Administrative procedures to guard data integrity, confidentiality, and availability on the matrix.

63 Fed. Reg. 43,242, 43,272 (Aug. 12, 1998)

Continuity of Signature Capability:

The public verification of a signature shall not compromise the ability of the signer to apply additional secure signatures at a later date. Part of digital signature on the matrix.

63 Fed. Reg. 43,242, 43,273 (Aug. 12, 1998)

Contrary:

When used to compare a provision of state law to a standard, requirement, or implementation specification adopted under this subchapter, means:

(1) A covered entity would find it impossible to comply with both the state and federal requirements; or

(2) The provision of State law stands as an obstacle to the accomplishment and execution of the full purposes and objectives of part C of title XI of the Act or section 264 of Pub. L. 104-191, as applicable.

45 C.F.R. §160.202

Correctional Institution:

Any penal or correctional facility, jail, reformatory, detention center, work farm, halfway house, or residential community program center operated by, or under contract to, the United States, a State, a territory, a political subdivision of a State or territory, or an Indian tribe, for the confinement or rehabilitation of persons charged with or convicted of a criminal offense or other persons held in lawful custody. Other persons held in lawful custody includes juvenile offenders adjudicated delinquent, aliens detained awaiting deportation, persons committed to mental institutions through the criminal justice system, witnesses, or others awaiting charges or trial.

45 C.F.R. §164.501

Counter Signatures:

It shall be possible to prove the order of application of signatures. This is analogous to the normal business practice of countersignatures, where some party signs a document that has already been signed by another party. Part of digital signature on the matrix.

63 Fed. Reg. 43,242, 43,273 (Aug. 12, 1998)

Covered Entity:

(1) A health plan.

(2) A health care clearinghouse.

(3) A health care provider who transmits any health information in electronic form in connection with a transaction covered by this subchapter.

45 C.F.R. §160.103

Covered Functions:

Means those functions of a covered entity the performance of which makes the entity a health plan, health care provider, or health care clearinghouse.

45 C.F.R. §164.501

Covered Health Care Provider:

A health care provider who transmits any health information in electronic form in connection with a transaction covered by Subchapter C—Administrative Data Standards and Related Requirements.

45 C.F.R. §162.402

D

Data:

A sequence of symbols to which meaning may be assigned.

63 Fed. Reg. 43,242, 43,273 (Aug. 12, 1998)

Data Aggregation:

With respect to protected health information created or received by a business associate in its capacity as the business associate of a covered entity, the combining of such protected health information by the business associate with the protected health information received by the business associate in its capacity as a business associate of another covered entity, to permit data analyses that relate to the health care operations of the respective covered entities.

45 C.F.R. §164.501

Data Authentication:

The corroboration that data has not been altered or destroyed in an unauthorized manner. Examples of how data corroboration may be assured include the use of a check sum, double keying, a message authentication code, or digital signature. Part of technical security services to control and monitor access to information on the matrix.

63 Fed. Reg. 43,242, 43,273 (Aug. 12, 1998)

Data Backup:

A retrievable, exact copy of information. Part of media controls on the matrix.

63 Fed. Reg. 43,242, 43,273 (Aug. 12, 1998)

Data Backup Plan:

A documented and routinely updated plan to create and maintain, for a specific period of time, retrievable exact copies of information. Part of contingency plans on the matrix.

63 Fed. Reg. 43,242, 43,273 (Aug. 12, 1998)

Data Condition:

The rule that describes the circumstances under which a covered entity must use a particular data element or segment.

45 C.F.R. §162.103

Data Content:

All the data elements and codes sets inherent to a transaction, and not related to the format of the transaction. Data elements that are related to the format are not data content.

45 C.F.R. §162.103

Data Element:

The smallest named unit of information in a transaction.

45 C.F.R. §162.103

Data Integrity:

The property that data has not been altered or destroyed in an unauthorized manner.

63 Fed. Reg. 43,242, 43,273 (Aug. 12, 1998)

Data Set:

A semantically meaningful unit of information exchanged between two parties to a transaction.

45 C.F.R. §162.103

Data Storage:

The retention of health care information pertaining to an individual in an electronic format. Part of media controls on the security matrix.

63 Fed. Reg. 43,242, 43,273 (Aug. 12, 1998)

Descriptor:

The text defining a code.

45 C.F.R. §162.103

Designated Record Set:

(1) A group of records maintained by or for a covered entity that is:

    (i) The medical records and billing records about individuals maintained by or for a covered health care provider;

(ii) The enrollment, payment, claims adjudication, and case or medical management record systems maintained by or for a health plan; or

(iii) Used, in whole or in part, by or for the covered entity to make decisions about individuals.

(2) For purposes of this paragraph, the term record means any item, collection, or grouping of information that includes protected health information and is maintained, collected, used, or disseminated by or for a covered entity.

45 C.F.R. §164.501

Designated Standard Maintenance Organization (DSMO):

An organization designated by the Secretary under §162.910(a).

45 C.F.R. §162.103

Digital Signature:

An electronic signature based upon cryptographic methods of originator authentication, computed by using a set of rules and a set of parameters such that the identity of the signer and the integrity of the data can be verified. (FDA Electronic Record; Electronic Signatures; Final Rule.) Part of electronic signature on the matrix.

63 Fed. Reg. 43,242, 43,273 (Aug. 12, 1998)

Direct Data Entry:

The direct entry of data (for example, using dumb terminals or Web browsers) that is immediately transmitted into a health plan's computer.

45 C.F.R. §162.103

Direct Treatment Relationship:

A treatment relationship between an individual and a health care provider that is not an indirect treatment relationship.

45 C.F.R. §164.501

Disaster Recovery:

The process whereby an enterprise would restore any loss of data in the event of fire, vandalism, natural disaster, or system failure. Part of physical access controls (limited access) on the matrix.

63 Fed. Reg. 43,242, 43,273 (Aug. 12, 1998)

Disaster Recovery Plan:

Part of an overall contingency plan. The plan for a process whereby an enterprise would restore any loss of data in the event of fire, vandalism, natural disaster, or system failure. Part of contingency plan on the matrix.

63 Fed. Reg. 43,242, 43,273 (Aug. 12, 1998)

Disclose/Disclosure:

Means the release, transfer, provision of access to, or divulging in any other manner of information outside the entity holding the information.

45 C.F.R. §164.501; American Recovery and Reinvestment Act of 2009, Pub. L. No. 111-5 §13400 (4)

Discretionary Access Control (DAC):

DAC is used to control access by restricting a subject's access to an object. It is generally used to limit a user's access to a file. In this type of access control, it is the owner of the file who controls other users' accesses to the file. A type of access control on the matrix.

63 Fed. Reg. 43,242, 43,273 (Aug. 12, 1998)

Disposal:

The final disposition of electronic data, and/or the hardware on which electronic data is stored. Part of media controls on the matrix.

63 Fed. Reg. 43,242, 43,273 (Aug. 12, 1998)

Documentation:

Written security plans, rules, procedures, and instructions concerning all components of an entity's security. Part of security configuration management on the matrix.

63 Fed. Reg. 43,242, 43,273 (Aug. 12, 1998)

E

EHR Module:

Any service, component, or combination thereof that can meet the requirements of at least one certification criterion developed by the Secretary.

45 C.F.R. § 170.102

EIN:

Stands for the employer identification number assigned by the Internal Revenue Service, U.S. Department of Treasury. The EIN is the taxpayer identifying number of an individual or other entity (whether or not an employer) assigned under one or the following:

(1) 26 U.S.C. [section] 6011(b), which is the portion of the Internal Revenue Code dealing with identifying the taxpayer in tax returns and statements, or corresponding provisions of prior law.

(2) 26 U.S.C. [section] 6109, which is the portion of the Internal Revenue Code dealing with identifying numbers in tax returns, statements, and other required documents.

45 C.F.R. §160.103

Electronic Data Interchange (EDI):

Intercompany, computer-to-computer transmission of business information in a standard format. For EDI purists, "computer-to-computer" means direct transmission from the originating application program to the receiving, or processing, application program, and an EDI transmission consists only of business data, not any accompanying verbiage or free-form messages. Purists might also contend that a standard format is one that is approved by a national or international standards organization, as opposed to formats developed by industry groups or companies.

63 Fed. Reg. 43,242, 43,273 (Aug. 12, 1998)

Electronic Health Record (EHR):

An electronic record of health-related information on an individual that is created, gathered, managed, and consulted by authorized health care clinicians and staff.

American Recovery and Reinvestment Act of 2009, Pub. L. No. 111-5 §13400 (5)

Electronic Media:

The mode of electronic transmission. It includes the Internet (wide-open), Extranet (using Internet technology to link a business with information only accessible to collaborating parties), leased lines, dial-up lines, private networks, and those transmissions that are physically moved from one location to another using magnetic tape, disk, or compact disk media.

45 C.F.R. §162.103

Electronic Protected Health Information:

Individually identifiable health information:

(1) Except as provided in paragraph (2) of this definition, that is:

(i) Transmitted by electronic media; or

(ii) Maintained in any medium described in the definition of electronic media at §162.103 of this subchapter.

(2) Protected health information excludes individually identifiable health information in:

(i) Education records covered by the Family Educational Right and Privacy Act, as amended, 20 U.S.C. [section] 1232g; and

(ii) Records described at 20 U.S.C. [section] 1232g(a)(4)(B)(iv).

45 C.F.R. §160.103

Electronic Signature:

The attribute that is affixed to an electronic document to bind it to a particular entity. An electronic signature process secures the user authentication (proof of claimed identity, such as by biometrics (fingerprints, retinal scans, hand-written signature verification, etc.), tokens, or passwords) at the time the signature is generated; creates the logical manifestation of signature (including the possibility for multiple parties to sign a document and have the order of application recognized and proven) and supplies additional information such as time stamp and signature purpose specific to that user; and ensures the integrity of the signed document to enable transportability, interoperability, independent verifiability, and continuity of signature capability. Verifying a signature on a document verifies the integrity of the document and associated attributes and verifies the identity of the signer. There are several technologies available for user authentication, including passwords, cryptography, and biometrics.

63 Fed. Reg. 43,242, 43,273 (Aug. 12, 1998)

Emergency Mode Operation:

Access controls in place that enable an enterprise to continue to operate in the event of fire, vandalism, natural disaster, or system failure. Part of physical access controls (limited access) on the matrix.

63 Fed. Reg. 43,242, 43,273 (Aug. 12, 1998)

Emergency Mode Operation Plan:

Part of an overall contingency plan. The plan for a process whereby an enterprise would be able to continue to operate in the event of fire, vandalism, natural disaster, or system failure. Part of contingency plan on the matrix.

63 Fed. Reg. 43,242, 43,273 (Aug. 12, 1998)

Employer:

Is defined as it is in 26 U.S.C. [Section] 3401(d).

45 C.F.R. §160.103

Encryption:

The use of an algorithmic process to transform data into a form in which there is a low probability of assigning meaning without use of a confidential process or key.

45 C.F.R. §164.304

Entity Authentication:

(1) The corroboration that an entity is the one claimed. Part of technical security services to control and monitor access to information on the matrix.

(2) A communications/network mechanism to irrefutably identify authorized users, programs, and processes, and to deny access to unauthorized users, programs and processes. Part of mechanisms to prevent unauthorized access to data that is transmitted over a communications network on the matrix.

63 Fed. Reg. 43,242, 43,273 (Aug. 12, 1998)

Equipment Control (Into and Out of Site):

Documented security procedures for bringing hardware and software into and out of a facility and for maintaining a record of that equipment. This includes, but is not limited to, the marking, handling, and disposal of hardware and storage media. Part of physical access controls (limited access) on the matrix.

63 Fed. Reg. 43,242, 43,273 (Aug. 12, 1998)

Event Reporting:

Network message indicating operational irregularities in physical elements of a network or a response to the occurrence of a significant task, typically the completion of a request for information. Part of mechanisms to prevent unauthorized access to data that is transmitted over a communications network on the matrix.

63 Fed. Reg. 43,242, 43,273 (Aug. 12, 1998)

F

Facility:

The physical premises and interior and exterior of a building(s).

45 C.F.R. §164.304

Facility Security Plan:

A plan to safeguard the premises and building(s) (exterior and interior) from unauthorized physical access, and to safeguard the equipment therein from unauthorized physical access, tampering, and theft. Part of physical access controls (limited access) on the matrix.

63 Fed. Reg. 43,242, 43,273 (Aug. 12, 1998)

Formal Mechanism for Processing Records:

Documented policies and procedures for the routine, and non-routine, receipt, manipulation, storage, dissemination, transmission, and/or disposal of health information. Part of administrative procedures to guard data integrity, confidentiality, and availability on the matrix.

63 Fed. Reg. 43,242, 43,273 (Aug. 12, 1998)

Format:

Those data elements that provide or control the enveloping or hierarchical structure, or assist in identifying data content of, a transaction.

45 C.F.R. §162.103

G

Group Health Plan:

An employee welfare benefit plan (as defined in section 3(1) of the Employee Retirement Income and Security Act of 1974 (ERISA), 29 U.S.C. [section] 1002(1)), including insured and self-insured plans, to the extent that the plan provides medical care (as defined in section 2791(a)(2) of the Public Health Service Act (PHS Act), 42 U.S.C. [section] 300gg-91(a)(2)), including items and services paid for as medical care, to employees or their dependents directly or through insurance, reimbursement, or otherwise, that:

(1) Has 50 or more participants (as defined in section 3(7) of ERISA, 29 U.S.C. [section] 1002(7)); or

(2) Is administered by an entity other than the employer that established and maintains the plan.

45 C.F.R. §160.103

H

Hardware/Software Installation & Maintenance Review and Testing for Security Features:

Formal, documented procedures for (1) connecting and loading new equipment and programs, (2) periodic review of the maintenance occurring on that equipment and programs, and (3) periodic security testing of the security attributes of that hardware/software. Part of security configuration management on the matrix.

63 Fed. Reg. 43,242, 43,274 (Aug. 12, 1998)

Health Care:

Care, services, or supplies furnished to an individual and related to the health of the individual. Health care includes the following:

(1) Preventive, diagnostic, therapeutic, rehabilitative, maintenance, or palliative care, and counseling, service, assessment, or procedure with respect to the physical or mental condition, or functional status, of an individual or affecting the structure or function of the body; and

(2) Sale or dispensing of a drug, device, equipment, or other item in accordance with a prescription.

45 C.F.R. §160.103

Health Care Clearinghouse:

Means a public or private entity, including a billing service, repricing company, community health management information system or community health information system, and "value added" networks and switches, that does either of the following functions:

(1) Processes or facilitates the processing of health information received from another entity in a nonstandard format or containing nonstandard data content into standard data elements or a standard transaction.

(2) Receives a standard transaction from another entity and processes or facilitates the processing of health information into nonstandard format or nonstandard data content for the receiving entity.

45 C.F.R. §160.103

Health Care Component:

A component or combination of components of a hybrid entity designated by the hybrid entity in accordance with §164.105 (a)(2)(iii)(c).

45 C.F.R. §164.103

Health Care Operations:

Any of the following activities of the covered entity to the extent that the activities are related to covered functions, and any of the following activities of an organized health care arrangement in which the covered entity participates:

(1) Conducting quality assessment and improvement activities, including outcomes evaluation and development of clinical guidelines, provided

that the obtaining of generalizable knowledge is not the primary purpose of any studies resulting from such activities; population-based activities relating to improving health or reducing health care costs, protocol development, case management and care coordination, contacting of health care providers and patients with information about treatment alternatives; and related functions that do not include treatment;

(2) Reviewing the competence or qualifications of health care professionals, evaluating practitioner and provider performance, health plan performance, conducting training programs in which students, trainees, or practitioners in areas of health care learn under supervision to practice or improve their skills as health care providers, training of non-health care professionals, accreditation, certification, licensing, or credentialing activities;

(3) Underwriting, premium rating, and other activities relating to the creation, renewal, or replacement of a contract of health insurance or health benefits, and ceding, securing, or placing a contract for reinsurance of risk relating to claims for health care (including stop-loss insurance and excess of loss insurance), provided that the requirements of §164.514(g) are met, if applicable;

(4) Conducting or arranging for medical review, legal services, and auditing functions, including fraud and abuse detection and compliance programs;

(5) Business planning and development, such as conducting cost-management and planning-related analyses related to managing and operating the entity, including formulary development and administration, development or improvement of methods of payment or coverage policies; and

(6) Business management and general administrative activities of the entity, including, but not limited to:

    (i) Management activities relating to implementation of and compliance with the requirements of this subchapter;

    (ii) Customer service, including the provision of data analyses for policy holders, plan sponsors, or other customers, provided that protected health information is not disclosed to such policy holder, plan sponsor, or customer;

    (iii) Resolution of internal grievances;

    (iv) Due diligence in connection with the sale or transfer of assets to a potential successor in interest, if the potential successor in interest is a covered entity or, following completion of the sale or transfer, will become a covered entity; and

    (v) Consistent with the applicable requirements of §164.514, creating de-identified health information, fundraising for the benefit of the covered entity, and marketing for which an individual authorization is not required as described in §164.514(e)(2).

45 C.F.R. §164.501

Health Care Provider:

A provider of services (as defined in section 1861(u) of the Act, 42 U.S.C. [section] 1395x(u)), a provider of medical or health services (as defined in section 1861(s) of the Act, 42 U.S.C. [section] 1395x(s)), and any other person or organization who furnishes, bills, or is paid for health care in the normal course of business.

45 C.F.R. §160.103 and HIPAA, Pub. L. No. 104-191, §262(a)

Health Information:

Any information, whether oral or recorded in any form or medium, that—

(1) Is created or received by a health care provider, health plan, public health authority, employer, life insurer, school or university, or health care clearinghouse; and

(2) Relates to the past, present, or future physical or mental health or condition of an individual; the provision of health care to an individual; or the past, present, or future payment for the provision of health care to an individual.

45 C.F.R. §160.103

Health Insurance Issuer:

As defined in Section 2791(b) (2) of the PHS Act, 42 U.S.C. [Section] 300gg-91(b) (2), and used in the definition of health plan in this section, means an insurance company, insurance service, or insurance organization (including an HMO) that is licensed to engage in the business of insurance in a state and is subject to state law that regulates insurance. Such term does not include a group health plan.

45 C.F.R. §160.103

Health Maintenance Organization (HMO):

A federally qualified HMO, an organization recognized as an HMO under state law, or a similar organization regulated for solvency under state law in the same manner and to the same extent as such an HMO.

45 C.F.R. §160.103

Health Oversight Agency:

An agency or authority of the United States, a state, a territory, a political subdivision of a state or territory, or an Indian tribe, or a person or entity acting under a grant of authority from or contract with such public agency, including the employees or agents of such public agency or its contractors or persons or entities to whom it has granted authority, that is authorized by law to oversee the health care system (whether public or private) or government programs in which health information is necessary to determine eligibility or compliance, or to enforce civil rights laws for which health information is relevant.

45 C.F.R. §164.501

Health Plan:

An individual or group plan that provides, or pays the cost of, medical care (as defined in section 2791(a)(2) of the PHS Act, 42 U.S.C. §300gg-91(a)(2)).

(1) *Health plan* includes the following, singly or in combination:

- (i) A group health plan, as defined in this section.
- (ii) A health insurance issuer, as defined in this section.
- (iii) An HMO, as defined in this section.
- (iv) Part A or Part B of the Medicare program under title XVIII of the Act.
- (v) The Medicaid program under title XIX of the Act, 42 U.S.C. §1396 *et seq.*
- (vi) An issuer of a Medicare supplemental policy (as defined in section 1882(g)(1) of the Act, 42 U.S.C. §1395ss(g)(1)).
- (vii) An issuer of a long-term care policy, excluding a nursing home fixed-indemnity policy.
- (viii) An employee welfare benefit plan or any other arrangement that is established or maintained for the purpose of offering or providing health benefits to the employees of two or more employers.
- (ix) The health care program for active military personnel under title 10 of the United States Code.
- (x) The veterans health care program under 38 U.S.C. chapter 17.
- (xi) The Civilian Health and Medical Program of the Uniformed Services (CHAMPUS) (as defined in 10 U.S.C. §1072(4).
- (xii) The Indian Health Service program under the Indian Health Care Improvement Act, 25 U.S.C. §1601 *et seq.*
- (xiii) The Federal Employees Health Benefits Program under 5 U.S.C. §8902 *et seq.*

(xiv) An approved State child health plan under title XXI of the Act, providing benefits for child health assistance that meet the requirements of section 2103 of the Act, 42 U.S.C. §1397 *et seq.*

(xv) The Medicare + Choice program under Part C of title XVIII of the Act, 42 U.S.C. §§1395w-21 through 1395w-28.

(xvi) A high-risk pool that is a mechanism established under State law to provide health insurance coverage or comparable coverage to eligible individuals.

(xvii) Any other individual or group plan, or combination of individual or group plans, that provides or pays for the cost of medical care (as defined in section 2791(a)(2) of the PHS Act, 42 U.S.C. §300gg-91(a)(2)).

(2) *Health plan* excludes:

(i) Any policy, plan, or program to the extent that it provides, or pays for the cost of, excepted benefits that are listed in section 2791(c)(1) of the PHS Act, 42 U.S.C. §300gg-91(c)(1); and

(ii) A government-funded program (other than one listed in paragraph (1)(i)—(xvi) of this definition):

(A) Whose principal purpose is other than providing, or paying the cost of, health care; or

(B) Whose principal activity is:

(1) The direct provision of health care to persons; or

(2) The making of grants to fund the direct provision of health care to persons.

45 C.F.R. §160.103

HCPCS:

The Health [Care Financing Administration] Common Procedure Coding System.

45 C.F.R. §162.103

HHS:

The Department of Health and Human Services.

45 C.F.R. §160.103

Hybrid Entity:

A single legal entity:

(1) That is a covered entity;

(2) Whose business activities include both covered and non-covered functions; and

(3) That designates health care components in accordance with paragraph §160.105(a) (2) (iii) (c).

45 C.F.R. §164.504

I

Implementation Specification:

Specific requirements or instructions for implementing a standard.

45 C.F.R. §160.103

Independent Verifiability:

The capability to verify a signature without the cooperation of the signer. Technically, it is accomplished using the public key of the signatory, and it is a property of all digital signatures performed with asymmetric key encryption. Part of digital signature on the matrix.

63 Fed. Reg. 43,242, 43,274 (Aug. 12, 1998)

Indirect Treatment Relationship:

A relationship between an individual and a health care provider in which:

(1) The health care provider delivers health care to the individual based on the orders of another health care provider; and

(2) The health care provider typically provides services or products, or reports the diagnosis or results associated with the health care directly to another health care provider, who provides the services or products or reports to the individual.

45 C.F.R. §164.501

Individual:

The person who is the subject of protected health information.

45 C.F.R. §164.501

Individually Identifiable Health Information:

Is information that is a subset of health information, including demographic information collected from an individual, and:

(1) Is created or received by a health care provider, health plan, employer, or health care clearinghouse; and

(2) Relates to the past, present, or future physical or mental health or condition of an individual; the provision of health care to an individual; or the past, present, or future payment for the provision of health care to an individual; and

(i) That identifies the individual; or

(ii) With respect to which there is a reasonable basis to believe the information can be used to identify the individual.

45 C.F.R. §160.103

Information:

Data to which meaning is assigned, according to context and assumed conventions.

63 Fed. Reg. 43,242, 43,274 (Aug. 12, 1998)

Information Access Control:

Formal, documented policies and procedures for granting different levels of access to health care information. Part of administrative procedures to ensure integrity and confidentiality on the matrix.

63 Fed. Reg. 43,242, 43,274 (Aug. 12, 1998)

Information System:

An interconnected set of information resources under the same direct management control that shares common functionality. A system normally includes hardware, software, information, data, applications, communications, and people.

45 C.F.R. §164.304

Inmate:

A person incarcerated in or otherwise confined to a correctional institution.

45 C.F.R. §164.501

Integrity:

The property that data or information have not been altered or destroyed in an unauthorized manner.

45 C.F.R. §164.304

Integrity Controls:

Security mechanism employed to ensure the validity of the information being electronically transmitted or stored. Part of mechanisms to prevent unauthorized access to data that is transmitted over a communications network on the matrix.

63 Fed. Reg. 43,242, 43,274 (Aug. 12, 1998)

Internal Audit:

The in-house review of the records of system activity (for example, logins, file accesses, security incidents) maintained by an organization. Part of administrative procedures to guard data integrity, confidentiality, and availability on the matrix.

63 Fed. Reg. 43,242, 43,274 (Aug. 12, 1998)

Interoperability:

The applications used on either side of a communication, between trading partners and/or between internal components of an entity, being able to read and correctly interpret the information communicated from one to the other. Part of digital signature on the matrix.

63 Fed. Reg. 43,242, 43,274 (Aug. 12, 1998)

Inventory:

Formal, documented identification of hardware and software assets. Part of security configuration management on the matrix.

63 Fed. Reg. 43,242, 43,274 (Aug. 12, 1998)

K

Key:

An input that controls the transformation of data by an encryption algorithm.

63 Fed. Reg. 43,242, 43,274 (Aug. 12, 1998)

L

Law Enforcement Official:

An officer or employee of any agency or authority of the United States, a state, a territory, a political subdivision of a state or territory, or an Indian tribe, who is empowered by law to:

(1) Investigate or conduct an official inquiry into a potential violation of law; or

(2) Prosecute or otherwise conduct a criminal, civil, or administrative proceeding arising from an alleged violation of law.

45 C.F.R. §164.501

M

Maintain or Maintenance:

Activities necessary to support the use of a standard adopted by the Secretary, including technical corrections to an implementation specification, and enhancements or expansion of a code set. This term excludes the activities related to the adoption of a new standard or implementation specification, or modification to an adopted standard or implementation specification.

45 C.F.R. §162.103

Maintenance of Record of Access Authorizations:

Ongoing documentation and review of the levels of access granted to a user, program, or procedure accessing health information. Part of personnel security on the matrix.

63 Fed. Reg. 43,242, 43,274 (Aug. 12, 1998)

Maintenance Records:

Documentation of repairs and modifications to the physical components of a facility, for example, hardware, software, walls, doors, locks. Part of physical access controls (limited access) on the matrix.

63 Fed. Reg. 43,242, 43,274 (Aug. 12, 1998)

Malicious Software:

Software, for example, a virus, designed to damage or disrupt a system.

45 C.F.R. §164.304

Mandatory Access Control (MAC):

A means of restricting access to objects that is based on fixed security attributes assigned to users and to files and other objects. The controls are mandatory in the sense that they cannot be modified by users or their programs. A type of access control on the matrix.

63 Fed. Reg. 43,242, 43,274 (Aug. 12, 1998)

Marketing:

(1) To make a communication about a product or service that encourages recipients of the communication to purchase or use the product or service, unless the communication is made:

   (i) To describe a health-related product or service (or payment for such product or service) that is provided by, or included in a plan of benefits of, the covered entity making the communication, including communications about the entities participating in a health care provider network or health plan network; replacement of, or enhancements to, a health plan; and health-related products or services available only to a health plan enrollee that add value to, but are not part of, a plan of benefits.

(ii) For treatment of the individual; or

(iii) For case management or care coordination for the individual, or to direct or recommend alternative treatments, therapies, health care providers, or settings of care to the individual.

(2) An arrangement between a covered entity and any other entity whereby the covered entity discloses protected health information to the other entity, in exchange for direct or indirect remuneration, for the other entity or its affiliate to make a communication about its own product or service that encourages recipients of the communication to purchase or use that product or service.

45 C.F.R. §164.501

Maximum Defined Data Set:

All of the required data elements for a particular standard based on a specific implementation specification.

45 C.F.R. §162.103

Media Controls:

Formal, documented policies and procedures that govern the receipt and removal of hardware/software (for example, diskettes, tapes) into and out of a facility. Part of physical safeguards to guard data integrity, confidentiality, and availability on the matrix.

63 Fed. Reg. 43,242, 43,274 (Aug. 12, 1998)

Message:

A digital representation of information.

63 Fed. Reg. 43,242, 43,274 (Aug. 12, 1998)

Message Authentication:

Ensuring, typically with a message authentication code, that a message received (usually via a network) matches the message sent. Part of mechanisms to prevent unauthorized access to data that is transmitted over a communications network on the matrix.

63 Fed. Reg. 43,242, 43,274 (Aug. 12, 1998)

Message Authentication Code:

Data associated with an authenticated message that allows a receiver to verify the integrity of the message.

63 Fed. Reg. 43,242, 43,274 (Aug. 12, 1998)

Message Integrity:

The assurance of unaltered transmission and receipt of a message from the sender to the intended recipient. Part of digital signature on the matrix.

63 Fed. Reg. 43,242, 43,274 (Aug. 12, 1998)

Modify or Modification:

Refers to a change adopted by the Secretary, through regulation, to a standard or an implementation specification.

45 C.F.R. §160.103

More Stringent:

Means, in the context of a comparison of a provision of state law and a standard, requirement, or implementation specification adopted under subpart E of part 164 of this subchapter, a state law that meets one or more of the following criteria:

(1) With respect to a use or disclosure, the law prohibits or restricts a use or disclosure in circumstances under which such use or disclosure otherwise would be permitted under this subchapter, except if the disclosure is:

　(i) Required by the Secretary in connection with determining whether a covered entity is in compliance with this sub-chapter; or

　(ii) To the individual who is the subject of the individually identifiable health information.

(2) With respect to the rights of an individual who is the subject of the individually identifiable health information of access to or amendment of individually identifiable health information, permits greater rights of access or amendment, as applicable; provided that, nothing in this subchapter may be construed to preempt any State law to the extent that it authorizes or prohibits disclosure of protected health information about a minor to a parent, guardian, or person acting in loco parentis of such minor.

(3) With respect to information to be provided to an individual who is the subject of the individually identifiable health information about a use, a disclosure, rights, and remedies, provides the greater amount of information.

(4) With respect to the form or substance of an authorization or consent for use or disclosure of individually identifiable health information, provides requirements that narrow the scope or duration, increase the privacy protections afforded (such as by expanding the criteria for), or reduce the coercive effect of the circumstances surrounding the authorization or consent, as applicable.

(5) With respect to recordkeeping or requirements relating to accounting of disclosures, provides for the retention or reporting of more detailed information or for a longer duration.

(6) With respect to any other matter, provides greater privacy protection for the individual who is the subject of the individually identifiable health information.

45 C.F.R. §160.202

Multiple Signatures:

It shall be possible for multiple parties to sign a document. Multiple signatures are conceptually simply appended to the document. Part of digital signature on the matrix.

63 Fed. Reg. 43,242, 43,274 (Aug. 12, 1998)

N

National Coordinator:

The head of the Office of the National Coordinator for Health Information Technology established under section 3001(a) of the Public Health Service Act, as added by section 13101.

American Recovery and Reinvestment Act of 2009, Pub. L. No. 111-5 §13400(9)

Need-to-Know Procedures for Personnel Access:

A security principle stating that a user should have access only to the data he or she needs to perform a particular function. Part of physical access controls (limited access) on the matrix.

63 Fed. Reg. 43,242, 43,274 (Aug. 12, 1998)

Nonrepudiation:

Strong and substantial evidence of the identity of the signer of a message and of message integrity, sufficient to prevent a party from successfully denying the origin, submission or delivery of the message and the integrity of its contents. Part of digital signature on the matrix.

63 Fed. Reg. 43,242, 43,274 (Aug. 12, 1998)

O

Organized Health Care Arrangement:

(1) A clinically integrated care setting in which individuals typically receive health care from more than one health care provider;

(2) An organized system of health care in which more than one covered entity participates, and in which the participating covered entities:

    (i) Hold themselves out to the public as participating in a joint arrangement; and

    (ii) Participate in joint activities that include at least one of the following:

        (A) Utilization review, in which health care decisions by participating covered entities are reviewed by other participating covered entities or by a third party on their behalf;

        (B) Quality assessment and improvement activities, in which treatment provided by participating covered entities is assessed by other participating covered entities or by a third party on their behalf; or

        (C) Payment activities, if the financial risk for delivering health care is shared, in part or in whole, by participating covered entities through the joint arrangement and if protected health information created or received by a covered entity is reviewed by other participating covered entities or by a third party on their behalf for the purpose of administering the sharing of financial risk.

(3) A group health plan and a health insurance issuer or HMO with respect to such group health plan, but only with respect to protected health information created or received by such health insurance issuer or HMO that relates to individuals who are or who have been participants or beneficiaries in such group health plan;

(4) A group health plan and one or more other group health plans each of which are maintained by the same plan sponsor; or

(5) The group health plans described in paragraph (4) of this definition and health insurance issuers or HMOs with respect to such group health plans, but only with respect to protected health information created or received by such health insurance issuers or HMOs that relates to individuals who are or have been participants or beneficiaries in any of such group health plans.

45 C.F.R. §164.501

P

PHR Identifiable Health Information:

Means individually identifiable health information, as defined in section 1171(6) of the Social Security Act (42 U.S.C. 1320d(6)), and includes, with respect to an individual, information—

(A) that is provided by or on behalf of the individual; and

(B) that identifies the individual or with respect to which there is a reasonable basis to believe that the information can be used to identify the individual.

American Recovery and Reinvestment Act of 2009, Pub. L. No. 111-5 §13407 (f)(3)

Password:

Confidential authentication information composed of a string of characters.

45 C.F.R. §164.304

Payment:

(1) The activities undertaken by:

    (i) A health plan to obtain premiums or to determine or fulfill its responsibility for coverage and provision of benefits under the health plan; or

    (ii) A covered health care provider or health plan to obtain or provide reimbursement for the provision of health care; and

(2) The activities in paragraph (1) of this definition relate to the individual to whom health care is provided and include, but are not limited to:

    (i) Determinations of eligibility or coverage (including coordination of benefits or the determination of cost sharing amounts), and adjudication or subrogation of health benefit claims;

    (ii) Risk adjusting amounts due based on enrollee health status and demographic characteristics;

    (iii) Billing, claims management, collection activities, obtaining payment under a contract for reinsurance (including stop-loss insurance and excess of loss insurance), and related health care data processing;

    (iv) Review of health care services with respect to medical necessity, coverage under a health plan, appropriateness of care, or justification of charges;

(v) Utilization review activities, including precertification and preauthorization of services, concurrent and retrospective review of services; and

(vi) Disclosure to consumer reporting agencies of any of the following protected health information relating to collection of premiums or reimbursement:

(A) Name and address;

(B) Date of birth;

(C) Social security number;

(D) Payment history;

(E) Account number; and

(F) Name and address of the health care provider and/or health plan.

45 C.F.R. §164.501

Periodic Security Reminders:

Employees, agents, and contractors should be made aware of security concerns on an ongoing basis. Part of training on the matrix.

63 Fed. Reg. 43,242, 43,274 (Aug. 12, 1998)

Person:

A natural person, trust or estate, partnership, corporation, professional association or corporation, or other entity, public or private.

45 C.F.R. §160.103

Personal Health Record:

An electronic record of PHR identifiable health information (as defined in section 13407(f)(2)) on an individual that can be drawn from multiple sources and that is managed, shared, and controlled by or primarily for the individual.

American Recovery and Reinvestment Act of 2009, Pub. L. No. 111-5 §13400(11)

Personal Identification Number (PIN):

A number or code assigned to an individual and used to provide verification of identity. Part of entity authentication on the matrix.

63 Fed. Reg. 43,242, 43,275 (Aug. 12, 1998)

Personnel Clearance Procedure:

A protective measure applied to determine that an individual's access to sensitive, unclassified automated information is admissible. The need for and extent of a screening process is normally based on an assessment of risk, cost, benefit, and feasibility as well as other protective measures in place. Effective screening processes are applied in such a way as to allow a range of implementation, from minimal procedures to more stringent procedures commensurate with the sensitivity of the data to be accessed and the magnitude of harm or loss that could be caused by the individual. Part of personnel security on the matrix.

63 Fed. Reg. 43,242, 43,274 (Aug. 12, 1998)

Personnel Security:

The procedures established to ensure that all personnel who have access to sensitive information have the required authority as well as appropriate clearances. Part of administrative procedures to guard data integrity, confidentiality, and availability on the matrix.

63 Fed. Reg. 43,242, 43,274 (Aug. 12, 1998)

Personnel Security Policy/Procedure:

Formal documentation of policies and procedures established to ensure that all personnel who have access to sensitive information have the required authority as well as appropriate clearances. Part of personnel security on the matrix.

63 Fed. Reg. 43,242, 43,274 (Aug. 12, 1998)

Physical Access Controls (Limited Access):

Those formal, documented policies and procedures to be followed to limit physical access to an entity while ensuring that properly authorized access is allowed. Part of physical safeguards to guard data integrity, confidentiality, and availability on the matrix.

63 Fed. Reg. 43,242, 43,274 (Aug. 12, 1998)

Physical Safeguards:

Physical measures, policies, and procedures to protect a covered entity's electronic information systems and related buildings and equipment, from natural and environmental hazards, and unauthorized intrusion.

45 C.F.R. §164.304

Plan Administration Functions:

Administration functions performed by the plan sponsor of a group health plan on behalf of the group health plan and excluding functions performed by the plan sponsor in connection with any other benefit or benefit plan of the plan sponsor.

45 C.F.R. §164.504

Plan Sponsor:

Is defined as set forth at section 3(16)(B) of ERISA, 29 U.S.C. [section] 1002(16)(B): The employer in the case of an employee benefit plan established or maintained by single employer; the employee organization in the case of a plan established or maintained by an employee organization; in the case of a plan established or maintained by two or more employers or jointly by one or more employers and one or more employee organizations, the association committee, joint board of trustees, or other similar group of representatives of the parties who establish or maintain the plan.

45 C.F.R. §164.501 and 29 U.S.C. §1002(16)(B)

Policy/Guideline on Work Station Use:

Documented instructions/procedures delineating the proper functions to be performed, the manner in which those functions are to be performed, and the physical attributes of the surroundings, of a specific computer terminal site or type of site, dependent upon the sensitivity of the information accessed from that site. Part of physical safeguards to guard data integrity, confidentiality, and availability on the matrix.

63 Fed. Reg. 43,242, 43,275 (Aug. 12, 1998)

Procedure for Emergency Access:

Documented instructions for obtaining necessary information during a crisis. Part of access control on the matrix.

63 Fed. Reg. 43,242, 43,275 (Aug. 12, 1998)

Procedures for Verifying Access Authorizations Prior to Physical Access:

Formal, documented policies and instructions for validating the access privileges of an entity prior to granting those privileges. Part of physical access controls (limited access) on the matrix.

63 Fed. Reg. 43,242, 43,275 (Aug. 12, 1998)

Protected Health Information:

Individually identifiable health information:

(1) Except as provided in paragraph (2) of this definition, that is:

    (i) Transmitted by electronic media;

    (ii) Maintained in any medium described in the definition of electronic media at §162.103 of this subchapter; or

(iii) Transmitted or maintained in any other form or medium.

(2) Protected health information excludes individually identifiable health information in:

(i) Education records covered by the Family Educational Right and Privacy Act, as amended, 20 U.S.C. [section] 1232g; and

(ii) Records described at 20 U.S.C. [section] 1232g(a)(4)(B)(iv).

45 C.F.R. §164.501

Psychotherapy Notes:

Notes recorded (in any medium) by a health care provider who is a mental health professional documenting or analyzing the contents of conversation during a private counseling session or a group, joint, or family counseling session and that are separated from the rest of the individual's medical record. Psychotherapy notes excludes medication prescription and monitoring, counseling session start and stop times, the modalities and frequencies of treatment furnished, results of clinical tests, and any summary of the following items: diagnosis, functional status, the treatment plan, symptoms, prognosis, and progress to date.

45 C.F.R. §164.501

Public Health Authority:

An agency or authority of the United States, a State, a territory, a political subdivision of a State or territory, or an Indian tribe, or a person or entity acting under a grant of authority from or contract with such public agency, including the employees or agents of such public agency or its contractors or persons or entities to whom it has granted authority, that is responsible for public health matters as part of its official mandate.

45 C.F.R. §164.501

Public Key:

One of the two keys used in an asymmetric encryption system. The public key is made public, to be used in conjunction with a corresponding private key.

63 Fed. Reg. 43,242, 43,275 (Aug. 12, 1998)

Q

Qualified EHR:

An electronic record of health-related information on an individual that:

(1) Includes patient demographic and clinical health information, such as medical history and problems list; and

(2) Has the capacity to:

  (i) To provide clinical decision support;

  (ii) To support physician order entry;

  (iii) To capture and query information relevant to health care quality; and

  (iv) To exchange electronic health information with, and integrate such information from other sources.

45 C.F.R. §170.102

R

Reasonable Cause:

Circumstances that would make it unreasonable for the covered entity, despite the exercise of ordinary business care and prudence, to comply with the administrative simplification provision violated.

45 C.F.R. § 160.401

Reasonable Diligence:

The business care and prudence expected from a person seeking to satisfy a legal requirement under similar circumstances.

45 C.F.R. §170.102

Relates to the Privacy of Individually Identifiable Health Information:

With respect to a state law, that the state law has the specific purpose of protecting the privacy of health information or affects the privacy of health information in a direct, clear, and substantial way.

45 C.F.R. §160.202

Removal from Access Lists:

The physical eradication of an entity's access privileges. Part of termination procedures on the matrix.

63 Fed. Reg. 43,242, 43,275 (Aug. 12, 1998)

Removal of User Account(s):

The termination or deletion of an individual's access privileges to the information, services, and resources for which they currently have clearance, authorization, and need to know when such clearance, authorization, and need-to-know no longer exists. Part of termination procedures on the matrix.

63 Fed. Reg. 43,242, 43,275 (Aug. 12, 1998)

Report Procedures:

The documented formal mechanism employed to document security incidents. Part of security incident procedures on the matrix.

63 Fed. Reg. 43,242, 43,275 (Aug. 12, 1998)

Required by Law:

A mandate contained in law that compels a covered entity to make a use or disclosure of protected health information and that is enforceable in a court of law. Required by law includes, but is not limited to, court orders and court-ordered warrants; subpoenas or summons issued by a court, grand jury, a governmental or tribal inspector general, or an administrative body authorized to require the production of information; a civil or an authorized investigative demand; Medicare conditions of participation with respect to health care providers participating in the program; and statutes or regulations that require the production of information, including statutes or regulations that require such information if payment is sought under a government program providing public benefits.

45 C.F.R. §164.501

Research:

A systematic investigation, including research development, testing, and evaluation, designed to develop or contribute to generalizable knowledge.

45 C.F.R. §164.501

Respondent:

A covered entity upon which the Secretary has imposed, or proposes to impose, a civil money penalty.

45 C.F.R. §160.302

Response Procedures:

The documented formal rules/instructions for actions to be taken as a result of the receipt of a security incident report. Part of security incident procedures on the matrix.

63 Fed. Reg. 43,242, 43,275 (Aug. 12, 1998)

Risk Analysis:

Risk analysis, a process whereby cost-effective security/control measures may be selected by balancing the costs of various security/control measures against the losses that would be expected if these measures were not in place. Part of the security management process on the matrix.

63 Fed. Reg. 43,242, 43,275 (Aug. 12, 1998)

Risk Management:

Risk is the possibility of something adverse happening. Risk management is the process of assessing risk, taking steps to reduce risk to an acceptable level and maintaining that level of risk. Part of the security management process on the matrix.

63 Fed. Reg. 43,242, 43,275 (Aug. 12, 1998)

Role-Based Access Control (RBAC):

Role-based access control is an alternative to traditional access control models (e.g., discretionary or non-discretionary access control policies) that permits the specification and enforcement of enterprise-specific security policies in a way that maps more naturally to an organization's structure and business activities. With RBAC, rather than attempting to map an organization's security policy to a relatively low-level set of technical controls (typically, access control lists), each user is assigned to one or more predefined roles, each of which has been assigned the various privileges needed to perform that role. Part of access control and authorization control on the matrix.

63 Fed. Reg. 43,242, 43,275 (Aug. 12, 1998)

S

Sanction Policy:

Organizations must have policies and procedures regarding disciplinary actions which are communicated to all employees, agents, and contractors, for example, verbal warning, notice of disciplinary action placed in personnel files, removal of system privileges, termination of employment and contract penalties. In addition to enterprise sanctions, employees, agents, and contractors must be advised of civil or criminal penalties for misuse or misappropriation of health information. Employees, agents, and contractors must be made aware that violations may result in notification to law enforcement officials and regulatory, accreditation and licensure organizations. Part of the security management process on the matrix.

63 Fed. Reg. 43,242, 43,275 (Aug. 12, 1998)

Secretary:

The Secretary of Health and Human Services or any other officer or employee of HHS to whom the authority involved has been delegated.

45 C.F.R. §160.103

Secure Work Station Location:

Physical safeguards to eliminate or minimize the possibility of unauthorized access to information, for example, locating a terminal used to access sensitive information in a locked room and restricting access to that room to authorized personnel, or not placing a terminal used to access patient information in any area of a doctor's office where the screen contents can be viewed from the reception area. Part of physical safeguards to guard data integrity, confidentiality, and availability on the matrix.

63 Fed. Reg. 43,242, 43,275 (Aug. 12, 1998)

Security or Security Measures:

Encompasses all of the administrative, physical, and technical safeguards in an information system.

45 C.F.R. §164.304

Security Awareness Training:

All employees, agents, and contractors must participate in information security awareness training programs. Based on job responsibilities, individuals may be required to attend customized education programs that focus on issues regarding use of health information and responsibilities regarding confidentiality and security. Part of physical safeguards to guard data integrity, confidentiality, and availability on the matrix.

63 Fed. Reg. 43,242, 43,275 (Aug. 12, 1998)

Security Configuration Management:

Measures, practices, and procedures for the security of information systems should be coordinated and integrated with each other and other measures, practices, and procedures of the organization so as to create a coherent system of security. Part of administrative procedures to guard data integrity, confidentiality, and availability on the matrix.

63 Fed. Reg. 43,242, 43,275 (Aug. 12, 1998)

Security Incident:

The attempted or successful unauthorized access, use, disclosure, modification, or destruction of information or interference with system operations in an information system.

45 C.F.R. §164.304

Security Incident Procedures:

Formal, documented instructions for reporting security breaches. Part of administrative procedures to guard data integrity, confidentiality, and availability on the matrix.

63 Fed. Reg. 43,242, 43,275 (Aug. 12, 1998)

Security Management Process:

A security management process encompasses the creation, administration, and oversight of policies to ensure the prevention, detection, containment, and correction of security breaches. It involves risk analysis and risk management, including the establishment of accountability, management controls (policies and education), electronic controls, physical security, and penalties for the abuse and misuse of its assets, both physical and electronic. Part of administrative procedures to guard data integrity, confidentiality and availability on the matrix.

63 Fed. Reg. 43,242, 43,275 (Aug. 12, 1998)

Security Policy:

The framework within which an organization establishes needed levels of information security to achieve the desired confidentiality goals. A policy is a statement of information values, protection responsibilities, and organization commitment for a system. The American Health Information Management Association recommends that security policies apply to all employees, medical staff members, volunteers, students, faculty, independent contractors, and agents. Part of the security management process on the matrix.

63 Fed. Reg. 43,242, 43,276 (Aug. 12, 1998)

Security Testing:

A process used to determine that the security features of a system are implemented as designed and that they are adequate for a proposed applications environment. This process includes hands-on functional testing, penetration testing, and verification. Part of security configuration management on the matrix.

63 Fed. Reg. 43,242, 43,276 (Aug. 12, 1998)

Segment:

A group of related data elements in a transaction.

45 C.F.R. §162.103

Sign-in for Visitors and Escort, if Appropriate:

Formal, documented procedure governing the reception and hosting of visitors. Part of physical access controls (limited access) on the matrix.

63 Fed. Reg. 43,242, 43,276 (Aug. 12, 1998)

Small Health Plan:

A health plan with annual receipts of $5 million or less.

45 C.F.R. §160.103

Standard:

The term "standard," when used with reference to a data element of health information or a transaction referred to in section 1173(a)(1), means any such data element or transaction that meets each of the standards and implementation specifications adopted or established by the Secretary with respect to the data element or transaction under sections 1172 through 1174.

HIPAA, Pub. L. No. 104-191, §262(a)

Standard:

A rule, condition, or requirement:

(1) Describing the following information for products, systems, services or practices:

(i) Classification of components;

(ii) Specification of materials, performance, or operations; or

(iii) Delineation of procedures; or

(2) With respect to the privacy of individually identifiable health information.

45 C.F.R. §160.103

Standard:

A technical, functional, or performance-based rule, condition, requirement, or specification that stipulates instructions, fields, codes, data, materials, characteristics, or actions.

45 C.F.R. §170.102

Standard Setting Organization (SSO):

An organization accredited by the American National Standards Institute that develops and maintains standards for information transactions or data elements, or any other standard that is necessary for, or will facilitate, the implementation of this part.

45 C.F.R. §160.103

State:

Refers to one of the following:

(1) For a health plan established or regulated by Federal law, *State* has the meaning set forth in the applicable section of the United States Code for such health plan.

(2) For all other purposes, *State* means each of the several States, the District of Columbia, the Commonwealth of Puerto Rico, the Virgin Islands, Guam, American Samoa, and the Northern Mariana Islands.

45 C.F.R. §160.103; American Recovery and Reinvestment Act of 2009, Pub. L. No. 111-5 §13400 (15)

State Law:

A constitution, statute, regulation, rule, common law, or other state action having the force and effect of law.

45 C.F.R. §160.202

Subject/Object Separation:

Access to a subject does not guarantee access to the objects associated with that subject.

Subject is defined as an active entity, generally in the form of a person, process, or device that causes information to flow among objects or changes the system state. Technically, a process/domain pair.

Object is defined as a passive entity that contains or receives information. Access to an object potentially implies access to the information it contains. Examples of objects are: records blocks, pages, segments, files, directories, directory trees, and programs, as well as bits, bytes, words, fields, processors, video displays, keyboards, clocks, printers, network nodes, etc.

A type of access control.

63 Fed. Reg. 43,242, 43,276 (Aug. 12, 1998)

Summary Health Information:

Information that may be individually identifiable health information, and:

A. That summarizes the claims history, claims expenses, or type of claims experienced by individuals for whom a plan sponsor has provided health benefits under a group health plan; and

B. From which the information described at §164.514(b)(2)(i) has been deleted, except that the geographic information described in §164.514(b)(2)(i)(B) need only be aggregated to the level of a five-digit ZIP code.

45 C.F.R. §164.504

T

Technical Safeguards:

The technology and the policy and procedures for its use that protect electronic protected health information and control access to it.

45 C.F.R. §164.304

Technical Security Mechanisms:

The processes that are put in place to guard against unauthorized access to data that is transmitted over a communications network. A section of the matrix.

63 Fed. Reg. 43,242, 43,276 (Aug. 12, 1998)

Technical Security Services:

The processes that are put in place: (1) to protect information and (2) to control and monitor individual access to information. A section of the matrix.

63 Fed. Reg. 43,242, 43,276 (Aug. 12, 1998)

Telephone Callback:

A method of authenticating the identity of the receiver and sender of information through a series of "questions" and "answers" sent back and forth establishing the identity of each. For example, when the communicating systems exchange a series of identification codes as part of the initiation of a session to exchange information, or when a host computer disconnects the initial session before the authentication is complete, and the host calls the user back to establish a session at a predetermined telephone number. Part of entity authentication on the matrix.

63 Fed. Reg. 43,242, 43,276 (Aug. 12, 1998)

Termination Procedures:

Formal, documented instructions, which include appropriate security measures, for the ending of an employee's employment, or an internal/external user's access. Part of administrative procedures to guard data integrity, confidentiality, and availability on the matrix.
63 Fed. Reg. 43,242, 43,276 (Aug. 12, 1998)

Testing and Revision:

(1) Testing and revision of contingency plans refer to the documented process of periodic testing to discover weaknesses in such plans and the subsequent process of revising the documentation if necessary. Part of contingency plan on the matrix.

(2) Testing and revision of programs should be restricted to formally authorized personnel. Part of physical access controls (limited access) on the matrix.

63 Fed. Reg. 43,242, 43,276 (Aug. 12, 1998)

Time-of-Day:

Access to data is restricted to certain time frames, e.g., Monday through Friday, 8:00 a.m. to 6:00 p.m. A type of access control on the matrix.

63 Fed. Reg. 43,242, 43,276 (Aug. 12, 1998)

Time-Stamp:

To create a notation that indicates, at least, the correct date and time of an action, and the identity of the person that created the notation.

63 Fed. Reg. 43,242, 43,276 (Aug. 12, 1998)

Token:

A physical item that is used to provide identity. Typically an electronic device that can be inserted in a door or a computer system to obtain access. Part of entity authentication on the matrix.

63 Fed. Reg. 43,242, 43,276 (Aug. 12, 1998)

Trading Partner Agreement:

An agreement related to the exchange of information in electronic transactions, whether the agreement is distinct or part of a larger agreement, between each party to the agreement. (For example, a trading partner agreement may specify, among other things, the duties and responsibilities of each party to the agreement in conducting a standard transaction.)

45 C.F.R. §160.103

Training:

Education concerning the vulnerabilities of the health information in an entity's possession and ways to ensure the protection of that information. Part of administrative procedures to guard data integrity, confidentiality, and availability on the matrix.

63 Fed. Reg. 43,242, 43,276 (Aug. 12, 1998)

Transaction:

The transmission of information between two parties to carry out financial or administrative activities related to health care. It includes the following types of information transmissions:

(1) Health care claims or equivalent encounter information.

(2) Health care payment and remittance advice.

(3) Coordination of benefits.

(4) Health care claim status.

(5) Enrollment and disenrollment in a health plan.

(6) Eligibility for a health plan.

(7) Health plan premium payments.

(8) Referral certification and authorization.

(9) First report of injury.

(10) Health claims attachments.

(11) Other transactions that the Secretary may prescribe by regulation.

45 C.F.R. §160.103

Transportability:

A signed document can be transported (over an insecure network) to another system, while maintaining the integrity of the document. Part of digital signature on the matrix.

63 Fed. Reg. 43,242, 43,276 (Aug. 12, 1998)

Treatment:

The provision, coordination, or management of health care and related services by one or more health care providers, including the coordination or management of health care by a health care provider with a third party; consultation between health care providers relating to a patient; or the referral of a patient for health care from one health care provider to another.

45 C.F.R. §164.501

Turn in Keys, Tokens, or Cards That Allow Access:

Formal, documented procedure to ensure all physical items that allow a terminated employee to access a property, building, or equipment are retrieved from that employee, preferably prior to termination. Part of termination procedures on the matrix.

63 Fed. Reg. 43,242, 43,276 (Aug. 12, 1998)

U

Unique User Identification:

The combination name/number assigned and maintained in security procedures for identifying and tracking individual user identity. Part of entity authentication on the matrix.

63 Fed. Reg. 43,242, 43,276 (Aug. 12, 1998)

Unsecured PHR Identifiable Health Information:

PHR identifiable health information that is not protected through the use of a technology or methodology specified by the Secretary in the guidance issued by the Secretary.

In the case that the Secretary does not issue guidance by the date required, for purposes of this section, the term "unsecured PHR identifiable health information" shall mean PHR identifiable health information that is not secured by a technology standard that renders protected health information unusable, unreadable, or indecipherable to unauthorized individuals and that is developed or endorsed by a standards-developing organization that is accredited by the American National Standards Institute.

American Recovery and Reinvestment Act of 2009, Pub. L. No. 111-5 §13407 (f)(3)

Unsecured Protected Health Information:

Protected health information that is not secured through the use of a technology or methodology specified by the Secretary in the guidance issued by the Secretary.

In the case that the Secretary does not issue guidance by the date required by this Act, the term "unsecured protected health information" shall mean protected health information that is not secured by a technology standard that renders protected health information unusable, unreadable, or indecipherable to unauthorized individuals and is developed or endorsed by a standards developing organization that is accredited by the American National Standards Institute.

American Recovery and Reinvestment Act of 2009, Pub. L. No. 111-5 §13401 (h)

Unsecured Protected Health Information:

Protected health information that is not rendered unusable, unreadable, or indecipherable to unauthorized individuals through the use of a technology or methodology specified by the Secretary in the guidance issued under section 13402(h)(2) of Public Law 111-5 on the HHS Web site.

45 C.F.R. §164.402

Use:

With respect to individually identifiable health information means, the sharing, employment, application, utilization, examination, or analysis of such information within an entity that maintains such information.

45 C.F.R. §164.501

User:

A person or entity with authorized access.

45 C.F.R. §164.304

User Authentication:

The provision of assurance of the claimed identity of an entity. Part of digital signature on the matrix.

63 Fed. Reg. 43,242, 43,276 (Aug. 12, 1998)

User-Based Access:

A security mechanism used to grant users of a system access based upon the identity of the user. Part of access control on the matrix. Part of authorization control on the matrix.

63 Fed. Reg. 43,242, 43,276 (Aug. 12, 1998)

User Education Concerning Virus Protection:

Training relative to user awareness of the potential harm that can be caused by a virus, how to prevent the introduction of a virus to a computer system, and what to do if a virus is detected. Part of training on the matrix.

63 Fed. Reg. 43,242, 43,276 (Aug. 12, 1998)

User Education in Importance of Monitoring Login Success/Failure, and How to Report Discrepancies:

Training in the user's responsibility to ensure the security of health care information. Part of training on the matrix.

63 Fed. Reg. 43,242, 43,276 (Aug. 12, 1998)

User Education in Password Management:

A type of user training in the rules to be followed in creating and changing passwords and the need to keep them confidential. Part of training on the matrix.

63 Fed. Reg. 43,242, 43,276 (Aug. 12, 1998)

V

Vendor of Personal Health Records:

An entity, other than a covered entity, that offers or maintains a personal health record.

American Recovery and Reinvestment Act of 2009, Pub. L. No. 111-5 §13400(18)

Violation or Violate:

Failure to comply with an administrative simplification provision.

45 C.F.R. §160.302

Virus Checking:

A computer program that identifies and disables:

(1) Another "virus" computer program, typically hidden, that attaches itself to other programs and has the ability to replicate. (Unchecked virus programs result in undesired side effects generally unanticipated by the user.)

(2) A type of programmed threat. A code fragment (not an independent program) that reproduces by attaching to another program. It may damage data directly, or it may degrade system performance by taking over system resources, which are then not available to authorized users.

(3) Code embedded within a program that causes a copy of itself to be inserted in one or more other programs. In addition to propagation, the virus usually performs some unwanted function. Part of security configuration management on the matrix.

63 Fed. Reg. 43,242, 43,276 (Aug. 12, 1998)

W

Willful Neglect:

Conscious, intentional failure or reckless indifference to the obligations to comply with the administrative simplification provisions violated.

45 C.F.R. §170.102

Workforce:

Employees, volunteers, trainees, and other persons whose conduct, in the performance of work for a covered entity, is under the direct control of such entity, whether or not they are paid by the covered entity.

45 C.F.R. §160.103

Workstation:

An electronic computing device, for example, a laptop or desktop computer, or any other device that performs similar functions, and electronic media stored in its immediate environment.

45 C.F.R. §164.304

Appendix E

Documenting the Deal [Forms]*

E-1	HIPAA Business Associate Agreement Forms.............................	769
	E-1.1 Business Associate Agreement [HIPAA Administrative Simplification Subtitle]: General Form	769
	E-1.2 Business Associate Agreement [HIPAA Administrative Simplification Subtitle]: Addendum	779
E-2	Resolution Agreement...	783
	E-2.1 Example of Resolution Agreement and Corrective Action Plan (Without External Monitoring) (Mass Gen RA and CAP)	787
	E-2.2 Example of Resolution Agreement and Corrective Action Plan (With External Monitoring) (Rite Aid RA and CAP)......	803

*These appendix documents are also available on the CD-ROM accompanying this volume.

Appendix E-1.1

Business Associate Agreement [HIPAA Administrative Simplification Subtitle]: General Form*

Source: Alan S. Goldberg, McLean, Virginia; Bradley G. Allen, Whiteman Osterman & Hanna LLP, Albany, New York; Adam H. Greene, Davis Wright Tremaine LLP, Washington, D.C.

Note on the Business Associate Agreement forms: The documents in Appendix F-4 in this Supplement replace the documents in Appendix F-4 in the Main Volume. This General Form may be used as a basis for preparing a Business Associate Agreement for either a Covered Entity (CE) or a Business Associate (BA). See Appendix F-4.3 in this Supplement for a similar form that also contains language addressing ethics issues, such as attorney-client privilege, and which a law firm might propose to a client, subject to applicable rules of professional responsibility. See Appendix F-4.4 in this Supplement for a sample form published by the HHS Office for Civil Rights (OCR).

BUSINESS ASSOCIATE AGREEMENT

[HIPAA Administrative Simplification subtitle]

This is a Business Associate Agreement ("Agreement") by and between:

"Covered Entity":   "Business Associate":

Intending to be legally bound, the parties to this Agreement identified above have executed this Agreement, consisting of this first page and all of the following pages through page [insert], effective as of the following "Effective Date"—[insert date].

---

*This appendix document is also available on the CD-ROM accompanying this volume.

Executed by duly authorized signatory for and in behalf of Covered Entity	Executed by duly authorized signatory for and in behalf of Business Associate
X_____	X_____
In behalf of Covered Entity	In behalf of Business Associate

Background

A. Business Associate and Covered Entity desire that Covered Entity achieve compliance with the Administrative Simplification subtitle of the federal Health Insurance Portability and Accountability Act of 1996, Public Law 104-191 ("HIPAA"), with respect to Covered Entity's engagement of Business Associate and Business Associate's Use and Disclosure of "Protected Health Information" (defined below) on Covered Entity's behalf, as more fully described below.

B. The purpose of this Agreement is to permit Covered Entity to Disclose "Protected Health Information" (defined below) to Business Associate, and to allow Business Associate to create or receive Protected Health Information on Covered Entity's behalf as and to the extent provided below, in a manner consistent with the requirements set forth in the HIPAA Administrative Simplification Provisions (defined below).

C. Consistent therewith, this Agreement is intended to set forth satisfactory assurances that Business Associate will appropriately safeguard such Protected Health Information.

D. Accordingly, in consideration of the mutual covenants set forth in this Agreement, and for other good and valuable consideration, the receipt and sufficiency of which are hereby acknowledged, the parties to this Agreement agree as follows:

I. Definitions.

Capitalized terms used, but not otherwise defined, in this Agreement shall have the same meaning as those terms in the HIPAA Administrative Simplification Provisions.

"Breach Notification Rule" means the regulations regarding Notification in the Case of Breach of Unsecured Protected Health Information at 45 CFR Part 160 and Part 164, subparts A and D.

"Business Associate" means the party identified above as Business Associate.

"Covered Entity" means the party identified above as Covered Entity.

"Disclose" means to make a disclosure of information, as the term "disclosure" is defined at 45 CFR § 160.103.

"Electronic Protected Health Information" shall have the same meaning as the term "electronic protected health information" in 45 CFR § 160.103, limited however to the information created or received by Business Associate from or on behalf of Covered Entity.

"HIPAA Administrative Simplification Provisions" means the regulations set forth at 45 C.F.R. Parts 160, 162, and 164, including the Privacy, Security, and Breach Notification Rules.

"Individual" means the person who is the subject of Protected Health Information, and shall include a person who qualifies as a personal representative in accordance with 45 CFR § 164.502(g).

"Privacy Rule" means the Standards for Privacy of Individually Identifiable Health Information at 45 CFR Part 160 and Part 164, subparts A and E.

"Protected Health Information" shall have the same meaning as the term "protected health information" in 45 CFR § 160.103, limited however to the information created or received by Business Associate from or on behalf of Covered Entity.

"Security Rule" means the Security Standards for the Protection of Electronic Protected Health Information in 45 CFR Part 160 and Part 164, subparts A and C.

II. Obligations and Activities of Business Associate

A. Business Associate agrees not to Use or Disclose Protected Health Information other than as permitted or required by this Agreement or as Required By Law.

B. Business Associate agrees to use appropriate safeguards to prevent Use or Disclosure of the Protected Health Information other than as provided for by or permitted under this Agreement.

C. Business Associate agrees to implement administrative, physical, and technical safeguards in accordance with the Security Rule that reasonably and appropriately protect the confidentiality, integrity, and availability of the Electronic Protected Health Information that Business Associate creates, receives, maintains, or transmits on behalf of Covered Entity.

D. [Recommended, but not required by HIPAA] Business Associate agrees to mitigate, to the extent practicable, any harmful effect that is known to Business Associate of a Use or Disclosure of Protected Health Information by Business Associate in violation of the requirements of this Agreement.

E. Business Associate agrees to report to Covered Entity any of the following of which Business Associate becomes aware: (1) any use or disclosure of the Protected Health Information by Business Associate not provided for by or permitted under this Agreement, and (2) any Security Incident. Such notification shall comply with the Breach Notification Rule at 45 CFR § 164.410, as applicable.

F. Business Associate agrees to ensure that any agents, including a subcontractor, to whom Business Associate provides Protected Health Information agrees to the same restrictions and conditions that apply through this Agreement to Business Associate with respect to such information.

G. If Business Associate has Protected Health Information in a Designated Record Set, Business Associate agrees to provide access, at the request of Covered Entity, to Protected Health Information in any such Designated Record Set, to Covered Entity or, as directed by Covered Entity, to an Individual in order to meet the requirements under 45 CFR § 164.524.

H. If Business Associate has Protected Health Information in a Designated Record Set, Business Associate agrees to make any amendments to Protected Health Information in any such Designated Record Set that Covered Entity directs or agrees to pursuant to 45 CFR § 164.526 at the request of Covered Entity.

I. Business Associate agrees to make its internal practices, books, and records, including policies and procedures and Protected Health Information, relating to the Use and Disclosure of Protected Health Information, available to the Secretary at the request of Covered Entity or the Secretary for purposes of the Secretary determining Covered Entity's compliance with the Privacy Rule. Business Associate agrees to notify Covered Entity promptly of: (1) any request by the Secretary to examine such internal practices, books, records, policies, procedures, and Protected Health Information, and (2) the results and disposition of any such request.

J. Business Associate agrees to document such Disclosures of Protected Health Information and information related to such Disclosures as would be required for Covered Entity to respond to a request by an Individual for an accounting of Disclosures of Protected Health Information in accordance with 45 CFR § 164.528.

K. Business Associate agrees to provide to Covered Entity or an Individual information collected in accordance with Section II(J) of this Agreement, to permit Covered Entity to respond to a request by an Individual for an accounting of Disclosures of Protected Health Information in accordance with 45 CFR § 164.528.

III. Permitted Uses and Disclosures by Business Associate

A. Except as otherwise limited in this Agreement, Business Associate may Use or Disclose Protected Health Information on behalf of, or to provide services to, Covered Entity for such purposes as may from time to time be specified in documents executed by Covered Entity and delivered to Business Associate (including the agreement between Covered Entity in force as of the date of this Agreement, under which Business Associate provides services to Covered Entity, which agreement's relevant provisions regarding, and the purposes of, such services are incorporated herein by this reference with the same force as if set forth herein at length), but only to the extent such Use or Disclosure of Protected Health Information would not violate (1) the Privacy Rule if done by Covered Entity.

B. Except as otherwise limited in this Agreement, Business Associate may Use Protected Health Information for the proper management and administration of Business Associate or to carry out the legal responsibilities of Business Associate.

C. Except as otherwise limited in this Agreement, Business Associate may Disclose Protected Health Information for the proper management and administration of Business Associate, provided that Disclosures are Required By Law, or Business Associate obtains reasonable assurances from the person to whom such information is disclosed that such information will remain confidential and used or further disclosed only as Required By Law or for the purpose for which such information was disclosed to such person, and such person notifies Business Associate of any instances of which such person is aware in which the confidentiality of such information has been breached.

D. Except as otherwise limited in this Agreement, Business Associate may Use Protected Health Information to provide "Data Aggregation" services to Covered Entity as permitted by 45 CFR § 164.504(e)(2)(i)(B).

E. Business Associate may Use or Disclose Protected Health Information as may be Required By Law or to report violations of law to appropriate Federal and State authorities, consistent with 45 CFR § 164.502(j)(1).

IV. Obligations of Covered Entity

A. Covered Entity shall notify Business Associate of any limitations in Covered Entity's notice of privacy practices in accordance with 45 CFR § 164.520, to the extent that any such limitation may affect Business Associate's Use or Disclosure of Protected Health Information.

B. Covered Entity shall notify Business Associate of any changes in, or revocation of, permission by any applicable Individual to Use or Disclose Protected Health Information, to the extent that any such change may affect Business Associate's Use or Disclosure of Protected Health Information.

C. Covered Entity shall notify Business Associate of any restriction to the Use or Disclosure of Protected Health Information that Covered Entity has agreed to in accordance with 45 CFR § 164.522, or otherwise, to the extent that any such restriction may affect Business Associate's Use or Disclosure of Protected Health Information.

V. Permissible Requests by Covered Entity

Covered Entity shall not request that Business Associate Use or Disclose Protected Health Information in any manner that would not be permissible under the Privacy Rule or the Security Rule if done by Covered Entity, unless expressly permitted in Sections III(B) through III(E) above.

VI. Term and Termination

A. Term. This Agreement shall be effective and enforceable by the parties to this Agreement as of the Effective Date first set forth above, and (notwithstanding anything contained in this Agreement to the contrary) may be terminated at any time by Covered Entity (for any reason or for no reason). This Agreement shall terminate when all of the Protected Health Information provided by Covered Entity to Business Associate, or created or received by Business Associate on behalf of Covered Entity, is destroyed or returned to Covered Entity, or if it is infeasible to return or destroy Protected Health Information, protections are extended to such information, in accordance with the termination provisions in this Section, or if, as, and when this Agreement is no longer required pursuant to the Privacy Rule and the Security Rule.

B. Termination for Cause. Upon Covered Entity's knowledge of a material breach by Business Associate, Covered Entity shall provide an opportunity for Business Associate to cure the breach or end the violation, and Covered Entity may terminate this Agreement if Business Associate does not cure the breach or end the violation within the time specified by Covered Entity, which shall in no event be less than a thirty (30)-day period beginning on the date Business Associate is so notified by Covered Entity that Covered Entity believes that such breach or violation occurred; alternatively, Covered Entity may immediately terminate this Agreement if Business Associate has breached a material term of this Agreement and cure is not possible. If neither termination nor cure in accordance with this Section are feasible, Covered Entity must report the violation of this Agreement to the Secretary (and if such report is so to be given, Covered Entity shall simultaneously provide a copy of any such report to Business Associate).

C. Effect of Termination.

1. Except as provided in paragraph 2 of this Section, upon termination of this Agreement, for any reason or for no reason, Business Associate shall return or destroy all Protected Health Information received from Covered Entity, or created or received by Business Associate on behalf of Covered Entity. This provision shall apply to Protected Health Information that is in the possession of subcontractors or agents of Business Associate. Business Associate shall not retain any copies of such Protected Health Information.

2. If Business Associate determines that returning or destroying the Protected Health Information is infeasible or in violation of law, Business Associate shall provide to Covered Entity notification of the conditions that make return or destruction infeasible. Upon mutual agreement of the parties to this Agreement that return or destruction of Protected Health Information is infeasible or in violation of law, Business Associate shall extend the protections of this Agreement to such Protected Health Information and limit further Uses and Disclosures of such Protected Health Information to those purposes that make the return or destruction infeasible or in violation of law, for so long as Business Associate maintains such Protected Health Information.

VII. Miscellaneous

A. Regulatory References. A reference in this Agreement to a section in the Privacy Rule or the Security Rule means the section as enforceable at the applicable time.

B. Amendment. The parties to this Agreement agree to take such action as is reasonably necessary to amend this Agreement from time to time as is necessary for Covered Entity to comply with the requirements of the Privacy Rule, the Security Rule, and HIPAA.

C. Interpretation. Any ambiguity in this Agreement shall be resolved to permit Covered Entity to comply with the Privacy Rule and the Security Rule. The word "including" as used in this Agreement shall be construed to mean "including, but not limited to."

D. No Third-Party Beneficiaries. The provisions of this Agreement shall be for the exclusive benefit of the parties to this Agreement, and no third party is an intended beneficiary of, or shall be entitled to rely on, the provisions of this Agreement. In amplification and not in limitation of the immediately preceding sentence, nothing expressed or implied in this Agreement is intended or shall be construed to confer upon or give any individual or entity other than the parties to this Agreement, and their respective successors and permitted assigns, any rights or remedies under this Agreement or by reason of this Agreement or any transaction or circumstance contemplated by this Agreement.

E. Entire Agreement. This Agreement constitutes the entire agreement of the parties to this Agreement with respect to the matters provided for in this Agreement, and there are no prior or contemporaneous oral or written agreements or commitments by or among such parties or their affiliates with respect to the subject matter of this Agreement, except as expressly set forth in this Agreement.

F. Counterparts. This Agreement may be executed in one or more counterparts, each of which shall be considered to be an original for all purposes and all of which together shall constitute one and the same instrument.

G. Waiver. No failure or delay by either Covered Entity or Business Associate in exercising any right, power, or privilege under this Agreement shall operate as a waiver thereof; nor shall any single or partial exercise thereof preclude any other or further exercise thereof or the exercise of any other right, power, or privilege.

H. No Joint Venture Relationship. This Agreement does not grant either party to this Agreement any authority to assume or to create any obligation on behalf of or in the name of the other. The parties to this Agreement expressly acknowledge that no franchise, partnership, or joint venture relationship exists or is intended to exist between the parties to this Agreement during the term or on account of this Agreement.

I. Notices. Any notice, request, instruction, or other document to be given under this Agreement by any party to this Agreement to the other of them shall be in writing and delivered personally or sent by a nationally recognized overnight courier service or by registered or certified mail, postage prepaid, to such party at such party's address first set forth above or at such other address for the party as shall be specified by like notice. Any notice that is delivered personally in the manner provided in this Agreement shall be considered to have been duly given to the party to this Agreement to which it is directed upon actual receipt by such party (or such party's agent for notices under this Agreement). Any notice that is addressed as provided in this Agreement and mailed by registered or certified mail shall be conclusively presumed to have been duly given to the party to this Agreement to which such notice is addressed at the close of business, local time of such party, on the fifth calendar day after the day such notice is so placed in the mail. Any notice that is addressed as provided in this Agreement and sent by a nationally recognized overnight courier service shall be conclusively presumed to have been duly given to the party to which such notice is addressed at the close of business, local time of such party, on the next business day following the deposit of any such notice with such courier service for next day delivery.

J. Governing Law. This Agreement and the legal relationship between the parties to this Agreement shall be governed and construed in accordance with applicable federal law and the substantive laws of [Name of State/Jurisdiction] without giving effect to the principles of conflict of laws thereof.

K. Severability. If any provision of this Agreement shall be held by a court of competent jurisdiction to be invalid, void, or unenforceable, such provision shall be construed in all respects as if such invalid or unenforceable provision were replaced with a valid and enforceable provision as similar as possible to the one replaced, and the remainder of this Agreement shall continue in full force and effect and shall not be invalidated impaired or otherwise affected.

L. Cooperation and Reasonableness. The parties to this Agreement acknowledge and agree that this Agreement is intended to address a complex series of rights and relationships, and that in the course of activity pursuant to this Agreement many matters may arise that require further clarification or memorialization in order to carry out the purposes and intentions of the parties to this Agreement as set forth in this Agreement; accordingly, the parties to this Agreement agree to negotiate in good faith with respect to such matters and to execute and deliver any and all documents and instruments reasonably necessary to effectuate such good-faith negotiation, in order to help Covered Entity comply with Covered Entity's obligations under the Privacy Rule and the Security Rule.

M. Force Majeure. Neither party to this Agreement shall be liable for, or be considered to be in breach of or default on account of, any delay or failure to perform as a result of any cause or condition beyond such party's reasonable control, including fire, casualty, storms, flood, and acts of God or the elements; court orders; acts, delays, and failures to act by civil, military or other governmental authority; strikes, lockouts, labor disputes, riots, insurrections, sabotage, and war; terrorism; breakdown or destruction of, or damage or casualty to, any equipment, facilities or other property; unavailability of materials, supplies, parts, equipment personnel, or other necessary items; interruption, suspension, curtailment, or other disruption of utilities and/or network or similar facilities; and acts or omissions of persons or entities other than the parties to this Agreement, as applicable.

N. Headings and Section References. The headings of the sections and paragraphs of this Agreement are included for convenience only and are not intended to be a part of, or to affect the meaning or interpretation of, this Agreement. All section references in this Agreement, unless otherwise clearly indicated, are to sections within this Agreement.

O. Compliance with State Law. Notwithstanding anything to the contrary in this Agreement, if any provision of the laws of [Name of State/Jurisdiction] applicable to Business Associate, because of Business Associate's relationship with Covered Entity, is contrary to and more stringent than an applicable requirement of the Privacy Rule, this Agreement shall be construed to permit Business Associate to comply with such provision of State law to the extent that Business Associate is required to comply with such provision and to the extent that such provision is not preempted by the Privacy Rule or other applicable preemptive federal law or regulation.

Appendix E-1.2

Business Associate Agreement [HIPAA Administrative Simplification Subtitle]: Addendum*

Source: Alan S. Goldberg, McLean, Virginia; Adam H. Greene, Davis Wright Tremaine LLP, Washington, D.C.

Note on the Business Associate Agreement forms: This Addendum to Business Associate Agreement should be used in combination with a Business Associate Agreement that only addresses the Privacy Rule. This Addendum need not be used in conjunction with the General Form, Appendix E-1.1, since the General Form incorporates the requirements of the Security Rule.

ADDENDUM TO BUSINESS ASSOCIATE AGREEMENT

[Insert Names of Covered Entity & Business Associate]

Dated:_____

This is an Addendum (Addendum) to a Business Associate Agreement by and [INSERT] (Covered Entity) and [INSERT] (Business Associate).

    A. The purpose of this Addendum is to amend a certain Business Associate Agreement dated [INSERT] (Business Associate Agreement) between Covered Entity and Business Associate (a true copy of the Business Associate Agreement is attached to this Addendum as Exhibit "A"), as required by the provisions of the Security Rule (defined below).

---

*This appendix document is also available on the CD-ROM accompanying this volume.

B. In consideration of the mutual covenants hereinafter set forth, and for other good and valuable consideration, the receipt and sufficiency of which are hereby acknowledged, the parties hereto agree as follows:

I. Definitions.

Capitalized terms used, but not otherwise defined, in this Addendum shall have the same meaning as those terms in the Business Associate Agreement or in the Security Rule.

"Business Associate" means the party first identified above as Business Associate.

"Covered Entity" means the party first identified above as Covered Entity.

"Electronic Protected Health Information" shall have the same meaning as the term "electronic protected health information" in 45 CFR § 160.103, limited however to the information received from Covered Entity or created or received by Business Associate on behalf of Covered Entity.

"Security Rule" means the Security Standards at 45 CFR Part 160 and Part 164, subparts A and C.

II. Obligations and Activities of Business Associate.

A. Business Associate agrees to implement administrative, physical, and technical safeguards in accordance with the Security Rule that reasonably and appropriately protect the confidentiality, integrity, and availability of the Electronic Protected Health Information that Business Associate creates, receives, maintains, or transmits on behalf of Covered Entity.

B. Business Associate agrees to report any Security Incident to Covered Entity.

C. Business Associate agrees to ensure that any agents, including a subcontractor, to whom it provides Electronic Protected Health Information agrees to implement reasonable and appropriate safeguards to protect such information in the manner set forth in Section II.A of this Addendum.

III. Termination.

Upon Covered Entity's knowledge of a material breach by Business Associate of this Addendum, Covered Entity shall provide an opportunity for Business Associate to cure the breach or end the violation, and Covered Entity may terminate the underlying Business Associate Agreement if Business Associate does not cure the breach or end the violation within the time specified by Covered Entity, which shall in no event be less than a thirty (30)-day period beginning on the date Business Associate is so notified by Covered Entity that Covered Entity believes that such breach or violation occurred; alternatively, Covered Entity may immediately terminate the underlying Business Associate Agreement if Business Associate has breached a material term of this Addendum and cure is not possible. If neither termination nor cure in accordance with this Section are feasible, Covered Entity must report the violation of this Agreement to the Secretary (and if such report is so to be given, Covered Entity shall simultaneously provide a copy of any such report to Business Associate).

IV. <u>Miscellaneous.</u>

A. <u>Regulatory References.</u> A reference in the Business Associate Agreement, as amended by this Addendum, to a Section in the Security Rule means the Section as enforceable at the applicable time.

B. <u>Amendment.</u> The Parties agree to take such action as is necessary to amend the Business Associate Agreement, as amended by this Addendum, from time to time as is necessary for Covered Entity to comply with the requirements of the Security Rule. In amplification and not in limitation of this Section B and upon the request of Covered Entity, Business Associate agrees from time to time to execute such amendments to the Business Associate Agreement, if, as and when required by HIPAA, in order to permit Covered Entity to comply with HIPAA.

C. <u>Interpretation.</u> Any ambiguity in the Business Associate Agreement, as amended by this Addendum, shall be resolved to permit Covered Entity to comply with the Privacy Rule and the Security Rule.

D. <u>Cooperation and Reasonableness.</u> The parties hereto acknowledge and agree that the Business Associate Agreement, as amended by this Addendum, is intended to address a complex series of rights and relationships, and that in the course of activity pursuant to the Business Associate Agreement many matters may arise that require further clarification or memorialization in order to carry out the purposes and intentions of the parties hereto as set forth in the Business Associate Agreement, as amended by this Addendum; accordingly, the parties hereto agree to negotiate in good faith with respect to such matters and to execute and deliver any and all documents and instruments reasonably necessary to effectuate such good faith negotiation, in order to help Covered Entity comply with Covered Entity's obligations under the Privacy Rule and the Security Rule.

E. <u>Headings and Section References.</u> The headings of the sections and paragraphs of this Addendum to the Business Associate Agreement are included for convenience only and are not intended to be a part of, or to affect the meaning or interpretation of, this Addendum or the Business Associate Agreement.

F. <u>Full Force and Effect.</u> As amended by this Addendum, the Business Associate Agreement is and shall remain in full force and effect, in accordance with its terms.

IN WITNESS WHEREOF, intending to be legally bound, the parties hereto have executed this Addendum as of the date first set forth above. The parties hereto further certify that the persons signing this Addendum are duly authorized to do so.

COVERED ENTITY:

[INSERT]

By:_____

Name:

Its: President

BUSINESS ASSOCIATE:

[INSERT]

By:_____

Name:

Hereunto duly authorized

Appendix E-2

Resolution Agreement*

Source: Department of Health & Human Services, Office of Civil Rights (July 9, 2008), *available at* http://www.hhs.gov/ocr/privacy/enforcement/agreement.pdf.

Resolution Agreement

I. Recitals

1. <u>Parties</u>. The Parties to this Resolution Agreement ("Agreement") are the United States Department of Health and Human Services, Office for Civil Rights and Centers for Medicare & Medicaid Services (hereafter collectively referred to as "HHS"), and Providence Health & Services ("PH&S"), a Washington non-profit corporation; Providence Health System—Oregon ("PHS-Oregon"), an Oregon nonprofit corporation; and Providence Hospice and Home Care ("PHHC"), a Washington non-profit corporation. PH&S, PHS-Oregon, and PHHC are collectively referred to in this Agreement as the "Covered Entities."

2. <u>Factual Background and Covered Incidents</u>.

   A. Authority of HHS

   HHS enforces the Federal standards that govern the privacy of individually identifiable health information (45 C.F.R. Part 160 and Subparts A and E of Part 164, the "Privacy Rule") and the Federal standards that govern the security of electronic individually identifiable health information (45 C.F.R. Part 160 and Subparts A and C of Part 164, the "Security Rule"). HHS has the authority to conduct investigations of complaints alleging violations of the Privacy and Security Rules by covered entities, and a covered entity must cooperate with HHS' investigation. 45 C.F.R. §160.306(c) and §160.310(b).

---

*This appendix document is also available on the CD-ROM accompanying this volume.

B. Covered Incidents

The following incidents are hereafter referred to as the "Covered Incidents":

(1) On or about December 30, 2005, electronic protected health information ("ePHI") on four backup tapes and two optical disks were left unattended overnight in the personal vehicle of an employee of one of the Covered Entities and were stolen. The employee took the disks and tapes from Providence Home and Community Services ("HCS"), a division of PHS-Oregon, pursuant to a practice followed at the time by HCS Information Staff with the knowledge of some HCS managers. The ePHI on the tapes and disks was not encrypted.

(2) On the following dates, laptops containing ePHI were left unattended and were stolen from members of the workforces of Covered Entities:

(a) September 29, 2005

(b) December 7, 2005

(c) February 27, 2006

(d) March 3, 2006

The ePHI on the stolen laptops was not encrypted.

3. <u>No Admission</u>. This Agreement is not an admission of liability by Covered Entities.

4. <u>No Concession</u>. This Agreement is not a concession by HHS that Covered Entities are not in violation of the Privacy and Security Rules and not liable for civil money penalties.

5. <u>Intention of Parties to Effect Resolution</u>. This Agreement is intended to resolve the complaints that were consolidated under Office for Civil Rights Complaint Nos. 06-47465 and 06-52268, Centers for Medicare & Medicaid Services Complaint Nos. 06-SEC00917 and 06-SEC00886, and any violations of the HIPAA Privacy and Security Rules related to the Covered Incidents. In consideration of the Parties' interest in avoiding the uncertainty, burden and expense of further investigation and formal proceedings, the Parties agree to resolve this matter according to the Terms and Conditions below.

II. Terms and Conditions

6. <u>Payment</u>. Covered Entities agree to pay HHS the amount of $ 100,000 ("Resolution Amount"). Covered Entities agree to pay the Resolution Amount: (1) by certified check made payable to "United States Department of Health and Human Services"; or (2) by electronic funds transfer pursuant to written instructions to be provided by HHS. Covered Entities agree to make this payment contemporaneously with their execution of this Agreement.

7. <u>Corrective Action Plan</u>. Covered Entities have entered into and agree to comply with the Corrective Action Plan ("CAP"), attached as Appendix A,

which is incorporated into this Agreement by reference. If any or all of Covered Entities breach the CAP, and fail to cure the breach as set forth in the CAP, then Covered Entities will be in breach of this Agreement and HHS will not be subject to the terms and conditions in the Release set forth in paragraph 8 of this Agreement.

8. Release by HHS. In consideration and conditioned upon Covered Entities' performance of their obligations under this Agreement, HHS releases Covered Entities from any actions it has or may have against Covered Entities under the Privacy and Security Rules arising out of or related to the Covered Incidents identified in paragraph "2" above. HHS does not release Covered Entities from, nor waive any rights, obligations, or causes of action other than those related to the Covered Incidents and referred to in this paragraph. This release does not extend to actions that may be brought under section 1177 of the Social Security Act, 42 U.S.C. §1320d-6.

9. Agreement by Released Parties. Covered Entities shall not contest the validity of their obligations to pay, nor the amount of, the Resolution Amount or any other obligations agreed to under this Agreement. Covered Entities waive all procedural rights granted under: Section 1128A of the Social Security Act (42 U.S.C. §1320a-7a) and Subpart E of 45 C.F.R. Part 160; and 45 C.F.R. Part 30, including, but not limited to, notice, hearing, and appeal with respect to the Resolution Amount.

10. Binding on Successors. This Agreement is binding on Covered Entities and their successors, heirs, transferees, and assigns.

11. Costs. Each Party to this Agreement shall bear its own legal and other costs incurred in connection with this matter, including the preparation and performance of this Agreement.

12. No Additional Releases. This Agreement is intended to be for the benefit of the Parties only. By this instrument the Parties do not release any claims against any other person or entity.

13. Effect of Agreement. This Agreement constitutes the complete agreement between the Parties. All material representations, understandings, and promises of the Parties are contained in this Agreement. Any modifications to this Agreement must be set forth in writing and signed by all Parties.

14. Execution of Agreement and Effective Date. The Agreement shall become effective (i.e., final and binding) upon the date of signing of both this Agreement and the CAP by the last signatory ("Effective Date").

15. Tolling of Statute of Limitations. Pursuant to 42 U.S.C. §1320a-7a(c)(l), a civil money penalty must be imposed within six years from the date of the occurrence of the violation. To ensure that this six-year period does not expire during the term of this agreement, Covered Entities agree that the time between the Effective Date of this Resolution Agreement (as set forth in paragraph 14) and the date same may be terminated by reason of Covered Entities' breach, plus one-year thereafter, will not be included in calculating the six (6) year statute of limitations applicable to the violations which are the

subject of this agreement. Covered Entities waive and will not plead any statute of limitations, laches, or similar defenses to any administrative action relating to the Covered Incidents identified in paragraph 2 that is filed by HHS within the time period set forth above, except to the extent that such defenses would have been available had an administrative action been filed on the Effective Date of this Resolution Agreement.

16. Disclosure. HHS places no restriction on the publication of the Agreement. This Agreement and information related to this Agreement may be made public by either party. In addition, HHS may be required to disclose this Agreement and related material to any person upon request consistent with the applicable provisions of the Freedom of Information Act, 5 U.S.C. §552, and its implementing regulations, 45 C.F.R. Part 5.

17. Execution in Counterparts. This Agreement may be executed in counterparts, each of which constitutes an original, and all of which shall constitute one and the same agreement.

18. Authorizations. The individual(s) signing this Agreement on behalf of Covered Entities represent and warrant that they are authorized by Covered Entities to execute this Agreement on their behalf. The individual(s) signing this Agreement on behalf of HHS represent and warrant that they are signing this Agreement in their official capacities and that they are authorized to execute this Agreement.

For Covered Entities

_____   _____
John Koster, M.D., Providence Health & Services   Date:

For Department of Health and Human Services

_____   _____
Tony Trenkle, Centers for Medicare & Medicaid Services   Date:

_____   _____
Linda Yuu Connor, Office for Civil Rights   Date:

Appendix E-2.1

Example of Resolution Agreement and Corrective Action Plan (Without External Monitoring)*

Source: Department of Health & Human Services, Office of Civil Rights (July 9, 2008), *available at* http://www.hhs.gov/ocr/privacy/hipaa/enforcement/examples/massgeneralracap.pdf.

RESOLUTION AGREEMENT

I. Recitals

1. <u>Parties</u>. The Parties to this Resolution Agreement ("Agreement") are the United States Department of Health and Human Services, Office for Civil Rights ("HHS"), and The General Hospital Corporation and Massachusetts General Physicians Organization, Inc. (hereinafter collectively referred to as Massachusetts General Hospital ("MGH")), each of which is a nonprofit corporation organized and operating under the laws of The Commonwealth of Massachusetts. MGH and HHS shall together be referred to as the "Parties."

2. <u>Factual Background and Covered Incident</u>.

   A. Authority of HHS

   HHS enforces the Federal standards that govern the privacy of individually identifiable health information (45 C.F.R. Part 160 and Subparts A and E of Part 164, the "Privacy Rule") and the Federal standards that govern the security of electronic individually identifiable health information (45 C.F.R. Part 160 and Subparts A and C of Part 164, the "Security Rule."). HHS has the authority to

---

*This appendix document is also available on the CD-ROM accompanying this volume.

conduct investigations of complaints alleging violations of the Privacy and Security Rules by covered entities, and covered entities must cooperate with HHS' investigation. 45 C.F.R. §160.306(c) and §160.310(b).

   B. Covered Incident

The following incident is hereafter referred to as the "Covered Incident":

(1) On March 6, 2009, an MGH employee removed from the MGH premises documents containing protected health information ("PHI"). The MGH employee removed the PHI from the MGH premises for the purpose of working on the documents from home. The documents consisted of billing encounter forms containing the name, date of birth, medical record number, health insurer and policy number, diagnosis and name of provider of 66 patients and the practice's daily office schedules for three days containing the names and medical record numbers of 192 patients.

(2) On March 9, 2009, while commuting to work on the subway, the MGH employee removed the documents containing PHI from her bag and placed them on the seat beside her. The documents were not in an envelope and were bound with a rubber band. Upon exiting the train, the MGH employee left the documents on the subway train and they were never recovered. These documents contained the PHI of 192 individuals.

   3. <u>No Admission.</u> This Agreement is not an admission, concession, or evidence of liability or wrongdoing by MGH or of any fact or any violation of any law, rule, or regulation, including any violation of HIPAA or the Privacy Rule. This Agreement is made without trial or adjudication of any alleged issue of fact or law and without any finding of liability of any kind, and MGH's agreement to undertake any obligation under this Agreement shall not be construed as an admission of any kind.

   4. <u>No Concession.</u> This Agreement is not a concession by HHS that MGH is not in violation of the Privacy and Security Rules and not liable for civil money penalties.

   5. <u>Intention of Parties to Effect Resolution</u>. This Agreement is intended to resolve the Office for Civil Rights Complaint No. 09-96024, and any violations of the HIPAA Privacy and Security Rules related to the Covered Incident. In consideration of the Parties' interest in avoiding the uncertainty, burden and expense of further investigation and formal proceedings, the Parties agree to resolve this matter according to the Terms and Conditions below.

II. <u>Terms and Conditions</u>

   6. <u>Payment</u>. MGH agrees to pay HHS the amount of $1,000,000 (Resolution Amount). MGH agrees to pay the Resolution Amount by (1) certified check made payable to "United States Department of Health and Human Services"; or (2) electronic funds transfer pursuant to written instructions to be provided by HHS. MGH agrees to make this payment contemporaneously with its execution of this Agreement.

7. Corrective Action Plan. MGH has entered into and agrees to comply with the Corrective Action Plan (CAP), attached as Appendix A, which is incorporated into this Agreement by reference. If MGH breaches the CAP, and fails to cure the breach as set forth in the CAP, then MGH will be in breach of this Agreement and HHS will not be subject to the terms and conditions in the Release set forth in paragraph 8 of this Agreement.

8. Release by HHS. In consideration of and conditioned upon MGH's performance of its obligations under this Agreement, HHS releases MGH and its successors, transferees, assigns, and subsidiaries, including its members, officers, agents, directors, affiliates and employees, from any claims and causes of action it has or may have against MGH under the Privacy and Security Rules arising out of or related to the Covered Incident identified in paragraph 2 above. HHS does not release MGH from, nor waive, any rights, obligations, or causes of action other than those arising out of or related to the Covered Incident and referred to in this paragraph. This release does not extend to actions that may be brought under section 1177 of the Social Security Act, 42 U.S.C. § 1320d-6.

9. Agreement by Released Party. MGH shall not contest the validity of its obligation to pay, nor the amount of, the Resolution Amount or any other obligations agreed to under this Agreement. MGH waives all procedural rights granted under Section 1128A of the Social Security Act (42 U.S.C. § 1320a- 7a) and 45 C.F.R. Part 160, subpart E; and 45 C.F.R. Part 30, including, but not limited to, notice, hearing, and appeal with respect to the Resolution Amount.

10. Binding on Successors. This Agreement is binding on MGH and its successors, transferees, and assigns.

11. Costs. Each Party to this Agreement shall bear its own legal and other costs incurred in connection with this matter, including the preparation and performance of this Agreement.

12. No Additional Releases. This Agreement is intended to be for the benefit of the Parties only. By this instrument, the Parties do not release any claims against any other person or entity.

13. Effect of Agreement. This Agreement constitutes the complete agreement between the Parties. All material representations, understandings, and promises of the Parties are contained in this Agreement. Any modifications to this Agreement must be set forth in writing and signed by both Parties. Nothing in this Agreement is intended to, or shall, be used as any basis for the denial of any license, authorization, approval, or consent that MGH may require under any law, rule, or regulation.

14. Execution of Agreement and Effective Date. The Agreement shall become effective (i.e., final and binding) upon the date of signing of both this Agreement and the CAP by the last signatory (Effective Date).

15. Tolling of Statute of Limitations. Pursuant to 42 U.S.C. § 1320a-7a(c)(1), a civil money penalty must be imposed within six years from the date of the occurrence of the violation. To ensure that this six-year period does not expire during the term of this Agreement, MGH agrees that the time between the Effective

Date of this Resolution Agreement (as set forth in paragraph 14) and the date same may be terminated by reason of MGH's breach, plus one-year thereafter, will not be included in calculating the six (6) year statute of limitations applicable to the violations which are the subject of this Agreement. MGH waives and will not plead any statute of limitations, laches, or similar defenses to any administrative action relating to the Covered Incident identified in paragraph 2 that is filed by HHS within the time period set forth above, except to the extent that such defenses would have been available had an administrative action been filed on the Effective Date of this Resolution Agreement.

16. <u>Disclosure</u>. HHS places no restriction on the publication of the Agreement. This Agreement and information related to this Agreement may be made public by either Party. In addition, HHS may be required to disclose this Agreement and related material to any person upon request consistent with the applicable provisions of the Freedom of Information Act, 5 U.S.C. § 552 (FOIA), and its implementing regulations, 45 C.F.R. Part 5; provided, however, that HHS will use its best efforts to prevent the disclosure of information, documents, and any other item produced by MGH to HHS as part of HHS' review, to the extent such items constitute trade secrets and/or confidential commercial or financial information that is exempt from turnover in response to a FOIA request under 45 C.F.R. § 5.65, or any other applicable exemption under FOIA and its implementing regulations.

17. <u>Execution in Counterparts</u>. This Agreement may be executed in counterparts, each of which constitutes an original, and all of which shall constitute one and the same agreement.

18. <u>Authorizations</u>. The individuals signing this Agreement on behalf of MGH represent and warrant that they are authorized by MGH to execute this Agreement on its behalf. The individual signing this Agreement on behalf of HHS represents and warrants that he is signing this Agreement in his official capacity and that he is authorized to execute this Agreement.

For The General Hospital Corporation

/s/ _____   _____
Peter L. Slavin, M.D.   Date
President

For Massachusetts General Physicians Organization, Inc.

/s/ _____   _____
David Torchiana, M.D.   Date
Chairman and Chief Executive Officer

For Department of Health and Human Services

/s/ _____   _____
Peter K. Chan   Date
Regional Manager, Region I Office for Civil Rights

Appendix A

CORRECTIVE ACTION PLAN BETWEEN THE DEPARTMENT OF HEALTH AND HUMAN SERVICES AND THE GENERAL HOSPITAL CORPORATION AND MASSACHUSETTS GENERAL PHYSICIANS ORGANIZATION, INC.

I. PREAMBLE

The General Hospital Corporation and Massachusetts General Physicians Organization, Inc. (hereinafter collectively referred to as Massachusetts General Hospital (MGH)) hereby enters into this Corrective Action Plan (CAP) with the United States Department of Health and Human Services, Office for Civil Rights (HHS). Contemporaneously with this CAP, MGH is entering into a Resolution Agreement (Agreement) with HHS, and this CAP is incorporated by reference into the Agreement as Appendix A. MGH enters into this CAP as part of the consideration for the release set forth in paragraph 8 of the Resolution Agreement.

II. CONTACT PERSONS AND SUBMISSIONS

A. Contact Persons

MGH has identified the following individuals as its authorized representatives and contact persons regarding the implementation of this CAP and for receipt and submission of notifications and reports:

Deborah Adair
Director, Health Information Services
Privacy Officer
The Massachusetts General Hospital
55 Fruit Street
Boston, MA 02114
Telephone: 617-726-2465

Brent L. Henry, Esq.
Vice President and General Counsel Partners HealthCare System, Inc. Office of the General Counsel
50 Staniford Street, 10th Floor
Boston, MA 02114 bhenry1@partners.org Telephone: 617-278-1115
Facsimile: 617-236-8563

For communications with the Monitor: Robert Damiano
Director, Internal Audit Services Partners HealthCare System, Inc. Internal Audit Services
529 Main Street, Suite 51
Charlestown, MA 02129 rdamiano@partners.org Telephone: 617-726-8126
Facsimile: 617-724-8039

HHS has identified the following individual as its contact person with whom MGH is to report information regarding the implementation of this CAP:

Susan Rhodes, Deputy Regional Manager Office for Civil Rights, Region I Department of Health and Human Services JFK Federal Building, Room 1875 Boston, MA 02203 susan.rhodes@hhs.gov Telephone: 617-565-1347 Facsimile: 617-565-3809

MGH and HHS agree to promptly notify each other of any changes in the contact persons or the other information provided above.

B. <u>Proof of Submissions</u>. Unless otherwise specified, all notifications and reports required by this CAP may be made by any means, other than email, including certified mail, overnight mail, or hand delivery, provided that there is proof that such notification was received. For purposes of this requirement, internal facsimile confirmation sheets do not constitute proof of receipt.

III. TERM OF CAP

The period of compliance obligations assumed by MGH under this CAP shall begin on the Effective Date and conclude 3 years from the Monitor Plan Approval Date pursuant to section V.E.2., except that after this period MGH shall be obligated to: (a) submit the Annual Report for the final Reporting Period, as set forth in section VI.B.; and (b) comply with the document retention requirement set forth in section VII. The Effective Date shall be calculated in accordance with paragraph 14 of the Resolution Agreement.

IV. TIME

In computing any period of time prescribed or allowed by this CAP, the day of the act, event, or default from which the designated period of time begins to run shall not be included. The last day of the period so computed shall be included, unless it is a Saturday, a Sunday, or legal holiday, in which event the period runs until the end of the next day that is not one of the aforementioned days.

V. CORRECTIVE ACTION OBLIGATIONS

MGH agrees to the following:

A. <u>Policies and Procedures</u>

1. MGH shall develop, maintain, and revise, as necessary, written policies and procedures governing (i) physical removal and transport of Protected Health Information (PHI), (ii) laptop encryption, and (iii) USB drive encryption (collectively, Policies and Procedures) that: (a) address the Covered Incident specified in paragraph 2 of the Agreement; and (b) are consistent with the Federal standards that govern the privacy of individually identifiable health information (45 C.F.R. Part 160 and Subparts A, C, and E of Part 164, the Privacy and Security Rules). Policies and Procedures shall include the minimum content set forth in section V.C. Policies and Procedures required under this CAP are in addition to, and may be incorporated into, any policies and procedures required by the Privacy and Security Rules.

2. MGH shall provide such Policies and Procedures, consistent with paragraph 1 above, to HHS within 90 days of the Effective Date for review and approval. Upon receiving any required changes to such Policies and Procedures from HHS, MGH shall have 60 days to revise such Policies and Procedures accordingly, and provide the revised Policies and Procedures to HHS for review and approval, which shall not be unreasonably withheld.

3. MGH shall fully implement its Policies and Procedures within 90 days of HHS' approval of the Policies and Procedures as described in section V.A.2. MGH's Policies and Procedures shall not be deemed fully implemented unless MGH has provided the specific training as required in the first paragraph of section V.D.1.

B. Distribution and Updating of Policies and Procedures

1. Within 30 days of HHS' approval of the Policies and Procedures identified in section V.A., MGH shall distribute such Policies and Procedures to all members of the workforce who have access to and use PHI. MGH shall distribute the Policies and Procedures to new members of the workforce who have access to and use PHI within 15 days of the workforce members beginning their service.

2. MGH shall document distribution of the Policies and Procedures and require, in connection with the distribution, workforce members to read and abide by such Policies and Procedures. Such documentation shall be retained by MGH and made available to HHS pursuant to sections V.E.5. and VII. MGH shall attest in the Implementation Report that the Policies and Procedures were distributed to the workforce members.

3. MGH shall assess, update, and revise, as necessary, the Policies and Procedures at least annually (and more frequently if appropriate). MGH shall provide such revised Policies and Procedures to HHS for review and approval. Upon receiving any required changes to such revised Policies and Procedures from HHS, MGH shall have 30 days to adopt such changes accordingly, and provide the revised Policies and Procedures to HHS for review and approval, which shall not be unreasonably withheld.

Within 30 days of HHS' approval of any substantive revisions, MGH shall distribute such revised Policies and Procedures to all members of its workforce who have access to and use PHI. MGH shall fully implement the revised Policies and Procedures within 60 days of its receipt of HHS' approval.

C. Minimum Content of the Policies and Procedures

The Policies and Procedures shall, at a minimum, include:

1. The administrative, physical, and technical safeguards in the Privacy and Security Rules that relate to the Policies and Procedures and reasonable protections for such PHI from any intentional or unintentional uses or disclosures in violation of the Privacy Rule.

2. If MGH determines that a member of their workforce has violated these Policies and Procedures, MGH shall notify in writing the Monitor de-

scribed in section V.E. within 30 days of its determination. Such violations shall be known as Reportable Events. The report to the Monitor shall include the following information:

> a. A complete description of the event, including the relevant facts, the persons involved, and the provision(s) of the Policies and Procedures implicated;
>
> b. A description of MGH's actions taken to mitigate any harm and any further steps MGH plans to take to address the matter and prevent it from recurring.

D. Training

1. Specific Training. Within 90 days of HHS' approval of the Policies and Procedures identified in section V.A., MGH shall provide specific training on the Policies and Procedures to all workforce members who have access to and use PHI.

After HHS' approval of the Policies and Procedures, MGH shall provide such training to new members of the workforce who are engaged in the above-referenced activities within 30 days of the workforce members beginning their service.

2. Training Certification. Each workforce member who is required to attend training shall certify, in writing or in electronic form, that the workforce member has received the required training. The training certification shall specify the date training was completed. All course materials shall be retained in compliance with section VII.

3. Annual Review of Training. MGH shall review the training annually, and update the training to reflect any new changes in federal law or HHS guidance or substantive revisions to the Policies and Procedures.

4. Prohibition on Removing PHI from Premises. Except as provided in section V.D.5., MGH shall prohibit any member of its workforce from physically removing PHI from MGH premises for use off-site and/or transporting PHI off-site if that workforce member has not completed a specified training certification required by section V.D.2.

5. Exception to Prohibition in V.D.4. MGH may permit workforce members to physically remove PHI from MGH premises for use or transport off-site provided that MGH, immediately following the Effective Date, has distributed a communication to its workforce members informing them that: (a) MGH has entered into this CAP with HHS; (b) pursuant to this CAP, MGH will be distributing new or revised Policies and Procedures relating to the physical removal of PHI from MGH premises and providing mandatory training to the workforce with respect to the Policies and Procedures; (c) workforce members may physically remove PHI from MGH premises only for the performance of their job duties and, when removing PHI, shall take reasonable and appropriate steps to safeguard its confidentiality; and (d) workforce members who fail to reasonably and appropriately safeguard such PHI are subject to sanctions (the

"Communication"). This exception to the prohibition in section V.D.4. expires on completion of the 90 day period or the specific training required by the first paragraph in section V.D.1., whichever is sooner, for those workforce members who have not completed a specified training certification required by section V.D.2.

6. Distribution of the Communication. The Communication, as described in section V.D.5., shall be distributed by email to the workforce members from the President or Chief Executive Officer of MGH with a copy to MGH's Privacy Officer. MGH shall provide a copy of the Communication to HHS promptly upon distribution. Department managers shall confirm to the Privacy Officer within a reasonable time following distribution of the Communication that workforce members under their supervision have received and read the Communication. The Privacy Officer then shall promptly provide a written attestation to HHS confirming that the Department managers have provided the confirmations described in the foregoing sentence.

E. Monitoring

1. Designation of Monitor. MGH shall designate the individual serving as the Director of Internal Audit Services of the Partners HealthCare System, Inc. at the time of the Effective Date as the Monitor under this CAP. The Monitor must certify in writing at the time of his designation, and must provide reasonable written documentation, to the effect that he has the requisite expertise and experience regarding the implementation of the Privacy and Security Rules and has the necessary resources and is otherwise able to perform the reviews described herein in a professionally independent fashion, taking into account any other business relationships or other engagements that the individual may have.

Upon reasonable notice, HHS may interview the individual who is designated by MGH as the Monitor. MGH shall provide the Monitor with convenient, timely access to any workforce members, policies, procedures, audit records, or other items or information that the Monitor deems necessary for the review and performance of the Monitor's duties.

2. Description of Monitor's Duties. The Monitor shall conduct assessments of implementation and compliance by MGH with the Corrective Action Obligations set forth in section V. hereof and prepare the plan and reports described below.

Within 45 days of the Effective Date, the Monitor shall submit to HHS and MGH a written plan, describing with adequate detail, the Monitor's plan for fulfilling the duties set forth in this section V.E. (Monitor Plan).

Within 45 days of its receipt of the Monitor Plan, HHS shall inform MGH and the Monitor of its approval or disapproval of the proposed Monitor Plan. If HHS does not approve the proposed Monitor Plan, HHS shall set forth in writing the reasons for its disapproval and required revisions to the proposed Monitor Plan, which shall be reasonable and consistent with this CAP. The Monitor then shall submit a revised

Monitor Plan to HHS, incorporating HHS' comments and required revisions, within 30 days of the date that HHS informed the Monitor of its disapproval of the proposed Monitor Plan. HHS shall inform MGH and the Monitor of its approval or disapproval of the revised Monitor Plan within 30 days of its receipt of the revised Monitor Plan (Monitor Plan Approval Date).

The Monitor shall review the Monitor Plan at least annually and shall provide HHS and MGH with a copy of any revisions to the Monitor Plan, before they are incorporated, for approval by HHS. HHS shall inform MGH and the Monitor of its approval or disapproval of the revisions. If HHS does not approve the proposed revisions, HHS shall set forth in writing the reasons for its disapproval and required modifications, which shall be reasonable and consistent with this CAP. The Monitor then shall timely incorporate the modifications into the Monitor Plan.

The Monitor shall begin implementation of the Monitor Plan immediately after the Monitor Plan Approval Date. Whenever the existing Monitor Plan is updated or revised and the updated or revised version has been approved by HHS and has then gone into effect, the updated or revised Monitor Plan shall supersede the prior Monitor Plan.

 a. The Monitor shall review MGH's compliance with this CAP and shall seek to validate that:

  i. All members of MGH's workforce are trained and familiar with the Policies and Procedures; and

  ii. All members of MGH's workforce are complying with the Policies and Procedures.

 b. The Monitor shall conduct his reviews and shall assess compliance by MGH with its obligations relative to the established processes and timeframes for satisfying such obligations under the CAP in accordance with the Monitor Plan. Monitor reviews shall include, but not be limited to:

  i. unannounced site inspections of MGH's locations/departments/practices referenced in section VI.A.4.;

  ii. interviews with any members of the workforce who use PHI;

  iii. interviews with any members of the workforce involved in implementing the safeguards required by this CAP;

  iv. inspection of a sample of laptops and USB flash drives that contain ePHI and are under the control of workforce members to ensure that such devices satisfy all applicable requirements of the Policies and Procedures; and

  v. inspection of relevant documents and interviews with workforce members for the purpose of confirming consistent training, implementation, and enforcement of the Policies and Procedures among workforce members.

c. <u>Semi-Annual Monitor Reports</u>. Within 180 days of the Monitor Plan Approval Date, and once every 6 month period thereafter, the Monitor shall prepare a written report based on the reviews the Monitor has performed and provide such report to HHS and MGH (Monitor Report). The Monitor Report shall describe Reportable Events in the manner set forth in sections V.C.2.a. and V.C.2.b. that relate to impermissible uses and disclosures of PHI. The Monitor Report shall include a summary of all other Reportable Events. MGH shall prepare a response to the Monitor Report and provide such response to HHS and the Monitor within 30 days of MGH's receipt of the Monitor Report.

d. <u>Monitor Reports Regarding Violation(s)</u>. The Monitor shall report any significant violations of the CAP to HHS and MGH within 10 business days of the Monitor's discovery of such violation. MGH shall prepare a response, including a plan of correction, and provide such response to HHS and the Monitor within 10 business days of its receipt of the Monitor's report of a significant violation.

e. <u>Documentation of Monitor Reviews</u>. The results of Monitor reviews shall be fully documented, including, but not limited to,

    i. Dates of unannounced site visits;

    ii. Summaries of results of interviews; and

    iii. Summaries of inspections of laptops and USB flash drives.

3. <u>Validation Review</u>. If HHS has reason to believe that (a) the Monitor's reviews or reports fail to conform to the requirements of this CAP or (b) the Monitor's report results are inaccurate, HHS may unilaterally conduct its own review to determine whether the Monitor reviews or reports complied with the requirements of the CAP and/or are inaccurate ("Validation Review").

4. <u>Monitor Replacement</u>.

a. <u>MGH Replaces Monitor</u>. If MGH intends to replace a Monitor during the term of this CAP, MGH shall immediately submit a notice explaining its reasons to HHS before doing so, unless exigent circumstances require immediate replacement. MGH shall propose a new internal Monitor without unreasonable delay and shall designate the new Monitor, subject to approval by HHS which shall not be unreasonably withheld.

b. <u>HHS Replaces Monitor</u>. If HHS has a reasonable basis to conclude that a Monitor does not possess the expertise, independence, or objectivity necessary to perform the duties under this CAP, or has failed to carry out the Monitor's responsibilities as set forth in this CAP, HHS shall notify MGH of its intent to replace the Monitor and provide a written explanation to MGH of its reasons for requiring MGH to designate a new Monitor. Within 15 days following MGH's receipt of such notice (or such additional period as the Parties may agree) (the "Period"), appropriate representative(s) of MGH and HHS shall meet to discuss in good faith and, if possible, resolve the concerns set forth in HHS' notice. If HHS' concerns are not resolved through this informal process, then at the conclusion of the Period, HHS may unilaterally require MGH to designate a new internal Monitor. In such event, MGH shall propose a new Monitor without unreasonable delay and shall designate a new Monitor, subject to approval by HHS which shall not be unreasonably withheld.

c. <u>HHS Approval Criteria</u>. HHS' approval of a new Monitor shall be based on the expertise and experience regarding the implementation of the Privacy and Security Rules and whether in HHS' determination the new Monitor has the necessary resources and is otherwise able to perform the reviews described herein in a professionally independent fashion, taking into account any other business relationships or other engagements that the individual may have.

d. <u>Monitor Certifies Credentials</u>. The Monitor must certify in writing at the time of his or her designation, and must provide reasonable written documentation, to the effect that he or she has the requisite expertise and experience regarding the implementation of the Privacy and Security Rules and has the necessary resources and is otherwise able to perform the reviews described herein in a professionally independent fashion, taking into account any other business relationships or other engagements that the individual may have.

e. MGH agrees to bear all of its costs incurred related to the Monitor, including, but not limited to, costs associated with a Monitor's replacement and the performance of a Monitor's duties under this CAP.

5 <u>Retention of Records</u>. The Monitor and MGH shall retain and promptly make available to HHS, upon request, all non-privileged work papers, supporting documentation, correspondence, and draft reports (those exchanged between the Monitor and MGH) related to the reviews by the Monitor in accordance with the CAP. If MGH asserts a claim of privilege with respect to any document that HHS requests MGH to make available for inspection and copying under this section, within a reasonable time of such request, MGH shall prepare a log identifying the document and the type of privilege asserted (e.g., attorney-client privilege, attorney work product, patient confidentiality, or other privilege). MGH shall make the log available to the Monitor, who shall provide it to HHS promptly upon request.

6. The use of a monitor does not affect HHS' authority to investigate complaints, or conduct compliance reviews or audits, or MGH's compliance with 45 C.F.R. Part 160, Subpart C.

VI.   IMPLEMENTATION REPORT AND ANNUAL REPORTS

A. <u>Implementation Report</u>. Within 120 days after receiving HHS' approval of the Policies and Procedures required by section V.A., MGH shall submit a written report to HHS and the Monitor summarizing the status of its implementation of the requirements of this CAP. This report, known as the "Implementation Report," shall include:

    1. An attestation signed by an officer of MGH attesting that the Policies and Procedures were fully implemented within 90 days of HHS' approval of the Policies and Procedures, which shall include a statement affirming that MGH distributed the Policies and Procedures to all appropriate members of the workforce within 30 days of HHS' approval;

    2. A copy of all training materials used for the training required by this CAP, a description of the training, including a summary of the topics covered, the length of the session(s) and a schedule of when the training session(s) were held;

    3. An attestation signed by an officer of MGH attesting that members of the workforce who were scheduled to complete the training required by section V.D.1. of this CAP by the date of this Implementation Report have completed such training and have executed the training certifications required by section V.D.2.;

    4. An attestation signed by an officer of MGH listing all MGH's locations/departments/practices (including mailing addresses), the name under which each location is doing business, the corresponding phone numbers and fax numbers, and attesting that each location is in compliance with the obligations of this CAP; and

    5. An attestation signed by an officer of MGH stating that he or she has reviewed the Implementation Report, has made a reasonable inquiry regarding its content and believes that, upon such inquiry, the information is accurate and truthful.

  B. Annual Reports. The one-year period after the Effective Date and each subsequent one-year period or portion thereof during the course of the period of compliance obligations shall be known as a "Reporting Period." MGH shall submit Annual Reports to the Monitor that reflect its status in complying with this CAP for each Reporting Period. Such Annual Reports shall be incorporated into the Monitor Reports to HHS. MGH shall submit each Annual Report to the Monitor no later than 60 days after the end of each corresponding Reporting Period. The Annual Report shall include:

    1. A copy of the schedule, topic outline, and materials for the training programs provided during the Reporting Period that is the subject of the report;

    2. An attestation signed by an officer of MGH attesting that MGH obtains and maintains written or electronic training certifications from all persons that must attend training, and that such training complies with the requirements established under this CAP;

    3. An attestation signed by an officer of MGH attesting that any revision(s) to the Policies and Procedures under section V.B.3. were fully implemented within 60 days of HHS' approval of the revision(s), which shall include a statement affirming that MGH distributed the revised Policies and Procedures

to all appropriate members of the workforce within 30 days of HHS' approval of the revision(s);

    4. A summary of Reportable Events (defined in section V.C.2.) that occurred during the Reporting Period and the status of any corrective and preventative action(s) relating to all such Reportable Events;

    5. A copy of reports generated by Monitor reviews pursuant to section V.E.2 and

    6. An attestation signed by an officer of MGH attesting that he or she has reviewed the Annual Report, has made a reasonable inquiry regarding its content and believes that, upon such inquiry, the information is accurate and truthful.

VII.   DOCUMENT RETENTION

The office(s) responsible for implementation of the obligations of the CAP shall maintain, for the individuals holding the titles set forth herein, for inspection and copying all non-privileged documents and records relating to compliance with this CAP for 6 years from the Effective Date. If MGH asserts a claim of privilege with respect to any document that HHS requests MGH to make available for inspection and copying under this section, within a reasonable time of such request, MGH shall prepare a log identifying the document and the type of privilege asserted (e.g., attorney-client privilege, attorney work product, patient confidentiality, or other privilege). MGH shall make the log available to the Monitor, who shall provide it to HHS promptly upon request.

VIII.   REQUESTS FOR EXTENSION AND BREACH PROVISIONS

MGH is expected to fully comply with all provisions contained in this CAP.

    A. <u>Timely Written Requests for Extensions</u>. MGH, through the Monitor, in advance of any due date set forth in this CAP, may submit a timely written request for an extension of time to perform any act or file any notification or report required by this CAP. A "timely written request" is defined as a request in writing received by HHS at least ten (10) business days prior to the date by which any act is due to be performed or any notification or report is to be filed and must contain a description of the facts giving rise to the request. HHS will consider such a request and make a reasonable determination as to whether to grant it.

    B. <u>Notice of Breach</u>. The Parties agree that an uncured breach of this CAP by MGH—meaning a breach of this CAP by The General Hospital Corporation or Massachusetts General Physicians Organization, Inc.—constitutes a breach of the Resolution Agreement. MGH agrees that actions or omissions of the Monitor in his or her performance of the duties set forth in section V.E.2. shall be deemed actions or omissions of MGH. Upon a determination by HHS that MGH has breached this CAP, HHS will notify MGH of MGH's breach thereof (this notification is hereinafter referred to as the "Notice of Breach").

C. <u>MGH Response</u>. MGH shall have 30 days from the date of receipt of the Notice of Breach to demonstrate to HHS' satisfaction that:

1. MGH is in compliance with the obligations of the CAP cited by HHS as the basis for the breach; or

2. the alleged breach has been cured; or

3. the alleged breach cannot be cured within the 30-day period, but that: (i) MGH has begun to take action to cure the breach; (ii) MGH is pursuing such action with due diligence; and (iii) MGH has provided to HHS a reasonable timetable for curing the breach.

D. <u>Imposition of CMP</u>. If at the conclusion of the 30-day period, MGH fails to meet the requirements of section VIII.C. to HHS' satisfaction, HHS may proceed to impose a civil money penalty (CMP) on MGH pursuant to 45 C.F.R. Part 160 for violations of the Privacy Rule related to the Covered Incident set forth in paragraph 2 of the Resolution Agreement and for any other act or failure to act that constitutes a violation of the Privacy Rule or Security Rule. HHS shall notify MGH in writing of its determination to proceed with the imposition of a CMP. MGH will retain all of the rights and obligations specified under 45 CFR Part 160, Subparts C through E, with respect to any determination by HHS that MGH has violated the Privacy Rule or the Security Rule and with respect to the imposition of a CMP under this paragraph.

/s/ _____   _____
Peter L. Slavin, M.D.   Date
President

For Massachusetts General Physicians Organization, Inc.

/s/ _____   _____
David Torchiana, M.D.   Date
Chairman and Chief Executive Officer

For Department of Health and Human Services

/s/ _____   _____
Peter K. Chan   Date
Regional Manager, Region I Office for Civil Rights

Appendix E-2.2

Example of Resolution Agreement and Corrective Action Plan (With External Monitoring)*

Source: Department of Health & Human Services, Office of Civil Rights (June 7, 2010), *available at* http://www.hhs.gov/ocr/privacy/hipaa/enforcement/examples/riteaidres.pdf.

RESOLUTION AGREEMENT

I. Recitals

1. Parties. The Parties to this Resolution Agreement (Agreement) are: (1) the United States Department of Health and Human Services' (HHS) Office for Civil Rights (OCR); and (2)(i) Rite Aid Corporation, a Delaware corporation, (Rite Aid) on behalf of its retail pharmacy store entities in the United States that meet the definition of a "covered entity" under 45 C.F.R. § 160.103, as a retail pharmacy "health care provider," as defined in 45 C.F.R. § 160.103; (ii) the forty (40) wholly-owned Rite Aid subsidiaries, listed in Exhibit 1 attached hereto, on behalf of each of their affiliated retail pharmacy store entities in the United States that meet the definition of a "covered entity" under 45 C.F.R. § 160.103, as a retail pharmacy "health care provider," as defined in 45 C.F.R. § 160.103; and, (iii) to the extent not already included in (i) or (ii), all entities owned or controlled by Rite Aid including, but not limited to, the entities listed in Exhibit 1 (which is current as of June 7, 2010), that meet the definition of a "covered entity" under 45 C.F.R. § 160.103, as a retail pharmacy "health care provider," as defined in 45 C.F.R. § 160.103 (collectively "Rite Aid Entities," and individually "Rite Aid Entity"). The descriptions of the Rite Aid Entities are only for purposes of this Agreement and the associated Corrective Action Plan of this same date (CAP) and have no impact regarding whether any Rite

---

*This appendix document is also available on the CD-ROM accompanying this volume.

Aid Entity or any Rite Aid Entities constitutes an "affiliated covered entity," as defined in 45 C.F.R. § 160.105(b). The term "Rite Aid Entities" shall also refer to any retail pharmacy legal entity that any Rite Aid Entity may originate, acquire, or over which it may obtain control at any time after the Effective Date of this Agreement for so long as this Agreement and the associated CAP are in force; provided that the entity meets the definition of a "covered entity" under 45 C.F.R. § 160.103; and further provided, that any such entity or entities acquired or over which a Rite Aid Entity obtained or obtains control on or after June 7, 2010 will not be subject to the terms of the Agreement and the CAP until the six-month anniversary of the date of the entity's or entities' origination, acquisition, or coming under control of a Rite Aid Entity.

As set forth in paragraph 6 below, each Rite Aid Entity has designated the same individual to act as its "Compliance Representative" for purposes of compliance with this Agreement and with the CAP of this same date, which is attached as Exhibit 2 hereto and the terms of which are incorporated by reference herein. All Rite Aid Entities shall satisfy their obligations under this Agreement and under the CAP directly or, when they so designate, through the actions of the Compliance Representative.

Attached hereto as Exhibit 1 and incorporated by reference herein is a list that contains: (1) the name and store number for each retail pharmacy store which any Rite Aid Entity owned and/or operated as of June 7, 2010; (2) the address of each such store; and (3) the date on which each such store was opened or acquired by a Rite Aid Entity.

2. Factual Background and Covered Conduct. OCR enforces the Federal standards that govern the privacy of individually identifiable health information (45 C.F.R. Part 160 and Subparts A and E of Part 164, the "Privacy Rule"). OCR has authority to conduct reviews of covered entities to determine if those entities are complying with the Privacy Rule. 45 C.F.R. § 160.308. Entities that are covered by the Privacy Rule must cooperate with OCR's compliance reviews. 45 C.P.R.§§ 160.308 and 160.310(a) and (b). The Rite Aid Entities that are Parties to this Agreement are required to comply with the Privacy Rule.

On September 27, 2007, OCR opened a review of the Rite Aid Entities' compliance with the Privacy Rule, pursuant to 45 C.F.R. § 160.308, based on media reports that protected health information (PHI) maintained by several retail pharmacy chains, including Rite Aid, was being disposed of in dumpsters that were potentially accessible to persons who were not authorized members of the pharmacy chains' workforces.

At the same time that OCR commenced its compliance review, the Federal Trade Commission (FTC) opened an investigation of the Rite Aid Entities in response to the media reports, pursuant to Section 5 of the FTC Act, 15 U.S.C. § 43, et seq. OCR and the FTC have conducted a collaborative review/investigation.

OCR's review indicates that the following conduct occurred ("Covered Conduct"): On several occasions between July 2006 and October 2006, some Rite Aid Entities disposed of nonelectronic PHI in open dumpsters potentially accessible to persons who were not authorized members of the Rite Aid Entities' workforces;

>(a) The policies and procedures establishing physical and administrative safeguards that the Rite Aid Entities adopted and have implemented, from the compliance date of the Privacy Rule through the date hereof, for their disposal of non-electronic PHI were and are not adequately designed to appropriately and reasonably safeguard such PHI;

>(b) The Rite Aid Entities did not maintain a sanctions policy for members of their workforces who failed to comply with the policies and procedures referenced in subparagraph (b) above;

>(c) From the compliance date of the Privacy Rule at least through the fall of 2008, the Rite Aid Entities did not provide and document training that was necessary and appropriate for the members of their workforces regarding the disposal of non-electronic PHI; thus, those workforce members responsible for disposal did not know how to dispose of non-electronic PHI consistent with the Privacy Rule.

3. *No Admission.* Execution of this Agreement does not constitute an admission of liability by any Rite Aid Entity, and the Rite Aid Entities expressly deny any violation of HIPAA or the Privacy Rule, and further deny any wrongdoing.

4. *No Concession.* Execution of this Agreement is not a concession by OCR that the Rite Aid Entities are in compliance with the Privacy Rule and are thus not liable for the imposition of civil money penalties (CMPs) by OCR pursuant to the Privacy Rule.

5. *Intention to Effect Resolution.* This Agreement is intended to resolve OCR Compliance Review No. 07-73377 regarding possible violations by the Rite Aid Entities of the Privacy Rule related to the Covered Conduct. As consideration for avoiding the uncertainty, burden, and expense of further investigation and formal proceedings, the Parties agree to resolve the issues raised in the compliance review according to the Terms and Conditions below.

At the same time, the Rite Aid Entities and the FTC are entering into an agreed order, resolving by consent the issues raised in the FTC's investigation (FTC Order). The proposed consent agreement will be presented to the Commission for its preliminary approval, and, after a public comment period, final approval.

II. Terms and Conditions

6. *Compliance Representative.* Each Rite Aid Entity shall designate an individual to serve as that Rite Aid Entity's Compliance Representative under this Agreement and under the CAP. The Rite Aid Entities hereby agree to appoint the same individual to serve as the Compliance Representative for each of them. The Compliance Representative shall be an individual who is knowledgeable about the Privacy Rule and about the disposal policies and practices of the Rite

Aid Entities with respect to non-electronic PHI. The Compliance Representative shall be responsible for assuring each Rite Aid Entity's compliance with this Agreement and the CAP and for arranging for the provision of such assistance as the Rite Aid Entities may require to comply with the Agreement and the CAP, including, but not limited to, arranging for and/or providing policies, procedures, training, and internal monitoring services.

The Rite Aid Entities, either individually or through Rite Aid Corporation in its capacity as their designee, shall provide OCR on the Effective Date with a written designation of a particular individual as the Compliance Representative, which designation shall be substantially in the form of Exhibit 3 hereto. If at any time while this Agreement and the CAP are in effect, the person designated as the Compliance Representative in Exhibit 3 shall no longer serve in that capacity, the Rite Aid Entities shall choose a new Compliance Representative within ten (10) business days of the conclusion of the former Compliance Representative's service and shall submit the name of the successor Compliance Representative to OCR within three (3) business days of choosing the successor Compliance Representative. Notification to OCR of the appointment of a successor Compliance Representative shall be made using a written designation, substantially in the form of Exhibit 3 hereto.

7. Payment. The Rite Aid Entities agree to pay HHS the aggregate amount of $1,000,000 (the Resolution Amount). The Rite Aid Entities shall pay $333,333.34 (Installment Payment #1) on the Effective Date of this Agreement. The Rite Aid Entities will pay the remaining balance of the Resolution Amount in two equal installments of $333,333.33, the first being due on the one year anniversary of the Effective Date (Installment Payment #2) and the second being due on the two-year anniversary of the Effective Date (Installment Payment #3). Each Installment Payment shall be paid by the Rite Aid Entities in the following manner. The Rite Aid Entities shall confirm that they have directed the Compliance Representative to pay the appropriate Installment Payment of the Resolution Amount either by: (1) certified check made payable to "United States Department of Health and Human Services" or (2) by electronic funds transfer, pursuant to written instructions to be provided by OCR. OCR and the Rite Aid Entities agree that that the Rite Aid Entities' obligation to make each of the Installment Payments of the Resolution Amount when due constitutes a Rite Aid obligation pursuant to the CAP in addition to an obligation under this Agreement. The Rite Aid Entities' failure to timely pay any of the Installment Payments of the Resolution Amount when due shall constitute a material breach of this Agreement and of the CAP and such breach shall be governed by section VIII.E. of the CAP.

8. Corrective Action Plan. The Rite Aid Entities hereby warrant that they have directed the Compliance Representative, on their behalf, to execute the CAP and to agree that the Rite Aid Entities will comply with the CAP in all respects. If an action or omission by any Rite Aid Entity or by the Compliance Representative constitutes a material breach of this Agreement and/or of the CAP and is not cured as provided in Section VIII.C or E of the CAP, then such action or omission shall also constitute a material breach of the Agreement and/

or the CAP by each of the Rite Aid Entities. In the event of an uncured material breach of this Agreement and/or of the CAP, the Rite Aid Entities will be deemed to have forfeited the benefits of the Release provided for in section 9 of this Agreement.

9. Release by HHS. In consideration of and conditioned upon the performance by the Rite Aid Entities of all of their obligations under this Agreement and under the CAP, OCR releases the Rite Aid Entities from any actions arising out of or related to the Covered Conduct identified in paragraph 2 of this Agreement. OCR does not, however, release the Rite Aid Entities from, nor waive any rights, obligations, or causes of action other than those specifically referred to in this paragraph. This release does not extend to actions that may be brought under section 1177 of the Social Security Act, 42 USC § 1320d-6.

10. Agreement by Released Parties. The Rite Aid Entities hereby waive any right to contest the validity of the obligation to pay, or to contest the amount of, the Resolution Amount or to contest any other obligations agreed to under this Agreement. The Rite Aid Entities also hereby waive all procedural rights available to them regarding the Resolution Amount, pursuant to Section 1128A of the Social Security Act (42 U.S.C. § 1320a-7a) and 45 C.F.R. Part 160 Subpart E, and pursuant to the HHS Claims Collection regulations at 45 C.F.R. Part 30, including, but not limited to, notice, hearing, and appeal.

11. Binding on Successors. This Agreement is binding on each of the Rite Aid Entities as well as their respective successors, heirs, transferees, and assigns.

12. Costs. Each Party to this Agreement shall bear its own legal and other costs incurred in connection with this matter, including the preparation and performance of this Agreement and the CAP.

13. No Additional Releases. This Agreement is intended to be for the benefit of the Parties only and by this instrument the Parties do not release any claims any of them may have against any other person or entity.

14. Effect of Agreement. This Agreement, including the CAP, constitutes the complete agreement between the Parties. All material representations, understandings, and promises of the Parties are contained in this Agreement. Any modifications to this Agreement must be set forth in writing and signed by all Parties to become effective.

15. Execution of Agreement and Effective Date. The Agreement and the CAP shall become effective (i.e., final and binding) upon the date of signing of this Agreement and the CAP by the last signatory (Effective Date).

16. Tolling of the Statute of Limitations. Pursuant to 42 U.S.C. § 1320a-7a(c)(1), a CMP must be imposed within six (6) years from the date of the occurrence of the violation. To ensure that this six-year period does not expire during the term of this Agreement, the Rite Aid Entities hereby stipulate that the time between the Effective Date of this Agreement (as set forth in paragraph 15) and the date that the Agreement may be terminated by reason of an uncured material breach committed by any Rite Aid Entity, plus one year thereafter, will not be included in calculating the six-year statute of limitations

applicable to the violations which are the subject of this Agreement. The Rite Aid Entities waive, and will, therefore, be barred from pleading, any statute of limitations, laches, or similar defenses in any administrative proceeding relating to the Covered Conduct identified in paragraph 2 of this Agreement that may be filed by HHS within the time period set forth above, except to the extent that such defenses would have been available had an administrative action been filed on or before the Effective Date of this Agreement.

17. Bankruptcy. In the event that any or all of the Rite Aid Entities commence, or is/are involuntarily placed in, bankruptcy or reorganization proceedings under Title 11 of the United States Code, the Rite Aid Entities agree not to contest or oppose any motion filed by HHS seeking relief from or modification of the automatic stay, 11 U.S.C. § 362. The Rite Aid Entities expressly acknowledge that this waiver of any rights they may have under the automatic stay is in consideration for final settlement of all issues, claims, or disputes arising between the Rite Aid Entities and OCR pertaining to any of the Covered Conduct, as set forth in Section 2 of this Agreement. The Rite Aid Entities further stipulate and agree that the Resolution Amount, and all installment payments thereof, payable by the Rite Aid Entities to OCR, are nondischargeable in bankruptcy by virtue of 11 U.S.C. § 523(a)(7) as a "fine, penalty, or forfeiture payable to and for the benefit of a governmental unit" that "is not compensation for a pecuniary loss." Further, the Rite Aid Entities agree that this Agreement and the CAP do not constitute an "executory contract" for purposes of 11 U.S.C. § 365 of the Bankruptcy Code in that OCR has no ongoing executory obligations to the Rite Aid Entities under either the Agreement or the CAP.

18. Disclosure. There are no restrictions on the publication of the Agreement. This Agreement and information related to this Agreement may be made public by any Party. In addition, OCR may be required to disclose this Agreement and related material to any person upon request consistent with the applicable provisions of the Freedom of Information Act, 5 U.S.C. § 552, et seq. (FOIA) and its implementing regulations, 45 C.P.R. Part 5; provided, however, that OCR will use its best efforts to prevent the disclosure of information, documents, CD-ROMs, photographs, tables, booklets, and any other item produced by any Rite Aid Entity to OCR as part of OCR's compliance review, to the extent that such items constitute trade secrets and/or confidential commercial or financial information that is exempt from turnover in response to a FOIA request under 45 C.P.R.§ 5.65, or any other applicable exemption under FOIA and its implementing regulations. In addition, OCR shall provide the Rite Aid Entities with prompt notice of any FOIA request which OCR receives pertaining to this compliance review, the Agreement, or the CAP.

19. Headings. The headings used in this Agreement are for the convenience of the Parties only and have no legal force or effect.

20. Execution in Counterparts. This Agreement may be executed in counterparts, each of which constitutes an original, and all of which shall constitute one and the same agreement.

21. Authorizations. The individual signing this Agreement and CAP on behalf of all of the Rite Aid Entities which are Parties to this Agreement and the CAP represents and warrants that: (a) s/he is the Compliance Representative provided for under paragraph 6 of this Agreement; (b) s/he is duly authorized by each Rite Aid Entity to execute this Agreement and the CAP; and (c) the Rite Aid Entities have agreed to be bound by the terms of this Agreement and the CAP. The individual signing this Agreement on behalf of HHS represents and warrants that she is signing this Agreement in her official capacity and that she is authorized to execute this Agreement by the Secretary of HHS or her designee.

For the Rite Aid Entities

_____   _____
Michael Yount   Date
Vice President- Regulatory Law
Compliance Representative

For the Department of Health and Human Services

_____   _____
Valerie Morgan-Alston   Date
Regional Manager, Region V
Office for Civil Rights

EXHIBIT 1
RITE AID ENTITIES/RETAIL STORES

EXHIBIT 2
CORRECTIVE ACTION PLAN

I. Preamble

The Parties to this Corrective Action Plan (CAP) are: (1) the United States Department of Health and Human Services (HHS) Office for Civil Rights (OCR); and (2) (i) Rite Aid Corporation, a Delaware corporation, (Rite Aid) on behalf of its retail pharmacy store entities in the United States that meet the definition of a "covered entity," under 45 C.P.R. § 160.103, as a retail pharmacy "health care provider," as defined in 45 C.P.R. § 160.103; (ii) the forty (40) wholly-owned Rite Aid subsidiaries, listed in Exhibit 1 attached hereto, on behalf of each of their affiliated retail pharmacy store entities in the United States that meet the definition of a "covered entity" under 45 C.P.R. § 160.103, as a retail pharmacy "health care provider" as defined in 45 C.F.R. § 160.103); and (iii) to the extent not already included in (i) or (ii), all entities owned or controlled by Rite Aid including, but not limited to the entities listed in Exhibit 1 (which is current as of June 7, 2010), that meet the definition of a "covered entity" under 45 C.P.R. § 160.103, as a retail pharmacy "health care provider," as defined in 45 C.P.R. § 160.103 (collectively "Rite Aid Entities," and individually "Rite Aid Entity"). The descriptions of the Rite Aid Entities are only for purposes of this CAP and the associated Agreement and have no impact regarding whether any Rite Aid Entity and/or any Rite Aid Entities is an "affiliated covered entity" as defined in 45 C.F.R. § 160.105(b). The term "Rite Aid Entity(ies)" shall also refer to any retail pharmacy legal entity that any Rite Aid Entity may originate, acquire, or over which it may obtain control or of which it may become a member and/or operating agent after the Effective Date of this CAP and the Resolution Agreement of this same date (Agreement) for so long as this CAP is in effect, provided that the entity meets the definition of a "covered entity" in 45 C.P.R.§ 160.103 and, further provided, that any such entity or entities originated, acquired, or over which a Rite Aid Entity shall have obtained control on or after June 7, 2010 will not be subject to the terms of this CAP until the six-month anniversary of the date of such entity's origination or acquisition by a Rite Aid Entity or the six-month anniversary of such entity coming under the control of a Rite Aid Entity.

As set forth in section II.A. of this CAP, each Rite Aid Entity has designated the same individual to act as its "Compliance Representative" for purposes of the Rite Aid Entity's compliance with this CAP and the Agreement. All Rite Aid Entities shall satisfy their obligations under this CAP, either directly or through the actions of the Compliance Representative. If an action or omission by the Compliance Representative constitutes a material breach of this CAP (or of the Agreement) and is not cured as provided in section VIII.C orE of this CAP, then such action or omission shall also constitute a material breach of the Agreement and/or the CAP by each of the Rite Aid Entities. The Rite Aid Entities enter into this CAP as consideration for the release from HHS that is set forth in paragraph 9 of the Agreement.

For purposes of this CAP, references to "Compliance Representative" shall mean the Compliance Representative designated by each Rite Aid Entity pursuant to paragraph 6 of the Agreement. The Compliance Representative may enlist the assistance of others, as appropriate, in fulfilling the obligations of the Compliance Representative under this CAP.

This CAP (along with the Agreement) is being entered into by the Parties to resolve a collaborative review conducted by OCR and the Federal Trade Commission (FTC).

Simultaneously with the execution of the Agreement and this CAP, the Rite Aid Entities and the FTC are entering into an agreed order, resolving by consent the issues raised in the FTC's investigation (FTC Order). The proposed consent agreement is between the FTC's staff and Rite Aid. It will be presented by the FTC's staff to the Commission for its preliminary approval, and, after a public comment period, final approval.

II. Compliance Representative and Submissions

A. <u>Compliance Representative as Contact Person</u>

The Compliance Representative designated by each Rite Aid Entity pursuant to paragraph 6 of the Agreement shall also serve as the Compliance Representative for purposes of this CAP and perform the duties regarding implementation of the CAP as set out in the CAP and in paragraph 6 of the Agreement.

The Compliance Representative, designated immediately below, shall also serve as the contact person on behalf of each Rite Aid Entity regarding the implementation of this CAP and for receipt and submission of notices and reports:

Michael Yount
Compliance Representative
Vice President – Regulatory Law
Rite Aid Corporate Headquarters
30 Hunter Lane
Camp Hill, PA 17011
Tel.# 717-761-2633
Fax# 717-975-5952
e-mail: Myount@riteaid.com

Any notices and/or reports provided by OCR to the Compliance Representative shall also be provided to counsel for the Rite Aid Entities:

Kathleen M. Sanzo
Partner
Morgan, Lewis & Bockius
1111 Pennsylvania Avenue, N.W Washington, DC 20004 ksanzo@morgan-lewis.com
(202) 739-5209

(202) 739-3001 (fax)

OCR has identified the following individual as its authorized representative and contact person with whom the Rite Aid Entities, through the Compliance Representative, are to report information regarding their implementation of this CAP:

Valerie Morgan-Alston Regional Manager Office for Civil Rights
U.S. Department of Health and Human Services
233 N. Michigan Avenue, Suite 240
Chicago, IL 60601
Valerie.Alston@hhs.gov
312-886-2359 (Voice Phone)
312-886-1807 (Fax)

OCR agrees to notify the Compliance Representative of any changes in the identity of its contact person or the other information provided above. Any changes in the identity of the contact person on behalf of the Rite Aid Entities shall only be made through the provisions set out in section 6 of the Agreement for the appointment of a successor Compliance Representative.

B. Proof of Submissions

Unless otherwise specified, all notices and reports required by this CAP may be made by any means, including certified mail, overnight mail, or hand delivery, provided that there is proof that such notification was received. For purposes of this requirement, internal facsimile confirmation sheets do not constitute proof of receipt.

III. Term of CAP

The period of compliance (Compliance Period) obligations assumed by the Rite Aid Entities under this CAP shall begin on the Effective Date of this CAP and shall end three (3) years from the date of the Assessor's approved appointment, as provided for in section V.E.2 below. After the expiration of the Compliance Period, the Compliance Representative shall still be obligated to do the following: (a) submit the Periodic Report for the final Reporting Period, as set forth in section VI.B below; (b) submit the response to the Third Year Assessor Report and a Supplemental Assessor Report if one is necessary, as set forth in section V.E.2.c below; and (c) comply with the document retention requirement set forth in section VII below. The Effective Date for this CAP shall be calculated in accordance with paragraph 15 of the Agreement.

IV. Time

In computing any period of time prescribed or allowed by this CAP, the day of the act, event, or default from which the designated period of time begins to run shall not be included. The last day of the period so computed shall be included, unless it is a Saturday, a Sunday, or a legal holiday, in which event the period runs until the end of the next business day.

V. Corrective Action Obligations

The Rite Aid Entities agree to the following:

A. Policies and Procedures

1. The Rite Aid Entities, directly or through the Compliance Representative, shall develop, maintain, and revise, as necessary, uniform, written policies and procedures ("Privacy Policies and Procedures") that: (a) address the Covered Conduct specified in paragraph 2 of the Agreement; and (b) are consistent with the Federal standards that govern the privacy of individually identifiable health information (45 C.F.R. Part 160 and Subparts A and E of Part 164, the "Privacy Rule"). The Rite Aid Entities' Privacy Policies and Procedures shall include, but not necessarily be limited to, the minimum content set forth in section V.C below.

2. The Compliance Representative shall submit the Rite Aid Entities' uniform Privacy Policies and Procedures, consistent with subparagraph 1 above, to OCR within ninety (90) days of the commencement of the Compliance Period for review and approval. OCR may provide any comments or recommended changes to the Compliance Representative. Upon receiving any recommended changes to such Privacy Policies and Procedures from OCR, the Rite Aid Entities, directly or through the Compliance Representative, shall have sixty (60) days in which to revise their Privacy Policies and Procedures accordingly and then have the Compliance Representative submit the revised Privacy Policies and Procedures to OCR for review and approval, which shall not be unreasonably withheld.

3. The Rite Aid Entities shall fully implement their Privacy Policies and Procedures within sixty (60) days of their receipt of OCR's approval.

B. Distribution and Updating of Privacy Policies and Procedures

1. The Rite Aid Entities shall either directly, or through the Compliance Representative, distribute the approved Privacy Policies and Procedures identified in section V.A. of this CAP and any subsequent revisions thereto, to all members of their workforces who have access to PHI, including duties pertaining to the disposal of PHI, within thirty (30) days of OCR's issuance of its written approval of the Privacy Policies and Procedures or of any revisions thereto. The Rite Aid Entities shall also distribute such documents, either directly or through the Compliance Representative, to new members of the workforce who have access to PHI, including duties pertaining to the disposal of PHI, of each Rite Aid Entity within ten (10) business days of the commencement of each such workforce member's engagement by a Rite Aid Entity.

2. Following the distribution of such Privacy Policies and Procedures or revisions thereto, the Rite Aid Entities shall require each member of their

workforce who receives the Policies and Procedures to submit a written or electronic compliance certification stating that the particular workforce member has received, read, understood, and agreed to abide by the Privacy Policies and Procedures. Such written or electronic certification must be received by the appropriate Rite Aid Entity within ten (10) business days of any workforce member's receipt of the Privacy Policies and Procedures and if such certification is not received that workforce member shall not be permitted to perform any services for any Rite Aid Entity that involve PHI until and unless such certification is received.

3. So long as this CAP is in effect, the Rite Aid Entities, directly or through the Compliance Representative, shall assess the Privacy Policies and Procedures required by this CAP, at least annually (and more frequently, if appropriate), and shall update and revise such Privacy Policy and Procedures as necessary.

C. **Minimum Content of the Privacy Policies and Procedures**

The Privacy Policies and Procedures to be adopted by the Rite Aid Entities shall, at minimum, provide for:

1. Administrative and physical safeguards for the disposal of all non-electronic PHI that appropriately and reasonably ensure that such PHI may not be used or disclosed in violation of the Privacy Rule. The administrative and physical safeguards for disposal shall be applicable to the final disposal of such PHI. Final disposal requires shredding, destroying or otherwise making such PHI unreadable or indecipherable.

2. Application of appropriate sanctions (which may include re-training or other instructive corrective action) against members of the Rite Aid Entities' workforces, including supervisors and managers, who fail to comply with the safeguards policies and procedures provided for in subparagraph (1) above.

3. Training, as required by the Privacy Rule, for members of the Rite Aid Entities' workforces who have access to PHI, including duties pertaining to the disposal of PHI, regarding how to implement and comply with the safeguards policies and procedures provided for in subparagraph (1) above. At a minimum, training shall include that which is necessary and appropriate for each member of the workforce of a Rite Aid Entity, who has access to PHI, including the disposal of PHI, to carry out that workforce member's function within the Rite Aid Entity pertaining to the safeguarding and/or disposal of non-electronic PHI.

4. Training, as required by the Privacy Rule, to appropriately and reasonably ensure that all appropriate members of the Rite Aid Entities' workforces who have access to PHI, including duties pertaining to the disposal of PHI, know how to implement and comply with the sanctions policies and procedures provided for in subparagraph (2) above. At a minimum, training shall be that which is necessary and appropriate for each such member of the

workforce who is in a position to implement or enforce the sanctions policy (e.g., any workforce member who has a duty to impose sanctions, or has a duty to report another workforce member whose actions may be cause for the imposition of sanctions).

D. Training

1. The Rite Aid Entities shall provide training to workforce members, who have access to PHI, including the disposal of PHI, as required by the Privacy Rule. The actual written and electronic evidence of training shall be made available for inspection by OCR and/or the Assessor, the appointment of whom is provided for in section V.E.2 below, during normal business hours, should either seek to inspect the documentary evidence that training was completed. So long as the CAP is in force, each Rite Aid Entity shall also provide such training to new members of its workforce, who have access to PHI, including duties pertaining to the disposal of PHI, within thirty (30) days of the new workforce members beginning their service. Each such Rite Aid Entity must also maintain written or electronic evidence of such training as described in the two previous sentences.

2. Each individual member of a Rite Aid Entity's workforce who is required to attend training shall certify, in writing or in electronic form, that the individual has received the required training no later than ten (10) business days after the training has been conducted. The training certification shall specify the date training was completed. All training certificates and course materials shall be retained by the Rite Aid Entity or the Compliance Representative in compliance with section VII.

3. Each Rite Aid Entity, directly or through the Compliance Representative, shall review the training materials annually and shall update the training materials to reflect any changes in policies or procedures being followed by the Rite Aid Entity, federal law, OCR guidance, and/or any material compliance issue(s) discovered during audits or reviews.

4. Each Rite Aid Entity shall prohibit any member of its workforce from using, disclosing, or disposing of PHI, if that workforce member has not completed the requisite training required by subparagraph (1) above.

E. Monitoring

1. <u>Internal Monitoring.</u> The Rite Aid Entities, through the Compliance Representative, shall submit to OCR within ninety (90) days of the Effective Date of this CAP, a written description of their plan to monitor internally their compliance with the Privacy Policies and Procedures required by this CAP (Internal Monitoring Plan). OCR may submit comments and recommendations, if any, for modifications to the Compliance Representative within 30 days of OCR's receipt of the Internal Monitoring Plan. In the event that OCR does submit comments and recommendations, the Rite Aid Entities, either directly or through the Compliance Representative, shall make the changes reasonably

requested by OCR, submit the revised Internal Monitoring Plan to OCR, and, having done so, place the Internal Monitoring Plan into effect.

While this CAP is in effect, the Rite Aid Entities may wish, or be required by changes in the law, technology, or otherwise, to update, revise or prepare a new Internal Monitoring Plan. The Rite Aid Entities, directly or through the Compliance Representative, shall be permitted to do so; provided, that the Rite Aid Entities, through the Compliance Representative, first submit any updated, revised, or new Internal Monitoring Plan to the Assessor, the appointment of whom is provided for in section V.E.2 below, and obtain the Assessor's approval before the Rite Aid Entities implement the revised version of the Internal Monitoring Plan; and, further provided, that the Rite Aid Entities, through the Compliance Representative, also submit any updated, revised, or new Internal Monitoring Plan to OCR for its 30-day review and comment, and obtain OCR's approval, before the Rite Aid Entities implement the revised Internal Monitoring Plan. Whenever the existing Internal Monitoring Plan is updated or revised and the updated or revised version has been approved by both the Assessor and OCR and has then gone into effect, the updated or revised Internal Monitoring Plan shall be deemed to have superseded the prior Internal Monitoring Plan.

2. Assessments.

(a) Selection and Engagement. The Rite Aid Entities shall engage a qualified, objective, independent third-party assessor (the Assessor) which may be the same entity or individual whom the Rite Aid Entities that are parties to the FTC Order engage as an assessor pursuant to Section III of the FTC Order. The Compliance Representative shall inform OCR in writing, within sixty (60) days of the Effective Date, of the name of an individual or entity which the Rite Aid Entities designate to serve as the Assessor. The Assessor may not currently be employed by or affiliated with Rite Aid Corporation or any other Rite Aid Entity and shall not have been employed by or affiliated with any Rite Aid Entity for at least five years prior to the Effective Date. The Compliance Representative shall also simultaneously submit to OCR the proposed Assessor's curriculum vitae or a statement of its expertise in the area of monitoring compliance with federal and/or state statutes and regulations, including privacy statutes and regulations.

Any individual or entity designated by the Compliance Representative to serve as the Assessor must certify in writing at the time of his, her or its designation, and must provide reasonable written documentation to the effect that he, she or it has the requisite expertise and experience regarding the implementation of the Privacy Rule and has the necessary resources and is otherwise able to perform the assessments and reviews described herein in a professionally independent fashion, taking into account any other business relationships or other engagements that the individual or entity may have. OCR shall be permitted to interview an individual who is designated by the Rite Aid Entities to serve as the Assessor or representatives of an entity which is designated. OCR shall either approve or disapprove of the designation in writing.

OCR's approval shall not be unreasonably withheld. If OCR does not approve the designation, OCR shall explain the basis of its disapproval in writing, and the process described above shall be repeated by the Rite Aid Entities, through the Compliance Representative, until OCR has approved a designated Assessor. Upon receiving OCR's approval, the Rite Aid Entities, directly or through the Compliance Representative, shall enter into a written contract with the Assessor for the performance of the assessments and reviews described herein.

(b) <u>Assessor's Duties.</u> The Assessor's duties shall be to conduct assessments of compliance by the Rite Aid Entities with the Corrective Action Obligations set forth in Sections V.A through V.E.1 above and prepare the Assessment Reports described below.

Within ninety (90) days of being approved for service by OCR, the Assessor shall submit to OCR and the Compliance Representative a written plan, describing with adequate detail, the Assessor's plan for fulfilling the duties set forth in this subsection (Assessor's Plan). Within thirty (30) days of its receipt of the Assessor's Plan, OCR shall inform the Compliance Representative of its approval or disapproval of the proposed Assessor Plan. If OCR does not approve the proposed Assessor Plan, OCR shall set forth in writing the reasons for its disapproval and recommendations for the necessary modifications to the proposed Assessor Plan. If the proposed Assessor Plan is not approved by OCR, the Assessor shall submit a revised Assessor Plan to OCR, incorporating OCR's comments and requested revisions, within thirty (30) days of OCR's issuance of its disapproval of the proposed Assessor Plan. The Assessor shall review the Plan at least annually and shall provide OCR and the Compliance Representative with a copy of any revisions to the Plan within ten (10) business days of the Assessor's making such revisions. OCR shall have a reasonable opportunity to comment and make recommendations regarding any revisions or modifications at any time while the CAP is in effect. The Assessor, in his, her, or its discretion, shall make such changes to the revisions as OCR may reasonably request.

(c) Assessor Reports. The Assessor shall prepare written reports (the Assessor Reports) based on the work that the Assessor performs as described in subparagraph (b) above. The Assessor shall provide such written reports to OCR and the Compliance Representative.

Assuming that the Rite Aid Entities do not employ the same Assessor under this CAP that they employ pursuant to the FTC Order, the first Assessor Report shall be due sixty (60) days after the one-year anniversary of OCR's issuance of its approval of the appointment of the Assessor, as provided in subsection (a) above (Assessor's First Year Report). The Assessor shall also submit reports within sixty (60) days of the second anniversary of the date of OCR's approval of the Assessor's appointment (Assessor's Second Year Report) and within sixty (60) days of the third anniversary of the date of OCR's approval of the Assessor's appointment (Assessor's Third Year Report).

In the event that the Rite Aid Entities do employ the same Assessor under this CAP that they employ pursuant to the FTC Order, the Assessor's First Year

Report to OCR shall be due sixty (60) days after the one-year anniversary of the date on which the FTC Order shall have been served by the FTC on the Rite Aid Entities, whether or not that date is earlier than or later than the date that the Assessor's First Year Report would otherwise be due; provided that the Compliance Representative must inform OCR in writing within thirty (30) days of OCR's approving the appointment of the Assessor that the Rite Aid Entities intend to employ the same Assessor pursuant to the FTC Order. In the event that the Rite Aid Entities employ the same Assessor under this CAP that they employ pursuant to the FTC Order, the Assessor's Second Year Report to OCR will be due on the one-year anniversary of the date on which the Assessor's First Year Report to OCR shall have become due pursuant to this CAP. In the event that the Rite Aid Entities employ the same Assessor under this CAP that they employ pursuant to the FTC Order, the Assessor's Third Year Report to OCR shall be due on the two-year anniversary of the date on which the Assessor's First Year Report to OCR shall have become due pursuant to this CAP. The Assessor's First Year Report and the Assessor's Third Year Report to be submitted to OCR may be the same written report that the Assessor submits to the FTC pursuant to Section III of the FTC Order; provided that the Assessor under this CAP is also the Assessor under the FTC Order; and, further provided, that the Assessor's First Year Report and Third Year Report include adequate descriptions of the Assessor's work under the CAP during the reporting period; and, further provided, that if the reporting period covered by the Assessor's First Year Report is less than one year, the Assessor shall be required to file a Supplemental Assessor Report with OCR sixty (60) days after the third anniversary of the date on which OCR approved the appointment of the Assessor, with such report covering work performed by the Assessor during the time between the three-year anniversary of the date on which the FTC Order was served on the Rite Aid Entities and the three-year anniversary of the date on which OCR approved the appointment of the Assessor.

Within sixty (60) days of his or her receipt of each Assessor Report, the Compliance Representative shall submit to OCR and the Assessor a written response to the report. OCR may, but is not required to, comment on any of the reports submitted by the Assessor and/or any response from the Compliance Representative.

The Assessor shall immediately report to the Compliance Representative, the affected Rite Aid Entity(ies), and to OCR on any significant violation of the CAP and/or of the Privacy Policies and Procedures which the Assessor identifies during the course of the performance of his, her or its duties. The Compliance Representative and the affected Rite Aid Entity shall prepare a written response, including, when appropriate, a plan(s) of correction, and provide such response to OCR and the Assessor, within ten (10) business days of the issuance of the Assessor's report of the significant violation.

(d) Retention of Records. The Assessor, the Compliance Representative, and each of the Rite Aid Entities shall retain and make available to OCR, upon OCR's request, all work papers, supporting documentation, correspondence, and draft reports (including those exchanged between the Assessor and the

Compliance Representative or any Rite Aid Entity) related to the Assessor's reviews.

3. Assessor Removal/Termination. The Rite Aid Entities may not terminate the Assessor except for cause and may only do so with OCR's consent, which shall not be unreasonably withheld. In the event that the Rite Aid Entities seek to terminate the Assessor, the Compliance Representative shall provide a written statement to OCR setting out in detail the basis for the request and OCR shall take those steps it deems appropriate in reviewing and deciding whether adequate cause actually exists for the termination of the Assessor. If OCR agrees that the current Assessor should be terminated, OCR will so inform the Compliance Representative in writing and the Rite Aid Entities will be authorized to terminate the services of the current Assessor. If such termination does occur, the Rite Aid Entities must engage a replacement Assessor in accordance with section V.E.2 of this CAP within thirty (30) days of the termination of the previous Assessor, subject to OCR's approval, as provided in Section V.B.2(a). If OCR concludes that cause does not exist for the removal of the original Assessor, it shall so inform the Compliance Representative in writing and the original Assessor shall remain in place and be authorized to function in all respects as if the Rite Aid Entities had never sought to remove the Assessor.

In the event that OCR determines that the Assessor does not possess the expertise, independence, competence, or objectivity required by this CAP, or has failed to carry out the duties and responsibilities set forth in this CAP for the Assessor, OCR may, at its sole discretion, require the Rite Aid Entities to terminate the original Assessor and to engage a replacement Assessor. Prior to requiring such action, OCR shall provide a written explanation to the Compliance Representative explaining the rationale for OCR's decision. In such event, the Rite Aid Entities must engage a replacement Assessor in accordance with section V.E.2 of this CAP within thirty (30) days of the termination of the previous Assessor.

In the event that the Assessor resigns while the CAP is in effect, the Rite Aid Entities, through the Compliance Representative, shall nominate a replacement Assessor, using the same process as described herein for appointing a replacement Assessor who is removed for cause at the instigation of either the Rite Aid Entities or OCR.

4. Validation Review. In the event OCR, in its discretion, determines or has reason to believe that: (a) one or more Assessor Reports fail to conform to the requirements of this CAP; or (b) one or more Assessor Reports are factually inaccurate or otherwise improper or incomplete, OCR may, in its sole discretion, conduct its own review to determine whether the Assessor Report(s) in question complied with the requirements of this CAP and/or are factually inaccurate, incorrect or otherwise improper ("Validation Review").

5. OCR's Authority Is Not Superseded. The use of internal monitoring by the Rite Aid Entities and the Rite Aid Entities' contracting for the services of the Assessor does not affect or limit, in any way, OCR's authority to in-

vestigate complaints against any Rite Aid Entity or conduct additional compliance reviews of any Rite Aid Entity under any applicable statute or regulation that OCR administers.

F. Internal Reporting

1. Procedure for Internal Reporting. The Rite Aid Entities shall require all members of their workforces who have access to PHI, including, but not limited to, responsibility for the disposal of PHI, to report to the Compliance Representative at the earliest possible time any violation of the Privacy Policies and Procedures of which they become aware. The procedure for such reporting shall be set out in the Internal Reporting Procedure which the Compliance Representative shall submit to OCR for its comment and approval within ninety (90) days of the Effective Date of this CAP. The review and approval process of the Internal Reporting Procedure shall be identical to that of the Internal Monitoring Plan, as set out in section V.E.1.

While the CAP is in effect, the Rite Aid Entities, directly or through the Compliance Representative, may determine from time to time to revise or amend the Internal Reporting Procedure; provided that such revisions or amendments may only take effect after the Compliance Representative has presented them to OCR for a 30-day review and made any changes that OCR may reasonably request.

Pursuant to the Internal Reporting Procedure, whenever a Rite Aid Entity or the Compliance Representative learns that a member of the workforce of a Rite Aid Entity who has access to PHI, including duties pertaining to the disposal of PHI, may have violated a relevant portion of the Privacy Policies and Procedures, the Compliance Representative, with the full cooperation of the Rite Aid Entity, shall promptly investigate the allegations raised and shall document each such investigation in writing. Written documents should include, but not necessarily be limited to, notes of all interviews of the affected Rite Aid Entity's employees and any other pertinent members of the Rite Aid Entity's workforce and maintenance of any relevant documents, including e-mails. An investigation shall be triggered whenever any Rite Aid Entity or the Compliance Representative receives a complaint of a specific violation of a relevant portion of the Privacy Policies and Procedures. An investigation by the Compliance Representative shall also be triggered whenever there are news reports of alleged specific violations of the relevant portions of the Privacy Policies and Procedures or complaints of an alleged specific violation of these provisions raised by any government agency; complaints raised by a consumer organization, such as the Better Business Bureau, regarding the disposal of PHI; or findings from the Rite Aid Entities' internal monitoring process that indicate a violation of the relevant provisions of the Privacy Policies and Procedures may have occurred. If a Rite Aid Entity determines that a member of its workforce who has access to PHI, including duties pertaining to the disposal of PHI, has failed to comply with the relevant portion(s) of the Privacy Policies and Procedures or if the Compliance Representative determines that one or more of the members of the workforce of a particular

Rite Aid Entity has violated the relevant provisions of the Privacy Policies and Procedures, the Compliance Representative shall notify both the Assessor and OCR in writing of the finding within thirty (30) business days. Such violation findings shall be known as "Reportable Events." The Compliance Representative's written report to OCR and the Assessor shall include the following information:

a. A complete description of the Reportable Event, including the relevant facts, the persons involved, the date, time and place on which the events occurred, and the provision(s) of the implicated requirement; and

b. A description of the actions taken by the affected Rite Aid Entity and/or the Compliance Representative to mitigate any harm and any further steps that they plan to take to address the problems that gave rise to the violation(s) and prevent them from recurring.

VI. Implementation Report and Periodic Reports

A. Implementation Report. Within 150 days after the receipt of OCR's approval of the Privacy Policies and Procedures and the other documents for which approval is required under this CAP, the Compliance Representative shall submit a written report to OCR and the Assessor summarizing the status of the implementation of the CAP by the Rite Aid Entities. This report, known as the "Implementation Report," shall include:

1. An attestation signed by the Compliance Representative attesting that to the best of his or her knowledge: (a) the portions of the Privacy Policies and Procedures that are required by this CAP are being implemented by each Rite Aid Entity; (b) the Privacy Policies and Procedures have been distributed to each member of the workforce of each Rite Aid Entity as required by this CAP; and (c) all of the compliance certifications required by section V.B.2 of this CAP have been obtained by the Rite Aid Entities, directly or through the Compliance Representative;

2. A copy of all training materials used for the training required by this CAP and a written description of the training, including a summary of the topics covered, the length of the session(s), and a schedule of when the training session(s) were held and/or the days during which on-line training was provided;

3. An attestation signed by the Compliance Representative, attesting that to the best of his or her knowledge members of the workforce of each Rite Aid Entity, who have access to PHI, including, but not limited to, responsibility for the disposal of PHI, have completed the initial training required by this CAP and have executed the training certifications required by section V.D.2;

4. An attestation signed by the Compliance Representative, listing all locations of the retail pharmacies of any Rite Aid Entity (including mailing addresses), the corresponding Rite Aid Entity for each location, the corresponding telephone numbers and fax numbers for each pharmacy location,

and attesting that to the best of his or her knowledge each such location has complied with all of the obligations required of Rite Aid Entities under this CAP, as of the date of the attestation; and

5. An attestation signed by the Compliance Representative, attesting that he or she has reviewed the Implementation Report, has made all reasonable inquiries regarding the thoroughness and accuracy of its contents, and based on such inquiries, believes, to the best of his or her knowledge, that all of the information contained in the Implementation Report is accurate and truthful.

B. Periodic Reports. The one-year period beginning on the date that OCR approves the Privacy Policies and Procedures pursuant to section V.A.2 of this CAP to the first anniversary of that date and each subsequent one-year periods during which this CAP is in effect shall be referred to as "the Reporting Period(s)." The Rite Aid Entities, through the Compliance Representative, shall submit to OCR a Periodic Report for each Reporting Period no later than ninety (90) days after the end of each corresponding Reporting Period, including the final Reporting Period which concludes with the expiration date of the CAP. The Periodic Report shall include:

1. A schedule, topic outline, and copies of the training materials for the training programs regarding the relevant portions of the Privacy Policies and Procedures that were conducted during the Reporting Period that is the subject of the report;

2. An attestation signed by the Compliance Representative, attesting that to the best of his or her knowledge each Rite Aid Entity has obtained and is maintaining written or electronic certifications from all persons that required training pursuant to this CAP during the Reporting Period that they did, in fact, receive the requisite training pursuant to the requirements set forth in this CAP;

3. A summary/description of all engagements between Rite Aid Corporation and/or any other Rite Aid Entity, on the one hand, and the Assessor, on the other hand, including, but not limited to, any outside financial audits, compliance program engagements, or reimbursement consulting, if different from what the Compliance Representative submitted to OCR as part of the Implementation Report;

4. A summary of Reportable Events (as defined in section V.F.1 of this CAP) identified during the Reporting Period, a thorough description of the facts regarding any such Reportable Event, if the Compliance Representative has not previously reported the event, and the status of any corrective and preventative action relating to each such Reportable Event; and

5. An attestation signed by the Compliance Representative, attesting that he or she has reviewed the Periodic Report, has made all reasonable inquiries regarding the thoroughness and accuracy of its contents and, based upon such

review and inquiry, believes, to the best of his or her knowledge, that all of the information contained in the Periodic Report is accurate and truthful.

VII. Document Retention

Each Rite Aid Entity and the Compliance Representative shall maintain for inspection and copying all documents and records relating to compliance with this CAP for six (6) years following the creation of the particular document. The term "document" shall be broadly construed to include, but not be limited to, letters, memoranda, brochures, bulletins, e-mails, CD ROMs, tapes, evidence of possible or alleged improper disclosure, affidavits, court pleadings, and the like.

VIII. Requests for Extensions and Breach Provisions

Each Rite Aid Entity is required to comply with all of their respective CAP obligations.

A. Timely Written Requests for Extensions

The Rite Aid Entities, through the Compliance Representative, in advance of any due date set forth in this CAP, may submit a timely written request for an extension of time to perform any act or file any notification or report required by this CAP. A "timely written request" is defined as a request in writing received by OCR at least ten (10) business days prior to the date by which any act is due to be performed or any notification or report is due to be filed and must contain a description of the facts giving rise to the request. OCR will consider such a request and make a reasonable determination as to whether to grant it, generally providing no more than one 30-day extension of time for a particular deadline without a showing of exigent circumstances.

B. Notice of Material Breach and Intent to Impose CMP

An uncured material breach of this CAP by any Rite Aid Entity, directly or through the acts or omissions of the Compliance Representative, constitutes a breach of the Agreement. Upon a finding by OCR that any Rite Aid Entity has materially breached this CAP, OCR will, pursuant to 45 C.F.R. Part 160, notify the Compliance Representative and the Assessor of the existence of the material breach ("Notice of Material Breach") and will indicate which Rite Aid Entity(ies) allegedly committed a material breach.

C. Response

The Rite Aid Entity(ies) shall have 35 days from the date of receipt of OCR's Notice of Material Breach, directly and through the Compliance Representative, to demonstrate to OCR's satisfaction, that:

1. The Rite Aid Entity(ies) identified in the Notice are in compliance with the obligations of the CAP cited by OCR as being the basis for OCR's declaration of a material breach;

2. The alleged material breach has been cured; or

3. The alleged material breach cannot be cured within the 35-day period, but: (i) the Rite Aid Entity(ies), directly and/or through the Compliance Representative, has/have begun to take the action(s) necessary to cure the breach; (ii) the Rite Aid Entity(ies), with the Compliance Representative's assistance, as appropriate, is/are pursuing an appropriate cure with due diligence; and (iii) the Rite Aid Entity(ies) has/have provided OCR with a written explanation as to why the Rite Aid Entity(ies) cannot cure the breach within 35 days and has/have provided OCR with a reasonable timetable during which the Rite Aid Entity(ies) will be able to cure the breach.

D. Imposition of CMP

If at the conclusion of the 35-day cure period or other time frame described in section VIII.C.3 above, the Rite Aid Entity(ies), with the assistance of the Compliance Representative, fail to meet the requirements of section VIII.C as determined by OCR, OCR may proceed with the imposition of a CMP against the Rite Aid Entities pursuant to 45 C.P.R. Part 160, for the Covered Conduct set forth in paragraph 2 of the Agreement and any other conduct that constitutes a violation of the Privacy Rule, including, but not necessarily limited to, the conduct giving rise to the material breach. OCR will notify the Compliance Representative and Rite Aid Entity(ies) involved in the breach of: OCR's intent to impose a CMP for: (a) the Covered Conduct set forth in paragraph 2 of the Agreement; and (b) the post-Effective Date conduct constituting the material breach, if the conduct constitutes a violation of the Privacy Rule. OCR and the Rite Aid Entities will retain all of the rights and obligations specified under 45 C.F.R. Part 160, Subparts C through E, with respect to the imposition of a CMP under this paragraph.

E. Failure to Pay an Installment of the Resolution Amount when Due

The Rite Aid Entities are required to pay each of the three installments of the Resolution Amount on or before the dates on which they are due, as set forth in paragraph 7 of the Agreement. The Rite Aid Entities' failure to make an Installment Payment by the due date shall be deemed a material breach of the CAP and of the Agreement. Should the Rite Aid Entities fail to pay timely any Installment Payment of the Resolution Amount, OCR may issue a Notice of Material Breach for Failure to Pay an Installment Payment, pursuant to 45 C.F.R. Part 160. In the event that OCR issues such a Notice of Material Breach for Failure to Pay an Installment Payment, the Rite Aid Entities shall have thirty (30) days in which to either: (a) prove that they made the requisite Installment Payment; or (b) make the requisite Installment Payment. 'If the Rite Aid Entities do not make an Installment Payment of the Resolution Amount by the expiration of the thirty-day cure period, OCR may, in its discretion, impose a civil money penalty upon the Rite Aid Entities pursuant to the terms of section VIII.D of this CAP above; provided that the cure period which would trigger OCR's right to impose such a civil money payment would be thirty (30) days for the Rite Aid Entities failure to pay an Installment Payment of the Resolution

Amount, rather than thirty-five (35) days as is otherwise provided for under section VIII.D of this CAP.

For the Rite Aid Entities

_____   _____
Michael Yount   Date
Vice President- Regulatory Law
Compliance Representative

For the Department of Health and Human Services

_____   _____
Valerie Morgan-Alston   Date
Regional Manager, Region V
Office for Civil Rights

Appendix F

Selected HIPAA Materials*

F-1 HHS, Security and Electronic Signature Standards;
     Proposed Rule, 63 Fed. Reg. 43,242 (Aug. 12, 1998) .... (on CD only)

F-2 HHS, Office of Civil Rights, Guidance on Risk Analysis
     Requirements Under the HIPAA Security Rule
     (July 14, 2010) .... (on CD only)

F-3 HHS, Educational Materials for State Attorney General
     Educational Event on Enforcement of Health Privacy
     Laws, etc. (2011) .... (on CD only)

---

*The materials in Appendix F are available only on the CD accompanying this volume.

Table of Cases

*References are to Chapter and footnote number (e.g., **13:** 153 refers to footnote 153 in Chapter 13). Alphabetization is letter-by-letter (e.g., "American Civil Liberties Union" precedes "America Online").*

A

A. v. B., 726 A.2d 924 (N.J. 1999)   **18:** 95, 96
Acara v. Banks, 470 F.3d 569 (5th Cir. 2006)   **8:** 43
Acosta v. Byrum, 638 S.E.2d 246 (N.C. Ct. App. 2006)   **8:** 220–22
Adams v. Commissioner, 170 F.3d 173 (3d Cir. 1999)   **8:** 104
Advanced Micro Devices, Inc. v. Intel Corp., No. 1:05-cv-00441-JJF, MDL No. 05-1717-JJF (D. Del. Sept. 25, 2007)   **17:** 68
Airline Tariff Publ'g Co.; United States v., No. Civ. A. 92-2854 (D.D.C. Nov. 2, 1993)   **14:** 36
Allen v. Wright, No. S06G2018 (Ga. May 14, 2007)   **8:** 229–31
Alliance Laundry Sys. v. Thyssenkrupp Mat'ls, 570 F. Supp. 2d 1061 (E.D. Wis. 2008)   **13:** 70
Allied Tube & Conduit Corp. v. Indian Head, 486 U.S. 492 (1988)   **14:** 89, 91, 92
Allison Engine Co. v. United States *ex rel.* Sanders, 553 U.S. 662 (2008)   **8:** 179
Alpha Capital Anstalt v. Qtrax, 2010 WL 841364 (N.Y. Sup. Ct. Feb. 1, 2010)   **13:** 70
ALS Scan, Inc. v. Digital Serv. Consultants, 293 F.3d 707, 63 USPQ2d 1389 (4th Cir. 2002)   **13:** 19
Aluminum Corp. of Am.; United States v., 148 F.2d 416 (2d Cir. 1945)   **14:** 17
Al-Yusr Townsend & Bottum Co. v. United Mid E. Co., No. Civ. A. 95-1168, 1995 U.S. Dist. LEXIS 14622 (E.D. Pa. 1995)   **18:** 121
American Civil Liberties Union v. Reno, 217 F.3d 162 (3d Cir. 2000)   **5:** 23
American Homecare Fed'n v. Paragon Scientific, 27 F. Supp. 2d 109 (D. Conn. 1998)   **13:** 29
America Online, Inc.
—v. AT&T Corp., 243 F.3d 812, 57 USPQ2d 1902 (4th Cir.), *cert. denied,* 534 U.S. 946 (2001)   **15:** 265; **16:** 24
—v. Booker, 781 So. 2d 423 (Fla. Dist. Ct. App. 2001)   **13:** 153
Anderson
—v. Bell, 234 P.3d 1147 (Utah 2010)   **13:** 72
—United States v.
—— 174 F.3d 515 (5th Cir. 1999)   **8:** 191, 192
—— No. 98-20030-JWL (D. Kan. July 15, 1998)   **18:** 60
Annie Oakley Enters. v. Sunset Tan Corporate & Consulting, 703 F. Supp. 2d 881 (N.D. Ind. 2010)   **13:** 41
Apple Computer, Inc. v. Microsoft Corp., 821 F. Supp. 616, 27 USPQ2d 1081 (N.D. Cal. 1993), *aff'd,* 35 F.3d 1435, 32 USPQ2d 1086 (9th Cir. 1994), *cert. denied,* 513 U.S. 1184 (1995)   **16:** 15
Ariad Pharms., Inc. v. Eli Lilly & Co., 598 F.3d 1336, 94 USPQ2d 1161 (Fed. Cir. 2010)   **15:** 326, 328
Arizona Retail Sys. v. Software Link., 831 F. Supp. 759 (D. Ariz. 1993)   **13:** 188
Arrow Fastener Co. v. Stanley Works, 59 F.3d 384, 35 USPQ2d 1449 (2d Cir. 1995)   **15:** 260
Arrowhead Indus. Water, Inc. v. Ecolochem, Inc., 846 F.2d 731, 6 USPQ2d 1685 (Fed. Cir. 1988)   **15:** 382, 385
Ashcroft
—v. American Civil Liberties Union
—— 532 U.S. 1037, 121 S. Ct. 1997 (2001)   **5:** 23
—— 535 U.S. 564, 122 S. Ct. 1700 (2002)   **5:** 23
—v. Iqbal, 129 S. Ct. 1937 (2009)   **14:** 46
Association of Am. Physicians & Surgeons, Inc. v. Department of Health & Human Servs., 224 F. Supp. 2d 1115 (S.D. Tex. 2002)   **8:** 33
Automated Marine Propulsion Sys., Inc. v. Sverdlin, No. 97-02103 (Tex. Dist. Ct. Oct. 27, 1998)   **18:** 88, 101
A.V. v. iParadigms, 544 F. Supp. 2d 473 (E.D. Va. 2008)   **13:** 167

B

Baldasarre v. Butler
—604 A.2d 112 (N.J. Super. Ct. App. Div. 1992)   **18:** 99
—625 A.2d 458 (N.J. 1993)   **18:** 99
Banks, *In re*, 584 P.2d 284 (Or. 1978)   **18:** 109
Baptist Mem'l Hosp. Sys. v. Sampson, 969 S.W.2d 945 (Tex. 1998)   **9:** 109–11, 113–18
Barden v. HarperCollins Publ'ns, Inc., 863 F. Supp. 41 (D. Mass. 1994)   **16:** 61

Barnett v. Network Solutions, 38 S.W.3d 200 (Tex. App. 2001) *13:* 170

Barwick v. Geico, 2011 WL 1198830 (Ark. Mar. 31, 2011) *13:* 72

Batzel v. Smith, 333 F.3d 1018 (9th Cir. 2003) *16:* 155

Bayer Co. v. United Drug Co., 272 F. 505 (S.D.N.Y. 1921) *15:* 285

Bell Atl. Corp. v. Twombly, 550 U.S. 544 (2007) *14:* 45

Bensusan Rest. Corp. v. King, 937 F. Supp. 295, 40 USPQ2d 1519 (S.D.N.Y. 1996) *13:* 27

Berger McGill, Inc., *In re*, 242 B.R. 413 (Bankr. S.D. Ohio 1999) *18:* 106

Best Van Lines v. Walker, 490 F.3d 239 (2d Cir. 2007) *13:* 21

Betts v. Allstate Ins. Co., 154 Cal. App. 3d 688 (Cal. App. 1984) *16:* 196

Bienz v. Central Suffolk Hosp., 557 N.Y.S.2d 139 (A.D. 2 Dep't 1990) *9:* 81

Bilski v. Kappos, 130 S. Ct. 3218, 177 L. Ed. 2d 792, 95 USPQ2d 1001 (2010) *15:* 307, 308

Bird v. Parsons, 289 F.3d 865, 62 USPQ2d 1905 (6th Cir. 2002) *13:* 28

Birmingham v. Fodor's Travel Publ'ns, Inc., 833 P.2d 70 (Haw. 1992) *16:* 60

Blake v. Murphy Oil USA, 2010 WL 3717245 (N.D. Miss. Sept. 14, 2010) *13:* 70, 95

Blue Cross & Blue Shield of Mich.; United States v., No. Civ. A. 2:10-cv-15155-DPH-MKM (E.D. Mich. 2010) *14:* 78, 79

Blue Cross & Blue Shield of Ohio v. Bingamin, 1996-2 Trade Cas. ¶71,600 (N.D. Ohio 1996) *14:* 76

Blusal Meats, Inc. v. United States, 638 F. Supp. 824 (S.D.N.Y. 1986) *8:* 194

Borjas v. Indiana, 946 N.E.2d 1230 (Ind. 2011) *13:* 70

Bowers v. Baystate Techs., 320 F.3d 1317 (Fed. Cir. 2003) *13:* 178, 196

Brand Name Prescription Drugs Antitrust Litig., *In re*, 94 C 897, MDL 997, 1995 WL 360526 (N.D. Ill. June 15, 1995) *17:* 71

Brooktree Corp. v. Advanced Micro Devices, Inc., 977 F.2d 1555, 24 USPQ2d 1401 (Fed. Cir. 1992) *15:* 192, 196

Brown Shoe Co. v. United States, 370 U.S. 294 (1962) *14:* 57

Brownstein, *In re*, 602 P.2d 655 (Or. 1979) *18:* 109

Burger King Corp. v. Rudzewicz, 471 U.S. 462 (1985) *13:* 10, 11, 44

Burks v. Meredith, 546 S.W.2d 366 (Tex. Civ. App. Waco 1977) *9:* 84

Business Elecs. Corp. v. Sharp Elecs. Corp., 485 U.S. 717 (1988) *14:* 9

Butler v. Kmart Corp., No. 2:05-CV-257-P-A, 2007 WL 2406982 (N.D. Miss. Aug. 20, 2007) *17:* 70, 88

Byrnie v. Town of Cromwell Bd. of Ed., 243 F.3d 93, 85 FEP Cases 323 (2d Cir. 2001) *17:* 53

C

Cacciola v. Nellhaus, 733 N.E.2d 133 (Mass. App. Ct. 2000) *18:* 120

Cafeteria Operators, *In re*, 299 B.R. 411 (N.D. Tex. 2003) *13:* 58

Cairo v. Crossmedia, 2005 WL 756610 (N.D. Cal. Apr. 1, 2005) *13:* 148

Calder v. Jones, 465 U.S. 783 (1984) *13:* 39

Caldwell v. Cheapcaribbean.com, 2010 U.S. Dist. LEXIS 93200 (E.D. Mich. Sept. 8, 2010) *13:* 32

Campbell v. General Dynamics Gov't Sys., 407 F.3d 546, 16 AD Cases 1361 (1st Cir. 2005) *13:* 58, 95

Carafano v. Metrosplash.com, 339 F.3d 1119 (9th Cir. 2003) *16:* 154

CareFirst of Md. v. CareFirst Pregnancy Ctrs., 334 F.3d 390, 67 USPQ2d 1243 (4th Cir. 2004) *13:* 26

Caspi v. Microsoft Network, 732 A.2d 528 (N.J. Super. Ct. App. Div. 1999) *13:* 165

CDN, Inc. v. Kapes, 197 F.3d 1256, 53 USPQ2d 1032 (9th Cir. 1999) *16:* 10

CEM v. Personal Chemistry AB, 192 F. Supp. 2d 438 (W.D.N.C. 2002) *13:* 28

Chemetron Corp. v. Jones, 72 F.3d 341 (3d Cir. 1995) *8:* 102

Chevron U.S.A., Inc. v. Natural Res. Def. Council, Inc., 467 U.S. 837 (1984) *8:* 39

Chocolate, *In re*, 641 F. Supp. 2d 367 (E.D. Pa. 2009) *13:* 43

Choiceparts v. General Motors, No. 01-cv-0067 (N.D. Ill. Jan. 4, 2001) *14:* 63, 64

Cianci v. New Times Publ'g Co., 639 F.2d 54 (2d Cir. 1980) *16:* 66

Citizens & S. Nat'l Bank; United States v., 422 U.S. 86 (1975) *14:* 43

Citizens for Health v. Thompson, No. Civ. A. 03-2267, 2004 WL 765356 (E.D. Pa. Apr. 2, 2004), *cert. denied*, 127 S. Ct. 43 (2006) *8:* 33

City of. *See name of city*

Clanton v. Von Haam, 340 S.E.2d 627 (Ga. Ct. App. 1990) *9:* 83

Cobell v. Kempthorne (formerly Cobell v. Norton), No. 96-1285 (D.D.C. Jan. 30, 2008) *17:* 113

Coleman (Parent) Holdings, Inc. v. Morgan Stanley & Co., No. 03 CA 5045 (Fla. S.D. Cir. Ct. Mar. 2005) *17:* 51

Collins
—v. Collins, No. 424017, 1999 Conn. Super. LEXIS 1803 (Conn. Super. Ct. July 12, 1999) *18:* 118
—v. Texas, 223 U.S. 288 (1912) *9:* 5

Columbia Pictures Indus. v. Bunnell, 2007 WL 2080419 (C.D. Cal. May 29, 2007) *17:* 67

Committee on Legal Ethics v. Frame, 433 S.E.2d 579 (W. Va. 1993) *18:* 109

CompuServe v. Patterson, 89 F.3d 1257 (6th Cir. 1996) *13:* 16

Consolidated Metal Prods. v. American Petroleum Insts., 846 F.2d 284 (5th Cir. 1988) *14:* 85

Container Corp. of Am.; United States v., 393 U.S. 333 (1969)   *14:* 40
Continental Grp., Inc. v. KW Prop. Mgmt., LLC, 622 F. Supp. 2d 1357 (S.D. Fla. 2009)   *15:* 159, 166
Cook, *In re*, 439 F.2d 730, 169 USPQ 298 (C.C.P.A. 1971)   *15:* 326
Corbis Corp. v. Integrity Wealth Mgmt., 2009 WL 3835976 (W.D. Wash. Nov. 16, 2009)   *13:* 159
Cossaboon v. Maine Med. Ctr., 600 F.3d 25 (1st Cir. 2010)   *13:* 20, 40
CoStar Realty Info., Inc. v. Field, 612 F. Supp. 2d 660 (D. Md. 2009)   *13:* 140
Cubby, Inc. v. CompuServe, Inc., 776 F. Supp. 135 (S.D.N.Y. 1991)   *16:* 71–77
CVS Caremark Corp. Complaint, Matter of, FTC (No. C-4259)   *8:* 203
Cybersell, Inc. v. Cybersell, 130 F.3d 414, 44 USPQ2d 1928 (9th Cir. 1997)   *13:* 17

D

Daniel v. American Bd. of Emergency Med., 802 F. Supp. 912 (W.D.N.Y. 1982)   *14:* 98, 99
Dartmouth-Hitchcock Med. Ctr.; Doe v., No. CIV. 00-1000-M, 2001 WL 873063 (D.N.H. July 19, 2001)   *15:* 168, 169
Davidson & Assocs. v. Jung, 422 F.3d 630, 76 USPQ2d 1287 (8th Cir. 2005)   *13:* 174
Day v. Persels, 2011 WL 1770300 (M.D. Fla. May 9, 2011)   *13:* 58
Delfino v. Agilent Techs., Inc., 145 Cal. App. 4th 790 (Cal. Ct. App. 2006)   *16:* 80, 81
Delta Dental Plan; United States v., 1995-1 Trade Cas. ¶71,048 (D. Ariz. 1995)   *14:* 80
Demuth Dev. Corp. v. Merck & Co., 432 F. Supp. 990 (E.D.N.Y. 1977)   *16:* 86–88
Dent v. West Va., 129 U.S. 114 (1889)   *9:* 5
Desktop Techs., Inc. v. Colorworks Reprod. & Design, Inc., 1999 WL 98572 (E.D. Pa. 1999)   *13:* 27
Diamond v. Chakrabarty, 447 U.S. 303, 206 USPQ 193 (1980)   *15:* 116
Doe v. *See name of opposing party*
Dolman v. Agee, 157 F.3d 708, 48 USPQ2d 1305 (9th Cir. 1998)   *16:* 185
Dominguez v. Kelly, 786 S.W.2d 749 (Tex. App. El Paso 1990)   *9:* 75, 76
Dougherty v. Gifford, 826 S.W.2d 668 (Tex. App. Texarkana 1992)   *9:* 86–91, 93
Downs; State v., 923 So. 2d 726 (La. Ct. App. 2005)   *8:* 224
Drew; United States v., 259 F.R.D. 449 (C.D. Cal. 2009)   *13:* 171

E

Eastern R.R. Presidents Conf. v. Noerr Motor Freight, Inc., 365 U.S. 127 (1961)   *14:* 90
Edberg v. Neogen, 17 F. Supp. 2d 104 (D. Conn. 1998)   *13:* 31
Edwards v. Garcia-Gregory, 866 S.W.2d 780 (Tex. App. Houston 14th Dist. 1993)   *9:* 106

Egilman v. Keller & Heckman, LLP, 401 F. Supp. 2d 105, 77 USPQ2d 1070 (D.D.C. 2005)   *15:* 183, 185
E.I. DuPont de Nemours & Co.; United States v., 353 U.S. 586 (1957)   *14:* 56
Eli Lilly & Co.
—Matter of, 120 F.T.C. 243 (1995)   *14:* 60
—v. Medtronic, Inc., 496 U.S. 661, 15 USPQ2d 1121 (1990)   *15:* 88, 105
EPCO Carbon Dioxide Prods. v. JP Morgan Chase Bank, 467 F.3d 466 (5th Cir. 2006)   *13:* 72
Erickson v. Commissioner, 172 B.R. 900 (Bankr. D. Minn. 1994)   *8:* 103

F

F.A. Davis Co. v. Wolters Kluwer Health, Inc., 413 F. Supp. 2d 507 (E.D. Pa. 2005)   *16:* 10
Federal Trade Comm'n. *See name of opposing party*
Feist Publ'ns, Inc. v. Rural Tel. Serv. Co., 499 U.S. 340, 111 S. Ct. 1282, 18 USPQ2d 1275 (1991)   *15:* 113, 115, 133, 139; *16:* 9
Feldman v. Google, 513 F. Supp. 2d 229 (E.D. Pa. 2007)   *13:* 170
Fenn v. Mleads Enters., 137 P.3d 706 (Utah 2006)   *13:* 30
Ferguson v. Lurie, 139 F.R.D. 362 (N.D. Ill. 1991)   *18:* 126
Fermata Int'l Melodies, Inc. v. Champions Golf Club, Inc., 712 F. Supp. 1257, 11 USPQ2d 1460 (S.D. Tex. 1989), *aff'd,* 915 F.2d 1567 (5th Cir. 1990)   *16:* 17
Ferrer; United States v., No. 0:06-cr-60261 (S.D. Fla. Sept. 7, 2006)   *8:* 176
FieldTurf, Inc. v. Triexe Mgmt. Grp., Inc., 2003 U.S. Dist. LEXIS 22280 (N.D. Ill. Dec. 10, 2003)   *16:* 49
Fiser v. Dell, 165 P.3d 328 (N.M. Ct. App. 2007)   *13:* 160
Fisher, *In re*, 427 F.2d 833, 166 USPQ 18 (C.C.P.A. 1970)   *15:* 321, 327
Flav-O-Rich, Inc. v. North Carolina Milk Comm'n, 593 F. Supp. 13 (D.N.C. 1983), *aff'd,* No. 83-2066, 734 F.2d 11 (4th Cir. Apr. 12, 1984), *cert. denied,* 469 U.S. 853, 105 S. Ct. 176 (1984)   *14:* 41, 42
Floyd v. WBTW, 2007 U.S. Dist. LEXIS 92482 (S.D. Cal. Dec. 17, 2007)   *16:* 50
FNS Mortg. Serv. Corp. v. Pacific Gen. Grp., Inc., 29 Cal. Rptr. 2d 916 (Cal. Ct. App. 1994)   *16:* 63, 64
Fogerty v. Fantasy, Inc., 510 U.S. 517, 114 S. Ct. 1023, 29 USPQ2d 1881 (1994)   *16:* 19
Fonovisa, Inc. v. Cherry Auction, Inc., 76 F.3d 259, 37 USPQ2d 1590 (9th Cir. 1996)   *16:* 16
Forrest v. Verizon Commc'ns, 805 A.2d 1007 (D.C. 2002)   *13:* 164
Forsyth v. First Trenton Indem., 2010 WL 2195996 (N.J. Super. Ct. App. Div. May 28, 2010)   *13:* 170
Fortson v. Winstead, McGuire, Sechrest & Minick, 961 F.2d 469 (4th Cir. 1992)   *18:* 125

Fractional Villas v. Tahoe Clubhouse, 2009 WL 465997 (S.D. Cal. Feb. 25, 2009) **13:** 77
Fruehauf Corp. v. FTC, 603 F.2d 345 (2d Cir. 1979) **14:** 58, 59
Fuchs; United States v., No. 3:02CR0369P (N.D. Tex. Feb. 23, 2005), *aff'd,* 467 F.3d 889 (5th Cir. 2006) **9:** 26

G

Gagnon v. Continental Casualty Co., 211 Cal. App. 3d 1598 (Cal. App. 1989) **16:** 196
Gaiman v. McFarlane, 360 F.3d 644, 69 USPQ2d 1946 (7th Cir. 2004) **15:** 122, 123
Galvan v. Downey, 933 S.W.2d 316 (Tex. App. Houston 14th Dist. 1996) **9:** 103
GeoCities, *In re,* No. C-3849, 1999 FTC LEXIS 17 (FTC Feb. 5, 1999) **16:** 136, 137
Georgia Dep't of Transp. v. Norris, 474 S.E.2d 216 (Ga. Ct. App. 1996), *rev'd,* 486 S.E.2d 826 (Ga. 1997) **18:** 23
Gibson; United States v., No. CR04-0374RSM, 2004 WL 2188280 (W.D. Wash. Aug. 19, 2004) **8:** 172
Goodman, *In re,* 11 F.3d 1046, 29 USPQ2d 2010 (Fed. Cir. 1993) **15:** 296
Gorman v. Ameritrade Holding Corp., 293 F.3d 506 (D.C. Cir. 2002) **13:** 22
Grand Jury Subpoenas, *In re,* 144 F.3d 653 (10th Cir. May 15, 1998) **18:** 60
Grand Union Co. v. United States, 696 F.2d 888 (11th Cir. 1983) **8:** 186
Granewich v. Harding, 329 Or. 47, 985 P.2d 788 (1999) **18:** 111
Greate Bay Hotel & Casino, Inc. v. City of Atl. City, 624 A.2d 102 (N.J. Super. Ct. Law Div. 1993) **18:** 122
Greber; United States v., 760 F.2d 68 (3d Cir. 1985) **8:** 182, 211
Green v. AOL, 318 F.3d 465 (3d Cir. 2003) **16:** 156
Greenberg v. National Geographic Soc'y, 244 F.3d 1267, 58 USPQ2d 1267 (11th Cir. 2001) **13:** 196
Griffin; United States v., 401 F. Supp. 1222 (S.D. Ind. 1975) **8:** 196
Griswold v. Connecticut, 381 U.S. 479 (1965) **5:** 10
Griva v. Davison, 637 A.2d 830 (D.C. 1994) **18:** 116
Groff v. America Online, 1998 WL 307001 (R.I. Super. Ct. May 27, 1998) **13:** 170
GTE New Media Servs. v. Ameritech, 21 F. Supp. 2d 27 (D.D.C. 1998) **13:** 32
Gulf Offshore Co. v. Mobil, 453 U.S. 473 (1981) **8:** 162
Gutter v. Dow Jones, Inc., 490 N.E.2d 898 (Ohio 1986) **16:** 59

H

Haas v. Four Seasons Campground, 952 A.2d 688 (Pa. Super. 2008) **13:** 28
Hagood, United States *ex rel.* v. Sonoma County Water Agency, 81 F.3d 1465 (9th Cir. 1996) **8:** 184
Hall v. Tomball Nursing Ctr., Inc., 926 S.W.2d 617 (Tex. App. Houston 14th Dist. 1996) **9:** 95
Hamilton; United States v., 413 F.3d 1138 (10th Cir. 2005) **17:** 104
Hangar One, Inc.; United States v., 563 F.2d 1155 (5th Cir. 1977) **8:** 186
Hanlester Network v. Shalala, 51 F.3d 1390 (9th Cir. 1995) **8:** 181
Harper & Row Publishers, Inc. v. Nation Enter., 471 U.S. 539, 105 S. Ct. 2218, 225 USPQ 1073 (1985) **15:** 116
Hart v. Van Zandt, 399 S.W.2d 791 (Tex. 1965) **9:** 95
Health Grades, Inc. v. Robert Wood Johnson Univ. Hosp., Inc., 634 F. Supp. 2d 1226, 92 USPQ2d 1583 (D. Colo. 2009) **16:** 12–14
Hearst v. Goldberger, 1997 WL 97097 (S.D. N.Y. 1997) **13:** 28
Hearst Trust
—Federal Trade Comm'n v., No. Civil 1:01CV00734 (D.D.C. Apr. 4, 2001), *consent judgment,* No. Civil 1:01CV00734 (D.D.C. Dec. 14, 2001) **14:** 32–34
—United States v., No. Civil 1:01CV02119 (D.D.C. Oct. 10, 2001) **14:** 34
Helicopteros Nacionales de Columbia v. Hall, 466 U.S. 408 (1984) **13:** 11
Hemi Grp.; State of Ill. v., 622 F.3d 754 (7th Cir. 2010) **13:** 22, 34
Henning v. Suarez, 713 F. Supp. 2d 459 (E.D. Pa. 2010) **13:** 34, 40
Henry v. United States, 73 F. Supp. 2d 1303 (N.D. Fla. 1999) **8:** 104
High Country Investor v. McAdams, 221 F. Supp. 2d 99 (D. Mass. 2002) **13:** 27
Hill v. Gateway 2000, 105 F.3d 1147 (7th Cir.), *cert. denied,* 522 U.S. 808 (1997) **13:** 158, 181–84, 192
Hindo v. University of Health Scis., 65 F.3d 608 (7th Cir. 1995) **8:** 184
Hines v. Overstock.com, Inc., 668 F. Supp. 2d 362 (E.D.N.Y. 2009), *aff'd,* 380 F. App'x 22, 2010 WL 2203030 (2d Cir. June 3, 2010) **13:** 138, 139
Hinners v. Robery, 336 S.W.3d 891 (Ky. 2011) **13:** 29
Hitachi v. Cain, 106 S.W.3d 776 (Tex. App. 2003) **13:** 30
Hoehling v. Universal City Studios, Inc., 618 F.2d 972, 205 USPQ 681 (2d Cir. 1980) **15:** 379, 380
Holowko; People v., 486 N.E.2d 877 (Ill. 1985) **17:** 102
Home Oxygen & Med. Equip. Co., *In re,* FTC Nos. 901-0109 & 901-0020 (1994) **14:** 55
Hood v. Phillips, 554 S.W.2d 160 (Tex. 1977) **9:** 95
Hopper v. Frank, 16 F.3d 92 (5th Cir. 1994) **18:** 116
Hotmail Corp. v. Van Money Pie, 1998 WL 388389 (N.D. Cal. Apr. 16, 1998) **13:** 152
Hubbert v. Dell, 835 N.E.2d 113 (Ill. App. Ct. 2005) **13:** 145

I

iLAN Sys. v. Netscout Serv. Level Corp., 183 F. Supp. 2d 328, 68 USPQ2d 1832 (D. Mass. 2002) *13:* 125, 172, 173

Illinois Wholesale Cash Register v. PCG Trading, 2008 WL 4924817 (N.D. Ill. Nov. 13, 2008) *13:* 188

I.M.S. Inquiry Mgmt. Sys., Ltd. v. Berkshire Info. Sys., Inc., 307 F. Supp. 2d 521, 70 USPQ2d 1105 (S.D.N.Y. 2004) *15:* 182, 184

Indiana Fed'n of Dentists; Federal Trade Comm'n v., 476 U.S. 447, 106 S. Ct. 2009 (1986) *14:* 11

In re. See name of party

International Airport Ctrs., LLC v. Citrin, 440 F.3d 418, 24 IER Cases 129 (7th Cir. 2006) *15:* 161

International Casings Grp. v. Premium Standard Farms, 358 F. Supp. 2d 863 (W.D. Mo. 2005) *13:* 74

International Shoe Co. v. Washington, 326 U.S. 310 (1945) *13:* 12, 44

I.S. v. Washington Univ., No. 4:11CV235SNLJ, 2011 WL 2433585 (E.D. Mo. June 14, 2011) *8:* 223

Island Software & Computer Serv., Inc. v. Microsoft Corp., 413 F.3d 257, 75 USPQ2d 1290 (2d Cir. 2005) *16:* 186

Ismoila; United States v., 100 F.3d 380 (5th Cir. 1996) *8:* 191

J

Jackson; United States v. No. CR-08-00430 (C.D. Cal. Apr. 9, 2008) (indictment) *8:* 176

Jain; United States v., 93 F.3d 436 (8th Cir. 1996) *8:* 181

Jallali v. National Bd. of Osteopathic Med. Exam'rs, 2009 WL 1818380 (Ind. Ct. App. May 28, 2010) *13:* 169

JDA Health Sys. v. Chap*in re*venue Cycle Mgmt., 2011 WL 2518938 (N.D. Ill. June 23, 2011) *13:* 34

Jefferson v. Best Buy, 2010 WL 1533107 (M.D. Ala. Mar. 18, 2010) *13:* 70, 95

Jefferson Parish Hosp. Dist. No. 2 v. Hyde, 466 U.S. 2, 104 S. Ct. 1551 (1984) *14:* 11

Jennings v. AC Hydraulic, 383 F.3d 546 (7th Cir. 2004) *13:* 20

Jesse v. Danforth, 169 Wis. 2d 229, 485 N.W.2d 63 (1992) *18:* 107, 108, 112

Johnson
—v. Superior Ct., 45 Cal. Rptr. 2d 312 (Cal. Ct. App. 1995) *18:* 126
—v. Whitehurst, 652 S.W.2d 441 (Tex. App. Houston 1st Dist. 1983) *9:* 84, 106

Johnston; United States v., 146 F.3d 785 (10th Cir. 1998) *8:* 195

Jones v. J. B. Lippincott Co., 694 F. Supp. 1216 (D. Md. 1988) *16:* 56–58

Juno Online Servs., LP v. June Lighting, Inc., 979 F. Supp. 684, 44 USPQ2d 1913 (N.D. Ill. 1997) *16:* 42

K

Kaminiski v. Land Tech, 2011 WL 1035533 (Cal. Ct. App. Mar. 23, 2011) *13:* 80

Kansas *ex rel.* Stovall v. Alivio, 61 P.3d 687 (Kan. 2003) *9:* 27

Karp v. Cooley, 493 F.2d 408 (5th Cir.), *cert. denied*, 419 U.S. 845 (1974) *9:* 102

Kats; United States v., 871 F.2d 105 (9th Cir. 1989) *8:* 182

K.C.P.L. v. Nash, 1998 WL 823657 (S.D.N.Y. 1998) *13:* 29

Kemmel; United States v., 160 F. Supp. 718 (M.D. Pa. 1958) *8:* 196

Kentucky Speedway, LLC v. National Ass'n of Stock Car Auto Racing, No. 05-138-WOB, 2006 WL 5097354 (E.D. Ky. Dec. 18, 2006) *17:* 83, 84

Kerr v. Dillard Store Servs., 2009 WL 385863 (D. Kan. Feb. 17, 2009) *13:* 77

Kewanee Oil Co. v. Bicron Corp., 416 U.S. 470, 181 USPQ 673 (1974) *15:* 340

King v. Flamm, 442 S.W.2d 679 (Tex. 1969) *9:* 84

Klocek v. Gateway, 104 F. Supp. 2d 1332 (D. Kan. 2000) *13:* 195

Kopituk; United States v., 690 F.2d 1289 (11th Cir. 1982) *8:* 218

Krause; United States v., 367 B.R. 740 (D. Kan. June 4, 2007) *17:* 66

Krizek; United States v., 909 F. Supp. 32 (D.D.C. 1995), *rev'd,* 111 F.3d 934 (D.C. Cir. 1997) *8:* 120–22

KSR Int'l Co. v. Teleflex, Inc., 550 U.S. 398, 127 S. Ct. 1727, 82 USPQ2d 1385 (2007) *15:* 318

L

LaHue; United States v., No. 97-20031-01-JWL (D. Kan. Indictment filed June 11, 1997) *18:* 60

Lakin v. Prudential Sec., 348 F.3d 704 (8th Cir. 2003) *13:* 19

Leegin Creative Leather Prods. v. PSKS, Inc., 551 U.S. 877 (2007) *14:* 12, 13

LeNotre v. Cohen, 979 S.W.2d 723 (Tex. App. Houston 1st Dist. 1998) *9:* 95

Lexmark Int'l v. Static Control Components, 387 F.3d 522, 72 USPQ2d 1839 (6th Cir. 2004) *13:* 196

Liberty Fin. Cos., *In re*, No. C-3891 (FTC Aug. 12, 1999) *16:* 138

Lieschke v. Realworks, 2000 WL 198424 (N.D. Ill. Feb. 11, 2000) *13:* 163

Lockheed Martin Corp. v. Network Solutions, Inc., 194 F.3d 980, 52 USPQ2d 1481 (9th Cir. 1999) *16:* 42

Logan v. Department of Veteran Affairs, 357 F. Supp. 2d 149 (D.D.C. 2004) *15:* 155

Loparex v. MPI Release Techs., 2011 WL 1326274 (S.D. Ind. Mar. 25, 2011) *13:* 95

Lorillard Tobacco Co. v. Reilly, 533 U.S. 525, 121 S. Ct. 2404 (2001) *16:* 83

Lorraine v. Markel Am. Ins. Co., No. PWG-06-1893, 241 F.R.D. 534 (D. Md. 2007) *17:* 99–110; *18:* 21

Luna v. Nering, 426 F.2d 95 (5th Cir. 1970) **9:** 103
Lunney v. Prodigy Servs. Co., 723 N.E.2d 539 (N.Y. 1999) **16:** 51
LVRC Holdings, LLC v. Brekka, 581 F.3d 1127, 29 IER Cases 1153 (9th Cir. 2009) **15:** 162
Lyman; United States v., 190 F. 414 (D. Or. 1911) **8:** 195

M

Magnetic Audiotape Antitrust Litig., *In re*, 171 F. Supp. 2d 179 (S.D.N.Y. 2001) **13:** 28
Magyar v. St. Joseph Reg'l Med. Ctr., 544 F.3d 766, 104 FEP Cases 449 (7th Cir. 2008) **13:** 128
Major v. McCakkister, 302 S.W.3d 227 (Mo. Ct. App. 2009) **13:** 148
M.A. Mortenson. v. Timberline Software, 998 P.2d 305 (Wash. 2000) (en banc) **13:** 154, 195
Manion v. Nagin, No. Civ. 00-238, 2004 WL 234402 (D. Minn. Feb. 5, 2004) **18:** 114
Manning v. Flannery, 2010 WL 55295 (E.D. Pa. Jan. 6, 2010) **13:** 42, 45
Manshul Constr. Corp., *In re*, 228 B.R. 532 (Bankr. S.D.N.Y. 1999) **18:** 106
Marcus, United States *ex rel.* v. Hess, 317 U.S. 537, 63 S. Ct. 379 (1943) **8:** 214
Maryland Cas. Co. v. Pacific Coal & Oil Co., 312 U.S. 270 (1941) **15:** 384
Marzocchi, *In re*, 439 F.2d 220, 169 USPQ 367 (C.C.P.A. 1971) **15:** 324
Matter of. *See name of party*
McBee v. Delica Co., 417 F.3d 107, 75 USPQ2d 1609 (1st Cir. 2005) **13:** 20
McCluskey v. Bedford High Sch., 2010 WL 5525153 (E.D. Mich. Dec. 30, 2010) **13:** 33
McDaniel v. Appraisal Inst., 117 F.3d 421 (9th Cir. 1997), *cert. denied*, 523 U.S. 1022 (1998) **14:** 88
McGee v. International Life Ins. Co., 355 U.S. 220 (1957) **13:** 44
McMunigal v. Bloch, 2010 WL 5399219 (N.D. Cal. Dec. 23, 2010) **13:** 95
McTyre Trucking Co., *In re*, 223 B.R. 588 (Bankr. M.D. Fla. 1998) **8:** 104
Mead Corp.; United States v., 533 U.S. 218 (2001) **8:** 39, 40
MedImmune, Inc. v. Genentech, Inc., 549 U.S. 118, 81 USPQ2d 1225 (2007) **15:** 383, 384
Merck KGaA v. Integra Lifesciences I, Ltd., 545 U.S. 193, 74 USPQ2d 1801 (2005) **15:** 106
Metallurgical Indus., Inc. v. Fourtek, Inc., 790 F.2d 1195, 229 USPQ 945 (5th Cir. 1986) **15:** 342
Microsoft Corp. v. i4i Ltd. P'ship, 131 S. Ct. 647 (2010) **15:** 319
Mid City Bowling Lanes & Sports Palace, Inc. v. Invercrest, Inc., 35 F. Supp. 2d 507 (E.D. La. 1999) **13:** 27
Mieczkowski v. Masco, 997 F. Supp. 782 (E.D. Tex. 1998) **13:** 33
Milbank, Tweed, Hadley & McCloy v. Boon, 13 F.3d 537 (2d Cir. 1994) **18:** 127

Miller v. Sullivan, 625 N.Y.S.2d 102 (A.D. 3d Dep't 1995) **9:** 83
Mine Workers v. Pennington, 381 U.S. 657 (1965) **14:** 90
Mink v. AAAA Dev., 190 F.3d 333, 52 USPQ2d 1218 (5th Cir. 1999) **13:** 17
Molnlycke Health Care v. Dumex Med. Surgical Prods., 64 F. Supp. 2d 448 (E.D. Pa. 1999) **13:** 45
Moore
—v. Lee, 109 Tex. 391, 211 S.W. 214 (1919) **9:** 84
—v. Microsoft Corp., 293 A.D.2d 587 (N.Y. App. Div. 2002) **13:** 166
Morgan Stanley & Co. v. Coleman (Parent) Holdings, Inc., No. 4D05-2606 (Fla. Dist. Ct. App. Mar. 12, 2007) **17:** 51
Morin v. Trupin, 711 F. Supp. 97 (S.D.N.Y. 1989) **18:** 125
Moseley v. V Secret Catalogue, Inc., 537 U.S. 418, 65 USPQ2d 1801 (2003) **15:** 278, 279
Motise v. America Online, 346 F. Supp. 2d 563 (S.D.N.Y. 2004) **13:** 140
Motorola, Inc. v. Fairchild Camera & Instrument Corp., 366 F. Supp. 1173, 177 USPQ 614 (D. Ariz. 1973) **15:** 341
Mount Hawley Ins. Co. v. Felman Prod., Inc., 271 F.R.D. 125 (S.D. W. Va. 2010) **18:** 11
Mruz v. Caring, Inc., 991 F. Supp. 701 (D.N.J. 1998) **18:** 90

N

Naldi v. Grunberg, 80 A.D.3d 1 (N.Y. App. Div. 2010) **13:** 58
Nelson; United States v., D.C. No. CR-01-142R (10th Cir. Sept. 20, 2004) **9:** 26
Neogen v. Neo Gen Screening, 282 F.3d 883, 61 USPQ2d 1845 (6th Cir. 2002) **13:** 19, 33
Net2Phone v. Superior Court, 135 Cal. Rptr. 2d 149 (2003) **13:** 144
Neuson v. Macy's, 249 P.3d 1054 (Wash. Ct. App. 2011) **13:** 81
Nevauex v. Park Place Hosp., Inc., 656 S.W.2d 923 (Tex. App. Beaumont 1983) **9:** 107, 108
New York v. Hernandez, 915 N.Y.S.2d 824 (N.Y. City Ct. 2011) **13:** 74
New York Times v. Sullivan, 376 U.S. 254 (1964) **16:** 82
Ni v. Slocum, 127 Cal. Rptr. 3d 620 (2011) **13:** 72
Northern Natural Gas Co. v. Federal Power Comm'n, 399 F.2d 953 (D.C. Cir. 1968) **14:** 51
Northern Pac. Ry. Co. v. United States, 356 U.S. 1, 78 S. Ct. 514 (1958) **14:** 10, 11
Northlake Med. Ctr., LLC v. Queen, 634 S.E.2d 486 (Ga. Ct. App. 2006) **8:** 231
Northwest Med. Labs. v. Blue Cross & Blue Shield, 775 P.2d 863 (Or. Ct. App. 1989), *aff'd*, 310 Or. 72 (1990) **14:** 67, 68
Northwest Wholesale Stationers v. Pacific Stationery & Printing Co., 472 U.S. 284 (1985) **14:** 47, 48

Norwalk Cmty. Coll.; Doe v., No. 3:04-cv-1976, 2007 WL 2066496 (D. Conn. July 16, 2007) *17:* 67

Novell v. Network Trade Ctr., 25 F. Supp. 2d 1218 (D. Utah 1997) *13:* 189, 190

Nujten, *In re*, 500 F.3d 1346, 84 USPQ2d 1495 (Fed. Cir. 2007) *15:* 308

N.Y. Mercantile Exch., Inc. v. IntercontinentalExchange, Inc., 497 F.3d 109, 83 USPQ2d 1609 (2d Cir. 2007) *16:* 11

O

O'Connell; United States v., 890 F.2d 563 (1st Cir. 1989) *8:* 186

Oldfield v. Pueblo De Bahia Lora, 558 F.3d 1210 (11th Cir. 2009) *13:* 19, 36–38

Opdyke v. Kent Liquor Mart, Inc., 181 A.2d 579 (Del. Ch. 1962) *18:* 109

Oppenheimer Fund, Inc. v. Sanders, 437 U.S. 340 (1978) *17:* 43

Ortiz v. Shah, 905 S.W.2d 609 (Tex. App. Houston 14th Dist. 1995) *9:* 76, 94

P

Pacific Bell Tel. Co. v. LinkLine Commc'ns, Inc., 555 U.S. 438 (2009) *14:* 66

Panavision Int'l LP v. Toeppen, 141 F.3d 1316, 46 USPQ2d 1511 (9th Cir. 1998) *15:* 277

Park; United States v., 421 U.S. 658 (1975) *16:* 106

Parker v. Flook, 437 U.S. 584, 198 USPQ 193 (1978) *15:* 116

Park Place Hosp. v. Estate of Milo, 909 S.W.2d 508 (Tex. 1995) *9:* 95

Parks Inns Int'l v. Pacific Plaza Hotels, 5 F. Supp. 2d 762 (D. Ariz. 1998) *13:* 34

Patrick v. Burget, 486 U.S. 94 (1988) *14:* 96, 97

Patriot Sys., Inc. v. C-Cubed Corp, 21 F. Supp. 2d 1318, 50 USPQ2d 1146 (D. Utah 1998) *13:* 27

Payment Card Interchange Fee & Merch. Disc. Antitrust Litig., *In re*, MD 05-1720 (JG) (JO), 2007 WL 121426 (E.D.N.Y. Jan. 12, 2007) *17:* 80–82

Penn-Olin Chem. Co.; United States v., 378 U.S. 158 (1964) *14:* 52

People v. *See name of opposing party*

Peskoff v. Faber, 240 F.R.D. 26 (D.D.C. 2007) *17:* 86

Peterson v. St. Cloud Hosp., 460 N.W.2d 635 (Minn. Ct. App. 1990) *9:* 90

Phillips; United States v., 477 F.3d 215 (5th Cir. 2007) *15:* 160

Pinehurst, Inc. v. Wick, 256 F. Supp. 2d 424, 66 USPQ2d 1610 (M.D.N.C. 2003) *16:* 48

Pitney Bowes, Inc. v. Hewlett-Packard Co., 182 F.3d 1298, 51 USPQ2d 1161 (Fed. Cir. 1999) *15:* 288

Pogue, United States *ex rel.* v. American Healthcorp., 914 F. Supp. 1507 (M.D. Tenn. 1996) *8:* 213

Polaroid Corp. v. Polarad Elecs. Corp., 287 F.2d 492, 128 USPQ 411 (2d Cir. 1961) *15:* 377

Pollstar v. Gigmania, 170 F. Supp. 2d 974 (E.D. Cal. 2000) *13:* 133, 147

Polygram Int'l Publ'g, Inc. v. Nevada/TIG, Inc., 855 F. Supp. 1314, 32 USPQ2d 1481 (D. Mass. 1994) *16:* 16

Powell v. Newton, 703 S.E.2d 723 (N.C. 2010) *13:* 74

Practice Mgmt. Info. Corp. v. American Med. Ass'n, 121 F.3d 516, 45 USPQ2d 1780 (9th Cir. 1997) *15:* 212–18

ProCD v. Zeidenberg, 86 F.3d 1447, 39 USPQ2d 1161 (7th Cir. 1996) *13:* 125, 158, 178–80, 196

Prometheus Labs. v. Mayo Collaboratives, 581 F.3d 1336, 92 USPQ2d 1075 (Fed. Cir. 2009) *15:* 309

Prudential Ins. Co. of Am.
—v. Dukoff, 674 F. Supp. 2d 401 (E.D.N.Y. 2009) *13:* 58
—v. Prusky, 413 F. Supp. 2d 489 (E.D. Pa. 2005) *13:* 61

Pucci v. Santi, 711 F. Supp. 916 (N.D. Ill. 1989) *18:* 126

Q

Quabaug Rubber Co. v. Fabiano Shoe Co., 567 F.2d 154, 195 USPQ 689 (1st Cir. 1977) *16:* 27

Qualitex Co. v. Jacobson Prods. Co., 115 S. Ct. 1300, 34 USPQ2d 1161 (1995) *15:* 256, 258

Quintel Corp., N.V. v. Citibank, N.A., 589 F. Supp. 1235 (S.D.N.Y. 1984) *18:* 125

Quirk, United States *ex rel.* v. Madonna Towers, Inc., 278 F.3d 765 (8th Cir. 2002) *8:* 183

R

Radio Steel & Mfg. Co. v. MTD Prods., Inc., 788 F.2d 1554, 229 USPQ 431 (Fed. Cir. 1986) *15:* 377

Rallis v. Cassady, 100 Cal. Rptr. 2d 763 (Cal. Ct. App. 2000) *18:* 102

RealPage v. EPS, 560 F. Supp. 2d 539 (E.D. Tex. 2007) *13:* 170, 175

Recursion Software v. Interactive Intelligence, 425 F. Supp. 2d 756 (N.D. Tex. 2006) *13:* 171

Register.com v. Verio, 356 F.3d 393, 69 USPQ2d 1545 (2d Cir. 2004) *13:* 133, 146

Reno, City of v. Reno Police Protective Ass'n, 59 P.3d 1212 (Nev. 2002), *modified on denial of reh'g*, 2003 Nev. LEXIS 25 (Nev. May 14, 2003) *18:* 12

Responsible Citizens v. Superior Ct., 20 Cal. Rptr. 2d 756 (Cal. Ct. App. 1993) *18:* 116

Revell v. Lidov, 317 F.3d 467 (5th Cir. 2002) *13:* 17

ReverseAuction.com, Inc.; Federal Trade Comm'n v., No. 000032 (D.D.C. Jan. 6, 2000) *16:* 138

Rhode Island Depositors Econ. Prot. Corp. v. Hayes, 64 F.3d 22 (1st Cir. 1995) *18:* 125

Rhone Poulenc Agro v. Dekalb Genetics, 284 F.3d 1323, 62 USPQ2d 1187, 62 USPQ2d 1188 (Fed. Cir. 2002) *13:* 125

Rice v. Strunk, 670 N.E.2d 1280 (Ind. 1996) *18:* 116

Richter v. Van Amberg, 97 F. Supp. 2d 1255 (D.N.M. 2000) *18:* 125

Rimkus Consulting Grp. v. Cammarata, 688 F. Supp. 2d 598 (S.D. Tex. 2010) *18:* 17

Rite Aid Corp. Complaint, Matter of, FTC (No. C-4308) *8:* 203

Roberts v. Heim, 123 F.R.D. 614 (N.D. Cal. 1988) *18:* 126

Roblor Mktg. Grp. v. GPS Indus., 645 F. Supp. 2d 1130 (S.D. Fla. 2009) *13:* 19

Roche Prods. v. Bolar Pharm. Co., 733 F.2d 858, 221 USPQ 937 (Fed. Cir. 1984) *15:* 103

Roe v. Wade, 410 U.S. 113 (1973) *5:* 11

Rogers v. Dell Computer Corp., 138 P.3d 826 (Mont. 2005) *13:* 155, 156

Roman v. New York City, 442 N.Y.S.2d 945 (N.Y. App. Div. 1981) *16:* 52–55

Rosefielde v. Falcon Jet Corp., 701 F. Supp. 1053 (D.N.J. 1988) *14:* 43

Roser v. Jackson & Perkins, 2010 WL 4823074 (N.D. Ill. Nov. 15, 2010) *13:* 34

Rosman v. Shapiro, 653 F. Supp. 1441 (S.D.N.Y. 1987) *18:* 109

Ross v. Sher, 483 S.W.2d 297 (Tex. Civ. App. Houston 14th Dist. 1972) *9:* 84

Roy, United States *ex rel.* v. Anthony, 914 F. Supp. 1504 (S.D. Ohio 1994) *8:* 213

RxCare of Tenn., Inc., *In re*, 121 F.T.C. 762 (1996) *14:* 75

S

St. John v. Pope, 901 S.W.2d 420 (Tex. 1995) *9:* 75, 76, 85

Salit v. Ruden, McClosky, Smith, Schuster & Russell, P.A., 742 So. 2d 381 (Fla. Dist. Ct. App. 1999) *18:* 106

Sallen v. Corinthians Licenciamentos LTDA, 273 F.3d 14, 60 USPQ2d 1941 (1st Cir. 2001) *16:* 44–46

Samara Bros. v. Wal-Mart Stores, Inc., 529 U.S. 205, 54 USPQ2d 1065 (2000) *15:* 259

Sanders, United States *ex rel.* v. Allison Engine Co., No. 1:95-cv-970 (S.D. Ohio Oct. 27, 2009) *8:* 179

Sanjuan v. American Bd. of Psychiatry & Neurology, 40 F.3d 247 (7th Cir. 1994), *cert. denied,* 516 U.S. 1159 (1996) *14:* 100, 101

Sattar v. Motorola, Inc., 138 F.3d 1164 (7th Cir. 1998) *17:* 69, 71

Sawyer v. Mills, 295 S.W.2d 79 (Ky. 2009) *13:* 57

Schaeffer v. Cohen, Rosenthal, Price, Mirkin, Jennings & Berg, PC, 541 N.E.2d 997 (Mass. 1989) *18:* 109

Schafer v. AT & T Wireless Servs., 2005 WL 850459 (S.D. Ill. Apr. 1, 2005) *13:* 157, 158

Schlesinger v. Herzog, 672 So. 2d 701 (La. Ct. App. 1996) *18:* 128

Schnabel v. Trilegiant, 2011 WL 797505 (D. Conn. Feb. 24, 2011) *13:* 176, 177

Scotts Co. LLC v. Liberty Mut. Ins. Co., No. 2:06-CV-899, 2007 WL 1723509 (S.D. Ohio June 12, 2007) *17:* 70

Seagate v. CIGNA, 2006 WL 1071881 (N.D. Cal. Apr. 21, 2006) *13:* 58

Seattle, City of v. State, 965 P.2d 619 (Wash. 1998) *7:* 154, 156

Securities & Exchange Comm'n v. Credit Bancorp, LTD, 96 F. Supp. 2d 357 (S.D.N.Y. 2000) *18:* 106

Security Bank v. Klicker, 418 N.W.2d 27 (Wis. Ct. App. 1987) *18:* 116

SF Hotel Co. v. Energy Invs., 985 F. Supp. 1032, 45 USPQ2d 1308 (D. Kan. 1997) *13:* 27

Sherman Coll. of Straight Chiropractic v. American Chiropractic Ass'n, 654 F. Supp. 716 (N.D. Ga. 1986), *aff'd,* 813 F.2d 349 (11th Cir.), *cert. denied,* 484 U.S. 854 (1987) *14:* 94, 95

SI Handling Sys., Inc. v. Heisley, 753 F.2d 1244, 225 USPQ 441 (3d Cir. 1985) *15:* 339

Silver Dunes Condo. v. Beggs & Lane, 763 So. 2d 1274 (Fla. Dist. Ct. App. 2000) *18:* 106

Silvestri v. General Motors, 271 F.3d 583 (4th Cir. 2001) *17:* 50, 52

Smallwood v. NCsoft Corp., 2010 WL 3064474 (D. Haw. Aug. 4, 2010) *13:* 168

Snap-On Bus. Solutions v. O'Neil, 708 F. Supp. 2d 669 (N.D. Ohio 2010) *13:* 151

Softman Prods. v. Adone Sys., 171 F. Supp. 2d 1075 (C.D. Cal. 2001) *13:* 141

Soma Med. Intern. v. Standard Chartered Bank, 196 F.3d 1292 (10th Cir. 1999) *13:* 20

Somerstein; United States v., 971 F. Supp. 736 (E.D.N.Y. 1997) *8:* 183

Sotelo v. DirectRevenue, 384 F. Supp. 2d 1219 (N.D. Ill. 2005) *13:* 142, 143

South Carolina Med. Ass'n v. Thompson, 327 F.3d 346 (4th Cir. 2003) *8:* 33

South Carolina State Ports Auth. v. Booz-Allen & Hamilton, Inc., 676 F. Supp. 346 (D.D.C. 1987) *16:* 83

Southwest Airlines v. BoardFirst, LLC, 2007 WL 4823761 (N.D. Tex. Sept. 12, 2007) *13:* 149–51

Specht v. Netscape Commc'ns Corp., 306 F.3d 17 (2d Cir. 2002) *13:* 58, 123–25, 134–37

Standard Oil Co. v. United States, 221 U.S. 1, 31 S. Ct. 502 (1911) *14:* 11

Starbucks Corp. v. Wolfe's Bourough Coffee, Inc., 588 F.3d 97, 92 USPQ2d 1769 (2d Cir. 2009) *15:* 283, 284

State v. *See name of opposing party*

State Oil Co. v. Khan, 522 U.S. 3 (1997) *14:* 14

Step-Saver Data Sys. v. Wyse Tech., 939 F.2d 91 (3d Cir. 1991) *13:* 185–87, 193, 194, 196

Stevens; United States v., No. RWT-10-694 (D. Md. May 10, 2011) *18:* 66, 68, 69

Stewart, United States *ex rel.* v. Louisiana Clinic, No. Civ. A. 99-1767, 2002 WL 31819130 (E.D. La. Dec. 12, 2002) *8:* 224

Stolle v. Baylor Coll. of Med., 981 S.W.2d 709 (Tex. App. Houston 1st Dist. 1998) *9:* 94

Surgidev Corp. v. ETI, Inc., 828 F.2d 452, 4 USPQ2d 1090 (8th Cir. 1987) *15:* 341

Sutherland; United States v., 143 F. Supp. 2d 609 (W.D. Va. 2001) **8:** 7
Swiss Am. Bank; United States v., 274 F.3d 610 (1st Cir. 2001) **13:** 18

T

Tadayon v. Saucon Indus., 2011 WL 1770172 (D. Md. May 9, 2011) **13:** 34
Teeven; United States v., 862 F. Supp. 1200 (D. Del. 1992) **8:** 214
Thompson
—v. Community Health Inv. Corp., 923 S.W.2d 569 (Tex. 1996) **9:** 94
—United States ex rel. v. Columbia/HCA Healthcare, 20 F. Supp. 2d 1017 (S.D. Tex. 1998) **8:** 213
Ticketmaster v. Tickets.com, 2003 WL 21406289 (C.D. Cal. Mar. 7, 2003) **13:** 133
Toysmart.com, LLC
—In re, No. 00-13995-CJK (Bankr. D. Mass. 2000) **5:** 26
—Federal Trade Comm'n v., No. 00-11341-RGS (D. Mass. 2000) **5:** 24, 26, 27
Toys "R" Us, Inc.
—v. Federal Trade Comm'n, 221 F.3d 928 (7th Cir. 2000) **14:** 70
—v. Step Two, 318 F.3d 446, 65 USPQ2d 1628 (3d Cir. 2003) **13:** 17
TracFone Wireless v. SND Cellular, 715 F. Supp. 2d 1246 (S.D. Fla. 2010) **13:** 197
Trintec Indus. v. Pedre Promotional Prods., 395 F.3d 1275, 73 USPQ2d 1587 (Fed. Cir. 2005) **13:** 20, 22
Tsoukas v. Lapid, 733 N.E.2d 823 (Ill. App. 1 Dist. 2000) **9:** 82
Turner v. U-Haul of Fla., 2008 WL 709107 (M.D. Fla. Mar. 14, 2005) **13:** 95
Two Pesos, Inc. v. Taco Cabana, Inc., 505 U.S. 763, 112 S. Ct. 2753 (1992) **15:** 261, 262; **16:** 22, 23

U

Unique Staff Licensing v. Onder, 2010 WL 5621289 (Tex. App. Dec. 9, 2010) **13:** 74
United States
—v. See name of opposing party
—ex rel. See name of related party
United States Gypsum Co.; United States v., 438 U.S. 422 (1978) **14:** 43
United States Ins. Co. v. Wilson, 18 A.3d 110 (Md. Ct. Spec. App. 2011) **13:** 88
University of Montreal Pension Comm. v. Banc of Am. Secs., 685 F. Supp. 2d 456 (S.D. N.Y. 2010) **18:** 17
U.S.H. Corp. of N.Y., In re, 223 B.R. 654 (Bankr. S.D.N.Y. 1998) **8:** 102
U.S. Healthcare, Inc. v. Healthsource, Inc., 986 F.2d 589 (1st Cir. 1993) **14:** 74

V

Vaeck, In re, 947 F.2d 488, 20 USPQ2d 1438 (Fed. Cir. 1991) **15:** 327
Verizon Commc'ns v. Trinko, 540 U.S. 398 (2004) **14:** 65
VGM Fin. Servs. v. Singh, 708 F. Supp. 2d 822 (N.D. Iowa 2010) **13:** 34
Viacom Int'l, Inc. v. YouTube, Inc., 718 F. Supp. 2d 514 (S.D.N.Y. 2010) **15:** 175, 177
Victor Stanley, Inc. v. Creative Pipe, Inc., 250 F.R.D. 251 (D. Md. 2008) **18:** 11
Vinhee, In re, 336 B.R. 437 (9th Cir. 2005) **17:** 98, 109–11
Virginia State Bd. of Pharmacy v. Virginia Consumer Council, 425 U.S. 748 (1976) **16:** 83
Vision Servs. Plan; United States v., 1996-1 Trade Cas. ¶71,404 (D.D.C. 1996) **14:** 80

W

Wachter Mgmt. v. Dexter & Chaney, 144 P.3d 747 (Kan. 2006) **13:** 191
Wall Data v. Los Angeles County Sheriff's Dep't, 447 F.3d 769, 78 USPQ2d 1728 (9th Cir. 2006) **13:** 196
Walters v. Rinker, 520 N.E.2d 468 (Ind. Ct. App. 1988) **9:** 90
Watchdog v. Schweiss, 2009 WL 276856 (S.D. Ind. Feb. 5, 2009) **13:** 39
Weber v. Jolly Hotels, 977 F. Supp. 327 (D.N.J. 1997) **13:** 27
Weinstein v. Todd Marine Enters., Inc., 115 F. Supp. 2d 668 (E.D. Va. 2000) **13:** 27
Weiss v. Weiss, 239 P.3d 123 (Mont. 2010) **13:** 70
Whalen v. Roe, 429 U.S. 589 (1977) **5:** 13, 14
Wilk v. American Med. Ass'n, 719 F.2d 207 (7th Cir. 1983) **14:** 93
Williams v. Sprint/United Mgmt. Co., 230 F.R.D. 640, 96 FEP Cases 1775 (D. Kan. Sept. 29, 2005) **17:** 83
Wilson v. Scott, 412 S.W.2d 299 (Tex. 1967) **9:** 98–101, 103
Winter v. G.P. Putnam's Sons, 938 F.2d 1033 (9th Cir. 1991) **16:** 84, 85
Woods v. Superior Ct., 197 Cal. Rptr. 185 (Cal. Ct. App. 1983) **18:** 109
World-Wide Volkswagen Corp. v. Woodson, 444 U.S. 286 (1980) **13:** 44
Wright, In re, 999 F.2d 1557, 27 USPQ2d 1510 (Fed. Cir. 1993) **15:** 327
W.W.W. Pharm. Co. v. Gillette Co., 984 F.2d 567, 25 USPQ2d 1593 (2d Cir. 1993) **15:** 377, 399

Y

Yamaha v. FTC, 657 F.2d 971 (8th Cir. 1981) **14:** 53, 54

Z

Zador Corp. v. Kwan, 37 Cal. Rptr. 2d 754 (Cal. Ct. App. 1995) *18:* 104, 105

Zavaletta v. American Bar Ass'n, 721 F. Supp. 96 (E.D. Va. 1989) *14:* 86, 87

Zippo Mfg. v. Zippo Dot Com, 952 F. Supp. 1119, 42 USPQ2d 1062 (W.D. Pa. 1997) *13:* 10, 13–16, 23–26

Zubulake v. UBS Warburg LLC, No. 1:02-CV-01243-SAS (S.D.N.Y. Mar. 16, 2005) *17:* 51, 54

Index

*References are to Chapter (number in bold) and section numbers (e.g., **15**: II.D.2 refers to section II.D.2 of Chapter 15).*

A

ABA (American Bar Association), 13: III.C
   Model Rules of Professional Conduct. *See* Ethics
Abandonment of patient, 9: IV.E
Abbreviated New Drug Applications, 15: II.D.2, II.D.3
Abuse. *See* Fraud and abuse
Access to information
   individual's right, **5:** III.B.1.b
Accountable care organizations (ACOs)
   generally, **3:** V
   antitrust and, **14:** I.A
   preliminary transactional agreements, **15:** IX.A.1.d
Accounting services
   business associates, HIPAA definitions, **5:** II.B.3.c.v
Accreditation
   JCAHO. *See* JCAHO (Joint Commission on Accreditation of Healthcare Organizations)
   professional licenses. *See* Licensed medical practitioners; Licenses
ACOs. *See* Accountable care organizations
ACPA (Anticybersquatting Consumer Protection Act of 1999), 16: II.A.1.b
Administrative law judges, 8: IV.F
Admissibility of evidence
   generally, **17:** I
   burdensomeness, **17:** IV.B
   development of rules and standards, **17:** II
   duty to preserve evidence, **17:** IV.A
   electronic health records, **17:** VI.A, VI.B
   electronic signatures, **17:** VI.A
   electronically stored information (ESI)
      generally, **17:** II
      authentication, **17:** V
      foundation for admission of, **17:** V
      hearsay, **17:** V
      independent analysis of, **17:** V
      production of, **17:** IV.B
   Federal Rules of Civil Procedure, 2006 Amendments, **17:** II, IV
   good faith standard, **17:** IV.A
   health information exchanges, **17:** VI.B
   historical background, **17:** II
   inadvertent disclosure, **17:** IV.C
   information ecosystem model, **17:** III
   metadata, **17:** IV.B
   paper records, **17:** II
   safe harbor, **17:** IV.A
   spoliation of evidence, **17:** IV.A
   two-tier approach, **17:** IV.B
Adulterated drugs, 16: II.B.1.a
Advertising
   due diligence, **12:** V.C
      asset-related review, **12:** VII.A
Agency for Healthcare Research and Quality (AHRQ), 1: III.B.1
Agents
   breach notification, **7:** III
   civil monetary penalties, **8:** IV.G.4
Aggravating factors for civil monetary penalties, 8: IV.G.5
Aggregation of data
   generally, **3:** VI.A
   interoperability and, **3:** VI.C
   issues with, **3:** VI.B
Aiding and abetting, 8: V.C
AIDS test results
   AMA guidelines, **5:** IV.A.1
   state disclosure laws, **5:** III.B.2.b
Alabama
   special licensing for medical practice privileges, **9:** II.E.4
Alaska
   breach notification laws, **7:** V.D
Alternative dispute resolution
   intellectual property litigation, managing exposure to, **15:** X.D.3
AMA. *See* American Medical Association
America Competes Reauthorization Act of 2010, 1: III.B.1
America Online
   browse wrap agreements, **13:** IV.A
American Bar Association (ABA), 13: III.C
   Model Rules of Professional Conduct. *See* Ethics
American Express, 16: III.F.3

839

American Health Information Community (AHIC), *3:* III.A
American Health Information Management Association (AHIMA), *3:* IV
American Hospital Association
    privacy, codes of conduct, *5:* IV.A.2
American Medical Association (AMA)
    Council on Ethical and Judicial Affairs, *2:* II.C.2
    e-content provider liability, *16:* II.A.2
    e-prescribing, liability for, *16:* II.B.1.a
    medical coding, *15:* V.A
    privacy, codes of conduct, *5:* IV.A.1
American Medical Informatics Association (AMIA), *3:* IV
American National Standards Institute (ANSI), *3:* III.A
American Recovery and Reinvestment Act of 2009 (ARRA), *2:* III.A; *12:* I
    incentive payments, *3:* III.A
    patient health care records, *4:* III.A
American Telemedicine Association, *10:* IV.A; *16:* II.D.4
Anticybersquatting Consumer Protection Act of 1999 (ACPA), *16:* II.A.1.b
Anti-kickback statute
    intent standard, *8:* V.B
Antitrust
    generally, *14:* I.B, VI
    boycotts, *14:* II.D
    business-to-business (B2B) exchanges, *14:* I.A, I.C, II.C.1, III.A, III.B
    collaboration with competitors, *14:* II
    collateral contractual restraint issues, *14:* I.A
    due diligence checklists, *12:* V.C
    in e-commerce setting, *14:* I.C
    electronic marketplace and, *14:* I.A
    exclusionary practices, *14:* IV
    exclusive use requirements, *14:* IV.B
    facilitating collusion, *14:* II.C
        circumstantial evidence, heightened standard for, *14:* II.C.3
        controlling risk, *14:* II.C.2
        inherent risks of sharing information, *14:* II.C.1
        issues, *14:* I.A
    group boycotts, *14:* II.D
    group purchasing and sales, *14:* II.E
        electronic marketplace and, *14:* II.E.2
        traditional analysis, *14:* II.E.1
    guidance, *14:* II.A
    market definition, *14:* II.B
    market structure issues, *14:* I.A
    most-favored-nation requirements, *14:* IV.C
    network effects, *14:* IV.A
    "per se" analysis, *14:* I.B
    resale price maintenance, *14:* I.B
    "rule of reason" analysis, *14:* I.B
    standards and certification, *14:* V
        historical background, *14:* V.B
        private standard-setting, *14:* V.B, V.C
        significance to e-health, *14:* V.A
    vertical integration, *14:* III
        competitor control of vertically related entity, *14:* III.A

        limitations of theory, *14:* III.B
Appeals of civil monetary penalties, *8:* IV.F
Apple, Inc.
    mobile applications, *1:* III.A.1
Arizona
    breach notification laws, *7:* V.D
Arkansas
    breach notification laws, *7:* V.D
Article 29 Working Party (EU), *6:* I.C, III.B, IV.C
Aspirin
    trademarks and service marks, *15:* VI.B.3
Attorney-client privilege
    crime-fraud exception, *18:* III.B.3.b
    due diligence, *12:* IV
    e-mail communications, *18:* II.A.2.c.i
    ethics, *18:* II.A.2.c.i, III.A
    joint confidences, *18:* IV.A.4
Attorneys
    business associates, HIPAA definitions, *5:* II.B.3.c.v
    disclosure of information, AMA guidelines, *5:* IV.A.1
    due diligence review
        reports, *12:* V.E
        team composition, *12:* IV
    ethics, *12:* II.A. *See also* Ethics
    fees. *See* Attorneys' fees
    privilege. *See* Attorney-client privilege
Attorneys' fees
    copyright infringement, *16:* II.A.1.a
    trademark or service mark infringement, *16:* II.A.1.b
Audit trails
    HIPAA security standards
        preemption, *5:* II.B.3.c.vii
Auditing of business associate contracts
    privacy issues, *13:* V.B.2.b
Authentication. *See also* Security policies
    electronic information, *17:* II
    electronically stored information (ESI), *17:* V
    paper records, *17:* II
    UCITA, *13:* III.C
Authorizations. *See* Consents and authorizations

B

Bankruptcy
    customer information, sale and disclosure, *5:* II.B.2.a
Beacon Community Cooperative Agreement Program, *1:* III.C
Berne Convention for the Protection of Literary and Artistic Works, *15:* III.D, III.F
Billing
    business associates, HIPAA definitions, *5:* II.B.3.c.v
Blackstone Group, *1:* III.B.2
Bluetooth 4.0
    mobile applications, *1:* III.A.1
Boycotts, *14:* II.D
Breach notification
    agents, *7:* III

business associate contracts
    data security issues, *13:* V.B.3.d
    requirements, *7:* III, IV
contact information, provision of, *11:* VI.C
contents of, *11:* VI.C
covered entities, *7:* III, IV
discovery rule, *11:* VI.A
draft guidance, *7:* IV
economic logic of, *7:* V.A
event, description of, *11:* VI.C
HIPAA provisions, *8:* III.B
HITECH Act amendments, *7:* III
identity theft and, *7:* V.A
intellectual property and, *15:* II.B.4
Internet, *11:* VI.B
mail delivery, *11:* VI.B
media, *11:* VI.B
method of providing, *11:* VI.B
mitigating actions, description of, *11:* VI.C
patient records. *See* Patient health care records
posting requirement, *11:* VI.B
precautionary steps, description of, *11:* VI.C
promulgation of rule, *8:* II.A
state laws and regulations, *7:* V
    analysis of representative law, *7:* V.C
    complexities of notification, *7:* V.C.2
    encryption and, *7:* V.C.1
    e-product providers, *16:* II.B.1.b.i
    E–SIGN Act, conformity with, *7:* V.C.2
    historical background, *7:* V.B
    immediate notice, *7:* V.C.2
    list of, *7:* V.D
    scope of regulation, *4:* VII.B; *7:* V.C.3
    substitute notice, *7:* V.C.2
subcontractors, *7:* III
time requirements, *11:* VI.A
type of information, description of, *11:* VI.C
unreasonable delay, *11:* VI.A
unsecured PHI, *7:* IV
writing requirement, *11:* VI.B
Breach of privacy or data security
generally, *11:* I, VIII
analysis of data protection technologies and methodologies prior to, *11:* II
compromise of privacy or data security as, *11:* I
defined, *11:* II, III
encryption obligation, *11:* II
exceptions to definition, *11:* IV
    determinations, *11:* I
    disclosed information not reasonably retained, *11:* IV.C
    good faith disclosure within scope of employment, *11:* IV.A
    inadvertent disclosure, *11:* IV.B
    limited data set excluding certain identifiers, *11:* IV.D
    unsecured protected health information, *11:* IV.B
HITECH Act
    generally, *11:* I
    civil penalties, *11:* VII.A
    criminal penalties, *11:* VII.B
    unsecured protected health information exception, *11:* IV.B
identity of breaching party, *11:* V
    business associate contracts, *11:* V.B
    multiple entities transferring protected health information, *11:* V.A
impermissible disclosure as, *11:* I
notification. *See* Breach notification
risk assessment obligation, *11:* III
    identity of any known recipient, *11:* III.B
    mitigating actions, *11:* III.C
    nature of breach, *11:* III.A
    small risk of individual harm, *11:* III.D
Breach reports, *8:* III.B
Browse wrap agreements, *13:* IV.A
Business associate contracts, *13:* V
generally, *13:* V.A
automatic amendment clauses, *13:* V.B.2.a
breach notification
    data security issues, *13:* V.B.3.d
    requirements, *7:* III, IV
business associate defined, *7:* II.E; *11:* V.B; *13:* V.B.1
data security issues, *13:* V.B.3
    generally, *7:* II.E
    additional responsibilities, *13:* V.B.3.e
    administrative safeguards, *13:* V.B.3.a
    breach notification, *13:* V.B.3.d
    civil monetary penalties, *13:* V.B.3.f
    physical safeguards, *13:* V.B.3.b
    technical safeguards, *13:* V.B.3.c
HIPAA safeguards, definitions,*5:* II.B.3.c.v
HITECH Act provisions, *5:* II.B.3.d.ii.c
identity of breaching party, *11:* V.B
privacy issues, *13:* V.B.2
    access to patient records, *13:* V.B.2.e
    fundraising and marketing, *13:* V.B.2.d
    logging and auditing, *13:* V.B.2.b
    minimum necessary rule, *13:* V.B.2.a
    restricted disclosures, *13:* V.B.2.c
    state law, role of, *13:* V.B.2.f
sample, *15:* IX.A.1.a
templates, *5:* II.B.3.c.v

C

California
breach notification laws, *7:* V.B, V.C, V.C.2, V.C.3, V.D
Health-Care Foundation (CHCF), *3:* IV.B
Pharmacy Act, *16:* II.B.1.a
unauthorized practice of medicine, *9:* II.B
Cancer Hope Network (e-content provider), *16:* II.A.1
Care providers. *See* E-care providers
CDA. *See* Communications Decency Act of 1996
CDC (Centers for Disease Control), *15:* IX.A.1
Cellular phones
ethics and, *18:* II.A.5
Census Bureau, *13:* I
Centers for Disease Control (CDC), *15:* IX.A.1

Centers for Medicare and Medicaid Services (CMS). *See also* Medicare and Medicaid
  attestation process, *1:* III.C
  authentication and, *17:* VI.A
  compliance audits, *8:* III.C
  data security guidance, *7:* II
  EHR use
    incentive program, *2:* III.A
    regulations regarding, *3:* III.B
  HIPAA administration, *8:* II.A
  incentive programs, achievement of meaningful use, *16:* II.E.2
  medical coding, *15:* V.A
  National Provider Identified Standard, *15:* II.A.3
  Office of E-Health Standards and Services, *7:* II.C; *16:* III.F.1
  Proposed Rule for Accountable Care Organizations, *15:* IX.A.1.d
  telemedicine credentialing, *16:* II.D.1
Centers for Medicare and Medicaid Services Electronic Health Record Incentive Program (EHR Incentive Program), *2:* III.A
Certificates of confidentiality
  clinical research, *5:* II.B.2.c
Certification
  JCAHO. *See* JCAHO (Joint Commission on Accreditation of Healthcare Organizations)
  pharmacies and pharmacists. *See* Verified Internet Pharmacy Practice Sites certification program
  professional licenses. *See* Licensed medical practitioners; Licenses
Certification Commission for Health Information Technology (CCHIT), *3:* III.A; *14:* V.A
CFAA (Computer Fraud and Abuse Act of 1986), *15:* IV.C
Checklists
  due diligence, *12:* V.C
Children
  disclosure and use restrictions, *5:* III.B.2.b
  online protection. *See* Children's Online Privacy Protection Act
Children's Health Insurance Programs
  privacy rule, applicability of, *15:* II.C.3
Children's Online Privacy Protection Act of 1998 (COPPA), *4:* VI.A.2; *16:* II.B.1.b.iii
  parental notice requirements, *5:* II.B.2.a
  privacy, impact on, *15:* IV.E.3
ChoicePoint (credit reporting agency), *7:* V.B
Circumstantial evidence and antitrust, *14:* II.C.3
Civil enforcement. *See* Enforcement
Civil monetary penalties, *8:* IV
  generally, *8:* IV.A
  agents, violations by, *8:* IV.G.4
  aggravating factors, *8:* IV.G.5
  appeals, *8:* IV.F
  business associate contracts, data security issues, *13:* V.B.3.f
  data security violations, *7:* II.D
  enforcement rule, *8:* IV.B
  HITECH Act, breach under, *11:* VII.A
  imposition of, *8:* IV.G.1
  industry-wide compliance, *8:* IV.E
  intellectual property and, *15:* II.B.5
  leniency provisions, *8:* IV.C
  letter of opportunity, *8:* IV.F
  limitations, *8:* IV.A, IV.C
  Medicare and Medicaid, *8:* VI.B
  mitigating factors, *8:* IV.G.5
  notice of proposed determination, *8:* IV.F
  number of violations, *8:* IV.D
  procedures, *8:* IV.F
  public notice, *8:* IV.G.2
  reasonable cause and, *8:* IV.C
  reasonable diligence and, *8:* IV.C
  state attorney general actions, *8:* IV.H
  statistical sampling, *8:* IV.G.3
  tiered increases, *8:* IV.A
  willful neglect and, *8:* IV.C
Claims processing
  fraud and abuse. *See* Fraud and abuse
  HIPAA defined standard transactions business associates, *5:* II.B.3.c.v
Clayton Act of 1914. *See also* Antitrust
  generally, *14:* I.B
  in e-commerce setting, *14:* I.C
  market definition, *14:* II.B
  vertical integration, *14:* III.A
Click-through agreements and click-wrap licenses, *13:* IV.B
  due diligence, *12:* VII.C
Client confidentiality rules, *18:* III.B.1
  assisting client's crime or fraud, *18:* III.B.2
  audits, *18:* III.B.3
  confidentiality, *18:* III.B.1
  investigations, *18:* III.B.3
  representing the organization, *18:* III.B.4
Clinical trials
  privacy protections, human subjects, *5:* II.B.2.b
Cloud computing
  generally, *1:* III.A.3
  due diligence, *5:* I; *12:* I
  ethics, *18:* II.A.6
  patient health care records and, *4:* III.C
CMS. *See* Centers for Medicare and Medicaid Services
Collaboration agreements, *15:* IX.A.2.a
Collusion, *14:* II.C. *See also* Antitrust
  circumstantial evidence, heightened standard for, *14:* II.C.3
  controlling risk, *14:* II.C.2
  inherent risks of sharing information, *14:* II.C.1
  issues, *14:* I.A
Colorado
  breach notification laws, *7:* V.D
Common law spoliation of evidence, *17:* IV.A
Communications Decency Act of 1996 (CDA), *16:* II.A.1.c, II.C.5, III.C.1
Complaint process, *8:* III.A
Compliance audits, *8:* III.C
Compliance plans to avoid enforcement actions, *8:* VIII
Compliance reviews, *8:* III.A
Computer Fraud and Abuse Act of 1986 (CFAA), *15:* IV.C
Computer privacy acts, *15:* IV.A

Computer programs. *See* Software
Computerized Provider-Order Entry (CPOE)
  e-health industry, **2:** II.E
Conditions of participation. *See also* Medicare and Medicaid
  human subjects in clinical trials, **5:** II.B.2.b
  Privacy. *See* Privacy
Confidentiality. *See also* Client confidentiality rules
  data security program development and management, **7:** II.A.1
  NDAs. *See* Nondisclosure agreements
  patient health care records, **4:** VII.A
  patient information. *See* Privacy
  RHIOs and, **16:** II.E.3
  state statutes, **4:** VII.A
  substance abuse and treatment records, **5:** II.B.1.b, III.B.2.b
  trade secrets. *See* Trade secrets
Conflicts of interest, 18: IV
  close corporations, **18:** IV.B
  general partnerships, **18:** IV.C.1
  joint representation, **18:** IV
    commercial negotiations, **18:** IV.A.6
    Ethics 2000 Commission, **18:** IV.A.2
    joint confidences, **18:** IV.A.4
    litigation, **18:** IV.A.8
    Model Rule 2.2, **18:** IV.A.1
    recommendation, **18:** IV.A.5
    Restatement, **18:** IV.A.3
    unintentional, **18:** IV.A.7
  limited partnerships, **18:** IV.C.2
  partnerships, **18:** IV.C
Connecticut
  breach notification laws, **7:** V.D
Connection providers. *See* E-connection providers
Consents and authorizations
  Children's Online Privacy Protection Act, **5:** II.B.2.a
  E-SIGN. *See* Electronic Signatures in Global and National Commerce Act
  HIPAA security requirements, **5:** II.B.3.c.iv
    required and permitted uses and disclosures, **5:** II.B.3.c.ii
  human subjects, privacy protections, **5:** II.B.2.b
  physician-patient relationship, **9:** IV.A, IV.C
  privacy
    federal agency prohibitions, **5:** II.B.3.a
    state laws and regulations, **5:** III.B.1.a
    unauthorized disclosures, cause of action, **5:** III.B.1.c
Conspiracy, 8: V.D
Constitution, U.S. *See also specific amendments*
  privacy protections, **5:** II
    Fourteenth Amendment, **5:** II.A.1
    Whalen v. Roe, **5:** II.A.2
Consultations
  licensure exception for physician licensed in one state to consult with licensed physician in another state, **9:** II.E.1
  telephone consults, **9:** IV.A
Consumer education, 10: II.A.2

Consumer protection
  EU Data Protection Directive and, **6:** X
  FTC. *See* Federal Trade Commission
  VIPPS certification program. *See* Verified Internet Pharmacy Practice Sites certification program
Content providers. *See* E-content providers
Contractors
  telemedicine and vicarious liability issues, **9:** IV.D
Contracts
  generally, **13:** I, VI
  browse wrap agreements, **13:** IV.A
  business associate contracts, HIPAA definitions, **5:** II.B.3.c.v
  capacity, **13:** IV
  click-wrap agreements, **13:** IV.B
  common principles, **13:** IV.D
  consideration, **13:** IV
  due diligence
    focus of review, **12:** VII
    liability review, **12:** VII.B
  E–SIGN Act, **13:** III.A
  fraud and abuse. *See* Fraud and abuse
  jurisdiction for e-health businesses, **13:** II
  legitimate purpose, **13:** IV
  offer and acceptance, **13:** IV
  preliminary transactional agreements, **15:** IX.A.1.a
  safe harbor regulations. *See* Fraud and abuse
  shrink wrap agreements, **13:** IV.C
  statutes, **13:** III
  Uniform Computer Information Transactions Act, **13:** III.B
  Uniform Electronic Transactions Act, **13:** III.B
Controlled substances. *See* Prescription drugs
Controlled Substances Act of 1970, 16: II.B.1.a
Cookies
  EU E-Privacy Directive and, **6:** VIII
COPPA. *See* Children's Online Privacy Protection Act of 1998
Copyright Act of 1976, 16: II.A.1.a
  computer programs, **15:** III.G
  copyright defined, **15:** III.A
  databases, **15:** III.H.2
  exclusive rights, **15:** III.B
Copyright infringement
  allocation of risk, **16:** III.A.2
  attorneys' fees, **16:** II.A.1.a
  contributory liability, **16:** II.A.1.a
  costs, **16:** II.A.1.a
  criminal penalties, **16:** II.A.1.a
  damages, **16:** II.A.1.a
  direct liability, **16:** II.A.1.a
  e-connection providers, **16:** II.C.1
  e-content providers, **16:** II.A.1.a
  injunctions, **16:** II.A.1.a
  mitigation of risk
    before claim, **16:** III.A.1
    upon claim, **16:** III.A.3
  prima facie case, **16:** II.A.1.a
  vicarious liability, **16:** II.A.1.a
  willful infringement for profit, **16:** II.A.1.a

Copyrights, 15: III. *See also* Proprietary rights
   Berne Convention for the Protection of Literary and Artistic Works, *15:* III.D, III.F
   compilations, *16:* II.A.1.a
   computer programs, *15:* III.G
   criminal penalties, *16:* II.A.1.a
   databases, *16:* II.A.1.a
     in European Union, *15:* III.H.2
     proprietary databases, *15:* III.I
     in United States, *15:* III.H.2
   defined, *15:* III.A
   derivative works, *15:* III.B, III.C
   due diligence and asset-related review, *12:* VII.A
   duration of protection, *15:* III.E
   exclusive rights, *15:* III.B
   fair use defense, *16:* II.A.1.a
   false representation in connection with application, *16:* II.A.1.a
   fraudulent use and removal of copyright notice, *16:* II.A.1.a
   infringement. *See* Copyright infringement
   medical documents and images, *15:* III.H.1
   obtaining, *15:* III.D
   public display, *15:* III.B
   public distribution, *15:* III.B
   public performance, *15:* III.B
   reproduction, *15:* III.B
   software, *15:* III.G
   substantial similarity, *15:* III.C
Corporate practice of medicine, *9:* II.B
Costs
   copyright infringement, *16:* II.A.1.a
   of health care, reducing, *1:* III
   trademark or service mark infringement, *15:* VI.A.2; *16:* II.A.1.b
Council of the European Union, *6:* I.A
Counterfeit drugs, *16:* II.B.1.a
Covered entities, HIPAA safeguards
   business associates, definitions, *5:* II.B.3.c.v
   required and permitted uses and disclosures, *5:* II.B.3.c.ii
Credit cards, data security and, *16:* III.F.3
Criminal enforcement, *8:* V
   generally, *8:* V.A
   aiding and abetting, *8:* V.C
   conspiracy, *8:* V.D
   data security violations, *7:* II.D
   indirect criminal liability of business associates, *8:* V.E
   intent standard, *8:* V.B
   knowingly standard, *8:* V.B
   penalties, *8:* V.A
   Sentencing Commission Guidelines for the Sentencing of Organizations, *8:* VIII
   statutes of limitations, *8:* V.F
Cross-licensing agreements, *15:* X.B.2
Cybersquatting, *16:* II.A.1.b

D

DailyData (mobile application), *1:* III.A.1
DailyStrength (e-content provider), *16:* II.A.1

Damages
   copyright infringement, *16:* II.A.1.a
   spoliation of evidence, *17:* IV.A
   trademark or service mark infringement, *15:* VI.A.2; *16:* II.A.1.b
Data administration
   business associates, HIPAA definitions, *5:* II.B.3.c.v
Data analysis, *3:* VI
   aggregation of data, *3:* VI.A
   interoperability, *3:* VI.C
   issues with aggregation of data, *3:* VI.B
   risks involved with, *3:* VI.D
Data collection and use policies, violations, *5:* II.B.2.a
Data controllers
   administrative requirements, *6:* VII
   defined, *6:* II.C
Data processors
   appointment, *6:* V
   defined, *6:* II.C
Data Protection Directive (EU)
   generally, *6:* I
   Article 29 Working Party, *6:* I.C, III.B, IV.C
   consent, *6:* IV.C
   consumer protection laws and, *6:* X
   data controllers
     administrative requirements, *6:* VII
     defined, *6:* II.C
   data processors
     appointment, *6:* V
     defined, *6:* II.C
   data security, *6:* IV.E
   data subject rights, *6:* IV.D
   explicit consent, *6:* IV.C
   export of personal data
     exceptions to prohibition, *6:* VI.C
     U.S. safe harbor, *6:* VI.A.2
   fair and lawful processing, *6:* IV.A
   human rights laws and, *6:* X
   jurisdiction
     EEA establishment, *6:* III.A
     non-EEA established entities, *6:* III.B
   national laws and, *6:* I.B
   personal data defined, *6:* II.A
   processing defined, *6:* II.B
   sensitive personal data, *6:* IV.B
Data security
   breach. *See* Breach of privacy or data security
   HIPAA Security Rule. *See* Security Rule
   Sentinel Initiative, *10:* V.C
Data Use and Reciprocal Support Agreements (DURSAs), *16:* III.F.2
Databases, copyrights and
   in EU, *15:* III.H.2
   proprietary databases, *15:* III.I
   in U.S., *15:* III.H.2
DEA. *See* Drug Enforcement Administration
Declaratory relief to determine proprietary rights, *15:* X.A.3
Defamation
   actionability, *16:* II.A.1.c
   allocation of risk, *16:* III.C.2

Index 845

dissemination of erroneous information, *16:* II.A.1.c
distributors, *16:* II.A.1.c
e-connection providers, *16:* II.C.5
e-content providers, *16:* II.A.1.c
falsity, *16:* II.A.1.c
fault, *16:* II.A.1.c
First Amendment issues, *16:* II.A.1.c
mitigation of risk
    before claim, *16:* III.C.1
    upon claim, *16:* III.C.3
publishers, *16:* II.A.1.c
unprivileged publication, *16:* II.A.1.c
Defense, Department of (DOD)
    mobile applications, *1:* III.A.1
Definitions
    account, *16:* II.B.1.b.iv
    accountability, *7:* II.A.3
    agent, *7:* III
    assisting client's crime or fraud, *18:* III.B.2
    breach, *11:* II, III
    business, *7:* V.C.3
    business associate, *7:* II.E; *11:* V.B; *13:* V.B.1
    business associate contract, HIPAA safeguards, *5:* II.B.3.c.v
    confidentiality, *7:* II.A.1
    covered account, *16:* II.B.1.b.iv
    customer, *7:* V.C.3
    data controller, *6:* II.C
    data processor, *6:* II.C
    disclosure, *11:* II
    discovered, *7:* IV
    distributor, *16:* II.A.1.c
    e-health, *1:* II
    e-health industry, *2:* I
    electronic health record, *1:* II
    electronic medical device, *1:* II
    electronic prescribing, *1:* II
    e-prescribing, *1:* II
    health insurance information, *7:* V.D
    individually identifiable health information, *5:* II.B.3.c
    meaningful use, *1:* III.C
    medical device, *10:* IV.C.1
    medical information, *7:* V.D
    mobile medical app manufacturer, *10:* IV.H.3
    patient health care record, *4:* II
    person, *8:* IV.D
    personal data, *6:* II.A
    personal information, *7:* V.D
    practice of medicine, *9:* II.A
    processing, *6:* II.B
    protected health information, *15:* II.C.2
    publisher, *16:* II.A.1.c
    subcontractor, *7:* III
    telehealth, *1:* II
    telemedicine, *1:* II
    tethered PHR, *4:* IV.A
    trade secret, *15:* VIII.B
    unsecured PHI, *7:* IV
    untethered PHR, *4:* IV.A
Delaware
    breach notification laws, *7:* V.D

Dell
    browse wrap agreements, *13:* IV.A
Derivative works, *15:* III.B, III.C
Diagnosis Related Groupings (DRG), *15:* V.C
Digital Millennium Copyright Act of 1998 (DMCA), *15:* IV.D
Digital signatures
    admissibility of evidence, *17:* VI.A
    E-SIGN. *See* Electronic Signatures in Global and National Commerce Act
Dilution, *15:* VI.A.4; *16:* II.A.1.b
Dilution Act. *See* Trademark Dilution Act
Direct Project, *3:* II, IV.A
Disclaimers
    telemedicine liability, *9:* IV.F.2
Disclosure. *See also* Privacy
    due diligence
        confidentiality agreements, *12:* V.B
        controls, *12:* VI.A
    personal information. *See* Privacy
    state laws and regulations, *5:* III.B.2
    telemedicine
        informed consent and duty to disclose, *9:* IV.C
Discover (credit card), *16:* III.F.3
Discovery. *See* Admissibility of evidence
Discovery rule, *11:* VI.A
Dispensing procedures for prescriptions drugs. *See* Prescription drugs
District of Columbia
    breach notification laws, *7:* V.D
    Department of Health, *3:* IV.A
DMCA (Digital Millennium Copyright Act of 1998), *15:* IV.D
Doctors. *See* Licensed medical practitioners
    prescribing and dispensing drugs. *See* Prescription drugs
Domain names
    trademarks and service marks
        protection of, *15:* VI.C.1
        securing, *15:* VI.C.2
DRG (Diagnosis Related Groupings), *15:* V.C
Drug Enforcement Administration (DEA), *10:* II.A.1; *16:* II.B.1.a
    Controlled Substances Act, *16:* II.B.1.a
Drug Price Competition and Patent Term Restoration Act of 1984. *See* Hatch–Waxman Act
Drugs. *See* Prescription drugs
DTC advertising. *See* Online direct-to-consumer advertising regulation
Due diligence, *15:* X.A
    accreditation issues, *12:* IX.B
    agreements review, *12:* VII.C
    American Recovery and Reinvestment Act (ARRA), *5:* I; *12:* VI.G
    asset review, *12:* VII.A
    audit committee activities, *12:* VI.C
    breach of fiduciary duty, *12:* VII.D
    certification issues, *12:* IX.B
    checklists, *12:* V.C
    cloud computing, *12:* I
    code of ethics, *12:* VI.D
    common pitfalls, *12:* VIII

Due Diligence—*Cont'd*
  conditions for reimbursement, *12:* IX.E
  confidentiality agreements, *12:* V.B
  data security, *12:* VI.H
    state laws, *12:* IX.C
  declaratory relief, *15:* X.A.3
  disclosure controls, *12:* VI.A
  EHR products, certification of, *12:* VI.G
  entity and operations, knowledge and
    understanding of, *12:* IX
  existing rights, identifying scope of, *15:* X.A.2
  focus of review, *12:* VII
  fraud and abuse laws, *12:* X
  grant considerations, *12:* IX.F
  HIPAA Act, *12:* IX.C, X
  HITECH Act, *12:* I, IX.C
  internal controls, *12:* VI.B
  interviews, *12:* VII.E
  laws and regulations, *12:* X
  liability review, *12:* VII.B
  licensure, *12:* X; *15:* X.A.3
  location, *12:* V.D
  materiality standard, *12:* III
  meaningful use, *12:* II, VI.G
  mistakes, *12:* VIII
  nature of process, *12:* II
  notification, *12:* IX.G
  off-balance-sheet transactions, *12:* VI.E
  overview, *12:* I
  Patient Protection and Affordable Care Act
    (PPACA), *12:* I
  permits, *12:* IX.D
  planning, *12:* IV, V.A
  potential rights holders, identifying, *15:* X.A.1
  privacy, *12:* VI.H
  protected information, *12:* IX.C
  purpose, *12:* II
  reimbursement, *12:* IX.E
  reports, *12:* V.E
  research considerations, *12:* IX.F
  review
    contents, *12:* VI
    procedure, *12:* V
  Sarbanes-Oxley Act, implications of, *12:* VI.F
  scope, *12:* III
  self-referral restrictions, *12:* X
  standard, *12:* III
  Stark Law, *12:* X
  state health planning approvals, *12:* IX.D
  tax law, *12:* X
  tax-exempt status, *12:* IX.A
  team composition, *12:* IV
  understanding of entity and operations, *12:* IX
  workarounds, *15:* X.A.3

E

EC Directives. *See* European Union
E-care providers, *16:* II.D
  data security, *16:* II.D.4
  malpractice, *16:* II.D.2
  practice of medicine, unlicensed or unauthorized,
    16: II.D.1
  privacy, *16:* II.D.4
  technology performance issues, *16:* II.D.3
  telemedicine, FDA regulation of, *16:* II.D.5
E-connection providers, *16:* II.C
  copyright infringement, *16:* II.C.1
  data security, *16:* II.C.4
  defamation, *16:* II.C.5
  privacy, *16:* II.C.4
  proprietary right infringement, *16:* II.C.3
  trademark and service mark infringement,
    16: II.C.2
Economic Espionage Act of 1996, *15:* VIII.A
E-content providers, *16:* II.A
  consumer-oriented e-content providers,
    16: II.A.1
  copyright infringement, *16:* II.A.1.a
  defamation, *16:* II.A.1.c
  practice of medicine, unlicensed or unauthorized,
    16: II.A.1.d
  provider-oriented e-content providers, *16:* II.A.2
  trademark and service mark infringement,
    16: II.A.1.b
**ECPA (Electronic Communications Privacy Act
  of 1986),** *4:* VI.A.2; *15:* IV.E.1
EEA (European Economic Area). *See* European
  Union
E-health industry
  generally, *1:* I, V
  antitrust. *See* Antitrust
  background, *2:* I
  business industry models, *2:* II.D
  challenges, *2:* II.G
  Computerized Provider-Order Entry (CPOE)
    adoption, state of, *2:* II.E
    improvements for e-health, *2:* II.F
  defined, *2:* I
  due diligence. *See* Due diligence
  electronic health records (EHR) systems, *2:* I
    adoption, state of, *2:* II.E
  e-prescribing, *2:* I
  ethics. *See* Ethics
  fraud and abuse. *See* Fraud and abuse
  government, role of, *2:* III
    American Recovery and Reinvestment Act
      (ARRA), *2:* III.A
    Centers for Medicare and Medicaid Services
      Electronic Health Record Incentive
      Program (EHR Incentive Program), *2:* III.A
    electronic health records (EHR) systems,
      2: III.B
    e-prescribing incentives, *2:* III.B
    health care reform, *2:* III.A
    HITECH Act, *2:* III.A
    key regulations, *2:* III.B
    Medicare Prescription Drug, Improvement
      and Modernization Act of 2003 (MMA),
      2: III.B
    Patient Protection and Affordable Care
      Act and the Health Care and Education
      Reconciliation Act of 2010 (PPACA),
      2: III.A
    payor, government as, *2:* III.C
    Stark exceptions and anti-kickback safe
      harbors, *2:* III.B

Hospital Corporation of America (HCA), *2:* II.A
improvements and, *2:* II.F
  health care delivery, *2:* IV
  Office of the National Coordinator for Health Information Technology (ONCHIT), *2:* II.F
jurisdictional issues. *See* Jurisdiction
medical devices, defined, *2:* I
participants, *2:* II.C
  AMA Council on Ethical and Judicial Affairs, *2:* II.C.2
  e-mail, *2:* II.C.2
  health information technology vendors, *2:* II.C
  Internet pharmacies, *2:* II.C.3
  National Association of Boards of Pharmacy (NABP), *2:* II.C.3
  providers, *2:* II.C.2
  vendors of health information technology, *2:* II.C.4
  Verified Internet Pharmacy Practice Sites (VIPPS) certification program, *2:* II.C.3
  Web site operators, *2:* II.C.1
privacy protections. *See* Privacy
technology, *2:* II.B
traditional health care delivery model, *2:* II.A
eHealthInsurance, *16:* II.A.1
EHR Incentive Programs, *1:* III.C; *3:* III.A
EHRs. *See* Electronic health records
Electronic Communications Privacy Act of 1986 (ECPA), *4:* VI.A.2; *15:* IV.E.1; *18:* II.A.2.c.ii
Electronic health records (EHRs)
barriers to adoption of, *3:* III.B
defined, *1:* II
development of standards, *3:* III.A
EHR Incentive Programs, *1:* III.C; *3:* III.A
FDA regulation, *10:* III
  authority, *10:* III.A
  collaboration with ONC, *10:* III.D
  FDA Working Group, *10:* III.C.1
  increased scrutiny and oversight, *10:* III.C
  legislative inquiries, *10:* III.C.2
  by ONC, *10:* III.B
patient health care records distinguished, *4:* IV.C
system providers, *16:* II.E
  data security, *16:* II.E.1
  health information exchanges, allocation of rights and obligations, *16:* II.E.3
  Medicare and Medicaid incentive programs, achievement of meaningful use, *16:* II.E.2
  privacy, *16:* II.E.1
Electronic medical devices
defined, *1:* II
Electronic medical records (EMRs)
admissibility of evidence, *17:* VI.A
exclusive use requirements, *14:* IV.B
patient health care records distinguished, *4:* IV.C
Electronic prescribing. *See* E-prescribing
Electronic Privacy Information Center (EPIC), *10:* V.C
Electronic Signatures in Global and National Commerce Act of 2000 (E–SIGN)
admissibility of evidence, *17:* II, VI.A
contracts, *13:* III.A
effect of, *13:* III.A
preemption, *13:* III.A
requirements, *13:* III.A
state breach notification laws, conformity of, *7:* V.C.2
UCITA compared, *13:* III.C
UETA compared, *13:* III.B
validity, general rule of, *13:* III.A
Electronically stored information (ESI)
generally, *17:* II
authentication, *17:* V
burdensomeness of production, *17:* IV.B
foundation for admission of, *17:* V
hearsay, *17:* V
HIPAA regulations, preemption, *5:* II.B.3.c.vii
independent analysis of, *17:* V
production of, *17:* IV.B
security of, *17:* V
two-tier approach, *17:* IV.B
E-mail
authorization. *See* Consents and authorizations
ethics
  confidentiality, *18:* II.A.1.a
  malpractice liability, *18:* II.A.2.c.iii
  metadata, *18:* II.A.2.e
  professional competence, *12:* II.A.1
  waiver of attorney-client privilege, *18:* II.A.2.c.ii
unsolicited e-mail, E-Privacy Directive (EU) and, *6:* VIII
Emdeon, Inc., *1:* III.B.2
Employment
good faith disclosure within scope of, *11:* IV.A
intellectual property litigation, managing exposure to
  existing employee education, *15:* X.C.1
  non-employee education, *15:* X.C.2
EMRs. *See* Electronic medical records
Encryption
electronic signatures and, *17:* VI.A
ethics, *18:* II.A.2.c
obligations, *11:* II
Endorsement for physician practice in second state, *9:* II.E.2, III.A
Enforcement
generally, *8:* I, IX
breach reports, *8:* III.B
civil monetary penalties. *See* Civil monetary penalties
complaint process, *8:* III.A
compliance audits, *8:* III.C
compliance plans to avoid enforcement actions, *8:* VIII
compliance reviews, *8:* III.A
criminal enforcement. *See* Criminal enforcement
False Claims Act, *8:* VI.B
Federal Trade Commission Act, *8:* VI.A
investigations, *8:* III.A
mail fraud, *8:* VI.C
privacy
  HIPAA security standards, *5:* II.B.3.c.vi; *8:* VI.E
  unauthorized disclosures, cause of action, *5:* III.B.1.c
private right of action, *8:* II.C

Enforcement—Cont'd
  RICO, **8:** VI.D
  voluntary compliance and resolution agreements, **8:** III.D
  wire fraud, **8:** VI.C
E-prescribing
  allocation of risk, **16:** III.E.2
  consumer-oriented e-product providers, **16:** II.B.1.a
  defined, **1:** II
  government role and incentives, **2:** III.B
  mitigation of risk, **16:** III.E.1
  Stark Law and, **16:** II.E.3
E-Privacy Directive (EU)
  generally, **6:** I
  cookies, **6:** VIII
  data security, **6:** IV.E
  unsolicited e-mail, **6:** VIII
E-product providers, 16: II.B
  business-oriented e-product providers, **16:** II.B.2
    employee access to health insurance accounts, **16:** II.B.2.a
    provider publication tools, **16:** II.B.2.b
  consumer-oriented e-product providers, **16:** II.B.1
    data security, **16:** II.B.1.b
    e-prescribing, **16:** II.B.1.a
    FTCA Section 5 actions, **16:** II.B.1.b.iii
    Payment Card Industry Data Security Standard, **16:** II.B.1.b.ii
    privacy, **16:** II.B.1.b
    Red Flags Rule, **16:** II.B.1.b.iv
    state breach notification statutes, **16:** II.B.1.b.i
  provider-oriented e-product providers, **16:** II.B.2
    employee access to health insurance accounts, **16:** II.B.2.a
    provider publication tools, **16:** II.B.2.b
Erroneous information. See Defamation
ESI. See Electronically stored information
E–SIGN. See Electronic Signatures in Global and National Commerce Act of 2000
Ethics
  attorney-client privilege, **18:** II.A.2.c.i, III.A
    crime-fraud exception, **18:** III.B.3.b
    due diligence, **12:** IV
    e-mail communications, **18:** II.A.2.c.i
  audits and investigations, **18:** III.B.3
    crime-fraud exception to attorney-client privilege, **18:** III.B.3.b
    hiring consultants, **18:** III.B.3.a
  cellular phones, use of, **18:** II.A.5
  client confidentiality rules, **18:** III.B
    assisting client's crime or fraud, **18:** III.B.2
    audits, **18:** III.B.3
    confidentiality, **18:** III.B.1
    investigations, **18:** III.B.3
    representing the organization, **18:** III.B.4
  cloud computing, **18:** II.A.6
  competence, **18:** II.A
    privacy issues, **18:** II.A
  confidentiality, **18:** II.A.1.a. See also client confidentiality rules, *this heading*
    backup, **18:** II.A.2.a
    deleting data, **18:** II.A.2.d.ii
    e-mail, **18:** II.A.2.c
    encryption, **18:** II.A.2.c
    hard drive, use of, **18:** II.A.2.d.1
    hardware risks, **18:** II.A.2.d
    HIPAA Act and compliance management, **18:** II.A.1.b
    HITECH Act and compliance management, **18:** II.A.1.b
    misdirected facsimiles or e-mails, **18:** II.A.1.a
    remote disk drive, use of, **18:** II.A.2.d.1
    viruses, **18:** II.A.2.
  conflicts of interest, **18:** IV
    close corporations, **18:** IV.B
    joint representation, **18:** IV.A
    limits partnerships, **18:** IV.C
    malpractice, **18:** IV.D
    partnerships, **18:** IV.C
  due diligence review, **18:** VI.D
  e-discovery, **18:** II.A.3.b
    scope of discovery, **18:** II.A.3.a
  electronic filings
    health care laws, affect on, **18:** II.A.4.b
    practice of law, affect on, **18:** II.A.4.a
  e-mail
    confidentiality, **18:** II.A.1.a
    HITECH Act violations, **18:** II.A.2.c.iv
    malpractice liability, **18:** II.A.2.c.iii
    metadata, **18:** II.A.2.e
    professional competence, **12:** II.A.1
    waiver of attorney-client privilege, **18:** II.A.2.c.ii
  investigations, **18:** III.B.3
  joint representation, **18:** IV.A
    commercial negotiations, **18:** IV.A.6
    Ethics 2000 Commission, **18:** IV.A.2
    joint confidences, **18:** IV.A.4
    litigation, **18:** IV.A.8
    Model Rule 2.2, **18:** IV.A.1
    recommendation, **18:** IV.A.5
    Restatement, **18:** IV.A.3
    unintentional, **18:** IV.A.7
  knowledge of client misconduct, **18:** III
    Stevens; United States v., **18:** III
    violations chart, **18:** III
  mobile devices, use of, **18:** II.A.5
  overview, **18:** I
  PDAs, use of, **18:** II.A.5
  privacy, **5:** IV
  representing the organization, **18:** III.B.4
    "climbing the corporate ladder," **18:** III.B.4.a
    discharge of constituent, **18:** III.B.4.c
    identity of client, **18:** III.B.4.b
  technology, **18:** II
    competence, **18:** II.A
    confidentiality, **18:** II.A.1
    corporate family conflict issues, **18:** II.B.3
    ex parte communications, **18:** II.C.3
    juror and witness, research of, **18:** II.C.2
    solicitation of business, **18:** II.C.1
    Web sites, use of, **18:** II.B.1
EU. See European Union
European Commission
  Article 29 Working Party, **6:** I.C

export of personal data
    findings of adequacy, **6:** VI.A.1
    Model Clauses, **6:** VI.B.1
  legislation, **6:** I.A
  national laws and, **6:** I.B
European Court of Justice, 6: I.C
European Economic Area (EEA). *See* European Union
European Parliament, 6: I.A
European Patent Convention, 15: VII.B.3
European Union (EU)
  generally, **6:** I
  Article 29 Working Party, **6:** I.C, III.B, IV.C
  consumer protection laws and, **6:** X
  cookies, **6:** VIII
  data controllers
    administrative requirements, **6:** VII
    defined, **6:** II.C
  data processors
    appointment, **6:** V
    defined, **6:** II.C
  Data Protection Directive. *See* Data Protection Directive
  data protection principles, **6:** IV
    data security, **6:** IV.E
    data subject rights, **6:** IV.D
    explicit consent, **6:** IV.C
    fair and lawful processing, **6:** IV.A
    sensitive personal data, **6:** IV.B
    valid consent, **6:** IV.C
  databases, copyright protection, **15:** III.H.2
  E-Privacy Directive
    generally, **6:** I
    cookies, **6:** VIII
    data security, **6:** IV.E
    unsolicited e-mail, **6:** VIII
  export of personal data, **6:** VI
    adequate level of protection, **6:** VI.A
    adequate safeguards, **6:** VI.B
    binding corporate rules, **6:** VI.B.2
    European Commission findings, **6:** VI.A.1
    exceptions to prohibition, **6:** VI.C
    flow chart, **6:** VI.D
    Model Clauses, **6:** VI.B.1
    U.S. safe harbor, **6:** VI.A.2
  human rights laws and, **6:** X
  jurisdiction
    EEA establishment, **6:** III.A
    non-EEA established entities, **6:** III.B
  legislation in, **6:** I.A
  national laws, **6:** I.B
  national regulators, **6:** I.C
  new proposals, **6:** IX
  personal data, **6:** II.A
  processing, **6:** II.B
  Unfair Commercial Practices Directive, **6:** X
  unsolicited e-mail, **6:** VIII
Evidence
  admissibility. *See* Admissibility of evidence
  attorney-client privilege. *See* Attorney-client privilege
  authentication. *See* Authentication
  circumstantial evidence, antitrust and, **14:** II.C.3
  disclosure. *See* Disclosure
  hearsay, **17:** V
  inadvertent disclosure, **17:** IV.C
  physician-patient privilege, **17:** IV.C
Ex parte communications
  technology, use of, **18:** II.C.3
Exclusionary practices. *See* Antitrust
Exclusive use requirements, 14: IV.B
Export of personal data from EEA, 6: VI
  adequate level of protection, **6:** VI.A
  adequate safeguards, **6:** VI.B
  binding corporate rules, **6:** VI.B.2
  European Commission findings, **6:** VI.A.1
  exceptions to prohibition, **6:** VI.C
  flow chart, **6:** VI.D
  Model Clauses, **6:** VI.B.1
  U.S. safe harbor, **6:** VI.A.2

F

Facebook, 1: III.A.2; **4:** III.C
Fair and Accurate Credit Transactions Act of 2007 (FACTA), 16: II.B.1.b.iv
Fair Credit Reporting Act of 1970, 16: II.B.1.b.iv
False Claims Act (FCA)
  barriers to adoption of EHR, **3:** III.B
  electronic health record system provider liability, **16:** II.E.3
  enforcement, **8:** VI.B
  intent standard, **8:** V.B
False statements, 8: VI.B
FDA. *See* Food and Drug Administration
FDAAA. *See* Food and Drug Administration Amendments Act of 2007
FDCA. *See* Food, Drug, and Cosmetic Act of 1938
Federal Bureau of Investigation (FBI), 10: II.A.1
Federal Communications Commission (FCC)
  telemedicine regulation, collaboration with FDA, **10:** IV.J
Federal Health Information Technology Strategic Plan (HIT Plan), 3: II
Federal Information Processing Standards, 7: IV
Federal Information Security Management Act of 2002 (FISMA), 10: V.C
Federal physician self-referral law. *See* Stark Law
Federal Rules of Civil Procedure
  admissibility of evidence, 2006 Amendments, **17:** IV
  generally, **17:** II
  duty to preserve evidence, **17:** IV.A
  inadvertent disclosure, **17:** IV.C
  production of electronically stored information (ESI), **17:** IV.B
  spoliation of evidence, **17:** IV.A
Federal Trade Commission (FTC)
  Antitrust Guidelines for Collaborations Among Competitors, **14:** I.A, II.A
  antitrust jurisdiction, **14:** I.B
  Competition Policy in the World of B2B Electronic Marketplaces, **14:** I.A, IV.A, IV.C
  COPPA. *See* Children's Online Privacy Protection Act
  standards and certification, **14:** V.B

Federal Trade Commission (FTC)—*Cont'd*
  Statements of Antitrust Enforcement Policy in Health Care, **14:** II.A, II.C.2, II.D.1, IV.B
Federal Trade Commission Act of 1914, 4: VI.E
  enforcement, **8:** VI.A
  e-prescribing, **16:** II.B.1.a
  e-product providers, **16:** II.B.1.b.iii
Federation of State Medical Boards (FSMB), 16: II.B.1.a
  Model Act to Regulate the Practice of Medicine Across State Lines, **9:** III.B
Fee-splitting, 9: II.B
Financial institutions
  business associates, HIPAA definitions, **5:** II.B.3.c.v
  privacy, Gramm–Leach–Bliley Financial Modernization Act, **5:** II.B.3.b
Fines. *See* Civil monetary penalties
First Amendment issues
  defamation, **16:** II.A.1.c
  e-discovery and social media, **18:** II.A.3.c.iii
Florida
  breach notification laws, **7:** V.D
FOIA (Freedom of Information Act)
  privacy protections, **5:** II.B.1.a
Food, Drug, and Cosmetic Act of 1938 (FDCA), 10: I, II.B
Food and Drug Administration (FDA)
  generally, **10:** I
  Abbreviated New Drug Applications, **15:** II.D.2, II.D.3
  Center for Devices and Radiological Health, **10:** II.B.2, III.C.1, IV.J
  Center for Drug Evaluation and Research, **10:** II.A.1
  Center for Food Safety and Applied Nutrition, **10:** II.A.1
  Cybersecurity for Networked Medical Devices Containing Off-the-Shelf (OTS) Software, **10:** IV.E.2
  Division of Drug Marketing, Advertising, and Communications, **10:** II.B
  Draft Guidance for Industry and Food and Drug Administration Staff: Mobile Medical Applications, **10:** IV.F, IV.I
  electronic health record regulation, **10:** III
    authority, **10:** III.A
    collaboration with ONC, **10:** III.D
    FDA Working Group, **10:** III.C.1
    legislative inquiries, **10:** III.C.2
    by ONC, **10:** III.B
    scrutiny and oversight, **10:** III.C
  FDA Final Rule on Medical Device Data Systems, **10:** IV.F
  FDCA. *See* Food, Drug, and Cosmetic Act
  General Principles of Software Validation: Final Guidance for Industry and FDA Staff, **10:** IV.E.1
  Guidance for Industry, FDA Reviewers and Compliance on Off-the-Shelf Software Use in Medical Devices, **10:** IV.E
  Guidance for the Content of Premarket Submissions for Software Contained in Medical Devices, **10:** IV.E.2
  Guidance for the Submission of Premarket Notifications for Medical Image Management Devices, **10:** IV.E.1
  human subjects, privacy protections, **5:** II.B.2.b
  Internet drug sale regulation, **10:** II.A
    consumer education, **10:** II.A.2
    enforcement, **10:** II.A.1
  Internet Drug Sales Action Plan, **10:** II
  Investigational New Drug Applications, **15:** II.D.5
  medical device data system regulation, **10:** IV.G
    exclusion of electronic medical records, **10:** IV.G.1
    uncertain applications, **10:** IV.G.2
  medical devices, definition, **2:** I
  mobile medical application regulation, **1:** III.A.1; **10:** IV.H
    classification of, **10:** IV.H.2
    manufacturer defined, **10:** IV.H.3
    scope of, **10:** IV.H.1
  mobile medical device regulation, **10:** IV.C
    generally, **10:** IV.C.1
    accessory and component devices, **10:** IV.C.2.a
    intended use, **10:** IV.C.2
    regulatory class, **10:** IV.C.2.b
  New Drug Applications, **15:** II.D.1, II.D.3
  Office of Device Evaluation, **10:** III.C.1
  Office of Regulatory Affairs, **10:** II.A.1
  Office of Science and Engineering Laboratories, **10:** III.C.1
  Office of Surveillance and Biometrics, **10:** III.C.1
  online activity regulation, **10:** II
  online direct-to-consumer advertising regulation, **10:** II.B
    genetic testing services, promotion of, **10:** II.B.2
    sponsored links, **10:** II.B.1
  prescription drugs. *See* Prescription drugs
  Sentinel Initiative, **10:** V
    generally, **3:** VI.B
    current status, **10:** V.B
    data security concerns, **10:** V.C
    future prospects, **10:** V.B
    privacy concerns, **10:** V.C
    structure and objective, **10:** V.A
  telemedicine regulation. *See* Telemedicine
Food and Drug Administration Amendments Act of 2007 (FDAAA), 3: VI.B; **10:** V, V.B, V.C
Forfeitures for trademark or service mark infringement, 16: II.A.1.b
Foundation for admission of electronically stored information, 17: V
Fourteenth Amendment issues
  privacy protections, **5:** II.A.1
Fourth Amendment issues
  e-discovery and social media, **18:** II.A.3.c.iii
France
  data controllers, administrative requirements, **6:** VII
Fraud and abuse
  due diligence reviews, **12:** X
  HIPAA security standards preemption, **5:** II.B.3.c.vii

mail fraud, *8:* VI.C
RHIOs and, *16:* II.E.3
wire fraud, *8:* VI.C
Freedom of Information Act (FOIA)
 privacy protections, *5:* II.B.1.a
FSMB. *See* Federation of State Medical Boards
FTC. *See* Federal Trade Commission
FTCA. *See* Federal Trade Commission Act of 1914
Fundraising and business associate contracts
 privacy issues, *13:* V.B.2.d

G

General Dynamics, *1:* III.B.2
General Services Administration (GSA),
 1: III.A.3
Generic drugs
 Hatch–Waxman Act, *15:* II.D.3
Genetic information
 disclosure and use restrictions, *5:* III.B.2.b
Genetic Information Nondiscrimination Act of 2008, *7:* III; *8:* I
Genetic testing services, *10:* II.B.2
Georgia
 breach notification laws, *7:* V.D
Germany
 data controllers, administrative requirements, *6:* VII
Ginger.io (mobile application), *1:* III.A.1
Good faith standard
 data security and, *7:* II.D
 exceptions to definition of breach
  disclosed information not reasonably retained, *11:* IV.C
  employment, disclosure within scope of, *11:* IV.A
 spoliation of evidence, *17:* IV.A
Google
 e-prescribing, *16:* II.B.1.a
 patient health care records and, *4:* III.C
 Terms of Service, *16:* III.A.2
Google Health, *1:* III.B.2
Government Accountability Office (GAO), *10:* V.C
Gramm–Leach–Bliley Financial Modernization Act of 1999, *5:* II.B.3.b; *7:* V.B
Group boycotts, *14:* II.D
Group health plans
 applicability of Privacy Rule, *15:* II.C.3
Group purchasing and sales, *14:* II.E
 electronic marketplace and, *14:* II.E.2
 traditional analysis, *14:* II.E.1
Growth of e-health industry, *1:* III
 cloud computing, *1:* III.A.3
 corporate transactions, *1:* III.B
 government investment in innovation, *1:* III.B.1
 government support, *1:* III.C
 mergers and acquisitions, *1:* III.B.2
 mobile applications, *1:* III.A.1
 product development, *1:* III.A
 social media, *1:* III.A.2
 venture capital investment in innovation, *1:* III.B.1
 wireless medical devices, *1:* III.A.1
GSA (General Services Administration), *1:* III.A.3

H

Hart–Scott–Rodino Act of 1976, *14:* II.B
Hatch–Waxman Act of 1984, *15:* II.D
 generally, *15:* II.D.1
 Abbreviated New Drug Applications, *15:* II.D.2, II.D.3
 generic drugs, *15:* II.D.3
 market exclusivity, *15:* II.D.5
 patent infringement, *15:* II.D.3
 patent term extension, *15:* II.D.5
 pioneer drug companies, *15:* II.D.5
 safe harbor, *15:* II.D.4
Hawaii
 breach notification laws, *7:* V.D
HCPCS/CPT (Health Care Financing Administration Common Procedure Coding System/Current Procedural Technology), *15:* V.A
Health and Human Services, U.S. Department of (HHS)
 audits, *8:* III.C
 breach notification. *See* Breach notification
 Centers for Medicare and Medicaid Services (CMS). *See* Centers for Medicare and Medicaid Services
 e-health defined by, *1:* II
 FDA. *See* Food and Drug Administration
 human subjects, privacy protections, *5:* II.B.2.b
 Office of Civil Rights. *See* Office of Civil Rights
 Office of Inspector General. *See* Office of Inspector General
 social media and, *1:* III.A.2
 voluntary compliance and resolution agreements, *8:* III.D
Health Care and Education Reconciliation Act, *2:* III.A
Health Information and Management Systems Society (HIMSS)
 e-health, proposed definition, *2:* I
Health Information Exchange Challenge Grant Program, *1:* III.B.1
Health information exchanges (HIEs). *See also* Regional health information organizations
 admissibility of evidence, *17:* VI.B
 antitrust and, *14:* I.A
 EHR system providers, allocation of rights and obligations, *16:* II.E.3
 preliminary transactional agreements, *15:* IX.A.1.b
Health information technology
 generally, *3:* I, VII
 accountable care organizations, *3:* V
 data analysis, *3:* VI
  aggregation of data, *3:* VI.A
  interoperability, *3:* VI.C
  issues with aggregation of data, *3:* VI.B
  risks involved with, *3:* VI.D
 government initiatives, *3:* II

Health information technology—Cont'd
  regional health information organizations, *3:* IV
    fragmentation of technology providers,
      3: IV.C
    implementation of, *3:* IV.A
    lessons learned from, *3:* IV.B
Health Information Technology for Economic and Clinical Health Act of 2009 (HITECH Act), *2:* III.A; *5:* II.B.3.d
  breach of privacy or data security
    generally, *5:* II.B.3.d.ii.b; *11:* I
    civil penalties, *11:* VII.A
    criminal penalties, *11:* VII.B
    notification. *See* Breach notification
    unsecured protected health information exception, *11:* IV.B
  business associate agreements, *5:* II.B.3.d.ii.c
  confidentiality and compliance management, *18:* II.A.1.b
  coordination with EHR use, *3:* III.B
  definitions, *5:* II.B.3.d.ii.a
  due diligence, *5:* I
  electronic health records (EHR) systems and prohibitions, *5:* II.B.3.d.ii.f
  email and encryption, violations concerning, *18:* II.A.2.c.iv
  enforcement. *See* Enforcement
  government support of e-health industry, *1:* III.C
  HIPAA privacy rule, amendments to, *5:* II.B.3.d.ii
  HIT Policy Committee, *3:* III.A
    recommendations, *10:* III.D.1, III.D.3
  HIT Standards Committee, *3:* III.A
  individual rights under HIPAA, changes to, *5:* II.B.3.d.ii.d
  intellectual property and, *15:* II.B
    generally, *15:* II.B.1
    breach notification, *15:* II.B.4
    health information technology standards, *15:* II.B.2
    incentive payments, *15:* II.B.3
    penalties, *15:* II.B.5
    privacy, *15:* II.B.4
  liability, *16:* I. *See also specific risk or entity*
  marketing and fundraising, changes to, *5:* II.B.3.d.ii.e
  notification of breach, *5:* II.B.3.d.ii.b
  ONC. *See* Office of the National Coordinator for Health IT
  privacy
    generally, *1:* IV
    business associate contracts. *See* Business associate contracts
    state law conflicts, *5:* II.B.3.c
  Promotion of Health Information Technology, *5:* II.B.3.d.i
  protected health information (PHI), prohibitions, *5:* II.B.3.d.ii.f
  subtitle A, summary of, *5:* II.B.3.d.i
  subtitle B, summary of, *5:* II.B.3.d.i
  subtitle C, summary of, *5:* II.B.3.d.i
  subtitle D, summary of, *5:* II.B.3.d.ii
  Testing of Health Information Technology, *5:* II.B.3.d.i
  unsecured protected health information (PHI), definition, *5:* II.B.3.d.ii.b
Health Information Technology Standards Panel (HITSP), *3:* III.A
Health Insurance Portability and Accountability Act of 1996 (HIPAA)
  administrative simplification, *8:* I, II.A, VI.B; *15:* II.A.1, II.A.5, II.B.5
  breach reports, *8:* III.B
  business associate contracts
    privacy protections, definitions, *5:* II.B.3.c.v
    safeguards, *5:* II.B.3.c.v
  complaint process, *8:* III.A
  compliance audits, *8:* III.C
  compliance plans, *8:* VIII
  compliance reviews, *8:* III.A
  confidentiality and compliance management, *18:* II.A.1.b
  coordination with EHR use, *3:* III.B
  due diligence, *12:* X
    liability review, *12:* VII.B
  enforcement. *See* Enforcement
  guidance, *8:* II.B
  individually identifiable health information, *5:* II.B.3.c.i
  intellectual property and, *15:* II.A
    generally, *15:* II.A.1
    data security, *15:* II.A.2
    enforcement rule, *15:* II.A.5
    National Provider Identifier Standard, *15:* II.A.3
    privacy, *15:* II.A.2
    transactions and code set (TCS) standards, *15:* II.A.4
  investigations, *8:* III.A
  liability under, *16:* I. *See also specific risk or entity*
  patents and, *15:* VII.D.2
  patient health care records
    breach notification. *See* Breach notification
    privacy, *4:* VI.A.1
  preemption, *8:* VII
  privacy protections
    business associates, definitions, *5:* II.B.3.c.v
    disclosures, required and permitted, *5:* II.B.3.c.ii
    enforcement, *5:* II.B.3.c.vi
    health information, definition, *5:* II.B.3.c
    "minimum necessary" standard, *5:* II.B.3.c.iii
    state law conflicts, *5:* II.B.3.c.vii
    uses, required and permitted, *5:* II.B.3.c.ii
  Privacy Rule. *See* Privacy Rule
  private right of action, *8:* II.C
  Security Rule. *See* Security Rule
  security standards
    consents and authorizations, *5:* II.B.3.c.iv
    de-identified information, *5:* II.B.3.c.iv
    disclosures, *5:* II.B.3.c.ii
    effective dates, *5:* II.B.3.c
    enforcement, *5:* II.B.3.c.vi
    health information, definition, *5:* II.B.3.c
    minimum necessary standard, *5:* II.B.3.c.iii
    required and permitted uses and disclosures, *5:* II.B.3.c.ii

state law conflicts, *5:* II.B.3.c.vii
as standard of care, *8:* II.A, VI.E
Standards for Electronic Transactions, *8:* II.A
state law conflicts with privacy protections,
5: II.B.3.c, II.B.3.c.vii
violations, *8:* II.C
voluntary compliance and resolution agreements,
8: III.D
Health maintenance organizations (HMOs)
exclusive use requirements, *14:* IV.B
privacy rule, applicability of, *15:* II.C.3
Health Privacy Project, *5:* III.B.1.a
Healthcare Common Procedure Coding System/ Current Procedural Technology (HCPCS/CPT), *15:* V.A
Healthcare Information and Management Systems Society, *8:* IV.E
HealthVault (mobile appolication), *1:* III.A.1
Hearsay, *17:* V
HHS. *See* Health and Human Services, U.S. Department of
HIMSS. *See* Health Information and Management Systems Society
HIPAA. *See* Health Insurance Portability and Accountability Act of 1996
HIT Policy Committee
generally, *3:* III.A
recommendations, *10:* III.D.1, III.D.3
HIT Standards Committee, *3:* III.A
HIT Startup Showcase, *1:* III.B.1
HITECH Act. *See* Health Information Technology for Economic and Clinical Health Act of 2009
HIV/AIDS test results
AMA guidelines, *5:* IV.A.1
state disclosure laws, *5:* III.B.2.b
Hospital Corporation of America (HCA), *2:* II.A
Hospitals
fair information practices, *5:* II.B.3.a
inadvertent disclosure, *11:* IV.B
Privacy Act of 1974, *5:* II.B.3.a
Hotmail
browse wrap agreements, *13:* IV.A
Human rights laws
EU Data Protection Directive and, *6:* X
Human subjects in clinical trials, *5:* II.B.2.b
privacy protections, *5:* II.B.2.b
Hypertext links. *See* Linking agreements

I

IBM, *1:* III.B.2
ICD-9-CM (International Classification of Diseases, Clinical Modification), *15:* V.B
Idaho
breach notification laws, *7:* V.D
Identity theft, *7:* V.A
iHealthBeat (e-content provider), *16:* II.A.2
IIHI. *See* Individually identifiable health information
Illinois
breach notification laws, *7:* V.D

**Imprisonment for breach under HITECH Act,
*11:*** VII.B
Inadvertent disclosure, *17:* IV.C
exceptions to definition of breach, *11:* IV.B
Independent contractors
telemedicine and vicarious liability issues,
9: IV.D
Indiana
breach notification laws, *7:* V.D
**Indirect criminal liability of business associates,
*8:*** V.E
**Individually identifiable health information,
*5:*** II.B.3.c.i; *15:* II.C
generally, *15:* II.C.1
administrative safeguards, *15:* II.C.5
definition, *5:* II.B.3.c
de-identified information, *5:* II.B.3.c.iv
disclosures, *15:* II.C.4
law enforcement purposes, *15:* II.C.4.b
marketing purposes, *15:* II.C.4.d
minimum necessary rule, *15:* II.C.4.e
oversight purposes, *15:* II.C.4.b
public health purposes, *15:* II.C.4.b
required disclosures, *15:* II.C.4.a
research purposes, *15:* II.C.4.c
enforcement, *5:* II.B.3.c.vi
HIPAA standards, preemption, *5:* II.B.3.c.vii
information protected, *15:* II.C.2
minimum necessary standard, *5:* II.B.3.c.iii
persons subject to, *15:* II.C.3
required and permitted uses and disclosures,
5: II.B.3.c.ii
Information ecosystem model, *17:* III
Information security. *See* Security policies
Informed consent. *See* Consents and authorizations
Infringement of proprietary rights
copyrights. *See* Copyright infringement
patents, *15:* II.D.3
trademarks and service marks. *See* Trademark or service mark infringement
Initiate Systems, *1:* III.B.2
Injunctions
copyright infringement, *16:* II.A.1.a
trademark or service mark infringement,
15: VI.A.2; *16:* II.A.1.b
Innovation, *1:* III.B.1
Inspections. *See* Enforcement
Institutional Review Board (IRB), *15:* II.C.4.c
human subjects, privacy protections, *5:* II.B.2.b
Intellectual property
copyrights. *See* Copyrights
due diligence. *See* Due diligence
Hatch–Waxman Act and. *See* Hatch–Waxman Act of 1984
HIPAA and. *See* Health Insurance Portability and Accountability Act of 1996
HITECH Act and. *See* Health Information Technology for Economic and Clinical Health Act of 2009
individually identifiable health information. *See* Individually identifiable health information
litigation. *See* Litigation
NDAs. *See* Nondisclosure agreements

Intellectual property—*Cont'd*
  patents. *See* Patents
  preliminary transactional agreements. *See*
    Preliminary transactional agreements
  trade secrets. *See* Trade secrets
  trademarks and service marks. *See* Trademarks
    and service marks
Intent
  criminal enforcement and, *8:* V.B
**International Classification of Diseases, Clinical
  Modification (ICD-9-CM), *15:* V.B**
International laws and standards. *See also*
    European Union
  overview of, *5:* I
Internet
  breach notification, *11:* VI.B
  Children's Online Privacy Protection Act,
    5: II.B.2.a
  domain names. *See* Domain names
  drug sale regulation, *10:* II.A
    consumer education, *10:* II.A.2
    enforcement, *10:* II.A.1
  e-mail. *See* E-mail
  ethics
    competence, *18:* II.A
    confidentiality, *18:* II.A.1
  jurisdiction over, *13:* II
  third-party Web pages, *12:* VII.C
**Internet Corporation for Assigned Names
  and Numbers (ICANN), *15:* VI.C.2;
  16: II.A.1.b, III.B.3**
Interoperability, *3:* VI.C
Interstate commerce
  physicians practicing in more than one state. *See*
    Licensed medical practitioners
Interviews
  due diligence, *12:* VII.E
Inventions. *See* Patents
Investigational New Drug Applications, *15:* II.D.5
Investigations, *8:* III.A. *See also* Enforcement
Iowa
  breach notification laws, *7:* V.D
iPad and iPhone
  mobile applications, *1:* III.A.1
IRB. *See* Institutional Review Board
iTouch
  mobile applications, *1:* III.A.1

J

**JCAHO (Joint Commission on Accreditation of
  Healthcare Organizations)**
  due diligence review, *12:* IX.B
  information management standards, *5:* IV.A.3
  patient rights standards, *5:* IV.A.3
Joint Working Group on Telemedicine, *9:* III.A
Journal of Medical Internet Research, **16:** II.A.2
**Judicial review of civil monetary penalties,
  8: IV.F**
Jurisdiction
  commercial nature of exchange of information,
    13: II
  contracts, *13:* II

effect test standard, *13:* II
European Union
  EEA establishment, *6:* III.A
  non-EEA established entities, *6:* III.B
level of interactivity, *13:* II
minimum contacts, *13:* II
over Internet, *13:* II
purposeful availment, *13:* II
sliding scale, *13:* II
Justice Department (DOJ)
  antitrust jurisdiction, *14:* I.B
  Office of Legal Counsel, *8:* V.A, V.B
  *Statements of Antitrust Enforcement Policy in
    Health Care,* *14:* II.A, II.C.2, II.D.1,
    IV.B

K

Kansas
  breach notification laws, *7:* V.D
Knowledge
  criminal enforcement, *8:* V.B

L

Lab tests
  physician-patient relationship with physician
    performing lab analysis, *9:* IV.A
Lanham Act of 1946
  codification of, *15:* VI.A.3
  dilution, *15:* VI.A.4
  e-content provider liability, *16:* II.A.1.b
  subject matter of mark, *15:* VI.A.1
Law enforcement
  disclosure of protected health information for,
    15: II.C.4.b
Letters of intent (LOI), *15:* IX
Liability
  generally, *16:* I
  Communications Decency Act immunity. *See*
    Communications Decency Act
Libel. *See* Defamation
Licensed medical practitioners
  certifications, *9:* VI.C
  definition of practice of medicine, *9:* II.A
  liability, *9:* VI.D
  Model Act to Regulate the Practice of Medicine
    Across State Lines (Federation of State
    Medical Boards), *9:* III.B
  overview, *9:* I
  physician-patient relationship, *9:* VI.A
  practice across state lines, *9:* I, II.E.1
    consultation exception, *9:* II.E.1, III.A
    endorsement, *9:* II.E.2, III.A
    proposed regulatory initiatives, *9:* III
    reciprocity, *9:* II.E.3
    special licensing, *9:* II.E.4
  prescribing drugs, *9:* IV.E. *See also* Prescription
    drugs
  standard of care, *9:* VI.B
  state regulation, *9:* II.A
  unauthorized practice of medicine, *9:* II.B

Licenses. *See also* Click-through agreements and click-wrap licenses
    due diligence, *12:* X; *15:* X.A.3
    Nurse Licensure Compact, *9:* III.C
    pharmacies and pharmacists. *See* Verified Internet Pharmacy Practice Sites certification program
    physicians. *See* Licensed medical practitioners
    privacy protections
        disclosure restrictions, *5:* III.B.2
        HIPAA security standards, preemption, *5:* II.B.3.c.vii
LifeLens
    mobile applications, *1:* III.A.1
Linking agreements
    click-wrap licenses, *12:* VII.C
    third-party Web pages, *12:* VII.C
Litigation
    intellectual property
        generally, *15:* X.E
        alternative dispute resolution, *15:* X.D.3
        cross-licensing agreements, *15:* X.B.2
        due diligence, *15:* X.A. *See also* Due diligence
        existing employee education, *15:* X.C.1
        independent contractor education, *15:* X.C.2
        industry and government outreach, *15:* X.D.2
        insurance, *15:* X.D.1
        non-employee education, *15:* X.C.2
        patent pools, *15:* X.B.2
        proper implementation of corporate policies, *15:* X.C.3
        strategic intellectual property filings, *15:* X.B.1
    joint representation, *18:* IV.A.8
    litigation holds, *17:* IV.A
Logging
    business associate contracts, privacy issues, *13:* V.B.2.b
Louisiana
    breach notification laws, *7:* V.D

M

Madrid Protocol, *15:* VI.A.3
Mail fraud, *8:* VI.C
Maine
    breach notification laws, *7:* V.D
Malpractice, *9:* IV
    allocation of risk, *16:* III.E.2
    "all-risk" coverage, *9:* IV.F.3.b
    conflicts of interest, *18:* IV.D
    disclaimers of liability, *9:* IV.F.2
    e-care providers, *16:* II.D.2
    e-mail communications, *18:* II.A.2.c.iii
    insurance and gaps, *9:* IV.F.1
    mitigation of risk, *16:* III.E.1
    "open-perils" coverage, *9:* IV.F.3.b
    recommendations, *9:* IV.F.3.c
    "specified-perils" coverage, *9:* IV.F.3.a
    "specified-risk" coverage, *9:* IV.F.3.a
    telemedicine, malpractice insurance coverage, *9:* IV.F.1

Market exclusivity, *15:* II.D.5
Marketing. *See also* Advertising
    business associate contracts, privacy issues, *13:* V.B.2.d
    disclosure of protected health information for, *15:* II.C.4.d
Maryland
    breach notification laws, *7:* V.D
Massachusetts
    breach notification laws, *7:* V.D
    unauthorized practice of medicine, *9:* II.B
Massachusetts e-Health Collaborative (MAeHC), *3:* IV.A
MasterCard, *16:* III.F.3
Materiality standard for due diligence reviews, *12:* III
Mayo Clinic, *16:* II.A.1
MDs. *See* Licensed medical practitioners; Practice of medicine
Media
    breach notification, *11:* VI.B
    disclosure of information, AMA guidelines, *5:* IV.A.1
Medicaid. *See* Medicare and Medicaid
Medical codings, *15:* V
    DRG, *15:* V.C
    HCPCS/CPT, *15:* V.A
    ICD-9-CM, *15:* V.B
    reidentification problem, *15:* V.D
Medical devices
    definition, *2:* I
    e-health applications, distinguished from, *2:* I
    FDA regulation of data systems, *10:* IV.G
        exclusion of electronic medical records, *10:* IV.G.1
        uncertain applications, *10:* IV.G.2
Medical records. *See also* Patient health care records
    electronic storage or transmission, HIPAA regulations preemption, *5:* II.B.3.c.vii
    privacy. *See* Privacy
    release. *See* Consents and authorizations
Medicare and Medicaid
    civil monetary penalties, *8:* VI.B
    conditions of participation, *5:* II.B.1.c
    due diligence reviews, *12:* IX.E
    fraud and abuse. *See* Fraud and abuse
    incentive programs, achievement of meaningful use, *15:* II.B.3; *16:* II.E.2
    international practice of medicine, *9:* V.C
    privacy of information
        conditions of participation, *5:* II.B.1.c
        privacy rule, applicability of, *15:* II.C.3
    Shared Savings Program, *14:* II.A
    Stark Law. *See* Stark Law
Medicare Prescription Drug, Improvement and Modernization Act of 2003 (MMA), *2:* III.B
Medicines. *See* Prescription drugs
Memoranda of understanding (MOU), *15:* IX
Mental health information
    disclosure and use restrictions, *5:* III.B.2.b

Mergers and acquisitions
  antitrust. *See* Antitrust
  growth of e-health industry and, *1:* III.B.2
Metadata, *17:* IV.B
  email, ethical considerations of, *18:* II.A.2.e
mHealth Regulatory Coalition, *10:* IV.B
mHealth technologies, *10:* IV.B
Michigan
  breach notification laws, *7:* V.D
Microsoft
  mergers and acquisitions, *1:* III.B.2
  mobile applications, *1:* III.A.1
  patient health care records and, *4:* III.C
Minimum contacts jurisdiction, *13:* II
Minimum necessary standard, *5:* II.B.3.c.iii; *13:* V.B.2.a; *15:* II.C.4.e
Minnesota
  breach notification laws, *7:* V.D
Minors
  disclosure and use restrictions, *5:* III.B.2.b
  online protection. *See* Children's Online Privacy Protection Act
Misbranded drugs, *16:* II.B.1.a
Missouri
  reciprocity for medical practice privileges, *9:* II.E.3
Mitigating actions
  contents of breach notification, *11:* VI.C
  risk assessment, *11:* III.C
Mitigating factors for civil monetary penalties, *8:* IV.G.5
Mobile devices and applications
  defined, *10:* IV.C.1
  development of, *1:* III.A.1
  ethics, *18:* II.A.5
  FDA regulation, *10:* IV.C, IV.H
    accessory and component devices, *10:* IV.C.2.a
    classification of, *10:* IV.H.2
    intended use, *10:* IV.C.2
    manufacturer defined, *10:* IV.H.3
    regulatory class, *10:* IV.C.2.b
    scope of, *10:* IV.H.1
Model laws, *5:* III.A
  Health Information Privacy Model Act, *5:* III.A.1
  Uniform Health Care Information Act, *5:* III.A.2
Modern-Healthcare.com, *16:* II.A.2
Monopoly. *See* Antitrust
Montana
  breach notification laws, *7:* V.D
Most-favored-nation requirements, *14:* IV.C

N

NABP (National Association of Boards of Pharmacy). *See* Verified Internet Pharmacy Practice Sites certification program
NAI Principles. *See* Network Advertising Initiative Fair Information Principles
National Ambulatory Medical Care Survey, *15:* IX.A.1
National Association of Boards of Pharmacy (NABP), *10:* II.A.2; *16:* II.B.1.a. *See also* Verified Internet Pharmacy Practice Sites certification program
National Center for Health Statistics, *15:* V.B
National Committee on Vital and Health Statistics (NCVHS), *4:* III.A
National Conference of Commissioners of Uniform State Laws (NCCUSL). *See specific Uniform Law*
National Conference of State Legislatures, *16:* III.F.3
National Council of State Boards of Nursing, *9:* III.C
National e-Health Collaborative (NeHC), *3:* III.A
National E-Health Innovation Series, *1:* III.B.1
National Health Information Technology Week, *1:* III.C
National Institute of Standards and Technology (NIST), *1:* IV; *7:* II, IV
National Provider Identified Standard, *15:* II.A.3
National Research Council, *10:* III.D.3
Nationwide Health Information Network (NHIN), *3:* II, IV.A, VI.C; *16:* III.F.2
NCCUSL (National Conference of Commissioners of Uniform State Laws). *See specific Uniform Law*
NDAs. *See* Nondisclosure agreements
Nebraska
  breach notification laws, *7:* V.D
Negligence. *See* Malpractice
Network effects, *14:* IV.A
Nevada
  breach notification laws, *7:* V.D
New Drug Applications, *15:* II.D.1, II.D.3
New England Journal of Medicine, *16:* II.A.2
New Hampshire
  breach notification laws, *7:* V.D
New Jersey
  breach notification laws, *7:* V.D
New York
  breach notification laws, *7:* V.D
  definition of practice of medicine, *9:* II.A
Nondisclosure agreements (NDAs), *15:* IX.B
  access to confidential information, *15:* IX.B.1
  nondisclosure of confidential information, *15:* IX.B.3
  nonsolicitation of customers and employees, *15:* IX.B.4
  reservation of proprietary rights, *15:* IX.B.5
  restricted use of confidential information, *15:* IX.B.2
North Carolina
  breach notification laws, *7:* V.D
North Dakota
  breach notification laws, *7:* V.D
Notice and notification
  breach notification. *See* Breach notification
  civil monetary penalties, *8:* IV.G.2
  due diligence, *12:* IX.G
Nurse Licensure Compact, *9:* III.C

O

OCILLA. *See* Online Copyright Infringement Liability Limitation Act of 1998
OECD. *See* Organization for Economic Cooperation and Development
Office of Civil Rights (OCR)
    breach reports, *8:* III.B
    complaint process, *8:* III.A
    data security, *7:* II.C, II.D
    enforcement activity, *1:* IV
    fines, *16:* II.E.1
    HIPAA administration, *8:* II.A
    intellectual property and, *15:* II.A.5
Office of E-Health Standards and Services, *7:* II.C
Office of Inspector General (OIG)
    civil monetary penalties, *8:* IV.F
    compliance audits, *8:* III.C
    data security, *7:* II.C
    EHR use, regulations on, *3:* III.B
Office of Legal Counsel (OLC), *8:* V.A, V.B
Office of National Drug Control and Policy (ONDCP), *10:* II.A.1
Office of the National Coordinator for Health IT (ONCHIT), *2:* II.F
    antitrust and, *14:* II.B
    electronic health record regulation
        generally, *10:* III.B
        collaboration with FDA, *10:* III.D
        concerns, *10:* III.D.2
        future collaboration with FDA, *10:* III.D.3
        HIT Policy Committee recommendations, *10:* III.D.1
    establishment of, *3:* II
    health information technology standards, *15:* II.B.2
    innovation, grants for, *1:* III.B.1
    standards for electronic health records, *3:* III.A
    support for electronic health records, *1:* III.C
Off-the-shelf software, *10:* IV.E
Ohio
    breach notification laws, *7:* V.D
    consultation exception for out-of-state physicians, *9:* II.E
Oklahoma
    breach notification laws, *7:* V.D
Online Copyright Infringement Liability Limitation Act of 1998 (OCILLA), *16:* II.C.1, III.A.1, III.A.3. *See also* Digital Millennium Copyright Act
Online direct-to-consumer advertising regulation, *10:* II.B
    genetic testing services, promotion of, *10:* II.B.2
    sponsored links, *10:* II.B.1
Oracle, *1:* III.B.2
Oregon
    breach notification laws, *7:* V.D

P

Patent and Trademark Office (PTO), *15:* VI.A.3, VII.A.1; *16:* III.B.1
Patent pools, *15:* X.B.2

Patents, *15:* VII. *See also* Proprietary rights
    acquisition of, *15:* VII.C.2
    applications, *15:* VII.A.1
    bringing product to market, *15:* VII.C
    due diligence and asset-related review, *12:* VII.A
    enablement, *15:* VII.B.2
        multiple configurations of drugs and materials, *15:* VII.D.1
    enforcement, *15:* VII.A.3
    filing, *15:* VII.C.2
    freedom to operate, *15:* VII.C.1
    HIPAA and, *15:* VII.D.2
    idea versus invention, *15:* VII.B.1
    infringement, *15:* II.D.3
        Hatch–Waxman Act, *15:* II.D.3
    invalidity, *15:* VII.B.5
    novelty, *15:* VII.B.4
    originality, *15:* VII.B.4
    privacy and, *15:* VII.D.2
    prosecutions, *15:* VII.A.2
    rights, *15:* VII.A.3
    statutory class of invention, *15:* VII.B.3
    term extension, *15:* II.D.5
    unobviousness, *15:* VII.B.5
    written description requirement, *15:* VII.B.2
Patient health care records (PHRs)
    generally, *4:* I, VIII
    attributes of, *4:* IV.B
    cloud computing and, *4:* III.C
    contents of breach notification, *4:* VI.C
    defined, *4:* II
    EHRs and EMRs distinguished from, *4:* IV.C
    electronic surveillance, *4:* V
    enforcement of breach notification requirements, *4:* VI.E
    HIPAA breach notification, *4:* VI.B.1
        breach defined, *4:* VI.B.1.a
        dual reporting obligations, *4:* VI.D
        enforcement, *4:* VI.B.1.d
        reporting requirements, *4:* VI.B.1.c
        threshold harm requirement, *4:* VI.B.1.b
    historical background, *4:* III
    HITECH breach notification, *4:* VI.B.2
        dual reporting obligations, *4:* VI.D
        FTC, reporting to, *4:* VI.B.2.b.iv
        individuals, reporting to, *4:* VI.B.2.b.ii
        media, reporting to, *4:* VI.B.2.b.iii
        reportable breach, *4:* VI.B.2.a
        third-party service providers, reporting to, *4:* VI.B.2.b.v
        vendors, reporting to, *4:* VI.B.2.b.i
    Internet, risks associated with, *4:* V
    market forces and, *4:* III.B
    paradigm shift, *4:* III.A
    privacy
        HIPAA entities, *4:* VI.A.1
        non-HIPAA vendors, *4:* VI.A.2
    recommendations, *4:* VIII
    social media and, *4:* III.C
    state statutes
        breach notification, *4:* VII.B
        confidentiality, *4:* VII.A
    tethered PHRs, *4:* IV.A
    types of, *4:* IV
    untethered PHRs, *4:* IV.A

Patient involvement and collaboration, *1:* III
Patient Protection and Affordable Care Act of 2010 (PPACA)
  accountable care organizations, *15:* IX.A.1.d
  health information technology development and, *12:* I
  HIPAA transactions and, *2:* III.A
  liability under, *16:* I. *See also specific risk or entity*
  privacy and, *15:* IV.A
  telemedicine and, *10:* IV.D.2
Patient records. *See also* Patient health care records (PHRs)
  electronic storage or transmission, HIPAA regulations
    preemption, *5:* II.B.3.c.vii
  privacy. *See* Privacy
  release. *See* Consents and authorizations
Patient rights
  Joint Commission on Accreditation of Healthcare Organizations standards, *5:* IV.A.3
  physician-patient relationship. *See* Practice of medicine
Patient Safety and Quality Improvement Act of 2005 (PSQIA), *8:* I
Patients Like Me (e-content provider), *16:* II.A.1
Payment Card Industry Data Security Standard, *16:* II.B.1.b.ii, III.F.1
PDAs (personal digital assistants), *18:* II.A.5
Penalties
  copyright infringement, *16:* II.A.1.a
  HITECH Act, breach under, *11:* VII.B
  unauthorized practice of medicine, *9:* II.B
Pennsylvania
  breach notification laws, *7:* V.D
  consultation exception for out-of-state physicians, *9:* II.E
Personal digital assistants (PDAs), *18:* II.A.5
Personalized Health Information Act of 2007, *4:* III.A
Phase Forward, *1:* III.B.2
Phoenix Health Systems, *8:* IV.E
PHRs. *See* Patient health care records
Physician self-referral law. *See* Stark Law
Physician-patient privilege, inadvertent disclosure, *17:* IV.C
Physicians. *See* Licensed medical practitioners; Practice of medicine
  prescribing and dispensing drugs. *See* Prescription drugs
Pioneer drug companies, *15:* II.D.5
PKI (Public key infrastructure), *17:* VI.A
Postal Service
  e-prescribing, *16:* II.B.1.a
Practice of medicine. *See also* Licensed medical practitioners
  corporate practice of medicine, *9:* II.B
  defined, *9:* II.A
  duty to disclose, *9:* IV.C
  electronic health information, *9:* VI
    certifications, *9:* VI.C
    liability, *9:* VI.D
    physician-patient relationship, *9:* VI.A

  standard of care, *9:* VI.B
  informed consent, *9:* IV.C
  insurance for telemedicine, *9:* IV.F
  international practice, *9:* V
    legal and licensing issues, *9:* V.D
    Medicaid and Medicare reimbursement, *9:* V.C
    medical tourism, *9:* V.B
    telemedicine, *9:* V.A
  legal duty to patient, *9:* IV.B
  malpractice, *9:* IV
    "all-risk" coverage, *9:* IV.F.3.b
    disclaimers of liability, *9:* IV.F.2
    insurance and gaps, *9:* IV.F.1
    "open-perils" coverage, *9:* IV.F.3.b
    recommendations, *9:* IV.F.3.c
    "specified-perils" coverage, *9:* IV.F.3.a
    "specified-risk" coverage, *9:* IV.F.3.a
  patient abandonment, *9:* IV.E
  physician-patient relationship, *9:* IV.A
  standard of care, *9:* IV.B
  unlicensed or unauthorized practice of medicine, *9:* II.B
    allocation of risk, *16:* III.D.2
    e-care providers, *16:* II.D.1
    e-content providers, *16:* II.A.1.d
    mitigation of risk, *16:* III.D.1
  vicarious liability, *9:* IV.D
Preemption
  E–SIGN Act, *13:* III.A
  HIPAA, *5:* II.B.3.c.vii; *8:* VII
Preliminary transactional agreements, *15:* IX.A
  accountable care organizations, *15:* IX.A.1.d
  contracts, *15:* IX.A.1.a
    foreign contractors, *15:* IX.A.1.a.iv
    regulatory compliance covenants, *15:* IX.A.1.a.iii
    software vendors, *15:* IX.A.1.a.i
    warranties, *15:* IX.A.1.a.ii
  EHRs, *15:* IX.A.1
  health information exchanges, *15:* IX.A.1.c
  health research, *15:* IX.A.1.b
  product development, *15:* IX.A.2
    collaboration agreements, *15:* IX.A.2.a
    trade secrets, *15:* IX.A.2.b
  protected health information, *15:* IX.A.1
Prescription drugs
  adulterated drugs, *16:* II.B.1.a
  Controlled Substances Act of 1970, *16:* II.B.1.a
  counterfeit drugs, *16:* II.B.1.a
  e-prescribing
    allocation of risk, *16:* III.E.2
    consumer-oriented e-product providers, *16:* II.B.1.a
    defined, *1:* II
    mitigation of risk, *16:* III.E.1
    Stark Law and, *16:* II.E.3
  Internet drug sale regulation, *10:* II.A
    consumer education, *10:* II.A.2
    enforcement, *10:* II.A.1
  medical products and devices. *See* Medical devices
  misbranded drugs, *16:* II.B.1.a
  online direct-to-consumer advertising regulation, *10:* II.B

genetic testing services, promotion of, *10:* II.B.2
sponsored links, *10:* II.B.1
prescribing drugs, regulation, *9:* IV.E
trademarks and service marks, *15:* VI.B.2
VIPPS certification program. *See* Verified Internet Pharmacy Practice Sites certification program
Preservation of evidence, *17:* IV.A
Privacy. *See also* Disclosure
access to information rights, *5:* III.B.1.b
breach. *See* Breach of privacy or data security
certificates of confidentiality, *5:* II.B.2.c
Children's Online Privacy Protection Act, *5:* II.B.2.a; *15:* IV.E.3
Computer Fraud and Abuse Act, *15:* IV.C
computer privacy acts, *15:* IV.A
Confidentiality of Records provisions, *5:* II.B.1.b, III.B.2.b
Constitution, U.S., *5:* II.A
scope of protections, *5:* II.A.3
Whalen v. Roe, 5: II.A.2
data collection and use policies, violations, *5:* II.B.2.a
development, *5:* I
Digital Millennium Copyright Act, *15:* IV.D
domestic laws and standards, overview of, *5:* I
due diligence
checklists, *12:* V.C
liability review, *12:* VII.B
understanding of entity and operations, *12:* X
Electronic Communications Privacy Act, *15:* IV.E.1
ethics
confidentiality, *18:* II.A.1
professional competence, *18:* II.A
in European Union. *See* European Union
federal prohibitions, *5:* II.B.3
federal protections, *5:* II
groups, *5:* II.B.2
health care industry, specific segments, *5:* II.B.3
laws and regulations, *5:* II.B
scope and limitations, *5:* II.B.1
Fourteenth Amendment protections, *5:* II.A.1
Freedom of Information Act (FOIA), *5:* II.B.1.a
FTC. *See* Federal Trade Commission
Gramm–Leach–Bliley Financial Modernization Act, *5:* II.B.3.b
HIPAA privacy regulations, *5:* II.B.3.c. *See also* Privacy Rule
business associate agreements, *5:* II.B.3.c.v
business associates, *5:* II.B.3.c.v
de-identified information, *5:* II.B.3.c.iv
disclosures, required and permitted, *5:* II.B.3.c.ii
enforcement, *5:* II.B.3.c.vi
individual rights, *5:* II.B.3.c.i
limited data sets, *5:* II.B.3.c.iv
"minimum necessary" standard, *5:* II.B.3.c.iii
state law conflicts, *5:* II.B.3.c.vii
uses, required and permitted, *5:* II.B.3.c.ii
HITECH Act, *5:* II.B.3.d
breach, *5:* II.B.3.d.ii.b

business associate agreements, *5:* II.B.3.d.ii.c
business associates, *5:* II.B.3.d.ii.c
definitions, *5:* II.B.3.d.ii.a
electronic health records (EHR) systems, prohibitions, *5:* II.B.3.d.ii.f
enforcement, improvements to, *5:* II.B.3.d.ii.g
individual rights under HIPAA, changes to, *5:* II.B.3.d.ii.d
marketing and fundraising, changes to, *5:* II.B.3.d.ii.e
notification of breach, *5:* II.B.3.d.ii.b
Privacy Rule, amendments to, *5:* II.B.3.d.ii
Promotion of Health Information Technology, *5:* II.B.3.d.i
protected health information (PHI), prohibitions, *5:* II.B.3.d.ii.f
subtitle A, summary of, *5:* II.B.3.d.i
subtitle B, summary of, *5:* II.B.3.d.i
subtitle C, summary of, *5:* II.B.3.d.i
subtitle D, summary of, *5:* II.B.3.d.ii
Testing of Health Information Technology, *5:* II.B.3.d.i
unsecured protected health information (PHI), definition, *5:* II.B.3.d.ii.b
impact of HIPAA, *15:* IV.B
medical coding and, *15:* V
DRG, *15:* V.C
HCPCS/CPT, *15:* V.A
ICD-9-CM, *15:* V.B
reidentification problem, *15:* V.D
Semiconductor Chip Protection Act, *15:* IV.E.2
Sentinel Initiative, *10:* V.C
state protections, *5:* III
Health Information Privacy Model Act, *5:* III.A.1
model privacy laws, *5:* III.A
Uniform Health Care Information Act, *5:* III.A.2
Privacy Act of 1974, *5:* II.B.3.a
Privacy Rule (HIPAA)
generally, *1:* IV
aggregation of data and, *3:* VI.B
allocation of risk, *16:* III.F.2
breach. *See* Breach of privacy or data security
breach notification. *See* Breach notification
business associate contracts, *13:* V.B.2
access to patient records, *13:* V.B.2.e
fundraising and marketing, *13:* V.B.2.d
logging and auditing, *13:* V.B.2.b
minimum necessary rule, *13:* V.B.2.a
restricted disclosures, *13:* V.B.2.c
state law, role of, *13:* V.B.2.f
Children's Health Insurance Programs, applicability of rule to, *15:* II.C.3
e-care providers, *16:* II.D.4
e-connection providers, *16:* II.C.4
EHR system providers, *16:* II.E.1
group health plans, applicability of rule to, *15:* II.C.3
HMOs, applicability to, *15:* II.C.3
inadvertent disclosure, *17:* IV.C
individually identifiable health information, *15:* II.C
generally, *15:* II.C.1

Privacy Rule (HIPAA)—*Cont'd*
   administrative safeguards, *15:* II.C.5
   disclosures, *15:* II.C.4
   information protected, *15:* II.C.2
   persons subject to, *15:* II.C.3
   intellectual property and
      HIPAA, *15:* II.A.2
      HITECH Act, *15:* II.B.4
   Medicare and Medicaid, applicability of rule to, *15:* II.C.3
   mitigation of risk
      before claim, *16:* III.F.1
      upon claim, *16:* III.F.3
   patents and, *15:* VII.D.2
   patient health care records, *4:* VI.A.1
      HIPAA entities, *4:* VI.A.1
      non-HIPAA vendors, *4:* VI.A.2
   RHIOs and, *16:* II.E.3, III.F.2
Private right of action, *8:* II.C
Private standard-setting, *14:* V.B, V.C
Privilege
   attorney-client privilege. *See* Attorney-client privilege
   inadvertent disclosure, *17:* IV.C
   physician-patient privilege, *17:* IV.C
Product providers. *See* E-product providers
Production of electronically stored information, *17:* IV.B
Professional codes of conduct, *5:* IV
   American Hospital Association, *5:* IV.A.2
   American Medical Association, *5:* IV.A.1
   ethics. *See* Ethics
   JCAHO/Joint Commission on Accreditation of Healthcare Organizations, *5:* IV.A.3
   privacy, *5:* IV
      American Hospital Association, *5:* IV.A.2
      American Medical Association, *5:* IV.A.1
      Joint Commission on Accreditation of Healthcare Organizations, *5:* IV.A.3
      other privacy protection guidelines, *5:* IV.B
Professional communications
   e-discovery
      admissibility, *18:* II.A.3.c.ii
      ethical considerations, *18:* II.A.3.c.i
      special issues, *18:* II.A.3.c.iii
Professional licenses. *See* Licenses
Program Fraud Civil Remedies Act of 1986, *8:* VI.B
Proprietary rights. *See also* Intellectual property
   copyrights. *See* Copyrights
   domain names. *See* Domain names
   e-connection providers, infringement, *16:* II.C.3
   infringement of, *15:* II.D.3
   letters of intent, *15:* IX
   memoranda of understanding, *15:* IX
   NDAs. *See* Nondisclosure agreements
   patents. *See* Patents
   preliminary transactional agreements. *See* Preliminary transactional agreements
   requests for proposals, *15:* IX
   trade secrets. *See* Trade secrets
   trademarks and service marks. *See* Trademarks and service marks
PTO. *See* Patent and Trademark Office

PTSD Coach (mobile application), *1:* III.A.1
Public health
   HIPAA security standards, preemption, *5:* II.B.3.c.vii
   state laws and federal privacy protections, *5:* II.B.3.c
Public Health Services Act (PHSA), *5:* II.B.2.c
Public key infrastructure (PKI), *17:* VI.A
Public Service Health Act of 1944, *8:* I
Puerto Rico
   breach notification laws, *7:* V.D
Punitive damages
   spoliation of evidence, *17:* IV.A
Purposeful availment, *13:* II

Q

Qui tam suits. *See* False Claims Act

R

Racketeer Influenced and Corrupt Organizations Act of 1970 (RICO), *8:* VI.D
Reasonable cause, *8:* IV.C
Reasonable diligence, *8:* IV.C
Reciprocity for medical practice in another state, *9:* II.E.3
Records. *See also* Patient health care records (PHRs)
   electronic storage or transmission, HIPAA regulations
      preemption, *5:* II.B.3.c.vii
   privacy. *See* Privacy
   release. *See* Consents and authorizations
Red Flags Rule, *16:* II.B.1.b.iv
Reducing costs of health care, *1:* III
Referrals
   liability of referring physician, *9:* IV.A
   self-referral law. *See* Stark Law
Refills of prescription drugs. *See* Prescription drugs
Regional health information organizations (RHIOs), *3:* IV
   closed systems, *3:* IV.A
   confidentiality, *16:* II.E.3
   data security, *16:* II.E.3, III.F.2
   electronic health record system providers, allocation of rights and obligations, *16:* II.E.3
   fragmentation of technology providers, *3:* IV.C
   fraud and abuse, *16:* II.E.3
   implementation of, *3:* IV.A
   lessons learned from, *3:* IV.B
   open systems, *3:* IV.A
   privacy, *16:* II.E.3, III.F.2
Registrar of Copyrights. *See* Copyrights
Registration
   VIPPS certification program. *See* Verified Internet Pharmacy Practice Sites certification program
Regulatory compliance covenants, *15:* IX.A.1.a.iii
Reidentification problem, *15:* V.D

Reimbursement
    Medicare and Medicaid. *See* Medicare and Medicaid
    self-referral laws. *See* Stark Law
Remedies. *See* Damages; Injunctions
Remuneration
    physician self-referral law. *See* Stark Law
Reporting requirements
    due diligence, *12:* V.E
    HIPAA security standards, preemption, *5:* II.B.3.c.vii
Requests for proposals (RFPs), *15:* IX
Resale price maintenance, *14:* I.B
Research
    certificates of confidentiality, *5:* II.B.2.c
    disclosure of protected health information for, *15:* II.C.4.c
    human subjects in clinical trials, *5:* II.B.2.b
    preliminary transactional agreements, *15:* IX.A.1.b
Restraint of trade. *See* Antitrust
RHIOs. *See* Regional health information organizations
Rhode Island
    breach notification laws, *7:* V.D
    unauthorized practice of medicine, *9:* II.B
RICO (Racketeer Influenced and Corrupt Organizations Act of 1970), *8:* VI.D
Risk assessment, *11:* III
    identity of any known recipient, *11:* III.B
    mitigating actions, *11:* III.C
    nature of breach, *11:* III.A
    small risk of individual harm, *11:* III.D

S

Safe harbors
    Digital Millennium Copyright Act, *15:* IV.D
    export of personal data from European Union, *6:* VI.A.2
    Hatch–Waxman Act, *15:* II.D.4
    intent standard, *8:* V.B
    spoliation of evidence, *17:* IV.A
    telemedicine, *16:* II.A.1.d
Sanctions. *See* Penalties
Santa Barbara County Care Data Exchange, *3:* IV.B
Sarbanes-Oxley Act of 2002
    due diligence review, *12:* VI
        audit committee activities, *12:* VI.C
        code of ethics, *12:* VI.D
        disclosure controls, *12:* VI.A
        implications of, *12:* VI.F
        internal controls, *12:* VI.B
        off-balance-sheet transactions, *12:* VI.E
SCPA (Semiconductor Chip Protection Act of 1984), *15:* IV.E.2
SEC. *See* Securities and Exchange Commission
Secrecy. *See* Privacy; Trade secrets
Secrecy agreements. *See* Nondisclosure agreements

Section 5 actions. *See* Federal Trade Commission Act of 1914
Security policies
    due diligence
        checklists, *12:* V.C
        liability review, *12:* VII.B
    HIPAA standards. *See* Health Insurance Portability and Accountability Act
    JCAHO information management standards, *5:* IV.A.3
Security Rule (HIPAA)
    generally, *1:* IV; *7:* I
    administrative safeguards, *7:* II; *13:* V.B.3.a
    allocation of risk, *16:* III.F.2
    breach. *See* Breach of privacy or data security
    breach notification. *See* Breach notification
    business associate contracts, *13:* V.B.3
        generally, *7:* II.E
        additional responsibilities, *13:* V.B.3.e
        administrative safeguards, *13:* V.B.3.a
        breach notification, *13:* V.B.3.d
        civil monetary penalties, *13:* V.B.3.f
        physical safeguards, *13:* V.B.3.b
        technical safeguards, *13:* V.B.3.c
    CMS guidance, *7:* II
    compliance functions, *7:* II.A
    covered entities, *7:* II
    credit cards, *16:* III.F.3
    criminal enforcement, *7:* II.D
    e-care providers, *16:* II.D.4
    e-connection providers, *16:* II.C.4
    EHR system providers, *16:* II.E.1
    electronic media, *7:* II
    false positives versus false negatives, *7:* II.A.3
    flexible approach, *7:* II
    gap analysis, *7:* II.B
    good faith standard, *7:* II.D
    high sensitivity information, *7:* II
    implementation of safeguards, *7:* II.B
    intellectual property and, *15:* II.A.2
    investigations, *7:* II.C
    low sensitivity information, *7:* II
    medium sensitivity information, *7:* II
    mitigation of risk
        before claim, *16:* III.F.1
        upon claim, *16:* III.F.3
    physical safeguards, *7:* II; *13:* V.B.3.b
    program development and management, *7:* II.A
        accountability, *7:* II.A.3
        balancing of objectives, *7:* II.A.4
        confidentiality, *7:* II.A.1
        integrity and availability, *7:* II.A.2
    promulgation of rule, *8:* II.A
    RHIOs and, *16:* II.E.3, III.F.2
    risk analysis, *7:* II
    risk management, *7:* II.A
    risk of penalties for violations, *7:* II.D
    scalability, *7:* II
    technical safeguards, *7:* II; *13:* V.B.3.c
    technology-neutral nature, *7:* II
    violations, civil monetary penalties, *7:* II.D
Self-referral law. *See* Stark Law

Self-regulation
  VIPPS certification program. *See* Verified Internet Pharmacy Practice Sites certification program
Semiconductor Chip Protection Act of 1984 (SCPA), *15:* IV.E.2
Sentencing Commission Guidelines for the Sentencing of Organizations, *8:* VIII
Sentillion Inc., *1:* III.B.2
Sentinel Initiative, *10:* V
  generally, *3:* VI.B
  current status, *10:* V.B
  data security concerns, *10:* V.C
  future prospects, *10:* V.B
  privacy concerns, *10:* V.C
  structure and objective, *10:* V.A
Service marks. *See* Trademarks and service marks
Shared Savings Program, *14:* II.A
Sherman Act of 1890. *See also* Antitrust
  generally, *14:* I.B
  in e-commerce setting, *14:* I.C
  facilitating collusion, *14:* II.C.1, II.C.2
  group boycotts, *14:* II.D
  most-favored-nation requirements, *14:* IV.C
Shrink wrap agreements, *13:* IV.C
Signatures, digital
  admissibility of evidence, *17:* VI.A
  E-SIGN. *See* Electronic Signatures in Global and National Commerce Act
Social media
  e-discovery
    admissibility, *18:* II.A.3.c.ii
    ethical considerations, *18:* II.A.3.c.i
    First Amendment issues, *18:* II.A.3.c.iii
  ethical issues
    attorneys and, *18:* II.B.2.f
    blogs and, *18:* II.B.2.a
    Facebook and, *18:* II.B.2.c
    LinkedIn and, *18:* II.B.2.d
    Myspace and, *18:* II.B.2.d
    Twitter and, *18:* II.B.2.e
    Wiki pages and, *18:* II.B.2.b
  growth of e-health industry in, *1:* III.A.2
  patient health care records and, *4:* III.C
Software
  copyrights, *15:* III.G
  preliminary transactional agreements, *15:* IX.A.1.a.i
South Carolina
  breach notification laws, *7:* V.D
Special-purpose licensing for medical practice privileges, *9:* II.E.4
Spoliation of evidence, *17:* IV.A
Standards of care, *1:* III
  physician standard of care, *9:* IV.B
Stark Law
  barriers to adoption of EHR, *3:* III.B
  due diligence, *12:* X
  e-prescribing and, *16:* II.E.3
  intellectual property and, *16:* II.E.3
  tax laws and, *16:* II.E.3
StartUp Health (strategic initiative), *1:* III.B.1

State boards of pharmacy. *See* Verified Internet Pharmacy Practice Sites certification program
State laws and regulations, *5:* III. *See also specific states*
  breach notification
    generally, *4:* VII.B
    analysis of representative law, *7:* V.C
    complexities of notification, *7:* V.C.2
    encryption and, *7:* V.C.1
    e-product providers, *16:* II.B.1.b.i
    E–SIGN Act, conformity with, *7:* V.C.2
    historical background, *7:* V.B
    immediate notice, *7:* V.C.2
    list of, *7:* V.D
    scope of regulation, *7:* V.C.3
    substitute notice, *7:* V.C.2
  business associate contracts, privacy issues, *13:* V.B.2.f
  civil monetary penalties, *8:* IV.H
  common protections, *5:* III.B.1
  confidentiality, *4:* VII.A
  entity, type of, *5:* III.B.2.c.a
  informed consent and duty to disclose, *9:* IV.C
  medical practice laws, *9:* II.A
    consultation exception for out-of-state physicians, *9:* II.E.1, III.A
    endorsement, *9:* II.E.2, III.A
    reciprocity, *9:* II.E.3
    unauthorized practice of medicine, *9:* II.B
  model privacy laws, *5:* III.A
  Nurse Licensure Compact, *9:* III.C
  preemption
    E–SIGN Act, *13:* III.A
    HIPAA, *8:* VII
  privacy protections, *5:* II.B.3.c, III
    common protections, *5:* III.B.1
    consents and authorizations, *5:* III.B.1.a
    disclosure restrictions, *5:* III.B.2
    Health Privacy Project, *5:* III.B.1.a
    HIPAA security standards, conflicts, *5:* II.B.3.c.vii
    individual's right of access, *5:* III.B.1.b
    mandatory versus permitted disclosures, *5:* III.B.2.c
    model privacy laws, *5:* III.A
    scope, *5:* III.B
    subpoenas, *5:* III.B.2.c
    unauthorized disclosures, cause for action, *5:* III.B.1.c
Uniform Computer Information Transactions Act. *See* Uniform Computer Information Transactions Act
Uniform Electronic Transactions Act. *See* Uniform Electronic Transactions Act
Statistical sampling and civil monetary penalties, *8:* IV.G.3
Statute of limitations
  criminal enforcement, *8:* V.F
Strategic intellectual property filings, *15:* X.B.1
Subcontractors
  breach notification, *7:* III

Subpoenas
  health information disclosures, *5:* III.B.2.c
Substance abuse and treatment records, *5:* II.B.1.b, III.B.2.b
  Confidentiality of Records provisions, *5:* II.B.1.b, III.B.2.b
Substantial similarity, *15:* III.C
Surgical products
  trademarks and service marks, *15:* VI.B.2

T

Taxation
  Stark Law, *16:* II.E.3
  tax-exempt status, *12:* IX.A, X
TDRA (Trademark Dilution Revision Act of 2006), *15:* VI.A.4
Telehealth defined, *1:* II
Telemedicine
  credentialing, *16:* II.D.1
  defined, *1:* II; *10:* IV.A
  FDA regulation, *10:* IV
    collaboration with FCC, *10:* IV.J
    early guidance, *10:* IV.E.1
    e-care providers, *16:* II.D.5
    future prospects, *10:* IV.I
    guidance documents, *10:* IV.E.1
    industry growth, *10:* IV.D.3
    legislative interest, *10:* IV.D.2
    medical device data systems, *10:* IV.G. *See also* Medical devices
    mobile devices and applications, *10:* IV.C, IV.H. *See also* Mobile devices and applications
    reasons for, *10:* IV.D
    recent developments, *10:* IV.F
    safety concerns, *10:* IV.D.1
  federal grants and contracts, *10:* IV.B
  informed consent and duty to disclose, *9:* IV.C
  insurance issues, *9:* IV.F
  international practice of medicine, *9:* V
  Joint Working Group on Telemedicine, *9:* III.A
  legal duty to patient, *9:* IV.B
  licenses, *9:* II.A
  medical software and devices. *See* Medical devices
  mHealth technologies, *10:* IV.B
  off-the-shelf software, *10:* IV.E
  patient abandonment, *9:* IV.E
  physician-patient relationship, *9:* IV.A
  practice across state lines, *9:* I, II.E.1. *See also* Licensed medical practitioners
  consultation exception for out-of-state physicians, *9:* II.E.1, III.A
  corporate practice of medicine, *9:* II.B
  endorsement, *9:* II.E.2, III.A
  included in state's definition of practice of medicine, *9:* II.A
  Model Act to Regulate the Practice of Medicine Across State Lines (Federation of State Medical Boards), *9:* III.B
  proposed regulatory initiatives, *9:* III
  reciprocity, *9:* II.E.3
  special licensing, *9:* II.E.4
  provision of services, *10:* IV.B
  reimbursement for services, *10:* IV.B
  safe harbors, *16:* II.A.1.d
  vicarious liability, *9:* IV.D
Tennessee
  breach notification laws, *7:* V.D
Tethered PHRs, *4:* IV.A
Texas
  breach notification laws, *7:* V.D
  definition of practice of medicine, *9:* II.A
  follow-up physician care when prescribing over Internet, *9:* IV.E
Third-party Web pages
  due diligence, business agreement review, *12:* VII.C
Thomson Reuters, *1:* III.B.2
Time requirements for breach notification, *11:* VI.A
Tort liability
  defamatory information. *See* Defamation
  malpractice. *See* Malpractice
Trade secrets, *15:* VIII. *See also* Proprietary rights
  establishing ownership of, *15:* VIII.C
    nature of information, *15:* VIII.C.1
    preserving secrecy, *15:* VIII.C.2
    proper and improper means of acquisition, *15:* VIII.C.3
  preliminary transactional agreements, *15:* IX.A.2.b
  sources of law, *15:* VIII.A
  Uniform Trade Secrets Act, *15:* VIII.A, VIII.B, IX.A.2.b
Trademark Act of 1946. *See* Lanham Act of 1946
Trademark and service mark infringement
  allocation of risk, *16:* III.B.2
  attorneys' fees, *16:* II.A.1.b
  costs, *15:* VI.A.2; *16:* II.A.1.b
  damages, *15:* VI.A.2; *16:* II.A.1.b
  e-connection providers, *16:* II.C.2
  e-content providers, *16:* II.A.1.b
  forfeitures, *16:* II.A.1.b
  injunctions, *15:* VI.A.2; *16:* II.A.1.b
  mitigation of risk
    before claim, *16:* III.B.1
    upon claim, *16:* III.B.3
  remedies, *15:* VI.A.2
Trademark Dilution Act of 1995, *15:* VI.A.4; *16:* II.A.1.b, II.C.2
Trademark Dilution Revision Act of 2006 (TDRA), *15:* VI.A.4
Trademark Trial and Appeal Board, *15:* VI.B.1
Trademarks and service marks, *15:* VI
  arbitrary marks, *15:* VI.A.1; *16:* II.A.1.b
  aspirin, *15:* VI.B.3
  colors, *15:* VI.B.1
  descriptive marks, *15:* VI.A.1; *16:* II.A.1.b
  dilution, *15:* VI.A.4; *16:* II.A.1.b
  distinctiveness, *16:* II.A.1.b
  domain names
    protection of, *15:* VI.C.1
    securing, *15:* VI.C.2
  due diligence
    asset-related review, *12:* VII.A

Trademarks and service marks—Cont'd
fanciful marks, *15:* VI.A.1; *16:* II.A.1.b
generic marks, *15:* VI.A.1, VI.B.3; *16:* II.A.1.b
infringement. *See* Trademark and service mark infringement
laws, *15:* VI.A.3
likelihood of confusion, *16:* II.A.1.b
Madrid Protocol, *15:* VI.A.3
medicines, *15:* VI.B.2
registration requirement, *16:* II.A.1.b
subject matter of mark, *15:* VI.A.1
suggestive marks, *15:* VI.A.1; *16:* II.A.1.b
surgical products, *15:* VI.B.2
Transactions and code set (TCS) standards, *15:* II.A.4
Transparency, *1:* III
Twitter, health care industry and, *1:* III.A.2

U

UCC. *See* Uniform Commercial Code
UCITA. *See* Uniform Computer Information Transactions Act
UETA. *See* Uniform Electronic Transactions Act
Unfair Commercial Practices Directive (EU), *6:* X
Uniform Commercial Code (UCC)
click-wrap agreements, *13:* IV.B
shrink wrap agreements, *13:* IV.C
transferable records, *13:* III.B
Uniform Computer Information Transactions Act (UCITA)
applicability of, *13:* III.C
attribution procedures, *13:* III.C
authentication, *13:* III.C
contracts, *13:* III.B
E–SIGN Act compared, *13:* III.C
licensing provisions, *13:* III.C
UETA compared, *13:* III.C
Uniform Domain Name Dispute Resolution of ICANN (Internet Corporation for Assigned Names and Numbers), *15:* VI.C.2; *16:* II.A.1.b, III.B.3
Uniform Electronic Transactions Act (UETA)
admissibility of evidence, *17:* II, VI.A
contracts, *13:* III.B
E–SIGN Act compared, *13:* III.B
objective of, *13:* III.B
receipt of records, *13:* III.B
sending of records, *13:* III.B
transferable records, *13:* III.B
UCITA compared, *13:* III.C
Uniform Health Care Information Act, *5:* III.A.2
Uniform Trade Secrets Act (UTSA), *15:* VIII.A, VIII.B, IX.A.2.b
United Kingdom
data controllers, administrative requirements, *6:* VII
Unlicensed or unauthorized practice of medicine, *9:* II.B
allocation of risk, *16:* III.D.2
e-care providers, *16:* II.D.1
e-content providers, *16:* II.A.1.d
mitigation of risk, *16:* III.D.1
Unreasonable restraint of trade. *See* Antitrust
Unsolicited e-mail
E-Privacy Directive (EU) and, *6:* VIII
Untethered PHRs, *4:* IV.A
Utah
breach notification laws, *7:* V.D
UTSA. *See* Uniform Trade Secrets Act

V

VA. *See* Veterans Affairs, Department of
Vangent Holding, *1:* III.B.2
Venture capitalists
investment in e-health innovation, *1:* III.B.1
Verified Internet Pharmacy Practice Sites (VIPPS) certification program, *10:* II.A.2; *16:* II.B.1.a, III.E.1
e-health industry and, *2:* II.C.3
Vermont
breach notification laws, *7:* V.D
Vertical integration, *14:* III
competitor control of vertically related entity, *14:* III.A
limitations of theory, *14:* III.B
Veterans Affairs, Department of (VA)
mobile applications, *1:* III.A.1
social media and, *1:* III.A.2
support of e-health industry, *1:* III.C
VISTA System, *3:* IV.A
Vicarious liability
copyright infringement, *16:* II.A.1.a
criminal enforcement, *8:* V.B
health care institution for physician's failure to obtain informed consent, *9:* IV.D
telemedicine, *9:* IV.D
VIPPS certification program. *See* Verified Internet Pharmacy Practice Sites certification program
Virginia
breach notification laws, *7:* V.D
VISA (credit card), *16:* III.F.3
Voluntary compliance and resolution agreements, *8:* III.D

W

Warranties
preliminary transactional agreements, *15:* IX.A.1.a.ii
Washington
breach notification laws, *7:* V.C, V.C.2, V.C.3, V.D
Web. *See* E-mail; Internet
WebMD, *16:* II.A.1, III.D.1
West Virginia
breach notification laws, *7:* V.D
Whistleblowers
ethics, unlawful discharges, *18:* III.B.4.c
False Claims Act. *See* False Claims Act
Willful neglect, *8:* IV.C

Wire fraud, *8:* VI.C
Wireless medical devices, *1:* III.A.1
Wiretap Act of 1968, *4:* VI.A.2
Wisconsin
   breach notification laws, *7:* V.D
Workarounds, *15:* X.A.3
Workplace
   good faith disclosure within scope of employment, *11:* IV.A
Wrap agreements, *13:* IV.B

   due diligence, *12:* VII.C
Written authorization. *See* Consents and authorizations
Wyoming
   breach notification laws, *7:* V.D

Y

YouTube, *1:* III.A.2; *4:* III.C

PLEASE READ BEFORE USING THIS CD-ROM

This is a legal agreement between you, the individual or entity using this software (the "User"), and BNA Books ("BNA"). Use of these software files ("Software") is governed by the terms of the following license agreement ("Agreement"). By proceeding to use this CD-ROM you agree to accept each of the terms, conditions, and covenants set forth herein. If you do not agree to each of the terms of this Agreement, promptly return the CD-ROM package and the accompanying items (including associated book and packaging) to BNA Books for a full refund or cancellation of all charges.

BNA BOOKS LICENSE AGREEMENT

1. *Grant of License.* BNA grants to User a nonexclusive limited license to use the Software on a single-user computer.

2. *Transfer of License.* You may not rent, loan, or lease the Software, but you may transfer the Software and the accompanying written materials on a permanent basis provided you transfer this Agreement to the recipient, retain no copies, and the recipient agrees in writing to comply with each of the terms set forth in this Agreement. If the Software is an update, any transfer must include the update and all prior versions.

3. *Other Restrictions.* You may not: reproduce, publish, distribute, sell, or otherwise use any material retrieved from or contained in the CD-ROM in any manner whatsoever that may infringe any copyright or proprietary interest of BNA; distribute, rent, sublicense, lease, transfer, or assign the product or the License Agreement; decompile, disassemble, or otherwise reverse-engineer the CD-ROM. Nothing herein, however, shall prevent you from using the material (electronic or written) in the normal course of business for which the material is intended.

4. *Copyright.* The Software is owned by BNA or its successors, assigns, or suppliers (as determined solely by BNA) and is protected by United States copyright laws and international treaty provisions.

Therefore, you must treat the Software like any other copyrighted material (e.g., a book or musical recording) except that you may either (a) make one copy of the Software solely for backup or archival purposes, or (b) transfer the Software to a single hard disk provided you keep the original solely for backup or archival purposes.

DISCLAIMER

This publication is designed to provide accurate and authoritative information in regard to the subject matter covered. In publishing this book, neither the authors and editors nor the American Bar Association, nor the Health Law Section, nor the publisher is engaged in rendering legal, accounting, or other professional service. If legal advice or other expert assistance is required, the services of a competent professional should be sought. Appendix documents may provide links to or refer to material on the Internet. While BNA and the author(s) have made every effort to provide the most current information available, users are cautioned that websites and documents on the Internet are subject to change without notice; users should consult specific websites identified in this publication for updates and for further information on topics of interest.

LIMITED WARRANTY

BNA warrants the physical media (i.e., CD-ROM) on which the Software is furnished to be free from defects in materials and workmanship under normal use for a period of one year from the date of delivery to you. This limited warranty gives you specific legal rights. You may have others, which vary from state to state. Some states do not allow the limitation or exclusion of some warranties, so the above limitation may not apply to you.

BNA does not warrant that the functions contained in the program will meet your requirements. You assume responsibility for the installation, use, and results obtained from the program.

THE ENCLOSED SOFTWARE IS PROVIDED "AS IS" WITHOUT WARRANTY OF ANY KIND, EITHER EXPRESS OR IMPLIED, INCLUDING BUT NOT LIMITED TO IMPLIED WARRANTIES OF MERCHANTABILITY AND FITNESS FOR A PARTICULAR PURPOSE, WITH RESPECT TO THE SOFTWARE AND ANY OTHER ACCOMPANYING MATERIALS.

LIMITATION OF REMEDIES

If for any reason the limited warranty provided by this agreement should be determined to be invalid or inapplicable to any claim that is based upon the quality or performance of the licensed Software, the aggregate liability of BNA and anyone else who has been involved in the creation, production, or delivery of the licensed Software nevertheless shall be limited to the amount paid by you to BNA for the original version of the Software.

IN NO EVENT WILL BNA BE LIABLE TO YOU FOR ANY DAMAGES, INCLUDING ANY LOST PROFITS, BUSINESS INTERRUPTION, LOST SAVINGS, LOSS OF BUSINESS INFORMATION OR OTHER INCIDENTAL OR CONSEQUENTIAL DAMAGES ARISING OUT OF THE USE OR INABILITY TO USE SUCH SOFTWARE EVEN IF BNA OR AN AUTHORIZED BNA DEALER HAS BEEN ADVISED OF THE POSSIBILITY OF SUCH DAMAGES. NOR SHALL BNA BE RESPONSIBLE FOR ANY CLAIM BY ANY OTHER PARTY ARISING FROM OR RELATED TO THE SOFTWARE.

SOME STATES DO NOT ALLOW THE LIMITATION OR EXCLUSION OF LIABILITY FOR INCIDENTAL OR CONSEQUENTIAL DAMAGES, SO THE ABOVE LIMITATION OR EXCLUSION MAY NOT APPLY TO YOU.

This Agreement is governed by the laws of the Commonwealth of Virginia. If any provision of this Agreement shall be determined to be invalid or otherwise unenforceable, the enforceability of the remaining provisions shall not be impaired thereby. The failure of BNA to exercise any right provided for herein shall not be deemed a waiver of any right hereunder. This Agreement sets forth the entire understanding of BNA and the User with respect to the issues addressed herein and may not be modified except by a writing executed by both parties.

The CD-ROM contains files in Microsoft® Word 2007* format and Adobe® Portable Document Format** (PDF) . These files will print on most printers; charts may not print without reformatting on some printers.

*Microsoft® and *Microsoft® Word 2007 are either registered trademarks or trademarks of Microsoft Corporation in the United States and/or other countries.
**Adobe® Portable Document Format (PDF) is a registered trademark of Adobe Systems Incorporated.

© Copyright 2011 The American Bar Association. No copyright claimed in U.S. government materials.